54th Annual Edition

Gun Digest® 2000

Edited by Ken Warner

— GUN DIGEST STAFF —

EDITOR-IN-CHIEF
Ken Warner

SENIOR STAFF EDITORS
Ken Ramage
Harold A. Murtz

CONTRIBUTING EDITORS

Bob Bell
Holt Bodinson
Raymond Caranta
Doc Carlson
Bill Hanus

John Malloy
Layne Simpson
Larry S. Sterett
Hal Swiggett

Editorial Comments and Suggestions

We're always looking for feedback on our books. Please let us know what you like about this edition. If you have suggestions for articles you'd like to see in future editions, please contact

Ken Ramage/Gun Digest
700 East State St.
Iola, WI 54990
email: ramagek@krause.com

Manuscripts, contributions and inquiries, including first class return postage, should be sent to the GUN DIGEST Editorial Offices, Krause Publications, 700 E. State Street, Iola, WI 54990-0001. All materials received will receive reasonable care, but we will not be responsible for their safe return. Material accepted is subject to our requirements for editing and revisions. Author payment covers all rights and title to the accepted material, including photos, drawings and other illustrations. Payment is at our current rates.

CAUTION: Technical data presented here, particularly technical data on handloading and on firearms adjustment and alteration, inevitably reflects individual experience with particular equipment and components under specific circumstances the reader cannot duplicate exactly. Such data presentations therefore should be used for guidance only and with caution. Krause Publications, Inc., accepts no responsibility for results obtained using this data.

Published by

krause publications

700 E. State Street • Iola, WI 54990-0001
Telephone: 715/445-2214
Web: www.krause.com

Please call or write for our free catalog.

Our toll-free number to place an order or obtain a free catalog is 800-258-0929 or please use our regular business telephone 715-445-2214 for editorial comment and further information.

Library of Congress Catalog Number: 44-32588

ISBN: 0-87341-752-6

JOHN T. AMBER LITERARY AWARD

*K*onrad F. Schreier

He's called Konnie Schreier by the hundreds who have worked with him, here and there, for 50 years. And for his "U.S. World War II Combat Riot Shotguns, " about a dozen of the top gun editors decided to call him the winner of the John T. Amber Award, the only juried award in outdoor sports-writing. Schreier's succinct six-page review covered all the bases from official sources, revealing the shotgun to have had a considerable importance in World War II.

Konrad Schreier is a military and technological historian. He has also consulted in the movie business on such films as *Patton* and *The Wind and the Lion.* Born in Illinois, he served in the CBI in World War II and in 1967 sneaked out of industry to do what he now does. He's a regular in *Gun Digest.*

Nominations for the award are made by Ken Warner, long-time Editor of *Gun Digest,* and are judged by a panel of some of the best-known editors in the gun field for what Warner calls "felicity of expression and illustration, origi-nality, scholarship and subject importance." This $1,000 prize replaced the Townsend Whelen Award, originated by the late John T. Amber and is, of course, named for him.

The year's Amber Award nominees, in addition to Schreier, were (in alphabetical order):

Geoffrey Boothroyd, "The Dickson Guns"
Jerry Burke, "Cowboy Shooting Now and Then"
Gene Gangarosa, Jr., "Germany's ULTRA Pistols"
Charles W. Karwan, "The Ljungmann AG42B
John Malloy, "The Wonderful Winchester 67"
Warren Peters, "Are 22 Pocket Pistols Practical?"
Carlos Schmidt, "Tropical Pistolas"
Konrad F. Schreier, Jr., "U.S. World War II Com-bat Riot Shotguns"
John Wallace, "James Paris Lee"
Marshall R. Williams, "The Interior Ballistics of Muzzle Loaders"

Schreier's work – and the work of the other nominees – was judged by the following gun publication editors:

John D. Acquilino, editor of *Inside Gun News*; Bob Bell, former editor-in-chief of *Pennsylvania Game News;* James W. Bequette, executive editor of *Shooting Times*; David Brennan, editor of *Precision Shooting;* Sharon Cunningham, director of Pioneer Press; Pete Dickey, retired technical edi-tor of *American Rifleman*; Robert Elman, former editor-in-chief of Winchester Press, now free-lance editor of Abenake and other publications; Jack Lewis, recently retired editor and publisher of *Gun World*; Bill Parkerson, former editor of *American Rifleman*, now director of research and informa-tion for the National Rifle Association and Dave Petzal, executive editor of *Field & Stream..*

THE R. W. LOVELESS PRIZE

With his first try at *Gun Digest*, Jon Love caught the idiosyncratic Loveless eye with *"How to Shoot A Boat Anchor."* Love's piece is short but it says a great deal about shooting and shooters and guns of all kinds. Loveless pre-fers writers who have something of their own to say.

Thus, Love gets a Loveless knife crafted just for him. This prize has been termed "a tribute from one very com-petent fellow to another."

This is the 12th such. The first 11 were awarded to the late Art Bevan, Paul A. Matthews, Charlie Smith, the late Francis E. Sell, Joe Wheeler, Carlos Schmidt, John Malloy, Howard McCord, Glen B. Ruh, Jim Foral and Raymond Caranta, *Gun Digest's* European correspondent. Loveless chooses the recipients as he does most things – independently.

About Our Covers...

It is the custom of *Gun Digest* to comment on the firearms that illustrate the covers of each edition. This year we can talk about not only several different handguns from Sturm, Ruger & Company, but also recognize the success and vitality of that company from its inception in October, 1949, to date, as it celebrates its 50th Anniversary.

The Big One—Ruger's Super Redhawk chambered for the 454 Casull and very nicely finished in the company's Target Grey.

Front Cover:

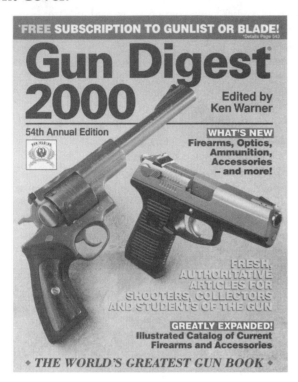

Ruger's first 45 ACP autoloader in the new P97 series, the KP97 with polymer frame.

Here you see the proven Ruger Super Redhawk Revolver, similar to earlier specimens except for the chambering. New for 1999—the Super Redhawk chambered in 454 Casull, in addition to the existing lineup. This is a heavy, well-built pistol with a strong, extended frame that includes integral scope mounts. Other features include interchangeable insert sight blades, adjustable rear sight and the comfortable Ruger "Cushioned Grip" of Santoprene panels with inset panels of Goncalvo Alves wood.

The 454 Casull cartridge deserves a bit of discussion, as well. According to *Cartridges of the World, 8th Edition*, it was developed in 1957 by Dick Casull and Jack Fulmer. Now available as factory ammunition, the cartridge is primarily a hunting round and is one of the most powerful revolver cartridges in the world. Planning to hunt big or dangerous game with a handgun? Ruger's Super Redhawk chambered in 454 Casull will do the job.

Paired with the Super Redhawk is one of the new autoloading P97 series pistols with polymer frame chambered, for the first time, in 45 ACP. This new series of autoloading pistols is available in either double-action-only or the conventional double-action operation system, with decocker. The sighting system is familiar: Drift-adjustable square notch rear sight with a square blade front sight. Slides are of stainless steel and ammunition capacity is eight rounds of 45 ACP, including one in the chamber.

Back Cover:

This is the gun that began it all—Ruger's 22 autoloader—and the 50th Anniversary version offered this year to commemorate the event. Two pistols are shown—hard to tell which is which, isn't it? The rear sight seems the most obvious difference and correctly identifies the pistol in the left background as the new Mark II 50th Anniversary model. Its companion is an original Ruger 22, kindly loaned to us for this cover photograph by Don Findley. Both pistols were photographed against a background of old Ruger literature provided by the company.

Specifications for the (MK4-50) 50th Anniversary Model are essentially the same as the standard Mk II. The blued ordnance steel receiver is machined to the same contour as that of the original pistols. The original pistols were shipped with an unblued steel bolt; to preserve this look, Ruger has substituted a stainless-steel bolt carrying the Ruger logo on the bolt cocking head.

Additionally, the top front portion of the receiver has been impressed with the attractive 50th Anniversary Ruger crest. The grips and magazine carry the Ruger medallion with a red background, instead of black. This last an exception to the use of a black medallion background ever since the untimely passing of Alex Sturm, cofounder of the company, in 1951. Finally, this 50th Anniversary pistol is shipped in a red Ruger commemorative case (lockable, with padlock).

Following the successful startup combining the firearms design genius and marketing savvy of Bill Ruger and the financial backing of Alex Sturm, the American shooting market took all the product the company could deliver. Alex Sturm left the picture all too soon and the story of Sturm, Ruger and Company from that point forward—through today—is clearly written by William Batterman Ruger, Sr.

The partners had been discussing their next product—a single action revolver similar to the classic Colt Single Action Army – but better. Bill Ruger had assumed sole direction of the company and carried forward with the new product plans. In the '50s he gave us the Single Six, another pistol. It was a single action, had fixed sights and strongly resembled a smaller, reproportioned Colt SAA—in 22LR. On the heels of the Single Six was the company's first centerfire single action revolver, the Blackhawk, introduced in 1955. Variations followed in the expanding product line, to include a small new 22 single action, the Bearcat.

By now—the early '50s—Bill Ruger had begun to pioneer the use of investment casting for firearms components and the company had grown considerably, relocating into larger quarters.

The '60s saw the introduction of the first rifle, the 44 Magnum Carbine (in 1960), the opening of a new and larger plant in New Hampshire and, in 1963, the company established its own foundry, Pine Tree Castings.

The Ruger line continued to expand. The 10/22 Rifle, exceptional for its 10-shot rotary magazine, was introduced in 1964. The Number One series of single shot rifles debuted in 1967 and, in 1968, the first Ruger bolt action rifle appeared, the M-77. Not all the product development activity was in rifles, though. A line of double action revolvers in 38 and 357 Magnum for the law enforcement market was introduced in 1969.

The 1970s brought us Ruger's blackpowder Old Army revolver—the company's only blackpowder gun until recently -- and the best cap 'n ball revolver on the market. The New Model Single Action revolvers followed in 1973, then the Mini-14 autoloading rifle and the Red Label over/under shotgun, initially offered only in 20 gauge; now in 12 and 28 gauge.

Growth continued and in the 1980's, the Ruger Redhawk 44 Magnum double-action revolver was introduced, followed by the Super Redhawk (one of our front cover guns). The New Hampshire plant was also busy turning out new rimfire and centerfire rifles and was joined by a new manufacturing facility in Prescott, Arizona, which was created to build a totally new line of autoloading pistols.

The early '90s saw the closure of the manufacturing facility in Southport, Connecticut, although corporate headquarters is still there, near the little red barn where the company began. Products from the Southport operation were assigned to the other two facilities that now produce all the Ruger line, including the recently introduced Vaquero single-action line and the 22/45 autoloading pistol in 22 LR.

Sturm, Ruger and Company is the only firearms manufacturer to make a complete line—rifles, pistols, revolvers and shotguns—entirely in the USA.   ●

The 50th Anniversary model MK 450 autoloading 22 LR pistol and its red Ruger commemorative case.

An original Ruger 22, the RST4.

Faithful—almost—to the original. This new 50th Anniversary model differs only for the better.

CONTENTS

Page 23

Page 38

Page 66

Page 81

REPORTS FROM THE FIELD

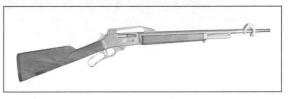

Page 142

Page 148

CATALOG OF ARMS AND ACCESSORIES

Just Another Millennium

By Ken Warner

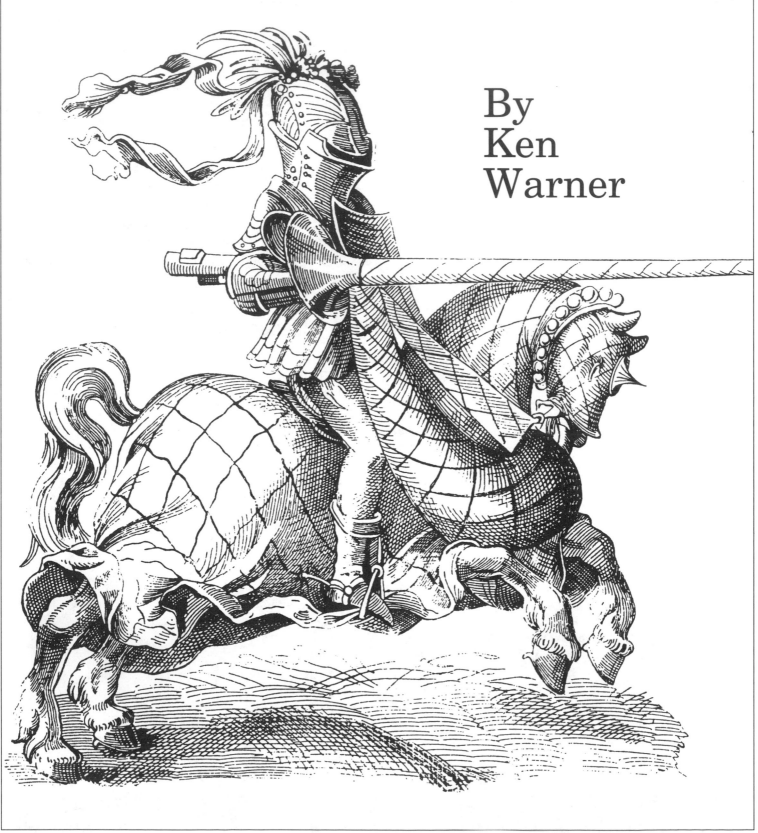

WE NOW ENTER another new age, they tell us. The millennium is the opportunity of our lifetimes perhaps, or we may be in a world of hurt, or maybe no one will notice. The only sure bet is that we all agree on the number that describes the New Year— it's to be the year 2000.

For the firearms fancy, it will be a new experience, this undue concern with a calendar date. When the last century turned, gun writing as a trade was just out of diapers, possibly up to toddling. Many of the important topics had been broached in print, but few were either explored or settled. The true cranks, as they called themselves, took little notice of our passage from the 19th Century to the 20th. (The last time there was a new millennium, of course, there weren't any firearms, let alone any rifle cranks (19th) or gun nuts (20th) and thus there were no publications on the subject, not in A. D. 999.)

A hundred years ago, however, there were a few notes of some interest. For them we are indebted to Jim Foral, and Mark Benenson and Russell Gilmore, GUN DIGEST writers all, and diligent diggers into our firearms past to boot. Some of this may surprise you.

The very first thing to note is our predecessors got the date wrong. There is a splendidly apocalyptic review of the progress of the 19th Century in Forest & Stream for December 29, 1900, and we are going to quote from it extensively even though we are, by its standards, a year early. That is, this present writing is being accomplished in 1999 for an issue dated 2000, and thus nearly 18 months shy of a full 100 years after Forest & Stream then published. Over the stretch of centuries, we can probably let that much time slide.

The best way to pass along the full flavor of Forest & Stream's turn-of-a-century remarks would be simply to reproduce them. However, we are faced with the insurmountable difficulty of the reproductive capacity being in one state and the material in another and the clock running very fast. So we must instead quote:

"The closing century has been marvelous in its discoveries, in its advance in civilization and in all that makes the living of life easier to civilized man." Forest & Stream pronounced. "It has been an age in which man has begun to understand certain of the forces of nature, to tame them to his own uses and to force them to work for him, as he ropes, saddles and breaks to ride the wild horse of the prairie. With the more easy life that has come from the chain-

ing of these forces and their adaptation to man's uses has come also a vast increase in the civilized population of the globe, and a corresponding decrease in its natural and uncivilized population.

"Nowhere has this change been more marked than in the territory of the United States. A century ago its population numbered 5,308,000 ... gathered in a little fringe of settlements ... the

There simply were no periodicals devoted wholly to firearms 100 years ago.

furthest limits of the West were the banks of the Mississippi River ... beyond was literally an unknown world ... the antelope, the white goat, the grizzly bear and a host of other species had not then been described ... and game and fish everywhere were as numerous as ever.

"Today, the population of the United States is nearly 76,000,000....industries have sent men far and wide over the land, threading the densest forests, penetrating the most remote nooks in the mountains. Each man who has done this work ... trapper, prospector, timber cruiser....has done his part in destroying nature and developing art in the place he visited ... which learned then there was in the world a new enemy to be feared...."

And with that, our 100-years-ago editorial friend launched into an even more distressing litany of the killing of the species, one after another, the slaughter almost a by-product of the presence of civilization. He cites authority and eyewitness 18th Century accounts, sorry announcements of the killing of "the last" of one species or another in one and another place, ever further West. In midstream, as it were, he concluded:

"...the man of today has pushed his resistless way everywhere, and where the civilized man comes there is no room for uncivilized creatures, whether they be men or beasts. We may try to preserve the game as much as we please; we may endeavor to make gradual the process of its extemination; but it is useless for us to try to fight against the laws of nature....the day is coming ... nay, it is almost here ... when to see big game we must look for it inside protected parks and preserves...."

And at this point, he goes on to suggest, with considerable prophetic accuracy, what should happen ... i.e., National Parks, Federal land protection, and so forth. In short, the man suggested in 1900 that we might still

set aside all that public property all Americans can today enjoy almost everywhere in this blessed Union and we have done what he suggested, perhaps more.

Our long-ago friend took one more prophetic giant step:

"With the changed game conditions has come a not less notable revolution of public sentiment regarding the game as a resource to be cared for and preserved. We have lost.....but we have gained an appreciation of what remains ... the outlook for the new century is not altogether one of discouragement. We shall take better care ... the period of indifference has passed by....the sportsmen of the twentieth century will have advantage, in a growing degree as the century shall progress, of a wiser system of game preservation."

Pretty good stuff, that. This writer thinks that writer would look at today's hunting picture and pronounce it more than he hoped for, prophet though he was. We are not, in these regards, quite where a lot of us would like, but we are far beyond what was hoped and even a casual review of our hunting seasons will reveal that sport hunting is alive and kicking.

There is more than that. Certain species are, one can contend, more numerous than ever. The whitetail deer and the woodchuck/groundhog are two cases in point, being forest animals that absolutely love the amount of edge and thick cover the clearing of the forests has provided, and, for the marmot, the lovely food the farmers grow. The ringneck pheasant has, you could say, caught on, though just now the gaudy roosters are trying to figure out how to live with excessively clean or no-till farming. Our two splendid big birds, the wild turkey and the Canada goose, have become genuinely renewable resources. There are, willy-nilly, still bears. There are wolves. There are cougars. There are more coyotes than anyone really needs and they are in places from which they were long gone 100 years ago.

There is, taken altogether, a large and ordered management effort, paid for mostly by sportsmen, to cherish and to control the wild game of our now-50 states on the authority of the very bedrock of our Revolution and on our founding documents and the resolve of our Founding Fathers which together have determined for us that all the game belongs to an the people. Thus we care for it—as an entire people, united.

I believe our friend at Forest & Stream would be pleased with us. In this regard, the story of the 20 th Century is worth boasting. Would that the other facets of the story of firearms in the 20th Century were so bright and so gleaming.

There will never ever be any problem in the future collecting data on the technical progress of firearms and ammunition in the 20th Century. And that is a new circumstance in great contrast with the 19th. There simply were no periodicals devoted wholly to firearms 100 years ago. So there are not many contemporary sources to quote from on the marvels of the 19th Century. One must glean and pick over to find much at all about what might then have been expected of the 20th Century and generally such remarks were made in books by people like Charles Askins, the elder, and Lt. Townsend Whelen much later. (And one does not envy that chap 100 years from now who must weave a rational discourse on this subject from the tens of thousands

of sources he will have to examine.) There they were, 100 and more years ago, with firearms changing exponentially about them and none noticed, not where that noticing would be easy to find now. Think of it.....the 19th Century began when every shot fired began with someone pouring powder down a tube, when armies lined up facing each

other at 50 or 100 yards, when flashes in the pan came every day, when swords were personal defense arms; and then, at that century's end, men in wars suffered accurate aimed fire at hundreds of yards, machine guns beat the killing grounds as McCormick reapers beat wheat, and a man with a good revolver at his belt and a sufficient resolve was someone the criminal classes left strictly

alone because, peaceful though he might be, he was dangerous in the sense he could defend himself against several attackers if given a half-second's notice, something not so generally so when the defense was a blade.

Over those ten decades we got the percussion cap and the revolving pistol and rifled muskets and Minie balls, then the cartridge and the repeating rifle and then many cartridges and many

Brown Bess, beloved workhorse of the world's best army in 1800, was the classic infantry flintlock musket—one shot at a time.

British SMLE kept the Union Jack fluttering all around the world in 1900—10 shots quick.

repeating rifles in rimfire and then pinfire and then center-fire and the long-range cartridge rifles and smokeless powder and a whole new round of repeaters, both handguns and shoulder arms. In 1801, the infantry projectile weighed an ounce and left the muzzle at 1200 feet per second or so;

One or another M-16, a full-auto high-velocity 22, closes this century out in the hands of U.S. and NATO forces—30 shots even quicker.

in 1899, it weighed about 200 grains and went out at 2200 or 2400 feet per second; and the knowledgeable can translate that to approximately the difference between plowing with a horse and plowing with a John Deere, a big John Deere.

So there was a lot to write about and nobody did, much. It wasn't because they were not paying attention to these matters; there was public discourse. In fact, as 1899 closed, Shooting and Fishing, edited by the redoubtable A. C. Gould, paid saccharine tribute to the "American Sportsman - 1900" in a fourparagraph Christmas Number epistle that called us (we are still American sportsmen, are we not?) " ... an unsurpassed type of manhood." That off his chest, Gould opened his campaign to resurrect the National Rifle Association, somewhat fallen on hard times, with the January 11, 1900 issue.

There were a series of suggested names for the group and organizational models and touted leaders. It began, that 11th of January, as the League of Military Riflemen, which was described then in plan to be an organization very like the National Rifle Association this writer joined in the late 1950s and served from 1971 to 1979. On February 3rd, it became the League of American Riflemen, and on February 22nd, they were still talking and it was still the League of American Riflemen.

The talk was probably either catching or alarming to some shooters, for on March 8th, the United States Revolver Association was announced as a done deal. Also on March 8th, and on the same page, Shooting and Fishing felt it important to define league as an alliance of organizations and association as a union of persons, which probably means a lot of letters were zipping back and forth. Subsequent events would reveal it to be so.

The background for much of this organizational activity involves the infantry rifle of the United States. The National Guard was not only stuck with singleshot 45-70 Springfield rifles shooting blackpowder loads as their issue arms (which, to their discomfiture, some of them had had to shoot at real enemies in Cuba not so many months earlier.) but they were not even getting a sniff at the Krag. And a renewed interest in handgun targetry had engendered a need for somebody—anybody—to run the matches. It was not all beer and skittles, shooting wasn't, not organizationally at any rate and regardless of what was going on the marketplace.

It all worked out, amid a blizzard of letters and a veritable circus of organizational maneuvering, the details of which are possibly best left to those who want to go to the source, which curiously enough is Shooting and Fishing which became Arms and the Man, which became The American Rifleman. At long last, on September 20th, 1900, Shooting and Fishing announced the National Rifle Association of America, a phoenix risen upon warm ashes kept so by Gen. George W. Wingate, who was both the last president of the first NRA (and one of its organizers) and the chairman of the committee which organized this one. It was all accomplished quite correctly and the organization turned out pretty well, most of us think.

And here we are, at the other end of that century, and what a century it has been. From one point of view, not a lot has happened; from another, it's a whole new world. In truth, where a hunter or soldier or even a duellist of the year 1800 would have been bumfoozled by a sudden entry into the year 1900, the rifle crank or shotgunner of 1900 wouldn't be pushed too far off-center on a sudden trip to the year 2000. Getting dropped into a Cowboy Match might give him a fit of the giggles, his own group having gone past that stuff a couple of decades earlier, but mostly he'd be OK. Still, we have more than meets the eye or would meet his at first glance.

First off, there's the sheer quantity of us and our guns and our ammo and all that. A century ago, we have had pointed out here, there were 76,000,000 Americans; a few short years ago, the National Rifle Association had something over 3,000,000 members for a while and it is by no means puny today. There's a whole lot of shooting going on.

To a degree, it's a different class of people in the shooting sports, as well. The way it is now, anybody can play. There's a shooting game for nearly any budget, and nearly any time schedule. No point in getting into lists, but a steady guy can make a fair showing at any of several handgunner sports with one solid gun and a lot of practice—about like golf. The same is true for the shotgunner in all of us—one good skeet gun and a lot of practice and a guy can compete at skeet and at sporting clays. If you can find a silhouette match or some cast bullet shooters, nearly any good rifle can play.

Things get pricey the harder you want to go at it, sure, but that's true of any sport, any pastime. These days, anyone who wants in on a gun sport can do it and that was not necessarily

...periodicals started crowding the stands, and soon enough there were gun magazines, and once there were more than two of them, the Rifleman apart, there were gun writers and publicity.

that easy as the century opened, when the venues were spread out, the money a little more important, and working guys thought a 40-hour week was a vacation.

There is more to work with, as well. The 20th Century started with 220-grain 30 caliber bullets going 2200 feet per second; now we have 180-grainers up to 3400 fps. That's a lot of difference. There are common match handguns now that shoot like rifles did; there are common hunting handguns that are a good bit more powerful than a lot of early-century rifles. The various new and often very specific disciplines have generated any number of new combinations of design features, from the all-out "race" guns of IPSC games to the heavy (recoil, you know) long-barreled sporting clays guns very few would take into tight coverts after birds. Games apart, there are also real-world specialties like police counter-sniper rifles, so-called "door" guns used to assist officers in sudden entries, "bean-field" rifles for very long-range shots on deer.

This, by the way, is not really new stuff. Fellow named Fitzgerald working for Colt in the 1920s designed some pretty special concealment sixguns and back then a "belly-shooter" was not a threat to society but a fellow who lay prone with a bull barrel and a 20x glass and tried put 22 rimfire bullets all in the same hole and a lot of them did it with rifles that suited no other earthly purpose.

Proliferation of design is one of the keys to understanding 20th Century firearms. The changes came at exponential pace, rivaling the annual changing of the fashion guard in couturier Paris. The purpose of the owners of the absolute latest thing was to win bigger, shoot further, lighten the load, sometimes stay alive. The purpose of the designers and the makers was to sell more guns and live a little better. There were very few parasites, but a lot of symbiotes. Taking in each others' washing is an honorable career in the firearms fancy.

For many historical purposes, the 20th Century is divided for examination into the four decades before that war and the five decades after it. For those of us interested in guns, the first four decades were pretty good in the sense there were plenty of guns, shooting was cheap and respected, and those who shot did a lot of shooting. After the war, there were even more guns, lots of them legitimate trophies of war—your reporter once spent an enthralled teen-age evening sprawled on the floor of a chum's living room emptying his paratrooper brother's dufflebag, just in from Germany. Apart from a tendency to jump out of airplanes, said brother had a lot of sense and had filled his bag with pistols—shiny, first quality, holstered pistols, the creme stripped from a defeated army....little Mausers and big, long Lugers and short, P-38s, and all manner of neat little guns, like Walther Sports and Walther PPs and Mauser HScs. Talk about fun all you want; I know where it was that night.

Probably the next most important thing was that a lot of those vets went to college which generally—back then, anyway—moved them closer to the idea of reading to discover stuff. It really was not very long before all sorts of periodicals started crowding the stands, and soon enough there were gun magazines, and once there were more than two of them, the Rifleman apart, there were gun writers and publicity. In one or another form, written gun history was in the making around the clock, around the years, from then on.

GUNS was the first to hit the stands and heady days they were for Bev Mann and Bill Edwards, presiding in Skokie, Illinois, over the beginning of a whole new thing. We're talking '50s here. Soon along came GUNS AND AMMO, curiously enough printed in brown ink

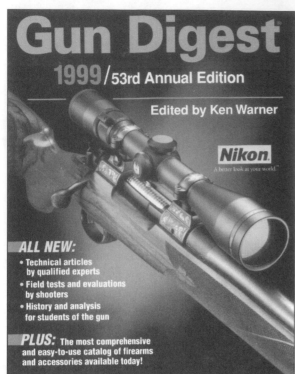

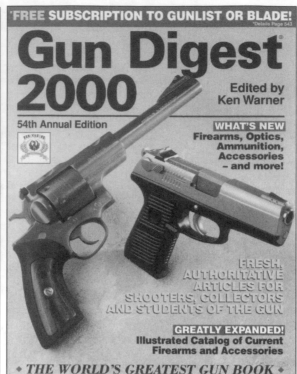

For over half this century, GUN DIGEST has chronicled the history of firearms, year by year.

and out of LA. And New Yorkers got on with GUNS AND HUNTING and others and pretty soon SHOOTING TIMES in tabloid format came out of Peoria. By 1967 or so, the field was so established this reporter could take a shot himself, and GUNfacts ran for 12 or so glorious months on a wing and a prayer with no gas in the tank.

And this now-venerable annual, this GUN DIGEST, was right in there. The idea of an annual in the gun business came out of a business necessity for an importer and wholesaler named Stoeger who needed a catalog and with marketing genius in full flower called that catalog The SHOOTERS BIBLE. Copies of that book from the '30s are bibles indeed to some collectors. Melding a different sort of catalog—a directory—with actual gunwriting was the idea of a different sort of fellow in the sporting goods business, Milton Klein, who called some slim volumes got out during World War 11 GUN DIGEST. When that idea fell to John T. Amber to improve in the '50s with Klein's backing, a single publication for the deposit of reams of firearms history came into being and you are reading its 54th Edition, now published by Krause Publications, Inc.

All of this played against a backdrop of the Cold War and the Space Age and some unparalleled grass-roots prosperity from 1950 until now, barring only a couple of small economic bumps. Americans took to the roads in new cars, to the suburbs in new houses, to the water in new boats, and to the woods and fields with new guns, very often all of it at once. They were heady decades in the sporting goods business, not the least in guns.

In part the boom was marketing driven, because when all else failed, something new would sell; a lot of it was technology, not least the successful search for cheaper ways to make effective guns; and there was a ton of entrepeneuring going on—men who made guns that would sell just because they could and thought that as good a way to create a company as any other.

The results? In terms of guns, we got a lot that shot farther and harder and a lot that shot quicker and quicker and even some that were better. The bolt action repeating rifle went to a stunning variety of models and sizes and capabilities; for a while, we nearly had the cartridge of the month as shooters and companies alike sought the magic bullets of competition or hunting or commerce and introduced variation upon variation—at this writing, there are, in common use, at least eight chamberings for 7mm tubes, eight factory chambers, that is.

In shotguns, the American-made double gun died, though one company born at mid-century resurrected it as an over-under, a company named Ruger. The repeating shotgun, however, stretched and heavied and shortened and lightened and then did it all at once. It has sprouted virtually invisible choke tubes and so now virtually every shotgun barrel is at least improved cylinder, modified or full at the shooter's immediate option. And the loads!! The modern shotshell is awesome; it is so good it can kill well with steel shot, a truly lousy projectile. And one gun can now, in 12 bore, go from one-ounce loads in 2 3/4-inch cases to 1 7/8 ounces in 3 1/2-inch cases. We shoot 3 1/4-1 1/4 loads now from 20s!!

One stands a chance to encapsulate the general picture of 20th Century sporting shoulder arms in a couple hundred words. That is not possible with modern handguns. We have seven-ounce 32 automatics and five pound revolvers; we have five-shot revolvers and 16-shot autoloaders. Each year brings new companies, new designs; they arrive and die; or they arrive and take over, which happened when Gaston Glock made an Austrian service pistol largely out of polymers and from a really clean piece of paper—he decided for a lot of us that our sidearm should be engineered more like a really good ballpoint pen than as a machine tool. And it works....very well. There is still room, of course, for all the other ways to build a pistol to survive and they do.

Not the least beneficiary of all this technical horsepower has been the military. The infantry arm's projectile now weighs 62 grains and proceeds at 3,100 feet per second. Twenty or thirty of them are carried in a seven-pound rifle. The rifle can fire in fully automatic mode and is, in fact, the logical extension of an idea from a mid-century war—the assault rifle, an arm that provides each soldier on the field with a machine gun and thus changes all the tactical options. Beyond this, there are tank guns that don't miss, smart bombs, grenade-firing shotguns—the 20th Century was a considerable upheaval in the ordnance business.

By the 80s, things were really looking good, examining the firearms business and the firearms fancy and field sports all together. They are not one and the same, we should note. Pontificators call them, all together, the "gun lobby" and pretend the "lobby" speaks with a single voice, but it's not so. Indeed, the differences between the separate interest groups are often as great as the differences between any of them and the great pontificators. The Na-

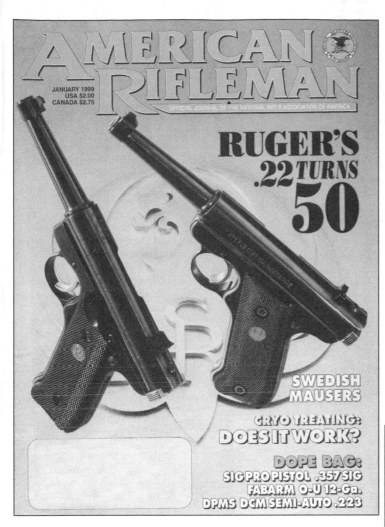

other and one kind of effort and then another. Pragmatic to the core, those various politically motivated anti-gun groups will do anything that works. Once they used race, then ethnicity, then location, then crime statistics, then all of those together. One small step at a time, settling for a quarter-loaf at each juncture, these frightened control freaks have continued on. Now they are attempting to accomplish in the civil courts what they could not accomplish in the legislatures—to punish firearms makers and sellers hard enough to make them go away.

And each bloody shirt that comes along serves their purpose. Whatever tragedy occurs involving firearms has a predictable result—within three hours there will be a solemn pronouncement by a person who commands an audience for these purposes that whatever happened would not have taken place except for the nation's unfortunate "preoccupation" with guns. Sadly, in today's news climate, such statements go largely unchallenged, they have gone unchallenged for over

tional Rifle Association is labeled a "tool of the gun manufacturers" and it is not, no more than the Player's Association is a tool of the National Basketball Association. Mostly, by working pretty hard at it, the NRA manages to sell advertising in its publications to the manufacturers of guns and to purveyors of a great many other things as well. That's about all the financial connection there is, and the advertising rates are competitive, not charitable. And independent (of NRA) publications quite often are more successful at these advertisement selling efforts.

Essentially, the NRA is a consumer group, and until the American Association of Retired People got going—and boy, has it gone—the NRA was the largest inclusive group there was. The American Medical Association was then larger, but no one has ever accused it of being inclusive. The NRA, on the other hand, had them all—young, old, professional, blue-collar, athletic, educated and less so. "We are the NRA" is a new advertising campaign based on a long-true reality.

For much of the 20th Century in the United States, there has been an effort to take guns out of the hands of citizens —first one kind of citizen and then an-

GUNS was the first national newsstand independent firearms magazine and it is still going.

Well-heeled shooters in the 21st Century will still acquire works of art like this 7x57 Mauser owned by Jan Billeb and made for her by the American Custom Gunmaker Guild.

much argument about its wording and the intent of the drafters and what they would have thought today and whether or not the Supreme Court ever ruled on the subject and on and on and on. And most of those who favor the untrammeled ownership of firearms jump right into the middle of that, in effect arguing about how much of their rights they should be allowed to keep.

Not enough of us point out that this nation was begun with a declaration that we—all of us—were endowed by our Creator with certain inalienable rights and that consequently those rights are the absolute foundation of our law. Distrustful of the future, some of those later involved in the creation of a Constitution to structure our future demanded, as the price of its passage through their states' legislatures, the enumeration of the rights of the Declaration as then understood. Those are the Bill of Rights and the Second of those is the right to be armed.

In short, citizens of the United States are born with those inalienable rights; the Constitution does not grant them, but guarantees them. This is not a popular view among lawyers, who believe in laws, not rights; nor do legislators like it, because they prefer to grant privilege, not suffer the rights of other citizens. It is, however, completely understood by people and that is the hope as this century closes....somehow, the law-abiding citizen who wishes to own a firearm for whatever purpose will have his right to do so once more set free of legislation and regulation as, for just one example, a man named Miranda had his rights to legal representation affirmed.

And in the 21stCentury? There will continue to be more and more of us with attendant impact on game populations, but we have become very good at managing that sort of thing and are getting better, so one can believe that Americans will hunt largely as they have for

50 years; and they are having a cumulative effect.

There is another ongoing reality that is having a cumulative effect, lesser, but real. And it's a good thing. A very large number of the states have passed what are called "must issue" concealed carry laws. That is, the law sets up standards that any law-abiding adult citizen can meet, and those who meet those standards must be permitted to carry a weapon concealed on their persons. In those places where such laws have gone into effect, the instant result is the lowering of significant numbers of crimes against persons—assault, rape, armed intrusion into houses. and such. It is so sensible, it would appear, that even a criminal can understand it. A resolute armed and law-abiding citizen is not someone to assault, and since one cannot reliably distinguish the armed from the unarmed in these circumstances, the safe approach is to avoid attacking citizens. The longer the carry law is in effect, the better the numbers. It's not something the anti-firearms crowd likes to talk about.

That is the best countervailing trend available. Enormous coverage of in-

credible tragedies inflicted on communities by deranged schoolchildren is having quite a different effect in the legislatures. Desperately hoping—as they have for half a century—the issue would just go away, those legislatures are getting themselves off the hook as fast as they can do so. The result is going to be more bad law creating more useless organizations to carry out impossible tasks in the areas of background checks, closing "loopholes" and a dozen other sound-bite panaceas. When one is a legislator and a law does not work, the obvious remedy is a new and different law. One does not, it seems, re-think the matter.

There is a pattern for this, unfortunately. Colin Greenwood, a British policeman of considerable repute, laid it out in black-and-white decades ago in a book. Simply enough, Greenwood traced Britons' right to arms from the Magna Carta to when the right disappeared. In terms of firearms, it took just about 120 years. The parallels with the United States are heartbreaking.

Sadly, these opportunities to disarm Americans ought not be available to those in opposition. There is much talk about the Second Amendment and the past 50 years over the next 100 years. They will travel farther, many of them, to do the simple homely things we do today—tramp the Smith place for a ringneck, spend a morning with the squirrels in Uncle Bud's woodlot, shoot doves over the corn harvest in the next county—and come to the realization that those things are as much the hunt as the pursuit of wapiti in Colorado or geese on Chesapeake Bay. The important thing is that all those things should be there, judging by what we now know.

There will be guns, surely. New guns, more useful and not necessarily more expensive, will be there for us. We will probably not see the end of specialization for decades, but it will come. During those decades, as better and better engineers and practitioners work harder and harder with better tools and materials, miracles will be commonplace. One wonders how they are going to find 300-yard ranges for benchresters when the 200-yard one-hole group—that is ten 6mm bullets, say, all going through one .243-inch hole in a piece of stiff paper—is easy and shoot-offs become boring. All the ingredients are at hand; in fact, they are all reported elsewhere in this very publication. It remains only to be seen how it works out.

"The closing century has been marvelous," said that other editor 100 years ago, "in its discoveries, in its advance in civilization and in all that makes the living of life easier....an age in which man has begun to understand certain forces of nature.. ..to tame them ... nowhere more marked than in the territory of the United States."

True then. True now. And the next century will be more of the same, but faster, much faster. There will be guns; there will be game; and the freedom to enjoy them will be up to us to secure for ourselves and for those who follow us and carry on into the 22nd Century. We should be about it.

H&R 1871 Inc. sees the future and these photos show it—the shooting family is the image and grandparents the vehicles.

HAVE YOU noticed? The bad guys shoot sideways!

To anyone who goes to the movies or watches television, it must seem as if all the bad guys in the make-believe worlds hold their pistols sideways when they shoot. It's the new thing in fictional shooting.

It probably was most noticeable in some recent "gangsta" flicks, but we see it on the screen almost all the time now. Almost invariably, the bad guys shoot sideways.

How did such a trend start?

The beginning is difficult to pin down. Perhaps the 1966 hit motion picture, THE GOOD, THE BAD, AND THE UGLY, has an influence. This was the last of Sergio Leone's Italian Westerns starring Clint Eastwood and Lee Van Cleef.

for today's TV and movie action features. Whatever the reason, today's fantasyland bad guys shoot sideways as often, maybe more often, as not.

Audience reaction probably varies. Some viewers undoubtedly must think, "Man, that's cool." Indeed, a number of real-life cases have been reported in which the miscreant held his pistol sideways. Criminals apparently go to the movies and watch TV, too, so perhaps this is an example of life imitating art.

Ordinary, upright citizens probably have a different reaction, particularly if they are knowledgeable about firearms, a reaction that may be summed up, "Boy, that's dumb."

But still, regardless of how dumb it looks, in the backs of the minds of those knowledgeable people grows the ques-

and opposite reaction. Centerfire handguns, being relatively light compared to the weight of their bullets, begin recoiling while the bullet is still in the bore. To compensate for this, most big-bore handguns have a line of bore that angles down, below the line of sight. Put another way, the line of sight angles up.

So, whichever way one prefers to look at it, before a conventional shot is fired, the barrel is pointing below the line of sight. As the shot is fired, the pistol rises so the line of bore comes closer to the original line of sight.

Obviously, then, the line of sight, the line of bore and the force of gravity must all be in the same plane—a vertical one going down through the center of the earth—for the sights to work as intended.

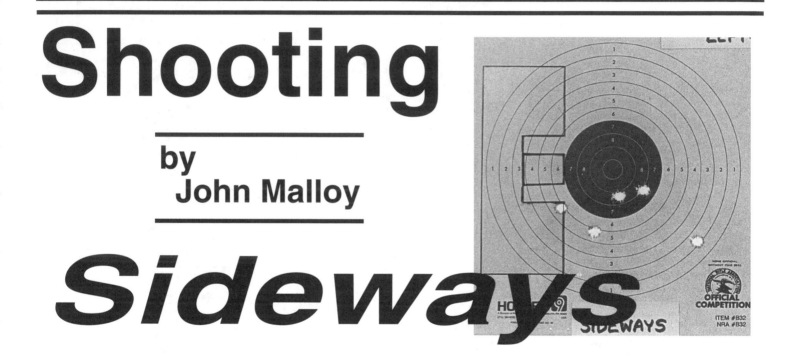

Shooting

by
John Malloy

Sideways

The film was a force in making the Spaghetti Western popular.

In one memorable scene, the Tuco Ramirez character, portrayed by Eli Wallach, is seated in a bathtub full of soapsuds when his adversary, played by veteran spaghetti actor Al Mullock, enters. Tuco, who has taken his revolver into the bath with him, shoots from the tub, his first shots knocking his opponent through a set of swinging doors. Rising from his tub, modestly covered with suds, Tuco walks to the doorway. He turns his also-suds-covered revolver sideways over the door and delivers the finishing shot.

That scene was played over three decades ago. Perhaps youngsters who watched that dramatic sideways shot are now in charge of coordinating scenes

tion: How does a handgun really perform when fired sideways?

Certain things must be considered when shooting a pistol sideways:

1. The law of gravity is still in effect. The bullets will begin to curve down to meet the earth as soon as they exit the muzzle, no matter in what orientation the pistol is held. This path is, of course, a bullet's trajectory.

Sights on handguns take this trajectory into account. A sight line is straight, but relates to the trajectory of a bullet curving in a plane that intersects the center of the earth. Any movement of the sights away from vertical adversely affects this relationship, and the shot will go astray.

2. The laws of physics are still in effect. For every action, there is an equal

To a film or TV actor, however, the sights may hold little importance, as he will not actually shoot at anything. Even in real life, many shots are taken with the point-shooting method, and the sights are not used. Indeed, at the close ranges at which inter-personal shooting generally takes place, deviation from the vertical plane may not be of great significance, even when the sights are used.

Thus, does the position of the sights really matter in close-range shooting?

Even if the position of the sights does not really matter, intuition suggests that recoil effect probably does.

In a normal vertical position, a shooter's grip stays more-or-less constant during recoil. The shooter's arm is in line with the vertical sight-bore-gravity plane. The gun rises in that plane during recoil, then gravity helps return it to its original position.

When held sideways, the gun would be expected to move within a system of complex force vectors that might twist the pistol in the hand. Recovery from recoil might be very much more difficult.

Holding a firearm in an orientation other than vertical had already been considered long before sideways shooting hit the tube and the big screen. In days prior to WWII, for instance, canting—leaning a rifle or pistol away from the vertical—was frowned upon. The experts considered any tilt a mistake and wanted the guns held upright.

Morris Fisher could probably be considered such an expert. A shooter of both rifle and handgun, Fisher in 1920 and 1924 earned a record five Olympic Gold Medals for the United States in rifle shooting. Writing books in 1930 on both rifle and pistol shooting, he stressed that the sights must be upright, and that canting could not be allowed with either rifle or pistol. A canted gun would throw the bullet off in the direction of the cant.

Other pre-war shooting authorities, such as Charles Askins, Jr., did not even mention canting. Their writings simply enough indicating that they expected the firearm to be held so that the sights were upright.

International shooting competition had ended in 1937, and with hints of world war approaching, military training became more important. During World War II, military trainers wanted the firearm held upright. Sighting and aiming exercises stressed a vertical position. Military-trained shooters and military techniques dominated the American shooting scene for some time after the war had ended.

Olympic competition, shut down during the war, resumed again in 1948. Although America may have had the greatest interest in shooting, our nation had only one vote on the International committee set up to standardize the shooting sports. The resulting shooting games were very different than traditional American shooting sports, and Americans were slow to adapt to the new ways of doing things.

The post-war Russian govenment was, in a way, instrumental in bringing about an acceptance of new techniques. The Soviet Union did not participate in the 1948 Olympics, but quickly saw the political and propaganda advantages to winning in International competition. The totalitarian state put considerable effort into the development of new equipment and techniques. In the 1952 Olympics and subsequent International shooting competition, the Soviet Union shooters constituted a force with which to contend. With political overtones attached to winning or losing, traditional ways of doing things began to change.

Positions for rifle shooting began to evolve. Writing in 1963, Gary Anderson—who was to win his first Olympic Gold Medal the following year—suggested that American shooters might try canting their rifles to allow a better head position. The rifle would be fired at a specific known distance, and the sights could be reset to compensate for the cant.

Also during the 1960s, the shooting press had reported that Olympic Rapid-Fire Pistol shooter William W. McMillan canted his pistol to the left. McMillan made the U.S. team for an amazing six Olympic contests, winning a Gold Medal in 1960. The stated reason for his cant was that it accommodated cross-dominance, allowing the champion to use his left eye while firing right-handed. If this were true, then it was still shooting at a specific range, allowing the sights to be set to accommodate the cant.

So, by the 1960s, at least a few shooters were leaning their guns at least a bit to the side. It would be assumed that canting was a technique for the experts, firing in competition at known ranges. The use of canting as a technique would seem to have little application for the deer hunter's rifle or the policeman's sidearm.

However, the 1960s also saw a big growth in what is now known as Practical Shooting. Buy the late 1970s, several academies had opened to teach people the techniques of practical pistol shooting.

At least one of these reportedly advises that a leftward tilt of the shooting hand (assuming a right-handed shooter) is not necessarily a bad thing for stabilizing a pistol. Sort of like pointing your finger, I imagine—few people naturally point their fingers with the hand upright; the hand is generally angled to the left. Reportedly, some law-enforcement agencies teach this sort of canted hold when an officer is shooting with one hand.

But even the tilted pistols of a few target shooters and some law-enforcement personnel do not compare with the horizontal sideways shooting of today's combatants on film.

With some obvious theoretical disadvantages, would anyone actually use sideways shooting in real life? Life, it seems, really might imitate what passes for art. Massad Ayoob, writing in January 1998, had already documented three actual cases in which sideways shooting had been used in violent confrontations.

The actual use of this method in real life brings up another point: Most of today's film bad guys use semiautomatic pistols, and the autoloader is now in common use by law officers, real bad guys and by us ordinary people. Most semiautomatic pistols are designed to work in a normal vertical position. In addition, virtually all autoloading pistols feed up-and-forward and eject up-and-right. Righ-hand ejection is almost universal because most people are right-handed. Statistically, one would assume most bad guys, including film bad guys, are also right-handed.

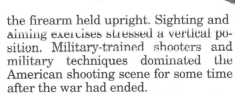

A sort of lunging thrust of the sideways pistol can shoot creditably at short ranges, but there are problems.

So, when a right-handed person fires a semiautomatic pistol horizontally instead of vertically, then the feed angle is changed from up-and-forward to left-and-forward; ejection angle is changed from up-and-right to up-and-left.

Will these changes create malfunctions—failures to feed or failures to eject?

With these aspects of functioning included, the questions about sideways shooting in our knowledgeable shooters' minds probably boil down to these two:

1. Can you hit anything?
2. Will the gun work?

The only way to find out, it seemed, was to try it.

How would one start out? Range should be short, for the sideways shooting method would only be used at relatively short range. Ten yards seemed about right, and at that range, the standard NRA 10-meter air pistol target (B32) would be an appropriate target. The horizontal and vertical lines of scoring-ring values would give an indication of deviation from a horizontal or vertical plane.

It seemed reasonable to eliminate as many variables as possible. All shooting would be done single-action, with the pistol held by only one hand. The sights would be used, and at 6 o'clock hold (3 o'clock for sideways shooting) would provide consistency.

This would not be a test of the accuracy of the gun or the ammunition (or, fortunately, of the ability of the shooter). The object would be to get representative groups in a relatively short time period. The cadence to be used would be about like that of a Rapid-Fire string in conventional pistol shooting—five shots in ten seconds.

The procedure would be to shoot groups with the pistol in the upright position, then record the group size and distance from the actual point of aim at the bottom edge of the bull. Then, the same pistol with the same ammunition would be fired sideways. Group size and distance from point of aim would be recorded. These figures could be compared.

Real-life guns would be used, just as they became available. Unless the pistol would not group on the paper with the ammunition at hand, sights would not be changed. If a pistol did not shoot to point of aim, it did not really matter. The object was to compare the relative size and position of the groups.

In addition, notes on failures to feed or eject would be made, and observations on recoil would be kept.

What gun to use?

Certainly, a Colt 1911 design should be included in any selection and perhaps should, indeed, lead off. The Browning-designed Colt 1911 design is considered one of the great pistols of all time. In this investigation, it was the first tried. The gun used was a Colt Government Model, Series 70, an unaltered 45 ACP commercial pistol.

The upright group from the Colt measured 2-1/2 inches center-to-center. The center of the group was about 1-1/2 inches low and left from the point of aim.

The 45 was then fired sideways at the 3 o'clock aiming point. The group opened up to 3-1/4 inches, perhaps because of my lack of familiarity with this hold. The group was slightly low and right of the point of aim; in other words, it was in about the same position relative to the bull and the sights as the upright group had been.

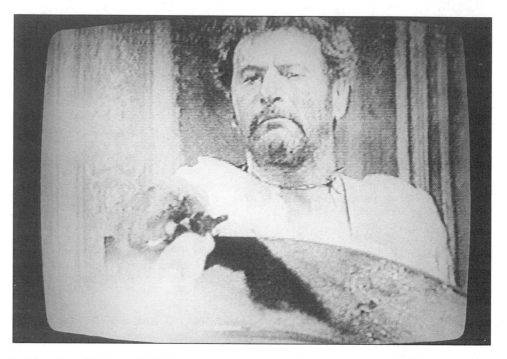

Is this where it all began? In this screen capture, Tuco (Eli Wallach) shoots sideways over a swinging door to finish off a film adversary in the 1966 hit motion picture, THE GOOD, THE BAD, AND THE UGLY.

With the sideways hold, I noted that the empties zip across the front of the shooter, angling down and to the left, and are a bit distracting. My first note on the recoil said it "feels funny."

I was beginning to learn things.

Could we favor the Colt without representing its archrival, Smith & Wesson? The next pistol tried was a S&W 645, using the same lot of ammunition that had been used in the Colt. The sights on the 645 put the upright group high and slightly left, running 2-3/8 inches in diameter and about 2-3/4 inches from point of aim.

The sideways group measured 3-1/4 inches, with the group (as would now be expected) low and left of the bull, with the center again about 2-3/4 inches from point of aim. The cases ejected also across the shooter down and to the left. Not a big distraction, they did take some attention away from the job at hand.

The 9mm Luger has become one of today's most popular handgun cartridges. To give us an idea of how a 9mm pistol behaves, I tried an Egyptian Helwan in that caliber. The open-slide Helwan is a remanufacture of the Beretta 951 (1951) single-action pistol. The rights of manufacture were transferred to Egypt when Beretta changed its production to the newer double-action, high-capacity pistols.

The Helwan shot a 2 inch upright group, mostly in the black, with center about an inch above point of aim. The sideways group was also a two incher and about an inch low and left of the 3 o'clock point of aim. All shots struck below the horizontal line of the target formed by the scoring ring numbers. Although this can not be considered of any great importance, it is a reminder that the force of gravity has an effect on the bullets, even at this short range.

By now, I had realized a basic difference of the sideways hold. In the upright hold, the sights are always above the hand. In the sideways hold, the hand moves around and up until the main portion of the hand is actually above the sights. This requires a break in the wrist so that the eye can see the sights. The absence of a straight wrist means that the recoil effect will try to break the wrist further, kicking down against the thumb. By the time I had finished with the Helwan, I was feeling the effects of the recoil on my thumb.

Up to now, I had fired three guns that had ejected up-and-right, so that when held sideways, the ejection port was up-and-left. They then ejected to the left across the shooter. It would be nice to evaluate a gun with ejection port down, but that would mean holding the pistol left-handed, which would add another variable.

Unless, of course, the gun ejected to the left when held upright!

The venerable Walther P38 is one of the few centerfire pistols that ejects to the left, so a P38 performed the next test.

The World War II pistol used, made by Walther in 1941, turned in a respectable two inch group, 1-1/4 inch above point of aim, which meant all shots were in the black. Sideways was not much worse at 2-1/2 inches with three shots in the black and two out at three o'clock. Cases flew down to hit the bench hard, at a diagonal in front of the shooter. By now, I didn't know if the cumulative effect of the strange recoil vectors was getting to me, but my right thumb felt the recoil noticeably. The gun felt as if it wanted to twist in my hand past the thumb.

The big three in centerfire pistol calibers in Ameria now are the 45 ACP, the 9mm Luger and the 40 Smith & Wesson. A newcomer introduced only in 1990, the 40 S&W has definitely carved a niche for itself in a short period of time. It appeals to, among others, those who can't make up their minds between the 45 and the 9. I needed to include a 40.

I used a Heritage Stealth C-4000, a 40-caliber pistol. In the interest of trying

several different actions as well as calibers, the Stealth fit perfectly. Unlike the previous four pistols, the slide is unlocked, but is retarded in its rearward movement by a gas delay system under the barrel.

The Stealth turned in the smallest group of the entire series, 1-3/8 inches in diameter and two inches above point of aim. Over on its side, the 3 o'clock hold put the bullets into a group of 2-5/8 inches. The group was 2-1/2 inches left of the point of aim.

The sideways hold with this light pistol allows the gun to kick noticeably down and left. The Pachmayr grip furnished with the gun may have helped, but my thumb still felt the recoil effect. In upright position, ejection was almost due right. When held sideways, cases

were launched almost straight up and hit the roof of the firing point shelter.

A blowback pistol had not been tried yet. A Bulgarian Makarov was called to duty to see how it would do. The Bulgarian Makarov is made by the Arsenal firm in Bulgaria. This one came in 9mm Makarov caliber, a cartridge that is actually slightly larger in diameter than a true 9mm. Because of the availability of the Makarov pistols, this cartridge has recently become something of a standard round for American shooters.

The upright group was a respectable 1-3/4 inches, printing about 3-1/2 inches above point of aim. The sideways group was not much different, measuring 1-5/8 inches (actually a slightly smaller group than that fired upright). It entered the target centered about 3 inches from point of aim. As noted with the Helwan, all shots fired sideways reached the target below the horizontal line formed by the score numbers.

You may recall that one of the things I planned to list for each pistol was functioning problems. I have not mentioned functioning with the individual pistols because my list was blank. Every pistol functioned fine, either upright or sideways. I had even fired the P38, a pistol that ejected from the opposite side, and it had presented no malfunctions.

True, though, they had all been fired from the right hand. Would shooting then from the left hand make a difference? Left-handed shooting would introduce another variable, but I would have to give it a try. I selected the Colt, the P38 and the Makarov to give me a vari-

ety of systems to try out from a left-hand hold.

The Colt, fired upright from my left hand, turned in a so-so group of 3 inches (four decent shots with one flyer), with the center of the group located about 2 inches from the 6 o'clock point of aim. Turning sideways, to the 9 o'clock

position now, the group opened up to a somewhat shameful 4-1/2 inches, with the center being about 1-1/2 inches high. I can blame the unfamiliar hold for the poor group, but noted that the placement of the group on the target was about what I had expected.

Recoil effect with this weak-hand sideways hold was very much in evidence. Subjectively, it felt much heavier than when the pistol was held and fired in the right hand.

Next, I prepared to fire the P38 with my left hand. Five upright rounds went into 2-1/4 inches, not much wider than the right-hand group. However, three clustered at the point of aim, while two went up into the black.

Sideways, now with a 9 o'clock hold, the group opened up to 3-3/8 inches, clustered about 1-1/2 inches low and right. It was getting to be repetitious, but I made a note that the recoil bothered my thumb, my left one this time.

The Makarov had its turn in the left hand next, and put five rounds into 2-3/4 inches, printing about 2 inches above point of aim. Turned sideways into a 9 o'clock hold, the Makarov interestingly produced a slightly smaller group, just as it had done during the right-hand shooting. Possibly the sideways position of the hand might have changed the position of my index finger on this particular trigger and somehow gave me better trigger control. I made a note to give

In a traditional hold a Colt Government Model 45's sights and barrel are aligned in the same plane as the shooter's wrist and forearm. The pull of gravity is also in the same plane.

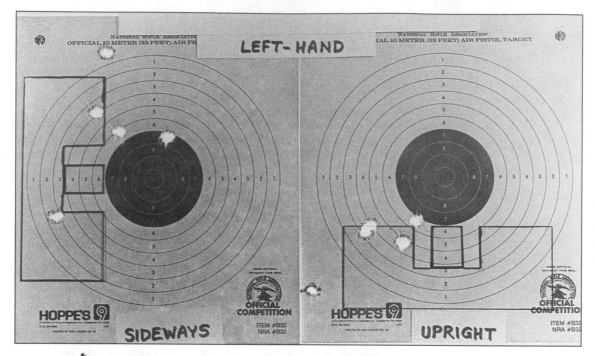

When the Colt Government Model was fired upright from the left hand, the grouping of the upright group (here, the right target) was not bad, if we discount the one wide shot. The left-hand sideways group was the widest of the series.

The first pistol tried with the sideways shooting technique was a Colt Government Model Series 70 45.

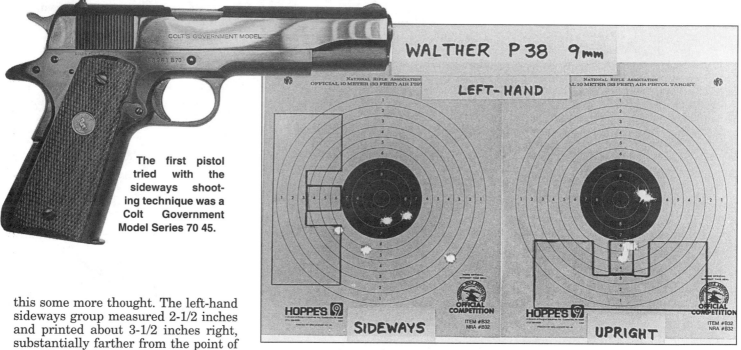

Left-hand shots with the Walther P38 had the same general point of impact on the target, but those fired sideways did not form as good a group as those fired upright. Neither group was as good as its counterpart fired with the right hand.

this some more thought. The left-hand sideways group measured 2-1/2 inches and printed about 3-1/2 inches right, substantially farther from the point of aim. Recoil during the firing of the Makarov sideways from the left-hand was very noticeable, kicking down (toward the ground) and right.

Again, there were no malfunctions with any of the pistols during the left-hand tests. However, recoil had begun to play a large role in this investigation when the sideways shooting began, and this factor deserves some thought.

Beginning pistol shooters are generally taught to keep the gun straight and in line with their forearm. However, with the pistol held sideways, the arm and wrist cannot be straight.

Careful measurements showed that with an erect head position and the pistol held sideways, the angle between this shooter's arm and the line

from the eye to the pistol is about 23 degrees.

Even with a low head position, the sort used in a sort of lunging crouch, pushing the gun forward, the wrist is still bent, with the arm at an angle of about 15 degrees to the line of sight and the pistol.

When shooting sideways, then, recoil thus operates in an unusual way.

The Walther P38 is one of the few centerfire pistols that ejects to the left. This World War II specimen was fired both right- and left-handed.

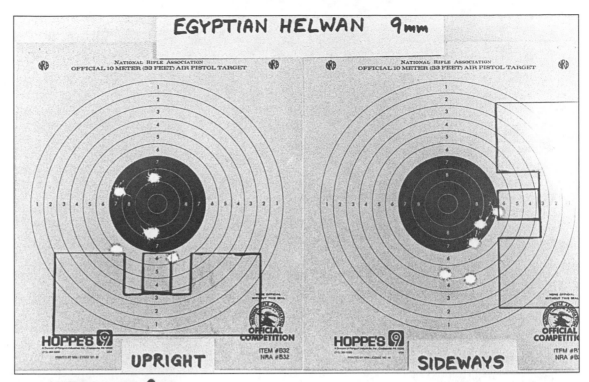

EGYPTIAN HELWAN 9mm

UPRIGHT

SIDEWAYS

The Helwan grouped just over the relative point of aim with both upright and sideways holds. The stringing of shots toward the ground on the sideways target is probably not due to gravity effect at this short range, but this sort of pattern might be expected at longer ranges.

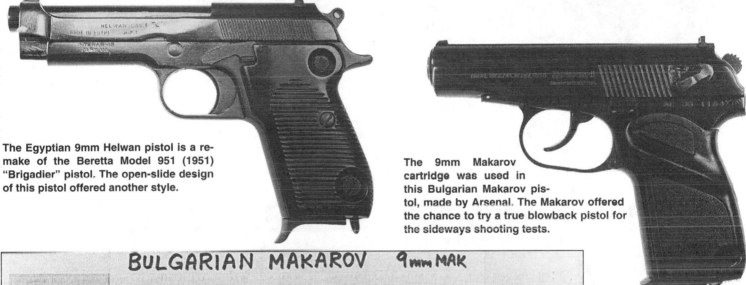

The Egyptian 9mm Helwan pistol is a remake of the Beretta Model 951 (1951) "Brigadier" pistol. The open-slide design of this pistol offered another style.

The 9mm Makarov cartridge was used in this Bulgarian Makarov pistol, made by Arsenal. The Makarov offered the chance to try a true blowback pistol for the sideways shooting tests.

BULGARIAN MAKAROV 9mm MAK

UPRIGHT

SIDEWAYS

The Makarov grouped high with the upright hold. As we would expect, the sideways group was to the left, or "high" relative to the sights. Surprisingly, the sideways group was smaller than the upright group.

The Smith & Wesson Model 645 45-caliber pistol's adjustable sights were not resighted for sideways shooting at 10 yards.

Instead of moving the pistol up and back, it attempts to move the sideways-shooting pistol (when held in the right hand) left and back. The rearward force vector puts more pressure on the already awkwardly-bent wrist, which then tends to "break" the angle to a larger one.

Added to this is the fact that gravity wants to pull the left side of the pistol down.

The result is a strange motion toward the ground that is resisted to a great extent by the thumb, because the hand and most of all the other fingers are on top of the grip.

It is difficult to recover rapidly from this unusual recoil pattern-a combination of rearward, leftward and downward forces. I was unable to consistently shoot the 5-shot sideways groups in the 10 seconds I had arbitrarily allotted. Within each five-shot sequence, my thumb was already beginning to notice

back to 1911 with that definition) apparently will work just as well sideways as upright, whether the ejection is up or down.

Yes, you can hit something. A single shot fired sideways is probably inherently as accurate as one fired from the traditional upright vertical hold. At short ranges on large targets, the difference in point of impact is measurable, but is probably of little consequence. In this informal testing, none of the pistols had been sighted in for this range. Yet, during the entire series, all shots hit the 7x8-inch targets; only six shots hit outside the 6-inch scoring rings. Even the largest group (left-hand sideways with the Colt 45) would have fit within the center ring of the Bianchi Cup D1 "tombstone" target.

For a specific longer range, the rear sight of an adjustable-sight handgun could be set to compensate. Eventually, the sight would run out of adjustment and be unable to compensate for the sideways position. I think most shooters would lose interest long before that point. Although the guns will work sideways and hit nearby targets, the sideways method has some other, not inconsiderable, drawbacks. For one, two-hand hold is pretty much out of the question, so that practical accuracy may be less without the two-hand option. Also, reloading the pistol is more difficult, and takes longer to accomplish, for the pistol must first be returned to the upright position to begin the traditional reloading procedures.

The biggest drawback is difficult recovery from recoil. A first shot might be fired with adequate accuracy, but successive aimed shots will take substantially more time than with the upright method. The need to hurry can create poor shooting.

The Heritage Stealth C-4000 offered a chance to try a pistol chambered for the 40 S&W cartridge. It also provided a new action type, a gas-delayed blowback system.

the punishment. In contrast, recovery with the upright groups was normal and painless, and shooting was able to stay within the time set.

So, now, on the basis of these simple tests of sideways shooting, what have we learned about this technique?

Yes, the gun will work sideways. Modern semiautomatic pistols (and I'm going

All in all, the sideways technique has no advantages for the average shooter over the traditional upright hold. And the disadvantages of shooting sideways could be serious, particularly in a life-and-death situation.

On reflection, though, maybe sideways shooting is not really such a bad thing. Perhaps we should be thankful that show business is portraying sideways shooting as something cool for their make-believe bad guys to do. Perhaps more real-life criminals will adopt the technique. That might give law-enforcement officers and the rest of us honest citizens a bit, at least a little bit, of an edge. •

Contemporary drawing of a "humane" mantrap in action, both device and drawing from 1890.

SET GUNS AND MANTRAPS IN OLD BLIGHTY

BETWEEN AROUND 1710 and 1820, rural life in Britain was obsessed with the defense of property. The property in question in the alleged democracy of the time was essentially landed estates and associated farmlands, and the game that abounded therein. Property was seen as the symbol of an ordered society, and harsh laws reflected a view that theft or trespass was not merely criminal but practically revolutionary. It was thus deemed acceptable that what we would now term "private security systems" need pay no heed to the life or limb of trespassers. In consequence, stately home and manor house alike, squire, farmer... even parson, took extraordinary measures to protect their private domains.

Gamekeepers, water bailiffs, and farmhands were not numerous enough to protect the larger estates which

By Mike Crow

might have boundaries miles long around thousands of acres. As a direct consequence and before long, they found unexpected assistance from a whole array of automatic devices which combined elements of surprise and ruthlessness. Many of these had much in common with the modern landmine and similar anti-personnel weapons.

The most extensively used device to protect woodlands, coverts, and estate lands generally, was the so-called "spring gun" or "trap gun". The main purpose was to protect game against human predators, though sanctimoniously it was sometimes claimed they could be used against vermin. Actually, this was quite correct since no essential differences were made between poachers and vermin anyway. Sometimes indeed relatively innocent trespassers did inadvertently become targets, but this was usually brushed aside on a "Well, he shouldn't have been there, anyway" basis.

Some of these unpleasant weapons were still in use in Britain in the late 1800s. They could be aimed along paths favoured by poachers, and normally were loaded with a charge equivalent to a modern 12-bore shotgun, usually based on powder and buckshot.

A drawing here shows a typical example from around 1810. The base spike was driven into the ground to anchor the device, and the trip wire (in practice often of considerable length, or having several strands fanned out) is passed via a support at the muzzle, back to the trigger lever, in a manner that any disturbance or pull on the wire would swivel the gun towards the source of the disturbance. This model fired with a percussion cap. Earlier models had flintlock mechanisms, but these were soon dis-

This 18th-Century flintlock spring gun swiveled to shoot wherever the wire was pulled - at least three different directions.

carded because the powder in the flashpan would inevitably be spoiled by damp. Barrels were the 'turn-off' type; that is, easily unscrewed for easy loading and cleaning.

The Trail Gun was another and smaller type, built on the scale of a miniature cannon, particularly favoured for setting up along woodland pathways. Variations included spring guns with barbed levers extending from the trigger mechanism, designed to catch in clothing and to react to the slightest touch. The iron rod "cannon ball" had a fearsome reputation as a close-quarter missile.

However, farmers, being perhaps a little less trigger-happy than the landowning gentry, soon discovered there were other ways of discouraging unwelcome visitors without planning their premature demise. By 1820, a range of explosive but non-lethal alarms was available. Their purpose was to make the maximum possible din accompanied by a flash of pyrotechnic dimensions, thus warning the farmer's household that something was amiss, and the intruder that it was time to depart.

These powder-operated alarms, triggered in much the same way as the spring guns were no doubt the forerunners of modern bird scarers, We show one of the many designs of the period. The heavy iron base could be screwed or chained to barn doors, gates or cowsheds. At one end is a substantial cylindrical chamber, fitted with an equally weighty iron hinged lid. The cylinder

would be filled with black powder, a percussion cap fitted, and the firing hammer and trigger mechanism cocked. The lid on the chamber would be closed. In the particular model illustrated, a trigger and separate trip

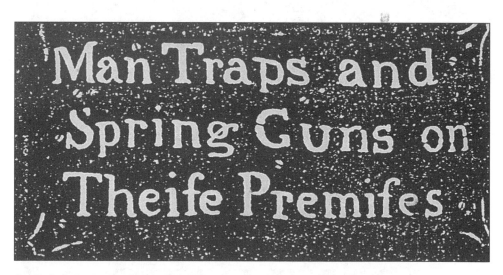

Such signs were actually posted. This one was still on a barn in Warwickshire in 1912 or so.

wire extended on both sides, for a second wire across a gate or doorway. Theoretically these devices were just alarms, but if an intruder were to be standing close to the very substantial explosion more than surprise could be inflicted. Some farmers were known to prime the powder with a few rusty nails as an extra discouragement. Many of these explosive gadgets have survived and are now collectors pieces.

A somewhat more delicate example of a security device was the once fairly common walking-stick gun, more usually known at the time as a cane gun. A personal armament this, not actuated by blind chance and a trip wire. Not used much by farmers, either, but a handy disguised weapon and comforting companion for our typical country squire of the time on lonely walks through his woods and estate. Some early versions date prior to 1760, and they were popular to c. 1880. Modern versions with overtones of James Bond are occasionally encountered, but these early examples were of very limited accuracy and range, and, of course, restricted to the single shot. They did

Simple real-world cane gun from later on - it shoots a centerfire cartridge, 24 gauge. No doubt quite useful.

present the user with one great advantage ... surprise. We illustrate one type. There were many variations. One, for example was most delicately designed so that the whole mechanism (lock, barrel, trigger, loaded with powder and shot) could be concealed wholly inside the cane itself, from which it could be drawn, when required, like a sword from its scabbard. The illustrated example is rather less elaborate, but is more typical.

The trigger normally lay flat against the cane's surface, ready to be lifted with a fingernail. This action would cock the gun. The tiny hammer, also

clogging of the barrel end when the cane was in normal use. One would presume that this was an accident waiting to happen, but I have no records of any disasters in this respect.

One of the most common, and certainly most barbaric, devices was the 17th-18th century man-trap. Right outside the orbit of trip-wire weapons, but extremely effective, and to use a modern phrase, cost-effective. Once set, all they needed was a regular inspection, to check if anything (or anyone!) was in the bag. Basically, they consisted of two curved, heavily toothed

the keeper himself carried the keys, that could have meant a long stay in the woods for the captive. Some of the toothed traps were up to 30 inches across the jaws, and required considerable force to set.

Even after 1820 there was considerable legal laxity about their legal prohibition. Could that possibly be be-

Cruder version of a spring gun, a little later, still follows the pattern, would shoot three ways—depending.

flush with the stem, could be similarly brought into firing position. On some types, this would cock the gun, instead of the trigger. The actual barrel would be of the turnoff type, removed earlier for priming with powder and shot before beginning an excursion. The open barrel end had a removable ferrule to take off before firing, thus preventing

Photos from Dorchester Museum. Rural History Centre, Birmingham University.

steel jaws, operated by powerful springs, suitably camouflaged, and set to lie open at ground level. Pressure on a flat metal plate at their center operated the trap. They were legal in Britain up to 1820.

Actually, in the early 19th century, a so-called humane man-trap was introduced. This was the same as the toothed version, in all respects, except that it had parallel steel bars without teeth. The snag was that it could in no way be opened, as it locked automatically in the closed position, and as only

cause the law-makers themselves were usually landowners? Even by 1827 the law regarded the use of this equipment only as a 'misdemeanor'...gentlemanly language reflecting some judicial smugness in the matter of poachers versus landowners. Not until 1861 was the big man-trap finally completely outlawed. We show a rather unusual version, with squared spiked jaws, instead of the more common toothed semicircular models.

These were indeed drastic measures, even for the 1700s and 1800s, but per-

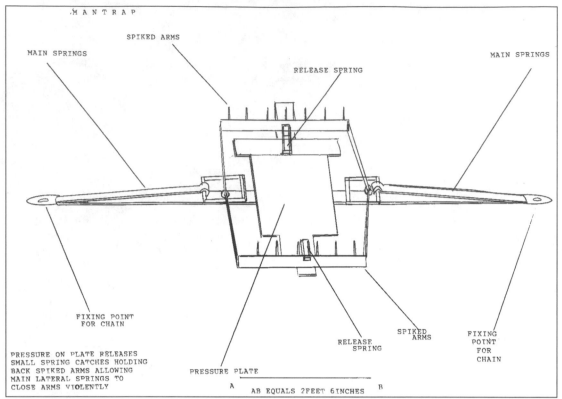

MANTRAP

MAIN SPRINGS
SPIKED ARMS
RELEASE SPRING
MAIN SPRINGS

FIXING POINT
FOR CHAIN

SPIKED
ARMS

FIXING
POINT
FOR
CHAIN

RELEASE
SPRING

PRESSURE ON PLATE RELEASES
SMALL SPRING CATCHES HOLDING
BACK SPIKED ARMS ALLOWING
MAIN LATERAL SPRINGS TO
CLOSE ARMS VIOLENTLY

PRESSURE PLATE

A AB EQUALS 2 FEET 6 INCHES B

Layout of the worst sort of mantrap, used in a different world.

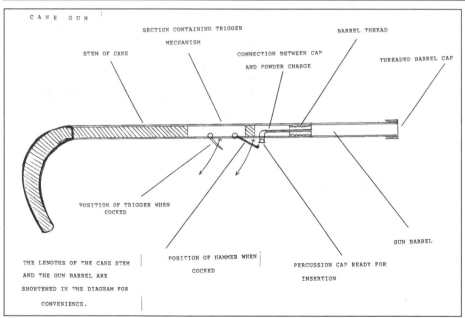

CANE GUN

SECTION CONTAINING TRIGGER
MECHANISM

BARREL THREAD

STEM OF CANE

CONNECTION BETWEEN CAP
AND POWDER CHARGE

THREADED BARREL CAP

POSITION OF TRIGGER WHEN
COCKED

GUN BARREL

THE LENGTHS OF THE CANE STEM
AND THE GUN BARREL ARE
SHORTENED IN THE DIAGRAM FOR
CONVENIENCE.

POSITION OF HAMMER WHEN
COCKED

PERCUSSION CAP READY FOR
INSERTION

How a percussion walking stick gun was laid out (some parts shortened). It does look like an accident in route to a site.

This is a humane mantrap since the jaws had no teeth and for the most part only break bones.

haps, as ever, it was natural for the "haves" to protect their property from the rest. Sometimes, of course, fate steps in to even things up. I have been reading a news story in a rural newspaper of the early 1800s. It tells the story of the gamekeeper on a local estate, who, whilst checking his traps, fouled one of his own trip wires. He had obviously done a good job in laying out his spring-guns and did not live to comment. There's nothing more I can add. ●

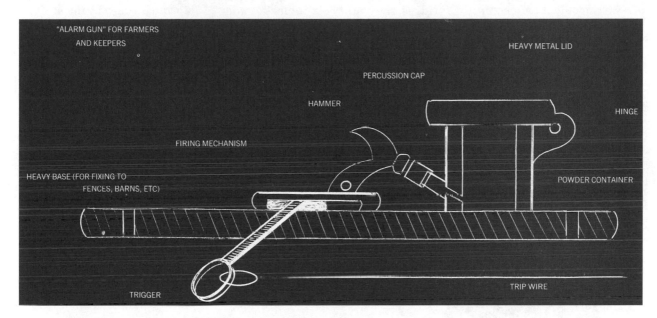

Alarm gun was not so positively lethal—sort of a permanent firecracker set off by a trip wire.

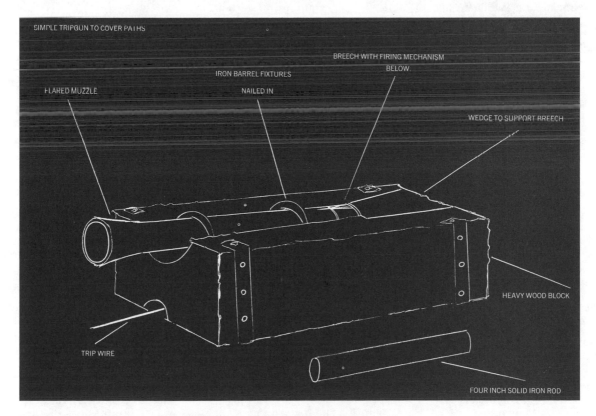

Trail gun—very simple and stout. The iron rod? That's what it shot!

BRITISH SPORTING rifle ammunition makers of the late 19th and early 20th century knew their business. Companies like Eley, Kynoch, and National Arms and Ammunition Company were providing sporting ammunition to a demanding and discerning clientele. These were the days of Empire when the British flag flew over a quarter of the earth's surface. The territories under British rule or patronage included the best hunting to be had in Africa, India, Canada, and other prime hunting areas. Game abounded and the British administrator or soldier had hunting opportunities which we can only imagine. Most took with them their battery of rifles, sometimes from top makers, but often from the lesser makers who could provide quality products for the less well off.

Britain was a democracy in those days and governments respected the Common Law right to keep arms. Railways had opened the Scottish highlands to deer stalkers and grouse

sway by an hysterical media. The number of gunmakers is now down to a few well-known names whose total annual production would have been exceeded in any week in the 1880s. British centerfire metallic ammunition is no more and handloaders must turn to the former colonies for their products and expertise.

Britain was to the fore in the development of breechloading sporting arms, though the repeating rifle owes more to the United States than to Britain. The key to the successful British ammunition was the design of cartridges, the quality of the blackpowder available, and the very sophisticated bullets developed to give the best results within the limitations of blackpowder cartridges.

Blackpowder rifles and their cartridges fell into fairly clear categories. At the lower end were the rook rifles, low powered rifles for use against rabbits, birds and smaller game animals.

Initially, there was no alternative to blackpowder so the term "Black Powder Express" was not used until nitro powders came along. After that there were three categories: "Black Powder Express," "Nitro for Black" and then "Nitro Express." Blackpowder rifles in good condition could be used with "nitro for black" cartridges, but the nitro express cartridges were properly reserved for rifles made for them.

Express cartridges used longer cases to provide additional velocity and energy. The 577 Express used a 3-inch case as opposed to the 2-inch pipsqueak used by the military in their 577 Snider rifle. With 167 grains of blackpowder, the Express pushed a 570-grain copper-tubed bullet along at 1725 feet per second. The 500 Express was usually in the 3-1/4-inch case pushing a 440-grain copper-tubed bullet at 1775 fps.

The most popular all-round Express was the 450 with its 3-1/4-inch

The Three Sixty Express

Alexander Henry's external hammer falling block rifle. This one has a left-hand lock with a safety bolt behind the hammer.

by Colin Greenwood

shooters, but even in lowland areas rifles were extensively used in pursuit of more humble quarry. An Englishman could buy and own whatever rifle he wanted and large numbers of them did. The idea that gun ownership was somehow limited to the "gentry" is dispelled by examining any gunmaker's catalogue of the day. All of them offered very low price rifles and shotguns as well as their "best" grades.

Today, the Empire has gone and democracy has been so far diminished that politicians facing an election can ban handguns in the hope of gaining a few more votes from a populace held in

They ran from .250-inch to .380-inch in calibre, but delivered pistol level energies. The 360 and 380 rook rifles were much used in India and Africa against the very smallest deer and antelope.

Express cartridges were designed to use blackpowder to its limits. A check of catalogues of the late 19th century will show that Express rifles were almost standardized to 360, 450, 500 and 577 calibres. Above them, at the top of the tree, came the really big boys, the 12-bore to 4-bore rifles used only against the largest game such as elephants.

case containing 120 grains of blackpowder and using bullets of from 120 grains to 270 grains. Three bullet designs were available. The copper-tubed bullet was for general use and reports in *The Field* in 1885 praised the effect of this 450 bullet against elk and grizzly bear as well as against smaller game. Bullets with a small hollow point were available for larger game against which the copper tubed bullet might over-expand, and solid lead bullets were available for penetration at short ranges.

The smallest of the true Express cartridges was the 360 Express or 360 x 2-1/4 inch which used 50 grains of blackpowder to push bullets of from 123 grains to 215 grains. This is one of the earliest centerfire sporting cartridges. An 1884 Kynoch catalogue[1], illustrates a drawn brass 360 Express, but a coiled brass version pre-dates that, possibly by 20 years. The early coiled brass cartridge used a very light 123-grain paper-covered (or paper-patched) bullet ahead of 50 grains of black. The bullet is hollow point, but has a wooden plug in the hollow point to aid expansion. Expansion of soft lead bullets, even with hollowpoints, has always been unpredictable at blackpowder velocities and this light bullet with its wood plugged point seems to be an early recognition of that.

When the cartridge settled down to its drawn brass version, we find three common loadings, each of them with 50 grains of blackpowder, but with a solid lead 215-grain bullet, a 190-grain copper-tubed bullet or a 155-grain hollowpoint.

The 360 Nitro for Black was most commonly available with 22 grains of cordite pushing a 190-grain bullet at 1650 feet per second. The bullet was of sophisticated design, being "metal based"—it used a gas check—and copper-tubed. The final version of this cartridge was the 360 x 2-1/4-inch Nitro Express which used a long "metal covered" (jacketed) soft-nosed or split-nosed bullet of 300 grains at 1650 feet per second.

Dimensionally the 360 x 2-1/4 inch was close to the 38-55 Winchester, the latter having a case about 1/8 inch shorter and having a thicker rim than the later 360s.

One of the most important features of all these Express cartridges was in the design of the bullets. The "copper-tubed" bullet was common to all the Express cartridges of this era and the importance of this bullet seems to be lost to modern students and manufacturers. Externally, the bullet seems to have a small cap of copper in its nose, but examination of a sectioned bullet shows just how clever this design was in the context of a bullet for the limited velocities attainable with blackpowder. The bullets have a nose cavity of enormous proportions and one that could not be sustained in its open form. The cavity is filled by a copper tube, open at the bottom end but finished at the top with a cap, the edges of which extend beyond the tube. This capped tube would deform the bullet in a predictable fashion, creating mushrooming which was probably as good as that of modern softpoints.

360 Express rifles were made in single and double barrel versions, the doubles and many of the singles being break-open but other singles using British falling block actions. The quality of the rifles varied from inexpensive break-open singles to the very best and most expensive doubles. In our examination of this cartridge, we looked at three rifles.

The first and earliest of the rifles was a single barrel break-open built on the Jones rotary under-level of 1859. The patent on this excellent early action was allowed to expire in 1862 and the system became public property and was widely used throughout the British gun trade on guns of all qualities. The rifle is marked on the top rib "H HOLLAND, 98 NEW BOND ST LONDON". Harris Holland set up as a gunmaker in 1853 and moved to the New Bond Street address in 1860. In 1867 the firm

ing on the sides of the action, lever, trigger guard and top strap. Whilst the rifle is sound, it was not of the "best" quality and would be relatively inexpensive. It has certainly seen a lot of use. External finish is well worn and it has a patina of age. The bore is pitted overall with a couple of quite rough places, but it has plenty of rifling left.

The only indication of calibre is the 105 stamped amongst the proof marks. This is "105 bore." That works out at 0.354 inch diameter for the tube before rifling. Slugging the barrel gave us a straight 0.370-inch groove diameter. As was common at the time, there is nothing to tell us which cartridge this was made for. There were several 360s

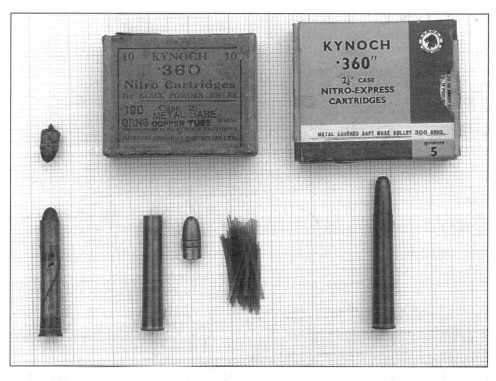

360 Express cartridges. The coiled brass case at left is an early example, uses a 123-grain paper patched bullet with a wooden plug in the hollow point. The box of 360 Express nitro for black cartridges shows one round intact, a second broken down to show the gas checked, copper-tubed bullet and the charge of cordite. The remaining load is the 360 Nitro Express with 300-grain jacketed soft point bullet.

became Holland and Holland. We can therefore date the rifle between 1862 when the Jones patent lapsed and 1867 with the change of name. It is probably toward the early part of that date bracket.

The rifle has pre-1887 Birmingham proof marks and these, together with the fact that the name was on the barrel but not on the lock, tell us that the gun was made in the Birmingham trade and retailed by Holland. It has a 28-inch slightly tapered octagonal barrel with a file-cut top surface, stand and two-fold rearsight and bead foresight. The action is a boxlock with an exposed central hammer. There is simple engrav-

about a little later, but a chamber cast made it clear that this was 360 x 2-1/4 inch. A check with coiled brass cartridges showed that this early rifle had used a thick rimmed case.

Our second rifle in 360 Express is a magnificent Alexander Henry falling block with its outside hammer. That rifle was patented in 1865 and a military version was submitted to the British War Office but failed against the Martini Henry, though it was adopted for military use elsewhere (New South Wales, for example). Sporting rifles were produced on this action in several calibers and qualities. The address shown on the rib is 12 South Street, An-

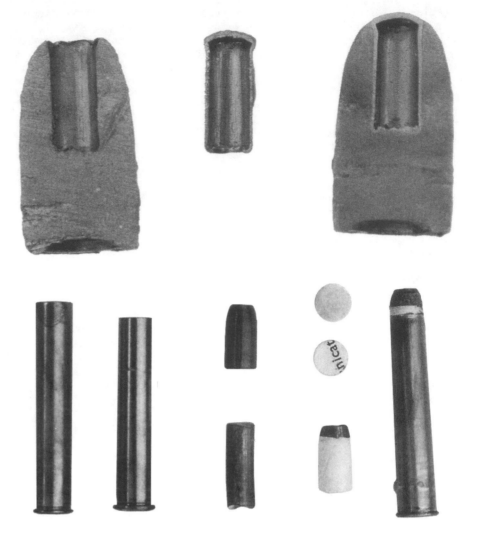

The copper-tubed bullet has an enormous cavity in the point and the tube is swaged into place. The tube is shown separately. Its cap extends beyond the hollow point. Expansion must have been excellent even at blackpowder velocities.

Left to right, a 360 x 2 inch case, a 38-55 case, a 190-grain lead core before swaging, the swaged core, the paper patched bullet and the loaded 360 Express nitro for black round.

drew Street, Edinburgh where Henry was until 1870. Jonathan Kirton in *The British Falling Block Breech Loading Rifle*[2] tells us that a rifle with a serial number one removed from ours was retailed in 1870, so we can be confident about the date of manufacture. The latest author to deal with these rifles, Walter G.Winfer[3], wrongly calls the 360 Express a rook rifle. There was a 360 Rook Rifle, a cartridge closely resembling 38 Special in size and power, but that is not an Express Rifle cartridge.

The Henry rifle is of top quality. It has a 25-inch octagonal barrel with a stand and two-fold rearsight and a tiny silver bead foresight. The action and lockplate are tastefully engraved overall and the hammer has a sliding bolt to lock it at half-cock. An original folding peepsight is fitted integral with the top tang, which is cut away for the adjusting wheel so that the sight lies flat

A magnificent Charles Lancaster double rifle originally made in 360 Express, possibly for his own extended cartridge. It has since been converted to 22 Hornet.

when folded. It has very pretty woodwork and everything about the rifle shouts quality. The rifle bears the Birmingham proof marks with 105 as the only indication of caliber. Checking with original cartridges shows that the action will not close on thick-rim cartridges, or on modern 38-55 rounds, but glides shut on original drawn brass 360 x 2-1/4 inch rounds and on the modern Bertram cases from Australia. The rifle has seen some ser-

vice and the barrel has lost much of its external finish to a patina of age, but the bore is still sound.

The third rifle is included for academic purposes only. It is a best quality double express non-ejector boxlock rifle built by Charles Lancaster in 1896. It has an assisted opening action. When the top lever is operated, spring loaded cams in the bottom of the action body kick the rifle fully open. Ejectors were available at the time, but many users preferred not to have them. Merely tipping the rifle sideways as it was opened threw the cases out of a non-ejector and the loud click which ejectors make was thought undesirable. The rifle's 26-inch barrels had Lancaster's patent oval bore rifling. It carries top quality engraving, even down to the Lyman peep sight which has been engraved *en suite*. The figured walnut stock has a cheekpiece, chequered rounded hand,

and integral buttplate. The safety has a locking bolt in the form of a tiny lever which must be pushed aside before the safety can be released. This is a very best quality double rifle built specifically for the 360 Express.

The Rules of Proof had changed when this rifle was built and the proof marks show it as a "360 Exp." The maker has added marks of his own showing that it is "360CF 2-3/8 case 72 grs No 6." Lancaster stressed in his catalogues that the correct powder was Curtis and Harvey's No 6, and we found that a 2-1/4 inch case filled to the top would hold only 64 grains of powder even using a long drop tube, but without compression. The extra powder in the 72-grain charge required another 3/16ths of an inch of case. We were using modern solid head cases and Lancaster might have been using balloon heads which would allow a bit more powder, but even allowing for that, Lancaster's charge could not have been loaded into a standard 2-1/4 inch case and must have been heavily compressed in Lancaster's longer case.

In his *The History and Development of Small Arms Ammunition, Vol III*[4], George Hoyem mentions the 360 x 3-3/4 and 360 x 2-7/16 as unusual variants of the 360 Express, but does not mention a 360 x 2-3/8. Perhaps, like so many gunsmiths of the period, Lancaster had his own slight variation of the standard cartridge. In any case, the standard 360 x 2-1/4 inch cartridge would have fired without problems and it was for that cartridge that the gun was proofed.

We say that this rifle is mentioned for academic reasons only because it has since been converted to 22 Hornet by Parkerifling. It remains a superb rifle and some might say it is more practical in 22 Hornet, but a piece of history has been lost by the process. For the purposes of this article, the rifle demonstrates that the very best quality rifles were built in 360 Express.

We therefore had two rifles to load for, the early Holland and the slightly later Henry. We acquired 360 x 2-1/4 inch cases from Bruce Bertram in Australia[5], via his UK agent.

We also acquired some Winchester 38-55 cases. The latter had thicker rims and would chamber in the Holland rifle, but not in the Henry. The 38-55s were therefore to be loaded with blackpowder for the Holland, whilst the Bertram 360s were used for the nitro for black loads in the Henry.

It would have been possible to use 38-55 dies, but we had a three-die set of 360 x 2-1/4 inch made by North Devon Firearms Services[6]. Paper patched bullets were to be used and a swaging die, also from NDFS, created .358-inch round-nosed bullets. When patched, they would measure 0.370-inch as required. We swaged bullets of 123 and 155 grains for the blackpowder loads and 190 grains for the Nitro for Black.

Paper patching is an art that was almost lost until a few enthusiasts revived it. The patch should have angled ends and go around the bullet precisely two or three times, according to the thickness of the paper, with no overlap or shortfall. The purists advise paper with a high cotton content but, following advice from Paul Matthews in *The Paper Jacket*[7], we used computer paper which served very well. The patches need to be damped and we used a very thin Alox lubricant, spread on the patches whilst they were on a board. This holds them down whilst they are rolled tightly around the bullet.

Having looked at Victorian factory practices, we are quite certain that the job of patching bullets would be allocated to women whose fingers are much more nimble than those of the clumsy male. A detailed explanation of this theory failed entirely to recruit female assistance and the art was, of necessity, soon learned.

The first blackpowder loads used 50 grains of C & H No 6 with a single card wad behind the 123-grain bullet. The crimping die would not touch the case mouth of the shorter 38-55 cases and, after some experimenting, we settled on using a 9mm taper crimp die which turned in the case mouth perfectly.

The best way to produce good loads is via a chronograph. If the loads give consistent readings within the desired limits, they are likely to shoot well. We normally chronograph loads in a barn, shooting through a ring of tires to cut down the noise. The first shot gave just over 400 feet per second and the next just under 4,000. It took a moment or two to realize what was happening and in the meantime, the chronograph looked set for a nervous breakdown.

The paper patch begins to leave the bullet as it emerges from the muzzle and the distance from the muzzle to the chronograph was such that the patch-

Henry Holland's break-open center-hammer 360 Express rifle, with Jones rotary under-lever. It was probably inexpensive.

Holland's trade label from the rifle case—everyone sold rifles then.

es were passing over the sensors, sometime over only one and sometimes over both. Outdoor testing with an increased distance gave positive readings and the result was a real joy. Ten rounds varied from a low of 1395 to a high of 1491 with an average of 1450 feet per second with this light bullet load. There were no signs of pressure on the cap or case and the gun felt sweet.

Moving onto the 50 yard target destroyed the theory that a good chronograph result can be relied on to indicate good accuracy. Groups ran to as much as 12 inches, though most were a little smaller. The short bullets were printing cleanly with no signs of tumbling.

Those results suggested that we needed to get serious about loading for this rifle. Re-slugging the bore and measuring the paper patched bullets indicated that they were a good fit. We changed to the 155-grain bullet which would have been standard soon after the rifle was made. We continued with the 50-grain C & H No 6 charge but this time topped it with two thin card wads, a 1/8th inch wad of pure beeswax and topped that with another card wad before loading the bullet. This meant that the charge was compressed but Express charges were normally compressed tightly.

This was an improvement, if groups running to 9 inches at 50 yards can be so called. About one bullet in 10 was tumbling when it hit the target and it may be that we had missed the tumbling with the 123-grain bullet because it was so short. Other remedies came to mind—a deep hollow base to the bullet, an over-size bullet, and so on. The truth was that the old rifle is shot out. To make it shoot accurately would involve considerable work on the bore. Lapping the barrel seems unlikely to be sufficient and it would probably have to be re-cut, enlarging the bore a little. That could be combined with a 0.380-inch diameter "heeled" bullet with a very good chance of producing an accurate rifle/cartridge combination. But that would not be a 360 Express and the collector's dilemma of how far to restore raises its head. For the time being, at least, the Holland goes back into the cupboard.

But the Nitro for Black load for the Henry rifle was a different story. After initial tests over the chronograph we settled on 28 grains of Reloder 7 behind the 190-grain paper-patched bullet. A 30-grain load felt too sharp in the rifle and had showed the first signs of primer flattening, whilst a 25-grain load felt distinctly sloppy and inconsistent. The 28-grain load gave us an average velocity of 1695 fps, just a touch over the 1650 shown

in a 1920s ICI catalogue. Wary of putting too much faith in the machine, we went to the 50 yard target and this time produced five-shot groups running a touch under 3 inches, center to center. But it was possible to sense that the load was not right. A combination of the feel of the rifle and the sound of the shot suggested some inconsistency that could be overcome. Such shooting from a 130-year-old rifle is not bad, but there was an inescapable feeling that things could be better.

The load was dropped to 27 grains and the powder was confined but not compressed by two thin card wads, topped by an 0.3-inch wad of pure wool felt which had been soaked in a very thin grease and then dried. A thin card wad was placed on top of that and the 190-grain bullet seated as before.

First tests were done at 40 yards and the results were pure magic. Shooting was done from a bench with a 6 o'clock aim on a black bull target so that the fine foresight had a white background. The last seven rounds of the first batch of reloads were shot into one group. Five shots went into a 3/4-inch group and the other two enlarged it to 1-1/2 inches, center to center. All were on point of aim. To take a 130-year-old rifle, re-create a load, and get results like this is a joy that anti-gunners could never understand. Later reloads give the same results and, consistently, any shot outside 2 inches at 50 yards is entirely the fault of the shooter.

The 360 Express is obsolete, but rifles chambered for it are still around and there is no reason why it can not be perfectly suitable for hunting smaller game or for shooting at a target. But, oh, for some copper-tubed bullets. They would really make this rifle sing and they would be a vast improvement in the various muzzleloading calibers. Surely some specialist maker will revive this forgotten piece of British ingenuity. ●

References:

1. 1884 Kynoch catalogue reproduced in *Gun Digest*, 9th Edition, 1955, Edited by John Amber.

2. Jonathan Kirton, *The British Falling Block Breechloading Rifle From 1865*, Armoury Publications, Tacoma, 1985.

3. Wal Winfer, *British Single Shot Rifles*, Vol. 1, Alexander Henry. R&R Books, Maynardville, 1998.

4. George A. Hoyem, *The History and Development of Small Arms Ammunition, Vol. III British Sporting Rifle*. Armoury Publications, Tacoma, 1985.

5. Bruce Bertram Bullet Co., PO Box 313, Seymour, Victoria 3660, Australia.

6. North Devon Firearm Services, 3 North Street, Barunton, N. Devon, EX33 1AJ, England.

7. Paul A. Matthews, *The Paper Jacket*, Wolfe Publishing, Prescott, Arizona, 1991.

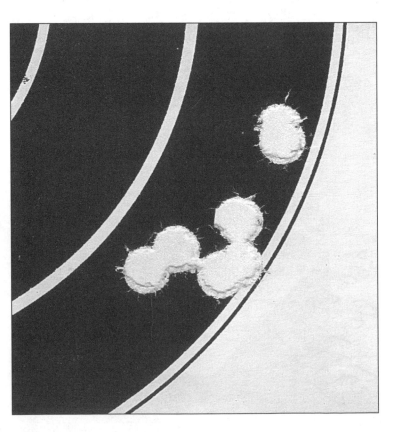

Pure magic. Seven shots at 40 yards—five in a 3/4-inch group and the seven into 1 1/2 inches (center to center).

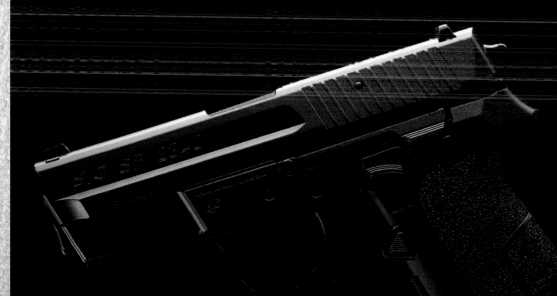

Still America's Original

THE MOSSBERG® MODEL 500®

Model 500
1970

Model 500
1998

Over four generations, the MOSSBERG family has produced affordable firearms, made in America for the American sportsman. MOSSBERG has continued to set the standards for reliability and durability, previously unheard of in production shotguns. Why?...Because firearms is our business and we proudly put our name on every one.

The MOSSBERG Model 500 continues to improve over time and still has the steel-to-steel lock up, dual cartridge stops, twin extractors and an ambidextrous top-tang safety, that was a first on any pump shotgun. In addition, MOSSBERG is still the only American made shotgun to meet U.S. government military specifications. New challenges have led to further innovation. **Many Model 500 barrels are factory ported** and feature a wide assortment of specialized choke tubes, stocks and finishes.

With models available in 12 ga., 20 ga. and .410, plus adult and youth versions, it's easy to see why the MOSSBERG Model 500 continues to be America's favorite pump shotgun.

12 ga. Model 500 Camo #52193

Safety and safe firearms handling is everyone's responsibility.

O.F. Mossberg & Sons, Inc. • 7 Grasso Avenue • P.O. Box 497 • North Haven, CT 06473-9844
An ISO 9001 registered company
Visit our website at: www.mossberg.com

WHEN I began collecting in the 1960s, I soon realized the vast majority of antique guns in decent condition had already disappeared permanently into major collections or were prohibitively overpriced. So I concentrated on "modern" cartridge arms, some in current production, some recently discontinued, that showed collector possibilities. The tactic worked well and many have appreciated significantly. I wanted that appreciation, of course, but I never bought strictly on a gun's investment potential; at minimum, I have to like the gun.

There were some setbacks, but none as extreme as the 1987 stock market crash. I've always been able to bounce back from reversals, and have managed to show a "paper" profit on my guns of around 30 percent. The pieces that actually cost me money are, for some reason, as memorable as my best investments. So, as we approach the new millennium, do investment grade firearms still exist among those guns in current production or which have been recently axed? The five specific areas reviewed in this article might enable current or would-be modern collectors to avoid some of the pitfalls.

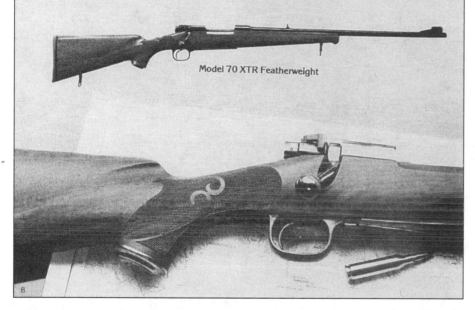

NEW FROM WINCHESTER!
MODEL 70 XTR FEATHERWEIGHT
Bolt Action Centerfire Rifle

The Gun: This is the newest featherweight bolt action centerfire rifle from Winchester . . . the first offered by Winchester in over 18 years. It is an answer to the requests of serious hunters for a lighter bolt action . . . for longer treks and tough terrain. At approximately 6¾ pounds, this new Model 70 XTR Featherweight rifle is designed for dependable performance with less weight. With all the reliability, features, and accuracy of Model 70 XTR Standard rifles, it is available in six calibers: 243, 270 and 308 Winchester, 30-06 Springfield, and the reintroduction of two highly regarded old favorites, the 257 Roberts and the 7 mm Mauser (7 X 57).

The Model 70 XTR Featherweight rifle is ideal for a broad range of game, especially in rough country or during lengthy hunts where its lighter weight becomes a noticeable advantage. Furthermore, this rifle has the high strength and durability that is characteristic of all Winchester Model 70 XTR rifles. This strength pays off in the ability to withstand hard use and rugged conditions through many hunting seasons.

Performance & Handling: Featherweight handling and carrying ease at only 6¾ pounds. Longer days in the field with less fatigue, quicker handling with the same Winchester dependability. The receiver recoil lug is epoxy bedded for greater accuracy and strength. The anti-bind bolt is precision-slotted for sure, smooth operation in any field situation. The slim, chromium molybdenum barrel is specially tapered and heat treated for light weight and strength.

Styling: This new Featherweight stock features a classic schnabel fore-end with checkering fashioned after early Model 70 custom rifle patterns for that traditional Winchester look. XTR satin finish protects the American walnut stock. High polish and blueing on metal surfaces. New red butt pad with black spacer.

Features: Featherweight, tapered 22" barrel. Hooded blade front sight and folding leaf rear sight. Stainless steel magazine follower. Three-position safety. Receiver drilled and tapped for scope. Detachable sling swivels.

The Ammunition: For every Model 70 XTR, Winchester Western Super-X Centerfire Rifle Cartridges assure top performance and compatibility. Both rifle and cartridge have been developed and tested as a compatible shooting system. Super-X cartridges are scientifically designed and precision-engineered to deliver maximum combined accuracy and energy, controlled expansion, and minimal lead loss. Available in a wide selection of calibers and bullet types for all kinds of game.

Model 70 XTR Featherweight

Author Brown took his greatest firearms loss during 1981 on a six gun set of the newly reintroduced Winchester Model 70 Featherweights.

PITFALLS FOR COLLECTORS...

Five easy ways you can lose money.

by Gary M. Brown

PITFALL ONE
Speculation that a manufacturer is going out of business.

I might as well begin with the worst beating I ever took. The year was 1981. Winchester (then owned and operated solely by the Olin Corporation) was on its last legs. Rumor had it the old firm might go completely bankrupt, but the company had introduced a Featherweight version of their Post-'64 Model 70 bolt action rifle. There had been no lightweight version of the M-70 offered for over 18 years. The six initial chamberings of the new Featherweights were intriguing. The seemingly obligatory 30-06, 270, 308 and 243 rounds were there, but also available were the 257 Roberts and the 7X57, two of the scarcer, more desirable cartridges offered in the Pre-'64 M-70.

These latter-day Featherweights were true gems. The sightless (prototypes had metallic sights) slim-barreled guns were gorgeous. Their classic stocks were adorned with deluxe pattern checkering, and were Schnabel-tipped. They certainly met my minimum criteria of liking them. They also seemed to have guaranteed investment potential, especially if "Winchester" had ceased operations. I acquired a six-gun set—all six chamberings.

As we now know, in hindsight, Olin licensed the use of the Winchester name and logo to a "new" company comprised mostly of former employees and shareholders. Thus, U.S. Repeating Arms Co. (dba "Winchester") rose like a phoenix from the ashes of the former Winchester Repeating Arms Co. (WRA Co.), The new firm went on to produce tens of thousands of identical Model 70 Featherweights (albeit in somewhat different chamberings). True, my six-gun set bore serial numbers indicating production by the "real" Winchester, and their box end-labels bore Olin/WRA Co. identification, but such subtleties would only have been appreciated by the most advanced collectors. None were available when I finally decided to take my beating and liquidate the group for whatever it would bring. The rifles had cost me over $400 each, but, if I'd chosen to piecemeal them out I believe I would have taken an even worse thrashing.

I finally found a "gentleman" who gave me $1,500.00 for the set. That comes out to $250.00 apiece, meaning I lost a bare minimum of $900.00. It was the last time I ever speculated on a business possibly going belly-up.

PITFALL TWO
Speculation on "discontinued" models by still active firms.

Here is yet another area virtually guaranteed to cost potential investors money. A perfect case in point is the famed Colt Single Action Army (SAA) revolver. I still have an April 13, 1981 letter from then Colt CEO C. E. Warner, trying to explain why his firm was yet again axing this legendary handgun. Warner's communication was in response to my letter solicited by *SHOOTING TIMES* Handgun Editor Charles "Skeeter" Skelton asking that the pistol be spared.

Although Warner did not spell it out, the real reason for Colt's discontinuation of this truly historic handgun was the myriad of product liability suits then endemic in the firearms industry. As Sturm, Ruger had discovered earlier, the first hammer notch of these guns (which had been the recommended position for carrying such weapons when fully-loaded dating back to the percussion era), was not perceived as a "safety" by today's litigious society. Never mind the fact that knowledgeable pistoleros had, for years, carried arms of this type with their hammers fully down, resting on an empty chamber, only inserting a sixth cartridge when danger was inevitable. Warner was, perhaps, prophetic ending his letter by saying: "Although we cannot foresee when, we are hopeful that at some point in the future we will be able to resume production of this famous gun."

Prices soared for nearly every configuration of the currently produced Third Generation SAAs (these guns had already been modified slightly from the originals to help reduce production costs). Certain of the scarcer SAA "plain-Jane" versions were being hawked at well over $1000.00, when "suggested retail" was around $600.00. Folks who had always wanted a single example found themselves vying for the remaining arms with both amateur and professional speculators.

By the early 1990s, however, the Single Action Army was again available (in the most popular "flavors") from the newly reconstituted Colt's Manufacturing Company. True, the pieces were accessible only through the auspices of the Custom Shop (at first in brightly polished Royal Blue or fully nickel plated only, with walnut grips), were prohibitively expensive (in the $1,100.00—$1,200.00 range), and were shipped with a disclaimer indicating that the mere firing of a single round would negatively affect their values. Dealer costs were in the mid-$800.00 area. Eventually, the revolvers were once again offered with the classic blue/case hardened finish and plastic "eagle" stocks. While some heavily into the earlier SAAs tried to denigrate both the physical appearance and the mechanical quality of the Custom Shop guns, many (including me) were financially bruised.

PITFALL THREE
Speculation based on manufacturers errors and/or mistakes.

Virtually every firearms knowledgeable individual is aware that William B. Ruger, originator of Sturm, Ruger, Inc., is a stickler for perfection. Many of his designs, along with extensive use of investment castings, helped revolutionize the modern firearms industry. But, like any human being, he has also come up with a few real lemons. Most notable of these, perhaps, was the nev-

An ad for the never-made Ruger XGI actually appeared in the firm's 1986 sales brochure. Owning an example of this "lemon" would have proved rewarding, but none were ever sold.

er-produced XGI (aka "Maxi-14") caliber 308 Winchester semi-automatic rifle. Although many would have taken the M14 battle rifle and modified it to sporting configuration, Bill Ruger insisted on a complete redesign—most notably to the new weapon's gas system. As pictured in this article, the company actually promoted the gun in their sales literature, one stating that the weapon was also available in 243 Winchester. A well-known gun value guide listed **used** prices for the piece in several of its editions. For whatever the reason (said to be a lack of reliability and/or accuracy), the XGI was made in experimental form **only**. There were **no** production examples. Here, at least, is a single instance where owning one of those lemons would have proven most rewarding!

Regardless, there have been several more examples of Ruger guns which were mistakes, that failed to become valuable collectibles (by the way, I'm certainly not "picking on" Bill Ruger who is one of my personal heroes—its just that his reputation of recalling and destroying faulty products best serves to illustrate this point). Among them, I point to the Blackhawk 357 Maximum revolver. This beefed-up New Model single action also featured an elongated cylinder necessary to accommodate the extended case of this powerful round (intended primarily for metallic silhouette shooting). Early-on, it was found that the cartridge had a nasty habit of flame-cutting guns in their upper-frame/rear-barrel area. Ruger, conceding the fact, ceased production. Speculators ran wild, driving prices for this model to well above current suggested retail. Today, however, the arms have drifted lower in value as many came to realize that a gun is simply a tool, and a defective tool is hardly worth having.

I lost money on another Ruger problem firearm. It was one of the first 500 "fully blued" Red Label **12 Gauge** Over/Under shotguns offered. Since I'd bought an early example of the initial **20 Gauge** Red Label (they were also fully blued), at its published retail price of $480.00, I wanted a similar 12 Gauge gun to complete my set. I knew I'd never get the matching "0249" serial number of my 20 Ga., but was thrilled when I found 12 Gauge number "0445" for sale in a Virginia gun shop at the suggested

Many a collector took a bath when the Colt Single Action Army was reintroduced (through the Colt Custom Shop) for the umpteenth time during the 1990s. Shown is the author's 1982 44-40 Sheriffs Model. Colt has not yet reprised this exact gun, it's value had dropped because of widespread availability and the (relatively) low price of the Custom Shop arms.

retail of $798.00. It seems that one of the 12 Ga. "all blue" examples had "doubled" (i.e. fired both barrels at once) during NRA testing. The NRA couldn't get the gun to double again, but once was enough for Bill Ruger who promptly tried to recall the ones which had been shipped.

It's a good thing I'd wanted #0445 as part of an ensemble, since those early 12 Gauge guns shortly wouldn't even fetch what the redesigned stainless steel receiver 12 Ga. O/Us were bringing. I finally traded the pair to a skeet shooter who had both fitted with Briley screw-in choke tubes, thereby assuring **neither** would ever be collectible!

1982 *WINCHESTER* SPORTING ARMS

U.S. *Repeating Arms Company*

Brown cautions against commemoratives as investments. The theme or person being commemorated has to have personal significance to the buyer, such as Winchester's Model 94 in long-discontinued caliber 32-40 celebrating American idol John Wayne.

The new Blackhawk SRM 357 Maximum single action revolver was boldly depicted in 1983 literature from the firm of Sturm, Ruger & Co. Those speculating on this one likely lost money.

sary Derringer. This arm celebrated the 125th birthday of that midwestern city. There were only 104 such guns made and they are currently worth about 25 times their original sale price of $28.00. Few would question that the above weapon was created to commemorate a specific date and/or event, and that 104 pieces certainly represents very limited production. The next two such firearms followed pretty closely in that mold. Today, the 1961-issued, three inch (without ejector rods or housings), Sheriff's Models in 45 Colt (478 blue/case hardened, 25 bright nickeled) are among the most sought after modern Colts by both "regular production" and "commemorative" collectors alike.

That same year, Colt also marked the 125th year of Single Action Army production with their 125th Anniversary Model SAA. Unfortunately, over 7,000 of these otherwise interesting guns were manufactured. Yes, they

PITFALL FOUR
Speculation on commemoratives and/or "special interest" guns.

One of the first commemorative firearms ever issued was the Colt 22 Short 1961 Geneseo, Illinois, 125th Anniver-

commemorated a historically significant event, but they were hardly of limited production. From that point many (if not most) such arms began to signify lesser dates, events or persons, and were produced in ever-increasing numbers.

Colt was not alone in creating this glut of instant collectibles. Winchester quickly caught on to what was perceived as being a completely new firearms market. They kicked off 1964 with their Wyoming Diamond Jubilee 94 Carbine, making just 1,501. By 1966, though, the temptation to exploit this apparently endless pool of buyers was too great and the firm produced over 102,000 Centennial '66 Rifles and Carbines. Such staid old-line firms as Marlin and Savage also succumbed to the commemorative racket. Initially, many bought every available issue, fearing to miss out on part of their matched sets.

I never got much involved in the commemorative scene. I can only remember actually buying two. The first was Smith & Wesson's 1977 Model 25-3 125th Anniversary Commemorative. The standard issue gun was sparingly adorned with gold lettering. I bought one because it was the first S & W since the mid-1950s to be chambered in 45 Colt. I needed a gun in that caliber to complete my collection containing a handgun in every chambering Smith had produced since the end of World War II. As soon as the company came out with their regular production Model 25-5, in 45 Colt, the commemorative took a back seat. My only other purchase of a similar arm was in 1982. This time, the gun's caliber and the man it celebrated combined to make it (at the time) a must! The piece in question was the Model 94 John Wayne Commemorative in 32-40 Winchester. Not only did the gun reintroduce a caliber Winchester which had not been offered since before WW II, but it also featured a large hoop lever made famous in Wayne's Western films.

I recall my particular arm carried a 2782JWC serial number. It was in a Winchester Repeating Arms Co./Olin carton, indicating production prior to the U.S. Repeating Arms Co. takeover. I still lost money on these commemoratives upon liquidating both prior to an ill-fated retail gun shop venture.

Let me be perfectly clear: I don't mean to rain on the parade of commemorative collectors. Any firearms-related endeavor that casts a positive light on guns is fine by me. Just remember several things: commemorative/special interest arms only have value if they are kept virtually untouched, absolutely unfired, in their original packaging with all related paperwork. If actually shot, they usually won't even command the price of a reg-

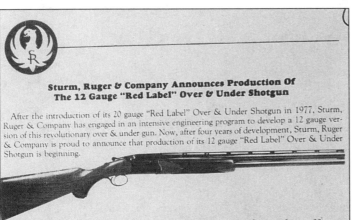

Sturm, Ruger & Company Announces Production Of The 12 Gauge "Red Label" Over & Under Shotgun

After the introduction of its 20 gauge "Red Label" Over & Under Shotgun in 1977, Sturm, Ruger & Company has engaged in an intensive engineering program to develop a 12 gauge version of this revolutionary over & under gun. Now, after four years of development, Sturm, Ruger & Company is proud to announce that production of its 12 gauge "Red Label" Over & Under Shotgun is beginning.

This first 12 gauge Over & Under Shotgun closely follows the lines of its now famous 20 gauge counterpart, and has been scaled up slightly to accommodate its larger bores. This 12 gauge "Red Label" plain grade gun incorporates traditional Ruger precision workmanship throughout, with a superior polish and finish. Curved shapes are geometrically accurate and plane surfaces are precision ground to be smooth and dead flat. All mechanical joints are fitted to minimum hairline clearances.

As is the case with the earlier 20 gauge Ruger Over & Under Shotgun, the action and frame of the 12 gauge gun have been designed for great strength and constructed of the finest materials. Hardened 4140 chrome-molybdenum and other alloy steels and music wire coil springs are used throughout. The distinctive styling and unusually low profile are the result of the compact mechanism, many parts of which are interchangeable with the 20 gauge Ruger Over & Under Shotgun.

The unique patented hammer and trigger mechanism and single selective trigger provide several positive safety features. The rebounding hammers and hammer interrupter help protect against accidental discharge when the hammers are cocked and the safety is engaged. With the safety off, the hammer interrupter is lifted clear of the hammers only by a deliberate pull of the single trigger. A deliberate, complete release of the single trigger is necessary to set it for firing the second shot.

The automatic top safety also serves as the selector that determines which of the two barrels is to be fired first. The conical, pointed firing pins are strongly proportioned and are virtually unbreakable. The smooth lines of the receiver are accentuated by the fact that there are no visible pins or screws whatsoever.

The barrels are hammer-forged 4130 chrome-molybdenum steel, stress relieved, contour ground, and precisely fitted and silver soldered to the finished mono-block. The dovetail hollow rib is automatically silver soldered to the top barrel. Unique machine-cut cross serrations in the top surface of the rib provide a matte, glare-free sighting plane. The front sight is a standard gold bead. Patented barrel side spacers are attached by simple mechanical means and can be left off if desired.

The stock and semi-beavertail forearm are carefully shaped from first quality straight grain American walnut, fully seasoned, with deep, hand-cut checkering of 20 lines to the inch. An improved method of forearm wood to metal assembly provides a broad, strong recoil surface

Bill Ruger is a genuine manufacturing hero, but over his illustrious career he has made a few lemons. For instance, one of the first 500 fully-blued 12 GA Red Label O/U Shotguns doubled during NRA testing. An immediate recall was issued.

ular production "shooter" because of their often garish, shiny finishes. Unless you are locked-in to requiring every one produced to keep an ensemble intact, try to limit your purchases to firearms depicting dates, events or persons that have real importance, and **never** put your money into guns of this type solely as an investment.

PITFALL FIVE

Speculation on early production examples of entirely new models.

Many collectors specialize in "first issue" guns bearing the lowest possible serial numbers. There is little doubt that low number Colt Single Action Army revolvers, especially those having so-called pinched-frames (referring to the shape of their rear-sight groove), regardless of their overall condition, command astronomical prices. Many similar examples abound, such as the 1 of 1,000 (and much rarer 1 of 100) Winchester Model 1873 rifles made in extremely limited quantities only during early production. This offering of supposedly perfect or nearly-perfect pieces was soon discontinued because it inferred to potential customers that some Winchesters were "better" than others.

Remember, however, that early features, while sometimes adding collector value, can also be negatives regarding functional reliability, accuracy, and even safety. One needs only to reflect on the recent Colt All American 2000 9x19mm semiautomatic pistol. Reports on these guns ranged from reporting them simply unreliable to actually being potentially dangerous.

The most recent firearm on which I took a bath, like several others I've mentioned, could be termed a "crossover" gun as it fell into more than one category. It was a M-84 Mini-Mauser bolt action rifle in 223 Remington made by Kimber **of Oregon**, Inc., in the late 1980s. The arm had a low serial number in the 12X range, and was bought just after the original firm went bankrupt.

In 1993, though, Kimber **of America**, Inc., reopened. That company is again producing nearly identical M-84s. My early address, and super-low serial number may someday make it worth slightly more than the newer guns, but, their **immediate** effect was to cut the value of my piece in half.

I'm not saying my pitfalls are the only ones likely to influence which guns may become collectible in the future. However, these five aspects of gun collecting merit careful attention. ●

The Colt All American™
Model 2000, Double Action
Semiautomatic Pistol

Buying early production guns on speculation that their values will be higher than arms produced later can boomerang. The defective (some even say dangerous) Colt All American 2000 9x19mm semiauto pistol is a good example of such.

The Model 84... a head locking, mini-Mauser sporter designed specifically for the .222 family of cartridges.

In 1985, Kimber introduced an all new rifle to its product line. The Model 84 is a "scaled down" Mauser type action and was designed specifically for the .222 family of cartridges. No other sporting bolt action rifle has ever been designed solely for this use.

The small, compact head locking action has enabled Kimber to utilize the same basic stock used on the Model 82 .22 rimfire sporter, thereby minimizing weight of the rifle. The Model 84 weighs just under 6¼ pounds (weight may vary slightly depending on the density of the walnut on each stock).

Like the Model 82, the design of this new model incorporates features which appeal to a classic rifle enthusiast. The extractor, for example, is the traditional Paul Mauser design. In addition to providing extremely reliable extraction, the Mauser extractor facilitates feeding of the cartridge in a "controlled" fashion. In other words, the cartridge head feeds up entirely into the bolt face as the bolt moves forward approximately midway. From there it feeds into the chamber horizontally.

Unlike most American centerfire rifles, the Model 84 utilizes a spring loaded ejector arm (similar to a pre '64 Winchester Model 70) which rides diagonally along the bottom section of the bolt head. Deviating from the true Mauser design, this feature precludes the need to split the left locking lug, as is the case on a Mauser. This feature ensures a stronger locking lug and provides the shooter with complete control over the cartridge case ejection process.

No compromises were made in choosing the material used in the

features of the Model 84 are outlined below.
• Head locking bolt with a Mauser type extractor.
• Spring-loaded ejector arm similar to pre '64 Model 70.
• 5 Shot magazine.
• Polished steel hinged floorplate & trigger guard.

• Rotary cam style safety.
• Adjustable trigger set for about 2½ pounds before it leaves the factory.
• Receiver and bolt machined from solid chrome moly steel bar stock.
• Chrome moly steel barrel.
• Round top receiver (new in 1986), drilled and tapped for Kimber scope mounts and bases.

In 1985, the Model 84 was first released in one chambering only, the very popular .223 Remington. For this new model year, six additional cartridges will join the family in response to many requests from Kimber enthusiasts and collectors.

Brown took his most recent financial beating on an early Kimber of Oregon Model 84 bolt action 223 "mini-Mauser" rifle (as shown in their 1986 catalog) because the revived Kimber of America is now producing nearly identical guns.

THE STRAIGHT GRIP

It was absolutely quiet, the thick, muffled quiet of snowbound woods at twilight. The abandoned logging trail wound uphill through dense conifer timber. Every bough was blanketed with six inches of freshly fallen snow. I was in N.W. Montana, and had been easing along the trail for a little over a mile, when an abrupt turn brought me to an opening of several acres in the gloomy conifers. Just as I stopped to look it over, a big whitetail buck entering the clearing from the other side snapped his head up. I think that we spotted each other at exactly the same instant. We stared in mutual surprise for a split second, and before I could raise my rifle, the buck whirled and bounded directly away into the dark timber.

There was no need to count points, this was unquestionably the largest whitetail I had ever seen. I found him in the scope, but all that was visible in

the shadowy timber was his raised white flag. In desperation, I briefly considered a Texas heart shot, something I had sworn that I would never attempt except at a wounded, escaping animal. Resisting that impulse, I watched his white flag slow and then finally stop. Just as it occurred to me that I might be able to try for his neck using the flag as a reference point, he lowered his tail and disappeared.

I was sure he was standing there somewhere, watching me, but I could not locate him, even with binoculars. I was heartsick, having missed a chance at the buck of a lifetime. Last light was fading fast, and soon, even in the open, it would be too dark to shoot. I could not think of anything else to do but to continue on down the trail through the clearing, as if nothing had happened, and then to double back and hope to catch him in the open on his original course. I was not optimistic.

I was 100 yards or so past the clearing, and thinking about stopping and sneaking back to watch it, when something caught my eye 125 yards downhill, off to my right. Silhouetted by the snow in a tiny opening, the big buck was standing broadside, looking at me. Had I been a few feet to one side or the other, he would not have been visible through the thick, snow covered timber. The old straight-gripped Springfield '03 came up smoothly, and the 150-grain CoreLokt found its mark. He was a majestic old buck, 7 or 8 years old by his worn teeth, high and wide, with double brow tines and 5 extra points around the antler bases. All in all, I felt incredibly lucky, and much better about passing up the earlier shot!

That old Springfield was my first straight-gripped rifle. But straight-gripped guns have interested me for a long time.

The very Springfield 30-06 and the Montana Whitetail buck discussed shown here on the scene.

I WAS in junior high when the 1967 Gun Digest was published. I remember being fascinated by a photo of three straight-gripped SxS double shotguns in the article by famed British author Gough Thomas, *"The Browning Legacy, Blessing Or Blight?"* The photo had full length views of a Purdey, a Westley Richards and an AyA, all straight-gripped and, to my mind, epitomes of grace and beauty in guns. I think that it may have been the first time that I was aware of the distinction between pistol-gripped and straight-gripped guns. They looked trim and fast!

Although it was the photograph that really caught my attention, I do vaguely recall being impressed by what Thomas had to say about the responsive, superbly balanced British-styled game guns. Some of it must have stuck with me, as I have been partial to straight-gripped guns ever since. I finally got my first one, 18 years later, when I restocked my pistol-gripped 20 bore Ithaca/SKB 200 E. It got a bit complicated, as the tangs had to be straightened and the angle of the drawbolt changed to fit the straight stock. While I was at it, I put on a new trigger guard with a long tang, and made a new, matching trigger. By hollowing out the buttstock and replacing the semi-beavertail

with a splinter forend, the weight was reduced from 6 1/4 to 5 1/2 pounds.

Over time, several more doubles found their way into my gun rack, a 5 pound C. Jeffery 20 bore and a tiny C & A Weston .410, both British boxlock nonejectors, with straight grips. These guns are easy to carry and very quick pointing, and they bolstered my interest in straight-gripped guns. And photos of exquisite straight-gripped rifles by Steve Billeb and Fred Wells, featured in the Custom Guns section of The Gun Digest, surely made an impression on me, as well.

Northern Michigan is my home, and I wanted a knockaround rifle to carry

Stalking Rifle

By Ken Ide

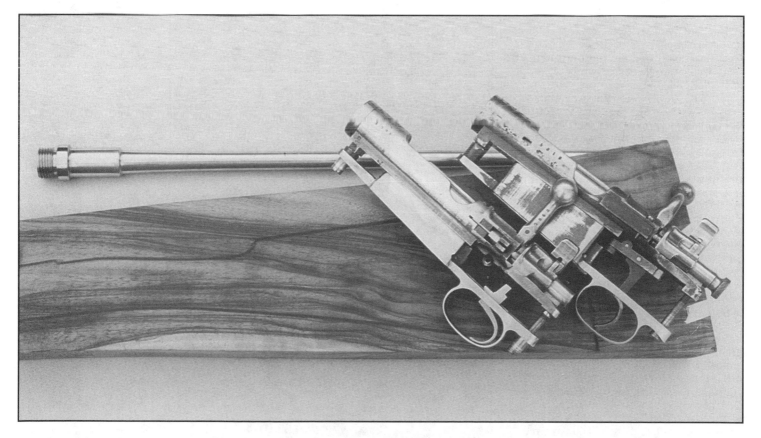

Note one of these Mexican Mausers (at left) has had the magazine depth reduced in a project to make a 7mm-08 for a friend.

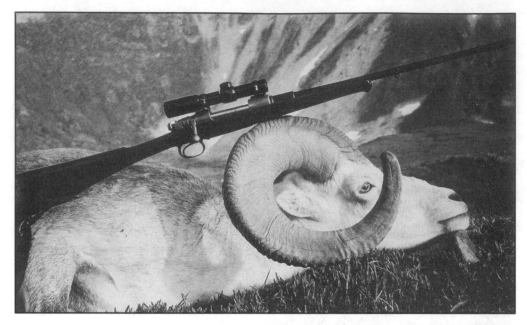

This beautiful Yukon Stone Ram was taken with the author's Mauser reworked to his favorite straight-gripped style.

while snowshoeing or cross-country skiing, in case there was an opportunity for a shot at a coyote or feral cat. Besides, it always seems more exhilarating to be in the woods when you are carrying a rifle, even if you are not likely to use it.

I found the old Springfield at a gun show about 10 years ago. It had a high number 1903 action, and a Williams Foolproof receiver sight. The forend of the original military style straight-gripped stock had been cut off in front of the barrel band, and a new sling loop installed. Otherwise, it was all military. The price was $80.00.

The '03 was a nice old rifle, very smooth to operate, and the firing mechanism was easy to disassemble and dry out, which came in handy when my skis or snowshoes snagged and tripped me into the snow. I never did get a shot at a coyote with it, but carrying it around for a while started me thinking about how it could be lightened up a bit, as it weighed almost 9 pounds.

A year or so later, friends invited me to go with them to coastal Alaska to fish for salmon and hunt Sitka Blacktail deer. Our destination was Montague Island, in Prince William Sound, and we read everything about the area that we could find. Of course, we read about brown bear, and at least one account of how the remote Montague was the Devils Island for bears, a place where problem bears that had been trapped elsewhere were released. We never did learn to what extent that took place, but it certainly did make our trip preparations interesting. Because of limitations on the weight of our baggage for the charter flight to the island, we each had to select a single firearm that would be suitable for both deer and charging brown bear.

Our research indicated that in early September the larger Sitka bucks were

Another 7x57 Mauser, this one built for a friend, next to a pre-64 M70 Featherweight. The Mauser is considerably trimmer.

supposed to be in the alpine country above timberline, and that taking one might involve some long range shooting. But in case of bear problems, we wanted a big, heavy bullet. The old '03 Springfield was the biggest bore rifle I had, and I

This view of the author's 7x57 sheep rifle, shows it to be indeed a lot like a classic English birdgun.

figured that a 220 grain 30-06 bullet would have to do for bear, and that once on top of the mountain, 150s would probably work for long shots at deer.

Thoughts of having that heavy rifle slung over my shoulder all of the time while fishing the stream, and of carrying it up past timberline, finally prompted me to trim off some of the excess wood and steel. Quite a bit was turned off of the barrel, and it was cut back to 21-inches. The issue stock had some plain sawn figure, and the grain ran pretty much parallel to the grip, so I decided to try and use it. Cutting a half an inch off the top of the magazine box, and inletting the barreled action further down into the wood raised the comb a little, and when excess wood was trimmed off the sides, some cast off was cut in.

With the Springfield's raised receiver bridge, the line of sight was still too high with a scope, so I constructed a mount for a Burris 2 3/4x Scout scope, low on the barrel ahead of the receiver ring, and put a compact peep sight on the bridge. With a Pilkington lever on the rotary dovetail style bases, it allowed the scope to go off and on in seconds. The plan was to mount the scope and change to 150's only when hunting deer up on top, where a bear could be seen well before it was too close for comfort. Everywhere else, it would be carried with iron sights and 220s in the magazine. It worked pretty well, too. We never had any bear problems, but did take a decent Sitka buck at around 225 yards after a memorable high country stalk.

The modified '03 carried and handled nicely, even with the Scout scope attached. It is trim enough so that you can wrap your hand all the way around the action. For me this was a rather novel and pleasant sensation in carrying a rifle, being used to conventionally mounted scopes that preclude such a hold. It felt very dynamic and, at six pounds, was fun to wander through the woods with. Before long it was my fa-

vorite rifle. My luck held, a couple of years later, in N.W. Montana, when the trimmed-down '03 accounted for the old buck mentioned at the beginning of this tale, as well as a spike elk.

Experience with the Springfield validated my interest in straight-gripped rifles. To me they looked good, felt right and worked well. And, of course, the fact that one had brought me good luck did not hurt. I cannot argue with the experts about the efficacy of a pistol grip, even the classic British stalking rifles were usually made with them. There are undoubtedly some good reasons for a pistol-gripped stock, possibly for better control of the rifle during recoil, and as an aid against canting. And perhaps the hand is more naturally positioned for squeezing the trigger. But I feel that this is more important for a target or varmint rifle, and do not feel handicapped with a straight-gripped stalking rifle. And in an ultralight rifle, doing without a pistol grip may save several ounces.

The straight grip has some other advantages, at least on a lightweight, moderate caliber rifle. I prefer to sling my rifles over my left shoulder, with the muzzle down. This allows you to get the rifle into action very quickly and smoothly. If the sling is properly adjusted, the bolt handle rides in the crook of your left elbow, and there is no pistol grip jabbing you in the side. It seems to me that the rifle comes up just a little more quickly without the pistol grip, too.

An alpine hunt for mountain sheep has been a lifelong dream of mine. Like so many others of my generation, I grew up reading Jack O'Connor's tales of the classic sheep hunt. But now the costs seem so high! One of my friends is a big game hunter of considerable experience, and he finally talked me in to going with him to the Yukon after Stone rams. His argument was persuasive "Yes, it is a lot of money, but it is something that you have always wanted to do, and we are not getting any younger". That was in 1995 and, at age 41, his advice struck a chord.

In due course, we were booked for the hunt of my lifetime, and I wanted

everything to be perfect, including my rifle. The old Springfield was functional, but I longed for something even lighter, with a really nice piece of wood and a conventionally mounted scope. With most of the components already on hand, all that was needed was a couple hundred hours to put them together.

The project began with a mint condition Brazilian M 1908 DWM 98 Mauser military rifle acquired a couple of years earlier. The actions of these rifles are beautifully machined. The 7mm bore was in perfect condition, so it seemed logical to use the military barrel, and keep it a 7x57. My experienced friend suggested a hotter cartridge, but because my plans were for a real lightweight, the 7x57, with its moderate recoil, seemed perfect. Besides, I was hoping for a classic sheep hunting experience, and the 7x57 is definitely a classic sheep cartridge!

Some of the lessons learned while building the Springfield came in handy, such as cutting off the top 1/2-inch of the magazine box to make a trimmer profile. This necessitated extensive modifications to the aftermarket trigger mechanism to shorten it enough to fit into the reduced space. The barrel was turned way down, to .485" at the muzzle, and cut off at 22-inches. The sides of the receiver ring were ground to small ring contour, and a little steel taken off of the recoil lug. A short, hollow knob bolt handle was welded on, a Dakota M 70-style safety fitted, and the action sent out for re-heat treatment. I cut, carved and glassed the military stock until it was what I wanted, and then sent it away for use as a pattern to cut a blank of nice California English. With the Burris Mini 4x mounted, it weighs exactly 5 3/4 lb., and comes up like a shotgun!

We had miserable weather in the Yukon, rain or snow for most of the ten-day hunt. On about the fifth day, we had a

The old Springfield after its final remodeling was the right rifle to pack in Alaska.

ram broadside at 60 yards, one that the guide estimated would go 36 to 37 inches around the curl, but I passed, and we never found a larger one. In fact, we never found another ram at all.

We went back the next year, hunting with outfitter Curt Thompson in the Pelly Mountains, and this time luck was on my side. After a rugged 7 1/2 hour climb and stalk, I was fortunate enough to take a 41 inch Stone ram. An absolutely magnificent animal, on a beautiful, bright, sunny day, up on the very top of the mountain. It was a classic sheep hunt, on horseback into sheep country and then on foot up the mountains to glass. The country is true wilderness, with vast, stunning vistas. There was no spotting of animals from aircraft, etc., just good, old fashioned hunting. It was an extraordinary experience, fulfilling a lifelong dream. And doing it with a rifle that I built myself was icing on the cake!

Is a straight-gripped rifle for everyone? Probably not. Beauty is in the eye of the beholder, and if you do not like the way that they look, don't bother. Rifles as trim as the ones that I have built for myself and my friends cannot be used as clubs if you run out of cartridges. A serious fall could break the stock at the wrist and even bend the barrel. The wood must be selected carefully, with the grain exactly parallel to the line of the grip for maximum strength. But if straight-gripped rifles do interest you, try to find one somewhere to handle. You may like it! ●

If there's a trail, I have...
TRAIL GUNS FOR COMPANY

The author had shot this buck the evening before. When Stephens went back to pack this buck out the next day, his kit gun went along, too!

By Ted Stephens

ALONG WITH my binoculars, a trail gun has always gone wherever I've gone. Such handguns have killed bayed wild pigs when we have found them while going about ranch work, taken many rattlesnakes when a rock or shovel wouldn't have been handy, fed our trackers rabbits and springhare in Africa, kept us in ptarmigan and grouse while looking for trophy bull moose and caribou in Alaska, supplied us sage and forest grouse while hunting the high mountains, and even dictated control and reclaimed the property a thug had stolen from my truck one day.

My interest in a trail gun started when I was about 8 or 9. My dad let me have his 1930s vintage H&R Sportsman nine-shot single action. I carried it everywhere we went. By the time I was 10, Dad had convinced the rest of our deer hunting party that I was a careful enough nimrod to carry the Sportsman on our group deer hunts. One day in our Redwood Grove Camp, one of the senior members was trying to free a threatening broken redwood branch about 30 feet above us with his early Model 1100 shotgun. When he couldn't bring it down with his shot loads, I went to work at the peppered limb with the Sportsman. About 10 shots later, it came tumbling down. The Sportsman was a very accurate handgun despite a really wide cylinder gap. I remember shooting from the sitting position in shorts as a kid and that cylinder gap sure would spray your legs! I eventually stopped carrying the Sportsman as it did not pack as well as some of my other revolvers and I thought then Colt and Smith & Wesson had a quality advantage.

Through the years, I have shot a lot of trail guns. From this, I have developed some opinions. I divide my trail guns into two groups: The ones I carry where I don't have to worry about using the trail gun to protect myself and those that serve a protection purpose.

As an example, in Alaska, my brother, Chris and I each carried 22 Kit Guns when we had our rifles. With those guns, we ate many a fine meal. Ptarmigan are pretty strong, but better than any chicken! When we were packing big loads of moose meat, sans rifle, and stepping in those big bear tracks going through the willows, we carried big bore handguns. (I had always said that with the right firearm, I wasn't worried about anything with fangs and claws. Then I saw those big bears. I am forever humbled. Big bore handgun, rifle, or shotgun, I hope I never have to use it to stop the charge of an Alaskan brown bear!)

In the light gun category, I have tried the following: The Sportsman, two Colt Diamondbacks, a Smith & Wesson Stainless Model 63 22 LR Kit Gun, a four-inch Smith & Wesson Model 10 in 38 Special, a Smith & Wesson Model 36 38 Special 3-inch heavy barrel, a long barreled Ruger Mark II Target Stainless, a S&W Stainless 32 H&R Magnum Kit Gun and a Browning FN/Challenger with a 4-1/2 inch barrel. My favorites are the S&W Kit Guns and the Browning FN Challenger. I like the 22s because they are cheap to feed, accurate and you can carry lots of ammo easily in your duffle. I like the revolvers because you can shoot them, and not have to worry about taking the shell out of the chamber. This is especially easy on your gun if you shoot a grouse or finish off your buck or bull on a rainy or snowy day. I also like the double-action revolver if you did have a bear on top of you that you didn't see coming and have to palm the gun and shoot for protection. The 32 kit gun is nice because a 32 S&W Long handloaded with a 90-grain lead semi-wadcutter at about 600 will kill a grouse better than any 22 and is very quiet. The 32 is also nice because you can have a 32 Magnum as a backup in the cylinder if you ever needed it. Last year while backpacking my Idaho bull out, I made a triple on forest grouse with the 32 kit gun that ate about as good as anything could eat back in the tent that night. All day, packing elk on my frame, I had hardly noticed the little kit gun on my side.

I like the Browning FN/Challenger 22 LR because it is so accurate and is built like a Swiss watch. Although I carry it a lot on my ranching duties, I usually don't take it in the backcountry because I am afraid a week of sweat, blood and weather will hurt it. I carry the Browning cocked, safety on, with an empty chamber. Like many Browning safeties, this one not only blocks the trigger but also cams the sear back. Although the internal hammer has never dropped, I would feel uncomfortable carrying a cartridge in the chamber. If you ever had a bear in your tent or got jumped in the backcountry, the time it took to use two hands to load the 22 auto might be a disadvantage compared to a doubleaction handgun where you could just pull the trigger.

I also wish I had ponied up the dough and bought a Walther PP DA 22LR auto when I had the chance. This might have been the perfect light trail carry gun.

In the big bore department, I have tried the following: Ruger Old Model Blackhawk 41 Magnum 4-5/8-inch, Colt New Frontier 44 Spl 7-1/2-inch bbl, Dan Wesson 357 Magnum 6 inch, S&W Model 66 357 4-inch, 45 Colt Auto, Browning High Power, and S&W 629 Classic 44 Magnum. My favorites are the S&W 66 and 629. With these you can kill grouse with 38 Specials, snakes with shotshells and have magnums ready for an attack. In fact, you can have them all handy in one cylinder! My 629 has a shot shell first round all snake season; if you need a solid, you simply cycle past it!

If you are packing meat in Big Bear Country, of course, the 41 and 44 Magnums get the nod! A 45 Colt or any of the super magnums would be in this camp, too.

Although I love the single action Browning-designed autos for personal protection, I find the magazines rattle on the trail. Also, if you want to shoot a different load in a hurry, it is nice to cycle through the revolver rather than shoot it out of the way with an auto.

The problem with the big bores is they are so big and heavy, you know you are carrying them. You also know you are packing the ammo! Fifty 44s in your duffle is like 500 22s. The other disadvantage if you are hunting big game and you want to shoot a grouse...the game knows you are shooting a big bore handgun! Big handguns are loud. The 32 H&R Magnum is loud, too.

This wild boar was taken with a single 240 grain SWC at about 1000 FPS—about the right medicine, all things considered.

The best holster for the trail gun is one that rides high and close to your body so your handgun doesn't flop around and beat you and it to death. For years we used Roy Baker Pancakes, having to modify them for the four-inch kit gun. The Bianchi 5 BHL has worked really well for our 32 kit guns. Custom leather maker Dick Murray of Murray Leather makes an excellent thumb break flap holster I use for my S&W 629. This holster is the ultimate for handgun protection and accessibility. Since production was limited and a long time ago, I made a pancake type holster for my Browning/FN Challenger.

If I could have only one trail gun, what would it be? Probably my Browning FN/Challenger 22 LR. Through the years, the 22 long rifle continues to amaze me. Here are a few of my experiences with it.

Once, when hunting wild boars on a neighboring ranch, the dogs took a big dry sow right down the hill on top of me.

An S&W 36 Kit Gun 22LR, the Browning 22LR and the S&W 631 32 Magnum Kit Gun alongside the author's 10 power Zeiss binoculars.

Holstering is important for the old Blackhawk and some Smiths. At center is a Dick Murray flap rig.

Two "bear country" meat-packing guns the author has confidence in: The S&W 629 44 Magnum and the Ruger 41 Magnum.

As my rifle was slung over my shoulder, as the pig just about touched me, I side-stepped and fired a single 22 LR from my Colt Diamondback into the top of the wild hog's skull. That pig, brained, piled up immediately. Usually, when I have to, I shoot pigs with the 22 below the ear. It works, but I do not recommend it, as the last thing any of us want is to wound game or make it suffer. A 44 Magnum is a much better handgun for pigs.

When I shot my first elk, I made a long stalk on a 6x6 herd bull. I had taken off my backpack for the utmost sneak-in and left my spare rifle ammo purposefully in the pack. But then, I was naive enough to think I would never need

more than the five 270s in the rifle magazine. Boy, have I learned a lot about elk! That time, when all the cows finally got up, I could only see pieces of the great bull. I hit him five times about the chest, but had to run him down and finish him with head shots with my 22!

Another time I shot a bull elk with the 270 that piled up in a strange fashion. When I walked up to him, I gave him one between the horns with a 22 hollow point just to make sure he was dead. That next spring, back home on the ranch porch, I was admiring the horns and noticed that 22 had broken, but had not entered the brain cavity. Would a solid have entered from up top?

I don't know, but I'm glad that bull really didn't need any more shooting.

Our 22s have also come in handy when hunting ducks and upland game. Our dogs always do their best to tree any feral cat or raccoon we happen upon, usually in a thorn thicket. The 22 is a pretty clean way to dispatch them without a big muzzle blast close to the dog's head. Also, when we jump lakes and knock down a bunch of ducks in short order, a 22 is a great way to line the dogs out for multiple retrieves. I've also killed a few cripples out of shotgun range with my kit gun.

Like I would feel naked without my pocket knife, the trail gun always goes along!

●

Winchester's 69

This is the full line of Winchester 22 rifles with the Model 69A action as offered at the height of their popularity in the early 1950's. They are, from left to right, the Model 75 target rifle, the Model 75 sporting rifle, the Model 72 tubular magazine rifle, the Model 47 single shot rifle and the Model 69A rifle.

A Class Act From 1938 to 1963

By Konrad F. Schreier, Jr.

LIKE MANY youngsters who learned to shoot in the 1930s I learned with a Winchester 22 rimfire bolt action Model 69 repeater. My grandmother gave it to me when she figured I was old and sensible enough to be taught how to use and take care of it. The grown-ups who taught me all thought my Model 69 was a pretty slick little rifle. Most of them had learned how to use firearms in World War I.

I learned to plink, hunt and shoot paper targets with my Winchester Model 69, and I even got to be a reasonably good shot. And my first Model 69 is still around. My younger brother has it, and he says it still shoots pretty well as it always has. And he taught his son to shoot with it.

The Model 69 was far from the first bolt action 22 rifle Winchester made. Their first were the little single shot Winchester-Brownings brought out in 1900 and made until the 1950s. There were many models and variations of this little John M. Browning-designed 22 bolt action rifle, and by the time it was discontinued about a million and a half had been made.

In 1919, right after World War I had vastly increased the interest in 22 rifle target shooting, Winchester introduced their superb Model 52 22 target rifle. It was a high-priced beautifully made magazine-loading 22 bolt action and it is still one of the best shooting 22 rifles ever made.

In 1926 Winchester filled out its 22 bolt action line by introducing the moderately priced 22 magazine-loading bolt action Model 56 Sporter and the Model 57 Target rifle. These rifles used some features adopted from the Winchester-Browning 22 bolt action single shot rifles and the excellent box magazine system developed for the Model 52 target rifle.

Both the Model 56 and Model 57 were introduced with a list price of about $12.50, over twice the list price of the Winchester-Browning single shot bolt action rifles at the time and about a quarter the list price of a Model 52 at the time.

The Model 56 and Model 57 weighed about 5 1/2 pounds. The Model 56 had a sporter stock and the Model 57 had a target stock with a barrel band and sling swivels. The Model 56 had open iron sights while the Model 57 had simple peep sights.

Although they were rifled for 22 long rifle cartridges both the Model 56 and Model 57 could fire both shorts and longs. The standard magazine held five long rifle cartridges. Special magazines to hold five 22 shorts could be purchased as could a special ten-shot 22 long rifle magazine. A blind magazine was also offered which allowed the rifles to be used as single shots.

Neither the Model 56 or Model 57 really caught on although some 27,500 were made before they were discontinued in 1938. However, both were good shooting and well-made little rifles. Their problem was that they were both small with 22 inch barrels, and both were considered rather expensive "boy's rifles."

At the height of the Great Depression, Winchester was looking for new products to encourage sales, and they brought out the Model 69 22 bolt action magazine-loader in 1935. The bolt action and magazine loading systems were both practically identical to those of the Model 56 and Model 57, but the Model 69 had a 28-inch barrel and a man-size stock. The Model 69 was about 42 1/2 inches long, the same length as the Model 1903 Springfield rifle. It weighed only some 5 1/2 pounds, but its size suited practically all shooters. So did its list price, about $12.50, the same as the Model 56 and Model 57. The Model 69 was an excellent shooter with an attractive design at a moderate price.

The Model 69 was a good seller, too. From its introduction until it was superceeded in 1938, some 25,000 were manufactured. The exact number, like the production numbers of the Model 56 and Model 57, is unknown because none of these rifles had serial numbers.

In the short time it was offered, a number of Model 69 variations were offered. There was the Model 69 Sporter, which had open iron sights. The Model 69 Target rifle had Winchester's simple peep sights for a dollar extra. For a few dollars more, it could be had with a

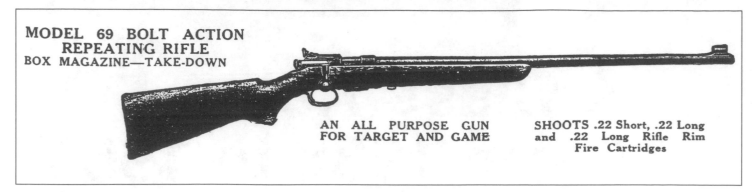

MODEL 69 BOLT ACTION REPEATING RIFLE
BOX MAGAZINE—TAKE-DOWN

AN ALL PURPOSE GUN FOR TARGET AND GAME

SHOOTS .22 Short, .22 Long and .22 Long Rifle Rim Fire Cartridges

This is the original Model 69 introduced in 1935. Its bolt action is practically identical to the Model 56 and Model 57, hoever it is a larger "man size" rifle.

Winchester 2 1/2 power or 5 power telescopic sight as well as iron sights. A very limited number were offered as the Model 697 which had telescopic sight only.

One feature shooters liked was its simple one-screw takedown system which dismounted the barrel and action from the stock and which had been carried over from the Model 56 and Model 57. For shooters who wanted a sling the factory would fit sling swivels for a dollar extra.

The Model 69 had sufficient accuracy for target shooting. Many shooters fitted lower-priced micrometer peep rear sights and globe front sights for target shooting, particularly for use by younger shooters. They did quite well in junior target matches.

In late 1938 the original Model 69 was superceded by the improved Model 69A. The Model 69A had a better bolt design which cocked on opening instead of on closing as Models 56, 57 and 69 did. It also had a new and improved safety located above its bolt handle instead of the older bolt head cocking piece safety. The original box magazine design was retained along with the trigger pull adjustment. The Model 69A's action was also the basis for the Model 75 and, in modified form, the Model 47 and Model 72.

The Model 69A was also successful from its introduction. Although very few were made during World War II, some 325,000 had been made by the time it was discontinued in 1963. The exact number is unknown since 69A's were not serial numbered, either.

Over its 25 years, the Model 69A was made in a large number of variations. The original basic $13.00 Model 69A Sporter was made with open iron sights. The Model 69A Target, which cost a dollar more, had Winchester's simple peep rear sight and hooded

MODEL 69 TARGET AND MATCH RIFLES

Model 69 Target and Match Rifles chambered for .22 Long Rifle Rim Fire cartridges only. Model 69 is also furnished in Target and Match styles with special sighting and army type leather sling strap. These are highly accurate rifles in the lower price bracket and provide excellent service for target shooting and for training for the use of the high precision match rifles used in the most exacting tournament shooting.

Model 69 Target Rifle (G6940R) above. This rifle has blade front sight and peep rear. Stock is same as standard rifle except butt end is specially shaped to give a 3 inch pitch. 1¼" Army type leather sling strap....:.........

Model 69 Match Rifle (G6941R). This rifle has blade front sight and Lyman 57E receiver sight with quarter minute click adjustments for windage and elevation. 1¼" Army type leather sling strap. Weight about 5½ lbs......

Extra 5 shot mag. ......
Extra 10 shot mag. .....

These are two of the many variations of the Model 69A rifle introduced in 1938. This rifle was also factory fitted with plain open iron sights and could be ordered fitted with these open sights and a telescopic sight.

WINCHESTER Model 69

Here is an up-to-date, all-purpose repeating rifle that is universally approved by camps, schools and clubs for Junior Marksmanship programs. Its smooth, fast-operating bolt is equipped with twin extractors. The quick, positive side lever safety . . . the Speed Lock with its crisp, clean trigger pull . . . and the graceful, well designed, full-sized walnut finish stock make the Model 69 an outstanding value.

SPECIFICATIONS — Caliber: 22 Short, Long and Long Rifle interchangeably. Capacity: 5 Short, Long or Long Rifle cartridges. Sights: Bead front, sporting rear. Receiver: Tapped for receiver sights and grooved for easy attachment of popular scopes. Barrel: 25"; twist: 1 turn in 16", right hand. Overall Length: 42". Stock Dimensions: Pull — 13⅝"; drop at comb — 1⅜"; at heel — 2¼". Weight: 5½ lbs.

Price: *$36.95*

The "H" stands for Henry

The "H" headstamp on Winchester rimfire ammunition honors B. Tyler Henry who developed the Henry lever action rifle and the 44 Henry rimfire cartridge. Henry was shop superintendent for the New Haven Arms Company, predecessor of Winchester Repeating Arms Company.

Model 69 Junior Target Shooter's Special

In addition to all the advantages of a standard Model 69, the Lyman 57 peep sight and blade type front sight on the Junior Target Shooter's Special gives you a clearer, finer sight picture. And when you add your sling to the forearm swivel you get the steadiness that means bullseyes, time and time again.

ADDED SPECIFICATIONS — Lyman 57 receiver sight, blade type front sight; 1¼" forearm sling swivel.

Price: *$47.95*

This Winchester ad from about 1950 shows the Model 69A standard and factory made Junior Target Shooter's Special Model 69. The Model 67 single shot also shown was the version of the original Browning design introduced in 1900 and still offered in 1950!

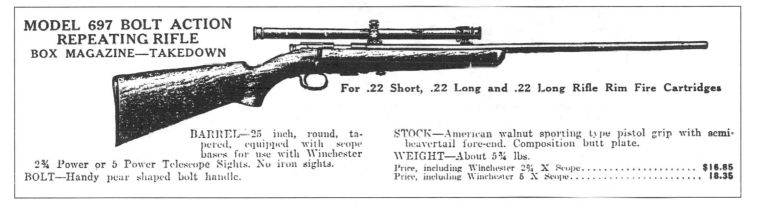

MODEL 697 BOLT ACTION REPEATING RIFLE
BOX MAGAZINE—TAKEDOWN

For .22 Short, .22 Long and .22 Long Rifle Rim Fire Cartridges

BARREL—25 inch, round, tapered, equipped with scope bases for use with Winchester 2¾ Power or 5 Power Telescope Sights. No iron sights.

BOLT—Handy pear shaped bolt handle.

STOCK—American walnut sporting type pistol grip with semi-beavertail fore-end. Composition butt plate.

WEIGHT—About 5¾ lbs.

Price, including Winchester 2¾ X Scope $16.85
Price, including Winchester 5 X Scope 18.35

The Winchester Model 697 was a variation of the Model 69 factory fitted with only a telescopic sight. This rifle was made with both the Model 69 and Model 69A actions before World War II, and it was never popular.

Model 56

Model 57

WINCHESTER
TRADE MARK

The Winchester Model 56 Sporting and Model 57 Target rifles shown here in the first ad for them which appeared in 1926. These are the rifles from which the Model 69 series was developed.

bead front sight. Right after World War II, Winchester added the Model 69A Match Rifle with a micrometer peep rear sight and a blade front sight which many shooters replaced with a commercial globe type front sight. There was also a post-World War II Model 69A Junior Target Shooter's Special version with a shortened stock and the same sights as the Model 69A Match Rifle.

The Model 69A could also be ordered with factory-fitted 2 1/2 power and 5 power telescopic sights either with or without open iron sights. This version was never very popular, although after World War II many shooters had gunsmiths fit Model 69A's with now readily available commercial telescopic sights.

In 1938, shortly after the Model 69A had been introduced, Winchester introduced the Model 75 Target rifle. The

Model 75 was a moderately priced target rifle often called "the poor man's Model 52" in tribute to that magnificent Winchester 22 rifle. The Model 75 Target is arguably one of the best moderate-priced 22 match rifles ever made. It cost about twice as much as a regular Model 69A and about half what a basic Model 52 brought.

The Model 75 Target had a medium weight 28-inch barrel, a somewhat

WINCHESTER
TRADE MARK

Chambered for .22 Long Rifle Rim Fire Cartridges Only

MODEL 75
BOLT ACTION

MODEL 75
Target Rifle

In the Model 75, Winchester presents a bolt action target rifle of fine design and high accuracy of lighter weight than the Model 52 and at materially lower price. It has 28" round tapered barrel, drilled and tapped for Winchester combination telescope sight bases. Winchester Speed Lock. Bolt is sturdy, simple, smooth operating with close tolerances. Thumb lever safety. Let-off is crisp without take-up or creep. Target type stock with pistol grip and semi-beavertail fore end of American walnut. Approx. length of pull 13¼"; drop at comb 1⅝", at heel 2¼". Steel butt plate, checkered. Adjustable sling swivel base. Winchester No. 105A quick detachable front sight with post and 3 extra apertures. Redfield 75HW micrometer receiver sight. Also furnished without sights. 1¼" Army type leather sling strap. Weight about 8 lbs. 10 oz.

The Winchester Model 75 target rifle which uses the same bolt action as the Model 69A which was introduced in 1938. This rifle is a perfect training rifle for 22 rimfire target shooters.

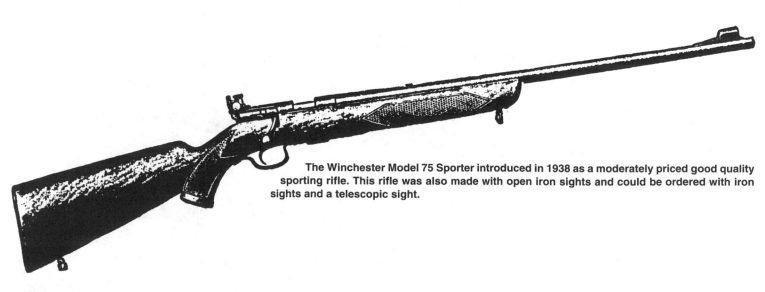

The Winchester Model 75 Sporter introduced in 1938 as a moderately priced good quality sporting rifle. This rifle was also made with open iron sights and could be ordered with iron sights and a telescopic sight.

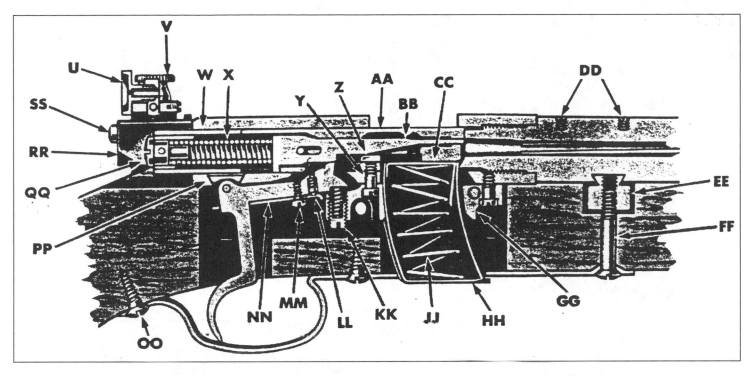

This cross section of a Winchester Model 75 action appeared in a World War II US Army manual on 22 rimfire training rifles. This action is the standard Model 69A type and shows the trigger adjusting screw "KK" which many Model 69A family rifle owners never knew they had.

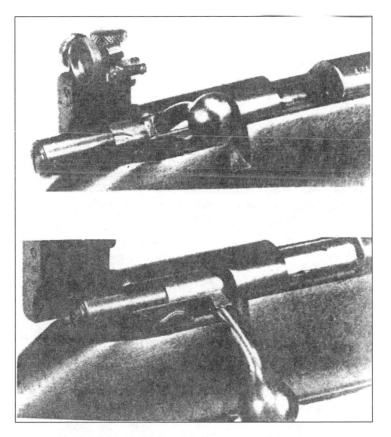

Close-up photographs of the Winchester Model 69A action also used on the Model 47, Model 72 and Model 75 rifles. Note the safety immediately behind the bolt handle.

This is the simple bolt head safety used on the Winchester Model 56, Model 57 and Model 69 rifles which was adapted from the Browning designed single shot bolt action 22 rifle Winchester introduced in 1900.

heavier stock than the 69A, and sling swivels were standard equipment. It weighed about 8 1/2 pounds. It was equipped with a micrometer peep rear sight and a globe-type front sight. After World War II, the Model 75 was offered with bases for telescopic sights if requested, and factory installed a beautifully made 7-pound rifle with a 24-inch barrel and a premium grade checkered walnut stock. Its standard sights were a micrometer peep rear and hooded bead front sight, and factory fitted telescopic sights and/or open iron sights were available on special order. The number of Model 75 Sporters made parts are the same as those of the Model 69A. By the time the Model 72 was discontinued in 1959, 161,000 had been manufactured. Again they were not serial numbered.

The Model 72 was built in three standard versions: The most common one was the basic Model 72 Sporter with

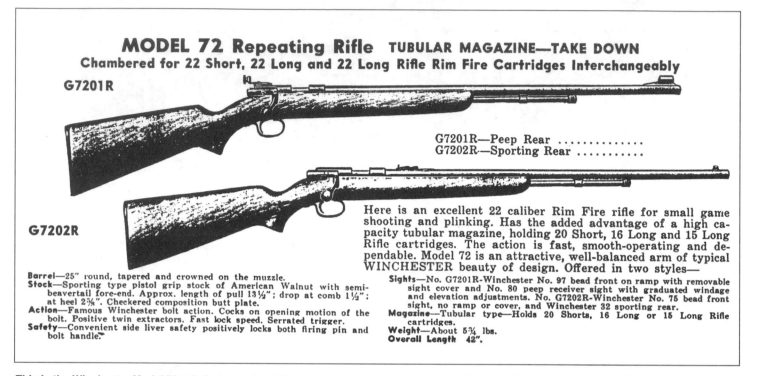

MODEL 72 Repeating Rifle TUBULAR MAGAZINE—TAKE DOWN
Chambered for 22 Short, 22 Long and 22 Long Rifle Rim Fire Cartridges Interchangeably

G7201R

G7201R—Peep Rear . . . .
G7202R—Sporting Rear . . . .

G7202R

Here is an excellent 22 caliber Rim Fire rifle for small game shooting and plinking. Has the added advantage of a high capacity tubular magazine, holding 20 Short, 16 Long and 15 Long Rifle cartridges. The action is fast, smooth-operating and dependable. Model 72 is an attractive, well-balanced arm of typical WINCHESTER beauty of design. Offered in two styles—

Barrel—25" round, tapered and crowned on the muzzle.
Stock—Sporting type pistol grip stock of American Walnut with semi-beavertail fore-end. Approx. length of pull 13½"; drop at comb 1¼"; at heel 2⅝". Checkered composition butt plate.
Action—Famous Winchester bolt action. Cocks on opening motion of the bolt. Positive twin extractors. Fast lock speed. Serrated trigger.
Safety—Convenient side liver safety positively locks both firing pin and bolt handle.

Sights—No. G7201R-Winchester No. 97 bead front on ramp with removable sight cover and No. 80 peep receiver sight with graduated windage and elevation adjustments. No. G7202R-Winchester No. 75 bead front sight, no ramp or cover, and Winchester 32 sporting rear.
Magazine—Tubular type—Holds 20 Shorts, 16 Long or 15 Long Rifle cartridges.
Weight—About 5¾ lbs.
Overall Length 42".

This is the Winchester Model 72 tubular magazine rifle which is a variation of the Model 69A rifle. The most common of this model is the lower one with the open iron sights. The Model 72 was introduced in 1938.

telescopic sights were also available, all extras, of course.

The US Army tested the Model 75 Target in 1939 and adopted it as an "alternate standard cal. 22 training rifle." During World War II the US Army procured about 25,000 Model 75 Target rifles from about 1941 to 1944. At the Army's request many of these were fitted with blade front sights, and some of them assembled during the war are Parkerized, not blued. Although the Model 75 Target is no longer a US Army "item of issue" because its parts are no longer available some can still be found in use in such places as the U.S. Army R.O.T.C. programs.

Although the Model 75 Target rifle is frequently encountered there is a also a Model 75 Sporter rifle which is quite rare. It was introduced about 1940 to fill shooters' desires for a high grade moderately priced 22 bolt action sporting rifle. The Model 75 Sporter is is unknown because records have never been analyzed to count them.

By the time the Model 75 was discontinued in 1958, 89,000 Target and Sporter models had been produced. They are the only rifles in the Model 69 family with sequential serial numbers. The Model 75s were as rugged, reliable and good shooting as any 22 in their class ever made. As a result of their popularity and capabilities, the Winchester factory and many gunsmiths modified them for shooters, and it is often impossible to tell which variation is factory-made and which a gunsmith job.

In 1938 Winchester introduced a tubular magazine version of the Model 69A rifle known as the Model 72 for shooters who preferred this magazine system. It took a number of changes in the basic Model 69A action to make the under-barrel tubular magazine Model 71. However, the barrel and many open iron sights which cost about the same as the basic 69A. There was also a Model 72 Target fitted with the simple Winchester peep rear sight and a hooded bead front sight. Sling swivels for either model had to be special-ordered from the factory for a dollar extra.

The Model 72 Gallery rifle was also made specifically for sale to shooting galleries which used to abound in amusement parks, carnivals and circus midways. This rifle was never fitted with a sling and always had open iron sights, and its barrel was the only one in the Model 96A family specifically rifled for 22 shorts instead of long rifle cartridges. The Model 72 Gallery was a special order version, and examples in good condition are seldom encountered.

The last rifle in the Model 69A family was the single shot Model 47. Some 43,000 were produced between 1949 and 1954. The Model 47 provided a

This Winchester Model 47 single shot version of the Model 69A was introduced in 1947.

moderate-priced good quality single shot bolt action 22 rifle. It was made by omitting the magazine opening from the bottom of the Model 69A receiver and the magazine provisions from the stock. There was a Model 47 Sporter with open iron sights and a Model 47 Target with a simple Winchester peep rear sight and hooded bead front sight. A shortened "junior" stock could be special ordered from the factory. The factory would also install a micrometer rear sight and globe front sight on special order. Like the shortened stocks, these were also frequently gunsmith done. The Model 47 is a rugged, reliable and good shooting. It was also the least popular and least successful of the Model 69A family.

When the last of the Model 69As was produced in 1963, a total of 620,000 Model 69As, Model 75s, Model 72s and Model 47s had been produced. It was a successful line with, except for the World War II years, some 32,000 produced a year.

Following the Model 69A family, Winchester made two much less successful 22 bolt action lines in the same class. One included Models 121, 131 and 1141 offered from 1967 to 1973. The other included Models 310 and 320, sold from 1972 to 1975. Not many shooters thought these models were as good shooting as the Model 69As, and by the time they were introduced, they faced competition from a profusion of 22 bolt action rifles on the market.

There are, fortunately, large numbers of the great old Winchester Model 69A family around, and they are still some of the best rifles in their class. Many of them are still in use, and, unless it is a factory new collector's example, there is no reason not to shoot them since modern good quality 22 ammunition will never wear a rifle out. It is, however, recommended that only long rifle 22s be used since shorts will damage the chamber if enough of them are fired.

I have a Model 69A Target with a micrometer peep rear sight and a target globe front sight which I purchased shortly after I returned from World War II. I taught both my boys to shoot with it, and we still shoot it once in a while. I am still delighted with its excellent accuracy at any range suitable for a 22, and I highly prize it. It is in good condition, and certainly a fine example of one of the many fine families of rifles Winchester has made.   •

A post-World War II target shooter aiming a Model 69-style 22 target rifle.

THE HAT TRICK

by Jack Collins

NO, THIS isn't about hockey. (That's another thing I don't understand.) What it is about is your eyes and shooting a handgun.

Do you have scopes on all your rifles? Do you wear bifocals? (Yes, it counts even if they don't have lines.) Are your kids in high school? If your answer to the first two questions is "no", but the answer to the third question is "yes", then it won't be long before you are changing your answers to the first two questions, because as sure as death and taxes, your eyes are gonna change. The result of this change is not pleasant, but it can be minimized, at least its impact on your ability to shoot a handgun.

"What's this gonna cost me?" you ask. Maybe $5.00 and 10 minutes; maybe nothing but your time. I discovered this phenomenon accidently, and since it cost me absolutely nothing, why, that's what I'm gonna charge you. The $5.00 is for you to buy a baseball-type cap. You already have one? Cool. If you are aware that the visor was intended to shade your eyes and not the back of your neck or one ear, then we already have one thing in common. Try this: Put it on, and pull it down as though you were trying to shade your eyes from a low-lying sun. You want to be able to see straight ahead, but not a lot higher. Pick up your handgun and look at the sights. Front sight a little fuzzy? There's good news and bad news. First, the bad news; it ain't gonna get any better. The only alternative to growing older is not acceptable, so they're gonna continue to get worse. Bifocals or even trifocals can postpone the problem, but in my case I found that their use mandated an uncomfortable head angle in order to sharpen the sights. The good news is that the $5.00 cap you are now wearing is the solution. No, it doesn't have to be a baseball cap; it can be a cowboy hat, a "Jones" cap or any other style of headware that has a brim. (No sir, I'm sorry, I haven't been able to adapt this method to a fez or a beret, but you give it a whirl if you like.)

Simply lower your head slowly until the brim of your cap begins to intrude into your line of sight. Notice that just before the cap brim blocks your view of the sights, the sights appear much sharper. Stop moving your head. The sights stay sharp. Raise your head and they go fuzzy again. Tilt your head downward again and, Voila! It only takes a few minutes practice and you will be able to produce this effect quickly and easily.

That's it. You know all you need to know in order to see your sights clearly. It works. I am not enough of a physicist to explain how (I think it has something to do with the wave nature of light.), but who cares? All we need to know is it works. It works for me at age 64, it works for my wife at a lesser age (I may be 64, but I'm not yet senile!), it works with glasses or without. It just works.

Don't thank me. Just go shooting more, and take a young person with you. Maybe they'll even start wearing their caps straight, but whether or not that happens, get them started shooting before they think that the only shooting is done in the "drive-by" mode. ●

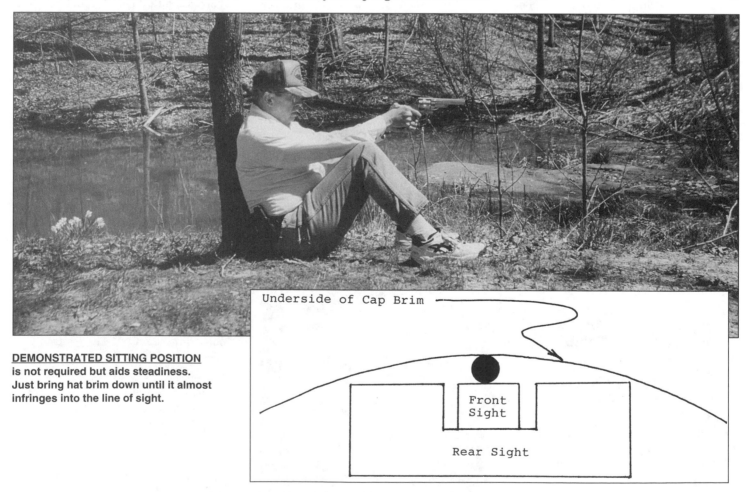

DEMONSTRATED SITTING POSITION is not required but aids steadiness. Just bring hat brim down until it almost infringes into the line of sight.

Underside of Cap Brim

Front Sight

Rear Sight

RESULTANT SIGHT PICTURE will look like this.

BY: RODERICK T. HALVORSEN

Try The 30/220/06..

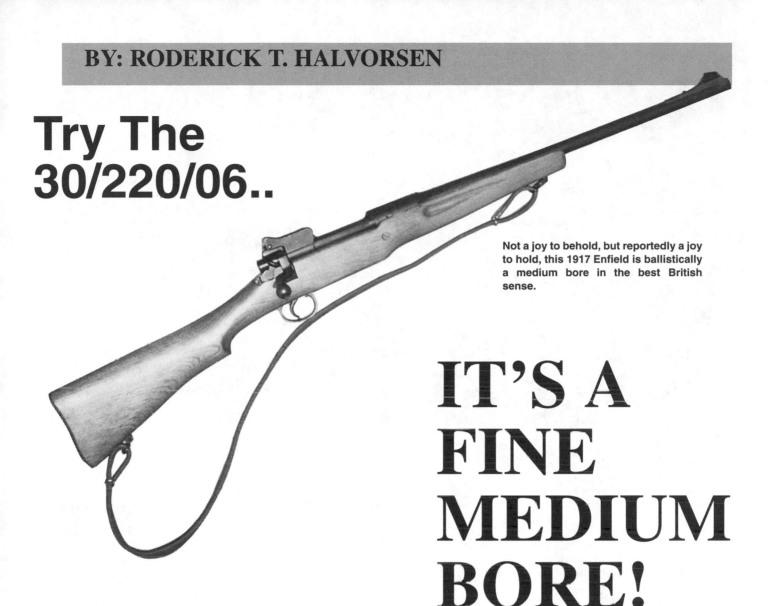

Not a joy to behold, but reportedly a joy to hold, this 1917 Enfield is ballistically a medium bore in the best British sense.

IT'S A FINE MEDIUM BORE!

WITH THE stealth and silence of a wrecking ball crashing through a tenement building, the bull bored through branch and brush on his way down the mountain. Needlessly straining my eyes, I watched the animal burst through the lodgepole pines, pull up and stop on the cut bank ten feet above the overgrown logging road. Just 200 yards away, and with the rising sun brilliantly outlining his immense bulk, there was no doubt in my mind that in his herd he was the only one that mattered.

The bull collapsed at the shot, the bullet taking him high on the shoulder, mashing the spine. Unable to rise, the animal lashed out with his rack when I approached him. With the number two tine on his right beam broken off at the base, and with all other points chipped and worn, he was a big fellow with a past, game to the end.

From no more than four feet away, a finisher was fired into his neck from above. It was this shot that started me on a quest that has included months of shooting tests and ballistic comparisons the results of which follow.

The rifle that day was my well-worn and utterly reliable left-hand Sako Finnbear. The caliber was the classic 375 Holland and Holland Magnum and the load was the super accurate 300 grain Hornady round nose. Propelled by 76 grains of IMR 4350, it chronographs 2450 fps at 15 feet from the business end of the 23-inch barrel. With its 4x Leupold scope, this combination has been for me the killing standard. With it I have taken various plains game in southern Africa and animals ranging from 80 pound whitetail does to 800-pound bull elk here at home in the states.

An elk taken at 180 long strides on a crystal clear day is an unlikely inspiration for a foul weather brush gun, but that is exactly what it was. More specifically, it was the coup de grace that did it. That shot penetrated only six inches of elk, albeit 4 inches of that was very tough and resilient vertebrae. The bullet never exited, but rather came to rest like a half-dissolved throat lozenge in the gullet of the big bull.

Many days of elk season here in the Pacific Northwest are spent mopping scope lenses with a sopping wet glove or peering through the tube into a blizzard of snow flakes at a murky brown ghost wafting through a clump of second-growth fir. Many are the days I have wished I had an iron-sighted rifle capable of instant use without regard for the downpour or snowstorm, yet one which if called upon would rise to the occasion to down an elk with certainty at 200 yards or even a bit more.

In the past I have always carried that scoped 375 because for me it has always delivered the deathblow of the Hammer of Thor. In the hunting game, when you find something that works it's a good idea not to try to fix it. However, the price for such ballistic certainty has been paid in really foul weather, when a wet scope has been a game-losing nuisance.

The bullet buster and the author's 30/220/06 tough weather gun, the one he thinks nearly matches his trusty 375.

The failure of the 300 grain Hornady to fully penetrate the neck of the bull elk, reminded me that even the great all-round caliber from Messers Holland and Holland has its limitations, and allowing my search for a foulweather gun to include some caliber other than three-seven-five would constitute no act of ballistic treason on my part.

Since I would be starting from scratch, so to speak, I wanted my foul weather gun to be shorter and lighter than my Sako, and chambered for a caliber that in such a configuration wouldn't stamp out my ability to hear the birds sing or back me out from under my sombrero when touched off. While my Marlin 45-70 lever-gun easily meets both the close-in power and lightness requirements, that big-bore cartridge just does not have what it takes for field shooting at ranges appreciably greater than John Elway can throw a football.

Thus, as I found out early on, the caliber was going to be the make or break factor in my choice of rifle. Of course, one further requirement had nothing to do with technical specifications at all. This came from the Secretary of the Treasury. Legally known as my wife, and colloquially as "yes, ma'am", her ruling made it clear that the new addition had to be of minimal investment value, that is, real cheap!

That last requirement effectively blotted out any plans I might otherwise have had to build a custom 375 complete with stainless barrel, express sights and a synthetic stock. In fact, at

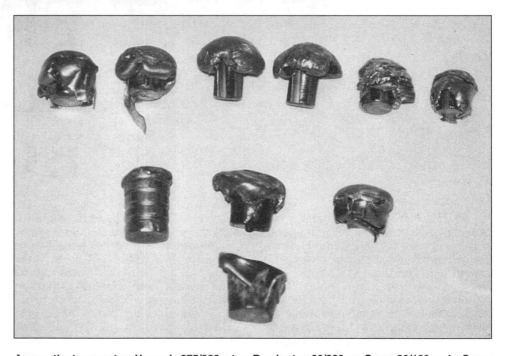

Across the top are: two Hornady 375/300s; two Remington 30/220s; a Speer 30/180 and a Speer 30/150. Below are a Lee 457/402; a Remington 45/450 (and jacket) and a Remington 45/300. Author believes they will all work.

the time, it eliminated the option of purchasing any additional rifle at all!

Just when I'd about given up and decided to try my old No. 5 Lee-Enfield carbine without alteration, I thought about the older Winchester-actioned 1917 Enfield "parts gun" reposing in my safe. With no real collector value to ruin, and possessing one of the finest actions available for a rough duty rifle, I spied it, I grabbed it and I set to work.

With Mauser-style controlled-round feeding and extractor, a safety I believe is superior to the Mauser's, and with an excellent and rugged rear sight arrangement, the unaltered 1917 action is perfect for my intended use. However, handiness is certainly not an adjective I would use to describe the rifle in its military guise. Thus, with a mitre saw, farrier's rasp and sandpaper the World War II birch replacement stock was whittled down to size. The barrel was lopped off a couple times till I found that 20-1/2 inches imparts superb handling characteristics to the rifle. A ramp front sight base was installed by a local gunsmith. Since I find beads useless, but couldn't locate a Sourdough or heavy blade, I used a bead as a base and with "JB Weld" built up a very serviceable and more importantly a highly visible square-topped, thick front sight.

Thus, in about two weeks and with very little cash outlay, the gun part of the equation was solved. With stout and weatherproof sights it is just made for foul weather, and with perfect balance and compact size it is a delight to carry. Though reeking a bit of 1950

"sporterization", I know of no commercial rifle with its positive features. Overall, I find my reworked '17 to be a fine addition to my rack and just as useful as a Stillson wrench in a fistfight.

Where the shootin' iron is basically a tool, the caliber has become a fascination.

Like any other patriotic American gun crank, I have a fairly long association with the hoary old US Caliber .30, Model 1906. That it has long been given nearly unanimous approval as an elk cartridge has not escaped me, though my experience with it has been limited to vermin and deer shooting. I guess familiarity bred comtempt, for I initially overlooked it as a contender against the

mountain range of reliability I have known in the 375. In fact, I originally planned on having the '17 rebored to some "more suitable" caliber like the 35 Whelen. I can now say that I am heartily glad I did not. Comparing my trusted 375 with my "new found" 30-06, I will spit it right out: performancewise, they ain't too far apart!

Against the gasps and guffaws of the arms-enlightened, let me say first that your garden-variety deer load from the '06 isn't dancing in the same nightclub as the 300 grain projectile from the 375. Yet neither am I saying that you need to take out a third mortgage for a box of custom 30 caliber bullets.

The loads I eventually settled on in my foul weather elk gun are simple to assemble, relatively inexpensive, ancient in the extreme and utterly, completely forgotten! The loads I now use take the 30-06 into lands trodden by such worthies as the 338-'06, 35 Whelen, 9.3x62 and yes, even the 375 Magnum. What's more, every 30-06 out there is a medium bore in disguise, deserving no apologies or caveats. All it takes is one bullet to do it—the big 220.

The 30-caliber 220 grain bullet predates the 30-06 by nearly 15 years, when it was the the standard projectile used in both of the 30-06's predecessors; the 30-40 Krag and the 30-03 service cartridges. Loaded to about 2000 fps in the Krag, and 2300 in the '03, the softnose version garnered an enviable reputation for almost boring dependability, penetrating deeply and holding together well in heavy game.

Recent developments have found the gun gurus enamored with long range super aerodynamic wonder bullets usually topping out in 30 caliber at 180 grains. One problem with such admittedly fine performing bullets is their cost. The price of a couple boxes of many so-called "custom" bullets would pay for a new dress for the wife and a nice dinner to take her to in it. I just can't get happily excited about paying that much for something that for the most part is going to end up in a dirt backstop. Moreover, I like to practice shooting with the same ammo I use hunting. I wonder how many hunters out there use "custom" bullets for hunting, but use their expense as an excuse not to practise much?

The big 220 round nose bullet has been derided for not possessing a ballistic coefficient conducive to long range shooting. In short, according to the pundits, it just slows down too much and thus has too looping a trajectory for modern use.

All of this is fine, well and good, but I don't ever plan to shoot farther than 200-to-225 yards with my foul weather gun. If a longer shot presents itself, I'll be happy to let the biggest bull in the woods go since the only time I'll be us-

Writer's rig allows him to compare known performers with new loads, but not without getting wet.

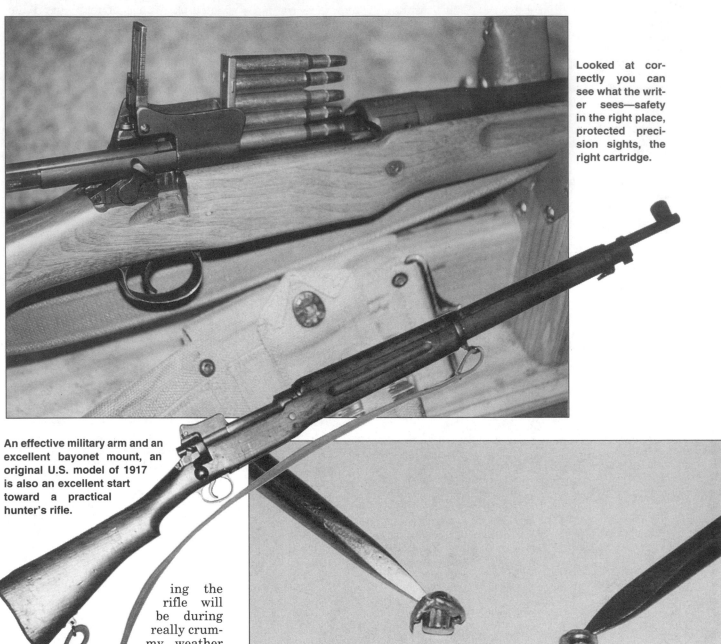

Looked at correctly you can see what the writer sees—safety in the right place, protected precision sights, the right cartridge.

An effective military arm and an excellent bayonet mount, an original U.S. model of 1917 is also an excellent start toward a practical hunter's rifle.

On the left is a Hornady 30/220 that demolished an elk leg; on the right a 30/150 that didn't do as well.

ing the rifle will be during really crummy weather which means with the scope I'd probably have to pass it up as well. I've walked away from animals before, and I'll do it again. Truth is, the trajectory of the 30/220/06 is just fine for 200-yard shooting. With a 3-inch high zero at 100 yards, no holdover or under is needed on elk-sized game out to 225 yards or so.

In one characteristic the 220 can not be beaten by any lighter bullet: sectional density, (sd). Now obviously, high sectional density does not equal fine performance, but having said that, when comparing traditionally constructed bullets (one lead core, one gilding metal jacket) it is an excellent place to start! The 30-caliber 220-grain bullet possesses the highest sectional density of any bullet currently loaded in commonly available sporting

ammunition from 375 caliber on down. The SD of the 30/220 even beats the 300-grain slug in 375 caliber!

Table 1 shows the weights needed in various calibers to equal the SD of the 220 grain .30 caliber. None of those weights are available in commonly

loaded ammunition or as normally available components. The closest is the 6.5 (.264) caliber where 160-grain Hornady slugs are available. The big 30/220 is available from Sierra and Hornady and, while I believe Remington no longer offers them as compo-

Leg Bone Test					
	Bullet	Velocity FPS	Recovered Diameter	Recovered Weight Grains	Retained Weight Percentage
Hornady	220 RN	2400	.571	84	38
Speer	150 SP	2850	.405	35	23

nents, Remington 220s can still be found from a number of sources as I write this. It is still available in loaded factory ammunition.

Table I

Bullet Weight Needed To Equal Sectional Density of .308 Caliber 220 Grain Bullet, (SD .331)

Caliber	Weight in Grains with SD .331
.224	116
.243	137
.257	153
.264	161
.277	177
.284	187
.311	224
.323	242
.338	265
.348	281
.358	297
.366	311
.375	326
.458	486

Some custom-made bullets in other calibers with sd's approaching the .331 of the standard 30/220 are available, and specially-made bullets are possible, but problems arise. First, obviously is the high cost. Second, standard rifling twist rates in many calibers will not stabilize bullets with sectional densities as high as that possessed by the 30 caliber 220. Third, for many of the calibers listed in Table 1, obtainable velocities fall several hundred feet below those with lighter bullets. Trajectories are heightened and terminal performance possibly lessened. The 30-06 just happens to be able to

launch and stabilize its heavyweight projectile at very satisfactory velocity for most game shooting. Furthermore, recoil from such loads is manageable indeed.

Of course, months-on-end spent in my study under a pile of calculators, slide rules and photostat copies of ballistics tables gleaned from "Hatcher's Notebook" prove nothing other than that I have not totally forgotten everything Mrs. Decuzzi taught me in 10th grade algebra. In the shooting game the proof is in the pudding, and in this case the pudding is made up of shattered bone and perforated muscle. Unfortunately elk season just ended when I began my quest, so some other form of "tissue" would have to suffice as a test medium.

I have played around with water-soaked phone books and recovery boxes and while both serve to stop bullets and shooting results in both can be duplicated, I don't like using either. First, collecting an adequate supply of phone books is difficult when the only town in the area doesn't even have one. Second, recovery boxes, almost regardless of what soil/sand/sawdust mixture is used are dirty and a pain in the neck to reset after shooting.

Discussing this dilemma with my son over oreo cookies and a glass of milk, I suddenly realized just how much of the stuff that kid drinks. In fact, in no time I had a mudroom full of plastic jugs waiting to be filled with something that would slow down a bullet. After much tinkering I settled on pure water. With old, wet cedar fence boards serving to provide "bone", the final "bullet buster" works like a charm. Where water-only provided a fine medium for producing classic mushrooms, the addition of one two-inch board between each jug served to tax the bullets just a bit, tearing the

expansion petals off some slugs. Results have been amazingly repeatable, and since my setup exists right next to a source of water (my creek), I have no trouble filling jugs. To be sure, at 21 feet the hydraulics are impressive, and I don't come home dry, but the bullets can be found and the buster rebuilt in no time.

Note: I have no doubt that high velocity small caliber cartridges such as the 25-06 and 270 Winchester can be and are used effectively on heavy game such as elk. However, only premium controlled expansion bullets should be used in such calibers. With such bullets there may indeed be some validity in using foot/pounds to make killing power comparisons. With such bullet construction high velocity can be used to advantage.

When using traditionally constructed bullets (one lead core, one gilding metal jacket), high velocity can cause problems, notably premature expansion, fragmentation and inadequate penetration. With such bullets I submit that the momentum and pounds/feet methods are the safest mathematical indicators of killing power in heavy game. These methods favor bullet weight, which is just right when traditional bullets are used.

However, all mathematical comparisons of one bullet type with another can be problematical, and will insure years of campfire arguments to come.

Personally, I don't get too dogmatic over any particular mathematical formula. I prefer to make direct comparisons in the media of the bullet buster, using a load (such as the 375/300) known to be effective on heavy game as a control. In such a way direct and accurate comparisons can be made

Table III: Killing Power Comparisons

Cartridge	Bullet Velocity	Weight	Foot/Pounds	Momentum	Pounds/Feet
375H&H	300	2450	3999	74	105
30'06	220	2405	2826	53	76
	180	2621	2746	47	67
	150	2878	2759	43	62
45-70	405	1600	2303	65	93
	402	1345	1615	54	77
	300	1586	1676	48	68

What is more, this method has provided me a means by which to compare the close-in performance of my pet 375/300 load and the 30/220/06. The results have been surprising. Table II lines them out.

It can be seen that many bullets (indeed, calibers) actually penetrate to

similar depths in the water/wood media. Effects on the bullets differ, however.

Comparing extremes, the 375/300 sheds more weight than the 30 caliber 150 grain bullet ends up with. However, the retained weight of the 375/300 is nonetheless nearly double that of the 150 grain pill! Remember, as long as

penetration is adequate, shed bullet weight results in ballistic fragments that can produce greater wounding effect. Remember also that bullets that fragment prematurely and do not get to the vitals do not bring home the bacon. It is this reality that makes heavy-for-caliber bullets reliable performers.

Comparing traditional 30 caliber competitors, we see that the Remington 220 beats out the Speer 180 in penetration, recovered diameter and weight. Indeed, the Hornady 220 ("soft" in comparison to the Remington) turns in a relatively low retained weight percentage though its actual recovered weight is nonetheless 10% greater than that of the 180 grain bullet! Recovered Remington 220s were nearly 90% heavier than recovered Speer 150s though the big 220 started out only 50% heavier.

Especially notable is the fact that the Remington 30/220, while starting off 80 grains lighter than the 375 bullet, ended up retaining more weight after penetrating the bullet buster. Indeed, recovered diameters were greater, too! There is no mistaking the fact that the 30/220/06 compares very favorably to the 375 H&H. And, while the closeup performance of the 45-70 is well-known, not shown in table 11 was the obviously greater violence of shots made with the 30/220/06 and the 375/300. Both of those actually shattered the pallet supporting the jugs and boards!

Comparisons in the bullet buster support the notion that heavy bullets with high sectional densities are highly dependable. In fact, dependability has long been the word associated with 220 grain bullets in the 30-06. While lighter bullets can at times turn in creditable results, the simple fact is that the more weight a bullet starts off with, the more it can afford to shed along its trip through bone and brawn.

One last test was made to explore this further. Two heavy hind elk legs were rescued from the marrow-hungry jaws of my dogs. Each was placed in front of the first jug of the bullet buster. One was shot with the 150 grain speer Spitzer (impact about 2850 FPS) and the other shot with the 220 grain Hornady round nose at about 2400 FPS. As these are really massive bones I felt they would severely stress the bullets. They did.

Total penetration was similar, both bullets having travelled through the bone, the first jug and the first board. Both were found in the second jug. Recovery weights, diameters and indeed destruction caused were very different. The big 220 simply did a better job, demonstrated by both the following data and the contrast in damage done to the bones. In regards to the latter, there was simply no comparison, as shown in the photo. The destruction caused by the 220 was massive. While the 150 did of course penetrate the bone, that's about all it did to it. The big 220 fractured and pulped it. Exit "wound" was massive.

Now I am still a real fan of the 375/300, with some real experience to back up my affinity for it, but facts are facts, and the fact here is that the

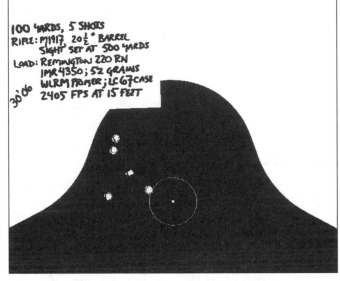

100 YARDS, 5 SHOTS
RIFLE: M1917, 20½" BARREL
SIGHT SET AT 500 YARDS
LOAD: REMINGTON 220 RN
IMR 4350; 52 GRAINS
WLRM PRIMER; LC 67 CASE
30.06
2405 FPS AT 15 FEET

Very tidy 5-shot group under three inches at 100 yards, iron-sighted; IMR4350, 220gr. Remington bullet, 2405FPS.

Table II: Close Range Performance

Cartridge	Bullet	Impact Velocity	Penetration Water	(Inches) Wood	Diameter Recovered Bullet	Weight (GR) Recovered Bullet	Retained Weight (%)
45-70	Lee 402 HP	1345	17.25	6	.557	327	81
45-70	Rem 405 JK	1600	11.5	4	.763	350	86
45-70	Rem 300 JK	1586	10	2	.658	256	85
30'06	Rem 220 RN	2405	11.5	3.5	.740	189	86
30'06	Horn 220 RN	2400	11.5	2.25	.655	151	69
30'06	Speer 180 SP	2621	11.5	2.25	.621	137	76
30'06	Speer 150 SP	2878	11.5	2.25	.524	95	63
375 HH	Horn 300 RN	2450	11.5	3.5	.65	178	59

All shots fired at 21 feet.
Lee 402 HP 45-70 bullet cast of wheel weights.
Rem 405 GR bullet from 45-70 completely shed its jacket. Jacket was found on the ground nearly intact and is not included in the recovered bullet weight.
Without boards in place, penetration increased dramatically. For example, the 220 grain Hornady penetrated 28.75 inches (5 jugs) of water and was found on the ground behind the last jug.

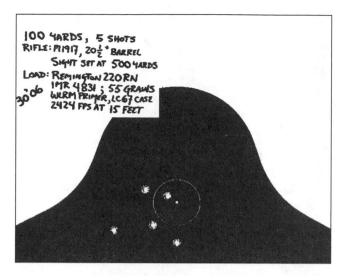

Handwritten on target:
100 YARDS, 5 SHOTS
RIFLE: P1917, 20½" BARREL
SIGHT SET AT 500 YARDS
LOAD: REMINGTON 220 RN
30°06   IMR 4831 ; 55 GRAINS
WLRM PRIMER, LC 67 CASE
2424 FPS AT 15 FEET

Deja vu all over again: 100 yards, under three inches for five shots, but IMR4831 and 2424FPS.

Foul Weather Rifle Specifications

US Rifle Model 1917

Weight empty	8.2 pounds
Barrel	20-1/2 inches
Overall length	41 inches
Magazine capacity	6 (1 in chamber)

Table IV: Sectional Densities of Widely Available Heavy-for-Caliber Bullets

Caliber	Weight	SD
.224	62	.177
.243	100	.242
.257	120	.260
.264	160	.328
.277	150	.279
.284	175	.310
.308	220	.301
.311	215	.317
.323	220	.301
.338	250	.313
.348	250	.295
.358	250	.279
.366	286	.305
.375	300	.305
.458	500	.341

Table VI: Loads Used in Chopped 1917-220 Grain Loads

Powder	Grains	Case	Primer	Velocity
IMR 4831	55	LC 67	WLRM	2424
IMR 4350	52	LC 67	WLRM	2405

* The above powders were chosen for the sake of tradition and easy local availability as much as for any other. So much work with the 220 grain bullet was done with these powders in days of yore that picking a good load is as easy as simply selecting one from any of a multitude of loadbooks.

Both of the above loads are comfortably under maximum in my rifle but obviously I can not speak for any other rifle. Normal "working up" procedures should be used, starting at 10% below the above-listed charges.

Working up loads with two powders is a hedge against the possibilty that one when needed may not be available nearby. The capabilities of both 4350 and 4831 with heavy bullets in the 30'06 are well known. Both are classics.

30/220/06 dances the tango with the 375/300, and in the same nightclub! With trajectories and terminal performance so similar, the quest is over.

Over the months I developed a respect for my weather gun and the 30/220/06 cartridge. The combination has won my confidence as a specialized elk rig. Next year when the snow flies and rain falls I'll grab my chopped '17 and stoke it with a fistful of big 220's, confident that it will get the job done. ●

These are all 30s—150 Speers on left, then 180 Speers, 220 Hornady's and 220 Remingtons. They illustrate the author's point.

QUALITY REPRODUCTIONS

By Ken Ramage

Introduced in 1973 and discontinued years later, Lyman's Plains Rifle is clearly related to today's Trade Rifle.

A Hardy Handful in Production for 20 Years!

REPLICA MUZZLELOADERS—copies of earlier muskets, revolvers and such—have been with us for nearly 50 years; generally available from one overseas manufacturer or another, through one importer or another. Muzzleloaders of proprietary design are a more recent phenomenon. A proprietary design being a unique model designed by, and manufactured to the specifications of, a manufacturer or importer and marketed exclusively by them. The clear patriarch of this branch of the muzzleloading family is the classic Thompson/Center Hawken Rifle.

Introduced in 1970, and still in full production today, this successful side-hammer design has had a widespread, and still-visible, effect on the market as others in the business—primarily Italian gunmakers—rushed their versions of the T/C Hawken into production. Soon, just about every importer had at least one variation of this rifle in his line. Often the only discernible difference between the guns from the various importers was the design of the brass

patchbox, although the guns were made by several manufacturers.

A few years later, January of '73 to be exact, I joined Lyman Products Corporation—the old "Lyman Gun Sight" founded in 1878. The company had its Italian-made half-stock rifle to introduce at the NSGA Show mid-month. The Lyman model was distinctive because of its very large, spacious brass patchbox. Otherwise, it was externally the same as the rest: Walnut stock, adjustable double set-triggers, brass furniture, 28-inch octagonal barrel measuring 15/16-inch across the flats with a rifling rate of one turn in 48 inches and a fully adjustable rear sight. It was the new Lyman Plains Rifle.

These were very good years for muzzleloaders. The Civil War Centennial was just past and the Revolutionary War Bicentennial was fast approaching. Muzzleloading guns increasingly appeared at shooting ranges across the country and re-enactors lined up to buy their Zouave and Brown Bess muskets. More companies jumped into the business with guns and accessories. Out West, a different area of muzzleloading enthusiasm had been gathering steam and was now drawing more notice...the fur trade era and its' mountain men.

Exploration of the West, fur-trapping...bring to mind cherished American icons of independence, self-sufficiency and adventure. The legendary rifle of choice was the half-stock Hawken, although other makers were clearly represented (and full-stock rifles were not uncommon). Back East, the big debates whirled around subjects like the correct color of thread with which to stitch the re-enactor's uniform while the correct choice of a properly pedigreed replica firearm was pretty clear. Not so out West.

What was an authentic Hawken – or mountain rifle, for that matter? Well, it certainly was not that gun from Thompson/Center—or all those copies of it, according to the self-styled purists. Further complicating the issue was the

industry standards, adapted to the muzzleloading system. Lots of helpful information came from that project. Concurrently, I was becoming well acquainted with our Italian gunmakers as well as the various U. S muzzleloading businesses, large and small.

During this period, Lyman briefly marketed a semi-custom Plains Rifle kit. Components of the kit included (as I recall) the coil-spring lock, adjustable set-triggers, sights and other fittings from the Italian gun. Also, a classically styled (Hawken) half-stock without patchbox, cut-rifling barrel and iron furniture (including toe plate) from the Sharon Rifle Barrel Company of Kalispell, Montana. The kit did not sell well, being perhaps too expensive for the market or requiring a bit too much critical work for the average home builder.

However, the seed of an idea was sown and, with the nod from the Front Office, I went to work on a new rifle.

shipped to Investarm, located in the northern Italian gun-making city of Brescia, and I soon followed on my annual visit.

Owned and operated by the Salvinelli family, Investarm (as it is now known) was spacious, engineering-oriented and equipped with machinery comparable to many of our U.S. companies. The prototype was routed through engineering for evaluation and any slight adjustments needed to adapt the design to machining and production requirements. However, not all the product specifications were to be found in the actual prototype.

You can say the barrel is the heart of a muzzleloader and, in this case, it was certainly true. First, the rate of twist was to be one turn in 66 inches—a true roundball twist delivering top accuracy at higher velocities. Second, and perhaps most importantly, was the requirement for a higher proof pressure level.

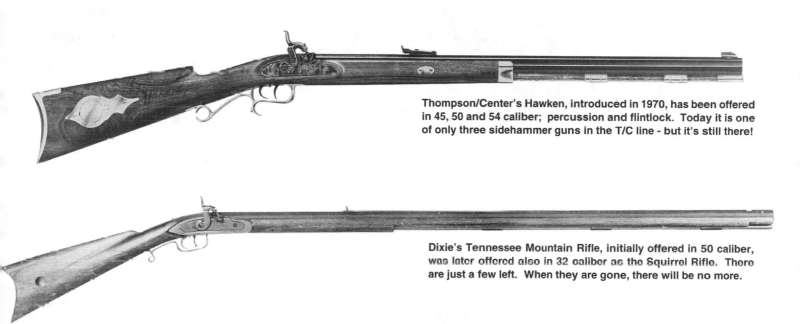

Thompson/Center's Hawken, introduced in 1970, has been offered in 45, 50 and 54 caliber; percussion and flintlock. Today it is one of only three sidehammer guns in the T/C line - but it's still there!

Dixie's Tennessee Mountain Rifle, initially offered in 50 caliber, was later offered also in 32 caliber as the Squirrel Rifle. There are just a few left. When they are gone, there will be no more.

fact that guns from the original fur trade era did indeed come in different shapes and sizes. You'll find the Hawken name—and the names of other established makers—on guns with both back-action and front-action locks, for example. And what about barrel diameter, length and rate of twist—or caliber? Whew! The debate raged hot and heavy.

About this time, the mid-70's, my responsibilities at Lyman expanded a bit to include management of the Technical Department and, later, the muzzleloading product line. We were just about to publish the *Black Powder Handbook*, the very first book containing extensive pressure-tested load data for muzzleloaders. The test fixtures were of our own design and fabrication; the test program modeled after current

Consultation with our Italian gunmakers gave a perspective of which parts were open for revision and which weren't. So I bundled up a set of key parts (all involving investment castings) from the current Plains Rifle—coil-spring percussion lock, tang, patent breech plug, a primitive-looking elevation-adjustable rear sight and double set-trigger assembly—and shipped them to Hall Sharon, at the Sharon Rifle Barrel Company, with instructions to build the prototype using classic Hawken-style iron furniture, a 32-inch octagonal barrel measuring 15/16-inchs across the flats, twin barrel wedges and a steel underrib with the steel (not brass) ferrules set into the rib—rather than atop it. The result was a graceful rifle that weighed under nine pounds. The finished prototype was

This latter consideration came about as the results of our blackpowder ballistics testing were collected, compiled and analyzed. In a nutshell, there was clearly a point of diminishing returns with higher charge levels; velocity increases slowed and peaked, while pressures continued to climb.

With this good internal ballistics data in hand, a pressure specification for the new Great Plains Rifle proofing was calculated using a service load/proof load pressure ratio similar to that used for modern cartridge guns. The resultant pressure was considerably higher than the proof level in place at the time. This required the Italian Proof House to make a new pressure testing fixture of the proper barrel length in order to set the new proof charge levels.

While there was nothing wrong with the earlier proof specification, the new specification for the Great Plains Rifle, and the engineering changes that it in turn drove, delivered an extremely safe, well-planned rifle from butt to muzzle. This same proof specification was part of the project for my next Lyman rifle—the Trade Rifle. The greatest benefit of this project might well be that, as I recall twenty years later, the Italian Proof House began applying this new proofing standard to all half-stock muzzleloaders passing through their facility.

Offhand Rifle aggregate....with his out-of-the-box Great Plains Rifle. The factory sights gave a good Patridge sight picture, just about perfect for muzzleloading ranges.

I set up one for hunting and for match shooting in the NMLRA Open Sight category. For the hunting application, I lowered the rear sight as far as it would go, then filed down the blade front sight until the ball hit point of aim at a hundred yards, using 100 grains of 3Fg. For target work, I reduced the charge to 70 grains of 3Fg and raised the rear sight as needed. A second Great Plains was

aesthetic sense—and a part of the product development cycle begun by the Great Plains Rifle. The mission here was to create a sturdy hunting rifle with an authentic appearance. Trade rifles of yore were simple, sturdy guns with a minimum of frills. The new Trade Rifle would be all of that—plus a more refined, rugged hunting gun.

The fundamentals of the rifle were sound, it was just the peripheral "trimmings" that needed adjustment. Any lingering ambivalence over the design revisions was erased by a blackpowder moose hunt in northern Ontario in Sep-

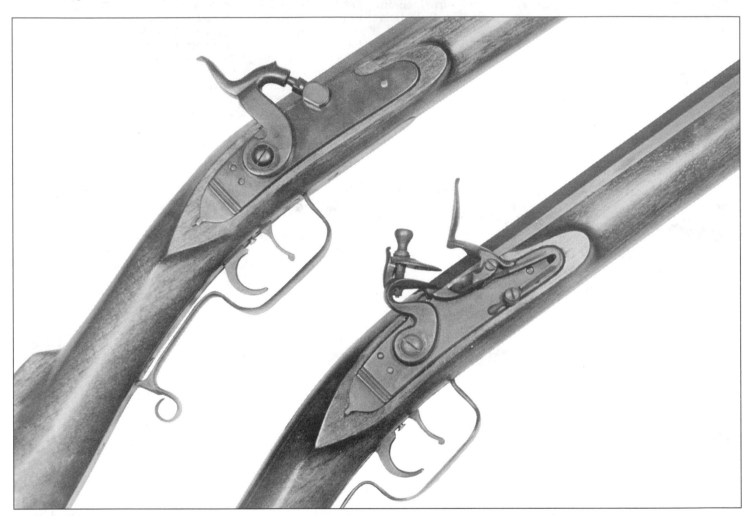

Faithfully capturing the lines of the Eastern "poor boy" rifle, Dixie's Tennessee Mountain Rifle could be converted from percussion to flint – or vice versa – using a kit from Dixie.

The Great Plains Rifle is among the oldest proprietary models still offered in 1999 catalogs. That is saying something, particularly in these times when the muzzleloading market is enthralled with in-line guns that look like modern bolt action rifles and fire plastic sabots carrying jacketed pistol bullets.

The Great Plains Rifle proved a fine rifle for competitive shooting or for hunting. Within a few years of its introduction, a letter arrived from Oklahoma. The writer reported that he had just won the Oklahoma State Muzzleloading Championship in, I think, the

set up for pure target work. An adjustable aperture rear sight was created from Lyman's #57 for the Savage 99 (safety on lever). A #17A globe sight, with its' family of changeable inserts, replaced the blade front sight. While I never won the benchrest matches (although I did place occasionally), I usually did pretty well in the One Rifle Aggregate that included both bench and offhand events out to 100 yards.

The next gun out, just a year later, was the Trade Rifle. Introduced in 1980, this was a design revision of the Plains Rifle in both the functional and

tember, 1979, using the 50-caliber Plains Rifle. A nice bull was taken using Lyman's #504617 ahead of 80 grains of GO 3Fg. The range was close —about 30 yards—and the conical passed through both lungs, stopping just under the hide on the far side. Experiences on this trip supported the planned design changes.

With its rugged stock and 28-inch barrel rifled one turn in 48 inches, the Plains Rifle was well suited to deliver ball or conical bullets at hunting ranges. However, the rear sight and triggers needed revision. Other modifications in-

Dial Monarch for
Long Distance

When long range hunting and varminting is your number, Nikon's newest full-featured variable is your calling card to performance.

Introducing the Nikon 5.5-16.5x44AO Monarch® UCC® with Handturn Reticle Adjustments

Featuring Nikon's all-new Handturn windage and elevation adjustments, the Monarch 5.5-16.5x44 offers reliable, repeatable,1/4 MOA reticle movements on the bench or in the field—even with gloved hands. The large 44mm adjustable objective lens, coupled with Nikon's advanced Ultra ClearCoat® lens coating system, maximizes light transmission, color rendition, clarity and optical precision in the most difficult situations. And Nikon's track record of 100% waterproof, fogproof, shockproof integrity will pull you through a lifetime of tough hunting conditions.

HOT SCOPE, COOL CAMO OFFER!
FREE Special Edition Realtree® Hardwoods™ insulated jacket when you buy any Monarch® UCC® scope from Aug. 1 to Dec. 31, 1999. See your dealer.

Nikon®

A better look at your world.™

ULTRA ClearCoat®

See the complete line of Nikon riflescopes at your dealer. For a free brochure: 1-800-248-6846.   www.nikonusa.com

THE MOST ACCLAIMED REVOLVER IN THE WORLD

Options and accessories available for all models.

Handgun Hunting—
Calibers in
 50 AE
 .475 Linebaugh
 454 Casull,
 .45 Colt Model 97
 .44 Magnum
 .41 Magnum
 .357 Magnum

Cowboy Action Shooting™—
Model 97 in
 .357 Magnum

Silhouette Shooting—Calibers in
 .44 Magnum
 .41 Magnum
 .357 Magnum, and
 22 Long Rifle

FREEDOM ARMS INC.
P.O. BOX 1776
FREEDOM, WYOMING 83120
307.883.2468
WEBSITE: WWW.FREEDOMARMS.COM
E-MAIL: FREEDOM@FREEDOMARMS.COM

THE NEW CITORI FEATHER: THE ONLY SHOTGUN THAT CAN COVER AS MUCH GROUND AS AN UPLAND BIRD.

SERIOUS RESULTS

Take a Citori Lightning Feather or a Citori Superlight Feather afield. Take your dog. Take a long walk. Take a limit of birds. Take a second to notice that your limit is heavier than your shotgun. Take five — if not for yourself, at least for the dog — after all, he had to work harder than you.

The new Feather series of Citori shotguns features everything you've come to expect from a Browning over and under — full-width hinge pin, tapered locking bolt, automatic ejectors — with the addition of a new, lightweight alloy receiver.

The result is the ultimate family of lightweight over and under shotguns.

BROWNING ®

Visit your Browning dealer for a
1999 Master Catalog or call 1-800-333-3504.
www.browning.com

On Duty. Off Duty.

Introducing the smallest large bore .45 caliber pistol Colt® has ever made. Packing the same fast, full-sized .45 ACP, but without the big kick. Perfect for use on or off-duty, or for concealed carry, the Defender has a snag-free design, low profile sights, a 7-round clip, and a small, lightweight stainless steel and alloy frame with a rust-resistant matte finish. Hogue finger-groove grips with a non-slip pebble grain finish fit perfectly in the hand of both male and female law enforcement officers, unlike some of the other top-of-the-line duty weapons.

This Defender never rests.

For more information, contact your nearest Colt dealer or dial 1-800-962-COLT. Colt's Manufacturing Company, Inc., P.O. Box 1868, Hartford, CT 06144-1868 ©1999

Warning: Never chamber a round until ready to shoot. Read and follow manual accompanying each firearm. Free manuals available on request.

cluded replacement of that anodized aluminum underrib with its screw-attached brass ferrules with a steel underrib (with inset steel thimbles) and the stock finish changed to oil, like the Great Plains Rifle. And that big brass patchbox had to go!

The carry balance point on the Plains Rifle was right at the rear sight. During a day in the woods the heel of your hand rubs up and down against the sight's elevation arm and, eventually, causes the spring-loaded adjustment screw to gradually back out, raising the rifle's point of impact. I remember one shot hitting nearly two feet above point of aim! The solution? Replace that sight with a primitive "file er' in" fixed rear sight and install the same traditional blade front sight used on the Great Plains Rifle. File in a wide Patridge notch, apply blue touchup -- and a crisp sight picture was at your disposal!

Next, the trigger. Double set triggers were all the rage, but not so good for cold weather hunters wearing gloves. I hunted with them a number of years, tending to

avoid using the triggers "set" because of the possibility of firing the rifle prematurely as I tried to wiggle a fat, gloved finger into place. Using the triggers "unset", a less temperamental mode, produced a long and definitely heavier trigger pull thanks to the geometry of the lock sear and trigger bar. To handle this challenge, the graceful single trigger and brass trigger guard from Sharon Rifle Barrel's English Fowler were selected. No prototype was created; the parts were sent to Investarms, with detailed instructions. The geometry between the lock sear

and the trigger bar worked out very well, giving the Trade Rifle an excellent single stage trigger pull.

The various engineering adjustments were easy and the first Trade Rifles were shipped in 1980.

I think it is the perfect sidehammer hunting rifle because the rifling rate of one turn in 48 inches accurately handles powerful charges behind ball or conical. Want a better sight picture? Install the Lyman #57 SML receiver sight and leave the front blade in place. I'd like to take a 54 back to Canada … and maybe I'll get the chance. There's an outfitter nearby offering muzzle-loading moose hunts and his rates seem reasonable....

With two new rifles of traditional design on deck, what's the next project? A pistol to accompany them—of tradition-

al "Hawken" design, naturally. Fewer existing key parts could be used—just the patent breech plug and the tang, shortened, since the barrel would be 15/16-inches across the

Arguably the best factory roundball rifle available today, Lyman's Great Plains is also stocked for lefties and takes a drop-in fast twist conversion barrel for determined conical shooters.

Target shooters using the Great Plains add a #57 SML receiver sight and a # 17A front sight to really dial in on the x-ring.

Designed for rugged, practical hunting service, Lyman's Trade Rifle has delivered the goods since 1980. Shown in flintlock, it is also available in percussion.

flats. A new, smaller coil-spring lock was built using almost all the existing internal parts and it, along with the other parts and instructions, was sent to a pistolmaker in Utah for the prototyping project. In due course, the finished gun was delivered and sent on its way to Investarm, by now accustomed to our methodology and adept at smoothing out manufacturing problems without affecting the lines of the gun.

Finally, the first production samples (three, I believe) arrived at the Lyman plant in Connecticut. We hurriedly opened the carton and lifted out the first Plains Pistol.

It was a beauty, the best-looking mountain pistol on the market. Massive, but sleek and well fitted. The authentically shaped oil-finished walnut halfstock included a belt hook on the off-side. The blued steel nosecap was perfectly fitted, as were the escutcheons, and the

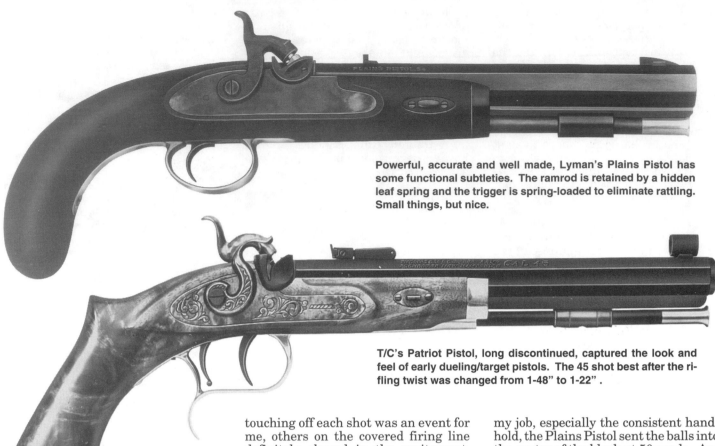

Powerful, accurate and well made, Lyman's Plains Pistol has some functional subtleties. The ramrod is retained by a hidden leaf spring and the trigger is spring-loaded to eliminate rattling. Small things, but nice.

T/C's Patriot Pistol, long discontinued, captured the look and feel of early dueling/target pistols. The 45 shot best after the rifling twist was changed from 1-48" to 1-22".

brass triggerguard blended gracefully with the inner curve of the grip.

The barrel was the same stock size as the rifles—15/16-inches across the flats, eight inches long. But there the resemblance ended. The rate of twist was a fast 1-30 for top accuracy in 50 and 54 calibers; this was no piece of cutoff rifle barrel delivering mediocre accuracy.

A rugged drift-adjustable primitive rear with a scaled-down blade front sight delivered a tight Patridge sight picture for target work. Not enough light getting through? A few minutes work with a needle file widens the rear notch to your satisfaction and a dab of touchup blue hides the bright metal.

By coincidence, these first pistols arrived just before the annual Blue Trail Rifle Frolic, held at the nearby Lyman family range. A field test was clearly in order! I entered the Single Shot Pistol Aggregate and reported to the firing line for the first relay —without having cleaned the pistol, let alone setting the target charge and filing-in the sights.

A few quick shots at the 25 yard sight-in target indicated a center hold —and 70 grains 3Fg behind the .530" patched ball. A stout pistol load, since the usual target charge ran more to 20-30 grains (in a 45 caliber pistol), but the balls drilled right in there. While

touching off each shot was an event for me, others on the covered firing line definitely shared in the excitement. The tremendous muzzle blast rattled the galvanized sheet metal roof the length of the line, providing a new competitive experience for most! When the smoke cleared, the Plains Pistol delivered excellent targets at 25 yards. Next, the 50 yard program and the acid test of the fast twist.

Again, a few quick sight-in shots revealed a different system was needed: Sights aligned in a classic Patridge six-o'clock hold, charge reduced to 50 grains 3Fg (to increase barrel time) and my handhold placed slightly higher on the stock (to encourage barrel flip). If I did

my job, especially the consistent handhold, the Plains Pistol sent the balls into the center of the black at 50 yards. Another set of good targets went to the scoring bench. As I recall, that day the untuned .54 caliber Plains Pistol placed first in the Pistol Aggregate. Not a bad showing for a brand new pistol not specifically designed for target work!

What does the future hold for these hardy sidelock muzzleloaders? I'm not sure—but I'm optimistic. While attending the 1999 SHOT Show, I stopped by the Lyman exhibit and the folks told me that orders for the Great Plains were pouring in. That's what is necessary to keep a muzzleloader—or any product—in the product line. ●

HARDY HALF-DOZEN

Year of Introduction	Brand & Model
1970	Thompson/Center Hawken
1976	CVA Mountain Rifle
1978	DixieTennessee Mountain Rifle
1979	Lyman Great Plains Rifle
1980	Lyman Trade Rifle
1981	Lyman Plains Pistol

Five Guns I'll Never Sell

by Harold A. Murtz

I SUPPOSE THERE are times in a collector's life when he should consider cleaning out the accumulated "stuff" he has scrounged over the years. Maybe even more than once. The true and dedicated collector, no matter how narrowly focused he is, always acquires gear that really doesn't fit his tidy plan to own an example of every variation of, say, the Trapdoor Springfield or the Broomhandle Mauser.

There is the unfocused collector—better termed a gatherer—who just buys neat stuff because it tickles his fancy at the moment. It's tough to keep on the straight and narrow when there are fantastic deals to be had.

However, when first smitten by the gun bug, and until one realizes he really wants to be a collector, our subspecies gathers a variety of pieces just because we like them. We are, at first, the unfocused collector. There is nothing wrong with this. Until you know just what it is you want to pursue, you should try to examine as many types and makes of guns as possible. Automatic pistols, for instance, is a pretty broad field. It's wise to narrow it down and we all try to do that but somehow get sidetracked.

So, there really are times when a housecleaning is in order, sometimes under duress, sometimes just to begin again in another direction. Equally there are those guns we simply can't part with because they have great sentimental value. That's what I'm confessing here.

This No.1 Mk III SMLE was the first of the author's Enfield collection, and was bought for $15. It's all there, original, and has matching numbers.

I have five guns I will never sell. I may someday decide to present them to a loved one, but never will I simply trade them for cash or other guns. I'm a sentimental kind of guy who has gotten a lot of enjoyment from these guns, the kind of memories that can't be replaced. So I'm keeping them, and I'm also going to tell you about them.

The Rolling Block

I don't know how many folks can claim to still have their very first real firearm, but I can. There's nothing real special about it except it is the first one I ever owned and that's good enough reason to be proud of it.

In my growing up years we had a neighbor, a very quiet and gentle man who made Kentuckys and Pennsylvania long rifles and was immensely proud of what he crafted. Sometimes he'd let my brother and me see a just-finished gun. We thought that was pretty neat, but what really got us bunched up were the World War II Mausers and a 1903 Springfield he had squirreled away in a corner.

We also spent a lot of time with a monthly wish book, The *American Rifleman*, the neighbor passed on to us. Just about that time, the war surplus ads began running in profusion and they drove me nuts. Here was a genuine

"U.S. Army Model 1917—Cal. 30-06" rifle that had just arrived at Ye Old Hunter's place "Virtually unfired. . . Fresh from Government Cases." Holy Cow! But they cost $27.95 and that was more than I could muster. However, down the page a little farther was something more my speed, the "Pancho Villa Specials," 7mm Remington rolling blocks, and the advertising hype was enough to get my blood boiling.

"Yes, here it is, the original 'gun crank condition' [whatever that was!] 7mm Remington. You can almost see the finger prints which the former fanatical owners pressed into the wood as they realized the jig was up. All guns practically complete. Pre-oiled and ready to clean up."

I was hooked. Especially since they were affordable—even for me—at the same price of hamburger then—92 cents per pound. That came to $8.28.

Well, I sold a lot of newspaper subscriptions that summer and did every thing I could to earn a couple of cents toward that rifle. I had to have it. Somehow I did manage to scrape together enough to order it, and waiting for the Railway Express truck to drop it at the

door was sheer torture. When it did arrive I was in ecstasy—my very own real gun with an intriguing history. Why, Pancho Villa himself probably held this very gun while riding through the desert with Black Jack Pershing hot on his tail.

I spent hours cleaning that gun and must have gone through 100 yards of emery cloth to get the rust and pitting to disappear. The ad copy writers didn't lie—it was "ready to clean up." And I hadn't even noticed that line about the guns being "practically complete." Fortunately, my own artifact seemed to have every part it was made with still firmly attached. The wood was nearly black from dirt and oil, but somehow I managed to get it light brown again, and filled in the worm holes and deeper gouges with Plastic Wood. A can of walnut wood stain served to even the color out, and what better thing to top it all off with than spar varnish! After all, those fancy new rifles were all shiny, so why not my newly restored prize?

Along the way I shot the old Remington quite a lot with penny-a-round, cracked-neck UMC ammo of uncertain vintage. I didn't know any better and most of it went "Bang!" with authority.

Author's first gun is this Remington rolling block in 7mm Mauser, bought mail order from Ye Old Hunter for under $10. After a lot of elbow grease and emery cloth the ol' gun shined up well and shot pretty good.

Those that didn't gave interesting pauses between the time the hammer fell and the gun went off. I spent many an hour cleaning and oiling the neat old gun, and rode many a trail with Pancho and his gang. This rifle is an old friend.

The Marlin Golden 39A

A year or two down the road, my thoughts turned to a 22, but not just any one would do, because now I was reading *Boys Life* magazine and in there spotted the Marlin Golden 39A lever-action rifle with a tube magazine. I was cutting grass for the neighborhood and earning a pretty good buck, so I figured I'd go for the Cadillac of 22s. I talked my Dad into buying it for me with my money—about $60—and, since the catalog house selling it was in Chicago, he brought it home on the train one evening.

What a prize I had, and it was brand spanking new! I cleaned and oiled that Marlin and worked the action until I knew all there was to know about the gun. A few months later, we spent a weekend at my great-grandmother's farm in Michigan and I got to take the

Golden 39A with me. My Dad bought some Long Rifles and, boy, did we have fun shooting at tin cans and other targets of opportunity! The smell of that much burned powder was intoxicating and one I'll never forget.

I shot my first game with that rifle on that same farm later that year. Now proficient with the gun, I was allowed to take it out to scout the sand dunes for Indians. I saw no Native Americans that afternoon, and the settlement seemed secure for a while longer. I did see a large mole running from hole to hole in the sandy soil. I waited for him to sit still long enough, and he did, and I touched one off and nailed him.

The Marlin was missing something and that was a scope, so I tried selling greeting cards because the Marlin-brand scope was a premium you could earn. It was amazing how many neighbors had just come from the drugstore where they'd bought cards just like those I was selling. And my parents and relatives didn't need any because there weren't any birthdays or holidays coming up soon.

In the end, my mother took pity on me after a few sale-less weeks and bought all the cards, bless her heart,

and I was able to get my scope. And that near-50-year-old Marlin won't be leaving this gun room.

The Mossberg 42MB

In the very late 1950s, when military surplus was really getting rolling, my brother and I got summer jobs at Klein's Sporting Goods in Chicago, working in the shipping room where we were needed.

Remember the little 310 Martini Cadet rifles? Klein's had them in spades—by the container-full, actually—and was selling them for $9.95 each. They were mostly in beautiful condition, but that wasn't very apparent when they first came into the store because they had been dipped in Cosmolene for long-term storage. My job periodically was to degrease the little guns to get them presentable for mail order sales or the gun racks out in the stores. Some appeared unfired and had only small bits of "rack rash" from storage. I sometimes wonder what happened to the thousands of those guns we shipped out, because you rarely see them these days.

One of the neater jobs we had was inspecting shipments of just-received guns from the prime importers, like the Mossberg Model 42MB bolt-action 22s that had been part of the U.S. Lend-Lease program just before World War II. This was a sturdy little clip-fed repeater, but many of them couldn't take the beating of training so many British troops over the years and the condition of the guns ranged from just Very Good to NRA Awful. Some had barrels bent nearly 90 degrees, many were missing parts like the stock or bolt, but on average most were complete. Two types of rear sights were in evidence, the standard barrel-mounted open leaf and a receiver sight made by Parker-Hale with micrometer adjust-

The First Enfield

When I finally got direction in my collecting, I settled on a line of guns no one I knew had any interest in—the "lowly" Lee-Enfield. They were then kind of the ugly ducklings of the gun collecting fraternity, what with that funny looking snout and ancient box-type magazine hanging down from the action. But I liked 'em and they were priced right. Others were paying $50 and $75 for their fancy Mausers and Springfields; I could buy four or five SMLEs for that kind of money. Well, almost.

My first No. 1 Mk. III cost $15 at a gun show, and it spawned a whole bunch of others. I eventually was col-

That first Enfield, however, an unremarkable 1918 BSA SMLE with fairly bad wood, started many years of collecting pleasure for me. Plain Jane as it is, I'll hold on to this one anyway.

The LeMay Pistol

One of the pleasures of working for the gun media is the occasional opportunity to test new and (sometimes) interesting guns. Back in 1978, Colt was celebrating an anniversary of some kind, and they introduced—re-introduced we should say—the Colt Service Model Ace autoloader, originally made from 1937 to 1945. The intent then was to train the military to shoot the Model 1911 pistol as cheaply as possible while retaining some realism. Because the 22

Marlin's Golden 39A was a lot of gun for about $60, even 40 years ago. Thousands of rounds have been fired through this one and the action is butter smooth.

ments. The company gave the mail-order customer his choice of sight—one or the other—and one of my jobs was to fit the type ordered and to make sure the gun was complete.

Some guns came out of the crates in pretty darned good condition and these were set aside to be sold at a premium. And since I was one of the inspectors and graders I picked out one of the nicer specimens for myself and outfitted it with both rear sights.

These guns were selling for around $15.95 plus shipping, but my price was about $9. The only way to get it home was on the train, so I wrapped a couple of rags around it and sat with it, enduring only a few inquisitive looks from fellow commuters.

I always liked this little gun because it shoots very well

lecting them fairly seriously and had more than 50 variations on that one theme. There was a profusion of Marks and stars to gather, and that, naturally, progressed into collecting the No. 4 rifles, then No. 5s.

One of my early Enfield prizes was picked off at Klein's Sporting Goods. That was the summer shipments of the No. 4, Mk. I (T) sniper rifles began and my brother and I were put in charge of unpacking the shipping crates, inspecting and grading them. We found an assortment of oddities. One was a number of the Canadian-made 22-caliber Cooey training rifles that somehow got packed in the sniper boxes. We also found a few Pattern 14 sniper rifles wedged into the crates but, unfortu-

rimfire round is so inexpensive, it was a natural choice, but it just didn't have the punch of the real thing. So the Service Model Ace came along, identical to the 45 ACP Model 1911A1 National Match, pistol except it shot 22 Long Rifles. In order to more closely simulate the recoil impulse of the 45, there was a "floating chamber" to magnify the "kick," the brainchild of David "Carbine" Williams (of M-1 Carbine fame). The gun does recoil a bit more than your garden variety 22 auto, but I don't think it comes close to feeling like the 45. That aside, the Service Model Ace became a collectible because not terribly many were produced, and it was fun to shoot. Colt had a good idea in resurrecting it.

and has a neat history attached to it. To attest to its wartime use, it has an abundance of British proof marks up and down the barrel that remind me of all the verbiage currently stamped on guns. There's nothing real special about this gun except it was one of those great bargains, I like it a lot, and I brought it home on the commuter train from Chicago and that gives me a chuckle these days.

It's a keeper, too.

nately, didn't think to buy them for ourselves. There were probably a half-dozen of these guns in all that showed up. Had I only known then . . .

I managed to pick out a near-new No. 4 sniper for myself for not much money, and I had that beautiful rifle until just a few years ago when it was stolen from me. If you ever see one with serial number K34280, let me know in care of *Gun Digest*. I'd love to have it back, and I still have the original, serial-numbered rifle and scope boxes for it.

There were thousands of these Mossberg Model 42M-Bs sold but very few are seen today. They were part of the pre-World War II U.S. Lend-Lease program to Britain and the British added a plethora of proof marks.

I got one of the early production examples and shot it for a test report in *Guns Illustrated* that year. The gun shot pretty well, but not great. Its reliability was not a factor as long as the floating chamber was kept clean. I got to liking the gun more and more as I

General Curtis LeMay with the author's Colt. He pronounced it an accurate and fun gun.

to the range. And in 1980, on an industry-sponsored prairie dog shoot in western Kansas, I broke out the Ace and a few boxes of Remington Target ammo and began pestering a not-too-distant dog mound with only fair results. And then none other than Gen. Curtis LeMay strolled over to see what I was shooting and seemed interested in trying his hand at it. He took a few well-aimed shots and enjoyed it so much he emptied the magazine! He proved to be a deadly shot with both rifle and handgun that day, and I enjoyed our all-too-brief visit. The fact that General LeMay took a liking to my Ace pistol makes it just a little more special to me, and I have a couple of photographs of him holding it and grinning approval. LeMay was a warm and friendly gentleman, and I am sorry I could not have spent more time with him.

Because I like the Colt Service Model Ace so well is one reason I won't part with it; the other is that Curtis LeMay shot it. Sounds corny, I know, but it means a lot to me.

A real collector of firearms, art, jewelry, or anything else, knows full well he is only a temporary custodian. They will be passed on eventually, but not always willingly. Some guns I can sell without too much remorse, but others, like these five, are simply too special. They're the guns I'll never sell. ●

Colt's 1978 re-issue of the Service Model Ace has become one of the author's favorite shooters. The floating chamber of the Ace gives the 22 LR some extra recoil for training purposes.

shot it. Each time I'd go out shooting, the little Ace went with me, but I really wasn't satisfied with the accuracy.

A gun writer named Art Blatt found he couldn't make a steady living at this game and went to work for Pachmayr in Los Angeles and Art soon offered to have my Ace accurized at the shop. He took a bunch of photos for me, gave me all the facts, and I reported on the accurizing results in the 1981 edition of *Guns Illustrated*.

Groups did shrink considerably after the work, and the gun felt like a finely tuned target gun. I'm very pleased with it still, and shoot it every time I go

I'VE ALWAYS had a fondness for cowboy guns. Actually, I've always had a fondness—an obsession, if you will—for all guns, but the Colt Single Action Army, especially in its 4 3/4-inch version, has been a perennial favorite of mine. Unfortunately, there have been some real drawbacks to this love affair that, until recently, have caused me untold frustration. You see, besides being a truly bona fide gun nut, I'm also somewhat of a perfectionist when it comes to my guns. Perhaps it is foolishly simple of me, but I expect—no—I DEMAND that my guns shoot where they point or, more precisely, where I point them.

This very seldom works out to be a successful relationship with an out-of-the-box Colt Single Action. I have owned, bought, sold, traded, and even ruined more single actions that I care to admit, in search of one that shot where I pointed it. It amazes me that a gun that usually costs more than a Colt Gold Cup or a Freedom Arms 454 Field Grade won't shoot within minute-of-bowling-ball of where one points it.

I recall one instance in my distant past when I acquired a beautiful second generation 4 3/4-inch 45 Colt with one-piece walnut grips. This wasn't my first experience with this genre of weapon,

by
Todd G. Lofgren

so it was with some trepidation that I gathered a multitude of different loads and headed for the range to see how it shot. Alas, as beautiful as it was, it shot like every other Single Action Army I had ever tried, nowhere near where I pointed it. An old gunsmith said he could "fix it" by turning the barrel a smidge, but that he might mark the

SIGHTING IN SINGLE-ACTIONS

The author sighting in one of his precious Colts.

Introducing elevation by bending the barrel, or at least the front portion of the barrel, upward. It is best to deal with windage and elevation in two separate bends.

This is a 12-ton hydraulic arbor press and the bending blocks pictured were fashioned out of aluminum round stock. Works great on revolver.

barrel if it slipped in the resin. Well, it did, and when I got my beautiful Colt back it had spiral scratches around what was once a flawlessly blued barrel and its front sight leaned precariously to one side. Needless to say, it shot closer to where it was supposed to, but was still unacceptable to me. I hate to admit what I did next, but remember this was in my younger years when sacrilege wasn't in my vocabulary. I ground off the front sight and had a Shorty Williams ramp sight screwed on. This was not a good plan either, as this combination not only didn't look right; it didn't shoot any better either. In a fit of frustration, I sold that Colt for a mere pittance of what it was worth—probably to someone who had more brains than I and a replacement barrel in waiting.

I eventually consulted all the gunsmiths in my area, but no acceptable solution ever surfaced. Often suggested were, and over the years I tried, lighter bullets, heavier bullets, different powders, different primers, filing the front sight, bending the front sight, and turning and switching barrels. Although some of these methods helped, none were entirely satisfactory. Besides, being a perfectionist, not only did I want my Colts to shoot where I pointed them, but I wanted my front sights original, unaltered, and straight up and down, to boot.

Lucky for me my shooting interests ran the gamut from trap shooting to IPSC, and there were great periods of time in my shooting years that I didn't even own a Colt SAA. Only recently,

with the advent of the cowboy shooting game, did my desire—my need, if you will—again surface for a straight-shooting Colt.

Colt Single Actions have never been cheap, but there was a time a couple of years back that one could pick up second-generation Colts that were built as NRA commemoratives. These were, it seemed, most commonly found in 357 Magnum configuration. These particular single actions also became popular for a short time as they were exempt from California's ever-changing gun laws and could be bought and sold among private parties as commemorative collectibles, while the non-commemorative Colts had to be registered and the transaction handled through a licensed FFL holder, subjecting the purchaser to California's 15-day waiting period and attendant fees.

Anyway, I managed to initially secure a 7 1/2-inch 357 Magnum NRA Colt from which to build my needed single action. Contact with John Kopec of Kopec Enterprises in Whitmore, California, revealed that John was offering rebored single action cylinders in 45 Colt with appropriately sized chamber mouths for greater accuracy potential. I selected a cylinder with a heavily beveled front edge, reminiscent of the Colts of the 1870s, and had it fitted along with a new 4 3/4-inch barrel in like caliber.

This pistol was later given a gunfighter action job by single action army gunsmith Eddie "Ned Six Killer" Janis of Peacemaker Specialists which gave it a feel one has to experience to appreciate. Kopec offered a sight-in package back then that consisted of rotating the barrel for windage adjustment, while the elevation factor was left to the gun's owner. Options for elevation modification included filing the front sight, or load modification,

neither of which resulted in—at least in my mind—a totally satisfactory solution to the shoot-where-it-points, doesn't look modified, front sight still straight up and down requirements that I had imposed on myself.

Discussing my dilemma with gunsmith and fellow cowboy shooter Larry Mears of Mears' Gunsmithing in Redding, California, one day was the first step to eventual solution to my single action sight-in problems. "Bend the bar-

bend a 357 barrel with little effort. Fortunately, this 12-ton press is portable enough that one merely takes it to the range along with a sufficient supply of ammo and goes at it.

I remember our first few attempts. This is not an exact science. First generation Colt barrels are much softer, therefore much easier to bend than, say, second or third generation barrels. Likewise, 45 Colt barrels bend much easier than 357 barrels, and long

This technique has also been successfully used on nickel guns, but the chances for creating a blemish always exists.

One of the author's Colts getting a windage adjustment. If the gun were turned minimally in the press, a slight amount of elevation could also be introduced.

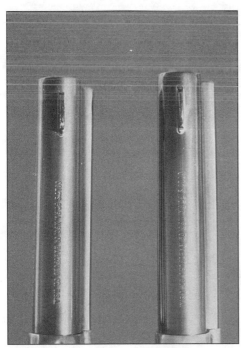

Can you tell if either of these barrels have been bent? Trust me—one of them has. If you guessed the one on the left—you're wrong.

rel," he said. "Say what?" was my response. "Bend the barrel where you want the gun to shoot." Larry explained that he had discussed this problem with his former gunsmithing instructor and the instructor's solution had been—one that he had used for years—to bend the barrel with an arbor press. Let me get this straight, I thought. I put one of my pristine, very expensive Colts into a piece of equipment normally used for things like pressing wheel bearings and apply several tons of pressure to it until its barrel bends. Yeah, right!!!

The more I thought about it, the more the idea appealed to me. If this worked, not only could I correct my guns for windage but I could correct any elevation problems at the same time. What was the worst that could happen? I'd wreck a barrel. It's not like I haven't done that before.

First step. Obtain an arbor press. My first acquisition was a one-ton press. A guy should be able to bend a Colt barrel under one ton of pressure, shouldn't he? Wrong. That press was returned and a 12-ton obtained. With that press, Larry and I were able to

barrels much easier than short ones. It turned out to be a game of feel and, to some extent, luck.

To sight in a Colt, one first assembles a sufficient quantity of ammunition of the bullet weight and powder charge desired. Once sighted in, it is doubtful that an SAA will shoot any other load to the same point of aim. Next, at least two, better three, groups are fired with this load off the bench at 25 yards to establish initial point of impact. Once these groups are fired, the ejector rod assembly is removed and the gun is placed under the press so that pressure from the press will bend the barrel where you want the bullet to go. That is, if the gun is shooting left, the barrel is positioned so that its front is bent to the right, thus moving bullet impact also to the right. Don't worry about the fact that you're also moving the front sight to the right, which should theoretically cause the gun to shoot further left. Bending the barrel in the direction you want the bullet to move works. Trust me, if you bend the front of the barrel to the right, it will shoot further to the right.

Five single actions, each with a group fired using the same load, hold, and point of aim. The center target was produced by firing one round from each of the guns pictured.

To avoid marring the barrel, support blocks made of aluminum round stock were fashioned and grooved to mate with the diameter of a barrel. Between these and the gun barrel itself, appropriately sized pieces of felt were inserted for further protection.

Now, pressure is applied to the barrel until there is a hint of movement or bend. Then a trial group is fired. The ejector rod housing is reinstalled during test firing to ensure that barrel or front end weight remains constant. Sometimes the group has moved in the right direction and sometimes it hasn't. It's trial and error until the desired results are obtained. Hopefully, this is accomplished without going too far in one direction. But, if this happens, one just applies tonnage in the opposite direction until groups move where they're supposed to be.

Does bending the barrel affect accuracy? I'd have to say yes. It makes the gun shoot where it should! Groups are as small as those from unaltered guns I've fired or seen fired, and the only difference I've noted is that my guns pleasantly put all of their bullets where they should be.

One of the last guns I worked on was a cute little New Thunderer recently re-

Two Colts sighted with the arbor press with their groups. Both Colts shot to the left requiring that their barrels be bent to the right. A 6 o'clock hold was used for all groups.

leased through Cimarron Arms. I was a little unsure if I could get this short barrel under the press and wondered how difficult it would be to bend if it did fit. Nothing ventured, nothing gained. The first groups out of this gun with my favorite cast load went low left. Not feeling I could get sufficient elevation using the arbor press, and being that the gun came with a real high front sight, I decided to raise the point of impact by filing down the front sight. Having brought the group up sufficiently using the file, I then walked the group to the right using the press.

This was one tough little barrel to bend, but bend it did. The feel I had somewhat developed on the several 4 3/4-inch Colt barrels I had previously adjusted didn't apply here. It took quite a bit of pressure to initially move the impact right, but when it moved, it really moved. After some disquieting moments, the group went where I wanted it.

My nickel Colt with factory ivories is one of my favorite cowboy guns. I hesitated for some time to subject it to the press, fearing that the nickel wouldn't take the stress of a bend or I'd get dents in the process. I originally was able to get this gun to shoot close by turning the barrel, but I just couldn't stand seeing the front sight listing to one side. Because of this, I seldom used this gun. Well, as it turned out, careful work with the press got this particular Colt to shoot as well as the rest without any damage to its finish. This is now my favorite Colt and it often goes with me to our local cowboy matches.

As can be seen in the accompanying photographs, each gun shoots well in its own right. But what pleases me the most is that they all shoot to the same place with the same load and the same sight picture. The composite group pictured was obtained by firing one shot with each gun using the same load, sight alignment, and hold on the target.

Most of the time I can make the necessary adjustments to a barrel without

creating a single blemish. The possibility does exist, though, of causing a slight indentation at one or two locations along the barrel caused by the tremendous focused pressure of the press. I'm considering the future use of hardwood blocks instead of the aluminum round stock to lessen or eliminate the possibility of this occurring. This process has also been found to be much more successful when applied to a 4 3/4-inch or 5 1/2-inch Colt barrel as opposed to its 7 1/2-inch version. Although I have used this technique to sight in guns with 7 1/2-inch barrels,

the bend, when applied over this length, has a greater chance of being noticeable.

I'm not recommending the arbor press technique to everyone. As a matter of fact, I'm not recommending it at all. I'm sure some of you readers out there must think I'm nuts for subjecting some real expensive handguns to what appears to be a drastic measure, but believe me when I say that this technique has allowed me to accomplish what no other technique ever had—all my beloved Colts now shoot where they look! ●

Both of these Colts shoot to the same place with the same hold. How often do you think that would happen with guns right out of the Colt factory?

Thunderer shot miserably right out of the box— eight inches low and five left at 25 yards. The group pictured was fired after sighting in this cute little SA with an arbor press.

DIRECTORY
Peacemaker Specialists
John A. Kopec Enterprises
Edward Janis, Proprietor
P.O. Box 157
Whitmore, CA 96096
Ph: (916) 472-3438

Larry Mears Gunsmithing
568 North Market Street
Redding, CA 96003
Ph: (916) 244-3213

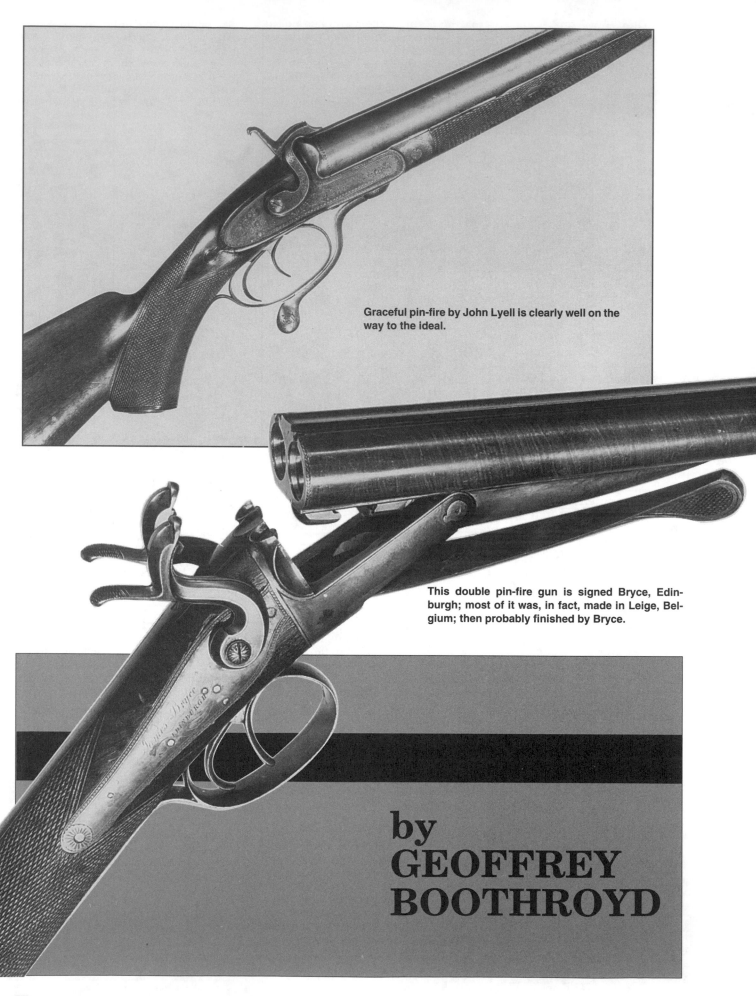

Graceful pin-fire by John Lyell is clearly well on the way to the ideal.

This double pin-fire gun is signed Bryce, Edinburgh; most of it was, in fact, made in Leige, Belgium; then probably finished by Bryce.

by
GEOFFREY BOOTHROYD

THE HISTORY, development and evolution of the British hammerless sporting shotgun has interested and intrigued me for well over half a century ever since, as a teenager, I first encountered a double hammer gun and later was allowed to use it. Over the years, as my knowledge and experience grew, I realized what a fascinating subject this was. Because of the way the British gun trade was organized, throughout the second half of the 19th century there was a vast outpouring of inventive and creative effort on the part of many of the relatively small gunmakers. Their combined efforts produced that article of

from my own experience, could be quite severe. I had a pin-fire shotgun which, when used with cartridges which had been reloaded several times, allowed enough gas to leak past the pin to bring the hammer back to half cock.

The other slight problem was the need to locate the pin

THE BRITISH SPORTING GUN

And how it grew

ultimate perfection, the center-fire, hammerless, breechloading ejector shotgun.

The story starts in France. Casimir Lefaucheux invented a crude breechloading shotgun with hinged drop down barrels in 1834. Originally, the cartridge used by Lefaucheux was ignited by an external percussion cap. Two years later, Lefaucheux patented a crude pin fire cartridge, later improved by another Frenchman, Houllier.

The classic Lefaucheux was made by several makers in Britain following the appearance of the Lefaucheux at the Great Exhibition in London in 1851. The Lefaucheux and the British guns made on the same principle were opened by means of a long lever extending along the fore-end. A typical center-fire example signed Bryce of Edinburgh is illustrated.

The pin-fire hammer shotgun was quite simple; later versions employed a lever which, instead of lying forward along the fore-end, curved backwards around the trigger guard. The pin-fire cartridges were reloadable, and tools to withdraw the pin, insert a new cap and correctly seat the pin were designed along with crimping machines.

One problem with the pin-fire cartridge was that after it had been reloaded several times there was a tendency for an escape of gas past the pin when the cartridge was fired. This,

in a slot in the barrel breech. Extraction was simple. If the finger nail was not strong enough to withdraw the fired cartridge a special simple tool with a small hole at one end was placed over the protruding pin and this would withdraw the fired case. The hammer was so shaped as to allow the pin, after firing, to protrude above the barrel for about an eighth of an inch.

The next development was to replace the pin-fire cartridge with the central-fire cartridge. In essentials, the new cartridges were much the same as those in use to-day.

The center-fire cartridge also originated in France and was in use in Britain by the late 1850's. Its introduction brought with it several problems which were speedily solved. The first was, lacking a pin, there was no means of withdrawing the fired case from the breech. This was overcome by the invention of the extractor. The other problem was that the firing pin because of the pressure exerted by the lock mainspring tended to remain in the indentation made in the cap, thus tying up the gun.

This difficulty was solved by the mechanical withdrawal of the firing pin when the hammer was brought back to half cock. Two of the several systems employed are illustrated. The system patented by Thomas Horsley, Gunmaker of York, em-

ployed a camming extension on the breast of the hammer which, when brought back to half cock, withdrew the firing pin by means of an internal linkage. Another system used by Griffiths of Manchester, seen on a very fine hammer gun, used a pin on the head of the firing pin which engaged a slot on the inside of the hammer.

The final solution was achieved by the use of a change in the locks which brought the lock to the half-cock position automatically by a modification to the main spring. This was combined with a spring around the striker. This brought the hammer gun to a high standard of perfection as can be seen in the top lever back action hammer gun by T.Hepplestone. Hammer guns continued to be built with the lever around the guard employing the Henry Jones patent No.2040 of 1859. Many of the interesting variations on barrel locking systems were not self-evident from a brief glance at the gun. An example is the Scott hammer gun with four lumps instead of the usual two. An example of an action where the barrels slide forward before dropping down, was that patented by the Glasgow gunmaker, James D.Dougall in 1860.

No sooner had the sportsman got a gun which withdrew the cartridges so he could remove them than he wanted a gun which would expel the fired case when the gun was opened.

Manchester maker W. Griffiths sleekly styled the hammers on this fine underlever centerfire gun. Note the fences.

This Hepplestone gun has back-action locks and a top lever. Note the quality of the engraving. This gun is a good one.

This Scott is different—it has twice as many barrel lumps as an ordinary gun for reasons we know not now.

The problem here was to devise a system which would only eject the fired case and not the live cartridge which was in the other barrel. A number of patents appeared which protected the gunmakers' ideas on what became known as selective ejectors.

The earliest of the more successful designs was that by Deeley, patented in 1886 and still used today. One of the rarest of these designs is illustrated. This ejector system was patented by William Anson in 1886. The cartridge is retained in the chamber by the tab on a lever under the barrel. (The tab on the right hand ejector is missing). This is the only example of this type of ejector I have ever encountered.

Before we leave the hammer gun, just have a look at an interesting device fitted to a hammer gun by one of the important Edinburgh gunmakers, James MacNaughton. This is something you could well miss on a merely cursory examination of the gun. The triggers have a small hook which can just be seen under the trigger plate. This hook is engaged by a lever which prevents the triggers being pulled and the gun fired until it is released by pressure from the hinged under lever. This was intended to prevent the gun from being fired if the opening lever was not fully closed.

The next important development was to move the hammers inside the lock plate or the action of the gun. As had happened with the introduction of the breech loader many men of the old school regarded this change with disfavour. One man stated that a gun without hammers was like a spaniel without ears!

Lacking external hammers a means of cocking the action had to be sought. The opening lever was one option employed by MacNaughton on his hammerless gun and by Alex Henry who employed a rotary under lever. The ultimate answer lay in employing the longest lever available, the barrels.

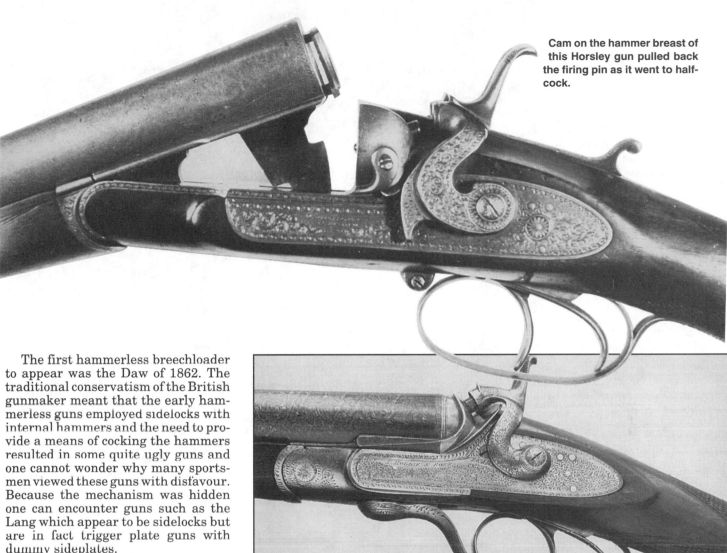

The first hammerless breechloader to appear was the Daw of 1862. The traditional conservatism of the British gunmaker meant that the early hammerless guns employed sidelocks with internal hammers and the need to provide a means of cocking the hammers resulted in some quite ugly guns and one cannot wonder why many sportsmen viewed these guns with disfavour. Because the mechanism was hidden one can encounter guns such as the Lang which appear to be sidelocks but are in fact trigger plate guns with dummy sideplates.

The classic sidelock hammerless gun was that introduced by Purdey in the 1880s with the Purdey under-bolt operated by a top lever and employing an action patented by Frederick Beesley in 1881.

The first significant departure from tradition was the Anson & Deeley action, the boxlock. Patented in 1875, the inventors, both of whom worked for the Birmingham gunmakers, Westley Richards, produced a gun delightful in its strength and simplicity. Guns with this action have probably been made in greater numbers than any other design of double shotgun and in all qualities from the appalling to the superb.

The basic action consists of but three limbs; the cocking lever or dog, the hammer and the sear. This plus three pins and two springs was all that was required. Later versions incorporated a number of improvements culminating in the Westley Richards "Hand Detachable Lock" an example of which with the left hand lock partially withdrawn is illustrated.

Tradition still exerted its strong influence and A&D actions will be encountered with plates let into the head

The bottom lever sidelock centerfire hammer gun in full flower.

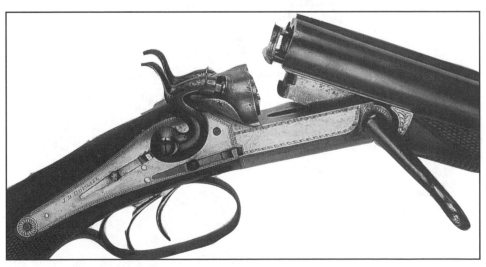

James D. Dougall of Glasgow was renowned for this extremely strong "Lockfast" action where the barrels move forward to unlock before opening.

Early William Anson ejector system, duly patented and the only one the writer ever saw.

of the stock and others with full length dummy side plates.

This has, of necessity, been but the briefest canter through the history of the British shotgun. Do take a careful look at any shotgun of British manufacture that you may come across. You will find a variety of levers on the top, side and underneath the gun for opening the gun for loading. The fences of the actions were made in a wide variety of styles and shapes. Those on many hammer guns still retain the vestigial fence which dates back to the days of the flintlock! If we then add to this, false sideplates there is enough of interest to delight the enquirer without recourse to a turn-screw (screwdriver) for those intrepid enough to extend their curiosity to the inside of their guns.

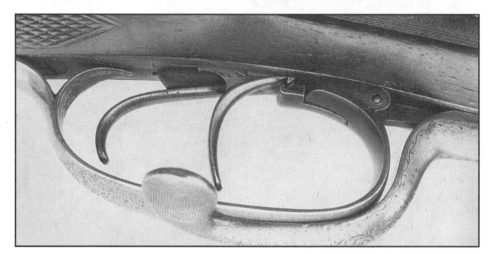

This additional safety device on the MacNaughton prevents the triggers being pulled unless the under lever is firmly 'home'. The lever hinged at the front of the guard engages the triggers when the operating lever is opened.

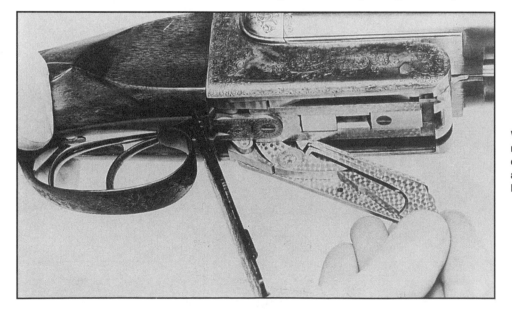

Westley Richards made numerous improvements to the basic Anson & Deeley action; one of the most famous is their "Hand Detachable" lock system seen here with the lefthand lock partially removed.

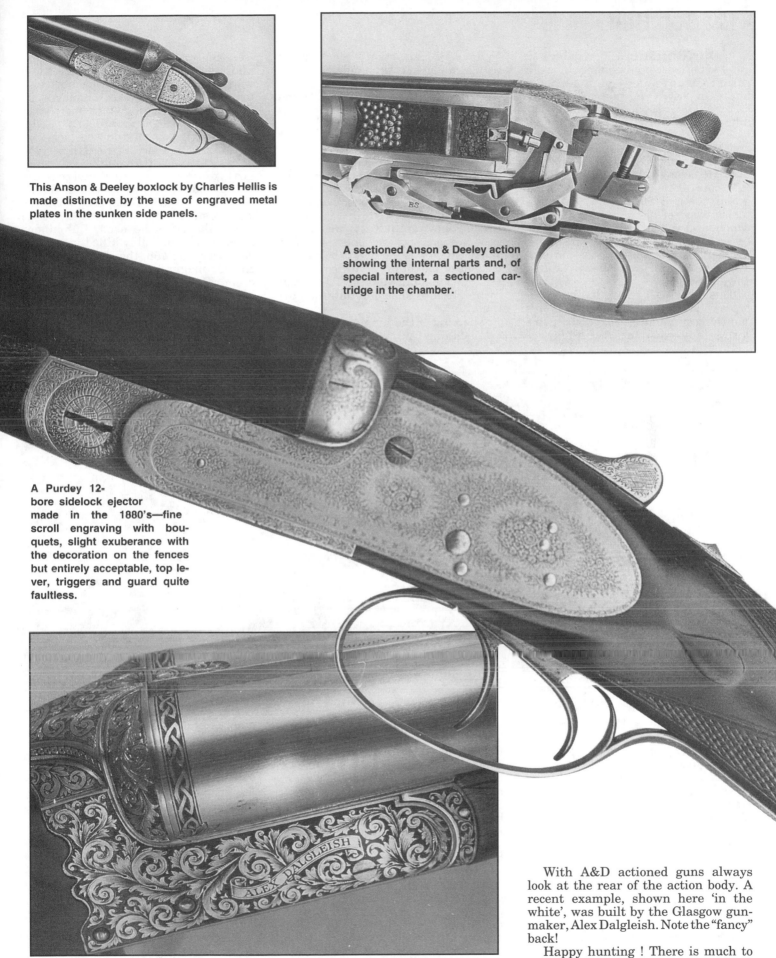

This Anson & Deeley boxlock by Charles Hellis is made distinctive by the use of engraved metal plates in the sunken side panels.

A sectioned Anson & Deeley action showing the internal parts and, of special interest, a sectioned cartridge in the chamber.

A Purdey 12-bore sidelock ejector made in the 1880's—fine scroll engraving with bouquets, slight exuberance with the decoration on the fences but entirely acceptable, top lever, triggers and guard quite faultless.

Dalgleish of Glasgow built this one with a "fancy back" and a lot of engraving.

With A&D actioned guns always look at the rear of the action body. A recent example, shown here 'in the white', was built by the Glasgow gunmaker, Alex Dalgleish. Note the "fancy" back!

Happy hunting ! There is much to seek. And to enjoy. ●

By Bob Bell

JOHN BUHMILLER probably had more experience on dangerous African game than any other non-professional hunter of post-WWII years, possibly of all time. Older shooters will remember him as one of the better known barrel-makers of that era, a friend of hunters and gunsmiths such as Elmer Keith, Jack O'Connor, C.M. O'Neil and the like. He belonged in their company.

According to a stack of letters from him in the mid '50s to mid '60s and a carbon copy of his fourth hunt diary which he gave me, he had by that time taken 235 "big critters" hunting either alone or with a few natives—no professional hunter, as they're called nowadays.

This is, at least to me, the most impressive part of Buhmiller's hunts. It's one thing to go after dangerous game with a fully experienced white hunter

Buhmiller's attention concentrated with a rifle in his own hands.

Of the 235 animals he had taken at that time, 165 were elephants, 53 Cape buffaloes, and 17 rhinos. There was also one hippo, which he listed as an afterthought. "Not counting one hippo," to quote him directly.

Hundreds of non-dangerous animals, mostly antelope of all sizes, also were shot for food, and a number of venomous snakes were killed incidentally, although no exact record was kept of these. There were at least three cobras, two puff adders, and one seven-foot snake which was thought to be a mamba. One of the cobras, a "little 5-footer" according to John, was killed in his bedroom. He also shot one nuisance python.

The king of the jungle never interested John much. "Never had any ob-

were aligned on head. At times I had an impression that animal was starting towards me, but too busy to pay much attention. Other times an animal was dropped when moving at an angle and not coming straight towards me, possibly leaving or going by some obstacle before coming straight at me—if charging. No way to know. Three of the eight rhinos taken in 1960 were definitely charging, all out. One was less than three steps distant when stopped, another was six steps."

On the rifles he used, Buhmiller said: "I have probably killed more big stuff with the 458 [the standard Winchester magnum cartridge] than any other rifle, simply because we had it as a second gun most of the time. It is not overly powerful, but will kill if pointed right, and one knows when using it that it is rather lacking in power and takes

BUHMILLER'S BIG BOOMERS

directing everything. His main responsibility is the client's safety, even more than getting him trophies, and if there's any likelihood of real danger, the guy who pays the expenses isn't going to be allowed to risk exposure,—if for no other reason than the reports that have to be filled out if something goes wrong.

Buhmiller, however, went into the bush a loner, with no one else giving him advice on possible problems or even armed with a rifle. **All** shooting depended on him, whether at 100 yards or 10 feet. Knowing he was hours on foot away from the farmhouse where he was staying, which was many miles from the nearest tiny town and much farther to whatever passed as a hospital in Tanganyika in the '50s, was enough to keep

session about lions," he wrote. "Have been around them to some extent, but they always behaved themselves, and I didn't feel like murdering any of them. Have come onto half a dozen in a day, but they always seemed so well-mannered I'd have felt like a heel to blast one. One year, they ate the trunks off nearly all the elephants I shot. Must have been hungry, or maybe they just like elephant trunk."

Regarding charges, a subject which always came up when speaking to groups, Buhmiller wrote: "On last trip at least one elephant was killed while making a charge, dropped eight steps distant. Others may have been coming or starting to come. On close up frontal shots I always fired the first time sights

more careful aim. Undoubtedly the best rifle I have ever used is the 510 Magnum, used on last trip loaded to approximate power of the 505 Gibbs. This wildcat can be loaded to over 8000 ft/lbs. energy—so can the Gibbs, but not so handily."

All of which brings us to the reason for this article—some of the wildcat cartridges which Buhmiller created, tested, loaded for and used on big stuff, mostly in Tanganyika, some in Kenya, Mozambique and elsewhere. Few hunters have used wildcats for such hunting, probably no one so many as Buhmiller.

Before we get into those, though, it might be worthwhile to tell how anyone could get so much dangerous game hunting in more or less modern time (Buhmiller's first African hunt was in 1955), much as the oldtimers had in the days before closely controlled bag limits and even the monitoring of cartridges used. As the September '59 issue of *Field & Tide* magazine put it:

"1. Try and arrange it so that you land in Tanganyika at the right spot just at the moment when the Game Department decides that several hundred elephants have to be destroyed in order to protect life and property;

"2. Make sure that you are able to convince the Game Warden that you are the right man for the job;

"3. Overcome several other obstacles in your way."

The article went on: Buhmiller's hunt was in the Manyara district of Tanganyika where large herds of elephant and buffalo, sheltered by dense and almost impenetrable forest, have for some considerable time been making farming a very precarious occupation."

Buhmiller goes into this some from a personal angle. After his third African trip he wrote: "I hunted in a newly organized farming area, where I had done three months shooting two years

previously. My first shooting there was in almost virginal territory. Buffaloes, rhinos, elephants and lesser game were there in abundance.

"Varmints were fairly well controlled at first by an electric fence that surrounded the cultivated fields. As time passed, this fence lost its effectiveness. Baboons and elephants became great pests. The baboon is difficult to deal with, but all his foraging is done by daylight, so watchmen can at least partially deal with him. The elephant comes by night, when it is nearly impossible to shoot effectively. He soon becomes used to all the noises, spotlighting and ineffective shots fired for his benefit, and by daylight may be ten miles away and still going. Appeals to the game department usually produce no results.

"... elephants were seldom molested unless they were found too near the crops, when a large herd could be easily forced through the electric fence by crowding from behind. Meat was shot for the farm laborers, numbering usually well toward one hundred, some with families.

Arriving on my third trip I found things vastly changed. The electric fence had become ineffective and had been allowed to go to pieces. Animals had left or become exceedingly wary. One of the main crops, maize (corn), from the time ears are formed until ripe, is a luscious tidbit for old Tembo, and trouble is on for two to three months. Elephants just can't pass up a juicy field of corn.

"The elephant is probably the worst varmint, from the farmer's standpoint. They go in herds up to fifty or more, and what such a horde will do to crops in one night is appalling." As an editor wrote after seeing one of John's slides, "The cornfield looked like a cyclone had hit it...the stalks all leveled ... worse than the neighbor kids in Mrs McGillicuddy's flower beds."

Describing a typical hunt, Buhmiller wrote: "We [John, his elephant guide Fundi, and sometimes several other natives] always took off at daybreak without breakfast, and would be gone until noon or later, when we would come in to eat and rest up for another jaunt in the evening. All hunting was done on foot. We sometimes used a truck to take us to the vicinity of our day's hunt to save so much walking. This area being made up of heavy brush and dense cover, I carried my own gun at all times, as a buffalo or a rhino might charge unexpectedly at close range."

This was a good habit as illustrated by a slide shown during a talk to an African service club. "The Cape buffalo you see there," John recounted, "was pretty close when I shot him. You can see the bullet hole just over his right eye."

A reporter who attended the talk later wrote: "John Buhmiller is a droll, small man but big with a rifle and one of the most knowledgeable persons in the US when it comes to guns and ammunition." Which shows that occasionally a newspaper story can be accurate.

Obviously, conditions in the post-WWII years in that part of Africa were more casual than recently. Another aspect which must be considered is that Buhmiller had managed to make arrangements for bed and board with a farmer many miles back in the bush in exchange for building and supplying some "varmint" rifles that would handle the critters that were bothering him. It may be hard for Americans, who think of woodchucks and prairie dogs and Swifts and 22-250s when speaking of varmints, to realize that in the mid '50s in Tanganyika the varmints were five-ton elephants and one-ton buffs, and the usual varmint rifle was of 458 Magnum class, but that's how it was.

In response to somebody's question during an informal slide lecture, Buhmiller explained: "The real purpose of this shooting was to test the killing pow-

Federal 500-gr. full patch factory load, left, shown for comparison with 450 Watts 400-gr. softpoint and Buhmiller's 450 Magnum made on full length Norma magnum case. Note straighter sides, small but steep neck, and cavity point of solid bullet on latter.

er of some rifles that I had made up. There is much controversy regarding the proper rifles for African use. I wanted firsthand know-ledge on the subject."

That's doubtless truer at least in part. But I have the feeling that Uncle John, as he often signed his letters, just wanted to go hunting in Africa. He also mentioned that the farmer on whose land he hunted a number of times had only a fraction of his land cleared, but this allowed him to put about 450 acres in corn, which yielded 15,000 bushels the year before; 80 acres in coffee; and

very close range before you know he is around. I have had a lot of rhino charges, in fact most that I have shot were charging...

"The elephant can hide himself so you can't see him. Get within reach of his trunk and then he has some 57 gruesome ways of pulling you apart or mashing you into the ground. I have never had one utter a sound when coming at me, but they are very determined. My best day's work was ten elephants with ten shots; another day I got another ten, but not in ten shots....

Then after going about thirty feet, where he was right into us, he was dead on his feet. Might mention that once, over several days hunting in dense bush, I got eleven buffaloes with thirteen shots. Shoulda done better, but one bullet hit a horn and ricocheted....

"Snakes are an ever present possibility, but not many are seen, since the grass is very heavy most everywhere ... most types seem interested only in getting away, except the adder; if stepped on he might bite through a leather boot, as he has very long fangs....

Buhmiller designed hunters' tools for the toughest job—stopping, and killing humanely, the globe's toughest game.

100 acres in papayas, a good cash crop when sold as a meat tenderizer. The elephants and baboons were extremely destructive to these crops, and this is the reason Buhmiller could arrange to do what was essentially control shooting.

To give some idea of what hunting in this style was like, consider some of Buhmiller's observations at different times:

"The rhino is easy except that you blunder onto him and get charged from

"But the damn buffalo is the tough one. Not one buff in ten will fall to your shot unless it's to the brain or spine, regardless of what gun you use. For anyone who doubts what it takes to kill a large mad bull buffalo, what we experienced would set them straight. I have seen one walk straight into five well-placed shots from the 5000 ft/lbs. class of big bore bullets without flinching or showing any indication of being hit.

"Insects? Lots of ticks, ants everywhere; during rainy season, plenty of mosquitoes (which carry malaria), tsetse flies, which are very annoying, harmless to man in most areas but kill cattle and horses. Houseflies are not too bad... "

About rifles: "In the old ivory hunting days many used the double very successfully. They used a matched pair, fired a right and left, then swung the empty gun over the shoulder and at the same time reached for the second gun with left hand. The gunbearer would grab the empty, reload and have it ready the instant the second gun was empty. This went on as long as the tuskers held out. As for me, I used a magazine always. A double rifle does not suit my requirements for this sort of shooting, where one should have five or six shots available without reloading. One time after I had just dropped two elephants, the third came for me. I was ready and dropped him without incident. With a double I'd been hard pressed to get it reloaded in time, and there is little use to run...."

Sights: Buhmiller repeatedly stated that the **best** sights for use in thick bush were the shallow-V rear and a wide front blade painted white, with the paint renewed often. He had better results with this style than with even a large peep (1/4-inch aperture), stressing that it was faster in the shadows and even accurate enough for rare shots up to 200 yards.

heavy bush where he usually found them, John wanted his doctored open sights. "I don't care if he is 20 feet away or nearly on top of you," he wrote.(Wow!)

As an example of the type of hunting he did, which sport hunters rarely if ever encounter on routine safaris, consider a shortened version of Buhmiller's May 5 entry in his 1960 diary about a strenuous day of elephant hunting on a wooded mountain and the night that followed:

"We kept going and going," he wrote, "and in about four hours we were nearing the top of the mountain and saw the last four elephants just before they went into some heavy timber. After some time we came onto two, but as I ran up they spooked and we followed them again for maybe an hour and a half." Buhmiller killed two with brain shots at that point, then followed the trail and occasional sounds of the others for hours. The elephants circled and zigzagged, always

458 Win Mag with Buhmiller's 510, 470, and 450 made on Norma's cylindrical magnum case. The 510 has a reduced heel on its bullet so it will seat in the case. These full length Norma cases have about 20 grains greater powder capacity than the shorter 458.

"We then took off for home," he wrote, "or at least I thought that is what the boys were doing, but I didn't watch them beyond checking the direction they took at the start. On the way down I saw a lone buffalo bull, which after some trouble I shot. We then resumed our homeward trek. I tried to hurry the boys but they had their gait and wouldn't go any faster. Somewhere, unnoticed by me, they had either accidentally or intentionally turned off the correct route. I wasn't paying attention, as these natives are supposed to have a sixth sense about direction. I never heard of even one getting lost, and I had four of them. We were in a stream bed and I thought we could plod along it and come out even if it was dark, risking twisted knees and banged heads. But by 7 pm it was full dark and had begun to rain. We kept going although I knew it was very dangerous in that terribly rough country, with snakes or a rhino likely to be anywhere. Rocks big and small, cliffs, and water. Lots of rain,

"A little later I partly fell into a sudden depression, except one leg caught above the knee on something. I immediately had a very lame knee. It was hard to walk, but I could sort of manage with the help of a stick. I was worn out, it hurt my sore knee just to move.

"About two hours later they left the stream bed and began climbing again. I bawled them out as I knew that was wrong. It was wrong to go up, but nothing could stop the idiots. Finally, about 10 pm when I no longer could walk without support on both sides, I was trembling with the cold and so exhausted that I was on the verge of vomiting. With nothing to eat since early morning, I could go no farther. Rain was pouring down, I was soaked, and by that time we were on a high place where all the wind could hit us. They stopped to sit under a tree till morning.

"I told them I was freezing. On top of being worn out by their crazy marching through the dark, I was so cold I was trembling all over and it was all I could do to speak. After a minute one said they could start a fire with his cigarette lighter. I couldn't imagine they could in that rain in watersoaked forest, but by bending over to shield the tiny flames, they did. It took two hours of hard blowing and piling on twigs to get any heat. We crowded around the fire, nobody talking, my knee throbbing, and spent the night in the rain. It was the most awful one I ever hope to spend. I'd wait what I thought was two hours and look at my watch and the hands had barely creeped fifteen minutes. Cold rainwater ran down my neck, face, arms, back, front ... everywhere. I had to move every few minutes to relieve agonizing cramps. I was sitting in a puddle of cold water, and every position I tried to get into was un-

For such chances he sometimes carried in his jacket a low-powered scope that could be immediately installed in Pike or Kesselring quick-detachable mounts. His choices were Weaver's K or J 2-1/2x models, due to their light weight, long eye relief, wide field and straight tubes. But for elephant, buffalo or rhino in the

just beyond sight. He and the natives would have to start home by 4 o'clock to get there by dark, Buhmiller figured, and it was close to that now. But then they heard the elephants up ahead and managed to get up to them, and before it was all over he had killed six more, making eight for the day.

comfortable. With no rest, no sleep, no food, I wondered if morning would ever come! But after an eternity it began to break daylight, and then I saw that the unspeakable knotheads had no intention of leaving until they got up on higher ground and located some landmark. Up where we were, clouds and fog usually stayed around to almost noon, making viewing impossible, but they insisted on going **up-UP**.

"I told the smartest boy in the group that if they wanted to get me home alive, they'd better quit going up. I said we must go down to get out, the only thing to do was follow the water. He seemed to agree, so he and I started down. After a bit the other three followed behind, reluctantly. After some miles, the youngster chopping a sort of path through the thick stuff with his panga as we followed ever larger streams and valleys, we got to territory we recognized and finally got to the farmhouse about noon. I was too exhausted to eat. All I wanted was a drink of tomato juice and then to lie in a bathtub with **hot** water all over me. In a few minutes I had both. The next day my farmer friends took me to Arusha to see the doctor. He gave me something to reduce the chances of pneumonia. Two days later, on May 9, I was hunting again."

Not too many hunters would want to go through something like that, but Uncle John was one tough cookie. As mentioned earlier, he wasn't a large man physically—he weighed but 127 pounds when he got home from his 1960 hunt—but he was all rawhide and spring steel and he had enough determination and guts for a platoon of Marines.

Every time he went to Africa—and he had eight solitary hunts over there from 1955 to 1964—he took an assortment of rifles which he had built himself, mostly on Brevex Magnum Mauser actions, some on 1917 Enfields, others on FN or 98 Mausers. Generally he favored the larger actions because of their greater magazine capacity. By tinkering with the Brevex he got the magazine to hold six of his cartridges built on the cylindrical Norma magnum case. He didn't like being restricted to the two shots in the big English doubles, though he once bought a beautiful 470 from a retiring white hunter along with considerable ammo. He recognized the power and romance of the doubles, and could see how they might be chosen by well-to-do clients who wanted only one animal at a time and were backed up by a white hunter. But for his own shooting, where he might want to drop half a dozen big critters as fast as he could shoot, he insisted a bolt action was superior.

I don't know every caliber that Buhmiller took to Africa. Those he mentioned repeatedly, and comments on them as assembled from different letters to me, follow:

Standard 458 Magnum, left, is noticeably smaller than the 450, 470, and 510 loads built on Weatherby's 378 case. In killing hundreds of elephants and buffalo, Buhmiller found that the larger the bore, the better it killed. But the big cartridges were a nuisance to carry and gave limited magazine capacity. Note that this 450 Mag utilizes a lathe-turned, cavity-pointed German silver bullet.

375 H&H Magnum John did not think this cartridge was overpowering enough to be used regularly in thick bush on dangerous game, but often used it for finishing shots on animals dropped by bigger calibers. He wrote: "If a second rifle is to be used for the smaller game **in the open**, you can look far and wide and never find anything better, if as good, as the old 375 H&H. Ammo can be bought anywhere and it will kill anything, but you must be careful on buffalo and larger game to place your bullet properly or **pass up the shot.**" (Emphasis added)

378 Weatherby Magnum "I never could see the logic of packing one to Africa. You don't shoot the big stuff with a 375-cal. softpoint. If you use a solid, the 375 H&H load is all you need in this caliber. Elephant and buffalo in the open, where you can get several shots into them, you can kill with the 375. The 378 can't do it much better."

416 (various case designs, both factory and wildcat); 400-gr. solid or softpoint at about 2400 fps. "This caliber got little use. It was okay, particularly for open shooting where shots could be well placed, but it didn't have the smashing power of the 45s and larger calibers, which may be needed in thick cover. It was used on one each, buffalo, rhino, and elephant, killing okay."

458 Winchester Magnum As mentioned earlier, Buhmiller killed many animals with this cartridge, simply because he had it along as a second rifle on most hunts and because it featured the excellent 500-gr. solids from Winchester or Hornady. His praise for these bullets was effusive. "They made the 458," he said, an observation that many others have come to agree with. "No other bullets compare with them. Their mantles are twice as heavy as in any English bullets I have seen, My full length 450 Mag will handle 458 factory cartridges and groups them near the same zero as full loads, which is an advantage.

"The 458 is effective, but not as good a killer as the 450 Magnum with 20 grains more powder. But it is all the ordinary hunter would need on safari where the bag of big stuff is small, and there is a white hunter close for protection. It has the advantages of short bolt throw and light recoil, and of course good factory ammo is readily available."

450 Magnum Called this to differentiate from the 458 Winchester Magnum, this one was based on the full length Norma magnum case before it was necked down for the 300 H&H. As a 450 Magnum the case had nearly straight sides and a slight shoulder, with a neck of about one-half inch. Buhmiller used Winchester and Hornady 500-gr. solids in this cartridge. Barrel twist was 1:20 to 1:24. Usual load was 85 to 90 grains of 4064 or 4320. If ammo supply was low, the always-available 458 Magnum factory load could be fired in this chamber, since the 458 case was long enough to reach into the rear end of the 450's neck. The

Barnes softpoints because the reversed slug wouldn't feed reliably.

The 450 Magnum was a favorite of John's and he used it on a number of hunts. He liked the extra capacity of a large action, the availability of good bullets, and noted that it was a significantly better killer than the 458.

470 Magnum "A marvelous elephant load, even on shoulder shots,"

a reduced heel so they would fit inside the case mouth. This made an odd looking centerfire cartridge, with the diameter of the visible part of the bullet as large as the outside of the case, but this is the same principle as the 22 Long Rifle, so shouldn't bother anyone.

"The 510 is a very satisfactory gun when loaded with 85 to 90 grains of 3031 and the 570-gr. Kynoch. I never needed

Buhmiller's elephants sometimes came in bunches—two down here—which surely affects gun choice. He wanted repeaters.

front end of the seated 458 bullet was well short of the 450's rifling, but this made no significant difference at the ranges Buhmiller was shooting. He particularly liked cartridges made up on this case because he could get six or seven in a Brevex action by widening the front of the magazine slightly.

Buhmiller preferred softpoints on buffalo because solids often went through on broadside shots and might wound another animal in a herd, unknown to the shooter, which could cause unexpected trouble in thick bush. He had good luck with Fred Barnes' 500-gr. heavy jacket, either a softpoint or the solid loaded hind end to in the chamber and the magazine filled with 600-gr.

was the way Buhmiller described this cartridge. It was based on the same Norma cylindrical magnum case—"a natural, as the case only needs slight sizing to hold the .475-diameter Kynoch Express bullet. In many ways this 470 makes the best wildcat of the whole lot with 500- or 600-gr. bullets. He usually used 90 grains of 4320 or 4064 in the 470 Magnum. While doing early testing, John fired a 500-gr. hard nose into some big wood blocks. It went through 39 inches before getting lost in a dirt bank.

510 Magnum This was even more impressive to John. It was full length made up on the same/Norma case as above, using .510 diameter bullets with

more than 90 grains. It killed better than the 505 Gibbs, because of the better bullet. Solids are okay—they have steel jackets with heavy points and will go through an elephant's head". Nuff said.

Buhmiller also made up a series of wildcat cartridges on the 1953-introduced 378 Weatherby Magnum case—416, 458, 470, and 510 calibers. These were made by simply opening up the neck. Interestingly, he was using the 458-378 in Africa in 1957, a full year before Weatherby announced the 460 Magnum as a commercial cartridge. I've no idea if Weatherby knew his blockbuster had an early workout, and it doesn't matter, of course. Wildcatters have often come up with cartridges

It doesn't take an NFL hero's physique. Buhmiller, at left, was outweighed by some African fish he caught.

which later were adopted commercially. Proves the old observation about great minds running in the same channels occasionally.

The 458-378 was a bruiser, and even more so were the 470 and 510 made on the Weatherby case. John killed considerable numbers of big stuff with them. Again the Kynoch 570-gr. Nitro Express bullet was favored in the 510, with the 500-gr. Kynoch or 600-gr. Barnes heavy jacket solid in the 470. In an interesting aside, he once wrote: "If necessary, you can pull the bullets of 470 NE cartridges (common in Africa) and use the cordite and bullets for reloading your empties.

Some countries, incidentally, had regulations against handloading, but I guess out where John was living, nobody checked or was interested. He even did routine gunsmithing when necessary, going so far as to change barrels on an action when he ran out of ammo for the first one. Through the years, he built up a fair amount of components, guns, gun parts and scopes over there.

Cartridges based on the necked-up 378 Weatherby case killed impressively, even on shoulder shots, but they

Walk-up-and shoot-'em hunting was Buhmiller's style and he had the only rifle in play.

Relative sizes of cartridges are obvious here. From left, Winchester's 458 Magnum; 450, 470, and 510 Magnum built on 378 Weatherby case; and 510, 470, and 450 Magnums on full length Norma magnum case. All wildcat cases were easy to form but some bullets were handmade; that's work, but paid off in the bush.

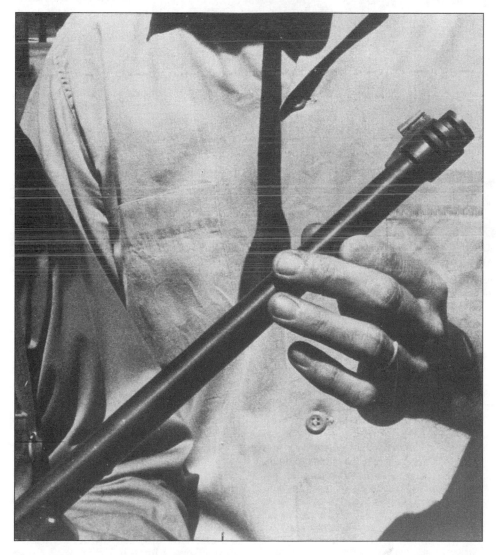

With "calluses on my ears," Buhmiller believed in muzzle brakes on his boomers.

had two drawbacks from Buhmiller's point of view—they were so large and heavy that carrying a number of them in his pockets was a nuisance, and rifles chambered for them had magazines of very limited capacity. Ultimately, he seemed to prefer cartridges based on Norma's full length magnum case. He could get six of these in a Brevex magazine plus one in the chamber, which was comforting when surrounded by a herd of elephants or buffalo. His usual maximum load in this case was about 90 grains of powder with a heavy bullet, which gave excellent killing power and considerable capacity without having to reload.

For special occasions when moving through thick cover where an individual cranky animal might be encountered unexpectedly, he made up a short light "blockbuster" which he could have in his hands at all times. Built on a Springfield-length action, it was a reduced-capacity 378 Weatherby case opened up to take a 500-gr. 470 bullet, and 107 grains of 4064. Not exactly a pipsqueak load, but well under what the full length 378 case would hold.

Buhmiller thought of it as his "stopper."

There's no doubt that Ol' Jawn was a pragmatist about things ballistic. He had a frontier approach to solving problems. When some of the big cartridges he was playing with showed symptoms of poor ignition—after all, sometimes he was using up to 125 grains of powder and magnum primers did not yet exist—he came up with his own solution: after dumping half the powder charge in the case, he dropped in a second primer and then finished off the charge. Doubtless today's experts would frown on such shenanigans, and magnum primers make the practice unnecessary now, but Buhmiller did it for years with no untoward results.

As with all experienced hunters, Buhmiller fully understood that, in the end, it's the bullet that does the killing. And 40-some years ago he was advocating the sweating of cores into jackets to hold them together on impact. "As now made," he wrote back in the '50s, "cores slip out of the jackets in a big percentage of shots on buff, while on lesser game they often slip through without upsetting...'"

Another time, of softpoints, he wrote: "...the forward part of the core should be soft lead, then toward the rear should be a core hardened enough to prevent breakup. But to get them, one would have to make up complete bullet making dies, a bothersome job. "This, of course, was long before Speer's Grand Slams and Tungsten Solids, before Corbin's bullet making dies.

Then a mild complaint:

"Bullet makers can sell whatever they make because the hunter has to have bullets ... no great reason the maker should worry about perfection when he can sell whatever he makes anyway." This should give younger hunters—the ones who have grown up during the time of premiums—some idea of how far things have progressed in the last few decades.

Buhmiller did get into some dies for altering the solids of his time. He got the feeling that the neat semi-round-nose profiles of many, while giving great penetration, should be giving more destruction. So he made up a die with an inner projection that would "bash" the nose back, giving a sort of cavity point to a solid. This seemed to work well.

Buhmiller preferred heavy soft-points for buffalo, and said that solids in such cartridges as his 450 Magnum were hardly to be recommended because the Winchester solid which he used for reloading "gave such penetration it will seldom stop in a buffalo unless it's a full length shot. Better to use the Barnes heavy jacket softpoints; I have used them with a 1/8-inch copper rivet through the rear end to pin the core inside the jacket. It works fairly well, but if the cores could be sweated inside the jackets they would be worth a dollar apiece to the occasional buffalo hunter." And this was in the '50s, when a dollar was worth a lot more than it is now.

Interestingly, a number of today's premium bullet makers routinely sweat or epoxy cores inside jackets, though offhand I can't recall hearing of anyone else riveting them together.

Buhmiller also pre-dated today's homogenous bullets by lathe-turning his own out of solid copper or German silver. He experimented with various point shapes here too, eventually seeming to prefer a sort of dished-out cavity on blunt-nosed slugs, believing they gave larger wound channels and had less tendency to veer when striking heavy bones than conventional solids, at the same time blowing flesh/bone debris out ahead of them rather

Three .510-inch-diameter bullets: 550-gr. cavity point, 570-gr. solid roundnose, heeled 560-gr. semi-roundnose solid removed from elephant; note rifling marks on latter.

than simply penetrating. In this way they acted much as his "bashed" solids.

At one time John spoke of building a barrel with a 50-cal. groove diameter so he could simply use half-inch solid copper rod as the basic bullet, cut to length and shaped. This would have saved him the expense and nuisance of importing Kynoch bullets or the work of lathe-turning larger diameter stock to .510, but I don't know if he ever got around to doing this.

Though he once said "My most effective rifle is the 510 Magnum loaded to the approximate power of the 505 Gibbs," he later wrote "There is little difference in killing effect of the 450 Mag using the full length Norma case and the 458-378 Weatherby, and the Norma case is cheaper, easier to make up, and magazine capacity is greater."

Another reason he liked the smaller 450 Magnum (if you can call any case using 90 grains of powder "small") was its lesser recoil. This was a subject John rarely mentioned, though he did make up and use different muzzlebrakes. These reduced recoil nearly 50 percent, but of course increased muzzle blast. John ignored this, as he did most nuisances, concentrating first and foremost on getting the job done, whatever it was. "I've got calloused ears," he said once when the subject came up.

Uncle John has been gone a long time now, since 1975, but I haven't heard of anyone who has matched his performance. The fact that many of today's premium bullet makers follow his suggestions and examples of decades ago shows the value of his actual field experiences and accurate observations. Few hunters have left more. ●

Buhmiller's cavity-pointed solid bullets flank a typical factory-loaded round nose solid. Cavity-points tended to blow bone and flesh debris out ahead of them instead of just slipping through as the traditional solid does.

The author's 10mm Cowboy outfit a Winchester 73 and a Bisley Colt, both in – you guessed, right? – 38-40.

The 10 Millimeter That Won the West

By Glen Ruh

COMPARED TO the 14mm Mississippi rifle or the 11.4mm trapdoor Springfield, the cowpuncher's 10mm was admittedly a latecomer to the American scene. Still, during the final years of the last century and well into the early part of this one, a lot of hunters, cattlemen, and other shooters packed a ten — in big Colt sixshooters, in Winchester and Marlin lever actions, or even in Colt and Remington slide-action rifles.

Of course, in the 19th century, they didn't know it as a 10-millimeter. Metric measure might have been used in scientific laboratories and far away places where English wasn't spoken, but not in the 30-some United States. Folks here called it the 38 Winchester centerfire (W.C.F.) or the 38-40. But 10 millimeters it was: a full .401 inch diameter lead bullet, inside lubricated, in a squat, slightly bottle-necked, balloon-head case necked down from the parent 44-40 Winchester. The ammunition company's marketing strategy for both cartridges was based in part on the convenience of using one cartridge in both a revolver and a rifle, and the major American gunmakers obliged with an array of suitable arms. The 44-40 was undeniably the most popular of the two, but for many years the 38-40 stayed a close second.

To put this cartridge in perspective, a little history is in order. In 1879, the year most authorities think the 38 W.C.F. was introduced, the standard military caliber was 45 in both sidearms and rifles. Colt's Single Action Army revolver fired a hefty 265-grain lead bullet behind 40 grains of black powder. For the standard-issue Springfield trapdoor shoulder arms, the 45 Government cartridge with 70 grains of black powder pushed a

500 grain slug in the rifle and 405 grains in the carbine loading.

In the decade after the Civil War, the civilian populace was served by an aggressively entrepreneurial firearms industry. Arms makers tended to develop proprietary rifle cartridges, and in 40-caliber, the choice included the 40-65 Winchester, both bottle-necked and tapered-case editions of the 40-70 Sharps, and a host of cartridges for Ballard, Maynard, Remington, Stevens, and other rifles. Yet until the 38 WCF appeared, in pistol calibers there was nothing between the

(left) The venerable 38-40 cartridge has been about the business for way over a century—it's a 10mm. (right) The 10mm auto, born to fanfare just years ago, is eclipsing already, stuck in the shade of the 40 S&W, another 10mm.

nominal 38s and the big 44s and 45s.

With the advent of the self-contained brass cartridge in the late 1860s, Colt and Remington percussion revolvers could be converted to take rim- and center-fire cylinders. After Smith & Wesson's patent on the bored-through cylinder ran out, more cartridge revolvers hit the market. Following Colt's lead, cartridge off-spring of the popular "Navy" caliber cap-and-ball revolvers were 36-inch in bore diameter, but they were called 38 caliber.

Just why those cartridge arms and the ammunition for them were designated 38s is a matter of some dispute. Why Winchester decided to further confuse the issue by calling its new 40 caliber bottlenecked round a 38 is even more of a mystery. To make matters even more puzzling, Colt used barrels of the same internal diameter for its 38-40 revolvers and for the 41 Long Colt (the early, inside-lubricated version, a 407-inch bullet backed by 21 grains of black powder). One modern loading manual contends that the designation actually reflects a 40 caliber bullet and the original loading of 38 grains of black powder. But if that were so, the name should logically have been the 40-38. A slogan arose to clarify everything: "All thirty-eights are thirty-sixes, except the thirty-eight-forty, which is a forty-one."

Confusing nomenclature aside, in the Winchester 1873 rifle and later in the Colt single-action Army revolver the 38-40 found much favor. It was commonly accepted that the 38 WCF black-powder round shot slightly harder and flatter than the 44 WCF, but in reality any difference in their decidedly parabolic trajectories was negligible. Of the 720,000 to a million-plus Model 1873s manufactured by Winchester, a large number were chambered in .38 W.C.F., as were

Model 1892 rifles and carbines that eventually replaced it.

Between 1873 and 1940 Colt produced more than 357,000 SAAs, and more than 50,000 of them were in 38-40. Colt factory shipping records reflect the cartridge's popularity from year to year: Introduced in the SAA in 1884, the 38-40 chambering soon ranked third behind 45 Colt and 44 WCF, and it stayed there for the next decade. In 1900 it overtook the 44-40 to gain second place, and from 1903 through 1908 annual production of the 38-40 out-stripped even the 45 Colt. In the Bisley models introduced in 1896, the .38-40 chambering was second only to the 32-20, with more than 12,000 manufactured, including 117 guns in the rare flattop Bisley target model. A respectable number of 38-40s were made in Colt's double-action Army model of 1877 and the swing-out cylinder New Service revolvers. Advertisements for all these arms advised that they were "suited to the 38 Winchester rifle cartridge." The 38-40 Colt Bisley illustrated here, numbered in the 261,000 serial number range, was shiny and new in 1905. You could have bought one in blued steel with gutta-percha grips from Sears, Roebuck that year for $15.50, with cartridges at $.73 the box of 50.

From 1909 and on through the 1920s, the 38-40 chambering in the Colt SAA gradually declined in popularity, being superseded in part by the straight-cased 38 and 44 Special cartridges pioneered by Smith and Wesson. Relatively few large-frame Smith and Wesson top-break revolvers were ever offered in 38-40, although the caliber was popular enough in the finely made but poorly marketed Merwin and Hulbert "automatic ejection" revolvers.

Sporting literature and gun catalogs from the 1880s through the the 1930s

The true Colt was made in its thousands in 10mm Cowboy—that is, 38-40. The writer shoots his, finds it fun and effective.

The Ruger is a Buckeye special. It has cylinders for both 38-40 and 10mm Auto and is special, indeed.

Fox Trapping, published in 1906, author A. R. Harding cites the experience of one I. W. Beardsley, a Connecticut fox hunter who pursued the wiley predator in a style of hunting no longer with us. "I was walking along the tracks of the Berkshire Division R.R. which was bounded by a fence three boards high, skirting the track. I noticed beneath the lower board the legs of a fox moving toward me some seventy-five yards away. I stopped between the rails, half raising my 38-40 Stevens, telescope mounted, and waited for a favorable shot. When some thirty yards away the fox crawled under the fence and trotted down the bank immediately in front of me, where I stood in plain view. He stopped in the middle of the tracks and looked toward me unconcernedly for several seconds, then swung his head down the tracks in the direction of a train which was rapidly approaching from the south. This was my chance. I brought the cross hairs to bear just back of his foreleg and pulled. With one mighty bound in the air he fell back across the tracks without a struggle, and I had to do some hustling to pull him out of the way before the train was upon us."

Even if the factory-loaded 38 W.C.F. in a rifle was limited to short-range hunting, there was no denying its utility as a heavy handgun load. A 180-grain round-nosed bullet leaving a pistol barrel at 900 feet a second works out to some 365 foot pounds of energy. The 40 S&W auto, the standard FBI cartridge of the 1990s, can't offer more. Handloaded with heavy blackpowder or smokeless loads, the 38-40 can be cranked up to every bit the equal of the 10mm auto. In the pre-magnum years of the 1920s, no less an authority than J. Henry Fitzgerald, the legendary "Fitz" of the Colt company, ranked the factory-loaded cartridge right up there with the 45 Colt and 44-40 for handgun hunting.

As much as he disparaged factory loads in almost any caliber, Elmer Keith allowed as how a handloaded 38-40 could deliver "fine accuracy and plenty of power." Never bashful about high pressure levels, he advised a full case of black pow-

consistently cite 38-40 rifles as suitable for game up to and including deer, and there is no doubt that they dropped many a whitetail. Although the 38-40 in a rifle would hardly be considered a deer-slayer by modern standards — even in its later smokeless powder loadings — it did the job nicely for great-grandad on small and medium sized game. For their

handiness and mild recoil, lever- and slide-action rifles and carbines in 38-40 stayed popular until eventually displaced by the 30-30 and other smokeless rounds that ushered in the first generation of high velocity cartridges around the turn of the 20th century.

The cartridge may have been at its best as a small game load. In his book

The 1892 Winchester was, in a long gun, the eventual darling of the 38-40 crowd.

der or startling quantities of DuPont #80 and Hercules 2400 behind 180 grain hard-cast bullets, claiming velocity and energy levels higher than the factory 357 Magnum. Keith's heavy-duty 38-40 recipe called for a large dose of 2400 pushing a 260-grain bullet, and he wrote of dropping a six-point elk with such a load. Another time, Keith tried to dispatch a wounded elk with 38-40 factory ammo. The first round bounced off the elk's skull, but Elmer's second shot was a 210-grain cast bullet over 40 grains of black powder. That one stopped the enraged animal just in time. Nonetheless Keith found the bottlenecked cartridge troublesome to reload. The thin case neck was given to undue buckling when being resized, he said, and it had poor crimping qualities. However, even qualified praise from Keith meant something.

Major Ned Roberts, one of America's foremost riflemen and decidedly a conservative compared to Keith, experimented with the 38-40 in a '73 Winchester rifle, looking for accuracy rather than stopping power. "I found the 38-40-180 [grain bullet] somewhat superior to the 44-40-200 cartridge, the velocity being greater and the trajectory lower. At known distances, this rifle shot very well indeed, closer than I could hold....

At 40 yards offhand I fired five shots that could be covered by a half dollar. I several times fired one hundred shots... and still obtained accurate shooting at 100 to 125 yards using reloaded ammunition. Everything considered, the Winchester 38-40 was the most practical and satisfactory rifle I had owned up to that time [1888], but it had some faults such

as high trajectory which caused many misses at ranges over 100 yards due to wrong estimation of distances."

An easy way to see what Roberts was talking about is to take a sound rifle and a box of modern factory loads out to a silhouette range. A good long-range sight makes hits possible at 100 and even 200 meters with the 30-40, but the allowance for elevation is significant. A 150-yard shot at a whitetail's lung area might just clip its toenails.

One version of the 38-40 is responsible for the demise of more renegade Injuns and bad men than George Custer or Bat Masterson could ever have imagined. For Hollywood, the ammunition makers turned out millions of the 5-in-1 blank, which for decades has sent clouds of black powder smoke across movie screens. Basically an elongated, crimped

The writer's '73, shortcomings not outstanding, lets him bang silhouettes with satisfying, if not work-winning, authority.

38-40 case, the rim and base dimentions of the 5-in-1 allows it to be used in 45 Colt, 44-40 and 38-40 re-volvers plus lever-action rifles in the last two calibers — hence the name 5-in-1. The current version uses a plastic case, presumably so it won't be confused with the real thing on a sound stage.

In many of his western films, when he wasn't wearing Army blue, John

action shooting began to gain popularity and old pistols were pressed into service.

In the late 1980s, a limited run of the Ruger Blackhawk appeared with interchangeable cylinders in 10mm and 38-40, courtesy of Buckeye Sports, a major distributor. The Colt factory also chambered some of its third generation SAAs in the old caliber, and some foreign makers of SAA clones have cautiously done

the round is once again appearing in new editions of some loading manuals.

In the days before smokeless powder, the convenience of one cartridge for both rifle and revolver may have made sense, at least for horsemen on long cattle drives or homesteaders far from a general store. Back then the standard 40-grain blackpowder load was also the maximum load. Now it's different. At

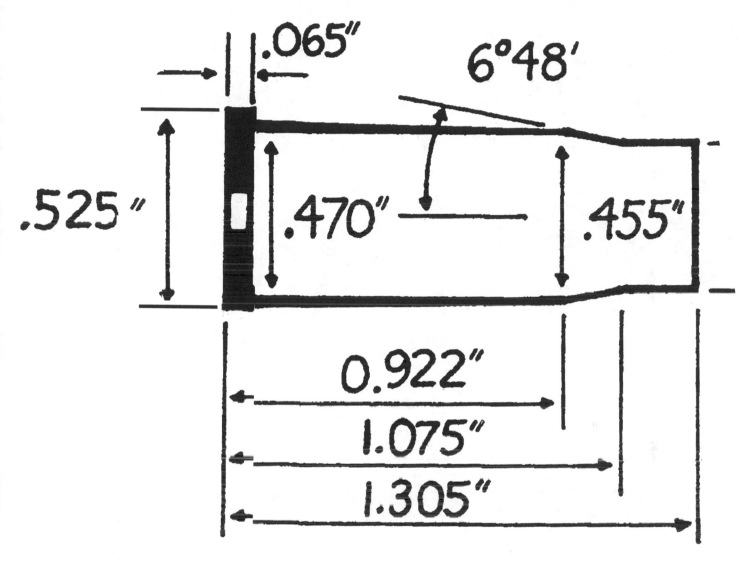

If your mystery cartridge comes close to these dimensions, it's a 38-40. And also, any observer would admit, a 10mm.

Wayne regularly packed the same well-worn 38-40 hogleg with a 4-3/4-inch barrel and stag grips. In the 1980s, Olin was inspired to issue a commemorative run of the cartridge in the Duke's memory, along with a similar issue of 32-40 rifle fodder for his trusty '94 Winchester carbine. So much for the one-round-for-two-guns legend.

After WW II, none of the U.S. arms makers offered either rifles or revolvers in 38 W.C.F. The cartridge had faded from reloading manuals by the 1960s, but continued to be factory loaded in relatively small runs. Modern interest in the cartridge was essentially nonexistent until a few years ago when cowboy

so as well. In one of my local gun shops there's a brand new, nickel-plated, 5-1/2-inch third generation Single Action from the Colt Custom Shop, complete with velvet-lined case, bargain priced in the very high three figures.

For years the situation was poor for handloaders. The better known bullet suppliers simply didn't list any cast or jacketed lead bullets in 40 caliber, and the mold manufacturers supplied only a few variations of 40 caliber cast pistol bullets. With the introduction of the 40 S&W and 10mm semiauto handguns, however, .401-inch cast and swaged bullets started to appear alongside jacketed bullets. Dies are available, and data for

present, the factory load, if you can find it, is a 180-grain jacketed soft-point with a listed velocity of 1160 fps from a rifle, giving 538 foot pounds of energy at the muzzle. But shooting factory smokeless loads in an elderly rifle or pistol isn't a great idea. For recreational shooting with guns made before 1900, it's prudent to stick with pistol reloads in the cast-bullet, 800 fps range. Unless you're packing a like-new Colt SAA or a Ruger Blackhawk, save the full-strength jacketed rounds for tight, well maintained long guns.

Tapered, bottle-necked cases have never been favored for handgun reloading, putting the 38-40 at a disadvantage from the outset. The 38-40's bad reputation may have started back when lighter-weight balloon-head cases were the norm. A commonly heard complaint is that the case necks tend to collapse in the loading process, and there's no doubt that the problem can occur. Modern solid-head cases, run though high-quality dies, however, should give the careful handloader no difficulty.

A sampling of modern solid-head Winchester-Western cases average around 96 grains in weight, with Remington-Peters cases running about 5 grains less. Water capacity runs 32 to 33 grains. By way of comparison, some old WRA cases (featuring small primer pockets) weigh only 76 grains; their Remington-UMC counterparts run about 81 grains. I haven't miked the neck-wall thickness, but the old case walls look slightly thinner than modern cases. It makes good sense to put old-style cases in the display case and reload only new, solid-head brass. If you're in doubt, shine a bright light into the case; primer cups in balloon head cases stand tall, while the inside of a solid-head case is flush at the bottom. Additionally, all my modern solid-head cases have an external extractor groove above the rim, a feature lacking in all the old balloon-head cases I've seen.

When I loaded my first batch of 38-40s, I decided Keith was right about troublesome cases. My Lee resizing die buckled several case necks in a row. Running them back through the expander straightened out all but one, but probably at the expense of case life. I also had problems getting the seating die to crimp bullets properly. On the advice of an experienced troubleshooter, I bought Lee's crimping die, which solved the problem forthwith. I find that 175-grain SWCs in front of a modest 7 grains of Unique and producing around 800 fps perfectly fine for paper targets or short-range silhouettes, and I'm sure the same applies to cowboy action shooting.

One doesn't bring out a retired gun without some trepidation. I admit to wincing at the first shot from the old Bisley, but without cause. The Bisley shoots to left of center with its blade sight and grooved frame, so Kentucky windage is necessary. But except for one called flier, I could cover a ten-round group at 25 yards with my hand—good enough for defensive work anytime. The Winchester came next. It's hard to imagine a flimsier bolt and lock-up than the system employed in the classic 1873 lever-action. The Browning-designed Model 1892, Marlin's lever actions—even slide-action Colt Lightning rifles—were far stronger. But Oliver Winchester was a salesman, not a gun designer, and he sold rings around his competitors anyway. The '73 feeding system was designed for round-nosed bullets, not for semi-wadcutters, so I had to help each new round into the chamber. Drawing a bead with big-eared, semi-buckhorn open sights makes you appreciate modern optics or even a good aperture sight. Still, the big spring steel rear sight was fully adjustable by tapping it side to side in its dovetail and using the stepped wedge. Without dumping too much lead into the berm, I was soon toppling silhouette pigs and rams at 50 and 100 yards with a satisfying clang. I scored tolerably well at close range on silhouettes with the Colt, too, using Keith's recommended two-hand hold and lots of front sight. And when the big slugs hit, they hit hard. Just the way they did for great granddad, Elmer, and Duke.

Did I say the 38-40 was back? You won't catch me taking my old guns afield, but anyone with a new Ruger convertible, a tight Winchester or Marlin lever action or a Remington 14 pump, plus the inclination to experiment with loads, can easily match 357 Magnum energy levels and more. I'm one of those people who believe that old guns are to enjoy, not just to look at. For anyone with a serviceable 38-40, you can't go wrong investing in a set of loading dies, a few boxes of new brass, and some 10mm cast bullets. You can have lots of fun plunking large lumps of lead downrange with one of America's all-time favorite cartridges—a 10mm at that. ●

Eastern togs and all, Ruh finds his 10mm Cowboy rifle a friendly plinker, a serious piece of history, and a lot of fun.

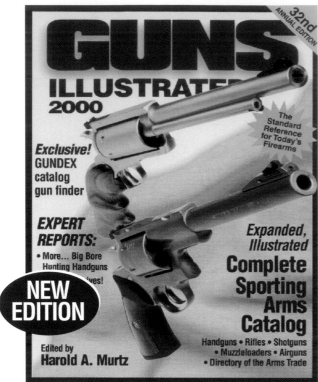
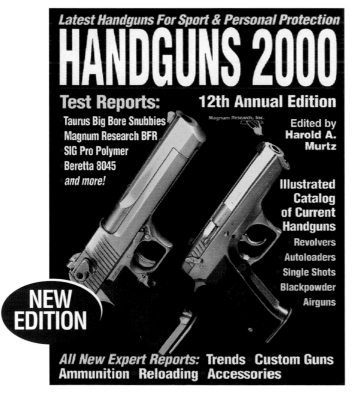

SERIOUS INNOVATION

INTRODUCING THE BROWNING BPR PUMP RIFLE: RELIABLE. FAST. ACCURATE.

The new Browning Pump Rifle (BPR) is true innovation. It's like no other pump rifle.

Pump the action and you will feel the difference — the unique camming forearm system operates quickly and easily because the forearm follows the natural movement of your hand. Its massive seven-lug rotary bolt design also handles magnum calibers.

It doesn't look like a pump — its lines are clean and sleek. The forearm hugs the receiver and the slide bars are totally hidden.

The BPR sets a new standard for pump-rifle strength, styling and reliability.

BROWNING®

Visit your Browning dealer for a
1999 Master Catalog or call 1-800-333-3504.
www.browning.com

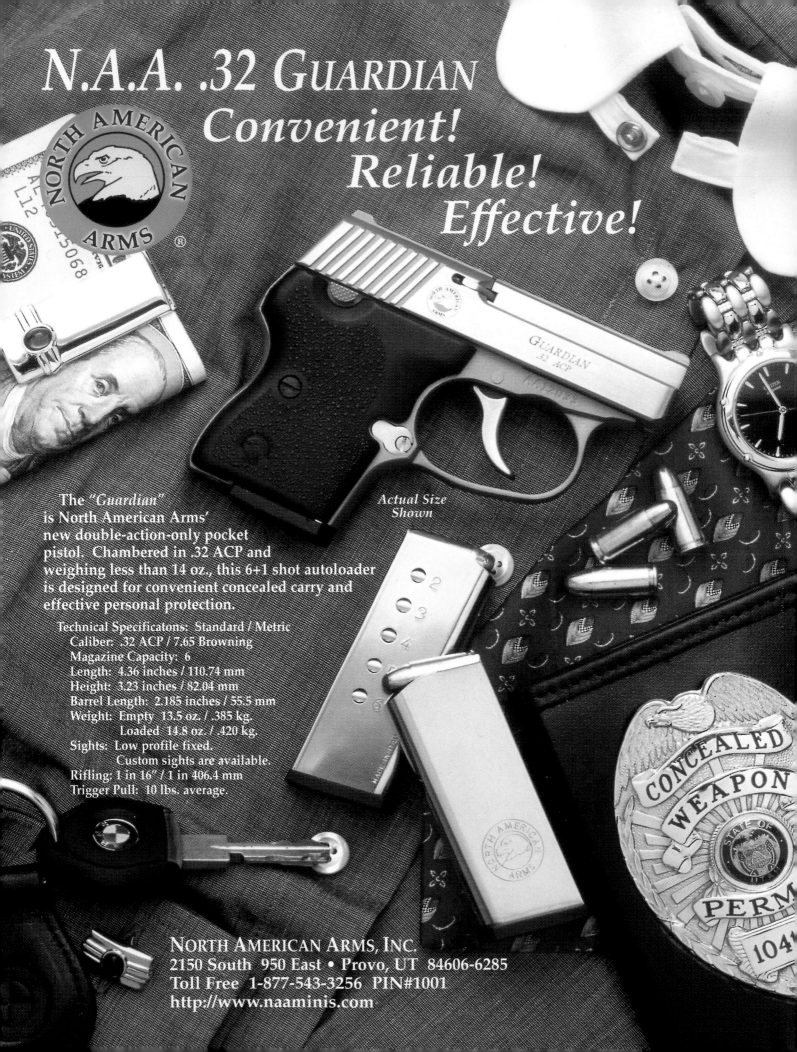

THE MYSTERY KRAG

By T.S. Wickens

Raised by an old horse trader (literally), I've seen some pretty sly deals and even made a few myself in my thirty years. Up until 1987, one of the best deals I ever saw was when we traded a psychopathic jenny mule for a 410 shotgun and a beagle hound. Neither the gun or dog were worth much, but the mule cost me several bruises and temporarily deprived one of our hounds of a roof over his head. But I digress.

You will see 1987 was important for two reasons: I graduated from North Dakota State University-Bottineau and I made a deal of legendary proportions, taking into my possession an elderly old beast of a rifle. It has since gone with me on many forays into the high deserts of Wyoming, the plains of North Dakota and the fields of Illinois. And it remains a mystery. Here is its story as I have been able to gather it.

Sometime in either 1898 or 1899, depending on which source you read, a rifle came off the production line at Springfield Armory. It was a U.S. Model of 1898 Krag-Jorgensen bolt action, in rifle configuration with 30 inch barrel and shotgun-style butt. The rifle's serial number is 158910.

The plot thickens sometime after the gun left Springfield Armory. I assume it was released from military stores at some point after the adoption of the 1903 Springfield and not before. When this occurred with this particular rifle I do not know, but could have been in 1905 when many of these guns were released to the public. What I do know is that sometime between 1898 and 1897 it fell into the hands of an absolute master gunsmith. The standard military rifle was turned into one of the finest custom sporters I have ever seen.

The person or persons who did the work did so with what resources were available:

The barrel was cut back to 24 inches, carefully re-crowned. The front sight is now a highly modified 1903 Springfield barrel band front sight. The military rear sight was removed and a Lyman Model 42 W receiver sight was added. The military stock was discarded to be replaced with a checkered walnut sporter stock, its pistol grip very hand-filling and curiously round in cross section. The front sling swivel was replaced with a barrel band sling swivel stud that drops through the forearm with the swivel itself screwing in from underneath. The trigger guard, buttplate and rear sling swivel are standard military issue. The knurled cocking knob of the Krag bolt has been completely removed and beveled off a la Mauser. The military two-stage trigger was polished to give a trigger pull of 2.5 pounds.

The rear sight gives an idea of the skill of the gunsmith and of the limited availability of aftermarket sights at the time, and more than anything else, puts a date on the gun. From Lyman, earlier this year, I learned this sight was originally made for a Hopkins and Allen 22 caliber bolt action target rifle

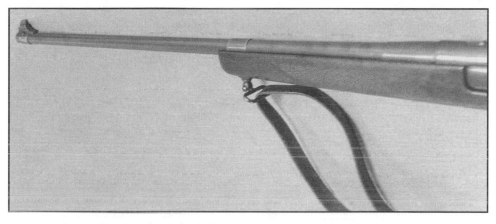

As you can see this is not the front end of a military Krag. The front sight is a modified 1903 Springfield sight. The sling swivel is attached to a barrel band. This was fairly common in custom guns of the era.

The bolt and magazine of the Krag open and ready to load. Note the lack of a cocking knob on the bolt. Although it looks better it makes disassembly a little tricky.

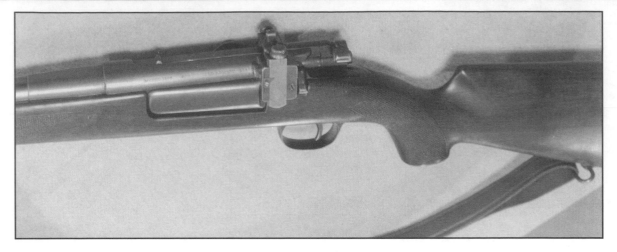

A view of the left side of the receiver showing the Lyman 42W sight which was originally made for a .22 rifle!

and was made in only one year, 1910. The later Lyman 48 receiver sight was not made, as I recall, until well into the 1920s. In order to get the sight to fit the Krag, the gunsmith silver soldered a half inch piece of bronze to the receiver, an alteration not visible without removing the sight. Judging by the even bluing on the barrel where the original rear sight used to be, the receiver sight has been in place since shortly after the gun was worked over.

The Krag still retains the swinging box magazine and magazine cutoff. This arrangement is fine by me since it allows for very positive functioning and makes the magazine much easier to top off. Some may think it looks uncomfortable to carry, but it has never bothered me because the width of the magazine distributes the weight of the gun in your hand. Also since the gun balances at the magazine it becomes even easier to carry in the field.

The magazine also makes the Krag very easy to load and unload thus making it very safe. Just take the number of shells you want, from one to five, make sure the cartridges are facing forward and just kind of shake them out of your palm into the magazine. It might not be as fast as a Mauser with a stripper clip, but it is alot faster to load than a tube magazine. To unload the magazine you just need to open it up and let them slide out. No need to worry about losing a clip or cycling the rounds through the action risking an accidental discharge.

The bolt is just as slick as the books say it is supposed to be. It doesn't bind and provides a positive lockup with front lug, bolt handle and guide rib. It may not be as strong as a Mauser, but it handles the standard 180-grain bullet at around 2400 feet per second nicely and has taken game up to and including elk and moose at ranges out to 250 yards.

In these days of stampings, plastics and polymers the Krag is an anachronism. All its metal parts are made from milled steel forgings. The bluing is very deep and still protects the gun after nearly 100 years. The hot bluing on my 1980s Winchester 94 XTR is nowhere near the same quality. Nor is the bluing on any standard factory guns of today.

How does it perform? Does it shoot 1/2 MOA ten shot groups at 100 yards? Of course not. It was made to be a serviceable combat rifle and it shoots three-shot groups of around 1 1/2 inches at 100 yards. The bullets do need to be between 165 and 220 grains in weight to get consistent accuracy and I usually try to use slightly reduced loads for prolonged shooting sessions. A 165 grain bullet at around 2400 feet per second works nicely. It is accurate, gives even lower recoil than normal and pretty much duplicates old 300 Savage ballistics.

This old Krag also handles like a dream. As I said, it balances at the magazine as a rifle should. Throw it to your shoulder and it is right on target. All of the time, and every time. Once, in order to check this capability, I waited until after dark then placed a gallon milk jug against our bulletstop. Pacing off twenty-five yards I turned, loaded the gun, shouldered it and fired. Without the sights I was able to put a round dead center through the jug and I was in love yet again.

Who customized the gun? I don't know. It looks much like a single shot 25-35 Griffin & Howe varmint rifle that I saw once. But the pistol grip and general style makes me think it might be the work of Louis Wundhammer or one of his apprentices. The time period of the rear sight should coincide with the period right before Wundhammer started working for Sedgeley, in the 1920s, I believe.

I can still remember that gun dealer. He said the gun had come out of Wisconsin and that the previous owner had used it as a target rifle. When my brother and I saw it we dead-panned immediately and when the gun dealer turned around, we mouthed the word "Sedgeley". When the fellow asked $180 dollars for the rifle and 200 rounds of reloaded ammo, I didn't even bat an eye.

From what dad says, the dealer is still trying to buy that gun back. I've

Full length view of the Mystery Krag. Showing all of the work done to it.

had people laugh at me for shooting the old Krag and I've seen people get jealous. If you are lucky to have a good Krag in shooting shape, shoot it and do so with pride. If you don't own one and see one for a reasonable price, buy it and you'll never be disappointed. they're all good guns.

THE WEBLEY MARK IV .38

By Edward R. Crews

The Webley Mark IV 38 gets little respect from gun writers. In more than 30 years of reading, I have seen few words of praise for this homely British pistol from World War II.

Criticism is wide ranging and few of its features get kind words. The negative adjectives pile up dark and thick: ugly, ungainly, inaccurate, and cursed with breaktop action and crude wartime fit and finish. Its 38 S&W cartridge is anemic, making it unfit for personal defense, critics say. And, it is plagued with a hard trigger pull.

I can't dispute all of that, but I believe my Webley Mark IV 38 is one good gun despite what detractors say. I bought it 20 years ago while a college student, and it has given me endless hours of pleasure at the range and in the field. It has proven to be rugged, reliable and cheap to shoot. It holds a special nostalgic place in my life being the first pistol I ever bought and the first for which I reloaded ammunition.

The Webley appeals to me in part because I always have enjoyed shooting old military weapons. I see them as historic touchstones and believe they give us a chance to get new insights into generals, battles and soldiers of bygone days. The Webley specifically came to my attention 23 years ago when I took a two-semester British history course in college. The Webley name continually appeared in reading I did on imperial expansion, World War I and World War II. I began to do a little research on Webley pistols and discovered that they had a long association with the British Army.

That army placed its first order with Webley in 1887 for 10,000 guns carrying the nomenclature—Pistol Breech-Loading, Revolver, WEBLEY (Mark I). British troops would carry several models thereafter, the best-known the Mark VI 455. Accepted by the army in May 1915, this pistol saw extensive service on the Western Front. That's not surprising. Because of their size and weight, pistols

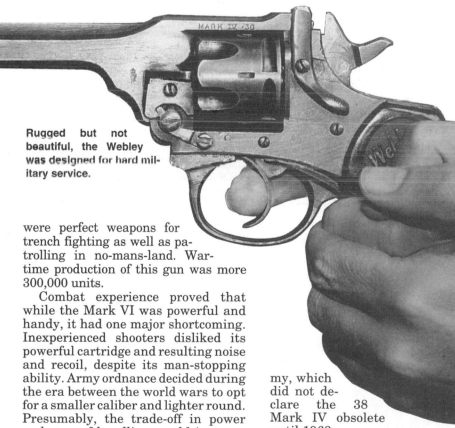

Rugged but not beautiful, the Webley was designed for hard military service.

were perfect weapons for trench fighting as well as patrolling in no-mans-land. Wartime production of this gun was more 300,000 units.

Combat experience proved that while the Mark VI was powerful and handy, it had one major shortcoming. Inexperienced shooters disliked its powerful cartridge and resulting noise and recoil, despite its man-stopping ability. Army ordnance decided during the era between the world wars to opt for a smaller caliber and lighter round. Presumably, the trade-off in power and ease of handling would increase accuracy. Accordingly, the British embraced the 38 S&W round. Official thinking was that the drop in power and bullet size would not put soldiers

at risk as the pistol was a very short-range weapon in British experience.

During World War II, Great Britain needed a huge number of pistols. Government orders for the Webley 38 Mark IV, the model I own, reached more than 100,000 units. The oft-repeated criticism of the 38 S&W round by modern day gun writers apparently was not a problem for the British Army, which did not declare the 38 Mark IV obsolete until 1963.

Twenty years ago, my research made me want a Webley pistol, but finding one of any caliber or age in the early 1970s proved difficult. I roamed

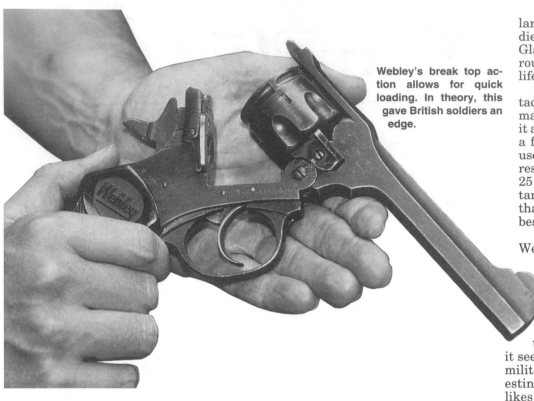

Webley's break top action allows for quick loading. In theory, this gave British soldiers an edge.

larly in garrison where most soldiers spend most of their careers. Glassy smooth trigger pulls in the rough-and-tumble world of military life invite innumerable accidents.

As to accuracy, the Webley is no tack-driver. A truly expert marksman can get solid performance from it at ranges up to 25 yards. I once let a former police firearms instructor use it, and he was able to obtain good results on a man-sized silhouette at 25 yards. Tight groups at more distant range are often more a dream than a reality even for some of the best competitive shooters I know.

One unintended benefit of the Webley is that I have found it to be a good ambassador for pistol marksmanship and gun ownership. Many of my friends have never fired a gun, and the low recoil Webley is a good introductory firearm. Unlike the 22, it is not so diminutive that it seems like a child's trainer, and its military associations make it an interesting object. Everyone who shoots it likes it. They are pleasantly surprised at how easy it is to shoot and several of them have started combing gun shops and shows for a similar pistol.

I'm quick to defend my Webley simply because it has given me so much pleasure. In the end, that's really the only rationale any shooter needs to feel a special kinship with any good gun.

gun shops and shows, searched diligently through classified ads, and asked friends to keep a lookout.

Then, one spring day in 1974, I got into a gun shop with my roommate. I was looking at rifles when I noticed him waving and tapping on a glass case filled with pistols. He had found a 38 Mark IV. According to the store owner, it had belonged to a retired American admiral who worked closely with the British Navy in World War II and brought the pistol home as a souvenir. The man had died and his widow wanted the gun out of the house. I don't recall haggling much about the price, which was around $30 and therefore affordable even for my budget.

I shot that pistol a lot during my last two years of college and even started reloading with a small Lee Loader hand kit. It was a fine first handgun and served me well until I put it away in 1980 and didn't shoot it for roughly a decade. There was never a decent place for shooting and rarely time. Then, in 1990, I joined a local gun club, then had a chance to buy a fair amount of 38 S&W ammo

for a good price. I did and got reacquainted with my old friend.

To appreciate the admittedly unlovely 38 Mark IV, you must accept it for what it is - a mass-produced military arm designed to fill a very narrow niche. It was never intended to serve as a match pistol or a collectable. It was supposed to be a light pistol with a light recoil for use only at extremely close ranges. It

Webley has served as an introductory gun for dozens of shooters.

had to be rugged and dependable, qualities that I have found my Webley to have. While it is true that large caliber bullets backed by powerful charges are manstoppers, I know from having been a police reporter that small-caliber rounds can prove deadly at short ranges.

The hard-pulling Webley trigger is a necessity in a military gun where safe handling has to be built into a weapon to prevent accidents, particu-

THE REMINGTON 742 in 308 Win.

By Dan Barton

In 1961 my great uncle Carroll Barton bought a new Remington 742 in 308 Winchester to take on a mule deer hunt in western Colorado. He brought back a nice eight-point buck, and he was pretty proud of his new gun.

Uncle Carroll was the hunter in my family. My dad and my grandfather would bird hunt on social occasions, but only Carroll was serious enough to make the long trips required in those days to get to good deer country. He bought me my first shotgun, took me along on hunting and fishing trips, and regaled me with stories of his adventures in Colorado and the brush country of south Texas. He worked in a sporting goods store and every Christmas he gave me some fancy piece of hunting or camping gear, but most of all he gave me a love of hunting and of wild country. When he died in 1971 he left me his rifle, and I hunt with it to this day.

The Remington has always been a safe and reliable gun, but it took me quite a while to get it to deliver really consistent accuracy. The first time I took it hunting after my uncle's death I sighted it in carefully at a local range. The point of impact seemed to rise drastically as the barrel heated up. Adjustments were easy and precise with the old Weaver K-4 scope, but the rifle seemed to want to string its shots vertically. I finally shot one fair group and declared it 'good enough'.

A friend had invited me along on a hunt in Llano County, a part of Texas where deer are numerous as rabbits and not much bigger. We got a whole day of shooting on a ranch whose owner cared as little for deer as he did for deer hunters. I took almost a dozen shots but the deer I shot at were completely unharmed. After the hunt I took the rifle back to the range and discovered that it was hitting a foot low at one

hundred yards. I reset the sights and wondered what the matter was. The next time I got a chance to hunt deer I took a different rifle. The Remington stood in my closet for years, carefully cleaned, but never going hunting.

The mid 80's in Texas were a tough time for woodworkers like me. The real estate market crashed and construction projects were few and far between. To keep solvent I ended up selling my whole gun collection, all but my uncle's 308. I just couldn't let it go. When an opportunity to go deer hunting came up, the old Remington was the only rifle I had.

Unfortunately, the story was the same as it was on my first hunt with the autoloader - a hard time sighting in, and a string of missed shots.

It was time to figure out what was wrong with the rifle, and get it to settle down and shoot straight. The K-4 was mounted in Weaver swing off mounts. Somehow the dull clicking sound the scope made when it was swung into sighting position didn't instill a lot of confidence. I replaced the old pivot mount with standard Weaver mounts and replaced the scope with a Bushnell 2.5, a better choice for quick shots at disappearing whitetails. As per the advice of Jack O'Connor, all base and

mount screws were fixed with Loctite. A trip to the range showed a drastic improvement. The rifle made much better groups, about two and a half inches at a hundred yards, but still had a tendency to shift point of impact as the barrel warmed up.

Relieving stock forend pressure always seems to help bolt action rifles with vertical grouping problems, so I tried to figure a way to do that with the Remington. The forend is held in place by a bolt that threads through a collar at the front of the forend and threads into a steel block attached to the bottom of the barrel which houses the gas take-off that powers the action. The threads that engage the two parts are separated by a rebated and unthreaded section that keeps the forend from being screwed down tight enough to damage the gas take-off. What was needed was a way to keep the forend firmly attached without applying pressure to the gas block or to the front of the receiver. Loctite had worked so well on the scope mounts I decided to try it on the forend. I assembled the forend loosely in place, applied Loctite to the threaded sections of the forend bolt, then threaded the bolt in until it was almost, but not quite tight. The next day I took the gun to the range and it shot like a target rifle.

Groups shrank to one and a half inches, not bad for factory ammunition and a 2.5X scope, and groups only started climbing after two or three clips at rapid fire. I've kept this rifle setup the same way for almost ten years now and it's become my favorite for hunting all big game. It's killed a dozen deer, a couple of javelinas, a big feral boar, a wild turkey and one particular nine point buck that was the biggest deer I'd ever seen in the wild. I'd kept the rifle for sentimental reasons, but I've learned to appreciate it for what it is-one good gun. ●

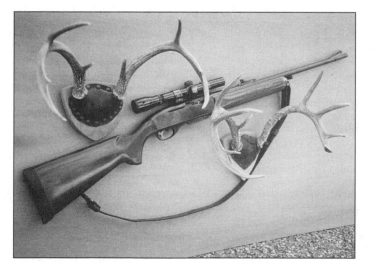

MUZZLE LOADING RIFLES ARE EASY....

...if you follow the directions on the box.

By Doc Carlson

Troy Hartman with his little buck—50 yards, center hit, clean and immediate kill with a Ruger.

WITH THE advent of reasonably priced, mass-produced guns, easily bought replica blackpowders, improved projectiles and a proliferation of muzzle-loader-only seasons, hunting with a muzzleloading rifle or shotgun has grown to the stature of bow hunting as a legitimate sub-division in the hunting hobby, and recently has begun a growth spurt that would do a skinny high school sophomore proud. Obviously, the fact that most states now have muzzleloading seasons has fueled this growth. However, great changes in equipment available for use by the beginning muzzleloading hunter has been at least as important, in my opinion.

Muzzleloading has always been easy to get into, at least in the view of those of us who have been doing it for a long time. The actual mechanics of the care and feeding of a muzzleloading firearm are relatively simple, when broken down to the basics. None of this has really changed. What has changed is the way that the average Joe out there, who has never tried the sport, views it.

It used to be that, when viewed from the standpoint of the cartridge gun hunter, called "suppository gun" shooters by some blackpowder purists, the sport appeared to be pretty complicated. The guns all had side-mounted, open hammers and a shape that looked like it would be difficult to shoot and handle comfortably. And they were right, at least to a point. The rifles tended to be longer than modern sporters and were much more barrel heavy. The shape of the buttstock on many of the rifles available didn't handle recoil very well.

And what is this business of wrapping a cloth patch around the bullet?

Then you had grease to add to the patch ball combination and cleaning was a real pain. Why, after a shooting session, a feller could be expected to spend the better part of a day with buckets of hot, soapy water cleaning the rifle. Took longer to clean the rifle than it did to cut up the deer.

Now, a great deal of this was certainly not true, as those of us shooting the old guns knew. There was a whole bunch of bad information on cleaning, loading and general handling of muzzleloading arms. Strangely, a lot of this came from some of the gun manufacturers themselves. Many of the instruction manuals left a great deal to be desired. Many of the myths, especially concerning cleaning, were repeated over and over, due, I believe, to two things. First, many of the

folks writing the instructions knew damn little about muzzleloading, and second, any deviation from accepted philosophy in the instructions might leave a company open to a lawsuit. I was, in fact, involved in a couple such that hinged upon whether universally accepted practices were followed—whether they made much sense or not.

Muzzleloading shooters and hunters themselves did little to debunk some of the hearsay, rumor, witchcraft and black magic that was associated with the sport. The mysterious aspect of the game added an aura of the occult. Muzzleloader shooters were "different," maybe even "weird" and they smelled funny.

All of that changed with a bang in the mid-1980s. Tony Knight brought out his "in-line" muzzleloader. Here, suddenly, was a muzzleloading rifle that looked and handled like a modern bolt action rifle. The balance and pointability were the same as the much used M-70 Winchester and the M-700 Remington. The guns used an action that had a striker that fell on a line with the barrel, like a bolt action. They had thumb-operated safeties and adjustable triggers. The breech plug screwed out so the shooter could clean from the breech with a patch and see through the barrel. The shooter could see if the bore was clean by looking through it, something that is nearly impossible with a traditional rifle without

modern shooter was familiar with. Plastic sabots (pronounced say-bow) that enclosed modern jacketed bullets came on the scene, as well as many different shapes and sizes of lead slug type bullets. All of these were used without the greased patch. Modern shooters understood this type of projectile—it looked familiar and was similar to what they had been shooting at targets and game with their breechloading suppository guns.

Cleaning was downplayed and relegated to its correct place, a fairly easy and straight forward process that takes very little time and creates a very small

get along when switching to the muzzleloader? To see how this worked out, I followed three hunters from their purchase of a rifle through their first deer season. All three were experienced deer hunters and all purchased inline type weapons, although all different models and makes. The three hunters were Ken Hochstein, Troy Hartman and Joel Stenberg. All three live and hunt in Northeastern Nebraska.

Ken is a Remington man. He shoots M-700 Remington rifles for most all of his rifle hunting. He likes the balance and feel of the M-700 series. He thinks the quality and accuracy potential of these rifles is just what he is looking for in a hunting rifle. With this mind set, it was almost a foregone conclusion that the new Remington 700ML would be his choice in a muzzleloading hunting rifle. This bolt action, inline gun is set into a black, synthetic stock. Ken bought the stainless version for ease of maintenance and cleaning, due to its natural rust resistance. He opted for a 50 caliber because that seemed to be the standard; at least, there is a wider variety of projectiles available for this caliber than any other at the present time. With the wide selection of projectiles of various weights and shapes in this caliber, Ken figured the 50 could handle most any hunting that he would be likely to engage in, including elk or moose.

Hochstein decided to use Pyrodex, primarily due to the lack of fouling buildup. He used CCI #11 caps and tried a couple of bullet types before settling on Hornady's 265 gr. 44caliber bullet in a plastic sabot. The instruction manual that Remington packs with the rifle provided the basic instruction in loading and cleaning that was needed to safely use the M-700ML. The manual provided the information necessary to lead the new shooter through load work up and loading techniques. A load of 90 gr. Pyrodex RS behind the Hornady bullet was used and 4-inch groups at 50 yards were produced quickly.

An experienced hunter and shooter, Ken had trouble with the relatively coarse open sights. As one who uses a scope for most of his shooting, the open sight seemed pretty crude by comparison. As Nebraska does not allow the use of scope sights for muzzleloading deer hunting, sighting in was done with the open sighting equipment that came with the rifle. In spite of the sights, all shots could be easily held on a 8-inch pie plate at 100 yards, adequate for deer hunting. With a scope mounted on the rifle, Hochstein felt he could have easily cut the group size by half. I would tend to agree.

He found the ramrod that is supplied with the rifle adequate for loading and cleaning. The cleaning process

Ken Hochstein with his nice buck killed up close with a Remington—cleanly taken.

some fairly sophisticated equipment. All in all, the new rifle was just more familiar and, therefore, more comfortable for the modern type shooter. Nothing had really changed except looks— even the ballistics were the same.

Other manufacturers followed the trail blazed by Knight rifles and inline actions sprouted like wild flowers after a spring rain. Many variations of the original idea were marketed and, finally, a bolt handle was added to the striker so the action operated like any other bolt action to cock the firing mechanism. The modern type muzzleloader had arrived. Hunters and shooters took to the new guns like mosquitoes to bikinis.

Along with the changes in guns came a proliferation of new projectiles. These moved away from the round ball and patch and utilized bullets that the

mess, when done correctly. Many of the "miracle" cleaners and bore lubes went the way of the stone ax and were replaced by "natural" cleaners and lubes that duplicated the old tried and proven tallow products, a move that cut down on fouling and "gunk" in the bore considerably and a change I'm proud to say I had a hand in.

The ready availability of Pyrodex, a replica blackpowder with the same shipping regulations as smokeless powder, was also a big factor. Ammunition was now easily available at most stores that handled smokeless powders. The regulations that many administrations impose upon storage and sale of blackpowder made it hard to get in some areas.

So, with all this change and simplification, how does the average hunter

Troy getting familiar with his Knight, It took one day at the range and he was ready.

The first two went low—next one hit up some—the last three were good enough. He was ready in six shots.

how the tape had drilled safety procedures and loading techniques into the new shooter. He had watched the tape through a couple of times and commented on how well it covered the subject and answered his questions.

After some experimentation Hartman settled on a load of 100 gr. Pyrodex behind a Hornady 245 gr. hollowpoint bullet in a sabot. With a minimum of practice, this experienced shooter could easily keep all his shots on an 8-inch pie plate at 100 yards, with most of the shots going into 4-inches or so. He too complained about the rather coarse open sights that his Knight came equipped with. He plans to change them for one of the so-called illuminated sight sets that have recently come on the market. The bright dots supplied by the optic fibers in these open sights certainly improve sight pictures, especially in poor light conditions.

Troy's hunt was relatively short. He connected on a small buck opening morning. The shot was head on at 80 yards. He hit the buck where the neck entered the chest. He said the deer flipped over backwards and never moved. "I've used a 7mm Remington Magnum for several years and have never seen anything kill any quicker or cleaner. I'm very impressed with the killing power of this rifle.", he said.

"I've never had so much fun hunting or getting ready to hunt as I've had with this rifle," he noted. "I'm absolutely sold that this is the only way to hunt deer. It's great! It puts the "hunt" back in the sport. With the 7mm, if I can see it, I can probably hit it. With the muzzleloader, it's different. You have to get close. It is

went well. The manual describes the process adequately and it was a simple, easy process.

Well, how did the hunting go? After a few shots at small bucks under less than ideal conditions, a decent buck was spotted on the last Sunday of the season. He bedded in a shelter belt roughly a mile long. Ken set up at the end of the belt with the wind in his face. His son went into the shelter belt on the upwind side and worked it down slowly. The buck slipped out the end of the copse of trees and came by the concealed hunter at 15 yards. The 265 gr. bullet did its job and the hunt was over. Ken stated that he had several chances to shoot from 75 yards out, but held his fire and let the buck come closer. He said that he was completely confident that he could have hit the deer at any time, however. His confidence in the gun and its accuracy and killing power was very high.

"This type of hunting is very much like bow hunting," he says, "It takes a lot of patience."

A successful hunt is very important to this hunter. He says that the muzzleloader will remain a part of his hunting arsenal, along with his bow and cartridge guns. The muzzleloader is of interest to him basically as a tool to hunt another season, one less crowded.

Our next hunter purchased one of the more common types of inline action rifles put out by Modern Muzzleloading Inc. Troy liked the look and feel of the Knight Wolverine rifle in 54 caliber. He like the light weight of the rifle and the double safety system that Modern Muzzleloading is famous for. The excellent instructional video that comes with each Knight rifle did a good job of giving him the basics of muzzleloader care and feeding. I watched him on one of his first outings with the rifle at the range and was impressed with sure more challenging and there's a great feeling of accomplishment. Next year I'll apply for a muzzleloader permit only. No more cartridge guns for deer!"

The last of the three bought the Ruger 77/50RS, a 50 caliber muzzleloading rifle based on the M77 bolt action. This gun, like the Remington, uses the bolt handle to open the nipple area and cock

well satisfied with the performance of the rifle on game and its ease of use. He says that he will definitely hunt with his muzzleloader next year, but not to the exclusion of hunting with a cartridge gun. He'll use both and hunt in each season—rifle and muzzleloader.

In summary, all three hunters were experienced with both shooting and deer

loaders in the modern marketplace do have pretty heavy, coarse open sights, but then, so do the majority of centerfire rifles that come so equipped.

Strangely, none of the three hunters even mentioned cleaning. Obviously, it is nowhere near the hassle that has been associated with it. I think the fact that the breech plug is easily removable so

Load work-up on the bench is the same for front-stuffers as cartridge guns except you stand up between shots.

the striker. The gun has a walnut stock with blued hardware. The look and feel of this one is the same as the smaller 22 caliber M77 Ruger. It's a nicely finished and well designed gun.

Joel used the Pyrodex pellets as the basis for his hunting load—two of the pellets behind a 240gr. hollow point Hornady saboted bullet with a CCI #11 percussion cap. The instructions that came with the gun got him on the right track as far as loading and cleaning were concerned and he shot one inch groups at 25 yards right "out of the box." Holding groups on the 8-inch pie plate at 100 yards was no problem.

Stenberg got his buck about midweek of the first week of the season. At 50 yards, a shot through both lungs ended the hunt successfully. He was

hunting, all having many years in the field behind them. The only new part of what they were doing was the firearm that they were using. All said that the instruction provided with the guns was adequate to get them started with a minimum of problems. All preferred Pyrodex to black powder, although none really gave a reason other than less fouling. I suspect that advertising and ease of purchase played a big part in the selection. All opted to use sabotted bullets. They cited ease of loading as the main reason, but, I'm sure, the familiar look of the bullets was part of it. All three mentioned the coarseness of the open sights. This isn't surprising, given that most hunters use scopes almost exclusively. By comparison, any open sight will tend to look pretty coarse. Muzzle-

that the gun can be cleaned clear through the barrel from the breech, is a great contributor to the comfort level that the centerfire shooter will feel with the inline action. Being able to see through the bore and determine that it is clean and shiny is a comfort to those who have little experience with corrosive propellants. Also the use of Pyrodex, with its' low level of fouling, contributes to ease of "gunk removal."

It would appear, at least from the limited research, that any experienced shooter will have little or no trouble in converting from centerfire firearms to muzzleloaders, especially if the familiar looking inline type is used. We are entering a whole new era of muzzleloading interest. I, for one, believe it will bode well for the sport. ●

IN THE good old days, military cartridges like the 30-06 served as the basis of several sporting cartridges. In the same way, many European military cartridges were converted to sporting cartridges with various bullet diameters. The 303 British and the 7mm Mauser-based versions are widely known, but also other military cartridges like the Russian 7.62x54R have been resized to accept a number of different diameter bullets. However, like the others, the 7.62x54R-based sporting cartridges are principally used in very limited geographic areas. In this case, the 7.62x54R-based sporting cartridges are virtually unknown outside Finland and Russia.

fles as well as machine guns were chambered for the 7.62x53R. A majority of sporting rifles were converted from various Finnish or Russian-made Mosin-Nagants, but also Japanese Arisakas, Swedish and German Mausers and even Winchester M1895 lever action rifles were cannibalized for new hunting rifles. Especially in the post-WWII period, bigger manufacturers like Valmet, Sako, Tampereen Asepaja as well as many Finnish gunsmiths built hunting rifles on military actions. Very few completely new sporting arms were ever chambered for the 7.62x53R or other rounds based on that cartridge.

Currently there exist at least nine 7.62x53R-based rifle cartridges devel-

quired a new barrel, but most popular ones were made by re-boring a worn-out 7.62mm caliber barrel to a new caliber. To be simple, the Finnish 7.62x53R-related cartridges can be put in two categories; those which are designed for fowling and those designed for big game, particularly for moose hunting. As one may notice, there exists no specific deer calibers. Deer-sized animals were virtually absent while the Mosin-Nagant variants were most diligently developed. Use of shotgun slugs in big game hunting was outlawed by the Hunting Act of 1932, and Finns were still more riflemen than shotgunners. In addition, the reloaded ammo for moose hunting

A full array of Finnish 7.62x53R-based cartridges, from left to right: The 5.7x53R, 6.3x53R, 7x53R (with round nosed 93 gr. bullet), 8.2x53 R, 9x53R, 9.3x53R, .375x52R (Jalonen), .416x53R (Helenius), 11.6x55R (Makinen).

CHILDREN OF THE

Two Soviet sporting rounds, the 6.5x54R for the Mosin-Nagant-based target rifles, and the 9x54R used with the Medved ('Bear') semi-automatic hunting rifle are recognized in the west whereas Finnish-developed variants are virtually unknown. Basic references like "Cartridges of the World" by F.C. Barnes and "The Cartridge Guide" by I.V. Hogg list only one example, the 6.3x53R Finnish.

The Finnish army has used the 7.62x54R cartridge as their standard service round since 1918. They call it the 7.62x53R, but it is the same cartridge. The Finnish variation is interchangeable with Soviet, Warsaw Pact and Chinese-made ones.

During these 80 years, a great number of Finnish military and sporting ri-

Photos by Tuomas Mäkelä

oped in Finland, including 5.7mm, 6.3mm, 7mm, 8.2mm, 9mm, 9.3mm, .375 (9.5mm), a .416 (10.5mm) and .458 (11.6mm) caliber versions. Furthermore, there exists the 12.0x75R gauge shotshell based on the 7.62x53R case.

While Finnish gunsmiths varied the 7.62x53R, they don't use the word "wildcat" for their brainchildren. In fact, most variations are not true wildcats because ammunition is (or was) produced commercially. There were basically two cartridge manufacturers, Valtion Patruunatehdas (VPT, later Lapua) at Lapua and Sako at Riihimaki which produced ammunition for both military and commercial sales.

Virtually all Finnish wildcat cartridges have developed from similar basis: Bullets of most common calibers were combined with the 7.62x53R cases which were both cheap and easily obtainable. Some conversions re-

was banned from 1962 to 1993. Hunters had to rely on factory-loaded big game ammunition.

Particularly for economic reasons, there were a lot of reloaders in Finland. Before American reloading tools entered the Finnish marketplace, Sako manufactured a hand-loading kit for rifle ammunition reloading. It was hammer-powered like the later Lee Loader, but has a full-length sizing-die and a unique hydraulic decapper for then-common Berdan primers.

THE 5.7x53R

Unlike other variants, the 5.7x53R was developed in the 1950s for running target shooting, not for hunting purposes. It is more "wildcat" in nature than most of its contemporaries and fires the common 5.69mm (.224) bullet, not a 5.79mm (.228) bullet as used with some other European high velocity 22s. The only proven load has a 50gr (3.2g) bullet loaded with 26.2gr (1.7g) of Vihtavouri N120 powder. This moderate load has a muzzle velocity of 3117fps (950 mps). Without doubt, if slower powders are used, higher velocities can be achieved; if loaded to its full potential, the 5.7x53R could be superior to the 22-250.

One time, the 5.7x53R ammunition was loaded by Sako in very limited quantities, but currently the 5.7x53R has almost disappeared as other small diameter calibers, particularly 222 Remington became common. Most of the 5.7x53R caliber rifles were built on fast-operated Swiss Schmidt-Rubin straight pull actions. Rifles chambered for this round are very rare and no commercial ammo or reloading tooling is available.

THE 6.3x53R

For some reason, the only Finnish-origin cartridge that western references recognize is the 6.3x53R. Time of development traces probably back

Factory loaded ammunition is usually fitted with light bullets weighing 70 - 90 gr. For example, a discontinued Sako load had a 70gr (4.5 g) bullet with muzzle velocity of 2936 fps (895 mps.)

THE 7x53R

Applications for the 7x53R are quite similar to ones for the 6.3x53R. A 7mm variation of the Mosin-Nagant cartridge likely attracted many Finnish shooters, because there was the 7x33mm Sako developed during the Second World War as an experimental assault rifle cartridge, but adapted after the war for the Sako L46 bolt action rifle which became popular in Finland. In the early 1930s, the

7x53R may easily exceed potential of the 7x57mm Mauser.

There exists a very similar cartridge also of Finnish design, the 7x54mm. It was made by necking up a 6.5x55mm Swedish Mauser case to 7mm. Like the 7x53R, also the 7x54mm would provide ballistics almost equal to 7x57mm, but rifles in this caliber have usually barrels with slow rifling and short bullet seats for light bullets. The 7x54mm modification was more popular than the 7x53R because a 7x54R caliber rifle was made from a used 6.5x55mm caliber Swedish Mauser by simply re-boring the barrel to its new caliber.

Still in military use—with a 100-year-plus history there—this rimmed 30-caliber cartridge has served many purposes and still does.

7.62 x54R

Text by Janne Pohojoispää

to the 1930s, but the 6.3x53R got its reputation post-WWII. In the late 1940s, and 1950s, it was used as a long-range cartridge for hunting large forest birds like wood grouse and black grouse. After Remington introduced the 222 Remington in 1950, it soon became popular in Finland, and superseded many Finnish hunting calibers like the 6.3x53R, 7x53R and 7x33 Sako.

The 6.3x53R is more powerful than the 25-35 Winchester which was also popular in Finland at that time. Factory loaded ammo has performance quite similar to the 250 Savage, but due to larger case volume, the 6.3x53R would provide higher velocities with heavy bullets, so it is more like the 257 Roberts. However, the 6.3x53R caliber rifles have barrels with short bullet seats and slow rifling suitable for light bullets only.

Finnish Army examined 7x57mm caliber Mauser 98 rifles, but never beyond the experimental stage.

The 7x53R caliber rifles were usually built over the Mosin-Nagant actions, and mostly fitted with barrels having slow twist and a short bullet seat. For example, a discontinued Lapua fowling load has a 6g (93gr) bullet fired with a velocity of 3100 fps (945 mps.) The 7x53R caliber barrel suitable for heavy bullets exists, too. A discontinued Sako big game load featured a 156gr bullet (10.1 g) fired with muzzle velocity of 2428 fps (740 mps.) Like the 6.3x53R, converting the 7.62mm Mosin-Nagant to fire the 7x53R cartridge was not particularly a budget-minded modification because it required a new barrel. If loaded to full potential with heavy bullets, the

THE 8.2x53R

The 8.2x53R is still the most common Finnish-made variation of the 7.62x53R. There exists no exact record of the 8.2x53R development, but probably it traces back to before WWII. In the 1930s, many members of the Finnish National Guard (Suojeluskunta) used their service rifles for hunting. Their headquarters became worried over this increased wear on state property, and the use of military rifles for hunting was banned. About the same time moose hunting was allowed in limited extent. (There was a long period from the late 1800s while the moose was practically killed to extinction.) A new hunting law, as issued in 1932, ruled the minimum caliber allowed for big game hunting to be 8mm. The 8mm bullet was an obvious choice.

Good quality 30 caliber big game bullets were scarce in Finland, but German-made 8mm (.323) bullets were widely available. In the post-WWII period, the 8mm variation provided also some political benefits. The 7.62x53R rifles were usually considered military firearms that required a special license, but sporterizing or amputating the forearm and changing the caliber created a politically correct solution. In most cases, the Mosin-Nagant chambered for the 8.2x53R was the most economical choice, too.

The 8.2x53R ammunition is still produced by Sako and Lapua. Cases can be made from 7.62x53R (or other Mosin-Nagant) brass by simply necking up to proper diameter. Except neck diameter and shoulder angle, the 8.2x53R case has other dimensions equal to the 7.62x53R.

The 8.2x53R delivers ballistics almost identical to the 8x57mm, except the 8mm Mauser can provide a bit more energy with heaviest loads. For example, the Lapua load with a 200gr (13 g) soft-point has muzzle velocity of 2460 fps (750 mps.)

THE 9x53R

Cartridges with 9mm (.355) bullets were once quite popular, but currently the 9mm rifle cartridges have disappeared completely.

The history of the 9x53R cartridge remains the most unique one. A Finnish wholesaler required 9.3mm caliber bullets, but by an accident placed an order to Sako for 9mm bullets. Sako manufactured more than 200,000 bullets otherwise similar to 9.3mm type 102D bullet, but with 9mm diameter.

After this accident appeared, most of these bullets were used by Sako for the 9x57mm cartridges, but the necked-up 7.62x53R case was also utilized to consume these bullets. The 9x53R caliber ammunition were loaded by a small company named Urheiluase located in Helsinki. Some rifles in this caliber still exist, but ammunition is very scarce. No further information is available, but ballistics are apparently very similar to the 9.3x53R.

THE 9.3x53R

Developed before the Second World War, the origins of the 9.3x53R are quite similar to the 8.2x53R as discussed above. At the time of birth of the 9.3mm (.366), calibers like 9.3x62mm and 9.3x74R were (and are still) popular in Europe. The German examples and availability of good quality big game bullets inspired to create a 9.3mm variation of the Mosin-Nagant.

Like the 8.2mm version, the 9.3x53R is a simple modification. It requires only necking up a 7.62x53R case to proper diameter.

A potential example for the 9.3x53R was a German 9.3x57mm. Ballistics of this Finnish cartridge are very similar to the 9.3x57mm or the American 358 Winchester. A Russian version, the 9x54R, is very similar in performance to the Finnish 9.3x53R. Despite the 9x54R designation, a Russian version fires also the 9.3mm caliber bullets. However, Russian and Finnish variants are not interchangeable.

The 9.3x53R caliber ammunition is still loaded by Sako. Their load fitted with a soft pointed bullet (type 102D)

weighing 256 gr (16.6 g) has muzzle velocity of 2330 fps (710 mps.)

THE 375x52R (9.5x52R)

A true wildcat, the 375 caliber variant of the 7.62x53R was developed by Jyri Jalonen for the Valmet 412-based double rifle. Jalonen is a custom gunsmith and better recognized for his match-grade rifle actions, but has also made other custom rifles.

Despite the resized neck, older variations have a case configuration similar to the original 7.62mm round. The

After WWII the Mosin-Nagant action served as basis for Finnish hunting rifles. Various barrel lengths and styles as well as stock configurations were employed. The scoped rifle in center is chambered for the 7x53R, others are in original 7.62x53R caliber.

Reloading tools of the 1950's: Sako-made kit contained separate bullet seating and resizing dies. The steel cup in front of powder tin is a priming tool. A unique feature was a hydraulic decapper, but there was a spike-type decapping tool, too.

.375x52R has a longer powder space and a shorter neck. For making the .375 cases from the 7.62mm caliber brass a sizing die is not enough, since fireforming is required.

Due to the improved case configuration, the 375x52R has a bit more potential than Finnish 9.3x53R or the discontinued 375 Winchester. A 57 gr (3.7 g) charge of Vihtavuori N540 will launch a 270 gr (17.5 g) bullet with muzzle velocity 2297 fps (721 mps.)

THE 416x53R (10.5x53R)

This 416-caliber wildcat was developed by Pekka Helenius for his highly modified Mosin-Nagant rifle conversion. Gunsmith Helenius has also developed other big bore wildcats and 50-caliber sniping rifles.

Due to a minimal difference of body and neck diameters, the 416x53R case has a short shoulder portion and sharp, Weatherby-type shoulder angle. It has greater powder space than, for instance, the 9.3x53R. It fires a 416 caliber bullet, which has become again popular after decades of oblivion.

The 416x53R has ballistic potential close to the 10.75x68 Mauser, although it fires a slightly smaller diameter projectile. A 50 gr (3.24 g) charge of N130 powder develops a muzzle velocity of 2330 fps (710 mps) for a 300 gr (19.4 g) bullet.

THE 11.6x55R

The 45-caliber variant of the 7.62x53R was developed by Erkki Mäkinen to meet or exceed ballistic capability of the 45-70 and provide ensured feeding with the Mosin-Nagant box magazines. The 45-70 is currently quite a popular big game cartridge in Finland. The "barrel-wizard" Mäkinen

manufactures high quality rifle barrels, and was amongst the very first Finnish gunsmiths who have built the 45-70 caliber rifles. His 45-70s have appeared in various configurations including bolt action, lever action and double barreled ones. When used in rifles with box magazines, the large rim of the 45-70 case requires excessive modifications, for example, to a Mosin-Nagant single row box magazine. A basic idea of the 11.6x55R is to create a cartridge similar to 45-70 that fits in the Mosin-Nagant magazine with minor modifications.

No expanded 7.62x53R cases were used for the 11.6x55R caliber wildcat cartridge. Because extended case length is needed, the 11.6x55R cases are turned from the 7.62x53R caliber case blanks manufactured by Sako. With this stronger case, hotter loads can be used with the 11.6x55R than the 45-70. For example, a 3.8 g (58.6 gr) charge of Vihtavuori N130 powder launches a 22.3 g (350 gr) bullet with muzzle velocity of 660 mps (2165 fps.)

While the 6.3x53R, 8.2x53R etc. are traditional chamberings, the wildcats developed by Jalonen, Helenius and Mäkinen are fairly recent developments.

MOSIN-NAGANT SHOTGUNS?

In the late 1800s and early 1900s, a considerable number of obsolescent

Acknowledgements: I would like to thank these indivdiuals who provided invaluable help for this article: Pekka Helenius, Jyri Jalonen, Erkki Kauppi of Sako Oy, P.T. Kekkonen, Erkki Mäkinen, Vesa Toivonen, Matti Virtanen.

military rifles were converted to fire small gauge shotshells like 20 ga, 24 ga, 28 ga or 36 ga. Modification was usually simple, a new smooth bore barrel was fitted and the bolt head and extractor were modified to accept shotshell base.

In 1945, Valtion Patruunatehdas (now Lapua) developed a small gauge shotshell derived from the 7.62x53R case blank. Called 12.0x75R, this tiny shotshell has an all-metal case with base and rim diameters equal to 7.62x53R. No factory-loaded ammo was ever available, but VPT offered virgin brass for reloaders. Ballistics of the 12.0x75R shotshell will slightly exceed the 410/3" magnum cartridge.

The 12.0x75R was nothing but a tailor-made cartridge for the Mosin-Nagant action. In the late 1940s, gunsmith Aarre Viitanen and some others manufactured small batches of single shot 12.0mm bolt action shotguns on the Mosin-Nagant actions. The 12.0x75R gauge shotguns were used for small game hunting, and most of them were retired by the 1970s.

The selection of Finnish sporting calibers now is a mixing of domestic and American ones, and American readers may find several familiar chamberings. For some reason, British-origin calibers are virtually unknown; neither were German sporting rounds popular in Finland. Especially nowadays, Finnish shooters and hunters rely on American calibers like the 222 Remington, 308 Winchester, 30-06, 45-70 and such. Currently the 308 Winchester is the most popular rifle chambering in Finland, but the 7.62x53R and its domestic variants are still in use and even gaining back their popularity.   ●

DEVELOPED BY three Soviet arms designers in the 1969-74 period, the Pistolet Samozaryadniy Malogabaritniy or PSM pistol resembles the Walther PP design. It is, however, not a copy.

Tikhon Ivanovich Lashnev, the head of the design team, was born in Tula in 1919 (died 1988). A designer-engineer in the Design Research Bureau in 1946, and later a section head,

trusions other than the fixed sights and the portion of the safety lever which protrudes behind the rear of the slide on the left side. The recoil spring surrounds the barrel.

The free-swinging hammer is housed in the conventional position in the upper rear of the frame. Below lies the springloaded sear and the strut connecting the hammer and mainspring. A cam on the sear interacts

the pistol can quickly be dismantled without tools. The substitution of the alloy for plastic or wood was to prevent deterioration under especially harsh conditions.

The weight of the PSM with an empty magazine is 16.22 ounces. With a loaded magazine, the weight increases to 17.99 ounces.

According to Anatoliy Simarin in one published report, the main diffi-

RUSSIA'S

he graduated from the Mechanical Institute in 1957. Among his works were a number of hunting and sporting guns used by Soviet shooters and sportmen in the Olympic Games and also in the field.

Anatoliy Alexeevich Simarin was born in 1936 (died 1991) in Krasnoye in the Tula district, and graduated from the Tula Mechanical Institute. In the early 1960s he participated in the design and production of the first USSR-manufactured pneumatic pistol. Later, he was part of the design-team responsible for the SMP3 cartridge-firing industrial pistol, which gained him a bronze medal. From the 1960s onward, until the PSM project started, he was part of a team which

with the safety lever, and a stud-and-rod assembly locks the trigger in the forward position when the slide-mounted safety is 'on.' The safety prevents the hammer from reaching the firing pin, and locks the slide and trigger in the forward position. When the safety is in the 'off' position, a hammer safety prevents the pistol from firing should it be dropped accidentally.

Placing the slide safety above the rear part of the slide permits the shooter to move the safety to the 'off' position and cock the hammer at the same time. This can be done with the firing hand or with the free hand.

A lug on the spring loaded trigger guard prevents the slide from moving off the frame when the slide moves to

culty in designing the PSM was how to produce a lightweight and thin pistol without protrusions on its sides. It had to be reliable under difficult conditions, such as cold, sand, dirt, etc., have good handling characteristics, high hit probability, excellent accuracy, and simple assembly. He attributed part of the achieved results to researcher-engineer E. F. Moiseev, whose assistance permitted the team to place the PSM into production rather rapidly.

That the team achieved their goal was attested to by the fact that the preproduction samples, all factory-produced rather than-hand assembled, passed both firing-range and field tests with excellent results and were

AND ITS

designed a semi-automatic target pistol for silhouette shooting. Some of the target pistol research provided solutions to problems encountered when the PSM was under development.

Lev Leonicovich Kulikov was born in Tula in 1931 and graduated from the S.I. Mosin Tula Mechanical-Technical College in 1950. In addition to participating in the creation, testing and production engineering of the PSM pistol, Kulikov helped design several other sporting arms and was awarded "Best Inventor in the Ministry" in 1982.

The PSM pistol features a flat frame with a rigidly attached 3.35 inch barrel, giving an overall pistol length of 6.10 inches. The barrel is rifled with 6 grooves. The slide is flat, with no pro-

its rearmost position. It also absorbs the impact of the slide as it moves rearward in recoil. As on the Walther PP and similar designs, the trigger guard is held to the frame by an axis pin through the frame at the rear of the guard.

The magazine capacity is eight rounds, and ports on the sides of the magazine indicate how many rounds remain. When the last round has been fired, a bolt or slide stop on the follower retains the slide in the rear position.

A distinguishing feature of the PSM is the flat light-alloy stock or grip plate assembly covering the sides of the grip. This assembly covers the sides and rear of the grip, retaining the axis or assembly pins. It is latched to the frame, rather than being screwed, and

immediately approved.

The PSM is chambered for a bottle-necked, rimless centerfire 5.45mm x 18 cartridge developed in 1979 by Aleksandr Bochin, according to Jane's. This date seems a bit off, since the pistol dates from at least five years prior to that. Another edition of Jane's states that the cartridge has existed since the mid 1970's, which seems more reasonable, but that little was known about it or the PSM pistol until 1983. Measuring 0.980-inch long, the 5.45mm cartridge features a bottle-necked case measuring 0.700-inch long. The rim diameter measures 0.297-inch. It has a loaded weight of 74.1 grains. The bullet measures 0.222-inch in diameter with a length of 0.563-inch, or approximately 2.5

calibers, and a weight of 38.5 grains. Featuring a flat tip, the bullet has a gilding metal jacket and a compound or dual core, consisting of a steel forward portion and a lead rear half. Loaded with 2.3 grains of powder the 5.45mm bullet exits the muzzle at 1,033 feet/second. Jane's states this cartridge has stopping power no better than the 6.35mm Browning, but one Finnish source states "this cartridge approaches the efficiency of the 9mm pattern." With 129 Joules of muzzle energy it would seem to be more comparable to the 32 Smith & Wesson, but less than the 32 Smith & Wesson Long.

The 5.45 x 18mm cartridge has apparently been chambered in at least two other pistols, although neither proved as reliable under service conditions as the PSM. One was the PP and the second was the "Makarov". Due to bulkiness and protruding components, among other shortcomings, both projects were dropped.

The PSM pistol and its cartridge are interesting. According to Russian sources, it is accurate and reliable. As such, due to its slimness, it would make an excellent second handgun for security people, including undercover police, or a dresser-drawer gun. ●

PSM PISTOL

By Larry S. Sterett

The Soviet PSM (Pistolet Samozaryadniy Malogabaritniy) pistol is a double-action, fixed barrel, blowback-operated design.

AMMO

Left to right: Federal 22 Long Rifle rimfire cartridge, 5.45mm x 18 Soviet centerfire cartridge for the PSM pistol, 22 JGR centerfire Canadian cartridge from the 1950-60 era, and a 9mm x 18 centerfire Makarov cartridge.

TESTFIRE
TESTFIRE
TESTFIRE

The Republic Arms Patriot Pistol

by John Malloy

The new variation of the Republic Arms Patriot has its stainless-steel slide covered with a black Melonite finish, producing a uniform flat-black appearance.

The Patriot grip is well designed, providing good recoil control and pointing characteristics.

THE REPUBLIC Arms Patriot is a light, compact 45-caliber pistol designed for personal protection use.

Right-to-carry legislation spread across the country in the last half of the 1990s, creating a new demand for concealable handguns. Most of the suitable semiautomatic pistols available when this trend began were 45s of substantial size and weight, or more compact pistols of smaller caliber.

The Patriot, introduced by Republic Arms of Chino, California in early 1997, filled a new niche. Weighing only 20 ounces including empty magazine, it fired the 45 ACP cartridge. The magazine held six rounds and an additional cartridge could be carried in the chamber. The lightweight 45 was offered as a two-tone pistol—stainless steel slide contrasting with the black polymer frame.

In early 1999, the California company introduced the first variation of the Patriot. Mechanically identical, the new variant has the stainless-steel slide covered with a black Melonite finish. Thus,

the pistol has a uniform flat black appearance, broken only by the bright finish barrel.

With an advertised three-inch barrel, the Patriot is only six inches long. Height without magazine is 4-3/4 inches. The magazines currently used have a removable base plate that adds about 1/4 inch to the height. Although considered a compact, the short overall length almost puts the pistol into the subcompact class.

The pistol is striker-fired. A firing-pin block prevents movement of the pin unless the trigger is actually pulled. The trigger mechanism is double-action-only (DAO). The trigger is much like a double-action revolver trigger in shape and feel. The trigger is not set by the movement of the slide; in case of a misfire, a cartridge can be tried again by pulling the trigger again. Firing the shot does not require bringing the trigger back to the frame—the let-off occurs about 1/2 inch forward of the projected front line of the grip. Many shooters like this geometry. The trigger pull itself is fairly heavy but smooth. It lets off the shot without any "jump" of the pistol.

The slide is flat-sided, with 10 wide grasping grooves on each side to aid

retraction.

The sights are low but wide, with a square Patridge sight picture. The rear sight is adjustable for windage, and is locked in place with a .050-inch Allen setscrew. When the setscrew is loosened, the sight can be drifted in its dovetail to either side.

The shape of the pistol's polymer frame is unique, yet shows elements of other designs. The rear of the grip has a shape a little bit like that of a CZ-75. The front of the grip has a single projection forming a finger groove below the trigger guard, reminiscent of the style introduced by M-S Safari Arms years ago. The result is a comfortable hand-filling grip that appears to be an aid in controlling recoil with this light pistol. The trigger guard provides ample space for the trigger finger. The front of the trigger guard is grooved to provide purchase for those who favor a hold with a finger on the guard.

Rails are formed in the polymer frame to mate with the slide rails. Checkering is moulded into the rear of the grip and the two sides of the grip.

Besides the trigger, the magazine release is the only external control on the pistol. The magazine release button is finely grooved and is recessed into the grip frame on the left side. Because no controls protrude, the pistol is very flat, with slide and frame essentially uniform in width. Width of the pistol is one inch. Note that this is only about twice the diameter of the cartridge.

The pistol functions as a locked-breech design in which the slide and barrel travel rearward, locked together, for about 1/4-inch to allow chamber pressure to subside. Locking and unlocking is by the tilting-barrel method. A single lug on the barrel locks into a recess in the inside of the slide that extends to the ejection port. A cam lug on the bottom of the barrel is acted on by the main (takedown) pin to accomplish tilting the barrel.

The barrel itself is advertised as three inches, but again, the company is being modest. The tested specimen's barrel actually measured about 3 1/4-inches from muzzle to breech face. It is rifled with ten lands and grooves, right-hand twist. The barrel is the only bright part on the new black finish Patriot. The muzzle is heavily beveled, apparently to prevent damage to the front edge of the rifling. The result for a defense pistol is impressive, for the muzzle is a shiny circle that looks very large. A friend of mine once said that if he ever had to draw his 45, he wanted it to be apparent just how big that hole really was.

The barrel is belled at the muzzle end, which fits tightly into the opening at the front of the slide. There is no barrel bushing. Lock-up appears very good, with no discernable play when the slide is in battery.

The recoil spring is a single-wind coil spring held captive under the barrel. The magazine is of single-column type holding six rounds, making the capacity of the Patriot 6+1. The magazine can be disassembled for cleaning, if necessary, by pressing a release button and sliding off the base-plate .

The takedown of the pistol for cleaning is unconventional, but simple. Before attempting takedown, the magazine should be removed and the chamber emptied. Then, retract the slide about inch and push the takedown pin out. At this point, pull the trigger and hold it to the rear. Slide the slide forward about inch until it stops, then release the trigger while sliding the slide off the rest of the way.

The captive recoil spring and the barrel can then be easily removed.

Shooting the Patriot was a pleasure, but my first session began with a problem. The magazine in the pistol gave several failures to feed within the first few rounds. Republic had provided three packaged extra magazines, so I tried them. They all fed flawlessly. What could have been the trouble with the first one?

A call to Republic netted a somewhat embarrassed answer. Before shipping my test pistol, the people there had tried out three magazines to go with it. Then someone realized my pistol no longer had a magazine. Another magazine on the bench was inserted and the pistol shipped. As fate would have it, that fourth one was a problem magazine sent back to the shop for inspection.

Republic stands behind their products, and I was told that if anyone has a magazine problem, he can get it replaced under warranty.

I numbered the other three magazines and rotated them during my test firing. The pistol functioned flawlessly with all three.

Because the pistol would probably be purchased for self-defense, it seemed appropriate to shoot at 10 yards on the Bianchi Cup "Tombstone" target. Two-hand 5-shot groups ranged from a so-so 3 inches down to an excellent 1-1/8 inches, using a variety of ammunition. The average of all groups fired was 2.3 inches. Recall that the center ring of the Bianchi Cup target is 4 inches in diameter; all groups were smaller.

At 25 yards, five-shot groups ran between 5 and 7 inches. While this will not get one into the Olympics, it shows that the pistol has practical defense accuracy to at least 25 yards.

A variety of 230-grain jacketed ammunition made by three different manufacturers was used, and some similar military surplus 230-grain "hardball" was also tried. Everything functioned well.

Republic literature warns that the use of handloads or +P ammunition will void the warranty. This is a fairly standard warning for the protection of the manufacturers. I did, however, want to try some of my moderate cast-bullet handloads to see if they would feed satisfactorily. They functioned perfectly, giving satisfactory accuracy at both 10 and 25 yards.

A Republic representative had mentioned that 1911 type magazines generally can be used in the Patriot with 230-grain ball ammunition. Such magazines stick out the bottom of the pistol, but many shooters have a supply of surplus GI 45 magazines, and this information could be useful to them. GI magazines can be variable in feeding, but the one I used in the Patriot fed not only the jacketed-bullet loads, but my semiwadcutter handloads, all without a hitch.

Does the Patriot have any faults? Yes. It has no slide lock. At the range, this lack was not a big problem. I simply used an empty cartridge case in the ejection port to hold the slide open. For defense use, absence of this feature would make little practical difference.

So, the Patriot is a pistol that weighs about half what a full-size 45 weighs. It costs about half what most other 45s cost. It is of a size and weight that allows comfortable carry in a belt pouch. It will also fit into a bathrobe pocket, and would be a comforting thing to have when answering the doorbell late at night.

The Republic Arms Patriot would seem to have satisfactory accuracy, reliability and power to appeal to those who are considering a lightweight 45 pistol for personal protection. ●

Malloy found that a good grip, a smooth (although heavy) trigger and a decent sight picture allowed good 10 and 25-yard groups with this light DAO 45.

"S&W's Centennial 5, 6 & 7-Shooters!"

by: Jerry Burke

In 1886, the factory dubbed it the "Safety Hammerless", although consumers received their handguns in Smith & Wesson boxes marked, "New Departure", and both descriptions were apt. It was D.B. Wesson's concern for child safety which was behind the development of this decidedly different pocket revolver. The gun's double-action-only firing mechanism and pivoting, backstrap-mounted grip safety both spoke to the safety issue. It certainly was a "new departure" for S&W. Later on the slick little DA-only revolver took on the moniker "lemon squeezer", as it continued in production through 1940. both a small-frame 32-caliber as well as a slightly larger version made to accommodate the 38 S&W cartridge were produced.

The ol' lemon squeezer didn't make the post-WWII cut, but soon thereafter Smith & Wesson engineers came up with a highly concealable 38 Special revolver. The "Chief's Special", was so dubbed at a Chiefs of Police convention in 1950. The Chief's was and is the quintessential, small-frame snub-nose revolver, but it was only

Whether the new AirLite Ti™ "L"-frame (top) or the smaller "J"-frame, there's a S&W Centennial™ Model for every concealed carry application.

the beginning and S&W took the J-frame concept a bit further, and in 1952, brought on the Centennial Model, so-named because it was introduced in the 100th year of the Smith & Wesson partnership, with its hammer completely enclosed, as with the Safety Hammerless. The grip safety was carried forward as well. The first frame was crafted from aircraft-quality aluminum alloy and anodized to match the carbon steel parts, and even the cylinder was aluminum alloy, producing a handgun which weighed only 14-1/4 ounces, with walnut grip panels. In 1954, the cylinder was changed to carbon steel for increased durability, and an all-steel version came into being as well.

The Centennial version of the J-frame remained in production through 1974, but was discontinued due to production costs and the increasing popularity of the 1955 Bodyguard Model.

Happily, the Centennial Model was reintroduced in 1990, sans grip safety, again giving handgunners their choice of all three J-frame configurations. And today, options abound with the Centennial Model alone. The 38 Special remains the best seller, with a 357 Magnum version now as well, both five-shooters. There's an all-stainless steel Centennial in 357 Magnum, and the ever popular Airweight, and now a 32 H&R Magnum Centennial, a six-shooter. And now it gets even more interesting.

Among new J-frame products are AirLite Ti models, with aluminum alloy frames and titanium cylinders. The titanium provides a 25% weight reduction from a comparable Airweight version. The AirLite Ti Centennial revolver weighs just 11.3 ounces in 38 Special with wood grips.

If that's not enough, S&W has two additional Centennial Models, these on the medium-size "L"-frame. Thus, the Centennial series now includes a 44 Special, a 5-shot, titanium/aluminum alloy DA-only revolver that weighs only 18.9 ounces. And, there's also a 38 Special L-Frame, a seven-shooter.

This all should take S&W nicely into the 21st Century. And perhaps even to S&W's Bi-Centennial.

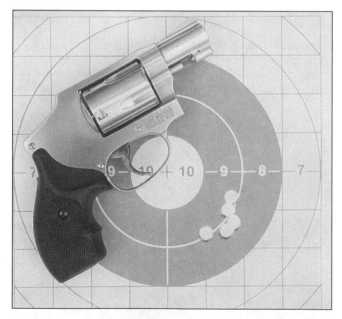

Experienced DA-shooters will have no trouble duplicating this offhand, 10-yard group with S&W's Centennial™ Model and Black Hills 38 Special wadcutters.

TESTFIRE
TESTFIRE
TESTFIRE

The Umarex-Beretta 92FS in its basic version with blued finish can be had with a choice of checkered plastic or wood grip panels. Either way this pistol is a dead ringer for the famous 9mm autoloader.

The Umarex-Beretta 92FS

by J. I. Galan

The Beretta 92 series of autopistols have been a runaway success since their introduction to the U.S. market some twenty-five years ago. Earning an enviable reputation for superb workmanship and rugged dependability, the big Beretta autoloader soon became a top choice with law enforcement and civilians alike, eventually being adopted by our military forces as well.

In light of the preceding, it is really not surprising that the German company Umarex has recently launched, under license from Beretta, a pellet-firing replica of the Model 92FS that's sure to become popular with handgun enthusiasts everywhere. The .177 caliber Umarex-Beretta 92FS is almost impossible to tell apart from the real thing, short of hands-on inspection. Even the Pietro Beretta name, model designation and initials are clearly visible on the left side of the dummy slide. In addition, the checkered plastic grip panels also carry the Beretta logo. One clue, however, is the "cal. .177/4.5 mm" legend on the "slide." The test sample came in a plastic carrying case bearing the Beretta logo as well. The case included one CO₂ cartridge, two pellet magazines, a tin of Walther match pellets, cleaning rod and comprehensive English instructions.

Since 1995 Umarex has produced a growing variety of CO2—powered pellet-firing clones of some of the most popular contemporary sidearms. Their first look-alike—still in production—was the Walther CP88, patterned after the 9mm Walther P88. This model was followed by the RWS C-225, a spittin' image of the SIG Sauer P225. In 1997, Umarex teamed up with none other than Colt to produce a CO₂ copy of the legendary Govt. Model autoloader. Besides the Beretta replica, Umarex has also recently unveiled replicas of the

Smith & Wesson 586/686 .357 Magnum revolvers, as well as of the famous Walther PPK pistol.

Outwardly, the Umarex-Beretta 92FS is basically an exact copy of the real McCoy. As far as weight, at around 2 pounds this pellet-shooting replica appears to be a bit heftier than the real Beretta, something that could still be advantageous when working on fast draw reflexes.

The Umarex 92FS utilizes the same 8-shot rotary pellet magazine common to that company's other replicas. This pellet magazine can be quickly installed by opening the "slide," which

Specifications	
Umarex-Beretta 92FS	
Caliber:	.177" (4.5mm) pellet
Action:	SA/DA repeater
Overall Length:	8" Standard model; 10" match model
Weight:	44 ounces Standard model; 48 ounces Match model
Power Plant:	12-gram CO2 cartridge
Barrel:	5", rifled steel
Magazine:	Rotary, 8-shot capacity
Sights:	Rear adj. for windage; blade front
Safety:	Manual; hammer block and trigger discount
Importer:	Interarms 10 Prince Street Alexandria, VA 22313 (703) 548-1400
Suggested Retail:	From about $188 for Standard blue model to $590 for satin-nickel Match "Trophy" model

snaps forward when the dummy take-down lever on the left side of the frame is pressed downward. Like Umarex's other models, the 92FS features double- as well as single-action operation. The trigger of the sample tested was as smooth as oiled marble in DA, releasing at around 9 pounds. In single action, the let-off was incredibly crisp, requiring a pressure of 4 pounds.

The main components of the Umarex 92FS appear to be constructed of zinc alloy castings, available in a choice of either polished blue or satin nickel finishes. All versions of this model, however, come with a 5-inch rifled steel barrel and can be had with either checkered plastic or checkered wood grip panels. A Match rendition – also available in either finish – comes with a slick-looking muzzle compensator that increases the pistol's overall length by about two inches.

The standard sights of the Umarex 92FS are rather basic. The rear sight is adjustable for windage only, via a small allen screw. For shooters wishing to pursue scaled-down IPSC-style action, the top-of-the-line 92FS Match "Trophy" comes with a Top Point optronic sight already installed and sighted in. The other versions of this pistol can also accept similar sights mounted on a special rail. Incidentally, a fully adjustable rear sight can also be ordered as an option. In fact, there is a wide assortment of useful accessories

available for this pistol, including a quick-draw "Speed Machine" IPSC-type holster.

Exhaustive testing of the Umarex 92FS revealed that my expectations were correct: This replica is a superb shooter! Slow-paced SA work produced groups averaging 5/8" across at ten yards. Various brands of wadcutter (match) pellets were tried, with similar results. As expected, switching to more spirited combat-style DA work widened the groups a bit. Still, most shots were well within the center chest area of a full-size combat silhouette target.

Folks used to the real Beretta's manual safety will find the replica's controls differing only slightly from those of the 9mm 92FS. Thumbing down the safety catch disconnects the trigger when the hammer is down, as in the real Beretta. With the hammer cocked, however, activating the safety won't decock the hammer. Pulling the trigger at that point will drop the hammer safely, as the "firing pin" (valve stem extension) will be rotated away from the hammer's path. In addition, opening the action locks the trigger automatically when the hammer is down.

The Umarex 92FS can be had in a Match version featuring a slick muzzle compensator. Notice checkered wood grips.

The standard 12-gram CO_2 cartridge that provides shooting power goes in the grip and is pierced by the camming action of the dummy magazine floor plate. Each CO_2 cartridge supplies enough gas for approximately 60 to 70 shots before a replacement is needed. With a fresh CO_2 cartridge the gun on test produced an average muzzle velocity of 413 fps for the first half-dozen or so shots in single action, using RWS Hobby pellets. The m.v. settled back to around 378 fps for the next two-dozen shots, dropping slightly through another string of about twenty shots.

Typically, in the DA mode, with its somewhat lighter hammer strike and correspondingly shorter valve opening, the m.v. was a bit lower, hovering around 351 fps. The instruction manual indicates a muzzle velocity of 393 fps, a figure that should be taken only as a general guide to this pistol's performance, given the multiple variables – such as pellet weight, shooting cadence and ambient temperature – that can affect the performance of a CO_2 gun.

Unquestionably, the Umarex-Beretta 92FS is a highly successful effort at producing a pellet-firing clone of the Beretta 92FS. This replica is so realistic that one alsmot expects the sharp blast and recoil of the centerfire Beretta, only to experience a soft "pop" and no recoil whatsoever. Folks who already own a Beretta 92 will find that this Umarex copy offers a highly economical way of keeping those defensive handgun skills in top shape, right at home. In addition, this CO_2 pistol is just plain lots of fun, any way you look at it.

At seven yards in rapid DA mode the Umarex 92FS printed outstanding groups in this Birchwood Casey "Shoot-N-C" combat silhouette target.

by JOHN MALLOY

HANDGUNS TODAY:

AUTOLOADERS

shooting and hunting industry is to our economy.

As the concealed-carry movement grows across the country, the demand for small but powerful handguns grows. The 45 ACP seems to be king of the hill, with a number of manufacturers introducing new scaled-down 45 pistols. A number of pistols originally introduced as 9mms are now also being offered in 40 S&W.

Somewhat strangely, in a parallel trend, the 32 ACP is developing a new following, after being essentially defunct. Smaller pistols and more choices of ammunition seem to have revived the caliber.

More polymer-frame pistols are now offered, many new for 1999. The synthetic material allows pistols to be lighter and cost less.

Pistols chambered for the 22 Long Rifle (22 LR) have been popular for most of the century, and new offerings are here, some for entry level shooters, some for competition. Conversion units have been introduced that will convert popular centerfire pistols to 22 LR also.

Some familiar pistols are still available, but are offered through new sources, as several companies have changed hands since last year.

We'll take a look at what the companies are doing:

AMT

Galena Industries of Irwindale, CA recently purchased the rights to produce most firearms developed by Arcadia Machine & Tool (AMT). Galena will continue to market the line of 1911-style pistols, the Automag II, III and IV line, and the stainless steel Backup pistols, under the AMT trade

Arms Moravia has introduced a new polymer-frame compact pistol, the CZ-G 2000. The trigger opening and guard give it a distinctive shape.

The CZ-G 2000, left view. The decocker is recessed into the slide and does not protrude.

At a time when commentators seem to have relegated us to a service economy, gunmakers are still making things. And manufacturers of autoloading handguns are among the most active.

To an objective observer, it must seem strange, then, that increasing numbers of meritless lawsuits are being filed against a productive segment of our economy. Big-city mayors and even private organizations seem to want to dip their hands into the money pot and destroy an industry they just seem not to like. They are filing or considering lawsuits against the firearms industry, in particular those companies that make semiautomatic pistols.

The latest SHOT Show, perhaps the largest trade show of firearms in the world, was held in Atlanta, Georgia in February, 1999. Incredibly, during that time, the mayor of Atlanta was attempting to initiate a suit against the firearms industry. A few manufacturers boycotted Atlanta, but the show went on as scheduled. About 30,000 people were involved, hopefully showing Atlantans just how important the

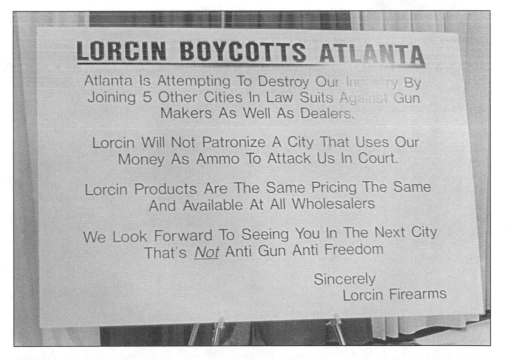

LORCIN BOYCOTTS ATLANTA

Atlanta Is Attempting To Destroy Our Industry By Joining 5 Other Cities In Law Suits Against Gun Makers As Well As Dealers.

Lorcin Will Not Patronize A City That Uses Our Money As Ammo To Attack Us In Court.

Lorcin Products Are The Same Pricing The Same And Available At All Wholesalers

We Look Forward To Seeing You In The Next City That's *Not* Anti Gun Anti Freedom

Sincerely
Lorcin Firearms

Some handgun manufacturers, such as Lorcin, chose not to attend the 1999 SHOT Show because of the suit against the firearms industry by Atlanta's mayor.

name. Galena will also manufacture the commemorative specimens of original Auto Mag pistols for a new corporate entity, Automag, Inc.

ARMS MORAVIA

The Czech Republic company has introduced a new pistol, the CZ-G2000. The compact polymer-frame pistol is conventional double action (DA) and is available in 9mm and 40 S&W. A tilting-barrel locking system is used. The decocking lever is nicely recessed into the slide for a trim package. The U.S. importer for the CZ-G2000 is Intrac Arms of Knox, TN.

AUTO-ORDNANCE

In mid-1998, Auto-Ordnance, the maker of 1911-type pistols as well as the famous Thompson guns, was put up for sale. By February 1999, the announcement was made that the company had been acquired by Kahr Arms.

AWT

Advanced Weapons Technologies, of Athens, Greece, has produced firearms for European sale as Zastava-Europe. Now the company is entering the U. S. market. Displayed for the first time at the 1999 SHOT Show was their new CZ 999 pistol. This interesting pistol looks a bit like a SIG, but there are differences. The most obvious is that a single style pretty much covers all bases, or, as AWT puts it, is "tactically universal." A control on the upper part of the slide allows the pistol to fill the niches of single-action (SA), conventional double-action (DA) or double-action-only (DAO) pistols. When used as a DAO, the hammer can still be cocked by the thumb. Because it is sometimes handy to know if you are low on ammunition, the CZ 999 has a "three-round-left" device. When the magazine is down to three rounds, a tiny rod protrudes through the right upper grip screw. It can be seen or felt, and provides a warning. Available in 9mm and 40 S&W, the CZ 999 has a 4 1/4-inch barrel, measures 5 1/2 x 7 1/2 inches, and weighs 34 ounces.

BERETTA

New variations of basic Model 92 and 96 designs already in the line constituted Beretta's new offerings for 1999. The Border Marshal has the heavier, reinforced "Brigadier" slide and a dovetailed moveable (or removeable) front sight. It is a 40 caliber pistol, similar to guns made under contract for the Border Patrol. The Tactical

The CZ 999 is offered by AWT. The control at the top of the slide, forward of the rear sight, can convert the pistol from single-action to double-action operation.

Stainless, besides the use of stainless steel, has night sights and a nickel magazine. The Elite Team guns, in 9 and 40, have the Brigadier slide, a shortened barrel, no lanyard loop and other features. Mechanically, the decocker lever on these pistols springs back instead of remaining in the down position. The Custom Carry pistols are more compact, in 9 and 40. They have a shorter grip height and a shorter slide and barrel. Compactness is aided by elimination of the right-side safety and trimming the other control levers.

BERSA

The Argentine-made Bersa line of blowback 32 and 380 autos remains mechanically much the same. However, just so no one has to have a gun that looks like that of his shooting companions, a number of cosmetic changes have been introduced.

One of Colt's new subcompacts, the Pocket Nine, with the writer's hand for scale.

Variations with polished and matte blue finishes, nickel, two-tone, and blue with contrasting nickel parts are available. Bersa pistols are handled by Eagle Imports.

BRILEY

Briley was known as a manufacturer of shotgun barrels and accessories, then got into the pistol

market with their 1911-type pistols. Now that the market for small 45s has expanded, Briley has introduced its Fantom, a polymer frame 45 with a 3 1/2-inch barrel. The new 45 is very flat, as separate grips are omitted.

BROLIN

Most of Brolin's previous pistol offerings have been suspended, and the company is concentrating on the Brolin Bantam. The small all-steel, conventional DA pistol is a Hungarian FEG design. It is available in 9mm or 40 S&W, and features a spurless hammer and ambidextrous safety. Capacity is 6+1.

BROWNING

Browning has introduced three new additions to its successful 22-caliber BuckMark line. The new Challenge pistol has a lightweight 5 1/2-inch barrel and-most noticeable-a smaller grip diameter. The smaller grip, together with adjustable sights and a 25 ounce weight would seem to aim at the market of the younger shooter or one with smaller hands. A 4-inch version, at 23 ounces, is called the Challenge Micro.

Beefing the BuckMark up with a 5 1/2-inch bull barrel and a matte finish boosts the weight to 34 ounces. This new variant is called the Camper.

Many have wondered why the Buck-Mark slide serrations were set in a concave portion of the slide, making them a little hard to grasp when it came time to pull back the slide. Beginning in 1999, most of the Browning 22 pistols will have projections on both sides of the rear end of the slide, to give greater purchase for slide retraction.

BUL

Bul Transmark, the Israeli maker of polymer-frame wide 1911-style pistols, has introduced a new pistol, the Bul Storm. A departure that almost seems to be bucking the trend, the Storm is Buls first all-steel gun. Based on the CZ-75 design, the steel Bul is available in 9mm, 40 and 45. Full-size and compact models are cataloged, with a subcompact apparently scheduled soon.

But polymer has been Bul's thing, and they have designed a new polymer-frame pistol, the Bul Impact. It has the basic CZ mechanism, but is set up to use the same double-column magazines as the original Bul 1911-style pistol.

CENTURY INTERNATIONAL

The 32 ACP M-74 and Carpati pistols, made in Romania, are now being imported into the U.S. by Century International Arms. Design is a slightly modified Walther PP, with a different shape to the grip and a heel-type magazine release.

Bersa has introduced a number of cosmetic changes. Allison Sodini displays a two-tone version.

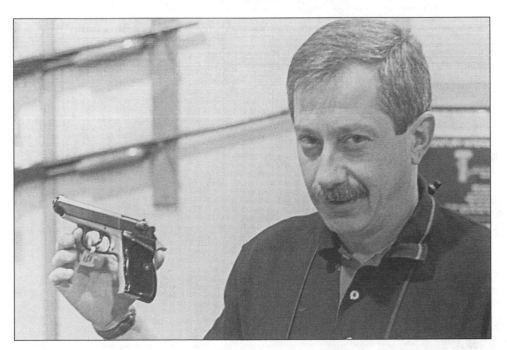

Steve Kehaya of Century International holds a new Carpati 32 ACP pistol, a modified PP design from Romania.

Century is also now the importer and distributor for Daewoo pistols in 9mm and 40 S&W. Recall that the Daewoo pistols are the ones that can be made safe by pushing the cocked hammer forward.

CHARLES DALY

The Charles Daly name was first applied to a pistol last year, when KBI introduced a modernized 1911 under that marking. Now, a Commander-size 45 has been introduced, with availability scheduled by mid-1999.

Also, a prototype of a high-capacity, polymer-frame pistol was at the 1999 SHOT Show, with introduction as yet unspecified.

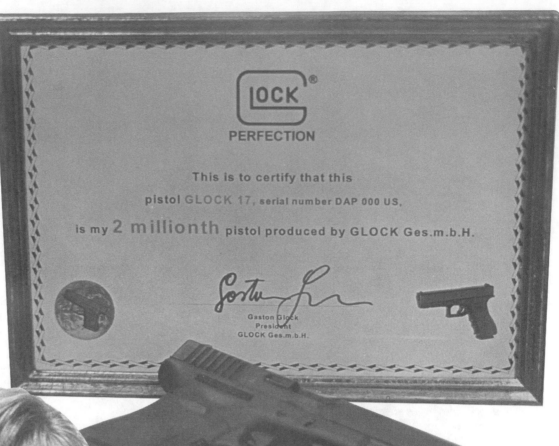

CIVIL DEFENCE

A high-capacity modified 1911-type pistol has been introduced by a British company, Civil Defence Supply. Called the PPW (Personal Protection Weapon) the pistol has a polymer frame with full forward section to match the slide length. It is a big pistol, measuring 8.7 x 5.9 inches, and weighing over 40 ounces. Perhaps the most noteworthy feature is the caliber—224 BOZ. The new round is basically a 10mm case shortened and necked down to 22 caliber. The 224 BOZ round is available in the U.S. through Anglo American, Inc. of Alexandria, VA. As are most British firearms developments nowadays, this one is designed for the government and not the citizenry.

COLT

Colt seems to be doing new things under new leadership. Two new semi-auto pistol offerings for 1999 were sub-compact 17-ounce 9mm pistols

Caroline Fleischer displays one of the first CZ 97B production pistols. The big new CZ is their first 45.

The Heckler & Koch USP Expert is the company's latest 45 ACP offering.

IAI is now offering full-size 1911-style pistols with 5-inch barrels.

Kel-Tec's little P 32 is a locked-breech 32 ACP that weighs just a bit over 6 1/2 ounces.

Kimber offers a 22 LR conversion kit for its line of centerfire 1911-style pistols.

Kimber is adding several compact pistols to their line. This is the 45-caliber Pro Carry.

designed for concealed carry. The pistols bear different names, but differ basically only in finish and sights. The Pocket Nine is stainless and has 3-dot sights. The TAC Nine has a black finish and Tritium night sights. Both are DAO, with bobbed hammers. Barrel length is 2-3/4 inches and overall length is 5 1/2 inches. The new small nines are equipped with wraparound rubber grips with front finger grooving.

Colt's 3-inch-barrel Defender, an abbreviated 45 introduced last year, has been well-received. Apparently, though, there are some people who, for whatever reason, would rather have a 40 than a 45. For 1999, the Defender was made available in 40 S&W.

Para-Ordnance's first double-action pistol is the LDA, a DAO 45 with a light trigger pull.

duced in prototype last year, and is now in production. The basic design is an enlarged CZ 75, but with full-length slide/frame contact. With a barrel length of about 5 inches, the big 45 measures about 8 1/2 x 5 1/2, a full-size pistol. Weight is about 40 ounces and capacity is 10+1.

At 40 ounces, the big 223 pistol from Professional Ordnance is, relatively speaking, very light.

CZ

CZ-USA is a new American company formed to handle the CZ line of Czech-designed firearms. The February 1999 SHOT Show was the first display of products handled by CZ-USA. Featured were the first production specimens of the CZ 97B. This pistol, CZ's first 45, was intro-

EAA

Is the 10mm cartridge dead in the water? European American Armory (EAA) doesn't think so. They are betting that the powerful round would have a bigger following if only it were available in the right pistol. They have introduced a steel-frame version of their full-size Tanfoglio-made Witness series. Just in case someone does not like the 10 as much as he thought he might, EAA can furnish conversion parts to make it a 9, 40, 45 or 38 Super.

The IMI Baby Eagle pistol, in 9 and 40, is back at Magnum Research. Here, Malloy tries out a 9mm.

GLOCK

Glock began making pistols in 1982, and has now passed the two million mark in pistol production. The two-millionth pistol was displayed at the February 1999 SHOT Show.

New at the show was Glock's Model 36, a new 45-caliber compact pistol. The small gun is the company's first single-column-magazine pistol ever marketed. For the concealed-carry market, the Glock 36 is a bit flatter than previous models, having a width of just about 1-1/8 inches. Barrel length is 3.78 inches and weight (with magazine) is about 22 ounces. Capacity is 6+1. The new Model 36 was scheduled for mid-1999 availability.

Mike Sodini's hand provides scale to show the size of the new scaled-down Llama 45.

Llama's entry in the niche of scaled-down 45s with 10+1 capacity is the Minimax 45 Sub-Compact.

GRIZZLY

A sad note for many: The big Grizzly pistol, the giant 1911-style handgun originally chambered for 45 Winchester Magnum, is no more; LAR, the manufacturer, has dropped it from its line. Of the 50 original Grizzly pistols recently made into commemoratives of the 50 states, only 21 were still left by the time of the February 1999 SHOT Show.

HECKLER & KOCH

HK is filling yet another niche in its USP line with the introduction of its new USP Expert pistol. Designed for IPSC and other competitive shooting, the new USP pistol has adjustable sights, a 5.2-inch barrel and, of course, a polymer frame. The pistol measures 8.75 x 5.9 inches, yet is light for its size, weighing only a bit over 30 ounces.

Realizing that the rights of gunowners are being challenged, Heckler & Koch pledged a dollar for every gun sold in 1999. The money, donated to the American Shooting Sports Council, will be used to help preserve our right to own firearms.

HERITAGE

Just a few subtle changes in the Heritage Stealth 9mm and 40 pistols for 1999, but in years to come, shooters and collectors will want to have this information.

The 40-caliber pistols have new magazines, with an improved floorplate that is more durable and actually makes it easier to load the full 10-round capacity.

Republic Arms' new black-finish 45 has been added to the company's line.

All the Stealth pistols now have shortened rear firing pin extensions that protrude just past flush when in the half-cock position. This still allows determining the condition by touch, but has less protrusion than before. To aid determination by sight, the firing pin extensions are now colored red.

HI-POINT

Hi-Point, the Ohio outfit that makes inexpensive pistols in 380, 9mm, 40 and 45 calibers, is quietly phasing in improvements such as adjustable sights and last-round hold-open for all models. Hi-Point's Charles Brown stresses their "no questions asked" lifetime warranty.

IAI

Israel Arms International (IAI) seems to have finally settled the name game. A few years ago, they were J.O. Arms, then changed to IAI. Last year, they resurrected the name of Firearms International. Now, they are back to IAI and it looks as if it will stick.

The former line of Browning HP-type and SIG-type pistols has been expanded to include a full line of 1911-style variants. New for 1999 were full-size 5-inch versions to join the 4 1/4-inch pistols in last years catalog. The new 1911-type pistols are available in 45 ACP and 9mm.

KAHR

Kahr has acquired Auto-Ordnance, and will add at least some of the A-O 1911-style pistols to its line.

Springfield now offers versions of its FBI-adopted 45 to the public. Formerly called the Bureau, it is now named the Professional Model.

Even without considering the A-O acquisition, though, Kahr has some interesting things coming up. A shortened new subcompact 40-caliber pistol, the Kahr MK 40, was displayed at the SHOT Show and was scheduled for availability by mid-1999. For those who want to impress their friends with their knowledge, think of the separate letters M and K as standing for "Micro Kahr" and don't call it a "Mark 40."

By the end of 1999, Kahr plans the introduction of a polymer-frame pistol. A rough prototype was available at the SHOT Show.

KEL-TEC

The 25-sized 32 market has had another entry. The Kel-Tec P-32 is a light, flat 32 ACP pistol introduced to the world at the February 1999 SHOT Show. The original DAO polymer-frame 9mm Kel-Tec pistol had set a new style in small defense pistols. So, as might be expected, the P-32 has a polymer frame and is DAO. As might not be expected, however, the diminutive 32 is a locked-breech pistol. The

The Ruger Standard Model pistol is having its 50th anniversary, and Ruger has brought out a commemorative version. Here, Malloy shows off a fairly decent 50-foot target he shot with his early Standard Model.

Saf-T-Hammer displayed a prototype of a new 40-caliber pistol that uses their detachable hammerhead system.

Llama decided "Yes." The new MiniMax Sub-Compact was introduced at the February 1999 SHOT Show. With a 3.14-inch barrel, the new 45 weights 31 ounces. Magazine is of the short double-column type and holds a full "legal limit" of ten rounds, giving the pistol 10+1 capacity.

MAGNUM RESEARCH

After an absence of three years, the "Baby" Eagle pistol has returned to Magnum Research. The pistols are made by IMI in Israel and are now in production as steel-frame guns in calibers 9mm and 40 S&W. Many are impressed with the design, in which the slide rides inside the frame rails. Poly-

tilting-barrel locking system allows a very light slide, and the little pistol weighs only 6.6 ounces. To make the little gun flatter, the external slide stop has been eliminated in favor of an internal one. Width of the P-32 is an exact 3/4 of an inch.

The P-32 was the star of Kel-Tec's display, but the company has also introduced a conversion kit for their original P-11 9mm pistol. For a little over half the price of a new pistol, the owner of a 9mm can now convert it to 40 S&W.

KIMBER

Kimber's big news is a small pistol. Kimber has entered the subcompact 45 market with their new Ultra Carry model. The new small 45 joins the newly introduced compact Pro Carry 45, and is even smaller, with a 3-inch barrel. The aluminum frame is shortened, but still holds a 7-round magazine, giving a weight of 25 ounces and a capacity of 7+1. The Ultra Carry is also available in stainless and also in 40 S&W.

Other Kimber pistols are now being offered in new configurations.

Also, for the first time, Kimber pistols are being offered in calibers other than 45 ACP. 9mm, 38 Super and 40 S&W versions are now available.

A 22 LR conversion kit for Kimber big-bore pistols is now available.

LLAMA

With the introduction last year of Para-Ordnance's scaled-down 45 with a 10-round magazine, probably every company that made a double-column 45 had to decide if they wanted to enter that market.

SIG Arms new Model P245 is 45-caliber, and is a compact, scaled-down version of their full-size P220 pistol.

A Philippine company, Shooters Arms Manufacturing, has introduced new 1911-type pistols, including some gussied-up versions.

mer frame variants and a steel-frame 45 ACP were scheduled to be introduced during 1999.

MOSSBERG

O.F. Mossberg & Sons is no longer in the pistol business. The three-year arrangement between Mossberg and IMI of Israel has come to an end. Uzi America, the Mossberg subsidiary that was set up to distribute and maintain the guns, no longer exists. The few people with O.F.M. or Uzi-marked IMI pistols now have interesting collector items.

PARA-ORDNANCE

The designers at Para-Ordnance have spent considerable time studying cam angles. The result is a new pistol with a light, smooth double-action pull. The company's first double-action pistol attracted a good deal of attention during its introduction at the 1999 SHOT Show. Dubbed the 14.45 LDA, the new pistol is a full-size, 5-inch-barrel model in 45 ACP. The mechanism operates DAO; the gun has an outside hammer, but it does not cock. The trigger pull is exceptionally light and smooth, and stacks somewhat just before let-off. The thumb safety operates by disconnecting the trigger, not by blocking it—the trigger

just "freewheels" while the pistol is on safe. Versions in 40 S&W and 9mm are also planned. In addition, a special version for law enforcement will have a high-capacity magazine, a spurless hammer and no safety thumbpiece. For the common folk, each new 14.45 LDA will come with a 10-round magazine, but also with a coupon allowing the buyer to purchase up to two of Para-Ordnance's grandfathered 14-round magazines.

PROFESSIONAL ORDNANCE

The Carbon 15 pistol is now offered with a slim stainless-steel barrel and a lighter weight. Design is basically AR-15, but with upper and lower receivers made of carbon fiber instead of metal. The result is a big pistol-19 1/2 x 7 inches--that only weighs 40 ounces. Caliber is 223 and barrel length is 7 1/4 inches.

REPUBLIC ARMS (SOUTH AFRICA)

The South African company, Republic Arms, now has in production an all-steel 40-caliber pistol, the RAP 440, which was introduced in prototype last year. With a 3 1/2-inch barrel, the pistol measures 6.5 x 4.75 inches and weighs 32 ounc-

es. A polymer-frame version of the RAP pistol is also being considered.

REPUBLIC ARMS (U.S)

The Republic Arms Patriot, a lightweight 20-ounce DAO polymer-frame pistol in 45 ACP, has been introduced in a new black Melonite finish. This is a black finish over the stainless-steel slide, and it makes the pistol all black and less easily observed.

For those who have wondered if plentiful 1911-type magazines will work in the Republic pistols, here is the definitive answer from Republic's Todd Smith: yes and no. The Republic magazine was very slightly redesigned to provide better feeding. Some 1911 magazines will work perfectly in the Republic, feeding everything; some will feed only 230-grain ball ammunition. The Republic magazines are not expensive, but some people already have a supply of 1911 magazines on hand.

The futuristic South African pistol, the Vektor CP-1, is displayed by Christine Danforth, wife of Vektor USA president Michael Danforth.

Horst Wesp (left), Walther P99 designer, explains the features of the Walther P99 and P990 pistols to Malloy.

RUGER

Sturm, Ruger & Company celebrated its 50th anniversary in 1999. What better way to commemorate the event than to bring out a 50th Anniversary version of the 1949-vintage 22 pistol that started it all? The anniversary model is designated MK4-50, and was scheduled for production only in 1999. Old-timers will see some

familiar features: the absence of relief cuts at the rear of the receiver and the red background of the Ruger crest on the grip panels. The Ruger crest is on the rear of the bolt of this special pistol, and a new 50th Anniversary crest is on the upper front portion of the receiver. Mechanically, the pistol is all modern, with the holdopen and bolt release of the current models.

A 22-caliber Makarov? A conversion kit was displayed by Pearce Grips and may be imported from Bulgaria.

Also new for 1999 were the P97 series pistols, Ruger's first 45 ACP pistols with polymer frames. Offered in DAO, and conventional DA with a decocker, the new 45s have stainless-steel slides and weigh 27 ounces. Capacity is 7+1.

SAF-T-HAMMER

A new name on the firearms scene, the Saf-T-Hammer corporation has introduced a safety device for autoloaders and revolvers with outside hammers. The device is a removable hammerhead-the gun can fire with the top of the hammer in place, cannot fire with it removed.

The company has also introduced a pistol that includes the Saf-T-Hammer device and a prototype was displayed at the SHOT Show. Called the STH 40-LE, the pistol is 40 caliber, DAO and has 10+1 capacity. A polymer frame is used, but the prototype also had wood grips. The STH pistol has a conventional tilting-barrel locking system, and measures 7.75 x 5.75 inches.

S.A.M.

A new manufacturer of 1911-type pistols, Shooters Arms Manufacturing (S.A.M.) made their first display of firearms in the United States in February 1999. The Philippine company began in 1992 and offers revolvers and shotguns as well as semiautomatic pistols. The 1911-style pistols are available in several different variants, and in calibers 9mm, 38 Super, 40 S&W and 45 ACP.

SIG ARMS

The full-size 45-caliber SIG P220 has been around for decades, and lived through the "wondernine" period, but never really got the recognition some felt it deserved. So, now, at

The Glock 36 is the company's first pistol with a single-column magazine, making a slimmer 45 for concealed carry.

The IMI double-action pistols are back under the Magnum Research name, imported as the Baby Eagle. Calibers are 9mm and 40 S&W.

a time when scaled-down 45s seem to be all the rage, what should SIG do? How about shortening it a half inch in both directions and bringing out a scaled-down version? The resulting new model P245 has a 3.9-inch barrel and measures 7.3 x 5 inches, good enough to put it into the Compact class. Weight is 30 ounces and capacity is 6+1.

Sig has also taken the P220 in the other direction, now offering the P220S, an adjustable-sight, compensated target version. With a 5.5-inch barrel and compensator, this new 45 measures a whopping 10 x 6 inches and weighs about 47 ounces. Polymer frames have now been introduced to the SIG line. The "Sig Pro" series guns are the SP2009 (9mm) and the SP2340 (40 and 357 SIG).

Although it didn't get the buildup the new centerfire pistols got, SIG's new Trailside 22 drew a lot of attention. In 22 LR, it is basically a Hammerli, dressed down to be a hunting, plinking or casual target pistol. Two versions—fixed sights and adjustable sights—are offered.

SMITH & WESSON

Some have looked askance at S&W's use of the traditional revolver name "Chiefs Special" on new small semiauto pistols, but the new autoloaders seemed well-received at the 1999 SHOT Show. The code is easy to break: Model CS9 is a 9mm, CS40 is a 40 S&W,

The Ruger MK4-50 will be made only in 1999 to commemorate the 50th anniversary of the company and its first product, the Standard Model 22 pistol.

Ruger's first polymer-frame 45, the KP 97, is available in conventional double action or DAO.

The Steyr Model M is a new polymer-frame pistol that sits low in the hand and has a number of interesting features. Calibers are 9mm and 40 S&W.

and CS45 is a 45 ACP. Black and stainless finishes are offered in all versions. The 9mm has a 3-inch barrel, while the larger calibers go 3 1/4. Weight is about 21 ounces for the 9, about 24 for the 40 and 45. Capacity is 6+1 for the 45, 7+1 for the 9 and 40.

The company has also made some changes to their Sigma line of polymer-frame pistols, and the new pistols form the Enhanced Sigma lineup. There are some mechanical changes, such as a shorter trigger pull. The ejection port has been enlarged and lowered. The checkering on the grip frames has been changed, and a bar has been moulded under the slide stop to prevent inadvertent engagement while shooting. Accessary grooves are now on the forward part of the frame. Sigmas are available in all black or two-tone, and in 9mm or 40 S&W.

It is not in the regular catalog, but the S&W Custom Shop offers the Model 945. This is a Smith & Wesson for the man who thinks every pistol ought to feel like a Colt 1911. Single action, and with the controls in the same positions as those on a 1911, it shows that S&W gives some thought to filling all available niches.

SPRINGFIELD

The Springfield 1911-type 45 pistol that was tested and adopted by the Federal Bureau of Investigation (FBI) was scheduled to be also offered to the shooting public, as the "Bureau" Model. The pistol is now available, but it no longer goes by that name. To avoid any idea of an endorsement by the FBI, the name of the pistol was changed to the "Professional" Model. Some pistols were made with the "Bureau" markings, and they should be interesting collector items.

STEYR

Steyr was a big name in the early days of the semiautomatic pistol, and now is introducing an innovative new pistol, the Model M. The new Steyr has a polymer frame designed to sit low in the hand, and the design is said to reduce felt recoil while enhancing natural pointing. To obtain this feel, the grip angle was set slantier than a 1911, but less so than a Luger. The new Steyr M pistol is available in 9mm or 40 S&W. Weight is 28 ounces, and the gun measures 5 x 7 inches, putting it in the compact category. Locking is by the conventional tilting barrel system.

Safeties are interestingly done. There is a little trigger set into the trigger, which, although of different shape, will be familiar enough to Glock users. A manual safety can also be set to protrude from the top of the trigger guard; pushing it up with the trigger finger will ready the gun to fire. The third safety is a key-lock safety; with a key, you can simply turn the gun "off" by way of a locking mechanism on the right side of the frame.

Sights on the Steyr M pistols will probably seem strange to all but Nambu shooters. A dovetail rear sight is used with a triangular front sight. Steyr calls this the triangle/trapezoid sight system and claims it leads the eye to the target for quicker and more accurate aiming.

TAURUS

The polymer-frame subcompact Millenium PT 111 in 9mm has now been joined by two new Taurus Millennium pistols. The PT 140 in 40 S&W is a logical addition. Taurus has also chosen to cover the other side, and the PT 138 is now available in 380. All versions have 3.25-inch barrels, weigh about 19 ounces, are DAO and have 10+1 capacity. The Millenium series pistols, although they are DAO, are equipped with a manual thumb safety and also have a key-lock safety to disable the pistol when not in use.

The Taurus compact line has two potent new additions. The PT 400 is in 400 Cor-Bon. The PT 957 is chambered for 357 SIG. Both of the new boomers are conventional DA, have 3.62-inch barrels and weigh about 28 ounces. Capacity is 10+1.

The Challenge Micro is a four-inch, 23-ounce, Benchmark.

In addition to the new pistols, Taurus has also brought out a 22 LR conversion kit for its full-size PT 92 and PT 96 pistols .

VEKTOR

A new Virginia company, Vektor USA, has been formed to import the South African line of Vektor pistols. The handguns were displayed for the first time in the U.S. at the February 1999 SHOT Show.

Vektor makes the Z88, a licensed copy of the 9mm Beretta 92, now in use by South African and German police forces. Their SP1 and SP2 pistols are "service pistols" in 9mm and 40 S&W, respectively. They also use the basic Beretta locking-block mechanism, but they don't look at all like Berettas. Instead of the open-top slide, the Vektors have full-coverage slides with ejection ports. Trigger guard shapes and grip frame contours are very different, too.

The real attention-getter at the Vektor display was the CPI. This 9mm "compact pistol" is a futuristic-looking polymer frame gun, with a Glock-type trigger mechanism. The rearward movement of the slide is gas-retarded by a piston that rides in a gas tube under the barrel. A special control in the front of the trigger guard acts as a manual safety and also as a device for quick disassembly.

WALTHER

The 9mm Walther P 99, introduced a short time ago, now has a 40 S&W variant in the family. How to tell them apart at a glance? The new 40 has a slightly heavier slide, accomplished by eliminating the recess at the front of the slide. The 9mm still has the recess.

Take a Benchmark to a 5 1/2-inch bull barrel and 34 ounces and you get the Camper.

The C59—the newest Chief's Special—has siblings in 40 and 45.

A new variant, the Walther P 990, is DAO, and is available in both 9mm and 40 S&W. The decocker, which blends nicely into the lines of the slide on the P 99, is completely absent on the new DAO P 990.

POSTSCRIPT

If a semiautomatic pistol is to be carried, a holster is a useful accessory. Many manufacturers make excellent holsters of various types. Sights of several types metallic, optical, electronic, laser-can be added by a shooter for various purposes. But the list of accessories for autoloading handguns goes well beyond holsters and sights.

Safety considerations are important and many companies make trigger locks and storage containers. An innovative approach by Saf-T-Hammer uses a retrofitted two-piece hammer. The top of the hammer can be removed for safe storage.

Some accessories are a convenience. Want to fill up the space in the rear of a Glock grip? LaPrade offers a block to close it off. Then the area can be used for storage of I.D., money, survival items, etc. To make a Glock easier to disassemble, Ranch Products offers an enlarged takedown bar.

Several manufacturers offer kits to change pistols of their make from one caliber to another. A new 22 LR conversion kit for the popular Makarow pistols was displayed by Pearce Grips, and may be imported.

Holsters, sights, extra magazines, magazine pouches, tools, cleaning equipment and supplies, conversion kits, safety devices, specialized accessories-I wonder if anyone has really thought about how much, just by themselves, aftermarket items for autoloading handguns help our economy. ●

It's an Enhanced Sigma—a lot of changes—in 40 and 9mm.

by HAL SWIGGETT

HANDGUNS TODAY:

SIXGUNS AND OTHERS

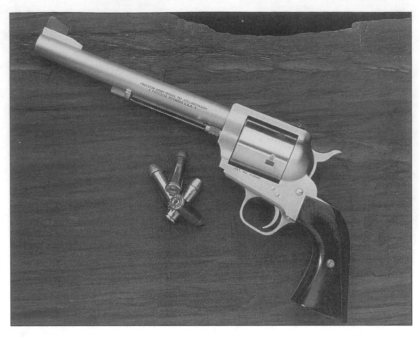

Freedom Arms Model 757 5-shot single action is of stainless steel construction, chambered 475 Linebaugh, and offered in barrel lengths of 4 3/4, 6 or 7 1/2 inches.

There are more than a few Sixguns and Others to report on this time around. However two stood out as tops in this handgun hunter/writer's eyes, so let's start with them in alphabetical order so we can't be accused of favoritism.

FREEDOM ARMS

Long known for many and varied innovations this newest is, by far, the best they have come up with: How about a 420-grain lead .475-inch flat-nose bullet at 1,300 fps from a 7 1/2-inch barrel in a stainless steel five-shooter single action?

It's the 475 Linebaugh, offered in two grades—Premier and Field. Both have adjustable sights and barrel lengths are 4 3/4, 6 or 7 1/2-inches. Premier Grade is stainless steel, brush finish and impregnated hardwood grips; Field Grade is matte finished with Pachmayr grips. The 7 1/2-incher weighs 51 ounces.

There is still another new one. A sort of miniature that was shown a year or so ago at the SHOT Show and is now in production. The Model 97 (because it was first shown in 1997) is in a choice of two flavors. It holds six 357 Magnums or five 45 Colt (or 45 ACP) rounds. Barrel lengths are 5 1/2 or 7 1/2 inches. Weight is 36 ounces chambered 45 and 39.5 ounces chambered 357.

Plus, in their brochure, on display during the SHOT Show, there was, for all to see, a Casull single action with an octagon barrel. And it looked good— mighty good.

MAGNUM RESEARCH

This Minnesota company has taken on Darwin and Maxine Carda's single action revolvers, which are now Mag-

Revealing the size of Freedom Arms' new cartridge, here it is with 44 Special, 44 Rem. Mag., 454 Casull and 475 Linebaugh—left to right.

num's B F R (Biggest Finest Revolver) MAXINE Models include 7 1/2 and 10-inch barrels chambered 45 Colt/410, 45-70 or 444 Marlin.

LITTLE MAX Models offer 454 Casull with 6 1/2, 7 1/2 or 10-inch barrels; 45 Colt +P barreled 6 1/2 or 7 1/2-inches; 22 Hornet 7 1/2 or 10-inch; and 50 AE in 7 1/2-inch.

Their "biggie" is built on an extended Ruger frame. Such a frame will then accept the lengthier cylinder to hold 45-

70 "cattiges", as a long-departed elderly friend used to call them. And I was allowed to devote an entire morning to one of their executives' "personal" 45-70 single actions, topped with a 2x Leupold in that company's mount. Barrel length was 10 inches and it was .825-inches in diameter.

Three factory loads were fired: Winchester 405 gr. SPs; Remington 405 gr. SPs; and Cor-Bon 350 gr. Bonded-Core Flat Points. All shot well, though Cor-

Freedom Arms had this octagon barreled revolver on display, in their booth, at the Atlanta SHOT Show. No info—just this revolver.

Bon's was both fastest and printed the tightest 5-shot groups. However ALL of the 5-shot groups could, easily, have been covered with one of those saucers that holds your morning coffee cup—at 100 yards!!

SMITH & WESSON

The new Model 296 Airlite Ti comes by its name easily. Manufactured with an aluminum alloy frame and barrel yoke and Titanium cylinder and stainless steel barrel liner, it has a concealed hammer. There are 2 1/2 inches of barrel, a 5-round capacity, with a "fixed notch" rear sight and up front a pinned black serrated ramp. The finish is Matte Alloy/Titanium and it weighs 18.9 ounces.

Chambering? How about 44 S&W Special?!?

Then there are Models 331 and 332, with 1 7/8-inch barrels chambered 32 H&R Magnum, followed by Models 337 and 342, same dimensions but chambered 38 Special +P.

Big bore shooters were not left out. S&W's Model 629 Mountain Gun is chambered 44 Remington Magnum with a 4-inch tapered barrel along and a 6-shot cylinder. This one lists its sights as "pinned black ramp front and micrometer click-adjustable black blade rear". Overall length is 9 1/2 inches; weight is 39.5 ounces. And it's stainless steel.

Smith & Wesson's Performance Center is offering their Model 629 V-Comp—a 4-inch custom barrel, unfluted cylinder with chamfered charge holes plus the added benefits/strength of ball-detent lock up.

Model 629 V-Comp wears a Hogue grip AND three port comp that is removable, along with a replacement muzzle to protect its crown should the shooter NOT want to take advantage of those recoil-reducing capabilities.

Model 629 V-Comp is delivered with a red ramp dovetailed up front and black micrometer adjustable click rear sights. Overall length is 8 1/2 inches; weight, empty, is 43.0 ounces.

The chambering? How about 45 ACP? Remember, please, this one is special-made from S&W's Performance Center.

One of my revolvers is a very elderly K-22. Bought it from a pawn shop in Laredo, Texas, give or take on 50 years ago. It had the letter P inset in its right side plate. A fine engraver friend of mine, Charlie Price, knew I was deeply involved with rattlesnakes at that time (a lengthy story here but for another time) so inlaid a gold rattlesnake where that letter was. And YES—it is a 6-shooter.

Smith & Wesson has upgraded their K-22 Masterpiece to a 10-shooter and offered with 4-, 6-, or 8 3/8-inch barrel. And, if I am reading their literature correctly, only in stainless steel with that lengthier barreled version weighing in at 52.5 ounces.

After nearly 150 years manufacturing handguns this company—S&W—is offering CO2 revolvers, double or single action, Model 586 in blue and Model 686 in nickel, 10-shot capacity, chambered (?) to accept .177 caliber pellets. There is more: interchangeable 4, 6 or

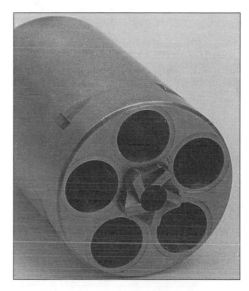

And yes—proof it is a five shooter ...

Magnum Research .45-70 is built on an extended Ruger frame with 10 inches of stainless steel barrel measuring .825" in diameter—front to back.

Hal's very elderly K 22 S&W with a gold-inlaid rattlesnake inside scroll engraving.

Close-up of the gold rattlesnake in Hal's S&W K 22.

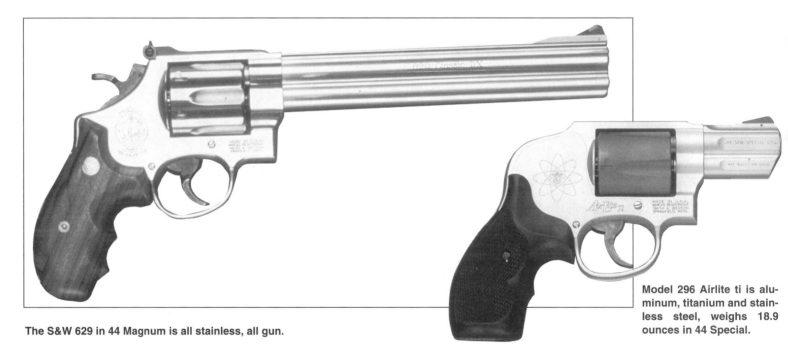

The S&W 629 in 44 Magnum is all stainless, all gun.

Model 296 Airlite ti is aluminum, titanium and stainless steel, weighs 18.9 ounces in 44 Special.

S&W 629 V-Comp has all the goodies, shoots the 45 ACP.

Ruger's BEARCAT is 4 inches of barrel, as was the original.

Its name is on the frame immediately under the cylinder.

8-inch barrels, a fully adjustable black blade rear sight and Patridge front.

TAURUS

This is, truly, a very active revolver company.

Total Titanium is their thing this time around. Their description, "The only substance strong enough to enclose nuclear guided-missile warheads and durable enough to fan flames inside hypersonic aircraft engines."

Six different chamberings including compact-frame 7-shot 357 Magnum, 5-shot 41 Magnum, 44 Special and 45 Colt, a small frame 5-shot 38 Special +P and a 6-shot 32 H&R Magnum.

Model 941 is stainless steel, with 2, 4, or 5-inch barrel, an 8-shot 22 WMR. There are adjustable sights, and choice of bright blue or polished stainless steel. Soft rubber grips are on the two shorter guns, wood on the 5-incher.

Model 617 and 817, bright blue or polished stainless, is 357 Magnum. Another version of Model 617 is with a concealed hammer, ported, in polished stainless steel. All are 7-shooters.

Raging Bull made its appearance in 454 Casull a few years back.

In fact, I had one of their first a few days and took a rather large, change that to really big, wild hog with it. Now that same Raging Bull is available chambered 44 Remington Magnum or 45 Colt. It is a 5-shooter in 454 but a 6-shooter when chambering 44 Magnum or 45 Colt cartridges. And one 8-shooter I'm going to have to try has a 10 inch barrel. It's a 22 Hornet delivered with a scope base attached to its vent rib. All that's necessary is to add a scope and fill its cylinder with cartridges.

And my answer is "YES!". This Savage on/off muzzle brake really does a fine job.

Savage STRIKER, with its bolt on the left side, makes it MUCH easier to handle for right-hand shooters. Topped with Burris' 3X-9X scope this one took at least its share of Prairie Dogs in western Kansas last year

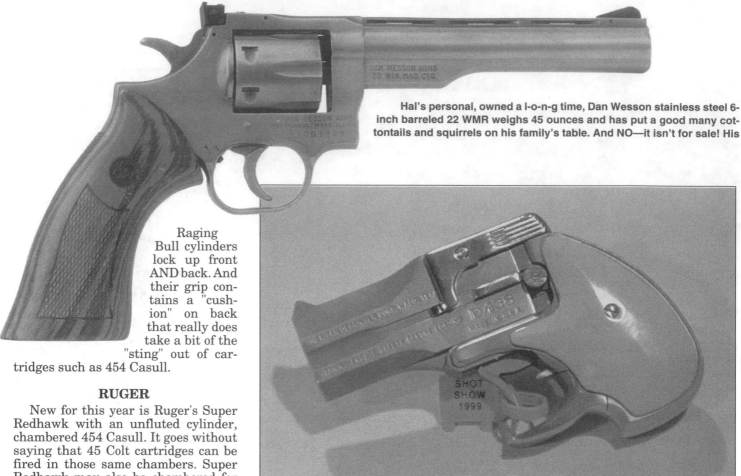

Hal's personal, owned a l-o-n-g time, Dan Wesson stainless steel 6-inch barreled 22 WMR weighs 45 ounces and has put a good many cottontails and squirrels on his family's table. And NO—it isn't for sale! His

Raging Bull cylinders lock up front AND back. And their grip contains a "cushion" on back that really does take a bit of the "sting" out of cartridges such as 454 Casull.

RUGER

New for this year is Ruger's Super Redhawk with an unfluted cylinder, chambered 454 Casull. It goes without saying that 45 Colt cartridges can be fired in those same chambers. Super Redhawk may also be chambered for the 44 Remington Magnum.

Redhawk revolvers come in 44 Remington Magnum caliber and 45 Colt. Both chamber six cartridges. Redhawk and Super Redhawks are designed to accept scope rings (blue or stainless) which are included with each revolver sold.

Their awfully cute little Ruger New Bearcat is fitted with a 4-inch barrel, same as the first. The only "real" difference, visible to the naked eye, is the lack of #1's brass trigger guard and much, much slimmer, narrower hammer. Weight? My elderly model weighs, on my postal scale, a hair-line below 17 ounces. The new one goes 24 ounces.

SAVAGE

A Striker, chambered 22-250, went to Western Kansas with me in early summer a year ago, topped with a 3X-9X Burris scope in Weaver mounts. It came along with five (5) cases of Winchester 40-grain Ballistic Tip ammunition. Less than half a case made the trip back to Texas.

One of the things I liked most, make that two, was the adjustable muzzle brake out front AND the bolt on the left side with right side ejection.

As rigged, scope and mount, it weighed an even seven (7) pounds. And it's a three-shooter—two in the magazine with one chambered. The trigger pull was mighty crisp at an even three (3) lbs. The black, synthetic, dual-pil-

Shown in American Derringer's booth at the SHOT Show was this double action only 38 Special. A right-fancy piece of craftsmanship.

lar-bedded stock I found to be extremely comfortable to shoot.

Other chamberings offered are 223 Remington, 243 Winchester, 7mm-08 Remington, 260 Remington and 308 Winchester.

CHARTER ARMS

It was GOOD to find Charter Arms back in production. There's only a single entry—but they're back.

Their brochure reads: "The new Charter Arms Undercover is now produced in limited quantities for the police, professional security and home defense markets".

Their entry is described as "Newly designed one piece barrel assembly". It is manufactured in stainless steel, chambered 38 Special, 2-inch barrel, 5-shot, 6 1/4 inches overall length, 4 1/4 inches high and weighing 18 oz.

Like old times, perhaps better.

COMPETITOR

Al Straitiff has made a few changes in his Competitor cannon-breeched pistol. First—there is a newly designed compound camming force to pull the tightest cases out with ease. This is a two-stage action. The first actually

takes up any free travel before full force of the cam acts on the cartridge case.

And now there's an adjustable trigger designed with fewer parts for greater strength and endurance.

Competitor's trigger has always fascinated this shooter. That tiny little "device" in its center causes the trigger to do its job and fire the pistol. Mine, chambered 284 Winchester, lets go, fires, at ONLY 1 1/2 lbs. of pull.

DAN WESSON

Described in their literature are two revolvers listed as NEW GENERATION SRS-1 and NEW GENERATION 445 VH4C. SRS-1 is chambered 445 SuperMag, 414 SuperMag, 44 Magnum, and 41 Magnum. These are satin brushed stainless steel or blue your choice. Barrel lengths are 4-, 6-, 8- or 10 inches. The 445 VH4C is chambered as above but with their DW Compensator System.

Dan Wesson revolvers are famous for their interchangeable barrel system, adjustable black Bomar competition target sights and inter-changeable, hooded, Patridge style sights. Laser engraving and Hogue rubber finger groove grips are a standard feature. Wood lam-

This cannon-like breech adds only 1 7/8 inches to Competitor's over-all length which is 17 7/8 inches, including muzzle brake.

less Steel. DW claims accuracy at distances over 200 meters (218 yards) on a consistent basis. For this they offer drilled and tapped versions for scope mounting. From personal knowledge: I have been shooting, for more than a few years, a stainless steel Dan Wesson 22WMR revolver with a 6-inch, vent-ribbed barrel. It has taken a whole bunch more than a few cottontails AND squirrels plus numerous jack rabbits.

BOND ARMS

This not very old company manufactures fine, sturdy, stainless steel derringers chambered in 410/45 Colt to 45 ACP, 44 Remington Magnum/44 Special, 40 S&W, 357 Maximum, 357 Magnum/38 Special, 9mm Parabellum and 32 H&R Magnum.

Their patented Rebounding Hammer prevents unintentional contact with firing pins for safer loading and unloading. And a patented spring loaded cammed locking lever provides faster, easier loading/unloading, and a tighter barrel/frame fit.

Bond Arms over/under derringers are unique in that their barrels ARE interchangeable. Plus they can be had with 3 or 3 1/2-inch barrels.

Another offering from Bond Arms is their Century 2000 Defender. Barrel length is 3 1/2-inches. Built to accept 3-inch 00 buck shot with five (5) pellets.

inate finger groove grips can be ordered as an additional feature.

DW's small frame series includes 22 Long Rifle, 22 WMR, 32 H&R Magnum. 32-20 and 357 Magnum. Rimfire barrel lengths are 2 1/2, 4, 6 or 8 inches. These are offered in Brite Blue or Satin Stain-

The single action 45 Colt seen here is built in Classic Arms shop, by Frank Turner. It IS a faithful reproduction of first generation single actions ...

Interestingly, barrels to be interchanged on a single frame. Barrel lengths are 3-inch or 3 1/2-inch, weight 21 ounces and length 5 inches. Grips are laminated black ash or rosewood. And there's a left-handed model.

ANSCHUTZ

The newest offering is the Model 64P, a sporter/target pistol chambered 22 Long Rifle or 22 WMR. The trigger is target style two stage factory set at 1 lb. 12 oz. and adjustable (by gunsmiths) from 1 lb. 5 oz. to 2 lbs.

...as can be seen here.

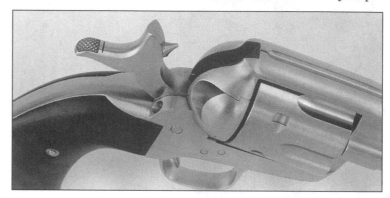

bered 22-250, 270 Winchester or 308 Winchester topped with their 2.5x-7x variable Recoil Proof Pistol Scope. It's a nice outfit.

Both Contender and Encore booklets include a bright yellow box—1/2 by 2 inches—reading "NOTE: 45/410 Barrels of Less Than 18 inches in Length Are Not Offered For Sale In California". Another reason to NOT live in that state.

RPM

I do own one of their first—with a 22 Long Rifle barrel AND a 44 Remington Magnum barrel. In fact, way back BG (before glasses), I killed more than a few cottontails for our table with that rimfire chambered barrel. Minus any scope.

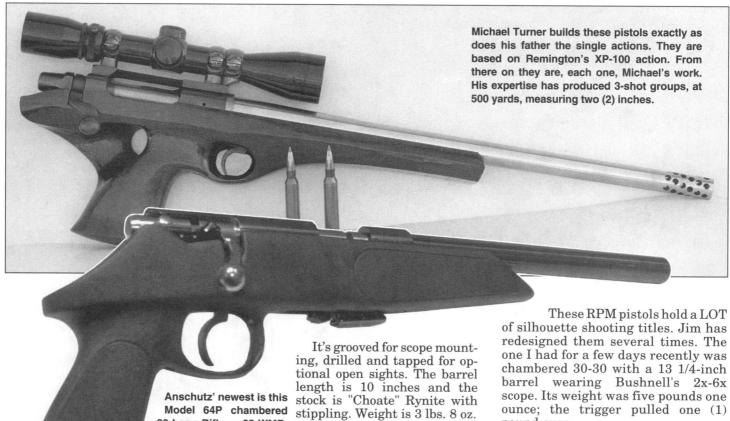

Michael Turner builds these pistols exactly as does his father the single actions. They are based on Remington's XP-100 action. From there on they are, each one, Michael's work. His expertise has produced 3-shot groups, at 500 yards, measuring two (2) inches.

Anschutz' newest is this Model 64P chambered 22 Long Rifle or 22 WMR. It is delivered from the factory with the two stage trigger set at 1 lb. 12 oz. It is grooved for scope mounting plus drilled and tapped for optional open sights.

It's grooved for scope mounting, drilled and tapped for optional open sights. The barrel length is 10 inches and the stock is "Choate" Rynite with stippling. Weight is 3 lbs. 8 oz. It will shoot.

THOMPSON/CENTER

The Encore line now includes a "Hunter" package: an Encore 15-inch pistol cham-

These RPM pistols hold a LOT of silhouette shooting titles. Jim has redesigned them several times. The one I had for a few days recently was chambered 30-30 with a 13 1/4-inch barrel wearing Bushnell's 2x-6x scope. Its weight was five pounds one ounce; the trigger pulled one (1) pound even.

How did it shoot?

Exactly like you would expect a pistol to perform that holds numerous records in silhouette shooting. Another way to put it, "A lot better than this typewriter jockey!"

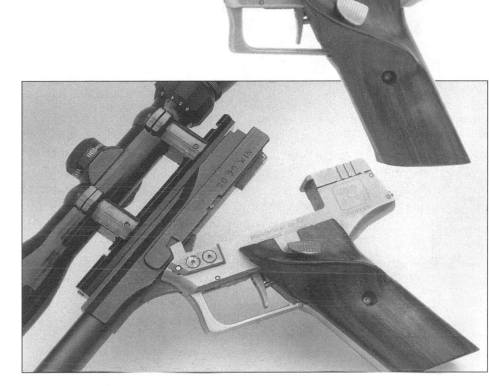

And yes—the new Jim Rock RPM pistol is more hand-some plus his added innovations.

.....and the barrel opens.

CLASSIC ARMS

This is a father and sons business. They custom-build the finest single action revolvers and bolt action pistol I've ever seen and been allowed to shoot. They do it one at a time.

Frank and son Michael build the guns on high-tech machines maintained by son Warren. Frank specializes in building what, really, is his own single action. It differs, several ways, from those manufactured on a mass-production basis.

Michael specializes in taking Ruger frames and turning them into custom 454 Casull five-shot single actions. These are manufactured from S7 tool steel heat treated to 45 RC for maximum strength. He uses a special fixture to hold the frame and cylinder blank during the machining process. This gives perfect alignment of the chambers. Forcing cones are lapped. Cylinder gap is .002inches. Triggers are set at a crisp two lbs. Barrel lengths can be from 4 5/8 to 12-inches and offered with, or without, muzzle brakes.

Michael builds his own single shot pistols too, based on Remington's XP-100 action. His ONLY chambering is 30-338 Magnum. The exhibition grade thumbhole stock blanks come from Richards Microfit.

Harrington & Richardson's Model 999 has been a favorite for a long, long time. Top quality and low priced.

His load is 76 grains of Winchester 760 with a 125 grain Nosler Ballistic Tip. Chronographed velocity is 3,400 fps. This load produces 2-inch, 3-shot, groups at, get this, 500 yards. (Yes—five hundred.)

Back to Frank's single action. Any user can, safely, carry six rounds in the cylinder. His design is such that the hammer cannot reach any cartridge unless its trigger is pulled. And there are still "four clicks". The one I saw and shot is chambered 45 Colt. He can, on order, build that same single action in 44-40, 44 Special or 38-40. Barrel lengths can be 4 3/4, 5 1/2 or 7 1/2 inches.

COLT

"We are putting the new Cowboy Single Action into full production." Those are the first eleven words in their new products release. Then it goes on to say, "It offers Cowboy Action Shooters the same fit and feel of the original with the accuracy and affordability only modern manufacturing can deliver." "Cowboy" is reissued with first generation grips and rich color-cased

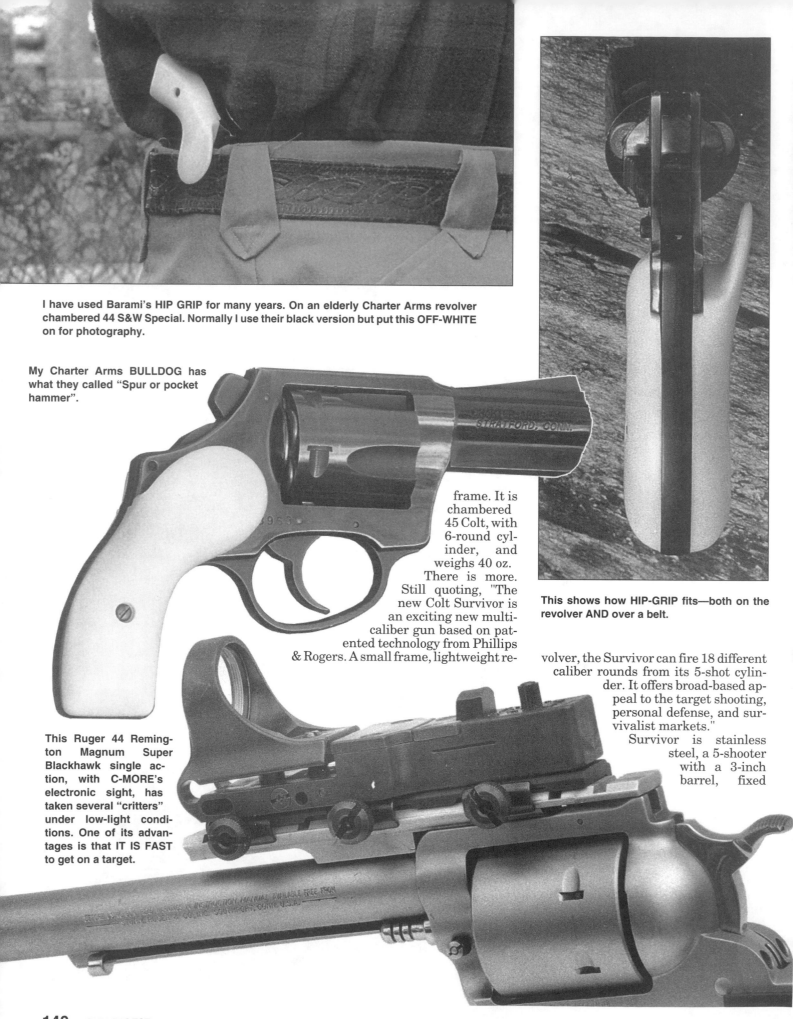

I have used Barami's HIP GRIP for many years. On an elderly Charter Arms revolver chambered 44 S&W Special. Normally I use their black version but put this OFF-WHITE on for photography.

My Charter Arms BULLDOG has what they called "Spur or pocket hammer".

This shows how HIP-GRIP fits—both on the revolver AND over a belt.

This Ruger 44 Remington Magnum Super Blackhawk single action, with C-MORE's electronic sight, has taken several "critters" under low-light conditions. One of its advantages is that IT IS FAST to get on a target.

frame. It is chambered 45 Colt, with 6-round cylinder, and weighs 40 oz. There is more. Still quoting, "The new Colt Survivor is an exciting new multi-caliber gun based on patented technology from Phillips & Rogers. A small frame, lightweight re-volver, the Survivor can fire 18 different caliber rounds from its 5-shot cylinder. It offers broad-based appeal to the target shooting, personal defense, and survivalist markets."

Survivor is stainless steel, a 5-shooter with a 3-inch barrel, fixed sights, rubber, combat style grip and weighs 22 oz. Cartridges accepted by Survivor include 9x18, 9x19, 9x23, 9mm Largo, 380, 38 Super, 38 Special, 38 Special Plus-P and 357 Magnum.

Python Elite is 357 Magnum, blue/color case, 4-inch barrel, 6-shot, target hammer, red ramp front sight, white outlined rear, serrated trigger, Hogue finger grip and weighs 43 1/2 oz.

One more: A 2-inch stainless steel, 6-shot 357 Magnum/38 Special with fixed sights, rubber, combat style grips and weighs 21 oz. This one is called Colt Magnum Carry.

NAVY ARMS

Val Forgett's company is the leader in imported "Old West" handguns—top break or single action.

Their catalog lists six top breaks including New Model Russian, Schofield Cavalry, Schofield Wells Fargo, 1875 Schofield Hideout, Deluxe 1875 Schofield and Engraved 1875 Schofield. There's a U.S. Cavalry holster, too.

Turning to the next pair of pages there are 12 single actions from the early "Pinched Frame" Colt "Peacemaker" through Navy, Cavalry, Artillery, Flat Top, Bisley, Remington and Shootist models.

Should you be interested in "authentic" old-style revolvers you need to contact this company.

One of my handiest items has been MTM's CASE-GARD handgun rest. It lives with my "paraphenalia" box and, believe it or not, I find it is useful regularly. Here it is with my SSK Industries 45-70

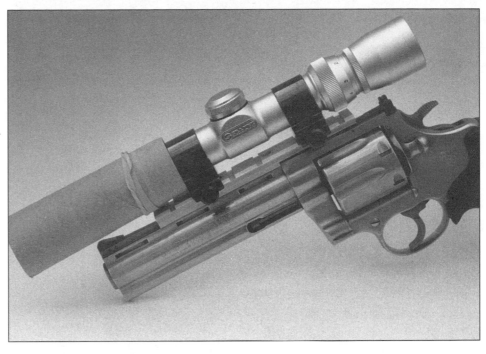

That 4 1/2-inch long cardboard center in a roll of bathroom tissue can come in MIGHTY handy when shooting into a rising—or setting— sun. Try it and find for yourself.

Grip on two of my short-barreled revolvers and carry one or the other often.

Designed especially for concealed carry the Hip-Grip replaces your handgun's original grips and allows it to be held inside your trousers by hooking over your belt. Models are offered for S&W Medium or K-Frame along with smaller J-Frame revolvers plus Colt Detective Special, Cobra, Agent or Diamond Back.

Also included in their line are models for Rossi Models 68 and 88, Charter Arms 38 Undercover, 22 Pathfinder, 32 Undercoverette and 44 Bulldog. And Taurus Model 85 revolvers.

These are good gear. ●

H & R 1873, Inc.

H & R guns have been, literally, my all-time favorite, since my discharge from the USAAF November 30, 1945. There were two reasons: their revolvers are top-quality and, at least as important, inexpensive.

I went on a campaign, a good many years back, collecting H & R Model 999 "Sportsman" revolvers. Ended up buying nine (9) in varied versions. One was a Model 199—same barrel length—looked like the 999, except it Is Single Action.

All I can say about these revolvers is that they are not only inexpensive but truly dependable.

HIP-GRIP

The Barami Corporation has been showing Hip-Grip for as far back as I can remember. In fact, I have their Hip-

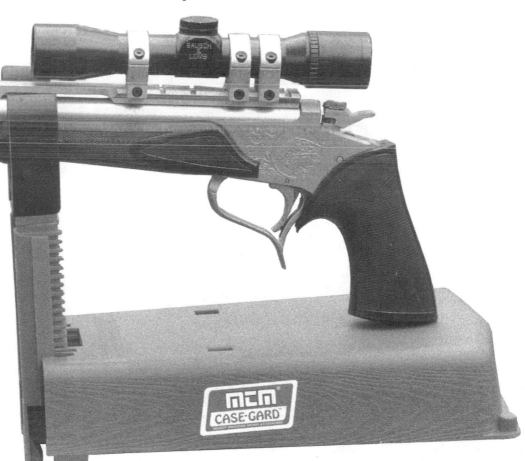

by RAYMOND CARANTA

THE GUNS OF EUROPE

gressively, gave way to bold, clean and innovative designs.

After World War II, the introduction of new manufacturing machinery tremendously increased the flexibility of work in modern gunsmithing, other generations of designers were able to carry into effect their most extravagant dreams; while a few imaginative engravers displayed unwonted art, mostly in Italy, Belgium, France and the Soviet Union. China being rightly considered Asian, the European countries reviewed here or below are limited to Austria, France, Germany and Italy, whose achievements are most familiar to this writer.

Austria is a very rich gunsmithing country, with highly inventive designers for industrial purposes, at Glock and Steyr, and top level

Since the Renaissance period, which, incidentally, coincided with the development of the first sophisticated firearms, Europe has been the seat of the modern civilization, with both its discoveries and fashions, generally along conventional lines. However, while most people stick with the accepted standards of their

A Marlin 444 restocked and fitted with redoubtable "battue" sights for the quickest of rifle shooting, by Ducros.

craftsmen in Ferlach. Nevertheless, all these productions are now well integrated into the globalized "establishment", which only leaves, for our purpose, the unique 5.7x26mm UCC semi-caseless ammunition from Voere (55-grain bullet @ x3300 fps) in limited production since 1991 for their bolt action "VEC91" rifle and the weird Wolf delayed blow-back pistol, for "Practical Shooting" designed in 1992 as the "Spowa", by a certain Mr Gabriel.

times, it is a constant that always some strong, and often talented, characters will set their own goals and turn aside from the beaten track and manage to set themselves against the whole world. Such people were particularly conspicuous, thanks to an exceptionally favorable environment, during the 19th century.

In this century, during the Roaring Twenties, as such individuals became partly doomed by the increasing circulation of efficient production items made for common people, the new 1925 "decorative arts" trend offered them a new opportunity to break off with the past. And since then, the delicate scrolls, flowered works and figurative ornaments were considered as antiquated to the eyes of the most daring amateurs and, pro-

Ducros fitted this highly visible front end on another 444 battue rifle.

Here, in France, in spite of the GIAT Industries contorted 5.56mm NATO "FA-MAS" assault rifle, conventional shotguns and hunting rifles by Chapuis, Gaucher and Verney-Carron, or top level custom doubles by Granger, are the rule, and we might well be poor in the field of talented eccentric achievements. Fortunately, Providence has sent to this blessed country, both Bouchet, with his pet 500 A-Square express over/under, entirely machined from the bar and engraved by himself, and Christian Ducros, a young unbridled stylist, an out-and-out apostle of cleanliness of lines, sharpness of edges, super-accurate fittings and ultra-smooth surface conditions.

In the Ducros, even the finest engraved scroll is a thing of the past, spoiling modern guns' appearance. Nevertheless, as far as engraving is concerned, Ducros reluctantly admits his weakness for the Italian master Manrico Torcoli, whose voluptuous ladies interlaced with snakes, horses, tigers and eagles, have placed him under the spell of their beauty.

As for more practical achievements, Frenchmen can proudly mention the fine PGM "Ultima Ratio" bolt action rifles with inter changeable super-accurate barrels, marketed in 1995, which constitute genuine masterpieces of the most modern gunmaking.

Christian Ducros' rendition of a Thompson gun "project" – a pistol version with remarkable handguards – demonstrates, at a minimum – distinctive flair.

Ducros' approach to the all-round shotgun includes minimum bulk, clearly expressed lines and, of all things, an abundance of bright yellow surfaces.

Bouchet, also French, unconventionally carves conventional actions from the block, seeking never-failing strength.

In Germany the master country of gun design, let us put aside Anschutz, Blazer, Feinwerkbau, Haenel, Hartmann & Weiss, Heckler-und-Koch, Heym, Krico, Krieghoff, Mauser, Merkel, Sauer & Sohn, Walther, Weihrauch and other international champions. We shall concentrate on unconventional wizards, such as Keppeler and Fritz, Korth and "Shorty" (Sommer & Ockenfuss).

Keppeler and Fritz are specialized in under-caliber barrels and top accuracy sporting and sniper rifles. Their line includes, among others, three outstanding bullpup long range rifles, the SKI (308 Win, 7-08 Rem, 8x75 JS, 300 Winchester Magnum, 6mm PPC, 222 Remington and 223 Remington), KSII and KSIII (308 Winchester, 300 Winchester Magnum and 338 Lapua Magnum).

Korth are mostly known for their highly expensive swing-out, double action revolvers. They have also, since 1988, produced a ten-shot automatic pistol chambered in 30 Luger, 9mm Luger, 9x21 IMI, 357 Sig and 40 S&W,

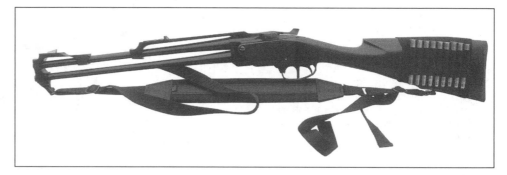

It's the quickest 9.3x62R double gun on Christian Ducros' block – nothing but shooter here.

with axially recoiling barrel, in limited production.

"Shorty", made by Sommer & Ockenfuss, is a very compact slide action rifle (length overall is 31 inches in the American Hunter version and 33.5 inches, for the Shorty Marksman) of clever design. They were the hit of all

the 1998 and 1999 international gun shows. Of course, the Shorty is currently imported in the United States.

If, in Austria and Germany, fine gun design can be properly regarded as a sort of national drug for these mechanically-minded people and in France as the exteriorization of an ardent passion, with little commercial consideration, in Italy, firearms design is actually one of the fine arts for dilet-

The Commando II of 1995, a PGM sniper in the latest of European "practical" layouts.

This Keppeler & Fritz KSIII bullpup sniper is yet another rendition of the unconventional becoming standard, but not ho-hum.

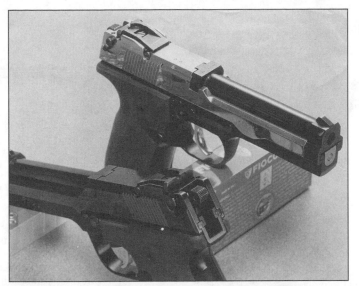

Prototypes of the Mateba Model 95, not yet in production, reveal the maker's penchant for its own drumbeat.

Again in the same generation is the flamboyant Renato Gamba, personifying better than anybody else the "Dolce Vita" epoch, with his riot of luxury and elegance. The reason for including him in this chronicle is not so much the style of his work, which can be grandiose, though always well conceived, conservative and in good taste, but his implication of a blessed economic period, when money was gushing forth and even the poorest was happy.

Emilio Ghisoni, from Mateba, the last of our Italian designers, is also a giant, well-known by the reader as, since 1983, he has designed several families of clever revolvers and an innovative 9mm automatic pistol. The first Mateba revolvers, "MTRB" and "MTR12", were 8- or 12-shot swing out hammerless models, chambered in 357 Magnum, featuring a side-cocking lever for single action shooting. The second generation, issued in 1986 as the "MTR6", were still six-shooters in the same caliber, but with a sliding double-action trigger and an inverted swing-out cylinder firing from the lower chamber, under its axis of rotation. They were fitted with sleeved interchangeable

The Mateba MTR Sport shoots very well, but holsters somewhat slowly.

Mateba's automatic revolver does not remind one of the Webley–Fosberg, now does it?

tantes eager to communicate their joy of living, love of perfection and the pleasure of creating something beautiful, which will be the pride of its owner. Even Beretta, who are in the very heart of the world gun business since the 1950s, have been able to save their soul, thanks to their original and well-made Model 92 pistol.

Amerigo Cosmi e Figlio, from Torette near Ancona, have made, in limited quantities, and beside superb custom side-lock doubles, since 1930, a dreamy folding-barrel automatic shotgun featuring an internal magazine located in the stock and a nice muzzle light balance, providing ideally fast aiming. The Cosmis are the worthy continuators of the pre-World War II highly personalized Italian designers, such as Marengoni, Scotti or Sosso.

Then, we cannot miss perhaps the greatest, in the "Italian miracle generation" of gunmakers, our late friend Mario Abbiatico, from FAMARS, famous for his reactive "Castore E.A.270" double self-cocking external hammer shotgun and his extraordinary four-barreled external hammer 28-gauge, an unnamed "Fucile a quattro canne".

Korth – conventional revolver designs most unconventionally finished and fitted – very top drawer.

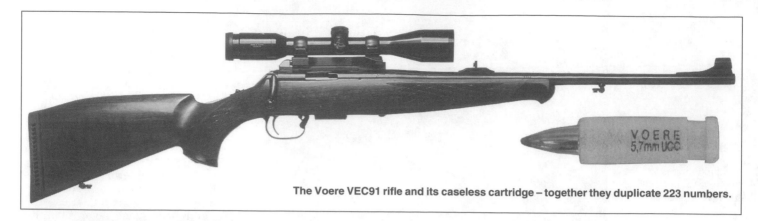

The Voere VEC91 rifle and its caseless cartridge – together they duplicate 223 numbers.

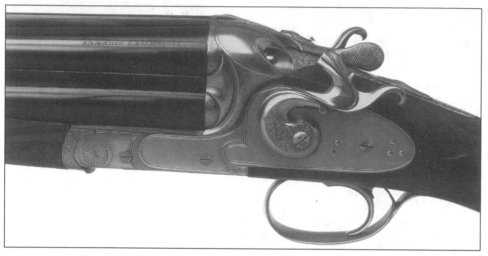

Abbiatico & Salvinelli's four-barrel gun—a 28-bore—hefted like a 20 double—almost.

barrels of different lengths.

When Mr. Ghisoni went back to more conventional pivoting triggers, in 1988, his revolvers became "MR2006". The current model is the "AutoRevolver 6 Unica", another 357 Magnum, swing-out six-shooter with interchangeable sleeved barrels, but featuring a modular lock-work entirely contained in the frame (leaving the grip free for shaping it as required) and recoil actuated. This futurist revolver is highly successful and, of course, imported in the United States. The Mateba model "95" automatic pistol is still a prototype with a selective double action pull and a 15-shot 9mm magazine, but fitted with a patented coaxial-feed.

In this short recoil system, the above round does not jump from the magazine into the barrel, but the barrel is swiveled downwards to its level during the recoil stroke for chambering and, then, upwards into battery. This unconventional pistol is now in course of development.

Manrico Torcoli is neither a gunmaker, nor a stylist, but an engraver.

Pupil of the famous Firmo Fracassi, his innovative works are present on such prestigious guns as those from Pietro Beretta, Bertuzzi, Beschi, Luciano Bosis, Ivo Fabbri, Famars (Abbiatico et Salvinelli), Renato Gamba, Perazzi and Fratelli Piotti.

The impeccable Manrico Torcoli creatively and masterfully fits nudes and horses and eagles together—on shotguns!

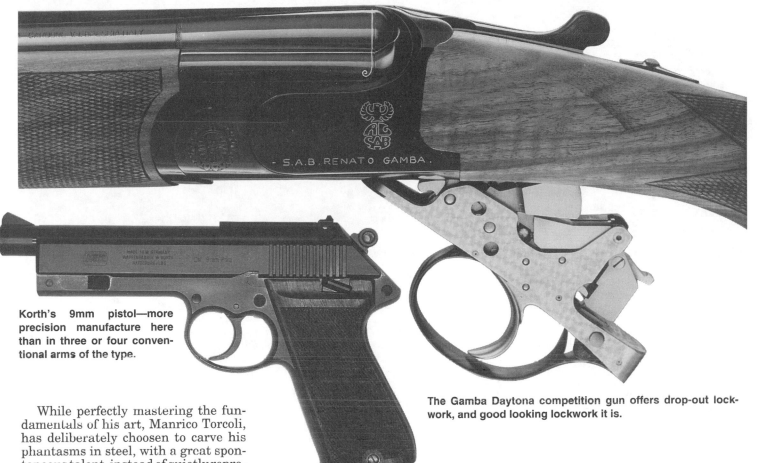

Korth's 9mm pistol—more precision manufacture here than in three or four conventional arms of the type.

The Gamba Daytona competition gun offers drop-out lockwork, and good looking lockwork it is.

Below: Cesare Giovanelli delineates the storming of the Bastille on this Gamba shotgun, made up for France's Bicentennial.

While perfectly mastering the fundamentals of his art, Manrico Torcoli, has deliberately choosen to carve his phantasms in steel, with a great spontaneous talent, instead of quietly reproducing scrolls, game and dogs...The result is striking!

What about these designers? Whoever they can be, Austrians, French, Germans or Italians, they obviously share a sincere love for the art they have freely choosen, often leading them to sacrifice the normality of an ordinary life, for the satisfaction of their yearnings.

Thus, for Voere, the incentive is obviously the quest of ballistical progress; for Gabriel, that of a typical European answer to the "Practical Shooting" challenge of the "Major" class; the Bouchet mammoth express rifles are an epidermic reaction to the sophistications of expensive conventional models, unfitted to the continuous firing of the most powerful modern calibers.

The young Ducros is a phenomenon by himself, with a strong faith in purity, similar to that of the first surrealists. PGMs Morier and Kepeller are the high priests of 300-meter accuracy, while Korth is that of mechanical perfection. Such a propensity is shared by Cosmi e Figlio, Mario Abbiatico, Renato Gamba and Emilio Ghisoni in Italy, but reinforced by their unerring Latin sense of beauty. In the different field of engraving, such is also the case for Manrico Torcoli, who is successfully uniting steel and dream, without betraying the classical rules of his art.

What about them? They are all alike in this: they seek to achieve perfection with their own hands.   •

A Gamba Daytona model celebrates, with Abbiattico engraving, the Discovery of America in period art style.

by LAYNE SIMPSON

RIFLE REVIEW

Although not as big as the brown bear, this Alaska black bear required more walking and climbing in steep country with the 300 Ultra Mag.

No doubt about it, composite barrels are here to stay and you are on the verge of reading about some of them in this report. But that's just the start of it. The oldest firearms company in America is finally getting around to introducing its own 300 magnum cartridge and my 358 STA wildcat is now available in a very famous rifle. The 444 Marlin hasn't exactly found a new home but the old shack has been overhauled a bit for 1999. We've got new super accurate rifles and we've got a new lightweight bolt gun with a titanium receiver. Make room for yet another family of proprietary cartridges and while you're at it, do the same for a new autoloading rifle in 22 WMR that will surely sell. Takedown rifles are back in style and two more companies have now responded to the growing demand. Last but certainly not least, a new and improved version of a not-so-old 22 rimfire will have you, me and many others like us reaching for our checkbooks.

Accuracy International

The English firm of Accuracy International Ltd. has been around since 1968 and as the name implies its specialty is precision rifles capable of match-winning accuracy. The bolt action rifles are imported to the U.S. by Accuracy International North America, Inc. of Oak Ridge, Tennessee. A number of different variations are available, including the PAL-MASTER which conforms to both NRA and UIT rules, the CISMASTER which was designed for slow- and rapid-fire

Layne took this Alaska brown bear at about 60 yards with a Model 700 BDL/SS chambered for Remington's New 300 Ultra Mag back in September of 98.

The 22 caliber Marlin 7000T autoloader has a red, white and blue laminated wood stock, a heavy barrel and should shoot quite accurately.

The Mountain Eagle from MRI comes in right- and left-hand action and with standard or varmint-weight barrel.

military rifle competition, the PERRY-MASTER for across the course competition and the VARMINT. Various chamberings such as 22 BR, 223, 22-250, 22-243, 6mm BR, 243, 6.5x55, 7.5x55, and 308 are available. Hammerli and Anschutz sights are standard equipment on some models, while others are set up for scope mounting. Tactical models in various calibers such as 308, 300 Winchester Magnum, 338 Lapua and 50 BMG are also offered. Options include adjustable cheekpiece and buttplate, hinged bipod and a folding buttstock. These rifles look like they would shoot like a house afire.

American Hunting Rifles

Seems like each time I turn around someone else has added a new line to an already crowded field of proprietary cartridges. Latest examples are those available in rifles built around Model 70 actions by American Hunting Rifles of Hamilton, MT. Whereas the trend among other shops has been to see who could burn the heaviest charges of powder in various bore sizes, the AHR fellows are offering a line of in-between cartridges cooked up by Ken Howell. Simply described, the new case is nothing more than the 30-06 case lengthened to 2.6 inches and given a 25 degree shoulder angle. What you get is a cartridge with possibly a wee bit more performance than the 30-06 Improved but without the recoil of the magnums. It doesn't shoot as flat as a genuine magnum nor does it deliver as much punch away out yonder, but it doesn't make as much noise either. For now, they say five calibers are available, 220, 270, 300, 340 and 350.

ArmaLite, Inc.

According to the ArmaLite representative I talked to, the new-old AR-10B is intended to bring back some of the flavor of the early AR-10 and AR-15 rifles. Some of its oldie moldy features include the tapered handguard, grip shape and short buttstock of the early M16, all in the original brown colora-

tion. Just as noticeable, the early bolt handle (which resembles an upside-down trigger fingerpiece at the inside front of the carrying handle) is back. Chambered to 7.62mm NATO, this one has a 20 inch barrel and weighs 9-1/2 pounds. Also back for another try is the ArmaLite AR-7 survival rifle in 22 Long Rifle. You'll remember this one; when its barreled action is stowed inside its synthetic stock the rig measures only 16-1/2 inches long and, just like Ivory soap, if you drop it overboard it will float. Moving on to bigger things, as its AR-50 model designation might imply, a new single shot bolt action rifle from ArmaLite is chambered for 50 BMG. It has a 31 inch barrel, weighs

Remington's 180-grain Partition loading of the new 300 Ultra Mag worked equally well on this Alaska moose at 265 paces.

Marlin's 444P Outfitter offers a lot of noise and firepower in a compact package.

Beretta

Beretta's Mato is now available with walnut and synthetic stocks. For the benefit of those who are not familiar with this particular turnbolt rifle I'll mention that it has a detachable box magazine, controlled cartridge feed and fully adjustable trigger. From a distance you'd swear the action came as a result of mating Remington's Model 700 with Winchester's Model 70. The result is a rifle that costs about three times as much as either of those. Its chamberings range from 270 to 375 H&H Magnum, the latter option also available with a muzzle brake.

Browning

The BAR Mark II autoloader is now available in three variations: Safari with high-gloss wood finish, Classic with a satin wood finish, and Lightweight with an aluminum receiver and 20 inch barrel (standard chamberings) or 24 inch barrel (magnums). Chambering options run from the 22-250 to the 338 Winchester Magnum. The new A-Bolt II Classic has a no-shine blue job, satin-finished Monte Carlo stock with palm swell, while the equally new Micro Hunter has a short length of pull for those with short arms. Another new A-Bolt variant is the White Gold Medallion, called that because it combines a high-gloss walnut stock with a stainless steel barreled action. Moving on to rifles that make less noise, a new member of the BL22 family is the Classic with its gold-colored trigger, satin wood finish and cut checkering.

Dakota

Except for two steel plates dividing its two-piece walnut stock just forward of the receiver ring, the new Traveler takedown rifle looks exactly like any other Dakota 76 and is available with a left- or right-handed action. Its length when taken down is whatever length the barrel happens to be since that's the longer of the two pieces. Removing the barrel and forearm does not disturb the scope so the rifle should come close to holding its zero when taken down and then put back together. The Traveler can be ordered with extra barrels, so long as all chamberings remain in the same family. In other words, if your first choice is, say, the 257 Roberts, you might want to consider the 338-06 for the second barrel. The 300 Winchester Magnum and 416 Remington Magnum would also be a very useful pair.

Kimber

I'm one of those fellows who makes the annual pilgrimage to the SHOT Show each year to see what's new in the way of firearms, ammunition and accessories. As far as I'm concerned the clear winner in the rifle department at the 1999 show was the new Kimber Model 82 in 22 Long Rifle. For starters, this is not a rehash of the previous Model 82. Rather, it is a totally new rifle with a number of design features usually seen only on centerfire rifles. One is a Model 70-style safety lever on the bolt shroud. Another is a nonrotating Mauser-style extractor. Yep, you read correctly; the new Kimber has inherit-

ed the controlled feed of the old 22 caliber Mauser Model 34. Then we have an eccentric action and barrel fit which allows the firing pin to remain concentric or centered in the bolt just like a centerfire design. The receiver is machined from a special 4140-class steel and then heat treated. The bolt is machined from chrome moly and its locking lugs are case-hardened for durability. The trigger is fully adjustable. Four variations will be available initially: Classic with blued steel, nice walnut with 18-line cut checkering, steel grip cap, pillar bedding and match chamber; SuperAmerica with more of the same plus triple-A Claro walnut, beaded cheekrest, ebony foreend tip and 22-line checkering; Short Varmint Target with heavy 18-inch stainless steel barrel with lightening flutes, laminated wood stock; and Hunter Silhouette with checkered walnut stock and medium-heavy 24-inch barrel.

Krieghoff

Even though a 12-gauge Krieghoff over/under with subgauge tubes in 20, 28 and 410 is my shotgun of choice for most of the clay target shooting I manage to squeeze into my schedule, not until recently did I did realize the same company also offers a fine side-by-side double rifle. I examined a couple back in January and they were indeed nice. One called Classic has a boxlock action with 23-1/2 inch chopper lump barrels and double triggers. Depending on caliber, it weighs from 7-1/4 to 8 pounds. Chamberings range from the 308 to the 9.3x74R and at just under $8000 the cost is about 80 percent less than that

Adjemian APH 3000 is a sport-model as a single-shot, a SWAT special as a repeater, a French-made dandy either way.

The hollow synthetic buttstock and forearm of NEF's new Survivor in 223 and 308 have plenty of room for storage of extra ammo and other survival gear.

NEF is offering both grownup and youth versions of its Sportster Handi-Rifle in 22 rimfire.

of a Beretta Model 455. Extra sets of rifle barrels and 20-gauge shotgun barrels are also available. Then we have the Big Five version from Krieghoff. Similar to the Classic but it has an articulated front trigger which is a good thing since it is offered in 375 Flanged Nitro Express, 500/416 N.E., 470 N.E. and 500 N.E.

Lazzeroni

According to John Lazzeroni his Model 2000ST-28 is one of the fastest big game rifles in the West since its 7.82 Warbird chambering pushes the Barnes 130-grain X-Bullet along at 4000 fps. Such extreme velocity from a 30 caliber big-game cartridge can be equaled only by other equally big numbers such as the 30-378 Weatherby Magnum and the 30-416 Rigby, the latter a wildcat. The L2000ST-28 wears a Schmidt & Bender 2.5-10X scope with multi-dot reticle.

I have long been impressed by the quality of Lazzeroni rifles but have never found the styles of their stocks to be overly exciting. Or at least this held true prior to the introduction of the L2000SA Lightweight with its stock of more conventional shape and form. It weighs less than seven pounds and is available in the five short-action cham-

berings from the 243 Spitfire to the 416 Maverick, and while I have not actually shot one I do like the way it looks.

Those who desire to own a factory rifle chambered for a Lazzeroni cartridge but cannot handle their high cost might find it of interest to know that the 308 Warbird is slated to become available in the Sako TRG-S during late 1999.

Magnum Research, Inc.

Like the older Lone Eagle the new Mountain Eagle is built around an action built for Magnum Research by the Finnish firm of Sako. It is also available in a left-hand version. The standard rifle has a H-S Precision synthetic stock, 24-inch Krieger barrel, weighs around eight pounds and is available in a variety of standard and belted magnum chamberings with the most recent addition being the 7mm STW. The varmint rifle has a heavy 26 inch fluted stainless steel barrel in 222 or 223. A muzzle brake is also available. Also new from MRI is an aftermarket graphite-encased 18-inch barrel for the Ruger 10/22. It weighs less than a pound compared to 3-1/2 pounds for a steel bull barrel of the same length.

Marlin

Last year Marlin introduced the Guide Gun, a snubnosed version of its Model 1895SS lever action in 45-70 Government. This year it is the Outfitter, an abbreviated version of the Model 444SS in 444 Marlin. Notable features include a ported 18-1/2 inch barrel with Ballard-style cut rifling and open sights, cut checkering on walnut stock and forearm and quick-detach sling swivel posts. The buttstock of the little 6-3/4 pound carbine has a straight grip and square finger lever, both of which I like. One of these rigs filled with six handloaded cartridges capable of pushing the Nosler 250 Partition HG along at maximum speed would handle about anything in North America so long as the range does not greatly exceed 100 long paces.

Latest variation of the Model 336 is the Cowboy with a tubular magazine that holds six 30-30 or 38-55 cartridges. Other neat things include checkered walnut, straight-grip buttstock with square finger lever, blued steel forearm cap, and 25-inch tapered octagon barrel. There's also a new Cowboy version of the 22 caliber Model 39AS with all of the features I just described for its Model 336C mate. Continuing on with things 22 rimfire, we have the new

Model 7000T autoloader with a heavy 18-inch Micro-Groove barrel and laminated wood stock with red, white and blue coloration. Possibly the most interesting new item from North Haven is the Model 250 "Garden Gun", a bolt action mini-shotgun with a smoothbore barrel chambered for the CCI 22 WMR shot load. It is built around Marlin's ever-popular 22 rimfire action and should be just the ticket for dragonfly wingshooting.

New England Firearms

To me at least, the most interesting new item from NEF is the Superlight Handi-Rifle in 22 rimfire. Called the Sportster Rimfire, it has a 20-inch barrel and a Monte Carlo style synthetic stock. A Youth version with a shorter length of pull is also slated for production. Through its partnership with the NRA, the company is also introducing what it calls Youth Endowment Edition shotguns based on the current Pardner Youth line. To be produced in 20, 28 and 410, this one will have a high-gloss blued receiver, walnut stock and special engraving which will include the logo of the NRA Foundation. Also new from NEF is the Survivor Rifle with a heavy 22-inch barrel in 223 or 308 and oversized buttstock and forearm replete with interior compartments for stowing items such as fishing line and hook, candy bars, extra ammo and

Lyman's new tang sight for the '86 Winchester is old stuff, but plenty welcome.

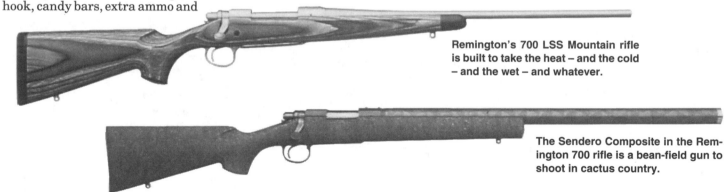

Remington's 700 LSS Mountain rifle is built to take the heat – and the cold – and the wet – and whatever.

The Sendero Composite in the Remington 700 rifle is a bean-field gun to shoot in cactus country.

a copy of "Rifle Review". Each rifle comes with a nylon carrying sling and quick-detach swivels. Last of all, the Handi-Rifle is now available in 357 Magnum.

Prairie Gun Works

Of all the rifles I have worked with during the past 12 months, one of the more impressive has been the Model T15 from the Canadian firm of Prairie Gun Works. Called the Model 15/T1 its action is quite similar in size and shape to the Remington Model 700 but its receiver is made of titanium. Use of the lightweight metal allows the builders of the rifle to put extra weight where it is

needed most, in the barrel. In other words, despite the fact that the rifle weighs less than 5-1/2 pounds, everything about it is full size. The 243 I've been shooting has a Krieger barrel and is extremely accurate. To date I have tried a dozen factory loads and those with bullets weighing 55 to 85 grains chalked up an overall aggregate of .823 inch while the various 100-grain deer loads averaged 1.095 inches. Best accuracy was with Federal's 70-grain Ballistic Tip and 60 grain hollowpoint loadings with respective averages of .492 and .440 inch. Needless to say, this is heavy-gun accuracy from a rifle light enough to tote up any steep mountain. I have chosen Prairie Gun Works to build the first rifle chambered for the next member of the STW family I'll be introducing during 1999. Called the 6.5

STW, you might see a report on rifle and cartridge right here next time we meet.

Remington

Biggest news from Remington for 1999 is the 300 Ultra Mag chambering. I got a sneak preview of the new cartridge and one of the rifles in which it will be available back in August of 1998 while hunting in Alaska with Art Wheaton and Jay Bunting of Remington. On that trip I took black bear, moose and a brown bear, the latter squaring only three inches shy of 10 feet. At the time, company officials were contemplating the introduction of two loads, 180-grain Nosler Partition and Remington Core-Lokt of the same weight, but later decided to only offer the former in 1999. The rifle I used was a Model 700 BDL/SS with a Leupold

2.5-8X scope and I took all my game with the Partition load. Ranges were inside 100 yards for the two bears and 265 long paces for the moose. Two bullets we managed to recover weighed 110.2 and 111.9 grains for over 60 percent weight retention. Overall length of the 300 Ultra Mag is the same as for full-length belted magnums such as the 300 H&H and 300 Weatherby but since it is basically a modified version of the 404 Jeffery case it has no belt and its body is considerably fatter. Even so, by modifying the magazine box of the Model 700, Remington engineers were able to squeeze four into the rifle, counting one in the chamber. Since the case has about 10 percent more capacity than that of the 300 Weatherby it will run about 100 fps faster than that cartridge when both are loaded to the same chamber pressure level. Unlike some of today's beltless magnums, you won't have to pay as much for a box of ammo as you paid for your scope; the cost will be about the same as a box of 300 Winchester Magnum ammo in Remington's Premier Safari Grade line. The new chambering is slated to become available in five standard production Model 700s- BDL, LSS, LSS/LH., Sendero SF and BDL/SS like the one I used in Alaska. The new chambering will also be available in the African Plains Rifles, Alaska Wilderness Rifle, Custom KS Mountain Rifle and Custom KS Stainless Mountain Rifle from Remington's custom shop.

Also big news from Remington is the introduction of a Model 700 with a composite barrel made by encasing a thin stainless steel rifled tube with epoxy-hardened graphite fiber. What we have here is an extremely thick barrel that's relatively light in weight but as rigid as an all-steel barrel weighing five times more, or so they say. In addition, the composite material is said to dissipate heat 10 times faster than steel which is good news to we varmint shooters. Two Model 700 variations will be available. Varmint Synthetic Composite in 223, 22-250 and 308 and Sendero Composite in 25-06, 7mm STW and 300 Winchester Magnum.

Remington began its limited edition series of Model 700 Classic rifles back in 1981 with the 7x57mm Mauser and followed that one with the 257 Roberts, 300 H&H Magnum, 250-3000 Savage, 350 Remington Magnum, 264 Winchester Magnum, 338 Winchester Magnum, 35 Whelen, 300 Weatherby Magnum, 25-06, 7mm Weatherby Magnum, 220 Swift, 222 Remington, 6.5x55mm Swedish, 300 Winchester Magnum, 375 H&H Magnum, 280 Remington, 8mm Remington Magnum. For 1999, it is the 17 Remington. About five years ago I got the jump on this year's offering by having the fellows in Remington's custom shop build for me a Model 700 Classic in 17 Remington. It shoots great with the Remington 25-grain factory load and even better with handloads that push Walt Berger's 30-grain moly-coated bullet along at 3900 fps or so.

Also new in the Model 700 lineup is the LSS Mountain Rifle with laminated wood stock and stainless steel barreled action in 260, 7mm-08, 270 and 30-06.

Robar

During a short visit with Robby Barrkman, president of Robar, a few weeks back, he showed me a line of custom big game rifles around various actions, including the Remington 700, Winchester 70 and Ruger 77. They are available in high-grade English or Claro walnut or synthetic with various finish colorations and the list of chamberings, both factory and wildcat is endless. This company also offers a variety of tactical rifles with one of the more interesting being the QR2 with its folding stock and half-minute-of-angle guarantee.

RND Manufacturing

Colt AR15 knock-offs are becoming quite common and one of the newest to be introduced is the 2000 from RND Manufacturing. Available in 223 and 308 it has CNC machined upper and lower receivers, a free-floating barrel, adjustable and quick-detachable buttstock, titanium firing pin, lightweight speed hammer, bolt buffer, black anodized Teflon finish, 3-1/2 pound trigger and laminated wood stock. Custom finishes are available, as are custom chamberings, including a 338 caliber wildcat.

Ruger

Lots of new stuff from Ruger for 1999. First there is a 10/22 autoloader with a steel receiver in 22 WMR. By making its bolt of a metal heavier than steel, Ruger technicians were able to control the increased backthrust of the 22 WMR with a blowback-operated action, and while this increased the toting weight of the rifle a bit its external dimensions are virtually the same as those of the regular 10/22 with its aluminum receiver. And since a new receiver had to be designed for the rifle anyhow, they went ahead and added Ruger's integral scope mounting base up top. The stock of the 10/22M is hardwood and it utilizes the same nine-round rotary magazine as the Model

This All-Weather version of the Ruger Mini-14 Ranch Rifle has a stainless steel barreled action and black synthetic stock.

The new Ruger 10/22M in 22 WMR has an integral scope mounting base on its steel receiver and will sell well.

77/22M. Also new are "All-Weather" variations of the Model 77, 77/44 and Mini 14, all with stainless steel barreled actions and synthetic stocks.

SIGARMS

One of the more unusual rifles I have examined lately is the Swedish-built SHR-970. The rifle is a switch-barrel design which may be a moot point for now since it is available only in 270 and 30-06. The addition of other options, mainly the 25-06 and possibly the 35 Whelen would make this particular outfit even more interesting. On the other hand, even if those never happen the detachable barrel is still not a bad idea since it allows the rifle to be taken down for more discreet carry through airports and other places where hunters must go.

Thompson/Center

T/C's Encore rifle family keeps growing with one of the newest additions having (guess what?) a stainless steel barreled action and black synthetic stock. Chambering options for that version as well as the blued-steel, wood-stocked gun range from 223 to 45-70 with 11 other possibilities between those two. One of these in 243, 260 or 7mm-08 would not be a bad choice for a youngster's first deer rifle.

Ultra Light Arms, Inc.

Sometime back a magazine editor who is reputed to never let accurate reporting stand in the way of a juicy story breathlessly stated that Ultra Light Arms had been sold to Colt. I asked Melvin Forbes about this and he says Colt is, in fact, negotiating to obtain a license to build a rifle with some of the features of his Model 20 but he had no intention of selling the company at that time. As I write this his plans are to continue building and selling the same line of fine lightweight rifles Ultra Light Arms has become famous for worldwide. They include the rifle that started it all, the 4-3/4 pound Model 20 in short chamberings ranging from 22 Hornet to 358 Winchester, the Model 24 for the 30-06 family of cartridges, the Model 28 in various short belted magnums and the Model 40 for really big guys like the 7mm STW, 30-378 Weatherby Magnum and 416 Rigby. And we must not overlook the Model 20RF which represents one of the finest 22 rimfires that can be bought for less than $1000.

USRAC

My old Model 70 Sporter, the one in 270 I used to bag the best mule deer of my life has now been replaced by the Sporter LT version. Actually, the only differences I see are thinner stock dimensions and a more open grip. But there's much more from USRAC. Between Marlin's Guide Gun and Outfitter versions of its Model 336 and USRAC's new Timber Carbine version of its Model 94, all bases are well covered when it comes down to slinging lead fast and making lots of noise. Available only in 444 Marlin, the new Timber Carbine has a whole covey of muzzle jump-reducing gas ports at the muzzle of its 17-3/4 inch barrel and a thin rubber pad out back. As interesting things from USRAC go, my gold star goes to the Model 1886 Takedown with its octagon barrel in 45-70. Come May I'll be hunting black bear on Vancouver Island and this might just be the rifle I'll take down into two pieces and stow in my duffel bag for that trip. I also like the looks of the new Model 92 Short Rifle with its full-length magazine and 20 inch barrel in 357 Magnum, 44-40 or 45 Colt. A new custom shop offering is the Model 70 Custom Safari Express in my own 358 Shooting Times Alaskan, a cartridge I used to take a nice brown bear some years ago. Other custom shop goodies include the Model 70 Ultimate Classic with numerous options such as round, fluted-round, half-round, half-octagon or full-octagon barrel, the Model 70 Ultra Light Mannlicher with its full-length stock and the Model 70 Custom African Express in magnum chamberings from the 340 Weatherby to the 458 Winchester. Each member of USRAC's family of compacts has a length of pull ranging from 12-1/2 to 13 inches and are just the ticket for those who find standard-length stocks too long. Regardless of whether your needs lean toward a Model 1300 scattergun, a Model 70 Classic or Model 70 Ranger or perhaps a Model 94, USRAC has a compact for you. Last but not least, all Winchester firearms made by or for USRAC will come with a cable-style lock that deters anyone without a key or cable cutter from shooting them.

Weatherby

Limited to a maximum of 700 rifles (with serial numbers ranging from 1 to 700), a special custom grade Mark V Sporter in 300 Weatherby Magnum will be available for purchase only at Friends of NRA events. Each rifle will be accompanied by Paco Young's "Too Close For Comfort" which has been chosen wildlife print of the year. Acid-etched in 24-karat gold, the floorplate depicts a game scene from the print. Other features include a 26 inch barrel, gold-plated quick-detach sling swivels, walnut stock with high-gloss finish and cut checkering, one-inch thick black recoil pad and matte blued metal finish. For the benefit of those who might not be aware, Friends of NRA is a grassroots fundraising program originated to support the mission of the NRA.

Also to be built in a limited quantity of 200 but for the Rocky Mountain Elk Foundation is a Mark V Accumark chambered for my own 7mm STW. This

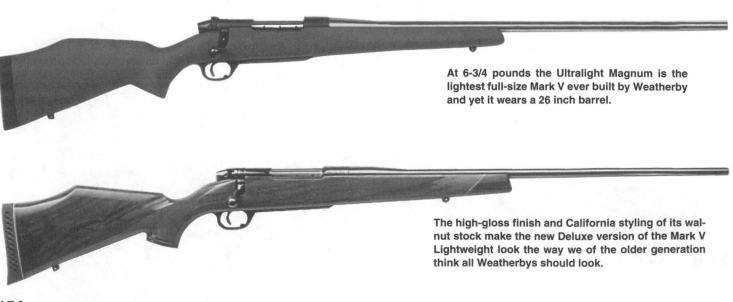

At 6-3/4 pounds the Ultralight Magnum is the lightest full-size Mark V ever built by Weatherby and yet it wears a 26 inch barrel.

The high-gloss finish and California styling of its walnut stock make the new Deluxe version of the Mark V Lightweight look the way we of the older generation think all Weatherbys should look.

one will have a 26-inch barrel and the RMEF logo laser-engraved on the body of its bolt.

Southpaw shooters are sure to become excited when they learn of Weatherby's announcement of a Mark V Accumark with its bolt handle over on their side of its action. This, by the way, is the first left-hand bolt gun the company has offered since production was moved from Japan to Maine back in 1985. The list of chambering options will include a lineup of Weatherby belted magnums ranging from the 257 Magnum to the 338-378 plus Remington's 7mm Magnum and Winchester's 300 Magnum.

As far as I know, the new Mark V Ultra Lightweight Magnum is the lightest standard-production bolt gun ever built by Weatherby on its full-length Mark V action. Its heft of only 6-3/4 pounds was accomplished by utilizing several ounce-trimming tricks, including flutes in the bolt shroud, wider and deeper flutes machined into barrel and bolt body and swiss-cheesed bolt handle. More ounces were trimmed away by replacing steel with aluminum in areas such as the magazine follower and trigger guard/floorplate assembly. The lightweight stock is a Kevlar/fiberglass composite and has an aluminum bedding block system. And yet, light as the rifle is, those clever engineers managed to retain the 26-inch barrel which is needed for squeezing maximum speed from cartridges such as Weatherby's 257, 270, 7mm and 300 Magnums as well as the 7mm Remington and 300 Winchester magnums.

A new version of the Mark V Lightweight has a Monte Carlo style walnut stock and yet it weighs less than seven pounds. Called the lightweight Deluxe, its chamberings are 22-250, 243, 7mm-08, 308, 25-06, 270, 280, 30-06 and 240 Weatherby Magnum. Sometime back I carried one of these on a hunt for mule deer and was impressed by the way its accuracy not to mention the we it handled. •

About Those Other Guns

Since I have reported only on new rifles in Gun Digest for the past couple of decades I'm sure some readers are not aware of the fact that I am just as involved in handgunning and shotgunning and write about those subjects as well. Fact of the matter is, I hold a Master rating in USPSA action pistol competition and hunt big game and varmints a great deal with various handguns. I enjoy shotgunning equally well, mostly for feathered targets but I also shoot a bit of trap, skeet and sporting clays. Sometime back I was asked what guns I would keep if I had to thin them down to just a few and two of the scatterguns that survived the weeding out were a 12-gauge Krieghoff over/under with subgauge tubes in 20, 28 and 410 for clay targets and a 1930s vintage 20-gauge Westley Richards side-by-side with 28-inch barrels, straight wrist and splinter forearm for about everything else.

I'm really lucky in a number of ways not the least of which is the amount of big game hunting I get to do and the 21-day hunt in Alaska with my good friends Art Wheaton and Jay Bunting I mentioned in this report was one of the very best. A fantastic trip! And if I had to pick a couple more recent hunts that ranked right up there at the top one would be the trip to Uruguay with Kent Cartridge to field test that company's new Tungsten Matrix nontoxic waterfowl loads. We shot ducks each morning and either partridge or spotted wing pigeon each afternoon and the rest of the time we ate. Great fun!

Then there was the Missouri cottontail rabbit hunt with a couple of other woods buddies by the name of Kevin Howard and Mike Jordan. I started out with a Browning Gold and finished up with Mike's little Winchester 42 in 410. But anybody who has done it knows that shooting rabbits ain't where the fun is in rabbit hunting; it's listening to a pack of beagles cry their little hearts out. Back when I was a youngster my father raised, trained and sold beagles so I grew up on rabbit hunting. Maybe that's why I still enjoy it so much today.

Layne Simpson

Simpson and a friend on a happy day afield

THE GUN DIGEST WEB DIRECTORY

By Holt Bodinson

Faster than a speeding bullet, the firearms industry has adopted the Internet as an essential vehicle for reaching its customer and dealer base. With 60,000 new Internet users going online each day, it's not hard to understand why.

The growth in firearm related Web sites over the last year has been phenomenal. Not only are most of the major players online with colorful presentations of their products and services, but there are now even subscription based, online, gun magazines as well as numerous chat rooms and interactive sites. As a measure of the impact the computer is having on our sport, Sierra Bullets just released the 4th edition of its reloading manuals and its new exterior ballistics program on a single computer CD disk. In truth, a computer is becoming as essential a part of the reloading bench as a progressive loading press.

The following index of current Web sites is offered to our readers as a convenient jumping-off point. The Internet is such a dynamic and changing environment that half the fun is just exploring what's out there. Considering that most of the Web sites have hot links to other firearm-related Web sites, the Internet trail just goes on-and-on once you've taken the initial step to go online.

Here are a few pointers:

If the web site you desire is not listed, try using the full name of the company, typed without spaces, between www.-and-.com, for example, www.krause.com. Probably 95% of current Web sites are based on this simple, self-explanatory format.

Try a variety of search engines like Microsoft Internet Explorer, Yahoo, HotBot, AltaVista, Lycos, Excite, InfoSeek and Webcrawler while using key words such as gun, firearm, rifle, pistol, shooting, hunting -- frankly, any word that relates to the sport. Sport's not a bad word either. Each search engine seems to comb through the World Wide Web in a different fashion and produces different results. And the results can be surprising. When using the keyword "shooting", InfoSeek came up with 1,311,428 references on the Web while Hot-Bot lead me to the shooting and hunting art collection of a prominent Parisian art dealer. Accessing the various search engines is simple. Just type www.yahoo.com for example, and you're on your way.

Finally, the best introduction to firearms-related Web sites is a large, specialized Web site like Shooter's Online Services located at www.shooters.com. There are enough firearm-related links at shooters.com to make your trip down the Internet highway a rewarding adventure.

Good surfing!

AMMUNITION AND COMPONENTS

3D Ammunition **www.3dammo.com**
4W Ammunition and Reloading Supplies **www.texans.com/texans**
Accurate Arms Co. Inc **www.accuratepowder.com**
ADCO/Nobel Sport Powder **www.adcosales.com**
All Purpose Ammunition **www.dragonbreath.com**
Alliant Powder **www.alliantpowder.com**
Ammo Depot **www.ammodepot.com**
Arizona Ammunition, Inc. **www.arizonaammunition.com**
Ballard Rifle & Cartridge LLC **www.ballardrifles.com**
Ballistic Products, Inc. **www.ballisticproducts.com**
Barnes Bullets **www.barnesbullets.com**
Berger Bullets, Ltd. **www.bergerbullets.com**
Berry's Mfg., Inc. **www.berrysmfg.com**
Bismuth Cartridge Co. **www.bismuth-notox.com**
Black Hills Ammunition, Inc. **www.black-hills.com**

Brenneke of America Ltd. **turpin@kih.net**
Bull-X inc. **www.bull-x.com**
CCI-Blount **www.blount.com**
Century Arms **www.centuryarms.com**
Cheaper Than Dirt **www.cheaperthandirt.com**
Clean Shot Powder **www.cleanshot.com**
Cor-Bon **www.cor-bon.com**
Denver Bullet Co. **denbullets@aol.com**
DKT, Inc. **www.expresspages.com/d/dktinc**
Dynamit Nobel RWS Inc. **www.shooters.com/rws**
Elephant Black Powder **www.elephantblackpowder.com**
Eley Ammunition **www.shooters.com/eley**
Eley Hawk Ltd. **www.eleyhawk.com**
Eley Limited **www.eley.co.uk**
Federal Cartridge Co. **www.federalcartridge.com**

WEB DIRECTORY

Fiocchi of America **www.fiocchiusa.com**
Fowler Bullets **www.benchrest.com/fowler**
Glaser Safety Slug, Inc. **www.safetyslug.com**
GOEX Inc. **www.goexpowder.com**
Graf & Sons **graf@email-pinet.net**
Hirtenberger **kengsfirearms@mindspring.com**
Hodgdon Powder **www.hodgdon.com**
Hornady **www.hornady.com**
Hull Cartridge **www.hullcartridge.com**
Huntington Reloading Products **www.huntingtons.com**
Impact Bullets **www.impactbullets.com**
IMR Smokeless Powders **www.imrpowder.com**
Keng's Firearms Specialty **kengsfirearms@mindspring.com**
Kynoch Ammunition **kynamco@aol.com**
Lapua **www.lapua-usa.com**
Laser-Cast **www.laser-cast.com**
Lazzeroni Arms Co. **www.lazzeroni.com**
Lightfield Slug Group **slugrp@bedford.net**
Lomont Precision Bullets **www.klomont.com/kent**
Lyman **www.lymanproducts.com**
Magnus Bullets **www.magnusbullets.com**
Mast Technology **www.bellammo.com**
Miltex, Inc. **www.miltexuas.com**
National Bullet Co. **www.nationalbullet.com**
Nobel Sport **www.adcosales.com**
Nosler Bullets Inc **www.nosler.com**

Old Western Scrounger **www.snowcrest.net/oldwest**
Oregon Trail/Laser-Cast Bullets **www.shooters.com/lasercast**
Pattern Control **www.patterncontrol.com**
PMC-Eldorado Cartridge **www.pmcammo.com**
Primex Technologies Inc. **ksstase11@primextech.com**
Pro Load Ammunition **www.proload.com**
Rainier Ballistics **www.rainierballistics.com**
Reloading Specialties Inc. **www.reloadingspecialties.com**
Remington **www.remington.com**
Sauvestre Slug **kengsfirearms@mindspring.com**
Sellier & Bellot USA Inc. **www.sb-usa.com**
Shilen **www.shilen.com**
Sierra **www.sierrabullets.com**
Slug Group Inc. **slugrp@bedford.net**
Speer-Blount **www.blount.com**
Sporting Supplies Int'l Inc. **www.ssiintl.com**
Starline **www.starlinebrass.com**
Triton Cartridge **www.triton-ammo.com**
Tru-Tracer **novasci@execpc.com**
Vihtavuori Lapua **kaltron@concentric.net**
Western Powders Inc. **www.westernpowders.com**
Widener's Reloading & Shooters Supply **www.wideners.com**
Winchester Ammunition **www.winchester. com**
Woodleigh Bullets **zedfield@apollo.ruralnet.net.au**
Zanders Sporting Goods **www.gzanders.com**

CASES, SAFES, GUN LOCKS, AND CABINETS

AG English Sales Co. **www.agenglish.com**
All Americas' Outdoors **www.innernet.net/gunsafe**
Alpine Cases **www.0800.co.za/alpine**
Aluma Sport by Dee Zee **www.deezee.com**
American Security Products **www.amsecusa.com**
Americase **www.americase.com**
Bear Track Cases **www.beartrackcases.com**
Boyt Harness Co. **sales@boytharness.com**
Bulldog Gun Safe Co. **www.gardall.com**
Cannon Safe Co. **www.cannonsafe.com**
Fort Knox Safes **www.ftknox.com**
Franzen Security Products **www.securecase.com**
Frontier Safe Co. **www.fronteirsafe.com**
Granite Security Products **www.granitesafe.com**
Gunlocker Phoenix USA Inc. **www.gunlocker.com**
GunVault **www.gunvault.com**
Hakuba USA Inc. **www.hakubausa.com**
Heritage Safe Co. **www.heritagesafecompany.com**
Hide-A-Gun **www.hide-a-gun.com**
Hunter Company **www.huntercompany.com**

Kolpin Mfg. Co. **www.kolpin.com**
Liberty Safe & Security **www.libertysafe.com**
Noble Security Systems Inc. **www.noble.co.ll**
Phoenix USA Inc. **www.gunlocker.com**
Rocky Mountain Safe Inc. **www.rockymountainsafe.com**
Saf-T-Hammer **www.saf-t-hammer.com**
Saf-T-Lok Corp. **www.saf-t-lok.com**
San Angelo All-Aluminum Products Inc. **sasptuld@x.net-com.com**
Securecase **www.securecase.com**
Shot Lock Corp. **www.shotlock.com**
Smart Lock Technology Inc. **www.smartlock.com**
Sportsmans Steel Safe Co. **www.sportsmansteelsafes.com**
Stack-On Products Co. **www.stack-on.com**
T.Z. Case Int'l **www.tz-case.com**
Treadlock Security Safes **www.treadlok.com**
Versatile Rack Co. **www.versatilegunrack.com**
V-Line Industries **www.vlineind.com**
Winchester Safes **www.fireking.com**
Ziegel Engineering **ziegel@aolcom**

CHOKE DEVICES, RECOIL REDUCERS, AND ACCURACY DEVICES

100 Straight Products **Bbowen999@aol.com**
Answer Products Co. **www.thewild.com/answer/**
Briley Mfg **www.briley.com**
Carlson's **www.carlsonschokes.com**

Colonial Arms www.**colonialarms.com**
Mag-Na-Port Int'l Inc. **www.magnaport.com**

WEB DIRECTORY

CHRONOGRAPHS

Competitive Edge Dynamics **www.cedhk.com**
Oehler Research Inc. **www.oehler-research.com**

PACT **www.pact.com**
Shooting Chrony Inc **www.pathcom.com/~chrony**

CLEANING PRODUCTS

Accupro **www.accupro.com**
Ballistol USA **www.ballistol.com**
Birchwood Casey **www.birchwoodcasey.com**
Bore Tech **www.boretech.com**
Break-Free, Inc. **break-free@worldnet.att.net**
G 96 **www.g96.com**
Hoppes **www.hoppes.com**
Kleen-Bore Inc. **www.kleen-bore.com**
L&R Mfg. **www.lrultrasonics.com**

Mpro 7 Gun Care **www.mp7.com**
National Tech Labs, Inc. **www.guncleaner.com**
Outers **www.blount.com**
Ok-Yoke Originals Inc. **www.oxyoke.com**
Sentry Solutions Ltd. **www.sentrysolutions.com**
Shooters Choice Gun Care **www.shooters-choice.com**
Silencio **www.silencio.com**
Tetra Gun **www.tetraproducts.com**
World's Fastest Gun Bore Cleaner **www.guncleaner.com**

FIREARM MANUFACTURERS AND IMPORTERS

AAR, Inc. **www.iar-arms.com**
Ace Custom 45's **www.acecustom45.com**
Advanced Weapons Technology **www.AWT-Zastava.com**
Aldo Uberti & Co. **uberti@lumetel.it**
American Derringer Corp. **www.amderringer.com**
AMT **www.amtguns.com**
Answer Products Co. **www.thewild.com/answer/**
AR-7 Industries, LLC **www.ar-7.com**
Armalite **www.armalite.com**
Arms Corp. of the Philippines **armscor@info.com.ph**
Arnold Arms **www.arnoldarms.com**
Autauga Arms, Inc. **autaugaarms@mindspring.com**
Axtell Rifle Co. **www.riflesmith.com**
Ballard Rifle & Cartridge LLC **www.ballardrifles.com**
Barrett Firearms Mfg. **www.barrettrifles.com**
Beeman Precision Airguns **www.beeman.com**
Benelli USA Corp. **www.benelliusa.com**
Benjamin Sheridan **www.crosman.com**
Beretta U.S.A. Corp. **www.berettausa.com**
Bill Hanus Birdguns **www.billhanusbirdguns.com**
Blackstar **www.benchrest.com/blackstar**
Bond Arms **www.bondarms.com**
Borden's Accuracy **www.benchrest.com/borden**
Bowen Classic Arms **www.bowenclassicarms.com**
Briley Mfg **www.briley.com**
BRNO Arms **www.zbrojouka.com**
Brolin Arms **www.shooters.com/brolin/**
Browning **www.browning.com**
BUL Transmark, Ltd. **www.aquanet.co.il/bul m5**
Bushmaster Firearms/Quality Parts **www.bushmaster.com**
Casull Arms Corp. **www.casullarms.com**
Century Arms **www.centuryarms.com**
Charles Daly **www.charlesdaly.com**
Christensen Arms **www.christensenarms.com**
Cimarron Firearms Co. **www.cimarron-firearm.com**
Clark Custom Guns **www.clarkcustomguns.com**

Colt Mfg Co. **www.colt.com**
Connecticut Valley Arms **www.cva.com**
CoonanArms **www.uslink.net/~cruzer/main/htm**
Cooper Firearms **www.cooperfirearms.com**
Crosman **www.crosman.com**
CZ USA **www.cz-usa.com**
    www.czub.cz
D.S.A., Inc. **www.dsarms.com**
Daisy Mfg Co. **www.daisy.com**
Dakota Arms Inc. **www.dakotaarms .com**
Davis Industries **www.davisindguns.com**
DZ Arms **www.tool-fix.com/dzarms.html**
Enterprise Arms **www.enterprise.com**
European American Armory Corp. **www.eaacorp.com**
Freedom Arms **www.cyberhighway.net/~freedom**
Gamo **www.gamo.com**
Gibbs Rifle Company **www.gibbsrifle.com**
Glock **www.glockworks.com**
Griffin & Howe **www.griffinhowe.com**
GSI Inc. **www.gsifirearms.com**
H&R 1871, Inc., New England Firearms, **H&R**
    hr1871@hr1871.com
Hammerli **www.hammerli.com**
Harris Gunworks **www.harrisgunworks.com**
Heavy Express, Inc. **www.heavyexpress.com**
Heckler and Koch **www.hecklerkoch-usa.com**
Henry Repeating Arms Co. **www.henryrepeating.com**
High Standard Mfg. **www.highstandard.com**
Hi-Point Firearms **www.hi-poinfirearms.com**
H-S Precision **www.hsprecision.com**
Interarms **www.interarms.com**
Intrac Arms International LLC **defence@dldnet.com**
Israel Arms **www.israelarms.com**
Ithaca Gun Co. **www.ithacagun.com**
JP Enterprises, Inc. **www.jpar15.com**
Kahr Arms **www.kahr.com**

WEB DIRECTORY

Kel-Tech CNC Ind., Inc. **www.kel-tec.com**
Kimber **www.kimberamerica.com**
Knight Mfg. Co. **kacsr25@aol.com**
Krieghoff GmbH **www.krieghoff.de**
Krieghoff Int'l **www.shootingsports.com**
LAR, Inc. **www.iar-arms.com**
Lazzeroni Arms Co. **www.lazzeroni.com**
Les Baer Custom, Inc. **www.lesbaer.com**
Magnum Research **www.magnumresearch.com**
Marksman Products **www.marksman.com**
Marlin **www.marlinfirearms.com**
McMillan Bros Rifle Co. **www.mcfamily.com**
Merkel **www.gsifirearms.com**
Miltext, Inc. **www.miltexusa.com**
Navy Arms **www.navyarms.com**
North American Arms **www.naaminis.com**
Nowlin Mfg. Inc. **www.nowlinguns.com**
O.F. Mossberg & Sons **www.mossberg.com**
Olympic Arms **www.olyarms.com**
Para-Ordnance **www.paraord.com**
Pedersoli Davide & Co. **www.davide-pedersoli.com**
Remington **www.remington.com**
Republic Arms Inc. **www.republicarmsinc.com**
Rogue Rifle Co. Inc. **www.chipmunkrifle.com**
Rossi Arms **www.rossiusa.com**
RPM **www.rpmxlpistols.com**
Sabatti SpA **info@sabatti.it**
Safari Arms **www.olyarms.com**

Samco Global Arms Inc. **www.samcoglobal.com**
Savage Arms Inc. **www.savagearms.com**
Scattergun Technologies Inc. **www.scattergun.com**
SIG Arms, Inc. **www.sigarms.com**
SKB Shotguns **www.skbshotguns.com**
Slug Group Inc. **slugrp@bedford.net**
Smith & Wesson **www.smith-wesson.com**
Springfield Armory **www.springfield-armory.com**
SSK Industries **www.shooters.com/ssk**
Steyr Mannlicher **www.gsifirearms.com**
STL Int'l **sales@sti-guns.com**
Strayer-Voight Inc. **strayer@airmail.net**
Sturm, Ruger & Company **www.ruger-firearms.com**
Taurus **www.taurususa.com**
The 1877 Sharps Co. **www.1877 sharps.com**
The Robar Co. **www.robarguns.com**
Thompson Center Arms **www.tcarms.com**
Traditions **www.traditionsmuzzle.com**
Uberti USA, Inc. **www.uberti.com**
United States Fire Arms Mfg. Co. **www.usfirearms.com**
Vektor USA **vektorusa@series2000.com**
Volquartsen Custom Ltd. **www.volquartsen.com**
Weatherby **www.weatherby.com**
Webley Scott Ltd. **www.webley.g.uk**
William Larkin Moore & Co. **www.doublegun.com**
Wilson Combat **www.wilsoncombat.com**
Wilson's Gun Shop Inc. **www.wilsoncombat.com**
Winchester Firearms **www.winchester-guns.com**

GUN PARTS, BARRELS, AFTER-MARKET ACCESSORIES

300 Below **www.300below.com**
Accuracy Speaks, Inc. **www.accuracyspeaks.com**
American Spirit Arms Corp. **www.gunkits.com**
Badger Barrels, Inc. **www.badgerbarrels.com**
Bar-Sto Precision Machine **barsto@eee.org**
Blackstar **www.benchrest.com/blackstar**
Buffer Technologies **www.buffertech.com**
Bushmaster Firearms/Quality Parts **www.bushmaster.com**
Butler Creek Corp **www.butler-creek.com**
Caspian Arms Ltd. **Caspianarm@aol.com**
Cheaper Than Dirt **www.cheaperthandirt.com**
Chestnut Ridge **www.chestnutridge.com**
Chip McCormick Corp **www.chipmccormickcorp.com**
Colonia Arms **www.colonialarms.com**
Cylinder & Slide Shop **www.cylinder-slide.com**
Dixie Gun Works **www.dixiegun.com**
DPMS **www.dpmsinc.com**
DSA, Inc. **www.dsarms.com**
Ed Brown Products **www.edbrown.com**
EFK Marketing/Fire Dragon Pistol Accessories **www.flmfire.com**
Federal Arms **www.fedarms.com**
Gun Parts Corp. **www.gunpartscorp.com**

Hastings Barrels **www.hastingsbarrels.com**
International Training Concepts Inc. **isub4itc@gvi.net**
J&T Distributing **www.jtsurplus.com**
Jonathan Arthur Ciener, Inc. **www.221rconversions.com**
JP Enterprises **www.jpar15.com**
King's Gunworks **www.kingsgunworks.com**
Les Baer Custom, Inc. **www.lesbaer.com**
Lilja Barrels **www.riflebarrels.com**
Lothar Walther Precision Tools Inc. **www.lothar-walther.de**
M&A Parts, Inc. **www.m-aparts.com**
MEC-GAR SrL **www.mec-gar.it**
Michaels of Oregon Co. **www.michaels-oregon.com**
Pachmayr **www.pachmayr.com**
Pac-Nor Barreling **www.pac-nor.com**
Para Ordinance Pro Shop **www.ltms.com**
Point Tech Inc. **pointec@ibm.net**
Promag Industries **www.promagindustries.com**
Rocky Mountain Arms **www.rockymountainarms.com**
Royal Arms Int'l **www.royalarms.com**
Sarco Inc. **www.webspan.net/~sarco/**
Scattergun Technologies Inc. **www.scattergun.com**
Shilen **www.shilen.com**

WEB DIRECTORY

Smith & Alexander Inc. **sa1911@gte.net**
Speed Shooters Int'l **www.shooternet.com/ssi**
Sprinco USA Inc. **sprinco@primenet.com**
SSK Industries **www.shooters.com/apg/members.htm**
Tapco **www.tapco.com**
Triple K Manufacturing Co. Inc. **www.triplek.com**
U.S.A. Magazines Inc. **www.usa-magazines.com**
Verney-Carron SA **www.verney-carron.com**

Volquartsen Custom Ltd. **www.volquartsen.com**
W.C. Wolff Co. **www.gunsprings.com**
Waller & Son **www.wallerandson.com**
Weigand Combat Handguns **www.weigandcombat.com**
Western Gun Parts **www.westerngunparts.com**
Wilson Combat **www.wilsoncombat.com**
Wisner's Inc. **www.localaccess.com/gunparts/**
Z-M Weapons **www.zmweapons.com/home.htm**

GUNSMITHING SUPPLIES AND INSTRUCTIONS

American Gunsmithing Institute **www.americangunsmith.com**
Brownells, Inc. **www.brownells.com**
B-Square Co. **www.b-square.com**
Clymer Mfg. Co. **www.clymertool.com**
Craftguard Metal Finishing **crftgrd@aol.com**
Du-Lite Corp. **www.dulite.com**

Dvorak Instruments **www.dvorakinstruments.com**
Gradiant Lens Corp. **www.gradiantlens.com**
JGS Precision Tool Mfg. LLC **jgstools@harborside.com**
Midway **www.midwayusa.com**
Olympus America Inc. **www.olympus.com**

HANDGUNS GRIPS

Ajax Custom Grips, Inc. **www.ajaxgrips.com**
Barami Corp. **www.baramihipgrip.com**
Eagle Grips **www.eaglegrips.com**
Fitz Pistol Grip Co. **johnpaul@snowcrest.net**
Hogue Grips **www.getgrip.com**

Lasergrips **www.crimsontrace.com**
Lett Custom Grips **www.lettgrips.com**
Pachmayr **www.pachmayr.com**
Pearce Grips **www.pearcegrips.com**
Uncle Mike's: **www.uncle-mikes.com**

HOLSTERS AND LEATHER PRODUCTS

Aker Leather Products **www.akerleather.com**
Alessi Distributor R&F Inc. **www.alessiholsters.com**
Bianchi **www.bianchiinternational.com**
Blackhills Leather **www.blackhillsleather.com**
BodyHugger Holsters **www.nikolais.com**
Brigade Gun Leather **www.brigadegunleather.com**
Chimere **www.chimere.com**
Classic Old West Styles **www.cows.com**
Conceal It **www.conceal-it.com**
Conceal 'N Draw **feminine.protection@airmail.net**
Coronado Leather Co. **www.coronadoleather.com**
Creedmoor Sports, Inc. **www.creedmoorsports.com**
Custom Leather Wear **www.customleatherwear.com**
Defense Security Products **www.thunderwear.com**
DeSantis Holster **www.desantisholster.com**
Dillon Precision **www.dillonprecision .com**
Don Hume Leathergoods, Inc. **www.donhume.com**
Ernie Hill International **www.erniehill.com**
First **www.first-inc.com**
Front Line Ltd. **frontlin@internet-zahav.net**
Galco **www.usgalco.com**
Gilmore's Sports Concepts **www.gilmoresports.com**
Gould & Goodrich **www.goulduse.com**
Gunmate Products **www.gun-mate.com**
Hellweg Ltd. **www.hellwegltd.com**
Hide-A-Gun **www.hide-a-gun.com**
Hunter Co. **www.huntercompany.com**

Kirkpatrick Leather Company **mjkmao@aol.com**
Kramer Leather **www.kraemerleather.com**
Law Concealment Systems **www.handgunconcealment.com**
Levy's Leathers Ltd. **www.levysleathers.com**
Michaels of Oregon Co. **www.michaels-oregon.com**
Mitch Rosen Extraordinary Gunleather **www.mitchrosen.com**
Old World Leather **www.gun-mate.com**
Pager pal **www.pagerpal.com**
Phalanx Corp. **www.phalanxarms.com**
PWL **www.pwlusa.com**
Rumanya Inc. **www.rumanya.com**
Safariland Ltd. Inc **www.safariland.com**
Safariland Ltd. Inc. **www.safariland.com**
Shooting Systems Group Inc. **www.shootingsystems.com**
Strictly Anything Inc. **www.strictlyanything.com**
Strong Holster Co. **www.strong-holster.com**
The Belt Co. **www.conceal-it.com**
The Leather Factory Inc. **lflandry@flash.net**
The Outdoor Connection **www.outdoorconnection.com**
Top-Line USA Inc. **www.toplineusa.com**
Triple K Manufacturing Co. **www.triplek.com**
Wilson Combat **www.wilsoncombat.com**

WEB DIRECTORY

MISCELLANEOUS SHOOTING PRODUCTS

10X Products Group www.10Xwear.com
Aero Peltor www.aearo.com
Dalloz Safety www.cdalloz.com
Deben Group Industries Inc. www.deben.com
E.A.R., Inc. www.earinc.com

Johnny Stewart Wildlife Calls www.stewartoutdoors.com
North Safety Products www.northsafety-brea.com
Second Chance Body Armor Inc. email@secondchance.com
Silencio www.silencio.com
Walker's Game Ear Inc. www.walkersgameear.com

MUZZLELOADING FIREARMS AND PRODUCTS

Austin & Halleck, Inc. austinhal@aol.com
Dixie Gun Works, Inc. www.dixiegun.com
Knight Rifles www.knightrifles.com
Lyman www.lymanproducts.com
Mountain State Muzzleloading muzzleloading@citynet.net
Muzzleloading Technologies, Inc. www.mtimuzzleloading.com

October Country Muzzleloading rifle@oct-country.com
Ox-Yoke Originals Inc. www.oxyoke.com
Rightnour Mfg. Co. Inc. www.rmcsports.com
Thompson Center Arms www.tcarms.com
Traditions Performance Muzzleloading www.traditionsmuzzle.com

PUBLICATIONS, VIDEOS, AND CD'S

Airgun Letter www.airgunletter.com
American Firearms Industry www.amfire.com
American Shooting Magazine www.americanshooting.com
American Shooting Magazine www.rust.net
Blacksmith bcbooks@glasscity.net
Blue Book Publications www.bluebookinc.com
Combat Handguns www.combathandguns.com
Countrywide Press www.countrysport.com
DBI Books/Krause Publications www.krause.com
Delta Force www.infogo.com/delta
Discount Gun Books www.discountgunbooks.com
Gun List www.krause.com
Gun Video www.gunvideo.com
Gunweb Magazine WWW Links www.imags.com
Harris Publications www.harrispublications.com
Heritage Gun Books www.gunbooks.com
Krause Publications www.krause.com
Munden Enterprises Inc. www.bob-munden.com
Outdoor Videos www.outdoorvideos.com
Precision Shooting www.precisionshooting .com
Rifle and Handloader Magazines www.riflemagazine.com

Rifle and Shotgun Magazine/Gun Journal www.natcom-publications.com
Safari Press Inc. www.safaripress.com
Shooters News www.shootersnews.com
Shooting Sports Retailer ssretailer@ad.com
Shotgun News www.shotgunnews.com
Shotgun Report www.shotgunreport.com
Shotgun Sports Magazine www.shotgun-sports.com
Small Arms Review www.smallarmsreview.com
Sporting Clays Web Edition www.sportingclays.com
Sports Afield www.sportsafield.com
Sports Trend www.sportstrend.com
Sportsmen on Film www.sportsmenonfilm.com
Tactical Shooter www.tacticalshooter.com
The Gun Journal www.shooters.com
The Shootin Iron www.off-road.com/4x4web/si/si.html
The Single Shot Exchange Magazine singleshot@earthlink.net
Voyageur Press www.voyageurpress.com
Vulcan Outdoors Inc. www.vulcanpub.com
Wolfe Publishing Co. wolfepub@bslnet.com

RELOADING TOOLS AND SUPPLIES

Ballisti-Cast Mfg. ballisti@ndak.net
Bruno Shooters Supply www.brunoshooters.com
Bullet Moulds www.bulletmolds.com
Corbin Mfg & Supply Co. www.corbins.com
Dillon Precision www.dillonprecision.com
Forster Precision Products www.forsterproducts.com
Harrell's Precision www.harrellsprec.com
Hornady www.hornady.com
Huntington Reloading Products www.huntingtons.com
J & J Products Co. www.jandjproducts.com
Lee Precision, Inc. www.leeprecision.com
Lyman www.lymanproducts.com

Mayville Engineering Co. (MEC) www.mayvl.com
Midway www.midwayusa.com
Moly-Bore www.molybore.com
MTM Case-Guard www.mtmcase-guard.com
Neil Jones Custom Products www.toolcity.bet/~njones/
Ponsness/Warren www.reloaders.com
Ranger Products www.pages.prodigy.com/rangerproducts.home.htm
Rapine Bullet Mold Mfg Co. www.bulletmolds.com
RCBS www.blount.com
Redding Reloading Equipment www.redding-reloading.com
Russ Haydon's Shooting Supplies www.shooters-supply.com

WEB DIRECTORY

Sinclair Int'l Inc. **www.sinclairintl.com**
Stony Point Products Inc **www.stonypoint.com**

The Hanned Line **www.hanned.com**
Thompson Bullet Lube Co. **www.vipersites.com/tbl**

RESTS – BENCH, PORTABLE, ATTACHABLE

Harris Engineering Inc. **www.cyberteklabs.com/harris/main/htm**
L Thomas Rifle Support **www.ltsupport.com**

Level-Lok **www.levellok.com**
Midway **www.midwayusa.com**
Versa-Pod **www.versa-pod.com**

SCOPES, SIGHTS, MOUNTS AND ACCESSORIES

ADCO **www.shooters.com/adco/index/htm**
Aimpoint **www.aimpointusa.com**
Aimtech Mount Systems **www.aimtech-mounts.com**
Alpec Team, Inc. **www.alpec.com**
American Technologies Network, Corp. **www.atncorp.com**
Ashley Outdoors, Inc. **sales@ashleyoutdoors.com**
ATN **www.atncorp.com**
BSA Optics **bsaoptics@bellsouth.net**
B-Square Company, Inc. **www.b-square.com**
Burris **www.burrisoptics.com**
Bushnell Corp. **www.bushnell.com**
Carl Zeiss Optical Inc. **www.zeiss.com**
C-More Systems **www.cmore.com**
Conetrol Scope Mounts **www.conetrol.com**
Crossfire L.L.C. **www.amfire.com/hesco/html**
DCG Supply Inc. **www.dcgsupply.com**
Decot Hy-Wyd Sport Glasses **www.sportglasses.com**
EasyHit, Inc. **www.easyhit.com**
Electro-Optics Technologies **www.eotechmdc.com/holosight**
Europtik Ltd. **www.europtik.com**
Gilmore Sports **www.gilmoresports.com**
Hitek Industries **www.nightsight.com**
HIVIZ **www.northpass.com**
Innovative Weaponry, Inc. **www.sarah.aimlv.com/ptnightsights/index.html**
Ironsighter Co. **www.ironsighter.com**
ITT Night Vision **www.ittnightvision.com**
Kowa Optimed Inc. **www.kowascope.com**
Laser Devices Inc. **sales@laserdevices.com**
Lasergrips **www.crimsontrace.com**

LaserMax Inc. **www.lasermax-inc.com**
Leapers, Inc. **www.leapers.com**
Leica Camera Inc. **carleica@aol.com**
Leupold **www.leupold.com**
Lyman **www.lymanproducts.com**
Millett **www.millettsights.com**
Miniature Machine Corp. **www.mmcsight.com**
NAIT **www.nait.com**
Newcon International Ltd. **newconsales@newcon-optik.com**
Night Owl Optics **www.jnltrading.com**
Nikon Inc. **www.nikonusa.com**
North American Integrated Technologies **www.nait.com**
O.K. Weber, Inc. **www.okweber.com**
Pentax Corp. **www.pentax.com**
Premier Reticle **www.premierreticles.com**
Schmidt & Bender **www.schmidt-bender.com**
Scopecoat **www.scopecoat.com**
Segway Industries **www.segway-industries.com**
Shepherd Scope Ltd. **www.shepherdscopes.com**
Simmons-Blount **www.blount.com**
Sure-Fire **www.surefire.com**
Swarovski/Kahles **www.swarovskioptik.com**
Swift Instruments Inc. **www.swift-optics.com**
Tasco **www.tascosales.com**
Trijicon Inc. **www.trijicon-inc.com**
Truglo Inc. **www.truglosights.com**
U.S. Optics Technologies Inc. **www.usoptics.com**
Weaver-Blount **www.blount.com**
Wilcox Industries Corp **www.wilcoxind.com**
Williams Gun Sight Co. **www.williamsgunsight.com**

SHOOTING ORGANIZATIONS, SCHOOLS AND RANGES

Amateur Trapshooting Assoc. **www.shootata.com**
American Gunsmithing Institute **www.americangunsmith.com**
American Shooting Sports Council **www.assc.com**
BATF **www.atf.ustreas.gov**

Blackwater Lodge and Training Center **www.blackwater-lodge.com**
Boone and Crockett Club **www.boone-crockett.org**
Buckmasters, Ltd. **www.buckmasters.com**
Citizens Committee for the Right to Keep & Bear Arms

www.ccrkba.org
Civilian Marksmanship Program **www.odcmp.com**
Ducks Unlimited **www.ducks.org**
Front Sight Firearms Training Institute **www.frontsight.com**
Gun Clubs **www.associatedgunclubs.org**
Gun Owners' Action League **www.goal.org**
Gun Owners of America **www.gunowners.org**
Gun Trade Assoc. Ltd. **www.brucepub.com/gta**
Gunsite Training Center, Inc. **www.gunsite.com**
International Defense Pistol Assoc. **www.idpa.com**

WEB DIRECTORY

International Hunter Education Assoc. **www.ihea.com**
National 4-H Shooting Sports **kesabo@nmsu.edu**
National Benchrest Shooters Assoc. **www.benchrest.com**
National Muzzle Loading Rifle Assoc. **www.nmlra.org**
National Reloading Manufacturers Assoc **www.reload-nrma.com**
National Rifle Assoc. **www.nra.org**
National Shooting Sports Foundation **www.nsssf.org**
National Skeet Shooters Association **www.nssa-nsca.com**
National Sporting Clays Assoc. **www.nssa-nsca.com**
National Wild Turkey Federation **www.hooks.com/nwtf**
North American Hunting Club **www.huntingclub.com**
Pennsylvania Gunsmith School **www.pagunsmith.com**
Quail Unlimited **www.qu.org**
Rocky Mountain Elk Foundation **www.rmef.org**
S&W Academy and Nat'l Firearms Trng. Center **www.smith-wesson.com/academy/index.html**
Second Amendment Foundation **www.saf.org**
Single Action Shooting Society **www.sassnet.com**
Ted Nugent United Sportsmen of America **www.outdoors.net/tednugent**
Thunder Ranch **www.thunderranchinc.com**
Trapshooters Homepage **www.trapshooters.com**
Trinidad State Junior College **www.tsjc.cccoes.edu**
U.S. Int'l Clay Target Assoc. **www.usicta.com**
United States Fish and Wildlife Service **www.fws.gov**
U.S. Practical Shooting Assoc. **www.uspsa.org**
USA Shooting Home Page **www.usashooting.edu**
USA Shooting **www.usashooting.org**
Wildlife Legislative Fund of America **www.wlfa.org**
Women's Shooting Sports Foundation **wssf@worldnet.att.net**

STOCKS

Bell & Carlsen, Inc. **www.users.pld.com/bacinc**
Boyd's Gunstock Industries, Inc. **office@boydboys.com**
Butler Creek Corp www.**butler-creek.com**
Great American Gunstocks **www.gunstocks.com**
M L Greene Precision Products **www.henge.com/~mlgreene**
McMillan Fiberglass Stocks **www.mcmfamily.com**
Pacific Research Laboratories **www.rimrockstocks.com**
Ram-Line Blount Inc. **www/blount.com**

TARGETS AND RANGE EQUIPMENT

Action Target Co. **www.actiontarget.com**
Advanced Interactive Systems **www.ais-sim.com**
Birchwood Casey **www.birchwoodcasey.com**
Caswell Detroit Armor Companies **www.bullettrap.com**
Newbold Target Systems **www.newboldtargets.com**
Range Management Services Inc. **www.casewellintl.com**
Reactive Target Systems Inc. **chrts@primenet.com**
Thompson Target Technology **www.cantorweb.com/thompson-targets**
Visible Impact Targets **www.crosman.com**
White Flyer **www.whiteflyer.com**

TRAP AND SKEET SHOOTING EQUIPMENT AND ACCESSORIES

10X Products Group **10X@10xwear.com**
Claymaster Traps **www.claymaster.com**
Laporte USA **lapoursa@netscope.nct**
Outers **www.blount.com**
Trius Products Inc. **www.triustraps.com**

TRIGGERS

Shilen **www.shilen.com**
Timney Triggers **www.timneytrigger.com**

MAJOR SHOOTING WEB SITES AND LINKS

All Outdoors **www.alloutdoors.com**
Alpha List of Gun Links **www.prairienet.org/guns/alphaO.htm**
Alphabetical Index of Links **www.gunsgunsguns.com**
Firearms Internet Database **www.savannahlane.com**
Gun Games Online **www.gungames.com**
Gun Index **www.gunindex.com**
Gun Talk **www.shooters.com/guntalkactivitiesframe.html**
GunLinks **www.gunlinks.com**
Guns For Sale **www.gunsamerica.com**
Gunweb **www.gunweb.com**
GunXchange **www.gunxchange.com**
Rec. Guns **www.recguns.com**
Shooters' Gun Calendar **www.guncalendar.com/index.cfm**
Shooter's Online Services **www.shooters.com**
Shooters Search **www.shooterssearch.com**
Shotgun Sports Resource Guide **www.shotgunsports.com**
The Hunting Net **www.huntingnet.com**
The Sportsman's Web **www.sportsmansweb.com**
Where To Shoot **www.wheretoshoot.com**

by BILL HANUS

SHOTGUN REVIEW

New shotgun reporter and Tootsie and friends afield.

The year 1999 is destined to go down in shotgun history as The Year Of The Magnum. The 3-1/2-inch 12 gauge magnum introduced a decade ago by Mossberg has finally captured the interest of the mainstream of shotgun manufacturers. For turkey and waterfowl hunters, the pleasant anguish of researching their next shotgun purchase can now begin with what looks like several excellent multiple choice answers to the "which one?" question.

Having, however, labored in the small gauge vineyard for lo, these many years it seemed incumbent on me to bring myself up to magnum speed by seeking out expert advice and opinion. My interview with Mike Larsen, Federal Cartridge Company's Manager of Industry Relations, almost

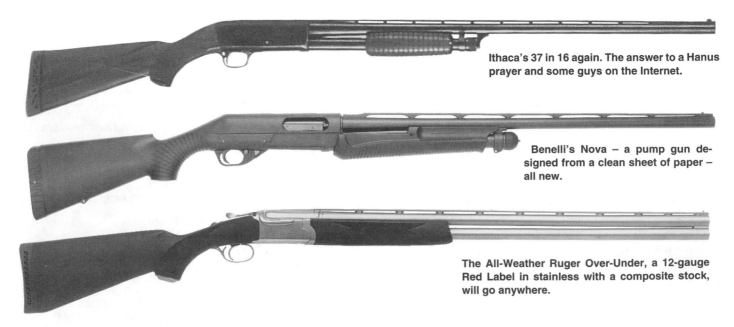

Ithaca's 37 in 16 again. The answer to a Hanus prayer and some guys on the Internet.

Benelli's Nova – a pump gun designed from a clean sheet of paper – all new.

The All-Weather Ruger Over-Under, a 12-gauge Red Label in stainless with a composite stock, will go anywhere.

foundered when it was discovered that we had English cocker spaniels in common. After we had traded information on his Emma and my Tootsie, however, we were able to get down to business.

With scarcely any difference between payloads of the 10 gauge and the 3-1/2-inch magnum, comparisons between the two are inevitable and will no doubt occupy shotgun writers well into the next millennium. Mike Larsen referred to the 3-1/2-inch 12 as the "ultimate for the one-gun guy". With the new crop of such magnums capable of handling everything from 1-1/8 oz. target loads to 2-1/4 oz. magnums, perhaps it is. It performs well on waterfowl, turkey and other upland game and is highly portable (when compared, for example, with Remington's SP-10, an 11-pounder).

However, the 12 gauge bore diameter does not handle larger pellet sizes as well as the 10 gauge, so if your primary target is going to be geese, pterodactyls or cloud-hopping Cessnas, you'd be better off sticking with the 10 gauge.

The three most interesting approaches to recoil suppression—a subject worth considering as the industry moves toward mass acceptance of the Magnum Force—I came across at the SHOT show came from Benelli, Fabarm and Mossberg. Most of the semi-automatic magnums rely upon the gas-operated cycling system to bleed off some of the recoil—a benefit well understood by competition clay target shooters.

F.A.I.R. 16 – another answer to a Hanus prayer – and a trim bird gun it is.

In February 1885, nobody batted an eye when Annie Oakley chose three 16 gauge hammer guns when she set out to establish the feat of shooting 5,000 targets in one day (pp. 49, October 1998, *The American Rifleman*). The moderate recoil and superior patterning characteristics of the 16 gauge were well-known and widely appreciated throughout the United States and Europe. U.S. history also records that skeet once was a 5-gun event —yep, it included the 16 gauge! Some even claim the 16 was better than either the 12 or the 20 at that game. It took Annie 9 hours to break 4,772 targets out of 5,000 thrown—a 95.4% record that any contemporary clay target buff would brag on—with her 16 gauge hammer doubles.

So it should come as no surprise that as the self-appointed poster boy of the 16 gauge rediscovery movement (the original Bill Hanus Birdgun was introduced in 16 gauge in 1988) I seek out kindred spirits wherever and whenever shotgunners gather. (EDITOR'S NOTE: This Bill Hanus is that same Bill Hanus of Birdgun notoriety.)

The 16 gauge newsmaker of 1999 is the F.A.I.R. (I.Rizzini) over/under built on a 16-gauge frame and imported exclusively by New England Arms. There are three brothers, an uncle and, I think, a cousin all making shotguns under the Rizzini name, so confusion comes easily when referring to a "Rizzini" shotgun. F.A.I.R. is the acronym for Fabbrica Armi Isidoro Rizzini which makes the M500 16 gauge O/U with choke tubes that I shot on last year's hunting trip to Nebraska. The five choke tubes, which I normally don't like to fuss with, really came in handy this time. Tootsie is 12 years old now and her hearing is getting kind of selective. Although she can hear a dinner plate being scraped the length of the house, a shouted command in the field sometimes goes unheard. As a result, I made a mid-morning switch from Cylinder/Improved Cylinder to Improved Cylinder/Modified and everyone was happy. Tootsie worked farther ahead than usual and my voice recovered nicely, thanks to F.A.I.R.'s thoughtfulness in providing this feature. Well, the birds weren't too happy about it, but you can't please everyone.

The weight of the 16 gauge F.A.I.R. is about 6 pounds 5 or 6 ounces and is a joy to behold, carry and shoot. It looks good and it shoots good. The pierced opening lever, the gold inlays and the Turkish walnut might add little to the shooting excellence that this gun enjoys, but it will make your heart skip a beat every time you take it out of the gun cabinet. Mine does. If you are a nut for nice wood, wait until you see the M600. This model has gold inlays on case-colored sideplates with even prettier wood and you can own it without selling the farm.

And another old 16 gauge friend we want to welcome back—the famous Ithaca 16 gauge Featherlight pump gun—now available with fixed or screw-in chokes. You would think the reintroduction of the 16 gauge by Ithaca would be a real "no-brainer." When I was gossiping with Ithaca's top folks they confided that they hoped to take orders for 250 guns at the show. You can imagine how delighted they were to approach the 500 mark by the third day of the show.

The 16 gauge—like the 28 gauge—is almost ballistically perfect in moderate loads. Both deliver superb patterns and have short shot strings -- a recipe for clean kills and/or more broken targets. They don't need to be hyped, tweaked or improved upon. That said, most makers try to imitate 12 gauge loadings that are mini-mags to the 16

The 512P Marlin is a 12-gauge bolt gun with everything for the modern deer hunter – 21-inch posted and rifled barrel, sights, pad, reinforced stock.

Marlin's Garden Gun, a bolt-action shoots 22 WRM shotshell – six pounds, 22-inch barrel, clip magazine.

gauge shooter who, they think, "needs all the help he can get." What a crock!

This year—1999—I discovered the perfect 16 gauge load! It's the Baschieri & Pellagri 16 gauge 2-2/3" F2 Classic—a 29 gram load (that's about 1-1/32 oz.) of 4% antimony shot with a 1320 fps velocity (measured 1 meter from the muzzle) and chamber pressures under 10,000 psi. This is an altogether superior product. Barry Davis writing in Shooting Sportsman describes wads used in Baschieri & Pellagri shells as the "most technically advanced wads made in the world today." Tom Roster, writing in Sporting Clays says: "In terms of pellet quality, uniformity, and sphericity, B&P ammo is outstanding and may well be at the top of the heap globally."

At last, a 16 gauge load with superb internals and outstanding downrange performance.

As it happens the owner of B & P America—Mike Dotson—is a friend of mine. If you call him at 972/726-9073 and identify yourself "as a

visited with Jack Rowe, the affable English gunsmith, and AYA's chief of warranty work in the U.S. In the course of our conversation he happened to mention that "these plastic snap caps are ruining our firing pins." Apparently the spring-loaded brass "primer" in the snap cap fights the spring-driven firing pin—and wins! Then, in a kind of deja vu flashback I remembered handing a set of these plastic snap caps to a friend, only to have him hand them back to me with a polite "No thanks." He explained that he put a pair in a gun and when he checked the gun three months after he had cleaned it—both chambers were wet."

With experts crawling out of every booth at the show, I decided to investigate. I learned that plastic "out gases"—it exudes a gas. You may have experienced this in a new car. The gases from the plastic inside the car combine with moisture and deposit a gunk

Montefeltro also has a left-hand model and is available in 12 and 20 gauge, both chambered for 2-3/4 and 3-inch shells. The Sport Model, available only in 12 gauge, is described as the first out-of-the-box gun that can be modified to provide a perfect fit. Each Sport comes equipped with two interchangeable carbon fiber ribs, a shim kit to adjust for drop and a removable recoil pad and optional spacers to set the length of pull.

Also new for 1999 are the 12 and 20 gauge Legacy and 12 gauge Executive models—each with a nickel-finished alloy lower receiver, nicely engraved. The Executive Type I and Type II models are hand-engraved by Bottega, Incisoni di Giovanelli and the Type III selectively gold-filled. All have high grade wood. The catalog describes these one-of-a-kind guns as "A Benelli finished to this level is without parallel in performance or appearance."

But the hottest item in the 1999

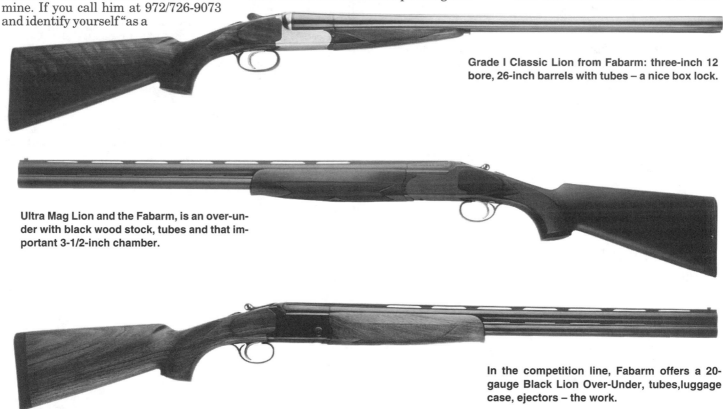

Grade I Classic Lion from Fabarm: three-inch 12 bore, 26-inch barrels with tubes – a nice box lock.

Ultra Mag Lion and the Fabarm, is an over-under with black wood stock, tubes and that important 3-1/2-inch chamber.

In the competition line, Fabarm offers a 20-gauge Black Lion Over-Under, tubes, luggage case, ejectors – the work.

friend of Bill Hanus" you will get the 40-case wholesale price (what are friends for?) and end up having the 16 gauge shot-shells of your dreams delivered to your doorstep by UPS anywhere in the U.S. for a smidgen over $6 a box. Our search for quality 16 gauge ammunition is over.

Snap caps are the perfect ending to a hunting season. You clean your guns, slip in snap caps, pull the triggers to take the gun off cock so it isn't stored cocked for 9 or 10 months. What could be simpler? Stooging around the AYA booth at the SHOT Show this year I

on the inside of the windshield. According to my friend, it was also deposited in the confined space of his shotgun chambers. That's not a place I want to use to collect moisture.

All that said, let the Year of the Magnum begin:

Benelli

There is a lot to like about the Benelli line of inertia recoil semi-automatics. The Super Black Eagle fires 3-1/2, 3 and 2-3/4-inch loads and, new for 1999 there's a left-hand version. The

Benelli line is not a semi-automatic shotgun. It's the all-new NOVA®—a new 3-1/2-inch pump-action shotgun! Benelli started with a blank piece of paper on this one. Molded (and sculpted) from glass-reinforced technopolymers with a steel cage embedded to house the receiver, these unique guns come in either camo or black synthetic finish. A twist of the recoil pad provides access to the buttstock, where the optional (and recommended) recoil reduction system is easily installed in this 8 pound shotgun. The forearm is a kind of reverse wedge shape so that your grip is tighter the harder you pull it. The longer forearm extends over the receiver area, making it virtually impossible to pinch your hand or fingers or get a glove jammed while operating the slide.

Benelli's NOVA slide-action is a ruggedly simple design that promises to be a reliable performer in the woods or on the water. It will be easy to use, easy to clean and will defy the elements.

Beretta

The Beretta AL-390 is the only semi-automatic shotgun with a fully adjustable stock that utilizes shims for quick ad-

justment of both vertical and horizontal angles to the shooter's individual requirements. It's available in 12 and 20 gauge plus a 20 gauge

Youth Model with a choice of gloss, matte, camo or synthetic stocks. Special purpose Turkey Models with high visibility TRUGLO sights and special Realtree X-tra Brown camo finish, Briley extended extra-full choke tube and 3-inch chambers.

IAR brings Cowboy guns to Capistrano – this one has 20-inch barrels and the Cowboy action shooter look.

Browning

Browning has added two camouflage patterns to its successful Gold and BPS shotgun lines. The Gold semi-automatic has the ability to handle all 2-3/4, 3 and 3-1/2-inch loads interchangeably. Its self-regulating gas system reportedly uses nearly all the gas from the smaller 2-3/4-inch load to operate the action,

while excess gases from larger 3 and 3-1/2-inch magnum loads are vented away. Joseph Rousseau, the gun's designer says "gas operated guns

are the preference of shooters who are concerned with recoil. If you're shooting 2-3/4" loads, it's simply a matter of personal taste. But to anyone shooting 3-1/2-inch magnum loads, it becomes a concern."

On the 10 gauge front, Browning announced a 10 gauge combo — a 26", 28" or 30" barrel for waterfowl and a 24" turkey barrel. Browning claims the 10-pound Gold with its advanced gas system tames recoil for greater comfort and enables the shooter to make quick recoveries for second and third shots. A ventilated style recoil which vents gases away from the receiver makes it cleaner operating, according to the maker.

Two new Gold models —the Gold Golden Clays transfers the Golden Clays motif from the Citori line and is available only in 12 gauge with 2-3/4-inch cham-

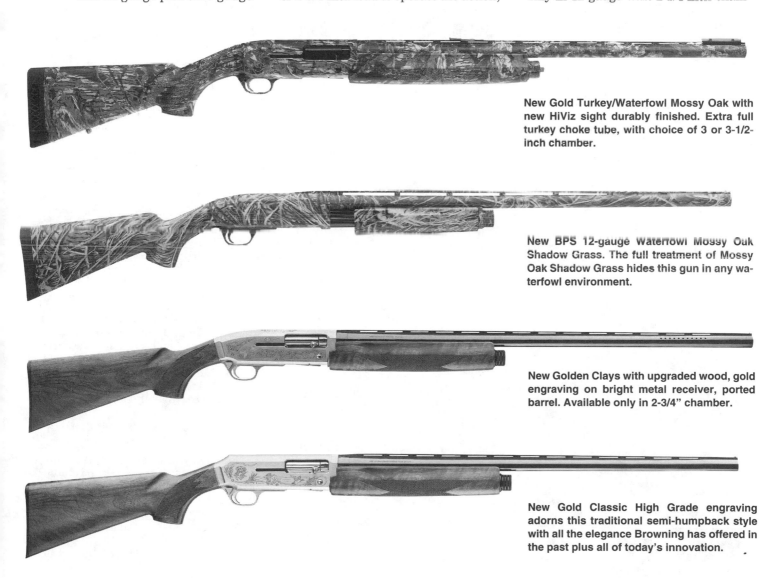

New Gold Turkey/Waterfowl Mossy Oak with new HiViz sight durably finished. Extra full turkey choke tube, with choice of 3 or 3-1/2-inch chamber.

New BPS 12-gauge Waterfowl Mossy Oak Shadow Grass. The full treatment of Mossy Oak Shadow Grass hides this gun in any waterfowl environment.

New Golden Clays with upgraded wood, gold engraving on bright metal receiver, ported barrel. Available only in 2-3/4" chamber.

New Gold Classic High Grade engraving adorns this traditional semi-humpback style with all the elegance Browning has offered in the past plus all of today's innovation.

bers and 28 or 30-inch ported barrels. A new Ladies/Youth Sporting Clays "designed by women for women" in 12 gauge with 2-3/4-inch chamber, 28-inch ported barrel and overall dimensions adjusted to fit women has been added to the Gold line this year.

It is also interesting to note the return of the 3-inch 12 and 20 gauge New Gold Classic Hunter with the squared receiver, magazine cut-off, adjustable comb and satin finish wood.

The 3-1/2-inch shell has made its way to the over/under side of the Browning aisle with the Citori Satin Hunter (matte finished barrels for duck blind work) and Citori Hunter so chambered. Browning's New Citori Superlight Feather and Lightning Feather are wisely chambered for only 2-3/4-inch ammunition.

Some nice embellishments among target guns—on some models an optional adjustable comb is available enabling the shooter to adjust drop, cast-off and cast-on and the Sporting Clays models have a Triple Trigger System that can adjust to three positions for length of pull. The BT-100 Thumbhole single barrel trap gun offers a thumbhole stock with a palm swell grip, adjustable trigger and ejector-selector features.

F.A.I.R.

This gun is unique—although offered in all gauges, the 16 gauge is the newsmaker. The gun is built on a true 16 gauge frame and not 16 gauge barrels beefed up at the breech and hung on a 12-gauge frame. Very nice Turkish walnut, scalloped fences, reliable inertial single trigger, case colored receiver, slender Schnabel forend, 24 lines-per-inch checkering, good standard stock dimensions with a bit of cast-off, a straight grip with a long tang, 28" barrels, ventilated rib, stainless steel screw-in chokes and

Remington's big guy, the SP-10, gussied up for the turkey woods and the far reach.

The awaited 11-87 20-bore is here, and it's trimmer than it might have been, a neat field gun.

Take the young'un when you can, suit him up with an 1100 Youth in camo.

The little Wingmasters are back, and here's the 410 Remington Model 870 to prove it.

Big Magnum benefits the N.W.T.F. – Harrington & Richardson 3-1/2-inch 12 has camo laminate stock, sling, an NWTF logo – and H&R 1871 donates part of the price.

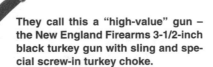
They call this a "high-value" gun – the New England Firearms 3-1/2-inch black turkey gun with sling and special screw-in turkey choke.

weight of about 6 pounds, 4 oz. The entire barrels are hard chrome lined, not just the chambers. Five stainless steel chokes are standard (C, IC, M, IM, F) and are steel-shot friendly in C and IC. This 16 gauge truly "carries like a 20 and hits like a 12." In addition to the M500, higher grades include the M600, Model 702 and Model 900. The F.A.I.R. line made by Isidoro Rizzini is imported exclusively by New England Arms.

Fabarm

Fabarm—Fabbrica Bresciana Armi— is a full-line Italian shotgun manufacturer, represented exclusively by Heckler & Koch, Inc. in the U.S. They offer a Gold Lion semi-automatic, a Max Lion over/under and Classic Lion side-by-side for both target and field applications. The shotguns are sold with a lifetime warranty—backed by Heckler & Koch—which is unusual in this day and age.

Of special interest is their proprietary Tri-Bore system, which they claim provides significant recoil reduction. The key elements to this system seem to be longer forcing cones, over-bored barrels and porting. An H&K official says that "The system changes the internal profile of the barrel. It's similar to back-boring in that it reduces felt recoil and improves patterns."

Bill Hanus Birdguns

Nobody else makes quality small gauge boxlock doubles on small gauge frames—where a 28 gauge weighs 5 pounds 2 oz., a 20 gauge 5 pounds 10 oz. and a 16 gauge 6 pounds 5 oz. -- that are designed to be user-friendly right out of the box. This is my own company remember.

Work has started on a prototype which follows the style set by the famous Boss round action. Both wood and action will be rounded to form a sleek and elegant shotgun. We'll make it in all gauges using AYA's No. 1 wood, built to each buyer's individual specifications.

Ithaca Classic Doubles

Ithaca Classic Doubles has licensed the Ithaca name and production has begun on reproducing several models—Special Field, 4E, 7E and Sousa Grade—for which Ithaca was justly famous. Initially in 20, 28 and .410; with 12 and yes, 16 gauge to follow. The plan is to have the guns made in Italy and then finished in the U.S.

Ithaca Gun

Ithaca is reintroducing the famous Model 37 16 gauge Featherlite due largely to research conducted by the company on the Internet! Hundreds of respondents gave these three reasons why they wanted the 16 gauge back: "the 16 gauge is superior to the 20 gauge and lighter than the 12...the 16 gauge has less recoil than the 12...the 16 gauge is the most versatile of all shotguns." Honestly, I couldn't have said it any better. Each Featherlite is made by hand from solid steel, hand milled and assembled in the U.S. using the finest American Walnut.

Merkel

With a solid product line to start with, Merkel has turned its attention to enhancement by featuring upgraded wood and engraved sideplates on "new" models—notably the 147EL, 122, 47SL, 147SL and 147SSL, in its side by-side line. Merkel is one of the very few makers that catalog 16 gauge side-by-side models. As near as I can tell, these are mounted on 12 gauge frames, weighing in at about 6-3/4 pounds. Curiously, Merkel is one of the very few makers to offer a true 28 gauge frame for their 28-gauge guns. They don't mount beefed up 28 gauge barrels on 20 gauge frames.

A 20-bore on the Montefeltro action, the Fabarm Legacy is a highly finished 20-bore autoloader.

Also on the autoloader side, Fabarm has a Red Lion, a three-inch 12 with tubes in 24, 26 or 28-inch barrel.

On the over/under rack, the 2000EL and 2000EL Sporter, 2002EL and 303EL all offer "Luxury Grade Walnut"—an otherwise $1,200 upgrad — and offering both traditional and new engraving styles. 12, 20 and 28 gauge are offered in the O/U line.

Merkel does not offer screw-in chokes as an option on any of their guns, but suggests Briley Manufacturing of Houston for those interested in adding after market screw-in chokes to their guns.

Of special interest is Merkel's catalog statement regarding the use of steel shot: "The extra hardness created by Merkel's cold hammer forging of the barrel _allows maximum choke_ life when using steel shot." The italics are mine. Note that "maximum choke life" does not mean eternal choke life. Over time, repeated use of steel shot is likely to pound out and expand the chokes in the strongest barrels or hardened choke tubes. This is true of all makers—not just Merkel. The trick is to frequently test the removal of choke tubes after steel shot is used. When they start to get difficult to remove THROW THEM AWAY! Once hardened steel tubes expand into the screw-in threads of the softer metal inside the barrel and "Freeze" the barrels are ruined. The responsibility to check on enlarged choke tubes is the owner's. Few manufacturers warranty their products against dumb.

Mossberg

Mossberg has an interesting working model display demonstrating how their new "Recoil Reducing Stock" works. They claim a 15% reduction in "Felt" recoil. Here's how Mossberg sees the problem: "With the onset of a wide diversity of 'high-performance shotshells,' we are now seeing a wide diversity of 'high-performance recoil.' We, as shooters, take the punishment given by these speed demons as payment for the extra performance."

The idea behind the Recoil Reducing Stock is to reduce the peak amount of rearward thrust — to spread out the recoil over a longer time frame — to get a soft push instead of a sharp hit. This feature is supposed to be available on selected models by the fall of 1999.

Perazzi

Perazzi has introduced an MX5 "entry level" line covering trap, skeet, sporting clays and game guns. The MX5 features a fixed trigger guard group, instead of the detachable feature common on higher grade Perazzi models. The MX5 is offered in 16 gauge. Visits to a Perazzi display are always a highlight and my admiration for the $75,000 Extra Gold Grade and the $300,000 Extra Gold 12-20-28-410 set remains, as always, unalloyed.

Remington

Lots of new stuff going on at Remington, much of it grist for our mill. In order of interest, here's what's happening: (1) The long-awaited 20-gauge version of the Model 11-87 autoloader has finally come to the marketplace with a choice of 26 or 28-inch barrels, ventilated rib, ivory front bead and metal mid-bead and Rem Chokes for field or target use. (2) The Model 870 28 gauge and 410 bore little darlings—they weigh only about 6 pounds—are back. The 28 has Rem Chokes, the 410 fixed Modified. (3) Two new Model 870 Super Magnum 3-1/2-inch as 12 gauge magnums each appropriately camouflaged for waterfowl or turkey hunters are examples of commitment to the magnum movement.

Emilio Rizzini

Emilio Rizzini makes a nice line of over/unders—in all gauges—that are imported exclusively by Tristan Sporting Arms. The 12s and 16s are on 12 gauge frames weighing 7-1/4 to 7-3/4 pounds; the small gauges all on 20 gauge frames weighing from 7 to 7-1/2 pounds. Available with either screw-in chokes and ejectors or fixed chokes and extractors.

In adition to several attractive target models, a 12 gauge with 3-1/2-inch chambers is offered with screw-in chokes.

The same importer brings in a line of side-by-side shotguns made by Luciana Rota. This year a new, upgraded line caught my eye — a single trigger, English grip with splinter forend, ejectors and some of the bells and whistles we all look for in a side-by-side. No 16 gauge, but a 28 gauge built on a 20 gauge frame that weighs in at 6-1/2 pounds.

Ruger

Ruger—celebrating their 50-year anniversary this year—proudly introduced the new All-Weather 12 gauge, 3-inch Red Label stainless steel/black synthetic pistol grip stock over/under shotgun. Impervious to corrosive saltwater spray, rain or mud Ruger feels this gun answers the need for a lightweight, durable over/under. Available in 26, 28 or 30-inch barrel lengths, single selective trigger, weighs 7-1/2 to 7-3/4 pounds, comes with 5 choke tubes—2 Skeet plus IC-M-F.

S.I.A.C.E.

Although hardly a household name in America, S.I.A.C.E. is yet another Italian niche shotgun manufacturer who has found a growing and largely untapped market on our shores. S.I.A.C.E. makes side-by-side hammer guns! The low end of their line (under $2,000) has become the signature gun for IAR, Inc.

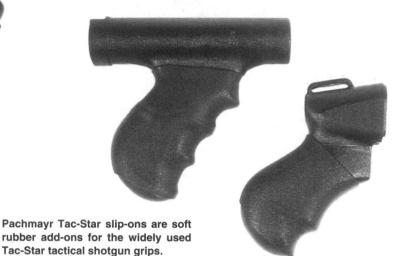

Thompson-Center's Encore 20-bore has 26-inch vent rib barrel, three choke tubes, rounds out the set – either as an extra barrel or a complete gun.

Pachmayr Tac-Star slip-ons are soft rubber add-ons for the widely used Tac-Star tactical shotgun grips.

of San Juan Capistrano, California who imports it in Cowboy and Gentry models in 12 and 20 gauge and which have proven to be exactly what Cowboy Action Shooters have long sought for the shotgun portion of their shooting discipline. As a curious aside, IAR, Inc. also imports used Swedish 12 and 16 gauge side-by-side shotguns with exposed hammers. Most are Husqvarna and feature the LeFaucheaux style underlever, top break action made from the 1870 until 1972. Amazing!

The top end of the S.I.A.C.E. exposed hammer line is imported by New England Arms of Kittery Point, Maine and made in the style of an elegant English game gun circa 1880 with fancy Turkish wood, a top-tang safety and a self-cocking feature that I had never seen before. The hammers cock on opening. Both the Addieville and Vin-

There's a Grade II Classic Lion Fabarm with sideplates, tubes, all the good stuff, and it looks like this.

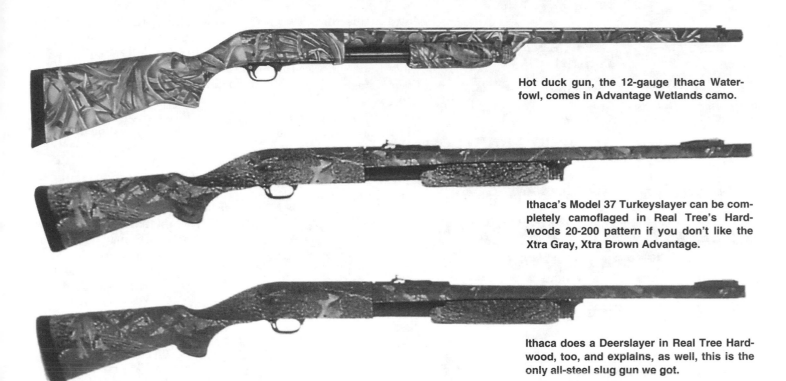

Hot duck gun, the 12-gauge Ithaca Waterfowl, comes in Advantage Wetlands camo.

Ithaca's Model 37 Turkeyslayer can be completely camoflaged in Real Tree's Hardwoods 20-200 pattern if you don't like the Xtra Gray, Xtra Brown Advantage.

Ithaca does a Deerslayer in Real Tree Hardwood, too, and explains, as well, this is the only all-steel slug gun we got.

tager models are offered in 12 and 20 gauge. Automatic ejectors and a single trigger are extra cost options.

SKB

SKB makes two side-by-side models—the M385 with scalloped receiver and the M485 with false sideplates. The M485 has better wood and more engraving on the sideplates. Both have the high-gloss polyurethane finish and are available with either pistol or English grip. New this year are M385 Field and Sporting Clays 20 and 28 gauge sets plus a M485 20 and 28 gauge Field set. I like the SKB line with these reservations: (1) they tend to run a bit on the chunky side; and, (2) they mount their 28 gauge barrels on a 20 gauge frame.

SKB makes three over/under models—785, 585 and 505. Best wood and engraving detail is on the top grade Model 785 and SKB offers various combination sets and features for field and target use.

Thompson/Center

The world's most versatile rifle — the single shot Thompson/Center Encore can now be converted to a shotgun with the addition of a 20 gauge, 26-inch ventilated rib shotgun barrel, supplied with three screw-in choke tubes—IC-M-F. The action breaks open by squeezing the trigger guard. Since the Encore is available as a pistol, centerfire rifle and muzzleloading rifle, the addition of the shotgun barrel fills out Thompson/Center's hand quite nicely and extends the flexibility of the system for owners.

Weatherby

Weatherby has added 12 and 20 gauge semi-automatic shotgun with screw-in chokes to their line. Designed by SKB and based on their considerable experience with semi-automatic shotguns, the SAS (semi-automatic shotgun) Model is offered with 28 and 30-inch barrel lengths in 12 gauge and 26 and 28-inch in 20 gauge, all with 3-inch chambers.

Winchester

Winchester is back in the shotgun business big time with the Super X2—a simple, reliable, versatile, easy-recoiling gas operated semi-automatic 3 and 3-1/2-inch shotgun and available in five different models. The Super X2 received rave notices from every outdoor writer who helped test the gun and it is easy to see why. Everything about it is good. The action is extremely reliable because it's simple and uncomplicated; it shoots anything from 2-3/4-inch target loads to the heaviest lead or steel waterfowl loads. The barrels are back-bored and the balance is right between the hands; the composite stock, the alloy receiver and the action design will take all kinds of weather and handling abuse. One editor told me he submerged the action of his Super X2 in muddy water and went right on killing ducks with water and mud dripping out of his Super X2's action!

About Zutz

Don Zutz, who filled this space for a good many years, died last year of cancer. He fought it hard and it took him pretty quick, and if you and I go to our ends with the class Zutz did, our families will be proud.

Bill Hanus knew Zutz and he knows guns and he's going to give this his best shot. I think he'll do well.

Ken Warner

by DOC CARLSON

BLACKPOWDER REVIEW

WHEN MOST states offered special muzzleloading big game seasons, the front-loader sport took off like the proverbial scalded cat. Black powder target and fun type shooting, in all its facets, has also grown by leaps and bounds, fueled by the popular long range black powder cartridge rifle shooting and cowboy matches using black powder-era rifles, shotguns and pistols. As is typical of the American entrepreneur spirit, if there is a market, it will be addressed.

Inline muzzleloaders remain strong in the market place, but there seems to be a resurgence of the traditional guns now. I suspect last year's ruling by Colorado that forbade the use of the inline type for hunting during muzzleloading seasons, had a lot to do with this shift. That rule was rescinded for the coming season, by the way, so inlines are legal in Colorado again. Be sure and check all local laws before hunting anywhere, of course. That aside, there does seem to be a growing number of hunters that want to use traditional sidehammer guns.

The demand for the inline is very much alive, however, and beginning muzzleloading hunters like its familiar look and feel.

A new outfit on the horizon with the modern name of **Millennium Designed Muzzleloaders, LTD.**, has an inline available for the hunter that incorporates most of the new thinking going on for this type of gun. The rifle is 50-caliber with a slightly oversize bore to allow for ease of reloading in a fouled bore, a good move in my opinion. Lead bullets and sabot type projectiles will easily upset enough on firing to take up the slight amount of oversize. The gun is stainless steel and is glass bedded into a synthetic stock utilizing two bedding lugs on the barreled action. This gives a solid bed for the rifle and should contribute to good accuracy. The barrel is offered in a 1 in 24 inch twist for use with slugs and sabot type bullets and is rated for three of the 50-grain Pyrodex pellets for 150 gr. black powder, a magnum loading. The muzzle has a deep crown to ease the job of starting the bullet down the bore straight and undeformed, again something that should contribute to accuracy.

The action is a straight pull type with a side mounted cocking handle that drops into a safety notch. This functions as a secondary safety which blocks the primary safety on the trigger group from moving unless the cocking handle is raised out of the safety notch. This double safety protection also makes it difficult to forget to take off both safeties when wishing to fire the gun. The M2K is available in either right or left hand models, and with your choice of a standard Spitfire nipple to accept a #11 percussion cap or the Spitfire Magnum nipple that takes a musket cap. The musket cap will provide three times the

Top: Crockett small game rifle, a 32, maybe only an early entry in a new small-bore trend.
Middle: Thompson Center's Black Mountain magnum is a no-nonsense heavy hitter in traditional layout.
Bottom: Markesbery's Black Bear offers in-line advantages - and power - without the bolt-gun look.

fire of a standard #11 cap and at 700 degrees hotter temperature—definitely a good idea in the field.

The customer has a choice of solid wood stock or laminated and the ramrod is made of nylon-type material that is unbreakable, at least in any use short of prying a pickup out of a mudhole. The rod has a cleaning jag on one end that screws off to reveal a bullet pulling worm-screw. The other end is tapped for the standard 10-32 line of accessories available on the market.

The trigger is fully adjustable and comes factory set at 3 1/2 pounds. The sights are a ramp front with a glow-type bead and a neat-looking aperture rear. The peep is very quick and accurate to use and will be especially well liked by those whose eyesight is not up to the standards that it once was. The receiver is drilled and tapped for scope mounts and the hole spacing of the scope mounts is the same as the rear sight giving one the choice of three different placements for the rear sight. That should fit just about everyone.

This appears to be a gun that combines the best features of several years of inline experience. Someone has done their homework and I suspect we'll be seeing a few of these in the woods.

Any time we look at what's available in the inline field, it's natural that we look at what **Modern Muzzleloading, Inc.** has to offer. This outfit is the brainchild of

Tony Knight, the inventor of the Knight MK85—the inline that started it all back in 1985. Beginning with the very advanced for its time MK85, Tony and Company have continued to bring out something innovative nearly every year since. This year their Disc Rifle is offered in either 24 or 26-inch barrel lengths and is recommended for use with three 50 gr. Pyrodex pellets or 150 gr. charges of loose powder under your favorite projectile, sabot or slug. A bit of good news is that the Bureau of Alcohol, Tobacco and Firearms has ruled that this rifle is no longer considered a firearm under the Gun Control Act of 1968 and does not have to be sold as a modern cartridge firearm. This means that it can be sold like any other muzzleloader and is not subject to recordkeeping requirements or confined to sale by licensed firearms dealers. This ruling clarifies that firearms that load from the muzzle, using powder and bullet, are classified as "antique firearms" regardless of what kind of primer they use. Good news, indeed.

Modern has also upgraded their straight pull type of gun with a longer 26-inch barrel and 150-grain magnum capabilities. Coupled with their

"Red Hot" nipple using musket caps for reliable ignition under most any circumstances, this is a very practical hunting rifle. The synthetic stock is available in Mossy Oak Break Up or Advantage camo patterns or basic black with either blued or stainless barrels in a 1 to 28-inch twist. The stock features a checkered pistol grip and forend for a sure grip in cold, wet conditions and has a rubber recoil pad. The Knight trigger is adjustable for windage and elevation and the receiver is drilled and tapped for scope mounts.

These rifles, coupled with several new accessories that have been added to the

Top: Millennium isn't fooling around. Their M2K goes straight at the new-to-muzzleloading crowd with inline system.
Middle: Thompson-Center plays the game both ways. This is the inline Black Diamond in a Rynite stock.
Bottom: Knight's Bighorn updates all the conveniences and power options the company pioneered.

Top: Given the Encore cartridge series, this muzzleloading 209x50 magnum was sure to follow and it has.
Middle: Blackbear's brothers, Grizzly and Brown (in camo), wear different coats but offer the same good stuff.
Bottom: The T/C Mountain magnum comes in 12-bore, too, and looks just like this.

line, shows that Tony Knight continues to innovate.

I was recently told by **Marlin** that they will be dropping their MLS inline muzzleloader this year. This rifle was available in 50 and 54 caliber. If you have an interest in one of these, this will be the last year they will be available and, I would imagine, availability will be dependent upon stocks on hand.

For those who can't decide if they like the traditional side lock gun or the inline, the **Markesbery Muzzleloader** may be the answer. This rifle utilizes a center hung hammer, similar to what is seen on single shot shotguns.

Because the barrel is seated to the rear of the receiver, the rifle is 4 to 5 inches shorter than the average inline with a similar 24-inch barrel. Barrels are interchangeable by simply loosening a screw on the bottom of the receiver, slipping the barrel from the receiver, slipping another in and re-tightening the screw. With the interchangeable barrels available, the system gives the shooter a choice of 36, 45, 50, or 54 caliber utilizing the same receiver and butt stock. Sights are attached to the barrel, so there is no need to resight-in when the barrel is changed.

As Markesbery notes, the hunter can have one barrel with open sights and one with a scope of the same caliber or not, as the shooter wishes, and be sure of having a rifle that will be legal in most any state.

The rifle is available with either cap and nipple ignition or the 400 SRP (small rifle primer) system. This is a closed system of ignition wherein a small rifle primer is placed in a recess in the base and the top half is threaded into place, covering the primer. The top part contains a floating firing pin which, when struck by the hammer, fires the primer igniting the main charge. According to the company, this gives up to 10 times the amount of fire that is produced by a standard #11 cap. The system is also sealed against the weather. The 400 SRP system is interchangeable with the standard nipple, requiring only a couple of minutes to convert from one to the other. Where legal, this system will give very reliable ignition.

The Markesbery is a short, fast handling rifle being only 38 inches long, with the balance point between the hands. The balance reminds one of the venerable '94 Winchester. Sights are an adjustable rear combined with a fiber optic, high visibility front. As noted, all barrels are drilled and tapped for scope mounts. The 50 and 54 caliber versions are recommended for loads of up to three Pyrodex 50 grain pellets or 150 grain loose powder giving velocities of 2000 fps with some saboted bullets. The stainless steel rifle can be had with a laminated wood stock or a thumbhole-type synthetic with either black or camo finish. A solid aluminum ramrod completes this solid little hunting gun.

With the prejudice that is shown by some state hunting agencies against the inline type of muzzleloader, it was a matter of time before the market began to use the inline type barrel in a traditional side-hammer gun. **Thompson Center Arms** has their new Black Mountain Magnum on the market this year. This gun is designed to give the inline type of performance in a traditional side-hammer style. It is designed to handle 150 grain loads of either loose powder or Pyrodex pellets. Most side-hammer guns do not handle the Pyrodex pellets very well. The configuration of their breech plugs gives erratic ignition of the pellets. T/C has redesigned their breech plug so that the pellets

can be seated well into the plug recess and ignition is as good as with the straight flash channels of the inlines. To further facilitate positive ignition, the gun uses a musket cap nipple. A spare nipple that will handle #11 caps is also included.

The 28-inch blued barrel has a 1 in 28 inch twist for use with conical projectiles. The barrel is equipped with T/C's QLA system, a deep crowned muzzle that allows for easy starting of conical bullets. Sights are fiber optic type and are fully adjustable for both windage and elevation. It is drilled and tapped for scope mounts also.

Stocks can be had in either composite or walnut and calibers can be either 54 or 50; a 12 gauge turkey gun is also available. The 12 gauge barrel is equipped with a screw-in, extra full choke tube and a standard bead front sight.

Thompson Center has also upgraded their popular inline Black Diamond rifle. The rifle is now provided with three interchangeable ignition systems utilizing musket caps, the standard #11 cap or a 209 shotgun primer. The two systems that use conventional cap/nipple combinations feature T/C's Flame Thrower nipples that reportedly direct 80% of the priming fire into the main charge of powder as opposed to something like 50% with a standard

nipple. The Flame Thrower nipple directs a ring of fire into the periphery of the powder charge simultaneously with a concentrated flame into the central core of the charge. All this translates into very reliable ignition under the most adverse circumstances.

In addition to the black Rynite standard stock, the Black Diamond is offered this year with a premium American walnut stock, the high quality wood stock that T/C has always been famous for. The rifle is available in either stainless steel or blued finish with the Rynite stock and blued only with the walnut. The sights of the Black Diamond have been upgraded to the fiber optic style that is becoming so popular with hunters. The fully adjustable rear sight features two orange dots that, when paired with the chartreuse ramp front bead,

give a very clear sight picture, even in poor light conditions. The sights are made of steel, rather than plastic, making them very durable and reliable.

The new aluminum ramrod completes the upgrades that are included with the Black Diamond. The rod has 1 1/2 inches of serration on one end for gripping and the standard 10x32 thread to take all standard accessories. It has a super hard, anodized finish.

The Black Diamond has a 22 1/2-inch barrel with a 1 in 28-inch twist and has the QLA loading system incorporated into the muzzle. It features rubber recoil pad, sling swivels and a patented sliding thumb safety. Since its debut last year, this has been a very popular rifle with hunters. The upgrades should make it even more so.

Seeing we are about to enter into the new millennium, T/C is offering a Limited Edition Black Diamond rifle that will include

a Leupold Vari-X II 3-9x40mm scope with a matching matte finish. The scope will be mounted with Leupold Quick Release mounts. Each rifle and scope in the Black Dia-

Top to bottom, we got the standard Lone Star rifle production rifle; the Standard Sporter with target sights; the Custom target with shotgun butt.

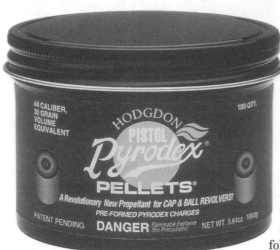

The new 30-grain Pyrodex pellets are packaged up 100 to the jar.

mond Millennium package will be consecutively serial numbered beginning with the number 2000. They will carry a lifetime guarantee good for the next millennium and beyond. Just think what that will be worth in the year 2100!

Many people are not aware that in 1998 T/C brought out the Encore 209x50 Magnum. This is a muzzleloading barrel that interchanges on the centerfire Encore rifle to convert it to a center hammer, inline type muzzleloader. The rifle can be had stocked in either walnut or Rynite and in stainless or blued finish. The gun is a top break action that is released by squeezing the trigger guard spur. It is offered in .50 cal and is designed for charges of 150 gr. of FFg black-powder or Pyrodex equivalent. It is fired by use of the 209 shotgun primer. When coupled with all the calibers that are available in the Encore centerfire rifle, this is a very versatile system for the hunter who wants one gun to "do it all."

T/C's Flame Thrower ignition systems pump up the impulse more than somewhat.

The Encore 209x50 Magnum comes with T/C's fiber optic sights and is drilled and tapped for scope mounts, of course. The 26-inch barrel is rifled with a 1 in 28-inch twist and has the T/C QLA easy loading system. The little rifle weighs in at a trim 7 pounds.

Thompson Center has added a folding handle ramrod accessory new this year. This folding handle can be added to T/C's aluminum rods and will fit many of the other companies standard ramrods. Called the Power Handle, the T-handle swings up to provide extra power for seating projectiles, cleaning or pulling projectiles. The handle then folds back into the ramrod, virtually disappearing. The rod can be carried in the thimbles of the rifle and looks like any other rod until the T-handle is unfolded. The attachment adds very little to the overall length of the ramrod and certainly makes the standard rod much more user friendly.

One of the problems with the nipples which use a musket cap, is the lack of an easy way to carry the larger musket caps. T/C is bringing out a musket size capper to handle this problem. The capper holds 8 musket caps, keeping one ready for instant use. The spring-loaded capper is made of clear plastic so the user can instantly see how many caps are available. It includes a lanyard tab so it can be hung around the neck or attached to horns or pouches. Reasonably priced, this should be a well received accessory.

Pedersoli is a well-known name in the blackpowder field. This Italian firm makes a fine assortment of black pow-

der reproduction firearms, both cartridge and muzzleloading type. The line is imported into this country by **Flintlocks Etc.**. New this year will be a side-by-side percussion shotgun, a couple of Sharps rifle reproductions and a reproduction German musket that is an interesting piece for those who like

something a bit different. The musket is a faithful reproduction of a long military rifle manufactured by the Gewehrfabrik in Oberndorf from 1857 until 1862. If Gewehrfabrik in Oberndorf sounds familiar, it should. That's the home of the Mauser rifle of WWI and WWII fame. The Infantry Wurttembergisch "Veirendsgewehr" 1857 model has a rifled barrel of 54 caliber with 5 grooves in a 1 in 55 inch right hand twist. The rifle musket is percussion and shows typical Germanic military lines.

The new rifle was reproduced especially to be a contender in the 100 meter "minie" match of International Muzzle Loading competitions. The rear sight is adjustable for wind-

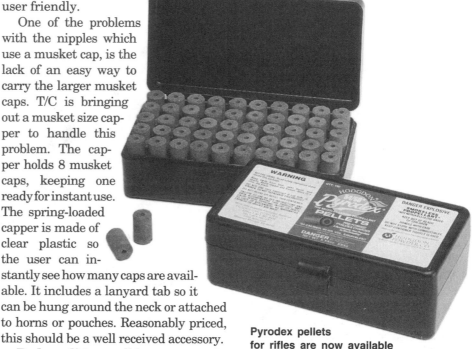

Pyrodex pellets for rifles are now available in 50 and 54-caliber.

age and elevation, as per the original gun. The stock is walnut and is equipped with three bright steel bands. The lock is case hardened and the barrel is polished steel, not blued or browned. Its a very nice looking gun different from run-of-the-mill musket reproductions.

It was adopted by the German states of Wurttemberg, Baden, and the Great Axia Dukedom, and while I know of no proof of this, it certainly could have been imported and used by some unit during the Civil War. This gun is being made in limited quantities so, if it sounds interesting, contact the folks at Flintlocks Etc. soon. I suspect these will sell out relatively fast. Flintlocks Etc. has a catalog that shows a very complete line of reproduction guns and is certainly worth a look.

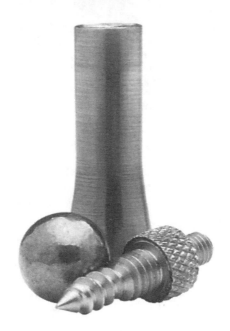

Remington gets up a brass bullet loading top and ball puller very nicely.

Another well known name in the muzzleloading business is developing a Germanic rifle for the hunter. **Dixie Gun Works** is in the development stages of a typical German Jaeger hunting rifle. The gun will be in 54 caliber with a fast twist barrel for use with conical projectiles. Plans are to have it available in either flint or percussion. The Jaeger rifle style was developed as a practical hunting gun and handles recoil well. They balance and point naturally, as a good hunting arm should. I'll look forward to seeing this gun come on the market. Dixie hopes to have it by the latter part of the year.

If our own shop is any indication, there is a growing interest in smaller caliber muzzleloaders for use in both target shooting and small game hunting. While there used to be a fair number of rifles available in the 30 to 40 caliber range, these have disappeared in recent years. They were a casualty of the phenomenal demand for big game hunting rifles, I suppose. With the renewed interest in the smaller calibers, some companies are beginning to bring them back.

Traditions Performance Firearms has introduced a very nice little 32 caliber rifle to fill this need. Called the Crockett, the trim Kentucky style half-stocked rifle is a very traditional type of gun. It features a walnut stained hardwood stock, fitted with polished brass furniture. The 32 inch barrel is ri-

fled 1 turn in 48 inches and is intended for round ball shooting. The lock is percussion with double set triggers. The gun utilizes a hook breech for ease of take down for cleaning, if the owner wishes. The overall length is 49 inches and it weighs a trim 6 1/2 pounds. A great little target and small game rifle.

In the blackpowder cartridge guns a name that commands a great deal of respect is **Lone Star Rifle Co.** This outfit has been making reproductions of the Remington rolling block rifles for some years, mostly on a custom basis. They are now making a standard line that includes three models: The Silhouette is made in 45/70 and 40/65 calibers with choice of 32 or 34-inch barrel; the #5 Sporting with 26-inch barrel in 30-40 Krag; and the Cowboy Action with 26-inch barrel in calibers 45/70, 40/65, 38/55, 32/40 or 45 Colt. All have round barrels of custom quality for top accuracy, single trigger and straight-grained walnut stocks with either a shotgun or crescent buttplate. The trim forend features a schnable tip that is very attractive. The actions are color case hardened using a bone pack process. Truly custom quality rifles that will be at home in the hunting

field as well as competitive at targets.

A couple of new reproduction blackpowders have come on the scene. **Clear Shot** is a blackpowder replacement from Clean Shot Technologies that is a greatly improved version of the old Black Canyon powder. It gives pressures similar to blackpowder with no fouling and is not corrosive. **Goex, Inc.**, the folks that took over the Dupont blackpowder factory and has made blackpowder for some years, has moved its operations to Louisiana and is just getting on the market with Clean Shot powder, a non-corrosive, non-fouling blackpowder replica powder. This new powder should be

available this year. This will allow the shooter to choose either a repro blackpowder or the real thing, both made by one of the oldest names in the blackpowder industry in the US.

Hodgdon Powder Co., the makers of Pyrodex, are adding 30-grain pellets to their 50-grain pellets made for 50 caliber guns and 54 caliber 60 grain pellets for rifles of that caliber. These various combinations should fit most every load in the two most popular hunting calibers. They will also have 30-grain pellets for use in 44 caliber percussion revolvers.

Several companies are making saboted bullets that contain no lead. These are mostly made of copper or copper compounds. This may well be a wave of the future. The U.S. Army recently announced that they will be using a bullet that contains no lead in their small arms. They are calling this a "green" bullet, meaning that it is "friendly" to the environment. With the present anti-lead hysteria that is rampant in the press, look for more and more pressure to eliminate the use of lead altogether in the shooting sports.

Brilliant Tru-G's sighting system for Thompson-Center makes full use of fiber optics.

While it is pretty basic science that metallic lead is relatively inert and does very little, if any, leaching into soil and water, I suspect that blackpowder shooters are going to be under more and more pressure to eliminate lead from our shooting activities. This bears watching and be sure and contact your legislators when this type of regulation comes up.

The blackpowder shooting sports in all their many forms seem to be in fine shape as we close out the twentieth century. It will be interesting to see what the next millennium will bring to our sport. ●

by BOB BELL

SCOPES AND MOUNTS

I GOT my first scope, a little Weaver 29-S, in the summer of 1937 when I was eleven, and gunsmith Ken Wright mounted it on my first cartridge rifle, a M72 Winchester bolt action 22. I put it that way because my dad had got me a Daisy air "rifle" for my fourth birthday and a Crosman pellet gun for my sixth, but they didn't shoot cartridges, of course.

Even then I'd been reading everything about scopes that I could lay my hands on, and really wanted one. I'm not sure why. I didn't know anyone who had one; I don't think I'd even seen one, but something convinced me they'd make shooting lots better. I didn't even know what kind I should have. So I wrote to Col. Whelen and asked.

I don't think he was a colonel then, and I don't know what he thought about getting such a letter from a kid, but he replied immediately; a single-spaced full page answer, the friendliest, non-patronizing letter imaginable. I've had a warm feeling toward the Colonel ever since, even though he's long gone.

Boiled down, his letter recommended the 29-S as the best rimfire scope of the day, so that's what I got. Actually, Dad must have bought it for me, just as he had the Winchester for my previous birthday (he often gave me a gun for a birthday present), for that was still the time of the Great Depression and I sure didn't have any money of my own. (He probably didn't have any to spare either, but he scraped it up for me; some kids are lucky enough to have fathers like that.)

So why am I telling you all this? Just so you'll know that I've been using scopes for well over 60 years, almost daily, which means I've seen quite a bit of their development. (I'm sure many other old geezers have done likewise, but I happen to be the one writing this article, so you're stuck with me.) Now, scopes were used long before 1937. Snipers used them for both the North and the South in the Civil War, many buffalo hunters had them on their big singleshots in the late 1800s, and German and English snipers used them in WWI, even a few Yanks.

But if you calculate the years from about 1860 to 1937, then '37 to the present, it's obvious that scope users of my age have been using glass sights for almost half the time they've been in fairly common use. I dunno if that means anything significant—except that we're getting old!—but maybe it also indicates that we've had some experience with them. At least it allows us to look back over a considerable amount of time and get some idea of the progress that's been made.

I think it's fair to say that practically every scope of current manufacture is better than the best pre-WWII model of its class. That is, I'm comparing hunting scopes to hunting scopes, target models to targets. Sure, it's nostalgic to look back to Bill Weaver's little 3/4-inch tube 330 and Lyman's Alaskan All-Weather and Unertl's big target jobs. They were the best of their day and many of them are still good if you happen to have

Schmidt & Bender 1.2-4x doesn't require enlarged objective, is Bell's favorite size for big game hunting.

Bausch & Lomb 1.5-6x36 Elite is intended to handle 95 percent of all big game hunting.

Like all 4200 Series Elites, this B&L 6-24x40 has the new RainGuard coating to make it usable in wet weather.

one. I have an original Alaskan and a 1 1/2-inch 12x Unertl that I wouldn't part with, but I can't explain my reasons for feeling that way; they're not really rational.

I should say that I've never (ever!) had the slightest trouble with this Unertl, but feel obligated to tell you that Carl Jarrett, a friend who was a sniper in the South Pacific during WWII, had an 8x 1 1/4-inch on an '03-A3 and it took on so much moisture that he removed it and went with the aperture sight. Of course, few hunters will ever experience an environment as bad as Carl did, and no hunting situation ever is as rough on equipment and the guys using it as combat. And the Unertl has been improved since WWII. But still, today's scopes are better than they were back then.

They should be. There's been over five decades of development by smart guys since that war. Lenses have gotten bigger and better, they've been installed with more perfection and in stronger housings; thanks to single and then multiple layer hard lens coating, light transmission is up from about 60 percent to some 95 percent (which is essentially perfect, for there has to be at least a 10 percent improvement for the human eye to be able to recognize any

change, various authorities have pointed out); weatherproofing is far advanced; adjustments are more precise and of better design; variables have become common and have reached a high state of perfection, making a single scope adaptable to a variety of uses and ranges; rangefinding reticles have been developed to prevent gross errors, and red dot reticles make it possible to aim precisely under the dimmest conditions. But when it's time to put a scope on a gun, optics are not the only consideration. Size and weight are also important. We do have to mount

Leupold's ARD (Anti-Reflective Device) is intended to reduce sunlight and glare in fixed 40mm objective scopes.

these things on firearms, not just admire them on an optical bench.

Today's scopes are also tougher, more durable. And don't think that isn't important. The stress a scope has to undergo when it is fired is unbelievable. Sitting above the receiver as it does, inertia tends to make it stand still when

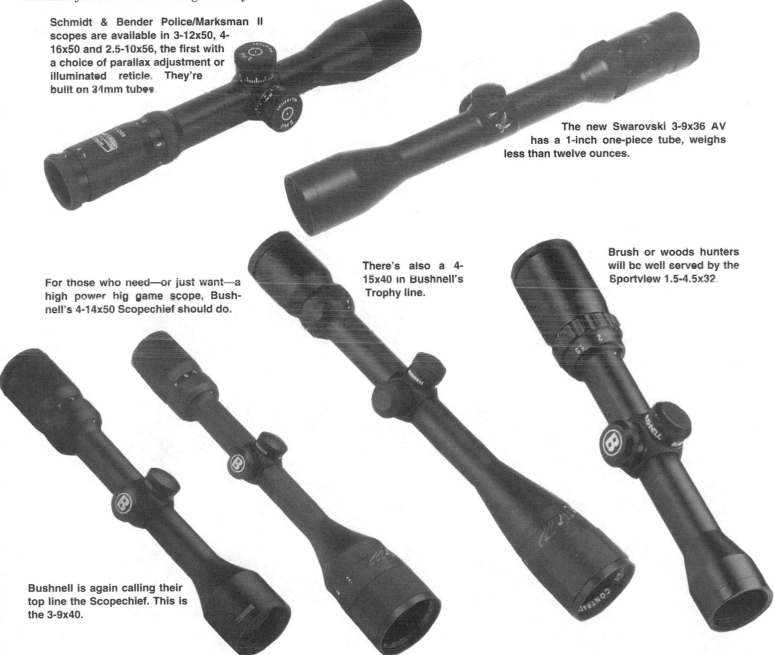

Schmidt & Bender Police/Marksman II scopes are available in 3-12x50, 4-16x50 and 2.5-10x56, the first with a choice of parallax adjustment or illuminated reticle. They're built on 34mm tubes.

The new Swarovski 3-9x36 AV has a 1-inch one-piece tube, weighs less than twelve ounces.

There's also a 4-15x40 in Bushnell's Trophy line.

Brush or woods hunters will be well served by the Sportview 1.5-4.5x32.

For those who need—or just want—a high power big game scope, Bushnell's 4-14x50 Scopechief should do.

Bushnell is again calling their top line the Scopechief. This is the 3-9x40.

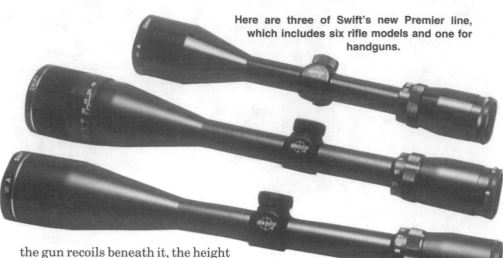

Here are three of Swift's new Premier line, which includes six rifle models and one for handguns.

tra dense flint? These glasses all refract light at different wavelengths throughout the spectrum, and changing any one has an effect on all the others. The optical engineer must keep in mind (actually, in his daily records) all of these glass characteristics when working out the lens combinations which will most nearly eliminate the aberrations in a given scope...and eliminating them is one of the primary goals of scope design. But doing all this is an expensive procedure, and different manufacturers go to different lengths and are willing to invest different amounts, and that's another reason for the difference in the

The Weaver V24 has a power spread of 6-24x, the most in the V-Series, which also includes the V3, V9, V10 and V16.

the gun recoils beneath it, the height of its mounts acting like levers to multiply the force on it. Everything inside the tube tries to move when all those g's hit it....the lenses, their mountings, adjustment mechanisms...everything. Even the apexes of the lenses tend to stay put for a fraction of a millisecend while their peripheries, supported by their mountings, first recoil. Only the inherent elasticity of the lenses themselves brings them back to their original shape and position. Nothing inside the scope tube may permanently move the tiniest measurable amount if the scope is to stay in zero. A thousandth of an inch is a lot in here.

A scope isn't subjected to this force only once. It has to take it every time the gun is fired, possibly thousands of times. Durability is one reason, maybe the most important reason, that some scope lines cost significantly more than others. These days computers do the calculations in lens design and interrelationships, answering questions in seconds which only a few decades ago

literally took years of personal computations. There are many, very smart optical engineers out there who know almost exactly what glass characteristics and dimensions

they want. So theoretically, at least, there should be very little difference between the best scopes and what we might call the second level. And I guess the difference is minuscule...but it is there. Just because a designer knows what he'd like to have doesn't mean he gets it. For instance, the cost of getting the ideal makeup of the glass for the lenses has to be considered. The basic question of whether crown or flint glass should be used, and should it be fluor, boro-silicate, zinc, medium or dense barium crown glass in a given lens, or extra light, light, dense, or ex-

prices of makes. The accuracy of lens grinding and installation is another area that's important, as are other factors that we all can think of, but we won't go into them here. Obviously, the manufacturer who goes to the furthest extreme is going to produce the best scope...and it's also going to be the most expensive.

So in the end, each of us has to ask himself "How good a scope do I need?" Sure, we'd all like to have the best, but do we have to have it to bang a little whitetail in Pennsylvania? No. But how about a bongo in a West Africa equatorial forest? You spent tens of thousands of dollars, maybe months of time, traveled halfway around the world for such a safari. Finally, you have your chance. But in the dense green wavering shadows, where any

This 2.5-10x50 is one of six new scopes in the Zeiss Diavari VW/V Series.

Biggest Zeiss Diavari VM/V scope is this 5-15x42.

light is a sometime thing, do you want any scope but the very best? Everyone has to make up his own mind, of course, but it seems to me there are times when I'd wish even the best was better.

But looking at the big picture, one quickly realizes that almost nobody goes for bongo but millions of us go for commoner critters. How to pick a scope

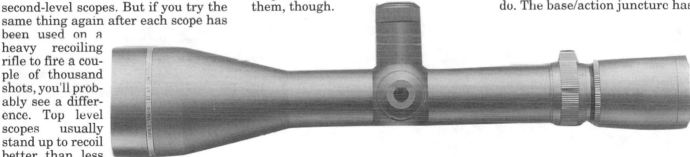

Leupold's new Vari-X III is a 3.5-10x40 addition to the Tactical line. Its 30mm maintube allows 65 minutes of w. and e. adjustment.

for these? Well, a simple way is to just tack up a sheet of newspaper at 100 yards, then study it with solidly supported scopes of different makes and prices. See how they compare with each other at resolving the various sizes and faces of type. That might not seem like a very sophisticated test, but it's a simple and effective way to actually see the differences in resolving power and other optical characteristics under identical atmospheric conditions.

Truth is, my eyes can't make out much difference between new first- and second-level scopes. But if you try the same thing again after each scope has been used on a heavy recoiling rifle to fire a couple of thousand shots, you'll probably see a difference. Top level scopes usually stand up to recoil better than less expensive ones.

I once read a government report that said the WWII military expected the 2 1/2x Lyman Alaskan then used on some sniper rifles to be servicable for 6000 shots. This was on a fairly heavy rifle (8-10 lbs.) chambered for the 30-06 cartridge, which doesn't have especially severe recoil—nothing like a hunter's 338 Magnum with 250-gr. bullet, the 375/300, or 458/500, say. Of course, it's not likely that the average hunter will ever fire several thousand rounds from his magnum,

even including load testing, zeroing, and casual shooting. Nevertheless, at some point durability has to be considered.

Some hunters will conclude it makes more sense to buy a second-level scope instead of the most expensive model, use it as long as it performs okay (which probably will be many years), then scrap it if it fails and get another of similar quality, rather than tie up a large amount of money in the top model, just because it might last longer.

There's a lot to be said for that kind of thinking, but at the same time we must realize that

a good percentage of hunters can afford the most expensive scopes available, and also that there are some who simply are not content unless at any given moment they have the most expensive gizmo in the world, be it a scope, rifle, sport utility vehicle, private jet, or whatever. It must be hell to be driven like that, but some guys are. I know a couple. I don't envy them, though.

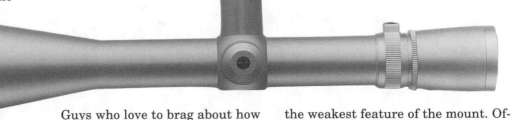

The Leupold 4.5-14x50 and 6.5-20x50 Long Range Target scopes are now offered with a silver finish to match stainless rifles.

Guys who love to brag about how much something cost them can have a good time with scopes nowadays. Consider their price relationships to the rifles they go on. A few minutes

ago, I took a look at GD 19, the 1965 edition, which happened to be handy. At that time, for the magnum calibers, a Remington M700 BDL cost $160, the M70 Winchester $155, and the Savage 110 $130, while the most expensive American hunting scopes were the B&L 2.5-8x at $100, Redfield 2-7x $95, and Leupold Vari-X II 3-9x $90. In other words, the rifle cost approximately 1/3 to 2/3 more than the scope. In GD53, the 1999 edition, the M700 and M70 prices had risen almost four times to over $600, and the Savage M111 was up three-plus times. However, the Leupold 3.5-10x, nearest equivalent to their early 3-9x, cost some eight and one-half times as much, and the B&L 2.5-10x and Redfield 2-7x Illuminator were up more than five and one-half times.

As a further comparison, whereas American hunting model scopes averaged under $100 in 1965, in 1999 one Weaver sold for $771, a Springfield Armory $769, a Leupold $1098, a McMillan $1250, and you could spend $4000 for a U.S. Optics. If you want a German/Austrian glass, it went as much as $1575 for a Zeiss, $1665 for Swarovski and $1199 for Kahles. So in many cases the scope now cost far more than the rifle. To say nothing of the mount, whose price isn't mentioned here but might as well be included, for without it you can't scope a rifle.

Speaking of mounts, incidentally, wouldn't it be nice if all riflemakers made their receivers with integral mount bases, as Sako and Ruger now do. The base/action juncture has to be the weakest feature of the mount. Often it doesn't have a recoil shoulder, so it depends on a few small screws for solidity...and that isn't truly enough. Personally, I like Sako's integral tapered dovetails, which are as low as scope mounts should be and get tighter if there's ring movement at all during recoil. This is especially important these days when so many scopes are so heavy.

I wish this upward weight trend would come to an end. There's no doubt that optical engineers working in a design room can keep coming up with ideas that improve scopes optically or reticlewise or whatever when they're tested in a lab, but every time they do the scope gets bigger and bulkier. That's no problem on an optical bench, but shooters gotta mount these things on a rifle and use them in the field. The designers and especially the military spec-setters who specify an indestructible scope for snipers, just seem to go on their merry way, with no thought to the person who's going to use it, often under abominable conditions. As a guy who's been there, I can tell you that for an infantryman or Marine who has to lug everything on his back in unimaginable conditions most of the time, everything is bloody heavy! It would be far simpler, at least in the case of the snipers, to specify a good scope of reasonable power and not over a pound in weight (we already have lots like that), use it as long as it's re-

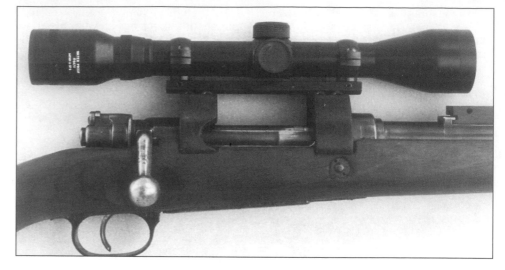

Here is S&K's raised bridge Insta-Mount which allows scope installation on a Mauser without altering the bolt or safety.

Bob Wise occasionally borrows Bell's 2.5x Leupold Compact-equipped Model 7 for whitetails. After all, he's only got forty or fifty rifles of his own.

liable, or if it fails, throw the damn thing away and install another one. Civilian hunters, of course, have the right to buy and carry anything they want, but I have a hunch that most of them will begin to see things my way once they get a mile away from a benchrest or Jeep.

Anyway, what all this boils down to after using scopes of many makes and prices for 60-some years now, which maybe qualifies me to have some opinions, is:

a) It's understandable if you want to get a scope from a longtime, well-

known manufacturer, but many new ones do their darndest to turn out a good product, knowing they have to do so to break into a highly competitive field, so deserve consideration.

b) Pick one to best serve your hunting conditions. Don't fall for the lure of too much magnification; 1 1/2x to 4x is plenty for most woods use, their big fields being more helpful than high power; a good 1-4x variable is the best choice for most big game hunting. A 6x or 8x will do for any long range mountain game, and will also serve for open country pronghorns, the critter that's

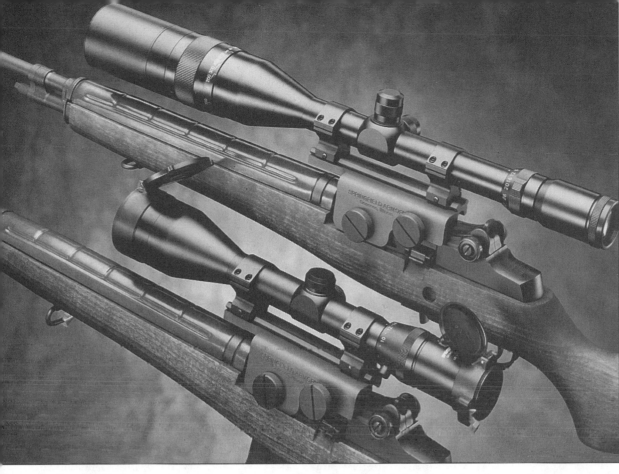

Shown here on military rifles, Springfield Armory Government Model scopes can also be used on hunting rigs.

usually shot at longer range than any other species. A 10x or 12x can usually be used on speedsters also, for field increases proportionately with range, so there's plenty of it at long distances. Higher powers such as 16x to 24x are best suited to long shots at small, indistinct targets like prairie dogs, while still higher magnifications are best reserved for benchrest shooting.

c) For all big game hunting, to be sure of a bright target image, make sure the scope has an exit pupil of at least 5mm diameter (unobstucted objective lens diameter divided by magnification), with 6-7mm being better if much hunting is done in poorest light, as at dawn or dusk. There's never any need to go above 7mm as the eye's entrance pupil never does, so won't admit it.

d) Install the mounts solidly, preferably in a rig whose bases have a recoil shoulder... and make sure it abuts the receiver.

e) Position scope as far forward as possible while maintaining a full field of view from the standing position while wearing hunting clothes. (Any other shooting position will move the eye closer to the scope, and you don't want that to wallop you.)

Consider these suggestions and you'll be in good shape.

Incidentally, I still have that Weaver 29-S.

Well, shoot, when I sat down here I didn't intend to get all hopped up and start preaching. So I'll quit that stuff. Here's what's new this year:

Bausch & Lomb has introduced a most interesting improvement to scopes this year, especially hunting models. They call it RainGuard. Consider: Since scopes were first used many decades ago, moisture was always a problem. Early models leaked a lot, so much so that some German models back in WWI days had holes drilled in the bottom of tubes to let them drain. One of the big attractions of the legendary 2-1/2x Lyman Alaskan of the '30s and early '40s was part of its name, "All-Weather." Following WWII all makes of scopes were improved until most were essentially waterproof, at least one being noted in ads for not leaking a drop after weeks of submersion in a lake. Anyone who had ever hunted in rain or snow quickly learned to appreciate their tight sealing.

Of course, the external lens surfaces could be affected by any kind of moisture. It was common to see circles of innertube stretched around a scope to protect the lenses-even a bandanna folded over the objective while a hunter huddled under a dripping hemlock, and various companies soon made commercial versions of the innertube approach, which could quickly be flipped off so a shot could be fired. But still that was an interruption in proceedings, just another thing to do when time was of the essence. Still, I never heard a hunter suggest any solution to this problem other than, jokingly, tiny windshield wipers. I did once suggest to an inventor that he

dream up some way of making lens covers flip up when the safety was shoved, but nothing ever came of this.

But B&L engineers have been thinking about the wet-lens problem for a long time (needless to say, they're smarter than I am), and after four years of research they developed a process that virtually eliminates external lens fogging. This water repellant coating system, called RainGuard, is applied to the outside of the objective and eyepiece lenses. It causes moisture from rain, fog or snow to form in tiny droplets and sheet off the lenses. The result is a much clearer sight picture.

At the moment, RainGuard is available only on the B&L Elite 4200 Series, five scopes that pretty much cover all shooting needs, 1.5-6x, 2.5-10x, 4-16x, 6-24x, and 36x.

Be nice if you and I could apply this process to the windshields of our 4x4s, wouldn't it?

B&L also has introduced a Command Post reticle in the 3-9x50. The twist of a selector ring gives the choice of thin crosshairs or a 3-post with crosshairs reticle, for use at dawn and dusk.

Bushnell has reintroduced the Scopechief name for their top line, one they used many years ago. I remember the satisfaction I got out of mounting a 10x Scopechief on a 6mm Cobra back in the early '50's. It was one of my deadliest varmint rigs, but the barrel has long been shot out and I don't know where the scope went. The new

Scopechiefs are greatly improved, of course. All have fully multicoated optics, 3.5-inch eye relief, wide fields, new rotating powerchange fast focus eyepiece, and a composite aspherical lens to improve resolution and flatness of field. The Scopechief line includes 1.5-6x32, 3-9x40, 3.5-10x42, 4-14x50, and 6-20x40 models.

Bushnell's Trophy line also has been expanded by a 4-15x40. At less than 14 inches and 19 oz., this one can be used for both big game and varmints. Like all Bushnell scopes for centerfires, it has 1/4 MOA clicks. Adjustments are in semi-turret target knobs, and the objective unit is adjustable to eliminate parallax, of course. In the Sportview line, two shotgun scopes have been added, 1.5-4.5x and 2.5x. Both have Circle-X reticles, ideal for either turkey hunting or deer in the woods.

A few years ago we mentioned Bushnell's Yardage Pro 400, a laser rangefinder which up to approximately a quarter-mile immediately told within ±1 yard how far a target was. Now the unit has been upgraded, with compact models that work the same way to 600 and 800 yards (much farther on highly reflective targets). And a 1000-yard model should be available by the time you read this.

The Yardage Pro 600 which we've been using recently is considerably shorter than the original and a lot lighter. So far we've had a chance to use it on varmints only, and admittedly, up to about 300 yards with a 22-250-class load a rangefinder might not be needed. But in the 300-500 yard bracket, where eyeballed range estimation can easily be off more than a little, this unit helps! And it sure will be appreciated by the pronghorn or sheep hunter when he's excited and needs a confidence builder.

Maybe a beginning varmint hunter can look at a unit like this Yardage Pro with a ho-hum attitude, but as a fellow who's spent decades trying—not too

successfully—to become proficient at range estimation, it's incredible. Just find the target, press a button, and there's the answer. It blows my mind every time I use it.

Leupold has a new Tactical scope this year and has reintroduced an old favorite of mine. The first is a 3.5-10x40 Vari-X III called the Long Range M1. It's built on a 30mm maintube, has a parallax adjustment conveniently located on the left side of the turret, and has a full 65 minutes of w. and e. adjustment in 1/4-MOA clicks which can be both felt and heard. They're resettable to zero after sighting in. The tube is aircraft grade aluminum, lenses have Multicoat 4 coating, and Duplex, Target Dot, and 3/4 Mil Dot reticles are standard choices. Finish is black matte, as serious riflemen want.

Leupold's other offering is the M8 2.5x20 Compact. I got one of these when it first came out years ago, and killed a dozen or more whitetails using it on my Model Seven 7mm-08. It's a perfect addition to that little rifle. The current one has a black matte finish and comes with Duplex, Heavy Duplex, or a new Turkey Ranger reticle, for those who want to mount it on their gobbler-banger. The TR reticle subtends 9 inches between the bottom post and crosswire at 40 yards, where it is parallax free. The Duplexes are adjusted for the usual 150 yards.

New and interesting is the Leupold Scopesmith 40mm ARD (Anti-Reflection Device). Useable on fixed 40mm objective scopes, this unit reduces sunlight and glare, much as a long lens shade does on an adjustable objective scope. The ARD simply snaps into place inside the rim of the objective unit; it protrudes less than a half-inch. A micro-channeled honeycomb structure which fits in front of the lens is an integral part of the ARD.

Also new are Leupold's Quick Install (QI) bases for rifles, shotguns, and

handguns. These use existing assembly holes, so no additional drilling or tapping is necessary. Numerous cross-slots in the mounting surface makes positioning of scope or red dot sight easy.

Pentax has added a Mil Dot reticle option to three of their current models, the 3-9x, 4-16x, and 6-24x Lightseeker scopes. It was earlier available on the 8-32x. The Mil Dot looks like a standard reticle to which 4 oval dots have been added to each crosshair radiating from the center. The distance from each dot to the next one subtends one mil, or one yard at 1000 yards. If the shooter knows the approximate size of his target, its distance can be calculated simply. Pentax scopes feature seven-layer Super Multi-Coating on all glass surfaces, and all are available with gloss, matte, or electroless finish.

Redfield, I'm sorry to report, a company which made sturdy, dependable mounts since early in this century and several lines of excellent scopes since shortly after WWII, is no more. But that doesn't mean this old line is completely gone. I've been told that Blount Inc. has bought the machinery and equipment, inventory, patents, trademark, etc., and will move the manufacturing operations from Denver to Onalaska, WI, a la Weaver. So it seems likely that shooters who have a soft place in their hearts for Redfield products (like me, for instance) will be able to go on getting them.

Swarovski Optik, you might be interested to know, was founded in 1949, and grew out of Swarovski, which was based on a precision grinding machine for precious stones in 1895 in the Tirolean town of Wattens. In 1935, Wilhelm Swarovski, eldest son of the firm's founder, developed the prototype of a pair of binoculars, and thereby laid the foundation for their optics department. The company has long been recognized worldwide for the excellence of its products.

Latest addition in its scope field is the 3-9x36 AV ultralight 1-inch riflescope. Weighing 11.8 oz., it has a 43-15 foot field and is waterproof/submersible even with the turret caps removed.

A new reticle now available in the Swarovski 3-12x50 and 3-9x36 was designed by retired Air Force Lt. Col. T.D. Smith. It functions directly with the 308 and 30-06 cartridges using 165-gr. and 175-gr. bullets respectively, though any loads of about the same ballistic coefficient that give similar velocities can be used. In use, the rifle is zeroed on the center crosshair. Beneath the intersection are four additional calibrated smaller crosshairs that correspond to 200, 300, 400, and 500 yards respectively. These are stacked in a pyramid format, the end of each crosshair corresponding to the compensation needed for a 10 mph perpendicular crosswind at that specific range.

Conetrol mounts are made in several finishes, including non-glare for cautious hunters.

Swarovski is also making two styles of red illuminated reticles for their Habicht 2.5-10x56, 3-12x50, 8x50, and 8x56 scopes. One illuminates the inner crosswires, the other is in effect a center dot. A brightness control allows infinitely variable adaptation to the surrounding light intensity, but prevents a swamping of the view. The red light does not affect the shooter's night vision.

Kahles, which has been building scopes for over 100 years, has just introduced a new American Hunter. A 3-9x42, it's built here in America using Kahles components from Austria. Tube diameter is 1 inch, to take most of our mounts. Since Kahles has for some years been a Swarovski company, it's not unusual that both have the same illuminated and T.D. Smith reticles, as well as other European styles. Like Swarovski, Kahles has a full line of hunting scopes, both fixed powers and variables.

Weaver scopes are made in more styles and powers and sizes that I have time to count, so I'll just say if you're looking for a new scope and don't want to check the whole market, try a Weaver; they'll have whatever you need. This outfit has sure come a long way since the 3/4-inch 330 and 29-S of the early '30s. It's interesting that the K2.5, the first 1-inch tube scope after WWII, is still available, albeit much updated. I still have one of the originals from the '40s. I dunno how many guns I've had it on, but it still works. That's worth thinking about when you've got a spare moment.

The K4 and K6 are still offered too, though they've been much revised. Both now have non-adjustable 38mm objectives, which is 10mm larger than anyone needs for a 4x, but what the hell. Probably simplifies parts inventory a bit. Weaver's Target and Varmint scopes are known for their super-accurate Micro-Trac adjustments, and the lower powered T6 has this system too, as well as an adjustable objective, all of which makes this scope a high favorite among hunter-benchrest competitors. I remember when 6x was all the magnification most varmint hunters thought they needed... which shows how old I'm gettin', huh? Of course, in those days nobody had to apologize if he was caught with a Hornet or Bee in the chuck meadows.

(Incidentally, for some time I've been using a Ruger No. 1 Hornet for much of my ordinary varmint shooting, and results have been great. It has a medium heavy barrel, 8x Leupold with small dot, and makes 5-shot groups of 1-1/4 inches, occasionally smaller. This means it takes chucks up to 200 yards with ease, so long as I do my part, and I've had some kills to about 235. It sure is a delight to shoot after so many years of big boomers.)

Nightforce continues to offer their line of six big variables and two fixed powers. The latter are 26x56 and 36x56, while the others range from a 1.75-6x42 to 12-42x56. Weights go from 22 to 38.5 oz., which is noticeable if you ever have to lug it cross country on a heavy varmint rifle, plus a sack of ammo, a big canteen of water, etc. Maybe in the Outback of Australia nobody has to get out of the Jeep, but that's usually illegal here in the States.

With scopes this heavy be sure to use the sturdiest mounts you can find and check your long range zero occasionally. A minute mount movement can cause a miss out yonder, even if you think you're sighted in because closer shots are still kills; actually, in such cases the size of the target just absorbs the error.

Unlike many other scopemakers who seem to be caught up in the

One of three new airgun scopes from Simmons, all of which feature 1/8-moa clicks.

American habit of change for change's sake, the Nightforce people just build the best models they can and stick with 'em. There's something to be said for that approach.

Springfield Armory scopes usually are thought of as military or police counter-terrorist sighting systems, and that seems to be their primary function. Nevertheless, the same qualities which make them suitable there can be useful to the long range hunter. In addition to top quality optics, Springfield Armory scopes are built to stand up to the recoil of rifles chambered for the 50-cal. BMG cartridge. (And that's a significant amount, I can tell you, after trying it.) There are eight scopes in the SA line, which is called the Government Model series. The 6x40 and 10x56 are the only fixed powers. Five are 4-14s, all but one with 56mm objectives, and the last is a 6-20x56.

All models have an Internal Bubble Level at the bottom of the field. One has a reticle which has aiming points calibrated for 5.56mm match ammo in hundred-yard units out to 700, others for the 7.62mm to 1000. Reticle features of known dimension allow direct view rangefinding when the target's approx-imate size is known. Stated simply, the shooter determines the range, chooses the aiming point that matches it, and shoots. If he has estimated or measured the wind properly, and used a known reticle measurement to hold off for it, and if he/gun/ammo are good enough, a hit will result. This reticle looks complex at first, and it does take a bit of time to use, but at long range you normally have time to get organized, so its aid to hitting is obvious.

A Mil Dot reticle is also offered, and can be used essentially the same way. Knowing the reticle measurements in mils and the target size in inches, a table which can be taped to the gun stock shows distance in meters where the target/reticle lines cross.

Conetrol is adding to its inventory two-piece bases made of stainless steel, with Huntur, Gunnur or Custom finishes. Currently available are bases to fit BSA, Hoya, McMillan, Sauer and Savage bolt actions, the drilled Kimber Big Game Rifle, Browning A-Bolt and BBR, Remington 700, Winchester 70, Weatherby Mark V, and large-ring Mausers. Other stainless bases will be added as more rifles of this material are produced.

For shooters who want to mount scopes with extraordinarily large ends, Conetrol has a line of extra-high horizontally split 1-inch rings in three heights. They fit all Conetrol bases, which have windage adjustment built in. Some one-piece bases without windage adjustment are made. They also offer the well known projectionless rings in three heights for scopes with 26mm, 26-1/2mm, and 30mm tubes.

S&K has long been renowned for their Insta-Mounts which make it easy to attach a scope to an unaltered military rifle without drilling or tapping, though occasionally some wood must be removed or the bolt ground a bit. A few of the rifles easily scoped are the '03-A3, M1 Carbine, M1 Garand, Krag, SMLE, 1917 and P14 Enfield. We've recently had a chance to examine a raised bridge design for the 98 Mauser. Made for either large or small ring receivers, it's just high enough to allow working

Varminter Ranging Reticle
(NP1-RR)

The Varminter Ranging Reticle is much easier to use than it may first appear. The brackets are based on 18 inch targets and the circles represent 9 inches at the stated yardage's located near the lower portion of the reticle. All ranging and use of hold over points must be done at the following power settings to maintain these values:

3.5-15x56	15x
5.5-22x56	22x
8-32x56	22x or the "R" (ranging) position on the power change ring.
12-42x56	22x or the "R" (ranging) position on the power change ring.

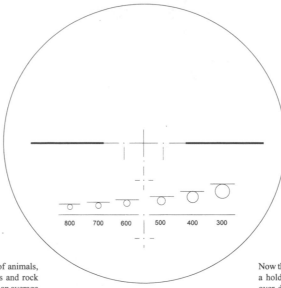

800 700 600   500 400 300

This reticle is capable of ranging a variety of animals, such as: elk, deer, coyotes, fox, prairie dogs and rock chucks to name a few. Deer, for example, have an average span of 18 inches from shoulder to brisket. Therefore, to range the animal, line up the solid line above the circles with the shoulder blade and the brisket with the solid line above the yard markings. Which ever one fits is the distance in yards.

Now that you know your targets range you simply choose a hold over point based on your ballistics. The hold over dots are provided at 4, 8, 15, and 20 m.o.a., you may also use the top or bottom of a post/line in between dots. The hold over points provided are based on flat shooting cartridges. Windage hold off points are also provided. A complete diagram showing all reference points is provided with the product.

---

of the unaltered bolt and safety. For those who want to get away from the military look, beautifully machined SKulptured mounts are available to blend with a fine sporter.

Ironsighter See-Thru mounts have long been popular with guys who still don't quite trust glass sights or often have to hunt in bad weather, so want the immediate option of metallics. They're made for most muzzleloaders as well as modern style firearms and can be had in regular height as well as raised, and to fit Kwik-Site and Weaver style bases.

Kwik-Site is another see-thru mount which this year has a design for blackpowder rifles in which the lower halves of the rings are made integral with a long base that has an open sight at its rear end. They also make a sort of triple decker mount that takes a small flashlight in the top, a scope in the middle, and permits a view of the iron sights through the bottom tunnel. Handy for night shooting of foxes, say, for the light's always in a perfect position.

Steiner's Hunting Z scopes come in three models at the moment, all variables, 1.5-5x, 2.5-8x, and 3.5-10x. They're made in the U.S. using German CAT/AC optics for crisp resolution and very high light trans-mission, and Leupold's precise adjustments and me-

chanical features. They have aircraft grade hardened aluminum 30 mm tubes with matte finish, 4-inch eye relief, and 1 cm. (about 1/3-minute) clicks. Duplex reticles are available in all (also Heavy Duplex in the 1.5-5x), as well as European #4, which looks like a HD without the 12 o'clock post. (I've often wondered what's supposed to be the advantage with this style reticle, as the top post never obscures your target, while at extremely long range the 6 o'clock post might. But doubtless some German optical expert could explain it.) I've often written that I prefer the smallest size variable for average shooting, but you can't go wrong with any size Steiner; they're all of top quality.

Simmons, who offers extensive lines of scopes for rifles and handguns, this year has added three models for airguns, the ProAir series. Included are a 4x32, 4-12x40, and 6-18x40. All have 1-inch tubes, black matte finish, and 1/8-MOA clicks. They're designed and built to withstand the unique recoil generated by airguns that most scopes can't tolerate. Anyone who questions the need for 1/8-minute scope clicks on an airgun has never shot one of the precision models. Within their range, they're more accurate than any cartridge gun I've shot. And you can spend several thousand dol-

lars to get one, so don't think we're talking about a kid's BB gun.

B-Square's Interlock mounts have been made to fit almost countless rifles, shotguns and handguns for a long time, with rings available for their own one-piece base or Weaver or tip-off styles. The rings can be either fixed or adjusted for w. and e. But there are an awful lot of guns out there to keep up

Kwik-Site see-thru mounts are made in several styles, including one that holds flashlight above scope and permits using metallic sights below.

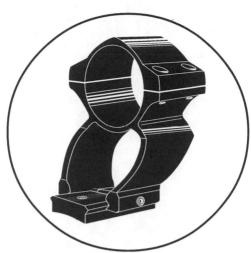

The standard Kwik-Site mount, in use for decades.

with, so mounts for additional ones are added constantly. New this year are those for the Taurus Raging Bull pistol; saddle mounts for the Rem. 870 Express, Browning Gold Series, and Beretta A390 shotguns. (Bases are now available for all predrilled shotguns and slug guns.) The AAA Vari-Clamp airgun mounts have adjustable w. and e. plus an adjustable base to fit any rail or grooved receiver from airguns to 22s. Also, to prevent canting in precision airgun shooting, a Bubble Level is offered for attaching to the mount. And for those into shooting military rifles, there's now a QD mount for the French MAS 49/56 and the Romanian AK, and Scout mount for Mauser and Mosin-Nagant.

Swift has a new line of hunting scopes this year called the Premier. It includes six rifle models and one for handguns. All are variables and all rifle scopes have 50mm objectives except one 3-9x40. Powers go from a 2.5-10x (which has a 30mm tube) to 6-18x. The handgun model is 1.25x4x28. All are hard anodized, waterproof, are multicoated, and have adjustable objectives.

Parsons Optical Co. is dedicated to the preservation of vintage optical sights, building reproductions and accessories, etc. For instance, they manufacture new Super Target Spots from Lyman's original blueprints; build the Parsons Long Scope, a 28 to 34-inch duplicate of a glass that buffalo hunters felt blessed to have on their big singleshot Sharps rifles; and make original style Stevens and Malcolm mounts, as well as many other items, all top quality.

BSA is an old British company that is now owned by the same Spanish group which builds GAMO airguns. Additionally, they now also offer three scope lines, the Platinum and Bronze for centerfires and the Blue for rimfires. The twelve Platinums go from a 1.5-6x to 3-12x, including fixed powers,

with objectives from 42 to 52mm. There are nine Bronze models in similar powers with somewhat smaller front ends. We've had a chance to use the 3.5-10x50 Platinum, which has a duplex style reticle (they call it 4-post), matte finish, diopter eyepiece focusing, and 1/4-minute clicks which can easily be adjusted by the fingertips. It's given excellent results.

Schmidt & Bender is making about two dozen scopes at the moment, the fixed powers with 1-inch steel tubes, all the

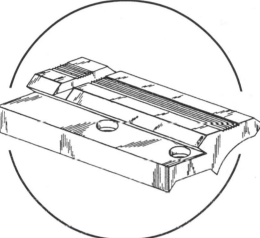

New offset bases for muzzleloaders look like this.

variables with hardened aluminum tubes of 30mm or 34mm diameter. Except for the 1.25-4x20, all have large objectives, topping out at 56mm. Many reticles are available, some illuminated. We've never talked about the Precision Hunter line before, so will give a bit of detail. Three scopes are included, 4-16x50, 3-12x50, and 2.5-10x56.

The 4-16x has a Mil Dot reticle, 5mm (1/5") clicks, and a parallax adjustment on the left side of the turret. The 3-12x is identical to the 4-16x, except its clicks are valued at 2/5" and it has no parallax adjustment; it is adjusted at the factory to be parallax free at 200 meters. The 2.5-10x also has 2/5" clicks and is made with their No. 9 Reticle, which has three conspicuous posts (none at 12 o'clock) overlying the crosshairs and extending inward far enough to contact a small open circle. The posts make this reticle conspicuous enough for hunting dangerous game at bottom power, while the open dot surrounding the CH intersection allows precision shooting at distant game. I've never used a Precision Hunter model, but have used several S&B scopes for years with perfect satisfaction. Optics and mechanics have always been top grade.

Zeiss has a line of six new scopes this year, the Diavari VM/Vs. The VMs have an integral mounting rail, the Vs

take conventional ring mounts, so maybe we could say there are actually twelve scopes, but since they differ only in mounting systems this seems simpler.

Smallest of the line is a 1.1-4x24 called the Varipoint. It's the only one with an unenlarged objective unit and features a battery illuminated red dot reticle. The dot is all the reticle there is. No crosshairs, no posts. When illumination is unnecessary, the dot appears black.

Other models are the 1.5-6x42, 2.5-10x50, 3-12x56, 3-9x42, and 5-15x42. All are built on 30mm tubes and lenses have the well known Zeiss T multicoating. (Zeiss, incidentally, was the company that developed lens coating, back in the '30s. Experts have declared this the biggest improvement in optics since the invention of lenses themselves). All VM/Vs have a minimum of 3.5 inches eye relief, which is comforting to know when you're shooting a magnum, and there's a big choice of reticles. Eyepieces have binocular focusing. Speaking of eye relief, we'll take a moment to again

So-called Weaver-style rings fit both Kwik-Site and Weaver bases.

remind everyone that all scopes should be mounted as far forward as possible while maintaining a full field of view. It's a good idea to keep the rear end of that tube from contacting your eyebrow during recoil. Take it from someone who learned the hard way decades ago. We used to call it the Mark of the Magnum. Now it probably should be called the Mark of the Stupid Shooter.

Since 1997 Zeiss has been offering the Diavari C 3-9x36, a high grade, popular magnification model which is built on a 1-inch tube as Americans like. It's a fine scope that has over 90 percent light transmission. Because it's produced here it sells for well under the price of models made in Germany. ●

by LARRY S. STERETT

HANDLOADING UPDATE

Known for their fly boxes, tackle cases, and decoys, **Flambeau Products** produces a bench ideal for handloaders short on space. Tabbed the Work Center Fold, it folds down against the wall for storage to take up only 4-1/2 inches of space. When raised and locked, using a bolt and spring system, it will support up to 300 pounds on its 38-inch long work surface. Two adjustable clamps on the work surface will hold any of several different brands of single stage shotshell or metallic cartridge reloading presses.

rifles or handguns. An optional oscilloscope output jack to record pressure curves is available, but it does require a computer and oscilloscope combination to function, which the peak chamber pressure measurement does not.

The gauge is reasonably simple to install and operate, and complete instructions are provided. The meter has two switches-on/off and balance/peak hold and two buttons-reset and test. The necessary formulas are included to estimate absolute chamber pressures in psi, and, by comparing with factory load pressure levels, The user can keep all handloads within safe limits.

Fabrique Scientific currently has available a STRAIN 2.0 computer program which allows estimation of chamber pressure from the strain. A second program under development will allow estimation of the pressure curve, given

Cowboy ACTION Shooting and Sporting Clays shooters are discovering what many hunters, including varmint and small/big game, and skeet/trap clay target shooters already knew. Handloading is not only fun, it can be economical once the initial cost is realized.

Colorado Shooter's Supply has a new Cast Bullet Guide with information about cast bullets and their design, and for reloading using cast bullets it's worth the price. This firm has the nosepour Hoch Custom Bullet Moulds in 2, 3, and 4 cavity models available in most standard calibers, with custom designs made to order.

Corbin, the premier manufacturer of bullet swaging equipment has a new priming tool for the 50 BMG cartridge. It's available to fit either the Mega-Mite press or the Hydro-Press, and consists of two separate assemblies. One part screws into the ram with the second screwing into the press head. Adjustment is such that primers can be set to a precise given depth without fear of crushing.

The SL 900 Shotshell Reloader by **Dillon Precision Products** is now out and loading, and it's a gem. Available only in 12 gauge at present, with other gauges to be introduced later, it has a number of great features including an electric case feeding system, automatic positive-feed priming system, and a 25-pound shot hopper. It comes with factory-adjusted dies, and accessories are available.

Owners of Dillon AT 500 or RL 550B metallic reloading presses who load long grain extruded powders in their rifle cartridges, might want to check out the new Powder Measure Adapter. It permits the use on the above presses of any manufacturer's powder measure having 7/8x14 threads, but does require a Dillon AT 500 or similar powder die.

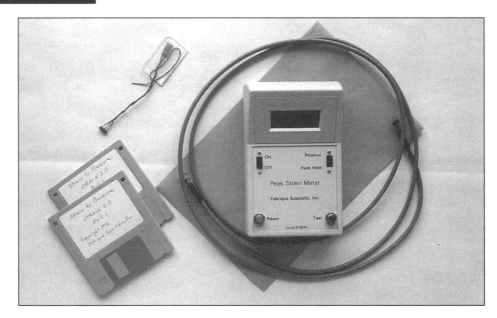

Fabrique Scientific's Peak Strain Meter and STRAIN 2.0 computer program allow estimation of chamber pressure.

Handloaders are frequently concerned about the pressures their reloads are producing, but have not had an economical means of determining such pressures. Three decades back, a lead crusher device was available to gauge relative pressure for rifle cartridges, but now a much better method is available. **Fabrique Scientific, Inc.** has introduced a Peak Strain Meter useful for measuring relative chamber pressures in shotguns,

Hodgdon's new No. 27 Data Manual has more than 750 pages, includes loading data on more than 150 different handgun and rifle cartridges from the 17 Bumble Bee and 17 Ackley to the 50 BMG and 500 Linebaugh.

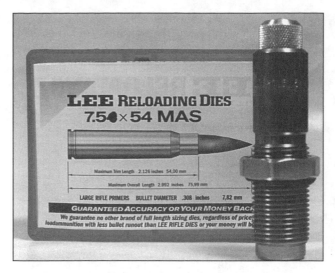

Lee Precision's new die sets include ones for the French 7.5 x 54 mm MAS cartridges; Starline will have brass cases this year.

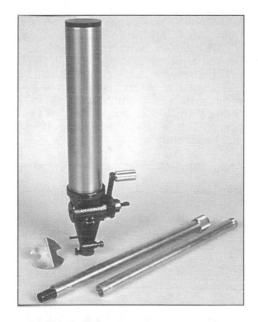

Lymon Products has a No. 55 Powder Measure specially designed for Cowboy Action Shooters loading black powder. It includes an aluminum non-sparking reservoir and brass metering sleeve.

a measured muzzle velocity, permitting handloaders to go a step further.

Forster Precision Products introduced the Classic 50 Case Trimmer and the 50 BMG Case Trimmer last year, but a couple of new items have been added. The Classic 50 is now available as a kit, which includes three collets and three pilots. Scaled to handle trimming of all the long English, U. S. and metric cartridge cases, the Classic 50 will accept nearly 300 different cases, according to Forster, from the smaller ones such as the 280 Nitro Express Rimmed Flanged to the larger 505 Gibbs and 12.17 x 44 Remington.

Another new Forster item is the Hand Outside Neck Turner for the 50 BMG case. This turner features a carbide neck thickness cutter, micrometer

adjustment knob accurate to 0.0005 inch and centerless ground pilots.

Hodgdon Powder Company has a new Data Manual. Number 27 contains more than 750 pages and is the most comprehensive manual the firm has produced, with historical information and detailed "how to" descriptions of cartridge assembly. Replacing the former hardbound editions, No. 27 offers a European-style ring binder that permits removal of individual data sheets. Most of the illustrations, with the major exception of the dimensioned cartridge drawings, are in full color, with the data page margins in attention-getting black.

Loading data covers golden oldies and new cartridges such as the 260 Remington, 30-378 Weatherby, 475 and 500 Linebaugh and others. There are 102 rifle cartridges from the 17 Ackley Bee to the 50 BMG, and 52 handgun cartridges from the 17 Bumble Bee to the 500 Linebaugh. With each set of data is a new three-dimensional cartridge case drawing and a complete listing of all components used in the development of the data for the specific cartridge.

In addition to Hodgdon powers, data for Alliant, IMR, and Winchester powers are included for the most popular cartridges, courtesy of those companies. Another feature is a set of exterior ballistic tables for bullets having ballistic coefficients ranging 0.12 to 0.56, providing velocity, energy, time of flight, and bullet path data. Short range tables provide data from 50 to 250 yards for bullets with coefficients of 0.39 or less, and long range tables provide data from 100 to 500 yards for bullets with coefficients from 0.14 to 0.56. Tabbed dividers separate the ten sections. An appropriate foreword with warning and mission statement is provided, along with an excellent Table of Contents, Tribute to Bruce Hodgdon and an index.

Hornady Manufacturing continues to expand the Lock-N-Load line with a new powder measure, featuring interchangeable standard, rifle, or pistol metering inserts. The latter two inserts are micrometer adjustable to 0.1 grain. A case-activated auto powder drop mechanism is available as an accessory or as a standard feature on the Lock-N-Load AP press. This drop automatically activates, dispensing a powder charge with every pull of the handle, but only when a case is present in the station. New Lock-N-Load bushing adapters and a Lock-N-Load drain metering insert are also available.

Another new item is the Cam-Lock bullet puller. It fits regular 7/8x14 die stations, and collets are available in 13

The New RCBS APS hand priming tool features a universal shell holder and the use of regular APS priming strips. For handloaders having a preference to 'feel' the primers being seated it is ideal.

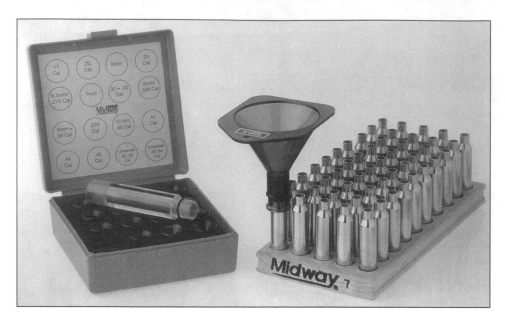

Midway USA's new Smarter Powder Funnel comes with a 3-inch drop tube and 16 different nozzles to fit calibers from .17 to .50, storable in a hinged-lid plastic case.

sizes to handle bullets ranging from 0.172-inch to 0.454-inch. With the puller installed and adjusted, just clamp down and the bullet is out.

Lee Precision, Inc. has a host of new products for handloaders, including fourteen new Deluxe three-die sets for rifle cartridges. These range from the 22 Hornet to the 303 British, and include the 220 Swift and 6.5x55mm Swedish. Lee also has dies for the 7.5x54mm French MAS cartridge, and Starline will be introducing reloadable brass cases for this cartridge about the time this appears in print. These cases will feature Boxer-type primer pockets.

Other new Lee products include a 7mm STW Factory Crimp Die and a limited production 2-die set for the 7mm STW cartridge, a Lube & Sizing Kit for .323-inch bullets, and two new 6-cavity Moulds: 401-175-TC and 358-158-RF to turn out cast bullets for 10mm and 38/357 handgun cartridges.

Lyman Products has been producing top quality reloading products for handloaders for more than six score years, and they continue to do so. The T-Mag and Crusher reloading presses have been reengineered and upgraded. Hi-tech iron frames with Silver Hammertone Powder Coat finishes, non-rust handles and links, and 'machined flat' bases for solid mounting, and left or right hand operation are standard features of the T-Mag II and Crusher II. And extra turrets are available for the T-Mag.

In the new die arena 50-90 and 45-120 sets are available in standard 7/8x14 3-die sets, and the 40-65 Winchester dies are available for the Lyman 310 Tool. Originally introduced in the last century as "The Ideal Tool", the 310 was known as the Tong Tool by many shooters.

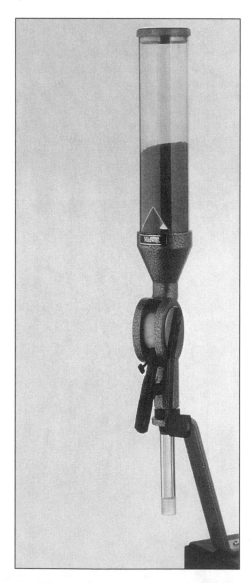

The Midway USA Indispensable Powder Dispenser is cast aluminum, has a laser-cut powder chamber and micrometer-adjustable metering chamber.

For big bore shooters there's a new Extra-Large Deburring Tool which will deburr the case mouths of cases up to 60 caliber, inside and out. The standard power trimmer has been improved with a new high torque motor for better trimming, and there's a manually operated 50 BMG Trimmer to take care of the 50 BMG cartridge.

A new version of the No. 55 Powder Measure is available. Designed especially for cowboy action shooters using black powder the 55 features an aluminum powder reservoir and a non-sparking brass metering sleeve. It comes with or without a 24-inch long drop tube (The tube is also available separately.) and mounts directly on the bench, a powder measure stand, or a press using a 7/8x14 adapter. A new powder measure baffle is available to fit all No. 55 measures, old or new.

Moly coating of bullets is becoming 'the way to go' with many handloaders, and Lyman has a Super Moly Tumble Coat Bullet Finishing Kit that contains a 1200 tumbler, extra coating bowl, Superfine Grade Moly, media and steel polishing media. A kit without the tumbler is available, and step-by-step instructions are naturally included. Super Moly Bore Cream, Spray and Superfine Grade Moly Powder are available separately.

The Midway USA Model 2009 single-stage reloading press will handle cases as long as the 470 Nitro Express, 460 Weatherby Magnum and similar lengths.

In the bullet mould department large handles for two-cavity moulds are available, in addition to moulds for several new or reintroduced designs. One of the most interesting is the limited edition (100 moulds only will be available) of the 145 grain 'collar button' bullet introduced originally in the late 1800's for the 45-70 Gov't. cartridge. The bullet weighs the same as a 45 round ball, the 'collar button' mould comes with a #130 top punch. Other moulds include the #311672 producing a 160 grain flatnose bullet for the 308 Winchester and similar cartridges; the #319247 producing a 165 grain flatnose for rifles such as the 32-40; the #323471 turning out a 210 grain 8mm bullet while the #457671 produces a 475 grain round nose bullet for rifles such as the 45-70, 45-90, and 45-120. All designs but the #319247 and the 45 "collar button" are for use with gas checks. Designs for cowboy action shooters include moulds #358665, #427666, #429667, and #452664, for 38, 44/40, 44 and 45 Colt, respectively. Black Powder Gold Bullet Lube and Super Moly Bullet Lube has also been introduced for these cast bullets designs.

Magma Engineering Company, the firm which produces automated bullet casting equipment, has purchased manufacturing rights to the Star Lubricator and Resizer and will be marketing it as the Magma Star Lube-sizer. This manually-operated sizer lubes straight through, dropping the sized/lubed bullet out the bottom ready to load. Additional

A cut-away view of one of the RCBS X-Die full length sizing dies, available for most bottleneck cartridges.

sizing dies, bullet feeder, heated base, and other accessories are available from Magma, as are parts for the older Star Machine Works Lubricator and Resizer.

Handloaders turning out large quantities of reloads of one particular cartridge using bottleneck cases, such as the 5.56mm (.223) or 7.62mm (.308) might want to consider the Gracey Case Trimmer from **Match Prep**. A bit pricey at just over two century notes it comes complete with one cartridge holder, and holders

Shotgunners will find the latest MTM Products Shotshell/Choke Tube case an excellent place to keep 50 or 100 reloads, depending on the shell length. With the slide-in choke tube case on top, it's off to the range.

One of eight new RCBS CAS two-cavity moulds for bullet casting, along with sizing die and top punch.

MTM Molded Products new P64-50-10 hinged-lid case will hold 64 loaded 50 A.E., 440 Cor-Bon, or similar size handgun cartridges.

for most bottleneck cartridges are available. It registers on the shoulder of the resized case and will completely trim, chamfer and deburr 500 cases per hour.

Midway USA is continuing to grow. Four new biggies include an Indispensable Powder Dispenser, a Model 2099 single-stage reloading press with enough clearance for loading 3-inch Sharps cases and most English Nitro Express cases, and a Smarter Powder Funnel with a 3-inch drop tube and 16 different nozzles to fit specific families of calibers from 17 to 50. Fourth is a shotshell reloading press which will initially be available to reload 12 gauge shells.

The Smarter Powder Funnel comes with a plastic storage case for the 16 nozzles, with the lid charted to indicate the specific caliber nozzle, and

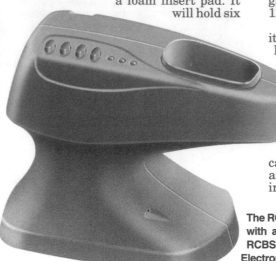

tures a handled container for shot shells with a separate slide-in choke tube case nestled on top. The choke tube case features see-thru plastic and a foam insert pad. It will hold six

extended tubes or nine standard tubes, along with most factory wrenches. The shotshell case will hold 100 standard (2-3/4") or magnum length (3") 12 gauge shells, or 50 of the 3-1/2" 10 or 12 gauge magnum shells.

The second new MTM Case-Gard item, the P64-50-10, is a plastic hinged-lid ammo box capable of holding 50 handgun cartridges of the 50 AE, 440 Cor-Bon, 475 and 500 Linebaugh class. Handloaders using new Starline brass, which is bulk packed, will find this new box ideal.

More and more shooters are beginning to reload the 50 BMG cartridge, and additional equipment and components are gradually becoming available. **NECO** has a couple of

The RCBS Electronic Powder Trickler is compatible with any type of powder, and will work with the RCBS Uniflow Powder Measure and Powder Pro Electronic Scale.

RCBS's new Cowboy Action Shooting or CAS loading dies are designed for loading lead bullets in 13 different revolver/carbine calibers 25-20 to 45 Colt.

is currently priced at just under a saw-buck. The Indispensable Powder Measure is of cast aluminum construction with a durable baked-on finish, clear powder hopper with baffle, and steel rotor arm and micrometer. The powder chamber is laser-cut and the micrometer-adjusted metering chamber locks into place to insure a precision charge every time. Two micrometers—pistol and rifle—are included with each Indispensable, along with a Smarter Powder Funnel system, and bench and shelf-mount brackets.

The Model 2009 single-stage reloading press is constructed of heat-treated cast aluminum, with steel ram, pins and lever. It features an 0-frame and will handle reloading of most metallic cartridges, including the 460 Weatherby Magnum, 470 Nitro Express and various Sharps cartridges, from depriming to case forming.

Midway has two new LoadMAP Manuals, bringing the current total to three, one each for the 45 ACP, 9mm, and 44 Remington Magnum. Unlike many other manuals, the Load-MAP manuals are in full color in graph form, and test results are given for each of the bullets of a particular caliber sold by Midway. Using ten of the most popular powders, Midway documented as much as a 20 percent variation in velocity using different brand bullets of the same weight with the same weight powder charge.

Shooters always seem to be in need of boxes or cases into which they can place their newly handloaded shot-shells or metallic cartridges. **MTM Molded Products** has a couple of new items along this line. The MTM Case-Gard Shotshell/Choke Tube case fea-

The new Speer Reloading Manual No. 13 has more than 700 pages featuring over 7,000 loads for pistol and rifle cartridges, includes cartridge drawings and ballistic tables as well.

The RCBS.Load V.288 computer software program contains the latest Speer reloading manual (No. 13), and the Accurate Reloading Guide No. 1, the RCBS Cast Bullet Manual, a Cartridge Designer tool, dimensional drawings and a host of other information useful to handloaders.

The Reloaders Delight, shown by Todd and Stephen Kolacz, the innovators, is a display case holding one-ounce bottles of forty of the most popular reloading powders.

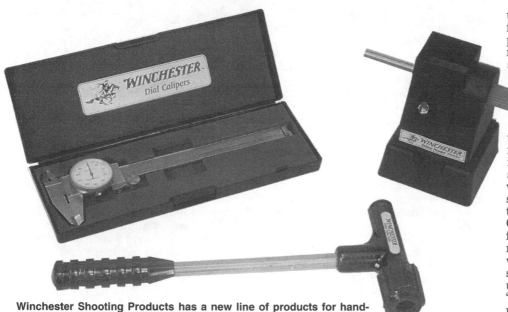

Winchester Shooting Products has a new line of products for hand-loaders, including a stainless steel dial caliper, a Deluxe Powder Trickler and an inertia bullet puller.

useful items, including a Case Holder for trimming the 50 BMG case in a drill press, and a Concentricity, Wall Thickness and Runout Gauge. The stainless steel Case Holder is designed to hold the 50 BMG case in an exact location on a drill press or milling machine table for trimming with a piloted counter-boring cutter. According to NECO the typical trimming cycle time using this holder is 2-3 seconds, not including deburring and chamfering. The Concentricity & etc. Gauge is similar to the regular NECO Gauge, but with an extra long base assembly and a special Chord Anvil Rod to accomodate the 50 BMG cartridge. This patented Case Gauge is designed to measure five features, including (1) the curved 'banana' shape of the case, (2) the relative wall thickness variation, (3) out-of-squareness of the case head, (4) individual 'out-of-round' or 'egg-shape' and/or 'banana' shape bullets, and (5) loaded round runout. Constructed of stainless steel and hard-anodized aluminum

Sierra's INFINITY Suite software Exterior Ballistics computer program is available in CD-ROM only. It contains the 4th Edition Rifle and Handgun Reloading Manuals, multiple trajectory charts, a Point Blank Range program, and much more.

To make sure the cases you reload are clean and bright and your bullets slick, Winchester has a new Deluxe Vibratory Tumbler, dry Moly Lubricant, a Brass/Media Separator, Brass Polish, and corn cob Brass Cleaning Media.

Every manufacturer of sporting powders for cartridge reloading generally introduces a small complimentary manual each year. This is some of this year's crop.

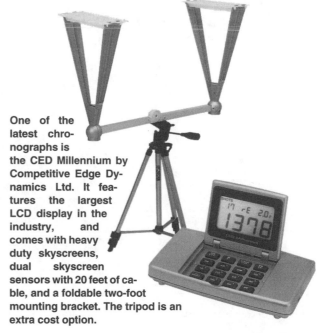

One of the latest chronographs is the CED Millennium by Competitive Edge Dynamics Ltd. It features the largest LCD display in the industry, and comes with heavy duty skyscreens, dual skyscreen sensors with 20 feet of cable, and a foldable two-foot mounting bracket. The tripod is an extra cost option.

components the gauge comes complete with a precision all-angle dial indicator, necessary accessories and an instruction manual.

Blount's **RCBS** line has been expanded to include a new AmmoMaster 50 BMG Pack, Electronic Powder Trickler, Cowboy Action Shooting Dies, and several new bullet moulds. The 50 BMG Pack includes a single stage AmmoMaster press rigged for 1-1/2" 50 BMG dies, a set of dies (full-length sizer and seater), ram priming unit, shell holder and a trim die. The only other items needed to turn out loaded 50 BMG cartridges are a powder scale and the components.

The Electronic Powder Trickler is compatible with any type of powder and will work with the Powder Pro Electronic Scale and the Uniflow Powder Measure by automatically adding powder to the pan until the memorized weight is reached. It has repeatable accuracy to 0.1 grain.

Now there's an APS hand Priming Tool with universal shell holder which will handle cases from the 32 ACP to the 45-70, without having to change shell holders. Constructed of cast metal with a grip shape modeled after the M1911 pistol it doesn't ride up during use. Regular APS priming strips holding 25 primers are used, and two primer plugs are provided to take care of the use of small or larger primers. For those reloaders with a preference to 'feel' the seating of primers this new hand tool should do the job, and well.

The new Cowboy Action Shooting or CAS loading dies are designed for loading lead bullets. The die bodies feature a case-hardened appearance with brass locking rings, and two and three-die sets are available, depending on the caliber.

Currently 13 revolver/carbine calibers are available, from the 25-20 Winchester to the 45 Colt.

The new X-Die is designed to control case growth during full length resizing, so trimming following each sizing is eliminated. The X-Dies are available for most popular bottleneck rifle cartridges from 223 Remington to 300 Winchester Magnum, as a set or the X-Sizer Die is available separately.

The new RCBS **CAS** dies now bring the die lines to seven. According to RCBS, at last count they could produce reloading dies for over 3,100 custom calibers. That's a lot of dies, anyway you count.

Eight CAS two-cavity moulds are available to cast bullets ranging from the 85-grain 25-20 to the 230 grain 45 Colt design. Another new 45 Colt mould is available to cast 270-grain flatnose bullets. For black powder silhouette shooters a new mould is available to cast 312-grain .378-in. diameter pointed bullets for 38-55 rifles/carbines. Members of the North-South Skirmish Association should find the new North-South Skirmish Bullet Moulds to their liking. Five Minie-type moulds are available to cast 0.500, 0.520, 0.576, 0.578 and 0.580-inch size bullets. The bullets feature two or three lube grooves depending on the size.

Speer Reloading Manual #13 contains over 700 pages of how-to information with over 9,000 loads. Bullet data, charts, cartridge drawings, detailed

ballistic tables, special tech sections, and even a problem solving section are features of the latest hardbound Speer Manual. It's also found in RCBS.LOAD V2.88, along with the RCBS Cast Bullet Manual and the Accurate Loading Guide No. 1. RCBS. LOAD V2.88 is a comprehensive software program which features a Cartridge Designer tool, Ballistic Coefficient Calculator, over 900 factory loads, a list of 1,137 component bullets and over 760 loads for standard and wildcat cartridges, in addition to a database of dimensional drawings for over 330 cartridges. It does require a 486DX PC with 16MB RAM and a color monitor with a capacity of 1024x768 pixel resolution recommended. Windows 95 or Windows NT is needed and a 5MB hard drive is required with up to 14MB recommended.

Although not exactly reloading equipment, **Reloaders Delight** could be handy for those shooters loading for many calibers and wanting to

Lyman's new X-Large deburring tool handles cases up to 60-caliber—and down to 17!

try a few loads without having to purchase conventional quantities. A hand-crafted display case holds a total of 160 bottles-four bottles each of the forty most popular powders. Each one-ounce bottle provides enough powder to load approximately 85 handgun cartridges or 8-10 rifle cartridges. (Dealers handling reloading components should be 'delighted' with this new product.) Currently, Accurate Arms, Alliant, Hodgdon, IMR, and Winchester powders are available, and refills can be purchased.

Rapine Bullet Mould Mfg. advertises the firm as having the world's largest selection of bullet moulds. Considering the number of moulds Lyman, RCBS, Saeco and others have available that's one big lot of moulds. Still, any handloader looking for a particular design might find it at Rapine. The firm also has a new Micro Graphite Mould Prep for use on moulds.

Reloading Specialties, Inc. has a new Steel Shotshell Reloading Handbook. Sub-titled "A Compendium on Reloading, Shooting and Hunting with Steel Shot", it is Volume VI, No. 1, and features the "World's Fastest" steel

This is the Gun Horse, from Store Horse, of course—a 14-pound shooting stand for range use.

shotshells (1,800 ft/sec at the muzzle.) Over 37 new loads are featured using Alliant "Steel" powder, especially formulated for use with steel shot. There are also a number of tables and articles dealing with the loading and use of steel shot, both for hunting and for all shotgun sports, including skeet and trap.

Competition Bullet Seating Dies for rifle calibers have been available from **Redding/Saeco** for a number of years. Now similar dies for handgun cartridges are available. With advanced bullet alignment, micrometer adjustable in 0.001-inch increments, the dies have a 'zero' set feature to permit returning to a particular setting. The dies are compatible with most progressive press designs, but do not have crimping capability.

Other new products from Redding include Competition Bullet Seating Dies for the 22 Hornet, and full length, neck and Deluxe die sets, Type S dies, and form dies for the 300 Remington Ultra Mag cartridge. New packaging for the Competition Shellholder set and a similar storage box that holds up to 15 neck sizing bushings for Redding Type S and Competition neck sizing dies are now available.

Sinclair International Inc. is known for top quality handloading equipment for precision shooters. New items from the Ft. Wayne firm include the 10th Edition of Precision Reloading and Shooting Handbook and a Neck Turning Tool Adjustment Fixture. The spiral-bound Handbook covers such topics as bullet coating technology, proper use of hand dies, best tools for best results, successful case preparation, load development for accurate shooting, and breaking in your barrel. Sinclair also has two spiral-bound log books for recording reloading data. The smaller book has space for over 300 loads, with the larger having space for 650 loads.

The Neck Turning Tool Adjustment Fixture is designed for use with Sinclair Neck Turning Tools and making setting the tool to a specific depth a snap. Employing a dial indicator to read the desired cutting depth directly, the fixture enables a cut to 0.0005-inch, using an indicator with 0.001-inch reading. For handloaders turning brass for use with several different rifles this fixture should be particularly handy. The Neck Turning Tool and dial indicator are sold separately, allowing handloaders already owning such tools to purchase the Adjustment Fixture separately.

Sierra, The Bulletsmiths in Sedalia, Missouri, offer a new INFINITY Suite software Exterior Ballistic computer program. It also contains the **4th Edition Rifle and Handgun Reloading Manuals**. Extremely user friendly, IN-FINITY is available in CD-ROM only, and requires 80486 or higher PC compatible, Win-95, Win-98, or Win-NT 4.0 with SP3, 8mb RAM (16mb is recommended), CDRom drive, VGA color vid-

eo, 5mb free hard drive space, pointing device, speakers or headset, and sound card. INFINITY offers multiple trajectory charts and graphics; Point Blank Range allows the user to calculate zero, uphill/downhill shooting, maximum range and more. (The bullet library section covers major bullet manufacturers and ammunition companies, and permits the addition of new and/or custom bullet designs.) INFINITY Suite carries a price tag of just under $60.00, plus shipping and handling, or without the 4th Edition manuals for $20.00 less, as this is written.

Handloaders wanting to do a bit of reloading at the range may find the Gun-Horse, GunBox, and StoreTable by StoreHorse handy. Manufactured in the U.S. from recycled material the products are weatherproof and backed by a no-nonsense warranty. The GunHorse weighs 14 pounds and folds to just two inches in width for carrying or storage. Opened, it can serve as a shooting rest for checking out handloads using the bucks supplied which are adjustable vertically and laterally. The GunBox has ample space to hold a supply of components and equipment, and the top can double as a field seat for use with the GunHorse. The StoreTable can be purchased as a complete unit, or the 20" x 30" top can be purchased separately to fit onto the GunHorse. The complete unit folds down to just three inches in width for storage or transporting. Braced against the legs of the GunHorse and fastened to the main platform, the table can handle most single stage loading presses used for reloading metallic handgun and rifle cartridges. It will also handle single stage presses for shotshell reloading, and would be handy where space is at a premium for a regular-size bench.

Sport Flite Manufacturing, Inc. produces bullet swaging die sets for turning out 22 and 6mm jacketed bullets, plus several handgun calibers up to 45 caliber. They also have core cutter and adjustable core moulds in addition to components.

Handloaders who use a variety of presses or have to remove a press for storage due to limited space, might be interested in the products of **Thompson Tool Mount**. This California firm manufactures bases which permit a tool or press to be snapped on or off a bench top in seconds. It's always possible to design a similar base on your own, but a ready-to-install base is much simpler, and Thompson Tool might just have it.

Winchester Shooting Products has introduced an extensive line of reloading products, including a Deluxe Reloading Stand, ideal for apartment dwellers with limited space, a Moly Dry Lubricant capable of treating thousands of bullets, See Through Ammo Boxes, A Deluxe Powder Trickler, Bullet Puller, Loading Trays, Vibratory Thumbler and Deluxe Brass/Media Separator, plus Ground Corn Cob Brass Cleaning Media and Brass Polish. The

new Spray-On Case Sizing Lubricant and Mica Case Neck Lubricant will ease case resizing, and a new stainless steel Dial Caliper (accurate to 0.001") with a range of 6 inches will allow handloaders to check case lengths.

The Winchester Deluxe Vibratory Tumbler will hold up to 350 small rifle or 600 handgun brass cases. Winchester Brass Polish coupled with corn cob or walnut brass cleaning media in the tumbler will insure thorough removal of the grime, stains and lubricants from dirty brass cases. An added plus is the pleasant citrus fragrance of the polish. Separating the media from the cases is simplified using the Brass/Media Separator which features a large hopper and a handle which can be installed for right or left-handed operation. A few cranks on the handle will leave the media in the bucket and the shiny clean cases in the separator. It's that simple.

The Reloading Stand needs only 2-1/2 square feet of floor space to set up. Both the base and upper working platform are removable for storage or transporting to the range. Complete with two component bins, this stand can be used with either shotshell or metallic case reloading.

One of the newest chronographs available to handloaders is the CED Millennium by **Competitive Edge Dynamics Ltd.** It has the largest LCD display in the industry with a full function custom display providing such information as current velocity, number of shots recorded in the string, and screen setting distance in feet or meters. Other standard features include an error warning indicator, PC interface, on/off control with no memory loss, permanent memory back-up, voice chip technology permitting results to be heard and seen, high, low, and average velocity, extreme spread, standard deviation, multiple skyscreen distance selection and 9 volt operation. It comes complete with heavy duty skyscreens, dual lens skyscreen sensors with 20 feet of shielded cable, a 2-foot foldable mounting bracket and instructions. An indoor lighting set and other accessories are available.

Handloaders appear to be increasing in number, along with an increase in new products for handloaders. A portion of this can be attributed to the current popularity in Cowboy Action Shooting and Sporting Clays, along with an increasing number of shooters reloading for the 50 BMG cartridge. This is great news for all reloaders, whether they load for the small bore varmint rifles, such as one of the 17s or 10 gauge shotguns. And, while this report has covered some of the newest products, others will no doubt be introduced by the time you open these pages. If handloaders continue to increase in number, so will the products to assist them in enjoyment of this sport.   ●

by HOLT BODINSON

AMMUNITION, BALLISTICS AND COMPONENTS

ADCO/NobelSport

ADCO is the U.S. importer and distributor of the Vectan line of handgun, shotgun and rifle powders under an arrangement with the NobelSport Div. of S.N.P.E. France. A full range of reloading manuals in the metric and U.S. measurement systems is available. The data covering a variety of popular metric calibers is particularly interesting. Reloading data and information on the current line-up of powders can be found at www.adcosales.com.

shotgun powder, but a superb powder for reduced rifle loads. For high volume reloaders, Alliant has introduced "Promo" shotgun powder in economical 8 lb. jugs. Promo is formulated to duplicate the reloading recipes and ballistics of Red Dot, but is cheaper and not as clean or consistent. www.alliantpowder.com

BALLISTIC PRODUCTS

Here's the source of the most intriguing assortment of shotshell reloading supplies on planet

Good old Red Dot has been given a cleaner burning formulation.

APPROACHING THE next millennium, the ammunition makers are revealing a bit of nostalgia in the products they're unveiling this year. The cowboy action scene is notably the fastest growing shooting sport that has come along since the sporting clays rage. The cowboys and cowgirls like lead bullets at low velocities packaged in authentic-looking boxes, and they're getting them in 32-20 Winchester, 38 Special, 357 Magnum, 38-40 Winchester, 44 Special, 44 Colt, 44 Russian, 44-40 Winchester, 45 Schofield, 45 Colt and even 30-30 Winchester and 45-70. In fact, the 45-70 Government seems to be experiencing something of a well-deserved revival with the introduction of Marlin's neat, little Guide Gun. There are at least four new 45-70 loads including Winchester's loading of a terrific 300-grain Nosler Partition Gold bullet at 1880 fps, and Randy Garrett's bone-crunching, 415-grain hard cast bullet at 1850 fps. Even the elderly 22 Hornet received a face lift this year with new loadings by Winchester and Hornady that push the little fellow over the 3000 fps mark. And, miracle-of-miracles, the Old Western Scrounger is reviving the 5mm Remington. It's been a good year for updated loading manuals by Hodgdon, Speer, and Sierra, which has issued their 4th Edition on a CD-ROM disk packaged with a new exterior ballistics program. Speaking about computers, the Internet is having a major impact on the industry with new and interesting Web sites being added daily, so be sure to peruse our new GUN DIGEST Web site directory.

Packaged in eight-pound jugs, Alliant's Promo shotgun powder, similar to old Red Dot, is ideal for high volume handloaders.

ALLIANT POWDER

That old favorite, Red Dot, has just been given a modern reformulation. It is 50% cleaner burning than the original 1932 formula and features improved flow and metering characteristics. Not only is Red Dot a great

Earth. Even if you don't ever plan on loading a single shotshell in your lifetime, you will enjoy reading Ballistic Products thoroughly informative and entertaining 55 page catalog. New this year is a series of 12-gauge Limited Bore Contact (LBC) wads that are compatible with steel or lead shot. The wad is ribbed thus reducing bore friction and providing lower pressures and higher velocities. BP observes that velocities produced by their LBC wads when teamed with Alliant's "Steel" powder are "jaw-dropping!" Ballistic Products is also introducing two new 28-gauge slugs, and six other new slug designs, one of which is fabricated to break into four pieces upon impact. And for lovers of the fine double, BP has added another well-written ti-

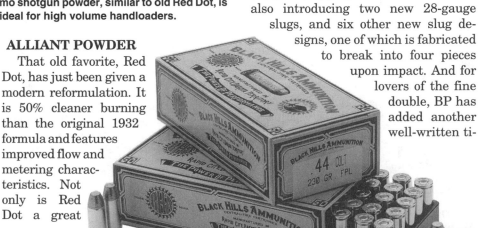

Black Hills' 44 Colt cowboy load was developed for the early percussion conversion replicas.

tle to its handbook series, this one, the "Care and Feeding of Fine Doubles." Among the many subjects covered is the performance and loading of 2, 2 1/4 and 2 1/2 inch 12-gauge shells. www.ballisticproducts.com

(A) Ballistic Products' LBC wads provide "jaw-dropping" velocities with Alliant's Steel powder. (B) Ballistic Products is the source of a variety of new Dangerous Game Slugs.

BARNES

Searching for a better coating than the widely adopted "moly," Barnes has added a high-tech, dry film lubricant to its popular X-Bullet line. The new XLC coating is baked on and blue in color. It is designed to reduce pressure, increase velocity, and extend the time between barrel cleanings. At least one bullet weight in each of the most popular calibers will be available immediately with XLC coating and that includes 40- and 50-grain .224 X-Bullets for the prairie dog hunters. New, too, in the X-Bullet line are a 250-grain 45-70 bullet and a 500-grain 470 Nitro bullet. Barnes continues to offer a complete line of jacketed softpoints in oddball calibers and bullet weights. www.barnesbullet.com

BELL BRASS

New for blackpowder shooters this year is 50-caliber, cylindrical, basic brass for the 3 1/4 inch Sharps and others; formed 50/70 and 50/90 brass and 45-caliber, cylindrical, 3 1/4 inch basic brass. New-formed cases include the 375 Flanged, 500/416, and 500 N.E. Coming soon will be 43 Mauser, 43 Spanish, 505 Gibbs, and 12-gauge brass. www.bellammo.com

In its 45-70 cowboy loads, Black Hills utilizes a heavy "ever-lasting" brass case.

BERGER BULLETS, LTD.

The maker of the ultra-accurate J-4 bullet jackets has purchased Berger and will continue to offer and expand the Berger line under its original name. The latest development is a Berger big game hunting bullet in 7mm and 30-caliber. The bullet named the "Berger-Lok" features a J-4 jacket that is locked to the lead core. Also coming soon is another first--a reloading manual featuring the full Berger bullet line. www.bergerbullets.com

BERTRAM BULLET CO.

This Aussie maker of rare and obsolete brass is adding the 351 WSL, 35 WSL and the 455 Webley to the line that now numbers over 110 calibers. In the U.S., Huntington is an excellent source for Bertram cases. bbertram@bigpond.com

BLACK HILLS AMMUNITION

Offering ammunition so accurate that it commands the match ammunition contracts of the U.S. Army and U.S. Marines, Black Hills Ammunition continues to flesh

It takes lots of draws to make a 416 Rigby case by Bell Brass.

out its cowboy and 223 loads. New this year are a 44 Colt load designed to fit black powder conversions featuring a 230-grain bullet at 730 fps--it fits and is useful, too, in 44 Special and 44 Magnum cowboy tools; a 45-70 cowboy/cowgirl loading consisting of a 405-grain cast slug at 1250 fps--this is a heavy "ever-lasting" case weighing 20-grains more than other commercial cases; and finally for 223 shooters, a 62-grain FMJ loading at 3150 fps that is offered in virgin brass or at a lesser cost, in once-fired military brass. I've shot literally hundreds of Black Hills' molycoated 223 loads put up in reprocessed military brass and have never seen a difference between virgin or carefully reprocessed cases from the standpoint of accuracy or reliability. Save money--shoot more--go Black Hills 223 reprocessed! www.black-hills.com

BRENNEKE

Producing over 10 million slugs annually in more designs than any other manufacturer, Brenneke has added a 7th design to its existing 12-gauge line. The new one ounce slug and loading, named the "K.O.", is designed to emulate the better qualities of the original Brenneke slug while offering some price competition to standard Foster-type slug ammunition. The "K.O.", which is compatible with smooth or rifled bores, features a deeply ribbed, hardened lead projectile with a one-piece plastic wad permanently attached to its base. Velocity is approximately 1600 fps, and the company claims it offers 1/3 more power and over twice the penetration of Foster-type slugs. Available now at your dealers for the big game season. Turpin@kih.net

BUFFALO BULLETS

Buffalo Bullets is the muzzleloaders' emporium for the widest selection of modern designed projectiles ever assembled under one roof. Whether it be round

Black Hills' new 62-grain FMJ load features virgin brass and economical target practice.

balls, conical bullets, ball-ets or sabots, Buffalo Bullets' products are unique and exhibit exceptional quality control. Responding to the growth of blackpowder silhouette competition, the company is adding a full line of 45-70 and 40-65 lubricated bullets in a variety of bullet weights and bullet tempers. Buflobulit@aol.com

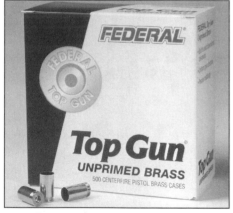

Federal now offers its premium Top Gun handgun brass as a handloading component.

BULL-X BULLETS

Using a proprietary dry film lubricant, BULL-X is now coating its complete cast bullet line that includes a variety of excellent rifle as well as pistol bullet designs. The improved line is called CSJ High Performance Bullets and according to our reports, the new coating seems to do just what the makers said it would do--eliminate leading, increase velocity, lower pressures and increase accuracy. www.bull-x.com

JAMES CALHOON

If bullet maker, James Calhoon, has his way, the 19-caliber will be the varmint caliber of the future. In fact, as two different cartridges-- the 19-223 Calhoon and the 19-Calhoon Hornet. Why 19? Calhoon indicates that during the NATO trials of 1977, the 4.85mm British cartridge (a 19-223) turned in superior levels of performance; however, the military 5.6mm (223) was so well entrenched by that time that the smaller bore cartridge didn't have a chance of being adopted. On the plus side, the longer 19-caliber bullet offers excellent sectional density in weights of 32, 36, 40 and 44-grains combined with Swift-like velocities from the parent 223 case. Calhoon offers a complete "re-barrel kit" that includes a chambered match grade 19-caliber barrel, Bonanza dies, bullets, instructions, loading data and two 19-caliber, Dewey bore brushes. (406) 395-4079

CLAYBUSTER/HARVESTER

C&D Special Products, that makes the excellent line of Claybuster shotgun wads, has developed a new muzzleloading component for 50- and 54-caliber rifles consisting of a very hard cast 44- or 45-caliber bullet encased in a proprietary plastic sabot. Called "Harvesters" the new components are furnished in bullet weights ranging from 280-to-400 grains. Penetration of the 44-or 45-caliber hardened bullets on game is said to be remarkable. (800) 922-6287

CCI-BLOUNT

Improved performance on a number of fronts highlights CCI's new offerings this year with a extra-hot musket cap; a Blazer 357 SIG load fea-

When you need an obsolete or odd-caliber bullet, DKT Bullets is the place to look.

turing the 125-grain Uni-Cor HP bullet; a target grade 22 LR Silhouette round featuring a 40-grain bullet at a zippy 1255 fps; a shotshell load for the 40 S&W; and a complete line of non-toxic, zinc core, handgun bullets in the Blazer line.

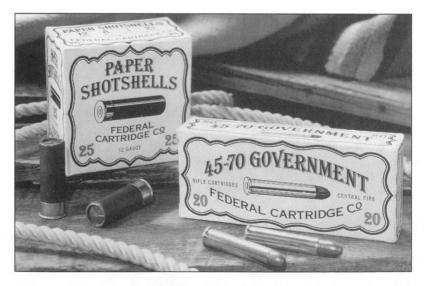

Supplying the Cowboy Action shooter with old-timey loads is big business as witnessed by Federal's latest paper shotshell and 45-70 loadings.

CLEAN SHOT POWDER

Another volume-to-volume replacement for blackpowder is on your dealers' shelves. The manufacturer claims that Clean Shot produces comparable velocities to black powder or Pyrodex when using the same rifle, bullet and powder charge without the fouling and sulfur corrosion experienced with blackpowder. The new powder is cartridge compatible and is gaining a rapid following in the cowboy action shooting world. Read about it at www.cleanshot.com

CORBON

Those long winter days in South Dakota have been particularly productive at CorBon which is introducing two new cartridges: the 440 CorBon Magnum, designed for semi-autos and having a case capacity of the 50AE, launches a 260-grain bullet at 1400 fps; and the 308 CorBon SuperMag, a short, fat, efficient case made from 404 Jeffery brass that will soon be seen chambered in single shot pistols. New, too, is a complete line of authentically packaged, blackpowder, cowboy ammunition; a line of rifle ammunition featuring CorBon's famous core bonded bullets; a Single Shot Hunt-

er line that combines bonded spitzers and fast burning powders to extract maximum performance from short barrels; and a variety of new bullets and loads for the 454 Casull, 44 Magnum and 357 Magnum.
www.cor-bon.com

DKT, Inc.

Need ammunition for the 14 Walker Hornet or the 300 (295) Rook or the 700 Nitro Express or a .266 diameter hunting bullet for the Italian 6.5mm Carcano? DKT will have it. This is a specialized, high quality ammunition

and bullet maker. I don't think you could ever stump them as long as your firearm has a chamber in it.
www.expresspages.com/d/dktinc

FEDERAL

Formerly a factory exclusive, Hydra-Shok and Nyclad bullets are being offered this year as reloading components. Hydra-Shok with its internal post delivers maximum expansion at handgun velocities while Nyclad's nylon-coated, soft, lead HP's eliminate leading, duplicate traditional factory bullet weights and expand very nicely. Try the 125-grain Nyclad HP in a S&W Chief's Special or any other snubnose. Another new reloading first is 500-case bulk lots of "Top Gun" pistol brass in 9mm, 38 Special, 357 Magnum, 40 S&W and 45 Auto. Top Gun brass is drawn to match standard dimensions and should be accurate and long lived under the sizing die. For the cowboys and cowgirls, Federal is introducing 12-gauge, paper shotgun shells loaded with 7/8 oz of shot plus a 45-70 load pushing a 405-grain lead bullet along at 1300 fps. Blackpowder buffs get a treat this year with Federal's new 50- and 54-caliber sabots loaded with

250 and 300-grain Trophy Bonded Bear Claw bullets. Turkey hunting is the fastest growing field sport in America, so this year Federal is producing a fast, high-

A black powder replacement, Goex's new Clear Shot powder, is non-corrosive and non-hygroscopic while offering black powder velocities and pressures.

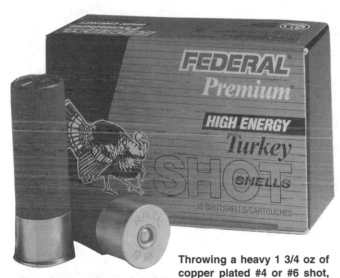

Throwing a heavy 1 3/4 oz of copper plated #4 or #6 shot, Federal's 12 ga. 3-inch Magnum loading will prove pure poison for turkeys.

Clean-shooting Nyclad handgun bullets are on Federal's latest reloading components list.

Combining 250- and 300-grain Trophy Bonded Bear Claw bullets with 50- and 54-caliber sabots, Federal has produced a superior big game load for the charcoal burners.

PMC now offers seven Cowboy Action calibers.

energy, 12-gauge 3 inch turkey load consisting of 1 3/4 ounces of copper plated # 4 or #6 shot with a muzzle velocity of 1300 fps. Finally, Federal is filling out its line of high energy rifle loads, adding Sierra and Speer bullets to its varmint line, and offering moly-coated as well as Barnes XLC coated X-Bullets in several loadings.

FIREQUEST

For the child in us all, there is Firequest--the complete source for the most outrageous mix of ammunition and pyrotechnics in the universe. How about a complete 37mm system that launches flare, bird bomb and smoke loads? Or 12-gauge "Blammo Boomers Blanks," "Pepper Buck," "Rhodesian Jungle Rounds," "Flechette Shot Shells," or " Macho Gaucho" loads? If you're curious, the "Macho Gaucho" round consists of two lead balls connected by a steel wire "which whirls during flight, devastating your target." www.firequest.com

GARRETT CARTRIDGES

When it comes to premium hunting loads for the 44 Magnum and 45-70, Randy Garrett is the world's specialist. Garrett loads are designed around super hard-cast lead bullets that are remarkable for their ability to penetrate game from stem-to-stern, break bones and deliver jacketed bullet velocities and accuracy. This year, Garrett has redesigned the whole bullet line to improve what was already some of the finest big game ammunition ever assembled. The two new 44 Magnum loads consist of a 310-grain Hammerhead slug at 1325 fps and a 330-grain Hammerhead at 1325 fps that is loaded "long" for the stretched cylinders of the Ruger Redhawk and Super Redhawk revolvers. The new 45-70 load features a 415-grain Hammerhead at 1850 fps. Garrett's new Hammerhead bullets feature a weight-forward design and a broad meplat that improve penetration while opening a larger wound

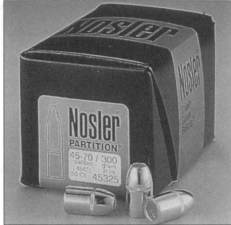

Nosler's new 300-grain Partition bullet for the 45-70 breaths new life into the old caliber. It's also good in the 458 Winchester.

Made with J-4 precision jackets, Nosler's 168-grain 30-caliber match bullet is ideal for big bore comptition.

Nosler Partition handgun bullets mated to 50- and 54-caliber muzzleloading sabots is a marriage made in heaven.

channel. Is it any surprise that Garrett ammunition is carried by the Wyoming Grizzly Bear Team? (360) 736-0702

GOEX

Maker of blackpowder and distributor of the Swiss line of blackpowder, GOEX has just released its own blackpowder replacement called "Clear Shot." The company points out that Clear Shot does not contain ascorbic acid or perchlorates, is non-corrosive and non-hygroscopic, has an indefinite shelf life and offers blackpowder velocities and pressures. Both FFg and FFFg granulations will be available this year. www.goex-powder.com

HODGDON

Building on its first generation of 50-caliber Pyrodex Pellets, Hodgdon is releasing a 30-grain, 44/45-caliber cap and ball revolver pellet, a 60-grain 54-caliber pellet, and a new 30-grain 50-caliber pellet that offers more loading options in that caliber. There's a new shotgun powder, too. Formulated to be perfect for the 410-gauge, LIL'GUN powder is also a flexible propellant for magnum pistol and small rifle cartridges. Finally, the

If you shoot a 454 Casull, you'll like the performance of Nosler's new 300-grain Partition bullet on big game.

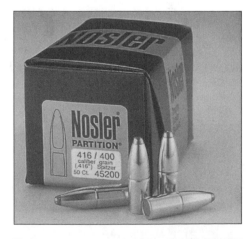

Nosler's 400-grain 416-caliber Partition bullet should be ideal for the African-bound hunter.

powder house has issued its 27th Edition Reloading Manual--all 800 pages are filled with new calibers, new powders, new loads and new ballistic tables. Bound in a European style binder, it's a classy looking book as well, and complements Hodgdon's exceptionally informative shotgun reloading manual. www.hodgdon.com

HORNADY

Celebrating 50 years of bullet making, Hornady is as innovative as ever and this year is introducing a 20-grain 17-caliber V-Max bullet plus a moly-coated, 25-grain 17-caliber HP—sure to please the micro-bore hunters. In the big game line, there is an exciting Light Magnum loading of a 130-grain SST bullet in the 270 Winchester that kicks up 3200 fps at the muzzle; a fast-stepping 500-grain FMJ load for the 458 Winchester Magnum doing 2260 fps; and a 300-grain XTP loading for the 454 Casull delivering 1775 fps. Big bore competitors will find a new 30

PMC's 12-gauge, 1 1/4 oz,1330 fps, Heavy Field Load is designed for heavy bodied upland game birds.

Combining 22- and 6mm-caliber MatchKing jackets with acetal resin tips, Sierra has introduced the BlitzKing – a true, match-quality varmint bullet.

caliber 178-grain A-Max bullet of interest. It has a BC of .495 and in the 308 Winchester remains supersonic at 1000 yards. Hornady is also introducing new cowboy bullets—a 140-grain 38 caliber and a 180-grain 44-caliber—and a deer slaying load for the 22-250 Remington consisting of a 60-grain SP at 3600 fps.

HUNTINGTON

We all mourn the loss of one of the great leaders in the reloading industry, Fred Huntington, founder of RCBS. Huntington's, run by his son, Buzz, is still the finest, single source of hard-to-find reloading components, RCBS tools and parts, in the world. For you owners of old drillings, Huntington has commissioned Norma to make an exclusive run of 9.3x72R brass this year and—lo and behold—Huntington has uncovered a nice supply of 303 Savage cases made by Winchester. www.huntingtons.com

KENG'S FIREARM SPECIALTY

If you're a shotgun slug shooter, you'll want to try the Sauvestre "Sledgehammer" load being imported by Keng's. Designed by Jean-Claude Sauvestre, who formerly headed the entire weapons development program for the French Defense Ministry, the high-tech projectile is a long, fin stabilized, 1.09 oz. 12-gauge slug encased in a discarding sabot. Velocity from a 2 3/4 inch case is 1640 fps and from the 3 inch magnum, 1900 fps! It will also be available in 16, and 20-gauge. Keng is importing a full line of Hirtenberger NATO-Match ammunition and brass in 223, 308, 9mm and 45

ACP as well as two hightech, self-defense loads for the 9mm. One, named the EMB-Monoblok, features a 77-grain JHP bullet at 1465 fps that expands to 0.63caliber in soft mediums yet "plugs up" and penetrates when impacting on hard mediums like glass. It's being touted as the "world's first smart bullet." See all of Keng's specialty items at www.kengsfirearms@mindspring.com

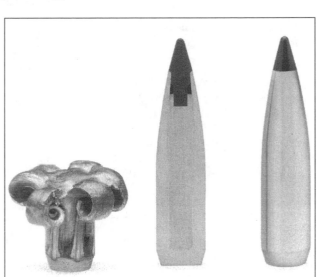

Swift's latest bullet, the Scirocco, features a bonded core and a sleek, polymer tipped, boat-tail profile.

LAZZERONI

John Lazzeroni just pushed the speed race up another notch with the release of a factory 308 Warbird load featuring a proprietary plated 130-grain Barnes-X bullet at 4000 fps. New this year is the release of Lazzeroni's own line of electroplated Barnes X, Nosler Partition, and Swift A-Frame bullets as handloading components. www.lazzeroni.com

LIBERTY/SHOOTING SUPPLIES

This small husband and wife operation is a quality source for some of the harder-to-find cast bullet calibers. Their latest listing includes such numbers as the 30 Mauser, 8mm Nambu, 41 Colt, 455 Webley, 22 Hi-Power, 310 Cadet, 41 Swiss and 43 Spanish. Lishsu@aol.com

MIDWAY

If there ever was a labor of love, it would have to be Midway's highly informative "LoadMap" loading guides to the most popular and most handloaded cartridges. Released this year are "Load-Map" guides for the 44 Magnum and 9mm Luger cartridges. What's unique about these guides is that they provide loading data for every brand and weight

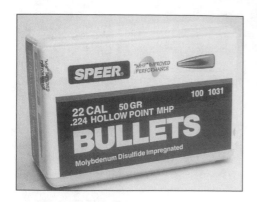

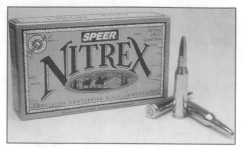

Speer's premium Nitrex line now offers a 140-grain loading for the 260 Remington.

Speer's TNT varmint bullets now wear a moly-coating.

Speer's Lawman ZNT handgun cartridge line features a zinc core bullet and Clean-Fire primer to moderate indoor range pollution.

of popular component bullet matched with the most suitable powders while taking velocities and pressures right up to the point of the industry's Maximum Average Pressure (MAP). The individual "LoadMaps" also include a fascinating history of each cartridge with photographs of the firearms currently chambered for them. www.midwayusa.com

NORTHERN PRECISION

Powdered tungsten core 30-caliber bullets! This was an idea hatched up by Corbin to achieve higher ballistic coefficients in normal length bullets. Bill Noody of Northern Precision is now applying the process to a 30-caliber line with bullet weights as high as 300-grains in conventional length jackets. As of this writing, no big game had been taken with the new bullet design. In response to the immediate popularity of Marlin's 45-70 Guide Gun, Northern Precision is offering a 400-grain, flat point, bonded core bullet designed to provide a perfect overall cartridge length for the compact new lever gun. Tel: 315-493-1711

NORMA

A lot of great new Norma component brass is headed our way--404 Jeffery, 45 Basic, 9.3x72 and 6.5/284 as well as a reintroduced powder, 203-B, useful in everything from 22-250 to 358 Norma Magnum.

NOSLER

Lining my 1895 Marlin up on a large cow femur imbedded in a block of ballistic gelatin, I let fly one of Nosler's new 300-grain 45-70 Partitions at 1880 fps. The bullet literally disintegrated the big bone and kept on going. Recovering the bullet, I found that, in true Partition form, the jacket had peeled back to the partition, the soft lead nose had wiped away, and the penetrating shank behind the partition was intact, weighing a full 230-grains. Truly impressive performance. Nosler will sell the component bullet while Winchester will load the 45-70 Partition Gold in its Supreme line. Other new Partitions being introduced this year include a 400-grain in the 416-caliber; a 300-grain Partition for the 454 Casull; and 50- and 54-caliber sabot rounds featuring the 300-grain 45-caliber Partition handgun bullets. Getting involved in the competition and sniper fields, Nosler is introducing a 168-grain 30-caliber HPBT match bullet featuring the benchrest quality J4 jacket. www.nosler.com

OLD WESTERN SCROUNGER

Remember the 5mm Remington rimfire with its little 38-grain bullet zipping along at 2100 fps? Probably not, but in many varminting circles, the 5mm was once highly regarded. Dangerous Dave, AKA The Old Western Scrounger, is going to surprise the world again this year by commissioning a special run of 5mm Remington rimfire ammunition. Break out those old Remington 591's and 592's, and T/C Contender barrels and relive the glorious 70's again. www.snowcrest.net/oldwest

OREGON TRAIL BULLET COMPANY

Makers of Laser-Cast bullets, considered by many the finest cast bullet line in the industry, Oregon Trail has released its first reloading manual, and it's a doozy! Containing great editorial content that even covers the specific firearm

and cartridge requirements for all the competitive sports such as Cowboy Action and Handgun Metallic Silhouette plus new cast bullet loading data for all popular handgun and many rifle cartridges, the Laser-Cast manual belongs on every reloading bench. www.laser-cast.com

PMC AMMUNITION

Cowboys and cowgirls, the industry is listening! PMC is bringing on six new Cowboy Action cartridges--the 44-40, 44 Special, 357 Magnum, 38 Special, 30-30 and 45-70--all are loaded with traditional lead bullets and at the moderate velocities required by Cowboy Action rules. For the chukar, pheasant, and sage grouse hunters, PMC is fielding a 12-gauge, heavy field load, featuring 1 1/4 ounces of hard shot at 1330 fps. www.pmcammo.com

REMINGTON

It was time for one of the majors to take off the belt, and Big Green did by introducing the 300 Remington Ultra Mag. This large beltless magnum, based on the 404 Jeffery, is capable of sending a 180-grain bullet down range at 3300 fps according to Remington. It won't be long, I suspect, before Big Green necks the basic case down to 7mm and up to 338- or 375-caliber. Other new developments at Remington include a Premier Nosler Partition line featuring some interesting loads like a 125-grain Partition for the 260 Remington at 2875 fps; Premier Nitro-Steel High Velocity waterfowl loads for the 12- and 10-gauge magnums that push velocities up to 1450 and 1500 fps; improved steel target loads; and a new 209 STS shotshell primer that is said to reduce high-to-low velocity spreads by up to 40 percent. www.remington.com

SABOT TECHNOLOGIES, INC.

Sabot Technologies is the latest member of the Slug Group, Inc. that includes Tar-Hunt Slug Guns, Inc. and Lightfield Sabot Slugs. When it comes to benchrest quality slug shooting, this is the group of companies that really knows its business. The latest product is the Sabot Pressure Wad (SPW). The SPW looks like a typical plastic shotgun wad, except for the shot cup portion that is designed to hold a variety of slugs 50-caliber in diameter. In flight, the SPW becomes a non-discarding sabot and together with the inserted slug becomes the actual projectile. Its simplicity makes it highly suited for handloading. In fact, the empty wad itself can be loaded in a shell, roll crimped, and then the payload—be it lead, copper, rubber bullets, incendiary, frangible--can be inserted as needed. Neat idea! Sabotech@bedford.net

SIERRA

Moly's "in" at Sierra. The Bulletsmiths now offer moly-coated bullets across their full lines of 22-, 6mm-, 6.5mm- and 30-caliber BlitzKings and MatchKings, giving the varmint hunter and big bore competitor the advantages of superior accuracy with reduced barrel fouling and cleaning. Meeting the varmint hunters demands is big business in the component field. Combining their

Extremely efficient in a 15-inch Encore barrel, SSK's Improved 30-06 line includes (L-R) the 280 JDJ, 30-06 JDJ, 338-06 JDJ, 35-06 JDJ, 375-06 JDJ and 416-06 JDJ.

22 and 6mm-caliber MatchKing jackets with an acetyl resin bullet tip, Sierra has introduced the BlitzKing--a true match-quality varmint bullet with superior ballistic qualities--and of course, the BlitzKing bullet tips are Sierra green. If you have a 486 or faster PC, Windows 95/98 or NT 4.0 with SP3, a minimum of 8mb ram, a CD-ROM drive, mouse, sound card, VGA color video and 5mb of free hard drive space, you're going to love Sierra's new INFINITY Suite exterior and interior ballistics program. The program combines Sierra's 4th Edition Rifle and Handgun Reloading Manuals with a ballistics program that has all the bells and whistles you'll ever need. The multimedia format even allows you to keep loading data table windows and exterior ballistic tables open on the desktop. Being thoroughly professional, Sierra has included the bullets of all ma-

jor manufacturers and ammunition companies in the program's bullet library. If you don't need the "manuals" side of the program, you can order the INFINITY ballistics program by itself. Finally, there's great information on bullets, advanced handloading techniques, and rifle tuning at their Web site: www.sierrabullets.com

SPEER

Speer has released the 13th Edition of their ever-popular Reloading Manual. It's an impressive 736-page work that includes data for up to 15 powders for some of the most popular cartridges. New editorial sections cover Cowboy Action Shooting and ballistic programs plus informative and personal "Lab Notes" written by the laboratory technicians that provide additional insight into the reloading process. Speer has joined the moly-coating club and is offering five of their explosive TNT bullets ranging in caliber from 22-to-270 plus a 168-grain 30-caliber match bullet with the molybdenum disulfide coating. The bullets will carry the "MHP" designation. Combining a copper jacket with a cast zinc alloy core, Speer has created a line of Lawman ZNT non-toxic indoor target loads for the 9mm Luger, 38 Special, 40 S&W and 45 ACP--all ignited with a Clean-Fire non-toxic

SSK offers a line of subsonic "Whisper" cartridges like the (L-R) 338-, 375- and 50-caliber Whispers shown here.

primer. Additionally, there are new Nitrex loadings for the 260 Rem., 7mmSTW and 7mm-08 Rem.; 50- and 54-caliber sabot loads featuring Speer's successful UNI-COR and Gold Dot handgun bullets; and for the decor of the shooter's den or trophy room, Speer is releasing three collectible bullet and cartridge boards displaying either the firm's 155 bullets, the complete 29 cartridge Nitrex line or the 78 cartridges contained in the CCI/Speer rimfire and handgun lines. www.blount.com

SSK INDUSTRIES

If you shoot a single shot handgun, you're going to love J.D. Jones' new cartridge line based on a radically improved 30-06 case. Velocities from a T/C Encore fitted with a 15" barrel are impressive. Here are just a few examples: 280 JDJ--140-grain bullet at 2900 fps; 30-06 JDJ--150-grain bullet at 2800 fps; 338 JDJ--200-grain bullet at 2800 fps. And for big bore lovers, there are the 358, 375 and 416 JDJ's. At the opposite end of the scale, there's J.D.'s "Whisper" series of efficient and quiet subsonic cartridges for M-16's, 308-caliber-size rifles, T/C Contenders and Encores, with or without suppressors. The "Whisper" series is made from 223 and 7mm BR brass necked out and sometimes shortened to accommodate loads such as the 300-grain MatchKing bullet in the 338 Whisper. The latest of J.D.'s creations is the 50 Whisper based on a very short H&H Magnum case. The little Whispers take just a pinch of powder to operate at 1050 fps. www.shooters.com

STARLINE, INC.

Lots of new and interesting brass coming forth from Starline this year including the 7.5 French Mas, 38 S&W, 41 Long Colt, 45-2.6 inch (45-100 & 45-90), 50-70, 38-55 as well as the 460 Rowland (the 45 ACP case lengthened to 0.957) and the 40 Super (an extended 400 Cor-Bon).

SWIFT BULLET COMPANY

It's called the "Scirocco" and it's an intriguing, new design by Swift. The Scirocco is a streamlined, boat-tailed, bonded-core, hunting bullet with a ballistically efficient, polymer, spitzer tip. Unlike previous Swift designs, the bullet is not constructed as an A-Frame. Instead, the heavy, pure copper jacket is progressively tapered to control expansion that is said to be excellent at veloc-

Sans the traditional H&H belt, Remington's modern looking 30-caliber Ultra Magnum is sure to be a hit with hunters.

"Get the lead out," and Remington did with a new line of steel target loads.

ities as low as 1440 fps. Swift will initially offer the Scirocco as a 180-grain, 30-caliber projectile with calibers ranging from 224-to-338 being added later in the year. Tel: (785) 754-3959

WINCHESTER AMMUNITION

Imagine a moly-coated, 34-grain JHP, 22 Hornet round clocking 3050 fps! Or a 250-grain JHP 454 Casull load throttled down to a user friendly 1300

loadings in calibers ranging from 223 to 300 Winchester Magnum carrying the "Supreme Power-Point Plus" label. Velocity increases over the popular Super-X Power-Point line average 100 fps. Even the 22 rimfire has been improved with the introduction of a Supreme 22LR Match round featuring an annealed and aged 40-grain bullet at a very consistent target velocity of

Moderating lead levels in indoor ranges is big business, and this year Winchester is introducing a complete line of value-priced, centerfire pistol ammunition in 9mm Luger, 38 Special,

Winchester's premium 22LR match ammunition sports a 40-grain, annealed and aged lead bullet at a very consistent 1080 fps.

Winchester's 250-grain JHP, 454 Casull load at 1300 fps is a gentle-recoiling, field load for light big game.

Featuring a 34-grain, moly-coated JHP, Winchester's 22 Hornet load rips along at an astonishing 3050 fps.

Breathing new life into the 45-70, Winchester offers a 300-grain Partition Gold bullet loaded for bear at 1880 fps.

fps! Or a thoroughly modern 45-70 hunting load featuring a 300-grain Partition Gold bullet at 1880 fps! Thanks to some heads-up design work at Winchester, they're here this year. And there's more.

There's a completely new line of moly-coated, Power-Point, big game

1080 fps. Responding to the needs of competitive target shooters and law enforcement units, Winchester and Nosler have jointly developed a 168-grain 308 Winchester competition load featuring HPBT match bullet made with a benchrest quality J4 jacket.

40 S&W, and 45 Auto under the Win-Clean label. The new line features a lead-free primer combined with a brass jacketed, truncated nose bullet. There's a new 5.56mm Super Clean NT (non-toxic) loading as well.
www.winchester.com   ●

Cartridge	Bullet Weight Grains	VELOCITY (fps)					ENERGY (ft. lbs.)					TRAJ. (in.)				Approx. Price per box
		Muzzle	100 yds.	200 yds.	300 yds.	400 yds.	Muzzle	100 yds.	200 yds.	300 yds.	400 yds.	100 yds.	200 yds.	300 yds.	400 yds.	
17 Remington	25	4040	3284	2644	2086	1606	906	599	388	242	143	+2.0	+1.7	-4.0	-17.0	$17
221 Fireball	50	2800	2137	1580	1180	988	870	507	277	155	109	0.0	-7.0	-28.0	NA	$14
22 Hornet	34	3050	2132	1415	1017	852	700	343	151	78	55	0.0	-6.6	-15.5	-29.9	NA
22 Hornet	35	3100	2278	1601	1135	929	747	403	199	100	67	2.75	0.0	-16.9	-60.4	NA
22 Hornet	45	2690	2042	1502	1128	948	723	417	225	127	90	0.0	-7.7	-31.0	NA	$27**
218 Bee	46	2760	2102	1550	1155	961	788	451	245	136	94	0.0	-7.2	-29.0	NA	$46**
222 Remington	40	3600	3117	2673	2269	1911	1151	863	634	457	324	+1.07	0.0	-6.13	-18.9	NA
222 Remington	50	3140	2602	2123	1700	1350	1094	752	500	321	202	+2.0	-0.4	-11.0	-33.0	$11
222 Remington	55	3020	2562	2147	1773	1451	1114	801	563	384	257	+2.0	-0.4	-11.0	-33.0	$12
22 PPC	52	3400	2930	2510	2130	NA	1335	990	730	525	NA	+2.0	1.4	-5.0	NA	NA
223 Remington	40	3650	3010	2450	1950	1530	1185	805	535	340	265	+2.0	+1.0	-6.0	-22.0	$14
223 Remington	40	3800	3305	2845	2424	2044	1282	970	719	522	371	0.84	0.0	-5.34	-16.6	NA
223 Remington	50	3300	2874	2484	2130	1809	1209	917	685	504	363	1.37	0.0	-7.05	-21.8	NA
223 Remington	52/53	3330	2882	2477	2106	1770	1305	978	722	522	369	+2.0	+0.6	-6.5	-21.5	$14
223 Remington	55	3240	2748	2305	1906	1556	1282	922	649	444	296	+2.0	-0.2	-9.0	-27.0	$12
223 Remington	60	3100	2712	2355	2026	1726	1280	979	739	547	397	+2.0	+0.2	-8.0	-24.7	$16
223 Remington	64	3020	2621	2256	1920	1619	1296	977	723	524	373	+2.0	-0.2	-9.3	-23.0	$14
223 Remington	69	3000	2720	2460	2210	1980	1380	1135	925	750	600	+2.0	+0.8	-5.8	-17.5	$15
223 Remington	75	2790	2554	2330	2119	1926	1296	1086	904	747	617	2.37	0.0	-8.75	-25.1	NA
222 Rem. Mag.	55	3240	2748	2305	1906	1556	1282	922	649	444	296	+2.0	-0.2	-9.0	-27.0	$14
225 Winchester	55	3570	3066	2616	2208	1838	1556	1148	836	595	412	+2.0	+1.0	-5.0	-20.0	$19
224 Wea. Mag.	55	3650	3192	2780	2403	2057	1627	1244	943	705	516	+2.0	+1.2	-4.0	-17.0	$32
22-250 Rem.	40	4000	3320	2720	2200	1740	1420	980	660	430	265	+2.0	+1.8	-3.0	-16.0	$14
22-250 Rem.	50	3725	3264	2641	2455	2103	1540	1183	896	669	491	0.89	0.0	-5.23	-16.3	NA
22-250 Rem.	52/55	3680	3137	2656	2222	1832	1654	1201	861	603	410	+2.0	+1.3	-4.0	-17.0	$13
22-250 Rem.	60	3600	3195	2826	2485	2169	1727	1360	1064	823	627	+2.0	+2.0	-2.4	-12.3	$19
220 Swift	40	4200	3678	3190	2739	2329	1566	1201	904	666	482	+0.51	0.0	-4.0	-12.9	NA
220 Swift	50	3780	3158	2617	2135	1710	1586	1107	760	506	325	+2.0	+1.4	-4.4	-17.9	$20
220 Swift	50	3850	3396	2970	2576	2215	1645	1280	979	736	545	0.74	0.0	-4.84	-15.1	NA
220 Swift	55	3800	3370	2990	2630	2310	1765	1390	1090	850	650	0.8	0.0	-4.7	-14.4	NA
220 Swift	55	3650	3194	2772	2384	2035	1627	1246	939	694	506	+2.0	+2.0	-2.6	-13.4	$19
220 Swift	60	3600	3199	2824	2475	2156	1727	1364	1063	816	619	+2.0	+1.6	-4.1	-13.1	$19
22 Savage H.P.	71	2790	2340	1930	1570	1280	1225	860	585	390	190	+2.0	-1.0	-10.4	-35.7	NA
6mm BR Rem.	100	2550	2310	2083	1870	1671	1444	1185	963	776	620	+2.5	-0.6	-11.8	NA	$22
6mm Norma BR	107	2822	2667	2517	2372	2229	1893	1690	1506	1337	1181	+1.73	0.0	-7.24	-20.6	NA
6mm PPC	70	3140	2750	2400	2070	NA	1535	1175	895	665	NA	+2.0	+1.4	-5.0	NA	NA
243 Winchester	55	4025	3597	3209	2853	2525	1078	1670	1257	994	779	+0.6	0.00	-4.0	-12.2	NA
243 Winchester	60	3600	3110	2660	2260	1890	1725	1285	945	680	475	+2.0	+1.8	-3.3	-15.5	$17
243 Winchester	70	3400	3040	2700	2390	2100	1795	1435	1135	890	685	1.1	0.0	-5.9	-18.0	NA
243 Winchester	75/80	3350	2955	2593	2259	1951	1993	1551	1194	906	676	+2.0	+0.9	-5.0	-19.0	$16
243 Winchester	85	3320	3070	2830	2600	2380	2080	1770	1510	1280	1070	+2.0	+1.2	-4.0	-14.0	$18
243 Winchester*	100	2960	2697	2449	2215	1993	1945	1615	1332	1089	882	+2.5	+1.2	-6.0	-20.0	$16
243 Winchester	105	2920	2689	2470	2261	2062	1988	1686	1422	1192	992	+2.5	+1.6	-5.0	-18.4	$21
243 Light Mag.	100	3100	2839	2592	2358	2138	2133	1790	1491	1235	1014	+1.5	0.0	-6.8	-19.8	NA
6mm Remington	80	3470	3064	2694	2352	2036	2139	1667	1289	982	736	+2.0	+1.1	-5.0	-17.0	$16
6mm Remington	100	3100	2829	2573	2332	2104	2133	1777	1470	1207	983	+2.5	+1.6	-5.0	-17.0	$16
6mm Remington	105	3060	2822	2596	2381	2177	2105	1788	1512	1270	1059	12.5	+1.1	-3.3	-15.0	$21
6mm Rem. Light Mag.	100	3250	2997	2756	2528	2311	2345	1995	1687	1418	1186	1.59	0.0	-6.33	-18.3	NA
6.17(.243) Spitfire	100	3350	3122	2905	2698	2501	2493	2164	1874	1617	1389	2.4	3.20	0	-8	NA
240 Wea. Mag.	87	3500	3202	2924	2663	2416	2366	1980	1651	1370	1127	+2.0	+2.0	-2.0	-12.0	$32
240 Wea. Mag.	100	3395	3106	2835	2581	2339	2559	2142	1785	1478	1215	+2.5	+2.8	-2.0	-11.0	$43
25-20 Win.	86	1460	1194	1030	931	858	407	272	203	165	141	0.0	-23.5	NA	NA	$32**
25-35 Win.	117	2230	1866	1545	1282	1097	1292	904	620	427	313	+2.5	-4.2	-26.0	NA	$24
260 Savage	100	2820	2504	2210	1936	1684	1765	1392	1084	832	630	+2.5	+0.4	0.0	-20.0	$17
257 Roberts	100	2980	2661	2363	2085	1827	1972	1572	1240	965	741	12.5	-0.8	-5.2	-21.6	$20
257 Roberts+P	117	2780	2411	2071	1761	1488	2009	1511	1115	806	576	+2.5	-0.2	-10.2	-32.6	$18
257 Roberts+P	120	2780	2560	2360	2160	1970	2060	1750	1480	1240	1030	+2.5	+1.2	-6.4	-23.6	$22
257 Roberts	122	2600	2331	2078	1842	1625	1831	1472	1169	919	715	+2.5	0.0	-10.6	-31.4	$21
257 Light Mag.	117	2940	2694	2460	2240	2031	2245	1885	1572	1303	1071	+1.7	0.0	-7.6	-21.8	NA
25-06 Rem.	87	3440	2995	2591	2222	1884	2286	1733	1297	954	686	+2.0	+1.1	-2.5	-14.4	$17
25-06 Rem.	90	3440	3043	2680	2344	2034	2364	1850	1435	1098	827	+2.0	+1.8	-3.3	-15.6	$17
25-06 Rem.	100	3230	2893	2580	2287	2014	2316	1858	1478	1161	901	+2.0	+0.8	-5.7	-18.9	$17
25-06 Rem.	117	2990	2770	2570	2370	2190	2320	2000	1715	1465	1246	+2.5	+1.0	-7.9	-26.6	$19
25-06 Rem.*	120	2990	2730	2484	2252	2032	2382	1985	1644	1351	1100	+2.5	+1.2	-5.3	-19.6	$17
25-06 Rem.	122	2930	2706	2492	2289	2095	2325	1983	1683	1419	1189	+2.5	+1.8	-4.5	-17.5	$23
257 Wea. Mag.	87	3825	3456	3118	2805	2513	2826	2308	1870	1520	1220	+2.0	+2.7	-0.3	-7.6	$32
257 Wea. Mag.	100	3555	3237	2941	2665	2404	2806	2326	1920	1576	1283	+2.5	+3.2	0.0	-8.0	$32
257 Scramjet	100	3745	3450	3173	2912	2666	3114	2643	2235	1883	1578	+2.1	+2.77	0.0	-6.93	NA
6.5x50mm Jap.	139	2360	2160	1970	1790	1620	1720	1440	1195	985	810	+2.5	-1.0	-13.5	NA	NA
6.5x50mm Jap.	156	2070	1830	1610	1430	1260	1475	1155	900	695	550	+2.5	-4.0	-23.8	NA	NA
6.5x52mm Car.	139	2580	2360	2160	1970	1790	2045	1725	1440	1195	985	+2.5	0.0	-9.9	-29.0	NA
6.5x52mm Car.	156	2430	2170	1930	1700	1500	2045	1630	1285	1005	780	+2.5	-1.0	-13.9	NA	NA
6.5x55mm Light Mag.	129	2750	2549	2355	2171	1994	2166	1860	1589	1350	1139	+2.0	0.0	-8.2	-23.9	NA
6.5x55mm Swe.	140	2550	NA	NA	NA	NA	2020	NA	NA	NA	NA	NA	NA	NA	NA	$18
6.5x55mm Swe.*	139/140	2850	2640	2440	2250	2070	2525	2170	1855	1575	1330	+2.5	+1.6	-5.4	-18.9	$18
6.5x55mm Swe.	156	2650	2370	2110	1870	1650	2425	1950	1550	1215	945	+2.5	0.0	-10.3	-30.6	NA
260 Remington	125	2875	2669	2473	2285	2105	2294	1977	1697	1449	1230	1.71	0.0	-7.4	-21.4	NA
260 Remington	140	2750	2544	2347	2158	1979	2351	2011	1712	1448	1217	+2.2	0.0	-8.6	-24.6	NA
6.71 (264) Phantom	120	3150	2929	2718	2517	2325	2645	2286	1969	1698	1440	+1.3	0.0	-6.0	-17.5	NA
6.5 Rem. Mag.	120	3210	2905	2621	2353	2102	2745	2248	1830	1475	1177	+2.5	+1.7	-4.1	-16.3	Disc.
264 Win. Mag.	140	3030	2782	2548	2326	2114	2854	2406	2018	1682	1389	+2.5	+1.4	-5.1	-18.0	$24

AVERAGE CENTERFIRE RIFLE CARTRIDGE BALLISTICS AND PRICES

Cartridge	Bullet Weight Grains	VELOCITY (fps)					ENERGY (ft. lbs.)					TRAJ. (in.)				Approx. Price per box
		Muzzle	100 yds.	200 yds.	300 yds.	400 yds.	Muzzle	100 yds.	200 yds.	300 yds.	400 yds.	100 yds.	200 yds.	300 yds.	400 yds.	
6.71 (264) Blackbird	140	3480	3261	3053	2855	2665	3766	3307	2899	2534	2208	+2.4	+3.1	0.0	-7.4	NA
270 Winchester	100	3430	3021	2649	2305	1988	2612	2027	1557	1179	877	+2.0	+1.0	-4.9	-17.5	$17
270 Winchester	130	3060	2776	2510	2259	2022	2702	2225	1818	1472	1180	+2.5	+1.4	-5.3	-18.2	$17
270 Win. Supreme	130	3150	2881	2628	2388	2161	2865	2396	1993	1646	1348	1.3	0.0	-6.4	-18.9	NA
270 Winchester	135	3000	2780	2570	2369	2178	2697	2315	1979	1682	1421	+2.5	+1.4	-6.0	-17.6	$23
270 Winchester*	140	2940	2700	2480	2260	2060	2685	2270	1905	1590	1315	+2.5	+1.8	-4.6	-17.9	$20
270 Win. Light Magnum	130	3215	2998	2790	2590	2400	2983	2594	2246	1936	1662	1.21	0.0	-5.83	-17.0	NA
270 Winchester*	150	2850	2585	2336	2100	1879	2705	2226	1817	1468	1175	+2.5	+1.2	-6.5	-22.0	$17
270 Win. Supreme	150	2930	2693	2468	2254	2051	2860	2416	2030	1693	1402	1.7	0.0	-7.4	-21.6	NA
270 Wea. Mag.	100	3760	3380	3033	2712	2412	3139	2537	2042	1633	1292	+2.0	+2.4	-1.2	-10.1	$32
270 Wea. Mag.	130	3375	3119	2878	2649	2432	3287	2808	2390	2026	1707	+2.5	-2.9	-0.9	-9.9	$32
270 Wea. Mag.*	150	3245	3036	2837	2647	2465	3507	3070	2681	2334	2023	+2.5	+2.6	-1.8	-11.4	$47
7mm BR	140	2216	2012	1821	1643	1481	1525	1259	1031	839	681	+2.0	-3.7	-20.0	NA	$23
7mm Mauser*	139/140	2660	2435	2221	2018	1827	2199	1843	1533	1266	1037	+2.5	0.0	-9.6	-27.7	$17
7mm Mauser	145	2690	2442	2206	1985	1777	2334	1920	1568	1268	1017	+2.5	+0.1	-9.6	-28.3	$18
7mm Mauser	154	2690	2490	2300	2120	1940	2475	2120	1810	1530	1285	+2.5	+0.8	-7.3	-23.5	$17
7mm Mauser	175	2440	2137	1857	1603	1382	2313	1774	1340	998	742	+2.5	-1.7	-16.1	NA	$17
7x57 Light Mag.	139	2970	2730	2503	2287	2082	2722	2301	1933	1614	1337	+1.6	0.0	-7.2	-21.0	NA
7x30 Waters	120	2700	2300	1930	1600	1330	1940	1405	990	685	470	+2.5	-0.2	-12.3	NA	$18
7mm-08 Rem.	120	3000	2725	2467	2223	1992	2398	1979	1621	1316	1058	+2.0	0.0	-7.6	-22.3	$18
7mm-08 Rem.*	140	2860	2625	2402	2189	1988	2542	2142	1793	1490	1228	+2.5	+0.8	-6.9	-21.9	$18
7mm-08 Rem.	154	2715	2510	2315	2128	1950	2520	2155	1832	1548	1300	+2.5	+1.0	-7.0	-22.7	$23
7mm-08 Light Mag.	139	3000	2790	2590	2399	2216	2777	2403	2071	1776	1515	+1.5	0.0	-6.7	-19.4	NA
7x64mm Bren.	140				Not Yet Announced											$17
7x64mm Bren.	154	2820	2610	2420	2230	2050	2720	2335	1995	1695	1430	+2.5	+1.4	-5.7	-19.9	NA
7x64mm Bren.*	160	2850	2669	2495	2327	2166	2885	2530	2211	1924	1667	+2.5	+1.6	-4.8	-17.8	$24
7x64mm Bren.	175				Not Yet Announced											$17
284 Winchester	150	2860	2595	2344	2108	1886	2724	2243	1830	1480	1185	+2.5	+0.8	-7.3	-23.2	$24
280 Remington	120	3150	2866	2599	2348	2110	2643	2188	1800	1468	1186	+2.0	+0.6	-6.0	-17.9	$17
280 Remington	140	3000	2758	2528	2309	2102	2797	2363	1986	1657	1373	+2.5	+1.4	-5.2	-18.3	$17
280 Remington*	150	2890	2624	2373	2135	1912	2781	2293	1875	1518	1217	+2.5	+0.8	-7.1	-22.6	$17
280 Remington	160	2840	2637	2442	2556	2078	2866	2471	2120	1809	1535	+2.5	+0.8	-6.7	-21.0	$20
280 Remington	165	2820	2510	2220	1950	1701	2913	2308	1805	1393	1060	+2.5	+0.4	-8.8	-26.5	$17
7x61mm S&H Sup.	154	3060	2720	2400	2100	1820	3200	2520	1965	1505	1135	+2.5	+1.8	-5.0	-19.8	NA
7mm Dakota	160	3200	3001	2811	2630	2455	3637	3200	2808	2456	2140	2.1	+1.9	-2.8	-12.5	NA
7mm Rem. Mag.*	139/140	3150	2930	2710	2510	2320	3085	2660	2290	1960	1670	+2.5	+2.4	-2.4	-12.7	$21
7mm Rem. Mag.	150/154	3110	2830	2085	2320	2085	3221	2667	2196	1792	1448	+2.5	+1.6	-4.6	-16.5	$21
7mm Rem. Mag.*	160/162	2950	2730	2520	2320	2120	3090	2650	2250	1910	1600	+2.5	+1.8	-4.4	-17.8	$34
7mm Rem. Mag.	165	2900	2699	2507	2324	2147	3081	2669	2303	1978	1689	+2.5	+1.2	-5.9	-19.0	$28
7mm Rem Mag.	175	2860	2645	2440	2244	2057	3178	2718	2313	1956	1644	+2.5	+1.0	-6.5	-20.7	$21
7mm Wea. Mag.	140	3225	2970	2729	2501	2283	3233	2741	2315	1943	1621	+2.5	+2.0	-3.2	-14.0	$35
7mm Wea. Mag.	154	3260	3023	2799	2586	2382	3539	3044	2609	2227	1890	+2.5	+2.8	-1.5	-10.8	$32
7mm Wea. Mag.*	160	3200	3004	2816	2637	2464	3637	3205	2817	2469	2156	+2.5	+2.7	-1.5	-10.6	$47
7mm Wea. Mag.	165	2950	2747	2553	2367	2189	3188	2765	2388	2053	1756	+2.5	+1.8	-4.2	-16.4	$43
7mm Wea. Mag.	175	2910	2693	2486	2288	2098	3293	2818	2401	2033	1711	+2.5	+1.2	-5.9	-19.4	$35
7.21(.284) Tomahawk	140	3300	3118	2943	2774	2612	3386	3022	2693	2393	2122	2.3	3.20	0	-7.7	NA
7mm STW	140	3325	3064	2818	2585	2364	3436	2918	2468	2077	1737	+2.3	+1.8	-3.0	-13.1	NA
7mm STW Supreme	160	3150	2894	2652	2422	2204	3526	2976	2499	2085	1727	1.3	0.0	-6.3	-18.5	NA
7mm Firehawk	140	3625	3373	3135	2909	2695	4084	3536	3054	2631	2258	+2.2	+2.9	0.0	-7.03	NA
30 Carbine	110	1990	1567	1236	1035	923	977	600	373	262	208	0.0	-13.5	NA	NA	$28**
303 Savage	190	1890	1612	1327	1183	1055	1507	1096	794	591	469	+2.5	-7.6	NA	NA	$24
30 Remington	170	2120	1822	1555	1328	1153	1696	1253	913	666	502	+2.5	-4.7	-26.3	NA	$20
30-30 Win.	55	3400	2693	2085	1570	1187	1412	886	521	301	172	+2.0	0.0	-10.2	-35.0	$18
30-30 Win.	125	2570	2090	1660	1320	1080	1830	1210	770	480	320	-2.0	-2.6	-19.9	NA	$13
30-30 Win.	150	2390	1973	1605	1303	1095	1902	1296	858	565	399	+2.5	-3.2	-22.5	NA	$13
30-30 Win. Supreme	150	2480	2095	1747	1446	1209	2049	1462	1017	697	487	0.0	-6.5	-24.5		NA
30-30 Win.	160	2300	1997	1719	1473	1268	1879	1416	1050	771	571	+2.5	-2.9	-20.2	NA	$18
30-30 PMC Cowboy	170	1300	1198	1121			638	474				.0	-27.0			NA
30-30 Win.*	170	2200	1895	1619	1381	1191	1827	1355	989	720	535	+2.5	-5.8	-23.6	NA	$13
300 Savage	150	2630	2354	2094	1853	1631	2303	1845	1462	1143	886	+2.5	-0.4	-10.1	-30.7	$17
300 Savage	180	2350	2137	1935	1754	1570	2207	1825	1496	1217	985	+2.5	-1.6	-15.2	NA	$17
30-40 Krag	180	2430	2213	2007	1813	1632	2360	1957	1610	1314	1064	+2.5	-1.4	-13.8	NA	$18
7.65x53mm Arg.	180	2590	2390	2200	2010	1830	2685	2280	1925	1615	1345	+2.5	0.0	-27.6	NA	NA
307 Winchester	150	2760	2321	1924	1575	1289	2530	1795	1233	826	554	+2.5	-1.5	-13.6	NA	Disc.
307 Winchester	180	2510	2179	1874	1599	1362	2519	1898	1404	1022	742	+2.5	-1.6	-15.6	NA	$20
7.5x55 Swiss	180	2650	2450	2250	2060	1880	2805	2390	2020	1700	1415	+2.5	+0.6	-8.1	-24.9	NA
308 Winchester	55	3770	3215	2726	2286	1888	1735	1262	907	638	435	-2.0	+1.4	-3.8	-15.8	$22
308 Winchester	150	2820	2533	2263	2009	1774	2648	2137	1705	1344	1048	+2.5	+0.4	-8.5	-26.1	$17
308 Winchester	165	2700	2440	2194	1963	1748	2670	2180	1763	1411	1199	+2.5	0.0	-9.7	-28.5	$20
308 Winchester	168	2680	2493	2314	2143	1979	2678	2318	1998	1713	1460	+2.5	0.0	-8.9	-25.3	$18
308 Winchester	178	2620	2415	2220	2034	1857	2713	2306	1948	1635	1363	+2.5	0.0	-9.6	-27.6	$23
308 Winchester*	180	2620	2393	2178	1974	1782	2743	2288	1896	1557	1269	+2.5	-0.2	-10.2	-28.5	$17
308 Light Mag.*	150	2980	2703	2442	2195	1964	2959	2433	1986	1606	1285	+1.6	0.0	-7.5	-22.2	NA
308 Light Mag.	165	2870	2658	2456	2263	2078	3019	2589	2211	1877	1583	+1.7	0.0	-7.5	-21.8	NA
308 High Energy	165	2870	2600	2350	2120	1890	3020	2485	2030	1640	1310	+1.8	0.0	-8.2	-24.0	NA
308 Light Mag.	168	2870	2658	2456	2263	2078	3019	2589	2211	1877	1583	+1.7	0.0	-7.5	-21.8	NA
308 High Energy	180	2740	2550	2370	2200	2030	3000	2600	2245	1925	1645	+1.9	0.0	-8.2	-23.5	NA
30-06 Spfd.	55	4080	3485	2965	2502	2083	2033	1483	1074	764	530	+2.0	+1.9	-2.1	-11.7	$22
30-06 Spfd.	125	3140	2780	2447	2138	1853	2736	2145	1662	1279	953	+2.0	+1.0	-6.2	-21.0	$17
30-06 Spfd.	150	2910	2617	2342	2083	1853	2820	2281	1827	1445	1135	+2.5	+0.8	-7.2	-23.4	$17
30-06 Spfd.	152	2910	2654	2413	2184	1968	2858	2378	1965	1610	1307	+2.5	+1.0	-6.6	-21.3	$23

AVERAGE CENTERFIRE RIFLE CARTRIDGE BALLISTICS AND PRICES

Cartridge	Bullet Weight Grains	VELOCITY (fps)					ENERGY (ft. lbs.)					TRAJ. (in.)				Approx. Price per box
		Muzzle	100 yds.	200 yds.	300 yds.	400 yds.	Muzzle	100 yds.	200 yds.	300 yds.	400 yds.	100 yds.	200 yds.	300 yds.	400 yds.	
30-06 Spfd.*	165	2800	2534	2283	2047	1825	2872	2352	1909	1534	1220	+2.5	+0.4	-8.4	-25.5	$17
30-06 Spfd.	168	2710	2522	2346	2169	2003	2739	2372	2045	1754	1497	+2.5	+0.4	-8.0	-23.5	$18
30-06 Spfd.	178	2720	2511	2311	2121	1939	2924	2491	2111	1777	1486	+2.5	+0.4	-8.2	-24.6	$23
30-06 Spfd.*	180	2700	2469	2250	2042	1846	2913	2436	2023	1666	1362	-2.5	0.0	-9.3	-27.0	$17
30-06 Spfd.	220	2410	2130	1870	1632	1422	2837	2216	1708	1301	988	+2.5	-1.7	-18.0	NA	$17
30-06 Light Mag.	150	3100	2815	2548	2295	2058	3200	2639	2161	1755	1410	+1.4	0.0	-6.8	-20.3	NA
30-06 Light Mag.	180	2880	2676	2480	2293	2114	3316	2862	2459	2102	1786	+1.7	0.0	-7.3	-21.3	NA
30-06 High Energy	180	2880	2690	2500	2320	2150	3315	2880	2495	2150	1845	+1.7	0.0	-7.2	-21.0	NA
7.82 (308) Patriot	150	3250	2999	2762	2537	2323	3519	2997	2542	2145	1798	+1.2	0.0	-5.8	-16.9	NA
308 Norma Mag.	180	3020	2820	2630	2440	2270	3645	3175	2755	2385	2050	+2.5	+2.0	-3.5	-14.8	NA
300 Dakota	200	3000	2824	2656	2493	2336	3996	3542	3131	2760	2423	+2.2	+1.5	-4.0	-15.2	NA
300 H&H Magnum*	180	2880	2640	2412	2196	1990	3315	2785	2325	1927	1583	+2.5	+0.8	-6.8	-21.7	$24
300 H&H Magnum	220	2550	2267	2002	1757	NA	3167	2510	1958	1508	NA	-2.5	-0.4	-12.0	NA	NA
300 Peterson	180	3500	3319	3145	2978	2817	4896	4401	3953	3544	3172	+2.3	+2.9	0.0	-6.8	NA
300 Win. Mag.	150	3290	2951	2636	2342	2068	3605	2900	2314	1827	1424	+2.5	+1.9	-3.8	-15.8	$22
300 Win. Mag.	165	3100	2877	2665	2462	2269	3522	3033	2603	2221	1897	+2.5	+2.4	-3.0	-16.9	$24
300 Win. Mag.	178	2900	2760	2568	2375	2191	3509	3030	2606	2230	1897	+2.5	+1.4	-5.0	-17.6	$29
300 Win. Mag.*	180	2960	2745	2540	2344	2157	3501	3011	2578	2196	1859	+2.5	+1.2	-5.5	-18.5	$22
300 W.M. High Energy	180	3100	2830	2580	2340	2110	3840	3205	2660	2190	1790	+1.4	0.0	-6.6	-19.7	NA
300 W.M. Light Mag.	180	3100	2879	2668	2467	2275	3840	3313	2845	2431	2068	+1.39	0.0	-6.45	-18.7	NA
300 Win. Mag.	190	2885	1691	2506	2327	2156	3511	3055	2648	2285	1961	+2.5	+1.2	-5.7	-19.0	$26
300 W.M. High Energy	200	2930	2740	2550	2370	2200	3810	3325	2885	2495	2145	+1.6	0.0	-6.9	-20.1	NA
300 Win. Mag.*	200	2825	2595	2376	2167	1970	3545	2991	2508	2086	1742	-2.5	+1.6	-4.7	-17.2	$36
300 Win. Mag.	220	2680	2448	2228	2020	1823	3508	2927	2424	1990	1623	?2.6	0.0	-9.5	-27.5	$23
300 Rem. Ultra Mag	180	3250	3037	2834	2640	2454	4221	3686	3201	2786	2407	2.4		-3.0	-12.7	NA
300 Wea. Mag.	100	3900	3441	3038	2652	2305	3714	2891	2239	1717	1207	+2.0	+2.6	-0.6	-8.7	$32
300 Wea. Mag.	150	3600	3307	3033	2776	2533	4316	3642	3064	2566	2137	+2.5	+3.2	0.0	-8.1	$32
300 Wea. Mag.	165	3450	3210	3000	2792	2593	4360	3796	3297	2855	2464	+2.5	+3.2	0.0	-7.8	NA
300 Wea. Mag.	178	3120	2902	2695	2497	2308	3047	3320	2870	2464	2104	+2.5	-1.7	-3.6	-14.7	$43
300 Wea. Mag.	180	3330	3110	2910	2710	2520	4430	3875	3375	2935	2540	+1.0	0.0	-5.2	-15.1	NA
300 Wea. Mag.	190	3030	2830	2638	2455	2279	3873	3378	2936	2542	2190	+2.5	+1.6	-4.3	-16.0	$38
300 Wea. Mag.	220	2850	2541	2283	1964	1736	3967	3155	2480	1922	1471	+2.5	+0.4	-8.5	-26.4	$35
300 Warbird	180	3400	3180	2971	2772	2582	4620	4042	3528	3071	2664	+2.59	+3.25	0.0	-7.95	NA
300 Pegasus	180	3500	3319	3145	2978	2817	4896	4401	3953	3544	3172	+2.28	+2.89	0.0	-6.79	NA
32-20 Win.	100	1210	1021	913	834	769	325	231	185	154	131	0.0	-32.3	NA	NA	$23**
303 British	150	2685	2441	2210	1992	1787	2401	1984	1627	1321	1064	+2.5	+0.6	-8.4	-26.2	$18
303 British	180	2460	2124	1817	1542	1311	2418	1803	1010	050	687	+2.5	-1.8	-16.8	NA	$18
303 Light Mag.	150	2830	2570	2325	2094	1884	2667	2199	1800	1461	1185	+2.0	0.0	-8.4	-24.6	NA
7.62x39mm Rus.	123/125	2300	2030	1780	1550	1350	1445	1125	860	655	500	+2.5	-2.0	-17.5	NA	$13
7.62x54mm Rus.	146	2950	2730	2520	2320	NA	2820	2415	2055	1740	NA	+2.5	+2.0	-4.4	-17.7	NA
7.62x54mm Rus.	180	2580	2370	2180	2000	1820	2650	2250	1900	1590	1100	+2.5	0.0	-9.8	-28.5	NA
7.7x58mm Jap.	180	2500	2300	2100	1920	1750	2490	2105	1770	1475	1225	+2.5	0.0	-10.4	-30.2	NA
8x57mm JS Mau.	165	2850	2520	2210	1930	1670	2965	2330	1795	1360	1015	+2.5	+1.0	-7.7	NA	NA
32 Win. Special	170	2250	1921	1626	1372	1175	1911	1393	998	710	521	+2.5	-3.5	-22.9	NA	$14
8mm Mauser	170	2360	1969	1622	1333	1123	2102	1464	993	671	476	+2.5	-3.1	-22.2	NA	$18
8mm Rem. Mag.	185	3080	2761	2464	2186	1927	3896	3131	2494	1963	1525	+2.5	+1.4	-5.5	-19.7	$30
8mm Rem. Mag.	220	2830	2581	2346	2123	1913	3912	3254	2688	2201	1787	+2.5	+0.6	7.6	-23.5	Disc.
338-06	200	2750	2553	2364	2184	2011	3358	2894	2482	2118	1796	+1.9	0.0	-8.22	-23.6	NA
330 Dakota	250	2900	2719	2545	2378	2217	4668	4103	3595	3138	2727	+2.3	+1.3	-5.0	-17.5	NA
338 Lapua	250	2963	2795	2640	2493	NA	4842	4341	3881	3458	NA	+1.9	0.0	-7.9	NA	NA
338 Win. Mag.	200	2960	2658	2375	2110	1862	3890	3137	2505	1977	1500	+2.5	+1.0	-6.7	-22.3	$27
338 Win. Mag.*	210	2830	2590	2370	2150	1940	3735	3130	2610	2155	1760	+2.5	+1.4	-6.0	-20.9	$33
338 Win. Mag.*	225	2785	2517	2266	2029	1808	3871	3165	2565	2057	1633	+2.5	+0.4	-8.5	-25.9	$27
338 W.M. Heavy Mag.	225	2920	2678	2449	2232	2027	4259	3583	2996	2489	2053	+1.75	0.0	-7.65	-22.0	NA
338 W.M. High Energy	225	2940	2690	2450	2230	2010	4320	3610	3000	2475	2025	+1.7	0.0	-7.5	-22.0	NA
338 Win. Mag.	230	2780	2573	2375	2186	2005	3948	3382	2881	2441	2054	+2.5	+1.2	-6.3	-21.0	$40
338 Win. Mag.*	250	2660	2456	2261	2075	1898	3927	3348	2837	2389	1999	+2.5	+0.2	-9.0	-26.2	$27
338 W.M. High Energy	250	2800	2610	2420	2250	2080	4350	3775	3260	2805	2395	+1.8	0.0	-7.8	-22.5	NA
8.59(.338) Galaxy	200	3100	2899	2707	2524	2347	4269	3734	3256	2829	2446	3	3.80	0	-9.3	NA
340 Wea. Mag.*	210	3250	2991	2746	2515	2295	4924	4170	3516	2948	2455	+2.5	+1.9	-1.8	-11.8	$56
340 Wea. Mag.*	250	3000	2806	2621	2443	2272	4995	4371	3812	3311	2864	+2.5	+2.0	-3.5	-14.8	$56
338 A-Square	250	3120	2799	2500	2220	1958	5403	4348	3469	2736	2128	+2.5	+2.7	-1.5	-10.5	NA
338-378 Wea. Mag.	225	3180	2974	2778	2591	2410	5052	4420	3856	3353	2902	3.1	3.80	0	-8.9	NA
338 Titan	225	3230	3010	2800	2600	2409	5211	4524	3916	3377	2898	+3.07	+3.80	0.0	-8.95	NA
338 Excalibur	200	3600	3361	3134	2920	2715	5755	5015	4363	3785	3274	+2.23	+2.87	0.0	-6.99	NA
338 Excalibur	250	3250	2922	2618	2333	2066	5863	4740	3804	3021	2370	+1.3	0.0	-6.35	-19.2	NA
348 Winchester	200	2520	2215	1931	1672	1443	2820	2178	1656	1241	925	+2.5	-1.4	-14.7	NA	$42
357 Magnum	158	1830	1427	1138	980	883	1175	715	454	337	274	0.0	-16.2	-33.1	NA	$25**
35 Remington	150	2300	1874	1506	1218	1039	1762	1169	755	494	359	+2.5	-4.1	-26.3	NA	$16
35 Remington	200	2080	1698	1376	1140	1001	1921	1280	841	577	445	+2.5	-6.3	-17.1	-33.6	$16
356 Winchester	200	2460	2114	1797	1517	1284	2688	1985	1434	1022	732	+2.5	-1.8	-15.1	NA	$31
356 Winchester	250	2160	1911	1682	1476	1299	2591	2028	1571	1210	937	+2.5	-3.7	-22.2	NA	$31
358 Winchester	200	2490	2171	1876	1619	1379	2753	2093	1563	1151	844	+2.5	-1.6	-15.6	NA	$31
358 STA	275	2850	2562	2292	2039	NA	4958	4009	3208	2539	NA	+1.9	0.0	-8.6	NA	NA
350 Rem. Mag.	200	2710	2410	2130	1870	1631	3261	2579	2014	1553	1181	+2.5	-0.2	-10.0	-30.1	$33
35 Whelen	200	2675	2378	2100	1842	1606	3177	2510	1958	1506	1145	+2.5	-0.2	-10.3	-31.1	$20
35 Whelen	225	2500	2300	2110	1930	1770	3120	2650	2235	1870	1560	+2.6	0.0	-10.2	-29.9	NA
35 Whelen	250	2400	2197	2005	1823	1652	3197	2680	2230	1844	1515	+2.5	-1.2	-13.7	NA	$20
358 Norma Mag.	250	2800	2510	2230	1970	1730	4350	3480	2750	2145	1655	+2.5	+1.0	-7.6	-25.2	NA
358 STA	275	2850	2562	229*2	2039	1764	4959	4009	3208	2539	1899	+1.9	0.0	-8.58	-26.1	NA
9.3x57mm Mau.	286	2070	1810	1590	1390	1110	2710	2090	1600	1220	955	+2.5	-2.6	-22.5	NA	NA

Cartridge	Bullet Weight Grains	VELOCITY (fps)					ENERGY (ft. lbs.)					TRAJ. (in.)				Approx. Price per box
		Muzzle	100 yds.	200 yds.	300 yds.	400 yds.	Muzzle	100 yds.	200 yds.	300 yds.	400 yds.	100 yds.	200 yds.	300 yds.	400 yds.	
9.3x62mm Mau.	286	2360	2089	1844	1623	NA	3538	2771	2157	1670	1260	+2.5	-1.6	-21.0	NA	NA
9.3x64mm	286	2700	2505	2318	2139	1968	4629	3984	3411	2906	2460	+2.5	+2.7	-4.5	-19.2	NA
9.3x74Rmm	286	2360	2089	1844	1623	NA	3538	2771	2157	1670	NA	+2.5	-2.0	-11.0	NA	NA
38-55 Win.	255	1320	1190	1091	1018	963	987	802	674	587	525	0.0	-23.4	NA	NA	$25
375 Winchester	200	2200	1841	1526	1268	1089	2150	1506	1034	714	527	+2.5	-4.0	-26.2	NA	$27
375 Winchester	250	1900	1647	1424	1239	1103	2005	1506	1126	852	676	+2.5	-6.9	-33.3	NA	$27
375 Dakota	300	2600	2316	2051	1804	1579	4502	3573	2800	2167	1661	+2.4	0.0	-11.0	-32.7	NA
375 N.E. 2-1/2"	270	2000	1740	1507	1310	NA	2398	1815	1362	1026	NA	+2.5	-6.0	-30.0	NA	NA
375 Flanged	300	2450	2150	1886	1640	NA	3998	3102	2369	1790	NA	+2.5	-2.4	-17.0	NA	NA
375 H&H Magnum	250	2670	2450	2240	2040	1850	3955	3335	2790	2315	1905	+2.5	-0.4	-10.2	-28.4	NA
375 H&H Magnum	270	2690	2420	2166	1928	1707	4337	3510	2812	2228	1747	+2.5	0.0	-10.0	-29.4	$28
375 H&H Magnum*	300	2530	2245	1979	1733	1512	4263	3357	2608	2001	1523	+2.5	-1.0	-10.5	-33.6	$28
375 H&H Hvy. Mag.	270	2870	2628	2399	2182	1976	4937	4141	3451	2150	1845	+1.7	0.0	-7.2	-21.0	NA
375 H&H Hvy. Mag.	300	2705	2386	2090	1816	1568	4873	3793	2908	2195	1637	+2.3	0.0	-10.4	-31.4	NA
375 Wea. Mag.	300	2700	2420	2157	1911	1685	4856	3901	3100	2432	1891	+2.5	-.04	-10.7	-	NA
378 Wea. Mag.	270	3180	2976	2781	2594	2415	6062	5308	4635	4034	3495	+2.5	+2.6	-1.8	-11.3	$71
378 Wea. Mag.	300	2929	2576	2252	1952	1680	5698	4419	3379	2538	1881	+2.5	+1.2	-7.0	-24.5	$77
375 A-Square	300	2920	2626	2351	2093	1850	5679	4594	3681	2917	2281	+2.5	+1.4	-6.0	-21.0	NA
38-40 Win.	180	1160	999	901	827	764	538	399	324	273	233	0.0	-33.9	NA	NA	$42**
450/400-3"	400	2150	1932	1730	1545	1379	4105	3316	2659	2119	1689	+2.5	-4.0	-9.5	-30.0	NA
416 Dakota	400	2450	2294	2143	1998	1859	5330	4671	4077	3544	3068	+2.5	-0.2	-10.5	-29.4	NA
416 Taylor	400	2350	2117	1896	1693	NA	4905	3980	3194	2547	NA	+2.5	-1.2	15.0	NA	NA
416 Hoffman	400	2380	2145	1923	1718	1529	5031	4087	3285	2620	2077	+2.5	-1.0	-14.1	NA	NA
416 Rigby	350	2600	2449	2303	2162	2026	5253	4661	4122	3632	3189	+2.5	-1.8	-10.2	-26.0	NA
416 Rigby	400	2370	2210	2050	1900	NA	4990	4315	3720	3185	NA	+2.5	-0.7	-12.1	NA	NA
416 Rigby	410	2370	2110	1870	1640	NA	5115	4050	3165	2455	NA	+2.5	-2.4	-17.3	NA	$110
416 Rem. Mag.*	350	2520	2270	2034	1814	1611	4935	4004	3216	2557	2017	+2.5	-0.8	-12.6	-35.0	$82
416 Rem. Mag.*	400	2400	2175	1962	1763	1579	5115	4201	3419	2760	2214	+2.5	-1.5	-14.6	NA	$80
416 Wea. Mag.*	400	2700	2397	2115	1852	1613	6474	5104	3971	3047	2310	+2.5	0.0	-10.1	-30.4	$96
10.57 (416) Meteor	400	2730	2532	2342	2161	1987	6621	5695	4874	4147	3508	+1.9	0.0	-8.3	-24.0	NA
404 Jeffrey	400	2150	1924	1716	1525	NA	4105	3289	2614	2064	NA	+2.5	-4.0	-22.1	NA	NA
425 Express	400	2400	2160	1934	1725	NA	5115	4145	3322	2641	NA	+2.5	-1.0	-14.0	NA	NA
44-40 Win.	200	1190	1006	900	822	756	629	449	360	300	254	0.0	-33.3	NA	NA	$36**
44 Rem. Mag.	210	1920	1477	1155	982	880	1719	1017	622	450	361	0.0	-17.6	NA	NA	$14
44 Rem. Mag.	240	1760	1380	1114	970	878	1650	1015	661	501	411	0.0	-17.6	NA	NA	$13
444 Marlin	240	2350	1815	1377	1087	941	2942	1753	1001	630	472	+2.5	-15.1	-31.0	NA	$22
444 Marlin	265	2120	1733	1405	1160	1012	2644	1768	1162	791	603	+2.5	-6.0	-32.2	NA	Disc.
45-70 Govt.	300	1810	1497	1244	1073	969	2182	1492	1031	767	625	0.0	-14.8	NA	NA	$21
45-70 Govt. Supreme	300	1880	1558	1292	1103	988	2355	1616	1112	811	651	0.0	-12.9	-46.0	-105	NA
45-70 Govt. CorBon	350	1800	1526	1296			2519	1810	1307			0.0	-14.6			NA
45-70 Govt.	405	1330	1168	1055	977	918	1590	1227	1001	858	758	0.0	-24.6	NA	NA	$21
45-70 Govt. PMC Cowboy	405	1550	1193				1639	1280				0.0	-23.9			NA
45-70 Govt. Garrett	415	1850					3150					3.0	-7.0			NA
458 Win. Magnum	350	2470	1990	1570	1250	1060	4740	3065	1915	1205	870	+2.5	-2.5	-21.6	NA	$43
458 Win. Magnum	400	2380	2170	1960	1770	NA	5030	4165	3415	2785	NA	+2.5	-0.4	-13.4	NA	$73
458 Win. Magnum	465	2220	1999	1791	1601	NA	5088	4127	3312	2646	NA	+2.5	-2.0	-17.7	NA	NA
458 Win. Magnum	500	2040	1823	1623	1442	1237	4620	3689	2924	2308	1839	+2.5	-3.5	-22.0	NA	$61
458 Win. Magnum	510	2040	1770	1527	1319	1157	4712	3547	2640	1970	1516	+2.5	-4.1	-25.0	NA	$41
450 Dakota	500	2450	2235	2030	1838	1658	6663	5544	4576	3748	3051	+2.5	-0.6	-12.0	-33.8	NA
450 N.E. 3-1/4"	465	2190	1970	1765	1577	NA	4952	4009	3216	2567	NA	+2.5	-3.0	-20.0	NA	NA
450 N.E. 3-1/4"	500	2150	1920	1708	1514	NA	5132	4093	3238	2544	NA	+2.5	-4.0	-22.9	NA	NA
450 No. 2	465	2190	1970	1765	1577	NA	4952	4009	3216	2567	NA	+2.5	-3.0	-20.0	NA	NA
450 No. 2	500	2150	1920	1708	1514	NA	5132	4093	3238	2544	NA	+2.5	-4.0	-22.9	NA	NA
458 Lott	465	2380	2150	1932	1730	NA	5848	4773	3855	3091	NA	+2.5	-1.0	-14.0	NA	NA
458 Lott	500	2300	2062	1838	1633	NA	5873	4719	3748	2960	NA	+2.5	-1.6	-16.4	NA	NA
450 Ackley Mag.	465	2400	2169	1950	1747	NA	5947	4857	3927	3150	NA	+2.5	-1.0	-13.7	NA	NA
450 Ackley Mag.	500	2320	2081	1855	1649	NA	5975	4085	3820	3018	NA	+2.5	-1.2	-15.0	NA	NA
460 Short A-Sq.	500	2420	2175	1943	1729	NA	6501	5250	4193	3319	NA	+2.5	-0.8	-12.8	-	NA
460 Wea. Mag.	500	2700	2404	2128	1869	1635	8092	6416	5026	3878	2969	+2.5	+0.6	-8.9	-28.0	$72
500/465 N.E.	480	2150	1917	1703	1507	NA	4926	3917	3089	2419	NA	+2.5	-4.0	-22.2	-	NA
470 Rigby	500	2150	1940	1740	1560	NA	5130	4170	3360	2695	NA	+2.5	-2.8	-19.4	NA	NA
470 Nitro Ex.	480	2190	1954	1735	1536	NA	5111	4070	3210	2515	NA	+2.5	-3.5	-20.8	NA	NA
470 Nitro Ex.	500	2150	1890	1650	1440	1270	5130	3965	3040	2310	1790	+2.5	-4.3	-24.0	NA	$177
475 No. 2	500	2200	1955	1728	1522	NA	5375	4243	3316	2573	NA	+2.5	-3.2	-20.9	NA	NA
505 Gibbs	525	2300	2063	1840	1637	NA	6166	4922	3948	3122	NA	+2.5	-3.0	-18.0	NA	NA
500 N.E.-3"	570	2150	1928	1722	1533	NA	5850	4703	3752	2975	NA	+2.5	-3.7	-22.0	NA	NA
500 N.E.-3"	600	2150	1927	1721	1531	NA	6158	4947	3944	3124	NA	+2.5	-4.0	-22.0	NA	NA\
495 A-Square	570	2350	2117	1896	1693	NA	5850	4703	3752	2975	NA	+2.5	-1.0	-14.5	NA	NA
495 A-Square	600	2280	2050	1833	1635	NA	6925	5598	4478	3562	NA	+2.5	-2.0	-17.0	NA	NA
500 A-Square	600	2380	2144	1922	1766	NA	7546	6126	4920	3922	NA	+2.5	-3.0	-17.0	NA	NA
500 A-Square	707	2250	2040	1841	1567	NA	7947	6530	5318	4311	NA	+2.5	-2.0	-17.0	NA	NA
500 BMG PMC	660	3080	2854	2639	2444	2248	13688		500 yd. zero			+3.1	+3.90	+4.7	+2.8	NA
577 Nitro Ex.	750	2050	1793	1562	1360	NA	6990	5356	4065	3079	NA	+2.5	-5.0	-26.0	NA	NA
577 Tyrannosaur	750	2400	2141	1898	1675	NA	9591	7633	5996	4671	NA	+3.0	0.0	-12.9	NA	NA
600 N.E.	900	1950	1680	1452	NA	NA	7596	5634	4212	NA	NA	+5.6	0.0	NA	NA	NA
700 N.E.	1200	1900	1676	1472	NA	NA	9618	7480	5774	NA	NA	+5.7	0.0	NA	NA	NA

Wea. Mag.= Weatherby Magnum. Spfd. = Springfield. A-A-Sq. = A-Square. N.E.=Nitro Express. Many manufacturers do not supply suggested retail prices. Others did not get their pricing to us before press time. All pricing can vary dependent on the exact brand and style of ammo selected and/or the retail outlet from which you make your purchase. Pricing has been rounded to the nearest dollar and represents our best estimate of average pricing. An * after the cartridge means these loads are available with Nosler Partition or Swift A-Frame bullets. Listed pricing may or may not reflect this bullet type.
** = these are packed 50 to box, all others are 20 to box.

Centerfire Handgun Cartridges — Ballistics & Prices

Caliber	Bullet Wgt. Grs.	VELOCITY (fps) MV	50 yds.	100 yds.	ENERGY (ft. lbs.) ME	50 yds.	100 yds.	Mid-Range Traj. (in.) 50 yds.	100 yds.	Bbl. Lgth. (in).	Est. Price/ box
221 Rem. Fireball	50	2650	2380	2130	780	630	505	0.2	0.8	10.5"	$15
25 Automatic	35	900	813	742	63	51	43	NA	NA	2"	$18
25 Automatic	45	815	730	655	65	55	40	1.8	7.7	2"	$21
25 Automatic	50	760	705	660	65	55	50	2.0	8.7	2"	$17
7.5mm Swiss	107	1010	NA	NA	240	NA	NA	NA	NA	NA	NEW
7.62mmTokarev	87	1390	NA	NA	365	NA	NA	0.6	NA	4.5"	NA
7.62 Nagant	97	1080	NA	NA	350	NA	NA	NA	NA	NA	NEW
7.63 Mauser	88	1440	NA	NA	405	NA	NA	NA	NA	NA	NEW
30 Luger	93†	1220	1110	1040	305	255	225	0.9	3.5	4.5"	$34
30 Carbine	110	1790	1600	1430	785	625	500	0.4	1.7	10"	$28
32 S&W	88	680	645	610	90	80	75	2.5	10.5	3"	$17
32 S&W Long	98	705	670	635	115	100	90	2.3	10.5	4"	$17
32 Short Colt	80	745	665	590	100	80	60	2.2	9.9	4"	$19
32 H&R Magnum	85	1100	1020	930	230	195	165	1.0	4.3	4.5"	$21
32 H&R Magnum	95	1030	940	900	225	190	170	1.1	4.7	4.5"	$19
32 Automatic	60	970	895	835	125	105	95	1.3	5.4	4"	$22
32 Automatic	60	1000	917	849	133	112	96			4"	NA
32 Automatic	65	950	890	830	130	115	100	1.3	5.6	NA	NA
32 Automatic	71	905	855	810	130	115	95	1.4	5.8	4"	$19
8mm Lebel Pistol	111	850	NA	NA	180	NA	NA	NA	NA	NA	NEW
8mm Steyr	112	1080	NA	NA	290	NA	NA	NA	NA	NA	NEW
8mm Gasser	126	850	NA	NA	200	NA	NA	NA	NA	NA	NEW
380 Automatic	60	1130	960	NA	170	120	NA	1.0	NA	NA	NA
380 Automatic	85/88	990	920	870	190	165	145	1.2	5.1	4"	$20
380 Automatic	90	1000	890	800	200	160	130	1.2	5.5	3.75"	$10
380 Automatic	95/100	955	865	785	190	160	130	1.4	5.9	4"	$20
38 Super Auto +P	115	1300	1145	1040	430	335	275	0.7	3.3	5"	$26
38 Super Auto +P	125/130	1215	1100	1015	425	350	300	0.8	3.6	5"	$26
38 Super Auto +P	147	1100	1050	1000	395	355	325	0.9	4.0	5"	NA
9x18mm Makarov	95	1000	NA	NA	NA	NA	NA	NA	NA	NA	NEW
9x18mm Ultra	100	1050	NA	NA	240	NA	NA	NA	NA	NA	NEW
9x23mm Largo	124	1190	1055	966	390	306	257	0.7	3.7	4"	NA
9x23mm Win.	125	1450	1249	1103	583	433	338	0.6	2.8	NA	NA
9mm Steyr	115	1180	NA	NA	350	NA	NA	NA	NA	NA	NEW
9mm Luger	88	1500	1190	1010	440	275	200	0.6	3.1	4"	$24
9mm Luger	90	1360	1112	978	370	247	191	NA	NA	4"	$26
9mm Luger	95	1300	1140	1010	350	275	215	0.8	3.4	4"	NA
9mm Luger	100	1180	1080	NA	305	255	NA	0.9	NA	4"	NA
9mm Luger	115	1155	1045	970	340	280	240	0.9	3.9	4"	$21
9mm Luger	123/125	1110	1030	970	340	290	260	1.0	4.0	4"	$23
9mm Luger	140	935	890	850	270	245	225	1.3	5.5	4"	$23
9mm Luger	147	990	940	900	320	290	265	1.1	4.9	4"	$26
9mm Luger +P	90	1475	NA	NA	437	NA	NA	NA	NA	NA	NA
9mm Luger +P	115	1250	1113	1019	399	316	265	0.8	3.5	4"	$27
9mm Federal	115	1280	1130	1040	420	330	280	0.7	3.3	4"V	$24
9mm Luger Vector	115	1155	1047	971	341	280	241	NA	NA	4"	NA
9mm Luger +P	124	1180	1089	1021	384	327	287	0.8	3.8	4"	NA
38 S&W	146	685	650	620	150	135	125	2.4	10.0	4"	$19
38 Short Colt	125	730	685	645	150	130	115	2.2	9.4	6"	$19
39 Special	100	950	900	NA	200	180	NA	1.3	NA	4"V	NA
38 Special	110	945	895	850	220	195	175	1.3	5.4	4"V	$23
38 Special	130	775	745	710	175	160	120	1.9	7.9	4"V	$22
38 Special Cowboy	140	800	767	735	199	183	168			7.5" V	NA
38 (Multi-Ball)	140	830	730	505	215	130	80	2.0	10.6	4"V	$10**
38 Special	148	710	635	565	165	130	105	2.4	10.6	4"V	$17
38 Special	158	755	725	690	200	185	170	2.0	8.3	4"V	$18
38 Special +P	95	1175	1045	960	290	230	195	0.9	3.9	4"V	$23
38 Special +P	110	995	925	070	240	210	185	1.2	5.1	4"V	$23
38 Special +P	125	975	929	885	204	238	218	1	5.2	4"	NA
38 Special +P	125	945	900	860	250	225	205	1.3	5.4	4"V	#23
38 Special +P	129	945	910	870	255	235	215	1.3	5.3	4"V	$11
38 Special +P	130	925	887	852	247	227	210	1.3	5.50	4"V	NA
38 Special +P	147/150(c)	884	NA	NA	264	NA	NA	NA	NA	4"V	$27
38 Special +P	158	890	855	825	280	255	240	1.4	6.0	4"V	$20
357 SIG	115	1520	NA	NA	593	NA	NA	NA	NA	NA	NA
357 SIG	124	1450	NA	NA	578	NA	NA	NA	NA	NA	NA
357 SIG	125	1350	1190	1080	510	395	325	0.7	3.1	4"	NA
357 SIG	150	1130	1030	970	420	355	310	0.9	4.0	NA	NA
356 TSW	115	1520	NA	NA	593	NA	NA	NA	NA	NA	NA
356 TSW	124	1450	NA	NA	578	NA	NA	NA	NA	NA	NA
356 TSW	135	1280	1120	1010	490	375	310	0.8	3.50	NA	NA
356 TSW	147	1220	1120	1040	485	410	355	0.8	3.5	5"	NA
357 Mag., Super Clean	105	1650									NA
357 Magnum	110	1295	1095	975	410	290	230	0.8	3.5	4"V	$25
357 (Med.Vel.)	125	1220	1075	985	415	315	270	0.8	3.7	4"V	$25
357 Magnum	125	1450	1240	1090	585	425	330	0.6	2.8	4"V	$25
357 (Multi-Ball)	140	1155	830	665	420	215	135	1.2	6.4	4"V	$11**
357 Magnum	140	1360	1195	1075	575	445	360	0.7	3.0	4"V	$25
357 Magnum	145	1290	1155	1060	535	430	360	0.8	3.5	4"V	$26
357 Magnum	150/158	1235	1105	1015	535	430	360	0.8	3.5	4"V	$25
357 Mag. Cowboy	158	800	761	725	225	203	185				NA
357 Magnum	165	1290	1189	1108	610	518	450	0.7	3.1	8-3/8"	NA
357 Magnum	180	1145	1055	985	525	445	390	0.9	3.9	4"V	$25
357 Magnum	180	1180	1088	1020	557	473	416	0.8	3.6	8"V	NA
357 Mag. CorBon F.A.	180	1650	1512	1386	1088	913	767	1.66	0.0		NA
357 Mag. CorBon	200	1200	1123	1061	640	560	500	3.19	0.0		NA
357 Rem. Maximum	158	1825	1590	1380	1170	885	670	0.4	1.7	10.5"	$14**
40 S&W	135	1140	1070	NA	390	345	NA	0.9	NA	4"	NA
40 S&W	155	1140	1026	958	447	362	309	0.9	4.1	4"	$14***
40 S&W	165	1150	NA	NA	485	NA	NA	NA	NA	4"	$18***
40 S&W	180	985	936	893	388	350	319	1.4	5.0	4"	$14***
40 S&W	180	1015	960	914	412	368	334	1.3	4.5	4"	NA
400 Cor-Bon	135	1450	NA	NA	630	NA	NA	NA	NA	5"	NA
10mm Automatic	155	1125	1046	986	436	377	335	0.9	3.9	5"	$26
10mm Automatic	170	1340	1165	1145	680	510	415	0.7	3.2	5"	$31
10mm Automatic	175	1290	1140	1035	650	505	420	0.7	3.3	5.5"	$11**
10mm Auto. (FBI)	180	950	905	865	361	327	299	1.5	5.4	4"	$16**
10mm Automatic	180	1030	970	920	425	375	340	1.1	4.7	5"	$16**
10mm Auto H.V.	180†	1240	1124	1037	618	504	430	0.8	3.4	5"	$27
10mm Automatic	200	1160	1070	1010	495	510	430	0.9	3.8	5"	$14**
10.4mm Italian	177	950	NA	NA	360	NA	NA	NA	NA	NA	NEW
41 Action Exp.	180	1000	947	903	400	359	326	0.5	4.2	5"	$13**
41 Rem. Magnum	170	1420	1165	1015	760	515	390	0.7	3.2	4"V	$33
41 Rem. Magnum	175	1250	1120	1030	605	490	410	0.8	3.4	4"V	$14**
41 (Med. Vel.)	210	965	900	840	435	375	330	1.3	5.4	4"V	$30
41 Rem. Magnum	210	1300	1160	1060	790	630	535	0.7	3.2	4"V	$33
44 S&W Russian	247	780	NA	NA	335	NA	NA	NA	NA	NA	NA
44 S&W Special	180	980	NA	NA	383	NA	NA	NA	NA	6.5"	NA
44 S&W Special	180	1000	935	882	400	350	311	NA	NA	7.5"V	NA
44 S&W Special	200†	875	825	780	340	302	270	1.2	6.0	6"	$13**
44 S&W Special	200	1035	940	865	475	390	335	1.1	4.9	6.5"	$13**
44 S&W Special	240/246	755	725	695	310	285	265	2.0	8.3	6.5"	$26
44-40 Win. Cowboy	225	750	723	695	281	261	242				NA
44 Rem. Magnum	180	1610	1365	1175	1035	745	550	0.5	2.3	4"V	$18**
44 Rem. Magnum	200	1400	1192	1053	870	630	492	0.6	NA	6.5"	$20
44 Rem. Magnum	210	1495	1310	1165	1040	805	635	0.6	2.5	6.5"	$18**
44 (Med. Vel.)	240	1000	945	900	535	475	435	1.1	4.8	6.5"	$17
44 R.M. (Jacketed)	240	1180	1080	1010	740	625	545	0.9	3.7	4"V	$18**
44 R.M. (Lead)	240	1350	1185	1070	970	750	610	0.7	3.1	4"V	$29
44 Rem. Magnum	250	1180	1100	1040	775	670	600	0.8	3.6	6.5"V	$21
44 Rem. Magnum	250	1230	1132	1057	840	711	620	0.8	2.9	6.5"V	NA
44 Rem. Magnum	275	1235	1142	1070	931	797	699	0.8	3.3	6.5"	NA
44 Rem. Magnum	300	1200	1100	1026	959	806	702	NA	NA	7.5"	$17
440 CorBon	260	1700	1544	1403	1669	1377	1136	1.58	NA	10	NA
450 Short Colt	226	830	NA	NA	350	NA	NA	NA	NA	NA	NEW
45 Automatic	165	1030	930	NA	385	315	NA	1.2	NA	5"	NA
45 Automatic	185	1000	940	890	410	360	325	1.1	4.9	5"	$28
45 Auto. (Match)	185	770	705	650	245	204	175	2.0	8.7	5"	$28
45 Auto. (Match)	200	940	890	840	392	352	312	2.0	8.6	5"	$20
45 Automatic	200	975	917	860	421	372	328	1.4	5.0	5"	$18
45 Automatic	230	830	800	675	355	325	300	1.6	6.8	5"	$27
45 Automatic	230	880	846	816	396	366	340	1.5	6.1	5"	NA
45 Automatic +P	165	1250	NA	NA	573	NA	NA	NA	NA	NA	NA
45 Automatic +P	185	1140	1040	970	535	445	385	0.9	4.0	5"	$31
45 Automatic +P	200	1055	982	925	494	428	380	NA	NA	5"	NA
45 Super	185	1300	1190	1108	694	582	504	NA	NA	5"	NA
45 Win. Magnum	230	1400	1230	1105	1000	775	635	0.6	2.8	5"	$14**
45 Win. Magnum	260	1250	1137	1053	902	746	640	0.8	3.3	5"	$16**
45 Win. Mag. CorBon	320	1150	1080	1025	940	830	747	3.47			NA
455 Webley MKII	262	850	NA	NA	420	NA	NA	NA	NA	NA	NA
45 Colt	200	1000	938	889	444	391	351	1.3	4.8	5.5"	$21
45 Colt	225	960	890	830	460	395	345	1.3	5.5	5.5"	$22
45 Colt + P CorBon	265	1350	1225	1126	1073	884	746	2.65	0.0		NA
45 Colt + P CorBon	300	1300	1197	1114	1126	956	827	2.78	0.0		NA
45 Colt	250/255	860	820	780	410	375	340	1.6	6.6	5.5"	$27
454 Casull	250	1300	1151	1047	938	735	608	0.7	3.2	7.5"V	NA
454 Casull	260	1800	1577	1301	1871	1436	1101	0.4	1.8	7.5"V	NA
454 Casull	300	1625	1451	1308	1759	1413	1141	0.5	2.0	7.5"V	NA
454 Casull CorBon	360	1500	1387	1286	1800	1640	1323	2.01	0.0		NA
50 Action Exp.	325	1400	1209	1075	1414	1055	835	0.2	2.3	6"	$24**

Notes: Blanks are available in 32 S&W, 38 S&W, and 38 Special. V after barrel length indicates test barrel was vented to produce ballistics similar to a revolver with a normal barrel-to-cylinder gap. Ammo prices are per 50 rounds except when marked with an ** which signifies a 20 round box; *** signifies a 25-round box. Not all loads are available from all ammo manufacturers. Listed loads are those made by Remington, Winchester, Federal, and others. DISC. is a discontinued load. Prices are rounded to nearest whole dollar and will vary with brand and retail outlet. † = new bullet weight this year; "c" indicates a change in data.

Rimfire Ammunition — Ballistics & Prices

Cartridge Type	Bullet Wt. Grs.	Velocity (fps) 22-1/2" Bbl. Muzzle	100 yds.	Energy (ft. lbs.) 22-1/2" Bbl. Muzzle	100 yds.	Mid-Range Traj. (in.) 100 yds.	Muzzle Velocity 6" Bbl.
22 Short Blank	—	—	—	—	—	—	—
22 Short CB	29	727	610	33	24	NA	706
22 Short Target	29	830	695	44	31	6.8	786
22 Short HP	27	1164	920	81	50	4.3	1077
22 Long CB	29	727	610	33	24	NA	706
22 Long HV	29	1180	946	90	57	4.1	1031
22 LR Ballistician	25	1100	760	65	30	NA	NA
22 LR Pistol Match	40	1070	890	100	70	4.6	940
22 LR Sub Sonic HP	38	1050	901	93	69	4.7	NA
22 LR Standard Velocity	40	1070	890	100	70	4.6	940
22 LR HV	40	1255	1016	140	92	3.6	1060
22 LR Silhoutte	42	1220	1003	139	94	3.6	1025
22 LR HV HP	40	1280	1001	146	89	3.5	1085
22 LR Hyper HP	32/33/34	1500	1075	165	85	2.8	NA
22 LR Stinger HP	32	1640	1132	191	91	2.6	1395
22 LR Shot #12	31	950	NA	NA	NA	NA	NA
22 Win. Mag.	30	2200	1373	322	127	1.4	1610
22 Win. Mag. JHP	34	2120	1435	338	155	1.4	NA
22 Win. Mag. JHP	40	1910	1326	324	156	1.7	1480
22 Win. Mag. FMJ	40	1910	1326	324	156	1.7	1480
22 Win. Mag. JHP	50	1650	1280	300	180	1.3	NA
22 Win. Mag. Shot #11	52	1000	—	NA	—	—	NA

Note: The actual ballistics obtained with your firearm can vary considerably from the advertised ballistics. Also, ballistics can vary from lot to lot with the same brand and type load.

SHOTSHELL LOADS AND PRICES

Dram Equiv.	Shot Ozs.	Load Style	Shot Sizes	Brands	Avg. Nom. Price/box	Velocity (fps)
10 Gauge 3-1/2" Magnum						
4-1/2	2-1/4	premium	BB, 2,4,5,6	Win., Fed., Rem.	$33	1205
4-1/4	2	high velocity	BB, 2, 4	Rem.	$22	1210
4-1/2	2-1/4	duplex	4x6	Rem.	$14*	1205
Max	18 pellets	premium	00 buck	Fed., Win.	$7**	1100
Max	1-7/8	Bismuth	BB, 2, 4	Win., Bis.	NA	1225
4-1/4	1-3/4	steel	TT, T, BBB, BB, 1, 2, 3	Win., Rem.	$27	1260
Mag	1-5/8	steel	T, BBB	Win.	$27	1285
4-5/8	1-5/8	steel	F, T, BBB	Fed.	$26	1350
Max	1-5/8	Tungsten - Iron	BBB, BB, 2, 4	Fed.		1300
Max	1-3/8	steel	T, BBB, BB, 2	Fed., Win.	NA	1450
Max	1-3/8	Tungsten - Iron	BBB, BB, 2, 4	Fed.		1450
Max	1-3/4	slug, rifled	slug	Fed.	NA	1280
12 Gauge 3-1/2" Magnum						
Max	2/14	premium	4, 5, 6	Fed., Rem., Win.	$13*	1150
Max	18 pellets	premium	00 buck	Fed., Win., Rem.	$7**	1100
Max	1-7/8	Bismuth	BB, 2, 4	Win., Bis.	NA	1225
4-1/8	1-9/16	steel	TT, F, T, BBB, BB, 1, 2	Rem., Win., Fed.	$22	1335
Max	1-3/8	steel	T, BBB, BB, 2, 4	Fed., Win.	NA	1450
Max	1-3/8	Tungsten - Iron	BBB, BB, 2, 4	Fed.	NA	1450
12 Gauge 3" Magnum						
4	2	premium	BB, 2, 4, 5, 6	Win., Fed., Rem.	$9*	1175
4	2	duplex	4x6	Rem.	$10	1175
4	1-7/8	premium	BB, 2, 4, 6	Win., Fed., Rem.	$19	1210
4	1-7/8	duple	4x6	Rem., Fio.	$9*	1210
Max	1-3/4	turkey	4, 5, 6	Fed., Rem., Win.	NA	1300
4-1/2	1-3/4	duplex	2x4, 4x6	Fio.	NA	1150
4	1-5/8	premium	2, 4, 5, 6	Win., Fed., Rem.	$18	1290
Max	1-5/8	Bismuth	BB, 2, 4, 5, 6	Win., Bis.	NA	1250
4	24 pellets	buffered	1 buck	Win., Fed., Rem.	$5**	1040
4	15 pellets	buffered	00 buck	Win., Fed., Rem.	$6**	1210
4	10 pellets	buffered	000 buck	Win., Fed., Rem.	$6**	1225
4	41 pellets	buffered	4 buck	Win., Fed., Rem.	$6**	1210
Max	1-3/8	Tungsten - Polymer	4, 6	Fed.	NA	1330
Max	1-3/8	slug	slug	Bren.	NA	1476
Max	1-1/4	slug, rifled	slug	Fed.	NA	1600
Max	1-3/16	saboted slug	copper slug	Rem.	NA	1500
Max	1-1/8	Tungsten - Iron	BBB, BB, 2, 4	Fed.	NA	1400
Max	1	steel	4, 6	Fed.		1330
Max	1	slug, rifled	slug, magnum	Win., Rem.	$5**	1760
Max	1	saboted slug	slug	Rem., Win., Fed.	$10**	1550
3-5/8	1-3/8	steel	TT, F, T, BBB, BB, 1, 2, 3, 4	Win., Fed., Rem.	$19	1275
Max	1-1/8	steel	T, BBB, BB, 2, 4, 5, 6	Fed., Win.	NA	1450
Max	1-1/8	steel	BB, 2	Fed.	NA	1400
4	1-1/4	steel	TT, F, T, BBB, BB, 1, 2, 3, 4, 6	Win., Fed., Rem.	$18	1375
12 Gauge 2-3/4"						
Max	1-5/8	magnum	4, 5, 6	Win., Fed.	$8*	1250
Max	1-3/8	turkey	4, 5, 6	Fio.	NA	1250
Max	1-3/8	duplex	2x4, 4x6	Fio.	NA	1200
Max	1-3/8	Bismuth	BB, 2, 4, 5, 6	Win., Bis.	NA	1280
3-3/4	1-1/2	magnum	BB, 2, 4, 5, 6	Win., Fed., Rem.	$16	1260
3-3/4	1-1/2	duplex	BBx4, 2x4, 4x6	Rem., Fio.	$9*	1260
3-3/4	1-1/4	high velocity	BB, 2, 4, 5, 6, 7-1/2, 8, 9	win., Fed., Rem., Fio.	$13	1330
Max	1-1/4	Tungsten - Polymer	4, 6	Fed.	NA	1330
3-1/2	1-1/4	mid velocity	7, 8, 9	Win.	Disc.	1275
3-1/4	1-1/4	standard velocity	6, 7-1/2, 8, 9	Win., Fed., Rem., Fio.	$11	1220
Max	1-1/4	Bismuth	4, 6	Win.		1220
3-1/4	1-1/8	standard velocity	4, 6, 7-1/2, 8, 9	Win., Fed., Rem., Fio.	$9	1255
Max	1	steel	BB, 2	Fed.	NA	1450
Max	1	Tungsten - Iron	BB, 2, 4	Fed.	NA	1450
3-1/4	1	standard velocity	6, 7-1/2, 8	Rem., Fed., Fio., Win.	$6	1290
3-1/4	1-1/4	target	7-1/2, 8, 9	Win., Fed., Rem.	$10	1220
3	1-1/8	spreader	7-1/2, 8, 8-1/2, 9	Fio.	NA	1200
3	1-1/8	duplex target	7-1/2x8	Rem.	NA	1200
3	1-1/8	target	7-1/2, 8, 9, 7-1/2x8	Win., Fed., Rem., Fio.	$7	1200
3	1-1/8	duplex clays	7-1/2x8-1/2	Rem.	NA	1200
2-3/4	1-1/8	target	7-1/2, 8, 8-1/2, 9, 7-1/2x8	Win., Fed., Rem., Fio.	$7	1145
2-3/4	1-1/8	duplex target	7-1/2x8	Rem.	NA	1145
2-3/4	1-1/8	low recoil	7-1/2, 8	Rem.	NA	1145
2-1/2	26 grams	low recoil	8	Win.	NA	980
2-1/4	1-1/8	target	7-1/2, 8, 8-1/2, 9	Rem., Fed.	$7	1080
Max	1	spreader	7-1/2, 8, 8-1/2, 9	Fio.	NA	1300
3-1/4	28 grams (1 oz)	target	7-1/2, 8, 9	Win., Fed., Rem., Fio.	$8	1290
3	1	target	7-1/2, 8, 8-1/2, 9	Win., Fio.	NA	1235
2-3/4	1	target	7-1/2, 8, 8-1/2, 9	Fed., Rem., Fio.	NA	1180
3-1/4	24 grams	target	7-1/2, 8, 9	Fed., Win., Fio.	NA	1325
3	7/8	light	8	Fio.	NA	1200
3-3/4	8 pellets	buffered	000 buck	Win., Fed., Rem.	$4**	1325
4	12 pellets	premium	00 buck	Win., Fed., Rem.	$5**	1290
3-3/4	9 pellets	buffered	00 buck	Win., Fed., Rem., Fio.	$19	1325
3-3/4	12 pellets	buffered	0 buck	Win., Fed., Rem.	$4**	1275
4	20 pellets	buffered	1 buck	Win., Fed., Rem.	$4**	1075
3-3/4	16 pellets	buffered	1 buck	Win., Fed., Rem.	$4**	1250
4	34 pellets	premium	4 buck	Fed., Rem.	$5**	1250
3-3/4	27 pellets	buffered	4 buck	Win., Fed., Rem., Fio.	$4**	1325
Max	1	saboted slug	slug	Win., Fed., Rem.	$10**	1450
Max	1-1/4	slug, rifled	slug	Fed.	NA	1520
Max	1-1/4	slug	slug	Lightfield		1440
Max	1	slug, rifled	slug, magnum	Rem., Fio.	$5**	1680
Max	1	slug, rifled	slug	Win., Rem.	$4**	1610
Max	1	sabot slug	slug	Sauvestre		1640
3	1-1/8	steel target	6-1/2, 7	Rem.	NA	1200
2-3/4	1-1/8	steel target	7	Rem.	NA	1145
3	1#	steel	7	Win.	$11	1235
3-1/2	1-1/8	steel	T, BBB, BB, 1, 2, 3, 4, 5, 6	Win., Fed., Rem.	$18	1275
3-3/4	1-1/8	steel	BB, 1, 2, 3, 4, 5, 6	Win., Fed., Rem., Fio.	$16	1365
3-3/4	1	steel	2, 3, 4, 5, 6, 7	Win., Fed., Rem., Fio.	$13	1390
Max	7/8	steel	7	Fio.	NA	1440
16 Gauge 2-3/4"						
3-1/4	1-1/4	magnum	2, 4, 6	Fed., Rem.	$16	1260
3-1/4	1-1/8	high velocity	4, 6, 7-1/2	Win., Fed., Rem., Fio.	$12	1295
Max	1-1/8	Bismuth	4, 5	Win., Bis.	NA	1200
2-3/4	1-1/8	standard velocity	6, 7-1/2, 8	Fed., Rem., Fio.	$9	1185
2-1/2	1	dove	6, 7-1/2, 8, 9	Fio., Win.	NA	1165
2-3/4	1		6, 7-1/2, 8	Fio.	NA	1200
Max	15/16	steel	2, 4	Fed., Rem.	NA	1300
Max	7/8	steel	2, 4	Win.	$16	1300
3	12 pellets	buffered	1 buck	Win., Fed., Rem.	$4**	1225
Max	4/5	slug, rifled	slug	Win., Fed., Rem.	$4**	1570
Max	.92	sabot slug	slug	Sauvestre		1560
20 Gauge 3" Magnum						
3	1-1/4	premium	2, 4, 5, 6, 7-1/2	Win., Fed., Rem.	$15	1185
3	1-1/4	turkey	4, 6	Fio.	NA	1200
Max	18 pellets	buck shot	2 buck	Fed.	NA	1200
Max	24 pellets	buffered	3 buck	Win.	$5**	1150
2-3/4	20 pellets	buck	3 buck	Rem.	$4**	1200
3-1/4	1	steel	1, 2, 3, 4, 5, 6	Win., Fed., Rem.	$15	1330
Max	7/8	Tungsten - Iron	2, 4	Fed.	NA	1375
Mag	5/8	saboted slug	275 gr.	Fed.	NA	1450
20 Gauge 2-3/4"						
2-3/4	1-1/8	magnum	4, 6, 7-1/2	Win., Fed., Rem.	$14	1175
2-3/4	1	high velocity	4, 5, 6, 7-1/2, 8, 9	Win., Fed., Rem., Fio.	$12	1220
Max	1	Bismuth	4, 6	Win., Bis.	NA	1200
2-1/2	1	standard velocity	6, 7-1/2, 8	Win., Rem., Fed., Fio.	$6	1165
2-1/2	7/8	clays	8	Rem.	NA	1200
2-1/2	7/8	promotional	6, 7-1/2, 8	Win., Rem., Fio.	$6	1210
2-1/2	1	target	8, 9	Win., Rem.	$8	1165
2-1/2	7/8	target	8, 9	Win., Fed., Rem.	$8	1200
2-1/2	7/8	steel - target	7	Rem.		1200
Max	20 pellets	buffered	3 buck	Win., Fed.	$4	1200
Max	5/8	slug, saboted	slug	Win.,	$9**	1400
2-3/4	5/8	slug, rifled	slug	Rem.	$4**	1580
Max	3/4	saboted slug	copper slug	Fed., Rem.	NA	1450
Max	3/4	slug, rifled	slug	Win., Fed., Rem., Fio.	$4**	1570
Max	.9	sabot slug	slug	Sauvestre		1480
Max	3/4	steel	2, 3, 4, 6	Win., Fed., Rem.	$14	1425
28 Gauge 2-3/4"						
2	1	high velocity	6, 7-1/2, 8	Win.	$12	1125
2-1/4	3/4	high velocity	6, 7-1/2, 8, 9	Win., Fed., Rem., Fio.	$11	1295
2	3/4	target	8, 9	Win., Fed., Rem.	$9	1200
Max	5/8	Bismuth	4, 6	Win., Bis.	NA	1250
410 Bore 3"						
Max	11/16	high velocity	4, 5, 6, 7-1/2, 8, 9	Win., Fed., Rem.	$10	1135
Max	9/16	Bismuth	4	Win., Bis.	NA	1175
410 Bore 2-1/2"						
Max	1/2	high velocity	4, 6, 7-1/2	Win., Fed., Rem.	$9	1245
Max	1/5	slug, rifled	slug	Win., Fed., Rem.	$4**	1815
1-1/2	1/2	target	8, 8-1/2, 9	Win., Fed., Rem., Fio.	$8	1200

NOTES: * = 10 rounds per box. ** = 5 rounds per box. Pricing variations and number of rounds per box can occur with type and brand of ammunition. Listed pricing is the average nominal cost for load style and box quantity shown. Not every brand is available in all shot size variations. Some manufacturers do not provide suggested list prices. All prices rounded to nearest whole dollar. The price you pay will vary dependent upon outlet of purchase. # = new load spec this year; "C" indicates a change in data.

CAUTION: PRICES SHOWN ARE SUPPLIED BY THE MANUFACTURER OR IMPORTER. CHECK YOUR LOCAL GUNSHOP.

SHOOTER'S MARKETPLACE

INTERESTING PRODUCT NEWS FOR THE ACTIVE SHOOTING SPORTSMAN.

The companies represented on the following pages will be happy to provide additional information – feel free to contact them.

SOLID STEEL RINGS & BASES

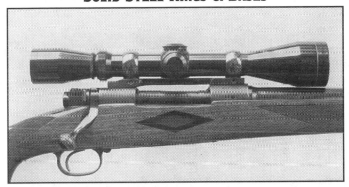

The World's Sleekest System! The only projectionless split-ring scope mount in the world. Cut from the solid. Not a cookie-cutter, detach-and-duck perversion of Conetrol's splendid concept, but the genuine original machine-cut rendition of a pristine one of a kind product. The strongest because muscle is packed into both rings. Others limit strength to one ring. Dual ring movement allows scope to be centered over gun after adjustment, not possible for other mount designs. Conetrol fits more high-power firearms than any other mount-maker - can provide mounting even for guns long obsolete.

Three basic styles - from matte to streamlined high gloss. Fluted bases. Teflon. Stainless steel or electroless nickel. Metric ring sizes.

CONETROL SCOPE MOUNTS
10225 Hwy. 123 South, Seguin, TX 78155
Phone: (800) CONETROL • Web: www.conetrol.com

Turn Your .380 Auto Into A .45!

Extreme-Performance Ammo

Rated Tops in the Strasbourg Tests, yet SAFEST for Home Use

---

call us for the name of the dealer nearest you

Phone (407) 834-9966
from 10 a.m. to 6 p.m.
Monday-Friday EST
24-Hour FAX (407) 834-8185

MAGSAFE AMMO, INC.
4700 South US Highway 17-92,
Casselberry, FL 32707 USA
Phone: 407-834-9966
Fax: 407-834-8185

MagSafe Ammo is available in all popular calibers:

.25 ACP
.32 ACP
.32 H&R Magnum
.380 ACP
9mm Makarov
9mm Luger
.357 SIG
.38 Special
.357 Magnum
10mm
.40 S&W
.44 Special
.44 Magnum
.45 ACP
.45 L. Colt
7.62 x 25 Tokarev
7.52 x 39 Russian
.30 M-1 Carbine

MAG-NA-PORT FOR SEMI-AUTOMATICS

Mag-na-port on the semi-automatic pistols provides a tactical advantage reducing recoil and muzzle climb without altering the gun's silhouette. The EDM (electrical discharge machining process pioneered by Larry Kelly) is superior to many of today's compensating systems. Trapezoidal ports cut into the barrel and slide meter gases without fouling. In a crucial situation where quick repeat shots are necessary, Mag-na-port might be enough to make a real difference.

Many law enforcement agencies allow the use of Mag-na-port on semi-autos and back up revolvers. The reduction in muzzle rise and felt recoil allow the firearms to be brought back on target in less time, which could be crucial in a firefight.

For information, call or write Mag-na-port International, Inc.

MAG-NA-PORT
41302 Executive Drive, Harrison Twp., MI 48045-1306
Phone: 810-469-6727 • Fax: 810-469-0425
Web: www.magnaport.com

SHOOTER'S MARKETPLACE

YOUTH CAMO LAMINATE TURKEY SHOTGUN

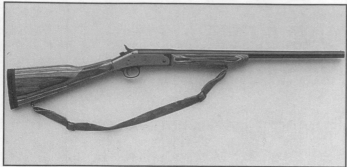

The new Harrington & Richardson® "NWTF Sponsored Edition Youth" shotgun is produced in 20 gauge with a 22" barrel with a modified choke for maximun versatility on turkeys and a variety of other game as well. The polished receiver is laser engraved with the NWTF logo. The stock and forend are hand checkered hardwood laminate with a green, brown and black pattern. Includes a ventilated recoil pad, sling swivels and a camo sling. The stock is dimensioned to properly fit young turkey hunters. This model uses the H&R 1871®, Inc. Transfer Bar System for hammer down safety.

As a "Sponsored Edition" this shotgun also provides a great benefit to the NWTF for their programs. With the sale of each gun H&R 1871® will make a donation to the NWTF.

H&R 1871, INC.
60 Industrial Rowe, Gardner, MA 01440
Phone: 978-632-9393 • Fax: 978-632-2300
Email: hr1871@hr1871.com

YOUTH GUN SALES FUND EDUCATION

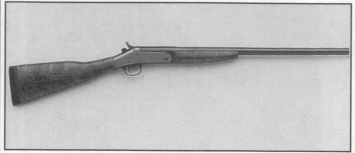

These new shotguns are based on the current Pardner® Youth shotguns in 20 ga., 28 ga. and .410 and feature polished blue receivers and real American Black Walnut stocks and forends. The engraving has both the NRA Foundation's logo and the inscription "Youth Endowment Edition."

Each of the NEF "Youth Endowment Edition" shotguns are specifically designed to properly fit young shooters and have a 22" barrel and are stocked at 12-1/2" length of pull, including a ventilated recoil pad. All include the patented NEF Transfer Bar System for a high level of hammer down safety. New England Firearms® shotguns using this system are currently in use by 37 states in their Hunter Safety Education programs, making these one of the most popular "beginner's" shotguns in the world.

H&R 1871, INC.
60 Industrial Rowe, Gardner, MA 01440
Phone: 978-632-9393 • Fax: 978-632-2300
Email: hr1871@hr1871.com

SURVIVAL SPECIALTY RIFLE

New for 1999 is a new heavy barrel 308 Winchester Survivor® in a matte blue finish to the line.

The 308 Winchester has an excellent reputation on most North American big game and is available in the most remote areas.

This new heavy barrel 308 Winchester model will include all of the features that have made the Survivor® rifle line so popular: a heavy weight 22-inch barrel, factory fitted with a Weaver style scope base. A hammer extension is included for cocking when the scope is mounted. The thumbhole stock and forend are high density polymer. The stock has a large storage compartment and the forend is removable for ammo storage as well. Sling swivels and a nylon sling are standard equipment.

The new 308 Survivor® can also accept a wide range of additional NEF rifle and shotgun barrels.

H&R 1871, INC.
60 Industrial Rowe, Gardner, MA 01440
Phone: 978-632-9393 • Fax: 978-632-2300
Email: hr1871@hr1871.com

ADULT RIMFIRE RIFLE

The new NEF Sportster™ Rimfire looks like the Superlight Handi-Rifle™ but in a pure rimfire format. The action is heat-treated steel with a properly offset firing pin, incorporating the well respected NEF transfer bar system. As a true rimfire, none of the current centerfire rifle or shotgun barrels in the NEF Accessory Barrel Program will function with this receiver.

The Sportster™ barrel is 20" long and fitted with a Weaver style scope base. An offset hammer extension is supplied for easy cocking when the scope is mounted. The overall finish on metal components is low visibility blue. The Monte Carlo stock and semi-beavertail forend are high density polymer with a textured non-slip finish, including a recoil pad and Uncle Mikes® sling swivel studs.

H&R 1871, INC.
60 Industrial Rowe, Gardner, MA 01440
Phone: 978-632-9393 • Fax: 978-632-2300
Email: hr1871@hr1871.com

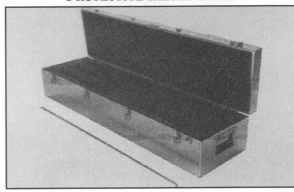
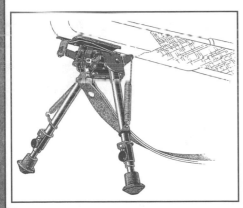
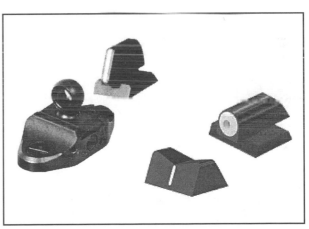

SHOOTER'S MARKETPLACE

NEW SCOPES FROM SWIFT

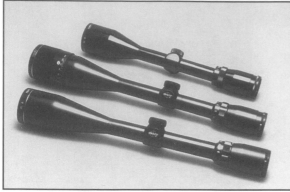

Swift reports that the new Swift Premier Line is brighter than comparable scopes, with generous eye relief. All are hard anodized, waterproof and have the Swift self-centering Quadraplex reticle.

This new line features objective adjustments for parallax, full saddle construction for strength, elevation and windage adjustments, multi-coated optics and Speed Focus, a feature that makes it quicker to focus.

Included are six new riflescope models: five 50mm scopes with variable power ranges from 2.5x to 18x, and a 40mm scope with a 3-9x zoom, plus one new pistolscope, (Model 679M) a 1.25 - 4x, 28mm.

SWIFT INSTRUMENTS, INC.
952 Dorchester Avenue, Dept: GD, Boston, MA 02125
Phone: 617-436-2960 • Fax: 617-436-3232
Email: swift1@tiac.net • Web: www.swift-optics.com

NEW BINOCULARS FOR HUNTERS

Swift 818R Trilyte: this 12 ounce roof prism, rubber armored, camouflage binocular is light enough to carry all day. Prisms use both BaK-4 and BaK-7 optical glass with magenta and aluminum coating. Multi-coating (green) is used on exterior objective and ocular lenses. It is supplied with both objective and eyepiece lens caps and a padded pouch-type case with belt strap.

For more information, contact:

SWIFT INSTRUMENTS, INC.
952 Dorchester Avenue, Dept. GD, Boston, MA 02125
Phone: 617-436-2960 • Fax: 617-436-3232
Email: swift1@tiac.net • Web: www.swift-optics.com

BALLARD RIFLE IS BACK!

The Ballard rifle is back in production after more than 100 years. At the Cody, Wyoming factory, we have made a firm commitment to honoring the Ballard tradition of superior quality, fit and finish. Our craftsmen focus on that goal every day as they make Ballard rifles from the patent, in all original configurations.

Whether your interest is hunting, target shooting or Schuetzen shooting, there is a Ballard rifle to perfectly fit your needs. Please send for our color catalog of rifles, sights, parts and obsolete brass.

BALLARD RIFLE & CARTRIDGE CO., LLC
113 W. Yellowstone Ave., Cody, WY 82414
Phone: 307-587-4914 • Fax: 307-527-6097
Email: ballard@wyoming.com

THE COMPETITOR

The Competitor® Single Shot Pistol is completely ambidextrous with interchangeable barrels available in over 330 calibers, ranging from small rimfire to large belted magnum. Competitor® barrels can be changed in less than three minutes and average accuracy exceeds most rifles.

Standard Competitor® pistols come with a 14" barrel, scope base, synthetic grip, adjustable trigger, and black oxide finish for under $415.00. Laminate or regular wooden grips, sights, muzzle brakes, nickel finish, and barrels from 10-1/2"-23" are optional.

All Competitor® Pistols are completely U.S. made, feature a patented cammed rotary ejection system and cock on opening: are low in cost, strong, reliable and have a 100% lifetime guarantee. Contact your local dealer or distributor.

COMPETITOR INC.
30 Tricnit Road, Unit 16, New Ipswich, NH 03071-0508
Phone: 603-878-3891 • Fax: 603: 878-3950

SHOOTER'S MARKETPLACE

SHOTSHELL / CHOKE TUBE CASE

Carry your shotshells and choke tubes in one convenient compact case. 12 gauge shell boxes can be left open for quick access in the field or at the range. Ideal for all shotgun shooting sports. Detachable choke tube case holds up to nine tubes, most factory wrenches and choke lube. Holds 100 rounds 2-3/4" or 3" 12 gauge or 50 rounds of 3-1/2" 12 or 10 gauge. Rugged polypropylene molding with large comfortable handle in camo (09) or forest green (11). Catalog no. SW100-.

Write for free catalog.

MTM CASE-GARD
P.O. Box 13117, Dayton, OH 45413
Phone: 937-890-7461 • Fax: 937-890-1747
Web: www.mtmcase-gard.com

RELOADING EQUIPMENT AND SUPPLIES

We offer fast, friendly service and fair prices.

100% processed rifle brass full length sized & trimmed. Ready to Load! 223...$42.99/1000; 308...$64.99/1000.

Processed Pistol Brass: 9MM...$29.99/1000; 38 SPL...$28.99/1000; 40 S&W...$34.99/1000.
Freight pre-paid with order of $25 or more, in 48 continuous states.
Machinery: Roller Mics pistol brass separation machines • Case Inspector/Auto Reamer • Scharch Roller Sizer • Ammunition Boxing Machine • Packaging Supplies • Black Plastic Trays with red or white boxes. Prices subject to change without notice. We accept all major credit cards.

SCHARCH MFG. INC.
10325 C. Rd. 120, Salida, CO 81201
Phone: 800-836-4683 • Email: scharch@csn.net • Web: www.scharch.com

---

GATLING GUN BUILDER'S PACKAGE

Complete plans for the 22-caliber Long Rifle Gatling are now available and have been fully adapted to incorporate obtainable materials and makeable parts. No castings are required.

The to-scale blueprints are fully dimensioned and toleranced. A 40-page instruction booklet lists materials and explains each part and how it is made.

The package includes drawings and instructions for making rifled barrels, wooden spoked wheels and all internal parts. The finished piece has 10 rifled barrels and is 3 feet long by 2 feet high. The plan package is $58.57; priority postage within the U.S. included. Overseas air add $14.00. Materials kits and finished parts also available. Major credit cards, check or money order accepted. Include a self-addressed card.

RG-G INC.
P.O. Box 935, Trinidad, CO 81082
Phone/Fax: 719-845-1436

CHAMBERING REAMERS * HEADSPACE GAUGES
SPECIAL TOOLING
NEW TOOLS FOR SIXGUNNERS & WILDCATTERS

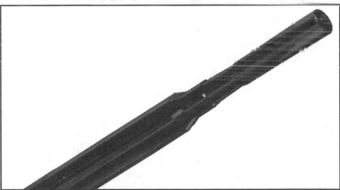

Clymer Manufacturing, a leader in its field, offers chambering reamers and headspace gauges for all popular rifle, pistol and shotgun calibers, plus technical assistance in the design and manufacture of specialized tooling.

Our new tooling includes a fixture designed to throat the cylinder chambers of single action sixguns in a concentric, straight manner for maximum accuracy (calibers 38 to 45) and a new process for forming wildcat cartridges.

Both a price list and catalog are available.

CLYMER MANUFACTURING COMPANY
1645 W. Hamlin Road, Rochester Hills, MI 48309-3312
Phone: 248-853-5555 • Fax: 248-853-1530
Email: clymer@clymertool.com • Web: www.clymertool.com

SHOOTER'S MARKETPLACE

BUY & SELL GUNS

Gun List is the nation's only indexed firearm paper devoted to helping the gun enthusiast find guns, parts, supplies and ammunition for most firearms. Gun List is an essential publication for buyers and sellers because it contains advertisements from the nation's top gun dealers and an extensive list of alphabetized classifieds. Every issue features more than 40,000 firearms for sale.

1 year (26 issues)...........$34.98	
2 years (52 issues).........$61.98	
3 years (78 issues).........$86.98	
Write for foreign rates	

KRAUSE PUBLICATIONS, INC.

700 East State Street, Iola, WI 54990-0001

Phone: 715-445-2214 • Web: www.krause.com

Manufacturing custom and production gunstocks for hundreds of models of rifles and shotguns—made from the finest stock woods and available in all stages of completion.

GREAT AMERICAN GUNSTOCK COMPANY

3420 Industrial Drive • Yuba City, CA 95993
(530)671-4570 • FAX: (530)671-3906
GUNSTOCK HOTLINE (800)784-GUNS(4867)
WEB SITE: www.gunstocks.com
E-MAIL: gunstox@oro.net

10-22® HAMMER AND SEAR PAC

Power Custom introduces a new Ruger 10-22® Matched Hammer & Sear to reduce the trigger pull weight for your 10-22®. This allows for a 2 1/2lb. trigger pull. Manufactured by the E.D.M. process out of carbon steel and heat treated to a 56-58 Rc and precision ground with honed engagement surfaces. Kit includes extra power hammer & sear disconnector spring, 2 precision trigger shims, 2 precision hammer shims, and a replacement trigger return spring. Price $55.95.

10-22® is a registered trademark of Sturm, Ruger & Co. Inc.

POWER CUSTOM, INC.

29739 Hwy J, Dept GD,
Gravois Mills. MO 65037

Phone: 573-372-5684 • Fax: 573-372-5799
Email: cwpowers@laurie.net

PERSONAL DEFENSE AMMUNITION

Manufacturers of state-of-the-art personal defense ammunition now available in two bullet styles. The GLASER BLUE is available in a full range of handgun calibers from the 25 ACP to 45 Colt (including the 9mm Makarov and 357 SIG) and four rifle calibers including the 223, 308, 30-06 and 7.62x39. The GLASER SILVER is available in a full range of handgun calibers from the 380 ACP to the 45 Colt.

Glaser accessories include the Delta cheekpiece and the new night vision Delta Star cheekpeice for the Colt AR-15 rifle, and the CAR-15 cheekpiece.

For further information and a free brochure, contact:

GLASER SAFETY SLUG, INC.

P.O. Box 8223, Foster City, CA 94404
Phone: 800-221-3489 • Fax: 510-785-6685
Email: safetyslug@best.com • Web: www.safetyslug.com

SHOOTER'S MARKETPLACE

KOWA OPTIMED GETS THE BIG PICTURE

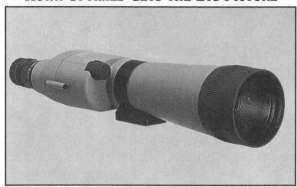

With over 30 year's experience in the manufacture of spotting scopes and other precision optical instruments, Kowa has acquired in-depth knowledge about the requirements for field use. The TSN-820 series is waterproof and offers state-of-the-art optics with unmatched quality and ease of use under all conditions. Full multi-coated optics and an 82mm objective lens produce the ultimate in bright, clear, high-definition imagery. The superb sharpness is especially noticeable at extended distances or under low-light conditions. We offer 82mm, 60mm and 50mm Spotting scopes, and binoculars. Call, write or send us an e-mail to receive a free brochure.

KOWA OPTIMED INC.
ATTN: Sporting Optics Division
20001 S. Vermont Ave., Torrance, CA 90502
Phone: 310-327-1913 • Fax: 310-327 4177
Email: scopekowa@kowa.com • Web: www.kowascope.com

PRECISION RIFLE REST

Bald Eagle Precision Machine Co. offers a rifle rest perfect for the serious benchrester or the dedicated varminter.

The rest is constructed of aircraft-quality aluminum or fine grain East iron weights 12 to 20lbs. Mariner wheel with bearings as a standard feature. It's finished with three coats of Imron Clear. Height adjustments are made with a rack and pinion and a mariner wheel. A fourth leg allows lateral movement on the bench.

Bald Eagle offers approximately 56 rest models to choose from, including windage adjustable, right or left hand, cast aluminum or cast iron. The Standard Windage Rest with rifle stop and bag is pictured above.

Prices: $165.00 to $335.00. For more information or a free brochure, contact Bald Eagle.

BALD EAGLE PRECISION MACHINE CO.
101-K Allison Street, Lock Haven, PA 17745
Phone: 570-748-6772 • Fax: 570-748-4443

RIMFIRE CARTRIDGE GAGE

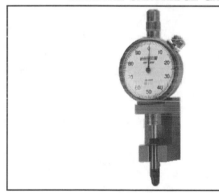

The Rimfire Cartridge Gage from Bald Eagle Precision Machine Co. can improve overall group size up to 25% by sorting rimfire ammo into uniform rim-thickness lots.

The more consistent the rim thickness, the more consistent the ignition of the primer and powder charge, and the firing pin travel remains uniform from shot-to-shot.

The Cartridge Gage is a snap to use—grab a box or two of rimfire ammo and start sorting. It is ideal for BR-50 benchrest competitors and serious small game hunters.

Normally $85.00, mention Shooter's Marketplace and it's only $80.00. Write Bald Eagle for a free brochure.

BALD EAGLE PRECISION MACHINE CO.
101-K Allison Street, Lock Haven, PA 17745
Phone: 570-748-6772 • Fax: 570-748-4443

NEW REPLACEMENT STOCKS

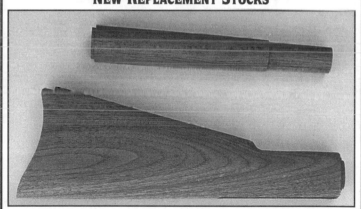

New replacement stocks for Winchester and Marlin rifles. In select straight grain American Black Walnut: $59 straight grip; $69 pistol grip; $39 forearms. Four fancy figured upgrades available.

Winchester Models Henry, 66, 67, 68, 71, 73, 76, 85, 86, 87, 90, 92, 94, 95, 01, 06, 62/A, 53, 55, 64, 65, 61, 97.

Marlin Models 20, 25, 27, 29, 30, 32, 38, 39/A, 81, 89, 92, 93, 94, 97, 98, 336, 375, 444.

Inletting .005-.0010" undersize for perfect fitting to your rifle. Complete stock finishing kit $19.95, catalog of hard-to-find Winchester parts $5.

Complete firearm restoration service available.

PRECISION GUN WORKS™
104 Sierra Road, Dept. GD, Kerrville, TX 78028
Phone: 830-367-4587 • Mon-Thurs 10 am - 5 pm
Web: www.precisiongunstocks.com

SHOOTER'S MARKETPLACE

TOP-QUALITY BULLET LUBE

Rooster Laboratories offers consistently high performance, professional high-melt cannelure bullet lubricants in a choice of two hardnesses. Both are available in 2"x 6"sticks for the commercial reloader, and 1"x 4" hollow and solid sticks.

With a 230°F melting point, both are ideal for indoor and outdoor shooting. Both bond securely to the bullet, remaining intact during shooting.

Zambini is a hard, tough lubricant designed primarily for pistols. **HVR** is softer, but still firm. Designed primarily for high-velocity rifles, **HVR** is easier to apply, and also excellent for pistols. Application requires that the lubesizer be heated.

Prices: 2"x6" sticks $4.00; 1"x4" sticks $135.00 per 100. Contact **Rooster Laboratories** for more information.

ROOSTER LABORATORIES
P.O. Box 412514, Kansas City, MO 64141
Phone: 816-474-1622

RIFLE AND PISTOL MAGAZINES

Forrest Inc. offers shooters one of the largest selections of standard and extended high-capacity magazines in the United States. Whether you're looking for a few spare magazines for that obsolete 22 rifle or pistol, or wish to replace a reduced-capacity ten-shot magazine with the higher-capacity pre-ban original, all are available from this California firm. They offer competitive pricing especially for dealers wanting to buy in quantity. Gun show dealers are our specialty.

Forrest Inc. also stocks parts and accessories for the Colt 1911 45 Auto pistol, the SKS and MAK-90 rifles as well as many U.S. military rifles. One of their specialty parts is firing pins for obsolete weapons.

Call or write Forrest Inc. for more information and a free brochure. Be sure and mention *Shooter's Marketplace*.

FORREST INC.
P.O. Box 326, Dept: #100, Lakeside, CA 92040
Phone: 619-561-5800 • Fax: 888-GUNMAGS
Email: sforr10675@aol.com

PRESSURE ♦ VELOCITY ♦ ACCURACY

You must know all three. For over thirty years, Oehler ballistic test equipment and software have been the standard for precision measurements. We invite comparison. and even make our systems compare to themselves. The patented *Proof Channel*™ uses three screens to make two velocity measurements on each shot. The Model 43 Personal Ballistics Lab provides shooters with accurate measurements of pressure, velocity, ballistic coefficient, and target information. Oehler instruments are used by military proving grounds and all major ammunition makers.

Phone for free catalog or technical help.

OEHLER RESEARCH, INC.
P.O. Box 9135, Austin, TX 78766
Phone: 800-531-5125 or 512-327-6900
Web: www.oehler-research.com

PERSONAL PROTECTION

The Century 2000 Defender is designed for self-defense.

This Derringer-style pistol has a 3-1/2" double barrel, rebounding hammer, retracting firing pins, crossbolt safety, cammed locking lever, spring-loaded extractor and interchangeable barrels. Choice of calibers are .410 with 3" chambers and .410/45 Colt with 2-1/2" chambers.

For further information, contact:

BOND ARMS, INC.
P.O. Box 1296, Granbury, TX 76048
Phone: 817-573-4445 • Fax: 817-573-5636
Email: bondarms@shooters.com • Web: www.bondarms.com

SHOOTER'S MARKETPLACE

NYLON COATED GUN CLEANING RODS

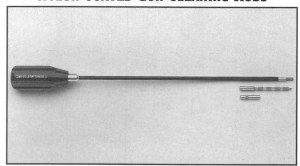

J. Dewey cleaning rods have been used by the U.S. Olympic shooting team and the benchrest community for over 20 years. These one-piece, spring-tempered, steel-base rods will not gall delicate rifling or damage the muzzle area of front-cleaned firearms. The nylon coating eliminates the problem of abrasives adhering to the rod during the cleaning operation. Each rod comes with a hard non-breakable plastic handle supported by ball-bearings, top and bottom, for ease of cleaning.

The brass cleaning jags are designed to pierce the center of the cleaning patch or wrap around the knurled end to keep the patch centered in the bore.

Coated rods are available from 17-caliber to shotgun bore size in several lengths to meet the needs of any shooter. Write for more information.

J. DEWEY MFG. CO., INC.
P.O. Box 2014, Southbury, CT 06488
Phone. 203-264-3064 • Fax: 203 262-6907

PROPELLANT FOR HANDLOADERS

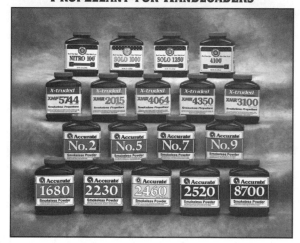

Accurate Powder offers a full line of rifle, pistol, and shotshell propellant for the handloader. Their disc, flake, ball, and extruded powders offer burning speeds for all popular cartridges. Complete specifications are included in the Accurate Reloading Manual, which has comprehensive data for rifle and pistol, plus data for obsolete cartridges, Schutzen cartridges and NRA high power.

For more information, or to order a free reloading booklet, call or visit our website.

ACCURATE ARMS COMPANY INC.
5891 Highway 230 West, McEwen, TN 37101
Phone: 800-416-3006 • Web: www.accuratepowder.com

HIGH QUALITY OPTICS

One of the best indicators of quality is a scope's resolution number. The smaller the number, the better. Our scope has a resolution number of 2.8 seconds of angle. This number is about 20% smaller (better) than other well-known scopes costing much more. It means that two .22 caliber bullets can be a hair's breath apart and edges of each still be clearly seen. With a Shepherd at 800 yards, you will be able to tell a four inch antler from a four inch ear and a burrowing owl from a prairie dog. Bird watchers will be able to distinguish a Tufted Titmouse from a Ticked-Off Field Mouse.

SHEPHERD ENTERPRISES, INC.
Box 189, Waterloo, NE 68069
Phone: 402-779-2424 • Fax: 402-779-4010
Email: shepherd@shepherdscopes.com • Web: www.shepherdscopes.com

VERSATILE CAMERA REST

The Magna-Pod weighs less than two pounds, yet firmly supports more than most expensive tripods. It will hold 50 pounds at its low nine inch height and over 10 pounds extended to 17 inches. It sets up in seconds where there is neither time nor space for a tripod and keeps your expensive equipment safe from knock-overs by kids, pets, pedestrians, or even high winds. It makes a great mono-pod for camcorders, etc., and its carrying box is less than 13" x 13" x 3-1/4" high for easy storage and access.

Attached to its triangle base it becomes an extremely stable table pod or rifle bench rest. The rifle yoke pictured in photo at left is included.

It's 5 pods in 1: Magna-Pod, Mono-Pod, Table-Pod, Shoulder-Pod and Rifle Rest.

SHEPHERD ENTERPRISES, INC.
Box 189, Waterloo, NE 68069
Phone: 402-779-2424 • Fax: 402-779-4010
Email: shepherd@shepherdscopes.com • Web: www.shepherdscopes.com

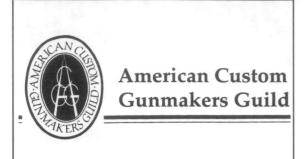
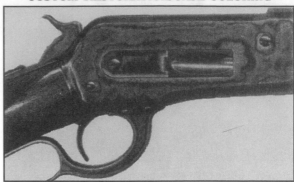
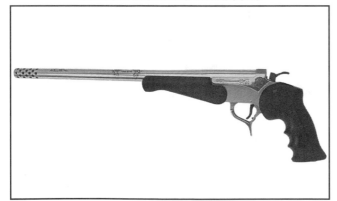
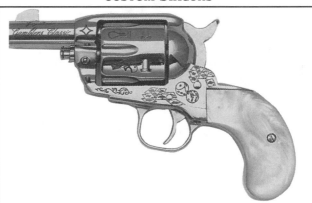

SHOOTER'S MARKETPLACE

FRIENDLY CLAY TARGET THROWERS

Model ST1

Trius Traps offers shotgunners low-cost, easy-cocking mechanical clay target traps. Lay-on loading of singles, doubles and piggyback doubles makes it possible to launch four birds in the air at one time. For the casual shooter, Trius offers four models: the Birdshooter, a quality trap at an affordable price; the Model 92 with high angle clip and can-thrower; the TrapMaster with sit-down comfort and pivoting action; and the New Trius 1-Step. The innovative 1-Step offers cocking and target release in one easy, effortless motion. Set the arm and place the targets on the arm without tension. Stepping on the trap's pedal puts tension on the arm and launches targets in one continuous motion. To receive a free catalog for more information on these models, contact Trius.

TRIUS TRAPS, INC.

Attn: Dept. SM'2000, P.O. Box 25 • Cleves, OH 45002
Phone: 513-941-5682 • Fax: 513-941-7970

THE JACKASS RIG RETURNS

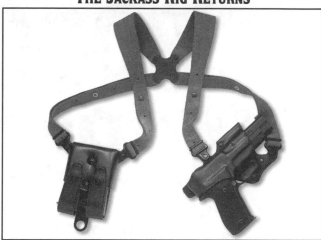

First introduced in 1969, this shoulder system features a horizontal holster with patented swivel connectors, a streamlined ammo carrier and a genuine suede leather harness for unparalleled concealment suitability. The suede harness has our trademarked clover-shaped flexalon backplate that allows greater adjustment and comfort. The Original Jackass Rig comes in Havana Brown, is available in right or left-handed designs and sells for an introductory price of $99.99 + S&H. All components also may be purchased separately. Tie downs are also available.

GALCO INTERNATIONAL

2019 W. Quail Ave. • Phoenix, AZ 85027
Phone: 602-258-8295 • 800-US-Galco (074-2526)
Fax: 800-737-1725 • Web: www.usgalco.com

PORTABLE PIVOT BENCHREST

The BR Pivot is the epitome of stability and portability in portable benchrests. Manufactured from high quality materials using CNC machinery, it is ideal for varmint and general bench shooting. Designed for a lifetime of use. The bench top, roomy enough for all your shooting gear, is made from edge-glued hardwood in butcher-block design. Individually adjustable legs for leveling, and a fully adjustable padded seat to ensure comfort for long shooting sessions. The entire upper assembly (top, post, seat) rotate 360° on synthetic bearings for varmint shooting. Sets up in one minute without tools. Ballistic nylon carry/storage bags available.

VARMINT MASTERS LLC

P.O. Box 6724, Bend, OR 97708
Phone/Fax: 541-318-7306

EXTRA-STRONG SCOPE RINGS

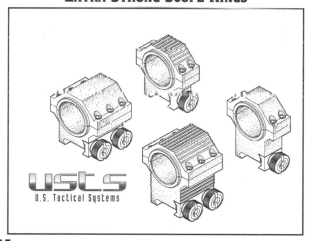

U.S. Tactical Systems

Machined using wire-EDM from a solid billet of 4140 steel for precision and strength. Designed for the US MIL-STD 1913 (Picatinny) dovetail - features flat-sided crossbolts for maximum contact with base cutouts. Rings are available in two heights and widths. LO handles up to a 45mm objective lens; HI up to a 60mm objective lens. Single width rings 1 crossbolt; dual width rings two crossbolts. Prices from $129.95 to $319.95 per pair.

U.S. TACTICAL SYSTEMS

c/o Keng's Firearms Specialty, Inc.
875 Wharton Drive (P.O. Box 44405) • Atlanta, GA 30336-1405
Phone: 404-691-7611 or 800-848-4671 • Fax: 404-505-8445
Email: kengsfirearms@mindspring.com

2000
GUN DIGEST
Complete Compact
CATALOG

GUNDEX

GUNDEX

HANDGUNS

RIFLES

SHOTGUNS

BLACKPOWDER

AIRGUNS

ACCESSORIES

REFERENCE

DIRECTORY OF THE ARMS TRADE

GUNDEX

GUNDEX

GUNDEX

GUNDEX

Includes models suitable for several forms of competition and other sporting purposes.

Accu-Tek BL-9

Accu-Tek XL9

Accu-Tek AT 380

Accu-Tek HC-380

AA ARMS AP9 MINI PISTOL

Caliber: 9mm Para., 10-shot magazine. **Barrel:** 3". **Weight:** 3.5 lbs. **Length:** 12" overall. **Stocks:** Checkered black synthetic. **Sights:** Post front adjustable for elevation, rear adjustable for windage. **Features:** Ventilated barrel shroud; blue or electroless nickel finish. Made in U.S. by AA Arms.

Price: 3" barrel, blue	$239.00
Price: 3" barrel, electroless nickel	$259.00
Price: Mini/5, 5" barrel, blue	$259.00
Price: Mini/5, 5" barrel, electroless nickel	$279.00

ACCU-TEK BL-9 AUTO PISTOL

Caliber: 9mm Para., 5-shot magazine. **Barrel:** 3". **Weight:** 22 oz. **Length:** 5.6" overall. **Stocks:** Black pebble composition. **Sights:** Fixed. **Features:** Double action only; black finish. Introduced 1997. Made in U.S. by Accu-Tek.

Price: $199.00

Accu-Tek Model AT-32SS Auto Pistol

Same as the AT-380SS except chambered for 32 ACP. Introduced 1991.
Price: Satin stainless $189.00

ACCU-TEK MODEL AT-380 AUTO PISTOL

Caliber: 380 ACP, 5-shot magazine. **Barrel:** 2.75". **Weight:** 20 oz. **Length:** 5.6" overall. **Stocks:** Grooved black composition. **Sights:** Blade front, rear adjustable for windage. **Features:** Stainless steel frame and slide. External hammer; manual thumb safety; firing pin block, trigger disconnect. Introduced 1991. Made in U.S. by Accu-Tek.

Price: Satin stainless $189.00

ACCU-TEK MODEL HC-380 AUTO PISTOL

Caliber: 380 ACP, 10-shot magazine. **Barrel:** 2.75". **Weight:** 26 oz. **Length:** 6" overall. **Stocks:** Checkered black composition. **Sights:** Blade front, rear adjustable for windage. **Features:** External hammer; manual thumb safety with firing pin and trigger disconnect; bottom magazine re-

lease. Stainless steel construction. Introduced 1993. Made in U.S. by Accu-Tek.

Price: Satin stainless $199.00

ACCU-TEK XL-9 AUTO PISTOL

Caliber: 9mm Para., 5-shot magazine. **Barrel:** 3". **Weight:** 24 oz. **Length:** 5.6" overall. **Stocks:** Black pebble composition. **Sights:** Three-dot system; rear adjustable for windage. **Features:** Stainless steel construction; double-action-only mechanism. Introduced 1999. Made in U.S. by Accu-Tek.

Price: $215.00

AMERICAN ARMS MATEBA AUTO/REVOLVER

Caliber: 357 Mag., 6-shot. **Barrel:** 4", 6", 8". **Weight:** 2.75 lbs. **Length:** 8.77" overall. **Stocks:** Smooth walnut. **Sights:** Blade on ramp front, adjustable rear. **Features:** Double or single action. Cylinder and slide recoil together upon firing. All-steel construction with polished blue finish. Introduced 1957. Imported from Italy by American Arms, Inc.

Price: $1,295.00
Price: 6" $1,349.00

AMT AUTOMAG II AUTO PISTOL

Caliber: 22 WMR, 9-shot magazine (7-shot with 3-3/8" barrel). **Barrel:** 3-3/8", 4-1/2", 6". **Weight:** About 23 oz. **Length:** 9-3/8" overall. **Stocks:** Grooved carbon fiber. **Sights:** Blade front, adjustable rear. **Features:** Made of stainless steel. Gas-assisted action. Exposed hammer. Slide flats have brushed finish, rest is sandblast. Squared trigger guard. Introduced 1986. From Galena Industries, Inc.

Price: $399.00

AMT AUTOMAG III PISTOL

Caliber: 30 Carbine, 8-shot magazine. **Barrel:** 6-3/8". **Weight:** 43 oz. **Length:** 10-1/2" overall. **Stocks:** Carbon fiber. **Sights:** Blade front, adjustable rear. **Features:** Stainless steel construction. Hammer-drop safe-

AMT 45 ACP Backup   **Auto-Ordnance Standard**   **Auto-Ordnance Deluxe**

ty. Slide flats have brushed finish, rest is sandblasted. Introduced 1989. From Galena Industries, Inc.
Price: $499.00

AMT AUTOMAG IV PISTOL
Caliber: 45 Winchester Magnum, 6-shot magazine. **Barrel:** 6.5". **Weight:** 46 oz. **Length:** 10.5" overall. **Stocks:** Carbon fiber. **Sights:** Blade front, adjustable rear. **Features:** Made of stainless st3578eel with brushed finish. Introduced 1990. Made in U.S. by Galena Industries, Inc.
Price: $599.00

AMT 45 ACP HARDBALLER II
Caliber: 45 ACP. **Barrel:** 5". **Weight:** 39 oz. **Length:** 8-1/2" overall. **Stocks:** Wrap-around rubber. **Sights:** Adjustable. **Features:** Extended combat safety, serrated matte slide rib, loaded chamber indicator, long grip safety, beveled magazine well, adjustable target trigger. All stainless steel. From Galena Industries, Inc.
Price: $425.00
Price: Government model (as above except no rib, fixed sights) . $399.00
Price: 400 Accelerator (400 Cor-Bon, 7" barrel)............... $549.00
Price: Commando (40 S&W, Government Model frame)....... $425.00

AMT 45 ACP HARDBALLER LONG SLIDE
Caliber: 45 ACP. **Barrel:** 7". **Length:** 10-1/2" overall. **Stocks:** Wrap-around rubber. **Sights:** Fully adjustable rear sight. **Features:** Slide and barrel are 2" longer than the standard 45, giving less recoil, added velocity, longer sight radius. Has extended combat safety, serrated matte rib, loaded chamber indicator, wide adjustable trigger. From Galena Industries, Inc.
Price: $499.00

AMT DAO BACKUP PISTOL
Caliber: 357 SIG (5-shot); 38 Super, 9mm Para. (6-shot); 40 S&W, 400 Cor-Bon; 45 ACP (5-shot). **Barrel:** 3". **Weight:** 23 oz. **Length:** 5-3/4" overall. **Stocks:** Checkered black synthetic. **Sights:** None. **Features:** Stainless steel construction; double-action-only trigger; dust cover over the trigger transfer bar; extended magazine; titanium nitride finish. Introduced 1992. Made in U.S. by AMT.
Price: 9mm, 40 S&W, 45 ACP $319.00
Price: 38 Super, 357 SIG, 400 Cor-Bon.................. $369.00

AMT 380 DAO Small Frame Backup
Similar to the DAO Backup except has smaller frame, 2-1/2" barrel, weighs 18 oz., and is 5" overall. Has 5-shot magazine, matte/stainless finish. Made in U.S. by AMT.
Price: $319.00

AUTO-ORDNANCE 1911A1 AUTOMATIC PISTOL
Caliber: 45 ACP, 7-shot magazine. **Barrel:** 5". **Weight:** 39 oz. **Length:** 8-1/2" overall. **Stocks:** Checkered plastic with medallion. **Sights:** Blade front, rear adjustable for windage. **Features:** Same specs as 1911A1 military guns—parts interchangeable. Frame and slide blued; each radius has non-glare finish. Made in U.S. by Auto-Ordnance Corp.
Price: 45 ACP, blue $425.00
Price: 45 ACP, Parkerized $399.00
Price: 45 ACP Deluxe (three-dot sights, textured rubber wraparound grips)..................................... $438.00

Auto-Ordnance 1911A1 Custom High Polish Pistol
Similar to the standard 1911A1 except has a Videki speed trigger, extended thumb safety, flat mainspring housing, Acurod recoil spring guide system, rosewood grips, custom combat hammer, beavertail grip safety.

Auto-Ordnance Pit Bull   **Baer Custom Carry**   **Baer Premium II**

High-polish blue finish. Introduced 1998. Made in U.S. by Auto-Ordnance Corp.
Price: $585.00

Auto-Ordnance ZG-51 Pit Bull Auto

Same as the 1911A1 except has 3-1/2" barrel, weighs 36 oz. and has an over-all length of 7-1/4". Available in 45 ACP only; 7-shot magazine. Introduced 1989.
Price: $470.00

AUTAUGA 32 AUTO PISTOL

Caliber: 32 ACP, 6-shot magazine. **Barrel:** 2". **Weight:** 11.3 oz. **Length:** 4.3" overall. **Stocks:** Black polymer. **Sights:** Fixed. **Features:** Double-action-only mechanism. Stainless steel construction. Uses Winchester Silver Tip ammunition.
Price: .... NA

BAER 1911 CUSTOM CARRY AUTO PISTOL

Caliber: 45 ACP, 7- or 10-shot magazine. **Barrel:** 5". **Weight:** 37 oz. **Length:** 8.5" overall. **Stocks:** Checkered walnut. **Sights:** Baer improved ramp-style dovetailed front, Novak low-mount rear. **Features:** Baer forged NM frame, slide and barrel with stainless bushing; fitted slide to frame; double serrated slide (full-size only); Baer speed trigger with 4-lb. pull; Baer deluxe hammer and sear, tactical-style extended ambidextrous safety, beveled magazine well; polished feed ramp and throated barrel; tuned extractor; Baer extended ejector, checkered slide stop; lowered and flared ejection port, full-length recoil guide rod; recoil buff. Made in U.S. by Les Baer Custom, Inc.
Price: Standard size, blued. $1,620.00
Price: Standard size, stainless $1,690.00
Price: Comanche size, blued $1,640.00
Price: Comanche size, stainless. $1,690.00
Price: Comanche size, aluminum frame, blued slide $1,890.00
Price: Comanche size, aluminum frame, stainless slide $1,995.00

Baer 1911 Concept III Auto Pistol

Same as the Concept I except has forged stainless frame with blued steel slide, Bo-Mar rear sight, 30 lpi checkering on front strap. Made in U.S. by Les Baer Custom, Inc.
Price: $1,520.00
Price: Concept IV (with Baer adjustable rear sight) $1,499.00

Price: Concept V (all stainless, Bo-Mar sight, checkered front strap)
.... $1,558.00
Price: Concept VI (stainless, Baer adjustable sight, checkered front strap) $1,558.00

BAER 1911 PREMIER II AUTO PISTOL

Caliber: 9x23, 38 Super, 400 Cor-Bon, 45 ACP, 7- or 10-shot magazine. **Barrel:** 5". **Weight:** 37 oz. **Length:** 8.5" overall. **Stocks:** Checkered rosewood, double diamond pattern. **Sights:** Baer dovetailed front, low-mount Bo-Mar rear with hidden leaf. **Features:** Baer NM forged steel frame and barrel with stainless bushing; slide fitted to frame; double serrated slide; lowered, flared ejection port; tuned, polished extractor; Baer extended ejector, checkered slide stop, aluminum speed trigger with 4-lb. pull, deluxe Commander hammer and sear, beavertail grip safety with pad, beveled magazine well, extended ambidextrous safety; flat mainspring housing; polished feed ramp and throated barrel; 30 lpi checkered front strap. Made in U.S. by Les Baer Custom, Inc.
Price: Blued $1,428.00
Price: Stainless. $1,558.00
Price: 6" model, blued, from $1,595.00

BAER 1911 S.R.P. PISTOL

Caliber: 45 ACP. **Barrel:** 5". **Weight:** 37 oz. **Length:** 8.5" overall. **Stocks:** Checkered walnut. **Sights:** Trijicon night sights. **Features:** Similar to the F.B.I. contract gun except uses Baer forged steel frame. Has Baer match barrel with supported chamber, Wolff springs, complete tactical action job. All parts Mag-na-fluxed; deburred for tactical carry. Has Baer Ultra Coat finish. Tuned for reliability. Contact Baer for complete details. Introduced 1996. Made in U.S. by Les Baer Custom, Inc.
Price: Government or Comanche length $2,990.00

BAER 1911 CONCEPT I AUTO PISTOL

Caliber: 45 ACP, 7-shot magazine. **Barrel:** 5". **Weight:** 37 oz. **Length:** 8.5" overall. **Stocks:** Checkered rosewood. **Sights:** Baer dovetail front, Bo-Mar deluxe low-mount rear with hidden leaf. **Features:** Baer forged steel frame, slide and barrel with Baer stainless bushing; slide fitted to frame; double serrated slide; Baer beavertail grip safety, checkered slide stop, tuned extractor, extended ejector, deluxe hammer and sear, match disconnector; lowered and flared ejection port; fitted recoil link; polished feed ramp, throated barrel; Baer fitted speed trigger, flat serrated mainspring housing. Blue finish. Made in U.S. by Les Baer Custom, Inc.

Beretta Model 92B

Beretta 96D

Price: **$1,390.00**
Price: Concept II (with Baer adjustable rear sight) **$1,390.00**

Baer 1911 Concept VII Auto Pistol

Same as the Concept I except reduced Comanche size with 4.25" barrel, weighs 27.5 oz., 7.75" overall. Blue finish, checkered front strap. Made in U.S. by Les Baer Custom, Inc.
Price: **$1,495.00**
Price: Concept VIII (stainless frame and slide, Baer adjustable
rear sight) **$1,547.00**

Baer 1911 Concept IX Auto Pistol

Same as the Comanche Concept VII except has Baer lightweight forged aluminum frame, blued steel slide, Baer adjustable rear sight. Chambered for 45 ACP, 7-shot magazine. Made in U.S. by Les Baer Custom, Inc.
Price: **$1,655.00**
Price: Concept X (as above with stainless slide) **$1,675.00**

Baer 1911 Prowler III Auto Pistol

Same as the Premier II except also has full-length guide rod, tapered cone stub weight and reverse recoil plug. Made in U.S. by Les Baer Custom, Inc.
Price: Standard size, blued............................. **$1,795.00**

BERETTA MODEL 92FS PISTOL

Caliber: 9mm Para., 10-shot magazine. **Barrel:** 4.9". **Weight:** 34 oz. **Length:** 8.5" overall. **Stocks:** Checkered black plastic. **Sights:** Blade front, rear adjustable for windage. Tritium night sights available. **Features:** Double action. Extractor acts as chamber loaded indicator, squared trigger guard, grooved front- and backstraps, inertia firing pin. Matte or blued finish. Introduced 1977. Made in U.S. and imported from Italy by Beretta U.S.A.
Price: With plastic grips **$629.00**
Price: Stainless, rubber grips **$691.00**

EW! ### Beretta Model 92FS/96 Brigadier Pistols

Similar to the Model 92FS/96 except with a heavier slide to reduce felt recoil and allow mounting removable front sight. Wrap-around rubber grips. Three-dot sights dovetailed to the slide, adjustable for windage. Weighs 35.3 oz. Introduced 1999.
Price: 9mm or 40 S&W, 10-shot........................ **$675.00**

Beretta Model 92FS 470th Anniversary Limited Edition

EW! Similar to the Model 92FS stainless except has mirror polish finish, smooth walnut grips with inlaid gold-plated medallions. Special and unique gold-filled engraving includes the signature of Beretta's president. The anniversary logo is engraved on the top of the slide and the back of the magazine. Each pistol identified by a "1 of 470" gold-filled number. Special chrome-plated magazine included. Deluxe lockable walnut case with teak inlays and engraving. Only 470 pistols will be sold. Introduced 1999.
Price: **$2,002.00**

Beretta Model 92FS Compact and Compact Type M Pistol

Similar to the Model 92FS except more compact and lighter: overall length 7.8"; 4.3" barrel; weighs 30.9 oz. Has Bruniton finish, chrome-lined bore, combat trigger guard, ambidextrous safety/decock lever. Single column 8-shot magazine (Type M), or double column 10-shot (Compact), 9mm only. Introduced 1998. Imported from Italy by Beretta U.S.A.
Price: Compact (10-shot) **$629.00**
Price: Compact Type M (8-shot) **$629.00**

Beretta Model 96 Pistol

Same as the Model 92FS except chambered for 40 S&W. Ambidextrous safety mechanism with passive firing pin catch, slide safety/decocking lever, trigger bar disconnect. Has 10-shot magazine. Available with three-dot sights. Introduced 1992.
Price: Model 96, plastic grips........................... **$629.00**
Price: Stainless, rubber grips **$691.00**

Beretta M9 Special Edition Pistol

Copy of the U.S. M9 military pistol. Similar to the Model 92FS except has special M9 serial number range; one 15-round (pre-ban) magazine; dot-and-post sight system; special M9 military packaging; Army TM 9-1005-317-10 operator's manual; M9 Special Edition patch; certificate of authenticity; Bianchi M12 holster, M1025 magazine pouch, and M1015 web pistol belt. Introduced 1998. From Beretta U.S.A.
Price: **$828.00**

BERETTA MODEL 80 CHEETAH SERIES DA PISTOLS

Caliber: 380 ACP, 10-shot magazine (M84); 8-shot (M85); 22 LR, 7-shot (M87). **Barrel:** 3.82". **Weight:** About 23 oz. (M84/85); 20.8 oz. (M87). **Length:** 6.8" overall. **Stocks:** Glossy black plastic (wood optional at extra cost). **Sights:** Fixed front, drift-adjustable rear. **Features:** Double action, quick takedown, convenient magazine release. Introduced 1977. Imported from Italy by Beretta U.S.A.
Price: Model 84 Cheetah, plastic grips.................... **$543.00**
Price: Model 84 Cheetah, wood grips **$572.00**
Price: Model 84 Cheetah, wood grips, nickel finish **$615.00**
Price: Model 85 Cheetah, plastic grips, 8-shot.............. **$513.00**
Price: Model 85 Cheetah, wood grips, 8-shot **$545.00**
Price: Model 85 Cheetah, wood grips, nickel, 8-shot **$573.00**
Price: Model 87 Cheetah, wood, 22 LR, 7-shot **$543.00**

Beretta Model 86 Cheetah

Similar to the 380-caliber Model 85 except has tip-up barrel for first-round loading. Barrel length is 4.4", overall length of 7.33". Has 8-shot magazine, walnut grips. Introduced 1989.
Price: **$545.00**

BERETTA MODEL 950 JETFIRE AUTO PISTOL

Caliber: 25 ACP, 8-shot. **Barrel:** 2.4". **Weight:** 9.9 oz. **Length:** 4.7" overall. **Stocks:** Checkered black plastic or walnut. **Sights:** Fixed. **Features:** Sin-

Beretta 950 Jetfire   Beretta M8000/8040 Cougar   Bersa Series 95   Bersa Thunder 380

gle action, thumb safety; tip-up barrel for direct loading/unloading, cleaning. From Beretta U.S.A.

Price: Jetfire plastic, blue	**$220.00**
Price: Jetfire plastic, nickel	**$300.00**
Price: Jetfire wood, EL	**$337.00**
Price: Jetfire plastic, matte finish	**$220.00**

Beretta Model 21 Bobcat Pistol

Similar to the Model 950 BS. Chambered for 22 LR or 25 ACP. Both double action. Has 2.4" barrel, 4.9" overall length; 7-round magazine on 22 cal.; 8 rounds in 25 ACP, 9.9 oz., available in nickel, matte, engraved or blue finish. Plastic or walnut grips. Introduced in 1985.

Price: Bobcat, 22-cal., blue	**$273.00**
Price: Bobcat, nickel, 22-cal.	**$316.00**
Price: Bobcat, 25-cal., blue	**$273.00**
Price: Bobcat, nickel, 25-cal.	**$316.00**
Price: Bobcat EL, 22 or 25	**$349.00**
Price: Bobcat plastic matte, 22 or 25	**$242.00**

BERETTA MODEL 3032 TOMCAT PISTOL

Caliber: 32 ACP, 7-shot magazine. **Barrel:** 2.45". **Weight:** 14.5 oz. **Length:** 5" overall. **Stocks:** Checkered black plastic. **Sights:** Blade front, drift-adjustable rear. **Features:** Double action with exposed hammer; tip-up barrel for direct loading/unloading; thumb safety; polished or matte blue finish. Imported from Italy by Beretta U.S.A. Introduced 1996.

Price: Blue	**$355.00**
Price: Matte	**$326.00**

BERETTA MODEL 8000/8040/8045 COUGAR PISTOL

Caliber: 9mm Para., 10-shot, 40 S&W, 10-shot magazine; 45 ACP, 8-shot. **Barrel:** 3.6". **Weight:** 33.5 oz. **Length:** 7" overall. **Stocks:** Checkered plastic. **Sights:** Blade front, rear drift adjustable for windage. **Features:** Slide-mounted safety; rotating barrel; exposed hammer. Matte black Bruniton finish. Announced 1994. Imported from Italy by Beretta U.S.A.

Price:	**$668.00**
Price: D model, 9mm, 40 S&W	**$646.00**
Price: D model, 45 ACP	**$719.00**

Beretta Model 8000/8040/8045 Mini Cougar

Similar to the Model 8000/8040 Cougar except has shorter grip frame and weighs 27.6 oz. Introduced 1998. Imported from Italy by Beretta U.S.A.

Price: 9mm or 40 S&W	**$668.00**
Price: 9mm or 40 S&W, DAO	**$646.00**
Price: 45 ACP, 6-shot	**$719.00**
Price: 45 ACP DAO	**$696.00**

BERSA SERIES 95 AUTO PISTOL

Caliber: 380 ACP, 7-shot magazine. **Barrel:** 3.5". **Weight:** 22 oz. **Length:** 6.6" overall. **Stocks:** Wrap-around textured rubber. **Sights:** Blade front, rear adjustable for windage; three-dot system. **Features:** Double action; firing pin and magazine safeties; combat-style trigger guard. Matte blue or satin nickel. Introduced 1992. Distributed by Eagle Imports, Inc.

Price: Matte blue	**$248.95**
Price: Satin nickel	**$264.95**

BERSA THUNDER 380 AUTO PISTOLS

Caliber: 380 ACP, 7-shot (Thunder 380 Lite), 9-shot magazine (Thunder 380 DLX). **Barrel:** 3.5". **Weight:** 25.75 oz. **Length:** 6.6" overall. **Stocks:** Black polymer. **Sights:** Blade front, notch rear adjustable for windage; three-dot system. **Features:** Double action; firing pin and magazine safeties. Available in blue or nickel. Introduced 1995. Distributed by Eagle Imports, Inc.

Price: Thunder 380, 7-shot, deep blue finish	**$274.95**

Browning 40 S&W Hi-Power Mark III Pistol

Similar to the standard Hi-Power except chambered for 40 S&W, 10-shot magazine, weighs 35 oz., and has 4-3/4" barrel. Comes with matte blue finish, low profile front sight blade, drift-adjustable rear sight, ambidextrous safety, moulded polyamide grips with thumb rest. Introduced 1993. Imported from Belgium by Browning.

Price: Mark III	**$579.00**

BROWNING FORTY-NINE AUTOMATIC PISTOL

Caliber: 40 S&W, 10-shot magazine. **Barrel:** 4.25". **Weight:** 26 oz. **Length:** 7.75" overall. **Stocks:** Integral; black nylon with pebble-grain texture. **Sights:** Dovetailed three-dot. **Features:** Has FN's patented RSS (Repeatable Secure Striker) firing system; extended modular slide rails;

Browning Capitan Hi-Power Browning Micro Buck Mark Standard Browning Buck Mark Challenge Browning Buck Mark Varmint

reversible magazine catch; stainless slide, black nylon frame. Introduced 1999. Imported by Browning.
Price: **$440.00**

BROWNING HI-POWER 9mm AUTOMATIC PISTOL

Caliber: 9mm Para., 40 S&W, 10-shot magazine. **Barrel:** 4-21/32". **Weight:** 32 oz. **Length:** 7-3/4" overall. **Stocks:** Walnut, hand checkered, or black Polyamide. **Sights:** 1/8" blade front; rear screw-adjustable for windage and elevation. Also available with fixed rear (drift-adjustable for windage) **Features:** External hammer with half-cock and thumb safeties. A blow on the hammer cannot discharge a cartridge; cannot be fired with magazine removed. Fixed rear sight model available. Imported from Belgium by Browning.
Price: Fixed sight model, walnut grips **$615.00**
Price: 9mm with rear sight adj. for w. and e., walnut grips **$668.00**
Price: Mark III, standard matte black finish, fixed sight, moulded grips, ambidextrous safety **$579.00**
Price: Silver chrome, adjustable sight, Pachmayr grips **$684.00**

Browning Capitan Hi-Power Pistol

Similar to the standard Hi-Power except has adjustable tangent rear sight authentic to the early-production model. Also has Commander-style hammer. Checkered walnut grips, polished blue finish. Reintroduced 1993. Imported from Belgium by Browning.
Price: 9mm only **$728.00**

Browning Hi-Power HP-Practical Pistol

Similar to the standard Hi-Power except has silver-chromed frame with blued slide, wrap-around Pachmayr rubber grips, round-style serrated hammer and removable front sight, fixed rear (drift-adjustable for windage). Available in 9mm Para. or 40 S&W. Introduced 1991.
Price: **$662.00**
Price: With fully adjustable rear sight **$717.00**

BROWNING BUCK MARK 22 PISTOL

Caliber: 22 LR, 10-shot magazine. **Barrel:** 5-1/2". **Weight:** 32 oz. **Length:** 9-1/2" overall. **Stocks:** Black moulded composite with checkering. **Sights:** Ramp front, Browning Pro Target rear adjustable for windage and

elevation. **Features:** All steel, matte blue finish or nickel, gold-colored trigger. Buck Mark Plus has laminated wood grips. Made in U.S. Introduced 1985. From Browning.
Price: Buck Mark, blue **$265.00**
Price: Buck Mark, nickel finish with contoured rubber stocks.... **$312.00**
Price: Buck Mark Plus **$324.00**

Browning Buck Mark Camper

Similar to the Buck Mark except 5-1/2" bull barrel. Weight is 34 oz. Available in matte blue. Introduced 1999. From Browning. **NEW!**
Price: **$234.00**

Browning Buck Mark Challenge, Challenge Micro

Similar to the Buck Mark except has a lightweight barrel and smaller grip **NEW!** diameter. Barrel length is 5-1/2", weight is 25 oz. Introduced 1999. From Browning.
Price: **$296.00**
Price: Challenge Micro (4" barrel) **$296.00**

Browning Micro Buck Mark

Same as the standard Buck Mark and Buck Mark Plus except has 4" barrel. Available in blue or nickel. Has 16-click Pro Target rear sight. Introduced 1992.
Price: Blue **$265.00**
Price: Nickel **$312.00**
Price: Buck Mark Micro Plus **$324.00**
Price: Buck Mark Micro Plus Nickel **$354.00**

Browning Buck Mark Varmint

Same as the Buck Mark except has 9-7/8" heavy barrel with .900" diameter and full-length scope base (no open sights); walnut grips with optional forend, or finger-groove walnut. Overall length is 14", weighs 48 oz. Introduced 1987.
Price: **$403.00**

CALICO M-110 AUTO PISTOL

Caliber: 22 LR. **Barrel:** 6". **Weight:** 3.7 lbs. (loaded). **Length:** 17.9" overall. **Stocks:** Moulded composition. **Sights:** Adjustable post front, notch rear.

Calico M-100

Charles Daly M-1911-A1P

Carbon-15

Colt 22 Target

Colt 1991 A1 Compact

Features: Aluminum alloy frame; flash suppressor; pistol grip compartment; ambidextrous safety. Uses same helical-feed magazine as M-100 Carbine. Introduced 1986. Made in U.S. From Calico.
Price: $432.00

CARBON-15 (Type 97) PISTOL

Caliber: 223, 10-shot magazine. **Barrel:** 7.25". **Weight:** 46 oz. **Length:** 20" overall. **Stock:** Checkered composite. **Sights:** Ghost ring. **Features:** Semi-automatic, gas-operated, rotating bolt action. Carbon fiber upper and lower receiver; chromemoly bolt carrier; fluted stainless match barrel; mil. spec. optics mounting base; uses AR-15-type magazines. Introduced 1992. From Professional Ordnance, Inc.
Price: $1,600.00
Price: Type 20 pistol (light-profile barrel, no compensator, weighs 40 oz.). $1,500.00

CHARLES DALY M-1911-A1P AUTOLOADING PISTOL

Caliber: 45 ACP, 7- or 10-shot magazine. **Barrel:** 5". **Weight:** 38 oz. **Length:** 8-3/4" overall. **Stocks:** Checkered. **Sights:** Blade front, rear drift adjustable for windage; three-dot system. **Features:** Skeletonized combat hammer and trigger; beavertail grip safety; extended slide release; over-size thumb safety; Parkerized finish. Introduced 1996. Imported from the Philippines by K.B.I., Inc.
Price: $449.00

COLT 22 TARGET AUTOMATIC PISTOL

Caliber: 22 LR, 10-shot magazine. **Barrel:** 4.5". **Weight:** 33 oz. **Length:** 8.62" overall. **Stocks:** Textured black polymer. **Sights:** Blade front, fully adjustable rear. **Features:** Stainless steel construction; ventilated barrel rib; single action mechanism; cocked striker indicator; push-button safety. Introduced 1995. Made in U.S. by Colt's Mfg. Co.
Price: $377.00

COLT MODEL 1991 A1 AUTO PISTOL

Caliber: 45 ACP, 7-shot magazine. **Barrel:** 5". **Weight:** 38 oz. **Length:** 8.5" overall. **Stocks:** Checkered black composition. **Sights:** Ramped blade front, fixed square notch rear, high profile. **Features:** Parkerized finish. Continuation of serial number range used on original G.I. 1911 A1 guns. Comes with one magazine and moulded carrying case. Introduced 1991.

Price: $556.00
Price: Stainless. $610.00

Colt Model 1991 A1 Compact Auto Pistol

Similar to the Model 1991 A1 except has 3-1/2" barrel. Overall length is 7", and gun is 3/8" shorter in height. Comes with one 6-shot magazine, moulded case. Introduced 1993.
Price: $556.00

COLT LIGHTWEIGHT COMMANDER AUTO PISTOL

Caliber: 45 ACP, 8-shot. **Barrel:** 4-1/4". **Weight:** 26 oz. **Length:** 7-3/4" overall. **Stocks:** Double diamond checkered rosewood. **Sights:** Fixed, glare-proofed blade front, square notch rear; three-dot system. **Features:** Brushed stainless slide, nickeled aluminum frame; McCormick elongated-slot enhanced hammer, McCormick two-cut adjustable aluminum hammer. Made in U.S. by Colt's Mfg. Co., Inc.
Price: 45, stainless. $610.00

COLT MUSTANG POCKETLITE

Caliber: 380 ACP, 7-shot magazine. **Barrel:** 2-1/4". **Weight:** 12-1/2 oz. **Length:** 5-1/2" overall. **Stocks:** Checkered composition. **Sights:** Ramp

Colt Lightweight Commander   Colt Mustang 380   Colt Pocket Nine   Colt Pony Pocketlite

front, square notch rear, fixed. **Features:** Scaled-down version of the 1911 A1 Colt G.M. Has thumb and internal firing pin safeties. Introduced 1983.
Price: Pocketlite 380, stainless........................ **$508.00**

COLT POCKET NINE DAO AUTOMATIC PISTOL

EW! **Caliber:** 9mm Para., 6-shot magazine. **Barrel:** 2-3/4". **Weight:** 17 oz. **Length:** 5-1/2" overall. **Stocks:** Wraparound rubber. **Sights:** White dot dovetailed post front, dovetailed no-snag white dot rear. **Features:** Double-action-only; aluminum frame, stainless slide; smooth combat trigger. Introduced 1999. Made in U.S. by Colt's Mfg., Inc.
Price: **$615.00**

Colt Tac Nine Auto Pistol

EW! Similar to the Pocket Nine except has enhanced trigger pull, black non-reflective finish, tritium three-dot sights. Introduced 1999. Made in U.S. by Colt's Mfg., Inc.
Price: .... **NA**

COLT PONY POCKETLITE AUTOMATIC PISTOL

Caliber: 380 ACP, 6-shot magazine. **Barrel:** 2-3/4". **Weight:** 13 oz. **Length:** 5-1/2" overall. **Stocks:** Black composition. **Sights:** Ramp front, fixed rear. **Features:** Aluminum frame, stainless slide. Double-action-only mechanism; recoil-reducing locked breech. Introduced 1997. Made in U.S. by Colt's Mfg. Co.
Price: **$529.00**

COLT DEFENDER

Caliber: 40 S&W, 45 ACP, 7-shot magazine. **Barrel:** 3". **Weight:** 22-1/2 oz. **Length:** 6-3/4" overall. **Stocks:** Pebble-finish rubber wraparound with finger grooves. **Sights:** White dot front, snag-free Colt competition rear. **Features:** Stainless finish; aluminum frame; combat-style hammer; Hi Ride grip safety, extended manual safety, disconnect safety. Introduced 1998. Made in U.S. by Colt's Mfg. Co.
Price: **$750.00**

Colt Model 1991 A1 Commander Auto Pistol

Similar to the Model 1991 A1 except has 4-1/4" barrel. Parkerized finish. 7-shot magazine. Comes in moulded case. Introduced 1993.
Price: **$556.00**

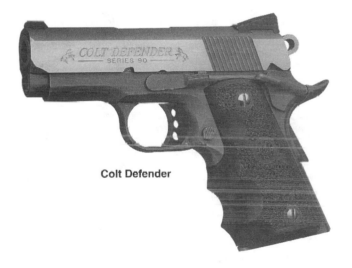

Colt Defender

Colt Concealed Carry Officer

Similar to the Combat Commander with stainless slide and aluminum Officers lightweight frame; matte stainless slide, satin frame; weighs 26 oz. Introduced 1998. Made in U.S. by Colt's Mfg. Co., Inc.
Price: **$610.00**

COONAN 357 MAGNUM, 41 MAGNUM PISTOLS

Caliber: 357 Mag., 41 Magnum, 7-shot magazine. **Barrel:** 5". **Weight:** 42 oz. **Length:** 8.3" overall. **Stocks:** Smooth walnut. **Sights:** Interchangeable ramp front, rear adjustable for windage. **Features:** Stainless steel construction. Unique barrel hood improves accuracy and reliability. Linkless barrel. Many parts interchange with Colt autos. Has grip, hammer, half-cock safeties, extended slide latch. Made in U.S. by Coonan Arms, Inc.
Price: 5" barrel, from................................. **$735.00**
Price: 6" barrel, from................................. **$768.00**
Price: With 6" compensated barrel..................... **$1,014.00**

CZ 75B 9mm   CZ 75B Decocker   CZ 75 Compact   CZ 85

Price: Classic model (Teflon black two-tone finish, 8-shot magazine, fully adjustable rear sight, integral compensated barrel) **$1,400.00**
Price: 41 Magnum Model, from **$825.00**

Coonan Compact Cadet 357 Magnum Pistol

Similar to the 357 Magnum full-size gun except has 3.9" barrel, shorter frame, 6-shot magazine. Weight is 39 oz., overall length 7.8". Linkless bull barrel, full-length recoil spring guide rod, extended slide latch. Introduced 1993. Made in U.S. by Coonan Arms, Inc.
Price: **$855.00**

CZ 75B AUTO PISTOL

Caliber: 9mm Para., 40 S&W, 10-shot magazine. **Barrel:** 4.7". **Weight:** 34.3 oz. **Length:** 8.1" overall. **Stocks:** High impact checkered plastic. **Sights:** Square post front, rear adjustable for windage; three-dot system. **Features:** Single action/double action design; firing pin block safety; choice of black polymer, matte or high-polish blue finishes. All-steel frame. Imported from the Czech Republic by CZ-USA.
Price: Black polymer.................................... **$459.00**
Price: Glossy blue....................................... **$472.00**
Price: Dual tone or satin nickel.......................... **$472.00**
Price: 22 LR conversion unit............................. **$279.00**

CZ 75B Decocker

NEW! Similar to the CZ 75B except has a decocking lever in place of the safety lever. All other specifications are the same. Introduced 1999. Imported from the Czech Republic by CZ-USA.
Price: 9mm, black polymer............................... **$467.00**

CZ 75B Compact Auto Pistol

Similar to the CZ 75 except has 10-shot magazine, 3.9" barrel and weighs 32 oz. Has removable front sight, non-glare ribbed slide top. Trigger guard is squared and serrated; combat hammer. Introduced 1993. Imported from the Czech Republic by CZ-USA.
Price: 9mm, black polymer............................... **$499.00**
Price: Dual tone or satin nickel.......................... **$513.00**
Price: Compact D, black polymer......................... **$526.00**

Coonan 357 Magnum

CZ 85B Auto Pistol

Same gun as the CZ 75 except has ambidextrous slide release and safety-levers; non-glare, ribbed slide top; squared, serrated trigger guard; trigger stop to prevent overtravel. Introduced 1986. Imported from the Czech Republic by CZ-USA.
Price: Black polymer.................................... **$419.00**
Price: Combat, black polymer **$475.00**
Price: Combat, dual tone **$487.00**
Price: Combat, glossy blue.............................. **$499.00**

CZ 85 Combat

Similar to the CZ 85B (9mm only) except has an adjustable rear sight, adjustable trigger for overtravel, free-fall magazine, extended magazine catch. Does not have the firing pin block safety. Introduced 1999. Imported from the Czech Republic by CZ-USA. **NEW**
Price: 9mm, black polymer............................... **$540.00**
Price: 9mm, glossy blue................................. **$559.00**
Price: 9mm, dual tone or satin nickel **$559.00**

CZ 85 Compact   CZ 83B   CZ 97B   CZ 75/85 Kadet

CZ 100

CZ 83B DOUBLE-ACTION PISTOL

Caliber: 9mm Makarov, 32 ACP, 380 ACP, 10-shot magazine. **Barrel:** 3.8". **Weight:** 26.2 oz. **Length:** 6.8" overall. **Stocks:** High impact checkered plastic. **Sights:** Removable square post front, rear adjustable for windage; three-dot system. **Features:** Single action/double action; ambidextrous magazine release and safety. Blue finish; non-glare ribbed slide top. Imported from the Czech Republic by CZ-USA.
Price: Blue $378.00
Price: Nickel $378.00

CZ 97B AUTO PISTOL

Caliber: 45 ACP, 10-shot magazine. **Barrel:** 4.85". **Weight:** 40 oz. **Length:** 8.34" overall. **Stocks:** Checkered walnut. **Sights:** Fixed. **Features:** Single action/double action; full-length slide rails; screw-in barrel bushing; linkless barrel; all-steel construction; chamber loaded indicator; dual transfer bars. Introduced 1999. Imported from the Czech Republic by CZ-USA.

Price: Black polymer. $599.00
Price: Glossy blue $619.00

CZ 75/85 KADET AUTO PISTOL

Caliber: 22 LR, 10-shot magazine. **Barrel:** 4.88". **Weight:** 36 oz. **Length:** NA. **Stocks:** High impact checkered plastic. **Sights:** Blade front, fully adjustable rear. **Features:** Single action/double action mechanism; all-steel construction. Duplicates weight, balance and function of the CZ 75 pistol. Introduced 1999. Imported from the Czech Republic by CZ-USA.
Price: Black polymer. $486.00

CZ 100 AUTO PISTOL

Caliber: 9mm Para., 40 S&W, 10-shot magazine. **Barrel:** 3.7". **Weight:** 24 oz. **Length:** 6.9" overall. **Sights:** Grooved polymer. **Sights:** Blade front with dot, white outline rear drift adjustable for windage. **Features:** Double action only with firing pin block; polymer frame, steel slide; has laser sight mount. Introduced 1996. Imported from the Czech Republic by CZ-USA.
Price: 9mm Para. $432.00
Price: 40 S&W $432.00

DAVIS P-380 AUTO PISTOL

Caliber: 380 ACP, 5-shot magazine. **Barrel:** 2.8". **Weight:** 22 oz. **Length:** 5.4" overall. **Stocks:** Black composition. **Sights:** Fixed. **Features:** Choice of chrome or black Teflon finish. Introduced 1991. Made in U.S. by Davis Industries.
Price: $98.00

DAVIS P-32 AUTO PISTOL

Caliber: 32 ACP, 6-shot magazine. **Barrel:** 2.8". **Weight:** 22 oz. **Length:** 5.4" overall. **Stocks:** Laminated wood. **Sights:** Fixed. **Features:** Choice of black Teflon or chrome finish. Announced 1986. Made in U.S. by Davis Industries.
Price: $87.50

DESERT EAGLE MAGNUM PISTOL

Caliber: 357 Mag., 9-shot; 44 Mag., 8-shot; 50 Magnum, 7-shot. **Barrel:** 6", 10", interchangeable. **Weight:** 357 Mag.—62 oz.; 44 Mag.—69 oz.; 50 Mag.—72 oz. **Length:** 10-1/4" overall (6" bbl.). **Stocks:** Rubber. **Sights:** Blade on ramp front, combat-style rear. Adjustable available. **Features:** Rotating three-lug bolt; ambidextrous safety; adjustable trigger. Military

Davis P-32

Davis P-38

Desert Eagle Magnum

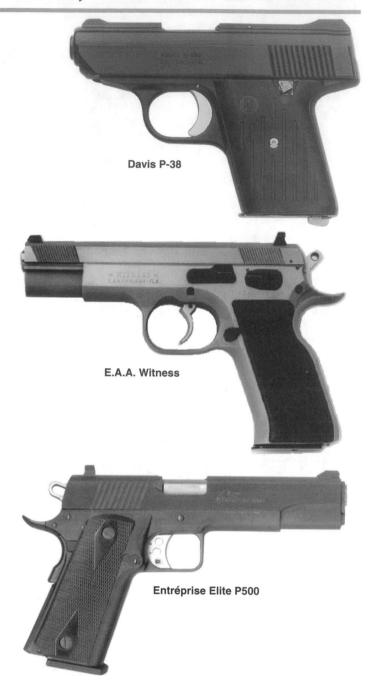

E.A.A. Witness

epoxy finish. Satin, bright nickel, hard chrome, polished and blued finishes available. Imported from Israel by Magnum Research, Inc.

Price: 357, 6" bbl., standard pistol **$1,099.00**
Price: 44 Mag., 6", standard pistol **$1,099.00**
Price: 50 Magnum, 6" bbl., standard pistol **$1,099.00**
Price: 440 Cor-Bon barrel, 6" **$399.00**

E.A.A. WITNESS DA AUTO PISTOL

Caliber: 9mm Para., 10-shot magazine; 38 Super, 40 S&W, 10-shot magazine; 45 ACP, 10-shot magazine. **Barrel:** 4.50". **Weight:** 35.33 oz. **Length:** 8.10" overall. **Stocks:** Checkered rubber. **Sights:** Undercut blade front, open rear adjustable for windage. **Features:** Double-action trigger system; round trigger guard; frame-mounted safety. Introduced 1991. Imported from Italy by European American Armory.

Price: 9mm, blue **$351.00**
Price: 9mm, Wonder finish **$366.00**
Price: 9mm Compact, blue, 10-shot **$351.00**
Price: As above, Wonder finish **$366.60**
Price: 40 S&W, blue **$366.60**
Price: As above, Wonder finish **$366.60**
Price: 40 S&W Compact, 9-shot, blue **$366.60**
Price: As above, Wonder finish **$366.60**
Price: 45 ACP, blue **$351.00**
Price: As above, Wonder finish **$366.60**
Price: 45 ACP Compact, 8-shot, blue **$351.00**
Price: As above, Wonder finish **$366.60**

E.A.A. EUROPEAN MODEL AUTO PISTOLS

Caliber: 32 ACP or 380 ACP, 7-shot magazine. **Barrel:** 3.88". **Weight:** 26 oz. **Length:** 7-3/8" overall. **Stocks:** European hardwood. **Sights:** Fixed blade front, rear drift-adjustable for windage. **Features:** Chrome or blue finish; magazine, thumb and firing pin safeties; external hammer; safety-lever takedown. Imported from Italy by European American Armory.

Price: Blue **$132.60**
Price: Wonder finish **$163.80**

Entréprise Elite P500

ENTRÉPRISE ELITE P500 AUTO PISTOL

Caliber: 45 ACP, 10-shot magazine. **Barrel:** 5". **Weight:** 40 oz. **Length:** 8.5" overall. **Stocks:** Black ultra-slim, double diamond, checkered synthetic. **Sights:** Dovetailed blade front, rear adjustable for windage; three-dot system. **Features:** Reinforced dust cover; lowered and flared ejection port; squared trigger guard; adjustable match trigger; bolstered front strap; high grip cut; high ride beavertail grip safety; steel flat mainspring housing; extended thumb lock; skeletonized hammer; match grade sear, disconnector; Wolff springs. Introduced 1998. Made in U.S. by Entréprise Arms.
Price: **$739.90**

Entréprise Boxer P500 Auto Pistol

Similar to the Medalist model except has adjustable Competizione "melded" rear sight with dovetailed Patridge front; high mass chiseled slide with sweep cut; machined slide parallel rails; polished breech face and barrel channel. Introduced 1998. Made in U.S. by Entréprise Arms.
Price: **$1,099.00**

Entréprise Boxer P500

Entréprise Tactical 500

FEG PJK-9HP

Felk MTF 450

Entréprise Medalist P500 Auto Pistol

Similar to the Elite model except has adjustable Competizione "melded" rear sight with dovetailed Patridge front; machined slide parallel rails with polished breech face and barrel channel; front and rear slide serrations; lowered and flared ejection port; full length one-piece guide rod with plug; National Match barrel and bushing; stainless firing pin; tuned match extractor, oversize firing pin stop; throated barrel and polished ramp; slide lapped to frame. Introduced 1998. Made in U.S. by Entréprise Arms.

Price: 45 ACP **$979.00**
Price: 40 S&W **$1,099.00**

Entréprise Tactical P500 Auto Pistol

Similar to the Elite model except has Tactical2 Ghost Ring sight or Novak lo- mount sight; ambidextrous thumb safety; front and rear slide serrations; full-length guide rod; throated barrel, polished ramp; tuned match extractor; fitted barrel and bushing; stainless firing pin; slide lapped to frame; dehorned. Introduced 1998. Made in U.S. by Entréprise Arms.

Price: **$979.00**
Price: Tactical Plus (full-size frame, Officer's slide) **$1,049.00**

ERMA KGP68 AUTO PISTOL

Caliber: 32 ACP, 6-shot, 380 ACP, 5-shot. **Barrel:** 4". **Weight:** 22-1/2 oz. **Length:** 7-3/8" overall. **Stocks:** Checkered plastic. **Sights:** Fixed. **Features:** Toggle action similar to original "Luger" pistol. Action stays open after last shot. Has magazine and sear disconnect safety systems. Imported from Germany by Mandall Shooting Supplies.

Price: **$499.95**

FEG PJK-9HP AUTO PISTOL

Caliber: 9mm Para., 10-shot magazine. **Barrel:** 4.75". **Weight:** 32 oz. **Length:** 8" overall. **Stocks:** Hand-checkered walnut. **Sights:** Blade front, rear adjustable for windage; three dot system. **Features:** Single action; polished blue or hard chrome finish; rounded combat-style serrated hammer. Comes with two magazines and cleaning rod. Imported from Hungary by K.B.I., Inc.

Price: Blue **$249.00**
Price: Hard chrome **$329.00**

FEG SMC-380 AUTO PISTOL

Caliber: 380 ACP, 6-shot magazine. **Barrel:** 3.5". **Weight:** 18.5 oz. **Length:** 6.1" overall. **Stocks:** Checkered composition with thumbrest. **Sights:** Blade front, rear adjustable for windage. **Features:** Patterned after the PPK pistol. Alloy frame, steel slide; double action. Blue finish. Comes with two magazines, cleaning rod. Imported from Hungary by K.B.I., Inc.

Price: **$209.00**

FELK MTF 450 AUTO PISTOL

Caliber: 9mm Para. (10-shot); 40 S&W (8-shot); 45 ACP (9-shot magazine). **Barrel:** 3.5". **Weight:** 19.9 oz. **Length:** 6.4" overall. **Stocks:** Checkered. **Sights:** Blade front; adjustable rear. **Features:** Double-action-only trigger, striker fired; polymer frame; trigger safety, firing pin safety, trigger bar safety; adjustable trigger weight; fully interchangeable slide/barrel to change calibers. Introduced 1998. Imported by Felk Inc.

Price: **$395.00**
Price: 45 ACP pistol with 9mm and 40 S&W slide/barrel
assemblies **$999.00**

FORT WORTH HSS

Caliber: 22 LR, 10-shot magazine. **Barrel:** 5-1/2" bull. **Weight:** 45 oz. **Length:** 10.25" overall. **Stocks:** Checkered walnut. **Sights:** Ramp front, slide-mounted square notch rear adjustable for windage and elevation. **Features:** Stainless steel construction. Military grip. Slide lock; smooth grip straps; push-button takedown; drilled and tapped for barrel weights. Introduced 1995. Made in U.S. by Fort Worth Firearms.

Price: **$379.95**

Gal Compact   Gal 7000   Glock 17C

FORT WORTH HSSK

Caliber: 22 LR, 10-shot magazine. **Barrel:** 4-1/2" or 6-3/4". **Weight:** 39 oz. (4-1/2" barrel). **Length:** 9" overall (4-1/2" barrel). **Stocks:** Checkered black plastic. **Sights:** Blade front, side-mounted rear adjustable for windage. **Features:** Stainless steel construction, military grip; standard trigger; push-button barrel takedown. Introduced 1995. Made in U.S. by Fort Worth Firearms.
Price: $312.95

GAL MODEL 5000 AUTO PISTOL

Caliber: 45 ACP, 8-shot magazine. **Barrel:** 4.25". **Weight:** 36 oz. **Length:** 7.75" overall. **Stocks:** Rubberized wrap-around. **Sights:** Low profile, fixed, three-dot system. **Features:** Forged steel frame and slide; competition trigger, hammer, slide stop magazine release, beavertail grip safety; front and rear slide grooves; blue or two-tone finish. Introduced 1996. Imported from Israel by Israel Arms International.
Price: $396.95

Gal Model 6000 Auto Pistol

NEW! Similar to the Gal Model 5000 except has 5" stainless barrel, beveled feed ramp, extended slide stop, safety and magazine release, fixed sights. Introduced 1999. From Israel Arms International.
Price: Blue or two-tone................................. $396.95

Gal Model 7000 Auto Pistol

NEW! Similar to the Gal Model 5000 except has wide frame for 10-shot magazine. Introduced 1999. From Israel Arms International.
Price: Blue or two-tone................................. $489.95

GLOCK 17 AUTO PISTOL

Caliber: 9mm Para., 10-shot magazine. **Barrel:** 4.49". **Weight:** 22.04 oz. (without magazine). **Length:** 7.32" overall. **Stocks:** Black polymer. **Sights:** Dot on front blade, white outline rear adjustable for windage. **Features:** Polymer frame, steel slide; double-action trigger with "Safe Action" system; mechanical firing pin safety, drop safety; simple takedown without tools; locked breech, recoil operated action. Adopted by Austrian armed forces 1983. NATO approved 1984. Imported from Austria by Glock, Inc.

Price: Fixed sight, with extra magazine, magazine loader, cleaning kit
.... $616.00
Price: Adjustable sight $644.00
Price: Model 17L (6" barrel) $800.00
Price: Model 17C, ported barrel $646.00

Glock 19 Auto Pistol

Similar to the Glock 17 except has a 4" barrel, giving an overall length of 6.85" and weight of 20.99 oz. Magazine capacity is 10 rounds. Fixed or adjustable rear sight. Introduced 1988.
Price: Fixed sight $616.00
Price: Adjustable sight $644.00
Price: Model 19C, ported barrel $646.00

Glock 20 10mm Auto Pistol

Similar to the Glock Model 17 except chambered for 10mm Automatic cartridge. Barrel length is 4.60", overall length is 7.59", and weight is 26.3 oz. (without magazine). Magazine capacity is 10 rounds. Fixed or adjustable rear sight. Comes with an extra magazine, magazine loader, cleaning rod and brush. Introduced 1990. Imported from Austria by Glock, Inc.
Price: Fixed sight $668.00
Price: Adjustable sight $697.00

Glock 21 Auto Pistol

Similar to the Glock 17 except chambered for 45 ACP, 10-shot magazine. Overall length is 7.59", weight is 25.2 oz. (without magazine). Fixed or adjustable rear sight. Introduced 1991.
Price: Fixed sight $668.00
Price: Adjustable sight $697.00

Glock 22 Auto Pistol

Similar to the Glock 17 except chambered for 40 S&W, 10-shot magazine. Overall length is 7.28", weight is 22.3 oz. (without magazine). Fixed or adjustable rear sight. Introduced 1990.
Price: Fixed sight $616.00
Price: Adjustable sight $644.00
Price: Model 22C, ported barrel $646.00

Glock 21

Glock 23C

Glock 26

Glock 23 Auto Pistol

Similar to the Glock 19 except chambered for 40 S&W, 10-shot magazine. Overall length is 6.85", weight is 20.6 oz. (without magazine). Fixed or adjustable rear sight. Introduced 1990.

Price: Fixed sight **$616.00**
Price: Model 23C, ported barrel **$646.00**
Price: Adjustable sight **$644.00**

GLOCK 26, 27 AUTO PISTOLS

Caliber: 9mm Para. (M26), 10-shot magazine; 40 S&W (M27), 9-shot magazine. **Barrel:** 3.46". **Weight:** 21.75 oz. **Length:** 6.29" overall. **Stocks:** Integral. Stippled polymer. **Sights:** Dot on front blade, fixed or fully adjustable white outline rear. **Features:** Subcompact size. Polymer frame, steel slide; double-action trigger with "Safe Action" system, three safeties. Matte black Tenifer finish. Hammer-forged barrel. Imported from Austria by Glock, Inc. Introduced 1996.

Price: Fixed sight **$616.00**
Price: Adjustable sight **$644.00**

GLOCK 29, 30 AUTO PISTOLS

Caliber: 10mm (M29), 45 ACP (M30), 10-shot magazine. **Barrel:** 3.78". **Weight:** 24 oz. **Length:** 6.7" overall. **Stocks:** Integral. Stippled polymer. **Sights:** Dot on front, fixed or fully adjustable white outline rear. **Features:** Compact size. Polymer frame steel slide; double-recoil spring reduces recoil; Safe Action system with three safeties; Tenifer finish. Two magazines supplied. Introduced 1997. Imported from Austria by Glock, Inc.

Price: Fixed sight **$668.00**
Price: Adjustable sight **$697.00**

Glock 31/31C Auto Pistols

Similar to the Glock 17 except chambered for 357 Auto cartridge; 10-shot magazine. Overall length is 7.32", weight is 23.28 oz. (without magazine). Fixed or adjustable sight. Imported from Austria by Glock, Inc.

Price: Fixed sight **$616.00**
Price: Adjustable sight **$644.00**
Price: Model 31C, ported barrel **$646.00**

Glock 35

Glock 32/32C Auto Pistols

Similar to the Glock 19 except chambered for the 357 Auto cartridge; 10-shot magazine. Overall length is 6.85", weight is 21.52 oz. (without magazine). Fixed or adjustable sight. Imported from Austria by Glock, Inc.

Price: Fixed sight **$616.00**
Price: Adjustable sight **$644.00**
Price: Model 32C, ported barrel **$646.00**

Glock 33 Auto Pistol

Similar to the Glock 26 except chambered for the 357 Auto cartridge; 9-shot magazine. Overall length is 6.29", weight is 19.75 oz. (without magazine). Fixed or adjustable sight. Imported from Austria by Glock, Inc.

Price: Fixed sight **$616.00**
Price: Adjustable sight **$644.00**

GLOCK 34, 35 AUTO PISTOLS

Caliber: 9mm Para. (M34), 40 S&W (M35), 10-shot magazine. **Barrel:** 5.32". **Weight:** 22.9 oz. **Length:** 8.15" overall. **Stocks:** Integral. Stippled polymer. **Sights:** Dot on front, fully adjustable white outline rear. **Fea-**

Glock 36

Heckler & Koch USP 45

Heckler & Koch USP 45 Tactical

tures: Polymer frame, steel slide; double-action trigger with "Safe Action" system; three safeties; Tenifer finish. Imported from Austria by Glock, Inc.

Price: Model 34, 9mm. **$760.00**
Price: Model 35, 40 S&W **$760.00**

GLOCK 36 AUTO PISTOL

Caliber: 45 ACP, 6-shot magazine. **Barrel:** 3.78". **Weight:** 20.11 oz. **Length:** 6.77" overall. **Stocks:** Integral. Stippled polymer. **Sights:** Dot on front, fully adjustable white outline rear. **Features:** Polymer frame, steel slide; double-action trigger with "Safe Action" system; three safeties; Tenifer finish. Imported from Austria by Glock, Inc.

Price: **$668.00**

HAMMERLI TRAILSIDE PL 22 TARGET PISTOL

NEW! Caliber: 22 LR, 10-shot magazine. **Barrel:** 4.5", 6". **Weight:** 28 oz. (4.5" barrel). **Length:** 7.75" overall. **Stocks:** Wood target-style. **Sights:** Blade front, rear adjustable for windage. **Features:** One-piece barrel/frame unit; two-stage competition-style trigger; dovetail scope mount rail. Introduced 1999. Imported from Switzerland by SIGARMS, Inc.

Price: . . . . **NA**

HECKLER & KOCH USP AUTO PISTOL

Caliber: 9mm Para., 10-shot magazine, 40 S&W, 10-shot magazine. **Barrel:** 4.25". **Weight:** 28 oz. (USP40). **Length:** 6.9" overall. **Stocks:** Non-slip stippled black polymer. **Sights:** Blade front, rear adjustable for windage. **Features:** New HK design with polymer frame, modified Browning action with recoil reduction system, single control lever. Special "hostile environment" finish on all metal parts. Available in SA/DA, DAO, left- and right-hand versions. Introduced 1993. Imported from Germany by Heckler & Koch, Inc.

Price: Right-hand **$655.00**
Price: Left-hand **$680.00**
Price: Stainless steel, right-hand **$701.00**
Price: Stainless steel, left-hand **$726.00**

Heckler & Koch USP Compact Auto Pistol

Similar to the USP except has 3.58" barrel, measures 6.81" overall, and weighs 1.60 lbs. (9mm). Available in 9mm Para. or 40 S&W with 10-shot magazine. Introduced 1996. Imported from Germany by Heckler & Koch, Inc.

Price: Blue **$685.00**
Price: Blue with control lever on right **$710.00**
Price: Stainless steel **$731.00**
Price: Stainless steel with control lever on right **$756.00**

Heckler & Koch USP45 Auto Pistol

Similar to the 9mm and 40 S&W USP except chambered for 45 ACP, 10-shot magazine. Has 4.13" barrel, overall length of 7.87" and weighs 30.4 oz. Has adjustable three-dot sight system. Available in SA/DA, DAO, left- and right-hand versions. Introduced 1995. Imported from Germany by Heckler & Koch, Inc.

Price: Right-hand **$717.00**
Price: Left-hand **$742.00**
Price: Stainless steel right-hand. **$763.00**
Price: Stainless steel left-hand. **$788.00**

Heckler & Koch USP45 Compact

Similar to the USP45 except has stainless slide; 8-shot magazine; modified and contoured slide and frame; extended slide release; 3.80" barrel, 7.09" overall length, weighs 1.75 lbs.; adjustable three-dot sights. Introduced 1998. Imported from Germany by Heckler & Koch, Inc.

Price: With control lever on left, stainless. **$747.00**
Price: As above, blue **$705.00**
Price: With control lever on right, stainless **$772.00**
Price: As above, blue **$730.00**

HECKLER & KOCH USP45 TACTICAL PISTOL

Caliber: 45 ACP, 10-shot magazine. **Barrel:** 4.92". **Weight:** 2.24 lbs. **Length:** 8.64" overall. **Stocks:** Non-slip stippled polymer. **Sights:** Blade front, fully adjustable target rear. **Features:** Has extended threaded barrel with rubber O-ring; adjustable trigger; extended magazine floorplate; adjustable trigger stop; polymer frame. Introduced 1998. Imported from Germany by Heckler & Koch, Inc.

Price: **$965.00**

Heckler & Koch USP Compact

Heritage Stealth

Heckler & Koch USP Expert

Hi-Point 45 ACP

HECKLER & KOCH MARK 23 SPECIAL OPERATIONS PISTOL

Caliber: 45 ACP, 10-shot magazine. **Barrel:** 5.87". **Weight:** 43 oz. **Length:** 9.65" overall. **Stocks:** Integral with frame; black polymer. **Sights:** Blade front, rear drift adjustable for windage; three-dot. **Features:** Polymer frame; double action; exposed hammer; short recoil, modified Browning action. Civilian version of the SOCOM pistol. Introduced 1996. Imported from Germany by Heckler & Koch, Inc.
Price: **$2,055.00**

Heckler & Koch USP Expert Pistol

Combines features of the USP Tactical and HK Mark 23 pistols with a new slide design. Chambered for 45 ACP; 10-shot magazine. Has adjustable target sights, 5.20" barrel, 8.74" overall length, weighs 1.87 lbs. Match-grade single- and double-action trigger pull with adjustable stop; ambidextrous control levers; elongated target slide; barrel O-ring that seals and centers barrel. Suited to IPSC competition. Introduced 1999. Imported from Germany by Heckler & Koch, Inc.
Price: **$1,369.00**

HECKLER & KOCH P7M8 AUTO PISTOL

Caliber: 9mm Para., 8-shot magazine. **Barrel:** 4.13". **Weight:** 29 oz. **Length:** 6.73" overall. **Stocks:** Stippled black plastic. **Sights:** Blade front, adjustable rear; three dot system. **Features:** Unique "squeeze cocker" in frontstrap cocks the action. Gas-retarded action. Squared combat-type trigger guard. Blue finish. Compact size. Imported from Germany by Heckler & Koch, Inc.
Price: P7M8, blued **$1,222.00**

HERITAGE STEALTH AUTO PISTOL

Caliber: 9mm Para., 40 S&W, 10-shot magazine. **Barrel:** 3.9". **Weight:** 20.2 oz. **Length:** 6.3" overall. **Stocks:** Black polymer; integral. **Sights:** Blade front, rear drift adjustable for windage. **Features:** Gas retarded blowback action; polymer frame, 17-4 stainless slide; frame mounted ambidextrous trigger safety, magazine safety. Introduced 1996. Made in U.S. by Heritage Mfg., Inc.
Price: **$289.95**
Price: Stainless or stainless/black **$329.95**

HERITAGE H25S AUTO PISTOL

Caliber: 25 ACP, 6-shot magazine. **Barrel:** 2.25". **Weight:** 13.5 oz. **Length:** 4.5" overall. **Stocks:** Smooth hardwood. **Sights:** Fixed. **Features:** Frame-mounted trigger safety, magazine disconnect safety. Made in U.S. by Heritage Mfg. Inc.
Price: Blue **$149.95**
Price: Nickel **$159.95**

HI-POINT FIREARMS 40 S&W AUTO

Caliber: 40 S&W, 8-shot magazine. **Barrel:** 4.5". **Weight:** 39 oz. **Length:** 7.72" overall. **Stocks:** Checkered acetal resin. **Sights:** Adjustable; low profile. **Features:** Internal drop-safe mechanism; alloy frame. Introduced 1991. From MKS Supply, Inc.
Price: Matte black. **$148.95**

HI-POINT FIREARMS 45 CALIBER PISTOL

Caliber: 45 ACP, 7-shot magazine. **Barrel:** 4.5". **Weight:** 39 oz. **Length:** 7.95" overall. **Stocks:** Checkered acetal resin. **Sights:** Adjustable; low profile. **Features:** Internal drop-safe mechanism; alloy frame. Introduced 1991. From MKS Supply, Inc.
Price: Matte black. **$148.95**
Price: Chrome slide, black frame **$152.95**

Hi-Point 9MM Comp   Hi-Point 380 Polymer   Kahr K9 Nickel   Kareen M1500

HI-POINT FIREARMS 9MM AUTO PISTOL

Caliber: 9mm Para., 9-shot magazine. **Barrel:** 4.5". **Weight:** 39 oz. **Length:** 7.72" overall. **Stocks:** Textured acetal plastic. **Sights:** Adjustable; low profile. **Features:** Single-action design. Scratch-resistant, non-glare blue finish, alloy frame. Introduced 1990. From MKS Supply, Inc.
Price: Matte black $139.95

Hi-Point Firearms 9mm Comp Pistol

Similar to the standard 9mm pistol except has 4" barrel, muzzle brake/compensator, 10-shot magazine, adjustable rear sight. Compensator is slotted for laser or flashlight mounting. Introduced 1998. From MKS Supply, Inc.
Price: $149.95

HI-POINT FIREARMS MODEL 9MM COMPACT PISTOL

Caliber: 9mm Para., 8-shot magazine. **Barrel:** 3.5". **Weight:** 29 oz. **Length:** 6.7" overall. **Stocks:** Textured acetal plastic. **Sights:** Combat-style adjustable three-dot system; low profile. **Features:** Single-action design; frame-mounted magazine release; polymer or alloy frame. Scratch-resistant matte finish. Introduced 1993. From MKS Supply, Inc.
Price: Black $124.95
Price: With polymer frame (29 oz.), non-slip grips $124.95
Price: Chrome with polymer frame $128.95

Hi-Point Firearms Model 380 Polymer Pistol

Similar to the 9mm Compact model except chambered for 380 ACP, 8-shot magazine, adjustable three-dot sights. Weighs 29 oz. Polymer frame. Introduced 1998. Made in U.S. From MKS Supply.
Price: $99.95
Price: Chrome slide, black frame $103.95

KAHR K9, K40 DA AUTO PISTOLS

Caliber: 9mm Para., 7-shot, 40 S&W, 6-shot magazine. **Barrel:** 3.5". **Weight:** 25 oz. **Length:** 6" overall. **Stocks:** Wrap-around textured soft polymer. **Sights:** Blade front, rear drift adjustable for windage; bar-dot combat style. **Features:** Trigger-cocking double-action mechanism with passive firing pin block. Made of 4140 ordnance steel with matte black finish. Contact maker for complete price list. Introduced 1994. Made in U.S. by Kahr Arms.
Price: 9mm $538.00

Price: Matte black, night sights 9mm $624.00
Price: Matte nickel finish 9mm $612.00
Price: Matte nickel, night sights 9mm $699.00
Price: Matte stainless steel, 9mm $588.00
Price: 40 S&W, matte black $552.00
Price: 40 S&W, matte black, night sights $638.00
Price: 40 S&W, matte stainless $602.00
Price: Lady K9, 9mm, matte black, from $545.00
Price: K9 Elite 98 (high-polish stainless slide flats, Kahr combat trigger), from $631.00
Price: As above, MK9 Elite 98, from $648.00
Price: As above, K40 Elite 98, from $646.00

Kahr MK9 Micro-Compact Pistol

Similar to the K9 except is 5.5" overall, 4" high, has a 3" barrel. Weighs 22 oz. Has snag-free bar-dot sights, polished feed ramp, dual recoil spring system, DA-only trigger. Comes with 6- and 7-shot magazines. Introduced 1998. Made in U.S. by Kahr Arms.
Price: Matte stainless $605.00
Price: Matte stainless, tritium night sights $692.00
Price: Duo-Tone (stainless frame, Black-T slide) $749.00
Price: Duo-Tone with tritium night sights $836.00

Kahr KS40 Small Frame Pistol

Same as standard K40 except 1/2" shorter grip. Comes with one 5-shot, one 6-shot magazine. Introduced 1998. Made in U.S. by Kahr Arms.
Price: $594.00
Price: With night sights. $677.00

KAREEN M-1500 AUTO PISTOL

Caliber: 9mm Para., 10-shot magazine. **Barrel:** 3.9". **Weight:** 32.2 oz. **Length:** 6" overall. **Stocks:** Textured composition. **Sights:** Blade front, rear adjustable for windage. **Features:** Single-action mechanism; ambidextrous external hammer safety; magazine safety; combat trigger guard. Two-tone finish. Introduced 1985. Imported from Israel by Israel Arms International.
Price: $411.95

HANDGUNS — AUTOLOADERS, SERVICE & SPORT

Kel-Tec P-11

Kel-Tec P-32

Kimber Custom 45

Kimber Custom

KEL-TEC P-11 AUTO PISTOL

Caliber: 9mm Para., 10-shot magazine. **Barrel:** 3.1". **Weight:** 14 oz. **Length:** 5.6" overall. **Stocks:** Checkered black polymer. **Sights:** Blade front, rear adjustable for windage. **Features:** Ordnance steel slide, aluminum frame. Double-action-only trigger mechanism. Introduced 1995. Made in U.S. by Kel-Tec CNC Industries, Inc.

Price: Blue **$309.00**
Price: Hard chrome. **$363.00**
Price: Parkerized **$350.00**

KEL-TEC P-32 AUTO PISTOL

Caliber: 32 ACP, 7-shot magazine. **Barrel:** 2.68". **Weight:** 6.6 oz. **Length:** 5.07" overall. **Stocks:** Checkered composite. **Sights:** Fixed. **Features:** Double-action-only mechanism with 6-lb. pull; internal slide stop. Textured composite grip/frame. Made in U.S. by Kel-Tec CNC Industries, Inc.

Price: **$295.00**

KIMBER CUSTOM AUTO PISTOL

Caliber: 45 ACP, 7-shot magazine. **Barrel:** 5", match grade. **Weight:** 38 oz. **Length:** 8.7" overall. **Stocks:** Checkered black rubber (standard), walnut, or rosewood. **Sights:** McCormick dovetailed front, low combat rear. **Features:** Slide, frame and barrel machined from steel forgings; match-grade barrel, chamber, trigger; extended thumb safety; beveled magazine well; beveled front and rear slide serrations; high-ride beavertail safety; checkered flat mainspring housing; kidney cut under trigger guard; high cut grip design; match-grade stainless barrel bushing; Commander-style hammer; lowered and flared ejection port; Wolff springs; bead blasted black oxide finish. Made in U.S. by Kimber Mfg., Inc.

Price: Custom. **$657.00**
Price: Custom Walnut (double-diamond walnut grips) **$670.00**
Price: Custom Stainless **$753.00**
Price: Custom Stainless 40 S&W, 9mm, 38 Super. **$780.00**
Price: Custom Stainless Target 45 ACP (stainless, adj. sight). . . . **$843.00**
Price: Custom Stainless 40 S&W, 9mm, 38 Super. **$870.00**

Kimber Compact Auto Pistol

Similar to the Custom model except has 4" bull barrel fitted directly to the slide without a bushing; full-length guide rod; grip is .400" shorter than full-size gun; no front serrations. Steel frame models weigh 34 oz., aluminum 28 oz. Introduced 1998. Made in U.S. by Kimber Mfg., Inc.

Price: 45 ACP, matte black **$677.00**
Price: Compact Cristobal 45 ACP (cristobal grips). **$690.00**
Price: Compact Stainless 45 ACP **$773.00**
Price: Compact Stainless 40 S&W **$800.00**
Price: Compact Stainless Cristobal 45 ACP. **$786.00**
Price: Compact Aluminum 45 ACP (aluminum frame, blue slide) . **$677.00**
Price: Compact Stainless Aluminum 45 ACP (aluminum frame, stainless slide) **$745.00**
Price: Compact Stainless Aluminum 40 S&W **$771.00**

Kimber Pro Carry Auto Pistol

Similar to the Compact model except has aluminum frame with full-length grip. Has 4" bull barrel fitted directly to the slide without bushing. Introduced 1998. Made in U.S. by Kimber Mfg., Inc.

Price: 45 ACP **$676.00**
Price: 40 S&W **$704.00**
Price: Stainless Pro Carry 45 ACP. **$745.00**
Price: Stainless Pro Carry 40 S&W **$771.00**

Kimber Ultra Carry Auto Pistol

Similar to the Compact Aluminum model except has 3" balljoint spherical bushingless cone barrel; aluminum frame; beveling at front and rear of ejection port; relieved breech face; tuned ejector; special slide stop; dual captured low-effort spring system. Weighs 25 oz. Introduced 1999. made in U.S. by Kimber Mfg., Inc.

Price: 45 ACP. **$676.00**
Price: 40 S&W **$704.00**
Price: Stainless, 45 ACP **$745.00**
Price: Stainless, 40 S&W **$771.00**

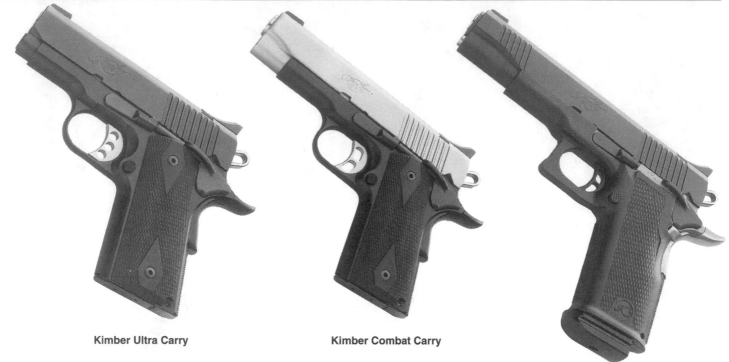

Kimber Ultra Carry   **Kimber Combat Carry**

Kimber High Capacity Polymer

Kimber Combat Carry Auto Pistol

NEW! Similar to the Compact Stainless Aluminum except all edges have been rounded; 30 lpi front strap checkering; tritium night sights; premium match-grade aluminum trigger; ambidextrous thumb safety; black oxide frame, natural stainless slide; special Custom Shop markings. Introduced 1999. Made in U.S. by Kimber Mfg., Inc.

Price: 45 ACP **$1,044.00**
Price: 40 S&W **$1,071.00**

KIMBER HIGH CAPACITY POLYMER PISTOL

Caliber: 45 ACP, 14-shot magazine. **Barrel:** 5". **Weight:** 34 oz. **Length:** 8.7" overall. **Stocks:** Integral; checkered black polymer. **Sights:** McCormick low profile front and rear. **Features:** Polymer frame with steel insert. Comes with pre-ban magazine. Checkered front strap and mainspring housing; polymer trigger; stainless high ride beavertail grip safety; hooked trigger guard. Introduced 1997. Made in U.S. by Kimber Mfg., Inc.

Price: Matte black finish **$814.00**
Price: Polymer Stainless (satin-finish stainless slide) **$881.00**
Price: Polymer Stainless 40 S&W, 9mm, 38 Super **$909.00**
Price: Polymer Pro Carry (compact slide, 4" bull barrel) **$814.00**
Price: Polymer Pro Carry Stainless **$881.00**

Kimber Gold Match Auto Pistol

Similar to the Custom model except has Kimber adjustable sight with rounded and blended edges; stainless steel match-grade barrel hand-fitted to spherical barrel bushing; premium aluminum trigger; extended ambidextrous thumb safety; hand-checkered double diamond rosewood grips. Hand-fitted by Kimber Custom Shop. Made in U.S. by Kimber Mfg., Inc.

Price: Gold Match 45 ACP **$1,019.00**
Price: Stainless Gold Match 45 ACP (highly polished flats) **$1,146.00**
Price: Stainless Gold Match 40 S&W, 9mm, 38 Super........ **$1,174.00**

Kimber Polymer Gold Match Auto Pistol

NEW! Similar to the Polymer model except has Kimber adjustable sight with rounded and blended edges; stainless steel match-grade barrel hand-fitted to spherical barrel bushing; premium aluminum trigger; extended ambidextrous thumb safety. Hand-fitted by Kimber Custom Shop. Introduced 1999. Made in U.S. by Kimber Mfg., Inc.

Price: **$1,085.00**
Price: Polymer Stainless Gold Match (polished stainless slide) . **$1,235.00**
Price: Polymer Stainless Gold Match 40 S&W, 9mm, 38 Super **$1,263.00**

Kimber Gold Combat Auto Pistol

NEW! Similar to the Gold Match except designed for concealed carry. Has two-piece extended and beveled magazine well, tritium night sights; premium aluminum trigger; 30 lpi front strap checkering; special Custom Shop markings; Kim Pro black finish. Introduced 1999. Made in U.S. by Kimber Mfg., Inc.

Price: 45 ACP **$1,481.00**
Price: Gold Combat Stainless (satin-finished stainless frame and slide, special Custom Shop markings)........................ **$1,426.00**

LASERAIM ARMS SERIES I AUTO PISTOL

Caliber: 10mm Auto, 8-shot, 40 S&W, 400 Cor-Bon, 45 ACP, 7-shot magazine. **Barrel:** 6", with compensator. **Weight:** 46 oz. **Length:** 9.75" overall. **Stocks:** Pebble-grained black composite. **Sights:** Blade front, fully adjustable rear. **Features:** Single action; barrel compensator; stainless steel construction; ambidextrous safety-levers; extended slide release; matte black Teflon finish; integral mount for laser sight. Introduced 1993. Made in U.S. by Laseraim Technologies, Inc.

Price: Standard, fixed sight **$349.00**
Price: Standard, Compact (4-3/8" barrel), fixed sight......... **$349.00**
Price: Adjustable sight **$349.00**
Price: Standard, fixed sight, Auto Illusion red dot sight system .. **$349.00**
Price: Standard, fixed sight, Laseraim Laser with Hotdot....... **$349.00**

Laseraim Arms Series II Auto Pistol

Similar to the Series I except without compensator, has matte stainless finish. Standard Series II has 5" barrel, weighs 43 oz., Compact has 3-3/8" barrel, weighs 37 oz. Blade front sight, rear adjustable for windage or fixed. Introduced 1993. Made in U.S. by Laseraim Technologies, Inc.

Price: Standard or Compact (3-3/8" barrel), fixed sight **$349.00**
Price: Adjustable sight, 5" only........................ **$349.00**
Price: Standard, fixed sight, Auto Illusion red dot sight **$349.00**
Price: Standard, fixed sight, Laseraim Laser **$349.00**

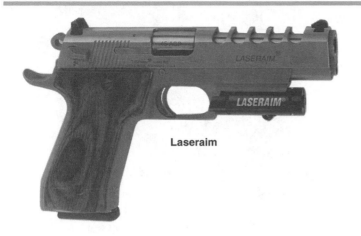

Laseraim

Llama Minimax

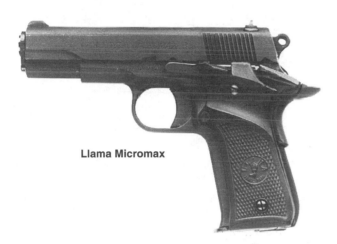

Llama Micromax

Llama Max-1

Laseraim Arms Series III Auto Pistol
Similar to the Series II except has 5" barrel only, with dual port compensator; weighs 43 oz.; overall length is 7-5/8". Choice of fixed or adjustable rear sight. Introduced 1994. Made by U.S. by Laseraim Technologies, Inc.
Price: Fixed sight **$349.00**
Price: Adjustable sight **$345.00**
Price: Fixed sight Dream Team Laseraim laser sight **$349.00**

LLAMA MICROMAX 380 AUTO PISTOL
Caliber: 32 ACP, 8-shot, 380 ACP, 7-shot magazine. **Barrel:** 3-11/16". **Weight:** 23 oz. **Length:** 6-1/2" overall. **Stocks:** Checkered high impact polymer. **Sights:** 3-dot combat. **Features:** Single-action design. Mini custom extended slide release; mini custom extended beavertail grip safety; combat-style hammer. Introduced 1997. Imported from Spain by Import Sports, Inc.
Price: Matte blue. **$246.95**
Price: Satin chrome (380 only) **$281.95**

LLAMA MINIMAX SERIES
Caliber: 9mm Para., 8-shot; 40 S&W, 7-shot; 45 ACP, 6-shot magazine. **Barrel:** 3-1/2". **Weight:** 35 oz. **Length:** 7-1/3" overall. **Stocks:** Checkered rubber. **Sights:** Three-dot combat. **Features:** Single action, skeletonized combat-style hammer, extended slide release, cone-style barrel, flared ejection port. Introduced 1996. Imported from Spain by Import Sports, Inc.
Price: Blue **$291.95**
Price: Duo-Tone finish (45 only) **$298.95**
Price: Satin chrome **$308.95**

Llama Minimax Sub Compact Auto Pistol
Similar to the Minimax except has 3.14" barrel, weighs 31 oz.; 6.8" overall length; has 10-shot magazine with finger extension; beavertail grip safety.

Introduced 1999. Imported from Spain by Import Sports, Inc.
Price: 9mm Para., 40 S&W, 45 ACP, matte blue **$308.95**
Price: As above, satin chrome **$324.95**
Price: Duo-Tone finish (45 only) **$314.95**

LLAMA MAX-I AUTO PISTOLS
Caliber: 45 ACP, 7-shot. **Barrel:** 5-1/8". **Weight:** 36 oz. **Length:** 8-1/2" overall. **Stocks:** Black rubber. **Sights:** Blade front, rear adjustable for windage; three-dot system. **Features:** Single-action trigger; skeletonized combat-style hammer; steel frame; extended manual and grip safeties. Introduced 1995. Imported from Spain by Import Sports, Inc.
Price: 45 ACP, 7-shot, Government model **$298.95**
Price: As above, satin chrome finish **$314.95**

LORCIN L-22 AUTO PISTOL
Caliber: 22 LR, 9-shot magazine. **Barrel:** 2.5". **Weight:** 16 oz. **Length:** 5.25" overall. **Stocks:** Black combat, or pink or pearl. **Sights:** Fixed three-dot system. **Features:** Available in chrome or black Teflon finish. Introduced 1989. From Lorcin Engineering.
Price: About **$89.00**

LORCIN L9MM AUTO PISTOL
Caliber: 9mm Para., 10-shot magazine. **Barrel:** 4.5". **Weight:** 31 oz. **Length:** 7.5" overall. **Stocks:** Grooved black composition. **Sights:** Fixed; three-dot system. **Features:** Matte black finish; hooked trigger guard; grip safety. Introduced 1994. Made in U.S. by Lorcin Engineering.
Price: **$159.00**

LORCIN L-25, LT-25 AUTO PISTOLS
Caliber: 25 ACP, 7-shot magazine. **Barrel:** 2.4". **Weight:** 14.5 oz. **Length:** 4.8" overall. **Stocks:** Smooth composition. **Sights:** Fixed. **Features:**

Lorcin L9MM

Para-Ordnance P12.45

One Pro .45

Available in choice of finishes: chrome, black Teflon or camouflage. Introduced 1989. From Lorcin Engineering.

Price: L-25 .... **$69.00**
Price: LT-25 .... **$79.00**

LORCIN L-32, L-380 AUTO PISTOLS

Caliber: 32 ACP, 380 ACP, 7-shot magazine. **Barrel:** 3.5". **Weight:** 27 oz. **Length:** 6.6" overall. **Stocks:** Grooved composition. **Sights:** Fixed. **Features:** Black Teflon or chrome finish with black grips. Introduced 1992. From Lorcin Engineering.

Price: L-32 32 ACP...................................... **$89.00**
Price: L-380 380 ACP................................... **$100.00**

NORTH AMERICAN ARMS GUARDIAN PISTOL

Caliber: 32 ACP, 6-shot magazine. **Barrel:** 2.1". **Weight:** 13.5 oz. **Length:** 4.36" overall. **Stocks:** Black polymer. **Sights:** Fixed. **Features:** Double-action-only mechanism. All stainless steel construction; snag-free. Introduced 1998. Made in U.S. by North American Arms.

Price: **$425.00**

OLYMPIC ARMS OA-96 AR PISTOL

Caliber: 223. **Barrel:** 6", 8", 4140 chrome-moly steel. **Weight:** 5 lbs. **Length:** 15-3/4" overall. **Stocks:** A2 stowaway pistol grip; no buttstock or receiver tube. **Sights:** Flat-top upper receiver, cut-down front sight base. **Features:** AR-15-type receivers with special bolt carrier; short aluminum hand guard; Vortex flash hider. Introduced 1996. Made in U.S. by Olympic Arms, Inc.

Price: **$858.00**

Olympic Arms OA-98 AR Pistol

NEW!

Similar to the OA-93 except has removable 7-shot magazine, weighs 3 lbs. Introduced 1999. Made in U.S. by Olympic Arms, Inc.

Price: **$990.00**

ONE PRO .45 AUTO PISTOL

Caliber: 45 ACP or 400 Cor-Bon, 10-shot magazine. **Barrel:** 3.75" **Weight:** 31.1 oz. **Length:** 7.04" overall. **Stocks:** Textured composition. **Sights:** Blade front, drift-adjustable rear; three-dot system. **Features:** All-steel construction; decocking lever and automatic firing pin lock; DA or DAO operation. Introduced 1997. Imported from Switzerland by Magnum Research, Inc.

Price: **$649.00**
Price: Conversion kit, 45 ACP/400, 400/45 ACP **$249.00**

ONE PRO 9 AUTO PISTOL

Caliber: 9mm Para., 10-shot magazine. **Barrel:** 3.01". **Weight:** 25.1 oz. **Length:** 6.06" overall. **Stocks:** Smooth wood. **Sights:** Blade front, rear adjustable for windage. **Features:** Rotating barrel; short slide; double recoil springs; double-action mechanism; decocking lever. Introduced 1998. Imported from Switzerland by Magnum Research.

Price: **$649.00**

PARA-ORDNANCE P-SERIES AUTO PISTOLS

Caliber: 9mm Para., 40 S&W, 45 ACP, 10-shot magazine. **Barrel:** 3", 3-1/2", 4-1/4", 5". **Weight:** From 24 oz. (alloy frame). **Length:** 8.5" overall. **Stocks:** Textured composition. **Sights:** Blade front, rear adjustable for windage. High visibility three-dot system. **Features:** Available with alloy, steel or stainless steel frame with black finish (silver or stainless gun). Steel and stainless steel frame guns weigh 40 oz. (P14.45), 36 oz. (P13.45), 34 oz. (P12.45). Grooved match trigger, rounded combat-style hammer. Beveled magazine well. Manual thumb, grip and firing pin lock safeties. Solid barrel bushing. Contact maker for full details. Introduced 1990. Made in Canada by Para-Ordnance.

Price: P14.45ER (steel frame) **$775.00**
Price: P14.45RR (alloy frame) **$740.00**
Price: P12.45RR (3-1/2" bbl., 24 oz., alloy) **$740.00**
Price: P13.45RR (4-1/4" barrel, 28 oz., alloy) **$740.00**
Price: P12.45ER (steel frame) **$750.00**
Price: P16.40ER (steel frame) **$875.00**
Price: P10-9RR (9mm, alloy frame) **$740.00**

Para-Ordnance Limited Pistols

Similar to the P-Series pistols except with full-length recoil guide system; fully adjustable rear sight; tuned trigger with overtravel stop; beavertail grip safety; competition hammer; front and rear slide serrations; ambidextrous safety; lowered ejection port; ramped match-grade barrel; dovetailed front sight. Introduced 1998. Made in Canada by Para-Ordnance.

Price: 9mm, 40 S&W, 45 ACP .... **$865.00** to **$899.00**

Para-Ordnance LDA Auto Pistols

Similar to the P-series except has double-action trigger mechanism. Steel frame with matte black finish, checkered composition grips. Available in 9mm Para., 40 S&W, 45 ACP. Introduced 1999. Made in Canada by Para-Ordnance.

NEW!

Price: **$775.00**

Para-Ordnance LDA   Phoenix Arms HP22   PSA-25 Auto   Republic Patriot

PHOENIX ARMS HP22, HP25 AUTO PISTOLS

Caliber: 22 LR, 10-shot (HP22), 25 ACP, 10-shot (HP25). **Barrel:** 3".
Weight: 20 oz. **Length:** 5-1/2" overall. **Stocks:** Checkered composition.
Sights: Blade front, adjustable rear. **Features:** Single action, exposed
hammer; manual hold-open; button magazine release. Available in satin
nickel, polished blue finish. Introduced 1993. Made in U.S. by Phoenix
Arms.
Price: With gun lock **$116.00**

PSA-25 AUTO POCKET PISTOL

Caliber: 25 ACP, 6-shot magazine. **Barrel:** 2-1/8". **Weight:** 9.5 oz. **Length:**
4-1/8" overall. **Stocks:** Checkered black polymer, ivory, checkered transparent carbon fiber filled polymer. **Sights:** Fixed. **Features:** All steel con-
struction; striker fired; single action only; magazine disconnector; cocking
indicator. Introduced 1987. Made in U.S. by Precision Small Arms, Inc.
Price: Traditional (polished black oxide)..................... **$269.00**
Price: Nouveau - Satin (brushed nickel)..................... **$269.00**
Price: Nouveau - Mirror (highly polished nickel).............. **$309.00**
Price: Featherweight (aluminum frame, nickel slide).......... **$405.00**
Price: Diplomat (black oxide with gold highlights, ivory grips) **$625.00**
Price: Montreaux (gold plated, ivory grips).................. **$692.00**
Price: Renaissance (hand engraved nickel, ivory grips)....... **$1,115.00**
Price: Imperiale (inlaid gold filligree over blue, scrimshawed
ivory grips) **$3,600.00**

REPUBLIC PATRIOT PISTOL

Caliber: 45 ACP, 6-shot magazine. **Barrel:** 3". **Weight:** 20 oz. **Length:** 6"
overall. **Stocks:** Checkered. **Sights:** Blade front, drift-adjustable rear.
Features: Black polymer frame, stainless steel slide; double-action-only
trigger system; squared trigger guard. Introduced 1997. Made in U.S. by
Republic Arms, Inc.
Price: About **$325.00**

ROCKY MOUNTAIN ARMS PATRIOT PISTOL

Caliber: 223, 10-shot magazine. **Barrel:** 7", with muzzle brake. **Weight:** 5
lbs. **Length:** 20.5" overall. **Stocks:** Black composition. **Sights:** None furnished. **Features:** Milled upper receiver with enhanced Weaver base;
milled lower receiver from billet plate; machined aluminum National Match

Ruger P89

handguard. Finished in DuPont Teflon-S matte black or NATO green.
Comes with black nylon case, one magazine. Introduced 1993. From
Rocky Mountain Arms, Inc.
Price: With A-2 handle top .... **$2,500.00** to **$2,800.00**
Price: Flat top model .... **$3,000.00** to **$3,500.00**

RUGER P89 AUTOLOADING PISTOL

Caliber: 9mm Para., 10-shot magazine. **Barrel:** 4.50". **Weight:** 32 oz.
Length: 7.84" overall. **Stocks:** Grooved black Xenoy composition.
Sights: Square post front, square notch rear adjustable for windage, both
with white dot inserts. **Features:** Double action with ambidextrous slide-
mounted safety-levers. Slide is 4140 chrome-moly steel or 400-series
stainless steel, frame is a lightweight aluminum alloy. Ambidextrous magazine release. Blue or stainless steel. Introduced 1986; stainless introduced 1990.

Ruger P93DAO

Ruger KP95DAO

Price: P89, blue, with extra magazine and magazine loading tool, plastic case with lock **$430.00**
Price: KP89, stainless, with extra magazine and magazine loading tool, plastic case with lock **$475.00**

Ruger P89D Decocker Autoloading Pistol

Similar to the standard P89 except has ambidextrous decocking levers in place of the regular slide-mounted safety. The decocking levers move the firing pin inside the slide where the hammer can not reach it, while simultaneously blocking the firing pin from forward movement—allows shooter to decock a cocked pistol without manipulating the trigger. Conventional thumb decocking procedures are therefore unnecessary. Blue or stainless steel. Introduced 1990.
Price: P89D, blue with extra magazine and loader, plastic case with lock **$430.00**
Price: KP89D, stainless, with extra magazine, plastic case with lock **$475.00**

Ruger P89 Double-Action-Only Autoloading Pistol

Same as the KP89 except operates only in the double-action mode. Has a spurless hammer, gripping grooves on each side of the rear of the slide; no external safety or decocking lever. An internal safety prevents forward movement of the firing pin unless the trigger is pulled. Available in 9mm Para., stainless steel only. Introduced 1991.
Price: With lockable case, extra magazine, magazine loading tool **$475.00**

RUGER P93 COMPACT AUTOLOADING PISTOL

Caliber: 9mm Para., 10-shot magazine. **Barrel:** 3.9". **Weight:** 31 oz. **Length:** 7.3" overall. **Stocks:** Grooved black Xenoy composition. **Sights:** Square post front, square notch rear adjustable for windage. **Features:** Front of slide is crowned with a convex curve; slide has seven finger grooves; trigger guard bow is higher for a better grip; 400-series stainless slide, lightweight alloy frame; also in blue. Decocker-only or DAO-only. Introduced 1993. Made in U.S. by Sturm, Ruger & Co.
Price: KP93DAO, double-action-only **$520.00**
Price: KP93D ambidextrous decocker, stainless **$520.00**
Price: P93D, ambidextrous decocker, blue **$421.50**

Ruger KP94 Autoloading Pistol

Sized midway between the full-size P-Series and the compact P93. Has 4.25" barrel, 7.5" overall length and weighs about 33 oz. KP94 is manual safety model; KP94DAO is double-action-only (both 9mm Para., 10-shot magazine); KP94D is decocker-only in 40-caliber with 10-shot magazine. Slide gripping grooves roll over top of slide. KP94 has ambidextrous safety-levers; KP94DAO has no external safety, full-cock hammer position or decocking lever; KP94D has ambidextrous decocking levers. Matte finish stainless slide, barrel, alloy frame. Also available in blue. Introduced 1994. Made in U.S. by Sturm, Ruger & Co.

Price: P94, P944, blue **$421.50**
Price: KP94 (9mm), KP944 (40-caliber).................... **$520.00**
Price: KP94DAO (9mm), KP944DAO (40-caliber) **$520.00**
Price: KP94D (9mm), KP9440 (40-caliber) **$520.00**

RUGER P90 SAFETY MODEL AUTOLOADING PISTOL

Caliber: 45 ACP, 7-shot magazine. **Barrel:** 4.50". **Weight:** 33.5 oz. **Length:** 7.87" overall. **Stocks:** Grooved black Xenoy composition. **Sights:** Square post front, square notch rear adjustable for windage, both with white dot inserts. **Features:** Double action with ambidextrous slide-mounted safety-levers which move the firing pin inside the slide where the hammer can not reach it, while simultaneously blocking the firing pin from forward movement. Stainless steel only. Introduced 1991.
Price: KP90 with extra magazine, loader, plastic case with lock . **$513.00**
Price: P90 (blue).. **$476.00**

Ruger P90 Decocker Autoloading Pistol

Similar to the P90 except has a manual decocking system. The ambidextrous decocking levers move the firing pin inside the slide where the hammer can not reach it, while simultaneously blocking the firing pin from forward movement—allows shooter to decock a cocked pistol without manipulating the trigger. Available only in stainless steel. Overall length 7.87", weighs 34 oz. Introduced 1991.
Price: P90D with lockable case, extra magazine, and magazine loading tool **$513.00**

RUGER P95 AUTOLOADING PISTOL

Caliber: 9mm Para., 10-shot magazine. **Barrel:** 3.9". **Weight:** 27 oz. **Length:** 7.3" overall. **Stocks:** Grooved; integral with frame. **Sights:** Blade front, rear drift adjustable for windage; three-dot system. **Features:** Moulded polymer grip frame, stainless steel or chrome-moly slide. Suitable for +P+ ammunition. Decocker or DAO. Introduced 1996. Made in U.S. by Sturm, Ruger & Co. Comes with lockable plastic case, spare magazine, loading tool.
Price: P95 DAO double-action-only **$351.00**
Price: P95D decocker only............................... **$351.00**
Price: KP95 stainless steel.............................. **$369.00**

RUGER MARK II STANDARD AUTOLOADING PISTOL

Caliber: 22 LR, 10-shot magazine. **Barrel:** 4-3/4" or 6". **Weight:** 25 oz. (4-3/4" bbl.). **Length:** 8-5/16" (4-3/4" bbl.). **Stocks:** Checkered plastic. **Sights:** Fixed, wide blade front, square notch rear adjustable for windage. **Features:** Updated design of the original Standard Auto. Has new bolt hold-open latch. 10-shot magazine, magazine catch, safety, trigger and new receiver contours. Introduced 1982.
Price: Blued (MK 4, MK 6) **$252.00**
Price: In stainless steel (KMK 4, KMK 6) **$330.25**

Ruger P4

Ruger MK-4B

Ruger KMK-4

Ruger KP512

Ruger MK10

Ruger MK-4B Compact Pistol

Similar to the Mark II Standard pistol except has 4" bull barrel, Patridge-type front sight, fully adjustable rear, and smooth laminated hardwood thumbrest stocks. Weighs 38 oz., overall length of 8-3/16". Comes with extra magazine, plastic case, lock. Introduced 1996. Made in U.S. by Sturm, Ruger & Co.

Price: **$336.50**

Ruger 22/45 Mark II Pistol

Similar to the other 22 Mark II autos except has grip frame of Zytel that matches the angle and magazine latch of the Model 1911 45 ACP pistol. Available in 4", 4-3/4" standard and 5-1/2" bull barrel. Comes with extra magazine, plastic case, lock. Introduced 1992.

Price: P4, 4", adjustable sights.......................... **$237.50**
Price: KP 4 (4-3/4" barrel) **$280.00**
Price: KP512 (5-1/2" bull barrel)........................ **$330.00**
Price: P512 (5-1/2" bull barrel, all blue) **$237.50**

Ruger 50th Anniversary Mark II Pistol

Similar to the Mark II Standard except receiver is contoured like the original pistol, bolt has Ruger logo at rear, grips and magazine have the Ruger medallion with red background. The top front of the receiver has 50th Anniversary crest. Comes in a red Ruger commemorative lockable case. Made only in 1999. Made in U.S. by Sturm, Ruger & Co.

Price: MK4-50.. **$287.00**

SAFARI ARMS ENFORCER PISTOL

Caliber: 45 ACP, 6-shot magazine. **Barrel:** 3.8", stainless. **Weight:** 36 oz. **Length:** 7.3" overall. **Stocks:** Smooth walnut with etched black widow spider logo. **Sights:** Ramped blade front, LPA adjustable rear. **Features:** Extended safety, extended slide release; Commander-style hammer; beavertail grip safety; throated, polished, tuned. Parkerized matte black or satin stainless steel finishes. Made in U.S. by Safari Arms.

Price: **$630.00**

SAFARI ARMS GI SAFARI PISTOL

Caliber: 45 ACP, 7-shot magazine. **Barrel:** 5", 416 stainless. **Weight:** 39.9 oz. **Length:** 8.5" overall. **Stocks:** Checkered walnut. **Sights:** G.I.-style blade front, drift-adjustable rear. **Features:** Beavertail grip safety; extended thumb safety and slide release; Commander-style hammer. Parkerized finish. Reintroduced 1996.

Price: **$439.00**

SAFARI ARMS CARRIER PISTOL

Caliber: 45 ACP, 7-shot magazine. **Barrel:** 6", 416 stainless steel. **Weight:** 30 oz. **Length:** 9.5" overall. **Stocks:** Wood. **Sights:** Ramped blade front, LPA adjustable rear. **Features:** Beavertail grip safety; extended controls; full-length recoil spring guide; Commander-style hammer. Throated, polished and tuned. Satin stainless steel finish. Introduced 1999. Made in U.S. by Safari Arms, Inc.

Price: **$714.00**

SAFARI ARMS COHORT PISTOL

Caliber: 45 ACP, 7-shot magazine. **Barrel:** 3.8", 416 stainless. **Weight:** 37 oz. **Length:** 8.5" overall. **Stocks:** Smooth walnut with laser-etched black widow logo. **Sights:** Ramped blade front, LPA adjustable rear. **Features:** Combines the Enforcer model, slide and MatchMaster frame. Beavertail grip safety; extended thumb safety and slide release; Commander-style hammer. Throated, polished and tuned. Satin stainless finish. Introduced 1996. Made in U.S. by Safari Arms, Inc.

Price: **$654.00**

SIG Sauer P220

SIG Arms P245 Compact

SIG Arms Pro 2009

SAFARI ARMS MATCHMASTER PISTOL

Caliber: 45 ACP, 7-shot. **Barrel:** 5" or 6", 416 stainless steel. **Weight:** 38 oz. (5" barrel). **Length:** 8.5" overall. **Stocks:** Smooth walnut. **Sights:** Ramped blade, LPA adjustable rear. **Features:** Beavertail grip safety; extended controls; Commander-style hammer; throated, polished, tuned. Parkerized matte-black or satin stainless steel. Made in U.S. by Olympic Arms, Inc.

Price: 5" barrel $594.00
Price: 6" barrel $654.00

Safari Arms Carry Comp Pistol

Similar to the Matchmaster except has Wil Schueman-designed hybrid compensator system. Made in U.S. by Olympic Arms, Inc.

Price: $1,067.00

SEECAMP LWS 32 STAINLESS DA AUTO

Caliber: 32 ACP Win. Silvertip, 6-shot magazine. **Barrel:** 2", integral with frame. **Weight:** 10.5 oz. **Length:** 4-1/8" overall. **Stocks:** Glass-filled nylon. **Sights:** Smooth, no-snag, contoured slide and barrel top. **Features:** Aircraft quality 17-4 PH stainless steel. Inertia-operated firing pin. Hammer fired double-action-only. Hammer automatically follows slide down to safety rest position after each shot—no manual safety needed. Magazine safety disconnector. Polished stainless. Introduced 1985. From L.W. Seecamp.

Price: $425.00

SIG P210-6 SERVICE PISTOL

Caliber: 9mm Para., 8-shot magazine. **Barrel:** 4-3/4". **Weight:** 32 oz. **Length:** 8-1/2" overall. **Stocks:** Checkered walnut. **Sights:** Blade front, notch rear drift adjustable for windage. **Features:** Mechanically locked, short-recoil operation; single action only; target trigger with adjustable stop; magazine safety; all-steel construction with matte blue finish. Optional 22 LR conversion kit consists of barrel, slide, recoil spring and magazine. Imported from Switzerland by SIGARMS, Inc.

Price: $2,100.00
Price: With 22LR conversion kit $2,400.00

SIG SAUER P220 SERVICE AUTO PISTOL

Caliber: 45 ACP, (7- or 8-shot magazine). **Barrel:** 4-3/8". **Weight:** 27.8 oz. **Length:** 7.8" overall. **Stocks:** Checkered black plastic. **Sights:** Blade front, drift adjustable rear for windage. Optional Siglite nightsights. **Features:** Double action. Decocking lever permits lowering hammer onto locked firing pin. Squared combat-type trigger guard. Slide stays open after last shot. Imported from Germany by SIGARMS, Inc.

Price: Blue SA/DA or DAO $750.00
Price: Blue, Siglite night sights $845.00
Price: K-Kote or nickel slide $795.00
Price: K-Kote or nickel slide with Siglite night sights $895.00

SIG Sauer P220 Sport Auto Pistol

Similar to the P220 except has 4.9" barrel, ported compensator, all-stainless steel frame and slide, factory-tuned trigger, adjustable sights, extended competition controls. Overall length is 9.9", weighs 43.5 oz. Introduced 1999. From SIGARMS, Inc.

Price: $1,320.00

SIG Sauer P245 Compact Auto Pistol

Similar to the P220 except has 3.9" barrel, shorter grip, 6-shot magazine, 7.28" overall length, and weighs 27.5 oz. Introduced 1999. From SIGARMS, Inc.

Price: Blue $750.00
Price: Blue, with Siglite sights $845.00
Price: Two-tone $795.00
Price: Two-tone with Siglite sights $895.00
Price: With K-Kote finish $795.00
Price: K-Kote with Siglite sights $895.00

SIG Sauer P229 DA Auto Pistol

Similar to the P228 except chambered for 9mm Para., 40 S&W, 357 SIG. Has 3.86" barrel, 7.08" overall length and 3.35" height. Weight is 30.5 oz. Introduced 1991. Frame made in Germany, stainless steel slide assembly made in U.S.; pistol assembled in U.S. From SIGARMS, Inc.

Price: $795.00
Price: With nickel slide $890.00
Price: Nickel slide Siglite night sights $935.00

SIG SAUER SP2340 SIG PRO AUTO PISTOL

Caliber: 9mm Para., 40 S&W, 10-shot magazine. **Barrel:** 3.86". **Weight:** 27.2 oz. **Length:** 7.36" overall. **Stocks:** Composite and rubberized one-piece. **Sights:** Blade front, rear adjustable for windage. Optional Siglite night sights. **Features:** Polymer frame, stainless steel slide; integral frame accessory rail; replaceable steel frame rails; left- or right-handed magazine release. Introduced 1999. From SIGARMS, Inc.

Price: SP2340 (40 S&W) $596.00
Price: SP2009 (9mm Para.) $596.00
Price: As above with Siglite night sights $655.00

SIG Sauer P229S

Smith & Wesson 457

SIG Sauer P229S

SIG Sauer P226 Service Pistol

Similar to the P220 pistol except has 4.4" barrel, and weighs 28.3 oz. 357 SIG or 40 S&W. Imported from Germany by SIGARMS, Inc.

Price: Blue SA/DA or DAO	$795.00
Price: With Siglite night sights	$890.00
Price: Blue, SA/DA or DAO 357 SIG	$795.00
Price: With Siglite night sights	$890.00
Price: K-Kote finish, 40 S&W only or nickel slide	$795.00
Price: K-Kote or nickel slide Siglite night sights	$890.00
Price: Nickel slide 357 SIG	$830.00
Price: Nickel slide, Siglite night sights	$930.00

SIG Sauer P229 Sport Auto Pistol

Similar to the P229 except available in 357 SIG only; 4.8" heavy barrel; 8.6" overall length; weighs 40.6 oz.; vented compensator; adjustable target sights; rubber grips; extended slide latch and magazine release. Made of stainless steel. Introduced 1998. From SIGARMS, Inc.

Price: $1,320.00

SIG SAUER P232 PERSONAL SIZE PISTOL

Caliber: 380 ACP, 7-shot. **Barrel:** 3-3/4". **Weight:** 16 oz. **Length:** 6-1/2" overall. **Stocks:** Checkered black composite. **Sights:** Blade front, rear adjustable for windage. **Features:** Double action/single action or DAO. Blowback operation, stationary barrel. Introduced 1997. Imported from Germany by SIGARMS, Inc.

Price: Blue SA/DA or DAO	$485.00
Price: In stainless steel	$525.00
Price: With stainless steel slide, blue frame	$505.00
Price: Stainless steel, Siglite night sights, Hogue grips	$560.00

SIG SAUER P239 PISTOL

Caliber: 9mm Para., 8-shot, 357 SIG 40 S&W, 7-shot magazine. **Barrel:** 3.6". **Weight:** 25.2 oz. **Length:** 6.6" overall. **Stocks:** Checkered black

composite. **Sights:** Blade front, rear adjustable for windage. Optional Siglite night sights. **Features:** SA/DA or DAO; blackened stainless steel slide, aluminum alloy frame. Introduced 1996. Made in U.S. by SIGARMS, Inc.

Price: SA/DA or DAO	$595.00
Price: SA/DA or DAO with Siglite night sights	$690.00
Price: Two-tone finish	$640.00
Price: Two-tone finish, Siglite sights	$735.00

SMITH & WESSON MODEL 22A SPORT PISTOL

Caliber: 22 LR, 10-shot magazine. **Barrel:** 4", 5-1/2", 7". **Weight:** 29 oz. **Length:** 8" overall. **Stocks:** Two-piece polymer. **Sights:** Patridge front, fully adjustable rear. **Features:** Comes with a sight bridge with Weaver-style integral optics mount; alloy frame; .312" serrated trigger; stainless steel slide and barrel with matte blue finish. Introduced 1997. Made in U.S. by Smith & Wesson.

Price: 4"	$230.00
Price: 5-1/2"	$255.00
Price: 7"	$289.00

SMITH & WESSON MODEL 457 TDA AUTO PISTOL

Caliber: 45 ACP, 7-shot magazine. **Barrel:** 3-3/4". **Weight:** 29 oz. **Length:** 7-1/4" overall. **Stocks:** One-piece Xenoy, wrap-around with straight backstrap. **Sights:** Post front, fixed rear, three-dot system. **Features:** Aluminum alloy frame, matte blue carbon steel slide; bobbed hammer; smooth trigger. Introduced 1996. Made in U.S. by Smith & Wesson.

Price: $515.00

SMITH & WESSON MODEL 908 AUTO PISTOL

Caliber: 9mm Para., 8-shot magazine. **Barrel:** 3-1/2". **Weight:** 26 oz. **Length:** 6-13/16". **Stocks:** One-piece Xenoy, wrap-around with straight backstrap. **Sights:** Post front, fixed rear, three-dot system. **Features:** Aluminum alloy frame, matte blue carbon steel slide; bobbed hammer; smooth trigger. Introduced 1996. Made in U.S. by Smith & Wesson.

Price: $466.00

SMITH & WESSON 9mm RECON AUTO PISTOL MODEL

Caliber: 9mm Para. **Barrel:** 3-1/2". **Weight:** 27 oz. **Length:** 7" overall. **Stocks:** Hogue wrap-around, finger-groove rubber. **Sights:** Three-dot Novak Low Mount, drift adjustable. **Features:** Traditional double-action mechanism. Tuned action, hand-crowned muzzle, polished feed ramp, hand-lapped slide, spherical barrel bushing. Checkered frontstrap. Introduced 1999. Made by U.S. by Smith & Wesson.

Price: $1,150.00

Smith & Wesson 4013 TSW

Smith & Wesson 3913 Ladysmith

SMITH & WESSON MODEL 2213, 2214 SPORTSMAN AUTOS

Caliber: 22 LR, 8-shot magazine. **Barrel:** 3". **Weight:** 18 oz. **Length:** 6-1/8" overall. **Stocks:** Checkered black polymer. **Sights:** Patridge front, fixed rear; three-dot system. **Features:** Internal hammer; serrated trigger; single action. Model 2213 is stainless with alloy frame, Model 2214 is blued carbon steel with alloy frame. Introduced 1990. Made in U.S. by Smith & Wesson.
Price: Model 2213. . . . . $340.00
Price: Model 2214. . . . . $292.00

SMITH & WESSON MODEL 4013, 4053 TSW AUTOS

Caliber: 40 S&W, 9-shot magazine. **Barrel:** 3-1/2". **Weight:** 26.4 oz. **Length:** 6-7/8" overall. **Stocks:** Xenoy one-piece wrap-around. **Sights:** Novak three-dot system. **Features:** Traditional double-action system; stainless slide, alloy frame; fixed barrel bushing; ambidextrous decocker; reversible magazine catch. Introduced 1997. Made in U.S. by Smith & Wesson.
Price: Model 4013 TSW $823.00
Price: Model 4053 TSW, double-action-only $823.00

Smith & Wesson Model 22S Sport Pistols

Similar to the Model 22A Sport except with stainless steel frame. Available only with 5-1/2" or 7" barrel. Introduced 1997. Made in U.S. by Smith & Wesson.
Price: 5-1/2" standard barrel. $312.00
Price: 5-1/2" bull barrel, wood target stocks with thumbrest. $379.00
Price: 7" standard barrel. $344.00
Price: 5-1/2" bull barrel, two-piece target stocks with thumbrest . . $353.00

SMITH & WESSON MODEL 410 DA AUTO PISTOL

Caliber: 40 S&W, 10-shot magazine. **Barrel:** 4". **Weight:** 28.5 oz. **Length:** 7.5 oz. **Stocks:** One-piece Xenoy, wrap-around with straight backstrap. **Sights:** Post front, fixed rear; three-dot system. **Features:** Aluminum alloy frame; blued carbon steel slide; traditional double action with left-side slide-mounted decocking lever. Introduced 1996. Made in U.S. by Smith & Wesson.
Price: $515.00

SMITH & WESSON MODEL 910 DA AUTO PISTOL

Caliber: 9mm Para., 10-shot magazine. **Barrel:** 4". **Weight:** 28 oz. **Length:** 7-3/8" overall. **Stocks:** One-piece Xenoy, wrap-around with straight backstrap. **Sights:** Post front with white dot, fixed two-dot rear. **Features:** Alloy frame, blue carbon steel slide. Slide-mounted decocking lever. Introduced 1995.
Price: Model 910. . . . . $466.00

SMITH & WESSON MODEL 3913 TRADITIONAL DOUBLE ACTION

Caliber: 9mm Para., 8-shot magazine. **Barrel:** 3-1/2". **Weight:** 26 oz. **Length:** 6-13/16" overall. **Stocks:** One-piece Delrin wrap-around, tex-

Smith & Wesson 3913 TSW

tured surface. **Sights:** Post front with white dot, Novak LoMount Carry with two dots, adjustable for windage. **Features:** Aluminum alloy frame, stainless slide (M3913) or blue steel slide (M3914). Bobbed hammer with no half-cock notch; smooth .304" trigger with rounded edges. Straight backstrap. Extra magazine included. Introduced 1989.
Price: $662.00

Smith & Wesson Model 3913-LS LadySmith Auto

Similar to the standard Model 3913 except has frame that is upswept at the front, rounded trigger guard. Comes in frosted stainless steel with matching gray grips. Grips are ergonomically correct for a woman's hand. Novak LoMount Carry rear sight adjustable for windage, smooth edges for snag resistance. Extra magazine included. Introduced 1990.
Price: $692.00

Smith & Wesson Model 3953 DAO Pistol

Same as the Model 3913 except double-action-only. Model 3953 has stainless slide with alloy frame. Overall length 7"; weighs 25.5 oz. Extra magazine included. Introduced 1990.
Price: $662.00

Smith & Wesson Model 3913TSW/3953TSW Auto Pistols

Similar to the Model 3913 and 3953 except TSW guns have tighter tolerances, ambidextrous manual safety/decocking lever, flush-fit magazine, delayed-unlock firing system; magazine disconnector. Compact alloy frame, stainless steel slide. Straight backstrap. Introduced 1998. Made in U.S. by Smith & Wesson.
Price: Single action/double action $694.00
Price: Double action only $694.00

Smith & Wesson 4506

Smith & Wesson 4553 TSW

Smith & Wesson Sigma SW40V

SMITH & WESSON MODEL 4006 TDA AUTO

Caliber: 40 S&W, 10-shot magazine. **Barrel:** 4". **Weight:** 38.5 oz. **Length:** 7-7/8" overall. **Stocks:** Xenoy wrap-around with checkered panels. **Sights:** Replaceable post front with white dot, Novak LoMount Carry fixed rear with two white dots, or micro. click adjustable rear with two white dots. **Features:** Stainless steel construction with non-reflective finish. Straight back-strap. Extra magazine included. Introduced 1990.

Price: With adjustable sights $822.00
Price: With fixed sight. $791.00
Price: With fixed night sights $906.00

Smith & Wesson Model 4043, 4046 DA Pistols

Similar to the Model 4006 except is double-action-only. Has a semi-bobbed hammer, smooth trigger, 4" barrel; Novak LoMount Carry rear sight, post front with white dot. Overall length is 7-1/2", weighs 28 oz. Model 4043 has alloy frame. Extra magazine included. Introduced 1991.

Price: Model 4043 (alloy frame) $772.00
Price: Model 4046 (stainless frame). $791.00
Price: Model 4046 with fixed night sights $906.00

SMITH & WESSON MODEL 4500 SERIES AUTOS

Caliber: 45 ACP, 8-shot magazine. **Barrel:** 5" (M4506). **Weight:** 41 oz. (4506). **Length:** 8-1/2" overall. **Stocks:** Xenoy one-piece wrap-around, arched or straight backstrap. **Sights:** Post front with white dot, adjustable or fixed Novak LoMount Carry on M4506. **Features:** M4506 has serrated hammer spur. All have two magazines. Contact Smith & Wesson for complete data. Introduced 1989.

Price: Model 4506, fixed sight $822.00
Price: Model 4506, adjustable sight $855.00
Price: Model 4566 (stainless, 4-1/4", traditional DA, ambidextrous safety, fixed sight). $822.00
Price: Model 4586 (stainless, 4-1/4", DA only) $822.00

SMITH & WESSON MODEL 4513TSW/4553TSW PISTOLS

Caliber: 45 ACP, 6-shot magazine. **Barrel:** 3-3/4". **Weight:** 28 oz. (M4513TSW). **Length:** 6-7/8 overall. **Stocks:** Checkered Xenoy; straight backstrap. **Sights:** White dot front, Novak Lo Mount Carry 2-Dot rear. **Features:** Model 4513TSW is traditional double action, Model 4553TSW is double action only. TSW series has tighter tolerances, ambidextrous manual safety/decocking lever, flush-fit magazine, delayed-unlock firing system; magazine disconnector. Compact alloy frame, stainless steel slide. Introduced 1998. Made in U.S. by Smith & Wesson.

Price: Model 4513TSW. $781.00
Price: Model 4553TSW. $781.00

SMITH & WESSON MODEL 5900 SERIES AUTO PISTOLS

Caliber: 9mm Para., 10-shot magazine. **Barrel:** 4". **Weight:** 28-1/2 to 37-1/2 oz. (fixed sight); 38 oz. (adjustable sight). **Length:** 7-1/2" overall. **Stocks:** Xenoy wrap-around with curved backstrap. **Sights:** Post front

with white dot, fixed or fully adjustable with two white dots. **Features:** All stainless, stainless and alloy or carbon steel and alloy construction. Smooth .304" trigger, .260" serrated hammer. Introduced 1989.

Price: Model 5906 (stainless, traditional DA, adjustable sight, ambidextrous safety) $788.00
Price: As above, fixed sight $751.00
Price: With fixed night sights $866.00
Price: Model 5946 DAO (as above, stainless frame and slide) . . $751.00

SMITH & WESSON ENHANCED SIGMA SERIES PISTOLS

Caliber: 9mm Para., 40 S&W, 10-shot magazine. **Barrel:** 4". **Weight:** 26 oz. **Length:** 7.4" overall. **Stocks:** Integral. **Sights:** White dot front, fixed rear; three-dot system. Tritium night sights available. **Features:** Ergonomic polymer frame; low barrel centerline; internal striker firing system; corrosion-resistant slide; Teflon-filled, electroless-nickel coated magazine. Introduced 1994. Made in U.S. by Smith & Wesson.

Price: SW9E, 9mm, 4" barrel, black finish, fixed sights $602.00
Price: SW9VE, 9mm, 4" barrel, satin stainless, fixed night sights $409.00
Price: SW40E, 40 S&W, 4" barrel, black finish, fixed sights. $602.00
Price: SW40VE, 40 S&W, 4" barrel, black polymer, fixed sights . $409.00

SMITH & WESSON SIGMA SW380 AUTO

Caliber: 380 ACP, 6-shot magazine. **Barrel:** 3". **Weight:** 14 oz. **Length:** 5.8" overall. **Stocks:** Integral. **Sights:** Fixed groove in the slide. **Features:** Polymer frame; double-action-only trigger mechanism; grooved/serrated front and rear straps; two passive safeties. Introduced 1995. Made in U.S. by Smith & Wesson.

Price: $328.00

Springfield 1911-A1 Standard **Springfield TRP** **Springfield N.R.A. PPC**

Smith & Wesson Model 6906 Double-Action Auto

Similar to the Model 5906 except with 3-1/2" barrel, 10-shot magazine, fixed rear sight, .260" bobbed hammer. Extra magazine included. Introduced 1989.

Price: Model 6906, stainless. **$720.00**
Price: Model 6906 with fixed night sights **$836.00**
Price: Model 6946 (stainless, DA only, fixed sights). **$720.00**

SMITH & WESSON MODEL CS9 CHIEFS SPECIAL AUTO

NEW! **Caliber:** 9mm Para., 7-shot magazine. **Barrel:** 3". **Weight:** 20.8 oz. **Length:** 6-1/4" overall. **Stocks:** Hogue wrap-around rubber. **Sights:** White dot front, fixed two-dot rear. **Features:** Traditional double-action trigger mechanism. Alloy frame, stainless or blued slide. Introduced 1999. Made in U.S. by Smith & Wesson.

Price: Blue or stainless. **$593.00**

Smith & Wesson Model CS40 Chiefs Special Auto

NEW! Similar to the CS9 except chambered for 40 S&W (7-shot magazine), has 3-1/4" barrel, weighs 24.2 oz., and measures 6-1/2" overall. Introduced 1999. Made in U.S. by Smith & Wesson.

Price: Blue or stainless. **$624.00**

Smith & Wesson Model CS45 Chiefs Special Auto

NEW! Similar to the CS40 except chambered for 45 ACP, 6-shot magazine, weighs 23.9 oz. Introduced 1999. Made in U.S. by Smith & Wesson.

Price: Blue or stainless. **$624.00**

SPRINGFIELD, INC. 1911A1 AUTO PISTOL

Caliber: 9mm Para., 9-shot; 38 Super, 9-shot; 45 ACP, 8-shot. **Barrel:** 5". **Weight:** 35.6 oz. **Length:** 8-5/8" overall. **Stocks:** Checkered plastic or walnut. **Sights:** Fixed three-dot system. **Features:** Beveled magazine well; lowered and flared ejection port. All forged parts, including frame, barrel, slide. All new production. Introduced 1990. From Springfield, Inc.

Price: Mil-Spec 45 ACP, Parkerized. **$519.00**
Price: Standard, 45 ACP, blued **$549.00**
Price: Standard, 45 ACP, stainless **$589.00**
Price: Lightweight (28.6 oz., matte finish). **$549.00**

Price: Standard, 9mm, 38 Super, blued **$549.00**
Price: Standard, 9mm, stainless steel **$599.00**

Springfield, Inc. N.R.A. PPC Pistol

Specifically designed to comply with NRA rules for PPC competition. Has custom slide-to-frame fit; polished feed ramp; throated barrel; total internal honing; tuned extractor; recoil buffer system; fully checkered walnut grips; two fitted magazines; factory test target; custom carrying case. Introduced 1995. From Springfield, Inc.

Price: **$1,469.00**

Springfield, Inc. TRP Pistols

Similar to the 1911A1 except 45 ACP only; has checkered front strap and mainspring housing; Novak combat rear sight and matching dovetailed front sight; tuned, polished extractor; oversize barrel link; lightweight speed trigger and combat action job; match barrel and bushing; extended ambidextrous thumb safety and fitted beavertail grip safety; Carry bevel on entire pistol; checkered cocobolo wood grips; comes with two Wilson 8-shot magazines. Frame is engraved "Tactical," both sides of frame with "TRP." Introduced 1998. From Springfield, Inc.

Price: Standard with Armory Kote finish. **$1,160.00**
Price: Standard, stainless steel **$1,160.00**
Price: Champion, Armory Kote. **$1,175.00**

Springfield, Inc. 1911A1 High Capacity Pistol

Similar to the Standard 1911A1 except available in 45 ACP with 10-shot magazine. Has Commander-style hammer, walnut grips, beveled magazine well, plastic carrying case. Introduced 1993. From Springfield, Inc.

Price: Mil-Spec 45 ACP **$659.00**
Price: 45 ACP Factory Comp **$1,075.00**
Price: 45 ACP Compact, Ultra **$689.00**
Price: As above, stainless steel **$759.00**

Springfield, Inc. 1911A1 Custom Carry Gun

Similar to the standard 1911A1 except has Novak low-mount sights, Videki speed trigger, match barrel and bushing; extended thumb safety, beavertail grip safety; beveled, polished magazine well, polished feed ramp

Springfield Ultra Compact V10

Taurus PT 22/PT 25

Stoeger American Eagle Luger

Taurus 92B

and throated barrel; match Commander hammer and sear, tuned extractor; lowered and flared ejection port; recoil buffer system, full-length spring guide rod; walnut grips. Comes with two magazines with slam pads, plastic carrying case. Available in all popular calibers. Introduced 1992. From Springfield, Inc.
Price: **$1,299.00**

Springfield, Inc. 1911A1 Factory Comp
Similar to the standard 1911A1 except comes with bushing-type dual-port compensator, adjustable rear sight, extended thumb safety, Videki speed trigger, and beveled magazine well. Checkered walnut grips standard. Available in 45 ACP, blue only. Introduced 1992.
Price: 45 ACP... **$947.00**

Springfield, Inc. 1911A1 Champion Pistol
Similar to the standard 1911A1 except slide is 4.025". Has low-profile three-dot sight system. Comes with skeletonized hammer and walnut stocks. Available in 45 ACP only; Parkerized or stainless. Introduced 1989.
Price: Parkerized **$549.00**
Price: Stainless....................................... **$579.00**
Price: Mil-Spec.. **$519.00**

Springfield, Inc. V10 Ultra Compact Pistol
Similar to the 1911A1 Compact except has shorter slide, 3.5" barrel, recoil reducing compensator built into the barrel and slide. Beavertail grip safety, beveled magazine well, "hi-viz" combat sights, Videki speed trigger, flared ejection port, stainless steel frame, blued slide, match grade barrel, walnut grips. Introduced 1996. From Springfield, Inc.
Price: V10 45 ACP **$675.00**
Price: Ultra Compact (no compensator), 45 ACP............ **$629.00**

STOEGER AMERICAN EAGLE LUGER
Caliber: 9mm Para., 7-shot magazine. **Barrel:** 4", 6". **Weight:** 32 oz. **Length:** 9.6" overall. **Stocks:** Checkered walnut. **Sights:** Blade front,

fixed rear. **Features:** Recreation of the American Eagle Luger pistol in stainless steel. Chamber loaded indicator. Introduced 1994. From Stoeger Industries.
Price: 4", or 6" Navy Model **$720.00**
Price: With matte black finish........................... **$798.00**

TAURUS MODEL PT 22/PT 25 AUTO PISTOLS
Caliber: 22 LR, 9-shot (PT 22); 25 ACP, 8-shot (PT 25). **Barrel:** 2.75". **Weight:** 12.3 oz. **Length:** 5.25" overall. **Stocks:** Smooth rosewood. **Sights:** Blade front, fixed rear. **Features:** Double action. Tip-up barrel for loading, cleaning. Blue or stainless. Introduced 1992. Made in U.S. by Taurus International.
Price: 22 LR or 25 ACP, blue, nickel or with duo-tone finish
with rosewood grips **$203.00**
Price: 22 LR or 25 ACP, blue with gold trim, rosewood grips.... **$219.00**
Price: 22 LR or 25 ACP, blue, nickel or duo-tone finish with checkered
wood grips **$180.00**

TAURUS MODEL PT 92B AUTO PISTOL
Caliber: 9mm Para., 15-shot magazine. **Barrel:** 4.92". **Weight:** 34 oz. **Length:** 8.54" overall. **Stocks:** Black rubber. **Sights:** Fixed notch rear. Three-dot sight system. **Features:** Double action, exposed hammer, chamber loaded indicator, ambidextrous safety, inertia firing pin. Imported by Taurus International.
Price: Blue **$508.00**
Price: Stainless steel **$523.00**

Taurus Model PT 99AF Auto Pistol
Similar to the PT-92 except has fully adjustable rear sight, smooth Brazilian walnut stocks and is available in stainless steel or polished blue. Introduced 1983.
Price: Blue **$531.00**
Price: Stainless steel **$547.00**

Taurus PT-911   Taurus PT 945   Taurus PT-957   Taurus PT-938

TAURUS MODEL PT-111 MILLENNIUM AUTO PISTOL

Caliber: 9mm Para., 10-shot magazine. **Barrel:** 3.30". **Weight:** 19 oz. **Length:** 6.0" overall. **Stocks:** Polymer. **Sights:** Fixed. Low profile, three-dot combat. **Features:** Double action only. Firing pin lock; polymer frame; striker fired; push-button magazine release. Introduced 1998. Imported by Taurus International.
Price: Blue $367.00
Price: Stainless. $383.00

TAURUS MODEL PT-911 AUTO PISTOL

Caliber: 9mm Para., 10-shot magazine. **Barrel:** 3.85". **Weight:** 28.2 oz. **Length:** 7.05" overall. **Stocks:** Black rubber. **Sights:** Fixed. Low profile, three-dot combat. **Features:** Double action, exposed hammer; ambidextrous hammer drop; chamber loaded indicator. Introduced 1997. Imported by Taurus International.
Price: Blue $453.00
Price: Stainless. $469.00

NEW! Taurus Model PT-138 Auto Pistol

Similar to the PT-911 except chambered for 380 ACP, with 10-shot magazine. Double-action-only mechanism. Has black polymer frame with blue or stainless slide. Introduced 1999. Imported by Taurus International.
Price: Blue $367.00
Price: Stainless. $383.00

TAURUS MODEL PT-945 AUTO PISTOL

Caliber: 45 ACP, 8-shot magazine. **Barrel:** 4.25". **Weight:** 29.5 oz. **Length:** 7.48" overall. **Stocks:** Black rubber. **Sights:** Drift-adjustable front and rear; three-dot system. **Features:** Double-action mechanism. Has manual ambidextrous hammer drop safety, intercept notch, firing pin block, chamber loaded indicator, last-shot hold-open. Introduced 1995. Imported by Taurus International.
Price: Blue $484.00
Price: Stainless. $500.00
Price: Blue, ported $523.00
Price: Stainless, ported. $539.00

Taurus Model PT-400 Auto Pistol

Similar to the PT-945 except chambered for 400 Cor-Bon cartridge. Conventional DA operation with exposed hammer, loaded chamber indicator, three-position safety. Ported barrel/slide. Introduced 1999. Imported by Taurus International.
Price: Blue $523.00
Price: Stainless. $539.00

TAURUS MODEL PT-957 AUTO PISTOL

Caliber: 357 SIG, 10-shot magazine. **Barrel:** 3 5/8". **Weight:** 28 oz. **Length:** 7" overall. **Stocks:** Checkered rubber. **Sights:** Fixed, low profile, three-dot combat. **Features:** Double action mechanism; exposed hammer; ported barrel/slide; three-position safety with decocking lever and ambidextrous safety. Introduced 1999. Imported by Taurus International.
Price: Blue $508.00
Price: Stainless. $523.00

TAURUS MODEL PT-938 AUTO PISTOL

Caliber: 380 ACP, 10-shot magazine. **Barrel:** 3.72". **Weight:** 27 oz. **Length:** 6.75" overall. **Stocks:** Black rubber. **Sights:** Fixed. Low profile, three-dot combat. **Features:** Double-action only. Chamber loaded indicator; firing pin block; ambidextrous hammer drop. Introduced 1997. Imported by Taurus International.
Price: Blue $453.00
Price: Stainless. $469.00

TAURUS MODEL PT-940 AUTO PISTOL

Caliber: 40 S&W, 10-shot magazine. **Barrel:** 3.35". **Weight:** 28.2 oz. **Length:** 7.05" overall. **Stocks:** Black rubber. **Sights:** Drift-adjustable front and rear; three-dot combat. **Features:** Double action, exposed hammer; manual ambidextrous hammer-drop; inertia firing pin; chamber loaded indicator. Introduced 1996. Imported by Taurus International.
Price: Blue $469.00
Price: Stainless steel $484.00

Taurus PT-940

Walther PP

Walther PPK/S

VEKTOR SP1 SPORT PISTOL

Caliber: 9mm Para., 10-shot magazine. **Barrel:** 5″. **Weight:** 38 oz. **Length:** 9 3/8″ overall. **Stocks:** Checkered black composition. **Sights:** Combat-type blade front, adjustable rear. **Features:** Single action only with adjustable trigger stop; three-chamber compensator; extended magazine release. Introduced 1999. Imported from South Africa by Vektor USA.
Price: **$729.95**

Vektor SP1 Tuned Sport Pistol

Similar to the Vektor Sport except has fully adjustable straight trigger, LPA three-dot sight system, and hard nickel finish. Introduced 1999. Imported from South Africa by Vektor USA.
Price: **$1,199.95**

VEKTOR SP1 Target Pistol

Similar to the Vektor Sport except has 5 7/8" barrel without compensator; weighs 40-1/2 oz.; has fully adjustable straight match trigger; black slide, bright frame. Introduced 1999. Imported from South Africa by Vektor USA.
Price: **$1,239.95**

Vektor SP1, SP2 Ultra Sport Pistols

Similar to the Vektor Target except has three-chamber compensator with three jet ports; strengthened frame with integral beavertail; lightweight polymer scope mount (Weaver rail). Overall length is 11", weighs 41-1/2 oz. Model SP2 is in 40 S&W. Introduced 1999. Imported from South Africa by Vektor USA.
Price: SP1 (9mm) **$2,149.95**
Price: SP2 (40 S&W) **$2,149.95**

VEKTOR SP1 AUTO PISTOL

Caliber: 9mm Para., 40 S&W (SP2), 10-shot magazine. **Barrel:** 4-5/8″. **Weight:** 35 oz. **Length:** 8-1/4″ overall. **Stocks:** Checkered black composition. **Sights:** Combat-type fixed. **Features:** Alloy frame, steel slide; traditional double-action mechanism; matte black finish. Introduced 1999. Imported from South Africa by Vektor USA.
Price: SP1 (9mm) **$599.95**
Price: SP1 with nickel finish **$629.95**
Price: SP2 (40 S&W) **$599.95**

Vektor SP1, SP2 Compact General's Model Pistol

Similar to the 9mm Para. Vektor SP1 except has 4" barrel, weighs 31-1/2 oz., and is 7-1/2" overall. Recoil operated. Traditional double-action mechanism. SP2 model is chambered for 40 S&W. Introduced 1999. Imported from South Africa by Vektor USA.
Price: SP1 (9mm Para.) **$649.95**
Price: SP2 (40 S&W) **$649.95**

VEKTOR CP-1 COMPACT PISTOL

Caliber: 9mm Para., 10-shot magazine. **Barrel:** 4″. **Weight:** 25.4 oz. **Length:** 7″ overall. **Stocks:** Textured polymer. **Sights:** Blade front adjust-able for windage, fixed rear; adjustable sight optional. **Features:** Ergonomic grip frame shape; stainless steel barrel; delayed gas-buffered blowback action. Introduced 1999. Imported from South Africa by Vektor USA.
Price: With black slide **$479.95**
Price: With nickel slide **$499.95**
Price: With black slide, adjustable sight **$509.95**
Price: With nickel slide, adjustable sight **$529.95**

WALTHER PP AUTO PISTOL

Caliber: 380 ACP, 7-shot magazine. **Barrel:** 3.86″. **Weight:** 23-1/2 oz. **Length:** 6.7″ overall. **Stocks:** Checkered plastic. **Sights:** Fixed, white markings. **Features:** Double action; manual safety blocks firing pin and drops hammer; chamber loaded indicator on 32 and 380; extra finger rest magazine provided. Imported from Germany by Carl Walther USA.
Price: 380 . . . . **$999.00**

Walther PPK/S American Auto Pistol

Similar to Walther PP except made entirely in the United States. Has 3.27″ barrel with 6.1″ length overall. Introduced 1980.
Price: 380 ACP only, blue **$540.00**
Price: As above, 32 ACP or 380 ACP, stainless **$540.00**

Walther PPK American Auto Pistol

Similar to Walther PPK/S except weighs 21 oz., has 6-shot capacity. Made in the U.S. Introduced 1986.
Price: Stainless, 32 ACP or 380 ACP. **$540.00**
Price: Blue, 380 ACP only **$540.00**

WALTHER MODEL TPH AUTO PISTOL

Caliber: 22 LR, 25 ACP, 6-shot magazine. **Barrel:** 2-1/4″. **Weight:** 14 oz. **Length:** 5-3/8″ overall. **Stocks:** Checkered black composition. **Sights:** Blade front, rear drift-adjustable for windage. **Features:** Made of stainless steel. Scaled-down version of the Walther PP/PPK series. Made in U.S. Introduced 1987. From Carl Walther USA.
Price: Blue or stainless steel, 22 or 25 . . . . **$440.00**

Walther PPK   Walther P99   Walther TPH   Wilkinson Sherry

WALTHER P88 COMPACT PISTOL
Caliber: 9mm Para., 10-shot magazine. **Barrel:** 3.93″. **Weight:** 28 oz. **Length:** NA. **Stocks:** Checkered black polymer. **Sights:** Blade front, drift adjustable rear. **Features:** Double action with ambidextrous decocking lever and magazine release; alloy frame; loaded chamber indicator; matte blue finish. Imported from Germany by Carl Walther USA.
Price: **$900.00**

WALTHER P99 AUTO PISTOL
Caliber: 9mm Para., 9x21, 40 S&W, 10-shot magazine. **Barrel:** 4″. **Weight:** 25 oz. **Length:** 7″ overall. **Stocks:** Textured polymer. **Sights:** Blade front (comes with three interchangeable blades for elevation adjustment), micrometer rear adjustable for windage. **Features:** Double-action mechanism with trigger safety, decock safety, internal striker safety; chamber loaded indicator; ambidextrous magazine release levers; polymer frame with interchangeable backstrap inserts. Comes with two magazines. Introduced 1997. Imported from Germany by Carl Walther USA.
Price: **$799.00**

Walther P990 Auto Pistol
NEW! Similar to the P99 except is double action only. Available in blue or silver tenifer finish. Introduced 1999. Imported from Germany by Carl Walther USA.
Price: **$749.00**

WALTHER P-5 AUTO PISTOL
Caliber: 9mm Para., 8-shot magazine. **Barrel:** 3.62″. **Weight:** 28 oz. **Length:** 7.10″ overall. **Stocks:** Checkered plastic. **Sights:** Blade front, adjustable rear. **Features:** Uses the basic Walther P-38 double-action mechanism. Blue finish. Imported from Germany by Carl Walther USA.
Price: **$900.00**

WILKINSON SHERRY AUTO PISTOL
Caliber: 22 LR, 8-shot magazine. **Barrel:** 2-1/8″. **Weight:** 9-1/4 oz. **Length:** 4-3/8″ overall. **Stocks:** Checkered black plastic. **Sights:** Fixed, groove. **Features:** Cross-bolt safety locks the sear into the hammer. Available in all blue finish or blue slide and trigger with gold frame. Introduced 1985.
Price: **$195.00**

WILKINSON LINDA AUTO PISTOL
Caliber: 9mm Para. **Barrel:** 8-5/16″. **Weight:** 4 lbs., 13 oz. **Length:** 12-1/4″ overall. **Stocks:** Checkered black plastic pistol grip, walnut forend. **Sights:** Protected blade front, aperture rear. **Features:** Fires from closed bolt. Semi-auto only. Straight blowback action. Cross-bolt safety. Removable barrel. From Wilkinson Arms.
Price: **$533.33**

Includes models suitable for several forms of competition and other sporting purposes.

Baer 1911 Ultimate Master

Beretta Model 89

Baer 1911 Bullseye Wadcutter

Beretta Model 96 Combat

BAER 1911 ULTIMATE MASTER COMBAT PISTOL

Caliber: 9x23, 38 Super, 400 Cor-Bon 45 ACP (others available), 10-shot magazine. **Barrel:** 5″, 6″; Baer NM. **Weight:** 37 oz. **Length:** 8.5″ overall. **Stocks:** Checkered rosewood. **Sights:** Baer dovetail front, low-mount Bo-Mar rear with hidden leaf. **Features:** Full-house competition gun. Baer forged NM blued steel frame and double serrated slide; Baer triple port, tapered cone compensator; fitted slide to frame; lowered, flared ejection port; Baer reverse recoil plug; full-length guide rod; recoil buff; beveled magazine well; Baer Commander hammer, sear; Baer extended ambidextrous safety, extended ejector, checkered slide stop, beavertail grip safety with pad, extended magazine release button; Baer speed trigger. Made in U.S. by Les Baer Custom, Inc.

Price: Compensated, open sights.	**$2,560.00**
Price: 6″ Model 400 Cor-Bon	**$2,590.00**
Price: Compensated, with Baer optics mount.	**$3,195.00**

Baer 1911 Ultimate Master Steel Special Pistol

Similar to the Ultimate Master except chambered for 38 Super with supported chamber (other calibers available), lighter slide, bushing-type compensator; two-piece guide rod. Designed for maximum 150 power factor. Comes without sights—scope and mount only. Hard chrome finish. Made in U.S. by Les Baer Custom, Inc.

Price:	**$2,980.00**

BAER 1911 NATIONAL MATCH HARDBALL PISTOL

Caliber: 45 ACP, 7-shot magazine. **Barrel:** 5″. **Weight:** 37 oz. **Length:** 8.5″ overall. **Stocks:** Checkered walnut. **Sights:** Baer dovetail front with undercut post, low-mount Bo-Mar rear with hidden leaf. **Features:** Baer NM forged steel frame, double serrated slide and barrel with stainless bushing; slide fitted to frame; Baer match trigger with 4-lb. pull; polished feed ramp, throated barrel; checkered front strap, arched mainspring housing; Baer beveled magazine well; lowered, flared ejection port; tuned extractor; Baer extended ejector, checkered slide stop; recoil buff. Made in U.S. by Les Baer Custom, Inc.

Price:	**$1,335.00**

Baer 1911 Bullseye Wadcutter Pistol

Similar to the National Match Hardball except designed for wadcutter loads only. Has polished feed ramp and barrel throat; Bo-Mar rib on slide; full-length recoil rod; Baer speed trigger with 3-1/2-lb. pull; Baer deluxe hammer and sear; Baer beavertail grip safety with pad; flat mainspring housing checkered 20 lpi. Blue finish; checkered walnut grips. Made in U.S. by Les Baer Custom, Inc.

Price: From.	**$1,495.00**
Price: With 6″ barrel, from	**$1,690.00**

BERETTA MODEL 89 GOLD STANDARD PISTOL

Caliber: 22 LR, 8-shot magazine. **Barrel:** 6″. **Weight:** 41 oz. **Length:** 9.5″ overall. **Stocks:** Target-type walnut with thumbrest. **Sights:** Interchangeable blade front, fully adjustable rear. **Features:** Single action target pistol. Matte black, Bruniton finish. Imported from Italy by Beretta U.S.A.

Price:	**$771.00**

BERETTA MODEL 96 COMBAT PISTOL

Caliber: 40 S&W, 10-shot magazine. **Barrel:** 4.9″ (5.9″ with weight). **Weight:** 34.4 oz. **Length:** 8.5″ overall. **Stocks:** Checkered black plastic. **Sights:** Blade front, fully adjustable target rear. **Features:** Uses heavier Brigadier slide with front and rear serrations; extended frame-mounted safety; extended, reversible magazine release; single-action-only with competition-tuned trigger with extra-short let-off and over-travel adjustment. Comes with tool kit. Introduced 1997. Imported from Italy by Beretta U.S.A.

Price:	**$1,593.00**
Price: 4.9" barrel.	**$1,341.00**
Price: 5.9" barrel.	**$1,634.00**
Price: Combo	**$1,599.00**

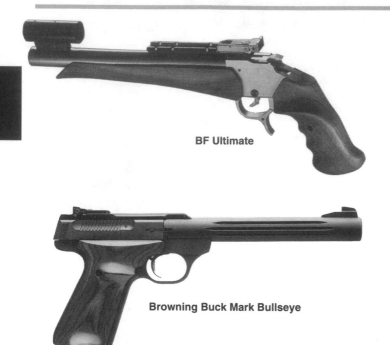

BF Ultimate

Browning Buck Mark Target 5.5

Browning Buck Mark Bullseye

Colt Gold Cup Trophy

Colt National Match

Beretta Model 96 Stock Pistol

Similar to the Model 96 Combat except is single/double action, with half-cock notch. Has front and rear slide serrations, rubber magazine bumper, replaceable accurizing barrel bushing, ultra-thin fine-checkered grips (aluminum optional), checkered front and back straps, radiused back strap, fitted case. Weighs 35 oz., 8.5″ overall. Introduced 1997. Imported from Italy by Beretta U.S.A.

Price: $1,407.00

BF ULTIMATE SINGLE SHOT PISTOL

Caliber: 7mm U.S., 22 LR Match and 100 other chamberings. **Barrel:** 10.75" Heavy Match Grade with 11° target crown. **Weight:** 3 lbs., 15 oz. **Length:** 16" overall. **Stocks:** Thumbrest target style. **Sights:** Bo-Mar/Bond ScopeRib I Combo with hooded post front adjustable for height and width, rear notch available in .032", .062", .080" and .100" widths; 1/2-MOA clicks. **Features:** Designed to meet maximum rules for IHMSA Production Gun. Falling block action gives rigid barrel-receiver mating. Hand fitted and headspaced. Etched receiver; gold-colored trigger. Introduced 1988. Made in U.S. by E.A. Brown Mfg.

Price: $895.00

BROWNING BUCK MARK SILHOUETTE

Caliber: 22 LR, 10-shot magazine. **Barrel:** 9-7/8″. **Weight:** 53 oz. **Length:** 14″ overall. **Stocks:** Smooth walnut stocks and forend, or finger-groove walnut. **Sights:** Post-type hooded front adjustable for blade width and height; Pro Target rear fully adjustable for windage and elevation. **Features:** Heavy barrel with .900″ diameter; 12-1/2″ sight radius. Special sighting plane forms scope base. Introduced 1987. Made in U.S. From Browning.

Price: $448.00

Browning Buck Mark Target 5.5

Same as the Buck Mark Silhouette except has a 5-1/2″ barrel with .900″ diameter. Has hooded sights mounted on a scope base that accepts an optical or reflex sight. Rear sight is a Browning fully adjustable Pro Target, front sight is an adjustable post that customizes to different widths, and can be adjusted for height. Contoured walnut grips with thumbrest, or finger-groove walnut. Matte blue finish. Overall length is 9-5/8″, weighs 35-1/2 oz. Has 10-shot magazine. Introduced 1990. From Browning.

Price: $425.00
Price: Target 5.5 Gold (as above with gold anodized frame and
top rib) $477.00
Price: Target 5.5 Nickel (as above with nickel frame and top rib) $477.00

Browning Buck Mark Field 5.5

Same as the Target 5.5 except has hoodless ramp-style front sight and low profile rear sight. Matte blue finish, contoured or finger-groove walnut stocks. Introduced 1991.

Price: $425.00

Browning Buck Mark Bullseye

Similar to the Buck Mark Silhouette except has 7-1/4″ heavy barrel with three flutes per side; trigger is adjustable from 2-1/2 to 5 lbs.; specially designed rosewood target or three-finger-groove stocks with competition-style heel rest, or with contoured rubber grip. Overall length is 11-5/16″, weighs 36 oz. Introduced 1996. Made in U.S. From Browning.

Price: With ambidextrous moulded composite stocks $389.00
Price: With rosewood stocks, or wrap-around finger groove $500.00

COLT GOLD CUP TROPHY MK IV/SERIES 80

Caliber: 45 ACP, 8-shot magazine. **Barrel:** 5″, with new design bushing. **Weight:** 39 oz. **Length:** 8-1/2″. **Stocks:** Checkered rubber composite with silver-plated medallion. **Sights:** Patridge-style front, Colt-Elliason rear adjustable for windage and elevation, sight radius 6-3/4″. **Features:** Arched or flat housing; wide, grooved trigger with adjustable stop; ribbed-top slide, hand fitted, with improved ejection port.

Price: Blue . . . . NA
Price: Stainless. . . . . NA

Competitor Single Shot

E.A.A. Witness Gold Team

Fort Worth HST

Fort Worth HSO

COLT NATIONAL MATCH PISTOL

Caliber: 45 ACP, 8-shot magazine. **Barrel:** 5″. **Weight:** 39 oz. **Length:** 8-1/2″ overall. **Stocks:** Double-diamond checkered rosewood. **Sights:** Dovetailed Patridge front, fully adjustable rear; three-dot system. **Features:** Adjustable two-cut aluminum trigger; Defender grip safety; ambidextrous manual safety. Introduced 1999. Made in U.S. by Colt's Mfg., Inc.
Price: .... **NA**

COMPETITOR SINGLE SHOT PISTOL

Caliber: 22 LR through 50 Action Express, including belted magnums. **Barrel:** 14″ standard; 10.5″ silhouette; 16″ optional. **Weight:** About 59 oz. (14″ bbl.). **Length:** 15.12″ overall. **Stocks:** Ambidextrous; synthetic (standard) or laminated or natural wood. **Sights:** Ramp front, adjustable rear. **Features:** Rotary canon-type action cocks on opening; cammed ejector; interchangeable barrels, ejectors. Adjustable single stage trigger, sliding thumb safety and trigger safety. Matte blue finish. Introduced 1988. From Competitor Corp., Inc.
Price: 14″, standard calibers, synthetic grip **$414.95**
Price: Extra barrels, from **$159.95**

CZ 75 CHAMPION COMPETITION PISTOL

Caliber: 9mm Para., 9x21, 40 S&W, 10-shot magazine. **Barrel:** 4.49″. **Weight:** 35 oz. **Length:** 9.44″ overall. **Stocks:** Black rubber. **Sights:** Blade front, fully adjustable rear. **Features:** Single-action trigger mechanism; three-port compensator (40 S&W, 9mm have two port) full-length guide rod; extended magazine release; ambidextrous safety; flared magazine well; fully adjustable match trigger. Introduced 1999. Imported from the Czech Republic by CZ USA.
Price: 9mm Para., 9x21, 40 S&W, dual-tone finish **1,484.00**

CZ 75 ST IPSC AUTO PISTOL

Caliber: 40 S&W, 10-shot magazine. **Barrel:** 5.12″. **Weight:** 2.9 lbs. **Length:** 8.86″ overall. **Stocks:** Checkered walnut. **Sights:** Fully adjustable rear. **Features:** Single-action mechanism; extended slide release and ambidextrous safety; full-length slide rail; double slide serrations. Introduced 1999. Imported from the Czech Republic by CZ-USA.
Price: Dual-tone finish **1,038.00**

E.A.A. WITNESS GOLD TEAM AUTO

Caliber: 9mm Para., 9x21, 38 Super, 40 S&W, 45 ACP. **Barrel:** 5.1″. **Weight:** 41.6 oz. **Length:** 9.6″ overall. **Stocks:** Checkered walnut, competition style. **Sights:** Square post front, fully adjustable rear. **Features:** Triple-chamber cone compensator; competition SA trigger; extended safety and magazine release; competition hammer; beveled magazine well; beavertail grip. Hand-fitted major components. Hard chrome finish. Match-grade barrel. From E.A.A. Custom Shop. Introduced 1992. From European American Armory.
Price: **$2,150.00**

E.A.A. Witness Silver Team Auto

Similar to the Witness Gold Team except has double-chamber compensator, oval magazine release, black rubber grips, double-dip blue finish. Comes with Super Sight and drilled and tapped for scope mount. Built for the intermediate competition shooter. Introduced 1992. From European American Armory Custom Shop.
Price: 9mm Para., 9x21, 38 Super, 40 S&W, 45 ACP **$968.00**

ENTRÉPRISE TOURNAMENT SHOOTER MODEL I

Caliber: 45 ACP, 10-shot magazine. **Barrel:** 6″. **Weight:** 40 oz. **Length:** 8.5″ overall. **Stocks:** Black ultra-slim double diamond checkered synthetic. **Sights:** Dovetailed Patridge front, adjustable Competizione "melded" rear. **Features:** Oversized magazine release button; flared magazine well; fully machined parallel slide rails; front and rear slide serrations; serrated top of slide; stainless ramped bull barrel with fully supported chamber; full-length guide rod with plug; stainless firing pin; match extractor; polished ramp; tuned match extractor; black oxide. Introduced 1998. Made in U.S. by Entréprise Arms.
Price: **$2,000.00**

FAS 607 MATCH PISTOL

Caliber: 22 LR, 5-shot. **Barrel:** 5.6″. **Weight:** 37 oz. **Length:** 11″ overall. **Stocks:** Walnut wrap-around; sizes small, medium, large or adjustable. **Sights:** Match. Blade front, open notch rear fully adjustable for windage and elevation. Sight radius is 8.66″. **Features:** Line of sight is only 11/32″ above centerline of bore; magazine is inserted from top; adjustable and removable trigger mechanism; single lever takedown. Full 5-year warranty. Imported from Italy by Nygord Precision Products.
Price: **$1,175.00**
Price: Model 603 (32 S&W) **$1,175.00**

FORT WORTH HST TARGET PISTOL

Caliber: 22 LR, 10-shot magazine. **Barrel:** 5-1/2″ bull or 7-1/4″ fluted. **Weight:** 44 oz. **Length:** 9.5″ overall. **Stocks:** Checkered hardwood with thumbrest. **Sights:** Undercut ramp front, frame-mounted micro-click rear adjustable for windage and elevation; drilled and tapped for scope mount-

Fort Worth Matchmaster Deluxe

Freedom Arms 252 Silhouette

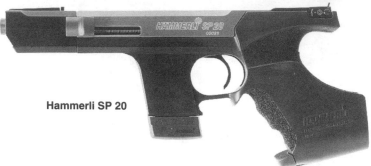

Hammerli SP 20

ing. **Features:** Gold-plated trigger, slide lock, safety-lever and magazine release; stippled front grip and backstrap; adjustable trigger and sear. Barrel weights optional. Introduced 1995. From Fort Worth Firearms.
Price: 5-1/2″ or 71/4″ right-hand $410.95
Price: 5-1/2″ left-hand $451.95

Fort Worth HSC Target Pistol

Same as the HST model except has nickel-plated trigger, slide lock, safety lever, magazine release, and has slightly heavier trigger pull. Has stippled front-grip and backstrap, checkered walnut thumbrest grips, adjustable trigger and sear. Matte finish. Drilled and tapped for scope mount and barrel weight. Introduced 1995. From Fort Worth Firearms.
Price: $388.95

FORT WORTH HSO AUTO PISTOL

Caliber: 22 Short, 10-shot magazine. **Barrel:** 6-3/4″ round tapered, with stabilizer and built-in muzzle brake. **Weight:** 40 oz. **Length:** 11-1/4″. **Stocks:** Checkered walnut with thumbrest. **Sights:** Undercut ramp front, frame-mounted click adjustable square notch rear. Drilled and tapped for scope mount. **Features:** Integral stabilizer with two removable weights. Trigger adjustable for pull and length of travel; stippled front and backstraps; push-button barrel takedown. Introduced 1995. Made in U.S. by Fort Worth Firearms.
Price: $599.95

FORT WORTH HSV TARGET PISTOL

Caliber: 22 LR, 10-shot magazine. **Barrel:** 4-1/2″ or 5-1/2″; push-button takedown. **Weight:** 46 oz. **Length:** 9.5″ overall. **Sights:** Checkered hardwood with thumbrest. **Stocks:** Undercut ramp front, micro-click rear adjustable for windage and elevation. Also available with scope mount, rings, no sights. **Features:** Stainless steel construction. Full-length vent rib. Gold-plated trigger, slide lock, safety-lever and magazine release; stippled front grip and backstrap; polished slide; adjustable trigger and sear. Comes with barrel weight. Introduced 1995. From Fort Worth Firearms.
Price: $472.95
Price: With Weaver rib $537.95
Price: With 8″ barrel, Weaver rib, custom grips, sights $616.95
Price: As above, 10″ barrel. $629.95

FORT WORTH MATCHMASTER STANDARD PISTOL

Caliber: 22 LR. **Barrel:** 3-7/8″, 4-1/2″, 5-1/2″, 7-1/2″, 10″. **Weight:** NA. **Length:** NA. **Stocks:** Checkered walnut. **Sights:** Ramp front, slide-mounted adjustable rear. **Features:** Stainless steel construction. Double extractors; trigger finger magazine release button and standard button; beveled magazine well; grip angle equivalent to M1911; low-profile frame. Introduced 1997. From Fort Worth Firearms.
Price: $388.95

Fort Worth Matchmaster Deluxe Pistol

Same as the Matchmaster Standard except comes with Weaver-style rib mount and integral adjustable rear sight system. Introduced 1997. From Fort Worth Firearms.
Price: $537.95

FREEDOM ARMS CASULL MODEL 252 SILHOUETTE

Caliber: 22 LR, 5-shot cylinder. **Barrel:** 10″. **Weight:** 63 oz. **Length:** 15.5″ overall. **Stocks:** Black micarta, western style. **Sights:** Adjustable front with bead, Iron Sight Gun Works silhouette rear, click adjustable for windage and elevation. **Features:** Stainless steel. Built on the Model 83. Two-point firing pin, lightened hammer for fast lock time. Trigger pull is 3 to 5 lbs. with pre-set overtravel screw. Introduced 1991. From Freedom Arms.

Price: Silhouette Class $1,578.00
Price: Extra fitted 22 WMR cylinder $264.00

GAUCHER GP SILHOUETTE PISTOL

Caliber: 22 LR, single shot. **Barrel:** 10″. **Weight:** 42.3 oz. **Length:** 15.5″ overall. **Stocks:** Stained hardwood. **Sights:** Hooded post on ramp front, open rear adjustable for windage and elevation. **Features:** Matte chrome barrel, blued bolt and sights. Other barrel lengths available on special order. Introduced 1991. Imported by Mandall Shooting Supplies.
Price: $425.00

HAMMERLI SP 20 TARGET PISTOL

Caliber: 22 LR, 32 S&W. **Barrel:** 4.6″. **Weight:** 34.6-41.8 oz. **Length:** 11.8″ overall. **Stocks:** Anatomically shaped synthetic Hi-Grip available in five sizes. **Sights:** Integral front in three widths, adjustable rear with changeable notch widths. **Features:** Extremely low-level sight line; anatomically shaped trigger; adjustable JPS buffer system for different recoil characteristics. Receiver available in red, blue, gold, violet or black. Introduced 1998. Imported from Switzerland by SIGARMS, Inc and Hammerli Pistols USA.
Price: . . . . NA

HARRIS GUNWORKS SIGNATURE JR. LONG RANGE PISTOL

Caliber: Any suitable caliber. **Barrel:** To customer specs. **Weight:** 5 lbs. **Stock:** Gunworks fiberglass. **Sights:** None furnished; comes with scope rings. **Features:** Right- or left-hand benchrest action of titanium or stainless steel; single shot or repeater. Comes with bipod. Introduced 1992. Made in U.S. by Harris Gunworks, Inc.
Price: $2,700.00

KIMBER SUPER MATCH AUTO PISTOL

Caliber: 45 ACP, 8-shot magazine. **Barrel:** 5″. **Weight:** 38 oz. **Length:** 18.7″ overall. **Sights:** Blade front, Kimber fully adjustable rear. **Features:** Guaranteed 3″ group at 50 yards. Stainless steel frame, black KimPro slide; two-piece magazine well; premium aluminum match-grade trigger; 30 lpi front strap checkering; stainless match-grade barrel; ambidextrous safety; special Custom Shop markings. Introduced 1999. Made in U.S. by Kimber Mfg., Inc.
Price: $1,699.00

MORINI MODEL 84E FREE PISTOL

Caliber: 22 LR, single shot. **Barrel:** 11.4″. **Weight:** 43.7 oz. **Length:** 19.4″ overall. **Stocks:** Adjustable match type with stippled surfaces. **Sights:** Interchangeable blade front, match-type fully adjustable rear. **Features:** Fully adjustable electronic trigger. Introduced 1995. Imported from Switzerland by Nygord Precision Products.
Price: $1,450.00

Ruger KMK678GC

Safari Arms Big Deuce

Smith & Wesson Model 41

PARDINI MODEL SP, HP TARGET PISTOLS

Caliber: 22 LR, 32 S&W, 5-shot magazine. **Barrel:** 4.7″. **Weight:** 38.9 oz. **Length:** 11.6″ overall. **Stocks:** Adjustable; stippled walnut; match type. **Sights:** Interchangeable blade front, interchangeable, fully adjustable rear. **Features:** Fully adjustable match trigger. Introduced 1995. Imported from Italy by Nygord Precision Products.
Price: Model SP (22 LR). **$950.00**
Price: Model HP (32 S&W). **$995.00**

PARDINI GP RAPID FIRE MATCH PISTOL

Caliber: 22 Short, 5-shot magazine. **Barrel:** 4.6″. **Weight:** 43.3 oz. **Length:** 11.6″ overall. **Stocks:** Wrap-around stippled walnut. **Sights:** Interchangeable post front, fully adjustable match rear. **Features:** Model GP Schuman has extended rear sight for longer sight radius. Introduced 1995. Imported from Italy by Nygord Precision Products.
Price: Model GP **$1,050.00**
Price: Model GP Schuman **$1,595.00**

PARDINI K50 FREE PISTOL

Caliber: 22 LR, single shot. **Barrel:** 9.8″. **Weight:** 34.6 oz. **Length:** 18.7″ overall. **Stocks:** Wrap-around walnut; adjustable match type. **Sights:** Interchangeable post front, fully adjustable match open rear. **Features:** Removable, adjustable match trigger. Barrel weights mount above the barrel. Introduced 1995. Imported from Italy by Nygord Precision Products.
Price: **$1,050.00**

RUGER MARK II TARGET MODEL AUTOLOADING PISTOL

Caliber: 22 LR, 10-shot magazine. **Barrel:** 6-7/8″. **Weight:** 42 oz. **Length:** 11 1/8″ overall. **Stocks:** Checkered hard plastic. **Sights:** .125″ blade front, micro-click rear, adjustable for windage and elevation. Sight radius 9-3/8″. Comes with lockable plastic case with lock.
Features: Introduced 1982.
Price: Blued (MK-678) **$310.50**
Price: Stainless (KMK-678) **$389.00**

Ruger Mark II Government Target Model

Same gun as the Mark II Target Model except has 6-7/8″ barrel, higher sights and is roll marked "Government Target Model" on the right side of the receiver below the rear sight. Identical in all aspects to the military model used for training U.S. armed forces except for markings. Comes with factory test target. Comes with lockable plastic case with lock. Introduced 1987.
Price: Blued (MK-678G) **$374.50**
Price: Stainless (KMK-678G) **$448.25**

Ruger Stainless Government Competition Model 22 Pistol

Similar to the Mark II Government Target Model stainless pistol except has 6-7/8″ slab-sided barrel; the receiver top is drilled and tapped for a Ruger scope base adaptor of blued, chrome moly steel; comes with Ruger 1″ stainless scope rings with integral bases for mounting a variety of optical sights; has checkered laminated grip panels with right-hand thumbrest. Has blued open sights with 9-1/4″ radius. Overall length is 11-1/8″, weight 45 oz. Comes with lockable plastic case with lock. Introduced 1991.
Price: KMK-678GC **$463.00**

Ruger Mark II Bull Barrel

Same gun as the Target Model except has 5-1/2″ or 10″ heavy barrel (10″ meets all IHMSA regulations). Weight with 5-1/2″ barrel is 42 oz., with 10″ barrel, 51 oz. Comes with lockable plastic case with lock.
Price: Blued (MK-512) **$310.50**
Price: Blued (MK-10) **$314.50**
Price: Stainless (KMK-10) **$393.00**
Price: Stainless (KMK-512) **$389.00**

SAFARI ARMS BIG DEUCE PISTOL

Caliber: 45 ACP, 7-shot magazine. **Barrel:** 6″, 416 stainless steel. **Weight:** 40.3 oz. **Length:** 9.5″ overall. **Stocks:** Smooth walnut. **Sights:** Ramped blade front, LPA adjustable rear. **Features:** Beavertail grip safety; extended thumb safety and slide release; Commander-style hammer. Throated, polished and tuned. Parkerized matte black slide with satin stainless steel frame. Introduced 1995. Made in U.S. by Safari Arms, Inc.
Price: **$714.00**

SMITH & WESSON MODEL 41 TARGET

Caliber: 22 LR, 10-shot clip. **Barrel:** 5-1/2″, 7″. **Weight:** 44 oz. (5-1/2″ barrel). **Length:** 9″ overall (5-1/2″ barrel). **Stocks:** Checkered walnut with modified thumbrest, usable with either hand. **Sights:** 1/8″ Patridge on ramp base; micro-click rear adjustable for windage and elevation. **Features:** 3/8″ wide, grooved trigger; adjustable trigger stop.
Price: S&W Bright Blue, either barrel **$801.00**

SMITH & WESSON MODEL 22A TARGET PISTOL

Caliber: 22 LR, 10-shot magazine. **Barrel:** 5-1/2″ bull. **Weight:** 38.5 oz. **Length:** 9-1/2″ overall. **Stocks:** Dymondwood with ambidextrous thumbrests and flared bottom or rubber soft touch with thumbrest. **Sights:** Patridge front, fully adjustable rear. **Features:** Sight bridge with Weaver-style integral optics mount; alloy frame, stainless barrel and slide; matte black finish. Introduced 1997. Made in U.S. by Smith & Wesson.
Price: **$320.00**

Smith & Wesson Model 22S Target Pistol

Similar to the Model 22A except has stainless steel frame. Introduced 1997. Made in U.S. by Smith & Wesson.
Price: **$379.00**

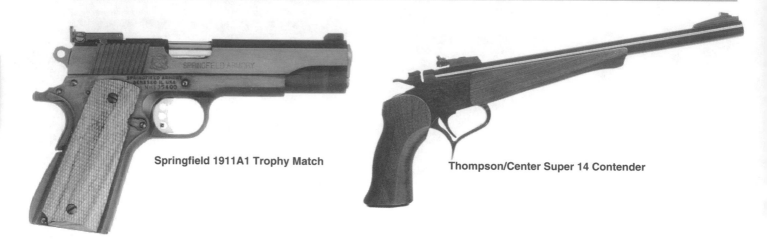

Springfield 1911A1 Trophy Match

Thompson/Center Super 14 Contender

Springfield, Inc. 1911A1 Trophy Match Pistol

Similar to the 1911A1 except factory accurized, Videki speed trigger, skeletonized hammer; has 4- to 5-1/2-lb. trigger pull, click adjustable rear sight, match-grade barrel and bushing. Comes with checkered walnut grips. Introduced 1994. From Springfield, Inc.

Price: Blue **$989.00**
Price: Stainless steel **$1,029.00**
Price: High Capacity (stainless steel, 10-shot magazine, front slide serrations, checkered slide serrations). **$1,118.00**

Springfield, Inc. Expert Pistol

Similar to the Competition Pistol except has triple-chamber tapered cone compensator on match barrel with dovetailed front sight; lowered and flared ejection port; fully tuned for reliability; fitted slide to frame; extended ambidextrous thumb safety, extended magazine release button; beavertail grip safety; Pachmayr wrap-around grips. Comes with two magazines, plastic carrying case. Introduced 1992. From Springfield, Inc.

Price: 45 ACP, Duotone finish **$1,724.00**
Price: Expert Ltd. (non-compensated) **$1,624.00**

Springfield, Inc. Distinguished Pistol

Has all the features of the 1911A1 Expert except is full-house pistol with deluxe Bo-Mar low-mounted adjustable rear sight; full-length recoil spring guide rod and recoil spring retainer; checkered frontstrap; S&A magazine well; walnut grips. Hard chrome finish. Comes with two magazines with slam pads, plastic carrying case. From Springfield, Inc.

Price: 45 ACP. **$2,445.00**
Price: Distinguished Limited (non-compensated). **$2,345.00**

SPRINGFIELD, INC. 1911A1 BULLSEYE WADCUTTER PISTOL

Caliber: 38 Super, 45 ACP. **Barrel:** 5″. **Weight:** 45 oz. **Length:** 8.59″ overall (5″ barrel). **Stocks:** Checkered walnut. **Sights:** Bo-Mar rib with undercut blade front, fully adjustable rear. **Features:** Built for wadcutter loads only. Has full-length recoil spring guide rod, fitted Videki speed trigger with 3.5-lb. pull; match Commander hammer and sear; beavertail grip safety; lowered and flared ejection port; tuned extractor; fitted slide to frame; recoil buffer system; beveled and polished magazine well; checkered front strap and steel mainspring housing (flat housing standard); polished and throated National Match barrel and bushing. Comes with two magazines with slam pads, plastic carrying case, test target. Introduced 1992. From Springfield, Inc.

Price: **$1,499.00**

Springfield, Inc. Basic Competition Pistol

Has low-mounted Bo-Mar adjustable rear sight, undercut blade front; match throated barrel and bushing; polished feed ramp; lowered and flared ejection port; fitted Videki speed trigger with tuned 3.5-lb. pull; fitted slide to frame; recoil buffer system; checkered walnut grips; serrated, arched mainspring housing. Comes with two magazines with slam pads, plastic carrying case. Introduced 1992. From Springfield, Inc.

Price: 45 ACP, blue, 5″ only. **$1,295.00**

Springfield, Inc. 1911A1 N.M. Hardball Pistol

Has Bo-Mar adjustable rear sight with undercut front blade; fitted match Videki trigger with 4-lb. pull; fitted slide to frame; throated National Match barrel and bushing, polished feed ramp; recoil buffer system; tuned extractor; Herrett walnut grips. Comes with two magazines, plastic carrying case, test target. Introduced 1992. From Springfield, Inc.

Price: 45 ACP, blue **$1,336.00**

STI EAGLE 5.1 PISTOL

Caliber: 9mm Para., 38 Super, 40 S&W, 45 ACP, 10-ACP, 10-shot magazine. **Barrel:** 5″, bull. **Weight:** 34 oz. **Length:** 8.62″ overall. **Stocks:** Checkered polymer. **Sights:** Bo-Mar blade front, Bo-Mar fully adjustable rear. **Features:** Modular frame design; adjustable match trigger; skeletonized hammer; extended grip safety with locator pad; match-grade fit of all parts. Many options available. Introduced 1994. Made in U.S. by STI International.

Price: **$1,792.00**

THOMPSON/CENTER SUPER 14 CONTENDER

Caliber: 22 LR, 222 Rem., 223 Rem., 7-30 Waters, 30-30 Win., 357 Rem. Maximum, 44 Mag., single shot. **Barrel:** 14″. **Weight:** 45 oz. **Length:** 17-1/4″ overall. **Stocks:** T/C "Competitor Grip" (walnut and rubber). **Sights:** Fully adjustable target-type. **Features:** Break-open action with auto safety. Interchangeable barrels for both rimfire and centerfire calibers. Introduced 1978.

Price: Blued **$495.00**
Price: Stainless steel **$550.00**
Price: Extra barrels, blued **$233.00**
Price: Extra barrels, stainless steel **$261.00**

Thompson/Center Super 16 Contender

Same as the T/C Super 14 Contender except has 16-1/4″ barrel. Rear sight can be mounted at mid-barrel position (10-3/4″ radius) or moved to the rear (using scope mount position) for 14-3/4″ radius. Overall length is 20-1/4″. Comes with T/C Competitor Grip of walnut and rubber. Available in, 223 Rem., 45-70 Gov't. Also available with 16″ vent rib barrel with internal choke, caliber 45 Colt/410 shotshell.

Price: Blue **$500.00**
Price: 45-70 Gov't., blue. **$506.00**
Price: Super 16 Vent Rib, blued. **$533.00**
Price: Extra 16″ barrel, blued **$238.00**
Price: Extra 45-70 barrel, blued **$243.00**
Price: Extra Super 16 vent rib barrel, blue **$270.00**

UNIQUE D.E.S. 32U TARGET PISTOL

Caliber: 32 S&W Long wadcutter. **Barrel:** 5.9″. **Weight:** 40.2 oz. **Stocks:** Anatomically shaped, adjustable stippled French walnut. **Sights:** Blade front, micrometer click rear. **Features:** Trigger adjustable for weight and position; dry firing mechanism; slide stop catch. Optional sleeve weights. Introduced 1990. Imported from France by Nygord Precision Products.

Price: Right-hand, about. **$1,350.00**
Price: Left-hand, about. **$1,380.00**

Unique D.E.S. 69U

Wichita Silhouette

UNIQUE D.E.S. 69U TARGET PISTOL

Caliber: 22 LR, 5-shot magazine. **Barrel:** 5.91". **Weight:** 35.3 oz. **Length:** 10.5" overall. **Stocks:** French walnut target-style with thumbrest and adjustable shelf; hand-checkered panels. **Sights:** Ramp front, micro. adjustable rear mounted on frame; 8.66" sight radius. **Features:** Meets U.I.T. standards. Comes with 260-gram barrel weight; 100, 150, 350-gram weights available. Fully adjustable match trigger; dry-firing safety device. Imported from France by Nygord Precision Products.
Price: Right-hand, about. $1,250.00
Price: Left-hand, about $1,290.00

UNIQUE MODEL 96U TARGET PISTOL

Caliber: 22 LR, 5- or 6-shot magazine. **Barrel:** 5.9". **Weight:** 40.2 oz. **Length:** 11.2" overall. **Stocks:** French walnut. Target style with thumbrest and adjustable shelf. **Sights:** Blade front, micrometer rear mounted on frame. **Features:** Designed for Sport Pistol and Standard U.I.T. shooting. External hammer; fully adjustable and movable trigger; dry-firing device. Introduced 1997. Imported from France by Nygord Precision Products.
Price: $1,350.00

WALTHER GSP MATCH PISTOL

Caliber: 22 LR, 32 S&W Long (GSP-C), 5-shot magazine. **Barrel:** 4.22". **Weight:** 44.8 oz. (22 LR), 49.4 oz. (32). **Length:** 11.8" overall. **Stocks:** Walnut. **Sights:** Post front, match rear adjustable for windage and elevation. **Features:** Available with either 2.2-lb. (1000 gm) or 3-lb. (1360 gm) trigger. Spare magazine, barrel weight, tools supplied. Imported from Germany by Nygord Precision Products.
Price: GSP, with case. $1,495.00
Price: GSP-C, with case. $1,595.00

WICHITA SILHOUETTE PISTOL

Caliber: 308 Win. F.L., 7mm IHMSA, 7mm-308. **Barrel:** 14-15/16". **Weight:** 4-1/2 lbs. **Length:** 21-3/8" overall. **Stock:** American walnut with oil finish. Glass bedded. **Sights:** Wichita Multi-Range sight system. **Features:** Comes with left-hand action with right-hand grip. Round receiver and barrel. Fluted bolt, flat bolt handle. Wichita adjustable trigger. Introduced 1979. From Wichita Arms.
Price: Center grip stock $1,800.00
Price: As above except with Rear Position Stock and target-type
Lightpull trigger $1,800.00

WICHITA CLASSIC SILHOUETTE PISTOL

Caliber: All standard calibers with maximum overall length of 2.800". **Barrel:** 11-1/4". **Weight:** 3 lbs., 15 oz. **Stocks:** AAA American walnut with oil finish, checkered grip. **Sights:** Hooded post front, open adjustable rear. **Features:** Three locking lug bolt, three gas ports; completely adjustable Wichita trigger. Introduced 1981. From Wichita Arms.
Price: $3,450.00

Includes models suitable for hunting and competitive courses for fire, both police and international.

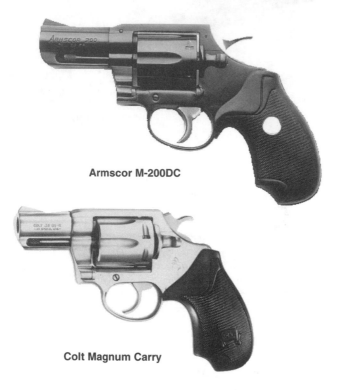

Armscor M-200DC

Colt Magnum Carry

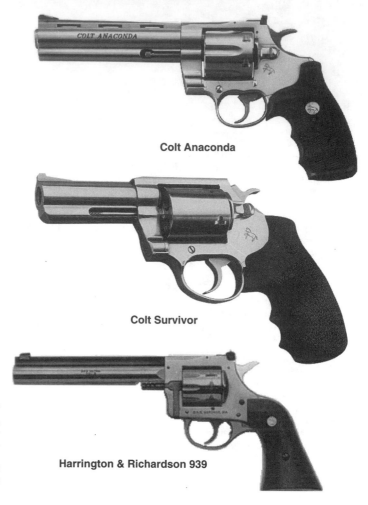

Colt Anaconda

Colt Survivor

Harrington & Richardson 939

ARMSCOR M-200DC REVOLVER

Caliber: 38 Spec., 6-shot cylinder. **Barrel:** 2-1/2", 4". **Weight:** 22 oz. (2-1/2" barrel). **Length:** 7-3/8" overall (2-1/2" barrel). **Stocks:** Checkered rubber. **Sights:** Blade front, fixed notch rear. **Features:** All-steel construction; floating firing pin, transfer bar ignition; shrouded ejector rod; blue finish. Reintroduced 1996. Imported from the Philippines by K.B.I., Inc.
Price: 2-1/2" **$199.99**
Price: 4" **$205.00**

COLT ANACONDA REVOLVER

Caliber: 44 Rem. Magnum, 45 Colt, 6-shot. **Barrel:** 4", 6", 8". **Weight:** 53 oz. (6" barrel). **Length:** 11-5/8" overall. **Stocks:** TP combat style with finger grooves. **Sights:** Red insert front, adjustable white outline rear. **Features:** Stainless steel; full-length ejector rod housing; ventilated barrel rib; offset bolt notches in cylinder; wide spur hammer. Introduced 1990.
Price: **$629.00**
Price: 45 Colt, 6", barrel only **$629.00**

COLT PYTHON ELITE REVOLVER

Caliber: 357 Magnum (handles all 38 Spec.), 6-shot. **Barrel:** 6", with ventilated rib. **Weight:** 43-1/2 oz. **Length:** 11-1/2" overall. **Stocks:** Walnut. **Sights:** 1/8" ramp front, adjustable notch rear. **Features:** Ventilated rib; grooved, crisp trigger; swing-out cylinder; target hammer.
Price: Stainless steel **$1,018.00**

COLT MAGNUM CARRY REVOLVER

Caliber: 357 Mag., 6-shot. **Barrel:** 2". **Weight:** 21 oz. **Length:** NA. **Stocks:** Combat-style rubber. **Sights:** Ramp front, fixed notch rear. **Features:** Stainless steel construction. Smooth combat trigger. Introduced 1998. Made in U.S. by Colt's Mfg. Co.
Price: **$460.00**

COLT SURVIVOR REVOLVER

NEW! **Caliber:** Multi-caliber; accepts 9x18, 9x19, 9x23, 9mm Largo, 380 ACP, 38 Super, 38 Spec. +P, 357 Mag.; 5-shot cylinder. **Barrel:** 3". **Weight:** 22 oz. **Length:** 7" overall. **Stocks:** Textured rubber, combat-style. **Sights:** Ramp front, fixed notch rear. **Features:** Stainless steel construction. Multi-cali-

ber cylinder, ejector system. Introduced 1999. Made in U.S. by Colt's Mfg., Inc.
Price: . . . . **NA**

E.A.A. STANDARD GRADE REVOLVERS

Caliber: 38 Spec., 6-shot; 357 magnum, 6-shot. **Barrel:** 2", 4". **Weight:** 38 oz. (22 rimfire, 4"). **Length:** 8.8" overall (4" bbl.). **Stocks:** Rubber with finger grooves. **Sights:** Blade front, fixed or adjustable on rimfires; fixed only on 32, 38. **Features:** Swing-out cylinder; hammer block safety; blue finish. Introduced 1991. Imported from Germany by European American Armory.
Price: 38 Special 2" **$180.00**
Price: 38 Special, 4" **$199.00**
Price: 357 Magnum, 2" **$199.00**
Price: 357 Magnum, 4" **$233.00**

HARRINGTON & RICHARDSON 939 PREMIER REVOLVER

Caliber: 22 LR, 9-shot cylinder. **Barrel:** 6" heavy. **Weight:** 36 oz. **Length:** NA. **Stocks:** Walnut-finished hardwood. **Sights:** Blade front, fully adjustable rear. **Features:** Swing-out cylinder with plunger-type ejection; solid barrel rib; high-polish blue finish; double-action mechanism; Western-style grip. Introduced 1995. Made in U.S. by H&R 1871, Inc.
Price: **$184.95**

HARRINGTON & RICHARDSON 929 SIDEKICK

Caliber: 22 LR, 9-shot cylinder. **Barrel:** 4" heavy. **Weight:** 30 oz. **Length:** NA. **Stocks:** Cinnamon-color laminated wood. **Sights:** Blade front, notch rear. **Features:** Double action; swing-out cylinder, traditional loading gate;

Harrington & Richardson Sportsman 999

New England Lady Ultra

Harrington & Richardson 949

New England Ultra

Ruger GP161

blued frame and barrel. Comes with lockable storage case, Uncle Mike's Sidekick holster. Introduced 1996. Made in U.S. by H&R 1871, Inc.
Price: **$159.95**

HARRINGTON & RICHARDSON SPORTSMAN 999 REVOLVER

Caliber: 22 Short, Long, Long Rifle, 9-shot. **Barrel:** 4", 6". **Weight:** 30 oz. (4" barrel). **Length:** 8.5" overall. **Stocks:** Walnut-finished hardwood. **Sights:** Blade front adjustable for elevation, rear adjustable for windage. **Features:** Top-break loading; polished blue finish; automatic shell ejection. Reintroduced 1992. From H&R 1871, Inc.
Price: **$279.95**

HARRINGTON & RICHARDSON 949 WESTERN REVOLVER

Caliber: 22 LR, 9-shot cylinder. **Barrel:** 5-1/2", 7-1/2". **Weight:** 36 oz. **Length:** NA. **Stocks:** Walnut-stained hardwood. **Sights:** Blade front, adjustable rear. **Features:** Color case-hardened frame and backstrap, traditional loading gate and ejector rod. Introduced 1994. Made in U.S. by H&R 1871, Inc.
Price: About **$184.95**

MEDUSA MODEL 47 REVOLVER

Caliber: Most 9mm, 38 and 357 caliber cartridges; 6-shot cylinder. **Barrel:** 2-1/2", 3", 4", 5", 6"; fluted. **Weight:** 39 oz. **Length:** 10" overall (4" barrel). **Stocks:** Gripper-style rubber. **Sights:** Changeable front blades, fully adjustable rear. **Features:** Patented extractor allows gun to chamber, fire and extract over 25 different cartridges in the .355- to .357 range, without half-moon clips. Steel frame and cylinder; match quality barrel. Matte blue finish. Introduced 1996. Made in U.S. by Phillips & Rogers, Inc.
Price: **$899.00**

NEW ENGLAND FIREARMS LADY ULTRA REVOLVER

Caliber: 32 H&R Mag., 5-shot. **Barrel:** 3". **Weight:** 31 oz. **Length:** 7.25" overall. **Stocks:** Walnut-finished hardwood with NEF medallion. **Sights:** Blade front, fully adjustable rear. **Features:** Swing-out cylinder; polished blue finish. Comes with lockable storage case. Introduced 1992. From New England Firearms.
Price: **$169.95**

NEW ENGLAND FIREARMS ULTRA REVOLVER

Caliber: 22 LR, 9-shot; 22 WMR, 6-shot. **Barrel:** 4", 6". **Weight:** 36 oz. **Length:** 10-5/8" overall (6" barrel). **Stocks:** Walnut-finished hardwood with NEF medallion. **Sights:** Blade front, fully adjustable rear. **Features:** Blue finish. Bull-style barrel with recessed muzzle, high "Lustre" blue/black finish. Introduced 1989. From New England Firearms.
Price: **$169.95**
Price: Ultra Mag 22 WMR. **$169.95**

NEW ENGLAND FIREARMS STANDARD REVOLVERS

Caliber: 22 LR, 9-shot; 32 H&R Mag., 5-shot. **Barrel:** 3", 4". **Weight:** 26 oz. (22 LR, 3"). **Length:** 8-1/2" overall (4" bbl.). **Stocks:** Walnut-finished American hardwood with NEF medallion. **Sights:** Fixed. **Features:** Choice of blue or nickel finish. Introduced 1988. From New England Firearms.
Price: 22 LR, 32 H&R Mag., blue **$134.95**
Price: 22 LR, 0", 4", nickel, 32 H&R Mag. 3" nickel **$144.95**

RUGER GP-100 REVOLVERS

Caliber: 38 Spec., 357 Mag., 6-shot. **Barrel:** 3", 3" heavy, 4", 4" heavy, 6", 6" heavy. **Weight:** 3" barrel—35 oz., 3" heavy barrel—36 oz., 4" barrel—37 oz., 4" heavy barrel—38 oz. **Sights:** Fixed; adjustable on 4" heavy, 6", 6" heavy barrels. **Stocks:** Ruger Santoprene Cushioned Grip with Goncalo Alves inserts. **Features:** Uses action and frame incorporating improvements and features of both the Security-Six and Redhawk revolvers. Full length and short ejector shroud. Satin blue and stainless steel.
Price: GP-141 (357, 4" heavy, adj. sights, blue) **$440.00**
Price: GP-160 (357, 6", adj. sights, blue) **$440.00**
Price: GP-161 (357, 6" heavy, adj. sights, blue) **$440.00**
Price: GPF-331 (357, 3" heavy), GPF-831 (38 Spec.) **$423.00**
Price: GPF-340 (357, 4"), GPF-840 (38 Spec.) **$423.00**
Price: GPF-341 (357, 4" heavy), GPF-841 (38 Spec.) **$423.00**
Price: KGP-141 (357, 4" heavy, adj. sights, stainless) **$474.00**
Price: KGP-160 (357, 6", adj. sights, stainless) **$474.00**
Price: KGP-161 (357, 6" heavy, adj. sights, stainless) **$474.00**
Price: KGPF-330 (357, 3", stainless), KGPF-830 (38 Spec.) **$457.00**
Price: KGPF-331 (357, 3" heavy, stainless), KGPF-831 (38 Spec.) **$457.00**
Price: KGPF-340 (357, 4", stainless), KGPF-840 (38 Spec.) **$457.00**
Price: KGPF-341 (357, 4" heavy, stainless), KGPF-841 (38 Spec.) **$457.00**

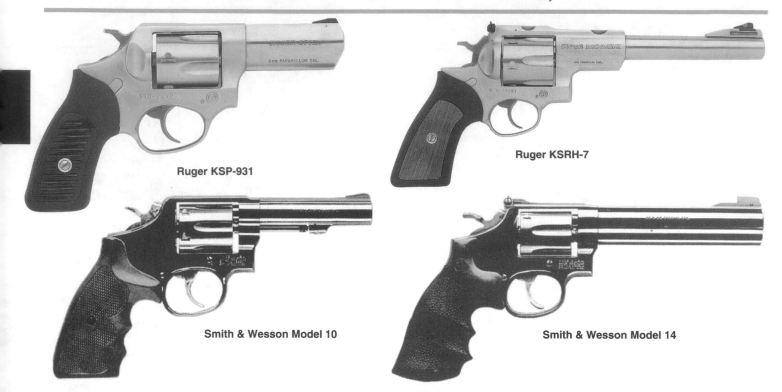

Ruger KSP-931

Ruger KSRH-7

Smith & Wesson Model 10

Smith & Wesson Model 14

Ruger SP101 Double-Action-Only Revolver

Similar to the standard SP101 except is double-action-only with no single-action sear notch. Has spurless hammer for snag-free handling, floating firing pin and Ruger's patented transfer bar safety system. Available with 2-1/4" barrel in 38 Special +P and 357 Magnum only. Weighs 25-1/2 oz., overall length 7.06". Natural brushed satin or high-polish stainless steel. Introduced 1993.

Price: KSP821L (38 Spec.), KSP321XL (357 Mag.) **$443.00**

RUGER SP101 REVOLVERS

Caliber: 22 LR, 32 H&R Mag., 6-shot, 9mm Para., 38 Spec. +P, 357 Mag., 5-shot. **Barrel:** 2-1/4", 3-1/16", 4". **Weight:** 2-1/4"—25 oz.; 3-1/16"—27 oz. **Sights:** Adjustable on 22, 32, fixed on others. **Stocks:** Ruger Santoprene Cushioned Grip with Xenoy inserts. **Features:** Incorporates improvements and features found in the GP-100 revolvers into a compact, small frame, double-action revolver. Full-length ejector shroud. Stainless steel only. Introduced 1988.

Price: KSP-821 (2-1/2", 38 Spec.) $443.00
Price: KSP-831 (3-1/16", 38 Spec.) $443.00
Price: KSP-221 (2-1/4", 22 LR) $443.00
Price: KSP-240 (4", 22 LR) $443.00
Price: KSP-241 (4" heavy bbl., 22 LR) $443.00
Price: KSP-3231 (3-1/16", 32 H&R) $443.00
Price: KSP-921 (2-1/4", 9mm Para.) $443.00
Price: KSP-931 (3-1/16", 9mm Para.) $443.00
Price: KSP-321 (2-1/4", 357 Mag.) $443.00
Price: KSP-331 (3-1/16", 357 Mag.) $443.00
Price: GKSP321X (2-1/4", 357 Mag.), high-gloss stainless $443.00
Price: GKSP331X (3-1/16", 357 Mag.), high-gloss stainless $443.00
Price: GKSP321XL (2-1/4", 357 Mag., spurless hammer, DAO) high-gloss stainless $443.00

RUGER REDHAWK

Caliber: 44 Rem. Mag., 45 Colt, 6-shot. **Barrel:** 5-1/2", 7-1/2". **Weight:** About 54 oz. (7-1/2" bbl.). **Length:** 13" overall (7-1/2" barrel). **Stocks:** Square butt Goncalo Alves. **Sights:** Interchangeable Patridge-type front, rear adjustable for windage and elevation. **Features:** Stainless steel, brushed satin finish, or blued ordnance steel. Has a 9-1/2" sight radius. Introduced 1979.

Price: Blued, 44 Mag., 5-1/2", 7-1/2" $515.00

Price: Blued, 44 Mag., 7-1/2", with scope mount, rings **$553.00**
Price: Stainless, 44 Mag., 5-1/2", 7-1/2". **$574.00**
Price: Stainless, 44 Mag., 7-1/2", with scope mount, rings **$618.00**
Price: Stainless, 45 Colt, 5-1/2", 7-1/2" **$574.00**
Price: Stainless, 45 Colt, 7-1/2", with scope mount **$618.00**

Ruger Super Redhawk Revolver

Similar to the standard Redhawk except has a heavy extended frame with the Ruger Integral Scope Mounting System on the wide topstrap. Also available in 454 Casull. The wide hammer spur has been lowered for better scope clearance. Incorporates the mechanical design features and improvements of the GP-100. Choice of 7-1/2" or 9-1/2" barrel, both with ramp front sight base with Redhawk-style Interchangeable Insert sight blades, adjustable rear sight. Comes with Ruger "Cushioned Grip" panels of Santoprene with Goncalo Alves wood panels. Satin stainless steel. Introduced 1987.

Price: KSRH-7 (7-1/2"), KSRH-9 (9-1/2") **$618.00**
Price: KSRH-7454 (7-1/2") 454 Casull **$745.00**

SMITH & WESSON MODEL 10 M&P HB REVOLVER

Caliber: 38 Spec., 6-shot. **Barrel:** 4". **Weight:** 33.5 oz. **Length:** 9-5/16" overall. **Stocks:** Uncle Mike's Combat soft rubber; square butt. **Sights:** Fixed; ramp front, square notch rear.

Price: Blue $420.00

SMITH & WESSON MODEL 14 FULL LUG REVOLVER

Caliber: 38 Spec., 6-shot. **Barrel:** 6", full lug. **Weight:** 47 oz. **Length:** 11-1/8" overall. **Stocks:** Hogue soft rubber. **Sights:** Pinned Patridge front, adjustable micrometer click rear. **Features:** Has .500" target hammer, .312" smooth combat trigger. Polished blue finish. Reintroduced 1991. Limited production.

Price: $498.00

SMITH & WESSON MODEL 15 COMBAT MASTERPIECE

Caliber: 38 Spec., 6-shot. **Barrel:** 4". **Weight:** 32 oz. **Length:** 9-5/16" (4" bbl.). **Stocks:** Uncle Mike's Combat soft rubber. **Sights:** Serrated ramp front, micro-click rear adjustable for windage and elevation.

Price: Blued $450.00

SMITH & WESSON MODEL 19 COMBAT MAGNUM

Caliber: 357 Mag. and 38 Spec., 6-shot. **Barrel:** 4". **Weight:** 36 oz. **Length:** 9-9/16" (4" bbl.). **Stocks:** Uncle Mike's Combat soft rubber; wood optional.

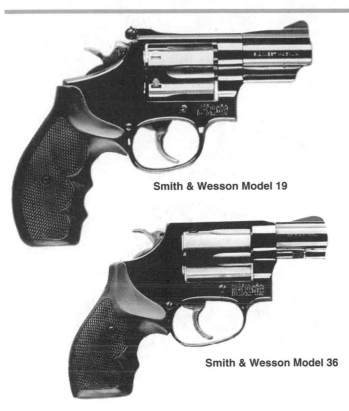

Smith & Wesson Model 19

Smith & Wesson Model 36

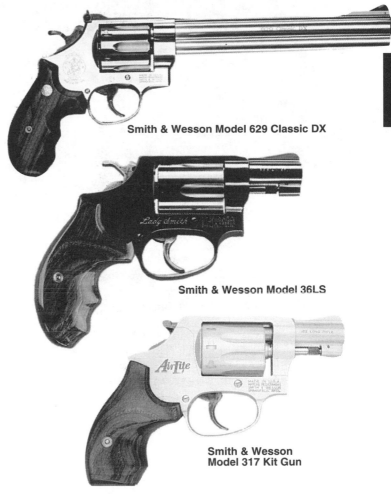

Smith & Wesson Model 629 Classic DX

Smith & Wesson Model 36LS

Smith & Wesson Model 317 Kit Gun

Sights: Red ramp front, micro-click rear adjustable for windage and elevation.
Price: 4" **$457.00**

SMITH & WESSON MODEL 629 REVOLVERS
Caliber: 44 Magnum, 6-shot. **Barrel:** 5", 6", 8-3/8". **Weight:** 47 oz. (6" bbl.). **Length:** 11-3/8" overall (6" bbl.). **Stocks:** Soft rubber; wood optional. **Sights:** 1/8" red ramp front, micro-click rear, adjustable for windage and elevation.
Price: Model 629 (stainless steel), 5" **$625.00**
Price: Model 629, 6" **$631.00**
Price: Model 629, 8-3/8" barrel **$646.00**

Smith & Wesson Model 629 Classic Revolver
Similar to the standard Model 629 except has full-lug 5", 6-1/2" or 8-3/8" barrel; chamfered front of cylinder; interchangeable red ramp front sight with adjustable white outline rear; Hogue grips with S&W monogram; the frame is drilled and tapped for scope mounting. Factory accurizing and endurance packages. Overall length with 5" barrel is 10-1/2"; weighs 51 oz. Introduced 1990.
Price: Model 629 Classic (stainless), 5", 6-1/2" **$670.00**
Price: As above, 8-3/8" **$691.00**

Smith & Wesson Model 629 Classic DX Revolver
Similar to the Model 629 Classic except offered only with 6-1/2" or 8-3/8" full-lug barrel; comes with five front sights: red ramp; black Patridge; black Patridge with gold bead; black ramp; and black Patridge with white dot. Comes with Hogue combat-style and wood round butt grip. Introduced 1991.
Price: Model 629 Classic DX, 6-1/2" **$860.00**
Price: As above, 8-3/8" **$888.00**

SMITH & WESSON MODEL 36, 37 CHIEFS SPECIAL & AIRWEIGHT
Caliber: 38 Spec.+P, 5-shot. **Barrel:** 1-7/8". **Weight:** 19-1/2 oz. (2" bbl.); 13-1/2 oz. (Airweight). **Length:** 6-1/2" (round butt). **Stocks:** Round butt soft rubber. **Sights:** Fixed, serrated ramp front, square notch rear.
Price: Blue, standard Model 36 . . . . **$406.00**
Price: Blue, Airweight Model 37 . . . . **$442.00**

Smith & Wesson Model 36LS, 60LS LadySmith
Similar to the standard Model 36. Available with 1-7/8" barrel, 38 Special. Comes with smooth, contoured rosewood grips with the S&W monogram. Has a speedloader cutout. Comes in a fitted carry/storage case. Introduced 1989.
Price: Model 36LS **$490.00**
Price: Model 60LS, as above except in stainless, 357 Magnum . **$494.00**

SMITH & WESSON MODEL 60 357 MAGNUM
Caliber: 357 Magnum, 5-shot. **Barrel:** 2-1/8" or 3". **Weight:** 24 oz. **Length:** 7-1/2 overall (3" barrel). **Stocks:** Uncle Mike's Combat. **Sights:** Fixed, serrated ramp front, square notch rear. **Features:** Stainless steel construction. Made in U.S. by Smith & Wesson.
Price: 2-1/8" barrel **$462.00**
Price: 3" barrel **$490.00**

SMITH & WESSON MODEL 65
Caliber: 357 Mag. and 38 Spec., 6-shot. **Barrel:** 3", 4". **Weight:** 34 oz. **Length:** 9-5/16" overall (4" bbl.). **Stocks:** Uncle Mike's Combat. **Sights:** 1/8" serrated ramp front, fixed square notch rear. **Features:** Heavy barrel. Stainless steel construction.
Price: **$458.00**

SMITH & WESSON MODEL 317 AIRLITE, 317 LADYSMITH REVOLVERS
Caliber: 22 LR, 8-shot. **Barrel:** 1-7/8" 3". **Weight:** 9.9 oz. **Length:** 6-3/16" overall. **Stocks:** Dymondwood Boot or Uncle Mike's Boot. **Sights:** Serrated ramp front, fixed notch rear. **Features:** Aluminum alloy, carbon and stainless steels, and titanium construction. Short spur hammer, smooth combat trigger. Clear Cote finish. Introduced 1997. Made in U.S. by Smith & Wesson.

Smith & Wesson Model 65LS

Smith & Wesson Model 625

Smith & Wesson Model 586, 686 Distinguished Combat

Price: With Uncle Mike's Boot grip **$465.00**
Price: With DymondWood Boot grip, 3" barrel **$491.00**
Price: Model 317 LadySmith (DymondWood only, comes
with display case). **$520.00**

Smith & Wesson Model 637 Airweight Revolver
Similar to the Model 37 Airweight except has alloy frame, stainless steel barrel, cylinder and yoke; rated for 38 Spec. +P; Uncle Mike's Boot Grip. Weighs 15 oz. Introduced 1996. Made in U.S. by Smith & Wesson.
Price: **$459.00**

SMITH & WESSON MODEL 64 STAINLESS M&P
Caliber: 38 Spec., 6-shot. **Barrel:** 2", 3", 4". **Weight:** 34 oz. **Length:** 9-5/16" overall. **Stocks:** Soft rubber. **Sights:** Fixed, 1/8" serrated ramp front, square notch rear. **Features:** Satin finished stainless steel, square butt.
Price: 2" **$446.00**
Price: 3", 4". **$454.00**

SMITH & WESSON MODEL 65LS LADYSMITH
Caliber: 357 Magnum, 6-shot. **Barrel:** 3". **Weight:** 31 oz. **Length:** 7.94" overall. **Stocks:** Rosewood, round butt. **Sights:** Serrated ramp front, fixed notch rear. **Features:** Stainless steel with frosted finish. Smooth combat trigger, service hammer, shrouded ejector rod. Comes with case. Introduced 1992.
Price: **$494.00**

SMITH & WESSON MODEL 66 STAINLESS COMBAT MAGNUM
Caliber: 357 Mag. and 38 Spec., 6-shot. **Barrel:** 2-1/2", 4", 6". **Weight:** 36 oz. (4" barrel). **Length:** 9-9/16" overall. **Stocks:** Soft rubber. **Sights:** Red ramp front, micro-click rear adjustable for windage and elevation. **Features:** Satin finish stainless steel.
Price: 2-1/2" **$499.00**
Price: 4", 6". **$505.00**

SMITH & WESSON MODEL 67 COMBAT MASTERPIECE
Caliber: 38 Special, 6-shot. **Barrel:** 4". **Weight:** 32 oz. **Length:** 9-5/16" overall. **Stocks:** Soft rubber. **Sights:** Red ramp front, micro-click rear adjustable for windage and elevation. **Features:** Stainless steel with satin finish. Smooth combat trigger, semi-target hammer. Introduced 1994.
Price: **$500.00**

SMITH & WESSON MODEL 242 AIRLITE Ti Revolver
NEW! **Caliber:** 38 Special, 7-shot. **Barrel:** 2-1/2". **Weight:** 18.9 oz. **Length:** 7-3/8" overall. **Stocks:** Uncle Mike's Boot grip. **Sights:** Serrated ramp front, fixed notch rear. **Features:** Alloy frame, yoke and barrel shroud; titanium cylinder; stainless barrel insert. Medium L-frame size. Introduced 1999. Made in U.S. by Smith & Wesson.
Price: **$658.00**

SMITH & WESSON MODEL 296 AIRLITE Ti REVOLVER
NEW! **Caliber:** 44 Spec. **Barrel:** 2-1/2". **Weight:** 18.9 oz. **Length:** 7-3/8" overall. **Stocks:** Uncle Mike's Boot grip. **Sights:** Serrated ramp front, fixed notch rear. **Features:** Alloy frame, yoke and barrel shroud; titanium cylinder;

stainless steel barrel insert. Medium, L-frame size. Introduced 1999. Made in U.S. by Smith & Wesson.
Price: **$658.00**

SMITH & WESSON MODEL 586, 686 DISTINGUISHED COMBAT MAGNUMS
Caliber: 357 Magnum. **Barrel:** 4", 6" (M 586); 2-1/2", 4", 6", 8-3/8" (M 686). **Weight:** 46 oz. (6"), 41 oz. (4"). **Stocks:** Soft rubber. **Sights:** Red ramp front, S&W micrometer click rear. Drilled and tapped for scope mount. **Features:** Uses L-frame, but takes all K-frame grips. Full-length ejector rod shroud. Smooth combat-type trigger, semi-target type hammer. Also available in stainless as Model 686. Introduced 1981.
Price: Model 586, blue, 4", from **$494.00**
Price: Model 586, blue, 6" **$499.00**
Price: Model 686, 6", ported barrel. **$564.00**
Price: Model 686, 8-3/8". **$550.00**
Price: Model 686, 2-1/2". **$514.00**

Smith & Wesson Model 686 Magnum PLUS Revolver
Similar to the Model 686 except has 7-shot cylinder, 2-1/2", 4" or 6" barrel. Weighs 34-1/2 oz., overall length 7-1/2" (2-1/2" barrel). Hogue rubber grips. Introduced 1996. Made in U.S. by Smith & Wesson.
Price: 2-1/2" barrel **$534.00**
Price: 4" barrel **$542.00**
Price: 6" barrel **$550.00**

SMITH & WESSON MODEL 625 REVOLVER
Caliber: 45 ACP, 6-shot. **Barrel:** 5". **Weight:** 46 oz. **Length:** 11.375" overall. **Stocks:** Soft rubber; wood optional. **Sights:** Patridge front on ramp, S&W micrometer click rear adjustable for windage and elevation. **Features:** Stainless steel construction with .400" semi-target hammer, .312" smooth combat trigger; full lug barrel. Introduced 1989.
Price: **$636.00**

SMITH & WESSON MODEL 640 CENTENNIAL
Caliber: 357 Mag., 5-shot. **Barrel:** 2-1/8". **Weight:** 25 oz. **Length:** 6-3/4" overall. **Stocks:** Uncle Mike's Boot Grip. **Sights:** Serrated ramp front, fixed notch rear. **Features:** Stainless steel. Fully concealed hammer, snag-proof smooth edges. Introduced 1995 in 357 Magnum.
Price: **$502.00**

Smith & Wesson Model 442

Smith & Wesson Model 649

Smith & Wesson Model 696

SMITH & WESSON MODEL 617 FULL LUG REVOLVER

Caliber: 22 LR, 6- or 10-shot. **Barrel:** 4", 6", 8-3/8". **Weight:** 42 oz. (4" barrel). **Length:** NA. **Stocks:** Soft rubber. **Sights:** Patridge front, adjustable rear. Drilled and tapped for scope mount. **Features:** Stainless steel with satin finish; 4" has .312" smooth trigger, .375" semi-target hammer; 6" has either .312" combat or .400" serrated trigger, .375" semi-target or .500" target hammer; 8-3/8" with .400" serrated trigger, .500" target hammer. Introduced 1990.

Price: 4" $534.00
Price: 6", target hammer, target trigger $524.00
Price: 6", 10-shot $566.00
Price: 8-3/8", 10 shot $578.00

SMITH & WESSON MODEL 610 CLASSIC HUNTER REVOLVER

Caliber: 10mm, 6-shot cylinder. **Barrel:** 6-1/2" full lug. **Weight:** 52 oz. **Length:** 12" overall. **Stocks:** Hogue rubber combat. **Sights:** Interchangeable blade front, micro-click rear adjustable for windage and elevation. **Features:** Stainless steel construction; target hammer, target trigger; unfluted cylinder; drilled and tapped for scope mounting. Introduced 1998.
Price: $684.00

SMITH & WESSON MODEL 331, 332 AIRLITE Ti Revolvers

Caliber: 32 H&R Mag., 6-shot. **Barrel:** 1-7/8". **Weight:** 11.2 oz. (with wood grip). **Length:** 6-15/16" overall. **Stocks:** Uncle Mike's Boot or Dymondwood Boot. **Sights:** Black serrated ramp front, fixed notch rear. **Features:** Aluminum alloy frame, barrel shroud and yoke; titanium cylinder; stainless steel barrel liner. Matte finish. Introduced 1999. Made in U.S. by Smith & Wesson.
Price: Model 331 Chiefs Special with Uncle Mike's Boot grip ... $624.00
Price: Model 331 Chiefs Special with Dymondwood Boot grip... $648.00
Price: Model 332 Centennial (shrouded hammer) with Uncle Mike's boot grip $640.00
Price: Model 332 Centennial with Dymondwood Boot grip...... $664.00

SMITH & WESSON MODEL 337 CHIEFS SPECIAL AIRLITE Ti

Caliber: 38 Spec., 5-shot. **Barrel:** 1-7/8". **Weight:** 11.2 oz. (Dymondwood grips). **Length:** 6-5/16" overall. **Stocks:** Uncle Mike's Boot or Dymondwood Boot. **Sights:** Black serrated front, fixed notch rear. **Features:** Aluminum alloy frame, barrel shroud and yoke; titanium cylinder; stainless

steel barrel liner. Matte finish. Introduced 1999. Made in U.S. by Smith & Wesson.
Price: With Uncle Mike's Boot grip $624.00
Price: With Dymondwood Boot grip $648.00

SMITH & WESSON MODEL 342 CENTENNIAL AIRLITE Ti

Caliber: 38 Spec., 5-shot. **Barrel:** 1-7/8". **Weight:** 11.3 oz. (Dymondwood stocks). **Length:** 6-15/16" overall. **Stocks:** Uncle Mike's Boot or Dymondwood Boot. **Sights:** Black serrated ramp front, fixed notch rear. **Features:** Aluminum alloy frame, barrel shroud and yoke; titanium cylinder; stainless steel barrel liner. Shrouded hammer. Matte finish. Introduced 1999. Made in U.S. by Smith & Wesson.
Price: With Uncle Mike's Boot grip $640.00
Price: With Dymondwood Boot grip $664.00

Smith & Wesson Model 442 Centennial Airweight

Similar to the Model 640 Centennial except has alloy frame giving weight of 15.8 oz. Chambered for 38 Special, 1-7/8" carbon steel barrel; carbon steel cylinder; concealed hammer; Uncle Mike's Boot grip. Fixed square notch rear sight, serrated ramp front. Introduced 1993.
Price: Blue $459.00

SMITH & WESSON MODEL 638 AIRWEIGHT BODYGUARD

Caliber: 38 Spec., 5-shot. **Barrel:** 1-7/8". **Weight:** 15 oz. **Length:** 6-15/16" overall. **Stocks:** Uncle Mike's Boot grip. **Sights:** Serrated ramp front, fixed notch rear. **Features:** Alloy frame, stainless cylinder and barrel; shrouded hammer. Introduced 1997. Made in U.S. by Smith & Wesson.
Price: With Uncle Mike's Boot grip $492.00

Smith & Wesson Model 642 Airweight Revolver

Similar to the Model 442 Centennial Airweight except has stainless steel barrel, cylinder and yoke with matte finish; Uncle Mike's Boot Grip; weighs 15.8 oz. Introduced 1996. Made in U.S. by Smith & Wesson.
Price: $474.00

Smith & Wesson Model 642LS LadySmith Revolver

Same as the Model 642 except has smooth combat wood grips, and comes with case; aluminum alloy frame, stainless cylinder, barrel and yoke; frosted matte finish. Weighs 15.8 oz. Introduced 1996. Made in U.S. by Smith & Wesson.
Price: $505.00

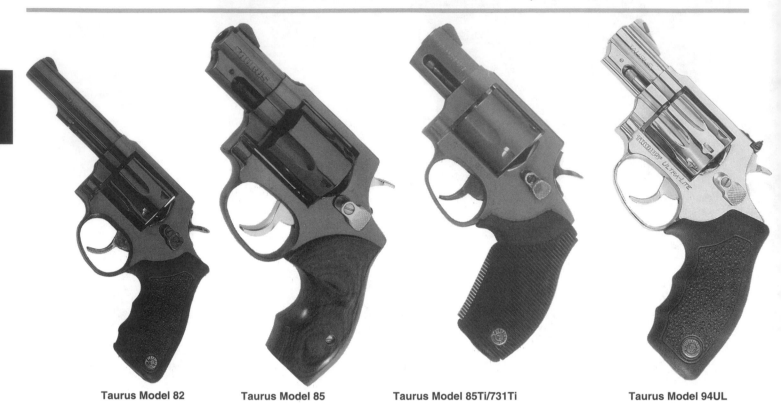

Taurus Model 82 Taurus Model 85 Taurus Model 85Ti/731Ti Taurus Model 94UL

SMITH & WESSON MODEL 649 BODYGUARD REVOLVER
Caliber: 357 Mag., 5-shot. **Barrel:** 2-1/8". **Weight:** 20 oz. **Length:** 6-5/16" overall. **Stocks:** Uncle Mike's Combat. **Sights:** Black pinned ramp front, fixed notch rear. **Features:** Stainless steel construction; shrouded hammer; smooth combat trigger. Made in U.S. by Smith & Wesson.
Price: $502.00

SMITH & WESSON MODEL 657 REVOLVER
Caliber: 41 Mag., 6-shot. **Barrel:** 6". **Weight:** 48 oz. **Length:** 11-3/8" overall. **Stocks:** Soft rubber. **Sights:** Pinned 1/8" red ramp front, micro-click rear adjustable for windage and elevation. **Features:** Stainless steel construction.
Price: $564.00

SMITH & WESSON MODEL 696 REVOLVER
Caliber: 44 Spec., 5-shot. **Barrel:** 3". **Weight:** 35.5 oz. **Length:** 8-1/4" overall. **Stocks:** Uncle Mike's Combat. **Sights:** Red ramp front, click adjustable white outline rear. **Features:** Stainless steel construction; round butt frame; satin finish. Introduced 1997. Made in U.S. by Smith & Wesson.
Price: $525.00

TAURUS MODEL 65 REVOLVER
Caliber: 357 Mag., 6-shot. **Barrel:** 4". **Weight:** 38 oz. **Length:** 10-1/2" overall. **Stocks:** Soft rubber. **Sights:** Serrated front, notch rear. **Features:** Solid rib barrel; +P rated. Imported by Taurus International.
Price: Blue $313.00
Price: Stainless...................................... $359.00

Taurus Model 66 Revolver
Same to the Model 65 except with 4" or 6" barrel, 7-shot cylinder, adjustable rear sight. Imported by Taurus International.
Price: Blue $359.00
Price: Stainless...................................... $406.00

TAURUS MODEL 82 HEAVY BARREL REVOLVER
Caliber: 38 Spec., 6-shot. **Barrel:** 4", heavy. **Weight:** 34 oz. (4" bbl.). **Length:** 9-1/4" overall (4" bbl.). **Stocks:** Soft black rubber. **Sights:** Serrated ramp front, square notch rear. **Features:** Imported by Taurus International.

Taurus Model 22H Raging Hornet

Price: Blue $297.00
Price: Stainless...................................... $344.00

TAURUS MODEL 85 REVOLVER
Caliber: 38 Spec., 5-shot. **Barrel:** 2", 3". **Weight:** 21 oz. **Stocks:** Black rubber, boot grip. **Sights:** Ramp front, square notch rear. **Features:** Blue finish or stainless steel. Introduced 1980. Imported by Taurus International.
Price: Blue, 2", 3" $286.00
Price: Stainless steel $327.00
Price: Blue, 2", ported barrel $305.00
Price: Stainless, 2", ported barrel...................... $345.00
Price: Blue, Ultra-Lite (17 oz.), 2".................... $311.00
Price: Stainless, Ultra-Lite (17 oz.), 2", ported barrel $342.00
Price: Blue with gold trim, ported $350.00

Taurus Model 85UL/Ti Revolver
Similar to the Model 85 except has titanium cylinder, aluminum alloy frame, and ported aluminum barrel with stainless steel sleeve. Weight is 13.5 oz. International.
Price: $515.00

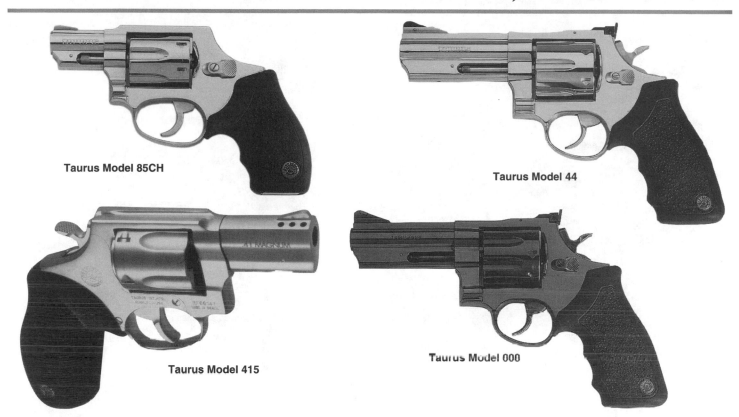

Taurus Model 85CH

Taurus Model 44

Taurus Model 415

Taurus Model 000

Taurus Model 85Ti, Model 731Ti Revolvers

Similar to the 2" Model 85 except has titanium frame, cylinder and ported barrel with stainless steel liner; yoke detent and extended ejector rod. Weight is 15.4 oz. Comes with soft, ridged Ribber grips. Available in Bright and Matte Spectrum blue, Matte Spectrum gold, and Steel Gray colors. Introduced 1999. Imported by Taurus International.
Price: Model 85Ti **$529.00**
Price: Model 731Ti (32 H&R mag., 6-shot). **$529.00**

Taurus Model 85CH Revolver

Same as the Model 85 except has 2" barrel only and concealed hammer. Soft rubber boot grip. Introduced 1991. Imported by Taurus International.
Price: Blue **$286.00**
Price: Stainless. **$327.00**
Price: Blue, ported barrel **$305.00**
Price: Stainless, ported barrel **$345.00**

TAURUS MODEL 94 REVOLVER

Caliber: 22 LR, 9-shot cylinder. **Barrel:** 2", 4", 5". **Weight:** 25 oz. **Stocks:** Soft black rubber. **Sights:** Serrated ramp front, click-adjustable rear for windage and elevation. **Features:** Floating firing pin, color case-hardened hammer and trigger. Introduced 1989. Imported by Taurus International.
Price: Blue **$308.00**
Price: Stainless. **$356.00**
Price: Model 94 UL, blue, 2", fixed sight, weighs 14 oz. **$342.00**
Price: As above, stainless **$391.00**

TAURUS MODEL 22H RAGING HORNET REVOLVER

Caliber: 22 Hornet, 8-shot cylinder. **Barrel:** 10". **Weight:** 50 oz. **Length:** 6.5" overall. **Stocks:** Soft black rubber. **Sights:** Patridge front, micrometer click adjustable rear. **Features:** Ventilated rib; 1:10: twist rifling; comes with scope base; stainless steel construction with matte finish. Introduced 1999. Imported by Taurus International.
Price: **$898.00**

TAURUS MODEL 44 REVOLVER

Caliber: 44 Mag., 6-shot. **Barrel:** 4", 6-1/2", 8-3/8". **Weight:** 44-3/4 oz. (4" barrel). **Length:** NA. **Stocks:** Soft black rubber. **Sights:** Serrated ramp front, micro-click rear adjustable for windage and elevation. **Features:**

Heavy solid rib on 4", vent rib on 6-1/2", 8-3/8". Compensated barrel. Blued model has color case-hardened hammer and trigger. Introduced 1994. Imported by Taurus International.
Price: Blue, 4". **$447.00**
Price: Blue, 6-1/2", 8-3/8". **$466.00**
Price: Stainless, 4" **$508.00**
Price: Stainless, 6-1/2", 8-3/8" **$530.00**

TAURUS MODEL 415 REVOLVER

Caliber: 41 Mag., 5-shot. **Barrel:** 2-1/2". **Weight:** 30 oz. **Length:** 7-1/8" overall. **Stocks:** Soft, ridged Ribber. **Sights:** Serrated front, notch rear. **Features:** Stainless steel construction; matte finish; ported barrel. Introduced 1999. Imported by Taurus International.
Price: **$452.00**

TAURUS MODEL 445, 445CH REVOLVERS

Caliber: 44 Special, 5-shot. **Barrel:** 2". **Weight:** 28.25 oz. **Length:** 6-3/4" overall. **Stocks:** Soft black rubber. **Sights:** Serrated ramp front, notch rear. **Features:** Blue or stainless steel. Standard or concealed hammer. Introduced 1997. Imported by Taurus International.
Price: Blue **$323.00**
Price: Blue, ported **$342.00**
Price: Stainless. **$370.00**
Price: Stainless, ported **$389.00**
Price: M445CH, concealed hammer, blue **$323.00**
Price: M445CH, blue, ported **$342.00**
Price: M445CH, stainless **$370.00**
Price: M445CH, stainless, ported. **$389.00**
Price: M445CH, Ultra-Lite, stainless, ported **$483.00**

TAURUS MODEL 605 REVOLVER

Caliber: 357 Mag., 5-shot. **Barrel:** 2-1/4", 3". **Weight:** 24.5 oz. **Length:** NA. **Stocks:** Soft black rubber. **Sights:** Serrated ramp front, fixed notch rear. **Features:** Heavy, solid rib barrel; floating firing pin. Blue or stainless. Introduced 1995. Imported by Taurus International.
Price: Blue **$303.00**
Price: Stainless. **$344.00**
Price: Model 605CH (concealed hammer) 2-1/4", blue **$303.00**

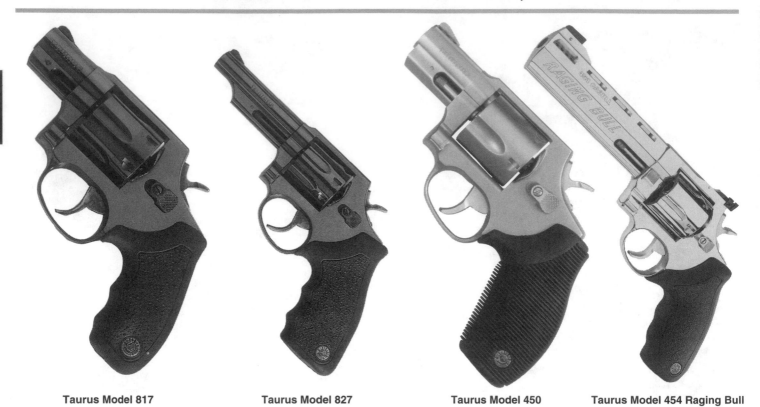

Taurus Model 817   Taurus Model 827   Taurus Model 450   Taurus Model 454 Raging Bull

Price: Model 605CH, stainless, 2-1/4" **$344.00**
Price: Blue, 2-1/4", ported barrel **$322.00**
Price: Stainless, 2-1/4", ported barrel. **$363.00**
Price: Blue, 2-1/4", ported barrel, concealed hammer **$322.00**
Price: Stainless, 2-1/4", ported barrel, concealed hammer **$363.00**

TAURUS MODEL 608 REVOLVER

Caliber: 357 Mag., 8-shot. **Barrel:** 4", 6-1/2", 8-3/8". **Weight:** 44 oz. **Length:** NA. **Stocks:** Soft black rubber. **Sights:** Serrated ramp front, fully adjustable rear. **Features:** Ventilated rib with built-in compensator on 6-1/2" barrel. Available in blue or stainless. Introduced 1995. Imported by Taurus international.
Price: Blue, 4". **$447.00**
Price: Blue, 6-1/2", 8-3/8" **$466.00**
Price: Stainless, 4" **$508.00**
Price: Stainless, 6-1/2", 8-3/8" **$530.00**

NEW! TAURUS MODEL 817 REVOLVER

Caliber: 38 Spec., 7-shot. **Barrel:** 2". **Weight:** 21 oz. **Length:** 6-1/2" overall. **Stocks:** Soft rubber. **Sights:** Serrated front, notch rear. **Features:** Compact alloy frame. Introduced 1999. Imported by Taurus International.
Price: Blue **$350.00**
Price: Blue, ported **$369.00**
Price: Stainless. **$389.00**
Price: Stainless, ported. **$408.00**

TAURUS MODEL 827 DOUBLE-ACTION REVOLVER

Caliber: 38 Special, 7-shot. **Barrel:** 4". **Weight:** 36 oz. **Length:** NA. **Stocks:** Finger-groove Santoprene. **Sights:** Serrated ramp front, notch rear. **Features:** Solid rib; shrouded ejector rod. Introduced 1998. Imported by Taurus International.
Price: Blue **$317.00**
Price: Stainless. **$364.00**

NEW! TAURUS MODEL 450 REVOLVER

Caliber: 45 Colt, 5-shot cylinder. **Barrel:** 2". **Weight:** 28 oz. **Length:** 6-5/8" overall. **Stocks:** Soft, ridged rubber. **Sights:** Serrated front, notch rear.

Taurus Model 454 Raging Bull

Features: Stainless steel construction; ported barrel. Introduced 1999. Imported by Taurus International.
Price: **$452.00**
Price: Ultra-Lite (alloy frame) **$483.00**

TAURUS MODEL 45, 444, 454 RAGING BULL REVOLVER

Caliber: 454 Casull, 5-shot. **Barrel:** 5", 6-1/2", 8-3/8". **Weight:** 53 oz. (6-1/2" barrel). **Length:** 12" overall (6-1/2" barrel). **Stocks:** Soft black rubber. **Sights:** Patridge front, micrometer click adjustable rear. **Features:** Ventilated rib; integral compensating system. Introduced 1997. Imported by Taurus International.
Price: 6-1/2", 8-3/8", blue **$750.00**
Price: 6-1/2", 8-3/8", stainless **$820.00**
Price: 5", 6-1/2", 8-1/2", matte stainless. **$820.00**
Price: 5", 6-1/2", 8-1/2", color case-hardened frame **$845.00**
Price: Model 45 (45 Colt), blue, 6-1/2", 8-3/8" **$545.00**
Price: Model 45, stainless, 6-1/2", 8-3/8" **$608.00**
Price: Model 444 (44 Mag.), blue, 6-1/2", 8-3/8" **$545.00**
Price: Model 444, stainless, 6-1/2", 8-3/8" **$608.00**

TAURUS MODEL 617, 606CH REVOLVER

Caliber: 357 Magnum, 7-shot. **Barrel:** 2". **Weight:** 29 oz. **Length:** 6-3/4" overall. **Stocks:** Soft black rubber. **Sights:** Serrated ramp front, notch

Taurus Model 617

Taurus Model 941

Dan Wesson Firearms Model 40, compenseated

rear. **Features:** Heavy, solid barrel rib, ejector shroud. Available with porting, concealed hammer. Introduced 1998. Imported by Taurus International.

Price: Blue, regular or concealed hammer $355.00
Price: Stainless, regular or concealed hammer $402.00
Price: Blue, ported $373.00
Price: Stainless, ported. $420.00
Price: Blue, concealed hammer, ported $373.00
Price: Stainless, concealed hammer, ported $420.00

Taurus Model 415Ti, 445Ti, 450Ti, 617Ti Revolvers

 Similar to the Model 617 except has titanium frame, cylinder, and ported barrel with stainless steel liner; yoke detent and extended ejector rod; +P rated; ridged Ribber grips. Available in Bright and Matte Spectrum Blue, Matte Spectrum Gold, and Stealth Gray. Introduced 1999. Imported by Taurus International.

Price: Model 617Ti, 357 Mag. $599.00
Price: Model 415Ti (41 Mag., 5-shot, 20.9 oz.) $599.00
Price: Model 450Ti (45 Colt, 5-shot, 19.2 oz.) $599.00
Price: Model 445Ti (44 Spec., 5-shot, 19.8 oz.) $599.00

TAURUS MODEL 941 REVOLVER

Caliber: 22 WMR, 8-shot. **Barrel:** 2", 4", 5". **Weight:** 27.5 oz. (4" barrel). **Length:** NA. **Stocks:** Soft black rubber. **Sights:** Serrated ramp front, rear adjustable for windage and elevation. **Features:** Solid rib heavy barrel with full-length ejector rod shroud. Blue or stainless steel. Introduced 1992. Imported by Taurus International.

Price: Blue $331.00
Price: Stainless. $384.00
Price: Model 941 UL, blue, 2", fixed sight, weighs 14 oz. $366.00
Price: As above, stainless $419.00

DAN WESSON FIREARMS MODEL 22 SILHOUETTE REVOLVER

Caliber: 22 LR, 6-shot. **Barrel:** 10", regular vent or vent heavy. **Weight:** 53 oz. **Stocks:** Combat style. **Sights:** Patridge-style front, .080" narrow notch rear. **Features:** Single action only. Available in blue or stainless. Reintroduced 1997. Made in U.S. by Dan Wesson Firearms.

Price: Blue, regular vent $474.00
Price: Blue, vent heavy. $492.00
Price: Stainless, regular vent $504.00
Price: Stainless, vent heavy $532.00

DAN WESSON FIREARMS MODEL 322/7322 TARGET REVOLVER

Caliber: 32-20, 6-shot. **Barrel:** 2.5", 4", 6", 8", standard vent, vent heavy. **Weight:** 43 oz. (6" VH). **Length:** 11.25" overall. **Stocks:** Checkered walnut. **Sights:** Red ramp interchangeable front, fully adjustable rear. **Features:** Bright blue or stainless. Reintroduced 1997. Made in U.S. by Dan Wesson Firearms.

Price: 6", vent heavy, blue $639.00
Price: 6", vent heavy, stainless. $743.00
Price: 8", vent heavy, blue $674.00
Price: 8", vent heavy, stainless. $787.00

DAN WESSON FIREARMS MODEL 40 SILHOUETTE

Caliber: 357 Maximum, 6-shot. **Barrel:** 4", 6", 8", 10". **Weight:** 64 oz. (8" bbl.). **Length:** 14.3" overall (8" bbl.). **Stocks:** Smooth walnut, target-style. **Sights:** 1/8" serrated front, fully adjustable rear. **Features:** Meets criteria for IHMSA competition with 8" slotted barrel. Blue or stainless steel. Made in U.S. by Dan Wesson Firearms.

Price: Blue, 4". $702.00
Price: Blue, 6". $749.00
Price: Blue, 8". $795.00
Price: Blue, 10". $858.00
Price: Stainless, 4" $834.00
Price: Stainless, 6" $892.00
Price: Stainless, 8" slotted $1,024.00
Price: Stainless, 10" $998.00
Price: 4", 6", 8" Compensated, blue . . . . $749.00 to $885.00
Price: As above, stainless . . . . $893.00 to $1,061.00

DAN WESSON FIREARMS MODEL 22 REVOLVER

Caliber: 22 LR, 22 WMR, 6-shot. **Barrel:** 2-1/2", 4", 6", 8"; interchangeable. **Weight:** 36 oz. (2-1/2"), 44 oz. (6"). **Length:** 9-1/4" overall (4" barrel).

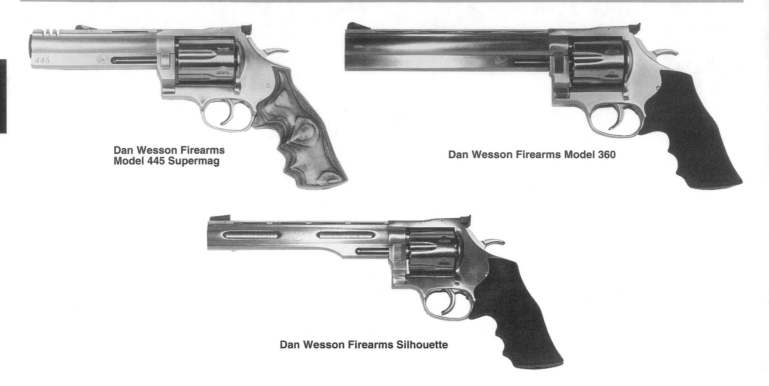

Dan Wesson Firearms
Model 445 Supermag

Dan Wesson Firearms Model 360

Dan Wesson Firearms Silhouette

Stocks: Checkered; undercover, service or over-size target. **Sights:** 1/8" serrated, interchangeable front, white outline rear adjustable for windage and elevation. **Features:** Built on the same frame as the Wesson 357; smooth, wide trigger with over-travel adjustment, wide spur hammer, with short double-action travel. Available in Brite blue or stainless steel. Reintroduced 1997. Contact Dan Wesson Firearms for complete price list.

Price: 2-1/2" bbl., blue $468.00
Price: As above, stainless $535.00
Price: With 4", vent heavy, blue $487.00
Price: As above, stainless $563.00
Price: Blue Pistol Pac, 22 LR $958.00

Dan Wesson Firearms Model 414, 445 SuperMag Revolvers

Similar size and weight as the Model 40 revolvers. Chambered for the 445 SuperMag cartridge, a longer version of the 44 Magnum and 414 Super-Mag. Barrel lengths of 4", 6", 8", 10". Contact maker for complete price list. Reintroduced 1997. Made in the U.S. by Dan Wesson Firearms.

Price: 4", vent heavy, blue $702.00
Price: As above, stainless $834.00
Price: 8", vent heavy, blue $795.00
Price: As above, stainless $950.00
Price: 10", vent heavy, blue $858.00
Price: As above, stainless $1,024.00
Price: 8", vent slotted, blue............................. $987.00
Price: As above, stainless $1,134.00
Price: 10", vent slotted, blue............................ $1,195.00
Price: As above, stainless $1,285.00
Price: 4", 6", 8" Compensated, blue .... $749.00 to $885.00
Price: As above, stainless .... $893.00 to $1,061.00

DAN WESSON FIREARMS MODEL 15 & 32 REVOLVERS

Caliber: 32-20, 32 H&R Mag. (Model 32), 357 Mag. (Model 15). **Barrel:** 2-1/2", 4", 6", 8" (M32), 2-1/2", 4", 6", 8", 10" (M15); vent heavy. **Weight:** 36 oz. (2-1/2" barrel). **Length:** 9-1/4" overall (4" barrel). **Stocks:** Checkered, interchangeable. **Sights:** 1/8" serrated front, fully adjustable rear. **Features:** New Generation Series. Interchangeable barrels; wide, smooth trigger, wide hammer spur; short double-action travel. Available in blue or stainless. Reintroduced 1997. Made in U.S. by Dan Wesson Firearms. Contact maker for full list of models.

Price: Model 15, blue, 2-1/2" $468.00
Price: Model 15, blue, 8" $552.00
Price: Model 15, stainless, 4".......................... $510.00
Price: Model 15, stainless, 6".......................... $546.00
Price: Model 15, blue, compensated .... $528.00 to $644.00
Price: Model 15, stainless, compensated........... $616.00 to $766.00
Price: Model 32, blue, 4" $553.00
Price: Model 32, blue, 8" $617.00
Price: Model 32, stainless, 2-1/2"...................... $593.00
Price: Model 32, stainless, 6"........................... $659.00

DAN WESSON FIREARMS MODEL 41V, 44V, 45V REVOLVERS

Caliber: 41 Mag., 44 Mag., 45 Colt, 6-shot. **Barrel:** 4", 6", 8", 10"; interchangeable; 4", 6", 8" Compensated. **Weight:** 48 oz. (4"). **Length:** 12" overall (6" bbl.) **Stocks:** Smooth. **Sights:** 1/8" serrated front, white outline rear adjustable for windage and elevation. **Features:** Available in blue or stainless steel. Smooth, wide trigger with adjustable over-travel; wide hammer spur. Available in Pistol Pac set also. Reintroduced 1997. Contact Dan Wesson Firearms for complete price list.

Price: 41 Mag., 4", vent heavy $558.00
Price: As above except in stainless $626.00
Price: 44 Mag., 4", blue $558.00
Price: As above except in stainless $626.00
Price: 45 Colt, 4", vent heavy............................ $555.00
Price: As above except in stainless $626.00
Price: Model 41, 44, 45, blue, 4", 6", 8" compensated . $633.00 to $727.00
Price: As above in stainless .... $752.00 to $868.00

DAN WESSON FIREARMS MODEL 360 REVOLVER

Caliber: 357 Mag. **Barrel:** 4", 6", 8", 10"; vent heavy. **Weight:** 64 oz. (8" barrel). **Length:** NA. **Stocks:** Hogue rubber finger groove. **Sights:** Interchangeable ramp or Patridge front, fully adjustable rear. **Features:** New Generation Large Frame Series. Interchangeable barrels and grips; smooth trigger, wide hammer spur. Blue or stainless. Introduced 1999. Made in U.S. by Dan Wesson Firearms.

Price: Blue, from.. $558.00
Price: Stainless, from $626.00

Dan Wesson Firearms Model 460

Dan Wesson Firearms
Super Ram Silhouette

DAN WESSON FIREARMS MODEL 460 REVOLVER

Caliber: 45 ACP and 460 Rowland. **Barrel:** 4", 6", 8", 10"; vent heavy. **Weight:** 49 oz. (4" barrel) **Length:** NA. **Stocks:** Hogue rubber finger groove; interchangeable. **Sights:** Interchangeable ramp or Patridge front, fully adjustable rear. **Features:** New Generation Large Frame Series. Shoots 45 ACP and 460 Rowland. Interchangeable barrels and grips. Available with non-fluted cylinder and Slotted Lightweight barrel shroud. Introduced 1999. Made in U.S. by Dan Wesson Firearms.
Price: .... **NA**

DAN WESSON FIREARMS STANDARD SILHOUETTE REVOLVER

Caliber: 357 SuperMag/Maxi, 41 Mag., 414 SuperMag, 445 SuperMag. **Barrel:** 8", 10" **Weight:** 64 oz. (8" barrel). **Length:** 14.3" overall (8" barrel). **Stocks:** Hogue rubber finger groove; interchangeable. **Sights:** Patridge front, fully adjustable rear. **Features:** Interchangeable barrels and grips; fluted or non-fluted cylinder; blue or stainless. Introduced 1999. Made in U.S. by Dan Wesson Firearms.

Price: 357 SuperMag/Maxi, 8", blue or stainless **$829.00**
Price: 41 Mag., 10", blue or stainless. **$929.00**
Price: 414 SuperMag., 8", blue or stainless **$949.00**
Price: 445 SuperMag., 8", blue or stainless **$949.00**

Dan Wesson Firearms Super Ram Silhouette Revolver

Similar to the Standard Silhouette except has 10 land and groove Laser Coat barrel, Bo-Mar target sights with hooded front, and special laser engraving. Fluted or non-fluted cylinder. Introduced 1999. Made in U.S. by Dan Wesson Firearms.

Price: 357 SuperMag/Maxi, 414 SuperMag., 445 SuperMag., 8", blue or stainless **$1,295.00**
Price: 41 Magnum, 44 Magnum, 8", blue or stainless **$1,149.00**
Price: 41 Magnum, 44 Magnum, 10", blue or stainless **$1,249.00**

Both classic six-shooters and modern adaptations for hunting and sport.

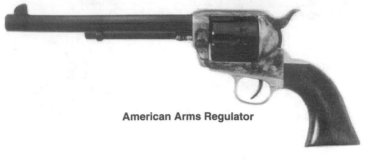

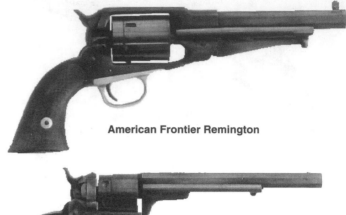

American Arms Regulator

American Frontier Remington

Armerican Frontier 1871-1872 Open-Top

American Frontier 1851 Mason

AMERICAN ARMS REGULATOR SINGLE-ACTIONS
Caliber: 357 Mag. 44-40, 45 Colt. **Barrel:** 4-3/4", 5-1/2", 7-1/2". **Weight:** 32 oz. (4-3/4" barrel). **Length:** 8-1/6" overall (4-3/4" barrel). **Stocks:** Smooth walnut. **Sights:** Blade front, groove rear. **Features:** Blued barrel and cylinder, brass trigger guard and backstrap. Introduced 1992. Imported from Italy by American Arms, Inc.
Price: Regulator, single cylinder $320.00
Price: Regulator Nickel (polished nickel finish) $375.00
Price: Storekeeper B/H Nickel (polished nickel finish, bird's head grip, 4" barrel, 44-40, 45 Colt $419.00
Price: Storekeeper Nickel (4" barrel, standard grip) $375.00
Price: Regulator Deluxe (steel backstrap and trigger guard) $365.00
Price: Silverado (brushed nickel finish, non-fluted cylinder, laminated stocks) $409.00

AMERICAN FRONTIER POCKET RICHARDS & MASON NAVY
Caliber: 32, 5-shot cylinder. **Barrel:** 4-3/4", 5-1/2". **Weight:** NA. **Length:** NA. **Stocks:** Varnished walnut. **Sights:** Blade front, fixed rear. **Features:** Shoots metallic-cartridge ammunition. Non-rebated cylinder; high-polish blue, silver-plated brass backstrap and trigger guard; ejector assembly; color case-hardened hammer and trigger. Introduced 1996. Imported from Italy by American Frontier Firearms Mfg.
Price: From $495.00

AMERICAN FRONTIER 1871-1872 POCKET MODEL REVOLVER
Caliber: 32, 5-shot cylinder. **Barrel:** 4-3/4", 5-1/2" round. **Weight:** NA. **Length:** NA. **Stocks:** Varnished walnut or Tiffany. **Sights:** Blade front, fixed rear. **Features:** Based on the 1862 Police percussion revolver converted to metallic cartridge. High polish blue finish with silver-plated brass backstrap and trigger guard, color case-hardened hammer. Introduced 1996. Imported from Italy by American Frontier Firearms Mfg.
Price: From $350.00

AMERICAN FRONTIER 1851 NAVY CONVERSION
Caliber: 38, 44. **Barrel:** 4-3/4", 5-1/2", 7-1/2", octagon. **Weight:** NA. **Length:** NA. **Stocks:** Varnished walnut, Navy size. **Sights:** Blade front, fixed rear. **Features:** Shoots metallic cartridge ammunition. Non-rebated cylinder; blued steel backstrap and trigger guard; color case-hardened hammer, trigger, ramrod, plunger; no ejector rod assembly. Introduced 1996. Imported from Italy by American Frontier Firearms Mfg.
Price: $695.00

AMERICAN FRONTIER 1871-1872 OPEN-TOP REVOLVERS
Caliber: 38, 44. **Barrel:** 4-3/4", 5-1/2", 7-1/2", 8" round. **Weight:** NA. **Length:** NA. **Stocks:** Varnished walnut. **Sights:** Blade front, fixed rear. **Features:** Reproduction of the early cartridge conversions from percussion. Made for metallic cartridges. High polish blued steel, silver-plated brass backstrap and trigger guard, color case-hardened hammer; straight non-rebated cylinder with naval engagement engraving; stamped with original patent dates. Does not have conversion breechplate. Introduced 1996. Imported from Italy by American Frontier Firearms Mfg.
Price: $795.00
Price: Tiffany model with Tiffany grips, silver and gold finish with engraving $995.00

AMERICAN FRONTIER REMINGTON NEW MODEL REVOLVER
Caliber: 38, 44. **Barrel:** 5-1/2", 7-1/2". **Weight:** NA. **Length:** NA. **Stocks:** Varnished walnut. **Sights:** Blade front, fixed rear. **Features:** Replica of the factory conversions by Remington between 1863 and 1875. High polish blue or silver finish with color case-hardened hammer; has original loading lever and no gate or ejector assembly. Introduced 1996. Imported from Italy by American Frontier Firearms Mfg.
Price: $695.00

AMERICAN FRONTIER RICHARDS 1860 ARMY
Caliber: 38, 44. **Barrel:** 4-3/4", 5-1/2", 7-1/2", round. **Weight:** NA. **Length:** NA. **Stocks:** Varnished walnut, Army size. **Sights:** Blade front, fixed rear. **Features:** Shoots metallic cartridge ammunition. Rebated cylinder; available with or without ejector assembly; high-polish blue including backstrap; silver-plated trigger guard; color case-hardened hammer and trigger. Introduced 1996. Imported from Italy by American Frontier Firearms Mfg.
Price: $695.00

AMERICAN FRONTIER REMINGTON NEW ARMY CAVALRY
Caliber: 38, 44, 45. **Barrel:** 5-1/2", 7-1/2", 8". **Weight:** NA. **Length:** NA. **Stocks:** Varnished walnut **Sights:** Blade front, fixed rear. **Features:** High polish blue finish; color case-hardened hammer. Has ejector assembly, loading gate. Government inspector's cartouche on left grip, sub-inspector's initials on various parts. Introduced 1997. Imported from Italy by American Frontier Firearms Mfg.
Price: Artillery model (5-1/2" barrel only) $795.00
Price: $795.00

American Frontier 1851 Navy Richards & Mason Conversion
Similar to the 1851 Navy Conversion except has Mason ejector assembly.

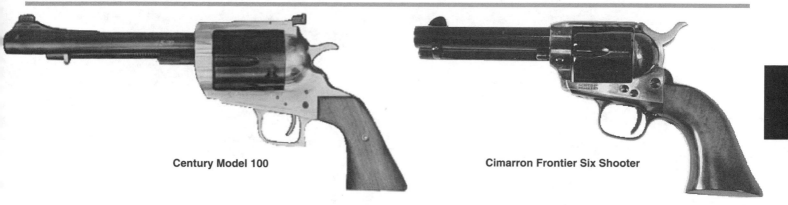

Century Model 100

Cimarron Frontier Six Shooter

Introduced 1996. Imported from Italy by American Frontier Firearms Mfg.
Price: $695.00

CENTURY GUN DIST. MODEL 100 SINGLE-ACTION
Caliber: 30-30, 375 Win., 444 Marlin, 45-70, 50-70. **Barrel:** 6-1/2" (standard), 8", 10". **Weight:** 6 lbs. (loaded). **Length:** 15" overall (8" bbl.). **Stocks:** Smooth walnut. **Sights:** Ramp front, Millett adjustable square notch rear. **Features:** Highly polished high tensile strength manganese bronze frame, blue cylinder and barrel; coil spring trigger mechanism. Calibers other than 45-70 start at $2,000.00. Contact maker for full price information. Introduced 1975. Made in U.S. From Century Gun Dist., Inc.
Price: 6-1/2" barrel, 45-70 .... $1,250.00

CIMARRON U.S. CAVALRY MODEL SINGLE-ACTION
Caliber: 45 Colt. **Barrel:** 7-1/2". **Weight:** 42 oz. **Length:** 13-1/2" overall. **Stocks:** Walnut. **Sights:** Fixed. **Features:** Has "A.P. Casey" markings; "U.S." plus patent dates on frame, serial number on backstrap, trigger guard, frame and cylinder, "APC" cartouche on left grip; color case-hardened frame and hammer, rest charcoal blue. Exact copy of the original. Imported by Cimarron F.A. Co.
Price: $499.00

Cimarron Rough Rider Artillery Model Single-Action
Similar to the U.S. Cavalry model except has 5-1/2" barrel, weighs 39 oz., and is 11-1/2" overall. U.S. markings and cartouche, case-hardened frame and hammer; 45 Colt only.
Price: $499.00

CIMARRON EL PISTOLERO SINGLE-ACTION REVOLVER
Caliber: 357 Mag., 45 Colt. **Barrel:** 4-3/4", 5-1/2", 7-1/2". **Weight:** 40 oz. **Length:** 10-1/4" overall (4-3/4" barrel). **Stocks:** Smooth walnut. **Sights:** Fixed. **Features:** Brass backstrap and trigger guard, blued barrel and cylinder, color case-hardened frame. Introduced 1999. Imported by Cimarron F.A. Co.
Price: $359.00

CIMARRON 1873 FRONTIER SIX SHOOTER
Caliber: 38 WCF, 357 Mag., 44 WCF, 44 Spec., 45 Colt. **Barrel:** 4-3/4", 5-1/2", 7-1/2". **Weight:** 39 oz. **Length:** 10" overall (4" barrel). **Stocks:** Walnut. **Sights:** Blade front, fixed or adjustable rear. **Features:** Uses "old model" blackpowder frame with "Bullseye" ejector or New Model frame. Imported by Cimarron F.A. Co.
Price: 4-3/4" barrel $469.00
Price: 5-1/2" barrel $469.00
Price: 7-1/2" barrel $469.00

Cimarron Bisley Model Single-Action Revolvers
Similar to the 1873 Frontier Six Shooter except has special grip frame and trigger guard, knurled wide-spur hammer, curved trigger. Available in 357 Mag., 44 WCF, 45 Schofield, 45 Colt. Introduced 1999. Imported by Cimarron F.A. Co.
Price: $499.00

Cimarron Flat Top Single-Action Revolvers
Similar to the 1873 Frontier Six Shooter except has flat top strap with windage-adjustable rear sight, elevation-adjustable front sight. Available

in 357 Mag., 44 WCF, 45 Schofield, 45 Colt; 4-3/4", 5-1/2", 7-1/2" barrel. Introduced 1999. Imported by Cimarron F.A. Co.
Price: $479.00

Cimarron Bisley Flat Top Revolver
Similar to the Flat Top revolver except has special grip frame and trigger guard, wide spur hammer, curved trigger. Introduced 1999. Imported by Cimarron F.A. Co.
Price: $509.00

CIMARRON 1851 RICHARDS CONVERSION REVOLVER
Caliber: 38 Spec., 38 Colt, 44 Colt. **Barrel:** 5-1/2", 7-1/2", 8" (Army model). **Weight:** NA. **Length:** NA. **Stocks:** Smooth walnut. **Sights:** Blade front, fixed rear. **Features:** Replica of the 1871 Richards cartridge conversion. Color case-hardened frame, silver-plated trigger guard, rest blued. Introduced 1999. From Cimarron F.A. Co.
Price: $549.00

CIMARRON 1860 ARMY RICHARDS CONVERSION REVOLVER
Caliber: 38 Spec., 44 Colt. **Barrel:** 5-1/2", 8". **Weight:** NA. **Length:** NA. **Stocks:** Smooth walnut. **Sights:** Brass blade front, fixed rear. **Features:** Replica of the 1871 Richards cartridge conversion. Color case-hardened frame, brass grip frame, silver-plated trigger guard, rest blued. Introduced 1999. From Cimarron F.A. Co.
Price: $549.00

CIMARRON THUNDERER REVOLVER
Caliber: 357 Mag., 44 WCF, 44 Spec., 45 Colt, 6-shot. **Barrel:** 3-1/2", 4-3/4", 5-1/2", 7-1/2", with ejector. **Weight:** 38 oz. (3-1/2" barrel). **Length:** NA. **Stocks:** Smooth walnut. **Sights:** Blade front, notch rear. **Features:** Thunderer grip; color case-hardened frame with balance blued. Introduced 1993. Imported by Cimarron F.A. Co.
Price: 3-1/2", 4-3/4", smooth grips $489.00
Price: As above, checkered grips......................... $524.00
Price: 5-1/2", 7-1/2", smooth grips $529.00
Price: As above, checkered grips......................... $564.00

CIMARRON 1872 OPEN-TOP REVOLVER
Caliber: 38 Spec., 38 Colt, 44 Spec., 44 Colt, 44 Russian, 45 Schofield. **Barrel:** 7-1/2". **Weight:** NA. **Length:** NA. **Stocks:** Smooth walnut. **Sights:** Blade front, fixed rear. **Features:** Replica of the original production. Color case-hardened frame, rest blued, including grip frame. Introduced 1999. Imported from Italy by Cimarron F.A. Co.
Price: $579.00

CIMARRON 1875 SCHOFIELD PATENT REVOLVER
Caliber: 44 Russian, 44 Special, 44 WCF, 45 Colt, 45 S&W Schofield. **Barrel:** 5", 7". **Weight:** 39 oz. **Length:** 10-3/4" overall (5" barrel). **Stocks:** Smooth walnut. **Sights:** Blade front, notch rear. **Features:** Authentic reproduction of the original. Single-action, top-break with automatic ejection. Wells Fargo has 5" barrel; U.S. Cavalry model has 7" barrel, military inspector markings and cartouche; civilian model has 7" barrel. Introduced 1999. Imported by Cimarron F.A. Co.
Price: $849.00

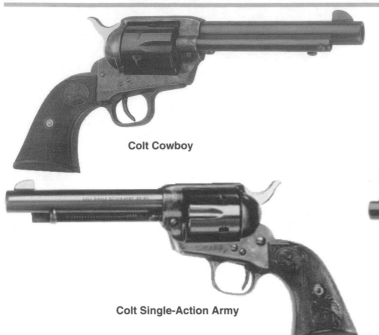

Colt Cowboy

Colt Single-Action Army

E.A.A. Bounty Hunter

EMF Hartford

EMF 1894 Bisley

COLT COWBOY SINGLE-ACTION REVOLVER
Caliber: 45 Colt, 6-shot. **Barrel:** 5-1/2". **Weight:** 42 oz. **Stocks:** Black composition, first generation style. **Sights:** Blade front, notch rear. **Features:** Dimensional replica of Colt's original Peacemaker with medium-size color case-hardened frame; transfer bar safety system; half-cock loading. Introduced 1998. Made in U.S. by Colt's Mfg. Co.
Price: About $599.00

COLT SINGLE-ACTION ARMY REVOLVER
Caliber: 44-40, 45 Colt, 6-shot. **Barrel:** 4-3/4", 5-1/2", 7-1/2". **Weight:** 40 oz. (4-3/4" barrel). **Length:** 10-1/4" overall (4-3/4" barrel). **Stocks:** Black Eagle composite. **Sights:** Blade front, notch rear. **Features:** Available in full nickel finish with nickel grip medallions, or Royal Blue with color case-hardened frame, gold grip medallions. Reintroduced 1992.
Price: $1,590.00

E.A.A. BOUNTY HUNTER SA REVOLVERS
Caliber: 22 LR/22 WMR, 357 Mag., 44 Mag., 45 Colt, 6-shot. **Barrel:** 4-1/2", 7-1/2". **Weight:** 2.5 lbs. **Length:** 11" overall (4-5/8" barrel). **Stocks:** Smooth walnut. **Sights:** Blade front, grooved topstrap rear. **Features:** Transfer bar safety; three position hammer; hammer forged barrel. Introduced 1992. Imported by European American Armory.
Price: Blue or case-hardened. $280.00
Price: Nickel $298.00
Price: 22LR/22WMR, blue $187.20
Price: As above, nickel. $204.36

EMF HARTFORD SINGLE-ACTION REVOLVERS
Caliber: 22 LR, 357 Mag., 32-20, 38-40, 44-40, 44 Spec., 45 Colt. **Barrel:** 4-3/4", 5-1/2", 7-1/2". **Weight:** 45 oz. **Length:** 13" overall (7-1/2" barrel). **Stocks:** Smooth walnut. **Sights:** Blade front, fixed rear. **Features:** Identical to the original Colts with inspector cartouche on left grip, original patent dates and U.S. markings. All major parts serial numbered using original Colt-style lettering, numbering. Bullseye ejector head and color case-hardening on frame and hammer. Introduced 1990. From E.M.F.
Price: $600.00
Price: Cavalry or Artillery $655.00
Price: Nickel plated. $725.00
Price: Engraved, nickel plated $840.00

EMF 1894 Bisley Revolver
Similar to the Hartford single-action revolver except has special grip frame and trigger guard, wide spur hammer; available in 45 Colt only, 5-1/2" or 7-1/2" barrel. Introduced 1995. Imported by E.M.F.

Price: Blue $680.00
Price: Nickel $805.00

EMF Hartford Pinkerton Single-Action Revolver
Same as the regular Hartford except has 4" barrel with ejector tube and birds head grip. Calibers 32-20, 38-40, 44-40, 44 Special, 45 Colt. Introduced 1997. Imported by E.M.F.
Price: $475.00

EMF Hartford Express Single-Action Revolver
Same as the regular Hartford model except uses grip of the Colt Lightning revolver. Barrel lengths of 4", 4-3/4", 5-1/2". Introduced 1997. Imported by E.M.F.
Price: $475.00

EMF 1875 OUTLAW REVOLVER
Caliber: 357 Mag., 44-40, 45 Colt. **Barrel:** 7-1/2". **Weight:** 46 oz. **Length:** 13-1/2" overall. **Stocks:** Smooth walnut. **Sights:** Blade front, fixed groove rear. **Features:** Authentic copy of 1875 Remington with firing pin in hammer; color case-hardened frame, blue cylinder, barrel, steel backstrap and brass trigger guard. Also available in nickel, factory engraved. Imported by E.M.F.
Price: All calibers $465.00
Price: Nickel $550.00
Price: Engraved $600.00
Price: Engraved nickel $710.00

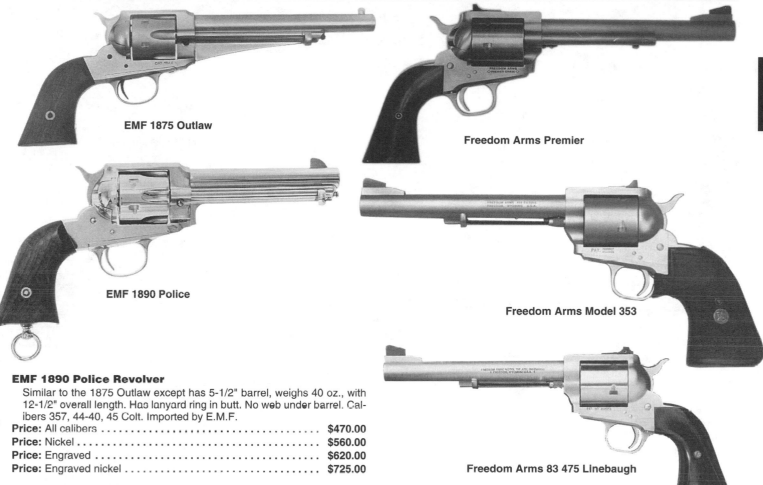

EMF 1875 Outlaw

Freedom Arms Premier

EMF 1890 Police

Freedom Arms Model 353

Freedom Arms 83 475 Linebaugh

EMF 1890 Police Revolver

Similar to the 1875 Outlaw except has 5-1/2" barrel, weighs 40 oz., with 12-1/2" overall length. Has lanyard ring in butt. No web under barrel. Calibers 357, 44-40, 45 Colt. Imported by E.M.F.

Price: All calibers **$470.00**
Price: Nickel **$560.00**
Price: Engraved **$620.00**
Price: Engraved nickel **$725.00**

FREEDOM ARMS MODEL 83 454 SINGLE-ACTION REVOLVER

Caliber: 357 Mag., 41 Rem. Mag., 44 Rem. Mag., 454 Casull, 50 AE, 5-shot. **Barrel:** 4-3/4", 6", 7-1/2", 10". **Weight:** 50 oz. **Length:** 14" overall (7-1/2" bbl.). **Stocks:** Impregnated hardwood (Premier grade), or Pachmayr (Field Grade). **Sights:** Blade front, notch or adjustable rear. **Features:** All stainless steel construction; sliding bar safety system. Lifetime warranty. Made in U.S. by Freedom Arms, Inc.

Price: Premier Grade, 454 Casull, 50 AE, adj. sight **$1,820.00**
Price: Premier Grade, 454 Casull, fixed sight. **$1,723.00**
Price: Field Grade, 454 Casull, 50 AE, adj. sight **$1,400.00**
Price: Field Grade, 454 Casull, fixed sight **$1,322.00**
Price: Premier Grade, 357 Mag., 41 Rem. Mag., 44 Rem. Mag.,
adj. sight **$1,760.00**
Price: Premier Grade, 44 Rem. Mag., fixed sight **$1,663.00**
Price: Field Grade, 357 Mag., 41 Rem. Mag., 44 Rem. Mag.,
adj. sight **$1,340.00**

Freedom Arms Model 83 353 Revolver

Made on the Model 83 frame. Chambered for 357 Magnum with 5-shot cylinder; 4-3/4", 6", 7-1/2" or 9" barrel. Weighs 59 oz. with 7-1/2" barrel. Field grade model has adjustable sights, matte finish, Pachmayr grips. Silhouette has 9" barrel, adjustable front sight blade with hood, Iron Sight Gun Works Silhouette adjustable rear, Pachmayr grips, trigger over-travel adjustment screw. All stainless steel. Introduced 1992.

Price: Field Grade. **$1,340.00**
Price: Premier Grade (brushed finish, impregnated hardwood grips,
Premier Grade sights) **$1,760.00**
Price: Silhouette (9", 357 Mag., 10", 44 Mag.) **$1,448.00**

Freedom Arms Model 83 654 Revolver

Made on the Model 83 frame. Chambered for 41 Magnum with 5-shot cylinder. Introduced 1998. Made in U.S. by Freedom Arms.

Price: Field Grade, adjustable sights **$1,400.00**
Price: Premier Grade, adjustable sights **$1,820.00**
Price: Silhouette **$1,440.00**

FREEDOM ARMS MODEL 83 475 LINEBAUGH REVOLVER

Caliber: 475 Linebaugh, 5-shot. **Barrel:** 4.75", 6", 7.5". **Weight:** NA. **Length:** NA. **Stocks:** Impregnated hardwood (Premier Grade) or Pachmayr (Field Grade). **Sights:** Removable ramp front, fully adjustable notch rear. **Features:** All stainless steel construction with brushed finish (Premier Grade) or matte finish (Field Grade); patented slide bar safety. Introduced 1999. Made in U.S. by Freedom Arms.

Price: Premier Grade **$1,820.00**
Price: Field Grade **$1,400.00**

Freedom Arms Model 83 555 Revolver

Made on the Model 83 frame. Chambered for the 50 A.E. (Action Express) cartridge. Offered in Premier and Field Grades with adjustable sights, 4-3/4", 6", 7-1/2" or 10" barrel. Introduced 1994. Made in U.S. by Freedom Arms, Inc.

Price: Premier Grade **$1,820.00**
Price: Field Grade **$1,400.00**

FREEDOM ARMS MODEL 97 MID FRAME REVOLVER

Caliber: 357 Mag., 6-shot cylinder; 45 Colt, 5-shot. **Barrel:** 5-1/2", 7-1/2". **Weight:** 40 oz. (5-1/2" barrel). **Length:** 10-3/4" overall (5-1/2" barrel). **Stocks:** Impregnated hardwood or black micanta optional. **Sights:** Blade on ramp front, fixed or fully adjustable rear. **Features:** Made of stainless steel; brushed finish. Introduced 1997. Made in U.S. by Freedom Arms.

Price: Adjustable sight **$1,492.00**
Price: Fixed sight **$1,391.00**

Freedom Arms Model 555

IAR Model 1873 Six Shooter

Freedom Arms Model 252 Varmint

IAR Model 1873 Frontier

Heritage Rough Rider

IAR Model 1873 Frontier Marshall

FREEDOM ARMS MODEL 252 VARMINT CLASS REVOLVER
Caliber: 22 LR, 5-shot. **Barrel:** 5.125", 7.5". **Weight:** 58 oz. (7.5" barrel). **Length:** NA. **Stocks:** Black and green laminated hardwood. **Sights:** Brass bead express front, express rear with shallow V-notch. **Features:** All stainless steel construction. Dual firing pins; lightened hammer; pre-set trigger stop. Built on Model 83 frame and accepts Model 83 Freedom Arms sights and/or scope mounts. Introduced 1991. Made in U.S. by Freedom Arms.
Price: **$1,527.00**
Price: Extra fitted 22 WMR cylinder **$264.00**

HERITAGE ROUGH RIDER REVOLVER
Caliber: 22 LR, 22 LR/22 WMR combo, 6-shot. **Barrel:** 2-3/4", 3-1/2", 4-3/4", 6-1/2", 9". **Weight:** 31 to 38 oz. **Length:** NA. **Stocks:** Exotic hardwood. **Sights:** Blade front, fixed rear. Adjustable sight on 6-1/2" only. **Features:** Hammer block safety. High polish blue or nickel finish. Introduced 1993. Made in U.S. by Heritage Mfg., Inc.
Price: . . . . **$119.95 to $174.95**
Price: 2-3/4", 3-1/2", 4-3/4" bird's-head grip . . . . **$139.95 to $174.95**

IAR MODEL 1873 SIX SHOOTER
Caliber: 22 LR/22 WMR combo. **Barrel:** 5-1/2". **Weight:** 36-1/2" oz. **Length:** 11-3/8" overall. **Stocks:** One-piece walnut. **Sights:** Blade front, notch rear. **Features:** A 3/4-scale reproduction. Color case-hardened frame, blued barrel. All-steel construction. Made by Uberti. Imported from Italy by IAR, Inc.
Price: **$360.00**

IAR MODEL 1873 FRONTIER REVOLVER
Caliber: 22 RL, 22 LR/22 WMR. **Barrel:** 4-3/4". **Weight:** 45 oz. **Length:** 10-1/2" overall. **Stocks:** One-piece walnut with inspector's cartouche. **Sights:** Blade front, notch rear. **Features:** Color case-hardened frame, blued barrel, black nickel-plated brass trigger guard and backstrap. Bright nickel and engraved versions available. Introduced 1997. Imported from Italy by IAR, Inc.
Price: **$395.00**
Price: Nickel-plated **$485.00**
Price: 22 LR/22WMR combo **$425.00**

IAR MODEL 1873 FRONTIER MARSHAL
Caliber: 357 Mag., 45 Colt. **Barrel:** 4-3/4", 5-1/2, 7-1/2". **Weight:** 39 oz. **Length:** 10-1/2" overall. **Stocks:** One-piece walnut. **Sights:** Blade front, notch rear. **Features:** Bright brass trigger guard and backstrap, color case-hardened frame, blued barrel and cylinder. Introduced 1998. Imported from Italy by IAR, Inc.
Price: **$395.00**

MAGNUM RESEARCH BFR SINGLE-ACTION REVOLVER
Caliber: 22 Hornet, 45 Colt +P, 454 Casull, 50 A.E. (Little Max, standard cylinder). **Barrel:** 7-1/2", 10". **Weight:** 4 lbs. **Length:** 11" overall with 7-1/2" barrel. **Stocks:** Uncle Mike's checkered rubber. **Sights:** Orange blade on ramp front, fully adjustable rear. **Features:** Stainless steel construction. Optional pearl and finger-groove grips available. Introduced 1997. Made in U.S. From Magnum Research, Inc.
Price: **$899.00**

MAGNUM RESEARCH LITTLE MAX REVOLVER
Caliber: 22 Hornet, 45 Colt, 454 Casull, 50 A.E. **Barrel:** 6-1/2", 7-1/2", 10". **Weight:** 45 oz. **Length:** 13" overall (7-1/2" barrel). **Stocks:** Rubber.

Navy Arms Flat Top   Navy Arms Pinched Frame   Navy Arms Bisley   Navy Arms 1873   Navy Arms Schofield

Sights: Ramp front, adjustable rear. **Features:** Single action; stainless steel construction. Announced 1998. Made in U.S. From Magnum Research.
Price: **$899.00**
Price: Maxline model (7-1/2", 10", 45 Colt, 45-70, 444 Marlin). . . **$899.00**

NAVY ARMS FLAT TOP TARGET MODEL REVOLVER
Caliber: 45 Colt, 6-shot cylinder. **Barrel:** 7-1/2". **Weight:** 40 oz. **Length:** 13-1/4" overall. **Stocks:** Smooth walnut. **Sights:** Spring-loaded German silver front, rear adjustable for windage. **Features:** Replica of Colt's Flat Top Frontier target revolver made from 1888 to 1896. Blue with color case-hardened frame. Introduced 1997. Imported by Navy Arms.
Price: **$430.00**

NAVY ARMS "PINCHED FRAME" SINGLE-ACTION REVOLVER
Caliber: 45 Colt, 6-shot. **Barrel:** 7-1/2". **Weight:** 37 oz. **Length:** 13" overall. **Stocks:** Smooth walnut **Sights:** German silver blade, notch rear. **Features:** Replica of Colt's original Peacemaker. Color case-hardened frame, hammer, rest charcoal blued. Introduced 1997. Imported by Navy Arms.
Price: **$415.00**

NAVY ARMS BISLEY MODEL SINGLE-ACTION REVOLVER
Caliber: 44-40 or 45 Colt, 6-shot cylinder. **Barrel:** 4-3/4", 5-1/2", 7-1/2". **Weight:** 40 oz. **Length:** 12-1/2" overall (7-1/2" barrel). **Stocks:** Smooth walnut. **Sights:** Blade front, notch rear. **Features:** Replica of Colt's Bisley Model. Polished blue finish, color case-hardened frame. Introduced 1997. Imported by Navy Arms.
Price: **$445.00**

Navy Arms Bisley Model Flat Top Target Revolver
Similar to the standard Bisley model except with flat top strap, 7-1/2" barrel only, and a spring-loaded German silver front sight blade, standing leaf rear sight adjustable for windage. Polished blue finish, color case-hardened frame. Introduced 1998. Imported by Navy Arms.
Price: **$480.00**

NAVY ARMS 1873 SINGLE-ACTION REVOLVER
Caliber: 357 Mag., 44-40, 45 Colt, 6-shot cylinder. **Barrel:** 4-3/4", 5-1/2", 7-1/2". **Weight:** 36 oz. **Length:** 10-3/4" overall (5-1/2" barrel). **Stocks:**

Smooth walnut. **Sights:** Blade front, notch rear. **Features:** Blue with color case-hardened frame. Introduced 1991. Imported by Navy Arms.
Price: **$385.00**
Price: 1873 U.S. Cavalry Model (7-1/2", 45 Colt, arsenal markings) **$455.00**
Price: 1895 U.S. Artillery Model (as above, 5-1/2" barrel) **$455.00**

NAVY ARMS SHOOTIST MODEL SINGLE-ACTION REVOLVER
Caliber: 357 Mag., 44-40, 45 Colt, 6-shot cylinder. **Barrel:** 4-3/4", 5-1/2", 7-1/2". **Weight:** 36 oz. **Length:** 11-1/4" overall (5-1/2" barrel). **Stocks:** Smooth walnut. **Sights:** Blade front, notch rear. **Features:** Replica of Colt's Single Action Army. Parts interchange with first and second generation Colts. Polished blue, color case-hardened frame. Introduced 1999. Imported by Navy Arms.
Price: **$385.00**

NAVY ARMS 1875 SCHOFIELD REVOLVER
Caliber: 44-40, 45 Colt, 6-shot cylinder. **Barrel:** 3-1/2", 5", 7". **Weight:** 39 oz. **Length:** 10-3/4" overall (5" barrel). **Stocks:** Smooth walnut. **Sights:** Blade front, notch rear. **Features:** Replica of Smith & Wesson Model 3 Schofield. Single-action, top-break with automatic ejection. Polished blue finish. Introduced 1994. Imported by Navy Arms.
Price: Hideout Model, 3-1/2" barrel **$695.00**
Price: Wells Fargo, 5" barrel. **$695.00**
Price: U.S. Cavalry model, 7" barrel, military markings **$695.00**

Navy Arms Deluxe 1875 Schofield Revolver
Similar to standard Schofield except has hand-cut "A" engraving and gold inlays, charcoal blue finish. Available in either Wells Fargo (5" barrel) or Cavalry (7" barrel) model. Introduced 1999. Imported by Navy Arms.
Price: **$1,875.00**

NAVY ARMS NEW MODEL RUSSIAN REVOLVER
Caliber: 44 Russian, 6-shot cylinder. **Barrel:** 6-1/2". **Weight:** 40 oz. **Length:** 12" overall. **Stocks:** Smooth walnut. **Sights:** Blade front, notch rear. **Features:** Replica of the S&W Model 3 Russian Third Model revolver. Spur trigger guard, polished blue finish. Introduced 1999. Imported by Navy Arms.
Price: **$745.00**

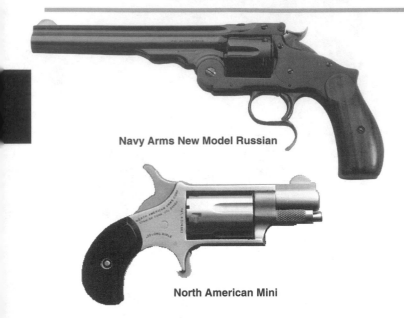

Navy Arms New Model Russian

North American Mini

Ruger Bisley Single-Action

Millett Low Profile fixed sights or Millett sight adjustable for elevation only. Overall length 5-7/8", weighs 8.8 oz. From North American Arms.
Price: Adjustable sight, 22 LR or 22 WMR **$269.00**
Price: As above with extra WMR/LR cylinder **$306.00**
Price: Fixed sight, 22 LR or 22 WMR **$251.00**
Price: As above with extra WMR/LR cylinder **$288.00**

NAVY ARMS 1851 NAVY CONVERSION REVOLVER

NEW! **Caliber:** 38 Spec., 38 Long Colt. **Barrel:** 5-1/2", 7-1/2". **Weight:** 44 oz. **Length:** 14" overall (7-1/2" barrel). **Stocks:** Smooth walnut. **Sights:** Bead front, notch rear. **Features:** Replica of Colt's cartridge conversion revolver. Polished blue finish with color case-hardened frame, brass trigger guard and backstrap. Introduced 1999. Imported by Navy Arms.
Price: **$360.00**

NAVY ARMS 1860 ARMY CONVERSION REVOLVER

NEW! **Caliber:** 38 Spec., 38 Long Colt. **Barrel:** 5-1/2", 7-1/2". **Weight:** 44 oz. **Length:** 13-1/2" overall (7-1/2" barrel). **Stocks:** Smooth walnut. **Sights:** Blade front, notch rear. **Features:** Replica of Colt's conversion revolver. Polished blue finish with color case-hardened frame, full-size 1860 Army grip with blued steel backstrap. Introduced 1999. Imported by Navy Arms.
Price: **$360.00**

NAVY ARMS 1861 NAVY CONVERSION REVOLVER

NEW! **Caliber:** 38 Spec., 38 Long Colt. **Barrel:** 5-1/2", 7-1/2". **Weight:** 44 oz. **Length:** 13-1/2" overall (7-1/2" barrel). **Stocks:** Smooth walnut. **Sights:** Blade front, notch rear. **Features:** Replica of Colt's cartridge conversion. Polished blue finish with color case-hardened frame, brass trigger guard and backstrap. Introduced 1999. Imported by Navy Arms.
Price: **$360.00**

NORTH AMERICAN MINI-REVOLVERS

Caliber: 22 Short, 22 LR, 22 WMR, 5-shot. **Barrel:** 1-1/8", 1-5/8". **Weight:** 4 to 6.6 oz. **Length:** 3-5/8" to 6-1/8" overall. **Stocks:** Laminated wood. **Sights:** Blade front, notch fixed rear. **Features:** All stainless steel construction. Polished satin and matte finish. Engraved models available. From North American Arms.
Price: 22 Short, 22 LR **$176.00**
Price: 22 WMR, 1-5/8" bbl. **$194.00**
Price: 22 WMR, 1-1/8" or 1-5/8" bbl. with extra 22 LR cylinder . . **$231.00**

NORTH AMERICAN MINI-MASTER

Caliber: 22 LR, 22 WMR, 5-shot cylinder. **Barrel:** 4". **Weight:** 10.7 oz. **Length:** 7.75" overall. **Stocks:** Checkered hard black rubber. **Sights:** Blade front, white outline rear adjustable for elevation, or fixed. **Features:** Heavy vent barrel; full-size grips. Non-fluted cylinder. Introduced 1989.
Price: Adjustable sight, 22 WMR or 22 LR **$299.00**
Price: As above with extra WMR/LR cylinder **$336.00**
Price: Fixed sight, 22 WMR or 22 LR **$281.00**
Price: As above with extra WMR/LR cylinder **$318.00**

North American Black Widow Revolver

Similar to the Mini-Master except has 2" heavy vent barrel. Built on the 22 WMR frame. Non-fluted cylinder, black rubber grips. Available with either

RUGER BLACKHAWK REVOLVER

Caliber: 30 Carbine, 357 Mag./38 Spec., 41 Mag., 45 Colt, 6-shot. **Barrel:** 4-5/8" or 5-1/2", either caliber; 7-1/2" (45 Colt only). **Weight:** 42 oz. (6-1/2" bbl.). **Length:** 12-1/4" overall (5-1/2" bbl.). **Stocks:** American walnut. **Sights:** 1/8" ramp front, micro-click rear adjustable for windage and elevation. **Features:** Ruger transfer bar safety system, independent firing pin, hardened chrome-moly steel frame, music wire springs throughout. Comes with plastic lockable case and lock.
Price: Blue 30 Carbine, 7-1/2" (BN31) **$380.00**
Price: Blue, 357 Mag., 4-5/8", 6-1/2" (BN34, BN36) **$380.00**
Price: As above, stainless (KBN34, KBN36) **$467.00**
Price: Blue, 357 Mag./9mm Convertible, 4-5/8", 6-1/2" (BN34X, BN36X) **$405.00**
Price: Blue, 41 Mag., 4-5/8", 6-1/2" (BN41, BN42) **$380.00**
Price: Blue, 45 Colt, 4-5/8", 5-1/2", 7-1/2" (BN44, BN455, BN45) **$380.00**
Price: Stainless, 45 Colt, 4-5/8", 7-1/2" (KBN44, KBN45) **$467.00**
Price: Blue, 45 Colt/45 ACP Convertible, 4-5/8", 5-1/2" (BN44X, BN455X)
. . . . **$405.00**

RUGER SUPER BLACKHAWK

Caliber: 44 Mag., 6-shot. Also fires 44 Spec. **Barrel:** 4-5/8", 5-1/2", 7-1/2", 10-1/2" bull. **Weight:** 48 oz. (7-1/2" bbl.), 51 oz. (10-1/2" bbl.). **Length:** 13-3/8" overall (7-1/2" bbl.). **Stocks:** American walnut. **Sights:** 1/8" ramp front, micro-click rear adjustable for windage and elevation. **Features:** Ruger transfer bar safety system, non-fluted cylinder, steel grip and cylinder frame, square back trigger guard, wide serrated trigger and wide spur hammer. Comes with plastic lockable case and lock.
Price: Blue, 4-5/8", 5-1/2", 7-1/2" (S458N, S45N, S47N) **$435.00**
Price: Blue, 10-1/2" (S411N) **$440.00**
Price: Stainless, 4-5/8", 5-1/2", 7-1/2" (KS458N, KS45N, KS47N). **$475.00**
Price: Stainless, 10-1/2" (KS411N) **$480.00**

RUGER VAQUERO SINGLE-ACTION REVOLVER

Caliber: 357 Mag., 44-40, 44 Mag., 45 Colt, 6-shot. **Barrel:** 4-5/8", 5-1/2", 7-1/2". **Weight:** 41 oz. **Length:** 13-3/8" overall (7-1/2" barrel). **Stocks:** Smooth rosewood with Ruger medallion. **Sights:** Blade front, fixed notch rear. **Features:** Uses Ruger's patented transfer bar safety system and loading gate interlock with classic styling. Blued model has color case-hardened finish on the frame, the rest polished and blued. Stainless model has high-gloss polish. Introduced 1993. From Sturm, Ruger & Co.
Price: 357 Mag. BNV34 (4-5/8"), BNV35 (5-1/2") **$455.00**
Price: 357 Mag. KBNV34 (4-5/8"), KBNV35 (5-1/2") stainless . . . **$455.00**
Price: BNV44 (4-5/8"), BNV445 (5-1/2"), BNV45 (7-1/2"), blue . . **$455.00**
Price: KBNV44 (4-5/8"), KBNV455 (5-1/2"), KBNV45 (7-1/2"), stainless **$455.00**

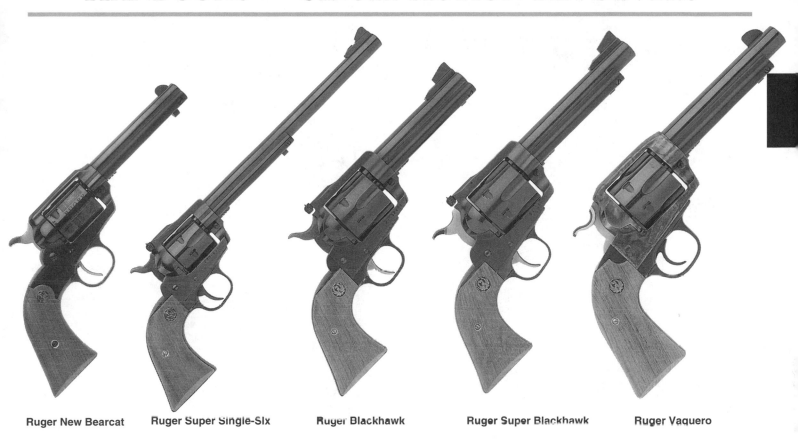

Ruger New Bearcat   **Ruger Super Single-Six**   **Ruger Blackhawk**   **Ruger Super Blackhawk**   **Ruger Vaquero**

Price: 44 Mag. BNV475IE (engraved cylinder, simulated ivory grips), blue, 5-1/2" **$604.00**
Price: 44 Mag. KBNV475IE (engraved cylinder, simulated ivory grips), stainless, 5-1/2" **$604.00**
Price: 45 Colt BNV455IE (engraved cylinder, simulated ivory grips), blue, 5 1/2" **$604.00**
Price: 45 Colt KBNV455IE (engraved cylinder, simulated ivory grips), stainless, 5-1/2" **$604.00**

Ruger Bisley-Vaquero Single-Action Revolver
Similar to the Vaquero except has Bisley-style hammer, grip and trigger and is available in 357 Magnum, 44 Magnum and 45 Colt only, with 5-1/2" barrel. Has smooth rosewood grips with Ruger medallion. Introduced 1997. From Sturm, Ruger & Co.
Price: Color case-hardened frame, blue grip frame, barrel and cylinder, RBNV-475, RBNV-455 .... **$472.00**
Price: High-gloss stainless steel, KRBNV-475, KRBNV-455 ..... **$512.00**
Price: For simulated ivory grips add **$36.00**
Price: 44-40 BNV40 (4-5/8"), BNV405 (5-1/2"), BNV407 (7-1/2") . **$455.00**
Price: 44-40 KBNV40 (4-5/8"), KBNV405 (5-1/2"), KBNV407 (7-1/2") stainless **$455.00**

RUGER NEW BEARCAT SINGLE-ACTION
Caliber: 22 LR, 6-shot. **Barrel:** 4". **Weight:** 23 oz. **Length:** 8-7/8" overall. **Stocks:** Smooth rosewood with Ruger medallion. **Sights:** Blade front, fixed notch rear. **Features:** Reintroduction of the Ruger Super Bearcat with slightly lengthened frame, Ruger patented transfer bar safety system. Available in blue only. Introduced 1993. Comes with plastic lockable case and lock. From Sturm, Ruger & Co.
Price: SBC4, blue **$330.00**

RUGER SUPER SINGLE-SIX CONVERTIBLE
Caliber: 22 LR, 6-shot; 22 WMR in extra cylinder. **Barrel:** 4-5/8", 5-1/2", 6-1/2", 9-1/2" (6-groove). **Weight:** 34-1/2 oz. (6-1/2" bbl.). **Length:** 11-13/16" overall (6-1/2" bbl.). **Stocks:** Smooth American walnut. **Sights:** Im-

proved Patridge front on ramp, fully adjustable rear protected by integral frame ribs; or fixed sight. **Features:** Ruger transfer bar safety system, gate-controlled loading, hardened chrome-moly steel frame, wide trigger, music wire springs throughout, independent firing pin.
Price: 4-5/8", 5-1/2", 6-1/2", 9-1/2" barrel, blue, fixed or adjustable sight (5-1/2", 6-1/2") **$335.00**
Price: 5-1/2", 6-1/2" bbl. only, stainless steel, adjustable sight .. **$415.00**

Ruger Bisley Small Frame Revolver
Similar to the Single-Six except frame is styled after the classic Bisley "flat top." Most mechanical parts are unchanged. Hammer is lower and smoothly curved with a deeply checkered spur. Trigger is strongly curved with a wide smooth surface. Longer grip frame designed with a hand-filling shape, and the trigger guard is a large oval. Adjustable dovetail rear sight; front sight base accepts interchangeable square blades of various heights and styles. Has an unfluted cylinder and roll engraving. Weighs about 41 oz. Chambered for 22 LR, 6-1/2" barrel only. Comes with plastic lockable case and lock. Introduced 1985.
Price: **$402.00**

Ruger Bisley Single-Action Revolver
Similar to standard Blackhawk except the hammer is lower with a smoothly curved, deeply checkered wide spur. The trigger is strongly curved with a wide smooth surface. Longer grip frame has a hand-filling shape. Adjustable rear sight, ramp-style front. Has an unfluted cylinder and roll engraving, adjustable sights. Chambered for 357, 44 Mags. and 45 Colt; 7-1/2" barrel; overall length of 13". Comes with plastic lockable case and lock. Introduced 1985.
Price: **$472.00**

TRADITIONS 1851 NAVY CONVERSION REVOLVER
Caliber: 38 Spec. **Barrel:** 7-1/2". **Weight:** 40 oz. **Length:** 14-1/2" overall. **Stocks:** Smooth walnut. **Sights:** Post front, hammer-notch rear. **Features:** Steel frame, brass trigger guard. Introduced 1998. From Traditions.
Price: **$395.00**

Traditions 1851 Navy

Traditions 1873

Traditions 1861 Navy

Traditions Sheriffs

TRADITIONS 1858 REMINGTON CONVERSION REVOLVER

NEW! **Caliber:** 38 Spec., 44 Colt. **Barrel:** 7-1/2". **Weight:** 2 lbs., 8 oz. **Length:** 14-1/2" overall. **Stocks:** Smooth walnut. **Sights:** Post front, notch rear. **Features:** Replica of converted Remington. Blued steel grip frame and trigger guard. Introduced 1999. Imported by Traditions.
Price: $410.00

TRADITIONS 1860 ARMY CONVERSION REVOLVER

NEW! **Caliber:** 38 Spec., 44 Colt. **Barrel:** 7-1/2". **Weight:** 44 oz. **Length:** 14-1/2" overall. **Stocks:** Smooth walnut. **Sights:** Blade front, notch rear. **Features:** Replica of Colt's conversion revolver. Polished blue finish with color case-hardened frame, full-size 1860 Army grip with blued steel backstrap. Introduced 1999. Imported by Traditions.
Price: $395.00

TRADITIONS 1861 NAVY CONVERSION REVOLVER

NEW! **Caliber:** 38 Spec., 44 Colt. **Barrel:** 7-1/2". **Weight:** 44 oz. **Length:** 14-1/2" overall. **Stocks:** Smooth walnut. **Sights:** Blade front, notch rear. **Features:** Replica of Colt's cartridge conversion. Polished blue finish with color case-hardened frame, brass trigger guard and backstrap. Introduced 1999. Imported by Traditions.
Price: $395.00

TRADITIONS 1872 OPEN-TOP CONVERSION REVOLVER

Caliber: 38 Spec., 44 Colt. **Barrel:** 8". **Weight:** 2 lbs. 8 oz. **Length:** 14-1/2" overall. **Stocks:** Smooth walnut. **Sights:** Blade front, fixed rear. **Features:** Replica of the original production. Color case-hardened frame, rest blued, including grip frame. Introduced 1999. Imported from Italy by Traditions.
Price: $395.00

TRADITIONS 1873 SINGLE-ACTION REVOLVER

Caliber: 22 LR, 357 Mag., 44-40, 45 Colt, 6-shot cylinder. **Barrel:** 4-3/4", 5-1/2", 7-1/2". **Weight:** 44 oz. **Length:** 10-3/4" overall (5-1/2" barrel). **Stocks:** Walnut. **Sights:** Blade front, groove in topstrap rear. **Features:** Blued barrel, cylinder, color case-hardened frame, blue or brass trigger guard. Nickel-plated frame with polished brass trigger guard available in 357 Mag., 44-40, 45 Colt. Introduced 1998. From Traditions.
Price: . . . . $345.00 to $395.00

Traditions Sheriffs Revolver

Similar to the 1873 single-action revolver except has special birds-head grip with spur, and smooth or checkered walnut grips. Introduced 1998. From Traditions.
Price: With smooth walnut grips $369.00
Price: With checkered walnut grips $429.00

Traditions 1875 Schofield

TRADITIONS 1875 SCHOFIELD REVOLVER

Caliber: 44-40, 45 Schofield, 45 Colt, 6-shot cylinder. **Barrel:** 5-1/2". **Weight:** 40 oz. **Length:** 11-1/4" overall. **Stocks:** Walnut. **Sights:** Blade front, notch rear. **Features:** Blue finish, case-hardened frame, hammer, trigger. Introduced 1998. From Traditions.
Price: $659.00

UBERTI 1873 CATTLEMAN SINGLE-ACTION

Caliber: 22 LR/22 WMR, 38 Spec., 357 Mag., 44 Spec., 44-40, 45 Colt/45 ACP, 6-shot. **Barrel:** 4-3/4", 5-1/2", 7-1/2"; 44-40, 45 Colt also with 3", 3-1/2", 4". **Weight:** 38 oz. (5-1/2" bbl.). **Length:** 10-3/4" overall (5-1/2" bbl.). **Stocks:** One-piece smooth walnut. **Sights:** Blade front, groove rear; fully adjustable rear available. **Features:** Steel or brass backstrap, trigger guard; color case-hardened frame, blued barrel, cylinder. Imported from Italy by Uberti U.S.A.
Price: Steel backstrap, trigger guard, fixed sights $435.00
Price: Brass backstrap, trigger guard, fixed sights $365.00
Price: Bisley model $435.00

HANDGUNS — SINGLE ACTION REVOLVERS

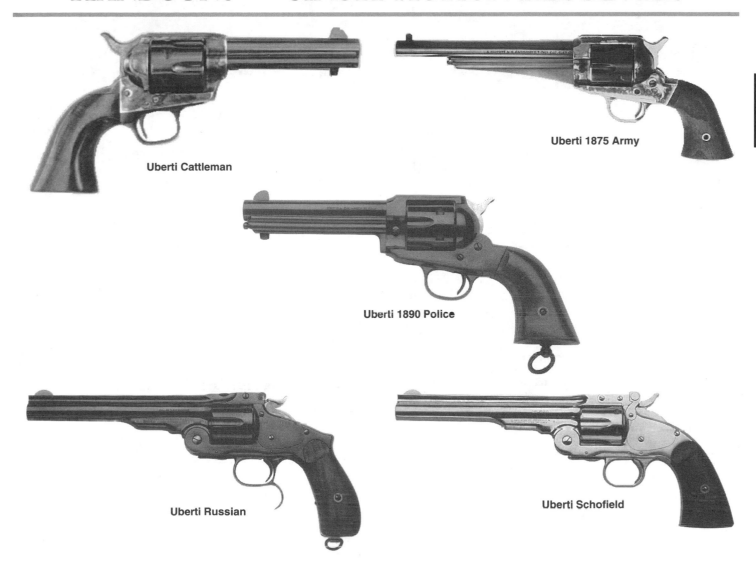

Uberti Cattleman

Uberti 1875 Army

Uberti 1890 Police

Uberti Russian

Uberti Schofield

Uberti 1873 Buckhorn Single-Action

A slightly larger version of the Cattleman revolver. Available in 44 Magnum or 44 Magnum/44-40 convertible, otherwise has same specs.
Price: Steel backstrap, trigger guard, fixed sights **$410.00**
Price: Convertible (two cylinders) **$475.00**

UBERTI 1875 SA ARMY OUTLAW REVOLVER

Caliber: 357 Mag., 44-40, 45 Colt, 45 Colt/45 ACP convertible, 6-shot. **Barrel:** 5-1/2", 7-1/2". **Weight:** 44 oz. **Length:** 13-3/4" overall. **Stocks:** Smooth walnut. **Sights:** Blade front, notch rear. **Features:** Replica of the 1875 Remington S.A. Army revolver. Brass trigger guard, color case-hardened frame, rest blued. Imported by Uberti U.S.A.
Price: **$435.00**
Price: 45 Colt/45 ACP convertible **$475.00**

UBERTI 1890 ARMY OUTLAW REVOLVER

Caliber: 357 Mag., 44-40, 45 Colt, 45 Colt/45 ACP convertible, 6-shot. **Barrel:** 5-1/2", 7-1/2". **Weight:** 37 oz. **Length:** 12-1/2" overall. **Stocks:** American walnut. **Sights:** Blade front, groove rear. **Features:** Replica of the 1890 Remington single-action. Brass trigger guard, rest is blued. Imported by Uberti U.S.A.
Price: **$435.00**
Price: 45 Colt/45 ACP convertible **$475.00**

UBERTI NEW MODEL RUSSIAN REVOLVER

Caliber: 44 Russian, 6-shot cylinder. **Barrel:** 6-1/2". **Weight:** 40 oz. **Length:** 12" overall. **Stocks:** Smooth walnut. **Sights:** Blade front, notch rear. **Features:** Replica of the S&W Model 3 Russian Third Model revolver. Spur trigger guard, polished blue finish. Introduced 1999. Imported by Uberti USA.
Price: **$775.00**

UBERTI 1875 SCHOFIELD REVOLVER

Caliber: 44-40, 45 Colt, 6-shot cylinder. **Barrel:** 5", 7". **Weight:** 39 oz. **Length:** 10-3/4" overall (5" barrel). **Stocks:** Smooth walnut. **Sights:** Blade front, notch rear. **Features:** Replica of Smith & Wesson Model 3 Schofield. Single-action, top-break with automatic ejection. Polished blue finish. Introduced 1994. Imported by Uberti USA.
Price: **$700.00**

UBERTI BISLEY MODEL SINGLE-ACTION REVOLVER

Caliber: 38-40, 357 Mag., 44 Spec., 44-40 or 45 Colt, 6-shot cylinder. **Barrel:** 4-3/4", 5-1/2", 7-1/2". **Weight:** 40 oz. **Length:** 12-1/2" overall (7-1/2" barrel). **Stocks:** Smooth walnut. **Sights:** Blade front, notch rear. **Features:** Replica of Colt's Bisley Model. Polished blue finish, color case-hardened frame. Introduced 1997. Imported by Uberti USA.
Price: **435.00**

Uberti Bisley Model Flat Top Target Revolver

Similar to the standard Bisley model except with flat top strap, 7-1/2" barrel only, and a spring-loaded German silver front sight blade, standing leaf rear sight adjustable for windage. Polished blue finish, color case-hardened frame. Introduced 1998. Imported by Uberti USA.
Price: **$455.00**

Uberti Bisley

Uberti Bisley Flattop

U.S. PATENT FIRE-ARMS SINGLE ACTION ARMY REVOLVER

Caliber: 22 LR, 22 WMR, 357 Mag., 44 Russian, 38-40, 44-40, 45 Colt, 6-shot cylinder. **Barrel:** 3", 4", 4-3/4", 5-1/2", 7-1/2", 10". **Length:** NA. **Stocks:** Smooth walnut. **Sights:** Blade front, notch rear. **Features:** Recreation of original guns; 3" and 4" have no ejector. Available with all-blue, blue with color case-hardening, or full nickel-plate finish. Made in Italy; available from United States Patent Fire-Arms Mfg. Co.

Price: 3" blue $600.00
Price: 4-3/4", blue/cased-colors $732.00
Price: 7-1/2", blue/case-colors $739.00
Price: 10", nickel $847.50

U.S. Patent Fire-Arms Nettleton Cavalry Revolver

Similar to the Single Action Army, except in 45 Colt only, with 7-1/2" barrel, color case-hardened/blue finish, and has old-style hand numbering, exact cartouche branding and correct inspector hand-stamp markings. Made in Italy; available from United States Patent Fire-Arms Mfg. Co.

Price: $950.00
Price: Artillery Model, 5-1/2" barrel $950.00

U.S. Patent Fire-Arms Bird Head Model Revolver

Similar to the Single Action Army except has bird's-head grip and comes with 3-1/2", 4" or 4-1/2" barrel. Made in Italy; available from United States Patent Fire-Arms Mfg. Co.

Price: 3-1/2", blue $635.50

Price: 4", blue with color case-hardening $735.00
Price: 4-1/2", nickel-plated $795.50

U.S. Patent Fire-Arms Flattop Target Revolver

Similar to the Single Action Army except 4-3/4", 5-1/2" or 7-1/2" barrel, two-piece hard rubber stocks, flat top frame, adjustable rear sight. Made in Italy; available from United States Patent Fire-Arms Mfg. Co.

Price: 4-3/4", blue, polished hammer $690.00
Price: 4-3/4", blue, case-colored hammer $813.00
Price: 5-1/2", blue, case-colored hammer $816.00
Price: 5-1/2", nickel-plated $765.00
Price: 7-1/2", blue, polished hammer $717.00
Price: 7-1/2", blue, case-colored hammer $822.00

U.S. PATENT FIRE-ARMS BISLEY MODEL REVOLVER

Caliber: 4 Colt, 6-shot cylinder. **Barrel:** 4-3/4", 5-1/2", 7-1/2", 10". **Weight:** 38 oz. (5-1/2" barrel). **Length:** NA. **Stocks:** Smooth walnut. **Sights:** Blade front, notch rear. **Features:** Available in all-blue, blue with color case-hardening, or full nickel plate finish. Made in Italy; available from United States Patent Fire-Arms Mfg. Co.

Price: 4-3/4", blue $652.00
Price: 5-1/2", blue/case-colors $750.50
Price: 7-1/2", blue/case-colors $756.00
Price: 10", nickel $862.50

Specially adapted single-shot and multi-barrel arms.

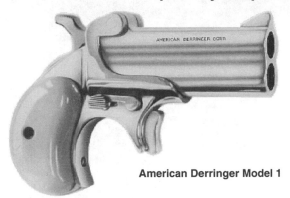

American Derringer Model 1

Bond Arms C2K Defender

AMERICAN DERRINGER MODEL 1

Caliber: 22 LR, 22 WMR, 30 Carbine, 30 Luger, 30-30 Win., 32 H&R Mag., 32-20, 380 ACP, 38 Super, 38 Spec., 38 Spec. shotshell, 38 Spec. +P, 9mm Para., 357 Mag., 357 Mag./45/410, 357 Maximum, 10mm, 40 S&W, 41 Mag., 38-40, 44-40 Win., 44 Spec., 44 Mag., 45 Colt, 45 Win. Mag., 45 ACP, 45 Colt/410, 45-70 single shot. **Barrel:** 3". **Weight:** 15-1/2 oz. (38 Spec.). **Length:** 4.82" overall. **Stocks:** Rosewood, Zebra wood. **Sights:** Blade front. **Features:** Made of stainless steel with high-polish or satin finish. Two-shot capacity. Manual hammer block safety. Introduced 1980. Available in almost any pistol caliber. Contact the factory for complete list of available calibers and prices. From American Derringer Corp.

Price: 22 LR	$260.00
Price: 38 Spec.	$260.00
Price: 357 Maximum	$285.00
Price: 357 Mag.	$275.00
Price: 9mm, 380,	$260.00
Price: 40 S&W	$275.00
Price: 44 Spec.	$338.00
Price: 44-40 Win., 45 Colt.	$338.00
Price: 30-30, 41, 44 Mags., 45 Win. Mag.	$400.00
Price: 45-70, single shot.	$327.00
Price: 45 Colt, 410, 2-1/2"	$365.00
Price: 45 ACP, 10mm Auto.	$280.00

American Derringer Model 4

Similar to the Model 1 except has 4.1" barrel, overall length of 6", and weighs 16-1/2 oz.; chambered for 357 Mag., 357 Maximum, 45-70, 3" 410-bore shotshells or 45 Colt or 44 Mag. Made of stainless steel. Manual hammer block safety. Introduced 1985.

Price: 3" 410/45 Colt.	$385.00
Price: 3" 410/45 Colt or 45-70 (Alaskan Survival model)	$400.00
Price: 44 Mag. with oversize grips	$445.00
Price: Alaskan Survival model (45-70 upper barrel, 410 or 45 Colt lower)	$400.00

American Derringer Model 6

Similar to the Model 1 except has 6" barrel chambered for 3" 410 shotshells or 22 WMR, 357 Mag., 45 ACP, 45 Colt; rosewood stocks; 8.2" o.a.l. and weighs 21 oz. Shoots either round for each barrel. Manual hammer block safety. Introduced 1986.

Price: 22 WMR	$365.00
Price: 357 Mag.	$365.00
Price: 45 Colt/410	$375.00
Price: 45 ACP	$365.00

American Derringer Model 7 Ultra Lightweight

Similar to Model 1 except made of high strength aircraft aluminum. Weighs 7-1/2 oz., 4.82" o.a.l., rosewood stocks. Available in 22 LR, 22 WMR, 32 H&R Mag., 380 ACP, 38 Spec., 44 Spec. Introduced 1986.

Price: 22 LR, WMR.	$265.00
Price: 38 Spec.	$265.00
Price: 380 ACP	$265.00

Price: 32 H&R Mag/32 S&W Long.	$265.00
Price: 44 Spec.	$505.00

American Derringer Model 10 Lightweight

Similar to the Model 1 except frame is of aluminum, giving weight of 10 oz. Stainless barrels. Available in 38 Spec., 45 Colt or 45 ACP only. Matte gray finish. Introduced 1989.

Price: 45 Colt	$325.00
Price: 45 ACP	$270.00
Price: 38 Spec.	$245.00

American Derringer Lady Derringer

Same as the Model 1 except has tuned action, is fitted with scrimshawed synthetic ivory grips; chambered for 32 H&R Mag. and 38 Spec.; 357 Mag., 45 Colt, 45/410. Deluxe Grade is highly polished; Deluxe Engraved is engraved in a pattern similar to that used on 1880s derringers. All come in a French fitted jewelry box. Introduced 1991.

Price: 32 H&R Mag.	$305.00
Price: 357 Mag.	$335.00
Price: 38 Spec.	$290.00
Price: 45 Colt, 45/410.	$365.00

American Derringer Texas Commemorative

A Model 1 Derringer with solid brass frame, stainless steel barrel and rosewood grips. Available in 38 Spec., 44-40 Win., or 45 Colt. Introduced 1987.

Price: 38 Spec.	$295.00
Price: 44-40 or 45 Colt.	$350.00
Price: Brass frame, 45 Colt	$380.00

AMERICAN DERRINGER DA 38 MODEL

Caliber: 22 LR, 9mm Para., 38 Spec., 357 Mag., 40 S&W. **Barrel:** 3". **Weight:** 14.5 oz. **Length:** 4.8" overall. **Stocks:** Rosewood, walnut or other hardwoods. **Sights:** Fixed. **Features:** Double-action only; two-shots. Manual safety. Made of satin-finished stainless steel and aluminum. Introduced 1989. From American Derringer Corp.

Price: 22 LR, 38 Spec.	$325.00
Price: 9mm Para.	$335.00
Price: 357 Mag., 40 S&W	$365.00

ANSCHUTZ MODEL 64P SPORT/TARGET PISTOL

Caliber: 22 LR, 22 WMR, 5-shot magazine. **Barrel:** 10". **Weight:** 3 lbs., 8 oz. **Length:** 18-1/2" overall. **Stock:** Choate Rynite. **Sights:** None furnished; grooved for scope mounting. **Features:** Right-hand bolt; polished blue finish. Introduced 1998. Imported from Germany by AcuSport.

Price: 22 LR	$455.95
Price: 22 WMR	$479.95

BOND ARMS TEXAS DEFENDER DERRINGER

Caliber: 9mm Para, 38 Spec./357 Mag., 40 S&W, 44 Spec./44 Mag., 45 Colt/410 shotshell. **Barrel:** 3", 3-1/2". **Weight:** 21 oz. **Length:** 5" overall. **Stocks:** Laminated black ash or rosewood. **Sights:** Blade front, fixed rear. **Features:** Interchangeable barrels; retracting firing pins; rebounding firing

Davis Big Bore

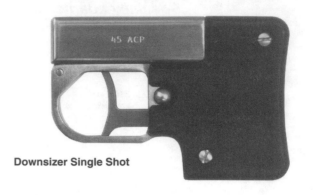

Downsizer Single Shot

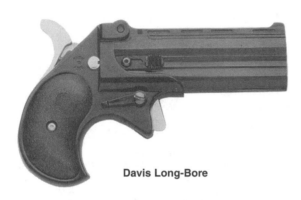

Davis Long-Bore

Gaucher GN1 Silhouette

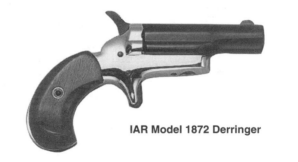

IAR Model 1872 Derringer

pins; cross-bolt safety; removable trigger guard; automatic extractor for rimmed calibers. Stainless steel construction with blasted/polished and ground combination finish. Introduced 1997. Made in U.S. by Bond Arms, Inc.

Price: $339.00
Price: Century 2000 Defender (410-bore, 3-1/2" barrels). $359.00

BROWN CLASSIC SINGLE SHOT PISTOL
Caliber: 17 Ackley Hornet through 45-70 Govt. **Barrel:** 15" airgauged match grade. **Weight:** About 3 lbs., 7 oz. **Stocks:** Walnut; thumbrest target style. **Sights:** None furnished; drilled and tapped for scope mounting. **Features:** Falling block action gives rigid barrel-receiver mating; hand-fitted and headspaced. Introduced 1998. Made in U.S. by E.A. Brown Mfg.
Price: $499.00

DAVIS BIG BORE DERRINGERS
Caliber: 22 WMR, 38 Spec., 9mm Para. **Barrel:** 2.75". **Weight:** 11.5 oz. **Length:** 4.65" overall. **Stocks:** Textured black synthetic. **Sights:** Blade front, fixed notch rear. **Features:** Alloy frame, steel-lined barrels, steel breech block. Plunger-type safety with integral hammer block. Chrome or black Teflon finish. Introduced 1992. Made in U.S. by Davis Industries.
Price: $98.00
Price: 9mm Para. $104.00

DAVIS LONG-BORE DERRINGERS
Caliber: 22 WMR, 38 Spec., 9mm Para. **Barrel:** 3.5". **Weight:** 13 oz. **Length:** 5.65" overall. **Stocks:** Textured black synthetic. **Sights:** Fixed. **Features:** Chrome or black Teflon finish. Larger than Davis D-Series models. Introduced 1995. Made in U.S. by Davis Industries.
Price: $104.00
Price: 9mm Para. $110.00
Price: Big-Bore models (same calibers, 3/4" shorter barrels). $98.00

DAVIS D-SERIES DERRINGERS
Caliber: 22 LR, 22 WMR, 25 ACP, 32 ACP. **Barrel:** 2.4". **Weight:** 9.5 oz. **Length:** 4" overall. **Stocks:** Laminated wood or pearl. **Sights:** Blade front, fixed notch rear. **Features:** Choice of black Teflon or chrome finish; spur trigger. Introduced 1986. Made in U.S. by Davis Industries.
Price: $75.00

DOWNSIZER WSP SINGLE SHOT PISTOL
Caliber: 9mm Para, 357 Magnum, 40 S&W, 45 ACP. **Barrel:** 2.10". **Weight:** 11 oz. **Length:** 3.25" overall. **Stocks:** Black polymer. **Sights:** None. **Features:** Single shot, tip-up barrel. Double action only. Stainless steel construction. Measures .900" thick. Introduced 1997. From Downsizer Corp.
Price: $354.00

GAUCHER GN1 SILHOUETTE PISTOL
Caliber: 22 LR, single shot. **Barrel:** 10". **Weight:** 2.4 lbs. **Length:** 15.5" overall. **Stocks:** European hardwood. **Sights:** Blade front, open adjustable rear. **Features:** Bolt action, adjustable trigger. Introduced 1990. Imported from France by Mandall Shooting Supplies.
Price: About $525.00
Price: Model GP Silhouette $425.00

IAR MODEL 1872 DERRINGER
Caliber: 22 Short. **Barrel:** 2-3/8". **Weight:** 7 oz. **Length:** 5-1/8" overall. **Stocks:** Smooth walnut. **Sights:** Blade front, notch rear. **Features:** Gold or nickel frame with blue barrel. Reintroduced 1996 using original Colt designs and tooling for the Colt Model 4 Derringer. Made in U.S. by IAR, Inc.
Price: $99.00
Price: Single cased gun $125.00
Price: Double cased set $215.00

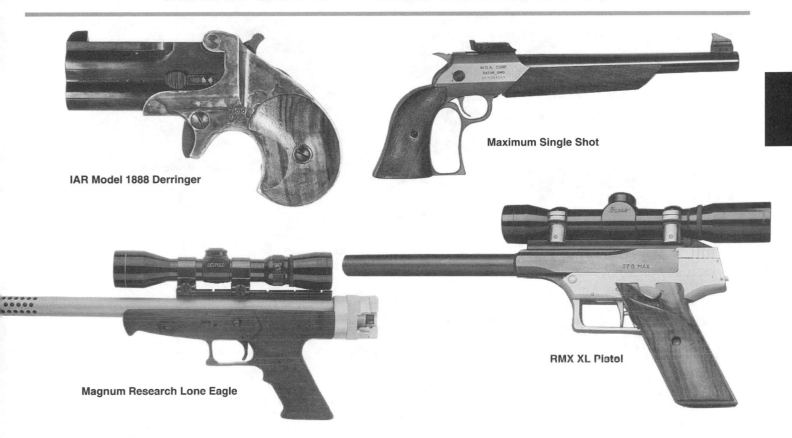

IAR Model 1888 Derringer

Maximum Single Shot

Magnum Research Lone Eagle

RMX XL Pistol

IAR MODEL 1888 DOUBLE DERRINGER
Caliber: 38 Special. **Barrel:** 2-3/4". **Weight:** 16 oz. **Length:** NA. **Stocks:** Smooth walnut. **Sights:** Blade front, notch rear. **Features:** All steel construction. Blue barrel, color case-hardened frame. Uses original designs and tooling for the Uberti New Maverick Derringer. Introduced 1999. Made in U.S. by IAR, Inc.
Price: $395.00

MAGNUM RESEARCH LONE EAGLE SINGLE SHOT PISTOL
Caliber: 22 Hornet, 223, 22-250, 243, 260 Rem., 7mm BR, 7mm-08, 30-30, 7.62x39, 308, 30-06, 357 Max., 35 Rem., 358 Win., 44 Mag., 444 Marlin, 440 Cor-Bon. **Barrel:** 14", interchangeable. **Weight:** 4 lbs., 3 oz. to 4 lbs., 7 oz. **Length:** 15" overall. **Stocks:** Ambidextrous. **Sights:** None furnished; drilled and tapped for scope mounting and open sights. Open sights optional. **Features:** Cannon-type rotating breech with spring-activated ejector. Ordnance steel with matte blue finish. Cross-bolt safety. External cocking lever on left side of gun. Muzzle brake optional. Introduced 1991. Available from Magnum Research, Inc.
Price: Complete pistol, black $438.00
Price: Barreled action only, black. $319.00
Price: Complete pistol, chrome. $478.00
Price: Barreled action, chrome $359.00
Price: Scope base $14.00
Price: Adjustable open sights $35.00

MANDALL/CABANAS PISTOL
Caliber: 177, pellet or round ball; single shot. **Barrel:** 9". **Weight:** 51 oz. **Length:** 19" overall. **Stock:** Smooth wood with thumbrest. **Sights:** Blade front on ramp, open adjustable rear. **Features:** Fires round ball or pellets with 22 blank cartridge. Automatic safety; muzzle brake. Imported from Mexico by Mandall Shooting Supplies.
Price: $139.95

MAXIMUM SINGLE SHOT PISTOL
Caliber: 22 LR, 22 Hornet, 22 BR, 22 PPC, 223 Rem., 22-250, 6mm BR, 6mm PPC, 243, 250 Savage, 6.5mm-35M, 270 MAX, 270 Win., 7mm TCU, 7mm BR, 7mm-35, 7mm INT-R, 7mm-08, 7mm Rocket, 7mm Super-

Mag., 30 Herrett, 30 Carbine, 30-30, 308 Win., 30x39, 32-20, 350 Rem. Mag., 357 Mag., 357 Maximum, 358 Win., 375 H&H, 44 Mag., 454 Casull. **Barrel:** 8-3/4", 10-1/2", 14". **Weight:** 61 oz. (10-1/2" bbl.); 78 oz. (14" bbl.). **Length:** 15", 18-1/2" overall (with 10-1/2" and 14" bbl., respectively). **Stocks:** Smooth walnut stocks and forend. Also available with 17" finger groove grip. **Sights:** Ramp front, fully adjustable open rear. **Features:** Falling block action; drilled and tapped for M.O.A. scope mounts; integral grip frame/receiver; adjustable trigger; Douglas barrel (interchangeable). Introduced 1983. Made in U.S. by M.O.A. Corp.
Price: Stainless receiver, blue barrel $740.00
Price: Stainless receiver, stainless barrel. $818.00
Price: Extra blued barrel. $235.00
Price: Extra stainless barrel $293.00
Price: Scope mount $60.00

REMINGTON MODEL XP-100R LONG RANGE PISTOL
Caliber: 22-250, 223, 260 Rem., 35 Rem., 4-shot magazine (5 in 223). **Barrel:** 14-1/2". **Weight:** 4-1/2 lbs. **Length:** NA. **Stocks:** Rear grip fiberglass composite. **Sights:** None furnished; drilled and tapped for scope mounting. **Features:** Blind magazine; blue finish. Reintroduced 1998. Made in U.S. by Remington.
Price: $665.00

RPM XL SINGLE SHOT PISTOL
Caliber: 22 LR through 45-70. **Barrel:** 8", 10-3/4", 12", 14". **Weight:** About 60 oz. **Length:** NA. **Stocks:** Smooth Goncalo Alves with thumb and heel rests. **Sights:** Hooded front with interchangeable post, or Patridge; ISGW rear adjustable for windage and elevation. **Features:** Barrel drilled and tapped for scope mount. Visible cocking indicator. Spring-loaded barrel lock, positive hammer-block safety. Trigger adjustable for weight of pull and over-travel. Contact maker for complete price list. Made in U.S. by RPM.
Price: Hunter model (stainless frame, 5/16" underlug, latch lever and positive extractor) $1,295.00
Price: Extra barrel, 8" through 10-3/4" $387.50
Price: Extra barrel with positive extractor, add $100.00
Price: Muzzle brake $100.00

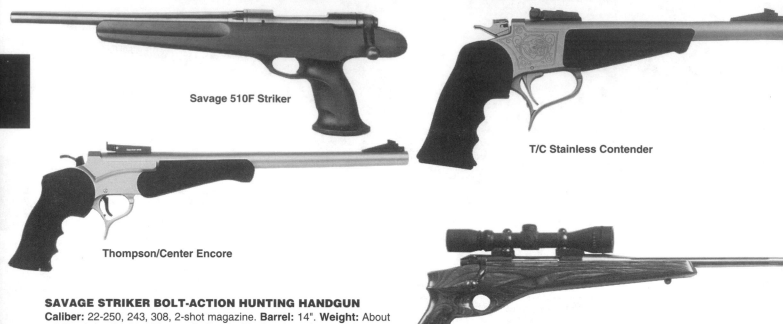

Savage 510F Striker

Thompson/Center Encore

T/C Stainless Contender

Weatherby Mark V CFP

SAVAGE STRIKER BOLT-ACTION HUNTING HANDGUN

Caliber: 22-250, 243, 308, 2-shot magazine. **Barrel:** 14". **Weight:** About 5 lbs. **Length:** 22-1/2" overall. **Stock:** Black composite ambidextrous mid-grip; grooved forend; "Dual Pillar" bedding. **Sights:** None furnished; drilled and tapped for scope mounting. **Features:** Short left-hand bolt with right-hand ejection; free-floated barrel; uses Savage Model 110 rifle scope rings/bases. Introduced 1998. Made in U.S. by Savage Arms, Inc.

Price: Model 510F (blued barrel and action) **$400.00**
Price: Model 516FSS (stainless barrel and action) **$450.00**
Price: Model 516FSAK (stainless, adjustable muzzle brake) **$500.00**

THOMPSON/CENTER ENCORE PISTOL

Caliber: 22-250, 223, 260 Rem., 7mm-08, 243, 308, 270, 30-06, 44 Mag., 454 Casull, 444 Marlin single shot. **Barrel:** 12", 15", tapered round. **Weight:** NA. **Length:** 21" overall with 12" barrel. **Stocks:** American walnut with finger grooves, walnut forend. **Sights:** Blade on ramp front, adjustable rear, or none. **Features:** Interchangeable barrels; action opens by squeezing the trigger guard; drilled and tapped for scope mounting; blue finish. Announced 1996. Made in U.S. by Thompson/Center Arms.

Price: **$534.00**
Price: Extra 10" barrels. **$235.00**
Price: Extra 15" barrels. **$243.00**
Price: 45 Colt/410 barrel, 12" **$258.00**
Price: 45 Colt/410 barrel, 15" **$274.00**

Thompson/Center Stainless Encore Pistol

Similar to the blued Encore except made of stainless steel and available wtih 15" barrel in 223, 22-250 7mm-08, 308. Comes with black rubber grip and forend. Made in U.S. by Thompson/Center Arms.

Price: **$591.00**

Thompson/Center Stainless Super 14

Same as the standard Super 14 and Super 16 except they are made of stainless steel with blued sights. Both models have black Rynite forend and finger-groove, ambidextrous grip with a built-in rubber recoil cushion that has a sealed-in air pocket. Receiver has a different cougar etching. Available in 22 LR Match, .223 Rem., 30-30 Win., 35 Rem. (Super 14), 45 Colt/410. Introduced 1993.

Price: **$550.00**
Price: 45 Colt/410, 14" **$584.00**

Thompson/Center Contender Shooter's Package

Package contains a 14" barrel without iron sights (10" for the 22 LR Match); Weaver-style base and rings; 2.5x-7x Recoil Proof pistol scope; and a soft carrying case. Calibers 22 LR, 223, 7-30 Waters, 30-30. Frame and barrel are blued; grip and forend are black composite. Introduced 1998. Made in U.S. by Thompson/Center Arms.

Price **$735.00**

THOMPSON/CENTER CONTENDER

Caliber: 7mm TCU, 30-30 Win., 22 LR, 22 WMR, 22 Hornet, 223 Rem., 270 Rem., 7-30 Waters, 32-20 Win., 357 Mag., 357 Rem. Max., 44 Mag., 10mm Auto, 445 SuperMag., 45/410, single shot. **Barrel:** 10", bull barrel and vent. rib. **Weight:** 43 oz. (10" bbl.). **Length:** 13-1/4" (10" bbl.). **Stock:** T/C "Competitor Grip." Right or left hand. **Sights:** Under-cut blade ramp front, rear adjustable for windage and elevation. **Features:** Break-open action with automatic safety. Single-action only. Interchangeable bbls., both caliber (rim & centerfire), and length. Drilled and tapped for scope. Engraved frame. See T/C catalog for exact barrel/caliber availability.

Price: Blued (rimfire cals.) **$484.00**
Price: Blued (centerfire cals.). **$484.00**
Price: Extra bbls. **$222.00**
Price: 45/410, internal choke bbl. **$245.00**

Thompson/Center Stainless Contender

Same as the standard Contender except made of stainless steel with blued sights, black Rynite forend and ambidextrous finger-groove grip with a built-in rubber recoil cushion that has a sealed-in air pocket. Receiver has a different cougar etching. Available with 10" bull barrel in 22 LR, 22 LR Match, 22 Hornet, 223 Rem., 30-30 Win., 357 Mag., 44 Mag., 45 Colt/410. Introduced 1993.

Price: **$539.00**
Price: 45 Colt/410. . . . . **$562.00**
Price: With 22 LR match chamber **$550.00**

UBERTI ROLLING BLOCK TARGET PISTOL

Caliber: 22 LR, 22 WMR, 22 Hornet, 357 Mag., 45 Colt, single shot. **Barrel:** 9-7/8", half-round, half-octagon. **Weight:** 44 oz. **Length:** 14" overall. **Stock:** Walnut grip and forend. **Sights:** Blade front, fully adjustable rear. **Features:** Replica of the 1871 rolling block target pistol. Brass trigger guard, color case-hardened frame, blue barrel. Imported by Uberti U.S.A.

Price: **$410.00**

WEATHERBY MARK V CFP PISTOL

Caliber: 22-250, 243, 7mm-08, 308. **Barrel:** 15" fluted stainless. **Weight:** NA. **Length:** NA. **Stock:** Brown laminate with ambidextrous rear grip. **Sights:** None furnished; drilled and tapped for scope mounting. **Features:** Uses Mark V lightweight receiver of chrome-moly steel, matte blue finish. Introduced 1998. Made in U.S. From Weatherby.

Price **$1,049.00**

CENTERFIRE RIFLES — AUTOLOADERS

Both classic arms and recent designs in American-style repeaters for sport and field shooting.

Armalite AR-10A4

Armalite M15A2

Auto-Ordnance 1927 A-1 Thompson

Barrett Model 82A-1

AA ARMS AR9 SEMI-AUTOMATIC RIFLE

Caliber: 9mm Para., 10-shot magazine. **Barrel:** 16". **Weight:** 6 lbs. **Length:** 31" overall. **Stock:** Fixed **Sights:** Post front adjustable for elevation, open rear for windage. **Features:** Blue or electroless nickel finish. Made in U.S. by AA Arms, Inc.

Price: Blue $695.00

ARMALITE M15A2 CARBINE

Caliber: 223, 7-shot magazine. **Barrel:** 16" heavy chrome lined; 1:9" twist. **Weight:** 7 lbs. **Length:** 35-11/16" overall. **Stock:** Green or black composition. **Sights:** Standard A2. **Features:** Upper and lower receivers have push-type pivot pin; hard coat anodized; A2-style forward assist; M16A2-type raised fence around magazine release button. Made in U.S. by ArmaLite, Inc.

Price: $930.00

ARMALITE AR-10A4 SPECIAL PURPOSE RIFLE

Caliber: 308 Win., 10-shot magazine. **Barrel:** 20" chrome-lined, 1:12" twist. **Weight:** 9.6 lbs. **Length:** 41" overall **Stock:** Green or black composition. **Sights:** Detachable handle, front sight, or scope mount available; comes with international style flattop receiver with Picatinny rail. **Features:** Proprietary recoil check. Forged upper receiver with case deflector. Receivers are hard-coat anodized. Introduced 1995. Made in U.S. by ArmaLite, Inc.

Price: $1,378.00

AUTO-ORDNANCE 1927 A-1 THOMPSON

Caliber: 45 ACP. **Barrel:** 16-1/2". **Weight:** 13 lbs. **Length:** About 41" overall (Deluxe). **Stock:** Walnut stock and vertical forend. **Sights:** Blade front, open rear adjustable for windage. **Features:** Recreation of Thompson Model 1927. Semi-auto only. Deluxe model has finned barrel, adjustable rear sight and compensator; Standard model has plain barrel and military sight. From Auto-Ordnance Corp.

Price: Deluxe $860.00

Price: 1927A1C Lightweight model (9-1/2 lbs.) $855.00

Auto-Ordnance Thompson M1

Similar to the 1927 A-1 except is in the M-1 configuration with side cocking knob, horizontal forend, smooth unfinned barrel, sling swivels on butt and forend. Matte black finish. Introduced 1985.

Price: $815.00

Auto-Ordnance 1927A1 Commando

Similar to the 1927A1 except has Parkerized finish, black-finish wood butt, pistol grip, horizontal forend. Comes with black nylon sling. Introduced 1998. Made in U.S. by Auto-Ordnance Corp.

Price: $850.00

BARRETT MODEL 82A-1 SEMI-AUTOMATIC RIFLE

Caliber: 50 BMG, 10-shot detachable box magazine. **Barrel:** 29". **Weight:** 28.5 lbs. **Length:** 57" overall. **Stock:** Composition with energy-absorbing recoil pad. **Sights:** Scope optional. **Features:** Semi-automatic, recoil op-

Browning Mark II Safari

Bushmaster M17S

Bushmaster XM15 E2S

erated with recoiling barrel. Three-lug locking bolt; muzzle brake. Adjustable bipod. Introduced 1985. Made in U.S. by Barrett Firearms.

Price: From **$6,800.00**

BROWNING BAR MARK II SAFARI SEMI-AUTO RIFLE

Caliber: 22-250, 243, 25-06, 270, 30-06, 308. **Barrel:** 22" round tapered. **Weight:** 7-3/8 lbs. **Length:** 43" overall. **Stock:** French walnut pistol grip stock and forend, hand checkered. **Sights:** Gold bead on hooded ramp front, click adjustable rear, or no sights. **Features:** Has new bolt release lever; removable trigger assembly with larger trigger guard; redesigned gas and buffer systems. Detachable 4-round box magazine. Scroll-engraved receiver is tapped for scope mounting. BOSS barrel vibration modulator and muzzle brake system available only on models without sights. Mark II Safari introduced 1993. Imported from Belgium by Browning.

Price: Safari, with sights **$760.00**
Price: Safari, no sights **$743.00**
Price: Safari, no sights, 270 Wea. Mag. **$797.00**
Price: Safari, no sights, BOSS **$803.00**

Browning BAR MARK II Lightweight Semi-Auto

Similar to the Mark II Safari except has lighter alloy receiver and 20" barrel. Available in 243, 308, 270, 30-06, 7mm Rem. Mag., 300 Win. Mag., 338 Win. Mag. Weighs 7 lbs., 2 oz.; overall length 41". Has dovetailed, gold bead front sight on hooded ramp, open rear click adjustable for windage and elevation. BOSS system optional. Introduced 1997. Imported from Belgium by Browning.

Price: 243, 308, 30-06 . . . . **$760.00**
Price: 7mm Rem. Mag., 300 Win. Mag., 338 Win. Mag **$814.00**
Price: As above with BOSS **$857.00**

Browning BAR Mark II Safari Magnum Rifle

Same as the standard caliber model, except weighs 8-3/8 lbs., 45" overall, 24" bbl., 3-round mag. Cals. 7mm Mag., 300 Win. Mag., 338 Win. Mag. BOSS barrel vibration modulator and muzzle brake system available only on models without sights. Introduced 1993.

Price: Safari, with sights **$814.00**
Price: Safari, no sights **$797.00**
Price: Safari, no sights, BOSS **$857.00**

BUSHMASTER M17S BULLPUP RIFLE

Caliber: 223, 10-shot magazine. **Barrel:** 21.5", chrome lined;1:9" twist. **Weight:** 8.2 lbs. **Length:** 30" overall. **Stock:** Fiberglass-filled nylon. **Sights:** Designed for optics—carrying handle incorporates scope mount rail for Weaver-type rings; also includes 25-meter open iron sights. **Features:** Gas-operated, short-stroke piston system; ambidextrous magazine release. Introduced 1993. Made in U.S. by Bushmaster Firearms, Inc./Quality Parts Co.

Price: **$720.00**

BUSHMASTER SHORTY XM15 E2S CARBINE

Caliber: 223,10-shot magazine. **Barrel:** 16", heavy; 1:9" twist. **Weight:** 7.2 lbs. **Length:** 34.75" overall. **Stock:** A2 type; fixed black composition. **Sights:** Fully adjustable M16A2 sight system. **Features:** Patterned after Colt M-16A2. Chrome-lined barrel with manganese phosphate finish. "Shorty" handguards. Has forged aluminum receivers with push-pin. Made in U.S. by Bushmaster Firearms Inc.

Price: **$912.50**

Bushmaster XM15 E2S Dissipator Carbine

Similar to the XM15 E2S Shorty carbine except has full-length "Dissipator" handguards. Weighs 7.6 lbs.; 34.75" overall; forged aluminum receivers with push-pin style takedown. Made in U.S. by Bushmaster Firearms, Inc.

Price **$925.00**

Bushmaster XM15 E25 AK Shorty Carbine

Similar to the XM15 E2S Shorty except has 14.5" barrel with an AK muzzle brake permanently attached giving 16" barrel length. Weighs 7.3 lbs. Introduced 1999. Made in U.S. by Bushmaster Firearms, Inc.

Price: **$937.50**

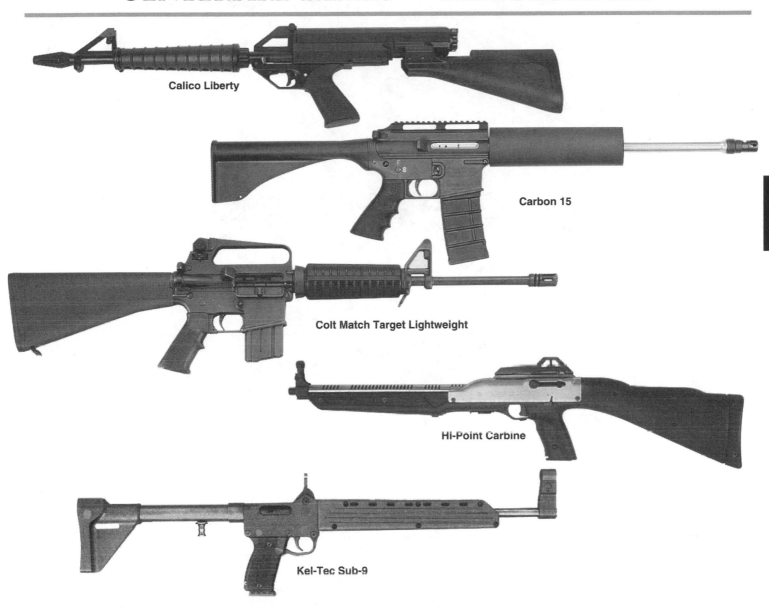

Calico Liberty

Carbon 15

Colt Match Target Lightweight

Hi-Point Carbine

Kel-Tec Sub-9

CALICO LIBERTY 50, 100 CARBINES

Caliber: 9mm Para. **Barrel:** 16.1". **Weight:** 7 lbs. **Length:** 34.5" overall. **Stock:** Glass-filled, impact resistant polymer. **Sights:** Adjustable front post, fixed notch and aperture flip rear. **Features:** Helical feed magazine; ambidextrous, rotating sear/striker block safety; static cocking handle; retarded blowback action; aluminum alloy receiver. Introduced 1995. Made in U.S. by Calico.

Price: Liberty 50 .... $648.00
Price: Liberty 100 .... $684.00

CARBON 15 (TYPE 97) AUTO RIFLE

Caliber: 223. **Barrel:** 16". **Weight:** 3.9 lbs. **Length:** 35" overall. **Stock:** Carbon fiber butt and forend, rubberized pistol grip. **Sights:** None furnished; optics base. **Features:** Carbon fiber upper and lower receivers; stainless steel match-grade barrel; hard-chromed bolt and carrier; quick-detachable compensator. Made in U.S. by Professional Ordnance Inc.

Price: $1,700.00
Price: Type 20 (light-profile stainless barrel, compensator optional) $1,550.00

COLT MATCH TARGET LIGHTWEIGHT RIFLE

Caliber: 9mm Para., 223 Rem., 5-shot magazine. **Barrel:** 16". **Weight:** 6.7 lbs. (223); 7.1 lbs. (9mm Para.). **Length:** 34.5" overall. **Stock:** Composition stock, grip, forend. **Sights:** Post front, rear adjustable for windage and elevation. **Features:** 5-round detachable box magazine, flash suppressor, sling swivels. Forward bolt assist included. Introduced 1991.

Price: $1,010.00

HI-POINT 9mm CARBINE

Caliber: 9mm Para., 40 S&W, 10-shot magazine. **Barrel:** 16-1/2" (17-1/2" for 40 S&W). **Weight:** 4-1/2 lbs. **Length:** 31-1/2" overall. **Stock:** Black polymer. **Sights:** Protected post front, aperture rear. Integral scope mount. **Features:** Grip-mounted magazine release. Black or chrome finish. Sling swivels. Introduced 1996. Made in U.S. by MKS Supply, Inc.

Price: Black or chrome, 9mm $189.00
Price: 40 S&W $209.00

KEL-TEC SUB-RIFLE AUTO RIFLE

Caliber: 9mm Para or 40 S&W. **Barrel:** 16.1". **Weight:** 4.6 lbs. **Length:** 30" overall (extended), 15.9" (closed). **Stock:** Metal tube; grooved rubber butt pad. **Sights:** Hooded post front, flip-up rear. Interchangeable grip assemblies allow use of most double-column high capacity pistol magazines. **Features:** Barrel folds back over the butt for transport and storage. Introduced 1997. Made in U.S. by Kel-Tec CNC Industries, Inc.

Price: 9mm $700.00
Price: 40 S&W $725.00

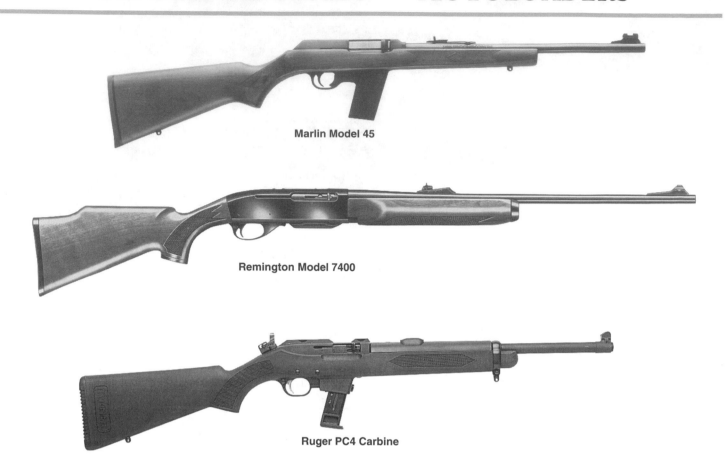

Marlin Model 45

Remington Model 7400

Ruger PC4 Carbine

LR 300 SR LIGHT SPORT RIFLE

Caliber: 223. **Barrel:** 16-1/4"; 1:9" twist. **Weight:** 7.2 lbs. **Length:** 36" overall (extended stock), 26-1/4" (stock folded). **Stock:** Folding, tubular steel, with thumbhold-type grip. **Sights:** Trijicon post front, Trijicon rear. **Features:** Uses AR-15 type upper and lower receivers; flattop receiver with weaver base. Accepts all AR-15/M-16 magazines. Introduced 1996. Made in U.S. from Z-M weapons.
Price: **$2,550.00**

MARLIN MODEL 9 CAMP CARBINE

Caliber: 9mm Para., 10-shot magazine. **Barrel:** 16-1/2", Micro-Groove® rifling. **Weight:** 6-3/4 lbs. **Length:** 35-1/2" overall. **Stock:** Press-checkered walnut-finished Maine birch; rubber butt pad; Mar-Shield™ finish; swivel studs. **Sights:** Ramp front with orange post, cutaway Wide-Scan™ hood, adjustable open rear. **Features:** Manual bolt hold-open; Garand-type safety, magazine safety; loaded chamber indicator; receiver drilled, tapped for scope mounting. Introduced 1985.
Price: **$443.00**

Marlin Model 45 Carbine

Similar to the Model 9 except chambered for 45 ACP, 7-shot magazine. Introduced 1986.
Price: **$443.00**

OLYMPIC ARMS CAR-97 RIFLES

Caliber: 223, 7-shot; 9mm Para., 45 ACP, 40 S&W, 10mm, 10-shot. **Barrel:** 16". **Weight:** 7 lbs. **Length:** 34.75" overall. **Stock:** A2 stowaway grip, telescoping-look butt. **Sights:** Post front, fully adjustable aperature rear. **Features:** Based on AR-15 rifle. Post-ban version of the CAR-15. Made in U.S. by Olympic Arms, Inc.
Price: 223 . . . . **$780.00**
Price: 9mm Para., 45 ACP, 40 S&W, 10mm **$840.00**
Price: PCR Eliminator (223, full-length handguards) **$803.00**

OLYMPIC ARMS PCR-4 RIFLE

Caliber: 223, 10-shot magazine. **Barrel:** 20". **Weight:** 8 lbs., 5 oz. **Length:** 38.25" overall. **Stock:** A2 stowaway grip, trapdoor buttstock. **Sights:** Post front, A1 rear adjustable for windage. **Features:** Based on the AR-15 rifle. Barrel is button rifled with 1:9" twist. No bayonet lug. Introduced 1994. Made in U.S. by Olympic Arms, Inc.
Price: **$792.00**

OLYMPIC ARMS PCR-6 RIFLE

Caliber: 7.62x39mm (PCR-6), 10-shot magazine. **Barrel:** 16". **Weight:** 7 lbs. **Length:** 34.75" overall. **Stock:** A2 stowaway grip, trapdoor buttstock. **Sights:** Post front, A1 rear adjustable for windage. **Features:** Based on the CAR-15. No bayonet lug. Button-cut rifling. Introduced 1994. Made in U.S. by Olympic Arms, Inc.
Price: **$828.00**

REMINGTON MODEL 7400 AUTO RIFLE

Caliber: 243 Win., 270 Win., 280 Rem., 308 Win., 30-06, 4-shot magazine. **Barrel:** 22" round tapered. **Weight:** 7-1/2 lbs. **Length:** 42-5/8" overall. **Stock:** Walnut, deluxe cut checkered pistol grip and forend. Satin or high-gloss finish. **Sights:** Gold bead front sight on ramp; step rear sight with windage adjustable. **Features:** Redesigned and improved version of the Model 742. Positive cross-bolt safety. Receiver tapped for scope mount. Comes with green Remington hard case. Introduced 1981.
Price: About **$573.00**
Price: Carbine (18-1/2" bbl., 30-06 only) **$573.00**
Price: With black synthetic stock, matte black metal, rifle or carbine **$473.00**

RUGER PC4, PC9 CARBINES

Caliber: 9mm Para., 40 S&W, 10-shot magazine. **Barrel:** 16.25". **Weight:** 6 lbs., 4 oz. **Length:** 34.75" overall. **Stock:** Black DuPont (Zytel) with checkered grip and forend. **Sights:** Blade front, open adjustable rear; integral Ruger scope mounts. **Features:** Delayed blowback action; manual

Ruger Mini 14/5

Springfield M1A

push-button cross bolt safety and internal firing pin block safety automatic slide lock. Introduced 1997. Made in U.S. by Sturm, Ruger & Co.

Price: PC4, 40 S&W **$555.00**
Price: PC9, 9mm Para **$555.00**
Price: PC4GR (40 S&W with ghost ring rear sight) **$580.00**
Price: PC9GR (9mm Para. with ghost ring rear sight) **$580.00**

RUGER MINI-14/5 AUTOLOADING RIFLE

Caliber: 223 Rem., 5-shot detachable box magazine. **Barrel:** 18-1/2". Rifling twist 1:9". **Weight:** 6.4 lbs. **Length:** 37-1/4" overall. **Stock:** American hardwood, steel reinforced. **Sights:** Ramp front, fully adjustable rear. **Features:** Fixed piston gas-operated, positive primary extraction. New buffer system, redesigned ejector system. Ruger S100RH scope rings included. 20-, 30-shot magazine available to police departments and government agencies only.

Price: Mini-14/5R, Ranch Rifle, blued, scope rings **$584.00**
Price: K-Mini-14/5R, Ranch Rifle, stainless, scope rings **$639.00**
Price: Mini-14/5, blued, no scope rings **$542.00**
Price: K-Mini-14/5, stainless, no scope rings **$597.00**
Price: K-Mini-14/5P, stainless, synthetic stock **$597.00**
Price: K-Mini-14/5RP, Ranch Rifle, stainless, synthetic stock **$639.00**

Ruger Mini Thirty Rifle

Similar to the Mini-14 Ranch Rifle except modified to chamber the 7.62x39 Russian service round. Weight is about 7 lbs., 3 oz. Has 6-groove barrel with 1:10″ twist, Ruger Integral Scope Mount bases and folding peep rear sight. Detachable 5-shot staggered box magazine. Blued finish. Introduced 1987.

Price: Blue **$584.00**
Price: Stainless. **$639.00**

SPRINGFIELD, INC. M1A RIFLE

Caliber: 7.62mm NATO (308), 5- or 10-shot box magazine. **Barrel:** 25-1/16" with flash suppressor, 22" without suppressor. **Weight:** 8-3/4 lbs. **Length:** 44-1/4" overall. **Stock:** American walnut with walnut-colored heat-resistant fiberglass handguard. Matching walnut handguard available. Also available with fiberglass stock. **Sights:** Military, square blade front, full click-adjustable aperture rear. **Features:** Commercial equivalent of the U.S. M-14 service rifle with no provision for automatic firing. From Springfield, Inc.

Price: M1A-A1, black fiberglass stock **$1,249.00**
Price: Standard M1A rifle, about **$1,381.00**
Price: National Match, about **$1,779.00**
Price: Super Match (heavy premium barrel), about **$2,479.00**
Price: M1A-A1 Collector, G.I. stock **$1,597.00**

STONER SR-15 M-5 RIFLE

Caliber: 223. **Barrel:** 20". **Weight:** 7.6 lbs. **Length:** 38" overall. **Stock:** Black synthetic. **Sights:** Post front, fully adjustable rear. **Features:** Modular weapon system. Black finish. Introduced 1998. Made in U.S. by Knight's Mfg.

Price: **$1,295.00**
Price: M-4 Carbine (16" barrel, 6.8 lbs) **$1,295.00**

STONER SR-25 CARBINE

Caliber: 7.62 NATO, 10-shot steel magazine. **Barrel:** 16 " free-floating **Weight:** 7-3/4 lbs. **Length:** 35.75" overall. **Stock:** Black synthetic. **Sights:** Integral Weaver-style rail. Scope rings, iron sights optional. **Features:** Shortened, non-slip handguard; removable carrying handle. Matte black finish. Introduced 1995. Made in U.S. by Knight's Mfg. Co.

Price: **$2,995.00**

STONER SR-50 LONG RANGE PRECISION RIFLE

Caliber: 50 BMG, 10-shot magazine. **Barrel:** 35.5". **Weight:** 31.5 lbs. **Length:** 58.37" overall. **Stock:** Tubular steel. **Sights:** Scope mount. **Features:** Gas-operated semi-automatic action; two-stage target-type trigger; M-16-type safety lever; easily removable barrel. Introduced 1996. Made in U.S. by Knight's Mfg. Co.

Price: **$6,995.00**

Both classic arms and recent designs in American-style repeaters for sport and field shooting.

American Arms/Uberti 1866 Sporting

American Arms/Uberti 1873 Sporting

Browning BPR

Browning Lightning BLR

AMERICAN ARMS/UBERTI 1873 SPORTING RIFLE
Caliber: 44-40, 45 Colt. **Barrel:** 24-1/4", 30", octagonal. **Weight:** 8.1 lbs. **Length:** 43-1/4" overall. **Stock:** Walnut. **Sights:** Blade front adjustable for windage, open rear adjustable for elevation. **Features:** Color case-hardened frame, blued barrel, hammer, lever, buttplate, brass elevator. Imported from Italy by American Arms, Inc.
Price: 24-1/4" barrel $860.00
Price: 30" barrel $940.00

AMERICAN ARMS/UBERTI 1866 SPORTING RIFLE, CARBINE
Caliber: 22 LR, 22 WMR, 38 Spec., 44-40, 45 Colt. **Barrel:** 24-1/4", octagonal. **Weight:** 8.1 lbs. **Length:** 43-1/4" overall. **Stock:** Walnut. **Sights:** Blade front adjustable for windage, rear adjustable for elevation. **Features:** Frame, buttplate, forend cap of polished brass, balance charcoal blued. Imported by American Arms, Inc.
Price: $730.00
Price: Yellowboy Carbine (19" round bbl.) $710.00

AMERICAN ARMS/UBERTI 1860 HENRY RIFLE
Caliber: 44-40, 45 Colt. **Barrel:** 24-1/4", half-octagon. **Weight:** 9.2 lbs. **Length:** 43-3/4" overall. **Stock:** American walnut. **Sights:** Blade front, rear adjustable for elevation. **Features:** Frame, elevator, magazine follower, buttplate are brass, balance blue. Imported by American Arms, Inc.
Price: $940.00
Price: 1860 Henry White (polished steel finish) $990.00

AMERICAN ARMS/UBERTI 1860 HENRY TRAPPER CARBINE
Similar to the 1860 Henry Rifle except has 18-1/2" barrel, measures 37-3/4" overall, and weighs 8 lbs. Introduced 1999. Imported from Italy by American Arms.

Price: Brass frame, blued barrel $940.00
Price: Henry Trapper White (brass frame, polished steel barrel) . . $990.00

BROWNING BPR PUMP RIFLE
Caliber: 243, 308 (short action); 270, 30-06, 7mm Rem. Mag., 300 Win. Mag., 4-shot magazine (3 for magnums). **Barrel:** 22"; 24" for magnum calibers. **Weight:** 7 lbs., 3 oz. **Length:** 43" overall (22" barrel). **Stock:** Select walnut with full pistol grip, high gloss finish. **Sights:** Gold bead on hooded ramp front, open click adjustable rear. **Features:** Slide-action mechanism cams forend down away from the barrel. Seven-lug rotary bolt; cross-bolt safety behind trigger; removable magazine; alloy receiver. Introduced 1997. Imported from Belgium by Browning.
Price: Standard calibers $718.00
Price: Magnum calibers $772.00

BROWNING LIGHTNING BLR LEVER-ACTION RIFLE
Caliber: 223, 22-250, 243, 7mm-08, 308 Win., 4-shot detachable magazine. **Barrel:** 20" round tapered. **Weight:** 6 lbs., 8 oz. **Length:** 39-1/2" overall. **Stock:** Walnut. Checkered grip and forend, high-gloss finish. **Sights:** Gold bead on ramp front; low profile square notch adjustable rear. **Features:** Wide, grooved trigger; half-cock hammer safety; fold-down hammer. Receiver tapped for scope mount. Recoil pad installed. Introduced 1996. Imported from Japan by Browning.
Price: $600.00

Browning Lightning BLR Long Action
Similar to the standard Lightning BLR except has long action to accept 30-06, 270, 7mm Rem. Mag. and 300 Win. Mag. Barrel lengths are 22" for 30-06 and 270, 24" for 7mm Rem. Mag. and 300 Win. Mag. Has six-

NEW!

CENTERFIRE RIFLES — LEVER AND SLIDE

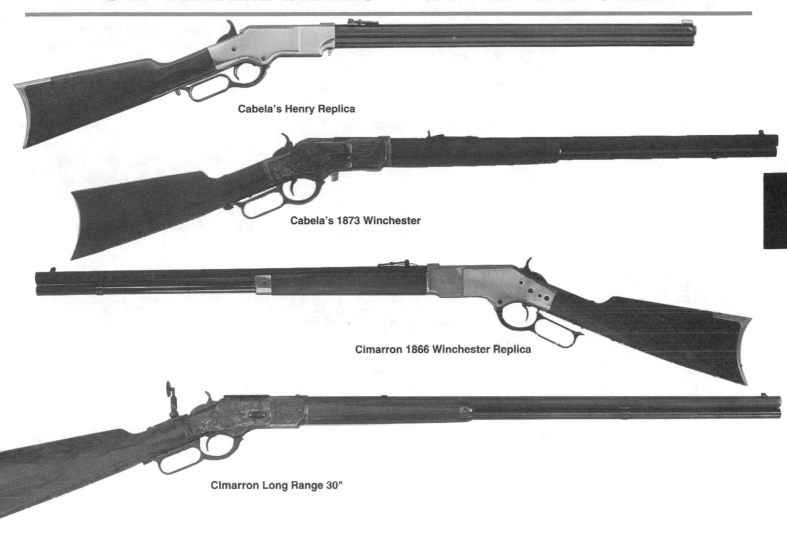

Cabela's Henry Replica

Cabela's 1873 Winchester

Cimarron 1866 Winchester Replica

Cimarron Long Range 30"

lug rotary bolt, bolt and receiver are full-length fluted. Fold-down hammer at half-cock. Weighs about 7 lbs., overall length 42-7/8" (22" barrel). Introduced 1000.
Price: $634.00

CABELA'S 1858 HENRY REPLICA
Caliber: 44-40, 45 Colt. **Barrel:** 24-1/4". **Weight:** 9.5 lbs. **Length:** 43" overall. **Stock:** European walnut. **Sights:** Bead front, open adjustable rear. **Features:** Brass receiver and buttplate. Uses original Henry loading system. Faithful to the original rifle. Introduced 1994. Imported by Cabela's.
Price: $749.99

CABELA'S 1866 WINCHESTER REPLICA
Caliber: 44-40, 45 Colt. **Barrel:** 24-1/4". **Weight:** 9 lbs. **Length:** 43" overall. **Stock:** European walnut. **Sights:** Bead front, open adjustable rear. **Features:** Solid brass receiver, buttplate, forend cap. Octagonal barrel. Faithful to the original Winchester `66 rifle. Introduced 1994. Imported by Cabela's.
Price: $759.99

CABELA'S 1873 WINCHESTER REPLICA
Caliber: 44-40, 45 Colt. **Barrel:** 24-1/4", 30". **Weight:** 8.5 lbs. **Length:** 43-1/4" overall. **Stock:** European walnut. **Sights:** Bead front, open adjustable rear; globe front, tang rear. **Features:** Color case-hardened steel receiver. Faithful to the original Model 1873 rifle. Introduced 1994. Imported by Cabela's.
Price: Sporting model, 30" barrel, 44-40, 45 Colt $749.99
Price: Sporting model, 24" or 25" barrel $729.99

CIMARRON 1860 HENRY REPLICA
Caliber: 44 WCF, 13-shot magazine. **Barrel:** 24-1/4" (rifle), 22" (carbine). **Weight:** 9-1/2 lbs. **Length:** 43" overall (rifle). **Stock:** European walnut. **Sights:** Bead front, open adjustable rear. **Features:** Brass receiver and buttplate. Uses original Henry loading system. Faithful to the original rifle. Introduced 1991. Imported by Cimarron F.A. Co.
Price: $1,029.00

CIMARRON 1866 WINCHESTER REPLICAS
Caliber: 22 LR, 22 WMR, 38 Spec., 44 WCF. **Barrel:** 24-1/4" (rifle), 19" (carbine). **Weight:** 9 lbs. **Length:** 43" overall (rifle). **Stock:** European walnut. **Sights:** Bead front, open adjustable rear. **Features:** Solid brass receiver, buttplate, forend cap. Octagonal barrel. Faithful to the original Winchester '66 rifle. Introduced 1991. Imported by Cimarron F.A. Co.
Price: Rifle $839.00
Price: Carbine... $829.00

CIMARRON 1873 SHORT RIFLE
Caliber: 22 LR, 22 WMR, 357 Mag., 44-40, 45 Colt. **Barrel:** 20" tapered octagon. **Weight:** 7.5 lbs. **Length:** 39" overall. **Stock:** Walnut. **Sights:** Bead front, adjustable semi-buckhorn rear. **Features:** Has half "button" magazine. Original-type markings, including caliber, on barrel and elevator and "Kings" patent. From Cimarron F.A. Co.
Price: $799.00

CIMARRON 1873 LONG RANGE RIFLE
Caliber: 22 LR, 22 WMR, 357 Mag., 38-40, 44-40, 45 Colt. **Barrel:** 30", octagonal. **Weight:** 8-1/2 lbs. **Length:** 48" overall. **Stock:** Walnut. **Sights:** Blade front, semi-buckhorn ramp rear. Tang sight optional. **Features:** Col-

Dixie 1873

IAR 1873 Revolver Carbine

Marlin 1894S
Lever-Action

Marlin 1894CS

or case-hardened frame; choice of modern blue-black or charcoal blue for other parts. Barrel marked "Kings Improvement." From Cimarron F.A. Co.
Price: **$999.00**

Cimarron 1873 Sporting Rifle
Similar to the 1873 Long Range except has 24″ barrel with half-magazine.
Price: **$949.00**
Price: 1873 Saddle Ring Carbine, 19" barrel **$949.00**

CIMARRON MODEL 1892 SPORTING RIFLE
NEW! Caliber: 44 WCF, 45 Colt. **Barrel:** 24" octagonal. **Weight:** NA. **Length:** NA. **Stock:** European walnut. **Sights:** Bead front, adjustable rear. **Features:** Replica of the Winchester Model 1892. Color case-hardened receiver, lever and forend cap, rest blued. Introduced 1999. Imported from Italy by Cimarron F.A. Co.
Price: **$649.00**

DIXIE ENGRAVED 1873 RIFLE
Caliber: 44-40, 11-shot magazine. **Barrel:** 20", round. **Weight:** 7-3/4 lbs. **Length:** 39" overall. **Stock:** Walnut. **Sights:** Blade front, adjustable rear. **Features:** Engraved and case-hardened frame. Duplicate of Winchester 1873. Made in Italy. From 21 Gun Works.
Price: **$1,295.00**
Price: Plain, blued carbine **$850.00**

E.M.F. 1860 HENRY RIFLE
Caliber: 44-40 or 44 rimfire. **Barrel:** 24.25". **Weight:** About 9 lbs. **Length:** About 43.75" overall. **Stock:** Oil-stained American walnut. **Sights:** Blade front, rear adjustable for elevation. **Features:** Reproduction of the original Henry rifle with brass frame and buttplate, rest blued. From E.M.F.
Price: Standard. **$1,100.00**

E.M.F. 1866 YELLOWBOY LEVER ACTIONS
Caliber: 38 Spec., 44-40. **Barrel:** 19" (carbine), 24" (rifle). **Weight:** 9 lbs. **Length:** 43" overall (rifle). **Stock:** European walnut. **Sights:** Bead front, open adjustable rear. **Features:** Solid brass frame, blued barrel, lever, hammer, buttplate. Imported from Italy by E.M.F.
Price: Rifle **$848.00**
Price: Carbine. **$825.00**

E.M.F. HARTFORD MODEL 1892 LEVER-ACTION RIFLE
Caliber: 45 Colt. **Barrel:** 24", octagonal. **Weight:** 7-1/2 lbs. **Length:** 43" overall. **Stock:** European walnut. **Sights:** Blade front, open adjustable rear. **Features:** Color case-hardened frame, lever, trigger and hammer with blued barrel, or overall blue finish. Introduced 1998. Imported by E.M.F.
Price: Standard. **$1,000.00**
Price: Deluxe **$1,085.00**
Price: Premier. **$1,250.00**

E.M.F. MODEL 73 LEVER-ACTION RIFLE
Caliber: 357 Mag., 44-40, 45 Colt. **Barrel:** 24". **Weight:** 8 lbs. **Length:** 43-1/4" overall. **Stock:** European walnut. **Sights:** Bead front, rear adjustable for windage and elevation. **Features:** Color case-hardened frame (blue on carbine). Imported by E.M.F.
Price: Rifle **$1,050.00**
Price: Carbine, 19" barrel. **$1,020.00**

IAR MODEL 1873 REVOLVER CARBINE
Caliber: 357 Mag., 45 Colt. **Barrel:** 18". **Weight:** 4 lbs., 8 oz. **Length:** 34" overall. **Stock:** One-piece walnut. **Sights:** Blade front, notch rear. **Features:** Color case-hardened frame, blue barrel, backstrap and triggerguard. Introduced 1998. Imported from Italy by IAR, Inc.
Price: Standard. **$490.00**

MARLIN MODEL 1894S LEVER-ACTION CARBINE
Caliber: 44 Spec./44 Mag., 10-shot tubular magazine. **Barrel:** 20" Micro-Groove®. **Weight:** 6 lbs. **Length:** 37-1/2" overall. **Stock:** Checkered American black walnut, straight grip and forend. Mar-Shield® finish. Rubber rifle butt pad; swivel studs. **Sights:** Wide-Scan hooded ramp front, semi-buckhorn folding rear adjustable for windage and elevation. **Features:** Hammer-block safety. Receiver tapped for scope mount, offset hammer spur, solid top receiver sand blasted to prevent glare.
Price: **$486.00**

Marlin Model 1894CS Carbine
Similar to the standard Model 1894S except chambered for 38 Spec./357 Mag. with full-length 9-shot magazine, 18-1/2″ barrel, hammer-block safety, hooded front sight. Introduced 1983.
Price: **$486.00**

Marlin 1894 Cowboy II

Marlin 444SS

Marlin 444P Outfitter

Marlin 1895SS

Marlin 336CS

MARLIN MODEL 1894 COWBOY, COWBOY II

Caliber: 357 Mag., 44 Mag., 44-40, 45 Colt, 10-shot magazine. **Barrel:** 24" tapered octagon, deep cut rifling. **Weight:** 7-1/2 lbs. **Length:** 41-1/2" overall. **Stock:** Straight grip American black walnut with cut checkering, hard rubber buttplate, Mar-Shield® finish. **Sights:** Marble carbine front, adjustable Marble semi-buckhorn rear. **Features:** Squared finger lever; straight grip stock; blued steel forend tip. Designed for Cowboy Shooting events. Introduced 1996. Made in U.S. by Marlin.
Price: Cowboy I, 45 Colt **$733.00**
Price: Cowboy II, 357 Mag., 44 Mag., 44-40 . . . . **$733.00**

MARLIN MODEL 444SS LEVER-ACTION SPORTER

Caliber: 444 Marlin, 5-shot tubular magazine. **Barrel:** 22" Micro-Groove®. **Weight:** 7-1/2 lbs. **Length:** 40-1/2" overall. **Stock:** Checkered American black walnut, capped pistol grip with white line spacers, rubber rifle butt pad. Mar-Shield® finish; swivel studs. **Sights:** Hooded ramp front, folding semi-buckhorn rear adjustable for windage and elevation. **Features:** Hammer-block safety. Receiver tapped for scope mount; offset hammer spur.
Price: **$566.00**

Marlin Model 444P Outfitter Lever-Action

Similar to the 444SS except has a ported 18-1/2" barrel with deep-cut Ballard-type rifling; weighs 6-3/4 lbs.; overall length 37". Available only in 444 Marlin. Introduced 1999. Made in U.S. by Marlin.
Price: **$572.00**

MARLIN MODEL 1895SS LEVER-ACTION RIFLE

Caliber: 45-70, 4-shot tubular magazine. **Barrel:** 22" round. **Weight:** 7-1/2 lbs. **Length:** 40-1/2" overall. **Stock:** Checkered American black walnut, full pistol grip. Mar-Shield® finish; rubber butt pad; quick detachable swivel studs. **Sights:** Bead front with Wide-Scan hood, semi-buckhorn folding rear adjustable for windage and elevation. **Features:** Hammer-block safety. Solid receiver tapped for scope mounts or receiver sights; offset hammer spur.
Price: **$566.00**

Marlin Model 1895G Guide Gun Lever Action

Similar to the Model 1895SS except has 18-1/2" ported barrel with deep-cut Ballard-type rifling; straight-grip walnut stock. Overall length is 37", weighs 6-3/4 lbs. Introduced 1998. Made in U.S. by Marlin.
Price: **$572.00**

MARLIN MODEL 336CS LEVER-ACTION CARBINE

Caliber: 30-30 or 35 Rem., 6-shot tubular magazine. **Barrel:** 20" Micro-Groove®. **Weight:** 7 lbs. **Length:** 38-1/2" overall. **Stock:** Checkered American black walnut, capped pistol grip with white line spacers. Mar-Shield® finish; rubber butt pad; swivel studs. **Sights:** Ramp front with Wide-Scan hood, semi-buckhorn folding rear adjustable for windage and elevation. **Features:** Hammer-block safety. Receiver tapped for scope mount, offset hammer spur; top of receiver sand blasted to prevent glare.
Price: **$474.00**

Marlin 30AS

Marlin 336W

Marlin 336CB Cowboy

Navy Arms Henry Trapper

Navy Arms Iron Frame Henry

Marlin Model 336CB Cowboy

Similar to the Model 336CS except chambered for 30-30 and 38-55 Win., 24" tapered octagon barrel with deep-cut Ballard-type rifling; straight-grip walnut stock with hard rubber buttplate; blued steel forend cap; weighs 7-1/2 lbs.; 42-1/2" overall. Introduced 1999. Made in U.S. by Marlin.
Price: **$658.00**

Marlin Model 30AS Lever-Action Carbine

Same as the Marlin 336CS except has cut-checkered, walnut-finished Maine birch pistol grip stock with swivel studs, 30-30 only, 6-shot. Hammer-block safety. Adjustable rear sight, brass bead front.
Price: **$405.00**
Price: With 4x scope and mount **$449.00**

Marlin Model 336W Lever-Action Rifle

Similar to the Model 336CS except has walnut-finished, cut-checkered Maine birch stock; blued steel barrel band has integral sling swivel; no front sight hood; comes with padded nylon sling; hard rubber butt plate. Introduced 1998. Made in U.S. by Marlin.
Price: **$411.00**
Price: With 4x scope and mount **$455.00**

NAVY ARMS MILITARY HENRY RIFLE

Caliber: 44-40 or 45 Colt, 12-shot magazine. **Barrel:** 24-1/4". **Weight:** 9 lbs., 4 oz. **Stock:** European walnut. **Sights:** Blade front, adjustable ladder-type rear. **Features:** Brass frame, buttplate, rest blued. Recreation of the model used by cavalry units in the Civil War. Has full-length magazine tube, sling swivels; no forend. Imported from Italy by Navy Arms.
Price: **$895.00**

Navy Arms Henry Carbine

Similar to the Military Henry rifle except has 22" barrel, weighs 8 lbs., 12 oz., is 41" overall; no sling swivels. Caliber 44-40. Introduced 1992. Imported from Italy by Navy Arms.
Price: **$875.00**

Navy Arms Henry Trapper

Similar to the Military Henry Rifle except has 16-1/2" barrel, weighs 7-1/2 lbs. Brass frame and buttplate, rest blued. Introduced 1991. Imported from Italy by Navy Arms.
Price: **$875.00**

Navy Arms Iron Frame Henry

Similar to the Military Henry Rifle except 44-40 only, receiver is blued or color case-hardened steel. Imported by Navy Arms.
Price: **$945.00**

CENTERFIRE RIFLES — LEVER AND SLIDE

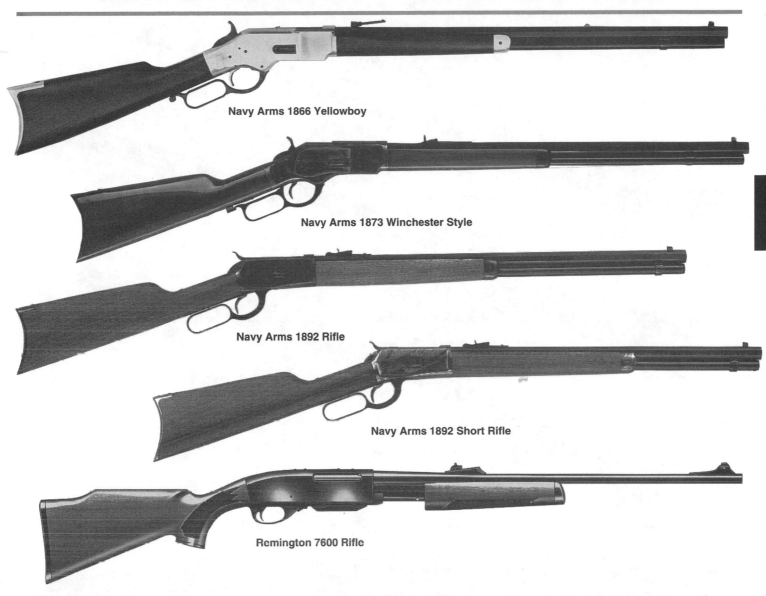

Navy Arms 1866 Yellowboy

Navy Arms 1873 Winchester Style

Navy Arms 1892 Rifle

Navy Arms 1892 Short Rifle

Remington 7600 Rifle

NAVY ARMS 1866 YELLOWBOY RIFLE

Caliber: 38 Spec., 44-40, 45 Colt, 12-shot magazine. **Barrel:** 24", full octagon. **Weight:** 8-1/2 lbs. **Length:** 42-1/2" overall. **Stock:** Walnut. **Sights:** Blade front, adjustable ladder-type rear. **Features:** Brass frame, forend tip, buttplate, blued barrel, lever, hammer. Introduced 1991. Imported from Italy by Navy Arms.

Price: $685.00
Price: Carbine, 19" barrel $675.00

NAVY ARMS 1873 WINCHESTER-STYLE RIFLE

Caliber: 357 Mag., 44-40, 45 Colt, 12-shot magazine. **Barrel:** 24-1/4". **Weight:** 8-1/4 lbs. **Length:** 43" overall. **Stock:** European walnut. **Sights:** Blade front, buckhorn rear. **Features:** Color case-hardened frame, rest blued. Full-octagon barrel. Imported by Navy Arms.

Price: $820.00
Price: Carbine, 19" barrel $800.00
Price: Border model, 20" octagon barrel $820.00

Navy Arms 1873 Sporting Rifle

Similar to the 1873 Winchester-Style rifle except has checkered pistol grip stock, 30″ octagonal barrel (24-1/4″ available). Introduced 1992. Imported by Navy Arms.

Price: 30" barrel $960.00
Price: 24-1/4" barrel $930.00

NAVY ARMS 1892 LEVER-ACTION RIFLE

Caliber: 357 Mag., 44-40, 45 Colt. **Barrel:** 24-1/4" octagonal. **Weight:** 7 lbs. **Length:** 42" overall. **Stock:** American walnut. **Sights:** Blade front, semi-buckhorn rear. **Features:** Replica of Winchester's early Model 1892 with octagonal barrel, forend cap and crescent buttplate. Blued or color case-hardened receiver; brass-frame model also available, in 44-40 or 45 Colt only. Introduced 1998. Imported by Navy Arms.

Price: $495.00

Navy Arms 1892 Carbine

Similar to the 1892 Rifle except has 20" round barrel, weighs 5-3/4 lbs., and is 37-1/2" overall. Introduced 1998. Imported by Navy Arms.

Price: $465.00

Navy Arms 1892 Short Rifle

Similar to the 1892 Rifle except has 20" octagonal barrel, weighs 6-1/4 lbs., and is 37-3/4" overall. Replica of the rare, special order 1892 Winchester nicknamed the "Texas Special." Blued or color case-hardened receiver and furniture. Introduced 1998. Imported by Navy Arms.

Price: $495.00

REMINGTON MODEL 7600 SLIDE ACTION

Caliber: 243, 270, 280, 30-06, 308. **Barrel:** 22" round tapered. **Weight:** 7-1/2 lbs. **Length:** 42-5/8" overall. **Stock:** Cut-checkered walnut pistol grip

Ruger Model 96/44

Traditions Model 1892

Winchester Model 1886

and forend, Monte Carlo with full cheekpiece. Satin or high-gloss finish. **Sights:** Gold bead front sight on matted ramp, open step adjustable sporting rear. **Features:** Redesigned and improved version of the Model 760. Detachable 4-shot clip. Cross-bolt safety. Receiver tapped for scope mount. Also available in high grade versions. Introduced 1981.

Price: **$540.00**
Price: Carbine (18-1/2" bbl., 30-06 only) **$540.00**
Price: With black synthetic stock, matte black metal, rifle or
carbine **$440.00**

RUGER MODEL 96/44 LEVER-ACTION RIFLE
Caliber: 44 Mag., 4-shot rotary magazine. **Barrel:** 18-1/2". **Weight:** 5-7/8 lbs. **Length:** 37-5/16" overall. **Stock:** American hardwood. **Sights:** Gold bead front, folding leaf rear. **Features:** Solid chrome-moly steel receiver. Manual cross-bolt safety, visible cocking indicator; short-throw lever action; integral scope mount; blued finish; color case-hardened lever. Introduced 1996. Made In U.S. by Sturm, Ruger & Co.
Price: **$440.00**

TRADITIONS MODEL 1892 LEVER-ACTION RIFLE
NEW! **Caliber:** 357 Mag., 44-40, 45 Colt. **Barrel:** 24" octagonal. **Weight:** 7 lbs. **Length:** 42" overall. **Stock:** Walnut. **Sights:** Blade front, semi-buckhorn rear. **Features:** Replica of Winchester's Model 1892 with octagonal barrel, forend cap, crescent buttplate. Antique silver, brass frame, or color case-hardened receiver. Introduced 1999. Imported by Traditions.
Price: Color case-hardened **$579.00**
Price: Antique silver **$629.00**
Price: Brass **$589.00**

Traditions Model 1892 Carbine
Similar to the 1892 Rifle except has 20" round barrel, saddle ring, weighs 6 lbs., and is 38" overall. Introduced 1999. Imported by Traditions.
Price: **$579.00**

VEKTOR H5 SLIDE-ACTION RIFLE
Caliber: 223 Rem., 5-shot magazine. **Barrel:** 18", 22". **Weight:** 9 lbs., 15 oz. **Length:** 42-1/2" overall (22" barrel). **Stock:** Walnut thumbhole. **Sights:** Comes with 1" 4x32 scope with low-light reticle. **Features:** Rotating bolt mechanism. Matte black finish. Introduced 1999. Imported from South Africa by Vektor USA.
Price: **$850.00**

WINCHESTER MODEL 1892 LEVER-ACTION RIFLE
Caliber: 357 Mag., 44-40, 44 Mag., 45 Colt, 11-shot magazine. **Barrel:** 24", round. **Weight:** 6-1/4 lbs. **Length:** 41-1/4" overall. **Stock:** Smooth walnut. **Sights:** Bead front, ramp-adjustable buckhorn-style rear. **Features:** Recreation of the Model 1892. Tang-mounted manual hammer stop; blued crescent buttplate; full magazine tube; straight-grip stock. Reintroduced 1997. From U.S. Repeating Arms Co., Inc.
Price: Grade I **$744.00**

WINCHESTER MODEL 1886 LEVER-ACTION RIFLE
Caliber: 45-70, 8-shot magazine. **Barrel:** 26", full octagon. **Weight:** 9-1/4 lbs. **Length:** 45" overall. **Stock:** Smooth walnut. **Sights:** Bead front, ramp-adjustable buckhorn-style rear. **Features:** Recreation of the Model 1886. Polished blue finish; crescent metal butt plate; metal forend cap; pistol grip stock. Reintroduced 1998. From U.S. Repeating Arms Co., Inc.
Price: **$1,148.00**

Winchester Model 94 Big Bore

Winchester 94 Side Eject

Winchester Model 94 Trapper

Winchester Model 94 Black Shadow

WINCHESTER MODEL 94 BIG BORE SIDE EJECT

Caliber: 307 Win., 356 Win., 444 Marlin, 6-shot magazine. **Barrel:** 20". **Weight:** 7 lbs. **Length:** 38-5/8" overall. **Stock:** American walnut. Satin finish. **Sights:** Hooded ramp front, semi-buckhorn rear adjustable for windage and elevation. **Features:** All external metal parts have Winchester's deep blue finish. Rifling twist 1:12". Rubber recoil pad fitted to buttstock. Introduced 1983. From U.S. Repeating Arms Co., Inc.

Price: **$416.00**

Winchester Timber Carbine

Similar to the Model 94 Big Bore. Chambered only for 444 Marlin; 17-3/4" barrel is ported; half-pistol grip stock with butt pad; checkered grip and forend. Introduced 1999. Made in U.S. by U.S. Repeating Arms Co., Inc.

Price: **$499.00**

WINCHESTER MODEL 94 WALNUT SIDE EJECT

Caliber: 30-30 Win., 44 Mag., 6-shot tubular magazine. **Barrel:** 20". **Weight:** 6-1/2 lbs. **Length:** 37-3/4" overall. **Stock:** Straight grip walnut stock and forend. **Sights:** Hooded blade front, semi-buckhorn rear. Drilled and tapped for scope mount. Post front sight on Trapper model. **Features:** Solid frame, forged steel receiver; side ejection, exposed rebounding hammer with automatic trigger-activated transfer bar. Introduced 1984.

Price: Checkered walnut. **$404.00**
Price: No checkering, walnut **$373.00**

Winchester Model 94 Trapper Side Eject

Same as the Model 94 Walnut Side Eject except has 16" barrel, 5-shot magazine in 30-30, 9-shot in 357 Mag., 44 Magnum/44 Special, 45 Colt. Has stainless steel claw extractor, saddle ring, hammer spur extension, walnut wood.

Price: 30-30 . . . . **$373.00**
Price: 44 Mag., 357 Mag., 45 Colt **$395.00**

Winchester Model 94 Trails End

Similar to the Model 94 Walnut except chambered only for 357 Mag., 44-40, 44 Mag., 45 Colt; 11-shot magazine. Available with standard lever loop. Introduced 1997. From U.S. Repeating Arms Co., Inc.

Price: With standard lever loop **$410.00**

Winchester Model 94 Black Shadow Lever-Action Rifle

Similar to the Model 94 Walnut except has black synthetic stock with higher comb for easier scope use, and fuller forend. Non-glare finish; recoil pad. Available in 30-30 with 20" or 24" barrel, 44 Mag. or as Big Bore model in 444 Marlin. Introduced 1998. Made in U.S. by U.S. Repeating Arms Co., Inc.

Price: Black Shadow, 30-30, 44 Mag. **$370.00**
Price: Black Shadow Big Bore, 444 Marlin **$370.00**

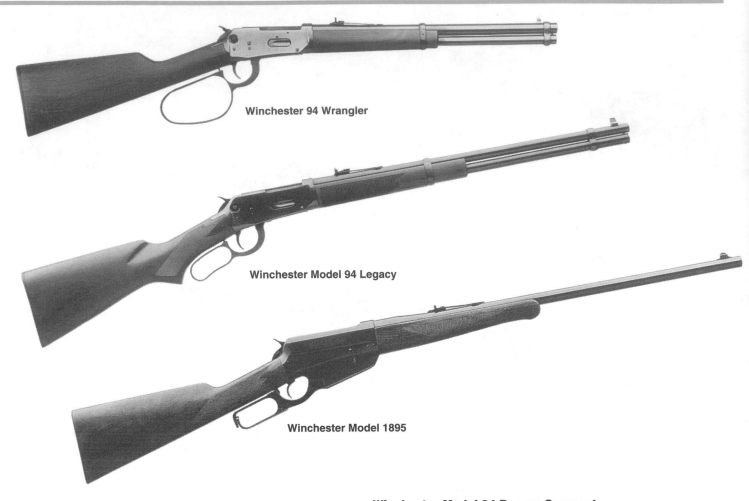

Winchester 94 Wrangler

Winchester Model 94 Legacy

Winchester Model 1895

Winchester Model 94 Wrangler Side Eject

Same as the Model 94 Walnut Side Eject except has 16″ barrel and large loop lever for large and/or gloved hands. Has 9-shot capacity (5-shot for 30-30), stainless steel claw extractor. Available in 30-30, 44 Magnum/44 Special, 45 Colt. Specially inscribed with "1894-1994" on the receiver. Reintroduced 1992.
Price: 30-30 . . . . $395.00
Price: 44 Magnum/44 Special, 45 Colt $416.00

Winchester Model 94 Legacy

Similar to the Model 94 Side Eject except has half-pistol grip walnut stock, checkered grip and forend. Chambered for 30-30, 357 Mag., 44 Mag., 45 Colt; 24″ barrel. Introduced 1995. Made in U.S. by U.S. Repeating Arms Co., Inc.
Price: With 24" barrel $419.00

Winchester Model 94 Ranger Side Eject Lever-Action Rifle

Same as Model 94 Side Eject except has 6-shot magazine, American hardwood stock and forend, post front sight. Introduced 1985.
Price: $329.00

Winchester Model 94 Ranger Compact

Similar to the Model 94 Ranger except has 16" barrel and 12-1/2" length of pull, rubber recoil pad, post front sight. Introduced 1998. Made in U.S. by U.S. Repeating Arms Co., Inc.
Price: 357 Mag. or 30-30 . . . . $349.00

WINCHESTER MODEL 1895 LEVER-ACTION RIFLE

Caliber: 30-06, 270, 4-shot magazine. **Barrel:** 24", round. **Weight:** 8 lbs. **Length:** 42" overall. **Stock:** American walnut. **Sights:** Gold bead front, buckhorn rear adjustable for elevation. **Features:** Recreation of the original Model 1895. Polished blue finish with Nimschke-style scroll engraving on receiver. Scalloped receiver, two-piece cocking lever, Schnabel forend, straight-grip stock. Introduced 1995. Only 4000 rifles made in 30-06 only. From U.S. Repeating Arms Co., Inc.
Price: Grade I $936.00

Winchester Model 1895 High Grade Rifle

Same as the Grade I except has silvered receiver with extensive engraving: right side shows two scenes portraying large big horn sheep; left side has bull elk and cow elk. Gold borders accent the scenes. Magazine and cocking lever also engraved. Has classic Winchester H-style checkering pattern on fancy grade American walnut. Only 4000 rifles made. Introduced 1995. From U.S. Repeating Arms Co., Inc.
Price: $1,400.00

Includes models for a wide variety of sporting and competitive purposes and uses.

Anschutz 1733D

Arnold Arms Alaskan

Arnold Arms Safari

ANSCHUTZ 1743D BOLT-ACTION RIFLE

Caliber: 222 Rem., 3-shot magazine. **Barrel:** 19.7". **Weight:** 6.4 lbs. **Length:** 39" overall. **Stock:** European walnut. **Sights:** Hooded blade front, folding leaf rear. **Features:** Receiver grooved for scope mounting; single stage trigger; claw extractor; sling safety; sling swivels. Imported from Germany by AcuSport Corp.
Price: **$1,588.95**

ANSCHUTZ 1740 MONTE CARLO RIFLE

Caliber: 22 Hornet, 5-shot clip; 222 Rem., 3-shot clip. **Barrel:** 24". **Weight:** 6-1/2 lbs. **Length:** 43.25" overall. **Stock:** Select European walnut. **Sights:** Hooded ramp front, folding leaf rear; drilled and tapped for scope mounting. **Features:** Uses match 54 action. Adjustable single stage trigger. Stock has roll-over Monte Carlo cheekpiece, slim forend with Schnabel tip, Wundhammer palm swell on grip, rosewood gripcap with white diamond insert. Skip-line checkering on grip and forend. Introduced 1997. Imported from Germany by AcuSport Corp.
Price: From. **$1,439.00**
Price: Model 1730 Monte Carlo, as above except in 22 Hornet . **$1,439.00**

Anschutz 1733D Rifle

Similar to the 1740 Monte Carlo except has full-length, walnut, Mannlicher-style stock with skip-line checkering, rosewood Schnabel tip, and is chambered for 22 Hornet. Weighs 6.4 lbs., overall length 39", barrel length 19.7". Imported from Germany by AcuSport Corp.
Price: **$1,588.95**

ARNOLD ARMS ALASKAN RIFLE

Caliber: 243 to 338 Magnum. **Barrel:** 22" to 26". **Weight:** NA. **Length:** NA. **Stock:** Synthetic; black, woodland or arctic camouflage. **Sights:** Optional; drilled and tapped for scope mounting. **Features:** Uses Apollo, Remington or Winchester action with controlled round feed or push feed; chromemoly steel or stainless; one-piece bolt, handle, knob; cone head bolt and breech; three-position safety; fully adjustable trigger. Introduced 1996. Made in U.S. by Arnold Arms Co.
Price: From. **$2,695.00**

Arnold Arms Alaskan Guide Rifle

Similar to the Alaskan rifle except chambered for 257 to 338 Magnum; choice of A-grade English walnut or synthetic stock; three-position safety; scope mount only. Introduced 1996. Made in U.S. by Arnold Arms Co.
Price: From. **$3,249.00**

Arnold Arms Grand Alaskan Rifle

Similar to the Alaskan rifle except has AAA fancy select or exhibition-grade English walnut; barrel band swivel; comes with iron sights and scope mount; 24" to 26" barrel; 300 Magnum to 458 Win. Mag. Introduced 1996. Made in U.S. by Arnold Arms Co.
Price: From. **$7,670.00**

Arnold Arms Alaskan Trophy Rifle

Similar to the Alaskan rifle except chambered for 300 Magnum to 458 Win. Mag.; 24" to 26" barrel; black synthetic or laminated stock; comes with barrel band on 375 H&H and larger; scope mount; iron sights. Introduced 1996. Made in U.S. by Arnold Arms Co.
Price: From. **$3,249.00**

ARNOLD ARMS SAFARI RIFLE

Caliber: 243 to 458 Win. Mag. **Barrel:** 22" to 26". **Weight:** NA. **Length:** NA. **Stock:** Grade A and AA Fancy English walnut. **Sights:** Optional; drilled and tapped for scope mounting. **Features:** Uses Apollo, Remington or Winchester action with controlled or push round feed; one-piece bolt, handle, knob; cone head bolt and breech; three-position safety; fully adjustable trigger; chrome-moly steel in matte blue, polished, or bead blasted stainless. Introduced 1996. Made in U.S. by Arnold Arms Co.
Price: From. **$6,495.00**

Arnold Arms African Trophy Rifle

Similar to the Safari rifle except has AAA Extra Fancy English walnut stock with wrap-around checkering; matte blue chrome-moly or polished or bead blasted stainless steel; scope mount standard or optional Express sights. Introduced 1996. Made in U.S. by Arnold Arms Co.
Price: Blued chrome-moly steel **$6,921.00**
Price: Stainless steel **$6,971.00**

A-Square Hannibal

Barrett Model 95

Beretta Mato Deluxe

Arnold Arms Grand African Rifle

Similar to the Safari rifle except has Exhibition Grade stock; polished blue chrome-moly steel or bead-blasted or Teflon-coated stainless; barrel band; scope mount, express sights; calibers 338 Magnum to 458 Win. Mag.; 24" to 26" barrel. Introduced 1996. Made in U.S. by Arnold Arms Co.

Price: Chrome-moly steel............................ **$8,172.00**
Price: Stainless steel **$8,022.00**

A-SQUARE CAESAR BOLT-ACTION RIFLE

Caliber: 7mm Rem. Mag., 7mm STW, 30-06, 300 Win. Mag., 300 H&H, 300 Wea. Mag., 8mm Rem. Mag., 338 Win. Mag., 340 Wea. Mag., 338 A-Square, 9.3x62, 9.3x64, 375 Wea. Mag., 375 H&H, 375 JRS, 375 A-Square, 416 Hoffman, 416 Rem. Mag., 416 Taylor, 404 Jeffery, 425 Express, 458 Win. Mag., 458 Lott, 450 Ackley, 460 Short A-Square, 470 Capstick, 495 A-Square. **Barrel:** 20" to 26" (no-cost customer option). **Weight:** 8-1/2 to 11 lbs. **Stock:** Claro walnut with hand-rubbed oil finish; classic style with A-Square Coil-Chek® features for reduced recoil; flush detachable swivels. Customer choice of length of pull. **Sights:** Choice of three-leaf express, forward or normal-mount scope, or combination (at extra cost). **Features:** Matte non-reflective blue, double cross-bolts, steel and fiberglass reinforcement of wood from tang to forend tip; three-position positive safety; three-way adjustable trigger; expanded magazine capacity. Right- or left-hand. Introduced 1984. Made in U.S. by A-Square Co., Inc.

Price: Walnut stock.................................. **$3,295.00**
Price: Synthetic stock............................... **$3,745.00**

A-SQUARE HANNIBAL BOLT-ACTION RIFLE

Caliber: 7mm Rem. Mag., 7mm STW, 30-06, 300 Win. Mag., 300 H&H, 300 Wea. Mag., 8mm Rem. Mag., 338 Win. Mag., 340 Wea. Mag., 338 A-Square Mag., 9.3x62, 9.3x64, 375 H&H, 375 Wea. Mag., 375 JRS, 375 A-Square Mag., 378 Wea. Mag., 416 Taylor, 416 Rem. Mag., 416 Hoffman, 416 Rigby, 416 Wea. Mag., 404 Jeffery, 425 Express, 458 Win. Mag., 458 Lott, 450 Ackley, 460 Short A-Square Mag., 460 Wea. Mag., 470 Capstick, 495 A-Square Mag., 500 A-Square Mag. 577 Tyrannosaur. **Barrel:** 20" to 26" (no-cost customer option). **Weight:** 9 to 11-3/4 lbs. **Stock:** Claro walnut with hand-rubbed oil finish; classic style with A-Square Coil-Chek®

features for reduced recoil; flush detachable swivels. Customer choice of length of pull. Available with synthetic stock. **Sights:** Choice of three-leaf express, forward or normal-mount scope, or combination (at extra cost). **Features:** Black matte Teflon coating, double cross-bolts, steel and fiberglass reinforcement of wood from tang to forend tip; Mauser-style claw extractor; expanded magazine capacity; two-position safety; three-way target trigger. Right-hand only. Introduced 1983. Made in U.S. by A-Square Co., Inc.

Price: Walnut stock.................................. **$3,295.00**
Price: Synthetic stock............................... **$3,745.00**

A-Square Hamilcar Bolt-Action Rifle

Similar to the A-Square Hannibal rifle except chambered for 25-06, 6.5x55, 270 Win., 7x57, 280 Rem., 30-06, 338-06, 9.3x62, 257 Wea. Mag., 264 Win. Mag., 270 Wea. Mag., 7mm Rem. Mag., 7mm Wea. Mag., 7mm STW, 300 Win. Mag., 300 Wea. Mag. Weighs 88-1/2 lbs. Introduced 1994. From A-Square Co., Inc.

Price: **$3,295.00**

BARRETT MODEL 95 BOLT-ACTION RIFLE

Caliber: 50 BMG, 5-shot magazine. **Barrel:** 29". **Weight:** 22 lbs. **Length:** 45" overall. **Stock:** Energy-absorbing recoil pad. **Sights:** Scope optional. **Features:** Bolt-action, bullpup design. Disassembles without tools; extendable bipod legs; match-grade barrel; high efficiency muzzle brake. Introduced 1995. Made in U.S. by Barrett Firearms Mfg., Inc.

Price: From.. **$4,700.00**

BERETTA MATO DELUXE BOLT-ACTION RIFLE

Caliber: 270, 280 Rem., 30-06, 7mm Rem. Mag., 300 Win. Mag., 338 Win. Mag., 375 H&H. **Barrel:** 23.6". **Weight:** 7.9 lbs. **Length:** 44.5" overall. **Stock:** XXX claro walnut with ebony forend tip, hand-rubbed oil finish. **Sights:** Bead on ramp front, open fully adjustable rear; drilled and tapped for scope mounting. **Features:** Mauser-style action with claw extractor; three-position safety; removable box magazine; 375 H&H has muzzle brake. Introduced 1998. From Beretta U.S.A.

Price: **$2,470.00**
Price: 375 H&H.................................... **$2,795.00**

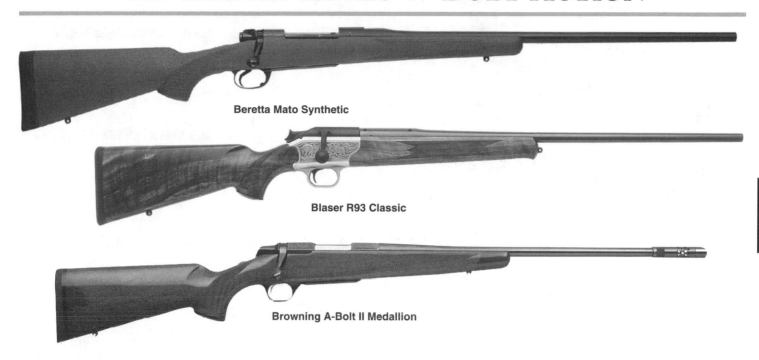

Beretta Mato Synthetic

Blaser R93 Classic

Browning A-Bolt II Medallion

Beretta Mato Synthetic Bolt-Action Rifle

Similar to the Mato except has fiberglass/Kevlar/carbon fiber stock in classic American style with shadow line cheekpiece, aluminum bedding block and checkering. Introduced 1998. From Beretta U.S.A.

Price: **$1,660.00**
Price: 375 H&H. **$2,015.00**

BLASER R93 BOLT-ACTION RIFLE

Caliber: 22-250, 243, 6.5x55, 270, 7x57, 7mm-08, 308, 30-06, 257 Wea. Mag., 7mm Rem. Mag., 300 Win. Mag., 300 Wea. Mag., 338 Win Mag., 375 H&H, 416 Rem. Mag. **Barrel:** 22" (standard calibers), 26" (magnum). **Weight:** 7 lbs. **Length:** 40" overall (22" barrel). **Stock:** Two piece European walnut. **Sights:** None furnished; drilled and tapped for scope mounting. **Features:** Straight pull-back bolt action with thumb-activated safety slide/cocking mechanism; interchangeable barrels and bolt heads. Introduced 1994. Imported from Germany by SIGARMS.

Price: R93 Classic **$3,495.00**
Price: R93 LX **$1,795.00**
Price: R93 Synthetic (black synthetic stock). **$1,495.00**
Price: R93 Safari Synthetic (416 Rem. Mag. only) **$2,285.00**
Price: R93 Grand Lux. **$4,675.00**
Price: R93 Attaché **$5,125.00**

BRNO 98 BOLT-ACTION RIFLE

Caliber: 7x64, 243, 270, 308, 30-06, 300 Win. Mag., 9.3x62. **Barrrel:** 23.6". **Weight:** 7.2 lbs. **Length:** 40.9" overall. **Stock:** European walnut. **Sights:** Blade on ramp front, open adjustable rear. **Features:** Uses Mauser 98-type action; polished blue. Announced 1998. Imported from the Czech Republic by Euro-Imports.

Price: Standard calibers **$507.00**
Price: Magnum calibers **$547.00**
Price: With set trigger, standard calibers **$615.00**
Price: As above, magnum calibers. **$655.00**
Price: With full stock, set trigger, standard calibers **$703.00**
Price: As above, magnum calibers. **$743.00**

BROWNING ACERA STRAIGHT-PULL RIFLE

Caliber: 30-06, 300 Win. Mag. **Barrel:** 22"; 24" for magnums. **Weight:** 6 lbs., 9 oz. **Length:** 41-1/4" overall. **Stock:** American walnut with high gloss finish. **Sights:** Blade on ramp front, open adjustable rear. **Features:** Straight-pull action; detachable box magazine; Teflon coated breechblock; drilled and tapped for scope mounting. Introduced 1999. Imported by Browning.

Price: 30-06, no sights **$845.00**
Price: 300 Win. Mag., no sights **$877.00**
Price: 30-06 with sights **$869.00**
Price: 300 Win. Mag., with sights **$901.00**
Price: 30-06, with BOSS. **$901.00**
Price: 300 Win. Mag., with BOSS. **$933.00**

BROWNING A-BOLT II RIFLE

Caliber: 25-06, 270, 30-06, 260 Rem., 280, 7mm Rem. Mag., 300 Win. Mag., 338 Win. Mag., 375 H&H Mag. **Barrel:** 22" medium sporter weight with recessed muzzle; 26" on mag. cals. **Weight:** 6-1/2 to 7-1/2 lbs. **Length:** 44-3/4" overall (magnum and standard); 41-3/4" (short action). **Stock:** Classic style American walnut; recoil pad standard on magnum calibers. **Features:** Short-throw (60°) fluted bolt, three locking lugs, plunger-type ejector; adjustable trigger is grooved and gold-plated. Hinged floorplate, detachable box magazine (4 rounds std. cals., 3 for magnums). Slide tang safety. Medallion has glossy stock finish, rosewood grip and forend caps, high polish blue. BOSS barrel vibration modulator and muzzle brake system not available in 375 H&H. Introduced 1985. Imported from Japan by Browning.

Price: Medallion, no sights **$662.00**
Price: Hunter, no sights **$557.00**
Price: Medallion, 375 H&H Mag., no sights **$767.00**
Price: For BOSS add **$60.00**

Browning A-Bolt II Short Action

Similar to the standard A-Bolt except has short action for 223, 22-250, 243, 257 Roberts, 260 Rem., 7mm-08, 284 Win., 308 chamberings. Available in Hunter or Medallion grades. Weighs 6-1/2 lbs. Other specs essentially the same. BOSS barrel vibration modulator and muzzle brake system optional. Introduced 1985.

Price: Medallion, no sights **$662.00**
Price: Hunter, no sights **$557.00**
Price: Composite stalker, no sights **$580.00**
Price: For BOSS, add. **$60.00**

Browning A-Bolt II Medallion Left-Hand

Same as the Medallion model A-Bolt except has left-hand action and is available in 25-06, 270, 280, 30-06, 7mm Rem. Mag., 300 Win. Mag., 338 Win. Mag., 375 H&H. Introduced 1987.

Price: **$688.00**
Price: With BOSS. **$748.00**

Browning A-Bolt II Micro Medallion

Browning A-Bolt II Eclipse M-1000

Charles Daly Superior

Browning A-Bolt II White Gold Medallion

Similar to the standard A-Bolt except has select walnut stock with brass spacers between rubber recoil pad and between the rosewood gripcap and forend tip; gold-filled barrel inscription; palm-swell pistol grip, Monte Carlo comb, 22 lpi checkering with double borders; engraved receiver flats. In 270, 30-06, 7mm Rem. Mag. only. Introduced 1988.

Price: $949.00
Price: For BOSS, add.................................... $60.00

Browning A-Bolt II Custom Trophy Rifle

Similar to the A-Bolt Medallion except has select American walnut stock with recessed swivel studs, octagon barrel, skeleton pistol gripcap, gold highlights, shadowline cheekpiece. Calibers 270, 30-06, 7mm Rem. Mag., 300 Win. Mag. Introduced 1998. Imported from Japan by Browning.

Price: $1,360.00

Browning A-Bolt II Eclipse

Similar to the A-Bolt II except has gray/black laminated, thumbhole stock, BOSS barrel vibration modulator and muzzle brake. Available in long and short action with standard weight barrel, or short-action Varmint with heavy barrel. Introduced 1996. Imported from Japan by Browning.

Price: Standard barrel, Hunter, with BOSS $941.00
Price: Varmint with BOSS............................... $969.00

Browning A-Bolt II Eclipse M-1000

Similar to the A-Bolt II Eclipse except has long action and heavy target barrel. Chambered only for 300 Win. Mag. Adjustable trigger, bench-style forend, 3-shot magazine; laminated thumbhold stock; BOSS system standard. Introduced 1997. Imported for Japan by Browning.

Price: $969.00

Browning A-Bolt II Varmint Rifle

Same as the A-Bolt II Hunter except has heavy varmint/target barrel, laminated wood stock with special dimensions, flat forend and palm swell grip. Chambered only for 223, 22-250, 308. Comes with BOSS barrel vibration modulator and muzzle brake system. Introduced 1994.

Price: With BOSS, gloss or matte finish.................. $853.00

NEW! Browning A-Bolt II Micro Hunter

Similar to the A-Bolt II Hunter except has 13-5/16" length of pull, 20" barrel, and comes in 260 Rem., 243, 308, 7mm-08, 22-250, 22 Hornet. Weighs 6 lbs., 1 oz. Introduced 1999. Imported by Browning.

Price: $557.00

Browning A-Bolt II Classic Series

Similar to the A-Bolt II Hunter except has low-luster bluing and walnut stock with Monte Carlo comb, pistol grip palm swell, double-border checkering. Available in 270, 30-06, 7mm Rem. Mag., 300 Win. Mag. Introduced 1999. Imported by Browning.

Price: $633.00

Browning A-Bolt II Stainless Stalker

Similar to the Hunter model A-Bolt except receiver and barrel are made of stainless steel; the rest of the exposed metal surfaces are finished with a durable matte silver-gray. Graphite-fiberglass composite textured stock. No sights are furnished. Available in 223, 22-250, 243, 308, 7mm-08, 270, 30-06, 7mm Rem. Mag., 375 H&H. Introduced 1987.

Price: $737.00
Price: With BOSS...................................... $797.00
Price: Left-hand, no sights $760.00
Price: With BOSS...................................... $820.00
Price: 375 H&H, with sights $839.00
Price: 375 H&H, left-hand, no sights $865.00

Browning A-Bolt II Composite Stalker

Similar to the A-Bolt II Hunter except has black graphite-fiberglass stock with textured finish. Matte blue finish on all exposed metal surfaces. Available in 223, 22-250, 243, 7mm-08, 308, 30-06, 270, 280, 25-06, 7mm Rem. Mag., 300 Win. Mag., 338 Win. Mag. BOSS barrel vibration modulator and muzzle brake system offered in all calibers. Introduced 1994.

Price: No sights $580.00
Price: No sights, BOSS $640.00

CHARLES DALY SUPERIOR BOLT-ACTION RIFLE

Caliber: 22 Hornet, 5-shot magazine. **Barrel:** 22.6". **Weight:** 6.6 lbs. **Length:** 41.25" overall. **Stock:** Walnut-finished hardwood with Monte Carlo comb and cheekpiece. **Sights:** Ramped blade front, fully adjustable open rear. **Features:** Receiver dovetailed for tip-off scope mount. Introduced 1996. Imported by K.B.I., Inc.

Price: $339.00

Charles Daly Empire Grade Rifle

Similar to the Superior except has oil-finished American walnut stock with 18 lpi hand checkering; black hardwood gripcap and forend tip; highly polished barreled action; jewelled bolt; recoil pad; swivel studs. Imported by K.B.I., Inc.

Price: $439.00

CZ 527

CZ 550 Lux

CZ 550 American Classic

COLT LIGHT RIFLE BOLT ACTION

Caliber: 243, 7x57, 7mm-08, 308 (short action); 25-06, 270, 280, 7mm Rem., Mag., 30-06, 300 Win. Mag. **Barrel:** 24" **Weight:** 5.4 to 6 lbs. **Length:** NA. **Stock:** Black synthetic. **Sights:** None furnished; low, medium, high scope mounts. **Features:** Matte black finish; three-position safety. Introduced 1999. Made in U.S. From Colt's Mfg., Inc.

Price: .... **NA**

COOPER MODEL 22 BOLT-ACTION RIFLE

Caliber: 22 BR, 22-250 Rem., 22-250 Ackley Imp., 243, 25-06, 25-06 Ackley Imp., 220 Swift, 257 Roberts, 257 Roberts Ackley Imp., 6mm Rem., 6mm PPC, 6mm BR, 7mm-08, single shot. **Barrel:** 24" stainless match grade. **Weight:** 7-3/4 to 8 lbs. **Stock:** AA Claro walnut, 20 lpi checkering. **Sights:** None furnished. **Features:** Uses three front locking lug system. Fully adjustable trigger. Many options available. Made in U.S. by Cooper Firearms.

Price: Classic	**$1,295.00**
Price: Varminter	**$1,195.00**
Price: Varmint Extreme	**$1,795.00**
Price: Custom Classic	**$1,995.00**
Price: Western Classic	**$2,195.00**

COOPER MODEL 21, 38 BOLT-ACTION RIFLES

Caliber: 17 Rem., 17 Mach IV, 17 Javelina, 19-223 Calhoon, 20 VarTag, 22 PPC, Model 21, 6mm PPC, 221 Fireball, 222 Rem., 222 Rem. Mag., 223 Rem., 223 Ackley Imp., 6x45, 6x47, single shot; Model 38—17 Squirrel, 17 HeBee, 17 Ackley Hornet, 22 Hornet, 22 K Hornet, 218 Mashburn Bee, 218 Bee, 22 Squirrel, single shot. **Barrel:** 24" stainless match grade. **Weight:** 6-1/2 to 7-1/4 lbs. **Stock:** AA Claro walnut; 20 l.p.i. checkering. **Sights:** None furnished. **Features:** Uses three front locking lug system. Fully adjustable trigger. Many options available. Contact maker for details. Made in U.S. by Cooper Firearms.

Price: Classic	**$995.00**
Price: Varminter	**$995.00**
Price: Varmint Extreme	**$1,750.00**
Price: Custom Classic	**$1,950.00**
Price: Western Classic	**$2,195.00**

COOPER ARMS MODEL 22 PRO VARMINT EXTREME

Caliber: 22-250, 220 Swift, 243, 25-06, 6mm PPC, 308, single shot. **Barrel:** 26"; stainless steel match grade, straight taper; free-floated. **Weight:** NA.

Length: NA. **Stock:** AAA Claro walnut, oil finish, 22 lpi wrap-around borderless ribbon checkering, beaded cheekpiece, steel gripcap, flared varminter forend, Pachmayr pad. **Sights:** None furnished; drilled and tapped for scope mounting. **Features:** Uses a three front locking lug system. Available with sterling silver inlaid medallion, skeleton gripcap, and French walnut. Introduced 1995. Made in U.S. by Cooper Arms.

Price: **$1,795.00**
Price: Benchrest model with Jewell trigger **$2,195.00**
Price: Black Jack model (McMillan synthetic stock) ... **$1,795.00**

CZ 527 LUX BOLT-ACTION RIFLE

Caliber: 22 Hornet, 222 Rem., 223 Rem., detachable 5-shot magazine. **Barrel:** 23-1/2"; standard or heavy barrel. **Weight:** 6 lbs., 1 oz. **Length:** 42-1/2" overall. **Stock:** European walnut with Monte Carlo. **Sights:** Hooded front, open adjustable rear. **Features:** Improved mini-Mauser action with non-rotating claw extractor; single set trigger; grooved receiver. Imported from the Czech Republic by CZ-USA.

Price: **$540.00**
Price: Model FS, full-length stock, cheekpiece **$607.00**

CZ 527 American Classic Bolt-Action Rifle

Similar to the CZ 527 Lux except has classic-style stock with 18 l.p.i. checkering; free-floating barrel; recessed target crown on barrel. No sights furnished. Introduced 1999. Imported from the Czech Republic by CZ-USA.

Price: 22 Hornet, 222 Rem., 223 Rem. **$540.00**

CZ 550 LUX BOLT-ACTION RIFLE

Caliber: 22-250, 243, 6.5x55, 7x57, 7x64, 308 Win., 9.3x62, 270 Win., 30-06. **Barrel:** 20.47". **Weight:** 7.5 lbs. **Length:** 44.68" overall. **Stock:** Turkish walnut in Bavarian style or FS (Mannlicher). **Sights:** Hooded front, adjustable rear. **Features:** Improved Mauser-style action with claw extractor, fixed ejector, square bridge dovetailed receiver; single set trigger. Imported from the Czech Republic by CZ-USA.

Price: Lux .... **$567.00 to $609.00**
Price: FS (full stock) **$645.00**

CZ 550 American Classic Bolt-Action Rifle

Similar to the CZ 550 Lux except has American classic-style stock with 18 l.p.i. checkering; free-floating barrel; recessed target crown. Has 25.6" barrel; weighs 7.48 lbs. No sights furnished. Introduced 1999. Imported from the Czech Republic by CZ-USA.

Price: .... **$576.00 to $609.00**

CZ 550 Magnum Bolt-Action Rifle

Similar to the CZ 550 Lux except has long action for 300 Win. Mag., 375 H&H, 416 Rigby, 458 Win. Mag. Overall length is 46.45"; barrel length

CZ 550 Magnum

Dakota 76 Classic

Dakota 76 Safari

Dakota Longbow

25"; weighs 9.24 lbs. Comes with hooded front sight, express rear with one standing, two folding leaves. Imported from the Czech Republic by CZ-USA.
Price: 300 Win. Mag., 375 H&H **$699.00**
Price: 416 Rigby, 458 Win. Mag. **$739.00**

DAKOTA TRAVELER TAKEDOWN RIFLE

NEW! **Caliber:** 257 Roberts, 25-06, 7x57, 270, 280, 30-06, 338-06, 35 Whelen (standard length); 7mm Rem. Mag., 300 Win. Mag., 338 Win. Mag., 416 Taylor, 458 Win. Mag. (short magnums); 7mm, 300, 330, 375 Dakota Magnums. **Barrel:** 23". **Weight:** 7-1/2 lbs. **Length:** 43-1/2" overall. **Stock:** Medium fancy-grade walnut in classic style. Checkered grip and forend; solid butt pad. **Sights:** None furnished; drilled and tapped for scope mounts. **Features:** Threadless disassembly—no threads to wear or stretch, no interrupted cuts, and headspace remains constant. Uses modified Model 76 design with many features of the Model 70 Winchester. Left-hand model also available. Introduced 1989. Made in U.S. by Dakota Arms, Inc.
Price: Classic **$3,995.00**
Price: Safari **$4,995.00**
Price: Extra barrels . . . . **$1,500.00** to **$1,700.00**

DAKOTA 76 CLASSIC BOLT-ACTION RIFLE

Caliber: 257 Roberts, 270, 280, 30-06, 7mm Rem. Mag., 338 Win. Mag., 300 Win. Mag., 375 H&H, 458 Win. Mag. **Barrel:** 23". **Weight:** 7-1/2 lbs. **Length:** 43-1/2" overall. **Stock:** Medium fancy grade walnut in classic style. Checkered pistol grip and forend; solid butt pad. **Sights:** None furnished; drilled and tapped for scope mounts. **Features:** Has many features of the original Model 70 Winchester. One-piece rail trigger guard assembly; steel gripcap. Model 70-style trigger. Many options available.

Left-hand rifle available at same price. Introduced 1988. From Dakota Arms, Inc.
Price: **$3,195.00**

Dakota 76 Classic Rifles

A scaled-down version of the standard Model 76. Standard chamberings are 22-250, 243, 6mm Rem., 250-3000, 7mm-08, 308, others on special order. Short Classic Grade has 21" barrel; Alpine Grade is lighter (6-1/2 lbs.), has a blind magazine and slimmer stock. Introduced 1989.
Price: Short Classic **$3,195.00**

DAKOTA 76 SAFARI BOLT-ACTION RIFLE

Caliber: 270 Win., 7x57, 280, 30-06, 7mm Dakota, 7mm Rem. Mag., 300 Dakota, 300 Win. Mag., 330 Dakota, 338 Win. Mag., 375 Dakota, 458 Win. Mag., 300 H&H, 375 H&H, 416 Rem. **Barrel:** 23". **Weight:** 8-1/2 lbs. **Length:** 43-1/2" overall. **Stock:** XXX fancy walnut with ebony forend tip; point-pattern with wrap-around forend checkering. **Sights:** Ramp front, standing leaf rear. **Features:** Has many features of the original Model 70 Winchester. Barrel band front swivel, inletted rear. Cheekpiece with shadow line. Steel gripcap. Introduced 1988. From Dakota Arms, Inc.
Price: Wood stock **$4,195.00**

Dakota 416 Rigby African

Similar to the 76 Safari except chambered for 404 Jeffery, 416 Rigby, 416 Dakota, 450 Dakota, 4-round magazine, select wood, two stock crossbolts. Has 24" barrel, weight of 9-10 lbs. Ramp front sight, standing leaf rear. Introduced 1989.
Price: **$4,695.00**

DAKOTA LONGBOW TACTICAL E.R. RIFLE

Caliber: 300 Dakota Magnum, 330 Dakota Magnum, 338 Lapua Magnum. **Barrel:** 28", .950" at muzzle **Weight:** 13.7 lbs. **Length:** 50" to 52" overall. **Stock:** Ambidextrous McMillan A-2 fiberglass, black or olive green color;

Dakota 97 Lightweight Hunter

Dakota Hunter

Harris Gunworks Alaskan

adjustable cheekpiece and buttplate. **Sights:** None furnished. Comes with Picatinny one-piece optical rail. **Features:** Uses the Dakota 76 action with controlled round food; three position firing pin block safety, claw extractor; Model 70-style trigger. Comes with bipod, case tool kit. Introduced 1997. Made in U.S. by Dakota Arms, Inc.
Price: **$4,250.00**

DAKOTA 97 VARMINT HUNTER
Caliber: 17 Rem., 222 Rem., 223 Rem., 220 Swift, 22-250, 22 BR, 22 PPC, 6mm BR. **Barrel:** 24". **Weight:** 8 lbs. **Length:** NA. **Stock:** X walnut; 13-5/8" length of pull. **Sights:** Optional. **Features:** Round short action; solid-bottom single shot; chrome-moly #4 barrel; adjustable trigger. Introduced 1998. Made in U.S. by Dakota Arms.
Price: **$1,795.00**

DAKOTA 97 LIGHTWEIGHT HUNTER
Caliber: 22-250 to 308. **Barrel:** 22"-24". **Weight:** 6.1-6.5 lbs. **Length:** 43" overall. **Stock:** Fiberglass. **Sights:** Optional. **Features:** Matte blue finish, black stock. Right-hand action only. Introduced 1998. Made in U.S. by Dakota Arms, Inc.
Price: **$1,795.00**

DAKOTA LONG RANGE HUNTER RIFLE
Caliber: 25-06, 257 Roberts, 270 Win., 280 Rem., 7mm Rem. Mag., 7mm Dakota Mag., 30-06, 300 Win. Mag., 300 Dakota Mag., 338 Win. Mag., 330 Dakota Mag., 375 H&H Mag., 375 Dakota Mag. **Barrel:** 24", 26", match-quality; free-floating. **Weight:** 7.7 lbs. **Length:** 45" to 47" overall. **Stock:** H-S Precision black synthetic, with one-piece bedding block system. **Sights:** None furnished. Drilled and tapped for scope mounting. **Features:** Cylindrical machined receiver controlled round feed; Mauser-style extractor; three-position striker blocking safety; fully adjustable match trigger. Right-hand action only. Introduced 1997. Made in U.S. by Dakota Arms, Inc.
Price: **$1,795.00**

HARRIS GUNWORKS SIGNATURE CLASSIC SPORTER
Caliber: 22-250, 243, 6mm Rem., 7mm-08, 284, 308 (short action); 25-06, 270, 280 Rem., 30-06, 7mm Rem. Mag., 300 Win. Mag., 300 Wea. (long action); 338 Win. Mag., 340 Wea., 375 H&H (magnum action). **Barrel:** 22", 24", 26". **Weight:** 7 lbs. (short action). **Stock:** Fiberglass in green, beige, brown or black. Recoil pad and 1" swivels installed. Length of pull up to 14-1/4". **Sights:** None furnished. Comes with 1" rings and bases. **Features:** Uses right- or left-hand action with matte black finish. Trigger pull set at 3 lbs. Four-round magazine for standard calibers; three for magnums. Aluminum floorplate. Wood stock optional. Introduced 1987. From Harris Gunworks, Inc.
Price: **$2,700.00**

Harris Gunworks Signature Classic Stainless Sporter
Similar to the Signature Classic Sporter except action is made of stainless steel. Same calibers, in addition to 416 Rem. Mag. Comes with fiberglass stock, right- or left-hand action in natural stainless, glass bead or black chrome sulfide finishes. Introduced 1990. From Harris Gunworks, Inc.
Price: **$2,900.00**

Harris Gunworks Signature Alaskan
Similar to the Classic Sporter except has match-grade barrel with single leaf rear sight, barrel band front, 1" detachable rings and mounts, steel floorplate, electroless nickel finish. Has wood Monte Carlo stock with cheekpiece, palm-swell grip, solid butt pad. Chambered for 270, 280

CENTERFIRE RIFLES — BOLT ACTION

Harris Gunworks Signature Titanium Mountain

Harris Gunworks Signature Super Varminter

Harris Gunworks Talon Safari

Howa Lightning

Rem., 30-06, 7mm Rem. Mag., 300 Win. Mag., 300 Wea., 358 Win., 340 Wea., 375 H&H. Introduced 1989.
Price: **$3,800.00**

Harris Gunworks Signature Titanium Mountain Rifle
Similar to the Classic Sporter except action made of titanium alloy, barrel of chrome-moly steel. Stock is of graphite reinforced fiberglass. Weight is 5-1/2 lbs. Chambered for 270, 280 Rem., 30-06, 7mm Rem. Mag., 300 Win. Mag. Fiberglass stock optional. Introduced 1989.
Price: **$3,300.00**
Price: With graphite-steel composite light weight barrel. **$3,700.00**

Harris Gunworks Signature Varminter
Similar to the Signature Classic Sporter except has heavy contoured barrel, adjustable trigger, field bipod and special hand-bedded fiberglass stock. Chambered for 223, 22-250, 220 Swift, 243, 6mm Rem., 25-06, 7mm-08, 7mm BR, 308, 350 Rem. Mag. Comes with 1" rings and bases. Introduced 1989.
Price: **$2,700.00**

HARRIS GUNWORKS TALON SAFARI RIFLE
Caliber: 300 Win. Mag., 300 Wea. Mag., 300 Phoenix, 338 Win. Mag., 30/378, 338 Lapua, 300 H&H, 340 Wea. Mag., 375 H&H, 404 Jeffery, 416 Rem. Mag., 458 Win. Mag. (Safari Magnum); 378 Wea. Mag., 416 Rigby, 416 Wea. Mag., 460 Wea. Mag. (Safari Super Magnum). **Barrel:** 24". **Weight:** About 9-10 lbs. **Length:** 43" overall. **Stock:** Gunworks fiberglass Safari. **Sights:** Barrel band front ramp, multi-leaf express rear. **Features:** Uses Harris Gunworks Safari action. Has quick detachable 1" scope mounts, positive locking steel floorplate, barrel band sling swivel. Match-

grade barrel. Matte black finish standard. Introduced 1989. From Harris Gunworks, Inc.
Price: Talon Safari Magnum. **$3,900.00**
Price: Talon Safari Super Magnum **$4,200.00**

HARRIS GUNWORKS TALON SPORTER RIFLE
Caliber: 22-250, 243, 6mm Rem., 6mm BR, 7mm BR, 7mm-08, 25-06, 270, 280 Rem., 284, 308, 30-06, 350 Rem. Mag. (long action); 7mm Rem. Mag., 7mm STW, 300 Win. Mag., 300 Wea. Mag., 300 H&H, 338 Win. Mag., 340 Wea. Mag., 375 H&H, 416 Rem. Mag. **Barrel:** 24" (standard). **Weight:** About 7-1/2 lbs. **Length:** NA. **Stock:** Choice of walnut or fiberglass. **Sights:** None furnished; comes with rings and bases. Open sights optional. **Features:** Uses pre-'64 Model 70-type action with cone breech, controlled feed, claw extractor and three-position safety. Barrel and action are of stainless steel; chrome-moly optional. Introduced 1991. From Harris Gunworks, Inc.
Price: **$2,900.00**

HOWA LIGHTNING BOLT-ACTION RIFLE
Caliber: 223, 22-250, 243, 270, 308, 30-06, 7mm Rem. Mag., 300 Win. Mag., 338 Win. Mag. **Barrel:** 22", 24" magnum calibers. **Weight:** 7-1/2 lbs. **Length:** 42" overall (22" barrel). **Stock:** Black Bell & Carlson Carbelite composite with Monte Carlo comb; checkered grip and forend. **Sights:** None furnished. Drilled and tapped for scope mounting. **Features:** Sliding thumb safety; hinged floorplate; polished blue/black finish. Introduced 1993. From Interarms/Howa.
Price: Blue, standard calibers. **$435.00**
Price: Blue, magnum calibers. **$455.00**
Price: Stainless, standard calibers **$485.00**
Price: Stainless, magnum calibers **$505.00**

CENTERFIRE RIFLES — BOLT ACTION

Howa M-1500 Hunter

Howa M-1500 PCS Police Counter Sniper

Howa M-1500 Varmint

L.A.R. Grizzly

Howa M-1500 Hunter Bolt-Action Rifle
Similar to the Lightning model except has walnut-finished hardwood stock. Polished blue finish or stainless steel. Introduced 1999. From Interarms/Howa.

Price: Blue, standard calibers $455.00
Price: Stainless, standard calibers $505.00
Price: Blue, magnum calibers $475.00
Price: Stainless, magnum calibers $525.00

Howa M-1500 PCS Police Counter Sniper Rifle
Similar to the M-1500 Lightning except chambered only for 308 Win., 24" hammer-forged heavy barrel. Trigger is factory set at 4 lbs. Available in blue or stainless steel, polymer or hardwood stock. Introduced 1999. Imported from Japan by Interarms/Howa.

Price: Blue, polymer stock $465.00
Price: Stainless, polymer stock........................... $525.00
Price: Blue, wood stock $485.00
Price: Stainless, wood stock............................. $545.00

Howa M-1500 Varmint Rifle
Similar to the M-1500 Lightning except has heavy 24" hammer-forged barrel. Chambered for 223 and 22-250. Weighs 9.3 lbs.; overall length 44.5". Introduced 1999. Imported from Japan by Interarms/Howa.

Price: Blue, polymer stock $465.00

Price: Stainless, polymer stock $525.00
Price: Blue, wood stock $485.00
Price: Stainless, wood stock............................. $545.00

L.A.R. GRIZZLY 50 BIG BOAR RIFLE
Caliber: 50 BMG, single shot. Barrel: 36". Weight: 28.4 lbs. Length: 45.5" overall. Stock: Integral. Ventilated rubber recoil pad. Sights: None furnished; scope mount. Features: Bolt-action bullpup design; thumb safety. All-steel construction. Introduced 1994. Made in U.S. by L.A.R. Mfg., Inc.
Price: $2,570.00

MARLIN MODEL MR-7 BOLT-ACTION RIFLE
Caliber: 22-250, 243, 25-06, 280, 308, 30-06, 4-shot detachable box magazine. Barrel: 22"; six-groove rifling. Weight: 7-1/2 lbs. Length: 43" overall. Stock: American black walnut with cut-checkered grip and forend, rubber butttpad, Mar-Shield® finish. Sights: Bead on ramp front, adjustable rear, or no sights. (25-06 only available without sights.) Features: Three-position safety; shrouded striker; red cocking indicator; adjustable 3-6 lb. trigger; quick-detachable swivel studs. Introduced 1996. Made in U.S. by Marlin.
Price: With sights $643.00
Price: No sights $603.00

Marlin Model MR-7B

Mountain Eagle Varmint

Raptor Bolt-Action

Remington 700 ADL Synthetic

Marlin Model MR-7B

Similar to the MR-7 except available in 270 or 30-06 with Maine birch stock with cut-checkered grip and forend. Blind magazine. Introduced 1998. Made in U.S.A. by Marlin.
Price: Without sights. **$483.00**

MOUNTAIN EAGLE RIFLE

Caliber: 222 Rem., 223 Rem. (Varmint); 270, 280, 30-06 (long action); 7mm Rem. Mag., 7mm STW, 300 Win. Mag., 338 Win. Mag., 300 Wea. Mag., 375 H&H, 416 Rem. Mag. (magnum action). **Barrel:** 24", 26" (Varmint); match-grade; fluted stainless on Varmint. Free floating. **Weight:** 7 lbs., 13 oz. **Length:** 44" overall (24" barrel). **Stock:** Kevlar-graphite with aluminum bedding block, high comb, recoil pad, swivel studs; made by H-S Precision. **Sights:** None furnished; accepts any Remington 700-type base. **Features:** Special Sako action with one-piece forged bolt, hinged steel floorplate, lengthened receiver ring; adjustable trigger. Krieger cut-rifled benchrest barrel. Introduced 1996. From Magnum Research, Inc.
Price: Right-hand **$1,499.00**
Price: Left-hand **$1,549.00**
Price: Varmint Edition. **$1,629.00**
Price: 375 H&H, 416 Rem., add **$300.00**

RAPTOR BOLT-ACTION RIFLE

Caliber: 270, 30-06, 243, 25-06, 308; 4-shot magazine. **Barrel:** 22". **Weight:** 7 lbs., 6 oz. **Length:** 42.5" overall. **Stock:** Black synthetic, fiberglass reinforced; checkered grip and forend; vented recoil pad; Monte

Carlo cheekpiece. **Sights:** None furnished; drilled and tapped for scope mounts. **Features:** Rust-resistant "Taloncote" treated barreled action; pillar bedded; stainless bolt with three locking lugs; adjustable trigger. Announced 1997. Made in U.S. by Raptor Arms Co., Inc.
Price: **$249.00**

REMINGTON MODEL 700 CLASSIC RIFLE

Caliber: 17 Rem. **Barrel:** 24". **Weight:** About 7-3/4 lbs. **Length:** 44-1/2" overall. **Stock:** American walnut, 20 lpi checkering on pistol grip and forend. Classic styling. Satin finish. **Sights:** None furnished. Receiver drilled and tapped for scope mounting. **Features:** A "classic" version of the M700 ADL with straight comb stock. Fitted with rubber recoil pad. Sling swivel studs installed. Hinged floorplate. Limited production in 1999 only.
Price: **$612.00**

REMINGTON MODEL 700 ADL BOLT-ACTION RIFLE

Caliber: 270, 308, 30-06 and 7mm Rem. Mag. **Barrel:** 22" or 24" round tapered. **Weight:** 7-1/4 to 7-1/2 lbs. **Length:** 41-5/8" to 44-1/2" overall. **Stock:** Walnut. Satin-finished pistol grip stock with fine-line cut checkering, Monte Carlo. **Sights:** Gold bead ramp front; removable, step-adjustable rear with windage screw. **Features:** Side safety, receiver tapped for scope mounts.
Price: From. **$492.00**

Remington Model 700 ADL Synthetic

Similar to the 700 ADL except has a fiberglass-reinforced synthetic stock with straight comb, raised cheekpiece, positive checkering, and black rub-

Remington 700 BDL

Remington 700 BDL DM

Remington 700 Safari KS

Remington 700 BDL Left Hand

ber butt pad. Metal has matte finish. Available in 22-250, 223, 243, 270, 308, 30-06 with 22" barrel, 300 Win. Mag., 7mm Rem. Mag. with 24" barrel. Introduced 1996.

Price: From **$425.00**

Remington Model 700 ADL Synthetic Youth
Similar to the Model 700 ADL Synthetic except has 1" shorter stock, 20" barrel. Chambered for 243, 308. Introduced 1998.

Price: **$425.00**

Remington Model 700 BDL Bolt-Action Rifle
Same as the 700 ADL except chambered for 222, 223 (short action, 24" barrel), 22-250, 25-06. (short action, 22" barrel), 243, 270, 30-06; skip-line checkering; black forend tip and gripcap with white line spacers. Matted receiver top, fine-line engraving, quick-release floorplate. Hooded ramp front sight; quick detachable swivels.

Price: From **$585.00**
Also available in 17 Rem., 7mm Rem. Mag., 300 Win. Mag. (long action, 24" barrel); 338 Win. Mag., (long action, 22" barrel); 300 Rem. Ultra Mag. (26" barrel). Overall length 44-1/2", weight about 7-1/2 lbs.

Price: From **$612.00**

Remington Model 700 Custom KS Mountain Rifle
Similar to the 700 BDL except custom finished with Kevlar reinforced resin synthetic stock. Available in both left- and right-hand versions. Chambered for 270 Win., 280 Rem., 30-06, 7mm Rem. Mag., 7mm STW, 300 Rem. Ultra Mag., 300 Win. Mag., 300 Wea. Mag., 35 Whelen, 338 Win. Mag., 8mm Rem. Mag., 375 H&H, with 24" barrel (except 300 Rem. Ultra Mag., 26"). Weighs 6 lbs., 6 oz. Introduced 1986.

Price: From **$1,193.00**

Remington Model 700 BDL DM Rifle
Same as the 700 BDL except has detachable box magazine (4-shot, standard calibers, 3-shot for magnums). Has glossy stock finish, fine-line en-

graving, open sights, recoil pad, sling swivels. Right-hand action calibers: 243, 270, 280, 7mm-08, 30-06, 7mm Rem. Mag., 300 Win. Mag., 338 Win. Mag.; left-hand calibers: 30-06, 7mm Rem. Mag. Introduced 1995.

Price: From **$639.00**

Remington Model 700 Safari
Similar to the 700 BDL except custom finished and tuned. In 8mm Rem. Mag., 375 H&H, 416 Rem. Mag. or 458 Win. Mag. calibers only with heavy barrel. Hand checkered, oil-finished stock in classic or Monte Carlo style with recoil pad installed.

Price: From **$1,197.00**
Price: Safari KS (Kevlar stock), from **$1,378.00**

Remington Model 700 AWR Alaskan Wilderness Rifle
Similar to the Model 700 BDL except has stainless barreled action with satin blue finish; special 24" Custom Shop barrel profile; matte gray stock of fiberglass and graphite, reinforced with DuPont Kevlar, straight comb with raised cheekpiece, magnum-grade black rubber recoil pad. Chambered for 7mm Rem. Mag., 7mm STW, 300 Rem. Ultra Mag., 300 Win. Mag., 300 Wea. Mag., 338 Win. Mag., 375 H&H. Introduced 1994.

Price: From **$1,445.00**

Remington Model 700 BDL Left Hand
Same as 700 BDL except mirror-image left-hand action, stock. Available in 270, 30-06, 7mm Rem. Mag.

Price: **$612.00**
Price: 7mm Rem. Mag. **$639.00**

Remington Model 700 APR African Plains Rifle
Similar to the Model 700 BDL except has magnum receiver and specially contoured 26" Custom Shop barrel with satin finish, laminated wood stock with raised cheekpiece, satin finish, black butt pad, 20 lpi cut checkering.

Remington 700 APR African Plains

Remington 700 BDL SS DM-B

Remington 700 BDL SS DM-B

Remington 700 VLS

Chambered for 7mm Rem. Mag., 300 Rem. Ultra Mag., 300 Win. Mag., 300 Wea. Mag., 338 Win. Mag., 375 H&H. Introduced 1994.
Price: **$1,554.00**

Remington Model 700 LSS Rifle
Similar to the 700 BDL except has stainless steel barreled action, gray laminated wood stock with Monte Carlo comb and cheekpiece. No sights furnished. Available in 7mm Rem. Mag., 300 Rem. Ultra Mag. and 300 Win. Mag., in right-hand, and 270, 7mm Rem. Mag., 30-06, 300 Rem. Ultra Mag., 300 Win. Mag. in left-hand model. Introduced 1996.
Price: From.. **$715.00**

Remington Model 700 MTN DM Rifle
Similar to the 700 BDL except weighs 6-1/2 to 6-5/8 lbs., has a 22" tapered barrel. Redesigned pistol grip, straight comb, contoured cheekpiece, hand-rubbed oil stock finish, deep cut checkering, hinged floorplate and magazine follower, two-position thumb safety. Chambered for 243, 260 Rem., 270 Win., 7mm-08, 25-06, 280 Rem., 30-06, 4-shot detachable box magazine. Overall length is 41-5/8"-42-1/2". Introduced 1995.
Price: About **$639.00**

Remington Model 700 BDL SS Rifle
Similar to the 700 BDL rifle except has hinged floorplate, 24" standard weight barrel in all calibers; magnum calibers have magnum-contour barrel. No sights supplied, but comes drilled and tapped. Has corrosion-resistant follower and fire control, stainless BDL-style barreled action with fine matte finish. Synthetic stock has straight comb and cheekpiece, textured

finish, positive checkering, plated swivel studs. Calibers—270, 30-06; magnums—7mm Rem. Mag., 300 Rem. Ultra Mag. (26" barrel) 300 Win. Mag., 338 Win. Mag., 375 H&H. Weighs 7-3/8 - 7-1/2 lbs. Introduced 1993.
Price: From... **$641.00**

Remington Model 700 BDL SS DM Rifle
Same as the 700 BDL SS except has detachable box magazine. Barrel, receiver and bolt made of #416 stainless steel; black synthetic stock, fine-line engraving. Available in 25-06, 260 Rem., 270, 280, 308, 30-06, 7mm Rem. Mag., 300 Win. Mag., 300 Wea. Mag., 338 Win. Mag. Introduced 1995.
Price: From.. **$702.00**

Remington Model 700 BDL SS DM-B
Same as the 700 BDL SS DM except has muzzle brake, fine-line engraving. Available only in 7mm Rem. Mag., 7mm STW, 300 Win. Mag., 300 Wea. Mag. Introduced 1996.
Price: **$789.00**

Remington Model 700 VLS Varmint Laminated Stock
Similar to the 700 BDL except has 26" heavy barrel without sights, brown laminated stock with beavertail forend, gripcap, rubber butt pad. Available in 223 Rem., 22-250, 6mm, 260 Rem., 7mm-08, 243, 308. Polished blue finish. Introduced 1995.
Price: From... **$625.00**

Remington Model 700 VS Varmint Synthetic Composite Rifles
Similar to the 700 BDL Varmint Laminated except has composite stock reinforced with DuPont Kevlar, fiberglass and graphite. Has aluminum bedding block that runs the full length of the receiver. Free-floating 26" barrel. Metal has black matte finish; stock has textured black and gray finish and swivel studs. Available in 223, 22-250, 308. Left-hand only. Introduced 1992.
Price: From... **$732.00**

Remington 700 Varmint Synthetic

Remington 700 VS Composite

Remington 700 VF SF

Remington 700 Sendero SF

Remington Model Seven

Remington Model 700 VS Composite Rifle

Similar to the Model 700 VS Varmint Synthetic except has a composite varmint-weight barrel, weighs 7-1/8 lbs., and is available in right-hand in 22-250, 223, 308 Win. Introduced 1999.
Price: **$1,692.00**

Remington Model 700 VS SF, VS SF-P Rifles

Similar to the Model 700 Varmint Synthetic except has satin-finish stainless barreled action with 26" fluted barrel, spherical concave muzzle crown, muzzle porting. Chambered for 223, 220 Swift, 22-250, 308. Introduced 1994.
Price: From **$852.00**

Remington Model 700 Sendero Rifle

Similar to the Model 700 Varmint Synthetic except has long action for magnum calibers. Has 26" heavy varmint barrel with spherical concave crown. Chambered for 25-06, 270, 7mm Rem. Mag., 300 Win. Mag. Introduced 1994.
Price: From **$705.00**

Remington Model 700 Sendero Composite Rifle

Similar to the Model 700 Sendero except has a composite barrel, and weighs 7-7/8 lbs. Available in 25-06, 7mm STW and 300 Win. Mag. with 26" barrel. Introduced 1999.
Price: **$1,692.00**

Remington Model 700 Sendero SF Rifle

Similar to the 700 Sendero except has stainless steel action and 26" fluted stainless barrel. Weighs 8-1/2 lbs. Chambered for 25-06, 7mm Rem.

Mag., 300 Wea. Mag., 7mm STW, 300 Rem. Ultra Mag., 300 Win. Mag. Introduced 1996.
Price: From **$852.00**

REMINGTON MODEL SEVEN BOLT-ACTION RIFLE

Caliber: 223 Rem. (5-shot); 243, 260 Rem., 7mm-08, 308 (4-shot). **Barrel:** 18-1/2". **Weight:** 6 1/4 lbs. **Length:** 37-3/4" overall. **Stock:** Walnut, with modified Schnabel forend. Cut checkering. **Sights:** Ramp front, adjustable open rear. **Features:** Short-action design; silent side safety; free-floated barrel except for single pressure point at forend tip. Introduced 1983.
Price: **$585.00**

Remington Model Seven KS

Similar to the Model Seven except has gray Kevlar reinforced stock with 1" black rubber recoil pad and swivel studs. Metal has black matte finish. No sights on 223, 260 Rem., 7mm-08, 308; 35 Rem. and 350 Rem. have iron sights.
Price: **$1,193.00**

Remington Model Seven SS

Similar to the Model Seven except has stainless steel barreled action and black synthetic stock, 20" barrel. Chambered for 223, 243, 260 Rem., 7mm-08, 308. Introduced 1994.
Price: **$641.00**

Remington Model Seven Custom MS Rifle

Similar to the Model Seven except has full-length Mannlicher-style stock of laminated wood with straight comb, solid black recoil pad, black steel forend tip, cut checkering, gloss finish. Barrel length 20", weighs 6-3/4 lbs. Available in 222 Rem., 223, 22-250, 243, 6mm Rem., 260 Rem., 7mm-08 Rem., 308, 350 Rem. Mag. Calibers 250 Savage, 257 Roberts, 35 Rem.

CENTERFIRE RIFLES — BOLT ACTION

Ruger 77/22 Hornet Varmint

Ruger M77 Mark II All-Weather

Ruger 77/44

available on special order. Polished blue finish. Introduced 1993. From Remington Custom Shop.

Price: From **$1,208.00**

Remington Model Seven Youth Rifle

Similar to the Model Seven except has hardwood stock with 12-3/16" length of pull and chambered for 243, 260 Rem., 7mm-08. Introduced 1993.

Price: **$479.00**

Ruger M77RSI International Carbine

Same as the standard Model 77 except has 18-1/2" barrel, full-length International-style stock, with steel forend cap, loop-type steel sling swivels. Integral-base receiver, open sights, Ruger 1" steel rings. Improved front sight. Available in 243, 270, 308, 30-06. Weighs 7 lbs. Length overall is 38-3/8".

Price: M77RSIMKII **$674.00**

RUGER M77 MARK II EXPRESS RIFLE

Caliber: 270, 30-06, 7mm Rem. Mag., 300 Win. Mag., 4-shot magazine. **Barrel:** 22", with integral steel rib; barrel-mounted front swivel stud; hammer forged. **Weight:** 7.5 lbs. **Length:** 42.125" overall. **Stock:** Hand-checkered medium quality French walnut with steel gripcap, black rubber butt pad, swivel studs. **Sights:** Ramp front, V-notch two-leaf express rear adjustable for windage mounted on rib. **Features:** Mark II action with three-position safety, stainless steel bolt, steel trigger guard, hinged steel floorplate. Introduced 1991.

Price: M77RSEXPMKII **$1,550.00**

RUGER 77/22 HORNET BOLT-ACTION RIFLE

Caliber: 22 Hornet, 6-shot rotary magazine. **Barrel:** 20". **Weight:** About 6 lbs. **Length:** 39-3/4" overall. **Stock:** Checkered American walnut, black rubber butt pad. **Sights:** Brass bead front, open adjustable rear; also available without sights. **Features:** Same basic features as the rimfire model except has slightly lengthened receiver. Uses Ruger rotary magazine. Three-position safety. Comes with 1" Ruger scope rings. Introduced 1994.

Price: 77/22RH (rings only) **$499.00**

Price: 77/22RSH (with sights) **$509.00**

Price: K77/22VHZ Varmint, laminated stock, no sights **$545.00**

RUGER M77 MARK II RIFLE

Caliber: 223, 243, 6mm Rem., 257 Roberts, 25-06, 6.5x55 Swedish, 270, 280 Rem., 308, 30-06, 7mm Rem. Mag., 300 Win. Mag., 338 Win. Mag., 4-shot magazine. **Barrel:** 20", 22"; 24" (magnums). **Weight:** About 7 lbs. **Length:** 39-3/4" overall. **Stock:** Hand-checkered American walnut; swivel studs, rubber butt pad. **Sights:** None furnished. Receiver has Ruger inte-

gral scope mount base, comes with Ruger 1" rings. Some models have iron sights. **Features:** Short action with new trigger and three-position safety. New trigger guard with redesigned floorplate latch. Left-hand model available. Introduced 1989.

Price: M77RMKII (no sights) **$599.00**

Price: M77RSMKII (open sights) **$667.00**

Price: M77LRMKII (left-hand, 270, 30-06, 7mm Rem. Mag.,300 Win. Mag.)

. . . . **$599.00**

Ruger M77 Mark II All-Weather Stainless Rifle

Similar to the wood-stock M77 Mark II except all metal parts are of stainless steel, and has an injection-moulded, glass-fiber-reinforced Du Pont Zytel stock. Also offered with laminated wood stock. Chambered for 223, 243, 270, 308, 30-06, 7mm Rem. Mag., 300 Win. Mag., 338 Win. Mag. Has the fixed-blade-type ejector, three-position safety, and new trigger guard with patented floorplate latch. Comes with integral Scope Base Receiver and 1" Ruger scope rings, built-in sling swivel loops. Introduced 1990.

Price: K77RPMKII **$599.00**

Price: K77RLPMKII Ultra-light, synthetic stock, rings, no sights . . **$599.00**

Price: K77LRBBZMKII, left-hand bolt, rings, no sights, laminated

stock **$636.00**

Price: K77RSPMKII, open sights **$667.00**

Price: K77RBZMKII, no sights, laminated wood stock, 223, 243, 270, 280 Rem., 7mm Rem. Mag., 30-06, 308, 300 Win. Mag., 338

Win. Mag. **$636.00**

Price: K77RSBZMKII, open sights, laminated wood stock, 243, 270, 7mm Rem. Mag., 30-06, 300 Win. Mag., 338 Win. Mag. **$700.00**

Ruger M77RL Ultra Light

Similar to the standard M77 except weighs only 6 lbs., chambered for 223, 243, 308, 270, 30-06, 257; barrel tapped for target scope blocks; has 20" Ultra Light barrel. Overall length 40". Ruger's steel 1" scope rings supplied. Introduced 1983.

Price: M77RLMKII **$640.00**

RUGER M77 MARK II MAGNUM RIFLE

Caliber: 375 H&H, 4-shot magazine; 416 Rigby, 3-shot magazine. **Barrel:** 26", with integral steel rib; hammer forged. **Weight:** 9.25 lbs. (375); 10.25 lbs. (416, 458). **Length:** 40.5" overall. **Stock:** Circassian walnut with hand-cut checkering, swivel studs, steel gripcap, rubber butt pad. **Sights:** Ramp front, two leaf express on serrated integral steel rib. Rib also serves as base for front scope ring. **Features:** Uses an enlarged Mark II action with three-position safety, stainless bolt, steel trigger guard and hinged steel floorplate. Controlled feed. Introduced 1989.

Price: M77RSMMKII **$1,620.00**

RUGER 77/44 BOLT-ACTION RIFLE

Caliber: 44 Magnum, 4-shot magazine. **Barrel:** 18-1/2". **Weight:** 6 lbs. **Length:** 38-1/4" overall. **Stock:** American walnut with rubber butt pad and

CENTERFIRE RIFLES — BOLT ACTION

Ruger M77VT Target

Sako TRG-S

Sako 75 Hunter

Sako 75 Deluxe

swivel studs or black polymer (stainless only). **Sights:** Gold bead front, folding leaf rear. Comes with Ruger 1" scope rings. **Features:** Uses same action as the Ruger 77/22. Short bolt stroke; rotary magazine; three-position safety. Introduced 1997. Made in U.S. by Sturm, Ruger & Co.
Price: Blue, walnut, 77/44RS $575.00
Price: Stainless, polymer, stock, K77/44RS $575.00

RUGER M77VT TARGET RIFLE
Caliber: 22-250, 220 Swift, 223, 243, 25-06, 308. **Barrel:** 26" heavy stainless steel with target gray finish. **Weight:** Approx. 9.25 lbs. **Length:** Approx. 44" overall. **Stock:** Laminated American hardwood with beavertail forend, steel swivel studs; no checkering or gripcap. **Sights:** Integral scope mount bases in receiver. **Features:** Ruger diagonal bedding system. Ruger steel 1" scope rings supplied. Fully adjustable trigger. Steel floorplate and trigger guard. New version introduced 1992.
Price: K77VTMKII $718.00

SAKO TRG-S BOLT-ACTION RIFLE
Caliber: 243, 7mm-08, 270, 6.5x55, 30-06, 7mm Rem. Mag., 300 Win. Mag., 338 Win. Mag., 270 Wea. Mag., 7mm Wea. Mag., 340 Wea. Mag., 375 H&H, 416 Rem. Mag., 5-shot magazine (4-shot for 375 H&H). **Barrel:** 22", 24" (magnum calibers). **Weight:** 7.75 lbs. **Length:** 45.5" overall. **Stock:** Reinforced polyurethane with Monte Carlo comb. **Sights:** None furnished. **Features:** Resistance-free bolt with 60-degree lift. Recoil pad adjustable for length. Free-floating barrel, detachable magazine, fully adjustable trigger. Matte blue metal. Introduced 1993. Imported from Finland by Stoeger.
Price: 243, 7mm-08, 270, 30-06 . . . . $854.00
Price: Magnum calibers $894.00

SAKO 75 HUNTER BOLT-ACTION RIFLE
Caliber: 22-250, 243, 7MM-08, 308 Win., 25-06, 270, 280, 30-06; 270 Wea. Mag., 7mm Rem. Mag., 7mm STW, 7mm Wea. Mag., 300 Win. Mag., 300 Wea. Mag., 338 Win. Mag., 340 Wea. Mag., 375 H&H, 416 Rem. Mag. **Barrel:** 22", standard calibers; 24", 26" magnum calibers. **Weight:** About 6 lbs. **Length:** NA. **Stock:** European walnut with matte lacquer finish. **Sights:** None furnished; dovetail scope mount rails. **Features:** New de-

sign with three locking lugs and a mechanical ejector; cold hammer-forged barrel is free-floating; two-position safety; hinged floorplate or detachable magazine that can be loaded from the top; short 70 degree bolt lift. Available in five action lengths. Introduced 1997. Imported from Finland by Stoeger Industries.
Price: Standard calibers $1,134.00
Price: Magnum Calibers $1,164.00

Sako 75 Stainless Synthetic Rifle
Similar to the 75 Hunter except all metal is of stainless steel, and the synthetic stock has soft composite panels moulded into the forend and pistol grip. Available in 22-250, 243, 308 Win., 25-06, 270, 30-06 with 22" barrel, 7mm Rem. Mag., 300 Win. Mag. with 24" barrel. Introduced 1997. Imported from Finland by Stoeger Industries.
Price: Standard calibers $1,221.00
Price: Magnum calibers $1,257.00

Sako 75 Deluxe Rifle
Similar to the 75 Hunter except has select wood rosewood gripcap and forend tip. Available in 25-06, 270, 280, 30-06; 270 Wea. Mag., 7mm Rem. Mag., 7mm STW, 7mm Wea. Mag., 300 Win. Mag., 300 Wea. Mag., 338 Win. Mag., 340 Wea. Mag., 375 H&H, 416 Rem. Mag. Introduced 1997. Imported from Finland by Stoeger Industries.
Price: Standard calibers $1,644.00
Price: Magnum calibers $1,674.00

Sako 75 Stainless Hunter Rifle
Similar to the Sako 75 Hunter except all metal is of stainless steel. Comes with walnut stock with matte lacquer finish, rubber butt pad. Introduced 1999. Imported from Finland by Stoeger Industries.
Price: 270, 30-06 . . . . $1,224.00
Price: 7mm Rem. Mag., 7mm STW, 300 Win. Mag., 300 Wea. Mag., 338 Win. Mag. $1,257.00

Sako 75 Varmint Stainless Rifle
Similar to the Sako 75 Hunter except chambered only for 222, 223, 22-250, 22 PPC USA, 6 PPC USA; has heavy 24" barrel with recessed crown; all metal is of stainless steel; has laminated wood stock with beavertail forend. Introduced 1999. Imported from Finland by Stoeger Industries.
Price: $1,474.00

NEW!

NEW!

Sako 75 Stainless Hunter

Sako 75 Varmint

Savage Model 10FM

Savage Model 10FP

Sako 75 Varmint Rifle

Similar to the Model 75 Hunter except chambered only for 17 Rem., 222 Rem., 223 Rem., 22-250 Rem.; 24" heavy barrel with recessed crown; beavertail forend. Introduced 1998. Imported from Finland by Stoeger Industries.

Price: **$1,299.00**

SAUER 202 BOLT-ACTION RIFLE

Caliber: Standard—243, 6.5x55, 270 Win., 308 Win., 30-06; magnum—7mm Rem. Mag., 300 Win. Mag., 300 Wea. Mag., 375 H&H. **Barrel:** 23.6" (standard), 26" (magnum). **Weight:** 7.7 lbs. (standard). **Length:** 44.3" overall (23.6" barrel). **Stock:** Select American Claro walnut with high-gloss epoxy finish, rosewood grip and forend caps; 22 lpi checkering. Synthetic also available. **Sights:** None furnished; drilled and tapped for scope mounting. **Features:** Short 60" bolt throw; detachable box magazine; six-lug bolt; quick-change barrel; tapered bore; adjustable two-stage trigger; firing pin cocking indicator. Introduced 1994. Imported from Germany by Sigarms, Inc.

Price: Standard calibers, right-hand...................... **$1,035.00**
Price: Magnum calibers, right-hand **$1,106.00**
Price: Standard calibers, synthetic stock **$985.00**
Price: Magnum calibers, synthetic stock **$1,056.00**

SAVAGE MODEL 110GXP3, 110GCXP3 PACKAGE GUNS

Caliber: 223, 22-250, 243, 250 Savage, 25-06, 270, 300 Sav., 30-06, 308, 7mm Rem. Mag., 7mm-08, 300 Win. Mag. (Model 110GXP3); 270, 30-06, 7mm Rem. Mag., 300 Win. Mag. (Model 110GCXP3). **Barrel:** 22" (standard calibers), 24" (magnum calibers). **Weight:** 7.25-7.5 lbs. **Length:** 43.5" overall (22" barrel). **Stock:** Monte Carlo-style hardwood with walnut finish, rubber butt pad, swivel studs. **Sights:** None furnished. **Features:** Model 110GXP3 has fixed, top-loading magazine; Model 110GCXP3 has detachable box magazine. Rifles come with a factory-mounted and bore-sighted 3-9x32 scope, rings and bases, quick-detachable swivels, sling. Left-hand models available in all calibers. Introduced 1991 (GXP3); 1994 (GCXP3). Made in U.S. by Savage Arms, Inc.

Price: Model 110GXP3, right- or left-hand **$420.00**
Price: Model 110GCXP3, right- or left-hand................ **$485.00**

Savage Model 111FXP3, 111FCXP3 Package Guns

Similar to the Model 110 Series Package Guns except with lightweight, black graphite/fiberglass composite stock with non-glare finish, positive checkering. Same calibers as Model 110 rifles, plus 338 Win. Mag. Model 111FXP3 has fixed top-loading magazine; Model 111FCXP3 has detachable box. Both come with mounted 3-9x32 scope, quick-detachable swivels, sling. Introduced 1994. Made in U.S. by Savage Arms, Inc.

Price: Model 111FXP3, right- or left-hand **$450.00**
Price: Model 111FCXP3, right- or left-hand **$495.00**

SAVAGE MODEL 110FM SIERRA ULTRA LIGHT WEIGHT RIFLE

Caliber: 243, 270, 308, 30-06. **Barrel:** 20"**Weight:** 6-1/4 lbs. **Length:** 41-1/2" overall. **Stock:** Graphite/fiberglass-filled composite. **Sights:** None furnished; drilled and tapped for scope mounting. **Features:** Comes with black nylon sling and quick-detachable swivels. Introduced 1996. Made in U.S. by Savage Arms, Inc.

Price: **$410.00**

Savage Model 10FM Sierra Ultra Light Rifle

Similar to the Model 110FM Sierra except has a true short action, chambered for 223, 243, 308; weighs 6 lbs. "Dual Pillar" bedding in black synthetic stock with silver medallion in gripcap. Comes with sling and quick-detachable swivels. Introduced 1998. Made in U.S. by Savage Arms, Inc.

Price: **$425.00**

SAVAGE MODEL 110FP TACTICAL RIFLE

Caliber: 223, 25-06, 308, 30-06, 300 Win. Mag., 7mm Rem. Mag., 4-shot magazine. **Barrel:** 24", heavy; recessed target muzzle. **Weight:** 8-1/2 lbs. **Length:** 45.5" overall. **Stock:** Black graphite/fiberglass composition; positive checkering. **Sights:** None furnished. Receiver drilled and tapped for scope mounting. **Features:** Pillar-bedded stock. Black matte finish on all metal parts. Double swivel studs on the forend for sling and/or bipod mount. Right or left-hand. Introduced 1990. From Savage Arms, Inc.

Price: Right- or left-hand **$429.00**

Savage Model 10FP Tactical Rifle

Similar to the Model 110FP except has true short action, chambered for 223, 308; black synthetic stock with "Dual Pillar" bedding. Introduced 1998. Made in U.S. by Savage Arms, Inc.

Price: **$446.00**
Price: Model 10FLP (left-hand) **$446.00**

CENTERFIRE RIFLES — BOLT ACTION

Savage Model 111FAK

Savage Model 10GY

Savage Model 11F

Savage Model 11G

Savage Model 114CE

SAVAGE MODEL 111 CLASSIC HUNTER RIFLES

Caliber: 223, 22-250, 243, 250 Sav., 25-06, 270, 300 Sav., 30-06, 308, 7mm Rem. Mag., 7mm-08, 300 Win. Mag., 338 Win. Mag. (Models 111G, GL, GNS, F, FL, FNS); 270, 30-06, 7mm Rem. Mag., 300 Win. Mag. (Models 111GC, GLC, FAK, FC, FLC). **Barrel:** 22", 24" (magnum calibers). **Weight:** 6.3 to 7 lbs. **Length:** 43.5" overall (22" barrel). **Stock:** Walnut-finished hardwood (M111G, GC); graphite/fiberglass filled composite. **Sights:** Ramp front, open fully adjustable rear; drilled and tapped for scope mounting. **Features:** Three-position top tang safety, double front locking lugs, free-floated button-rifled barrel. Comes with trigger lock, target, ear puffs. Introduced 1994. Made in U.S. by Savage Arms, Inc.

Price: Model 111FC (detachable magazine, composite stock, right- or left-hand) **$420.00**

Price: Model 111F (top-loading magazine, composite stock, right- or left-hand) **$380.00**

Price: Model 111FNS (as above, no sights, right-hand only).... **$372.00**

Price: Model 111G (wood stock, top-loading magazine, right- or left-hand) **$360.00**

Price: Model 111GC (as above, detachable magazine), right- or left-hand **$410.00**

Price: Model 111GNS (wood stock, top-loading magzine, no sights, right-hand only).. **$353.00**

Price: Model 111FAK Express (blued, composite stock, top loading magazine, Adjustable muzzle brake) **$450.00**

Savage Model 11 Hunter Rifles

Similar to the Model 111F except has true short action, chambered for 223, 22-250, 243, 308; black synthetic stock with "Dual Pillar" bedding, positive checkering. Introduced 1998. Made in U.S. by Savage Arms, Inc.

Price: Model 11F **$395.00**
Price: Model 11FL (left-hand)................................ **$395.00**
Price: Model 11FNS (right-hand, no sights)................... **$387.00**
Price: Model 11G (wood stock) **$371.00**
Price: Model 11GL (as above, left-hand) **$374.00**
Price: Model 11GNS (wood stock, no sights)................. **$367.00**

Savage Model 10GY, 110GY Rifle

Similar to the Model 111G except weighs 6.3 lbs., is 42-1/2" overall, and the stock is scaled for ladies, small-framed adults and youths. Chambered for 223, 243, 270, 308. Ramp front sight, open adjustable rear; drilled and tapped for scope mounts. Made in U.S. by Savage Arms, Inc.

Price: Model 110GY..................................... **$360.00**
Price: Model 10GY (short action, calibers 223, 243, 308) **$374.00**

SAVAGE MODEL 114C CLASSIC RIFLE

Caliber: 270, 30-06, 7mm Rem. Mag., 300 Win. Mag.; 4-shot detachable box magazine in standard calibers, 3-shot for magnums. **Barrel:** 22" for standard calibers, 24" for magnums. **Weight:** 7-1/8 lbs. **Length:** 45-1/2" overall. **Stock:** Oil-finished American walnut; checkered grip and forend. **Sights:** None furnished; drilled and tapped for scope mounting. **Features:** High polish blue on barrel, receiver and bolt handle; Savage logo laser-etched on bolt body; push-button magazine release. Introduced 1996. Made in U.S. by Savage Arms, Inc.

Price: **$525.00**

Savage Model 114CE Classic European

Similar to the Model 114C except the oil-finished walnut stock has a Schnabel forend tip, cheekpiece and skip-line checkering; bead on blade

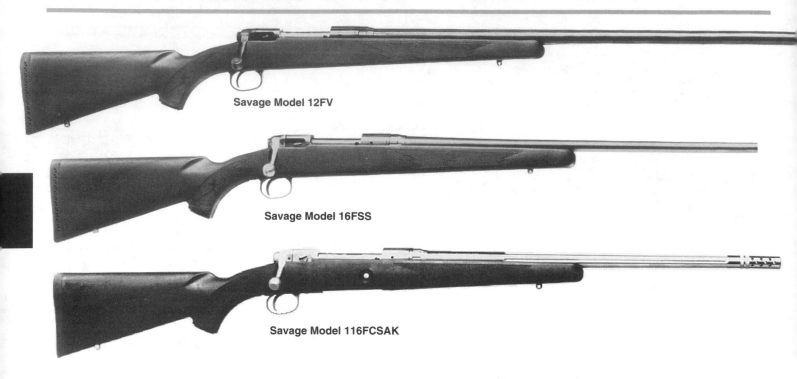

Savage Model 12FV

Savage Model 16FSS

Savage Model 116FCSAK

front sight, fully adjustable open rear; solid red butt pad. Chambered for 270, 30-06, 7mm Rem. Mag., 300 Win. Mag. Introduced 1996. Made in U.S. by Savage Arms, Inc.

Price: $600.00

SAVAGE MODEL 112 LONG RANGE RIFLES

Caliber: 22-250, 223, 5-shot magazine. **Barrel:** 26" heavy. **Weight:** 8.8 lbs. **Length:** 47.5" overall. **Stock:** Black graphite/fiberglass filled composite with positive checkering. **Sights:** None furnished; drilled and tapped for scope mounting. **Features:** Pillar-bedded stock. Blued barrel with recessed target-style muzzle. Double front swivel studs for attaching bipod. Introduced 1991. Made in U.S. by Savage Arms, Inc.

Price: Model 112FV $410.00
Price: Model 112FVSS (cals. 223, 22-250, 25-06, 7mm Rem. Mag., 300 Win. Mag., stainless barrel, bolt handle, trigger guard), right- or left-hand $515.00
Price: Model 112FVSS-S (as above, single shot) $515.00
Price: Model 112BVSS (heavy-prone laminated stock with high comb, Wundhammer swell, fluted stainless barrel, bolt handle, trigger guard) $540.00
Price: Model 112BVSS-S (as above, single shot) $540.00

Savage Model 12 Long Range Rifles

Similar to the Model 112 Long Range except with true short action, chambered for 223, 22-250, 308. Models 12FV, 12FVSS have black synthetic stocks with "Dual Pillar" bedding, positive checkering, swivel studs; model 12BVSS has brown laminated stock with beavertail forend, fluted stainless barrel. Introduced 1998. Made in U.S. by Savage Arms, Inc.

Price: Model 12FV (223, 22-250 only, blue) $429.00
Price: Model 12FVSS (blue action, fluted stainless barrel) $534.00
Price: Model 12FLVSS (as above, left-hand) $534.00
Price: Model 12FVSS-S (blue action, fluted stainless barrel, single shot) $534.00
Price: Model 12BVSS (laminated stock) $560.00
Price: Model 12BVSS-S (as above, single shot) $560.00

SAVAGE MODEL 116SE SAFARI EXPRESS RIFLE

Caliber: 300 Win. Mag., 338 Win. Mag., 425 Express, 458 Win. Mag. **Barrel:** 24". **Weight:** 8.5 lbs. **Length:** 45.5" overall. **Stock:** Classic-style select walnut with ebony forend tip, deluxe cut checkering. Two cross bolts; internally vented recoil pad. **Sights:** Bead on ramp front, three-leaf ex-

press rear. **Features:** Controlled-round feed design; adjustable muzzle brake; one-piece barrel band stud. Satin-finished stainless steel barreled action. Introduced 1994. Made in U.S. by Savage Arms, Inc.

Price: $900.00

Savage Model 116US Ultra Stainless Rifle

Similar to the Model 116SE except chambered for 270, 30-06, 7mm Rem. Mag., 300 Win. Mag.; stock has high-gloss finish; no open sights. Stainless steel barreled action with satin finish. Introduced 1995. Made in U.S. by Savage Arms, Inc.

Price: $700.00

SAVAGE MODEL 116 WEATHER WARRIORS

Caliber: 223, 243, 270, 30-06, 7mm Rem. Mag., 300 Win. Mag., 338 Win. Mag. (Model 116FSS); 270, 30-06, 7mm Rem. Mag., 300 Win. Mag. (Models 116FCSAK, 116FCS); 270, 30-06, 7mm Rem. Mag., 300 Win. Mag., 338 Win. Mag. (Models 116FSAK, 116FSK). **Barrel:** 22", 24" for 7mm Rem. Mag., 300 Win. Mag., 338 Win. Mag. (M116FSS only). **Weight:** 6.25 to 6.5 lbs. **Length:** 43.5" overall (22" barrel). **Stock:** Graphite/fiberglass filled composite. **Sights:** None furnished; drilled and tapped for scope mounting. **Features:** Stainless steel with matte finish; free-floated barrel; quick-detachable swivel studs; laser-etched bolt; scope bases and rings. Left-hand models available in all models, calibers at same price. Models 116FCS, 116FSS introduced 1991; Model 116FSK introduced 1993; Model 116FCSAK, 116FSAK introduced 1994. Made in U.S. by Savage Arms, Inc.

Price: Model 116FSS (top-loading magazine) $495.00
Price: Model 116FCS (detachable box magazine) $560.00
Price: Model 116FCSAK (as above with Savage Adjustable Muzzle Brake system) $650.00
Price: Model 116FSAK (top-loading magazine, Savage Adjustable Muzzle Brake system) $585.00
Price: Model 116FSK Kodiak (as above with 22" Shock-Suppressor barrel) $554.00

Savage Model 16FSS Rifle

Similar to the Model 116FSS except has true short action, chambered for 223, 243, 308; 22" free-floated barrel; black graphite/fiberglass stock with "Dual Pillar" bedding. Introduced 1998. Made in U.S. by Savage Arms, Inc.

Price: $515.00
Price: Model 16FLSS (left-hand) $515.00

Sigarms SHR 970

Steyr Mannlicher SBS

Steyr SBS Forester

Steyr SBS Prohunter

Steyr Scout Rifle

SIGARMS SHR 970 SYNTHETIC RIFLE

Caliber: 270, 30-06. **Barrel:** 22". **Weight:** 7.2 lbs. **Length:** 41.9" overall. **Stock:** Textured black fiberglass or walnut. **Sights:** None furnished; drilled and tapped for scope mounting. **Features:** Quick takedown; interchangeable barrels; removable box magazine; cocking indicator; three-position safety. Introduced 1998. Imported by Sigarms, Inc.

Price: Synthetic stock $499.00
Price: Walnut stock $530.00

STEYR MANNLICHER SBS RIFLE

Caliber: 243, 25-06, 308, 6.5x55, 6.5x57, 270, 7x64 Brenneke, 7mm-08, 7.5x55, 30-06, 9.3x62, 6.5x68, 7mm Rem. Mag., 300 Win. Mag., 8x685, 4-shot magazine. **Barrel:** 23.6" standard; 26" magnum; 20" full stock standard calibers. **Weight:** 7 lbs. **Length:** 40.1" overall. **Stock:** Hand-checkered fancy European oiled walnut with standard forend. **Sights:** Ramp front adjustable for elevation, V-notch rear adjustable for windage. **Features:** Single adjustable trigger; 3-position roller safety with "safe-bolt" setting; drilled and tapped for Steyr factory scope mounts. Introduced 1997. Imported from Austria by GSI, Inc.

Price: Half-stock, standard calibers $2,795.00
Price: Half-stock, magnum calibers $2,995.00
Price: Full-stock, standard calibers $2,995.00

STEYR SBS FORESTER RIFLE

Caliber: 243, 25-06, 270, 7mm-08, 308 Win., 30-06, 7mm Rem. Mag., 300 Win. Mag. Detachable 4-shot magazine. **Barrel:** 23.6", standard calibers; 25.6", magnum calibers. **Weight:** 7.5 lbs. **Length:** 44.5" overall (23.6" barrel). **Stock:** Oil-finished American walnut with Monte Carlo cheekpiece. Pachmayr 1" swivels. **Sights:** None furnished. Drilled and tapped for Browning A-Bolt mounts. **Features:** Steyr Safe Bolt systems, three-position ambidextrous roller tang safety, for Safe, Loading Fire. Matte finish on barrel and receiver; adjustable trigger. Rotary cold-hammer forged barrel. Introduced 1997. Imported by GSI, Inc.

Price: Standard calibers $899.00
Price: Magnum calibers $1,045.00

Steyr SBS Prohunter Rifle

Similar to the SBS Forester except has ABS synthetic stock with adjustable butt spacers, straight comb without cheekpiece, palm swell, Pachmayr 1" swivels. Special 10-round magazine conversion kit available. Introduced 1997. Imported by GSI.

Price Standard calibers $799.00
Price Magnum calibers $899.00

STEYR SCOUT BOLT-ACTION RIFLE

Caliber: 308 Win., 5-shot magazine. **Barrel:** 19", fluted. **Weight:** NA. **Length:** NA. **Stock:** Gray Zytel. **Sights:** None furnished; comes with Leupold M8 2.5x28 IER scope on Picatinny optic rail with Steyr mounts. **Fea-**

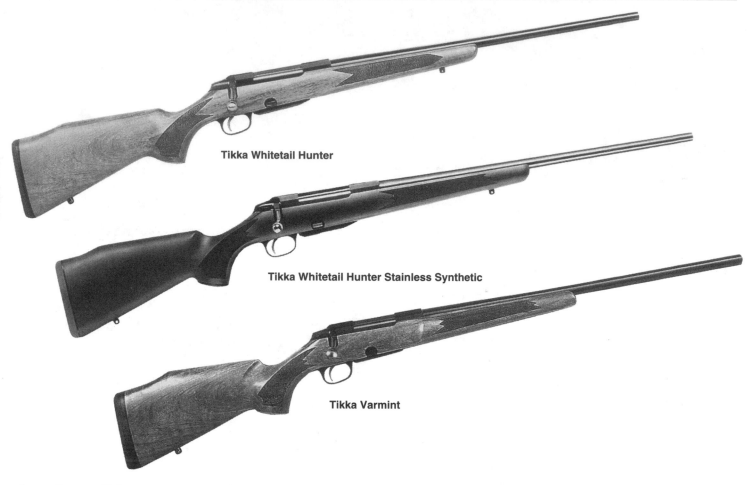

Tikka Whitetail Hunter

Tikka Whitetail Hunter Stainless Synthetic

Tikka Varmint

tures: Comes with luggage case, scout sling, two stock spacers, two magazines. Introduced 1998. From GSI.
Price: From $2,595.00

STEYR SSG BOLT-ACTION RIFLE

Caliber: 308 Win., detachable 5-shot rotary magazine. **Barrel:** 26" **Weight:** 8.5 lbs. **Length:** 44.5" overall. **Stock:** Black ABS Cycolac with spacers for length of pull adjustment. **Sights:** Hooded ramp front adjustable for elevation, V-notch rear adjustable for windage. **Features:** Sliding safety; NATO rail for bipod; 1" swivels; Parkerized finish; single or double-set triggers. Imported from Austria by GSI, Inc.
Price: SSG-PI, iron sights. $2,195.00
Price: SSG-PII, heavy barrel, no sights $2,195.00
Price: SSG-PIIK, 20" heavy barrel, no sights $2,195.00
Price: SSG-PIV, 16.75" threaded heavy barrel with flash hider . $2,660.00

TIKKA WHITETAIL HUNTER BOLT-ACTION RIFLE

Caliber: 22-250, 223, 243, 7mm-08, 25-06, 270, 308, 30-06, 7mm Rem. Mag., 300 Win. Mag., 338 Win. Mag. **Barrel:** 22-1/2" (std. cals.), 24-1/2" (magnum cals.). **Weight:** 7-1/8 lbs. **Length:** 43" overall (std. cals.). **Stock:** European walnut with Monte Carlo comb, rubber butt pad, checkered grip and forend. **Sights:** None furnished. **Features:** Detachable four-shot magazine (standard calibers), three-shot in magnums. Receiver dovetailed for scope mounting. Reintroduced 1996. Imported from Finland by Stoeger Industries.
Price: Standard calibers $609.00
Price: Magnum calibers $639.00

Tikka Continental Varmint Rifle

Similar to the standard Tikka rifle except has 26" heavy barrel, extra-wide forend. Chambered for 22-250, 223, 308. Reintroduced 1996. Made in Finland by Sako. Imported by Stoeger.
Price: $709.00

Tikka Whitetail Hunter Deluxe Rifle

Similar to the Whitetail Hunter except has select walnut stock with rollover Monte Carlo comb, rosewood grip cap and forend tip. Has adjustable trigger, detachable magazine, free-floating barrel. Same calibers as the Hunter. Introduced 1999. Imported from Finland by Stoeger Industries.
Price: Standard calibers $734.00
Price: Magnum calibers $764.00

Tikka Whitetail Hunter Synthetic Rifle

Similar to the Whitetail Hunter except has black synthetic stock; calibers 223, 308, 25-06, 270 Win., 30-06, 7mm Rem. Mag., 300 Win. Mag., 338 Win. Mag. Introduced 1996. Imported from Finland by Stoeger.
Price: Standard calibers $609.00
Price: Magnum calibers $639.00

Tikka Continental Long Range Hunting Rifle

Similar to the Whitetail Hunter except has 26" heavy barrel. Available in 25-06, 270 Win., 7mm Rem. Mag., 300 Win. Mag. Introduced 1996. Imported from Finland by Stoeger.
Price: 25-06, 270 Win. $709.00
Price: 7 Rem. Mag., 300 Win. Mag. $739.00

Tikka Whitetail Hunter Stainless Synthetic

Similar to the Whitetail Hunter except all metal is of stainless steel, and it has a black synthetic stock. Available in 22-250, 243, 25-06, 308, 30-06, 7mm Rem. Mag., 300 Win. Mag., 338 Win. Mag. Introduced 1997. Imported from Finland by Stoeger.
Price: Standard calibers $669.00
Price: Magnum calibers $699.00

ULTRA LIGHT ARMS MODEL 20 RIFLE

Caliber: 17 Rem., 22 Hornet, 222 Rem., 223 Rem. (Model 20S); 22-250, 6mm Rem., 243, 257 Roberts, 7x57, 7x57 Ackley, 7mm-08, 284 Win., 308

CENTERFIRE RIFLES — BOLT ACTION

Ultra Light Arms Model 20

Weatherby Mark V Euromark

Weatherby Mark V Lazermark

Savage. Improved and other calibers on request. **Barrel:** 22" Douglas Premium No. 1 contour. **Weight:** 4-1/2 lbs. **Length:** 41-1/2" overall. **Stock:** Composite Kevlar, graphite reinforced. DuPont imron paint colors—green, black, brown and camo options. Choice of length of pull. **Sights:** None furnished. Scope mount included. **Features:** Timney adjustable trigger; two-position three-function safety. Benchrest quality action. Matte or bright stock and metal finish. 3" magazine length. Shipped in a hard case. Made in U.S. by Colt Rifles, Inc.

Price: Right-hand **$2,500.00**
Price: Model 20 Left Hand (left-hand action and stock) **$2,600.00**
Price: Model 24 Long Action (25-06, 270, 7mm Express, 30-06, 3-3/8"
   magazine length) **$2,600.00**
Price: Model 24 Long Action Left Hand (left-hand action and
   stock) **$2,700.00**

Ultra Light Arms Model 28, Model 40 Rifle

Similar to the Model 20 except in 264, 7mm Rem. Mag., 300 Win. Mag., 338 Win. Mag. (Model 28), 300 Wea. Mag., 416 Rigby (Model 40). Both use 24" Douglas Premium No. 2 contour barrel. Weighs 5-1/2 lbs., 45" overall length. KDF or ULA recoil arrestor built in. Any custom feature available on any ULA product can be incorporated. Made in U.S. by Colt Rifles, Inc.

Price: Right-hand, Model 28 or 40 . . . . **$2,900.00**
Price: Left-hand, Model 28 or 40 . . . . **$3,000.00**

VEKTOR LYTTELTON BOLT-ACTION RIFLE

Caliber: 243, 308, 7x57, 7x64 Brenneke, 270 Win., 30-06, 300 Win. Mag., 300 H&H, 9.3x62. **Barrel:** 22"-26". **Weight:** NA. **Length:** NA. **Stock:** Turkish walnut with wrap-around hand checkering. **Sights:** Blade on ramp front, fixed standing leaf rear. **Features:** Combines the best features of the Mauser 98 and Winchester 70 actions. Controlled-round feed; Mauser-type extractor; no cut-away through the bolt locking lug; M70-type three-position safety; Timney-type adjustable trigger. Introduced 1999. Imported from South Africa by Vektor USA.

Price: **$1,295.00**

VEKTOR MODEL 98 BOLT-ACTION RIFLE

Caliber: 243, 308, 7x57, 7x64 Brenneke, 270 Win., 30-06, 300 Win. Mag., 300 H&H, 375 H&H, 9.3x62. **Barrel:** 22"-26". **Weight:** NA. **Length:** NA. **Stock:** Turkish walnut with hand-checkered grip and forend. **Sights:** None furnished; drilled and tapped for scope mounting. **Features:** Bolt has guide rib; non-rotating, long extractor enhances positive feeding; polished blue finish. Updated Mauser 98 action. Introduced 1999. Imported from South Africa by Vektor USA.

Price: **$995.00**

WEATHERBY MARK V DELUXE BOLT-ACTION RIFLE

Caliber: All Weatherby calibers plus 22-250, 243, 25-06, 270 Win., 280 Rem., 7mm-08, 308 Win. **Barrel:** 26" round tapered. **Weight:** 8-1/2 to 10-1/2 lbs. **Length:** 46-5/8" to 46-3/4" overall. **Stock:** Walnut, Monte Carlo with cheekpiece; high luster finish; checkered pistol grip and forend; recoil pad. **Sights:** None furnished. **Features:** Cocking indicator; adjustable trigger; hinged floorplate, thumb safety; quick detachable sling swivels. Made in U.S. From Weatherby.

Price: 257, 270, 7mm. 300, 340 Wea. Mags., 26" barrel **$1,449.00**
Price: 416 Wea. Mag. with Accubrake, 26" barrel **$1,875.00**
Price: 460 Wea. Mag. with Accubrake, 26" barrel **$2,193.00**

Weatherby Mark V Lazermark Rifle

Same as Mark V Deluxe except stock has extensive oak leaf pattern laser carving on pistol grip and forend. Introduced 1981.

Price: 257, 270, 7mm Wea. Mag., 300, 340, 26" **$1,699.00**
Price: 378 Wea. Mag., 26" **$1,007.00**
Price: 416 Wea. Mag., 26", Accubrake **$1,986.00**
Price: 460 Wea. Mag., 26", Accubrake **$2,233.00**

Weatherby Mark V Sporter Rifle

Same as the Mark V Deluxe without the embellishments. Metal has low-luster blue, stock is Claro walnut with high-gloss epoxy finish, Monte Carlo comb, recoil pad. Introduced 1993.

Price: 257, 270, 7mm, 300, 340 Wea. Mags., 26" **$999.00**
Price: 375 H&H, 24" **$999.00**
Price: 7mm Rem. Mag., 300 Win. Mag., 338 Win. Mag., 24", . . . **$999.00**

Weatherby Mark V Euromark Rifle

Similar to the Mark V Deluxe except has raised-comb Monte Carlo stock with hand-rubbed oil finish, fine-line hand-cut checkering, ebony grip and forend tips. All metal has low-luster blue. Right-hand only. Uses Mark V action. Introduced 1995. Made in U.S. From Weatherby.

Price: 257, 270, 7mm, 300, 340 Wea. Mags., 26" barrel **$1,599.00**
Price: 378 Wea. Mag., 26" barrel **$1,692.00**
Price: 416 Wea. Mag., 26" barrel **$1,875.00**
Price: 7mm Rem. Mag., 300 Win. Mag., 338 Win. Mag.,375 H&H, 24"
   barrel **$1,599.00**

Weatherby Mark V Stainless Rifle

Similar to the Mark V Deluxe except made of 400-series stainless steel. Also available in 30-378 Wea. Mag. Has lightweight injection-moulded synthetic stock with raised Monte Carlo comb, checkered grip and forend, custom floorplate release. Right-hand only. Introduced 1995. Made in U.S. From Weatherby.

Price: 257, 270, 7mm, 300, 340 Wea. Mags., 26" barrel **$899.00**

CENTERFIRE RIFLES — BOLT ACTION

Weatherby Mark V Stainless

Weatherby Mark V Lightweight

Weatherby Mark V Lightweight Stainless

Weatherby Mark V Synthetic

Price: 7mm Rem. Mag., 300, 338 Win. Mags., 24" barrel **$999.00**
Price: 375 H&H, 24" barrel **$999.00**
Price: 30-378 Wea. Mag. **$1,149.00**

Weatherby Mark V SLS Stainless Laminate Sporter

Similar to the Mark V Stainless except all metalwork is 400 series stainless with a corrosion-resistant black oxide bead-blast matte finish. Action is hand-bedded in a laminated stock with a 1" recoil pad. Weighs 8-1/2 lbs. Introduced 1997. Made in U.S. From Weatherby.
Price: 257, 270, 7mm, 300, 340 Wea. Mag., 26" barrel **$1,249.00**
Price: 7mm Rem. Mag., 300 Win. Mag., 338 Win. Mag., 24" barrel
. . . . **$1,249.00**

Weatherby Mark V Eurosport Rifle

Similar to the Mark V Deluxe except has raised-comb Monte Carlo stock with hand-rubbed satin oil finish, low-luster blue metal. No gripcap or forend tip. Right-hand only. Introduced 1995. Made in U.S. From Weatherby.
Price: 257, 270, 7mm, 300, 340 Wea. Mags., 26" barrel **$999.00**
Price: 7mm Rem. Mag., 300, 338 Win. Mags., 24" barrel **$999.00**
Price: 375 H&H, 24" barrel **$999.00**

WEATHERBY MARK V SPORTER BOLT ACTION RIFLE

Caliber: 22-250, 243, 25-06, 270, 7MM-08, 280, 30-06, 308, 240 Wea. Mag. **Barrel:** 24". **Weight:** 6-3/4 lbs. **Length:** 44" overall. **Stock:** Claro walnut. Monte Carlo with cheekpiece; high luster finish, checkered pistol grip and forend, recoil pad. **Sights:** None furnished. Drilled and tapped for scope mounting. **Features:** Cocking indicator; adjustable trigger; hinged floorplate; thumb safety; six locking lugs; quick detachable swivels. Introduced 1997. Made in U.S. from Weatherby.
Price: **$899.00**

Weatherby Mark V Stainless

Similar to the Sporter except made of 400 series stainless steel; injection moulded synthetic stock with Monte Carlo comb, checkered grip and forend. Weighs 6-1/2 lbs. Introduced 1997. Made in U.S. From Weatherby.
Price: **$899.00**
Price: Stainless Carbine (as above with 20" barrel, 243 Win., 7mm-08 Rem., 308 Win.), weighs 6 lbs. **$899.00**

Weatherby Mark V Synthetic

Similar to the Mark V Stainless except made of matte finished blued steel. Injection moulded synthetic stock. Weighs 6-1/2 lbs., 24" barrel. Available in 22-250, 240 Wea. Mag., 243, 25-06, 270, 7mm-08, 280, 30-06, 308. Introduced 1997. Made in U.S. From Weatherby.
Price: **$699.00**

Weatherby Mark V Synthetic Rifle

Similar to the Mark V except has synthetic stock with raised Monte Carlo comb, dual-taper checkered forend. Low-luster blued metal. Weighs 8 lbs. Uses Mark V action. Right-hand only. Also available in 30-378 Wea. Mag. Introduced 1995. Made in U.S. From Weatherby.
Price: 257, 270, 7mm, 300, 340 Wea. Mags., 26" barrel **$699.00**
Price: 7mm Rem. Mag., 300, 338 Win. Mags., 24" barrel **$799.00**
Price: 375 H&H, 24" barrel **$799.00**

Weatherby Mark V Carbine

Similar to the Mark V Synthetic except has 20" barrel; injection moulded synthetic stock. Available in 243, 7mm-08, 308. Weighs 6 lbs.; overall length 40". Introduced 1997. Made in U.S. From Weatherby.
Price: **$699.00**

WEATHERBY MARK V ACCUMARK RIFLE

Caliber: 257, 270, 7mm, 300, 340 Wea. Mags., 338-378 Wea. Mag., 30-378 Wea. Mag., 7mm STW, 7mm Rem. Mag., 300 Win. Mag. **Barrel:** 26". **Weight:** 8-1/2 lbs. **Length:** 46-5/8" overall. **Stock:** H-S Precision Pro-Series synthetic with aluminum bedding plate. **Sights:** None furnished.

Weatherby Accumark

Weatherby Accumark Lightweight

Wilderness Explorer

Drilled and tapped for scope mounting. **Features:** Uses Mark V action with heavy-contour stainless barrel with black oxidized flutes, muzzle diameter of .705". Introduced 1996. Made in U.S. From Weatherby.

Price: **$1,499.00**
Price: 30-378 Wea. Mag., 338-378 Wea. Mag., 20", Accubrake **$1,549.00**
Price: Accumark Left-Hand 257, 270, 7mm, 300, 340 Wea. Mag., 7mm Rem. Mag., 7mm STW, 300 Win. Mag. **$1,399.00**
Price: Accumark Left-Hand 30-378, 333-378 Wea. Mags...... **$1,599.00**

Weatherby Mark V Accumark Ultra Light Weight Rifle

Similar to the Mark V Accumark except weighs 5-3/4 lbs.; free-floated 24" fluted barrel with recessed target crown; hand-laminated stock with CNC-machined aluminum bedding plate and faint gray "spider web" finish. Available in 257, 270, 7mm, 300 Wea. Mags., 243, 240 Wea. Mag., 25-06, 270 Win., 280 Rem., 7mm-08, 7mm Rem. Mag., 30-06, 308, 300 Win. Mag. Introduced 1998. Made in U.S. from Weatherby.

Price: **$1,199.00**

Weatherby Mark V Accumark Rifle

Similar to the Mark V Accumark except chambered for 22-250, 243, 240 Wea. Mag., 25-06, 270, 280 Rem., 7mm-08, 30-06, 308; fluted 24" heavy-contour stainless barrel; hand-laminated Monte Carlo-style stock with aluminum bedding plate. Weighs 7 lbs.; 44" overall. Introduced 1998. Made in U.S. From Weatherby.

Price: **$1,199.00**

WICHITA VARMINT RIFLE

Caliber: 222 Rem., 222 Rem. Mag., 223 Rem., 22 PPC, 6mm PPC, 22-250, 243, 6mm Rem., 308 Win.; other calibers on special order. **Barrel:** 20-

1/8". **Weight:** 9 lbs. **Length:** 40-1/8" overall. **Stock:** AAA Fancy American walnut. Hand-rubbed finish, hand checkered, 20 lpi pattern. Hand-inletted, glass bedded, steel gripcap. Pachmayr rubber recoil pad. **Sights:** None. Drilled and tapped for scope mounts. **Features:** Right- or left-hand Wichita action with three locking lugs. Available as a single shot only. Checkered bolt handle. Bolt is hand fitted, lapped and jeweled. Side thumb safety. Firing pin fall is 3/16". Non-glare blue finish. From Wichita Arms.

Price: Single shot **$2,695.00**

WICHITA CLASSIC RIFLE

Caliber: 17-222, 17-222 Mag., 222 Rem., 222 Rem. Mag., 223 Rem., 6x47; other calibers on special order. **Barrel:** 21-1/8". **Weight:** 8 lbs. **Length:** 41" overall. **Stock:** AAA Fancy American walnut. Hand-rubbed and checkered (20 lpi). Hand-inletted, glass bedded, steel gripcap. Pachmayr rubber recoil pad. **Sights:** None. Drilled and tapped for scope mounting. **Features:** Available as single shot only. Octagonal barrel and Wichita action, right- or left-hand. Checkered bolt handle. Bolt is hand-fitted, lapped and jeweled. Adjustable trigger is set at 2 lbs. Side thumb safety. Firing pin fall is 3/16". Non-glare blue finish. From Wichita Arms.

Price: Single shot **$3,495.00**

WILDERNESS EXPLORER MULTI-CALIBER CARBINE

Caliber: 22 Hornet, 218 Bee, 44 Magnum, 50 A.E. (interchangeable). **Barrel:** 18", match grade. **Weight:** 5.5 lbs **Length:** 38-1/2" overall. **Stock:** Synthetic or wood. **Sights:** None furnished; comes with Weaver-style mount on barrel. **Features:** Quick-change barrel and bolt face for caliber switch. Removable box magazine; adjustable trigger with side safety; detachable swivel studs. Introduced 1997. Made in U.S. by Phillips & Rogers, Inc.

Price: **$995.00**

Winchester Model 70 Classic

Winchester Model 70 Classic Stainless

Winchester Model 70 Classic Laminated

Winchester Model 70 Classic Featherweight

Winchester Model 70 Classic Compact

WINCHESTER MODEL 70 CLASSIC SPORTER LT

Caliber: 25-06, 270 Win., 270 Wea., 30-06, 264 Win. Mag., 7mm STW, 7mm Rem. Mag., 300 Win. Mag., 300 Wea. Mag., 338 Win. Mag., 3-shot magazine; 5-shot for 25-06, 270 Win., 30-06. **Barrel:** 24", 26" for magnums. **Weight:** 7-3/4 lbs. **Length:** 44-3/4" overall. **Stock:** American walnut with cut checkering and satin finish. Classic style with straight comb. **Sights:** Optional hooded ramp front, adjustable folding leaf rear. Drilled and tapped for scope mounting. **Features:** Uses pre-64-type action with controlled round feeding. Three-position safety, stainless steel magazine follower; rubber butt pad; epoxy bedded receiver recoil lug. From U.S. Repeating Arms Co.
Price: Without sights. **$630.00**
Price: Left-hand, 270, 30-06, 7mm Rem. Mag., 7mm STW, 300 Win. Mag., 338 Win. Mag. **$659.00**

Winchester Model 70 Classic Stainless Rifle

Same as the Model 70 Classic Sporter except has stainless steel barrel and pre-64-style action with controlled round feeding and matte gray finish, black composite stock impregnated with fiberglass and graphite, contoured rubber recoil pad. Available in 22-250, 243, 308, 270 Win., 270 Wea. Mag., 30-06, 7mm Rem. Mag., 300 Win. Mag., 300 Wea. Mag., 338 Win. Mag., 375 H&H Mag. (24" barrel), 3- or 5-shot magazine. Weighs 6.75 lbs. Introduced 1994.

Price: Without sights. **$693.00**
Price: 375 H&H Mag., with sights. **$758.00**
Price: Classic Laminated Stainless (gray laminated stock, 270, 30-06, 7mm Rem. Mag., 300 Win. Mag., 338 Win. Mag. **$745.00**

Winchester Model 70 Classic Featherweight

Same as the Model 70 Classic except has claw controlled-round feeding system; action is bedded in a standard-grade walnut stock. Available in 22-250, 243, 6.5x55, 308, 7mm-08, 270 Win., 280 Rem., 30-06. Drilled and tapped for scope mounts. Weighs 7.25 lbs. Introduced 1992.
Price: **$639.00**
Price: Classic Featherweight Stainless, as above except made of stainless steel, and available in 22-250, 243, 270, 308, 30-06, 7mm Rem. Mag., 300 Win. Mag. **$737.00**

Winchester Model 70 Classic Compact

Similar to the Classic Featherweight except scaled down for smaller shooters. Has 20" barrel, 12-1/2" length of pull. Pre-'64-type action. Available in 243, 308 or 7mm-08. Introduced 1998. Made in U.S. by U. S. Repeating Arms Co.
Price: **$640.00**

Winchester Model 70 Ranger

Winchester Model 70 Stealth

Winchester Model 70 Classic Super Grade

Winchester Model 70 Laredo

WINCHESTER RANGER RIFLE

Caliber: 223, 22-250, 243, 270, 30-06, 7mm Rem. Mag. **Barrel:** 22". **Weight:** 7-3/4 lbs. **Length:** 42" overall. **Stock:** Stained hardwood. **Sights:** Hooded blade front, adjustable open rear. **Features:** Three-position safety; push feed bolt with recessed-style bolt face; polished blue finish; drilled and tapped for scope mounting. Introduced 1985. From U.S. Repeating Arms Co.

Price: $496.00
Price: Ranger Compact, 22-250, 243, 7mm-08, 308 only,
scaled-down stock $496.00

Winchester Model 70 Black Shadow

Similar to the Ranger except has black composite stock, matte blue barrel and action. Push-feed bolt design; hinged floorplate. Available in 270, 30-06, 7mm Rem. Mag., 300 Win. Mag. Made in U.S. by U.S. Repeating Arms Co.

Price: $462.00

WINCHESTER MODEL 70 STEALTH RIFLE

Caliber: 223, 22-250, 308 Win. **Barrel:** 26". **Weight:** 10-3/4 lbs. **Length:** 46" overall. **Stock:** Kevlar/fiberglass/graphite Pillar Plus Accu-Block with full-length aluminum bedding block. **Sights:** None furnished. **Features:** Push-feed bolt design; matte finish. Introduced 1999. Made in U. S. by U.S. Repeating Arms Co.

Price: 223 .... $786.00
Price: 22-250, 308 Win. $764.00

WINCHESTER MODEL 70 CLASSIC SUPER GRADE

Caliber: 270, 30-06, 5-shot magazine; 7mm Rem. Mag., 7mm STW, 300 Win. Mag., 338 Win. Mag., 3-shot magazine. **Barrel:** 24", 26" for mag-

nums. **Weight:** About 7-3/4 lbs. to 8 lbs. **Length:** 44-1/2" overall (24" bbl.) **Stock:** Walnut with straight comb, sculptured cheekpiece, wrap-around cut checkering, tapered forend, solid rubber butt pad. **Sights:** None furnished; comes with scope bases and rings. **Features:** Controlled round feeding with stainless steel claw extractor, bolt guide rail, three-position safety; all steel bottom metal, hinged floorplate, stainless magazine follower. Introduced 1994. From U.S. Repeating Arms Co.

Price: $865.00

WINCHESTER MODEL 70 CLASSIC LAREDO

Caliber: 7mm Rem. Mag., 7mm STW, 300 Win. Mag., 3-shot magazine. **Barrel:** 26" heavy; 1:10" (300), 1:9.5" (7mm). **Weight:** 9-1/2 lbs. **Length:** 46-3/4" overall. **Stock:** H-S Precision gray, synthetic with "Pillar Plus Accu-Block" bedding system, wide beavertail forend. **Sights:** None furnished; drilled and tapped for scope mounting. **Features:** Pre-64-style, controlled round action with claw extractor, receiver-mounted blade ejector; matte blue finish. Introduced 1996. Made in U.S. by U.S. Repeating Arms Co.

Price: $787.00

WINCHESTER MODEL 70 CLASSIC SAFARI EXPRESS MAGNUM

Caliber: 375 H&H Mag., 416 Rem. Mag., 458 Win. Mag., 3-shot magazine. **Barrel:** 24". **Weight:** 8-1/4 to 8-1/2 lbs. **Stock:** American walnut with Monte Carlo cheekpiece. Wrap-around checkering and finish. **Sights:** Hooded ramp front, open rear. **Features:** Controlled round feeding. Two steel cross bolts in stock for added strength. Front sling swivel stud mounted on barrel. Contoured rubber butt pad. From U.S. Repeating Arms Co.

Price: $927.00
Price: Left-hand, 375 H&H only $960.00

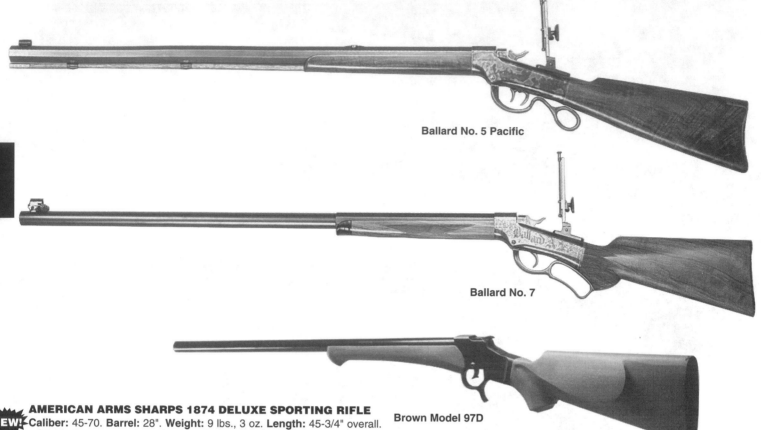

Ballard No. 5 Pacific

Ballard No. 7

Brown Model 97D

AMERICAN ARMS SHARPS 1874 DELUXE SPORTING RIFLE

NEW! **Caliber:** 45-70. **Barrel:** 28". **Weight:** 9 lbs., 3 oz. **Length:** 45-3/4" overall. **Stock:** European walnut; checkered grip and forend. **Sights:** Brass blade front, ladder-type adjustable rear. **Features:** Double-set triggers. Color case-hardened receiver, hammer, lever, browned barrel. Introduced 1999. Imported by American Arms, Inc.

Price: **$705.00**
Price: With blued barrel **$685.00**

American Arms Sharps Cavalry, Frontier Carbines

NEW! Similar to the 1874 Sporting RIfle except with 22" barrel. The Cavalry Carbine has double-set triggers; single trigger on Frontier, which also has a barrel band. Introduced 1999. Imported by American Arms, Inc.

Price: Cavalry carbine **$660.00**
Price: Frontier carbine **$675.00**

AMERICAN ARMS/UBERTI 1885 SINGLE SHOT

Caliber: 45-70. **Barrel:** 28". **Weight:** 8.75 lbs. **Length:** 44.5" overall. **Stock:** European walnut. **Sights:** Bead on blade front, open step-adjustable rear. **Features:** Recreation of the 1885 Winchester. Color case-hardened receiver and lever, blued barrel. Introduced 1998. Imported from Italy by American Arms. Inc.

Price: **$810.00**

ARMSPORT 1866 SHARPS RIFLE, CARBINE

Caliber: 45-70. **Barrel:** 28", round or octagonal. **Weight:** 8.10 lbs. **Length:** 46" overall. **Stock:** Walnut. **Sights:** Blade front, folding adjustable rear. Tang sight set optionally available. **Features:** Replica of the 1866 Sharps. Color case-hardened frame, rest blued. Imported by Armsport.

Price: **$865.00**
Price: With octagonal barrel **$900.00**
Price: Carbine, 22" round barrel **$850.00**

BALLARD NO. 5 PACIFIC SINGLE-SHOT RIFLE

NEW! **Caliber:** 32-40, 38-55, 40-65, 40-90, 40-70 SS, 45-70 Govt., 45-110 SS, 50-70 Govt., 50-90 SS. **Barrel:** 30", or 32" octagonal. **Weight:** 10-1/2 lbs. **Length:** NA. **Stock:** High-grade walnut; rifle or shotgun style. **Sights:** Blade front, Rocky Mountain rear. **Features:** Standard or heavy barrel;

double-set triggers; under-barrel wiping rod; ring lever. Introduced 1999. Made in U.S. by Ballard Rifle & Cartridge Co.

Price: **$2,475.00**

BALLARD NO. 7 LONG RANGE RIFLE

Caliber: 32-40, 38-55, 40-65, 40-70 SS, 45-70 Govt., 45-90, 45-110. **Barrel:** 32", 34" half-octagon. **Weight:** 11-3/4 lbs. **Length:** NA. **Stock:** Fancy walnut; checkered pistol grip shotgun butt, ebony forend cap. **Sights:** Globe front. **Features:** Designed for shooting up to 1000 yards. Standard or heavy barrel; single or double-set trigger; hard rubber or steel buttplate. Introduced 1999. Made in U.S. by Ballard Rifle & Cartridge Co. **NEW!**

Price: From **$2,750.00**

BALLARD NO. 8 UNION HILL RIFLE

Caliber: 22 LR, 32-40, 38-55, 40-65 Win., 40-70 SS. **Barrel:** 30" half-octagon. **Weight:** About 10-1/2 lbs. **Length:** NA. **Stock:** Fancy walnut; pistol grip butt with cheekpiece. **Sights:** Globe front. **Features:** Designed for 200-yard offhand shooting. Standard or heavy barrel; double-set triggers; full loop lever; hook Schuetzen buttplate. Introduced 1999. Made in U.S. by Ballard Rifle & Cartridge Co. **NEW!**

Price: From **$2,750.00**

BARRETT MODEL 99 SINGLE SHOT RIFLE

Caliber: 50 BMG. **Barrel:** 33". **Weight:** 25 lbs. **Length:** 50.4" overall. **Stock:** Anodized aluminum with energy-absorbing recoil pad. **Sights:** None furnished; integral M1913 scope rail. **Features:** Bolt action; detachable bipod; match-grade barrel with high-efficiency muzzle brake. Introduced 1999. Made in U.S. by Barrett Firearms. **NEW!**

Price: From **$2,800.00**

BROWN MODEL 97D SINGLE SHOT RIFLE

Caliber: 17 Ackley Hornet through 45-70 Govt. **Barrel:** Up to 26", air gauged match grade. **Weight:** About 5 lbs., 11 oz. **Stock:** Sporter style with pistol grip, cheekpiece and Schnabel forend. **Sights:** None furnished;

Browning Model 1885 Traditional Hunter

Browning Model 1885 Low Wall

Cabela's Sharps

drilled and tapped for scope mounting. **Features:** Falling block action gives rigid barrel-receiver matting; polished blue/black finish. Hand-fitted action. Made in U.S. by E. A. Brown Mfg.
Price: **$599.00**

BROWNING MODEL 1885 HIGH WALL SINGLE SHOT RIFLE

Caliber: 22-250, 30-06, 270, 7mm Rem. Mag., 454 Casull, 45-70. **Barrel:** 28". **Weight:** About 8-1/2 lbs. **Length:** 43-1/2" overall. **Stock:** Walnut with straight grip, Schnabel forend. **Sights:** None furnished; drilled and tapped for scope mounting. **Features:** Replica of J.M. Browning's high-wall falling block rifle. Octagon barrel with recessed muzzle. Imported from Japan by Browning. Introduced 1985.
Price: **$987.00**

Browning Model 1885 BPCR Rifle

Similar to the 1885 High Wall rifle except the ejector system and shell deflector have been removed; chambered only for 40-65 and 45-70; color case-hardened full-tang receiver, lever, buttplate and gripcap; matte blue 30" part octagon, part round barrel. The Vernier tang sight has indexed elevation, is screw adjustable windage, and has three peep diameters. The hooded front sight has a built-in spirit level and comes with sight interchangeable inserts. Adjustable trigger. Overall length 46 1/8", weighs about 11 lbs. Introduced 1996. Imported from Japan by Browning.
Price: **$1,749.00**
Price: BPCR Creedmoor (45-90, 34" barrel with wind gauge sight) **$1,764.00**

Browning Model 1885 Traditional Hunter

Similar to the Model 1885 High Wall except chambered for 357 Mag., 44 Mag., 45 Colt, 30-30, 38-55 and 45-70 only; steel crescent buttplate; 1/16" gold bead front sight, adjustable buckhorn rear, and tang-mounted peep sight with barrel-type elevation adjuster and knob-type windage adjustments. Barrel is drilled and tapped for a Browning scope base. Oil-finished select walnut stock with swivel studs. Introduced 1997. Imported for Japan by Browning.
Price: High Wall **$1,208.95**
Price: Low Wall. **$1,276.00**

Browning Model 1885 Low Wall Rifle

Similar to the Model 1885 High Wall except has trimmer receiver, thinner 24" octagonal barrel. Forend is mounted to the receiver. Adjustable trigger. Walnut pistol grip stock, trim Schnabel forend with high-gloss finish. Available in 22 Hornet, 223 Rem., 243 Win., 260 Rem. Overall length 39-1/2", weighs 6 lbs., 4 oz. Rifling twist rates: 1:16" (22 Hornet); 1:12" (223); 1:10" (243). Polished blue finish. Introduced 1995. Imported from Japan by Browning.
Price: **$987.00**

BRNO ZBK 110 SINGLE SHOT RIFLE

Caliber: 222 Rem., 5.6x52R, 22 Hornet, 5.6x50 Mag., 6.5x57R, 7x57R, 8x57JRS. **Barrel:** 23.6". **Weight:** 5.9 lbs. **Length:** 40.1" overall. **Stock:** European walnut. **Sights:** None furnished; drilled and tapped for scope mounting. **Features:** Top tang opening lever; cross-bolt safety; polished blue finish. Announced 1998. Imported from The Czech Republic by Euro-Imports.
Price: Standard calibers **$223.00**
Price: 7x57R, 8x57JRS **$245.00**
Price: Lux model, standard calibers **$311.00**
Price: Lux model, 7x57R, 8x57JRS **$333.00**

CABELA'S SHARPS SPORTING RIFLE

Caliber: 40-65, 45-70. **Barrel:** 32", tapered octagon. **Weight:** 9 lbs. **Length:** 47-1/4" overall. **Stock:** Checkered walnut. **Sights:** Blade front, open adjustable rear. **Features:** Color case-hardened receiver and hammer, rest blued. Introduced 1995. Imported by Cabela's.
Price: **$799.99**

CIMARRON BILLY DIXON 1874 SHARPS SPORTING RIFLE

Caliber: 40-65, 45-70. **Barrel:** 32" tapered octagon. **Weight:** NA. **Length:** NA. **Stock:** European walnut. **Sights:** Blade front, Creedmoor rear. **Features:** Color case-hardened frame, blued barrel. Hand-checkered grip and forend; hand-rubbed oil finish. Introduced 1999. Imported by Cimarron F.A. Co.
Price: **$1,495.00**

CIMARRON MODEL 1885 HIGH WALL RIFLE

Caliber: 38-55, 40-65, 45-70, 45-90. **Barrel:** 30" octagonal. **Weight:** NA. **Length:** NA. **Stock:** European walnut. **Sights:** Bead front, semi-buckhorn rear. **Features:** Replica of the Winchester 1885 High Wall rifle. Color case-hardened receiver and lever, blued barrel. Curved buttplate. Introduced 1999. Imported by Cimarron F.A. Co.
Price: **$995.00**

CIMARRON CREEDMOOR ROLLING BLOCK RIFLE

Caliber: 40-65, 45-70. **Barrel:** 30" tapered octagon. **Weight:** NA. **Length:** NA. **Stock:** European walnut. **Sights:** Globe front, fully adjustable rear. **Features:** Color case-hardened receiver, blued barrel. Hand-checkered pistol grip and forend; hand-rubbed oil finish. Introduced 1999. Imported by Cimarron F.A. Co.
Price: **$1,295.00**

CUMBERLAND MOUNTAIN PLATEAU RIFLE

Caliber: 40-65, 45-70. **Barrel:** Up to 32"; round. **Weight:** About 10-1/2 lbs. (32" barrel). **Length:** 48" overall (32" barrel). **Stock:** American walnut. **Sights:** Marble's bead front, Marble's open rear. **Features:** Falling block action with underlever. Blued barrel and receiver. Stock has lacquer finish,

Cumberland Mountain Plateau

Dakota Single Shot

Dixie 1874 Sharps Silhouette

H&R Ultra Hunter

crescent buttplate. Introduced 1995. Made in U.S. by Cumberland Mountain Arms, Inc.

Price: $1,085.00

DAKOTA SINGLE SHOT RIFLE

Caliber: Most rimmed and rimless commercial calibers. **Barrel:** 23". **Weight:** 6 lbs. **Length:** 39-1/2" overall. **Stock:** Medium fancy grade walnut in classic style. Checkered grip and forend. **Sights:** None furnished. Drilled and tapped for scope mounting. **Features:** Falling block action with under-lever. Top tang safety. Removable trigger plate for conversion to single set trigger. Introduced 1990. Made in U.S. by Dakota Arms.

Price: $3,195.00
Price: Barreled action $2,050.00
Price: Action only $1,675.00
Price: Magnum calibers $3,495.00
Price: Magnum barreled action. $2,050.00
Price: Magnum action only. $1,775.00

DIXIE 1874 SHARPS BLACKPOWDER SILHOUETTE RIFLE

Caliber: 45-70. **Barrel:** 30"; tapered octagon; blued; 1:18" twist. **Weight:** 10 lbs., 3 oz. **Length:** 47-1/2" overall. **Stock:** Oiled walnut. **Sights:** Blade front, ladder-type hunting rear. **Features:** Replica of the Sharps #1 Sporter. Shotgun-style butt with checkered metal buttplate; color case-hardened receiver, hammer, lever and buttplate. Tang is drilled and tapped for tang sight. Double-set triggers. Meets standards for NRA blackpowder cartridge matches. Introduced 1995. Imported from Italy by Dixie Gun Works.

Price: $995.00

Dixie 1874 Sharps Lightweight Hunter/Target Rifle

Same as the Dixie 1874 Sharps Blackpowder Silhouette model except has a straight-grip buttstock with military-style buttplate. Based on the 1874 military model. Introduced 1995. Imported from Italy by Dixie Gun Works.

Price: $995.00

E.M.F. SHARPS RIFLE

Caliber: 45-70. **Barrel:** 28", octagon. **Weight:** 10-3/4 lbs. **Length:** NA. **Stock:** Oiled walnut. **Sights:** Blade front, flip-up open rear. **Features:** Replica of the 1874 Sharps Sporting rifle. Color case-hardened lock; double-set trigger; blue finish. Imported by E.M.F.

Price: $950.00
Price: With browned finish $1,000.00
Price: Carbine (round 22" barrel, barrel band) $860.00

HARRINGTON & RICHARDSON ULTRA VARMINT RIFLE

Caliber: 223, 243. **Barrel:** 24", heavy. **Weight:** About 7.5 lbs. **Length:** NA. **Stock:** Hand-checkered laminated birch with Monte Carlo comb. **Sights:** None furnished. Drilled and tapped for scope mounting. **Features:** Break-open action with side-lever release, positive ejection. Comes with scope mount. Blued receiver and barrel. Swivel studs. Introduced 1993. From H&R 1871, Inc.

Price: $254.95

Harrington & Richardson Ultra Hunter Rifle

Similar to the Ultra Varmint rifle except chambered for 25-06 with 26" barrel, or 308 Win., 357 Rem. Max. with 22" barrel. Stock and forend are of

Model 1885 High Wall

Navy Arms 1885 High Wall

Navy Arms 1874 Sharps

Navy Arms 1873 Springfield

cinnamon-colored laminate; hand-checkered grip and forend. Introduced 1995. Made in U.S. by H&R 1871, Inc.

Price: $249.95

Harrington & Richardson Ultra Comp Rifle
Similar to the Ultra Varmint except chambered for 270 or 30-06; has compensator to reduce recoil; camo-laminate stock and forend; blued, highly polished frame; scope mount. Made in U.S. by H&R 1071, Inc.
Price: $289.95

HARRIS GUNWORKS ANTIETAM SHARPS RIFLE
Caliber: 40-65, 45-75. **Barrel:** 30", 32", octagon or round, hand-lapped stainless or chrome-moly. **Weight:** 11.25 lbs. **Length:** 47" overall. **Stock:** Choice of straight grip, pistol grip or Creedmoor with Schnabel forend; pewter tip optional. Standard wood is A Fancy; higher grades available. **Sights:** Montana Vintage Arms #111 Low Profile Spirit Level front, #108 mid-range tang rear with windage adjustments. **Features:** Recreation of the 1874 Sharps sidehammer. Action is color case-hardened, barrel satin black. Chrome-moly barrel optionally blued. Optional sights include #112 Spirit Level Globe front with windage, #107 Long Range rear with windage. Introduced 1994. Made in U.S. by Harris Gunworks.
Price: $2,400.00

MODEL 1885 HIGH WALL RIFLE
Caliber: 30-40 Krag, 32-40, 38-55, 40-65 WCF, 45-70. **Barrel:** 26" (30-40), 28" all others. Douglas Premium #3 tapered octagon. **Weight:** NA. **Length:** NA. **Stock:** Premium American black walnut. **Sights:** Marble's standard ivory bead front, #66 long blade top rear with reversible notch and elevator. **Features:** Recreation of early octagon top, thick-wall High Wall with Coil spring action. Tang drilled, tapped for High Wall tang sight. Receiver, lever, hammer and breechblock color case-hardened. Introduced 1991. Available from Montana Armory, Inc.
Price: $1,095.00

NAVY ARMS 1874 SHARPS CAVALRY CARBINE
Caliber: 45-70. **Barrel:** 22". **Weight:** 7 lbs., 12 oz. **Length:** 39" overall. **Stock:** Walnut. **Sights:** Blade front, military ladder-type rear. **Features:** Replica of the 1874 Sharps military carbine. Color case-hardened receiver and furniture. Imported by Navy Arms.
Price: $935.00

Navy Arms 1874 Sharps Sniper Rifle
Similar to the Navy Arms Sharps Carbine except has 30" barrel, double-set triggers; weighs 8 lbs., 8 oz., overall length 46-3/4". Introduced 1984. Imported by Navy Arms.
Price: $1,115.00
Price: 1874 Sharps Infantry Rifle (three-band) $1,060.00

NAVY ARMS 1885 HIGH WALL RIFLE
Caliber: 45-70; others available on special order. **Barrel:** 28" round, 30" octagonal. **Weight:** 9.5 lbs. **Length:** 45-1/2" overall (30" barrel). **Stock:** Walnut. **Sights:** Blade front, globe front, Vernier tang-mounted peep rear. **Features:** Replica of Winchester's High Wall designed by Browning. Color case-hardened receiver, blued barrel. Introduced 1998. Imported by Navy Arms.
Price: 28", round barrel, buckhorn sights $745.00
Price: As above, target sights. $845.00
Price: 30" octagonal barrel, buckhorn sight $815.00
Price: As above, target sights. $915.00

NAVY ARMS 1873 SPRINGFIELD CAVALRY CARBINE
Caliber: 45-70. **Barrel:** 22". **Weight:** 7 lbs. **Length:** 40-1/2" overall. **Stock:** Walnut. **Sights:** Blade front, military ladder rear. **Features:** Blued lockplate and barrel; color case-hardened breechblock; saddle ring with bar. Replica of 7th Cavalry gun. Imported by Navy Arms.
Price: $870.00

Navy Arms #2 Creedmoor

Navy Arms Sharps Buffalo

Navy Arms Sharps Plains

New England Firearms Handi-Rifle

Navy Arms 1873 Springfield Infantry Rifle

Same action as the 1873 Springfield Cavalry Carbine except in rifle configuration with 32-1/2" barrel, three-band full-length stock. Introduced 1997. Imported by Navy Arms.

Price: **$995.00**

NAVY ARMS ROLLING BLOCK BUFFALO RIFLE

Caliber: 45-70. **Barrel:** 26", 30". **Stock:** Walnut. **Sights:** Blade front, adjustable rear. **Features:** Reproduction of classic rolling block action. Available with full-octagon or half-octagon-half-round barrel. Color case-hardened action, steel fittings. From Navy Arms.

Price: **$765.00**

Navy Arms #2 Creedmoor Rolling Block Rifle

Similar to the Navy Arms Rolling Block Buffalo Rifle except has 30" tapered octagon barrel, checkered full-pistol grip stock, blade front sight, open adjustable rear sight and Creedmoor tang sight. Imported by Navy Arms.

Price: **$930.00**

NAVY ARMS 1874 SHARPS BUFFALO RIFLE

Caliber: 45-70, 45-90. **Barrel:** 28" heavy octagon. **Weight:** 10 lbs., 10 oz. **Length:** 46" overall. **Stock:** Walnut; checkered grip and forend. **Sights:** Blade front, ladder rear; tang sight optional. **Features:** Color case-hardened receiver, blued barrel; double-set triggers. Imported by Navy Arms.

Price: **$1,090.00**

Navy Arms Sharps Plains Rifle

Similar to the Sharps Buffalo rifle except 45-70 only, has 32" medium-weight barrel, weighs 9 lbs., 8 oz., and is 49" overall. Imported by Navy Arms.

Price: **$1,055.00**

Navy Arms Sharps Sporting Rifle

Same as the Navy Arms Sharps Plains Rifle except has pistol grip stock. Introduced 1997. Imported by Navy Arms.

Price: 45-70 only **$1,090.00**

NEW ENGLAND FIREARMS HANDI-RIFLE

Caliber: 22 Hornet, 223, 243, 7x57, 7x64 Brenneke, 30-30, 270, 280 Rem., 308, 30-06, 44 Mag., 45-70. **Barrel:** 22", 24"; 26" for 280 Rem. **Weight:** 7 lbs. **Stock:** Walnut-finished hardwood; black rubber recoil pad. **Sights:** Ramp front, folding rear (22 Hornet, 30-30, 45-70). Drilled and tapped for scope mount; 223, 243, 270, 280, 30-06 have no open sights, come with scope mounts. **Features:** Break-open action with side-lever release. The 223, 243, 270 and 30-06 have recoil pad and Monte Carlo stock for shooting with scope. Swivel studs on all models. Blue finish. Introduced 1989. From New England Firearms.

Price: **$209.95**

Price: 7x57, 7x64 Brenneke, 24" barrel **$211.95**

Price: 280 Rem., 26" barrel **$214.95**

Price: Synthetic Handi-Rifle (black polymer stock and forend, swivels, recoil pad). **$219.95**

Price: Handi-Rifle Youth (223, 243) **$209.95**

New England Firearms Super Light Rifle

Similar to the Handi-Rifle except has new barrel taper, shorter 20" barrel with recessed muzzle and special lightweight synthetic stock and forend. No sights are furnished on the 223 and 243 versions, but have a factory-mounted scope base and offset hammer spur; Monte Carlo stock; 22 Hornet has ramp front, fully adjustable open rear. Overall length is 36", weight is 5.5 lbs. Introduced 1997. Made in U.S. by New England Firearms.

Price: 22 Hornet, 223 Rem. or 243 Win. **$219.95**

New England Firearms Super Light

New England Firearms Survivor

Remington No. 1 Mid-Range

Ruger No. 1B

NEW ENGLAND FIREARMS SURVIVOR RIFLE

Caliber: 223, 357 Mag., single shot. **Barrel:** 22". **Weight:** 6 lbs. **Length:** 36" overall. **Stock:** Black polymer, thumbhole design. **Sights:** Blade front, fully adjustable open rear. **Features:** Receiver drilled and tapped for scope mounting. Stock and forend have storage compartments for ammo, etc.; comes with integral swivels and black nylon sling. Introduced 1996. Made in U.S. by New England Firearms.
Price: Blue **$219.95**
Price: Electroless nickel **$234.95**

REMINGTON NO. 1 ROLLING BLOCK MID-RANGE SPORTER

Caliber: 30-30, 444 Marlin, 45-70. **Barrel:** 30" round. **Weight:** 8-3/4 lbs. **Length:** 46-1/2" overall. **Stock:** American walnut with checkered pistol grip and forend. **Sights:** Beaded blade front, adjustable center-notch buckhorn rear. **Features:** Recreation of the original. Polished blue metal finish. Many options available. Introduced 1998. Made in U.S. by Remington.
Price: **$1,278.00**

RUGER NO. 1B SINGLE SHOT

Caliber: 218 Bee, 22 Hornet, 220 Swift, 22-250, 223, 243, 6mm Rem., 25-06, 257 Roberts, 270, 280, 30-06, 7mm Rem. Mag., 300 Win. Mag., 338 Win. Mag., 270 Wea., 300 Wea. **Barrel:** 26" round tapered with quarter-rib; with Ruger 1" rings. **Weight:** 8 lbs. **Length:** 43-3/8" overall. **Stock:** Walnut, two-piece, checkered pistol grip and semi-beavertail forend. **Sights:** None, 1" scope rings supplied for integral mounts. **Features:** Under-lever, hammerless falling block design has auto ejector, top tang safety.
Price: **$719.00**
Price: Barreled action **$488.00**

Ruger No. 1A Light Sporter

Similar to the No. 1B Standard Rifle except has lightweight 22" barrel, Alexander Henry-style forend, adjustable folding leaf rear sight on quarter-rib, dovetailed ramp front with gold bead. Calibers 243, 30-06, 270 and 7x57. Weighs about 7-1/4 lbs.
Price: No. 1A **$719.00**
Price: Barreled action **$488.00**

Ruger No. 1V Special Varminter

Similar to the No. 1B Standard Rifle except has 24" heavy barrel. Semi-beavertail forend, barrel tapped for target scope block, with 1" Ruger scope rings. Calibers 22-250, 220 Swift, 223, 25-06. Weight about 9 lbs.
Price: No. 1V **$719.00**
Price: Barreled action **$488.00**

Ruger No. 1 RSI International

Similar to the No. 1B Standard Rifle except has lightweight 20" barrel, full-length International-style forend with loop sling swivel, adjustable folding leaf rear sight on quarter-rib, ramp front with gold bead. Calibers 243, 30-06, 270 and 7x57. Weight is about 7-1/4 lbs.
Price: No. 1 RSI **$734.00**
Price: Barreled action **$488.00**

Ruger No. 1 RSI

C. Sharps New Model 1875 Old Reliable

C. Sharps New Model 1874

C. Sharps
New Model 1885

Ruger No. 1H Tropical Rifle

Similar to the No. 1B Standard Rifle except has Alexander Henry forend, adjustable folding leaf rear sight on quarter-rib, ramp front with dovetail gold bead, 24" heavy barrel. Calibers 375 H&H, 416 Rem. Mag. (weighs about 8-1/4 lbs.), 416 Rigby, and 458 Win. Mag. (weighs about 9 lbs.).

Price: No. 1H **$719.00**
Price: Barreled action.................................. **$488.00**

Ruger No. 1S Medium Sporter

Similar to the No. 1B Standard Rifle except has Alexander Henry-style forend, adjustable folding leaf rear sight on quarter-rib, ramp front sight base and dovetail-type gold bead front sight. Calibers 218 Bee, 7mm Rem. Mag., 338 Win. Mag., 300 Win. Mag. with 26" barrel, 45-70 with 22" barrel. Weighs about 7-1/2 lbs. In 45-70.

Price: No. 1S **$719.00**
Price: Barreled action.................................. **$488.00**

C. SHARPS ARMS NEW MODEL 1875 OLD RELIABLE RIFLE

Caliber: 22LR, 32-40 & 38-55 Ballard, 38-56 WCF, 40-65 WCF, 40-90 3-1/4", 40-90 2-5/8", 40-70 2-1/10", 40-70 2-1/4", 40-70 2-1/2", 40-50 1-11/16", 40-50 1-7/8", 45-90, 45-70, 45-100, 45-110, 45-120. Also available on special order only in 50-70, 50-90, 50-140. **Barrel:** 24", 26", 30" (standard), 32", 34" optional. **Weight:** 8-12 lbs. **Stock:** Walnut, straight grip, shotgun butt with checkered steel buttplate. **Sights:** Silver blade front, Rocky Mountain buckhorn rear. **Features:** Recreation of the 1875 Sharps rifle. Production guns will have case colored receiver. Available in Custom Sporting and Target versions upon request. Announced 1986. From C. Sharps Arms Co. and Montana Armory, Inc.

Price: 1875 Carbine (24" tapered round bbl.)............... **$810.00**
Price: 1875 Saddle Rifle (26" tapered oct. bbl.)............. **$910.00**
Price: 1875 Sporting Rifle (30" tapered oct. bbl.)........... **$975.00**
Price: 1875 Business Rifle (28" tapered round bbl.)......... **$860.00**

C. Sharps Arms 1875 Classic Sharps

Similar to the New Model 1875 Sporting Rifle except has 26", 28" or 30" full octagon barrel, crescent buttplate with toe plate, Hartford-style forend with cast German silver nose cap. Blade front sight, Rocky Mountain buckhorn rear. Weighs 10 lbs. Introduced 1987. From C. Sharps Arms Co. and Montana Armory, Inc.

Price: **$1,185.00**

C. Sharps Arms New Model 1875 Target & Long Range

Similar to the New Model 1875 except available in all listed calibers except 22 LR; 34" tapered octagon barrel; globe with post front sight, Long Range Vernier tang sight with windage adjustments. Pistol grip stock with cheek rest; checkered steel buttplate. Introduced 1991. From C. Sharps Arms Co. and Montana Armory, Inc.

Price: **$1,535.00**

C. SHARPS ARMS NEW MODEL 1874 OLD RELIABLE

Caliber: 40-50, 40-70, 40-90, 45-70, 45-90, 45-100, 45-110, 45-120, 50-70, 50-90, 50-140. **Barrel:** 26", 28", 30" tapered octagon. **Weight:** About 10 lbs. **Length:** NA. **Stock:** American black walnut; shotgun butt with checkered steel buttplate; straight grip, heavy forend with Schnabel tip. **Sights:** Blade front, buckhorn rear. Drilled and tapped for tang sight. **Features:** Recreation of the Model 1874 Old Reliable Sharps Sporting Rifle. Double set triggers. Reintroduced 1991. Made in U.S. by C. Sharps Arms. Available from Montana Armory, Inc.

Price: **$1,175.00**

C. SHARPS ARMS NEW MODEL 1885 HIGHWALL RIFLE

Caliber: 22 LR, 22 Hornet, 219 Zipper, 25-35 WCF, 32-40 WCF, 38-55 WCF, 40-65, 30-40-Krag, 40-50 ST or BN, 40-70 ST or BN, 40-90 ST or BN, 45-70 2-1/10" ST, 45-90 2-4/10" ST, 45-100 2-6/10" ST, 45-110 2-7/8" ST, 45-120 3-1/4" ST. **Barrel:** 26", 28", 30", tapered full octagon. **Weight:** About 9 lbs., 4 oz. **Length:** 47" overall. **Stock:** Oil-finished American walnut; Schnabel-style forend. **Sights:** Blade front, buckhorn rear. Drilled and tapped for optional tang sight. **Features:** Single trigger; octagonal receiver top; checkered steel buttplate; color case-hardened receiver and buttplate, blued barrel. Many options available. Made in U.S. by C. Sharps Arms Co. Available from Montana Armory, Inc.

Price: From....................................... **$1,195.00**

Thompson/Center Contender

Thompson/Center Encore

SHARPS 1874 RIFLE
Caliber: 45-70. **Barrel:** 28", octagonal. **Weight:** 9-1/4 lbs. **Length:** 46" overall. **Stock:** Checkered walnut. **Sights:** Blade front, adjustable rear. **Features:** Double set triggers on rifle. Color case-hardened receiver and buttplate, blued barrel. Imported from Italy by E.M.F.
Price: Rifle or carbine $950.00
Price: Military rifle, carbine $860.00
Price: Sporting rifle $860.00

SHILOH SHARPS 1874 LONG RANGE EXPRESS
Caliber: 40-50 BN, 40-70 BN, 40-90 BN, 45-70 ST, 45-90 ST, 45-110 ST, 50-70 ST, 50-90 ST, 50-110 ST, 32-40, 38-55, 40-70 ST, 40-90 ST. **Barrel:** 34" tapered octagon. **Weight:** 10-1/2 lbs. **Length:** 51" overall. **Stock:** Oil-finished semi-fancy walnut with pistol grip, shotgun-style butt, traditional cheek rest, Schnabel forend. **Sights:** Globe front, sporting tang rear. **Features:** Recreation of the Model 1874 Sharps rifle. Double set triggers. Made in U.S. by Shiloh Rifle Mfg. Co.
Price: $1,434.00
Price: Sporting Rifle No. 1 (similar to above except with 30" bbl., blade front, buckhorn rear sight) $1,408.00
Price: Sporting Rifle No. 3 (similar to No. 1 except straight-grip stock, standard wood) $1,304.00
Price: 1874 Hartford model $1,474.00

Shiloh Sharps 1874 Montana Roughrider
Similar to the No. 1 Sporting Rifle except available with half-octagon or full-octagon barrel in 24", 26", 28", 30", 34" lengths; standard supreme or semi-fancy wood, shotgun, pistol grip or military-style butt. Weight about 8-1/2 lbs. Calibers 30-40, 30-30, 40-50x1-11/16"BN, 40-70x2-1/10" BN, 45-70x2-1/10"ST. Globe front and tang sight optional.
Price: Standard supreme $1,304.00
Price: Semi-fancy $1,414.00

Shiloh Sharps 1874 Business Rifle
Similar to No. 3 Rifle except has 28" heavy round barrel, military-style buttstock and steel buttplate. Weight about 9-1/2 lbs. Calibers 40-50 BN, 40-70 BN, 40-90 BN, 45-70 ST, 45-90 ST, 50-70 ST, 50-100 ST, 32-40, 38-55, 40-70 ST, 40-90 ST.
Price: $1,310.00
Price: 1874 Saddle Rifle (similar to Carbine except has 26" octagon barrel, semi-fancy shotgun butt) $1,362.00

THOMPSON/CENTER CONTENDER CARBINE
Caliber: 22 LR, 22 Hornet, 223 Rem., 7x30 Waters, 30-30 Win. **Barrel:** 21". **Weight:** 5 lbs., 2 oz. **Length:** 35" overall. **Stock:** Checkered American walnut with rubber butt pad. Also with Rynite stock and forend. **Sights:** Blade front, open adjustable rear. **Features:** Uses the T/C Contender action. Eleven interchangeable barrels available, all with sights, drilled and tapped for scope mounting. Introduced 1985. Offered as a complete Carbine only.
Price: Rifle calibers $540.00
Price: Extra barrels, rifle calibers, each $243.00

THOMPSON/CENTER ENCORE RIFLE
Caliber: 22-250, 223, 243, 25-06, 270, 7mm-08, 308, 30-06, 7mm Rem. Mag., 300 Win. Mag. **Barrel:** 24", 26". **Weight:** 6 lbs., 12 oz. (24" barrel). **Length:** 38-1/2" (24" barrel). **Stock:** American walnut. Monte Carlo style; Schnabel forend or black composite. **Sights:** Ramp-style white bead front, fully adjustable leaf-type rear. **Features:** Interchangeable barrels; action opens by squeezing trigger guard; drilled and tapped for T/C scope mounts; polished blue finish. Introduced 1996. Made in U.S. by Thompson/Center Arms.
Price: $573.00
Price: Extra barrels $250.00
Price: With black composite stock and forend $555.00

Thompson/Center Stainless Encore Rifle
Similar to the blued Encore except made of stainless steel with blued sights, and has black composite stock and forend. Available in 22-250, 223, 7mm-08, 30-06, 308. Introduced 1999. Made in U.S. by Thompson/Center Arms.
Price: $619.00

UBERTI ROLLING BLOCK BABY CARBINE
Caliber: 22 LR, 22 WMR, 22 Hornet, 357 Mag., single shot. **Barrel:** 22". **Weight:** 4.8 lbs. **Length:** 35-1/2" overall. **Stock:** Walnut stock and forend. **Sights:** Blade front, fully adjustable open rear. **Features:** Resembles Remington New Model No. 4 carbine. Brass trigger guard and buttplate; color case-hardened frame, blued barrel. Imported by Uberti USA Inc.
Price: $490.00

WESSON & HARRINGTON BUFFALO CLASSIC RIFLE
Caliber: 45-70. **Barrel:** 32" heavy. **Weight:** 9 lbs. **Length:** 52" overall. **Stock:** American black walnut. **Sights:** None furnished; drilled and tapped for peep sight; barrel dovetailed for front sight. **Features:** Color case-hardened Handi-Rifle action with exposed hammer; color case-hardened crescent buttplate; 19th century checkering pattern. Introduced 1995. Made in U.S. by H&R 1871, Inc.
Price: About $349.95

Wesson & Harrington 38-55 Target Rifle
Similar to the Buffalo Classic rifle except chambered for 38-55 Win., has 28" barrel. The barrel and steel furniture, including steel trigger guard and forend spacer, are highly polished and blued. Color case-hardened receiver and buttplate. Barrel is dovetailed for a front sight, and drilled and tapped for receiver sight or scope mount. Introduced 1998. Made in U.S. by H&R 1871, Inc.
Price: $389.95

Designs for sporting and utility purposes worldwide.

Beretta Express SSO

Beretta Model 455 SxS

Charles Daily Superior

NEW! **AMERICAN ARMS SILVER EXPRESS O/U DOUBLE RIFLE**
Caliber: 8x57 JRS, 9.3x74R. **Barrel:** 24". **Weight:** 7 lbs., 14 oz. **Length:** 41-1/4" overall. **Stock:** European walnut. **Sights:** Ramped high-visibility front, standing leaf rear on rib. **Features:** Boxlock action with single trigger, extractors; engraved, silvered receiver; blued barrels; no barrel center rib. Introduced 1999. Imported by American Arms, Inc.
Price: **$1,949.00**

BERETTA EXPRESS SSO O/U DOUBLE RIFLES
Caliber: 375 H&H, 458 Win. Mag., 9.3x74R. **Barrel:** 25.5". **Weight:** 11 lbs. **Stock:** European walnut with hand-checkered grip and forend. **Sights:** Blade front on ramp, open V-notch rear. **Features:** Sidelock action with color case-hardened receiver (gold inlays on SSO6 Gold). Ejectors, double triggers, recoil pad. Introduced 1990. Imported from Italy by Beretta U.S.A.
Price: SSO6 . . . . **$21,000.00**
Price: SSO6 Gold **$23,500.00**

BERETTA MODEL 455 SxS EXPRESS RIFLE
Caliber: 375 H&H, 458 Win. Mag., 470 NE, 500 NE 3", 416 Rigby. **Barrel:** 23-1/2" or 25-1/2". **Weight:** 11 lbs. **Stock:** European walnut with hand-checkered grip and forend. **Sights:** Blade front, folding leaf V-notch rear. **Features:** Sidelock action with easily removable sideplates; color case-hardened finish (455), custom big game or floral motif engraving (455EELL). Double triggers, recoil pad. Introduced 1990. Imported from Italy by Beretta U.S.A.
Price: Model 455. . . . . **$36,000.00**
Price: Model 455EELL **$47,000.00**

BRNO 500 COMBINATION GUNS
Caliber/Gauge: 12 (2-3/4" chamber) over 5.6x52R, 5.6x50R, 222 Rem., 243, 6.x55, 308, 7x57R, 7x65R, 30-06. **Barrel:** 23.6". **Weight:** 7.6 lbs. **Length:** 40.5" overall. **Stock:** European walnut. **Sights:** Bead front, V-notch rear; grooved for scope mounting. **Features:** Boxlock action; double set trigger; blue finish with etched engraving. Announced 1998. Imported from The Czech Republic by Euro-Imports.
Price: **$1,023.00**
Price: O/U double rifle, 7x57R, 7x65R, 8x57JRS. **$1,125.00**

BRNO ZH 300 COMBINATION GUN
Caliber/Gauge: 22 Hornet, 5.6x50R Mag., 5.6x52R, 7x57R, 7x65R, 8x57JRS over 12, 16 (2-3/4" chamber). **Barrel:** 23.6". **Weight:** 7.9 lbs.

Length: 40.5" overall. **Stock:** European walnut. **Sights:** Blade front, open adjustable rear. **Features:** Boxlock action; double triggers; automatic safety. Announced 1998. Imported from The Czech Republic by Euro-Imports.
Price: **$724.00**

BRNO ZH Double Rifles
Similar to the ZH 300 combination guns except with double rifle barrels. Available in 7x65R, 7x57R and 8x57JRS. Announced 1998. Imported from The Czech Republic by Euro-Imports.
Price: **$1,125.00**

CHARLES DALY SUPERIOR COMBINATION GUN
Caliber/Gauge: 12 ga. over 22 Hornet, 223 Rem., 22-250, 243 Win., 270 Win., 308 Win., 30-06. **Barrel:** 23.5", shotgun choked Imp. Cyl. **Weight:** About 7.5 lbs. **Stock:** Checkered walnut pistol grip buttstock and semi-beavertail forend. **Features:** Silvered, engraved receiver; chrome-moly steel barrels; double triggers; extractors; sling swivels; gold bead front sight. Introduced 1997. Imported from Italy by K.B.I. Inc.
Price: **$1,209.00**

Charles Daly Empire Combination Gun
Same as the Superior grade except has deluxe wood with European-style comb and cheekpiece; slim forend. Introduced 1997. Imported from Italy by K.B.I., Inc.
Price: **$1,729.00**

CZ 584 SOLO COMBINATION GUN
Caliber/Gauge: 7x57R; 12, 2-3/4" chamber. **Barrel:** 24.4". **Weight:** 7.37 lbs. **Length:** 45.25" overall. **Stock:** Circassian walnut. **Sights:** Blade front, open rear adjustable for windage. **Features:** Kersten-style double lump locking system; double-trigger Blitz-type mechanism with drop safety and adjustable set trigger for the rifle barrel; auto safety, dual extractors; receiver dovetailed for scope mounting. Imported from the Czech Republic by CZ-USA.
Price: **$850.00**

GARBI EXPRESS DOUBLE RIFLE
Caliber: 7x65R, 9.3x74R, 375 H&H. **Barrel:** 24-3/4". **Weight:** 7-3/4 to 8-1/2 lbs. **Length:** 41-1/2" overall. **Stock:** Turkish walnut. **Sights:** Quarter-rib with express sight. **Features:** Side-by-side double; H&H-pattern sidelock ejector with reinforced action; chopper lump barrels of Boehler steel; double triggers; fine scroll and rosette engraving, or full coverage ornamental; coin-finished action. Introduced 1997. Imported from Spain by Wm. Larkin Moore.
Price: **$21,800.00**

Hoenig Round Action

Krieghoff Classic Double Rifle

Merkel Model 210E

HOENIG ROTARY ROUND ACTION DOUBLE RIFLE

Caliber: Most popular calibers from 225 Win. to 9.3x74R. **Barrel:** 22"-26". **Weight:** NA. **Length:** NA. **Stock:** English Walnut; to customer specs. **Sights:** Swivel hood front with button release (extra bead stored in trap door gripcap), express-style rear on quarter-rib adjustable for windage and elevation; scope mount. **Features:** Round action opens by rotating barrels, pulling forward. Has inertia extractor system; rotary safety blocks the strikers; single lever quick-detachable scope mount. Simple takedown without removing forend. Introduced 1997. Made in U.S. by George Hoenig.
Price: **$19,980.00**

KRIEGHOFF CLASSIC DOUBLE RIFLE

Caliber: 7x65R, 308 Win., 30-06, 30R Blaser, 8x57 JRS, 8x75RS, 9.3x74R. **Barrel:** 23.5". **Weight:** 7.3 to 8 lbs. **Length:** NA. **Stock:** High grade European walnut. Standard has conventional rounded cheekpiece, Bavaria has Bavarian-style cheekpiece. **Sights:** Bead front with removable, adjustable wedge (375 H&H and below), standing leaf rear on quarter-rib. **Features:** Boxlock action; double triggers; short opening angle for fast loading; quiet extractors; sliding, self-adjusting wedge for secure bolting, Purdey-style barrel extension; horizontal firing pin placement. Many options available. Introduced 1997. Imported from Germany by Krieghoff International.
Price: With small Arabesque engraving **$7,850.00**
Price: With engraved sideplates. **$9,800.00**
Price: For extra barrels. **$4,500.00**
Price: Extra 20-ga., 28" shotshell barrels **$3,200.00**

Krieghoff Classic Big Five Double Rifle

Similar to the standard Classic except available in 375 Flanged Mag. N.E., 500/416 N.E., 470 N.E., 500 N.E. 3". Has hinged front trigger, non-removable muzzle wedge (larger than 375-caliber), Universal Trigger System, Combi Cocking Device, steel trigger guard, specially weighted stock bolt for weight and balance. Many options available. Introduced 1997. Imported from Germany by Krieghoff International.
Price: **$9,450.00**
Price: With engraved sideplates. **$11,400.00**

LEBEAU - COURALLY EXPRESS RIFLE SxS

Caliber: 7x65R, 8x57JRS, 9.3x74R, 375 H&H, 470 N.E. **Barrel:** 24" to 26". **Weight:** 7-3/4 to 10-1/2 lbs. **Stock:** Fancy French walnut with cheekpiece. **Sights:** Bead on ramp front, standing left express rear on quarter-rib. **Features:** Holland & Holland-type sidelock with automatic ejectors; double triggers. Imported from Belgium by Wm. Larkin Moore.
Price: **$51,000.00**

MERKEL OVER/UNDER COMBINATION GUNS

Caliber/Gauge: 12, 16, 20 (2-3/4" chamber) over 22 Hornet, 5.6x50R, 5.6x52R, 222 Rem., 243 Win., 6.5x55, 6.5x57R, 7x57R, 7x65R, 308 Win., 30-06, 8x57JRS, 9.3x74R. **Barrel:** 25.6". **Weight:** About 7.6 lbs. **Length:** NA. **Stock:** Oil-finished walnut; pistol grip, cheekpiece. **Sights:** Bead front, fixed rear. **Features:** Kersten double cross-bolt lock; scroll-engraved, color case-hardened receiver; Blitz action; double triggers. Imported from Germany by GSI.
Price: Model 210E **$6,195.00**
Price: Model 211E (silver-grayed receiver, fine hunting scene engraving). **$7,495.00**

MERKEL DRILLINGS

Caliber/Gauge: 12, 20, 3" chambers; 16, 2-3/4" chambers; 22 Hornet, 5.6x50R Mag., 5.6x52R, 222 Rem., 243 Win., 6.5x55, 6.5x57R, 7x57R, 7x65R, 308, 30-06, 8x57JRS, 9.3x74R, 375 H&H. **Barrel:** 25.6". **Weight:** 7.9 to 8.4 lbs. depending upon caliber. **Stock:** Oil-finished walnut with pistol grip; cheekpiece on 12-, 16-gauge. **Sights:** Blade front, fixed rear. **Features:** Double barrel locking lug with Greener cross-bolt; scroll-engraved, case-hardened receiver; automatic trigger safety; Blitz action; double triggers. Imported from Germany by GSI.
Price: Model 95S (selective sear safety), from. **$7,995.00**
Price: Model 95K (manually cocked rifle system), from **$8,595.00**
Price: Model 96K (manually cocked rifle system), from **$5,895.00**

MERKEL OVER/UNDER DOUBLE RIFLES

Caliber: 22 Hornet, 5.6x50R Mag., 5.6x52R, 222 Rem., 243 Win., 6.5x55, 6.5x57R, 7x57R, 7x65R, 308, 30-06, 8x57JRS, 9.3x74R. **Barrel:** 25.6". **Weight:** About 7.7 lbs, depending upon caliber. **Length:** NA. **Stock:** Oil-finished walnut with pistol grip, cheekpiece. **Sights:** Blade front, fixed rear. **Features:** Kersten double cross-bolt lock; scroll-engraved, case-hardened receiver; Blitz action with double triggers. Imported from Germany by GSI.
Price: Model 221 E (silver-grayed receiver finish, hunting scene engraving). **$10,895.00**

MERKEL MODEL 160 SIDE-BY-SIDE DOUBLE RIFLE

Caliber: 22 Hornet, 5.6x50R Mag., 5.6x52R, 222 Rem., 243 Win., 6.5x55, 6.5x57R, 7x57R, 7x65R, 308, 30-06, 8x57JRS, 9.3x74R, 375 H&H. **Bar-**

Navy Arms Kodiak MK IV

Rizzini Express

Savage 24F Predator

Springfield M6 Scout

rel: 25.6". **Weight:** About 7.7 lbs, depending upon caliber. **Length:** NA. **Stock:** Oil-finished walnut with pistol grip, cheekpiece. **Sights:** Blade front on ramp, fixed rear. **Features:** Sidelock action. Double barrel locking lug with Greener cross-bolt; fine engraved hunting scenes on sideplates; Holland & Holland ejectors; double triggers. Imported from Germany by GSI.
Price: From **$13,295.00**

Merkel Boxlock Double Rifles

Similar to the Model 160 double rifle except with Anson & Deely boxlock action with cocking indicators, double triggers, engraved color case-hardened receiver. Introduced 1995. Imported from Germany by GSI.
Price: Model 140-1, from **$5,895.00**
Price: Model 140-1.1 (engraved silver-gray receiver), from **$6,795.00**
Price: Model 150-1 (false sideplates, silver-gray receiver, Arabesque engraving), from **$7,495.00**
Price: Model 150-1.1 (as above with English Arabesque engraving), from **$8,695.00**

NAVY ARMS KODIAK MK IV DOUBLE RIFLE

Caliber: 45-70. **Barrel:** 24". **Weight:** 10 lbs., 3 oz. **Length:** 39-3/4" overall. **Stock:** Checkered European walnut. **Sights:** Bead front, folding leaf express rear. **Features:** Blued, semi-regulated barrels; color case-hardened receiver and hammers; double triggers. Replica of Colt double rifle 1879-1885. Introduced 1996. Imported by Navy Arms.
Price: **$3,125.00**
Price: Engraved satin-finished receiver, browned barrels **$4,000.00**

RIZZINI EXPRESS 90L DOUBLE RIFLE

Caliber: 30-06, 7x65R, 9.3x74R. **Barrel:** 24". **Weight:** 7-1/2 lbs. **Length:** 40" overall. **Stock:** Select European walnut with satin oil finish; English-style cheekpiece. **Sights:** Ramp front, quarter-rib with express sight. **Features:** Color case-hardened boxlock action; automatic ejectors; single se-

lective trigger; polished blue barrels. Extra 20-gauge shotshell barrels available. Imported for Italy by Wm. Larkin Moore.
Price: With case **$4,500.00**

SAVAGE 24F PREDATOR O/U COMBINATION GUN

Caliber/Gauge: 22 Hornet, 223, 30-30 over 12 (24F-12) or 22 LR, 22 Hornet, 223, 30-30 over 20-ga. (24F-20); 3" chambers. **Action:** Takedown, low rebounding visible hammer. Single trigger, barrel selector spur on hammer. **Barrel:** 24" separated barrels; 12-ga. has Full, Mod., Imp. Cyl. choke tubes, 20-ga. has fixed Mod. choke. **Weight:** 8 lbs. **Length:** 40-1/2" overall. **Stock:** Black Rynite composition. **Sights:** Ramp front, rear open adjustable for elevation. Grooved for tip-off scope mount. **Features:** Removable butt cap for storage and accessories. Introduced 1989.
Price: 24F-12 . . . . **$425.00**
Price: 24F-20 . . . . **$415.00**

Savage 24F-12/410 Combination Gun

Similar to the 24F-12 except comes with "Four-Tenner" adaptor for shooting 410-bore shotshells. Rifle barrel chambered for 22 Hornet, 223 Rem., 30-30 Win. Introduced 1998. Made in U.S. by Savage Arms, Inc.
Price: **$475.00**

SPRINGFIELD, INC. M6 SCOUT RIFLE/SHOTGUN

Caliber/Gauge: 22 LR or 22 Hornet over 410-bore. **Barrel:** 18.25". **Weight:** 4 lbs. **Length:** 32" overall. **Stock:** Folding detachable with storage for 15 22 LR, four 410 shells. **Sights:** Blade front, military aperture for 22; V-notch for 410. **Features:** All-metal construction. Designed for quick disassembly and minimum maintenance. Folds for compact storage. Introduced 1982; reintroduced 1996. Imported from the Czech Republic by Springfield, Inc.
Price: Parkerized **$176.00**
Price: Stainless steel **$208.00**

Designs for hunting, utility and sporting purposes, including training for competition

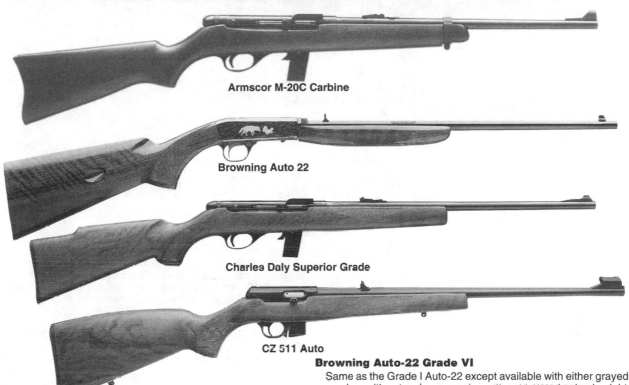

Armscor M-20C Carbine

Browning Auto 22

Charles Daly Superior Grade

CZ 511 Auto

AR-7 EXPLORER CARBINE

Caliber: 22 LR, 8-shot magazine. **Barrel:** 16". **Weight:** 2-1/2 lbs. **Length:** 34-1/2" / 16-1/2" stowed. **Stock:** Moulded Cycolac; snap-on rubber butt pad. **Sights:** Square blade front, aperture rear. **Features:** Takedown design stores barrel and action in hollow stock. Light enough to float. Reintroduced 1999. From AR-7 Industries, LLC.
Price: $150.00

ARMSCOR MODEL AK22 AUTO RIFLE

Caliber: 22 LR, 10-shot magazine. **Barrel:** 18.5". **Weight:** 7.5 lbs. **Length:** 38" overall. **Stock:** Plain mahogany. **Sights:** Adjustable post front, leaf rear adjustable for elevation. **Features:** Resembles the AK-47. Matte black finish. Introduced 1987. Imported from the Philippines by K.B.I., Inc.
Price: About $209.00

ARMSCOR M-1600 AUTO RIFLE

Caliber: 22 LR, 10-shot magazine. **Barrel:** 18.25". **Weight:** 6.2 lbs. **Length:** 38.5" overall. **Stock:** Black finished mahogany. **Sights:** Post front, aperture rear. **Features:** Resembles Colt AR-15. Matte black finish. Introduced 1987. Imported from the Philippines by K.B.I., Inc.
Price: About $189.00

ARMSCOR M-20C AUTO CARBINE

Caliber: 22 LR, 10-shot magazine. **Barrel:** 18.25". **Weight:** 6.5 lbs. **Length:** 38" overall. **Stock:** Walnut-finished mahogany. **Sights:** Hooded front, rear adjustable for elevation. **Features:** Receiver grooved for scope mounting. Blued finish. Introduced 1990. Imported from the Philippines by K.B.I., Inc.
Price: $149.00

BROWNING AUTO-22 RIFLE

Caliber: 22 LR, 11-shot. **Barrel:** 19-1/4". **Weight:** 4-3/4 lbs. **Length:** 37" overall. **Stock:** Checkered select walnut with pistol grip and semi-beavertail forend. **Sights:** Gold bead front, folding leaf rear. **Features:** Engraved receiver with polished blue finish; cross-bolt safety; tubular magazine in buttstock; easy takedown for carrying or storage. Imported from Japan by Browning.
Price: Grade I $415.00

Browning Auto-22 Grade VI

Same as the Grade I Auto-22 except available with either grayed or blued receiver with extensive engraving with gold-plated animals; right side pictures a fox and squirrel in a woodland scene; left side shows a beagle chasing a rabbit. On top is a portrait of the beagle. Stock and forend are of high-grade walnut with a double-bordered cut checkering design. Introduced 1987.
Price: Grade VI, blue or gray receiver $860.00

BRNO ZKM 611 AUTO RIFLE

Caliber: 22 WMR, 6- or 10-shot magazine. **Barrel:** 20.4". **Weight:** 5.9 lbs. **Length:** 38.9" overall. **Stock:** European walnut. **Sights:** Hooded blade front, open adjustable rear. **Features:** Removable box magazine; polished blue finish; cross-bolt safety; grooved receiver for scope mounting; easy takedown for storage. Imported from The Czech Republic by Euro-Imports.
Price: $475.00

CALICO M-100FS CARBINE

Caliber: 22 LR. **Barrel:** 16.25". **Weight:** 5 lbs. **Length:** 36" overall. **Stock:** Glass-filled, impact-resistant polymer. **Sights:** Adjustable post front, notch rear. **Features:** Has helical-feed magazine; aluminum receiver; ambidextrous safety. Made in U.S. by Calico.
Price: $504.00

CHARLES DALY FIELD GRADE AUTO RIFLE

Caliber: 22 LR, 10-shot magazine. **Barrel:** 20-3/4". **Weight:** 6.5 lbs. **Length:** 40-1/2" overall. **Stock:** Walnut-finished hardwood with Monte Carlo. **Sights:** Hooded front, adjustable open rear. **Features:** Receiver grooved for scope mounting; blue finish; shell deflector. Introduced 1998. Imported by K.B.I.
Price: $124.00
Price: Superior Grade (cut checkered stock, fully adjustable sight) . $199.00

Charles Daly Empire Grade Auto Rifle

Similar to the Field Grade except has select California walnut stock with 24 l.p.i. hand checkering, contrasting forend and gripcaps, damascened bolt, high-polish blue. Introduced 1998. Imported by K.B.I.
Price: $369.00

CZ 511 AUTO RIFLE

Caliber: 22 LR, 8-shot magazine. **Barrel:** 22.2". **Weight:** 5.39 lbs. **Length:** 38.6" overall. **Stock:** Walnut with checkered pistol grip. **Sights:** Hooded

Henry U.S. Survival

Marlin Model 60 SSK

Marlin Model 922

front, adjustable rear. **Features:** Polished blue finish; detachable magazine; sling swivel studs. Imported from the Czech Republic by CZ-USA.
Price: **$349.00**

HENRY U.S. SURVIVAL RIFLE .22

Caliber: 22 LR, 8-shot magazine. **Barrel:** 16" steel lined. **Weight:** 2.5 lbs. **Stock:** ABS plastic. **Sights:** Blade front on ramp, aperture rear. **Features:** Takedown design stores barrel and action in hollow stock. Light enough to float. Silver, black or camo finish. Comes with two magazines. Introduced 1998. From Henry Repeating Arms Co.
Price: **$165.00**

MAGTECH MT 7022 AUTO RIFLE

Caliber: 22 LR, 10-shot magazine. **Barrel:** 18". **Weight:** 4.8 lbs. **Length:** 37" overall. **Stock:** Brazilian hardwood. **Sights:** Hooded blade front, fully adjustable open rear. **Features:** Cross-bolt safety; last-shot bolt hold-open; alloy receiver is drilled and tapped for scope mounting. Introduced 1998. Imported from Brazil by Magtech Ammunition Co.
Price: **$100.00**

MARLIN MODEL 60 SELF-LOADING RIFLE

Caliber: 22 LR, 14-shot tubular magazine. **Barrel:** 22" round tapered. **Weight:** About 5-1/2 lbs. **Length:** 40-1/2" overall. **Stock:** Press-checkered, walnut-finished Maine birch with Monte Carlo, full pistol grip; Mar-Shield® finish. **Sights:** Ramp front, open adjustable rear. **Features:** Matted receiver is grooved for scope mount. Manual bolt hold-open; automatic last-shot bolt hold-open.
Price: **$168.00**
Price: With 4x scope. **$173.00**

Marlin Model 60SS Self-Loading Rifle

Same as the Model 60 except breech bolt, barrel and outer magazine tube are made of stainless steel; most other parts are either nickel-plated or coated to match the stainless finish. Monte Carlo stock is of black/gray Maine birch laminate, and has nickel-plated swivel studs, rubber butt pad. Introduced 1993.

Price: **$265.00**
Price: Model 60SSK (black fiberglass-filled stock). **$229.00**
Price: Model 60SSK with 4x scope. **$243.00**
Price: Model 60SB (walnut-finished birch stock) **$212.00**
Price: Model 60SB with 4x scope. **$225.00**

MARLIN 70PSS STAINLESS RIFLE

Caliber: 22 LR, 7-shot magazine. **Barrel:** 16-1/4" stainless steel, Micro-Groove® rifling. **Weight:** 3-1/4 lbs. **Length:** 35-1/4" overall. **Stock:** Black fiberglass-filled synthetic with abbreviated forend, nickel-plated swivel studs, moulded-in checkering. **Sights:** Ramp front with orange post, cut-

away Wide Scan® hood; adjustable open rear. Receiver grooved for scope mounting. **Features:** Takedown barrel; cross-bolt safety; manual bolt hold-open; last shot bolt hold-open; comes with padded carrying case. Introduced 1986. Made in U.S. by Marlin.
Price: **$272.00**

MARLIN MODEL 922 MAGNUM SELF-LOADING RIFLE

Caliber: 22 WMR, 5-shot magazine. **Barrel:** 20.5". **Weight:** 6.5 lbs. **Length:** 39.75" overall. **Stock:** Checkered American black walnut with Monte Carlo comb, swivel studs, rubber butt pad. **Sights:** Ramp front with bead and removable Wide-Scan® hood, adjustable folding semi-buckhorn rear. **Features:** Action based on the centerfire Model 9 Carbine. Receiver drilled and tapped for scope mounting. Automatic last-shot bolt hold-open; magazine safety. Introduced 1993.
Price: **$429.00**

MARLIN MODEL 995SS SELF-LOADING RIFLE

Caliber: 22 LR, 7-shot clip magazine. **Barrel:** 18" Micro-Groove®; stainless steel. **Weight:** 5 lbs. **Length:** 37" overall. **Stock:** Black fiberglass-filled synthetic with nickel-plated swivel studs, moulded-in checkering. **Sights:** Ramp front with orange post and cut-away Wide-Scan® hood; screw-adjustable open rear. **Features:** Stainless steel breech bolt and barrel. Receiver grooved for scope mount; bolt hold-open device; cross-bolt safety. Introduced 1979.
Price: **$255.00**

MARLIN MODEL 7000 SELF-LOADING RIFLE

Caliber: 22 LR, 10-shot magazine **Barrel:** 18" heavy target with 12-groove Micro-Groove® rifling, recessed muzzle. **Weight:** 5-1/2 lbs. **Length:** 37" overall. **Stock:** Black fiberglass-filled synthetic with Monte Carlo combo, swivel studs, moulded-in checkering. **Sights:** None furnished; comes with ring mounts. **Features:** Automatic last-shot bolt hold-open; manual bolt hold-open; cross-bolt safety; steel charging handle; blue finish, nickel-plated magazine. Introduced 1997. Made in U.S. by Marlin Firearms Co.
Price: **$225.00**

Marlin Model 795 Self-Loading Rifle

Similar to the Model 7000 except has standard-weight 18" barrel with 16-groove Micro-Groove rifling. Comes with ramp front sight with brass bead, screw adjustable open rear. Receiver grooved for scope mount. Introduced 1997. Made in U.S. by Marlin Firearms Co.
Price: **$159.00**
Price: With 4x scope. **$165.00**

REMINGTON MODEL 552 BDL SPEEDMASTER RIFLE

Caliber: 22 S (20), L (17) or LR (15) tubular mag. **Barrel:** 21" round tapered. **Weight:** 5-3/4 lbs. **Length:** 40" overall. **Stock:** Walnut. Checkered grip and forend. **Sights:** Bead front, step open rear adjustable for windage and elevation. **Features:** Positive cross-bolt safety, receiver grooved for tip-off mount.
Price: **$340.00**

Remington 597

Ruger 10/22 International

Savage Model 64FV

REMINGTON 597 AUTO RIFLE

Caliber: 22 LR, 10-shot clip. **Barrel:** 20". **Weight:** 5-1/2 lbs. **Length:** 40" overall. **Stock:** Gray synthetic. **Sights:** Bead front, fully adjustable rear. **Features:** Matte black finish, nickel-plated bolt. Receiver is grooved and drilled and tapped for scope mounts. Introduced 1997. Made in U.S. by Remington.

Price: $159.00
Price: Model 597 Magnum, 22 WMR, 8-shot clip............. $305.00
Price: Model 597 Magnum LS (laminated stock) $359.00
Price: Model 597 Sporter (22 LR, wood stock)............... $199.00
Price: Model 597 SS (22 LR, stainless steel, black synthetic stock) $212.00

Remington 597 LSS Auto Rifle

Similar to the Model 597 except has satin-finish stainless barrel, gray-toned alloy receiver with nickel-plated bolt, and laminated wood stock. Receiver is grooved and drilled and tapped for scope mounting. Introduced 1997. Made in U.S. by Remington.

Price: $265.00

RUGER 10/22 AUTOLOADING CARBINE

Caliber: 22 LR, 10-shot rotary magazine. **Barrel:** 18-1/2" round tapered. **Weight:** 5 lbs. **Length:** 37-1/4" overall. **Stock:** American hardwood with pistol grip and barrel band. **Sights:** Brass bead front, folding leaf rear adjustable for elevation. **Features:** Detachable rotary magazine fits flush into stock, cross-bolt safety, receiver tapped and grooved for scope blocks or tip-off mount. Scope base adaptor furnished with each rifle.

Price: Model 10/22 RB (blue) $225.00
Price: Model K10/22RB (bright finish stainless barrel) $268.00
Price: Model 10/22RP (blue, synthetic stock)............... $225.00

Ruger 10/22 International Carbine

Similar to the Ruger 10/22 Carbine except has full-length International stock of American hardwood, checkered grip and forend; comes with rubber butt pad, sling swivels. Reintroduced 1994.

Price: Blue (10/22RBI) $262.00
Price: Stainless (K10/22RBI) $282.00

Ruger 10/22 Deluxe Sporter

Same as 10/22 Carbine except walnut stock with hand checkered pistol grip and forend; straight buttplate, no barrel band, has sling swivels.
Price: Model 10/22 DSP................................ $274.00

Ruger 10/22T Target Rifle

Similar to the 10/22 except has 20" heavy, hammer-forged barrel with tight chamber dimensions, improved trigger pull, laminated hardwood stock dimensioned for optical sights. No iron sights supplied. Introduced 1996. Made in U.S. by Sturm, Ruger & Co.
Price: 10/22T $392.50
Price: K10/22T, stainless steel............................ $440.00

Ruger K10/22RP All-Weather Rifle

Similar to the stainless K10/22/RP except has black composite stock of thermoplastic polyester resin reinforced with fiberglass; checkered grip and forend. Brushed satin, natural metal finish with clear hardcoat finish. Weighs 5 lbs., measures 36-3/4" overall. Introduced 1997. From Sturm, Ruger & Co.
Price: $268.00

RUGER 10/22 MAGNUM AUTOLOADING CARBINE

Caliber: 22 WMR, 10-shot rotary magazine. **Barrel:** 18-1/2". **Weight:** 5-1/2 lbs. **Length:** 37-1/4" overall. **Stock:** Birch. **Sights:** Gold bead front, folding rear. **Features:** All-steel receiver has integral Ruger scope bases for the included 1" rings. Introduced 1999. Made in U.S. by Sturm, Ruger & Co.
Price: $425.00

SAVAGE MODEL 64G AUTO RIFLE

Caliber: 22 LR, 10-shot magazine. **Barrel:** 20". **Weight:** 5-1/2 lbs. **Length:** 40" overall. **Stock:** Walnut-finished hardwood with Monte Carlo-type comb, checkered grip and forend. **Sights:** Bead front, open adjustable rear. Receiver grooved for scope mounting. **Features:** Thumb-operated rotating safety. Blue finish. Side ejection, bolt hold-open device. Introduced 1990. Made in Canada, from Savage Arms.
Price: $123.00
Price: Model 64F, black synthetic stock $115.00
Price: Model 64GXP Package Gun includes 4x15 scope and mounts $129.00
Price: Model 64FXP (black stock, 4x15 scope) $120.00

Savage Model 64FV Auto Rifle

Similar to the Model 64F except has heavy 21" barrel with recessed crown; no sights provided—comes with Weaver-style bases. Introduced 1998. Imported from Canada by Savage Arms, Inc.
Price: $149.00

WINCHESTER MODEL 63 AUTO RIFLE

Caliber: 22 LR, 10-shot magazine. **Barrel:** 23". **Weight:** 6-1/4 lbs. **Length:** 39" overall. **Stock:** Walnut. **Sights:** Bead front, open adjustable rear. **Features:** Recreation of the original Model 63. Magazine tube loads through a port in the buttstock; forward cocking knob at front of forend; easy takedown for cleaning, storage; engraved receiver. Reintroduced 1997. From U.S. Repeating Arms Co.
Price: Grade I $678.00
Price: High grade, select walnut, cut checkering, engraved scenes with gold accents on receiver (made in 1997 only) $1,083.00

Classic and modern models for sport and utility, including training.

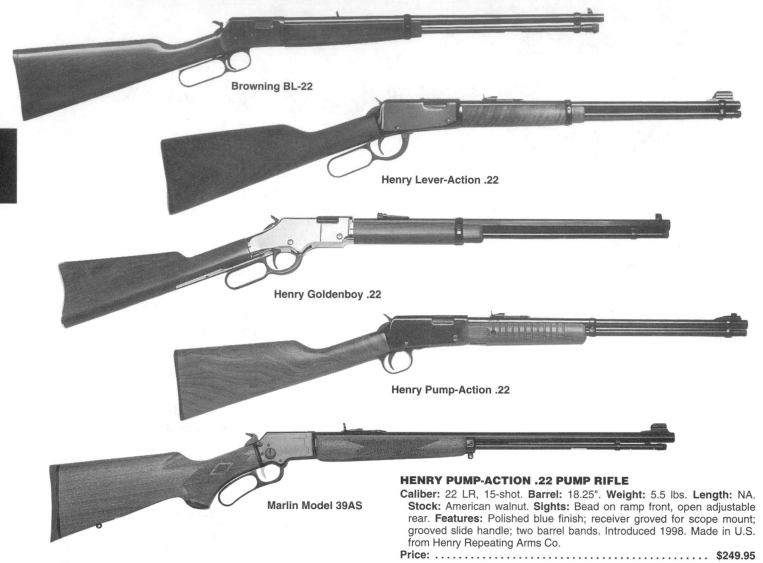

Browning BL-22

Henry Lever-Action .22

Henry Goldenboy .22

Henry Pump-Action .22

Marlin Model 39AS

BROWNING BL-22 LEVER-ACTION RIFLE
Caliber: 22 S (22), L (17) or LR (15), tubular magazine. **Barrel:** 20" round tapered. **Weight:** 5 lbs. **Length:** 36-3/4" overall. **Stock:** Walnut, two-piece straight grip Western style. **Sights:** Bead post front, folding-leaf rear. **Features:** Short throw lever, half-cock safety, receiver grooved for tip-off scope mounts. Imported from Japan by Browning.
Price: Grade I **$360.00**
Price: Grade II (engraved receiver, checkered grip and forend) . **$412.00**

HENRY LEVER-ACTION .22
Caliber: 22 Long Rifle (15-shot). **Barrel:** 18-1/4" round. **Weight:** 5-1/2 lbs. **Length:** 34" overall. **Stock:** Walnut. **Sights:** Hooded blade front, open adjustable rear. **Features:** Polished blue finish; full-length tubular magazine; side ejection; receiver grooved for scope mounting. Introduced 1997. Made in U.S. by Henry Repeating Arms Co.
Price: **$239.95**
Price: Youth model (33" overall, 11-rounds 22 LR) **$229.95**

HENRY GOLDENBOY .22 LEVER-ACTION RIFLE
Caliber: 22 LR, 16-shot. **Barrel:** 20" octagonal. **Weight:** 6.25 lbs. **Length:** 38" overall. **Stock:** American walnut. **Sights:** Blade front, open rear. **Features:** Brasslite receiver, brass buttplate, blued barrel and lever. Introduced 1998. Made in U.S. from Henry Repeating Arms Co.
Price: **$329.95**

HENRY PUMP-ACTION .22 PUMP RIFLE
Caliber: 22 LR, 15-shot. **Barrel:** 18.25". **Weight:** 5.5 lbs. **Length:** NA. **Stock:** American walnut. **Sights:** Bead on ramp front, open adjustable rear. **Features:** Polished blue finish; receiver groved for scope mount; grooved slide handle; two barrel bands. Introduced 1998. Made in U.S. from Henry Repeating Arms Co.
Price: **$249.95**

MARLIN MODEL 39AS GOLDEN LEVER-ACTION RIFLE
Caliber: 22 S (26), L (21), LR (19), tubular magazine. **Barrel:** 24" Micro-Groove®. **Weight:** 6-1/2 lbs. **Length:** 40" overall. **Stock:** Checkered American black walnut with white line spacers at pistol gripcap and buttplate; Mar-Shield® finish. Swivel studs; rubber butt pad. **Sights:** Bead ramp front with detachable Wide-Scan™ hood, folding rear semi-buckhorn adjustable for windage and elevation. **Features:** Hammer-block safety; rebounding hammer. Takedown action, receiver tapped for scope mount (supplied), offset hammer spur; gold-plated steel trigger.
Price: **$481.00**

Marlin Model 1897CB Cowboy Lever Action Rifle
Similar to the Model 39AS except it has straight-grip stock with hard rubber buttplate; blued steel forend cap; 24" tapered octagon barrel with Micro-Groove® rifling; adjustable Marble semi-buckhorn rear sight, Marble carbine front with brass bead; overall length 40". Introduced 1999. Made in U.S. by Marlin.
Price: **$648.00**

REMINGTON 572 BDL FIELDMASTER PUMP RIFLE
Caliber: 22 S (20), L (17) or LR (14), tubular magazine. **Barrel:** 21" round tapered. **Weight:** 5-1/2 lbs. **Length:** 40" overall. **Stock:** Walnut with checkered pistol grip and slide handle. **Sights:** Blade ramp front; sliding ramp rear adjustable for windage and elevation. **Features:** Cross-bolt

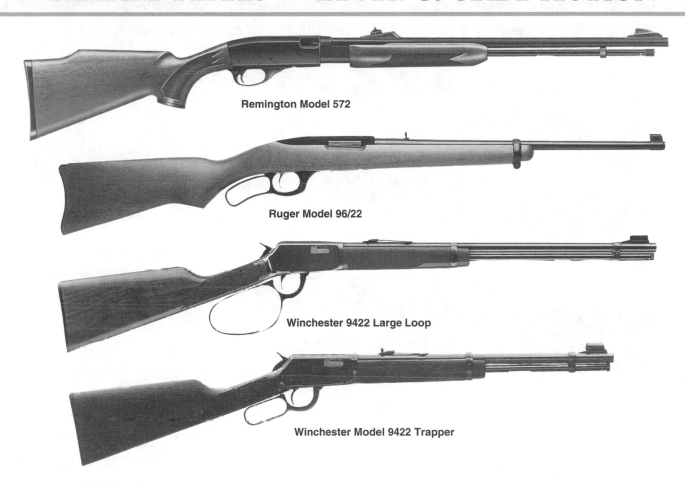

Remington Model 572

Ruger Model 96/22

Winchester 9422 Large Loop

Winchester Model 9422 Trapper

safety; removing inner magazine tube converts rifle to single shot; receiver grooved for tip-off scope mount.
Price: $353.00

RUGER MODEL 96/22 LEVER-ACTION RIFLE

Caliber: 22 LR, 10-shot rotary, magazine; 22 WMR, 9-shot rotary magazine. **Barrel:** 18-1/2". **Weight:** 5-1/4 lbs. **Length:** 37-1/4" overall. **Stock:** American hardwood. **Sights:** Gold bead front, folding leaf rear. **Features:** Cross-bolt safety, visible cocking indicator; short-throw lever action. Screw-on dovetail scope base. Introduced 1996. Made in U.S. by Sturm, Ruger & Co.
Price: 96/22 (22 LR) $327.50
Price: 96/22M (22 WMR) $345.00

TAURUS MODEL 62R PUMP RIFLE

Caliber: 22 LR, 13-shot. **Barrel:** 23" round. **Weight:** 5-3/4 lbs. **Length:** 39" overall. **Stock:** Walnut-finished hardwood, straight grip, grooved forend. **Sights:** Fixed front, adjustable rear. **Features:** Blue finish; bolt-mounted safety; quick takedown. Imported from Brazil by Interarms.
Price: .... NA

Taurus Model 62C Pump Carbine

Same as standard model except 22 LR, has 16-1/2" barrel. Magazine holds 12 cartridges.
Price: .... NA

WINCHESTER MODEL 9422 LEVER-ACTION RIFLE

Caliber: 22 LR, 22 WMR, tubular magazine **Barrel:** 20-1/2". **Weight:** 6-1/4 lbs. **Length:** 37-1/8" overall. **Stock:** American walnut, two-piece, straight grip (no pistol grip). **Sights:** Hooded ramp front, adjustable semi-buckhorn rear. **Features:** Side ejection, receiver grooved for scope mounting, takedown action. From U.S. Repeating Arms Co.
Price: Walnut $419.00
Price: With WinTuff laminated stock. $419.00
Price: With large lever loop $442.00
Price: Model 9422 Legacy (semi-pistol grip stock, 22 LR and 22 WMR)
.... $449.00

Winchester Model 9422 Magnum Lever-Action Rifle

Same as the 9422 except chambered for 22 WMR cartridge, has 11-round mag. capacity.
Price: Walnut $437.00

Winchester Model 9422 Trapper

Similar to the Model 9422 with walnut stock except has 16-1/2" barrel, overall length of 33-1/8", weighs 5-1/2 lbs. Magazine holds 15 Shorts, 12 Longs, 11 Long Rifles. Introduced 1996.
Price: $419.00
Price: 22 WMR, 8-shot $437.00

Includes models for a variety of sports, utility and competitive shooting.

Anschutz 1518D Luxus

Anschutz 1710D

Charles Daly Field Grade

ANSCHUTZ 1416D/1516D CLASSIC RIFLES

Caliber: 22 LR (1416D), 5-shot clip; 22 WMR (1516D), 4-shot clip. **Barrel:** 22-1/2". **Weight:** 6 lbs. **Length:** 41" overall. **Stock:** European hardwood with walnut finish; classic style with straight comb, checkered pistol grip and forend. **Sights:** Hooded ramp front, folding leaf rear. **Features:** Uses Match 64 action. Adjustable single stage trigger. Receiver grooved for scope mounting. Imported from Germany by AcuSport Corp.

Price: 1416D, 22 LR $755.95
Price: 1516D, 22 WMR. $779.95
Price: 1416D Classic left-hand $679.95

Anschutz 1416D/1516D Walnut Luxus Rifles

Similar to the Classic models except have European walnut stocks with Monte Carlo cheekpiece, slim forend with Schnabel tip, cut checkering on grip and forend. Introduced 1997. Imported from Germany by AcuSport Corp.

Price: 1416D (22 LR) $755.95
Price: 1516D (22 WMR) $779.95

ANSCHUTZ 1518D LUXUS BOLT-ACTION RIFLE

Caliber: 22 WMR, 4-shot magazine. **Barrel:** 19-3/4". **Weight:** 5-1/2 lbs. **Length:** 37-1/2" overall. **Stock:** European walnut. **Sights:** Blade on ramp front, folding leaf rear. **Features:** Receiver grooved for scope mounting; single stage trigger; skip-line checkering; rosewood forend tip; sling swivels. Imported from Germany by AcuSport Corp.

Price: $1,186.95

ANSCHUTZ 1710D CUSTOM RIFLE

Caliber: 22 LR, 5-shot clip. **Barrel:** 24-1/4". **Weight:** 7-3/8 lbs. **Length:** 42-1/2" overall. **Stock:** Select European walnut. **Sights:** Hooded ramp front, folding leaf rear; drilled and tapped for scope mounting. **Features:** Match 54 action with adjustable single-stage trigger; roll-over Monte Carlo cheekpiece, slim forend with Schnabel tip, Wundhammer palm swell on pistol grip, rosewood gripcap with white diamond insert; skip-line checkering on grip and forend. Introduced 1988. Imported from Germany by AcuSport Corp.

Price: $1,289.95

CABANAS MASTER BOLT-ACTION RIFLE

Caliber: 177, round ball or pellet; single shot. **Barrel:** 19-1/2". **Weight:** 8 lbs. **Length:** 45-1/2" overall. **Stocks:** Walnut target-type with Monte Carlo. **Sights:** Blade front, fully adjustable rear. **Features:** Fires round ball or pellet with 22-cal. blank cartridge. Bolt action. Imported from Mexico by Mandall Shooting Supplies. Introduced 1984.

Price: $189.95
Price: Varmint model (has 21-1/2" barrel, 4-1/2 lbs., 41" overall length, varmint-type stock) $119.95

Cabanas Leyre Bolt-Action Rifle

Similar to Master model except 44" overall, has sport/target stock.

Price: $149.95
Price: Model R83 (17" barrel, hardwood stock, 40" o.a.l.) $79.95
Price: Mini 82 Youth (16-1/2" barrel, 33" overall length, 3-1/2 lbs.) . $69.95
Price: Pony Youth (16" barrel, 34" overall length, 3.2 lbs.) $69.95

Cabanas Espronceda IV Bolt-Action Rifle

Similar to the Leyre model except has full sporter stock, 18-3/4" barrel, 40" overall length, weighs 5-1/2 lbs.

Price: $134.95

CABANAS LASER RIFLE

Caliber: 177. **Barrel:** 19". **Weight:** 6 lbs., 12 oz. **Length:** 42" overall. **Stock:** Target-type thumbhole. **Sights:** Blade front, open fully adjustable rear. **Features:** Fires round ball or pellets with 22 blank cartridge. Imported from Mexico by Mandall Shooting Supplies.

Price: $159.95

CHARLES DALY SUPERIOR BOLT-ACTION RIFLE

Caliber: 22 LR, 10-shot magazine. **Barrel:** 22-5/8". **Weight:** 6.7 lbs. **Length:** 41.25" overall. **Stock:** Walnut-finished mahogany. **Sights:** Bead front, rear adjustable for elevation. **Features:** Receiver grooved for scope mounting. Blued finish. Introduced 1998. Imported by K.B.I., Inc.

Price: $179.00

Charles Daly Field Grade Rifle

Similar to the Superior except has short walnut-finished hardwood stock for small shooters. Introduced 1998. Imported by K.B.I., Inc.

Price: $124.00
Price: Field Youth (17.5" barrel) $136.00

Chipmunk Deluxe

CZ 452 American Classic

Kimber 22 Classic

Charles Daly Superior Magnum Grade Rifle

Similar to the Superior except chambered for 22 WMR. Has 22.6" barrel, double lug bolt, checkered stock, weighs 6.5 lbs. Introduced 1987.
Price: About **$199.00**

Charles Daly Empire Magnum Grade Rifle

Similar to the Superior Magnum except has oil-finished American walnut stock with 18 lpi hand checkering; black hardwood gripcap and forend tip; highly polished barreled action; jewelled bolt; recoil pad; swivel studs. Imported from the Philippines by K.B.I., Inc.
Price: **$349.00**

Charles Daly Empire Grade Rifle

Similar to the Superior except has oil-finished American walnut stock with 18 lpi hand checkering; black hardwood gripcap and forend tip; highly polished barreled action; jewelled bolt; recoil pad; swivel studs. Imported by K.B.I., Inc.
Price: **$329.00**

CHARLES DALY TRUE YOUTH BOLT-ACTION RIFLE

Caliber: 22 LR, single shot. **Barrel:** 16-1/4". **Weight:** About 3 lbs. **Length:** 32" overall. **Stock:** Walnut-finished hardwood. **Sights:** Blade front, adjustable rear. **Features:** Scaled-down stock for small shooters. Blue finish. Introduced 1998. Imported by K.B.I., Inc.
Price: **$143.00**

CHIPMUNK SINGLE SHOT RIFLE

Caliber: 22, S, L, LR, single shot. **Barrel:** 16-1/8". **Weight:** About 2-1/2 lbs. **Length:** 30" overall. **Stocks:** American walnut. **Sights:** Post on ramp front, peep rear adjustable for windage and elevation. **Features:** Drilled and tapped for scope mounting using special Chipmunk base ($13.95). Made in U.S. Introduced 1982. From Rogue Rifle Co., Inc.
Price: Standard **$194.25**
Price: Deluxe (better wood, checkering) **$246.95**
Price: With black, brown or camouflage laminate stock **$209.95**
Price: With black polyurethane-coated wood stock **$183.95**
Price: Bull barrel models of above, add **$16.00**

CZ 452 M 2E LUX BOLT-ACTION RIFLE

Caliber: 22 LR, 22 WMR, 5-shot detachable magazine. **Barrel:** 24.8". **Weight:** 6.6 lbs. **Length:** 42.63" overall. **Stock:** Walnut with checkered pistol grip. **Sights:** Hooded front, fully adjustable tangent rear. **Features:** All-steel construction; adjustable trigger; polished blue finish. Imported from the Czech Republic by CZ-USA.
Price: 22 LR **$337.00**
Price: 22 WMR **$378.00**
Price: Synthetic stock, nickel finish, 22 LR **$344.00**

CZ 452 M 2E Varmint Rifle

Similar to the Lux model except has heavy 20.8" barrel; stock has beavertail forend; weighs 7 lbs.; no sights furnished. Available only in 22 LR. Imported from the Czech Republic by CZ-USA.
Price: **$369.00**

CZ 452 American Classic Bolt-Action Rifle

Similar to the CZ 452 M 2E Lux except has classic-style stock of Circassian walnut; 22.5" free-floating barrel with recessed target crown; receiver dovetail for scope mounting. No open sights furnished. Introduced 1999. Imported from the Czech Republic by CZ-USA.
Price: 22 LR **$337.00**
Price: 22 WMR **$378.00**

KIMBER 22 CLASSIC BOLT-ACTION RIFLE

Caliber: 22 LR, 5-shot magazine. **Barrel:** 22" Kimber match grade; 11-degree target crown. **Weight:** About 6.5 lbs. **Length:** 40.5" overall. **Stock:** Classic style in Claro walnut with 18 l.p.i. hand-cut checkering; satin finish; steel gripcap; swivel studs. **Sights:** None furnished; Kimber sculpted bases available that accept all rotary dovetail rings. **Features:** All-new action with Mauser-style full-length claw extractor; two-position in M70-type safety; fully adjustable trigger set at 2 lbs.; pillar-bedded action with recoil lug, free-floated barrel. Introduced 1999. Made in U.S. by Kimber Mfg., Inc.
Price: **$919.00**

Kimber 22 SuperAmerica Bolt-Action Rifle

Similar to the 22 Classic except has AAA Claro walnut stock with wrap-around 22 l.p.i. hand-cut checkering, ebony forened tip, beaded cheekpiece. Introduced 1999. Made in U.S. by Kimber Mfg., Inc.
Price: **$1,493.00**

Kimber 22 SVT Bolt-Action Rilfe

Similar to the 22 Classic except has 18" stainless steel, fluted bull barrel, gray laminated, high-comb target-style stock with deep pistol grip, high comb, and beavertail forend with bipod stud. Weighs 7.5 lbs., overall

Kimber 22 SVT

Kimber 22 HS

Marlin Model 15YN

Marlin Model 880SS

Marlin 880SQ Squirrel

length 36.5". Matte finish on action. Introduced 1999. Made in U.S. by Kimber Mfg., Inc.
Price: **$915.00**

NEW! Kimber 22 HS (Hunter Silhouette) Bolt-Action Rifle
Similar to the 22 Classic except has 24" medium sporter match-grade barrel with half-fluting; high comb, walnut, Monte Carlo target stock with 18 l.p.i. checkering; matte blue metal finish. Introduced 1999. Made in U.S. by Kimber Mfg., Inc.
Price: **$748.00**

MARLIN MODEL 15YN "LITTLE BUCKAROO"
Caliber: 22 S, L, LR, single shot. **Barrel:** 16-1/4" Micro-Groove®. **Weight:** 4-1/4 lbs. **Length:** 33-1/4" overall. **Stock:** One-piece walnut-finished, press-checkered Maine birch with Monte Carlo; Mar-Shield® finish. **Sights:** Ramp front, adjustable open rear. **Features:** Beginner's rifle with thumb safety, easy-load feed throat, red cocking indicator. Receiver grooved for scope mounting. Introduced 1989.
Price: **$188.00**
Price: Model 15N (full-sized stock) **$188.00**

MARLIN MODEL 880SS BOLT-ACTION RIFLE
Caliber: 22 LR, 7-shot clip magazine. **Barrel:** 22" Micro-Groove®. **Weight:** 6 lbs. **Length:** 41" overall. **Stock:** Black fiberglass-filled synthetic with nickel-plated swivel studs and moulded-in checkering. **Sights:** Ramp front with orange post and cutaway Wide-Scan™ hood, adjustable semi-buckhorn folding rear. **Features:** Stainless steel barrel, receiver, front breech bolt and striker; receiver grooved for scope mounting. Introduced 1994. Made in U.S. by Marlin.
Price: **$280.00**

Marlin Model 81TS Bolt-Action Rifle
Same as the Marlin 880SS except blued steel, tubular magazine, holds 17 Long Rifle cartridges. Weighs 6 lbs.
Price: **$187.00**
Price: With 4x scope. **$193.00**

Marlin Model 880SQ Squirrel Rifle
Similar to the Model 880SS except uses the heavy target barrel of Marlin's Model 2000L target rifle. Black synthetic stock with moulded-in checkering; double bedding screws; matte blue finish. Comes without sights, but has plugged dovetail for a rear sight, filled screw holes for front; receiver grooved for scope mount. Weighs 7 lbs. Introduced 1996. Made in U.S. by Marlin.
Price: **$294.00**

Marlin 883SS

Remington 541-T HB

Ruger K77/22 Varmint

Marlin Model 25N Bolt-Action Repeater
Similar to Marlin 880, except walnut-finished p.g. stock, adjustable open rear sight, ramp front.
Price: $189.00
Price: With 4x scope................................. $196.00

Marlin Model 25MN Bolt-Action Rifle
Similar to the Model 25N except chambered for 22 WMR. Has 7-shot clip magazine, 22" Micro-Groove® barrel, checkered walnut-finished Maine birch stock. Introduced 1989.
Price: $216.00
Price: With 4x scope................................. $223.00

Marlin Model 882 Bolt-Action Rifle
Same as the Marlin 880 except 22 WMR cal. only with 7-shot clip magazine; weight about 6 lbs. Comes with swivel studs.
Price: $286.00
Price: Model 882L (laminated hardwood stock) $304.00

Marlin Model 883 Bolt-Action Rifle
Same as Marlin 882 except tubular magazine holds 12 rounds of 22 WMR ammunition.
Price: $298.00

Marlin Model 882SS Bolt-Action Rifle
Same as the Marlin Model 882 except has stainless steel front breech bolt, barrel, receiver and bolt knob. All other parts are either stainless steel or nickel-plated. Has black Monte Carlo stock of fiberglass-filled polycarbonate with moulded-in checkering, nickel-plated swivel studs. Introduced 1995. Made in U.S. by Marlin Firearms Co.
Price: $305.00

Marlin Model 882SSV Bolt-Action Rifle
Similar to the Model 882SS except has selected heavy 22" stainless steel barrel with recessed muzzle, and comes without sights; receiver is grooved for scope mount and 1" ring mounts are included. Weighs 7 lbs. Introduced 1997. Made in U.S. by Marlin Firearms Co.
Price: $301.00

Marlin Model 883SS Bolt-Action Rifle
Same as the Model 883 except front breech bolt, striker knob, trigger stud, cartridge lifter stud and outer magazine tube are of stainless steel; other parts are nickel-plated. Has two-tone brown laminated Monte Carlo stock with swivel studs, rubber butt pad. Introduced 1993.
Price: $317.00

REMINGTON 541-T
Caliber: 22 S, L, LR, 5-shot clip. Barrel: 24". Weight: 5-7/8 lbs. Length: 42-1/2" overall. Stock: Walnut, cut-checkered p.g. and forend. Satin finish. Sights: None. Drilled and tapped for scope mounts. Features: Clip repeater. Thumb safety. Reintroduced 1986.
Price: About $465.00

Remington 541-T HB Bolt-Action Rifle
Similar to the 541-T except has a heavy target-type barrel without sights. Receiver is drilled and tapped for scope mounting. American walnut stock with straight comb, satin finish, cut checkering, black checkered buttplate, black gripcap and forend tip. Weight is 6-1/2 lbs. Introduced 1993.
Price: $492.00

REMINGTON MODEL 581-S SPORTSMAN
Caliber: 22 LR, 5-shot clip. Barrel: 24". Weight: 5-7/8 lbs. Length: 42-1/2" overall. Stock: Stained hardwood. Sights: Bead on blade front, open adjustable rear. Features: Polished blue finish. Comes with single-shot adapter. Receiver grooved for scope mounting.
Price: $230.00

RUGER K77/22 VARMINT RIFLE
Caliber: 22 LR, 10-shot, 22 WMR, 9-shot detachable rotary magazine. Barrel: 24", heavy. Weight: 7.25 lbs. Length: 43.25" overall. Stock: Laminated hardwood with rubber butt pad, quick-detachable swivel studs. No checkering or gripcap. Sights: None furnished. Comes with Ruger 1" scope rings. Features: Made of stainless steel with target gray finish. Three-position safety, dual extractors. Stock has wide, flat forend. Introduced 1993.
Price: K77/22VBZ, 22 LR............................. $509.00
Price: K77/22VMBZ, 22 WMR $509.00

RUGER 77/22 RIMFIRE BOLT-ACTION RIFLE
Caliber: 22 LR, 10-shot rotary magazine; 22 WMR, 9-shot rotary magazine. Barrel: 20". Weight: About 5-3/4 lbs. Length: 39-3/4" overall. Stock: Checkered American walnut or injection-moulded fiberglass-reinforced DuPont Zytel with Xenoy inserts in forend and grip, stainless sling swivels. Sights: Brass bead front, adjustable folding leaf rear or plain barrel with 1" Ruger rings. Features: Mauser-type action uses Ruger's 10-shot rotary magazine. Three-position safety, simplified bolt stop, patented bolt locking system. Uses the dual-screw barrel attachment system of the 10/22 rifle. Integral scope mounting system with 1" Ruger rings. Blued model introduced in 1983. Stainless steel model and blued model with the synthetic stock introduced in 1989.
Price: 77/22R (no sights, rings, walnut stock) $483.00
Price: 77/22RS (open sights, rings, walnut stock) $491.00
Price: K77/22RP (stainless, no sights, rings, synthetic stock) ... $483.00

Ruger 77/22R

Sako Finnfire

Savage Mark II-FXP

Price: K77/22RSP (stainless, open sights, rings, synthetic stock) . **$491.00**
Price: 77/22RM (22 WMR, blue, walnut stock). **$483.00**
Price: K77/22RSMP (22 WMR, stainless, open sights, rings, synthetic stock) **$491.00**
Price: K77/22RMP (22 WMR, stainless, synthetic stock) **$483.00**
Price: 77/22RSM (22 WMR, blue, open sights, rings, walnut stock) **$491.00**

SAKO FINNFIRE BOLT-ACTION RIFLE

Caliber: 22 LR, 5-shot magazine. **Barrel:** 22". **Weight:** 5.25 lbs. **Length:** 40" overall. **Stock:** European walnut with checkered grip and forend. **Sights:** Hooded blade front, open adjustable rear. **Features:** Adjustable single-stage trigger; has 50-degree bolt lift. Introduced 1994. Imported from Finland by Stoeger Industries.
Price: **$789.00**
Price: With heavy barrel **$884.00**

SAKO FINNFIRE SPORTER RIFLE

Caliber: 22 LR. **Barrel:** 22"; heavy, free-floating. **Weight:** NA. **Length:** NA. **Stock:** Match style of European walnut; adjustable cheekpiece and buttplate; stippled pistol grip and forend. **Sights:** None furnished; has 11mm integral dovetail scope mount. **Features:** Based on the Sako P45S action with two bolt locking lugs, 50-degree bolt lift and 30mm throw; adjustable trigger. Introduced 1999. Imported from Finland by Stoeger Industries.
Price: **$924.00**

SAVAGE MARK I-G BOLT-ACTION RIFLE

Caliber: 22 LR, single shot. **Barrel:** 20-3/4". **Weight:** 5-1/2 lbs. **Length:** 39-1/2" overall. **Stock:** Walnut-finished hardwood with Monte Carlo-type comb, checkered grip and forend. **Sights:** Bead front, open adjustable rear. Receiver grooved for scope mounting. **Features:** Thumb-operated rotating safety. Blue finish. Rifled or smooth bore. Introduced 1990. Made in Canada, from Savage Arms Inc.
Price: Mark I, rifled or smooth bore, right- or left-handed **$119.00**
Price: Mark I-GY (Youth), 19" barrel, 37" overall, 5 lbs. **$119.00**

SAVAGE MARK II-G BOLT-ACTION RIFLE

Caliber: 22 LR, 10-shot magazine. **Barrel:** 20-1/2". **Weight:** 5-1/2 lbs. **Length:** 39-1/2" overall. **Stock:** Walnut-finished hardwood with Monte Carlo-type comb, checkered grip and forend. **Sights:** Bead front, open ad-

justable rear. Receiver grooved for scope mounting. **Features:** Thumb-operated rotating safety. Blue finish. Introduced 1990. Made in Canada, from Savage Arms, Inc.
Price: **$126.00**
Price: Mark II-GY (youth), 19" barrel, 37" overall, 5 lbs. **$126.00**
Price: Mark II-GL, left-hand **$126.00**
Price: Mark II-GLY (youth) left-hand. **$126.00**
Price: Mark II-GXP Package Gun (comes with 4x15 scope), right- or left-handed **$131.00**
Price: Mark II-FXP (as above except with black synthetic stock) . . **$125.00**
Price: Mark II-F (as above, no scope) **$119.00**

Savage Mark II-LV Heavy Barrel Rifle

Similar to the Mark II-G except has heavy 21" barrel with recessed target-style crown; gray, laminated hardwood stock with cut checkering. No sights furnished, but has dovetailed receiver for scope mounting. Overall length is 39-3/4", weight is 6-1/2 lbs. Comes with 10-shot clip magazine. Introduced 1997. Imported from Canada by Savage Arms, Inc.
Price: **$200.00**
Price: Mark II-FV, with black graphite/polymer stock **$174.00**

Savage Mark II-FSS Stainless Rifle

Similar to the Mark II-G except has stainless steel barreled action and graphite/polymer filled stock; free-floated barrel. Weighs 5 lbs. Introduced 1997. Imported from Canada by Savage Arms, Inc.
Price: **$150.00**

Savage Model 93FVSS Magnum Rifle

Similar to the Model 93FSS Magnum except has 21" heavy barrel with recessed target-style crown; satin-finished stainless barreled action; black graphite/fiberglass stock. Drilled and tapped for scope mounting; comes with Weaver-style bases. Introduced 1998. Imported from Canada by Savage Arms, Inc.
Price: **$201.00**

SAVAGE MODEL 93G MAGNUM BOLT-ACTION RIFLE

Caliber: 22 WMR, 5-shot magazine. **Barrel:** 20-3/4". **Weight:** 5-3/4 lbs. **Length:** 39-1/2" overall. **Stock:** Walnut-finished hardwood with Monte Carlo-type comb, checkered grip and forend. **Sights:** Bead front, adjust-

NEW!

Savage Model 93G

Ultra Light Arms Model 20

Winchester Model 52B

able open rear. Receiver grooved for scope mount. **Features:** Thumb-operated rotary safety. Blue finish. Introduced 1994. Made in Canada, from Savage Arms.
Price: About **$145.00**
Price: Model 93F (as above with black graphite/fiberglass stock) . **$139.00**

Savage Model 93FSS Magnum Rifle

Similar to the Model 93G except has stainless steel barreled action and black synthetic stock with positive checkering. Weighs 5-1/2 lbs. Introduced 1997. Imported from Canada by Savage Arms, Inc.
Price: **$175.00**

ULTRA LIGHT ARMS MODEL 20 RF BOLT-ACTION RIFLE

Caliber: 22 LR, single shot or 5-shot repeater. **Barrel:** 22" Douglas Premium, #1 contour. **Weight:** 5 lbs., 3 oz. **Length:** 41-1/2" overall. **Stock:**

Composite Kevlar, graphite reinforced. DuPont Imron paint; 13-1/2" length of pull. **Sights:** None furnished. Drilled and tapped for scope mounting. **Features:** Available as either single shot or repeater with 5-shot removable magazine. Comes with scope mounts. Left-hand model available. Introduced 1993. Made in U.S. by Colt Rifles, Inc.
Price: Single shot **$800.00**
Price: Repeater **$850.00**

WINCHESTER MODEL 52B BOLT-ACTION RIFLE

Caliber: 22 Long Rifle, 5-shot magazine. **Barrel:** 24". **Weight:** 7 lbs. **Length:** 41-3/4" overall. **Stock:** Walnut with checkered grip and forend. **Sights:** None furnished; grooved receiver and drilled and tapped for scope mounting. **Features:** Has Micro Motion trigger adjustable for pull and over-travel; match chamber; detachable magazine. Reintroduced 1997. From U.S. Repeating Arms Co.
Price: **$654.00**

*Includes models for classic American and ISU target competition
and other sporting and competitive shooting.*

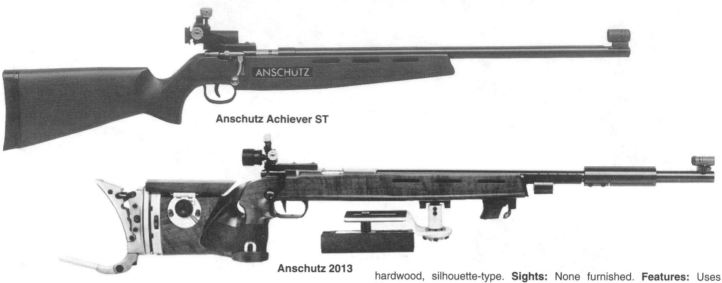

Anschutz Achiever ST

Anschutz 2013

ANSCHUTZ 1451R SPORTER TARGET RIFLE

Caliber: 22 LR, 5-shot magazine. **Barrel:** 22" heavy match. **Weight:** 6.4 lbs. **Length:** 39.75" overall. **Stock:** European hardwood with walnut finish. **Sights:** None furnished. Grooved receiver for scope mounting or Anschutz micrometer rear sight. **Features:** Sliding safety, two-stage trigger. Adjustable buttplate; forend slide rail to accept Anschutz accessories. Imported from Germany by AcuSport Corp.
Price: **$549.00**

ANSCHUTZ ACHIEVER ST SUPER TARGET RIFLE

Caliber: 22 LR, single shot. **Barrel:** 22", .75" diameter. **Weight:** About 6.5 lbs. **Length:** 38.75" to 39.75" overall. **Stock:** Walnut-finished European hardwood with hand-stippled panels on grip and forend; 13.5" accessory rail on forend. **Sights:** Optional. Receiver grooved for scope mounting. **Features:** Designed for the advanced junior shooter with adjustable length of pull from 13.25" to 14.25" via removable butt spacers. Two-stage #5066 adjustable trigger factory set at 2.6 lbs. Introduced 1994. Imported from Germany by Gunsmithing, Inc.
Price: **$329.95**
Price: #6834 Match Sight Set **$185.00**

ANSCHUTZ 1808D-RT SUPER RUNNING TARGET RIFLE

Caliber: 22 LR, single shot. **Barrel:** 32-1/2". **Weight:** 9.4 lbs. **Length:** 50.5" overall. **Stock:** European walnut. Heavy beavertail forend; adjustable cheekpiece and buttplate. Stippled grip and forend. **Sights:** None furnished. Grooved for scope mounting. **Features:** Designed for Running Target competition. Nine-way adjustable single-stage trigger, slide safety. Introduced 1991. Imported from Germany by Accuracy International, Gunsmithing, Inc.
Price: Right-hand . . . . **$1,300.10 to $1,410.00**

ANSCHUTZ 1903 MATCH RIFLE

Caliber: 22 LR, single shot. **Barrel:** 25", .75" diameter. **Weight:** 8.6 lbs. **Length:** 43.75" overall. **Stock:** Walnut-finished hardwood with adjustable cheekpiece; stippled grip and forend. **Sights:** None furnished. **Features:** Uses Anschutz Match 64 action and #5098 two-stage trigger. A medium weight rifle for intermediate and advanced Junior Match competition. Introduced 1987. Imported from Germany by Accuracy International, Gunsmithing, Inc.
Price: Right-hand . . . . **$720.40 to $775.00**
Price: Left-hand . . . . **$757.90 to $815.00**

ANSCHUTZ 64-MSR SILHOUETTE RIFLE

Caliber: 22 LR, 5-shot magazine. **Barrel:** 21-1/2", medium heavy; 7/8" diameter. **Weight:** 8 lbs. **Length:** 39.5" overall. **Stock:** Walnut-finished hardwood, silhouette-type. **Sights:** None furnished. **Features:** Uses Match 64 action. Designed for metallic silhouette competition. Stock has stippled checkering, contoured thumb groove with Wundhammer swell. Two-stage #5091 trigger. Slide safety locks sear and bolt. Introduced 1980. Imported from Germany by AcuSport Corp., Accuracy International, Gunsmithing, Inc.
Price: 64-MSR . . . . **$725.00 to $1,129.95**

ANSCHUTZ 2013 BENCHREST RIFLE

Caliber: 22 LR, single shot. **Barrel:** 19.75". **Weight:** About 11 lbs. **Length:** 37.75" to 42.5" overall. **Stock:** Benchrest style of European hardwood. Stock length adjustable via spacers and buttplate. **Sights:** None furnished. Receiver grooved for mounts. **Features:** Uses the Anschutz 2013 target action, #5018 two-stage adjustable target trigger factory set at 3.9 oz. Introduced 1994. Imported from Germany by Accuracy International, Gunsmithing, Inc.
Price: . . . . **$1,725.00 to $2,405.10**

Anschutz 2007 Match Rifle

Uses same action as the Model 2013, but has a lighter barrel. European walnut stock in right-hand, true left-hand or extra-short models. Sights optional. Available with 19.6" barrel with extension tube, or 26", both in stainless or blue. Introduced 1998. Imported from Germany by Gunsmithing, Inc., Accuracy International.
Price: Right-hand, blue, no sights . . . . **$1,697.00 to $1,725.00**
Price: Right-hand, blue, no sights, extra-short stock **$1,655.70**
Price: Left-hand, blue, no sights . . . . **$1,783.40 to $1,795.00**

ANSCHUTZ 1827B BIATHLON RIFLE

Caliber: 22 LR, 5-shot magazine. **Barrel:** 21-1/2". **Weight:** 8-1/2 lbs. with sights. **Length:** 42-1/2" overall. **Stock:** European walnut with cheekpiece, stippled pistol grip and forend. **Sights:** Optional globe front specially designed for Biathlon shooting, micrometer rear with hinged snow cap. **Features:** Uses Super Match 54 action and nine-way adjustable trigger; adjustable wooden buttplate, Biathlon butthook, adjustable hand-stop rail. Introduced 1982. Imported from Germany by Accuracy International, Gunsmithing, Inc.
Price: Right-hand, with sights, about . . . . **$1,500.50 to $1,555.00**

Anschutz 1827BT Fortner Biathlon Rifle

Similar to the Anschutz 1827B Biathlon rifle except uses Anschutz/Fortner system straight-pull bolt action, stainless steel barrel. Introduced 1982. Imported from Germany by Accuracy International, Gunsmithing, Inc.
Price: Right-hand, with sights . . . . **$2,155.10 to $2,210.00**
Price: Left-hand, with sights . . . . **$2,350.00 to $2,395.00**
Price: Right-hand, sights, stainless barrel (Gunsmithing, Inc.) **$2,295.00**

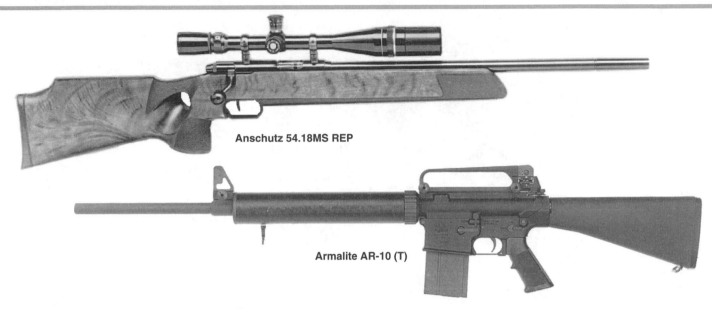

Anschutz 54.18MS REP

Armalite AR-10 (T)

ANSCHUTZ SUPER MATCH SPECIAL MODEL 2013 RIFLE
Caliber: 22 LR, single shot. **Barrel:** 19.75" (26" with tube installed). **Weight:** 15.5 lbs. **Length:** 43" to 45.5" overall. **Stock:** European walnut; target adjustable. **Sights:** Optional. Uses #7020/20 sight set. **Features:** Improved Super Match 54 action, #5018 trigger give fastest consistent lock time for a production target rifle. Barrel is micro-honed; trigger has nine points of adjustment, two stages. Slide safety. Comes with test target. Introduced 1992. Imported from Germany by Accuracy International, Gunsmithing, Inc.
Price: Right-hand .... $2,405.10 to $2,495.00
Price: Left-hand .... $2,526.00 to $2,610.00

ANSCHUTZ 1808 MSR SILHOUETTE RIFLE
Caliber: 22 LR, 5-shot magazine. **Barrel:** 22.4" match; detachable muzzle tube. **Weight:** 7.9 lbs. **Length:** 40.9" overall. **Stock:** European walnut, thumbhole design. **Sights:** None furnished. **Features:** Uses Anschutz 54.18 barreled action with two-stage match trigger. Introduced 1997. Imported from Germany by Accuracy International, AcuSport Corp.
Price: .... $1,425.00 to $2,219.95

ANSCHUTZ 1911 PRONE MATCH RIFLE
Caliber: 22 LR, single shot. **Barrel:** 27-1/4". **Weight:** 11 lbs. **Length:** 46" overall. **Stock:** Walnut-finished European hardwood; American prone-style with adjustable cheekpiece, textured pistol grip, forend with swivel rail and adjustable rubber buttplate. **Sights:** None furnished. Receiver grooved for Anschutz sights (extra) **Features:** Two-stage #5018 trigger adjustable from 2.1 to 8.6 oz. Extremely fast lock time. Stainless or blue barrel. Imported from Germany by Accuracy International, Gunsmithing, Inc.
Price: Right-hand, no sights .... $1,656.20 to $2,094.95

Anschutz 1913 Super Match Rifle
Same as the Model 1911 except European walnut International-type stock with adjustable cheekpiece, or color laminate, both available with straight or lowered forend, adjustable aluminum hook buttplate, adjustable hand stop, weighs 15.5 lbs., 46" overall. Stainless or blue barrel. Imported from Germany by Accuracy International, Gunsmithing, Inc.
Price: Right-hand, blue, no sights, walnut stock... $2,139.00 to $2,175.00
Price: Right-hand, blue, no sights, color laminate stock....... $2,199.40
Price: Right-hand, blue, no sights, walnut, lowered forend $2,181.80
Price: Right-hand, blue, no sights, color laminate, lowered forend.. $2,242.20
Price: Left-hand, blue, no sights, walnut stock.... $2,233.10 to $2,275.00

Anschutz 54.18MS REP Deluxe Silhouette Rifle
Same basic action and trigger specifications as the Anschutz 1913 Super Match but with removable 5-shot clip magazine, 22" barrel extendable to 30" using optional extension and weight set. Receiver drilled and tapped for scope mounting. Walnut Silhouette stock. Introduced 1990. Imported from Germany by Accuracy International, Gunsmithing, Inc.
Price: .... $1,140.00 to $1,151.70

Anschutz 1907 ISU Standard Match Rifle
Same action as Model 1913 but with 7/8" diameter 26" barrel (stainless or blue). Length is 44.5" overall, weighs 10 lbs. Choice of stock configurations. Vented forend. Designed for prone and position shooting ISU requirements; suitable for NRA matches. Also available with walnut flat-forend stock for benchrest shooting. Imported from Germany by Accuracy International, Gunsmithing, Inc.
Price: Right-hand, blue, no sights, hardwood stock . $1,253.40 to $1,299.00
Price: Right-hand, blue, no sights, colored laminated stock .... $1,316.10 to $1,375.00
Price: Right-hand, blue, no sights, walnut stock... $1,299.30 to $1,355.00
Price: Left-hand, blue barrel, no sights, hardwood stock.................................... $1,320.00 to $1,375.00

ANSCHUTZ 1909 MATCH RIFLE
Caliber: 22 LR, single shot. **Barrel:** 26" match. **Weight:** 14.3 lbs. **Length:** 44.8" overall. **Stock:** European beechwood, thumbhole design with hook buttplate, hand stop with swivel. **Sights:** None furnished. **Features:** Uses Match 54 action. Adjustable comb, buttplate; forend rail accepts Anschutz adjustable palm rest. Imported from Germany by Gunsmithing, Inc.
Price: $1,724.50

ARMALITE AR-10 (T) RIFLE
Caliber: 308, 10-shot magazine. **Barrel:** 24" target-weight Rock 5R custom. **Weight:** 10.4 lbs. **Length:** 43.5" overall. **Stock:** Green or black compostion; N.M. fiberglass handguard tube. **Sights:** Detachable handle, front sight, or scope mount available. Comes with international-style flat-top receiver with Picatinny rail. **Features:** National Match two-stage trigger. Forged upper receiver. Receivers hard-coat amodized. Introduced 1995. Made in U.S. by ArmaLite, Inc.
Price: $2,075.00
Price: AR-10 (T) Carbine, lighter 16" barrel, single stage trigger, weighs 8.8 lbs. $1,970.00

ARMALITE M15A4 (T) EAGLE EYE RIFLE
Caliber: 223, 7-shot magazine. **Barrel:** 24" heavy stainless; 1:8" twist. **Weight:** 9.2 lbs. **Length:** 42-3/8" overall. **Stock:** Green or black butt, N.M. fiberglass handguard tube. **Sights:** One-piece international-style flattop receiver with Weaver-type rail, including case deflector. **Features:** Detachable carry handle, front sight and scope mount (30mm or 1") available. Upper and lower receivers have push-type pivot pin, hard coat anodized. Made in U.S. by ArmaLite, Inc.
Price: $1,378.00

Bushmaster XM15 E2S Target

Bushmaster V-Match

Bushmaster DCM

ARMALITE M15A4 ACTION MASTER RIFLE

Caliber: 223, 7-shot magazine. **Barrel:** 20" heavy stainless; 1:9" twist. **Weight:** 9 lbs. **Length:** 40-1/2" overall. **Stock:** Green or black plastic; N.M. fiberglass handguard tube. **Sights:** One-piece international-style flattop receiver with Weaver-type rail. **Features:** Detachable carry handle, front sight and scope mount available. National Match two-stage trigger group; Picatinny rail; upper and lower receivers have push-type pivot pin; hard coat anodized finish. Made in U.S. by ArmaLite, Inc.
Price: **$1,175.00**

BLASER R93 LONG RANGE RIFLE

Caliber: 308 Win., 10-shot detachable box magazine. **Barrel:** 24". **Weight:** 10.4 lbs. **Length:** 44" overall. **Stock:** Aluminum with synthetic lining. **Sights:** None furnished; accepts detachable scope mount. **Features:** Straight-pull bolt action with adjustable trigger; fully adjustable stock; quick takedown; corrosion resistant finish. Introduced 1998. Imported from Germany by Sigarms.
Price: **$2,130.00**

BUSHMASTER XM15 E2S TARGET MODEL RIFLE

Caliber: 223. **Barrel:** 20", 24", 26"; 1:9" twist; heavy. **Weight:** 8.3 lbs. **Length:** 38.25" overall (20" barrel). **Stock:** Black composition; A2 type. **Sights:** Adjustable post front, adjustable aperture rear. **Features:** Patterned after Colt M-16A2. Chrome-lined barrel with manganese phosphate exterior. Forged aluminum receivers with push-pin takedown. Made in U.S. by Bushmaster Firearms Co./Quality Parts Co.
Price: 20" match heavy barrel **$925.00**

Bushmaster DCM Competition Rifle

Similar to the XM15 E2S Target Model except has 20" extra-heavy (1" diameter) barrel with 1.8" twist for heavier competition bullets. Weighs about 12 lbs. with balance weights. Has special competition rear sight with interchangeable apertures, extra-fine 1/2- or 1/4-MOA windage and elevation adjustments; specially ground front sight post in choice of three widths. Full-length handguards over free-floater barrel tube. Introduced 1998. Made in U.S. by Bushmaster Firearms, Inc.
Price: **$1,495.00**

BUSHMASTER XM15 E2S V-MATCH RIFLE

Caliber: 223. **Barrel:** 20", 24", 26"; 1:9" twist; heavy. **Weight:** 8.1 lbs. **Length:** 38.25" overall (20" barrel). **Stock:** Black composition. A2 type. **Sights:** None furnished; upper receiver has integral scope mount base. **Features:** Chrome-lined .950" heavy barrel with counterbored crown, manganese phosphate finish; free-floating aluminum handguard; forged aluminum receivers with push-pin takedown, hard anodized mil-spec finish. Competition trigger optional. Made in U.S. by Bushmaster Firearms, Inc.
Price: 20" Match heavy barrel **$995.00**
Price: 24" Match heavy barrel **$1,010.00**
Price: 26" Match heavy barrel **$1,025.00**
Price: V-Match Carbine (16" barrel) **$985.00**

COLT MATCH TARGET MODEL RIFLE

Caliber: 223 Rem., 8-shot magazine. **Barrel:** 20". **Weight:** 7.5 lbs. **Length:** 39" overall. **Stock:** Composition stock, grip, forend. **Sights:** Post front, aperture rear adjustable for windage and elevation. **Features:** Five-round detachable box magazine, standard-weight barrel, sling swivels. Has forward bolt assist. Military matte black finish. Model introduced 1991.
Price: **$1,040.00**
Price: With compensator **$1,150.00**

Colt Accurized Rifle

Similar to the Colt Match Target Model except has 24" stainless steel heavy barrel with 1.9" rifling, flattop receiver with scope mount and 1" rings, weighs 9.25 lbs. Introduced 1998. Made in U.S. by Colt's Mfg. Co., Inc.
Price: **$1,295.00**

Colt Match Target HBAR

Harris Gunworks Long Range

Harris Gunworks M-86

Colt Match Target HBAR Rifle

Similar to the Target Model except has heavy barrel, 800-meter rear sight adjustable for windage and elevation. Introduced 1991.

Price: $1,085.00

Colt Match Target Competition HBAR Rifle

Similar to the Sporter Target except has flat-top receiver with integral Weaver-type base for scope mounting. Counter-bored muzzle, 1:9" rifling twist. Introduced 1991.

Price: Model R6700 .... $1,090.00

Colt Match Target Competition HBAR II Rifle

Similar to the Match Target Competition HBAR except has 16.1" barrel, weighs 7.1 lbs., overall length 34.5"; 1:9" twist barrel. Introduced 1995.

Price: $1,065.00

E.A.A./HW 660 MATCH RIFLE

Caliber: 22 LR. Barrel: 26". Weight: 10.7 lbs. Length: 45.3" overall. Stock: Match-type walnut with adjustable cheekpiece and buttplate. Sights: Globe front, match aperture rear. Features: Adjustable match trigger; stippled pistol grip and forend; forend accessory rail. Introduced 1991. Imported from Germany by European American Armory.

Price: About $951.60
Price: With laminate stock $998.40

HARRIS GUNWORKS NATIONAL MATCH RIFLE

Caliber: 7mm-08, 308, 5-shot magazine. Barrel: 24", stainless steel. Weight: About 11 lbs. (std. bbl.). Length: 43" overall. Stock: Fiberglass with adjustable buttplate. Sights: Barrel band and Tompkins front; no rear sight furnished. Features: Gunworks repeating action with clip slot, Canjar trigger. Match-grade barrel. Available in right-hand only. Fiberglass

stock, sight installation, special machining and triggers optional. Introduced 1989. From Harris Gunworks, Inc.

Price: $3,500.00

HARRIS GUNWORKS LONG RANGE RIFLE

Caliber: 300 Win. Mag., 7mm Rem. Mag., 300 Phoenix, 338 Lapua, single shot. Barrel: 26", stainless steel, match-grade. Weight: 14 lbs. Length: 46-1/2" overall. Stock: Fiberglass with adjustable buttplate and cheekpiece. Adjustable for length of pull, drop, cant and cast-off. Sights: Barrel band and Tompkins front; no rear sight furnished. Features: Uses Gunworks solid bottom single shot action and Canjar trigger. Barrel twist 1:12". Introduced 1989. From Harris Gunworks, Inc.

Price: $3,620.00

HARRIS GUNWORKS M-86 SNIPER RIFLE

Caliber: 308, 30-06, 4-shot magazine; 300 Win. Mag., 3-shot magazine. Barrel: 24", Gunworks match-grade in heavy contour. Weight: 11-1/4 lbs. (308), 11-1/2 lbs. (30-06, 300). Length: 43-1/2" overall. Stock: Specially designed McHale fiberglass stock with textured grip and forend, recoil pad. Sights: None furnished. Features: Uses Gunworks repeating action. Comes with bipod. Matte black finish. Sling swivels. Introduced 1989. From Harris Gunworks, Inc.

Price: $2,700.00

HARRIS GUNWORKS M-89 SNIPER RIFLE

Caliber: 308 Win., 5-shot magazine. Barrel: 28" (with suppressor). Weight: 15 lbs., 4 oz. Stock: Fiberglass; adjustable for length; recoil pad. Sights: None furnished. Drilled and tapped for scope mounting. Features: Uses Gunworks repeating action. Comes with bipod. Introduced 1990. From Harris Gunworks, Inc.

Price: Standard (non-suppressed) $3,200.00

Marlin Model 2000L

Marlin Model 7000T

Olympic PCR-1

HARRIS GUNWORKS COMBO M-87 SERIES 50-CALIBER RIFLES

Caliber: 50 BMG, single shot. **Barrel:** 29, with muzzle brake. **Weight:** About 21-1/2 lbs. **Length:** 53" overall. **Stock:** Gunworks fiberglass. **Sights:** None furnished. **Features:** Right-handed Gunworks stainless steel receiver, chrome-moly barrel with 1:15" twist. Introduced 1987. From Harris Gunworks, Inc.

Price: $3,885.00
Price: M87R 5-shot repeater $4,000.00
Price: M-87 (5-shot repeater) "Combo" $4,300.00
Price: M-92 Bullpup (shortened M-87 single shot with bullpup stock) $4,770.00
Price: M-93 (10-shot repeater with folding stock, detachable magazine)..................................... $4,150.00

MARLIN MODEL 2000L TARGET RIFLE

Caliber: 22 LR, single shot. **Barrel:** 22" heavy, Micro-Groove® rifling, match chamber, recessed muzzle. **Weight:** 8 lbs. **Length:** 41" overall. **Stock:** Laminated black/gray with ambidextrous pistol grip. **Sights:** Hooded front with ten aperture inserts, fully adjustable target rear peep. **Features:** Buttplate adjustable for length of pull, height and angle. Aluminum forend rail with stop and quick-detachable swivel. Two-stage target trigger; red cocking indicator. Five-shot adaptor kit available. Introduced 1991. From Marlin.

Price: $656.00

MARLIN MODEL 7000T SELF-LOADING RIFLE

NEW! **Caliber:** 22 LR, 10-shot magazine. **Barrel:** 18" heavy target with Micro-Groove® rifling. **Weight:** 7-1/2 lbs. **Length:** 37" overall. **Stock:** Laminated red, white and blue hardwood with ambidextrous pistol grip, adjustable buttplate, aluminum forend rail. **Sights:** None furnished; grooved receiver for scope mounting. **Features:** Trigger stop; last-shot bolt hold-open; blue finish; scope mounts included. Introduced 1999. Made in U.S. by Marlin.

Price: $442.00

OLYMPIC ARMS PCR-SERVICEMATCH RIFLE

Caliber: 223, 10-shot magazine. **Barrel:** 20", broach-cut 416 stainless steel. **Weight:** About 10 lbs. **Length:** 39.5" overall. **Stock:** A2 stowaway grip and trapdoor buttstock. **Sights:** Post front, E2-NM fully adjustable aperture rear. **Features:** Based on the AR-15. Conforms to all DCM standards. Free-floating 1:8.5" or 1:10" barrel; crowned barrel; no bayonet lug. Introduced 1996. Made in U.S. by Olympic Arms, Inc.

Price: $1,062.00

OLYMPIC ARMS PCR-1 RIFLE

Caliber: 223, 10-shot magazine. **Barrel:** 20", 24"; 416 stainless steel. **Weight:** 10 lbs., 3 oz. **Length:** 38.25" overall with 20" barrel. **Stock:** A2 stowaway grip and trapdoor butt. **Sights:** None supplied; flattop upper receiver, cut-down front sight base. **Features:** Based on the AR-15 rifle. Broach-cut, free-floating barrel with 1:8.5" or 1:10" twist. No bayonet lug. Crowned barrel; fluting available. Introduced 1994. Made in U.S. by Olympic Arms, Inc.

Price: $1,038.00

Olympic Arms PCR-2, PCR-3 Rifles

Similar to the PCR-1 except has 16" barrel, weighs 8 lbs., 2 oz.; has post front sight, fully adjustable aperture rear. Model PCR-3 has flattop upper receiver, cut-down front sight base. Introduced 1994. Made in U.S. by Olympic Arms, Inc.

Price: $958.00

REMINGTON 40-XB RANGEMASTER TARGET CENTERFIRE

Caliber: 15 calibers from 220 Swift to 300 Win. Mag. **Barrel:** 27-1/4". **Weight:** 11-1/4 lbs. **Length:** 47" overall. **Stock:** American walnut, laminated thumbhole or Kevlar with high comb and beavertail forend stop. Rubber non-slip buttplate. **Sights:** None. Scope blocks installed. **Features:** Adjustable trigger. Stainless barrel and action. Receiver drilled and tapped for sights.

Price: Standard single shot $1,529.00
Price: Repeater $1,645.00

REMINGTON 40-XBBR KS

Caliber: Five calibers from 22 BR to 308 Win. **Barrel:** 20" (light varmint class), 24" (heavy varmint class). **Weight:** 7-1/4 lbs. (light varmint class); 12 lbs. (heavy varmint class). **Length:** 38" (20" bbl.), 42" (24" bbl.). **Stock:** Kevlar. **Sights:** None. Supplied with scope blocks. **Features:** Unblued stainless steel barrel, trigger adjustable from 1-1/2 lbs. to 3-1/2 lbs. Special 2-oz. trigger at extra cost. Scope and mounts extra.

Price: With Kevlar stock $1,702.00

Sako TRG-21

Savage Model 112BT

Savage Model 900TR

Springfield, Inc. M1A Super Match

REMINGTON 40-XC TARGET RIFLE

Caliber: 7.62 NATO, 5-shot. **Barrel:** 24", stainless steel. **Weight:** 11 lbs. without sights. **Length:** 43-1/2" overall. **Stock:** Kevlar, with palm rail. **Sights:** None furnished. **Features:** Designed to meet the needs of competitive shooters. Stainless steel barrel and action.
Price: **$1,702.00**

REMINGTON 40-XR KS RIMFIRE POSITION RIFLE

Caliber: 22 LR, single shot. **Barrel:** 24", heavy target.
Weight: 10 lbs. **Length:** 43" overall. **Stock:** Kevlar. Position-style with front swivel block on forend guide rail. **Sights:** Drilled and tapped. Furnished with scope blocks. **Features:** Meets all ISU specifications. Deep forend, buttplate vertically adjustable, wide adjustable trigger.
Price: **$1,585.00**

SAKO TRG-21 BOLT-ACTION RIFLE

Caliber: 308 Win., 10-shot magazine. **Barrel:** 25.75". **Weight:** 10.5 lbs. **Length:** 46.5" overall. **Stock:** Reinforced polyurethane with fully adjustable cheekpiece and buttplate. **Sights:** None furnished. Optional quick-detachable, one-piece scope mount base, 1" or 30mm rings. **Features:** Resistance-free bolt, free-floating heavy stainless barrel, 60-degree bolt lift. Two-stage trigger is adjustable for length, pull, horizontal or vertical pitch. Introduced 1993. Imported from Finland by Stoeger Industries.
Price: **$2,699.00**
Price: Model TRG-41, as above except in 338 Lapua Mag **$3,099.00**

SAVAGE MODEL 900TR TARGET RIFLE

Caliber: 22 LR, 5-shot magazine. **Barrel:** 25". **Weight:** 8 lbs. **Length:** 43-5/8" overall. **Stock:** Target-type, walnut-finished hardwood. **Sights:** Target front with inserts, peep rear with 1/4-minute click adjustments. **Features:** Comes with shooting rail and hand stop. Introduced 1991. Made in Canada, from Savage Arms Inc.
Price: Right- or left-hand **$415.00**

SAVAGE MODEL 112BT COMPETITION GRADE RIFLE

Caliber: 223, 308, 5-shot magazine, 300 Win. Mag., single shot. **Barrel:** 26", heavy contour stainless with black finish; 1:9" twist (223), 1:10" (308). **Weight:** 10.8 lbs. **Length:** 47.5" overall. **Stock:** Laminated wood with straight comb, adjustable cheek rest, Wundhammer palm swell, ventilated forend. Recoil pad is adjustable for length of pull. **Sights:** None furnished; drilled and tapped for scope mounting and aperture target-style sights. Recessed target-style muzzle has .812" diameter section for universal target sight base. **Features:** Pillar-bedded stock, matte black alloy receiver. Bolt has black titanium nitride coating, large handle ball. Has alloy accessory rail on forend. Comes with safety gun lock, target and ear puffs. Introduced 1994. Made in U.S. by Savage Arms, Inc.
Price: **$1,000.00**
Price: 300 Win. Mag. (single shot 112BT-S) **$1,000.00**

SPRINGFIELD, INC. M1A SUPER MATCH

Caliber: 308 Win. **Barrel:** 22", heavy Douglas Premium. **Weight:** About 10 lbs. **Length:** 44.31" overall. **Stock:** Heavy walnut competition stock with

Springfield, Inc. M1A/M-21

longer pistol grip, contoured area behind the rear sight, thicker butt and forend, glass bedded. **Sights:** National Match front and rear. **Features:** Has figure-eight-style operating rod guide. Introduced 1987. From Springfield, Inc.
Price: About **$2,479.00**

Springfield, Inc. M1A/M-21 Tactical Model Rifle
Similar to the M1A Super Match except has special sniper stock with adjustable cheekpiece and rubber recoil pad. Weighs 11.2 lbs. From Springfield, Inc.
Price: **$2,204.00**

STONER SR-15 MATCH RIFLE
Caliber: 223. **Barrel:** 20". **Weight:** 7.9 lbs. **Length:** 38" overall. **Stock:** Black synthetic. **Sights:** None furnished; flat-top upper receiver for scope mounting. **Features:** Short Picatinny rail; two-stage match trigger. Introduced 1998. Made in U.S. by Knight's Mfg.Co.
Price: **$1,595.00**

STONER SR-25 MATCH RIFLE
Caliber: 7.62 NATO, 10-shot steel magazine, 5-shot optional. **Barrel:** 24" heavy match; 1:11.25" twist. **Weight:** 10.75 lbs. **Length:** 44" overall. **Stock:** Black synthetic AR-15A2 design. Full floating forend of Mil-spec synthetic attaches to upper receiver at a single point. **Sights:** None furnished. Has integral Weaver-style rail. Rings and iron sights optional. **Features:** Improved AR-15 trigger; AR-15-style seven-lug rotating bolt. Gas block rail mounts detachable front sight. Introduced 1993. Made in U.S. by Knight's Mfg. Co.
Price: **$2,995.00**
Price: SR-25 Lightweight Match (20" medium match target contour barrel, 9.5 lbs., 40" overall) **$2,995.00**

TANNER 50 METER FREE RIFLE
Caliber: 22 LR, single shot. **Barrel:** 27.7". **Weight:** 13.9 lbs. **Length:** 44.4" overall. **Stock:** Seasoned walnut with palm rest, accessory rail, adjustable

hook buttplate. **Sights:** Globe front with interchangeable inserts, Tanner micrometer-diopter rear with adjustable aperture. **Features:** Bolt action with externally adjustable set trigger. Supplied with 50-meter test target. Imported from Switzerland by Mandall Shooting Supplies. Introduced 1984.
Price: About **$3,900.00**

TANNER STANDARD UIT RIFLE
Caliber: 308, 7.5mm Swiss, 10-shot. **Barrel:** 25.9". **Weight:** 10.5 lbs. **Length:** 40.6" overall. **Stock:** Match style of seasoned nutwood with accessory rail; coarsely stippled pistol grip; high cheekpiece; vented forend. **Sights:** Globe front with interchangeable inserts, Tanner micrometer-diopter rear with adjustable aperture. **Features:** Two locking lug revolving bolt encloses case head. Trigger adjustable from 1/2 to 6-1/2 lbs.; match trigger optional. Comes with 300-meter test target. Imported from Switzerland by Mandall Shooting Supplies. Introduced 1984.
Price: About **$4,700.00**

TANNER 300 METER FREE RIFLE
Caliber: 308 Win., 7.5 Swiss, single shot. **Barrel:** 27.58". **Weight:** 15 lbs. **Length:** 45.3" overall. **Stock:** Seasoned walnut, thumbhole style, with accessory rail, palm rest, adjustable hook butt. **Sights:** Globe front with interchangeable inserts, Tanner-design micrometer-diopter rear with adjustable aperture. **Features:** Three-lug revolving-lock bolt design; adjustable set trigger; short firing pin travel; supplied with 300-meter test target. Imported from Switzerland by Mandall Shooting Supplies. Introduced 1984.
Price: About **$4,900.00**

TIKKA SPORTER RIFLE
Caliber: 223, 22-250, 308, detachable 5-shot magazine. **Barrel:** 23-1/2" heavy. **Weight:** 9 lbs. **Length:** 43-5/8" overall. **Stock:** European walnut with adjustable comb, adjustable buttplate; stippled grip and forend. **Sights:** None furnished; drilled and tapped for scope mounting. **Features:** Buttplate is adjustable for distance, angle, height and pitch; adjustable trigger; free-floating barrel. Introduced 1998. Imported from Finland by Stoeger Industries.
Price: **$939.00**

Includes a wide variety of sporting guns and guns suitable for various competitions.

Benelli Legacy

Benelli M1 Super 90 Camouflage

Benelli Super Black Eagle

AMERICAN ARMS PHANTOM AUTO SHOTGUNS

Gauge: 12, 3" chamber. **Barrel:** 24", 26", 28" (Imp. Cyl., Mod., Full choke tubes). **Stock:** European walnut or black synthetic. **Features:** Gas-operated action; blued barrel; checkered pistol grip and forend; vent rib barrel. Introduced 1999. Imported by American Arms, Inc.

Price: . . . . **NA**

BENELLI LEGACY AUTO SHOTGUN

Gauge: 12, 20, 3" chamber. **Barrel:** 26", 28" (Full, Mod., Imp. Cyl., Imp. Mod., Skeet choke tubes). Mid-bead sight. **Weight:** 7.1 to 7.6 lbs. **Length:** 49-5/8" overall (26" barrel). **Stock:** European walnut with high-gloss finish. Special competition stock comes with drop adjustment kit. **Features:** Uses the Montefeltro rotating bolt inertia recoil operating system with a two-piece steel/aluminum etched receiver (bright on lower, blue upper). Drop adjustment kit allows the stock to be custom fitted without modifying the stock. Black lower receiver finish, blued upper. Introduced 1998. Imported from Italy by Heckler & Koch, Inc.

Price: **$1,320.00**

Benelli Sport Shotgun

Similar to the Legacy model except has matte blue receiver, two carbon fiber interchangeable ventilated ribs, adjustable butt pad, adjustable buttstock, and functions with ultra-light target loads. Walnut stock with satin finish. Introduced 1997. Imported from Italy by Benelli U.S.A.

Price: **$1,315.00**

BENELLI M1 FIELD AUTO SHOTGUN

Gauge: 12, 3" chamber. **Barrel:** 21", 24", 26", 28" (choke tubes). **Weight:** 7 lbs., 4 oz. **Stock:** High impact polymer; wood on 26", 28". **Sights:** Metal bead front. **Features:** Sporting version of the military & police gun. Uses the rotating Montefeltro bolt system. Ventilated rib; blue finish. Comes with set of five choke tubes. Imported from Italy by Benelli U.S.A.

Price: **$900.00**
Price: Wood stock version **$915.00**
Price: 24" rifled barrel, polymer stock. **$980.00**

Benelli M1 Super 90 Camouflage Field Shotgun

Similar to the M1 Super 90 Field except is covered with Realtree Xtra brown camouflage. Available with 24", 26", 28" barrel, polymer stock. Introduced 1997. Imported from Italy by Benelli U.S.A.

Price: **$990.00**

Benelli Montefeltro 90 Shotgun

Similar to the M1 Super 90 except has checkered walnut stock with high-gloss finish. Uses the Montefeltro rotating bolt system with a simple inertia recoil design. Full, Imp. Mod., Mod., Imp. Cyl. choke tubes. Weighs 7 - 7-1/2 lbs. Finish is matte black. Introduced 1987.

Price: 24", 26", 28" **$925.00**
Price: Left-hand, 26", 28" **$945.00**
Price: 20-ga., Montefeltro, 24", 26", 5-3/4 lbs. **$925.00**

Benelli Montefeltro 20-Gauge Shotgun

Similar to the 12-gauge Montefeltro Super 90 except chambered for 3" 20-gauge, 24" or 26" barrel (choke tubes), weighs 5 lbs., 12 oz. Has drop-adjustable walnut stock with gloss finish, blued receiver. Overall length 47.5". Introduced 1993. Imported from Italy by Benelli U.S.A.

Price: 24" and 26" barrels. **$925.00**
Price: 26", camouflage finish **$1,010.00**

BENELLI SUPER BLACK EAGLE SHOTGUN

Gauge: 12, 3-1/2" chamber. **Barrel:** 24", 26", 28" (Imp. Cyl., Mod., Imp. Mod., Full choke tubes). **Weight:** 7 lbs., 5 oz. **Length:** 49-5/8" overall (28" barrel). **Stock:** European walnut with satin finish, or polymer. Adjustable for drop. **Sights:** Bead front. **Features:** Uses Montefeltro inertia recoil bolt system. Fires all 12-gauge shells from 2-3/4" to 3-1/2" magnums. Introduced 1991. Imported from Italy by Benelli U.S.A.

Price: With 26" and 28" barrel, wood stock **$1,215.00**
Price: With 24", 26" barrel, polymer stock **$1,200.00**
Price: Left-hand, 24", 26", 28" **$1,225.00**

Benelli Super Black Eagle Slug Gun

Similar to the Benelli Super Black Eagle except has 24" rifled barrel with 3" chamber, and comes with scope mount base. Uses the Montefeltro inertia recoil bolt system. Matte-finish receiver. Weight is 7.5 lbs., overall length 45.5". Wood or polymer stocks available. Introduced 1992. Imported from Italy by Benelli U.S.A.

Price: With wood stock. **$1,255.00**
Price: With polymer stock. **$1,245.00**

Benelli Super Black Eagle Camouflage Shotgun

Similar to the Super Black Eagle except covered with Realtree Xtra Brown camouflage pattern and synthetic stock. Available with 24", 26", 28" barrel. Introduced 1997. Imported from Italy by Benelli U.S.A.

Price: **$1,300.00**
Price: **$1,310.00**

Benelli Executive Series Shotguns

Similar to the Super Black Eagle except has grayed steel lower receiver, hand-engraved and gold inlaid (Type III), and has highest grade of walnut

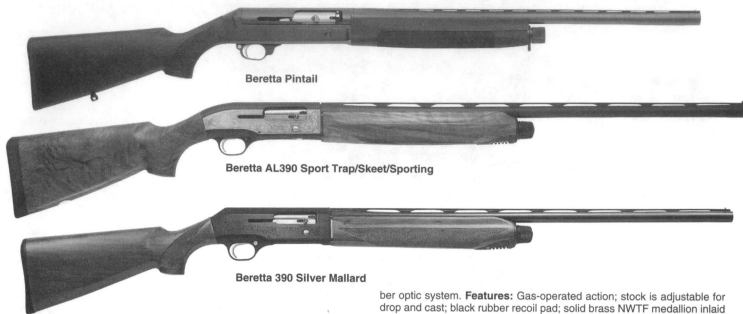

Beretta Pintail

Beretta AL390 Sport Trap/Skeet/Sporting

Beretta 390 Silver Mallard

stock with drop adjustment kit. Barrel lengths of 21", 24", 26", 28"; 3" chamber. **Special order only.** Introduced 1995. Imported from Italy by Benelli U.S.A.

Price: Type I (about two-thirds engraving coverage) **$4,950.00**
Price: Type II (full coverage engraving) **$5,600.00**
Price: Type III (full coverage, gold inlays). **$6,550.00**

BERETTA PINTAIL SYNTHETIC AUTO SHOTGUN

Gauge: 12, 3" chamber. **Barrel:** 24", 26" (choke tubes). **Weight:** 7.3 lbs. **Stock:** Synthetic. **Features:** Montefeltro-type short recoil action. Matte finish on stock and metal. Comes with sling swivels. Introduced 1993. Imported from Italy by Beretta U.S.A.
Price: **$815.00**

Beretta Pintail Rifled Slug Shotgun

Similar to the Pintail except has 24" fully rifled barrel with 1:28" twist; upper receiver drilled and tapped for scope mounting, and permanently joined for rigidity. Has removable rifle-type sights. Introduced 1998. Imported from Italy by Beretta U.S.A.
Price: **$985.00**

BERETTA AL390 SPORT SPORTING AUTO SHOTGUN

Gauge: 12, 20, 3" chamber. **Barrel:** 28", 30", choke tubes. **Weight:** 7.6 lbs. (12-ga.), 6.8 lbs. (20-ga.). **Stock:** Checkered select walnut. Adjustable drop and cast. **Features:** Low-contour, rounded receiver; gas operated; matte wood finish, matte receiver. Introduced 1995. Imported From Italy by Beretta U.S.A.
Price: 12 or 20 . . . . **$925.00**
Price: With ported barrel. **$995.00**
Price: Sport Sporting Collection (multi-colored stock, forend). **$965.00**
Price: As above, Youth model (13.5" stock) **$965.00**
Price: Sport Gold Sporting (silver-sided receiver with gold engraved decorations) **$1,145.00**

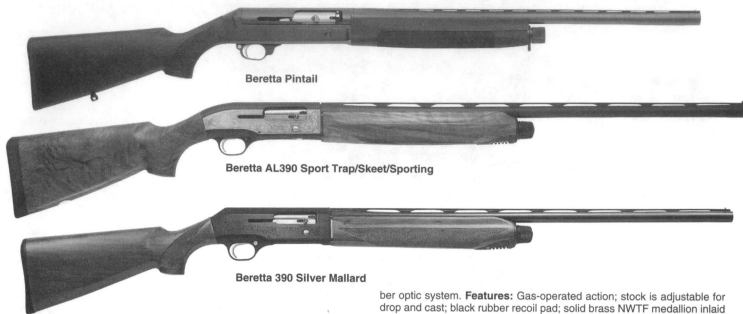Beretta AL390 Sport Diamond Sporting Auto Shotgun

Similar to the AL390 Sport Sporting except has silver-sided receiver with gold engraved decorations; highly select "EELL" quality walnut with oil finish; matte barrel with white front bead; oval stock plate insert; spare trigger group and flourescent orange front sight beads. Comes with ABS case. Introduced 1999. Imported from Italy by Beretta U.S.A.
Price: **$3,075.00**

BERETTA AL390 NWTF SPECIAL AUTO SHOTGUNS

Gauge: 12, 3" chambers. **Barrel:** 24" MC3 and Briley extended Extra-Full. **Weight:** 7.2 lbs. **Stock:** Synthetic, checkered. **Sights:** Truglo three-dot fi-

ber optic system. **Features:** Gas-operated action; stock is adjustable for drop and cast; black rubber recoil pad; solid brass NWTF medallion inlaid into bottom of pistol grip; padded sling. Introduced 1999. Imported from Italy by Beretta U.S.A.

Price: Realtree X-tra Brown camouflage finish overall **$1,105.00**
Price: Black stock and metal **$970.00**
Price: NWTF Special Youth (walnut stock, forend, matte black metal, 13.5" stock) **$910.00**

BERETTA ES100 NWTF SPECIAL AUTO SHOTGUN

Gauge: 12, 3" chamber. **Barrel:** 24", MC3 tubes and Briley extended Extra-Full Turkey. **Weight:** 7.3 lbs. **Stock:** Synthetic, checkered. **Sights:** Truglo fiber optic front and rear three-dot system. **Features:** Short recoil inertia operation. Mossy Oak Break-Up camouflage finish on stock and forend, black matte finish on all metal. Comes with camouflage sling. Introduced 1999. Imported from Italy by Beretta U.S.A.
Price: **$945.00**

BERETTA AL390 SILVER MALLARD AUTO SHOTGUN

Gauge: 12, 20, 3" chamber. **Barrel:** 24", 26", 28", 30", Mobilchoke choke tubes. **Weight:** 6.4 to 7.2 lbs. **Stock:** Select walnut. Adjustable drop and cast. **Features:** Gas-operated action with self-compensating valve allows shooting all loads without adjustment. Alloy receiver, reversible safety; chrome-plated bore; floating vent. rib. Matte-finish models for turkey/waterfowl and Deluxe with gold, engraving; camo models have Advantage finish. Youth models in 20-gauge and slug model available. Introduced 1992. Imported from Italy by Beretta U.S.A.
Price: Walnut or synthetic, 12 gauge **$860.00**
Price: 12-gauge, synthetic stock **$885.00**
Price: Gold Mallard, 12 and 20. . . . . **$1,055.00**
Price: 20-gauge, 20-gauge Youth **$885.00**
Price: Camouflage model. **$1,020.00**

Beretta AL390 Sport Trap/Skeet Shotguns

Similar to the AL390 Silver Mallard except has lower-contour, rounded receiver. Available with ported barrel. Trap has 30", 32" barrel (Full, Imp. Mod., Mod. choke tubes); Skeet has 26", 28" barrel (fixed Skeet). Introduced 1995. Imported from Italy by Beretta U.S.A.
Price: AL390 Sport Trap. **$925.00**
Price: Trap, ported 30", 32" barrel **$1,010.00**
Price: As above, fixed Full choke **$890.00**
Price: AL390 Sport Skeet. **$890.00**
Price: Skeet, ported 28" barrel **$995.00**

Beretta A390 Sport Super Skeet Shotgun

Similar to the AL390 Silver Mallard except has adjustable-comb stock that allows height adjustments via interchangeable comb inserts. Rounded recoil pad system allows adjustments for length of pull. Stepped tapered rib.

SHOTGUNS — AUTOLOADERS

Browning Gold Deer Hunter

Browning Gold Sporting Golden Clays

Browning Gold Waterfowl

Factory ported barrel in 28" (fixed Skeet) Weighs 8.1 lbs. In 12-gauge only, with 3" chamber. Introduced 1993. Imported from Italy by Beretta U.S.A.
Price: **$1,160.00**

BROLIN SAS12 AUTO SHOTGUN
Gauge: 12, 3" chamber, 3-round detachable magazine. **Barrel:** 24"; choke tubes. **Weight:** About 7-1/2 lbs. **Stock:** Black polymer. **Features:** Satin blue finish. Introduced 1998. Imported by Brolin Arms.
Price: **$499.00**

BROWNING GOLD HUNTER AUTO SHOTGUN
Gauge: 12, 20, 3" chamber. **Barrel:** 12-ga.—26", 28", 30", Invector Plus choke tubes; 20-ga.—26", 30", Invector choke tubes. **Weight:** 7 lbs., 9 oz. (12-ga.), 6 lbs., 12 oz. (20 ga.). **Length:** 46-1/4" overall (20-ga., 26" barrel). **Stock:** 14"x1-1/2"x2-1/3"; select walnut with gloss finish; palm swell grip. **Features:** Self-regulating, self-cleaning gas system shoots all loads; lightweight receiver with special non-glare deep black finish; large reversible safety button; large rounded trigger guard, gold trigger. The 20-gauge has slightly smaller dimensions; 12-gauge have back-bored barrels, Invector Plus tube system. Introduced 1994. Imported by Browning
Price: 12- or 20-gauge **$772.00**
Price: Extra barrels **$290.00**

Browning Gold Deer Hunter Auto Shotgun
Similar to the Gold Hunter except 12-gauge only, 22" rifled or smooth Standard Invector barrel with 5" rifled choke tube, cantilever scope mount, extra-thick recoil pad. Weighs 7 lbs., 12 oz., overall length 42-1/2". Sling swivel studs fitted on the magazine cap and butt. Introduced 1997. Imported by Browning.
Price: **$839.00**
Price: With Mossy Oak Break-up camouflage **$909.00**

Browning Gold Deer Stalker

Similar to the Gold Deer Hunter except has black composite stock and forend, fully rifled barrel, cantilever scope mount. Introduced 1999. Imported by Browning.
Price: **$839.00**

Browning Gold Sporting Clays Auto
Similar to the Gold Hunter except 12-gauge only with 28" or 30" barrel; front and center beads on tapered ventilated rib; ported and back-bored Invector Plus barrel; 2-3/4" chamber; satin-finished stock with solid, radiused recoil pad with hard heel insert; non-glare black alloy receiver has

"Sporting Clays" inscribed in gold. Introduced 1996. Imported from Japan by Browning.
Price: **$798.00**

Browning Gold Sporting Golden Clays
Similar to the Sporting Clays except has silvered receiver with gold engraving, high grade wood. Introduced 1999. Imported by Browning.
Price: **$1,267.00**

Browning Gold Ladies/Youth Sporting Clays Auto
Similar to the Gold Sporting Clays except has stock dimensions of 14-1/4"x1-3/4"x2" for women and younger shooters. Introduced 1999. Imported by Browning.
Price: **$798.00**

Browning Gold Stalker Auto Shotgun
Similar to the Gold Hunter except has black composite stock and forend. Choice of 3" or 3-1/2" chamber.
Price: With 3" chamber **$772.00**
Price: With 3-1/2" chamber **$929.00**

Browning Gold Waterfowl Shotgun
Similar to the Gold Hunter except 12-gauge only, completely covered with Mossy Oak Shadow Grass comouflage. Choice of 3" or 3-1/2" chamber. Introduced 1999. Imported by Browning.
Price: 26", 28" **$999.00**

Browning Gold Classic Hunter Auto Shotgun
Similar to the Gold Hunter 3" except has semi-hump back receiver, magazine cut-off, adjustable comb, and satin-finish wood. Introduced 1999. Imported by Browning.
Price: 12-gauge **$772.00**
Price: 20-gauge **$772.00**
Price: High Grade (silvered, gold engraved receiver, high grade wood) **$1,427.00**

Browning Gold Classic Stalker
Similar to the Gold Classic Hunter except has adjustable composite stock and forend. Introduced 1999. Imported by Browning.
Price: **$772.00**

Browning Gold Turkey/Waterfowl Hunter Auto
Similar to the Gold Hunter except available with 3" or 3-1/2" chamber; has 24" barrel with Hi-Viz front sight. Introduced 1999. Imported by Browning.
Price: **$929.00**

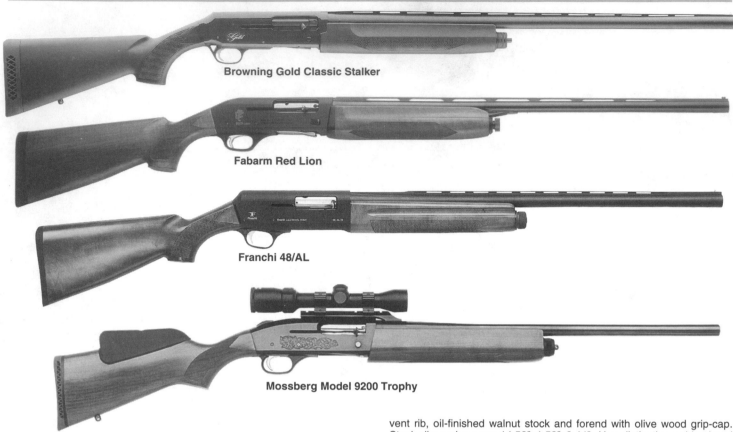

Browning Gold Classic Stalker

Fabarm Red Lion

Franchi 48/AL

Mossberg Model 9200 Trophy

Browning Gold Turkey/Waterfowl Camo Shotgun

NEW! Similar to the Gold Turkey/Waterfowl Hunter except 12-gauge only, 3" or 3-1/2" chamber, 24" barrel with Extra-Full Turkey choke tube, Hi-Viz front sight. Completely covered with Mossy Oak Breakup camouflage. Introduced 1999. Imported by Browning.

Price: $929.00
Price: Turkey/Waterfowl Stalker (black stock and metal) $949.00

BROWNING GOLD 10 AUTO SHOTGUN

Gauge: 10, 3-1/2" chamber, 5-shot magazine. **Barrel:** 26", 28", 30" (Imp. Cyl., Mod., Full standard Invector). **Weight:** 10 lbs. 7 oz. (28" barrel). **Stock:** 14-3/8"x1-1/2"x2-3/8". Select walnut with gloss finish, cut checkering, recoil pad. **Features:** Short-stroke, gas-operated action, cross-bolt safety. Forged steel receiver with polished blue finish. Introduced 1993. Imported by Browning.

Price: $1,007.95
Price: Extra barrel. $276.00

Browning Gold 10-Gauge Auto Combo

NEW! Similar to the Gold 10 except comes with 24" and 26" barrels with Imp. Cyl., Mod., Full Invector choke tubes. Introduced 1999. Imported by Browning.

Price: $1,059.00

FABARM RED LION AUTO SHOTGUN

Gauge: 12, 3" chamber. **Barrel:** 24", 26", 28", choke tubes. **Weight:** 7 lbs. **Length:** 45.5" overall. **Stock:** European walnut with gloss finish. **Features:** Reversible safety; nickel-plated trigger and carrier release button; leather-covered rubber recoil pad. Introduced 1998. Imported from Italy by Heckler & Koch, Inc.

Price: $804.00
Price: Gold Lion (as above except gold-plated trigger, carrier release button, olive wood gripcap) $914.00

NEW! Fabarm Sporting Clays Lion Auto Shotgun

Similar to the Red Lion except has 28" TriBore ported barrel with interchangeable colored front-sight beads, mid-rib bead, 10mm channeled vent rib, oil-finished walnut stock and forend with olive wood grip-cap. Stock dimensions are 14.58"x1.58"x2.44". Has distinctive gold-colored receiver logo. Available in 12-gauge only, 3" chamber. Introduced 1999. Imported from Italy by Heckler & Koch, Inc.

Price: $959.00

Fabarm Camo Lion Auto Shotgun

Similar to the Red Lion except has 24", 26" or 28" ported TriBore barrel **NEW** system with five choke tubes, and is completely covered with Wetlands camouflage pattern. Has red front sight bead and mid-rib bead. Introduced 1999. Imported from Italy by Heckler & Koch, Inc.

Price: $978.00

FRANCHI AL 48 SHOTGUN

Gauge: 12, 20 or 28, 2-3/4" chamber. **Barrel:** 24", 26", 28" (Franchoke Imp. Cyl., Mod., Full choke tubes), 28 ga. has fixed Imp. Cyl. Vent. rib. **Weight:** 5.2 lbs. (20-gauge). **Length:** NA **Stock:** 14-1/4"x1-5/8"x2-1/2". Walnut with checkered grip and forend. **Features:** Recoil-operated action. Chrome-lined bore; cross-bolt safety. Imported from Italy by Benelli U.S.A.

Price: 12, 20 . . . . $560.00
Price: 28 ga. $667.00

FRANCHI 612VS AUTO SHOTGUN

Gauge: 12, 3" chamber. **Barrel:** 24", 26", 28", Franchoke tubes. **Weight:** 7 lbs., 2 oz. **Length:** 47-1/2" overall. **Stock:** 14-1/4"x1-1/2"x2-1/2". European walnut. **Features:** Alloy frame with matte black finish; gas-operated with Variopress System; four-lug rotating bolt; loaded chamber indicator. Introduced 1996. Imported from Italy by Benelli U.S.A.

Price: $595.00
Price: 612VS Camo (Realtree Extra Brown camo) $657.00
Price: 612VS Synthetic (black synthetic stock, forend) $579.00
Price: 620VS (20-gauge, 24", 26", 28") $595.00

MOSSBERG MODEL 9200 CROWN GRADE AUTO SHOTGUN

Gauge: 12, 3" chamber. **Barrel:** 24" (rifled bore), 24", 28" (Accu-Choke tubes); vent. rib. **Weight:** About 7.5 lbs. **Length:** 48" overall (28" bbl.). **Stock:** Walnut with high-gloss finish, cut checkering. **Features:** Shoots all 2-3/4" or 3" loads without adjustment. Alloy receiver, ambidextrous top safety. Introduced 1992.

Mossberg 9200 Viking

Remington Model 11-87 Premier

Remington Model 11-87 SPS Camo

Price: 28", vent. rib **$552.00**
Price: Trophy, 24" with scope base, rifled bore, Dual-Comb stock **$552.00**
Price: 24", Fiber Optic or standard rifle sights, rifled bore **$517.00**

Mossberg Model 9200 Viking
Similar to the Model 9200 Crown Grade except has black matte metal finish, moss-green synthetic stock and forend; 28" Accu-Choke vent. rib barrel with Imp. Cyl, Full and Mod. tubes. Made in U.S. by Mossberg. Introduced 1996.
Price: **$429.00**

Mossberg Model 9200 Camo Shotgun
Same as the Model 9200 Crown Grade except completely covered with Mossy Oak Tree Stand, Mossy Oak Shadowbranch, Realtree AP gray or OFM camouflage finish. Available with 24" barrel with Accu-Choke tubes. Has synthetic stock and forend. Introduced 1993.
Price: Turkey, 24" vent. rib, Mossy Oak or Realtree finish **$595.00**
Price: 28" vent. rib, Accu-Chokes, Woodlands camo finish **$516.00**

Mossberg Model 9200 Special Hunter
Similar to the Model 9200 Crown Grade except with 28" vent rib barrel with Accu choke set, Parkerized finish, black synthetic stock and forend, and sling and swivels. Introduced 1998. Made in U.S. by Mossberg.
Price: **$471.00**

Mossberg Model 9200 Custom Grade Sporting Shotgun
Same as the Model 9200 Crown Grade except has custom engraved receiver. Comes with 28" vent. rib barrel with Accu-Choke tubes (including Skeet), cut-checkered walnut stock and forend. Introduced 1993.
Price: **$590.00**

Mossberg Model 9200 Bantam
Same as the Model 9200 Crown Grade except has 1" shorter stock, 22" vent. rib barrel with three Accu-Choke tubes. Made in U.S. by Mossberg. Introduced 1996.
Price: **$552.00**

REMINGTON MODEL 11-87 PREMIER SHOTGUN
Gauge: 12, 20, 3" chamber. **Barrel:** 26", 28", 30" Rem Choke tubes. Light Contour barrel. **Weight:** About 7-3/4 lbs. **Length:** 46" overall (26" bbl.).

Stock: Walnut with satin or high-gloss finish; cut checkering; solid brown buttpad; no white spacers. **Sights:** Bradley-type white-faced front, metal bead middle. **Features:** Pressure compensating gas system allows shooting 2-3/4" or 3" loads interchangeably with no adjustments. Stainless magazine tube; redesigned feed latch, barrel support ring on operating bars; pinned forend. Introduced 1987.
Price: **$705.00**
Price: Left-hand **$759.00**
Price: Premier Cantilever Deer Barrel, sling, swivels, Monte Carlo stock **$785.00**

Remington Model 11-87 Premier Trap
Similar to 11-87 Premier except trap dimension stock with Monte Carlo comb; select walnut with satin finish and Tournament-grade cut checkering; 30" barrel with Rem Chokes (Trap Full, Trap Extra Full, Trap Super Full). Gas system set for 2-3/4" shells only. Introduced 1987.
Price: With Monte Carlo stock **$833.00**

Remington Model 11-87 Premier Skeet
Similar to 11-87 Premier except Skeet dimension stock with cut checkering, satin finish, two-piece buttplate; 26" barrel with Skeet or Rem Chokes (Skeet, Imp. Skeet). Gas system set for 2-3/4" shells only. Introduced 1987.
Price: **$765.00**

Remington Model 11-87 Special Purpose Magnum
Similar to the 11-87 Premier except has dull stock finish, Parkerized exposed metal surfaces. Bolt and carrier have dull blackened coloring. Comes with 26" or 28" barrel with Rem Chokes, padded Cordura nylon sling and quick detachable swivels. Introduced 1987.
Price: **$705.00**
Price: With synthetic stock and forend (SPS) **$692.00**
Price: Magnum-Turkey with synthetic stock (SPS-T) **$705.00**

Remington Model 11-87 SPS Special Purpose Synthetic Camo
Similar to the 11-87 Special Purpose Magnum except has synthetic stock and all metal (except bolt and trigger guard) and stock covered with Mossy Oak Break-Up camo finish. In 12-gauge only, 26", Rem Choke. Comes with camo sling, swivels. Introduced 1992.
Price: **$767.00**

Remington Model 11-87 SPS-T Turkey Camo

Remington Model 11-87 SC NP

Remington Model 1100 Youth Turkey Camo

Remington Model 11-87 SPS-T Turkey Camo NWTF Shotgun

Similar to the 11-87 Special Purpose Magnum except with synthetic stock, 21" vent. rib barrel with Super-Full Turkey (.665" diameter with knurled extension) tube. Completely covered with Mossy Oak Break-Up Brown camouflage. Bolt body, trigger guard and recoil pad are non-reflective black. Introduced 1993.

Price: **$832.00**
Price: Model 11-87 SPS-T Camo (as above with rifled
choke tube).. **$805.00**

Remington Model 11-87 SPS-Deer Shotgun

Similar to the 11-87 Special Purpose Camo except has fully-rifled 21" barrel with rifle sights, black non-reflective, synthetic stock and forend, black carrying sling. Introduced 1993.

Price: **$725.00**
Price: With wood stock (Model 11-87 SP Deer gun) **$685.00**

Remington Model 11-87 SPS Cantilever Shotgun

Similar to the 11-87 SPS except has fully rifled barrel; synthetic stock with Monte Carlo comb; cantilever scope mount deer barrel. Comes with sling and swivels. Introduced 1994.

Price: **$772.00**

REMINGTON MODEL 11-87 PREMIER SPORTING CLAYS

Gauge: 12, 2-3/4" chamber. **Barrel:** 26", 28", vent. rib, Rem Choke (Skeet, Imp. Cyl., Mod., Full); Light Contour barrel. Medium height rib. **Weight:** 7.5 lbs. **Length:** 46.5" overall (26" barrel). **Stock:** 14-3/16"x1-1/2"x2-1/4". Walnut, with cut checkering; sporting clays butt pad. **Features:** Top of receiver, barrel and rib have matte finish; shortened magazine tube and forend; lengthened forcing cone; ivory bead front sight; competition trigger. Special no-wrench choke tubes marked on the outside. Comes in two-barrel fitted hard case. Introduced 1992.

Price: **$779.00**

Remington Model 11-87 SC NP Shotgun

Similar to the Model 11-87 Sporting Clays except has low-luster nickel-plated receiver with fine-line engraving, and ported 28" or 30" Rem choke barrel with matte finish. Tournament-grade American walnut stock measures 14-3/16"x2-1/4"x1-1/2". Sporting Clays choke tubes have knurled extensions. Introduced 1997. Made in U.S. by Remington.

Price: **$905.00**

REMINGTON MODEL 1100 SYNTHETIC LT-20 AUTO

Gauge: 20. **Barrel:** 25" (Full, Mod.), 26" Rem Chokes. **Weight:** 6-3/4 lbs. **Stock:** 14"x1-1/2"x2-1/2". Black synthetic, checkered pistol grip and forend. **Features:** Quickly interchangeable barrels. Matted receiver top with scroll work on both sides of receiver. Cross-bolt safety.

Price: **$505.00**
Price: Youth Gun LT-20 (21" Rem Choke)................. **$505.00**

Remington Model 1100 Special Field

Similar to Standard Model 1100 except 12- and 20-ga. only, comes with 23" Rem Choke barrel. LT-20 version 6-1/2 lbs.; has straight-grip stock, shorter forend, both with cut checkering. Comes with vent. rib only; matte finish receiver without engraving. Introduced 1983.

Price: 12- and 20-ga., 23" Rem Choke..................... **$665.00**

Remington Model 1100 Synthetic

Similar to the 1100 LT magnum except in 12- or 20-gauge, and has black synthetic stock; vent. rib 28" barrel on 12-gauge, 26" on 20, both with Mod. Rem Choke tube. Weighs about 7-1/2 lbs. Introduced 1996.

Price: **$505.00**

Remington Model 1100 Youth Synthetic Turkey Camo

Similar to the Model 1100 LT-20 except has 1" shorter stock, 21" vent rib barrel with Full Rem Choke tube; 3" chamber; synthetic stock and forend are covered with RealTree Advantage camo, and barrel and receiver have non-reflective, black matte finish. Introduced 1999.

Price: **$565.00**

Remington Model 1100 LT-20 Synthetic FR RS Shotgun

Similar to the 1100 LT-20 except has 21" fully rifled barrel with rifle sights, 2-3/4" chamber, and fiberglass-reinforced synthetic stock. Introduced 1997. Made in U.S. by Remington.

Price: **$539.00**

Remington Model 1100 Sporting 28

Similar to the 1100 LT-20 except in 28-gauge with 25" barrel; comes with Skeet, Imp. Cyl., Light Mod., Mod. Rem Choke tubes. Fancy walnut with gloss finish, Sporting rubber butt pad. Made in U.S. by Remington. Introduced 1996.

Price: **$799.00**

Remington Model 1100 Sporting 20 Shotgun

Similar to the Model 1100 LT-20 except has tournament-grade American walnut stock with gloss finish and sporting-style recoil pad, 28" Rem

SHOTGUNS — AUTOLOADERS

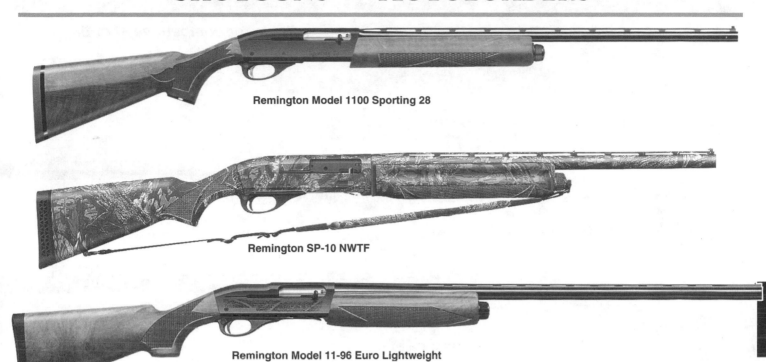

Remington Model 1100 Sporting 28

Remington SP-10 NWTF

Remington Model 11-96 Euro Lightweight

Weatherby SAS

Choke barrel for Skeet, Imp. Cyl., Light Modified and Modified. Introduced 1998.
Price: **$799.00**

Remington Model 1100 Synthetic FR CL Shotgun
Similar to the Model 1100 LT-20 except 12-gauge, has 21" fully rifled barrel with cantilever scope mount and fiberglass-reinforced synthetic stock with Monte Carlo comb. Introduced 1997. Made in U.S. by Remington.
Price: **$585.00**

REMINGTON MODEL SP-10 MAGNUM AUTO SHOTGUN
Gauge: 10, 3-1/2" chamber, 2-shot magazine. **Barrel:** 26", 30" (Full and Mod. Rem Chokes). **Weight:** 10-3/4 to 11 lbs. **Length:** 47-1/2" overall (26" barrel). **Stock:** Walnut with satin finish. Checkered grip and forend. **Sights:** Twin bead. **Features:** Stainless steel gas system with moving cylinder; 3/8" ventilated rib. Receiver and barrel have matte finish. Brown recoil pad. Comes with padded Cordura nylon sling. Introduced 1989.
Price: **$1,116.00**
Price: SP-10 Magnum Turkey Camo (23" vent rib barrel, Turkey Extra-Full Rem Choke tube) **$1,229.00**

Remington Model SP-10 Magnum Camo Auto Shotgun
Similar to the SP-10 Magnum except buttstock, forend, receiver, barrel and magazine cap are covered with Mossy Oak Break-Up camo finish; bolt body and trigger guard have matte black finish. Comes with Extra-Full Turkey Rem Choke tube, 26" vent. rib barrel with mid-rib bead and Bradley-style front sight, swivel studs and quick-detachable swivels, and a non-slip Cordura carrying sling in the same camo pattern. Introduced 1993.
Price: **$1,229.00**

Remington Model SP-10 Turkey Camo NWTF
Similar to the SP-10 Magnum Camo except has 23" barrel with Turkey Extra Full Rem Choke tube, Truglo fiber optic front sight, and N.W.T.F. 25th Anniversary logo on left side of receiver. Introduced 1998.
Price: **$1,229.00**

REMINGTON MODEL 11-96 EURO LIGHTWEIGHT AUTO SHOTGUN
Gauge: 12, 3" chamber. **Barrel:** 26", 28", Rem Chokes. **Weight:** 6-7/8 lbs. (26" barrel). **Length:** 46" overall (26" barrel). **Stock:** Semi-fancy Claro walnut with cut checkering; solid rubber butt pad. **Features:** Pressure-compensating gas system allows shooting 2-3/4" or 3" loads interchangeably with no adjustments. Lightweight steel receiver with scroll-engraved panels; stainless steel magazine tube; 6mm ventilated rib on light contour barrel. Introduced 1996. Made in U.S. by Remington.
Price: **$852.00**

WEATHERBY SAS AUTO SHOTGUN
Gauge: 12, 20, 2-3/4" or 3" chamber. **Barrel:** 26", 28" (20-ga.); 26", 28", 30" (12-ga.); Briley Multi-Choke tubes. **Weight:** 6-3/4 to 7-3/4 lbs. **Stock:** 14-1/4"x2-1/4"x1-1/2". Claro walnut. **Features:** Alloy receiver with matte finish; gold-plated trigger; magazine cut-off. Introduced 1999. Imported by Weatherby.
Price: 12 or 20-ga. **$749.00**

WINCHESTER SUPER X2 AUTO SHOTGUN
Gauge: 12, 3", 3-1/2" chamber. **Barrel:** 24", 26", 28"; Invector Plus choke tubes. **Weight:** 7-1/4 to 7-1/2 lbs. **Stock:** 14-1/4"x1-3/4"x2". Walnut or black synthetic. **Features:** Gas-operated action shoots all loads without adjustment; vent. rib barrels. Introduced 1999. Made in U.S. by U.S. Repeating Arms Co.
Price: Field, walnut or synthetic stock, 3". **$725.00**
Price: Camo Waterfowl, 3-1/2", Mossy Oak Shadow Grass. **$938.00**
Price: Turkey, 3-1/2", synthetic stock, 24" **$867.00**
Price: Magnum, 3-1/2", synthetic stock **$855.00**

Includes a wide variety of sporting guns and guns suitable for competitive shooting.

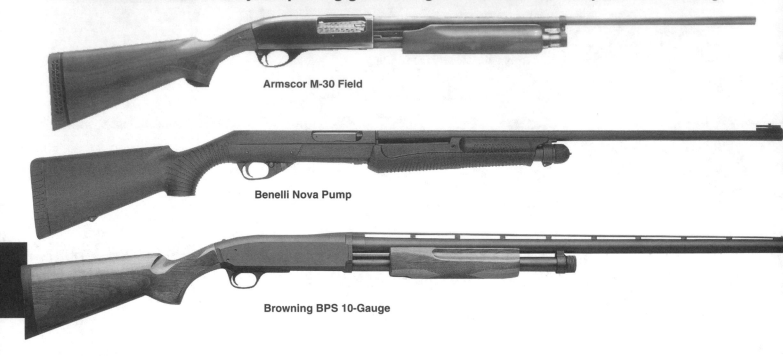

Armscor M-30 Field

Benelli Nova Pump

Browning BPS 10-Gauge

ARMSCOR M-30F FIELD PUMP SHOTGUN

Gauge: 12, 3" chamber. **Barrel:** 28" fixed Mod., or with Mod. and Full choke tubes. **Weight:** 7.6 lbs. **Stock:** Walnut-finished hardwood. **Features:** Double action slide bars; blued steel receiver; damascened bolt. Introduced 1996. Imported from the Philippines by K.B.I., Inc.
Price: With fixed choke. $239.00
Price: With choke tubes $269.00

BENELLI NOVA PUMP SHOTGUN

NEW! **Gauge:** 12, 3-1/2" chamber. **Barrel:** 24", 26", 28"; chrome lined, vent rib; choke tubes. **Weight:** 8 lbs. **Length:** 47.5" overall. **Stock:** Black polymer. **Features:** Montefeltro rotating bolt design with dual action bars; magazine cut-0ff; synthetic trigger assembly. Introduced 1999. Imported from Italy by Benelli USA.
Price: With black stock $357.00
Price: With Camo finish $425.00

Benelli Nova Pump Slug Gun

NEW! Similar to the Nova except has 18.5" barrel with adjustable rifle-type sights; weighs 7.2 lbs.; black synthetic stock. Introduced 1999. Imported from Italy by Benelli USA.
Price: $285.00

BROWNING BPS PUMP SHOTGUN

Gauge: 10, 12, 3-1/2" chamber; 12 or 20, 3" chamber (2-3/4" in target guns), 28, 2-3/4" chamber, 5-shot magazine. **Barrel:** 10-ga.—24" Buck Special, 28", 30", 32" Invector; 12-, 20- ga.—22", 24", 26", 28", 30", 32" (Imp. Cyl., Mod. or Full). Also available with Invector choke tubes, 12- or 20-ga.; Upland Special has 22" barrel with Invector tubes. BPS 3" and 3-1/2" have back-bored barrel. **Weight:** 7 lbs., 8 oz. (28" barrel). **Length:** 48-3/4" overall (28" barrel). **Stock:** 14-1/4"x1-1/2"x2-1/2". Select walnut, semi-beavertail forend, full pistol grip stock. **Features:** All 12-gauge 3" guns except Buck Special and game guns have back-bored barrels with Invector Plus choke tubes. Bottom feeding and ejection, receiver top safety, high post vent. rib. Double action bars eliminate binding. Vent. rib barrels only. All 12- and 20-gauge guns with 3" chamber available with fully engraved receiver flats at no extra cost. Each gauge has its own unique game scene. Introduced 1977. Imported from Japan by Browning.
Price: 10-ga., Hunting, Invector $532.00
Price: 12-ga., 3-1/2" Mag., Hunting, Invector Plus $532.00
Price: 12-, 20-ga., Hunting, Invector Plus. $444.00

Price: 12-ga. Buck Special $408.00
Price: 28-ga., Hunting, Invector $444.00

Browning BPS 10-Gauge Turkey

Similar to the BPS Hunter except has 24" barrel with Hi-Viz front sight for turkey hunting. Available with either walnut or black composite stock and forend. Introduced 1999. Imported by Browning.
Price: Hunter (walnut). $532.00
Price: Stalker (composite) $532.00

Browning BPS 10-Gauge Camo Pump

Similar to the BPS 10-gauge Hunter except completely covered with Mossy Oak Shadow Grass camouflage. Available with 24", 26", 28" barrel. Introduced 1999. Imported by Browning.
Price: $602.00

Browning BPS Waterfowl Camo Pump Shotgun

Similar to the BPS Hunter except completely covered with Mossy Oak Shadow Grass camouflage. Available in 12-gauge, with 24", 26" or 28" barrel, 3" chamber. Introduced 1999. Imported by Browning.
Price: $514.00

Browning BPS Game Gun Deer Special

Similar to the standard BPS except has newly designed receiver/magazine tube/barrel mounting system to eliminate play, heavy 20.5" barrel with rifle-type sights with adjustable rear, solid receiver scope mount, "rifle" stock dimensions for scope or open sights, sling swivel studs. Gloss or matte finished wood with checkering, polished blue metal. Introduced 1992.
Price: $516.00

Browning BPS Game Gun Turkey Special

Similar to the standard BPS except has satin-finished walnut stock and dull-finished barrel and receiver. Receiver is drilled and tapped for scope mounting. Rifle-style stock dimensions and swivel studs. Has Extra-Full Turkey choke tube. Introduced 1992.
Price: $482.00

Browning BPS Stalker Pump Shotgun

Same gun as the standard BPS except all exposed metal parts have a matte blued finish and the stock has a durable black finish with a black

SHOTGUNS — SLIDE ACTIONS

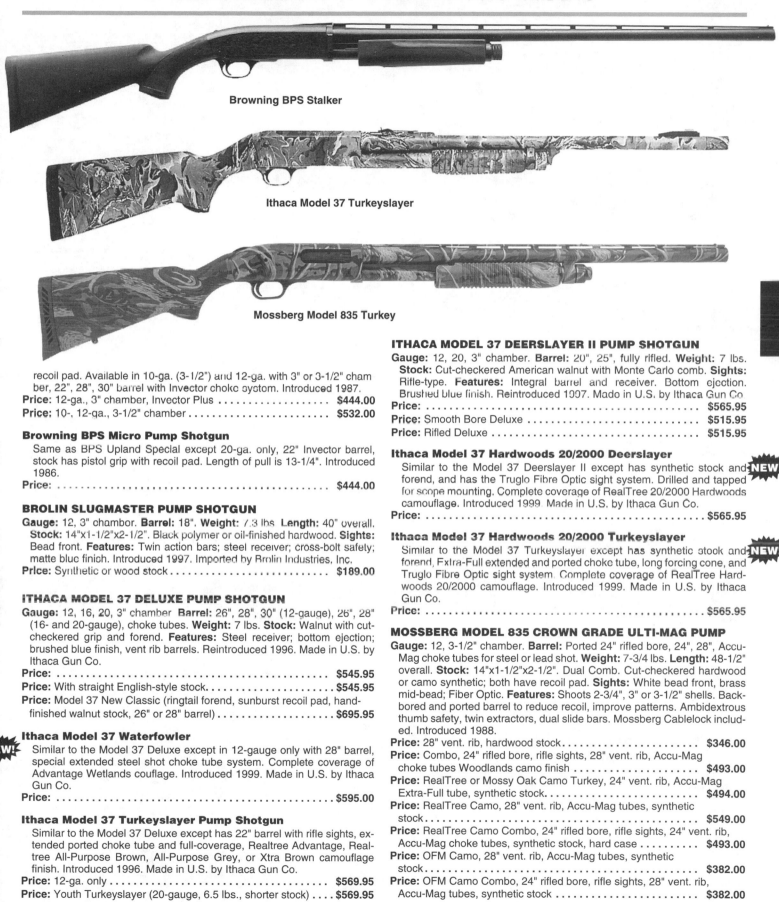

Browning BPS Stalker

Ithaca Model 37 Turkeyslayer

Mossberg Model 835 Turkey

recoil pad. Available in 10-ga. (3-1/2") and 12-ga. with 3" or 3-1/2" chamber, 22", 28", 30" barrel with Invector choke system. Introduced 1987.
Price: 12-ga., 3" chamber, Invector Plus **$444.00**
Price: 10-, 12-ga., 3-1/2" chamber **$532.00**

Browning BPS Micro Pump Shotgun
Same as BPS Upland Special except 20-ga. only, 22" Invector barrel, stock has pistol grip with recoil pad. Length of pull is 13-1/4". Introduced 1986.
Price: **$444.00**

BROLIN SLUGMASTER PUMP SHOTGUN
Gauge: 12, 3" chamber. **Barrel:** 18". **Weight:** 7.3 lbs. **Length:** 40" overall. **Stock:** 14"x1-1/2"x2-1/2". Black polymer or oil-finished hardwood. **Sights:** Bead front. **Features:** Twin action bars; steel receiver; cross-bolt safety; matte blue finish. Introduced 1997. Imported by Brolin Industries, Inc.
Price: Synthetic or wood stock **$189.00**

ITHACA MODEL 37 DELUXE PUMP SHOTGUN
Gauge: 12, 16, 20, 3" chamber. **Barrel:** 26", 28", 30" (12-gauge), 26", 28" (16- and 20-gauge), choke tubes. **Weight:** 7 lbs. **Stock:** Walnut with cut-checkered grip and forend. **Features:** Steel receiver; bottom ejection; brushed blue finish, vent rib barrels. Reintroduced 1996. Made in U.S. by Ithaca Gun Co.
Price: **$545.95**
Price: With straight English-style stock **$545.95**
Price: Model 37 New Classic (ringtail forend, sunburst recoil pad, hand-finished walnut stock, 26" or 28" barrel) **$695.95**

Ithaca Model 37 Waterfowler
Similar to the Model 37 Deluxe except in 12-gauge only with 28" barrel, special extended steel shot choke tube system. Complete coverage of Advantage Wetlands couflage. Introduced 1999. Made in U.S. by Ithaca Gun Co.
Price: **$595.00**

Ithaca Model 37 Turkeyslayer Pump Shotgun
Similar to the Model 37 Deluxe except has 22" barrel with rifle sights, extended ported choke tube and full-coverage, Realtree Advantage, Realtree All-Purpose Brown, All-Purpose Grey, or Xtra Brown camouflage finish. Introduced 1996. Made in U.S. by Ithaca Gun Co.
Price: 12-ga. only **$569.95**
Price: Youth Turkeyslayer (20-gauge, 6.5 lbs., shorter stock) **$569.95**

ITHACA MODEL 37 DEERSLAYER II PUMP SHOTGUN
Gauge: 12, 20, 3" chamber. **Barrel:** 20", 25", fully rifled. **Weight:** 7 lbs. **Stock:** Cut-checkered American walnut with Monte Carlo comb. **Sights:** Rifle-type. **Features:** Integral barrel and receiver. Bottom ejection. Brushed blue finish. Reintroduced 1997. Made in U.S. by Ithaca Gun Co.
Price: **$565.95**
Price: Smooth Bore Deluxe **$515.95**
Price: Rifled Deluxe **$515.95**

Ithaca Model 37 Hardwoods 20/2000 Deerslayer
Similar to the Model 37 Deerslayer II except has synthetic stock and forend, and has the Truglo Fibre Optic sight system. Drilled and tapped for scope mounting. Complete coverage of RealTree 20/2000 Hardwoods camouflage. Introduced 1999. Made in U.S. by Ithaca Gun Co.
Price: **$565.95**

Ithaca Model 37 Hardwoods 20/2000 Turkeyslayer
Similar to the Model 37 Turkeyslayer except has synthetic stock and forend, Extra-Full extended and ported choke tube, long forcing cone, and Truglo Fibre Optic sight system. Complete coverage of RealTree Hardwoods 20/2000 camouflage. Introduced 1999. Made in U.S. by Ithaca Gun Co.
Price: **$565.95**

MOSSBERG MODEL 835 CROWN GRADE ULTI-MAG PUMP
Gauge: 12, 3-1/2" chamber. **Barrel:** Ported 24" rifled bore, 24", 28", Accu-Mag choke tubes for steel or lead shot. **Weight:** 7-3/4 lbs. **Length:** 48-1/2" overall. **Stock:** 14"x1-1/2"x2-1/2". Dual Comb. Cut-checkered hardwood or camo synthetic; both have recoil pad. **Sights:** White bead front, brass mid-bead; Fiber Optic. **Features:** Shoots 2-3/4", 3" or 3-1/2" shells. Back-bored and ported barrel to reduce recoil, improve patterns. Ambidextrous thumb safety, twin extractors, dual slide bars. Mossberg Cablelock included. Introduced 1988.
Price: 28" vent. rib, hardwood stock **$346.00**
Price: Combo, 24" rifled bore, rifle sights, 28" vent. rib, Accu-Mag choke tubes Woodlands camo finish **$493.00**
Price: RealTree or Mossy Oak Camo Turkey, 24" vent. rib, Accu-Mag Extra-Full tube, synthetic stock. **$494.00**
Price: RealTree Camo, 28" vent. rib, Accu-Mag tubes, synthetic stock **$549.00**
Price: RealTree Camo Combo, 24" rifled bore, rifle sights, 24" vent. rib, Accu-Mag choke tubes, synthetic stock, hard case **$493.00**
Price: OFM Camo, 28" vent. rib, Accu-Mag tubes, synthetic stock **$382.00**
Price: OFM Camo Combo, 24" rifled bore, rifle sights, 28" vent. rib, Accu-Mag tubes, synthetic stock **$382.00**

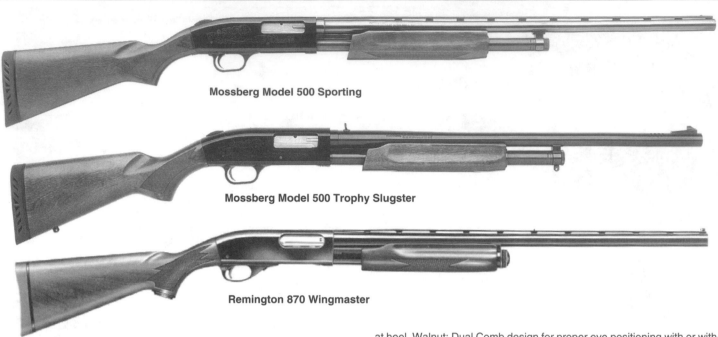

Mossberg Model 500 Sporting

Mossberg Model 500 Trophy Slugster

Remington 870 Wingmaster

Mossberg American Field Model 835 Pump Shotgun

Same as the Model 835 Crown Grade except has walnut-stained hardwood stock and comes only with Modified choke tube, 28" barrel. Introduced 1992.

Price: $331.00

Mossberg Model 835 Special Hunter

Similar to the Model 835 Crown Grade except with 24" or 28" ported barrel with Accu-Mag Mod. choke tube, Parkerized finish, black synthetic stock and forend; comes with sling and swivels. Introduced 1998. Made in U.S. by Mossberg.

Price: $347.00

MOSSBERG MODEL 500 SPORTING PUMP

Gauge: 12, 20, 410, 3" chamber. **Barrel:** 18-1/2" to 28" with fixed or Accu-Choke, plain or vent. rib. **Weight:** 6-1/4 lbs. (410), 7-1/4 lbs. (12). **Length:** 48" overall (28" barrel). **Stock:** 14"x1-1/2"x2-1/2". Walnut-stained hardwood. Cut-checkered grip and forend. **Sights:** White bead front, brass mid-bead; Fiber Optic. **Features:** Ambidextrous thumb safety, twin extractors, disconnecting safety, dual action bars. Quiet Carry forend. Many barrels are ported. Mossberg Cablelock included. From Mossberg.

Price: From about. $322.00

Price: Sporting Combos (field barrel and Slugster barrel), from . . $382.00

Mossberg Model 500 Bantam Pump

Same as the Model 500 Sporting Pump except 20-gauge only, 22" vent. rib Accu-Choke barrel with Mod. choke tube; has 1" shorter stock, reduced length from pistol grip to trigger, reduced forend reach. Introduced 1992.

Price: $322.00

Price: With full Woodlands camouflage finish. $399.00

Mossberg Model 500 Camo Pump

Same as the Model 500 Sporting Pump except 12-gauge only and entire gun is covered with special camouflage finish. Receiver drilled and tapped for scope mounting. Comes with quick detachable swivel studs, swivels, camouflage sling, Mossberg Cablelock.

Price: From about. $348.00

Price: Camo Combo (as above with extra Slugster barrel), from

about. $422.00

MOSSBERG MODEL 500 SLUGSTER

Gauge: 12, 20, 3" chamber. **Barrel:** 24", ported rifled bore. Integral scope mount. **Weight:** 7-1/4 lbs. **Length:** 44" overall. **Stock:** 14" pull, 1-3/8" drop

at heel. Walnut; Dual Comb design for proper eye positioning with or without scoped barrels. Recoil pad and swivel studs. **Features:** Ambidextrous thumb safety, twin extractors, dual slide bars. Comes with scope mount. Mossberg Cablelock included. Introduced 1988.

Price: Rifled bore, with integral scope mount, Dual-Comb stock, 12 or 20

. . . . $352.00

Price: Fiber Optic, rifle sights $382.00

Price: Rifled bore, rifle sights $382.00

Price: 20 ga., Standard or Bantam, from $353.00

REMINGTON MODEL 870 WINGMASTER LC

Gauge: 12, 3" chamber. **Barrel:** 26", 28", 30" (Rem Chokes). Light Contour barrel. **Weight:** 7-1/4 lbs. **Length:** 46-1/2" overall (26" bbl.). **Stock:** 14"x2-1/2"x1". American walnut with satin or high-gloss finish, cut-checkered pistol grip and forend. Rubber butt pad. **Sights:** Ivory bead front, metal mid-bead. **Features:** Double action bars; cross-bolt safety; blue finish. Introduced 1986.

Price: $532.00

Remington Model 870 TC Trap Gun

Similar to the 870 Wingmaster except has tournament-grade, satin-finished American walnut stock with or Monte Carlo comb, over-bored 30" vent. rib barrel with 2-3/4" chamber, over-bore-matched Rem Choke tubes. Made in U.S. by Remington. Reintroduced 1996.

Price: With Monte Carlo stock $680.00

Remington Model 870 Marine Magnum

Similar to the 870 Wingmaster except all metal is plated with electroless nickel and has black synthetic stock and forend. Has 18" plain barrel (Cyl.), bead front sight, 7-shot magazine. Introduced 1992.

Price: $513.00

Remington Model 870 Wingmaster LW Small-Bore

Similar to the Model 870 Wingmaster except in 28-gauge and 410-bore only, 25" vent rib barrel with Rem Choke tubes, high-gloss wood finish. Reintroduced 1999.

Price: 410-bore. $559.00

Price: 28-gauge $612.00

Remington Model 870 Express

Similar to the 870 Wingmaster except has a walnut-toned hardwood stock with solid, black recoil pad and pressed checkering on grip and forend. Outside metal surfaces have a black oxide finish. Comes with 26" or 28" vent. rib barrel with a Mod. Rem Choke tube. Introduced 1987.

Price: 12 or 20 . . . . $305.00

Remington Model 879 Express Super Magnum

Remington Model 870 Express Rifle-Sighted Deer Gun

Remington 870 SPS Super Slug Deer Gun

Price: Express Combo, 12-ga., 26" vent rib with Mod. Rem Choke and 20" fully rifled barrel with rifle sights **$439.00**
Price: Express 20-ga., 26" or 28" with Mod. Rem Choke tubes . . **$305.00**
Price: Express L-H (left-hand), 12-ga., 28" vent rib with Mod. Rem Choke tube. **$332.00**
Price: Express Synthetic. **$312.00**
Price: Express Combo (20-ga.) with extra Deer rifled barrel **$439.00**

Remington Model 870 Express Super Magnum
Similar to the 870 Express except has 28" vent. rib barrel with 3-1/2" chamber, vented recoil pad. Introduced 1998.
Price: **$345.00**
Price: Super Magnum Synthetic. **$352.00**
Price: Super Magnum Turkey Camo (Turkey Extra Full Rem Choke, full-coverage RealTree Advantage camo) **$465.00**
Price: Super Magnum Combo (26" with Mod. Rem Choke and 20" fully rifled deer barrel with 3" chamber and rifle sights; wood stock) **$479.00**

Remington Model 870 Express Youth Gun
Same as the Model 870 Express except comes with 13" length of pull, 21" barrel with Mod. Rem Choke tube. Hardwood stock with low-luster finish. Introduced 1991.
Price: 20-ga. Express Youth (1" shorter stock), from **$305.00**
Price: 20-ga. Youth Deer **$339.00**

Remington Model 870 Express Rifle-Sighted Deer Gun
Same as the Model 870 Express except comes with 20" barrel with fixed Imp. Cyl. choke, open iron sights, Monte Carlo stock. Introduced 1991.
Price: **$300.00**
Price: With fully rifled barrel **$339.00**
Price: Expres Synthetic Deer (black synthetic stock, black matte metal) **$259.00**

Remington Model 870 Express Turkey
Same as the Model 870 Express except comes with 3" chamber, 21" vent. rib turkey barrel and Extra-Full Rem Choke Turkey tube; 12-ga. only. Introduced 1991.
Price: **$319.00**

Price: Express Turkey Camo stock has RealTree Advantage camo, matte black metal **$372.00**
Price: Express Super Magnum Turkey (3-1/2" chamber, 23" barrel, synthetic stock, matte black metal). **$365.00**
Price: Express Youth Turkey camo (as above with 1" shorter length of pull). **$372.00**

Remington Model 870 Express Synthetic
Similar to the 870 Express with 18" barrel except has synthetic stock and forend. Introduced 1994.
Price: **$292.00**

Remington Model 870 SPS Super Slug Deer Gun
Similar to the Model 870 Express Synthetic except has 23" rifled, modified contour barrel with cantilever scope mount. Comes with black synthetic stock and forend with swivel studs, black Cordura nylon sling. Introduced 1999.
Price: **$520.00**

Remington Model 870 Special Purpose Synthetic Camo
Has synthetic stock and all metal (except bolt and trigger guard) and stock covered with Mossy Oak Break-Up camo finish In 12-gauge only, 26" vent. rib, Rem Choke. Comes with camo sling, swivels. Introduced 1992.
Price: **$532.00**
Price: Model 870 SPS Super Magnum Camo (3-1/2" chamber) . . **$532.00**
Price: Model 870 SPS-T Super Magnum Camo (3-1/2" chamber). **$532.00**

Remington Model 870 SPS Cantilever Shotgun
Has rifled barrel; synthetic stock with Monte Carlo comb; cantilever scope mount deer barrel. Comes with sling and swivels. Introduced 1994.
Price: With fully rifled barrel **$520.00**

TRISTAR MODEL 1887 LEVER-ACTION SHOTGUN
Gauge: 12, 2-3/4" chamber, 5-shot magazine. **Barrel:** 30" (Full). **Weight:** 8 lbs. **Length:** 48" overall. **Stocks:** 12-3/4" pull. Rounded-knob pistol grip; walnut with oil finish; blued, checkered steel buttplate. Dimensions duplicate original WRA Co. specifications. **Sights:** Brass, bead front. **Features:** Recreation of Browning's original 1885 patents and design as made by Win-

Winchester 1300 Black Shadow Field Gun

Winchester 1300 Ranger

chester Repeating Arms. External hammer with half- and full-cock positions; has original-type WRA Co. logo on left side of receiver; two-piece walnut forend. Announced 1997. Imported by Tristar Sporting Arms.

Price: .... **NA**

WINCHESTER MODEL 1300 WALNUT PUMP

Gauge: 12, 20, 3" chamber, 5-shot capacity. **Barrel:** 26", 28", vent. rib, with Full, Mod., Imp. Cyl. Winchoke tubes. **Weight:** 6-3/8 lbs. **Length:** 42-5/8" overall. **Stock:** American walnut, with deep cut checkering on pistol grip, traditional ribbed forend; high luster finish. **Sights:** Metal bead front. **Features:** Twin action slide bars; front-locking rotary bolt; roll-engraved receiver; blued, highly polished metal; cross-bolt safety with red indicator. Introduced 1984. From U.S. Repeating Arms Co., Inc.

Price: **$361.00**
Price: Deer Gun (22" rifled barrel, 12-gauge)................ **$425.00**

NEW! **Winchester Model 1300 Upland Special Pump Gun**

Similar to the Model 1300 Walnut except has straight-grip stock, 24" barrel. Introduced 1999. Made in U.S. by U.S. Repeating Arms Co.

Price: **$361.00**

Winchester Model 1300 Black Shadow Field Gun

Similar to the Model 1300 Walnut except has black composite stock and forend, matte black finish. Has vent. rib 26" or 28" barrel, 3" chamber, comes with Mod. Winchoke tube. Introduced 1995. From U.S. Repeating Arms Co., Inc.

Price: 12- or 20-gauge **$310.00**

Winchester Model 1300 Black Shadow Deer Gun

Similar to the Model 1300 Black Shadow Turkey Gun except has ramp-type front sight, fully adjustable rear, drilled and tapped for scope mount-ing. Black composite stock and forend, matte black metal. Smoothbore 22" barrel with one Imp. Cyl. WinChoke tube; 12-gauge only, 3" chamber. Weighs 7-1/4 lbs. Introduced 1994. From U.S. Repeating Arms Co., Inc.

Price: **$310.00**
Price: With rifled barrel................................ **$334.00**

WINCHESTER MODEL 1300 RANGER PUMP GUN

Gauge: 12, 20, 3" chamber, 5-shot magazine. **Barrel:** 26", 28" vent. rib with Full, Mod., Imp. Cyl. Winchoke tubes. **Weight:** 7 to 7-1/4 lbs. **Length:** 48-5/8" to 50-5/8" overall. **Stock:** Walnut-finished hardwood with ribbed forend. **Sights:** Metal bead front. **Features:** Cross-bolt safety, black rubber recoil pad, twin action slide bars, front-locking rotating bolt. From U.S. Repeating Arms Co., Inc.

Price: Vent. rib barrel, Winchoke **$325.00**
Price: Model 1300 Compact, 20-ga., 22" vent. rib **$325.00**

Winchester Model 1300 Ranger Pump Gun Combo & Deer Gun

Similar to the standard Ranger except comes with two barrels: 22" (Cyl.) deer barrel with rifle-type sights and an interchangeable 28" vent. rib Winchoke barrel with Full, Mod. and Imp. Cyl. choke tubes. Drilled and tapped; comes with rings and bases. Available in 12- and 20-gauge 3" only, with recoil pad. Introduced 1983.

Price: Deer Combo with two barrels..................... **$399.00**
Price: Rifled Deer Combo (22" rifled and 28" vent. rib barrels, 12- or 20-ga.) **$422.00**

Winchester Model 1300 Black Shadow Turkey Gun

Similar to the Model 1300 RealTree® Turkey except synthetic stock and forend are matte black, and all metal surfaces finished matte black. Drilled and tapped for scope mounting. In 12- or 20-gauge, 3" chamber, 22" vent. rib barrel; comes with one Extra-Full Winchoke tube (20-gauge has Full). Introduced 1994. From U.S. Repeating Arms Co., Inc.

Price: **$310.00**

Includes a variety of game guns and guns for competitive shooting.

American Arms Silver Sporting

Beretta 682 Gold Skeet

Borotta 682 Gold Sporting

AMERICAN ARMS SILVER I O/U

Gauge: 12, 20, 28, 410, 3" chamber (28 has 2-3/4"). **Barrel:** 26" (Imp. Cyl. & Mod., all gauges), 28" (Mod. & Full, 12, 20). **Weight:** About 6-3/4 lbs. **Stock:** 14-1/8"x1-3/8"x2-3/8". Checkered walnut. **Sights:** Metal bead front. **Features:** Boxlock action with scroll engraving, silver finish. Single selective trigger, extractors. Chrome-lined barrels. Manual safety. Rubber recoil pad. Introduced 1987. Imported from Italy by American Arms, Inc.
Price: 12- or 20-gauge **$649.00**
Price: 28 or 410 . . . . **$679.00**

American Arms Silver II Shotgun

Similar to the Silver I except 26" barrel (Imp. Cyl., Mod., Full choke tubes, 12- and 20-ga.), 28" (Imp. Cyl., Mod., Full choke tubes, 12-ga. only), 26" (Imp. Cyl. & Mod. fixed chokes, 28 and 410), automatic selective ejectors. Weight is about 6 lbs., 15 oz. (12-ga., 26").
Price: **$765.00**
Price: 28, 410 . . . . **$815.00**
Price: Two-barrel sets **$1,239.00**

AMERICAN ARMS SILVER SPORTING O/U

Gauge: 12, 2-3/4" chambers, 20 3" chambers. **Barrel:** 28", 30" (Skeet, Imp. Cyl., Mod., Full choke tubes). **Weight:** 7-3/8 lbs. **Length:** 45-1/2" overall. **Stock:** 14-3/8"x1-1/2"x2-3/8". Figured walnut, cut checkering; Sporting Clays quick-mount buttpad. **Sights:** Target bead front. **Features:** Boxlock action with single selective mechanical trigger, automatic selective ejectors; special broadway channeled rib; vented barrel rib; chrome bores. Chrome-nickel finish on frame, with engraving. Introduced 1990. Imported from Italy by American Arms, Inc.
Price: **$965.00**

AMERICAN ARMS WS/OU 12, TS/OU 12 SHOTGUNS

Gauge: 12, 3-1/2" chambers. **Barrel:** WS/OU—28" (Imp. Cyl., Mod., Full choke tubes); TS/OU—24" (Imp. Cyl., Mod., Full choke tubes). **Weight:** 6 lbs., 15 oz. **Length:** 46" overall. **Stock:** 14-1/8"x1-1/8"x2-3/8". European walnut with cut checkering, black vented recoil pad, matte finish. **Features:** Boxlock action with single selective trigger, automatic selective ejectors; chrome bores. Matte metal finish. Imported by American Arms, Inc.
Price: **$799.00**
Price: With Mossy Oak Break-Up camo **$885.00**

American Arms WT/OU 10 Shotgun

Similar to the WS/OU 12 except chambered for 10-gauge 3-1/2" shell, 26" (Full & Full, choke tubes) barrel. Single selective trigger, extractors. Non-reflective finish on wood and metal. Imported by American Arms, Inc.
Price: **$995.00**

BERETTA SERIES S682 GOLD SKEET, TRAP OVER/UNDERS

Gauge: 12, 2-3/4" chambers. **Barrel:** Skeet—28"; trap—30" and 32", Imp. Mod. & Full and Mobilchoke; trap mono shotguns—32" and 34" Mobilchoke; trap top single guns—32" and 34" Full and Mobilchoke; trap combo sets—from 30" O/U, to 32" O/U, 34" top single. **Stock:** Close-grained walnut, hand checkered. **Sights:** White Bradley bead front sight and center bead. **Features:** Receiver has Greystone gunmetal gray finish with gold accents. Trap Monte Carlo stock has deluxe trap recoil pad. Various grades available; contact Beretta U.S.A. for details. Imported from Italy by Beretta U.S.A.
Price: S682 Gold Skeet **$2,850.00**
Price: S682 Gold Skeet, adjustable stock **$3,410.00**
Price: S682 Gold Trap **$3,000.00**
Price: S682 Gold Trap Top Combo **$3,845.00**
Price: S682 Gold Trap with adjustable stock **$3,510.00**
Price: S686 Silver Pigeon Trap **$1,795.00**
Price: S686 Silver Pigeon Trap Top Mono **$1,795.00**
Price: S686 Silver Pigeon Skeet (28") **$1,760.00**
Price: S687 EELL Diamond Pigeon Trap **$4,815.00**
Price: S687 EELL Diamond Pigeon Skeet **$4,790.00**
Price: S687 EELL Diamond Pigeon Skeet, adjustable stock . . . **$5,810.00**
Price: S687 EELL Diamond Pigeon Trap Top
Mono . . . . **$5,055.00** to **$5,105.00**
Price: ASE Gold Skeet **$12,060.00**
Price: ASE Gold Trap **$12,145.00**
Price: ASE Gold Trap Combo **$16,055.00**

BERETTA MODEL S686 WHITEWING O/U

Gauge: 12, 3" chambers. **Barrel:** 26", 28", Mobilchoke tubes (Imp. Cyl., Mod., Full). **Weight:** 6.7 lbs. **Length:** 45.7" overall (28" barrels). **Stock:** 14.5"x2.2"x1.4". American walnut; radiused black buttplate. **Features:** Matte chrome finish on receiver, matte blue barrels; hard-chrome bores; low-profile receiver with dual conical locking lugs; single selective trigger, ejectors. Introduced 1999. Imported from Italy by Beretta U.S.A.
Price: **$1,255.00**

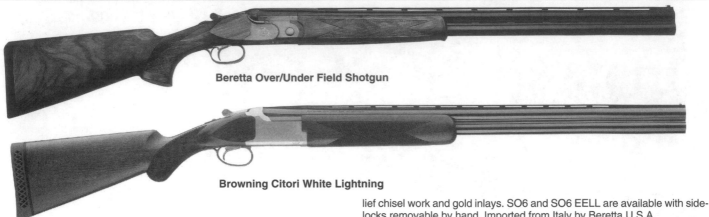

Beretta Over/Under Field Shotgun

Browning Citori White Lightning

BERETTA S686 ONYX SPORTING O/U SHOTGUN

NEW! **Gauge:** 12, 3" chambers. **Barrel:** 28", 30" (Mobilchoke tubes). **Weight:** 7.7 lbs. **Stock:** Checkered American walnut. **Features:** Intended for the beginning Sporting Clays shooter. Has wide, vented 12.5mm target rib, radiused recoil pad. Polished black finish on receiver and barrels. Introduced 1993. Imported from Italy by Beretta U.S.A.
Price: **$1,575.00**

BERETTA ULTRALIGHT OVER/UNDER

Gauge: 12, 2-3/4" chambers. **Barrel:** 26", 28", Mobilchoke choke tubes. **Weight:** About 5 lbs., 13 oz. **Stock:** Select American walnut with checkered grip and forend. **Features:** Low-profile aluminum alloy receiver with titanium breech face insert. Electroless nickel receiver with game scene engraving. Single selective trigger; automatic safety. Introduced 1992. Imported from Italy by Beretta U.S.A.
Price: **$1,795.00**

Beretta Ultralight Deluxe Over/Under Shotgun

NEW! Similar to the Ultralight except has matte electroless nickel finish receiver with gold game scene engraving; matte oil-finished, select walnut stock and forend. Introduced 1999. Imported from Italy by Beretta U.S.A.
Price: **$1,985.00**

BERETTA OVER/UNDER FIELD SHOTGUNS

Gauge: 12, 20, 28, and 410 bore, 2-3/4", 3" and 3-1/2" chambers. **Barrel:** 26" and 28" (Mobilchoke tubes). **Stock:** Close-grained walnut. **Features:** Highly-figured, American walnut stocks and forends, and a unique, weather-resistant finish on barrels. The S686 Onyx bears a gold P. Beretta signature on each side of the receiver. Silver designates standard 686, 687 models with silver receivers; 686 Silver Pigeon has enhanced engraving pattern, Schnabel forend; 686 Silver Essential has matte chrome finish; Gold indicates higher grade 686EL, 687EL models with full sideplates; Diamond is for 687EELL models with highest grade wood, engraving. Case provided with Gold and Diamond grades. Silver Gold, Diamond grades introduced 1994. Imported from Italy by Beretta U.S.A.
Price: S686 Onyx **$1,520.00**
Price: S686 Silver Pigeon two-bbl. set **$2,485.00**
Price: S686 Silver Pigeon. **$1,795.00**
Price: S687 Silver Pigeon. **$2,185.00**
Price: S687 Silver Pigeon II (deep relief game scene engraving, oil finish wood, 12-ga. only) **$2,050.00**
Price: S687EL Gold Pigeon (gold inlays, sideplates) **$3,935.00**
Price: S687EL Gold Pigeon, 410, 26", 28-ga., 28". **$4,105.00**
Price: S687EELL Diamond Pigeon (engraved sideplates) **$5,375.00**
Price: S687EELL Diamond Pigeon Combo, 20- and 28-ga., 26" **$5,995.00**

BERETTA MODEL SO5, SO6, SO9 SHOTGUNS

Gauge: 12, 2-3/4" chambers. **Barrel:** To customer specs. **Stock:** To customer specs. **Features:** SO5—Trap, Skeet and Sporting Clays models SO5; SO6—SO6 and SO6 EELL are field models. SO6 has a case-hardened or silver receiver with contour hand engraving. SO6 EELL has hand-engraved receiver in a fine floral or "fine English" pattern or game scene, with bas-relief chisel work and gold inlays. SO6 and SO6 EELL are available with sidelocks removable by hand. Imported from Italy by Beretta U.S.A.
Price: SO5 Trap, Skeet, Sporting **$13,000.00**
Price: SO6 Trap, Skeet, Sporting **$17,500.00**
Price: SO6 EELL Field, custom specs **$28,000.00**
Price: SO9 (12, 20, 28, 410, 26", 28", 30", any choke) **$31,000.00**

BERETTA SPORTING CLAYS SHOTGUNS

Gauge: 12 and 20, 2-3/4" and 3" chambers. **Barrel:** 28", 30", 32" Mobilchoke. **Stock:** Close-grained walnut. **Features:** Equipped with Beretta Mobilchoke flush-mounted screw-in choke tube system. Dual-purpose O/U for hunting and Sporting Clays.12- or 20-gauge, 28", 30" Mobilchoke tubes (four, Skeet, Imp. Cyl., Mod., Full). Wide 12.5mm top rib with 2.5mm center groove; 686 Silver Pigeon has silver receiver with scroll engraving; 687 Silver Pigeon Sporting has silver receiver, highly figured walnut; 687 EL Pigeon Sporting has game scene engraving with gold inlaid animals on full sideplate. Introduced 1994. Imported from Italy by Beretta U.S.A.
Price: 682 Gold Sporting, 28", 30", 31" (with case) **$3,000.00**
Price: 682 Gold Sporting, 28", 30", ported, adj. l.o.p. **$3,135.00**
Price: 686 Silver Pigeon Sporting. **$1,850.00**
Price: 686 Silver Pigeon Sporting (20-gauge) **$1,850.00**
Price: 687 Silver Pigeon Sporting. **$2,270.00**
Price: 687 Silver Pigeon Sporting (20 gauge) **$2,270.00**
Price: 687 Diamond Pigeon EELL Sporter (hand engraved sideplates, deluxe wood) **$5,515.00**
Price: ASE Gold Sporting Clay. **$12,145.00**

Beretta S687EL Gold Pigeon Sporting O/U

Similar to the S687 Silver Pigeon Sporting except has sideplates with gold inlay game scene, vent. side and top ribs, bright orange front sight. Stock and forend are of high grade walnut with fine-line checkering. Available in 12-gauge only with 28" or 30" barrels and Mobilchoke tubes. Weight is 6 lbs., 13 oz. Introduced 1993. Imported from Italy by Beretta U.S.A.
Price: **$4,015.00**

BRNO ZH 300 OVER/UNDER SHOTGUN

Gauge: 12, 2-3/4" chambers. **Barrel:** 26", 27-1/2", 29" (Skeet, Imp. Cyl., Mod., Full). **Weight:** 7 lbs. **Length:** 44.4" overall. **Stock:** European walnut. **Features:** Double triggers; automatic safety; polished blue finish engraved receiver. Announced 1998. Imported from the Czech Republic by Euro-Imports.
Price: ZH 301, field. **$594.00**
Price: ZH 302, Skeet **$608.00**
Price: ZH 303, 12-ga. trap **$608.00**
Price: ZH 321, 16-ga. **$595.00**

BRNO 501.2 OVER/UNDER SHOTGUN

Gauge: 12, 2-3/4" chambers. **Barrel:** 27.5" (Full & Mod.). **Weight:** 7 lbs. **Length:** 44" overall. **Stock:** European walnut. **Features:** Boxlock action with double triggers, ejectors; automatic safety; hand-cut checkering. Announced 1998. Imported from The Czech Republic by Euro-Imports.
Price: **$850.00**

BROWNING CITORI O/U SHOTGUN

Gauge: 12, 20, 28 and 410. **Barrel:** 26", 28" in 28 and 410. Offered with Invector choke tubes. All 12- and 20-gauge models have back-bored barrels

Browning Citori Ultra Sporter

and Invector Plus choke system. **Weight:** 6 lbs., 8 oz. (26" 410) to 7 lbs., 13 oz. (30" 12-ga.). **Length:** 43" overall (26" bbl.). **Stock:** Dense walnut, hand checkered, full pistol grip, beavertail forend. Field-type recoil pad on 12-ga. field guns and trap and Skeet models. **Sights:** Medium raised beads, German nickel silver. **Features:** Barrel selector integral with safety, automatic ejectors, three-piece takedown. Imported from Japan by Browning. Contact Browning for complete list of models and prices.

Price: Grade I, Hunting, Invector, 12 and 20 . . . . **$1,388.00**
Price: Grade I, Lightning, 28 and 410, Invector **$1,489.00**
Price: Grade III, Lightning, 28 and 410, Invector **$2,377.00**
Price: Grade VI, 28 and 410 Lightning, Invector. **$3,344.00**
Price: Grade I, Lightning, Invector Plus, 12, 20 . . . . **$1,432.00**
Price: Grade I, Hunting, 28", 30" only, 3-1/2", Invector Plus. . . . **$1,489.00**
Price: Grade I, Lightning, Invector, 12, 20 . . . . **$2,127.00**
Price: Grade VI, Lightning, Invector, 12, 20 . . . . **$3,095.00**
Price: Gran Lightning, 26", 28", Invector, 12, 20 . . . . **$1,963.00**
Price: Gran Lightning, 28, 410 . . . . **$2,068.00**
Price: White Lightning (silver nitride receiver with engraved scroll and rosette, 12-ga., 26", 28") **$1,478.00**
Price: Citori Satin Hunter (12-ga., satin-finished wood, matte-finished barrels and receiver) 3" chambers **$1,318.00**
Price: As above, 3-1/2" chambers **$1,420.00**

Browning Superlight Citori Over/Under
Similar to the standard Citori except available in 12, 20 with 24", 26" or 28" Invector barrels, 28 or 410 with 26" barrels choked Imp. Cyl. & Mod. or 28" choked Mod. & Full. Has straight grip stock, Schnabel forend tip. Superlight 12 weighs 6 lbs., 9 oz. (26" barrels); Superlight 20, 5 lbs., 12 oz. (26" barrels). Introduced 1982.
Price: Grade I only, 28 or 410, Invector **$1,511.00**
Price: Grade III, Invector, 12 . . . . **$2,127.00**
Price: Grade VI, Invector, 12 or 20, gray or blue **$3,095.00**
Price: Grade VI, 28 or 410, Invector, gray or blue **$3,304.00**
Price: Grade I Invector, 12 or 20 . . . . **$1,442.00**
Price: Grade I Invector, Upland Special (24" bbls.), 12 or 20. . . **$1,442.00**
Price: Citori Superlight Feather (12-ga., alloy receiver, 6 lbs. 6 oz.) **$1,592.00**

Browning Citori O/U Special Skeet
Similar to standard Citori except 26", 28" barrels, ventilated side ribs, Invector choke tubes; stock dimensions of 14-3/8"x1-1/2"x2", fitted with Skeet-style recoil pad; conventional target rib and high post target rib.
Price: Grade I Invector, 12-, 20-ga., Invector Plus (high post rib)
. . . . **$1,658.00**
Price: Grade I, 28 and 410 (high post rib) **$1,629.00**
Price: Grade III, 28, 410 (high post rib) **$2,316.00**
Price: Golden Clays,12, 20. . . . . **$3,434.00**
Price: Golden Clays, 28, 410 . . . . **$3,356.00**
Price: Grade III, 12, 20, Invector Plus. **$2,310.00**
Price: Adjustable comb stock, add **$210.00**

Browning Citori Special Trap Models
Similar to standard Citori except 12 gauge only; 30", 32" ported or non-ported (Invector Plus); Monte Carlo cheekpiece (14-3/8"x1-3/8"x1-3/8"x2"); fitted with trap-style recoil pad; high post target rib, ventilated side ribs.
Price: Grade I, Invector Plus, ported bbls. **$1,658.00**
Price: Grade III, Invector Plus Ported. **$2,310.00**
Price: Golden Clays **$3,434.00**

Price: Grade I, adjustable stock **$1,878.00**
Price: Grade III, adjustable stock **$2,530.00**
Price: Golden Clays, adjustable stock **$3,654.00**

Browning Citori XT Trap Over/Under
Similar to the Citori Special Trap except has engraved silver nitride receiver with gold highlights, vented side barrel rib. Available in 12-gauge with 30" or 32" barrels, Invector-Plus choke tubes. Introduced 1999. Imported by Browning.
Price: **$1,834.00**
Price: With adjustable-comb stock **$2,054.00**

Browning Micro Citori Lightning
Similar to the standard Citori 20-ga. Lightning except scaled down for smaller shooter. Comes with 24" Invector Plus back-bored barrels, 13-3/4" length of pull. Weighs about 6 lbs., 3 oz. Introduced 1991.
Price: Grade I **$1,486.00**

Browning Citori Lightning Feather O/U
Similar to the 12-gauge Citori Grade I except has 2-3/4" chambers, rounded pistol grip, Lightning-style forend, and lighweight alloy receiver. Weighs 7 lbs. 9 oz. with 26" barrels. Silvered, engraved receiver. Introduced 1999. Imported by Browning.
Price: **$1,582.00**

Browning Citori Ultra Sporter
Similar to the Citori Hunting except has slightly grooved, semi-beavertail forend, satin-finish stock, radiused rubber butt pad. Has three interchangeable trigger shoes, trigger has three length of pull adjustments. Ventilated rib tapers from 13mm to 10mm, 28" or 30" barrels (ported or non-ported) with Invector Plus choke tubes. Ventilated side ribs. Introduced 1989.
Price: With ported barrels, gray or blue receiver **$1,800.00**
Price: Golden Clays **$3,396.00**

Browning Citori Sporting Hunter
Similar to the Citori Hunting I except has Sporting Clays stock dimensions, a Superposed-style forend, and Sporting Clays butt pad. Available in 12-gauge with 3" chambers, back-bored 26", 28", all with Invector Plus choke tube system. Introduced 1998. Imported from Japan by Browning.
Price: 12-gauge, 3-1/2" **$1,595.00**
Price: 12-, 20-gauge, 3" **$1,500.00**

Browning Citori XS Sporting Clays
Similar to the Citori Grade I except has silver nitride receiver with gold accents, stock dimensions of 14-3/4"x1-1/2"x2-1/4" with satin finish, right-hand palm swell, Schnabel forend. Comes with Modified, Imp. Cyl. and Skeet Invector-Plus choke tubes. Back-bored barrels; vented side ribs. Introduced 1999. Imported by Browning.
Price: 12, 20-ga. **$2,011.00**
Price: 28-ga., 410-bore. **$2,077.00**

Browning Special Sporting Clays
Similar to the Citori Ultra Sporter except has full pistol grip stock with palm swell, gloss finish, 28", 30" or 32" barrels with back-bored Invector Plus chokes (ported or non-ported); high post tapered rib. Also available as 28" and 30" two-barrel set. Introduced 1989.
Price: With ported barrels. **$1,636.00**
Price: As above, adjustable comb **$1,856.00**

Browning Lightning Sporting Clays
Similar to the Citori Lightning with rounded pistol grip and classic forend. Has high post tapered rib or lower hunting-style rib with 30" back-bored Invector Plus barrels, ported or non-ported, 3" chambers. Gloss stock fin-

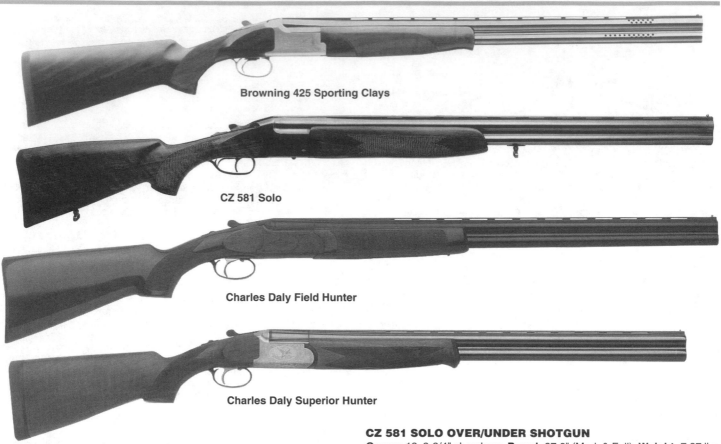

Browning 425 Sporting Clays

CZ 581 Solo

Charles Daly Field Hunter

Charles Daly Superior Hunter

ish, radiused recoil pad. Has "Lightning Sporting Clays Edition" engraved and gold filled on receiver. Introduced 1989.
Price: Low-rib, ported **$1,564.00**
Price: High-rib, ported. **$1,636.00**

BROWNING LIGHT SPORTING 802 ES O/U
Gauge: 12, 2-3/4" chambers. **Barrel:** 28", back-bored Invector Plus. Comes with flush-mounted Imp. Cyl. and Skeet; 2" extended Imp. Cyl. and Mod.; and 4" extended Imp. Cyl. and Mod. tubes. **Weight:** 7 lbs., 5 oz. **Length:** 45" overall. **Stock:** 14-3/8" x 1/8" x 1-9/16" x 1-3/4". Select walnut with radiused solid recoil pad, Schnabel-type forend. **Features:** Trigger adjustable for length of pull; narrow 6.2mm ventilated rib; ventilated barrel side rib; blued receiver. Introduced 1996. Imported from Japan from Browning.
Price: **$1,965.00**

BROWNING 425 SPORTING CLAYS
Gauge: 12, 20, 2-3/4" chambers. **Barrel:** 12-ga.—28", 30", 32" (Invector Plus tubes), back-bored; 20-ga.—28", 30" (Invector Plus tubes). **Weight:** 7 lbs., 13 oz. (12-ga., 28"). **Stock:** 14-13/16" (1/8")x1-7/16"x2-3/16" (12-ga.). Select walnut with gloss finish, cut checkering, Schnabel forend. **Features:** Grayed receiver with engraving, blued barrels. Barrels are ported on 12-gauge guns. Has low 10mm wide vent rib. Comes with three interchangeable trigger shoes to adjust length of pull. Introduced in U.S. 1993. Imported by Browning.
Price: Grade I, 12-, 20-ga., Invector Plus **$1,855.00**
Price: Golden Clays, 12-, 20-ga., Invector Plus **$3,507.00**
Price: With adjustable comb stock, add **$2,075.00**

Browning 425 WSSF Shotgun
Similar to the 425 Sporting Clays except in 12-gauge only, 28" barrels, has stock dimensions specifically tailored to women shooters (14-1/4"x1-1/2"x1-1/2"); top lever and takedown lever are easier to operate. Stock and forend have teal-colored finish or natural walnut with Women's Shooting Sports Foundation logo. Weighs 7 lbs., 4 oz. Introduced 1995. Imported by Browning.
Price: **$1,855.00**

CZ 581 SOLO OVER/UNDER SHOTGUN
Gauge: 12, 2-3/4" chambers. **Barrel:** 27.6" (Mod. & Full). **Weight:** 7.37 lbs. **Length:** 44.5" overall. **Stock:** Circassian walnut. **Features:** Automatic ejectors; double triggers; Kersten-style double lump locking system. Imported from the Czech Republic by CZ-USA.
Price: **$799.00**

CHARLES DALY SUPERIOR TRAP AE MC
Gauge: 12, 2-3/4" chambers. **Barrel:** 30" choke tubes. **Weight:** About 7 lbs. **Stock:** Checkered walnut; pistol grip, semi-beavertail forend. **Features:** Silver engraved receiver, chrome moly steel barrels; gold single selective trigger; automatic safety, automatic ejectors; red bead front sight, metal bead center; recoil pad. Introduced 1997. Imported from Italy by K.B.I., Inc.
Price: **$1,219.00**

CHARLES DALY FIELD HUNTER OVER/UNDER SHOTGUN
Gauge: 12, 20, 28 and 410 bore (3" chambers, 28 ga. has 2-3/4"). **Barrel:** 28" Mod & Full, 26 " Imp. Cyl. & Mod (410 is Full & Full). **Weight:** About 7 lbs. **Length:** NA. **Stock:** Checkered walnut pistol grip and forend. **Features:** Blued engraved receiver, chrome moly steel barrels; gold single selective trigger; automatic safety; extractors; gold bead front sight. Introduced 1997. Imported from Italy by K.B.I., Inc.
Price: 12 or 20 ga. **$749.00**
Price: 28 ga. **$809.00**
Price: 410 bore **$849.00**

Charles Daly Field Hunter AE Shotgun
Similar to the Field Hunter except 28-gauge and 410-bore only; 26" (Imp. Cyl. & Mod., 28-gauge), 26" (Full & Full, 410); automatic; ejectors. Introduced 1997. Imported from Italy by K.B.I., Inc.
Price: 28 . . . . **$889.00**
Price: 410 . . . . **$929.00**

Charles Daly Superior Hunter AE Shotgun
Similar to the Field Hunter AE except has silvered, engraved receiver. Introduced 1997. Imported from Italy by F.B.I., Inc.
Price: 28-ga. **$1,059.00**
Price: 410 bore **$1,099.00**

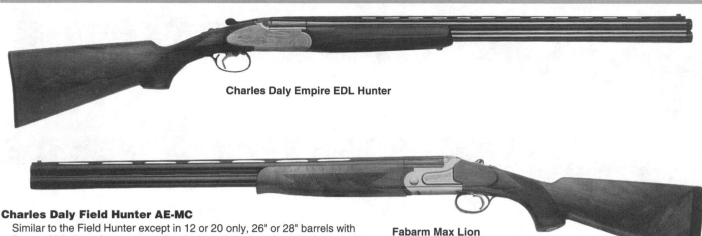

Charles Daly Empire EDL Hunter

Fabarm Max Lion

Charles Daly Field Hunter AE-MC
Similar to the Field Hunter except in 12 or 20 only, 26" or 28" barrels with five multichoke tubes; automatic ejectors. Introduced 1997. Imported from Italy by K.B.I., Inc.
Price: 12 or 20 . . . . $949.00

Charles Daly Superior Sporting O/U
Similar to the Field Hunter AE-MC except 28" or 30" barrels; silvered, engraved receiver; five choke tubes; ported barrels; red bead front sight. Introduced 1997. Imported from Italy by K.B.I., Inc.
Price: $1,219.00

CHARLES DALY EMPIRE TRAP AE MC
Gauge: 12, 2-3/4" chambers. **Barrel:** 30" choke tubes. **Weight:** About 7 lbs. **Stock:** Checkered walnut; pistol grip, semi-beavertail forend. **Features:** Silvered, engraved, reinforced receiver; chrome moly steel barrels; gold single selective trigger; automatic safety, automatic ejector; red bead front sight, metal bead center; recoil pad. Introduced 1997. Imported from Italy by K.B.I., Inc.
Price: $1,489.00

CHARLES DALY DIAMOND REGENT GTX DL HUNTER O/U
Gauge: 12, 20, 410, 3" chambers, 28, 2-3/4" chambers. **Barrel:** 26", 28", 30" (choke tubes), 26" (Imp. Cyl. & Mod. in 28, 26" (Full & Full) in 410. **Weight:** About 7 lbs. **Stock:** Extra select fancy European walnut with 24" hand checkering, hand rubbed oil finish. **Features:** Boss-type action with internal side lumps. Deep cut hand-engraved scrollwork and game scene set in full sideplates. GTX detachable single selective trigger system with coil springs; chrome moly steel barrels; automatic safety, automatic ejectors, white bead front sight, metal bead center sight. Introduced 1997. Imported from Italy by K.B.I., Inc.
Price: 12 or 20 . . . . $22,299.00
Price: 28 . . . . $22,369.00
Price: 410 . . . . $22,419.00
Price: Diamond Regent GTX EDL Hunter (as above with engraved scroll and birds, 10 gold inlays), 12 or 20 . . . . $26,249.00
Price: As above, 28 . . . . $26,499.00
Price: As above, 410 . . . . $26,549.00

CHARLES DALY EMPIRE EDL HUNTER O/U
Gauge: 12, 20, 410, 3" chambers, 28-ga., 2-3/4". **Barrel:** 26", 28" (12, 20, choke tubes), 26" (Imp. Cyl. & Mod., 28-ga.), 26" (Full & Full, 410). **Weight:** About 7 lbs. **Stocks:** Checkered walnut pistol grip buttstock, semi-beavertail forend; recoil pad. **Features:** Silvered, engraved receiver; chrome moly barrels; gold single selective trigger; automatic safety; automatic ejectors; red bead front sight, metal bead middle sight. Introduced 1997. Imported from Italy by K.B.I., Inc.
Price: Empire EDL (dummy sideplates) 12 or 20 . . . . $1,549.00
Price: Empire EDL, 28 . . . . $1,569.00
Price: Empire EDL, 410 . . . . $1,569.00

Charles Daly Empire Sporting O/U
Similar to the Empire EDL Hunter except 12- or 20-gauge only, 28", 30" barrels with choke tubes; ported barrels; special stock dimensions. Introduced 1997. Imported from Italy by K.B.I., Inc.
Price: $1,449.00

CHARLES DALY DIAMOND GTX SPORTING O/U SHOTGUN
Gauge: 12, 20, 3" chambers. **Barrel:** 28", 30" with choke tubes. **Weight:** About 8.5 lbs. **Stock:** Checkered deluxe walnut; Sporting clays dimensions. Pistol grip; semi-beavertail forend; hand rubbed oil finish. **Features:** Chromed, hand-engraved receiver; chrome moly steel barrels; GTX detachable single selective trigger system with coil springs, automatic safety; automatic ejectors; red bead front sight; ported barrels. Introduced 1997. Imported from Italy by K.B.I., Inc.
Price: $5,269.00

CHARLES DALY DIAMOND GTX TRAP AE-MC O/U SHOTGUN
Gauge: 12, 2-3/4" chambers. **Barrel:** 30" (Full & Full). **Weight:** About 8.5 lbs. **Stock:** Checkered deluxe walnut; pistol grip; trap dimensions; semi-beavertail forend; hand rubbed oil finish. **Features:** Silvered, hand-engraved receiver; chrome moly steel barrels; GTX detachable single selective trigger system with coil springs, automatic safety, automatic-ejectors, red bead front sight, metal bead middle; recoil pad. Introduced 1997. Imported from Italy by K.B.I., Inc.
Price: $6,429.00

CHARLES DALY DIAMOND GTX DL HUNTER O/U
Gauge: 12, 20, 410, 3 " chambers, 28, 2-3/4"chambers. **Barrel:** 26", 28", choke tubes in 12 and 20 ga., 26" (Imp. Cyl. & Mod.), 26" (Full & Full) in 410-bore. **Weight:** About 8.5 lbs. **Stock:** Select fancy European walnut stock, with 24 lpi hand checkering; hand-rubbed oil finish. **Features:** Boss-type action with internal side lugs, hand-engraved scrollwork and game scene. GTX detachable single selective trigger system with coil springs; chrome moly steel barrels, automatic safety, automatic ejectors, red bead front sight, recoil pad. Introduced 1997. Imported from Italy by K.B.I., Inc.
Price: 12 or 20 . . . . $12,399.00
Price: 28 . . . . $12,489.00
Price: 410 . . . . $12,529.00
Price: GTX EDL Hunter (with gold inlays), 12, 20 . . . . $15,999.00
Price: As above, 28 . . . . $16,179.00
Price: As above, 410 . . . . $16,219.00

FABARM MAX LION OVER/UNDER SHOTGUNS
Gauge: 12, 3" chambers, 20, 3" chambers. **Barrel:** 26", 28", 30" (12-ga.); 26", 28" (20-ga.), choke tubes. **Weight:** 7.4 lbs. **Length:** 47.5" overall (26" barrel). **Stock:** European walnut; leather-covered recoil pad. **Features:** Boxlock action with single selective trigger, manual safety, automatic ejectors; chrome-lined barrels; adjustable trigger. Silvered, engraved receiver. Comes with locking, fitted luggage case. Introduced 1998. Imported from Italy by Heckler & Koch, Inc.
Price: 12 or 20 . . . . $1,807.00
Price: With TriBore barrel stystem $1,373.00

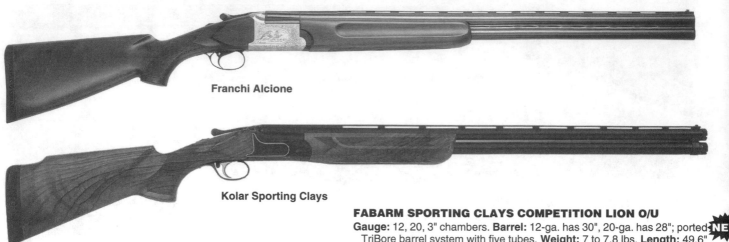

Franchi Alcione

Kolar Sporting Clays

Fabarm Black Lion Competition O/U Shotguns

Similar to the Max Lion except has black receiver finish, deluxe European walnut stock and forend. Introduced 1998. Imported from Italy by Heckler & Koch, Inc.

Price: 12 or 20 .... $1,529.00
Price: With TriBore barrel system......................... $1,595.00

FABARM ULTRA MAG LION O/U SHOTGUN

Gauge: 12, 3-1/2" chambers. **Barrel:** 28" (Cyl., Imp. Cyl., Mod., Imp. Mod., Full, SS-Mod., SS-Full choke tubes). **Weight:** 7.9 lbs. **Length:** 50" overall. **Stock:** Black-colored walnut. **Features:** Matte finished metal surfaces; single selective trigger; non-auto ejectors; leather-covered recoil pad. Comes with locking hard plastic case. Introduced 1998. Imported from Italy by Heckler & Koch, Inc.

Price: $1,120.00

Fabarm Ultra Camo Mag Lion O/U Shotgun

NEW! Similar to the Ultra Mag Lion except completely covered with Wetlands camouflage pattern, has the ported TriBore barrel system, and a mid-rib bead. Chambered for 3-1/2" shells. Stock and forend are walnut. Introduced 1999. Imported from Italy by Heckler & Koch, Inc.

Price: $1,295.00

FABARM SILVER LION OVER/UNDER SHOTGUNS

Gauge: 12, 3" chambers, 20, 3" chambers. **Barrel:** 26", 28", 30" (12-ga.); 26", 28" (20-ga.), choke tubes. **Weight:** 7.2 lbs. **Length:** 47.5" overall (26" barrels). **Stock:** Walnut; leather-covered recoil pad. **Features:** Boxlock action with single selective trigger; silvered receiver with engraving; automatic ejectors. Comes with locking hard plastic case. Introduced 1998. Imported from Italy by Heckler & Koch, Inc.

Price: 12 or 20 .... $1,146.00
Price: Super Light Lion (12-ga. only, 24" barrels, weighs 6.5 lbs.).. $1,053.00
Price: With TriBore barrel system....................... $1,264.00

Fabarm Silver Lion Youth Model O/U

NEW! Similar to the Silver Lion except has 12.5" length of pull, is in 20-gauge only (3-1/2" chambers), and comes with 24" TriBore barrel system. Weight is 6 lbs. Introduced 1999. Imported from Italy by Heckler & Koch, Inc.

Price: $1,331.00
Price: Super Light Lion Youth (12-ga. only, 6 lbs., blued receiver) $1,053.00

FABARM CAMO TURKEY MAG O/U SHOTGUN

NEW! **Gauge:** 12, 3-1/2" chambers. **Barrel:** 20" TriBore (Ultra-Full ported tubes). **Weight:** 7.5 lbs. **Length:** 46" overall. **Stock:** 14.5"x1.5"x2.29". Walnut. **Sights:** Front bar, Picatinny rail scope base. **Features:** Completely covered with Xtra Brown camouflage finish. Unported barrels. Introduced 1999. Imported from Italy by Heckler & Koch, Inc.

Price: $1,295.00

FABARM SPORTING CLAYS COMPETITION LION O/U

NE **Gauge:** 12, 20, 3" chambers. **Barrel:** 12-ga. has 30", 20-ga. has 28"; ported TriBore barrel system with five tubes. **Weight:** 7 to 7.8 lbs. **Length:** 49.6" overall (20-ga.). **Stock:** 14.50"x1.38"x2.17" (20-ga.); deluxe walnut; leather-covered recoil pad. **Features:** Single selective trigger, auto ejectors; recoil reducer installed in buttstock; 10mm channeled rib; silvered, engraved receiver. Introduced 1999. Imported from Italy by Heckler & Koch, Inc.

Price: $1,365.00

FRANCHI ALCIONE OVER/UNDER SHOTGUN

Gauge: 12, 3" chambers. **Barrel:** 26", 28"; Franchoke tubes. **Weight:** 7.5 lbs. **Length:** 43" overall with 26" barrels. **Stock:** European walnut. **Features:** Boxlock action with ejectors; barrel selector is mounted on the trigger; silvered, engraved receiver; vent center rib; automatic safety. Imported from Italy by Benelli USA.

Price: $947.00

Franchi Alcione Sport O/U Shotgun

Similar to the Alcione except has 2-3/4" chambers, elongated forcing cones and porting for Sporting Clays shooting, 10mm vent rib, tightly curved pistol grip, manual safety, removeable sideplates. Imported from Italy by Benelli USA.

Price: $1,227.00

KOLAR SPORTING CLAYS O/U SHOTGUN

Gauge: 12, 2-3/4" chambers. **Barrel:** 28", 30", 32"; extended choke tubes. **Stock:** 14-5/8"x2-1/2"x1-7/8"x1-3/8". French walnut. **Features:** Single selective trigger, detachable, adjustable for length; overbored barrels with long forcing cones; flat tramline rib; matte blue finish. Made in U.S. by Kolar.

Price: Standard. $7,250.00
Price: Elite $10,050.00
Price: Elite Gold $11,545.00
Price: Legend $13,045.00
Price: Custom Gold $24,750.00

Kolar AAA Competition Trap Over/Under Shotgun

Similar to the Sporting Clays gun except has 32" O/U / 34" Unsingle or 30" O/U / 34" Unsingle barrels as an over/under, unsingle, or combination set. Stock dimensions are 14-1/2"x2-1/2"x1-1/2"; American or French walnut; step parallel rib standard. Contact maker for full listings. Made in U.S. by Kolar.

Price: Over/under, choke tubes, Standard $7,025.00
Price: Unsingle, choke tubes, Standard $7,775.00
Price: Combo (30"/34", 32"/34"), Standard. $10,170.00

Kolar AAA Competition Skeet Over/Under Shotgun

Similar to the Sporting Clays gun except has 28" or 30" barrels with Kolarite AAA sub-gauge tubes; stock of American or French walnut with matte finish; flat tramline rib; under barrel adjustable for point of impact. Many options available. Contact maker for complete listing. Made in U.S. by Kolar.

Price: Standard, choke tubes $8,645.00
Price: Standard, choke tubes, two-barrel set $10,710.00

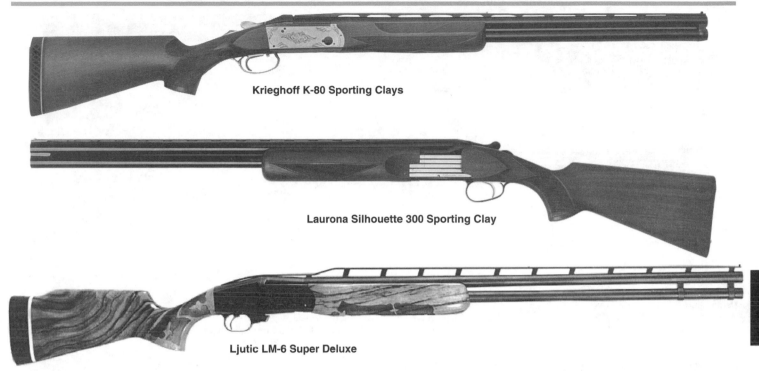

Krieghoff K-80 Sporting Clays

Laurona Silhouette 300 Sporting Clay

Ljutic LM-6 Super Deluxe

KRIEGHOFF K-80 SPORTING CLAYS O/U

Gauge: 12. **Barrel:** 28", 30" or 32" with choke tubes. **Weight:** About 8 lbs. **Stock:** #3 Sporting stock designed for gun-down shooting. **Features:** Choice of standard or lightweight receiver with satin nickel finish and classic scroll engraving. Selective mechanical trigger adjustable for position. Choice of tapered flat or 8mm parallel flat barrel rib. Free-floating barrels. Aluminum case. Imported from Germany by Krieghoff International, Inc.
Price: Standard grade with five choke tubes, from $8,150.00

KRIEGHOFF K-80 SKEET SHOTGUN

Gauge: 12, 2-3/4" chambers. **Barrel:** 28" (Skeet & Skeet, optional Tula or choke tubes). **Weight:** About 7-3/4 lbs. **Stock:** American Skeet or straight Skeet stocks, with palm-swell grips. Walnut. **Features:** Satin gray receiver finish. Selective mechanical trigger adjustable for position. Choice of ventilated 8mm parallel flat rib or ventilated 8-12mm tapered flat rib. Introduced 1980. Imported from Germany by Krieghoff International, Inc.

Price: Standard, Skeet chokes $6,900.00
Price: As above, Tula chokes $7,825.00
Price: Lightweight model (weighs 7 lbs.), Standard $6,900.00
Price: Two-Barrel Set (tube concept), 12-ga., Standard $11,840.00
Price: Skeet Special (28", tapered flat rib, Skeet & Skeet choke
tubes) $7,575.00

Krieghoff K-80 Four-Barrel Skeet Set

Similar to the Standard Skeet except comes with barrels for 12, 20, 28, 410. Comes with fitted aluminum case.
Price: Standard grade. $16,950.00

Krieghoff K-80 International Skeet

Similar to the Standard Skeet except has 1/2" ventilated Broadway-style rib, special Tula chokes with gas release holes at muzzle. International Skeet stock. Comes in fitted aluminum case.
Price: Standard grade. $7,825.00

KRIEGHOFF K-80 O/U TRAP SHOTGUN

Gauge: 12, 2-3/4" chambers. **Barrel:** 30", 32" (Imp. Mod. & Full or choke tubes). **Weight:** About 8-1/2 lbs. **Stock:** Four stock dimensions or adjustable stock available; all have palm swell grips. Checkered European walnut. **Features:** Satin nickel receiver. Selective mechanical trigger, adjustable for position. Ventilated step rib. Introduced 1980. Imported from Germany by Krieghoff International, Inc.
Price: K-80 O/U (30", 32", Imp. Mod. & Full), from $7,375.00

Price: K-80 Unsingle (32", 34", Full), Standard, from $7,950.00
Price: K-80 Combo (two-barrel set), Standard, from $9,975.00

LAURONA SUPER MODEL OVER/UNDERS

Gauge: 12, 20, 2-3/4" or 3" chambers. **Barrel:** 26", 28" (Multichoke), 29" (Multichokes and Full). **Weight:** About 7 lbs. **Stock:** European walnut. Dimensions may vary according to model. Full pistol grip. **Features:** Boxlock action, silvered with engraving. Automatic selective ejectors; choke tubes available on most models; single selective or twin single triggers; black chrome barrels. Has 5-year warranty, including metal finish. Imported from Spain by Galaxy Imports.
Price: Model 83 MG, 12- or 20-ga. $1,215.00
Price: Model 84S Super Trap (fixed chokes) $1,340.00
Price: Model 85 Super Game, 12- or 20-ga. $1,215.00
Price: Model 85 MS Super Trap (Full/Multichoke) $1,390.00

LAURONA SILHOUETTE 300 SPORTING CLAYS

Gauge: 12, 2-3/4" or 3" chambers. **Barrel:** 28", 29" (Multichoke tubes, flush-type or knurled). **Weight:** 7 lbs., 12 oz. **Stock:** 14-3/8"x1-3/8"x2-1/2". European walnut with full pistol grip, beavertail forend. Rubber butt pad. **Features:** Selective single trigger, automatic selective ejectors. Introduced 1988. Imported from Spain by Galaxy Imports.
Price: $1,250.00
Price: Silhouette Ultra-Magnum, 3-1/2" chambers $1,365.00

Laurona Silhouette 300 Trap

Same gun as the Silhouette 300 Sporting Clays except has 29" barrels, trap stock dimensions of 14-3/8"x1-7/16"x1-5/8", weighs 7 lbs., 15 oz. Available with flush or knurled Multichokes.
Price: $1,310.00

LEBEAU - COURALLY BOSS-VEREES O/U

Gauge: 12, 20, 2-3/4" chambers. **Barrel:** 25" to 32". **Weight:** To customer specifications. **Stock:** Exhibition-quality French walnut. **Features:** Boss-type sidelock with automatic ejectors; single or double triggers; chopper lump barrels. A custom gun built to customer specifications. Imported from Belgium by Wm. Larkin Moore.
Price: From $81,000.00

LJUTIC LM-6 SUPER DELUXE O/U SHOTGUN

Gauge: 12. **Barrel:** 28" to 34", choked to customer specs for live birds, trap, International Trap. **Weight:** To customer specs. **Stock:** To customer specs. Oil finish, hand checkered. **Features:** Custom-made gun. Hollow-

SHOTGUNS — OVER/UNDERS

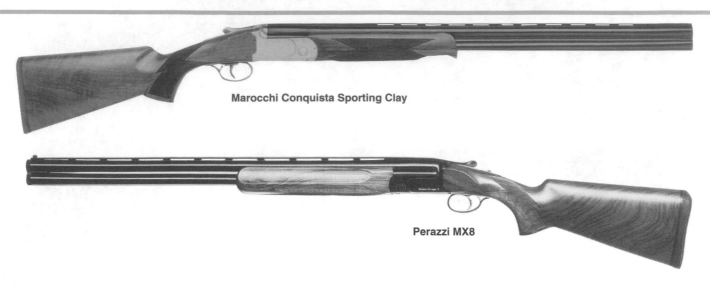

Marocchi Conquista Sporting Clay

Perazzi MX8

milled rib, pull or release trigger, pushbutton opener in front of trigger guard. From Ljutic Industries.

Price: Super Deluxe LM-6 O/U......................... **$17,995.00**
Price: Over/under Combo (interchangeable single barrel, two trigger guards, one for single trigger, one for doubles) **$24,995.00**
Price: Extra over/under barrel sets, 29"-32"................ **$5,995.00**

MAROCCHI CONQUISTA SPORTING CLAYS O/U SHOTGUNS

Gauge: 12, 2-3/4" chambers. **Barrel:** 28", 30", 32" (ContreChoke tubes); 10mm concave vent. rib. **Weight:** About 8 lbs. **Stock:** 14-1/2"-14-7/8"x2-3/16"x1-7/16"; American walnut with checkered grip and forend; Sporting Clays butt pad. **Sights:** 16mm luminescent front. **Features:** Has lower monoblock and frame profile. Fast lock time. Ergonomically-shaped trigger is adjustable for pull length. Automatic selective ejectors. Coin-finished receiver, blued barrels. Comes with five choke tubes, hard case. Also available as true left-hand model—opening lever operates from left to right; stock has left-hand cast. Introduced 1994. Imported from Italy by Precision Sales International.

Price: Grade I, right-hand............................ **$1,995.00**
Price: Grade I, left-hand............................. **$2,120.00**
Price: Grade II, right-hand........................... **$2,330.00**
Price: Grade II, left-hand............................ **$2,685.00**
Price: Grade III, right-hand, from **$3,599.00**
Price: Grade III, left-hand, from **$3,995.00**

Marocchi Lady Sport O/U Shotgun

Ergonomically designed specifically for women shooters. Similar to the Conquista Sporting Clays model except has 28" or 30" barrels with five Contrechoke tubes, stock dimensions of 13-7/8"-14-1/4"x1-11/32"x2-9/32"; weighs about 7-1/2 lbs. Also available as left-hand model—opening lever operates from left to right; stock has left-hand cast. Also available with colored graphics finish on frame and opening lever. Introduced 1995. Imported from Italy by Precision Sales International.

Price: Grade I, right-hand............................ **$2,120.00**
Price: Left-hand, add (all grades)....................... **$101.00**
Price: Lady Sport Spectrum (colored receiver panel)........ **$2,199.00**
Price: Lady Sport Spectrum, left-hand **$2,300.00**

Marocchi Conquista Trap Over/Under Shotgun

Similar to the Conquista Sporting Clays model except has 30" or 32" barrels choked Full & Full, stock dimensions of 14-1/2"- 14-7/8"x1-11/16"x1-9/32"; weighs about 8-1/4 lbs. Introduced 1994. Imported from Italy by Precision Sales International.

Price: Grade I, right-hand............................ **$1,995.00**
Price: Grade II, right-hand **$2,330.00**
Price: Grade III, right-hand, from **$3,599.00**

Marocchi Conquista Skeet Over/Under Shotgun

Similar to the Conquista Sporting Clays except has 28" (Skeet & Skeet) barrels, stock dimensions of 14-3/8"- 14-3/4"x2-3/16"x1-1/2". Weighs

about 7-3/4 lbs. Introduced 1994. Imported from Italy by Precision Sales International.

Price: Grade I, right-hand.............................. **$1,995.00**
Price: Grade II, right-hand **$2,330.00**
Price: Grade III, right-hand, from **$3,599.00**

MAROCCHI CLASSIC DOUBLES MODEL 92 SPORTING CLAYS O/U SHOTGUN

Gauge: 12, 3" chambers. **Barrel:** 30"; back-bored, ported (ContreChoke Plus tubes); 10 mm concave ventilated top rib, ventilated middle rib. **Weight:** 8 lbs. 2 oz. **Stock:** 14-1/4"- 14-5/8"x 2-1/8"x1-3/8"; American walnut with checkered grip and forend; Sporting Clays butt pad. **Features:** Low profile frame; fast lock time; automatic selective ejectors; blued receiver and barrels. Comes with three choke tubes. Ergonomically shaped trigger adjustable for pull length without tools. Barrels are back-bored and ported. Introduced 1996. Imported from Italy by Precision Sales International.

Price: **$1,598.00**

MERKEL MODEL 2001 EL O/U SHOTGUN

Gauge: 12, 20, 3" chambers, 28, 2-3/4" chambers. **Barrel:** 12—28"; 20, 28-ga.—26-3/4". **Weight:** About 7 lbs. (12-ga.). **Stock:** Oil-finished walnut; English or pistol grip. **Features:** Self-cocking Blitz boxlock action with cocking indicators; Kersten double cross-bolt lock; silver-grayed receiver with engraved hunting scenes; coil spring ejectors; single selective or double triggers. Imported from Germany by GSI, Inc.

Price: 12, 20.. **$5,895.00**
Price: 28-ga... **$6,495.00**
Price: Model 2000EL (scroll engraving, 12 or 20) **$4,995.00**

Merkel Model 303 EL O/U Shotgun

Similar to the Model 2001 EL except has Holland & Holland-style sidelock action with cocking indicators; English-style Arabesque engraving. Available in 12, 20 gauge. Imported from Germany by GSI, Inc.

Price: **$19,995.00**

Merkel Model 2002 EL O/U Shotgun

Similar to the Model 2001 EL except has dummy sideplates, Arabesque engraving with hunting scenes; 12, 20-gauge. Imported from Germany by GSI, Inc.

Price: **$9,995.00**

PERAZZI MX8 SPECIAL SPORTING O/U

Gauge: 12, 2-3/4" chambers. **Barrel:** 28-3/8" (Imp. Mod. & Extra Full), 29-1/2" (choke tubes). **Weight:** 7 lbs., 12 oz. **Stock:** Special specifications. **Features:** Has single selective trigger; flat 7/16"x5/16" vent. rib. Many options available. Imported from Italy by Perazzi U.S.A., Inc.

Price: **$9,600.00**

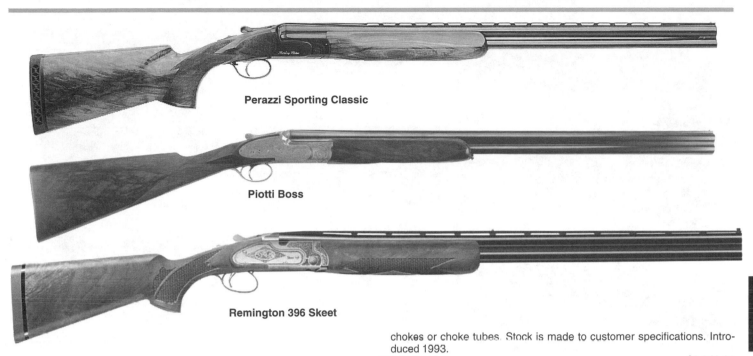

Perazzi Sporting Classic

Piotti Boss

Remington 396 Skeet

chokes or choke tubes. Stock is made to customer specifications. Introduced 1993.
Price: From.. **$9,340.00**

Perazzi MX8 Special Four-Gauge Skeet
Similar to the MX8 except has Skeet dimensions, interchangeable, adjustable four-position trigger assembly. Comes with four barrel sets in 12, 20, 28, 410, flat 5/16"x5/16" rib.
Price: From.. **$21,330.00**

PERAZZI MX10 OVER/UNDER SHOTGUN
Gauge: 12, 2-3/4" chambers. **Barrel:** 29.5", 31.5" (fixed chokes). **Weight:** NA. **Stock:** Walnut; cheekpiece adjustable for elevation and cast. **Features:** Adjustable rib; vent. side rib. Externally selective trigger. Available in single barrel, combo, over/under trap, Skeet, pigeon and sporting models. Introduced 1993. Imported from Italy by Perazzi U.S.A., Inc.
Price: From.. **$11,030.00**

PERAZZI MX28, MX410 GAME O/U SHOTGUNS
Gauge: 28, 2-3/4" chambers, 410, 3" chambers. **Barrel:** 26" (Imp. Cyl. & Full). **Weight:** NA. **Stock:** To customer specifications. **Features:** Made on scaled-down frames proportioned to the gauge. Introduced 1993. Imported from Italy by Perazzi U.S.A., Inc.
Price: From.. **$17,330.00**

PIOTTI BOS S OVER/UNDER SHOTGUN
Gauge: 12, 20. **Barrel:** 26" to 32", chokes as specified. **Weight:** 6.5 to 8 lbs. **Stock:** Dimensions to customer specs. Best quality figured walnut. **Features:** Essentially a custom-made gun with many options. Introduced 1993. Imported from Italy by Wm. Larkin Moore.
Price: From.. **$39,200.00**

REMINGTON 396 SKEET O/U
Gauge: 12, 2-3/4" chambers. **Barrel:** 28", 30" (Skeet & Imp. Skeet Rem. Choke tubes). **Weight:** 8 lbs. **Stock:** 14-3/16"x1-1/2"x2-1/4". Fancy, figured American walnut. Target-style forend, larger-radius comb, grip palm swell. **Features:** Boxlock action with removable sideplates. Barrels have lengthened forcing cones; 10mm non-stepped, parallel rib; engraved receiver, sideplates, trigger guard, top lever, forend iron are finished with gray nitride. Made in U.S. by Remington. Introduced 1996.
Price: **$1,993.00**

Remington 396 Sporting O/U
Similar to the 396 Skeet except the 28", 30" barrels are factory ported, and come with Skeet, Imp. Skeet, Imp. Cyl. and Mod. Rem Choke tubes. Made in U.S. by Remington. Introduced 1996.
Price: **$2,126.00**

Perazzi Sporting Classic O/U
Same as the Special Sporting except is deluxe version with select wood and engraving. Available with flush mount choke tubes, 29.5" barrels. Introduced 1993.
Price: From.. **$10,950.00**

PERAZZI MX12 HUNTING OVER/UNDER
Gauge: 12, 2-3/4" chambers. **Barrel:** 26", 27-5/8", 28-3/8", 29-1/2" (Mod. & Full); choke tubes available in 27-5/8", 29-1/2" only (MX12C). **Weight:** 7 lbs., 4 oz. **Stock:** To customer specs; Interchangeable. **Features:** Single selective trigger; coil springs used in action; Schnabel forend tip. Imported from Italy by Perazzi U.S.A., Inc.
Price: From.. **$8,670.00**
Price: MX12C (with choke tubes), from **$9,290.00**

Perazzi MX20 Hunting Over/Under
Similar to the MX12 except 20-ga. frame size. Available in 20, 28, 410 with 2-3/4" or 3" chambers. 26" standard, and choked Mod. & Full. Weight is 6 lbs., 6 oz.
Price: From.. **$8,670.00**
Price: MX20C (as above, 20-ga. only, choke tubes), from **$9,290.00**

PERAZZI MX8/MX8 SPECIAL TRAP, SKEET
Gauge: 12, 2-3/4" chambers. **Barrel:** Trap—29-1/2" (Imp. Mod. & Extra Full), 31-1/2" (Full & Extra Full). Choke tubes optional. Skeet—27-5/8" (Skeet & Skeet). **Weight:** About 8-1/2 lbs. (Trap); 7 lbs., 15 oz. (Skeet). **Stock:** Interchangeable and custom made to customer specs. **Features:** Has detachable and interchangeable trigger group with flat V springs. Flat 7/16" ventilated rib. Many options available. Imported from Italy by Perazzi U.S.A., Inc.
Price: From.. **$8,670.00**
Price: MX8 Special (adj. four-position trigger), from **$8,670.00**
Price: MX8 Special Combo (o/u and single barrel sets), from . **$12,460.00**

Perazzi MX8 Special Skeet Over/Under
Similar to the MX8 Skeet except has adjustable four-position trigger, Skeet stock dimensions.
Price: From.. **$9,340.00**

Perazzi MX8/20 Over/Under Shotgun
Similar to the MX8 except has smaller frame and has a removable trigger mechanism. Available in trap, Skeet, sporting or game models with fixed

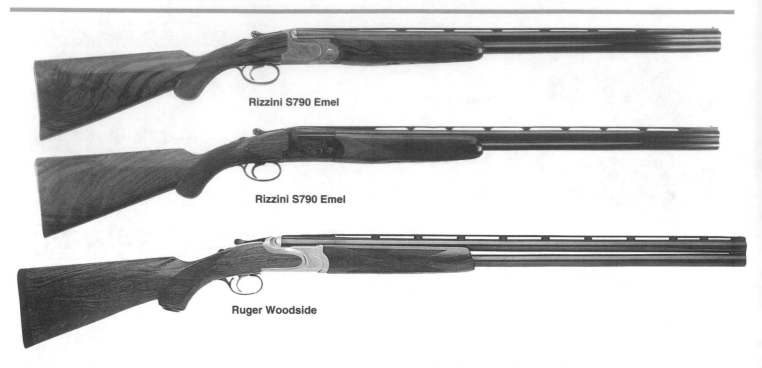

Rizzini S790 Emel

Rizzini S790 Emel

Ruger Woodside

RIZZINI S790 EMEL OVER/UNDER SHOTGUN

Gauge: 20, 28, 410. **Barrel:** 26", 27.5" (Imp. Cyl. & Imp. Mod.). **Weight:** About 6 lbs. **Stock:** 14"x1-1/2"x2-1/8". Extra-fancy select walnut. **Features:** Boxlock action with profuse engraving; automatic ejectors; single selective trigger; silvered receiver. Comes with Nizzoli leather case. Introduced 1996. Imported from Italy by Wm. Larkin Moore & Co.
Price: From $9,600.00

Rizzini S792 EMEL Over/Under Shotgun

Similar to the S790 EMEL except has dummy sideplates with extensive engraving coverage. Comes with Nizzoli leather case. Introduced 1996. Imported from Italy by Wm. Larkin Moore & Co.
Price: From $9,400.00

RIZZINI S790 SPORTING EL OVER/UNDER

Gauge: 12, 2-3/4" chambers. **Barrel:** 28", 29.5", Imp. Mod., Mod., Full choke tubes. **Weight:** 8.1 lbs. **Stock:** 14-1/2"x1-1/2"x2-1/4". Extra-fancy select walnut. **Features:** Boxlock action; automatic ejectors; single selective trigger; 10mm top rib. Comes with case. Introduced 1996. Imported from Italy by Wm. Larkin Moore & Co.
Price: $6,250.00

RIZZINI UPLAND EL OVER/UNDER SHOTGUN

Gauge: 12, 16, 20, 28, 410. **Barrel:** 26", 27-1/2", Mod. & Full, Imp. Cyl. & Imp. Mod. choke tubes. **Weight:** About 6.6 lbs. **Stock:** 14-1/2"x1-1/2"x2-1/4". **Features:** Boxlock action; single selective trigger; ejectors; profuse engraving on silvered receiver. Comes with fitted case. Introduced 1996. Imported from Italy by Wm. Larkin Moore & Co.
Price: From $3,500.00

Rizzini Artemis Over/Under Shotgun

Same as the Upland EL model except has dummy sideplates with extensive game scene engraving. Fancy European walnut stock. Comes with fitted case. Introduced 1996. Imported from Italy by Wm. Larkin Moore & Co.
Price: From $2,375.00

RIZZINI S782 EMEL OVER/UNDER SHOTGUN

Gauge: 12, 2-3/4" chambers. **Barrel:** 26", 27.5" (Imp. Cyl. & Imp. Mod.). **Weight:** About 6.75 lbs. **Stock:** 14-1/2"x1-1/2"x2-1/4". Extra fancy select walnut. **Features:** Boxlock action with dummy sideplates; extensive engraving with gold inlaid game birds; silvered receiver; automatic ejectors; single selective trigger. Comes with Nizzoli leather case. Introduced 1996. Imported from Italy by Wm. Larkin Moore & Co.
Price: From $12,250.00

ROTTWEIL PARAGON OVER/UNDER

Gauge: 12, 2-3/4" chambers. **Barrel:** 28", 30", five choke tubes. **Weight:** 7 lbs. **Stock:** 14-1/2"x1-1/2"x2-1/2"; European walnut. **Features:** Boxlock action. Detachable trigger assembly; ejectors can be deactivated; convertible top lever for right- or left-hand use; trigger adjustable for position. Imported from Germany by Dynamit Nobel-RWS, Inc.
Price: $5,995.00

RUGER WOODSIDE OVER/UNDER SHOTGUN

Gauge: 12, 3" chambers. **Barrel:** 26", 28" (Full, Mod., Imp. Cyl. and two Skeet tubes), 30" (Mod., Imp. Cyl. and two Skeet tubes). **Weight:** 7-1/2 to 8 lbs. **Stock:** 14-1/8"x1-1/2"x2-1/2". Select Circassian walnut; pistol grip or straight English grip. **Features:** Has a newly patented Ruger cocking mechanism for easier, smoother opening. Buttstock extends forward into action as two side panels. Single selective mechanical trigger, selective automatic ejectors; serrated free-floating rib; back-bored barrels with stainless steel choke tubes. Blued barrels, stainless steel receiver. Engraved action available. Introduced 1995. Made in U.S. by Sturm, Ruger & Co.
Price: $1,758.00
Price: Woodside Sporting Clays (30" barrels) $1,758.00
Price: Engraved Woodside $2,805.00

RUGER RED LABEL O/U SHOTGUN

Gauge: 12, 20, 3" chambers; 28 2-3/4" chambers. **Barrel:** 26", 28" (Skeet [two], Imp. Cyl., Full, Mod. screw-in choke tubes). Proved for steel shot. **Weight:** About 7 lbs. (20-ga.); 7-1/2 lbs. (12-ga.). **Length:** 43" overall (26" barrels). **Stock:** 14"x1-1/2"x2-1/2". Straight grain American walnut or black synthetic. Checkered pistol grip and forend, rubber butt pad. **Features:** Stainless steel receiver. Single selective mechanical trigger, selective automatic ejectors; serrated free-floating vent. rib. Comes with two Skeet, one Imp. Cyl., one Mod., one Full choke tube and wrench. Made in U.S. by Sturm, Ruger & Co.
Price: Red Label with pistol grip stock $1,276.00
Price: English Field with straight-grip stock $1,276.00
Price: All-Weather Red Label with black synthetic stock $1,276.00
Price: Factory engraved models . . . . $2,552.00 to $2,742.00

Ruger Sporting Clays O/U Shotgun

Similar to the Red Label except 30" back-bored barrels, stainless steel choke tubes. Weighs 7.75 lbs., overall length 47". Stock dimensions of 14-1/8"x1-1/2"x2-1/2". Free-floating serrated vent. rib with brass front and mid-rib beads. No barrel side spacers. Comes with two Skeet, one Imp.

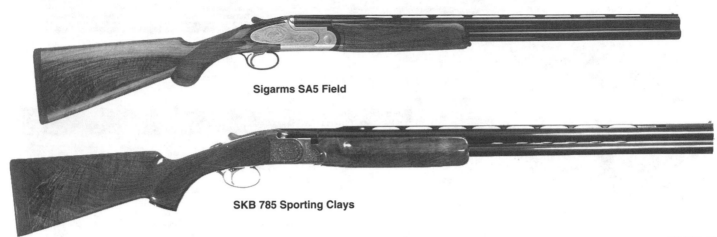

Sigarms SA5 Field

SKB 785 Sporting Clays

Cyl., one Mod. choke tubes. Full and Extra-Full available at extra cost. 12 ga. introduced 1992, 20 ga. introduced 1994.

Price: 12 or 20 . . . . **$1,415.00**
Price: All-Weather with black synthetic stock **$1,415.00**

SIGARMS SA5 OVER/UNDER SHOTGUN

Gauge: 12, 20, 3" chamber. **Barrel:** 26-1/2", 27" (Full, Imp. Mod., Mod., Imp. Cyl., Cyl. choke tubes). **Weight:** 6.9 lbs. (12-gauge), 5.9 lbs. (20-gauge). **Stock:** 14-1/2" x 1-1/2" x 2-1/2". Select grade walnut; checkered 20 l.p.i. at grip and forend. **Features:** Single selective trigger, automatic ejectors; hand-engraved detachable sideplated; matte nickel receiver, rest blued; tapered bolt lock-up. Introduced 1997. Imported by Sigarms, Inc.

Price: Field, 12-gauge **$2,670.00**
Price: Sporting Clays **$2,800.00**
Price: Field 20-gauge **$2,670.00**

SKB Model 505 Shotguns

Similar to the Model 585 except blued receiver, standard bore diameter, standard Inter-Choke system on 12, 20, 28, different receiver engraving. Imported from Japan by G.U. Inc.

Price: Field, 12 (26", 28"), 20 (26" only) **$1,049.00**
Price: Sporting Clays, 12 (20", 30") **$1,149.00**

SKB Model 585 Gold Package

Similar to the Model 585 Field except has gold-plated trigger, two gold-plated game inlays, and Schnabel forend. Silver or blue receiver. Introduced 1998. Imported from Japan by G.U. Inc.

Price: 12-, 20-ga. **$1,489.00**
Price: 28, 410 . . . . **$1,539.00**

SKB MODEL 785 OVER/UNDER SHOTGUN

Gauge: 12, 20, 3"; 28, 2-3/4"; 410, 3". **Barrel:** 26", 28", 30", 32" (Inter-Choke tubes). **Weight:** 6 lbs., 10 oz. to 8 lbs. **Stock:** 14-1/8"x1-1/2"x2-3/16" (Field). Hand-checkered American black walnut with high-gloss finish; semi-beavertail forend. Target stocks available in standard or Monte Carlo styles. **Sights:** Metal bead front (Field), target style on Skeet, trap, Sporting Clays models. **Features:** Boxlock action with Greener-style cross bolt; single selective chrome-plated trigger, chrome-plated selective ejectors; manual safety. Chrome-plated, over-size, back-bored barrels with lengthened forcing cones. Introduced 1995. Imported from Japan by G.U. Inc.

Price: Field, 12 or 20 . . . . **$1,949.00**
Price: Field, 28 or 410 . . . . **$2,029.00**
Price: Field set, 12 and 20 . . . . **$2,829.00**
Price: Field set, 20 and 28 or 28 and 410 . . . . **$2,929.00**
Price: Sporting Clays, 12 or 20 . . . . **$2,099.00**
Price: Sporting Clays, 28 . . . . **$2,169.00**
Price: Sporting Clays set, 12 and 20 . . . . **$2,999.00**
Price: Skeet, 12 or 20 . . . . **$2,029.00**
Price: Skeet, 28 or 410 . . . . **$2,069.00**
Price: Skeet, three-barrel set, 20, 28, 410 . . . . **$4,089.00**
Price: Trap, standard or Monte Carlo **$2,029.00**
Price: Trap combo, standard or Monte Carlo **$2,829.00**

SKB MODEL 585 OVER/UNDER SHOTGUN

Gauge: 12 or 20, 3"; 28, 2-3/4"; 410, 3". **Barrel:** 12-ga.—26", 28", 30", 32", 34" (Inter-Choke tube); 20-ga.—26", 28" (Inter-Choke tube); 28—26", 28" (Inter-Choke tube); 410—26", 28" (Imp. Cyl. & Mod., Mod. & Full). Ventilated side ribs. **Weight:** 6.6 to 8.5 lbs. **Length:** 43" to 51-3/8" overall. **Stock:** 14-1/8"x1-1/2"x2-3/16". Hand checkered walnut with high-gloss finish. Target stocks available in standard and Monte Carlo. **Sights:** Metal bead front (field), target style on Skeet, trap, Sporting Clays. **Features:** Boxlock action; silver nitride finish with Field or Target pattern engraving; manual safety, automatic ejectors, single selective trigger. All 12-gauge barrels are back-bored, have lengthened forcing cones and longer choke tube system. Sporting Clays models in 12-gauge with 28" or 30" barrels available with optional 3/8" step-up target-style rib, matte finish, nickel center bead, white front bead. Introduced 1992. Imported from Japan by G.U., Inc.

Price: Field **$1,329.00**
Price: Two-barrel Field Set, 12 & 20 . . . . **$2,129.00**
Price: Two-barrel Field Set, 20 & 28 or 28 & 410 . . . . **$2,179.00**
Price: Trap, Skeet **$1,429.00**
Price: Two-barrel trap combo **$2,129.00**
Price: Sporting Clays model . . . . **$1,149.00** to **$1,529.00**
Price: Skeet Set (20, 28, 410) **$0,000.00**

STOEGER/IGA CONDOR I OVER/UNDER SHOTGUN

Gauge: 12, 20, 3" chambers. **Barrel:** 26" (Imp. Cyl. & Mod. choke tubes), 28" (Mod. & Full choke tubes). **Weight:** 6-3/4 to 7 lbs. **Stock:** 14-1/2"x1-1/2"x2-1/2". Oil-finished hardwood with checkered pistol grip and forend. **Features:** Manual safety, single trigger, extractors only, ventilated top rib. Introduced 1983. Imported from Brazil by Stoeger Industries.

Price: With choke tubes **$559.00**
Price: Condor Supreme (same as Condor I with single trigger, choke tubes, but with auto. ejectors), 12- or 20-ga., 26", 28" **$629.00**

Stoeger/IGA Condor Waterfowl O/U

Similar to the Condor I except has Advantage camouflage on the barrels, stock and forend; all other metal has matte black finish. Comes only with 30" choke tube barrels, 3" chambers, automatic ejectors, single trigger and manual safety. Designed for steel shot. Introduced 1997. Imported from Brazil by Stoeger.

Price: **$729.00**

Stoeger/IGA Turkey Model O/U

Similar to the Condor I model except has Advantage camouflage on the barrels stock and forend. All exposed metal and recoil pad are matte black. Has 26" (Full & Full) barrels, single trigger, manual safety, 3" chambers. Introduced 1997. Imported from Brazil by Stoeger.

Price: **$729.00**

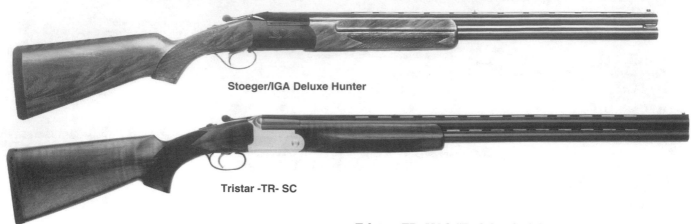

Stoeger/IGA Deluxe Hunter

Tristar -TR- SC

Stoeger/IGA Trap Model O/U

Similar to the Condor I except 30" barrels with Imp. Mod. & Full choke tubes, single selective trigger, automatic ejectors. Introduced 1998. Imported from Brazil by Stoeger Industries.
Price: $699.00

Stoeger/IGA Deluxe Hunter Clays O/U

Similar to the Condor Supreme except 12-gauge only with 28" choke tube barrels, select semi-fancy American walnut stock with black Pachmayr target-style recoil pad, high luster blued barrels, gold-plated trigger, red bead front and mid-rib sights. Introduced 1997. Imported from Brazil by Stoeger.
Price: $699.00

TRISTAR-TR-SC "EMILLIO RIZZINI" OVER/UNDER

Gauge: 12, 20, 2-3/4" chambers. **Barrel:** 28", 30" (Imp. Cyl., Mod., Full choke tubes). **Weight:** 7-1/2 lbs. **Length:** 46" overall (28" barrel). **Stock:** 1-1/2"x2-3/8"x14-3/8". Semi-fancy walnut; pistol grip with palm swell; semi-beavertail forend; black Sporting Clays recoil pad. **Features:** Silvered boxlock action with Four Locks locking system, auto ejectors, single selective (inertia) trigger, auto safety. Hard chrome bores. Vent. 10mm rib with target-style front and mid-rib beads, vent. spacer rib. Introduced 1998. Imported from Italy by Tristar Sporting Arms, Ltd.
Price: $949.00
Price: 20-ga. $1,022.00

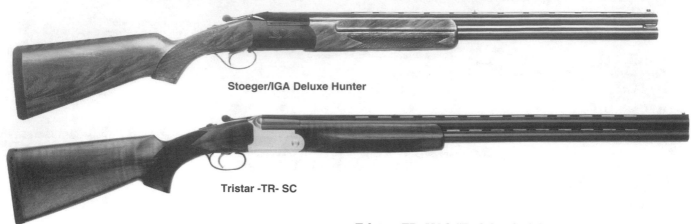 **Tristar TR-Royal Emilio Rizzini Over/Under**

Similar to the TR- SC except has special parallel stock dimensions (1-1/2"x1-5/8"x14-3/8") to give low felt recoil; Rhino ported, extended choke tubes; solid barrel spacer; has "TR-Royal" gold engraved on the silvered receiver. Available in 12-gauge (28", 30") 20- and 28-gauge (28" only). Introduced 1999. Imported from Italy by Tristar Sporting Arms, Ltd.
Price:12-ga. $1,277.00
Price: 20-, 28-ga. $1,345.00

Tristar -TR- L "Emillio Rizzinni" Over/Under

Similar to the TR- SC except has stock dimensions designed for female shooters (1-1/2" x 3" x 13-1/2"). Standard grade walnut. Introduced 1998. Imported from Italy by Tristar Sporting Arms, Ltd.
Price: $966.00

TRISTAR-TR- I, II "EMILLIO RIZZINI" OVER/UNDERS

Gauge: 12, 20, 3" chambers (TR-I); 12, 16, 20, 28, 410 3" chambers (except 28, 2-3/4"). **Barrel:** 12-ga., 26" (Imp. Cyl. & Mod.), 28" (Mod. & Full); 20-ga., 26" (Imp. Cyl. & Mod.), fixed chokes. **Weight:** 7-1/2 lbs. **Stock:** 1-1/2"x2-3/8"x14-3/8". Walnut with palm swell pistol grip, hand checkering, semi-beavertail forend, black recoil pad. **Features:** Boxlock action with blued finish, Four Locks® locking system, gold single selective (inertia) trigger system, automatic safety, extractors. Introduced 1998. Imported from Italy by Tristar Sporting Arms, Ltd.
Price: TR- I $654.00
Price: TR- II (automatic ejectors, choke tubes) 12-, 16-ga. $852.00
Price: 20-, 28-ga., 410 .... $880.00

Tristar -TR- MAG "Emillio Rizzini" Over/Under

Similar to the TR- I except 12-gauge, 3-1/2" chambers; choke tubes; 24" or 28" barrels with three choke tubes; extractors; auto safety. Matte blue finish on all metal, non-reflective wood finish. Introduced 1998. Imported from Italy by Tristar Sporting Arms, Ltd.
Price: $728.00

TRISTAR TR-CLASS SL EMILIO RIZZINI O/U

Gauge: 12, 2-3/4" chambers. **Barrel:** 28", 30", (Imp. Cyl., Mod., Full choke tubes). **Weight:** 7-1/2-7-3/4 lbs. **Stock:** 1-1/2"x1-3/8"x14-1/4". Fancy walnut with palm swell, hand checkering, semi-beavertail forend, black recoil pad, gloss finish. **Features:** Boxlock action with silvered, engraved sideplates; Four Lock locking system; automatic ejectors; hard chrome bores; vent tapered 7mm rib with target-style front bead. hand-fitted gun. Introduced 1999. Imported from Italy by Tristar Sporting Arms, Ltd.
Price: $1,690.00

VERONA LX501 HUNTING O/U SHOTGUNS

Gauge: 12, 20, (3" chambers), 28, 410 (2-3/4"). **Barrel:** 28"; 12-, 20-ga. have Interchoke tubes, 28-ga. and 410 have fixed Full & Mod. **Weight:** 6-7 lbs. **Stock:** Matte-finished walnut with machine-cut checkering. **Features:** Gold-plated single-selective trigger; ejectors; engraved, blued receiver, non-automatic safety; coil spring-operated firing pins. Introduced 1999. Imported from Italy by B.C. Outdoors .
Price: 12- and 20-ga. $720.00
Price: 28-ga. and 410 .... $755.00

Verona LX692 Gold Hunting Over/Under Shotguns

Similar to tthe Verona LX501 except has engraved, silvered receiver with false sideplates showing gold-inlaid bird hunting scenes on three sides; Schnabel forend tip; hand-cut checkering; black rubber butt pad. Available in 12- and 20-gauge only, with five InterChoke tubes. Introduced 1999. Imported from Italy by B.C. Outdoors.
Price: $1,295.00

Verona LX680 Sporting Over/Under Shotguns

Similar to the Verona LX501 except has engraved, silvered receiver; ventilated middle rib; beavertail forend; hand-cut checkering; available in 12- or 20-gauge only with 2-3/4" chambers. Introduced 1999. Imported from Italy by B.C. Outdoors.
Price: $1,020.00

Verona LX680 Skeet/Sporting, Trap O/U Shotguns

Similar to the Verona LX501 except with Skeet or trap stock dimensions; beavertail forend, palm swell on pistol grip; ventilated center barrel rib. Introduced 1999. Imported from Italy by B.C. Outdoors.
Price: $1,130.00
Price: Gold Competition (false sideplates with gold-inlaid hunting scenes) $1,500.00

Verona LX692 Gold Sporting Over/Under Shotguns

Similar to the Verona LX680 except with false sideplates that have gold-inlaid bird hunting scenes on three sides; red high-visibility front sight. Introduced 1999. Imported from Italy by B.C. Outdoors.
Price: $1,365.00

SHOTGUNS — OVER/UNDERS

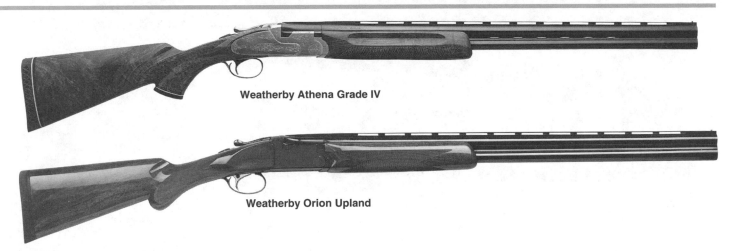

Weatherby Athena Grade IV

Weatherby Orion Upland

WEATHERBY ATHENA GRADE IV O/U SHOTGUNS

Gauge: 12, 20, 3" chambers. **Action:** Boxlock (simulated sidelock) top lever break-open. Selective auto ejectors, single selective trigger (selector inside trigger guard). **Barrel:** 26", 28", IMC Multi-Choke tubes. **Weight:** 12-ga., 7-3/8 lbs.; 20-ga. 6-7/8 lbs. **Stock:** American walnut, checkered pistol grip and forend (14-1/4"x1-1/2"x2-1/2"). **Features:** Mechanically operated trigger. Top tang safety, Greener cross bolt, fully engraved receiver, recoil pad installed. IMC models furnished with three interchangeable flush-fitting choke tubes. Imported from Japan by Weatherby. Introduced 1982.
Price: 12-ga., IMC, 26", 28" **$2,259.00**
Price: 20-ga., IMC, 26", 28" **$2,259.00**

Weatherby Ahtena Grade V Classic Field O/U

Similar to the Athena Grade IV except has rounded pistol grip, slender forend, oil-finished Claro walnut stock with fine-line checkering, Old English recoil pad. Sideplate receiver has rose and scroll engraving. Available in 12-gauge, 26", 28", 20-gauge, 26", 28", all with 3" chambers. Introduced 1993.
Price: **$2,599.00**

WEATHERBY ORION GRADE III FIELD O/U SHOTGUNS

Gauge: 12, 20, 3" chambers. **Barrel:** 26", 28", IMC Multi-Choke tubes. **Weight:** 6-1/2 to 9 lbs. **Stock:** 14-1/4"x1-1/2"x2-1/2". American walnut, checkered grip and forend. Rubber recoil pad. **Features:** Selective automatic ejectors, single selective inertia trigger. Top tang safety, Greener cross bolt. Has silver-gray receiver with engraving and gold duck/pheasant. Imported from Japan by Weatherby.
Price: Orion III, Field, 12, IMC, 26", 28" **$1,699.00**
Price: Orion III, Field, 20, IMC, 26", 28" **$1,699.00**

Weatherby Orion Grade III Classic Field O/U

Similar to the Orion III Field except the stock has a rounded pistol grip, satin oil finish, slender forend, Old English recoil pad. Introduced 1993. Imported from Japan by Weatherby.
Price: **$1,699.00**

Weatherby Orion Grade II Classic Field O/U

Similar to the Orion III Classic Field except stock has high-gloss finish, and the bird on the receiver is not gold. Available in 12-gauge, 26", 28", 30" barrels, 20-gauge, 26" 28", both with 3" chambers, 28-gauge, 26", 2-3/4" chambers. All have IMC choke tubes. Imported from Japan by Weatherby.
Price: **$1,399.00**

Weatherby Athena III Classic Field O/U

Has Grade III Claro walnut with oil finish, rounded pistol grip, slender forend; silver nitride/gray receiver has rose and scroll engraving with gold-overlay upland game scenes. Introduced 1999. Imported from Japan by Weatherby.
Price: **$1,849.00**

Weatherby Orion Grade I Field O/U

Similar to the Orion Grade III Field except has blued receiver with engraving, and the bird is not gold. Available in 12-gauge, 26", 28", 30", 20-gauge, 20", 28", both with 3" chambers and IMC choke tubes. Imported from Japan by Weatherby.
Price: **$1,329.00**

Weatherby Orion Upland O/U

Similar to the Orion Grade I. Plain blued receiver, gold W on the trigger guard; rounded pistol grip, slender forend of Claro walnut with high-gloss finish; black butt pad. Available in 12- and 20-gauge with 26" and 28" barrels. Introduced 1999. Imported from Japan by Weatherby.
Price: **$1,059.00**

WEATHERBY ORION SSC OVER/UNDER SHOTGUN

Gauge: 12, 3" chambers. **Barrel:** 28", 30", 32" (Skeet, SC1, Imp. Cyl., SC2, Mod. IMC choke tubes). **Weight:** About 8 lbs. **Stock:** 14-3/4"x2-1/4"x1-1/2". Claro walnut with satin oil finish; Schnabel forend tip; Sporter-style pistol grip; Pachmayr Decelerator recoil pad. **Features:** Designed for Sporting Clays competition. Has lengthened forcing cones and back-boring; ported barrels with 12mm grooved rib with mid-bead sight; mechanical trigger is adjustable for length of pull. Introduced 1998. Imported from Japan by Weatherby.
Price: **$1,749.00**

Weatherby Orion III English Field O/U

Similar to the Orion III Classic Field except has straight grip English-style stock. Available in 12-gauge (28"), 20 gauge (26", 28") with IMC Multi-Choke tubes. Silver/gray nitride receiver is engraved and has gold-plate overlay. Introduced 1997. Imported from Japan by Weatherby.
Price: **$1,699.00**

Weatherby Orion Grade II Classic Sporting O/U

Similar to the Orion II Classic Field except in 12 gauge only with (3" chambers), 28", 30" barrels with Skeet, SC1, SC2 Imp. Cyl., Mod. chokes. Weighs 7.5-8 lbs. Competition center vent rib; middle barrel and enlarged front beads. Rounded grip; high gloss stock. Radiused heel recoil pad. Receiver finished in silver nitride with acid-etched, gold-plate clay pigeon monogram. Barrels have lengthened forcing cones. Introduced 1993. Imported by Weatherby.
Price: **$1,499.00**

Weatherby Orion Grade II Sporting Clays

Similar to the Orion II Classic Sporting except has traditional pistol grip with diamond inlay, and standard full-size forend. Available in 12-gauge only, 28", 30" barrels with Skeet, Imp. Cyl., SC2, Mod. Has lengthened forcing cones, back-boring, stepped competition rib, radius heel recoil pad, hand-engraved, silver/nitride receiver. Introduced 1992. Imported by Weatherby.
Price: **$1,499.00**

Variety of models for utility and sporting use, including some competitive shooting.

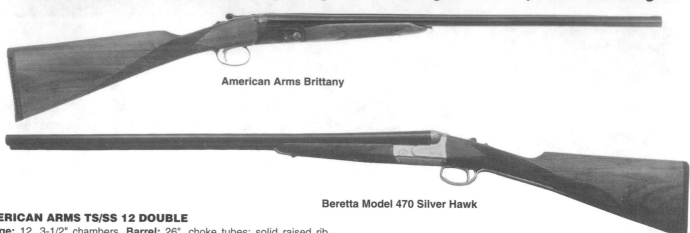

American Arms Brittany

Beretta Model 470 Silver Hawk

AMERICAN ARMS TS/SS 12 DOUBLE

Gauge: 12, 3-1/2" chambers. **Barrel:** 26", choke tubes; solid raised rib. **Weight:** 7 lbs., 6 oz. **Stock:** Walnut; cut-checked grip and forend. **Features:** Non-reflective metal and wood finishes; boxlock action; single trigger; extractors. Imported by American Arms, Inc.
Price: **$799.00**

AMERICAN ARMS WT/SS 10 DOUBLE

Gauge: 10, 3-1/2" chambers. **Barrel:** 28", choke tubes. **Weight:** 10 lbs., 3 oz. **Length:** 45" overall. **Stock:** 14-1/4"x1-1/8"x2-3/8"; walnut. **Features:** Boxlock action with extractors; single selective trigger; non-reflective wood and metal finishes. Imported by American Arms, Inc.
Price: **$860.00**

AMERICAN ARMS GENTRY DOUBLE SHOTGUN

Gauge: 12, 20, 410, 3" chambers; 28 ga. 2-3/4" chambers. **Barrel:** 26" (Imp. Cyl. & Mod., all gauges), 28" (Mod., & Full, 12 and 20 gauges). **Weight:** 6-1/4 to 6-3/4 lbs. **Stock:** 14-1/8"x1-3/8"x2-3/8". Hand-checkered walnut with semi-gloss finish. **Sights:** Metal bead front. **Features:** Boxlock action with English-style scroll engraving, color case-hardened finish. Single trigger, extractors. Independent floating firing pins. Manual safety. Five-year warranty. Introduced 1987. Imported from Spain by American Arms, Inc.
Price: 12 or 20 .... **$750.00**
Price: 28 or 410 .... **$795.00**

AMERICAN ARMS BRITTANY SHOTGUN

Gauge: 12, 20, 3" chambers. **Barrel:** 12-ga.—27"; 20-ga.—25" (Imp. Cyl., Mod., Full choke tubes). **Weight:** 6 lbs., 7 oz. (20-ga.). **Stock:** 14-1/8"x1-3/8"x2-3/8". Hand-checkered walnut with oil finish, straight English-style with semi-beavertail forend. **Features:** Boxlock action with case-color finish, engraving; single selective trigger, automatic selective ejectors; rubber recoil pad. Introduced 1989. Imported from Spain by American Arms, Inc.
Price: **$885.00**

ARRIETA SIDELOCK DOUBLE SHOTGUNS

Gauge: 12, 16, 20, 28, 410. **Barrel:** Length and chokes to customer specs. **Weight:** To customer specs. **Stock:** 14-1/2"x1-1/2"x2-1/2 (standard dimensions), or to customer specs. Straight English with checkered butt (standard), or pistol grip. Select European walnut with oil finish. **Features:** Essentially a custom gun with myriad options. Holland & Holland-pattern hand-detachable sidelocks, selective automatic ejectors; double triggers (hinged front) standard. Some have self-opening action. Finish and engraving to customer specs. Imported from Spain by Wingshooting Adventures.
Price: Model 557, auto ejectors, from **$2,750.00**
Price: Model 570, auto ejectors, from **$3,380.00**
Price: Model 578, auto ejectors, from **$3,740.00**
Price: Model 600 Imperial, self-opening, from **$4,990.00**
Price: Model 601 Imperial Tiro, self-opening, from **$5,750.00**
Price: Model 801, from **$7,950.00**
Price: Model 802, from **$7,950.00**
Price: Model 803, from **$5,850.00**

Price: Model 871, auto ejectors, from **$4,290.00**
Price: Model 872, self-opening, from **$9,790.00**
Price: Model 873, self-opening, from **$6,850.00**
Price: Model 874, self-opening, from **$7,950.00**
Price: Model 875, self-opening, from **$12,950.00**

BERETTA MODEL 470 SILVER HAWK SHOTGUN

Gauge: 12, 20, 3" chambers. **Barrel:** 26" (Imp. Cyl. & Imp. Mod.), 28" (Mod. & Full). **Weight:** 5.9 lbs. (20-gauge). **Stock:** Select European walnut, straight English grip. **Features:** Boxlock action with single selective trigger; selector provides automatic ejection or extraction; silver-chrome action and forend iron with fine engraving; top lever highlighted with gold inlaid hawk's head. Comes with ABS case. Introduced 1997. Imported from Italy by Beretta U.S.A.
Price: 12-ga. **$3,630.00**
Price: 20-ga. **$3,755.00**

CHARLES DALY SUPERIOR HUNTER DOUBLE SHOTGUN

Gauge: 12, 20, 3" chambers, 28, 2-3/4" chambers. **Barrel:** 28" (Mod. & Full) 26" (Imp. Cyl. & Mod.). **Weight:** About 7 lbs. **Stock:** Checkered walnut pistol grip buttstock, splinter forend. **Features:** Silvered, engraved receiver; chrome-lined barrels; gold single trigger; automatic safety; extractors; gold bead front sight. Introduced 1997. Imported from Italy by K.B.I., Inc.
Price: **$999.00**
Price: 28-ga., 26" **$1,049.00**

Charles Daly Empire Hunter Double Shotgun

Similar to the Superior Hunter except has deluxe wood, game scene engraving, automatic ejectors. Introduced 1997. Imported from Italy by K.B.I., Inc.
Price: 12 or 20 .... **$1,299.00**

CHARLES DALY DIAMOND REGENT DL DOUBLE SHOTGUN

Gauge: 12, 20, 410, 3" chambers, 28, 2-3/4" chambers. **Barrel:** 28" (Mod. & Full), 26" (Imp. Cyl. & Mod.), 26" (Full & Full, 410). **Weight:** About 5-7 lbs. **Stock:** Special select fancy European walnut, English-style butt, splinter forend; hand-checkered; hand-rubbed oil finish. **Features:** Drop-forged action with gas escape valves; demiblock barrels of chrome-nickel steel with concave rib; selective automatic-ejectors; hand-detachable, double-safety H&H sidelocks with demi-relief hand engraving; H&H pattern easy-opening feature; hinged trigger; coin finished action. Introduced 1997. Imported from Spain by K.B.I., Inc.
Price: 12 or 20 .... **$19,999.00**
Price: 28 .... **$20,499.00**
Price: 410 .... **$20,499.00**

CHARLES DALY FIELD HUNTER DOUBLE SHOTGUN

Gauge: 10, 12, 20, 28, 410 (3" chambers; 28 has 2-3/4"). **Barrel:** 32" (Mod. & Mod.), 28, 30" (Mod. & Full), 26" (Imp. Cyl. & Mod.) 410 (Full & Full).

Charles Daly Field Hunter

Fabarm Classic Lion

A.H. Fox DE Grade

Garbi Model 100

Weight: 6 lbs. to 11.4 lbs. **Stock:** Checkered walnut pistol grip and forend. **Features:** Silvered, engraved receiver; gold single selective trigger in 10-, 12-, and 20-ga.; double triggers in 28 and 410; automatic safety; extractors; gold bead front sight. Introduced 1997. Imported from Spain by K.B.I., Inc.

Price: 10-ga.	$949.00
Price: 12- or 20-ga.	$789.00
Price: 28-ga.	$829.00
Price: 410-bore	$829.00
Price: As above, 12 or 20	$899.00

CHARLES DALY DIAMOND DL DOUBLE SHOTGUN

Gauge: 12, 20, 410, 3" chambers, 28, 2-3/4" chambers. **Barrel:** 28" (Mod. & Full), 26" (Imp. Cyl. & Mod.), 26" (Full & Full, 410). **Weight:** About 5-7 lbs. **Stock:** Select fancy European walnut, English-style butt, beavertail forend; hand-checkered, hand-rubbed oil finish. **Features:** Drop-forged action with gas escape valves; demiblock barrels with concave rib; selective automatic ejectors; hand-detachable double safety sidelocks with hand-engraved rose and scrollwork. Hinged front trigger. Color case-hardened receiver. Introduced 1997. Imported from Spain by K.B.I., Inc.

Price: 12 or 20	$6,749.00
Price: 28	$7,049.00
Price: 410	$7,049.00

FABARM CLASSIC LION DOUBLE SHOTGUN

Gauge: 12, 3" chambers. **Barrel:** 26" (Cyl., Imp. Cyl., Mod., Imp. Mod., Full choke tubes). **Weight:** 7.2 lbs. **Length:** 47.6" overall. **Stock:** Oil-finished European walnut. **Features:** Boxlock action with single selective trigger, automatic ejectors, automatic safety. Introduced 1998. Imported from Italy by Heckler & Koch, Inc.

Price: Grade I	$1,488.00
Price: Grade II (sidelock action)	$2,110.00

A.H. FOX SIDE-BY-SIDE SHOTGUNS

Gauge: 16, 20, 28, 410. **Barrel:** Length and chokes to customer specifications. Rust-blued Chromox or Krupp steel. **Weight:** 5-1/2 to 6-3/4 lbs.

Stock: Dimensions to customer specifications. Hand-checkered Turkish Circassian walnut with hand-rubbed oil finish. Straight, semi- or full pistol grip; splinter, Schnabel or beavertail forend; traditional pad, hard rubber buttplate or skeleton butt. **Features:** Boxlock action with automatic ejectors; double or Fox single selective trigger. Scalloped, rebated and color case-hardened receiver; hand finished and hand-engraved. Grades differ in engraving, inlays, grade of wood, amount of hand finishing. Add $1,000 for 28 or 410-bore. Introduced 1993. Made in U.S. by Connecticut Shotgun Mfg.

Price: CE Grade	$9,500.00
Price: XE Grade	$11,000.00
Price: DE Grade	$13,500.00
Price: FE Grade	$18,500.00
Price: Exhibition Grade	$26,000.00
Price: 28/410 CE Grade	$8,200.00
Price: 28/410 XE Grade	$9,700.00
Price: 28/410 DE Grade	$13,800.00
Price: 28/410 FE Grade	$14,700.00
Price: 28/410 Exhibition Grade	$26,000.00

GARBI MODEL 100 DOUBLE

Gauge: 12, 16, 20, 28. **Barrel:** 26", 28", choked to customer specs. **Weight:** 5-1/2 to 7-1/2 lbs. **Stock:** 14-1/2"x2-1/4"x1-1/2". European walnut. Straight grip, checkered butt, classic forend. **Features:** Sidelock action, automatic ejectors, double triggers standard. Color case-hardened action, coin finish optional. Single trigger; beavertail forend, etc. optional. Five other models are available. Imported from Spain by Wm. Larkin Moore.

Price: From $4,600.00

Garbi Model 200 Side-by-Side

Similar to the Garbi Model 100 except has heavy-duty locks, magnum proofed. Very fine Continental-style floral and scroll engraving, well figured walnut stock. Other mechanical features remain the same. Imported from Spain by Wm. Larkin Moore.

Price: $10,000.00

Garbi Model 101 Side-by-Side

Similar to the Garbi Model 100 except is hand engraved with scroll engraving, select walnut stock. Better overall quality than the Model 100. Imported from Spain by Wm. Larkin Moore.

Price: From $5,950.00

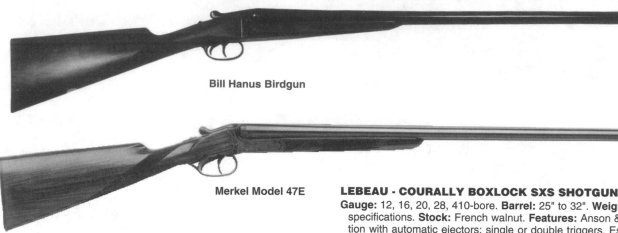

Bill Hanus Birdgun

Merkel Model 47E

Garbi Model 103A, B Side-by-Side
Similar to the Garbi Model 100 except has Purdey-type fine scroll and rosette engraving. Better overall quality than the Model 101. Model 103B has nickel-chrome steel barrels, H&H-type easy opening mechanism; other mechanical details remain the same. Imported from Spain by Wm. Larkin Moore.
Price: Model 103A, from................................. **$7,400.00**
Price: Model 103B, from.............................. **$10,400.00**

BILL HANUS BIRDGUN
Gauge: 16, 20, 28. **Barrel:** 27", 20- and 28-ga.; 28", 16-ga. (Skeet 1 & Skeet 2). **Weight:** 5 lbs., 4 oz. to 6 lbs., 4 oz. **Stock:** 14-3/8"x1-1/2"x2-3/8", with 1/4" cast-off. Select walnut. **Features:** Boxlock action with ejectors; splinter forend, straight English grip; checkered butt; English leather-covered handguard included. Made by AYA. Introduced 1998. Imported from Spain by Bill Hanus Birdguns.
Price: **$1,895.00**

IAR COWBOY SHOTGUNS
Gauge: 12. **Barrel:** 20", 28". **Weight:** 7 lbs. (20" barrel). **Length:** 36-7/8" overall (20" barrel). **Stock:** Walnut. **Features:** Exposed hammers; blued or brown barrels; double triggers. Introduced 1997. Imported from Italy by IAR, Inc.
Price: Gentry model, 20" or 28", engraved, bright-finished locks, blue barrels **$1,895.00**
Price: Cowboy model, 20" or 28", no engraving on color case-hardened locks, brown patina barrels.......................... **$1,895.00**

ITHACA CLASSIC DOUBLES SPECIAL FIELD GRADE SxS
NEW! **Gauge:** 20, 28, 2-3/4" chambers, 410, 3". **Barrel:** 26", 28", 30", fixed chokes. **Weight:** 5 lbs., 14 oz. (20-gauge). **Stock:** 14-1/2"x2-1/4"x1-3/8". High-grade American black walnut, hand-rubbed oil finish; splinter or beavertail forend, straight or pistol grip. **Features:** Double triggers, ejectors; color case-hardened, engraved action body with matted top surfaces. Introduced 1999. Made in U.S. by Ithaca Classic Doubles.
Price: From... **$3,150.00**

NEW! Ithaca Classic Doubles Grade 4E SxS Shotgun
Similar to the Special Field Grade except has gold-plated triggers, jeweled barrel flats and hand-turned locks. Feather crotch and flame-grained black walnut is hand-checkered 28 lpi with fleur de lis pattern. Action body is engraved with three game scenes and bank note scroll, and color case-hardened. Introduced 1999. Made in U.S. by Ithaca Classic Doubles.
Price: From.. **$4,199.00**

NEW! Ithaca Classic Doubles Grade 7E SxS Shotgun
Similar to the Special Field Grade except engraved with bank note scroll and flat 24k gold game scenes: gold setter and gold pointer on opposite action sides, and an American bald eagle is inlaid on the bottom plate. Hand-timed, polished, jeweled ejectors and locks. Exhibition grade American black walnut stock and forend with eight-panel fleur de lis borders. Introduced 1999. Made in U.S. by Itaca Classic Doubles.
Price: From.. **$8,399.00**

LEBEAU - COURALLY BOXLOCK SXS SHOTGUN
Gauge: 12, 16, 20, 28, 410-bore. **Barrel:** 25" to 32". **Weight:** To customer specifications. **Stock:** French walnut. **Features:** Anson & Deely-type action with automatic ejectors; single or double triggers. Essentially a custom gun built to customer specifications. Imported from Belgium by Wm. Larkin Moore.
Price: From..................................... **$23,000.00**

LEBEAU - COURALLY SIDELOCK SXS SHOTGUN
Gauge: 12, 16, 20, 28, 410-bore. **Barrel:** 25" to 32". **Weight:** To customer specifications. **Stock:** Fancy French walnut. **Features:** Holland & Holland-type action with automatic ejectors; single or double triggers. Essentially a custom gun built to customer specifications. Imported from Belgium by Wm. Larkin Moore.
Price: From..................................... **$47,000.00**

MERKEL MODEL, 47E SIDE-BY-SIDE SHOTGUNS
Gauge: 12, 3" chambers, 16, 2-3/4" chambers, 20, 3" chambers. **Barrel:** 12-, 16-ga.—28"; 20-ga.—26-3/4" (Imp. Cyl. & Mod., Mod. & Full). **Weight:** About 6-3/4 lbs. (12-ga.). **Stock:** Oil-finished walnut; straight English or pistol grip. **Features:** Anson & Deely-type boxlock action with single selective or double triggers, automatic safety, cocking indicators. Color case-hardened receiver with standard Arabesque engraving. Imported from Germany by GSI.
Price: Model 47E (H&H ejectors) **$2,695.00**
Price: Model 147 (extractors, silver-grayed receiver with hunting scenes).. **$2,995.00**
Price: Model 147E (as above with ejectors).............. **$3,195.00**
Price: Model 122 (as above with false sideplates, fine engraving)
.... **$4,995.00**

Merkel Model 47SL, 147SL Side-by-Sides
Similar to the Model 122 except with Holland & Holland-style sidelock action with cocking indicators, ejectors. Silver-grayed receiver and sideplates have Arabesque engraving, engraved border and screws (Model 47S), or fine hunting scene engraving (Model 147S). Imported from Germany by GSI.
Price: Model 47SL **$5,295.00**
Price: Model 147SL **$6,695.00**
Price: Model 247SL (English-style engraving, large scrolls) ... **$6,995.00**
Price: Model 447SL (English-style engraving, small scrolls) ... **$8,995.00**

PARKER REPRODUCTIONS SIDE-BY-SIDE SHOTGUN
Gauge: 12, 16/20 combo, 20, 28, 2-3/4" and 3" chambers. **Barrel:** 26" (Skeet 1 & 2, Imp. Cyl. & Mod.), 28" (Mod. & Full, 2-3/4" and 3", 12, 20, 28; Skeet 1 & 2, Imp. Cyl. & Mod., Mod. & Full 16-ga. only). **Weight:** 6-3/4 lbs. (12-ga.) **Stock:** Checkered (26 lpi) AAA fancy California English or Claro walnut, skeleton steel and checkered butt. Straight or pistol grip, splinter or beavertail forend. **Features:** Exact reproduction of the original Parker—parts interchange. Double or single selective trigger, selective ejectors, hard-chromed bores, designed for steel shot. One, two or three (16-20, 20) barrel sets available. Hand-engraved snap caps included. Introduced 1984. Made by Winchester. Imported from Japan by Parker Division, Reagent Chemical.
Price: D Grade, one-barrel set **$3,370.00**
Price: Two-barrel set, same gauge **$4,200.00**
Price: Two-barrel set, 16/20 .... **$4,870.00**

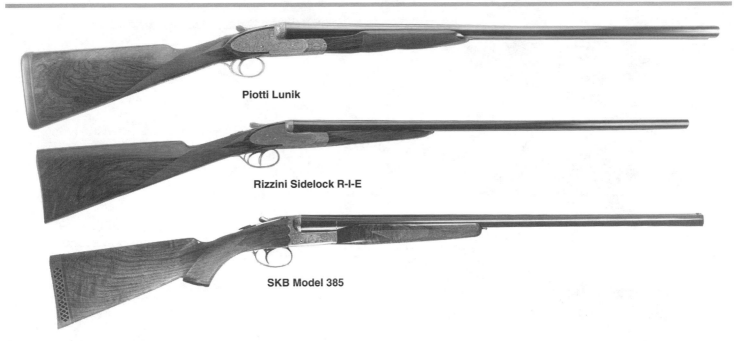

Piotti Lunik

Rizzini Sidelock R-I-E

SKB Model 385

Price: Three-barrel set, 16/20/20 . . . . $5,630.00
Price: A-1 Special two-barrel set $11,200.00
Price: A-1 Special three-barrel set $13,200.00

PIOTTI KING NO. 1 SIDE-BY-SIDE

Gauge: 12, 16, 20, 28, 410. **Barrel:** 25" to 30" (12-ga.), 25" to 28" (16, 20, 28, 410). To customer specs. Chokes as specified. **Weight:** 6-1/2 lbs. to 8 lbs. (12-ga. to customer specs.). **Stock:** Dimensions to customer specs. Finely figured walnut; straight grip with checkered butt with classic splinter forend and hand-rubbed oil finish standard. Pistol grip, beavertail forend, satin luster finish optional. **Features:** Holland & Holland pattern sidelock action, automatic ejectors. Double trigger with front trigger hinged standard, non-selective single trigger optional. Coin finish standard; color case-hardened optional. Top rib; level, file-cut standard; concave, ventilated optional. Very fine, full coverage scroll engraving with small floral bouquets, gold crown in top lever, name in gold, and gold crest in forend. Imported from Italy by Wm. Larkin Moore.
Price: From. $25,600.00

Piotti King Extra Side-by-Side

Similar to the Piotti King No. 1 except highest quality wood and metal work. Choice of either bulino game scene engraving or game scene engraving with gold inlays. Engraved and signed by a master engraver. Exhibition grade wood. Other mechanical specifications remain the same. Imported from Italy by Wm. Larkin Moore.
Price: From. $31,800.00

Piotti Lunik Side-by-Side

Similar to the Piotti King No. 1 in overall quality. Has Renaissance-style large scroll engraving in relief, gold crown in top lever. Best quality Holland & Holland-pattern sidelock ejector double with chopper lump (demibloc) barrels. Other mechanical specifications remain the same. Imported from Italy by Wm. Larkin Moore.
Price: From. $27,500.00

PIOTTI PIUMA SIDE-BY-SIDE

Gauge: 12, 16, 20, 28, 410. **Barrel:** 25" to 30" (12-ga.), 25" to 28" (16, 20, 28, 410). **Weight:** 5-1/2 to 6-1/4 lbs. (20-ga.). **Stock:** Dimensions to customer specs. Straight grip stock with walnut checkered butt, classic splinter forend, hand-rubbed oil finish are standard; pistol grip, beavertail forend, satin luster finish optional. **Features:** Anson & Deeley boxlock ejector double with chopper lump barrels. Level, file-cut rib, light scroll and rosette engraving, scalloped frame. Double triggers with hinged front standard, single non-selective optional. Coin finish standard, color case-hardened optional. Imported from Italy by Wm. Larkin Moore.
Price: From. $13,400.00

RIZZINI SIDELOCK SIDE-BY-SIDE

Gauge: 12, 16, 20, 28, 410. **Barrel:** 25" to 30" (12-, 16-, 20-ga.), 25" to 28" (28, 410). To customer specs. Chokes as specified. **Weight:** 6-1/2 lbs. to 8 lbs. (12-ga. to customer specs). **Stock:** Dimensions to customer specs. Finely figured walnut; straight grip with checkered butt with classic splinter forend and hand-rubbed oil finish standard. Pistol grip, beavertail forend, satin luster finish optional. **Features:** Holland & Holland pattern sidelock action, auto ejectors. Double triggers with front trigger hinged optional; non-selective single trigger standard. Coin finish standard. Top rib level, file cut standard; concave optional. Imported from Italy by Wm. Larkin Moore.
Price: 12-, 20-ga., from. $45,000.00
Price: 28, 410 bore, from $50,000.00

SKB Model 385 Sporting Clays

Similar to the Field Model 385 except 12-gauge only; 28" barrel with choke tubes; raised ventilated rib with metal middle bead and white front. Stock dimensions 14-1/4"x1-7/16"x1-7/8". Introduced 1998. Imported from Japan by G.U. Inc.
Price: $1,899.00
Price: Sporting Clays set, 20-, 28-ga.. . . . . $2,699.00

SKB MODEL 385 SIDE-BY-SIDE

Gauge: 12, 20, 3" chambers; 28, 2-3/4" chambers. **Barrel:** 26" (Imp. Cyl., Mod., Skeet choke tubes). **Weight:** 6-3/4 lbs. **Length:** 42-1/2" overall. **Stock:** 14-1/8"x1-1/2"x2-1/2" American walnut with straight or pistol grip stock, semi-beavertail forend. **Features:** Boxlock action. Silver nitrided receiver with engraving; solid barrel rib; single selective trigger, selective automatic ejectors, automatic safety. Introduced 1996. Imported from Japan by G.U. Inc.
Price: $1,799.00
Price: Field Set, 20-, 28-ga., 26", English or pistol grip $2,579.00

SKB Model 485 Side-by-Side

Similar to the Model 385 except has dummy sideplates, extensive upland game scene engraving, semi-fancy American walnut English or pistol grip stock. Imported from Japan by G.U. Inc.
Price: $2,439.00
Price: Field set, 20-, 28-ga., 26". $3,479.00

STOEGER/IGA UPLANDER SIDE-BY-SIDE SHOTGUN

Gauge: 12, 20, 28, 2-3/4" chambers; 410, 3" chambers. **Barrel:** 26" (Full & Full, 410 only, Imp. Cyl. & Mod.), 28" (Mod. & Full). **Weight:** 6-3/4 to 7 lbs. **Stock:** 14-1/2"x1-1/2"x2-1/2". Oil-finished hardwood. Checkered pistol grip and forend. **Features:** Automatic safety, extractors only, solid matted

Stoeger/IGA Deluxe Uplander

Stoeger/IGA Turkey

Tristar Model 411

barrel rib. Double triggers only. Introduced 1983. Imported from Brazil by Stoeger Industries.

Price: **$434.00**
Price: With choke tubes **$474.00**
Price: Coach Gun, 12, 20, 410, 20" bbls.................. **$415.00**
Price: Coach Gun, nickel finish, black stock............. **$464.00**
Price: Coach Gun, engraved stock....................... **$479.00**

Stoeger/IGA Ladies Side-by-Side
Similar to the Uplander except in 20-ga. only with 24" barrels (Imp. Cyl. & Mod. choke tubes), 13" length of pull, ventilated rubber recoil pad. Has extractors, double triggers, automatic safety. Introduced 1996. Imported from Brazil by Stoeger.
Price: **$485.00**

Stoeger/IGA Turkey Side-by-Side
Similar to the Uplander Model except has Advantage camouflage on stock, forend and barrels; 12-gauge only with 3" chambers, and has 24" choke tube barrels. Overall length 40". Introduced 1997. Imported from Brazil by Stoeger.
Price: **$559.00**

Stoeger/IGA English Stock Side-by-Side
Similar to the Uplander except in 410-bore only with 24" barrels (Mod. & Mod.), straight English stock and beavertail forend. Has automatic safety, extractors, double triggers. Intro 1996. Imported from Brazil by Stoeger.
Price: **$434.00**

Stoeger/IGA Youth Side-by-Side
Similar to the Uplander except in 410-bore with 24" barrels (Mod. & Full), 13" length of pull, ventilated recoil pad. Has double triggers, extractors, auto safety. Intro 1996. Imported from Brazil by Stoeger.
Price: **$446.00**

Stoeger/IGA Deluxe Coach Gun
Similar to the Uplander except 12- or 20-gauge, 20" barrels, choked Imp. Cyl. & Mod., 3" chambers; select semi-fancy American walnut pistol grip stock with checkering; double triggers; extractors. Introduced 1997. Imported form Brazil by Stoeger.
Price: **$499.00**

Stoeger/IGA Deluxe Uplander Shotgun
Similar to the Uplander except with semi-fancy American walnut with thin black Pachmayr rubber recoil pad, matte lacquer finish. Choke tubes and 3" chambers standard 12- and 20-gauge; 28-gauge has 26", 3" chokes, fixed Mod. & Full. Double gold plated triggers; extractors. Introduced 1997. Imported from Brazil by Stoeger.
Price: 12, 20... **$559.00**
Price: 28, 410.. **$519.00**

TRISTAR MODEL 411 SIDE-BY-SIDE
Gauge: 12, 16, 20, 410, 3" chambers; 28, 2-3/4". **Barrel:** 12-ga., 26", 28"; 16-, 20-, 28-ga., 410-bore, 26"; 12- and 20-ga. have three choke tubes, 16, 28 (Imp. Cyl. & Mod.), 410 (Mod. & Full) fixed chokes. **Weight:** 6-6-3/4 lbs. **Stock:** 14-3/8" l.o.p. Standard walnut with pistol grip, splinter-style forend; hand checkered. **Features:** Engraved, color case-hardened boxlock action; double triggers, extractors; solid barrel rib. Introduced 1998. Imported from Italy by Tristar Sporting Arms, Ltd.
Price: **$808.00**

Tristar Model 411D Side-by-Side
Similar to the model 411 except has automatic ejectors, straight English-style stock, single trigger. Solid barrel rib with matted surface; chrome bores; color case-hardened frame; splinter forend. Introduced 1999. Imported from Italy by Tristar Sporting Arms, Ltd. **NEW**
Price: **$1,057.00**

Tristar Model 411R Coach Gun Side-by-Side
Similar to the Model 411 except in 12- or 20-gauge only with 20" barrels and fixed chokes (Cyl. & Cyl.). Has double triggers, extractors, choke tubes. Introduced 1999. Imported from Italy by Tristar Sporting Arms, Ltd. **NEW**
Price: **$705.00**

Variety of designs for utility and sporting purposes, as well as for competitive shooting.

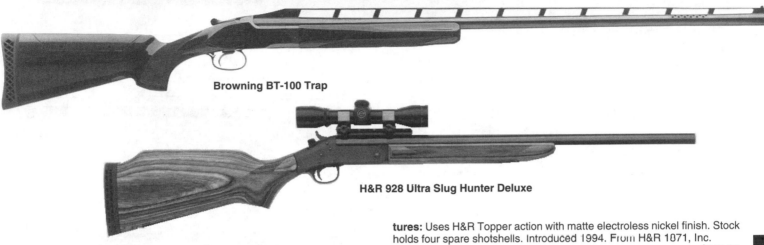

Browning BT-100 Trap

H&R 928 Ultra Slug Hunter Deluxe

BRNO ZBK 100 SINGLE BARREL SHOTGUN
Gauge: 12 or 20. **Barrel:** 27.5". **Weight:** 5.5 lbs. **Length:** 44" overall. **Stock:** Beech. **Features:** Polished blue finish; sling swivels. Announced 1998. Imported from The Czech Republic by Euro-Imports.
Price: $185.00

BROWNING BT-100 TRAP SHOTGUN
Gauge: 12, 2-3/4" chamber. **Barrel:** 32", 34" (Invector Plus); back-bored; also with fixed Full choke. **Weight:** 8 lbs. **Length:** 48-1/2" overall (32" barrel). **Stock:** 14-3/8"x1-9/16"x1-7/16x2" (Monte Carlo); 14-3/8"x1-3/4"x1-1/4"x2-1/8" (thumbhole). Walnut with high gloss finish; cut checkering. Wedge-shaped forend with finger groove. **Features:** Available in stainless steel or blue. Has drop-out trigger adjustable for weight of pull from 3-1/2 to 5-1/2 lbs., and for three length postions; Ejector-Selector allows ejection or extraction of shells. Available with adjustable comb stock and thumbhole stylo. Introduced 1995. Imported from Japan by Browning.
Price: Grade I, blue, Monte Carlo, Invector Plus $2,095.00
Price: As above, fixed Full choke $2,046.00
Price: With low-luster wood.......................... $1,667.00
Price: Stainless steel, Monte Carlo, Invector Plus $2,536.00
Price: As above, fixed Full choke $2,487.00
Price: Thumbhole stock, blue, Invector Plus $2,384.00
Price: Thumbhole stock, stainless, Invector Plus............ $2,825.00
Price: Thumbhole stock, blue, fixed choke................. $2,337.00
Price: Thumbhole stock, stainless, fixed choke $2,778.00
Price: BT-100 Satin (no ejector-selector, satin finish wood, metal) $1,667.00

HARRINGTON & RICHARDSON SB2-980 ULTRA SLUG
Gauge: 12, 20, 3" chamber. **Barrel:** 22" (20 ga. Youth) 24", fully rifled. **Weight:** 9 lbs. **Length:** NA. **Stock:** Walnut-stained hardwood. **Sights:** None furnished; comes with scope mount. **Features:** Uses the H&R 10-gauge action with heavy-wall barrel. Monte Carlo stock has sling swivels; comes with black nylon sling. Introduced 1995. Made in U.S. by H&R 1871, Inc.
Price: $209.95

Harrington & Richardson Model 928 Ultra Slug Hunter Deluxe
Similar to the SB2-980 Ultra Slug except uses 12-gauge action and 12-gauge barrel blank bored to 20-gauge, then fully rifled with 1:35" twist. Has hand-checkered camo laminate Monte Carlo stock and forend. Comes with Weaver-style scope base, offset hammer extension, ventilated recoil pad, sling swivels and camo nylon sling. Introduced 1997. Made in U.S. by H&R 1871 Inc.
Price: $239.95

HARRINGTON & RICHARDSON TAMER SHOTGUN
Gauge: 410, 3" chamber. **Barrel:** 19-1/2" (Full). **Weight:** 5-6 lbs. **Length:** 33" overall. **Stock:** Thumbhole grip of high density black polymer. **Fea-**

tures: Uses H&R Topper action with matte electroless nickel finish. Stock holds four spare shotshells. Introduced 1994. From H&R 1871, Inc.
Price: $124.95

HARRINGTON & RICHARDSON TOPPER MODEL 098
Gauge: 12, 16, 20, 28 (2-3/4"), 410, 3" chamber. **Barrel:** 12 ga.—28" (Mod., Full); 16 ga.— 28" (Mod.); 20 ga.—26" (Mod.); 28 ga.—26" (Mod.); 410 bore—26" (Full). **Weight:** 5-6 lbs. **Stock:** Black-finish hardwood with full pistol grip; semi-beavertail forend. **Sights:** Gold bead front. **Features:** Break-open action with side-lever release, automatic ejector. Satin nickel frame, blued barrel. Reintroduced 1992. From H&R 1871, Inc.
Price: $114.95
Price: Topper Junior 098 (as above except 22" barrel, 20-ga. (Mod.), 410-bore (Full), 12-1/2" length of pull) $119.95

Harrington & Richardson Topper Deluxe Model 098
Similar to the standard Topper 098 except 12-gauge only with 3-1/2" chamber, 28" barrel with choke tube (comes with Mod. tube, others optional). Satin nickel frame, blued barrel, black-finished wood. Introduced 1992. From H&R 1871, Inc.
Price: $134.95

Harrington & Richardson Topper Junior Classic Shotgun
Similar to the Topper Junior 098 except available in 20-gauge (3", Mod.), 410-bore (Full) with 3" chamber; 28-gauge, 2-3/4" chamber (Mod.); all have 22" barrel. Stock is American black walnut with cut-checkered pistol grip and forend. Ventilated rubber recoil pad with white line spacers. Blued barrel, blued frame. Introduced 1992. From H&R 1871, Inc.
Price: $144.95

Harrington & Richardson Topper Deluxe Rifled Slug Gun
Similar to the 12-gauge Topper Model 098 except has fully rifled and ported barrel, ramp front sight and fully adjustable rear. Barrel twist is 1:35". Nickel-plated frame, blued barrel, black-finished stock and forend. Introduced 1995. Made in U.S. by H&R 1871, Inc.
Price: $169.95

KRIEGHOFF K-80 SINGLE BARREL TRAP GUN
Gauge: 12, 2-3/4" chamber. **Barrel:** 32" or 34" Unsingle; 34" Top Single. Fixed Full or choke tubes. **Weight:** About 8-3/4 lbs. **Stock:** Four stock dimensions or adjustable stock available. All hand-checkered European walnut. **Features:** Satin nickel finish with K-80 logo. Selective mechanical trigger adjustable for finger position. Tapered step vent. rib. Adjustable point of impact on Unsingle.
Price: Standard grade full Unsingle, from.................. $7,950.00
Price: Standard grade full Top Single combo (special order), from $9,975.00
Price: RT (removable trigger) option, add $1,000.00

KRIEGHOFF KS-5 TRAP GUN
Gauge: 12, 2-3/4" chamber. **Barrel:** 32", 34"; Full choke or choke tubes. **Weight:** About 8-1/2 lbs. **Stock:** Choice of high Monte Carlo (1-1/2"), low Monte Carlo (1-3/8") or factory adjustable stock. European walnut. **Fea-**

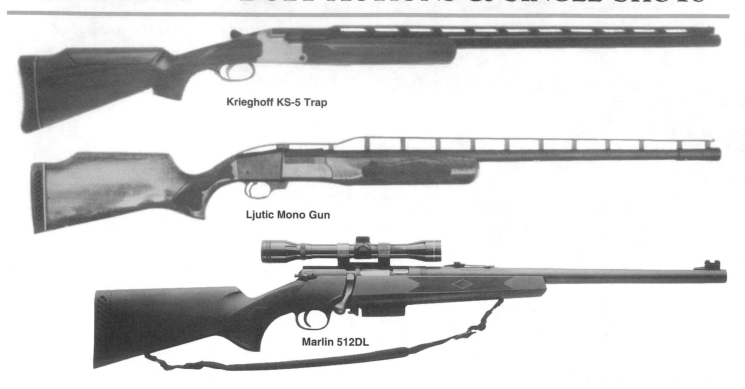

Krieghoff KS-5 Trap

Ljutic Mono Gun

Marlin 512DL

tures: Ventilated tapered step rib. Adjustable trigger or optional release trigger. Satin gray electroless nickel receiver. Comes with fitted aluminum case. Introduced 1988. Imported from Germany by Krieghoff International, Inc.
Price: Fixed choke, cased $3,695.00
Price: With choke tubes $4,120.00

Krieghoff KS-5 Special
Same as the KS-5 except the barrel has a fully adjustable rib and adjustable stock. Rib allows shooter to adjust point of impact from 50%/50% to nearly 90%/10%. Introduced 1990.
Price: $4,695.00

LJUTIC MONO GUN SINGLE BARREL
Gauge: 12 only. **Barrel:** 34", choked to customer specs; hollow-milled rib, 35-1/2" sight plane. **Weight:** Approx. 9 lbs. **Stock:** To customer specs. Oil finish, hand checkered. **Features:** Totally custom made. Pull or release trigger; removable trigger guard contains trigger and hammer mechanism; Ljutic pushbutton opener on front of trigger guard. From Ljutic Industries.
Price: With standard, medium or Olympic rib, custom 32"-34" bbls., and fixed choke $5,495.00
Price: As above with screw-in choke barrel $5,795.00

Ljutic LTX Super Deluxe Mono Gun
Super Deluxe version of the standard Mono Gun with high quality wood, extra-fancy checkering pattern in 24 lpi, double recessed choking. Available in two weights: 8-1/4 lbs. or 8-3/4 lbs. Extra light 33" barrel; medium-height rib. Introduced 1984. From Ljutic Industries.
Price: $6,495.00
Price: With three screw-in choke tubes $6,895.00

MARLIN MODEL 55GDL GOOSE GUN BOLT-ACTION SHOTGUN
Gauge: 12 only, 2-3/4" or 3" chamber. **Action:** Bolt action, thumb safety, detachable two-shot clip. Red cocking indicator. **Barrel:** 36" (Full) with burnished bore for lead or steel shot. **Weight:** 8 lbs. **Length:** 56-3/4" overall. **Stock:** Black fiberglass-filled synthetic with moulded-in checkering and swivel studs; ventilated recoil pad. **Sights:** Brass bead front, U-groove rear. **Features:** Brushed blue finish; thumb safety; red cocking indicator; 2-shot detachable box magazine. Introduced 1997. Made in U.S. by Marlin Firearms Co.
Price: $385.00

Marlin Model 50DL Bolt-Action Shotgun
Similar to the Model 55DL except has 28" barrel with Mod. choke. Weighs 7-1/2 lbs., measures 48-3/4" overall. Introduced 1997. Made in U.S. by Marlin Firearms Co.
Price: $330.00

MARLIN MODEL 25MG GARDEN GUN SHOTGUN
Gauge: 22 WMR shotshell, 7-shot magazine. **Barrel:** 22" smoothbore. **Weight:** 6 lbs. **Length:** 41" overall. **Stock:** Press-checkered hardwood. **Sights:** High-visibility bead front. **Features:** Bolt action; thumb safety; red cocking indicator. Introduced 1999. Made in U.S. by Marlin.
Price: $223.00

MARLIN MODEL 512 SLUGMASTER SHOTGUN
Gauge: 12, 3" chamber; 2-shot detachable box magazine. **Barrel:** 21", rifled (1:28" twist). **Weight:** 8 lbs. **Length:** 44-3/4" overall. **Stock:** Walnut-finished, press-checkered Maine birch with Mar-Shield® finish, ventilated recoil pad. **Sights:** Ramp front with brass bead and removable Wide-Scanô hood, adjustable folding semi-buckhorn rear. Drilled and tapped for scope mounting. **Features:** Uses Model 55 action with thumb safety. Designed for shooting saboted slugs. Comes with special Weaver scope mount. Introduced 1994. Made in U.S. by Marlin Firearms Co.
Price: $361.00

Marlin Model 512P Slugmaster Shotgun
Similar to the Model 512 except has black fiberglass-filled synthetic stock with moulded-in checkering, swivel studs; ventilated recoil pad; padded black nylon sling. Has 21" fully rifled and ported barrel with 1:28" rifling twist. Introduced 1997. Made in U.S. by Marlin Firearms Co.
Price: $366.00

MOSSBERG MODEL 695 SLUGSTER
Gauge: 12, 3" chamber. **Barrel:** 22"; fully rifled, ported. **Weight:** 7-1/2 lbs. **Stock:** Black synthetic, with swivel studs and rubber recoil pad. **Sights:** Blade front, folding rifle-style leaf rear; Fiber Optic. Comes with Weaver-style scope bases. **Features:** Matte metal finish; rotating thumb safety; detachable 2-shot magazine. Mossberg Cablelock. Made in U.S. by Mossberg. Introduced 1996.
Price: $330.00
Price: With Fiber Optic rifle sights $353.00
Price: Scope Combo Model includes Protecto case and Bushnell 1.5-4.5x scope $461.00

Tar-Hunt Mountaineer

NEW ENGLAND FIREARMS TRACKER SLUG GUN

Gauge: 12, 20, 3" chamber. **Barrel:** 24" (Cyl.). **Weight:** 6 lbs. **Length:** 40" overall. **Stock:** Walnut-finished hardwood with full pistol grip, recoil pad. **Sights:** Blade front, fully adjustable rifle-type rear. **Features:** Break-open action with side-lever release; blued barrel, color case-hardened frame. Introduced 1992. From New England Firearms.
Price: Tracker **$129.95**
Price: Tracker II (as above except fully rifled bore) **$139.95**

NEW ENGLAND FIREARMS TURKEY AND GOOSE GUN

Gauge: 10, 3-1/2" chamber. **Barrel:** 28" (Full), 32" (Mod.). **Weight:** 9.5 lbs. **Length:** 44" overall. **Stock:** American hardwood with walnut, or matte camo finish; ventilated rubber recoil pad. **Sights:** Bead front. **Features:** Break-open action with side-lever release; ejector. Matte finish on metal. Introduced 1992. From New England Firearms.
Price: Walnut-finish wood **$149.95**
Price: Camo finish, sling and swivels **$159.95**
Price: Camo finish, 32", sling and swivels **$179.95**
Price: Black matte finish, 24", Turkey Full choke tube, sling and swivels
. . . . **$184.95**

NEW ENGLAND FIREARMS SURVIVOR

Gauge: 12, 20, 410/45 Colt, 3" chamber. **Barrel:** 22" (Mod.); 20" (410/45 Colt, rifled barrel, choke tube). **Weight:** 6 lbs. **Length:** 36 overall. **Stock:** Black polymer with thumbhole/pistol grip, sling swivels; beavertail forend. **Sights:** Bead front. **Features:** Buttplate removes to expose storage for extra ammunition; forend also holds extra ammunition. Black or nickel finish. Introduced 1993. From New England Firearms.
Price: Black. **$129.95**
Price: Nickel **$145.95**
Price: 410/45 Colt, black. **$145.95**
Price: 410/45 Colt, nickel **$164.95**

NEW ENGLAND FIREARMS STANDARD PARDNER

Gauge: 12, 20, 410, 3" chamber; 16, 28, 2-3/4" chamber. **Barrel:** 12-ga.—28" (Full, Mod.), 32" (Full); 16-ga.—28" (Full), 32" (Full); 20-ga.—26" (Full, Mod.); 28-ga.—26" (Mod.); 410-bore—26" (Full). **Weight:** 5-6 lbs. **Length:** 43" overall (28" barrel). **Stock:** Walnut-finished hardwood with full pistol grip. **Sights:** Bead front. **Features:** Transfer bar ignition; break-open action with side-lever release. Introduced 1987. From New England Firearms.
Price: **$99.95**
Price: Youth model (12-, 20-, 28-ga., 410, 22" barrel, recoil pad) **$109.95**
Price: 12-ga., 32" (Full). **$104.95**

PERAZZI TMX SPECIAL SINGLE TRAP

Gauge: 12, 2-3/4" chamber. **Barrel:** 32" or 34" (Extra Full). **Weight:** 8 lbs., 6 oz. **Stock:** To customer specs; interchangeable. **Features:** Special high rib; adjustable four-position trigger. Also available with choke tubes. Imported from Italy by Perazzi U.S.A., Inc.
Price: From **$6,790.00**

ROSSI MODEL 12-G SHOTGUN

Gauge: 12, 20, 2-3/4" chamber; 410, 3" chamber. **Barrel:** 28". **Weight:** 5 lbs. **Length:** NA. **Stock:** Stained hardwood. **Features:** Spur hammer; integral safety; ejector; spur hammer. Imported from Brazil by BrazTech.
Price: **$119.00**
Price: Youth (shorter stock, 22" barrel) **$119.00**

SAVAGE MODEL 210F MASTER SHOT SLUG GUN

Gauge: 12, 3" chamber; 2-shot magazine. **Barrel:** 24" 1:35" rifling twist. **Weight:** 7-1/2 lbs. **Length:** 43.5" overall. **Stock:** Glass-filled polymer with positive checkering. **Features:** Based on the Savage Model 110 action; 60 bolt lift; controlled round feed; comes with scope mount. Introduced 1996. Made in U.S. by Savage Arms.
Price: **$380.00**

Savage Model 210FT Master Shot Shotgun

Similar to the Model 210F except has smoothbore barrel threaded for Winchoke-style choke tubes (comes with one Full tube); Advantage camo pattern covers the stock; pillar-bedded synthetic stock; bead front sight, U-notch rear. Introduced 1997. Made in U.S. by Savage Arms, Inc.
Price: **$440.00**

SNAKE CHARMER II SHOTGUN

Gauge: 410, 3" chamber. **Barrel:** 18-1/4". **Weight:** About 3-1/2 lbs. **Length:** 28-5/8" overall. **Stock:** ABS grade impact resistant plastic. **Features:** Thumbhole-type stock holds four extra rounds. Stainless steel barrel and frame. Reintroduced 1989. From Sporting Arms Mfg., Inc.
Price: **$149.00**
Price: Snake Charmer II Field Gun (as above except has conventional wood buttstock with 14" length of pull, 24" barrel 410 or 28-ga.) . **$160.00**
Price: New Generation Snake Charmer (as above except with black carbon steel bbl.) **$139.00**

TAR-HUNT RSG-12 PROFESSIONAL RIFLED SLUG GUN

Gauge: 12, 2-3/4" chamber, 1-shot magazine. **Barrel:** 21-1/2"; fully rifled, with muzzle brake. **Weight:** 7-3/4 lbs. **Length:** 41-1/2" overall. **Stock:** Matte black McMillan fiberglass with Pachmayr Decelerator pad. **Sights:** None furnished; comes with Leupold windage bases only. **Features:** Uses rifle-style action with two locking lugs; two-position safety; Shaw barrel; single-stage, trigger; muzzle brake. Many options available. Right- and left-hand models at same prices. Introduced 1991. Made in U.S. by Tar-Hunt Custom Rifles, Inc.
Price: Professional model , right- or left hand **$1,395.00**
Price: Matchless model (400-grit gloss metal finish, McMillan Fibergrain stock), right- or left-hand. **$1,873.00**
Price: Peerless model NP-3 nickel/Teflon metal finish, McMillan Fibergrain stock, right- or left-hand **$2,072.00**

Tar-Hunt RSG-20 Mountaineer Slug Gun

Similar to the RSG-12 Professional except chambered for 20-gauge (2-3/4") shells; 21" Shaw rifled barrel, with muzzle brake; two-lug bolt; one-shot blind magazine; matte black finish; McMillan fiberglass stock with Pachmayr Decelerator pad; receiver drilled and tapped for Rem. 700 bases. Weighs 6-1/2 lbs. Introduced 1997. Made in U.S. by Tar-Hunt Custom Rifles, Inc.
Price: **$1,295.00**

WESSON & HARRINGTON LONG TOM CLASSIC SHOTGUN

Gauge: 12, 3" chamber. **Barrel:** 32", (Full). **Weight:** 7-1/2 lbs. **Length:** 46" overall. **Stock:** 14"x1-3/4"x2-5/8". American black walnut with hand-checkered grip and forend. **Features:** Color case-hardened receiver and crescent steel buttplate, blued barrel. Receiver engraved with the National Wild Turkey Federation logo. Introduced 1998. Made in U.S. by H&R 1871, Inc.
Price: **$349.95**

Designs for utility, suitable for and adaptable to competitions and other sporting purposes.

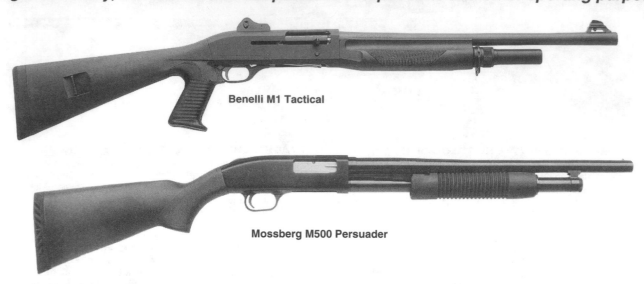

Benelli M1 Tactical

Mossberg M500 Persuader

AMERICAN ARMS PHANTOM HP AUTO SHOTGUN
Gauge: 12, 3" chamber. **Barrel:** 19"; threaded for external choke tubes. **Stock:** Black synthetic. **Sights:** Bead front. **Features:** Gas-operated action; blue/black finish; five-shot extended magazine tube. Imported by American Arms, Inc.
Price: .... **NA**

BENELLI M3 PUMP/AUTO SHOTGUN
Gauge: 12, 3" chamber, 7-shot magazine. **Barrel:** 19-3/4" (Cyl.). **Weight:** 7 lbs., 8 oz. **Length:** 41" overall. **Stock:** High-impact polymer with sling loop in side of butt; rubberized pistol grip on stock. **Sights:** Post front, buckhorn rear adjustable for windage. Ghost ring system available. **Features:** Combination pump/auto action. Alloy receiver with inertia recoil rotating locking lug bolt; matte finish; automatic shell release lever. Introduced 1989. Imported by Benelli USA.
Price: With standard stock **$1,040.00**
Price: With Ghost Ring sight system, standard stock **$1,080.00**

BENELLI M1 TACTICAL SHOTGUN
Gauge: 12, 3", 5-shot magazine. **Barrel:** 18.5", choke tubes. **Weight:** 6.5 lbs. **Length:** 39.75" overall. **Stock:** Black polymer. **Sights:** Rifle type with Ghost Ring system, tritium night sights optional. **Features:** Semi-auto inertia recoil action. Cross-bolt safety; bolt release button; matte-finish metal. Introduced 1993. Imported from Italy by Benelli USA.
Price: With rifle sights, standard stock **$905.00**
Price: With Ghost Ring rifle sights, standard stock **$905.00**
Price: As above with pistol grip stock **$950.00**

BERETTA MODEL 1201FP GHOST RING AUTO SHOTGUN
Gauge: 12, 3" chamber. **Barrel:** 18" (Cyl.). **Weight:** 6.3 lbs. **Stock:** Special strengthened technopolymer, matte black finish. **Stock:** Fixed rifle type. **Features:** Has 5-shot magazine. Adjustable Ghost Ring rear sight, tritium front. Introduced 1988. Imported from Italy by Beretta U.S.A.
Price: **$860.00**

BROLIN HP9 LAWMAN PUMP SHOTGUN
Gauge: 12, 3" chamber. **Barrel:** 18.5" (Cyl.). **Weight:** 7 lbs. **Length:** 38.5" overall. **Stock:** Black polymer or wood. **Sights:** Bead front. **Features:** Twin action bars; steel receiver; cross-bolt safety. Introduced 1997. Imported by Brolin Industries, Inc.
Price: Royal blue finish. **$189.00**
Price: Satin blue **$189.00**
Price: Hard chrome. **$219.00**

CROSSFIRE SHOTGUN/RIFLE
Gauge/Caliber: 12, 2-3/4" chamber 4-shot/223 Rem. (5-shot). **Barrel:** 20" (shotgun), 18" (rifle). **Weight:** About 8.6 lbs. **Length:** 40" overall. **Stock:**

Composite. **Sights:** Meprolight night sights. Integral Weaver-style scope rail. **Features:** Combination pump-action shotgun, rifle; single selector, single trigger; dual action bars for both upper and lower actions; ambidextrous selector and safety. Introduced 1997. Made in U.S. From Hesco.
Price: About **$1,895.00**
Price: With camo finish................................ **$1,995.00**

FABARM FP6 PUMP SHOTGUN
Gauge: 12, 3" chamber. **Barrel:** 20" (Cyl.); accepts choke tubes. **Weight:** 6.6 lbs. **Length:** 41.25" overall. **Stock:** Black polymer with textured grip, grooved slide handle. **Sights:** Blade front. **Features:** Twin action bars; anodized finish; free carrier for smooth reloading. Introduced 1998. Imported from Italy by Heckler & Koch, Inc.
Price: **$499.00**
Price: With flip-up front sight, Picatinny rail with rear sight, oversize safety button **$499.00**

MOSSBERG MODEL 500 PERSUADER SECURITY SHOTGUNS
Gauge: 12, 20, 410, 3" chamber. **Barrel:** 18-1/2", 20" (Cyl.). **Weight:** 7 lbs. **Stock:** Walnut-finished hardwood or black synthetic. **Sights:** Metal bead front. **Features:** Available in 6- or 8-shot models. Top-mounted safety, double action slide bars; swivel studs, rubber recoil pad. Blue, Parkerized, Marinecote finishes. Mossberg Cablelock included. From Mossberg.
Price: 12- or 20-ga., 18-1/2", blue, wood or synthetic stock, 6-shot
.... **$293.00**
Price: Cruiser, 12- or 20-ga., 18-1/2", blue, pistol grip, heat shield **$293.00**
Price: As above, 410-bore **$290.00**

Mossberg Model 500, 590 Mariner Pump
Similar to the Model 500 or 590 Security except all metal parts finished with Marinecote metal finish to resist rust and corrosion. Synthetic field stock; pistol grip kit included. Mossberg Cablelock included.
Price: 6-shot, 18-1/2" barrel **$425.00**
Price: 9-shot, 20" barrel **$440.00**

Mossberg Model HS410 Shotgun
Similar to the Model 500 Security pump except chambered for 20 gauge or 410 with 3" chamber; has pistol grip forend, thick recoil pad, muzzle brake and has special spreader choke on the 18.5" barrel. Overall length is 37.5", weight is 6.25 lbs. Blue finish; synthetic field stock. Mossberg Cablelock and video included. Introduced 1990.
Price: HS 410 .... **$304.00**

Mossberg Model 500, 590 Ghost-Ring Shotguns
Similar to the Model 500 Security except has adjustable blade front, adjustable Ghost-Ring rear sight with protective "ears." Model 500 has 18.5"

Tactical Response TR-870

Winchester Model 1300 Defender

(Cyl.) barrel, 6-shot capacity; Model 590 has 20" (Cyl.) barrel, 9-shot capacity. Both have synthetic field stock. Mossberg Cablelock included. Introduced 1990. From Mossberg.

Price: Model 500, blue **$343.00**
Price: As above, Parkerized **$399.00**
Price: Model 590, blue **$353.00**
Price: As above, Parkerized **$406.00**
Price: Parkerized Speedfeed stock **$497.00**

MOSSBERG MODEL 9200A1 JUNGLE GUN

Gauge: 12, 2-3/4" chamber; 5-shot magazine. **Barrel:** 18-1/2" (Cyl.). **Weight:** About 7 lbs. **Length:** 38-1/2" overall. **Stock:** Black synthetic. **Sights:** Bead front. **Features:** Designed to function only with 2-3/4" 00 Buck loads; Parkerized finish; mil-spec heavy wall barrel; military metal trigger housing; ambidextrous metal tang safety. Introduced 1998. Made in U.S. by Mossberg.
Price: **$676.00**

MOSSBERG MODEL 590 SHOTGUN

Gauge: 12, 3" chamber. **Barrel:** 20" (Cyl.). **Weight:** 7-1/4 lbs. **Stock:** Synthetic field or Speedfeed. **Sights:** Metal bead front. **Features:** Top-mounted safety, double slide action bars. Comes with heat shield, bayonet lug, swivel studs, rubber recoil pad. Blue, Parkerized or Marinecote finish. Mossberg Cablelock included. From Mossberg.
Price: Blue, synthetic stock **$353.00**
Price: Parkerized, synthetic stock **$406.00**
Price: Parkerized, Speedfeed stock **$441.00**

TACTICAL RESPONSE TR-870 STANDARD MODEL SHOTGUN

Gauge: 12, 3" chamber, 7-shot magazine. **Barrel:** 18" (Cyl.). **Weight:** 9 lbs. **Length:** 38" overall. **Stock:** Fiberglass-filled polypropolene with non-snag recoil absorbing butt pad. Nylon tactical forend houses flashlight. **Sights:** Trak-Lock ghost ring sight system. Front sight has tritium insert. **Features:** Highly modified Remington 870P with Parkerized finish. Comes with nylon three-way adjustable sling, high visibility non-binding follower, high performance magazine spring, Jumbo Head safety, and Side Saddle extended 6-shot shell carrier on left side of receiver. Introduced 1991. From Scattergun Technologies, Inc.
Price: Standard model **$815.00**
Price: FBI model **$770.00**

Price: Patrol model **$595.00**
Price: Border Patrol model **$605.00**
Price: K-9 model (Rem. 11-87 action) **$995.00**
Price: Urban Sniper, Rem. 11-87 action **$1,290.00**
Price: Louis Awerbuck model **$705.00**
Price: Practical Turkey model **$725.00**
Price: Expert model **$1,350.00**
Price: Professional model **$815.00**
Price: Entry model **$840.00**
Price: Compact model **$635.00**
Price: SWAT model **$1,195.00**

WINCHESTER MODEL 1300 DEFENDER PUMP GUN

Gauge: 12, 20, 3" chamber, 5- or 8-shot capacity. **Barrel:** 18" (Cyl.). **Weight:** 6-3/4 lbs. **Length:** 38-5/8" overall. **Stock:** Walnut-finished hardwood stock and ribbed forend, or synthetic; or pistol grip. **Sights:** Metal bead front. **Features:** Cross-bolt safety, front-locking rotary bolt, twin action slide bars. Black rubber butt pad. From U.S. Repeating Arms Co.
Price: 8-shot, wood or synthetic stock **$305.00**
Price: 5-shot, wood stock **$305.00**
Price: Camp Defender, 22" barrel with Winchoke tubes, rifle sights, synthetic stock, 5-shot **$345.00**

Winchester 8-Shot Pistol Grip Pump Security Shotgun

Same as regular Defender Pump but with pistol grip and forend of high-impact resistant ABS plastic with non-glare black finish. Introduced 1984.
Price: Pistol Grip Defender **$305.00**

Winchester Model 1300 Stainless Marine Pump Gun

Same as the Defender except has bright chrome finish, stainless steel barrel, rifle-type sights only. Phosphate coated receiver for corrosion resistance. Pistol grip optional.
Price: **$485.00**

Winchester Model 1300 Lady Defender Pump Gun

Similar to the Model 1300 Defender except in 20-gauge only, weighs 6-1/4 lbs. Available with synthetic full stock or synthetic pistol grip only. Introduced 1997. From U.S. Repeating Arms Co.
Price: **$305.00**

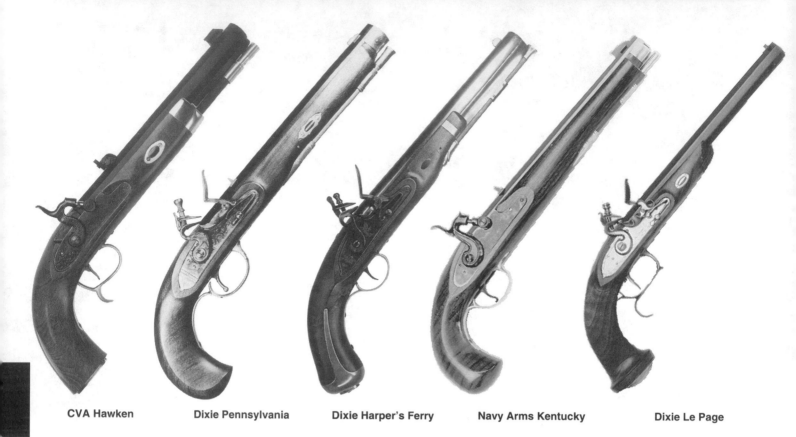

CVA Hawken   Dixie Pennsylvania   Dixie Harper's Ferry   Navy Arms Kentucky   Dixie Le Page

CVA HAWKEN PISTOL

Caliber: 50. **Barrel:** 9-3/4"; 15/16" flats. **Weight:** 50 oz. **Length:** 16-1/2" overall. **Stocks:** Select hardwood. **Sights:** Beaded blade front, fully adjustable open rear. **Features:** Color case-hardened lock, polished brass wedge plate, instep, ramrod thimble, trigger guard, grip cap. Imported by CVA.
Price: $149.95
Price: Kit $109.95

DIXIE PENNSYLVANIA PISTOL

Caliber: 44 (.430" round ball). **Barrel:** 10", (7/8" octagon). **Weight:** 2-1/2 labs. **Stocks:** Walnut-stained hardwood. **Sights:** Blade front, open rear drift-adjustable for windage; brass. **Features:** Available in flint only. Brass trigger guard, thimbles, instep, wedge plates; high-luster blue barrel. Imported from Italy by Dixie Gun Works.
Price: Finished $195.00
Price: Kit $185.00

FRENCH-STYLE DUELING PISTOL

Caliber: 44. **Barrel:** 10". **Weight:** 35 oz. **Length:** 15-3/4" overall. **Stocks:** Carved walnut. **Sights:** Fixed. **Features:** Comes with velvet-lined case and accessories. Imported by Mandall Shooting Supplies.
Price: $295.00

HARPER'S FERRY 1806 PISTOL

Caliber: 58 (.570" round ball). **Barrel:** 10". **Weight:** 40 oz. **Length:** 16" overall. **Stocks:** Walnut. **Sights:** Fixed. **Features:** Case-hardened lock, brass-mounted browned barrel. Replica of the first U.S. Gov't.-made flintlock pistol. Imported by Navy Arms, Dixie Gun Works.
Price: . . . . $275.00 to $405.00
Price: Kit (Dixie) $249.00
Price: Cased set (Navy Arms) $355.00

KENTUCKY FLINTLOCK PISTOL

Caliber: 44, 45. **Barrel:** 10-1/8". **Weight:** 32 oz. **Length:** 15-1/2" overall. **Stocks:** Walnut. **Sights:** Fixed. **Features:** Specifications, including caliber, weight and length may vary with importer. Case-hardened lock, blued barrel; available also as brass barrel flint Model 1821. Imported by Navy Arms, The Armoury.
Price: . . . . $145.00 to $235.00
Price: In kit form, from . . . . $90.00 to $112.00
Price: Single cased set (Navy Arms) $360.00
Price: Double cased set (Navy Arms) $590.00

Kentucky Percussion Pistol

Similar to flint version but percussion lock. Imported by The Armoury, Navy Arms, CVA (50-cal.).
Price: . . . . $129.95 to $225.00
Price: Steel barrel (Armoury) $179.00
Price: Single cased set (Navy Arms) $355.00
Price: Double cased set (Navy Arms) $600.00

LE PAGE PERCUSSION DUELING PISTOL

Caliber: 44. **Barrel:** 10", rifled. **Weight:** 40 oz. **Length:** 16" overall. **Stocks:** Walnut, fluted butt. **Sights:** Blade front, notch rear. **Features:** Double-set triggers. Blued barrel; trigger guard and buttcap are polished silver. Imported by Dixie Gun Works.
Price: $259.95

LYMAN PLAINS PISTOL

Caliber: 50 or 54. **Barrel:** 8"; 1:30" twist, both calibers. **Weight:** 50 oz. **Length:** 15" overall. **Stocks:** Walnut half-stock. **Sights:** Blade front, square notch rear adjustable for windage. **Features:** Polished brass trigger guard and ramrod tip, color case-hardened coil spring lock, spring-loaded trigger, stainless steel nipple, blackened iron furniture. Hooked patent breech, detachable belt hook. Introduced 1981. From Lyman Products.
Price: Finished $229.95
Price: Kit $184.95

Lyman Plains Pistol   Pedersoli Mang   Dixie Queen Anne   Traditions Pioneer   Traditions William Parker

PEDERSOLI MANG TARGET PISTOL

Caliber: 38. **Barrel:** 10.5", octagonal; 1:15" twist, **Weight:** 2.5 lbs. **Length:** 17.25" overall. **Stocks:** Walnut with fluted grip. **Sights:** Blade front, open rear adjustable for windage.
Features: Browned barrel, polished breech plug, rest color case-hardened. Imported from Italy by Dixie Gun Works.
Price: **$786.00**

QUEEN ANNE FLINTLOCK PISTOL

Caliber: 50 (.490" round ball). **Barrel:** 7-1/2", smoothbore. **Stocks:** Walnut. **Sights:** None. **Features:** Browned steel barrel, fluted brass trigger guard, brass mask on butt. Lockplate left in the white. Made by Pedersoli in Italy. Introduced 1983. Imported by Dixie Gun Works.
Price: **$225.00**
Price: Kit. **$175.00**

TRADITIONS BUCKHUNTER PRO IN-LINE PISTOL

Caliber: 50, 54. **Barrel:** 9-1/2", round. **Weight:** 48 oz. **Length:** 14" overall. **Stocks:** Smooth walnut or black epoxy coated grip and forend. **Sights:** Beaded blade front, folding adjustable rear. **Features:** Thumb safety; removable stainless steel breech plug; adjustable trigger, barrel drilled and tapped for scope mounting. From Traditions.
Price: With walnut grip **$219.00**
Price: Nickel with black grip **$234.00**
Price: With walnut grip and 12-1/2" barrel **$234.00**

TRADITIONS KENTUCKY PISTOL

Caliber: 50. **Barrel:** 10"; octagon with 7/8" flats; 1:20" twist. **Weight:** 40 oz. **Length:** 15" overall. **Stocks:** Stained beech. **Sights:** Blade front, fixed rear. **Features:** Birds-head grip; brass thimbles; color case-hardened lock. Percussion only. Introduced 1995. From Traditions.
Price: Finished **$131.00**
Price: Kit. **$101.00**

TRADITIONS PIONEER PISTOL

Caliber: 45. **Barrel:** 9-5/8"; 13/16" flats, 1:16" twist. **Weight:** 31 oz. **Length:** 15" overall. **Stocks:** Beech. **Sights:** Blade front, fixed rear. **Features:** V-type mainspring. Single trigger. German silver furniture, blackened hardware. From Traditions.

Traditions Buckhunter Pro

Price: **$140.00**
Price: Kit. **$116.00**

TRADITIONS TRAPPER PISTOL

Caliber: 50. **Barrel:** 9-3/4"; 7/8" flats; 1:20" twist. **Weight:** 2-3/4 lbs. **Length:** 16" overall. **Stocks:** Beech. **Sights:** Blade front, adjustable rear. **Features:** Double-set triggers; brass buttcap, trigger guard, wedge plate, forend tip, thimble. From Traditions.
Price: Percussion **$183.00**
Price: Flintlock **$197.00**
Price: Kit. **$139.00**

TRADITIONS WILLIAM PARKER PISTOL

Caliber: 50. **Barrel:** 10-3/8"; 15/16" flats; polished steel. **Weight:** 37 oz. **Length:** 17-1/2" overall. **Stocks:** Walnut with checkered grip. **Sights:** Brass blade front, fixed rear. **Features:** Replica dueling pistol with 1:20" twist, hooked breech. Brass wedge plate, trigger guard, cap guard; separate ramrod. Double-set triggers. Polished steel barrel, lock. Imported by Traditions.
Price: **$256.00**

BLACKPOWDER REVOLVERS

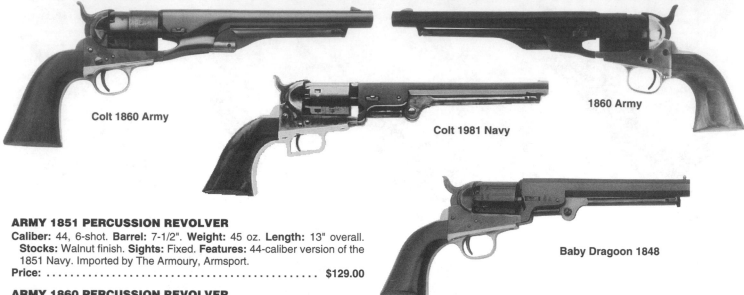

Colt 1860 Army

Colt 1981 Navy

1860 Army

Baby Dragoon 1848

ARMY 1851 PERCUSSION REVOLVER

Caliber: 44, 6-shot. **Barrel:** 7-1/2". **Weight:** 45 oz. **Length:** 13" overall. **Stocks:** Walnut finish. **Sights:** Fixed. **Features:** 44-caliber version of the 1851 Navy. Imported by The Armoury, Armsport.
Price: **$129.00**

ARMY 1860 PERCUSSION REVOLVER

Caliber: 44, 6-shot. **Barrel:** 8". **Weight:** 40 oz. **Length:** 13-5/8" overall. **Stocks:** Walnut. **Sights:** Fixed. **Features:** Engraved Navy scene on cylinder; brass trigger guard; case-hardened frame, loading lever and hammer. Some importers supply pistol cut for detachable shoulder stock, have accessory stock available. Imported by Cabela's (1860 Lawman), E.M.F., Navy Arms, The Armoury, Cimarron, Dixie Gun Works (half-fluted cylinder, not roll engraved), Euroarms of America (brass or steel model), Armsport, Traditions (brass or steel), Uberti U.S.A. Inc., United States Patent Fire-Arms.
Price: About . . . . **$92.95** to **$395.00**
Price: Hartford model, steel frame, German silver trim,
cartouches (E.M.F.) **$215.00**
Price: Single cased set (Navy Arms) **$300.00**
Price: Double cased set (Navy Arms). **$490.00**
Price: 1861 Navy: Same as Army except 36-cal., 7-1/2" bbl., weighs 41 oz., cut for shoulder stock; round cylinder (fluted available), from Cabela's, CVA (brass frame, 44-cal.), United States Patent Fire-Arms
. . . . **$99.95** to **$385.00**
Price: Steel frame kit (E.M.F., Euroarms). . . . . **$125.00** to **$216.25**
Price: Colt Army Police, fluted cyl., 5-1/2", 36-cal. (Cabela's) . . . **$124.95**
Price: With nickeled frame, barrel and backstrap, gold-tone fluted cylinder, trigger and hammer, simulated ivory grips (Traditions) **$199.00**

BABY DRAGOON 1848, 1849 POCKET, WELLS FARGO

Caliber: 31. **Barrel:** 3", 4", 5", 6"; seven-groove; RH twist. **Weight:** About 21 oz. **Stocks:** Varnished walnut. **Sights:** Brass pin front, hammer notch rear. **Features:** No loading lever on Baby Dragoon or Wells Fargo models. Unfluted cylinder with stagecoach holdup scene; cupped cylinder pin; no grease grooves; one safety pin on cylinder and slot in hammer face; straight (flat) mainspring. From Armsport, Dixie Gun Works, Uberti U.S.A. Inc.
Price: 6" barrel, with loading lever (Dixie Gun Works) **$254.95**
Price: 4" (Uberti USA Inc.) **$335.00**

COLT 1860 ARMY PERCUSSION REVOLVER

Caliber: 44. **Barrel:** 8", 7-groove, left-hand twist. **Weight:** 42 oz. **Stocks:** One-piece walnut. **Sights:** German silver front sight, hammer notch rear. **Features:** Steel backstrap cut for shoulder stock; brass trigger guard. Cylinder has Navy scene. Color case-hardened frame, hammer, loading lever. Reproduction of original gun with all original markings. From Colt Blackpowder Arms Co.
Price: **$399.95**

COLT 1848 BABY DRAGOON REVOLVER

Caliber: 31, 5-shot. **Barrel:** 4". **Weight:** About 21 oz. **Stocks:** Smooth walnut. **Sights:** Brass pin front, hammer notch rear. **Features:** Color case-hardened frame; no loading lever; square-back trigger guard; round bolt

cuts; octagonal barrel; engraved cylinder scene. Imported by Colt Blackpowder Arms Co.
Price: **$389.95**

Uberti 1861 Navy Percussion Revolver

Similar to 1851 Navy except has round 7-1/2" barrel, rounded trigger guard, German silver blade front sight, "creeping" loading lever. Available with fluted or round cylinder. Imported by Uberti U.S.A. Inc.
Price: Steel backstrap, trigger guard, cut for stock. **$300.00**

Colt 1860 "Cavalry Model" Percussion Revolver

Similar to the 1860 Army except has fluted cylinder. Color case-hardened frame, hammer, loading lever and plunger; blued barrel, backstrap and cylinder, brass trigger guard. Has four-screw frame cut for optional shoulder stock. From Colt Blackpowder Arms Co.
Price: **$399.95**

COLT 1851 NAVY PERCUSSION REVOLVER

Caliber: 36. **Barrel:** 7-1/2", octagonal; 7-groove left-hand twist. **Weight:** 40-1/2 oz. **Stocks:** One-piece oiled American walnut. **Sights:** Brass pin front, hammer notch rear. **Features:** Faithful reproduction of the original gun. Color case-hardened frame, loading lever, plunger, hammer and latch. Blue cylinder, trigger, barrel, screws, wedge. Silver-plated brass backstrap and square-back trigger guard. From Colt Blackpowder Arms Co.
Price: **$399.95**

COLT 1861 NAVY PERCUSSION REVOLVER

Caliber: 36. **Barrel:** 7-1/2". **Weight:** 42 oz. **Length:** 13-1/8" overall. **Stocks:** One-piece walnut. **Sights:** Blade front, hammer notch rear. **Features:** Color case-hardened frame, loading lever, plunger; blued barrel, backstrap, trigger guard; roll-engraved cylinder and barrel. From Colt Blackpowder Arms Co.
Price: **$399.95**

COLT 1849 POCKET DRAGOON REVOLVER

Caliber: 31. **Barrel:** 4". **Weight:** 24 oz. **Length:** 9-1/2" overall. **Stocks:** One-piece walnut. **Sights:** Fixed. Brass pin front, hammer notch rear. **Features:** Color case-hardened frame. No loading lever. Unfluted cylinder with engraved scene. Exact reproduction of original. From Colt Blackpowder Arms Co.
Price: **$389.95**

COLT 1862 POCKET POLICE "TRAPPER MODEL" REVOLVER

Caliber: 36. **Barrel:** 3-1/2". **Weight:** 20 oz. **Length:** 8-1/2" overall. **Stocks:** One-piece walnut. **Sights:** Blade front, hammer notch rear. **Features:** Has separate 4-5/8" brass ramrod. Color case-hardened frame and ham-

BLACKPOWDER REVOLVERS

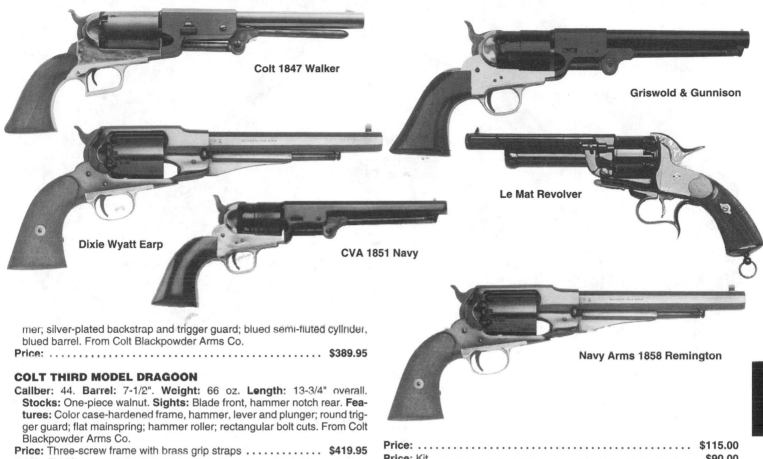

Colt 1847 Walker

Griswold & Gunnison

Dixie Wyatt Earp

CVA 1851 Navy

Le Mat Revolver

Navy Arms 1858 Remington

mer; silver-plated backstrap and trigger guard; blued semi-fluted cylinder, blued barrel. From Colt Blackpowder Arms Co.

Price: **$389.95**

COLT THIRD MODEL DRAGOON
Caliber: 44. **Barrel:** 7-1/2". **Weight:** 66 oz. **Length:** 13-3/4" overall. **Stocks:** One-piece walnut. **Sights:** Blade front, hammer notch rear. **Features:** Color case-hardened frame, hammer, lever and plunger; round trigger guard; flat mainspring; hammer roller; rectangular bolt cuts. From Colt Blackpowder Arms Co.
Price: Three-screw frame with brass grip straps **$419.95**
Price: First Dragoon (oval bolt cuts in cylinder, square-back trigger
guard) **$419.95**
Price: Second Dragoon (rectangular bolt cuts in cylinder, square-back
trigger guard) **$419.95**

Colt Walker 150th Anniversary Revolver
Similar to the standard Walker except has original-type "A Company No. 1" markings embellished in gold. Serial numbers begin with 221, a continuation of A Company numbers. Imported by Colt Blackpowder Arms Co.
Price: **$599.95**

COLT 1847 WALKER PERCUSSION REVOLVER
Caliber: 44. **Barrel:** 9", 7-groove; right-hand twist. **Weight:** 73 oz. **Stocks:** One-piece walnut. **Sights:** German silver front sight, hammer notch rear. **Features:** Made in U.S. Faithful reproduction of the original gun, including markings. Color case-hardened frame, hammer, loading lever and plunger. Blue steel backstrap, brass square-back trigger guard. Blue barrel, cylinder, trigger and wedge. From Colt Blackpowder Arms Co.
Price: **$419.95**

DIXIE WYATT EARP REVOLVER
Caliber: 44. **Barrel:** 12", octagon. **Weight:** 46 oz. **Length:** 18" overall. **Stocks:** Two-piece walnut. **Sights:** Fixed. **Features:** Highly polished brass frame, backstrap and trigger guard; blued barrel and cylinder; case-hardened hammer, trigger and loading lever. Navy-size shoulder stock ($45) will fit with minor fitting. From Dixie Gun Works.
Price: **$150.00**

GRISWOLD & GUNNISON PERCUSSION REVOLVER
Caliber: 36 or 44, 6-shot. **Barrel:** 7-1/2". **Weight:** 44 oz. (36-cal.). **Length:** 13" overall. **Stocks:** Walnut. **Sights:** Fixed. **Features:** Replica of famous Confederate pistol. Brass frame, backstrap and trigger guard; case-hardened loading lever; rebated cylinder (44-cal. only). Rounded Dragoon-type barrel. Imported by Navy Arms as Reb Model 1860.

Price: **$115.00**
Price: Kit. **$90.00**
Price: Single cased set. **$235.00**
Price: Double cased set **$365.00**

LE MAT REVOLVER
Caliber: 44/65. **Barrel:** 6-3/4" (revolver); 4-7/8" (single shot). **Weight:** 3 lbs., 7 oz. **Stocks:** Hand-checkered walnut. **Sights:** Post front, hammer notch rear. **Features:** Exact reproduction with all-steel construction; 44-cal. 9-shot cylinder, 65-cal. single barrel; color case-hardened hammer with selector; spur trigger guard; ring at butt; lever-type barrel release. From Navy Arms.
Price: Cavalry model (lanyard ring, spur trigger guard) **$595.00**
Price: Army model (round trigger guard, pin-type barrel release) **$595.00**
Price: Naval-style (thumb selector on hammer) **$595.00**
Price: Engraved 18th Georgia cased set **$795.00**
Price: Engraved Beauregard cased set **$1,000.00**

NAVY ARMS DELUXE 1858 REMINGTON-STYLE REVOLVER
Caliber: 44. **Barrel:** 8". **Weight:** 2 lbs., 13 oz. **Stocks:** Smooth walnut. **Sights:** Dovetailed blade front. **Features:** First exact reproduction—correct in size and weight to the original, with progressive rifling; highly polished with blue finish. From Navy Arms.
Price: Deluxe model **$415.00**

NAVY MODEL 1851 PERCUSSION REVOLVER
Caliber: 36, 44, 6-shot. **Barrel:** 7-1/2". **Weight:** 44 oz. **Length:** 13" overall. **Stocks:** Walnut finish. **Sights:** Post front, hammer notch rear. **Features:** Brass backstrap and trigger guard; some have 1st Model squareback trigger guard, engraved cylinder with navy battle scene; case-hardened frame, hammer, loading lever. Imported by The Armoury, Cabela's, Navy Arms, E.M.F., Dixie Gun Works, Euroarms of America, Armsport, CVA (44-cal. only), Traditions (44 only), Uberti U.S.A. Inc., United States Patent Fire-Arms.
Price: Brass frame .... **$99.95** to **$385.00**

BLACKPOWDER REVOLVERS

Uberti 1858

Ruger Old Army

North American Companion

Euroarms Rogers & Spencer

Pocket Police 1862

Price: Steel frame. . . . . $130.00 to $285.00
Price: Kit form. . . . . $110.00 to $123.95
Price: Engraved model (Dixie Gun Works). $159.95
Price: Single cased set, steel frame (Navy Arms) $280.00
Price: Double cased set, steel frame (Navy Arms). $455.00
Price: Confederate Navy (Cabela's). $89.99
Price: Hartford model, steel frame, German silver trim,
cartouche (E.M.F.) $190.00

NEW MODEL 1858 ARMY PERCUSSION REVOLVER

Caliber: 36 or 44, 6-shot. **Barrel:** 6-1/2" or 8". **Weight:** 38 oz. **Length:** 13-1/2" overall. **Stocks:** Walnut. **Sights:** Blade front, groove-in-frame rear. **Features:** Replica of Remington Model 1858. Also available from some importers as Army Model Belt Revolver in 36-cal., a shortened and lightened version of the 44. Target Model (Uberti U.S.A. Inc., Navy Arms) has fully adjustable target rear sight, target front, 36 or 44. Imported by Cabela's, CVA (as 1858 Army, brass frame, 44 only), Dixie Gun Works, Navy Arms, The Armoury, E.M.F., Euroarms of America (engraved, stainless and plain), Armsport, Traditions (44 only), Uberti U.S.A. Inc.
Price: Steel frame, about . . . . $99.95 to $280.00
Price: Steel frame kit (Euroarms, Navy Arms) . . . . . . $115.95 to $150.00
Price: Single cased set (Navy Arms) $290.00
Price: Double cased set (Navy Arms). $480.00
Price: Stainless steel Model 1858 (Euroarms, Uberti U.S.A. Inc., Cabela's, Navy Arms, Armsport, Traditions) . . . . $169.95 to $380.00
Price: Target Model, adjustable rear sight (Cabela's, Euroarms, Uberti U.S.A. Inc., Stone Mountain Arms). . . . . $95.95 to $399.00
Price: Brass frame (CVA, Cabela's, Traditions, Navy Arms) . . . . $79.95 to $125.00
Price: As above, kit (Dixie Gun Works, Navy Arms). . $145.00 to $188.95
Price: Buffalo model, 44-cal. (Cabela's) $119.99
Price: Hartford model, steel frame, German silver trim,
cartouche (E.M.F.). $215.00

NORTH AMERICAN COMPANION PERCUSSION REVOLVER

Caliber: 22. **Barrel:** 1-1/8". **Weight:** 5.1 oz. **Length:** 4-5/10" overall. **Stocks:** Laminated wood. **Sights:** Blade front, notch fixed rear. **Features:** All stainless steel construction. Uses standard #11 percussion caps. Comes with bullets, powder measure, bullet seater, leather clip holster,

gun rug. Long Rifle or Magnum frame size. Introduced 1996. Made in U.S. by North American Arms.
Price: Long Rifle frame. $191.00

North American Magnum Companion Percussion Revolver

Similar to the Companion except has larger frame. Weighs 7.2 oz., has 1-5/8" barrel, measures 5-7/16" overall. Comes with bullets, powder measure, bullet seater, leather clip holster, gun rag. Introduced 1996. Made in U.S. by North American Arms.
Price: $209.00

POCKET POLICE 1862 PERCUSSION REVOLVER

Caliber: 36, 5-shot. **Barrel:** 4-1/2", 5-1/2", 6-1/2", 7-1/2". **Weight:** 26 oz. **Length:** 12" overall (6-1/2" bbl.). **Stocks:** Walnut. **Sights:** Fixed. **Features:** Round tapered barrel; half-fluted and rebated cylinder; case-hardened frame, loading lever and hammer; silver or brass trigger guard and backstrap. Imported by Dixie Gun Works, Navy Arms (5-1/2" only), Uberti U.S.A. Inc. (5-1/2", 6-1/2" only), United States Patent Fire-Arms.
Price: About . . . . $139.95 to $335.00
Price: Single cased set with accessories (Navy Arms) $365.00
Price: Hartford model, steel frame, German silver trim,
cartouche (E.M.F.). $215.00

ROGERS & SPENCER PERCUSSION REVOLVER

Caliber: 44. **Barrel:** 7-1/2". **Weight:** 47 oz. **Length:** 13-3/4" overall. **Stocks:** Walnut. **Sights:** Cone front, integral groove in frame for rear. **Features:** Accurate reproduction of a Civil War design. Solid frame; extra large nipple cut-out on rear of cylinder; loading lever and cylinder easily removed for cleaning. From Dixie Gun Works, Euroarms of America (standard blue, engraved, burnished, target models), Navy Arms.
Price: . . . . $160.00 to $299.95
Price: Nickel-plated $215.00
Price: Engraved (Euroarms). $287.00
Price: Kit version . . . . $245.00 to $252.00
Price: Target version (Euroarms) . . . . $239.00 to $270.00
Price: Burnished London Gray (Euroarms) . . . . $245.00 to $270.00

RUGER OLD ARMY PERCUSSION REVOLVER

Caliber: 45, 6-shot. Uses .457" dia. lead bullets. **Barrel:** 7-1/2" (6-groove; 16" twist). **Weight:** 46 oz. **Length:** 13-3/4" overall. **Stocks:** Smooth walnut.

BLACKPOWDER REVOLVERS

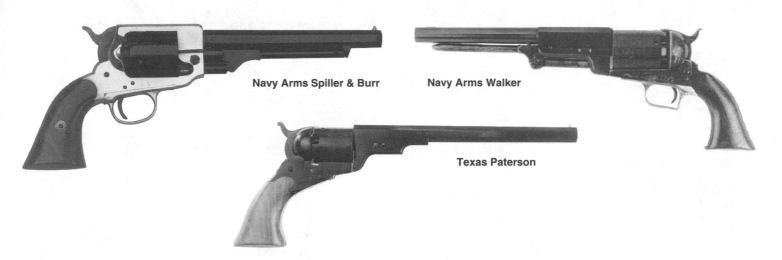

Navy Arms Spiller & Burr

Navy Arms Walker

Texas Paterson

Sights: Ramp front, rear adjustable for windage and elevation; or fixed (groove). **Features:** Stainless steel; standard size nipples, chrome-moly steel cylinder and frame, same lockwork as in original Super Blackhawk. Also available in stainless steel. Made In USA. From Sturm, Ruger & Co.
Price: Stainless steel (Model KBP-7) $475.00
Price: Blued steel (Model BP-7) $435.00
Price: Blued steel, fixed sight (BP-7F) $435.00
Price: Stainless steel, fixed sight (KBP-7F) $475.00

SHERIFF MODEL 1851 PERCUSSION REVOLVER
Caliber: 36, 44, 6-shot. **Barrel:** 5". **Weight:** 40 oz. **Length:** 10-1/2" overall. **Stocks:** Walnut. **Sights:** Fixed. **Features:** Brass backstrap and trigger guard; engraved navy scene; case-hardened frame, hammer, loading lever. Imported by E.M.F.
Price: Steel frame $172.00
Price: Brass frame $140.00

SPILLER & BURR REVOLVER
Caliber: 36 (.375" round ball). **Barrel:** 7", octagon. **Weight:** 2 1/2 lbs. **Length:** 12-1/2" overall. **Stocks:** Two piece walnut. **Sights:** Fixed. **Features:** Reproduction of the C.S.A. revolver. Brass frame and trigger guard. Also available as a kit. From Dixie Gun Works, Navy Arms.
Price: . . . . $89.95 to $199.00
Price: Kit form (Dixie) $149.95
Price: Single cased set (Navy Arms) $270.00
Price: Double cased set (Navy Arms) $430.00

TEXAS PATERSON 1836 REVOLVER
Caliber: 36 (.375" round ball). **Barrel:** 7-1/2". **Weight:** 42 oz. **Stocks:** One-piece walnut. **Sights:** Fixed. **Features:** Copy of Sam Colt's first commercially-made revolving pistol. Has no loading lever but comes with loading tool. From Dixie Gun Works, Navy Arms, Uberti U.S.A. Inc.
Price: About . . . . $310.00 to $395.00
Price: With loading lever (Uberti U.S.A. Inc.) $450.00
Price: Engraved (Navy Arms) $485.00

TRADITIONS 1858 STARR REVOLVER
Caliber: 44. **Barrel:** 6". **Weight:** 42 oz. **Length:** 11-3/4" overall. **Stocks:** Smooth. **Sights:** Blade front, grooved topstrap rear. **Features:** Double-action mechanism; blue finish. Introduced 1998. From Traditions.
Price: $395.00

UBERTI 1st MODEL DRAGOON
Caliber: 44. **Barrel:** 7-1/2", part round, part octagon. **Weight:** 64 oz. **Stocks:** One-piece walnut. **Sights:** German silver blade front, hammer notch rear. **Features:** First model has oval bolt cuts in cylinder, square-back flared trigger guard, V-type mainspring, short trigger. Ranger and Indian scene roll-engraved on cylinder. Color case-hardened frame, loading lever, plunger and hammer; blue barrel, cylinder, trigger and wedge. Available with old-time charcoal blue or standard blue-black finish. Polished

brass backstrap and trigger guard. From Uberti U.S.A. Inc., United States Patent Fire-Arms, Navy Arms.
Price: . . . . $325.00 to $435.00

Uberti 2nd Model Dragoon Revolver
Similar to the 1st Model except distinguished by rectangular bolt cuts in the cylinder. From Uberti U.S.A. Inc., United States Patent Fire-Arms, Navy Arms.
Price: . . . . $325.00 to $435.00

Uberti 3rd Model Dragoon Revolver
Similar to the 2nd Model except for oval trigger guard, long trigger, modifications to the loading lever and latch. Imported by Uberti U.S.A. Inc., United States Patent Fire-Arms.
Price: Military model (frame cut for shoulder stock, steel backstrap) . . . . $330.00 to $435.00
Price: Civilian (brass backstrap, trigger guard) $325.00

UBERTI 1862 POCKET NAVY PERCUSSION REVOLVER
Caliber: 36, 5-shot. **Barrel:** 5-1/2", 6-1/2", octagonal, 7-groove, LH twist. **Weight:** 27 oz (5-1/2" barrel), **Length:** 10-1/2" overall (5-1/2" bbl.). **Stocks:** One-piece varnished walnut. **Sights:** Brass pin front, hammer notch rear. **Features:** Rebated cylinder, hinged loading lever, brass or silver-plated backstrap and trigger guard, color-cased frame, hammer, loading lever, plunger and latch, rest blued. Has original-type markings. From Uberti U.S.A. Inc.
Price: With brass backstrap, trigger guard $310.00

U.S. PATENT FIRE-ARMS 1862 POCKET NAVY
Caliber: 36. **Barrel:** 4-1/2", 5-1/2", 6-1/2". **Weight:** 27 oz. (5-1/2" barrel). **Length:** 10-1/2" overall (5-1/2" barrel). **Stocks:** Smooth walnut. **Sights:** Brass pin front, hammer notch rear. **Features:** Blued barrel and cylinder, color case-hardened frame, hammer, lever; silver-plated backstrap and trigger guard. Imported from Italy; available from United States Patent Fire-Arms Mfg. Co.
Price: $335.00

WALKER 1847 PERCUSSION REVOLVER
Caliber: 44, 6-shot. **Barrel:** 9". **Weight:** 84 oz. **Length:** 15-1/2" overall. **Stocks:** Walnut. **Sights:** Fixed. **Features:** Case-hardened frame, loading lever and hammer; iron backstrap; brass trigger guard; engraved cylinder. Imported by Cabela's, Navy Arms, Dixie Gun Works, Uberti U.S.A. Inc., E.M.F., Cimarron, Traditions, United States Patent Fire-Arms.
Price: About . . . . $225.00 to $445.00
Price: Single cased set (Navy Arms) $405.00
Price: Deluxe Walker with French fitted case (Navy Arms) $540.00
Price: Hartford model, steel frame, German silver trim, cartouche (E.M.F.) $295.00

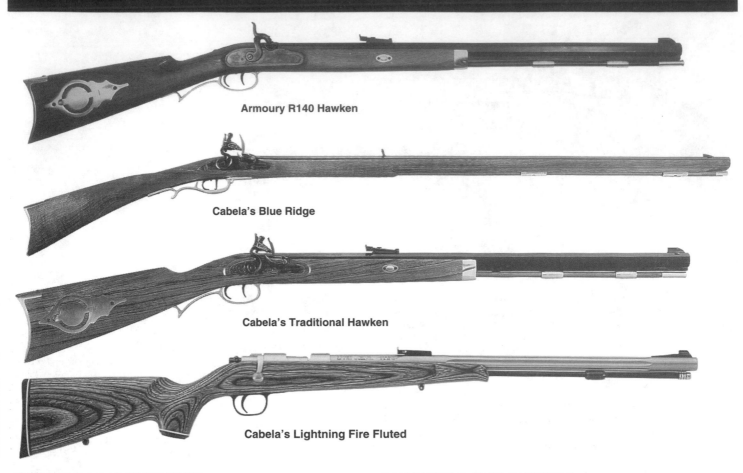

Armoury R140 Hawken

Cabela's Blue Ridge

Cabela's Traditional Hawken

Cabela's Lightning Fire Fluted

ARMOURY R140 HAWKEN RIFLE
Caliber: 45, 50 or 54. **Barrel:** 29". **Weight:** 8-3/4 to 9 lbs. **Length:** 45-3/4" overall. **Stock:** Walnut, with cheekpiece. **Sights:** Dovetail front, fully adjustable rear. **Features:** Octagon barrel, removable breech plug; double set triggers; blued barrel, brass stock fittings, color case-hardened percussion lock. From Armsport, The Armoury.
Price: .... $225.00 to $245.00

Austin & Halleck Model 320 LR In-Line Rifle
Similar to the Model 420 LR except has black resin synthetic stock with checkered grip and forend. Introduced 1998. Made in U.S. by Austin & Halleck.
Price: Blue $455.00
Price: Electroless nickel $506.00

AUSTIN & HALLECK MODEL 420 LR IN-LINE RIFLE
Caliber: 50. **Barrel:** 26", 1" octagon to 3/4" round; 1:28" twist. **Weight:** 7-7/8 lbs. **Length:** 47-1/2" overall. **Stock:** Lightly figured maple in Classic or Monte Carlo style. **Sights:** Ramp front, fully adjustable rear. **Features:** Blue or electroless nickel finish; in-line percussion action with removable weather shroud; Timney adjustable target trigger with sear block safety. Introduced 1998. Made in U.S. by Austin & Halleck.
Price: Blue $619.00
Price: Electroless nickel $689.00
Price: Blue, hand-select highly figured wood $729.00

AUSTIN & HALLECK MOUNTAIN RIFLE
Caliber: 50. **Barrel:** 32"; 1:66" twist; 1" flats. **Weight:** 7-1/2 lbs. **Length:** 49" overall. **Stock:** Curly maple. **Sights:** Silver blade front, buckhorn rear. **Features:** Available in percussion or flintlock; double throw adjustable set triggers; rust brown finish. Made in U.S. by Austin & Halleck.
Price: Flintlock $499.00
Price: Percussion $499.00
Price: Fancy wood $599.00

BOSTONIAN PERCUSSION RIFLE
Caliber: 45. **Barrel:** 30", octagonal. **Weight:** 7-1/4 lbs. **Length:** 46" overall. **Stock:** Walnut. **Sights:** Blade front, fixed notch rear. **Features:** Color case-hardened lock, brass trigger guard, buttplate, patchbox. Imported from Italy by E.M.F.
Price: $285.00

CABELA'S TRADITIONAL HAWKEN
Caliber: 50, 54. **Barrel:** 29". **Weight:** About 9 lbs. **Stock:** Walnut. **Sights:** Blade front, open adjustable rear. **Features:** Flintlock or percussion. Adjustable double-set triggers. Polished brass furniture, color case-hardened lock. Imported by Cabela's.
Price: Percussion, right-hand $189.99
Price: Percussion, left-hand $199.99
Price: Flintlock, right-hand $224.99

CABELA'S BLUE RIDGE RIFLE
Caliber: 32, 36, 45, 50. **Barrel:** 39", octagonal. **Weight:** About 7-3/4 lbs. **Length:** 55" overall. **Stock:** American black walnut. **Sights:** Blade front, rear drift adjustable for windage. **Features:** Color case-hardened lockplate and cock/hammer, brass trigger guard and buttplate, double set, double-phased triggers. From Cabela's.
Price: Percussion $399.99
Price: Flintlock $429.99

CABELA'S LIGHTNING FIRE FLUTED RIFLE
Caliber: 50. **Barrel:** 24", fluted; 1:32" twist; muzzle brake. **Weight:** 7 lbs. **Length:** NA. **Stock:** Black synthetic or laminated wood. **Sights:** Blade front, open fully adjustable rear. **Features:** Bolt-action in-line ignition uses musket caps. Introduced 1999. From Cabela's.
Price: Blue, black stock $239.99
Price: Stainless, laminated stock $329.99
Price: Nickel barrel, black stock $259.99
Price: Nickel barrel with muzzle brake, black stock $279.99

BLACKPOWDER MUSKETS & RIFLES

Cabela's Timber Ridge

Cabela's Lightning Fire Sidelock

Cook & Brother

CABELA'S LIGHTNING FIRE SIDELOCK RIFLE

Caliber: 50. **Barrel:** 28-3/4"; 1:32" twist. **Weight:** 7.85 lbs. **Length:** NA. **Stock:** Walnut-stained hardwood. **Sights:** Fiber optic front and rear. **Features:** Uses musket cap ignition. Comes with sling swivels, rubber recoil pad, color case-hardened lock. Introduced 1999. From Cabela's.
Price: $249.99

CABELA'S TIMBER RIDGE RIFLE

Caliber: 50, 54. **Barrel:** 24"; 1:32" twist (50-cal.), 1:48" twist (54-cal.). **Weight:** 7-1/2 lbs. **Length:** 42" overall. **Stock:** Composite; black or Advantage camo. **Sights:** Bead on ramp front, open adjustable rear. **Features:** In-line ignition system; sling swivel studs; synthetic ramrod; stainless steel breech plug. Introduced 1999. From Cabela's.
Price: Black stock....................................... $129.99
Price: Advantage camo stock........................... $159.99

Cabela's Sporterized Hawken Hunter Rifle

Similar to the Traditional Hawken's except has more modern stock style with rubber recoil pad, blued furniture, sling swivels. Percussion only, in 50- or 54-caliber.
Price: Carbine or rifle, right-hand $219.99

COLT MODEL 1861 MUSKET

Caliber: 58. **Barrel:** 40". **Weight:** 9 lbs., 3 oz. **Length:** 56" overall. **Stock:** Oil-finished walnut. **Sight:** Blade front, adjustable folding leaf rear. **Features:** Made to original specifications and has authentic Civil War Colt markings. Bright-finished metal, blued nipple and rear sight. Bayonet and accessories available. From Colt Blackpowder Arms Co.
Price: $569.95

COOK & BROTHER CONFEDERATE CARBINE

Caliber: 58. **Barrel:** 24". **Weight:** 7-1/2 lbs. **Length:** 40-1/2" overall. **Stock:** Select walnut. **Features:** Recreation of the 1861 New Orleans-made artillery carbine. Color case-hardened lock, browned barrel. Buttplate, trigger guard, barrel bands, sling swivels and nosecap of polished brass. From Euroarms of America.
Price: $447.00
Price: Cook & Brother rifle (33" barrel)................... $480.00

CUMBERLAND MOUNTAIN BLACKPOWDER RIFLE

Caliber: 50. **Barrel:** 26", round. **Weight:** 9-1/2 lbs. **Length:** 43" overall. **Stock:** American walnut. **Sights:** Bead front, open rear adjustable for windage. **Features:** Falling block action fires with shotshell primer. Blued receiver and barrel. Introduced 1993. Made in U.S. by Cumberland Mountain Arms, Inc.
Price: $931.50

CVA COLORADO MUSKET MAG 100 RIFLE

Caliber: 50, 54 **Barrel:** 26"; 1:32" twist. **Weight:** 7-1/2 lbs. **Length:** 42" overall. **Stock:** Synthetic; black, Hardwoods or X-Tra Brown camo. **Sights:** Illuminator front and rear. **Features:** Sidelock action uses musket caps for ignition. Introduced 1999. From CVA.
Price: With black stock.................................. $184.95
Price: With camo stock.................................. $219.95

CVA YOUTH HUNTER RIFLE

Caliber: 50. **Barrel:** 24"; 1:48" twist, octagonal. **Weight:** 5-1/2 lbs. **Length:** 38" overall. **Stock:** Stained hardwood. **Sights:** Bead front, Williams adjustable rear. **Features:** Oversize trigger guard; wooden ramrod. Introduced 1999. From CVA.
Price: $129.95

BLACKPOWDER MUSKETS & RIFLES

CVA Firebolt

CVA St. Louis Hawken

CVA Accubolt Pro

CVA BOBCAT RIFLE

Caliber: 50 and 54. **Barrel:** 26"; 1:48" twist. **Weight:** 6-1/2 lbs. **Length:** 40" overall. **Stock:** Dura-Grip synthetic. **Sights:** Blade front, open rear. **Features:** Oversize trigger guard; wood ramrod; matte black finish. Introduced 1995. From CVA.

Price: **$125.95**

CVA ECLIPSE IN-LINE RIFLE

Caliber: 50, 54. **Barrel:** 24" round; 1:32" rifling. **Weight:** 7 lbs. **Length:** 42" overall. **Stock:** Black Advantage camo synthetic. **Sights:** Illuminator Fiber Optic Sight System; drilled and tapped for scope mounting. **Features:** Inline action uses modern trigger with automatic safety; stainless percussion bolt; swivel studs. From CVA.

Price: 50 or 54, blue, black stock **$154.95**
Price: 50 or 54, blue, X-Tra Brown camo stock **$179.95**
Price: 50 or 54, Hardwoods camo **$179.95**

CVA Staghorn Rifle

Similar to the Eclipse except has standard open sights, manual safety, black DuraGrip stock and ramrod. From CVA.

Price: 50 or 54 . . . . **$134.95**

CVA MOUNTAIN RIFLE

Caliber: 50. **Barrel:** 32"; 1:66" rifling. **Weight:** 8-1/2 lbs. **Length:** NA **Stock:** American hard maple. **Sights:** Blade front, buckhorn rear. **Features:** Browned steel furniture; German silver wedge plates; patchbox. Made in U.S. From CVA.

Price: **$499.95**

CVA ST. LOUIS HAWKEN RIFLE

Caliber: 50, 54. **Barrel:** 28", octagon; 15/16" across flats; 1:48" twist. **Weight:** 8 lbs. **Length:** 44" overall. **Stock:** Select hardwood. **Sights:** Beaded blade front, fully adjustable open rear. **Features:** Fully adjustable double-set triggers; synthetic ramrod (kits have wood); brass patchbox, wedge plates, nosecap, thimbles, trigger guard and buttplate; blued barrel; color case-hardened, engraved lockplate. V-type mainspring. Button breech. Introduced 1981. From CVA.

Price: St. Louis Hawken, finished (50-, 54-cal.) **$199.95**
Price: Left-hand, percussion. **$234.95**
Price: Flintlock, 50-cal. only **$234.95**
Price: Flintlock, left-hand **$249.95**
Price: Percussion kit (50-cal., blued, wood ramrod). **$169.95**

CVA Monster Buck Rifle

Similar to the Firebolt Rifle except has Realtree X-Tra Brown camo finish stock with a rubber coating. Has CVA's Illuminator Fiber Optic Sight System, Bullet Guiding Muzzle. Available in 50- or 54-caliber. From CVA.

Price: **$289.95**

CVA HunterBolt MusketMag Rifle

Similar to the Firebolt except has standard open sights, black DuraGrip synthetic stock. Available in camo X-Tra Brown and Hardwoods camo. From CVA.

Price: 50 or 54 . . . . **$189.95** to **$229.95**

CVA FIREBOLT MUSKETMAG BOLT-ACTION IN-LINE RIFLES

Caliber: 50, 54. **Barrel:** 24". **Weight:** 7 lbs. **Length:** NA. **Stock:** DuraGrip synthetic; thumbhole, traditional, camo. **Sights:** CVA Illuminator Fiber Optic Sight System. **Features:** Bolt-action, in-line ignition system. Stainless steel or matte blue barrel; removable breech plug; trigger-block safety. Introduced 1997. From CVA.

Price: Stainless barrel, traditional stock **$309.00**
Price: Matte blue barrel, camo stock **$279.95**
Price: Matte blue barrel, traditional stock **$249.95**
Price: Left-hand, 50-caliber only, hardwood stock **$299.95**

BLACKPOWDER MUSKETS & RIFLES

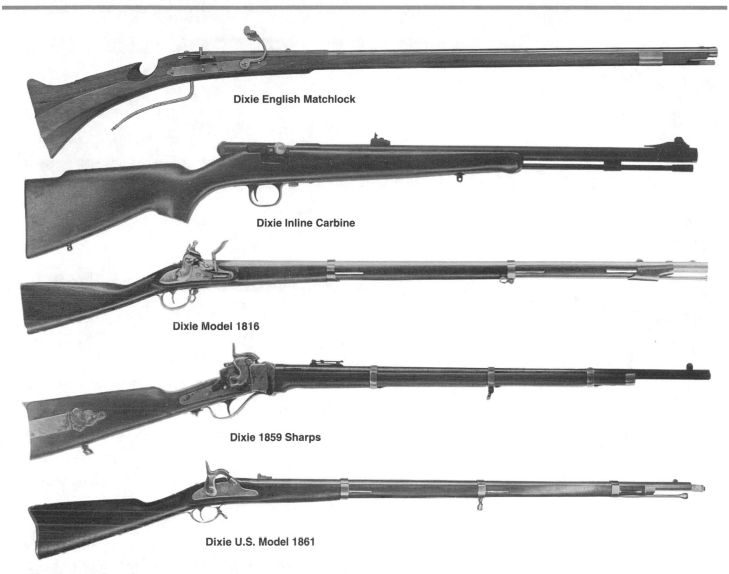

Dixie English Matchlock

Dixie Inline Carbine

Dixie Model 1816

Dixie 1859 Sharps

Dixie U.S. Model 1861

Price: With Teflon finish, black stock $279.95
Price: As above, synthetic Sniper stock $299.95
Price: As above, synthetic Advantage camo stock $299.95

DIXIE ENGLISH MATCHLOCK MUSKET

Caliber: 72. **Barrel:** 44". **Weight:** 8 lbs. **Length:** 57.75" overall. **Stock:** Walnut with satin oil finish. **Sights:** Blade front, open rear adjustable for windage. **Features:** Replica of circa 1600-1680 English matchlock. Getz barrel with 11" octagonal area at rear, rest is round with cannon-type muzzle. All steel finished in the white. Imported by Dixie Gun Works.
Price: $895.00

DIXIE DELUX CUB RIFLE

Caliber: 40. **Barrel:** 28". **Weight:** 6-1/2 lbs. **Stock:** Walnut. **Sights:** Fixed. **Features:** Short rifle for small game and beginning shooters. Brass patchbox and furniture. Flint or percussion. From Dixie Gun Works.
Price: Finished $415.00
Price: Kit $375.00
Price: Super Cub (50-caliber) $367.00

DIXIE 1863 SPRINGFIELD MUSKET

Caliber: 58 (.570" patched ball or .575" Minie). **Barrel:** 50", rifled. **Stock:** Walnut stained. **Sights:** Blade front, adjustable ladder-type rear. **Features:** Bright-finish lock, barrel, furniture. Reproduction of the last of the regulation muzzleloaders. Imported from Japan by Dixie Gun Works.

Price: Finished $595.00
Price: Kit $525.00

DIXIE INLINE CARBINE

Caliber: 50, 54. **Barrel:** 24"; 1:32" twist. **Weight:** 6.5 lbs. **Length:** 41" overall. **Stock:** Walnut-finished hardwood with Monte Carlo comb. **Sights:** Ramp front with red insert, open fully adjustable rear. **Features:** Sliding "bolt" fully encloses cap and nipple. Fully adjustable trigger, automatic safety. Aluminum ramrod. Imported from Italy by Dixie Gun Works.
Price: $349.95

DIXIE SHARPS NEW MODEL 1859 MILITARY RIFLE

Caliber: 54. **Barrel:** 30", 6-groove; 1:48" twist. **Weight:** 9 lbs. **Length:** 45-1/2" overall. **Stock:** Oiled walnut. **Sights:** Blade front, ladder-style rear. **Features:** Blued barrel, color case-hardened barrel bands, receiver, hammer, nosecap, lever, patchbox cover and buttplate. Introduced 1995. Imported from Italy by Dixie Gun Works.
Price: $895.00

DIXIE U.S. MODEL 1816 FLINTLOCK MUSKET

Caliber: 69. **Barrel:** 42", smoothbore. **Weight:** 9.75 lbs. **Length:** 56.5" overall. **Stock:** Walnut with oil finish. **Sights:** Blade front. **Features:** All metal finished "National Armory Bright"; three barrel bands with springs; steel ramrod with button-shaped head. Imported by Dixie Gun Works.
Price: $725.00

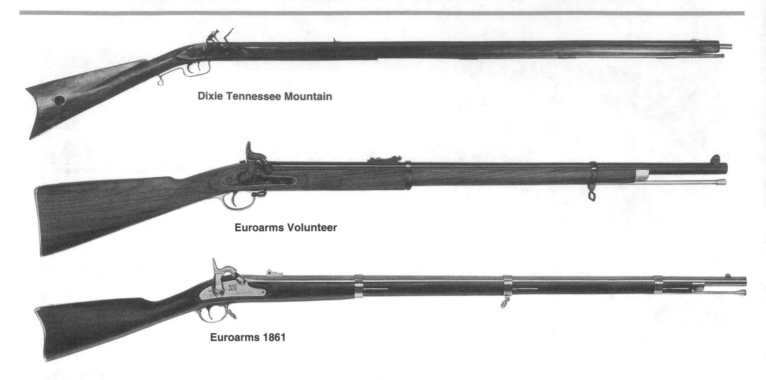

Dixie Tennessee Mountain

Euroarms Volunteer

Euroarms 1861

DIXIE U.S. MODEL 1861 SPRINGFIELD

Caliber: 58. **Barrel:** 40". **Weight:** About 8 lbs. **Length:** 55-13/16" overall. **Stock:** Oil-finished walnut. **Sights:** Blade front, step adjustable rear. **Features:** Exact recreation of original rifle. Sling swivels attached to trigger guard bow and middle barrel band. Lockplate marked "1861" with eagle motif and "U.S. Springfield" in front of hammer; "U.S." stamped on top of buttplate. From Dixie Gun Works.

Price:	$595.00
Price: From Stone Mountain Arms	$599.00
Price: Kit	$525.00

DIXIE TENNESSEE MOUNTAIN RIFLE

Caliber: 32 or 50. **Barrel:** 41-1/2", 6-groove rifling, brown finish. **Length:** 56" overall. **Stock:** Walnut, oil finish; Kentucky-style. **Sights:** Silver blade front, open buckhorn rear. **Features:** Recreation of the original mountain rifles. Early Schultz lock, interchangeable flint or percussion with vent plug or drum and nipple. Tumbler has fly. Double-set triggers. All metal parts browned. From Dixie Gun Works.

Price: Flint or percussion, finished rifle, 50-cal.	$575.00
Price: Kit, 50-cal.	$495.00
Price: Left-hand model, flint or percussion	$575.00
Price: Left-hand kit, flint or perc., 50-cal.	$495.00
Price: Squirrel Rifle (as above except in 32-cal. with 13/16" barrel flats), flint or percussion	$575.00
Price: Kit, 32-cal., flint or percussion	$495.00

EUROARMS BUFFALO CARBINE

Caliber: 58. **Barrel:** 26", round. **Weight:** 7-3/4 lbs. **Length:** 42" overall. **Stock:** Walnut. **Sights:** Blade front, open adjustable rear. **Features:** Shoots .575" round ball. Color case-hardened lock, blue hammer, barrel, trigger; brass furniture. Brass patchbox. Imported by Euroarms of America.

Price:	$440.00

E.M.F. 1863 SHARPS MILITARY CARBINE

Caliber: 54. **Barrel:** 22", round. **Weight:** 8 lbs. **Length:** 39" overall. **Stock:** Oiled walnut. **Sights:** Blade front, military ladder-type rear. **Features:** Color case-hardened lock, rest blued. Imported by E.M.F.

Price:	$860.00

EUROARMS VOLUNTEER TARGET RIFLE

Caliber: .451. **Barrel:** 33" (two-band), 36" (three-band). **Weight:** 11 lbs. (two-band). **Length:** 48.75" overall (two-band). **Stock:** European walnut with checkered wrist and forend. **Sights:** Hooded bead front, adjustable rear with interchangeable leaves. **Features:** Alexander Henry-type rifling with 1:20" twist. Color case-hardened hammer and lockplate, brass trigger guard and nosecap, rest blued. Imported by Euroarms of America.

Price: Two-band	$720.00
Price: Three-band	$773.00

EUROARMS 1861 SPRINGFIELD RIFLE

Caliber: 58. **Barrel:** 40". **Weight:** About 10 lbs. **Length:** 55.5" overall. **Stock:** European walnut. **Sights:** Blade front, three-leaf military rear. **Features:** Reproduction of the original three-band rifle. Lockplate marked "1861" with eagle and "U.S. Springfield." Metal left in the white. Imported by Euroarms of America.

Price:	$530.00

FORT WORTH FIREARMS SABINE RIFLE

Caliber: 22. **Barrel:** 16-1/4". **Weight:** 3-1/2 lbs. **Length:** 32" overall. **Stock:** Walnut-finished hardwood. **Sights:** Hooded blade front, open adjustable rear. **Features:** In-line design with side-cocking lever. Positive click safety; blued finish. Introduced 1997. From Fort Worth Firearms.

Price:	$189.95

FORT WORTH FIREARMS PECOS RIFLE

Caliber: 50. **Barrel:** 22", stainless; 1:24" twist. **Weight:** 6-1/2 lbs. **Length:** 39" overall. **Stock:** Black or camo composite with checkered grip and forend. **Sights:** Ramped blade front, open adjustable rear. Drilled and tapped for scope mounting. **Features:** In-line design with stainless steel barrel and receiver; fully adjustable trigger; synthetic Delron ramrod. Introduced 1997. From Fort Worth Firearms.

Price:	$457.95
Price: Blue barrel, Weaver scope bases	$438.30
Price: As above with open sights	$500.57
Price: Blue barrel, Weaver scope bases, peep sight	$510.19
Price: Stainless barrel, Weaver scope bases	$562.25
Price: As above with open sights	$603.04
Price: Stainless barrel, Weaver scope bases, peep sight	$609.76

FORT WORTH FIREARMS RIO GRANDE RIFLE

Caliber: 45, 50. **Barrel:** 22"; 1:22" twist. **Weight:** 6-1/2 lbs. **Length:** 39" overall. **Stock:** Black composite; checkered grip and forend; swivel studs; recoil pad. **Sights:** Ramped blade front, open adjustable rear. Drilled and tapped for scope mounting. **Features:** Bolt-action design with stainless

Gonic Model 93 Mountain Classic

Great American Sporting

Harper's Ferry 1803

Navy Arms J.P. Murray

barrel and receiver. Flash diffuser protects optics from blow-by. Fully adjustable trigger with safety; synthetic Delron ramrod. Introduced 1996. From Fort Worth Firearms.

Price: **$457.95**

GONIC MODEL 93 M/L RIFLE

Caliber: 50. **Barrel:** 26"; 1·24" twist. **Weight:** 6-1/2 to 7 lbs. **Length:** 43" overall. **Stock:** American hardwood with black finish. **Sights:** Hooded post front, fully adjustable open or aperture rear. **Features:** Adjustable trigger with side safety; unbreakable ram rod; comes with scope bases installed. Introduced 1993. Made in U.S. by Gonic Arms, Inc.

Gonic Model 93 Deluxe M/L Rifle

Similar to the Model 93 except has gray laminated wood stock. Introduced 1998. Made in U.S. by Gonic Arms, Inc.

Price: Blue barrel, scope bases $619.45
Price: As above with open sights $660.24
Price: Blue barrel, scope bases, peep sight $666.69
Price: Stainless barrel, scope bases $715.65
Price: As above with open sights $756.44
Price: Stainless barrel, scope bases, peep sight $763.16

Gonic Model 93 Mountain Classic, Thumbhole M/L Rifles

Similar to the Model 93 except classic model has high-grade walnut or gray laminate stock with extensive hand-checkered panels; integral muzzle brake. Thumbhole model has roll-over Monte Carlo cheekpiece, beavertail forend and palms well grip. Introduced 1998. Made in U.S. by Gonic Arms, Inc.

Price: Blue or stainless, walnut or gray laminate stock, Classic or
Thumbhole model **$2,132.00**

Gonic Model 93 Safari Classic M/L Rifle

Similar to the Model 93 except has classic-style walnut or laminated stock

with cheekpiece and hand-checkered grip and forend; integral muzzle brake. Introduced 1998. Made in U.S. by Gonic Arms, Inc.

Price: Blue or stainless barrel, walnut or gray laminate stock .. **$1,612.00**

GREAT AMERICAN SPORTING RIFLE

Caliber: 69. **Barrel:** 28", 1-1/4" octagon to 1·1/8" round. **Weight:** 10 lbs. **Length:** NA **Stock:** Walnut. **Sights:** Silver blade front, adjustable semi-buckhorn rear. **Features:** Hooked, patent Manton-style breech plug; iron furniture; bedded barrel; brown finish. Made in U.S. by October Country Muzzleloading, Inc.

Price: **$1,495.00**

HARPER'S FERRY 1803 FLINTLOCK RIFLE

Caliber: 54 and 58. **Barrel:** 35". **Weight:** 9 lbs. **Length:** 59-1/2" overall. **Stock:** Walnut with cheekpiece. **Sights:** Brass blade front, fixed steel rear. **Features:** Brass trigger guard, sideplate, buttplate; steel patchbox. Imported by Euroarms of America, Navy Arms (54-cal. only), Cabela's.

Price: .... **$495.95 to $729.00**
Price: 54-cal. (Navy Arms) **$625.00**
Price: 54-caliber (Cabela's) **$599.99**

HAWKEN RIFLE

Caliber: 45, 50, 54 or 58. **Barrel:** 28", blued, 6-groove rifling. **Weight:** 8-3/4 lbs. **Length:** 44" overall. **Stock:** Walnut with cheekpiece. **Sights:** Blade front, fully adjustable rear. **Features:** Coil mainspring, double-set triggers, polished brass furniture. From Armsport, Navy Arms, E.M.F.

Price: .... **$220.00 to $345.00**

J.P. MURRAY 1862-1864 CAVALRY CARBINE

Caliber: 58 (.577" Minie). **Barrel:** 23". **Weight:** 7 lbs., 9 oz. **Length:** 39" overall. **Stock:** Walnut. **Sights:** Blade front, rear drift adjustable for windage. **Features:** Browned barrel, color case-hardened lock, blued swivel and band springs, polished brass buttplate, trigger guard, barrel bands. From Navy Arms, Euroarms of America.

Price: .... **$405.00 to $453.00**

BLACKPOWDER MUSKETS & RIFLES

Navy Arms Kentucky Flintlock

Knight T-Bolt M/L

Knight Disc M/L

Knight Bighorn In/Line

J.P. HENRY TRADE RIFLE
Caliber: 54. **Barrel:** 34"; 1" flats. **Weight:** 8-1/2 lbs. **Length:** 45" overall. **Stock:** Premium curly maple. **Sights:** Silver blade front, fixed buckhorn rear. **Features:** Brass buttplate, side plate, trigger guard and nosecap; browned barrel and lock; L&R Large English percussion lock; single trigger. Made in U.S. by J.P. Gunstocks, Inc.
Price: $965.50

KENTUCKIAN RIFLE
Caliber: 44. **Barrel:** 35". **Weight:** 7 lbs. (Rifle), 5-1/2 lbs. (Carbine). **Length:** 51" overall (Rifle), 43" (Carbine). **Stock:** Walnut stain. **Sights:** Brass blade front, steel V-ramp rear. **Features:** Octagon barrel, case-hardened and engraved lockplates. Brass furniture. Imported by Dixie Gun Works.
Price: Flintlock $269.95
Price: Percussion $259.95

Kentucky Percussion Rifle
Similar to flintlock except percussion lock. Finish and features vary with importer. Imported by Navy Arms, The Armoury, CVA.
Price: About $259.95
Price: 45- or 50-cal. (Navy Arms) $425.00
Price: Kit, 50-cal. (CVA) $189.95

KNIGHT T-BOLT M/L RIFLE
Caliber: 50. **Barrel:** 22", 26"; 1:28" twist. **Weight:** 6 lbs. **Length:** 41" overall. **Stock:** Composite black, Mossy Oak Break-Up or Advantage camo. **Sights:** Bead on ramp front, fully adjustable rear; drilled and tapped for scope mounts. **Features:** Straight-pull T-Bolt action with double-safety system, removable hammer, removable stainless steel breech plug; adjustable trigger. Introduced 1998. Made in U.S. by Knight Rifles.
Price: Blue or stainless. $399.95 to $489.95

KENTUCKY FLINTLOCK RIFLE
Caliber: 44, 45, or 50. **Barrel:** 35". **Weight:** 7 lbs. **Length:** 50" overall. **Stock:** Walnut stained, brass fittings. **Sights:** Fixed. **Features:** Available in carbine model also, 28" bbl. Some variations in detail, finish. Kits also available from some importers. Imported by Navy Arms, The Armoury.
Price: About . . . . $217.95 to $345.00
Price: Flintlock, 45 or 50-cal. (Navy Arms) $435.00

KNIGHT DISC M/L RIFLE
Caliber: 50. **Barrel:** 24", 26". **Weight:** 7 lbs., 14 oz. **Length:** 43" overall (24" barrel). **Stock:** Checkered synthetic with palm swell grip, rubber recoil pad, swivel studs; black, Advantage or Mossy Oak Break-Up camouflage. **Sights:** Bead on ramp front, fully adjustable open rear. **Features:** Bolt-action in-line system uses #209 shotshell primer for ignition; primer is held in plastic drop-in Primer Disc. Available in blued or stainless steel. Made in U.S. by Knight Rifles.
Price: . . . . $449.95 to $569.95

KNIGHT BIGHORN IN-LINE RIFLE
Caliber: 50. **Barrel:** 22", 26"; 1:28" twist. **Weight:** 7 lbs. **Length:** 41" overall (22" barrel). **Stock:** Synthetic; black Advantage or Mossy Oak Break-Up camouflage. Black rubber recoil pad. **Sights:** Bead on ramp front, full adjustable open rear. **Features:** Patented double safety system; adjustable trigger; comes with #11 Red Hot Nipple. Available in blue or stainless steel. Made in U.S. by Knight Rifles.
Price: . . . . $329.95 to $469.95

KNIGHT MK-86 IN-LINE SHOTGUN
Gauge: 12. **Barrel:** 24", screw-in choke tubes. **Weight:** 7 lbs. **Length:** 43" overall. **Stock:** Black composition. **Features:** Patented double safety; Sure-Fire in-line percussion ignition. Receiver drilled and tapped for scope mounting. Blued barrel. Made in U.S. by Knight Rifles.
Price: $599.95

London Armory 1861

Lyman Cougar In/Line

Knight LK-93 Wolverine

KNIGHT AMERICAN KNIGHT M/L RIFLE

Caliber: 50. **Barrel:** 22"; 1:28" twist. **Weight:** 6 lbs. **Length:** 41" overall. **Stock:** Black composite. **Sights:** Bead on ramp front, open fully adjustable rear. **Features:** Double safety system; one-piece removable hammer assembly; drilled and tapped for scope mounting. Introduced 1998. Made in U.S. by Knight Rifles.
Price: $199.95

KNIGHT MK-85 RIFLE

Caliber: 50, 54. **Barrel:** 24". **Weight:** 6-3/4 lbs. **Stock:** Walnut, laminated or composition. **Sights:** Hooded blade front on ramp, open adjustable rear. **Features:** Patented double safety; Sure-Fire in-line percussion ignition; Timney Featherweight adjustable trigger; aluminum ramrod; receiver drilled and tapped for scope bases. Made in U.S. by Knight Rifles.
Price: Hunter, walnut stock. $549.95
Price: Stalker, laminated or composition stock. $569.95
Price: Predator (stainless steel), laminated or composition stock $649.95
Price: Knight Hawk, blued, composition thumbhole stock $769.95
Price: As above, stainless steel $769.95

KNIGHT LK-93 WOLVERINE RIFLE

Caliber: 50, 54. **Barrel:** 22", blued. **Weight:** 6 lbs. **Stock:** Black Advantage; Mossy Oak Break-Up camo. **Sights:** Bead front on ramp, open adjustable rear. **Features:** Patented double safety system; removable breech plug; Sure-Fire in-line percussion ignition system. Made in U.S. by Knight Rifles.
Price: From. $269.95
Price: LK-93 Stainless, from. $339.95
Price: LK-93 Thumbhole, from $309.95
Price: Youth model, blued, 50-cal. only $279.95

LONDON ARMORY 2-BAND 1858 ENFIELD

Caliber: .577" Minie, .575" round ball. **Barrel:** 33". **Weight:** 10 lbs. **Length:** 49" overall. **Stock:** Walnut. **Sights:** Folding leaf rear adjustable for eleva-

tion. **Features:** Blued barrel, color case-hardened lock and hammer, polished brass buttplate, trigger guard, nosecap. From Navy Arms, Euroarms of America, Dixie Gun Works.
Price: .... $385.00 to $531.00

LONDON ARMORY 1861 ENFIELD MUSKETOON

Caliber: 58, Minie ball. **Barrel:** 24", round. **Weight:** 7 - 7-1/2 lbs. **Length:** 40-1/2" overall. **Stock:** Walnut, with sling swivels. **Sights:** Blade front, graduated military-leaf rear. **Features:** Brass trigger guard, nosecap, buttplate, blued barrel, bands, lockplate, swivels. Imported by Euroarms of America, Navy Arms.
Price: .... $300.00 to $427.00
Price: Kit. .... $365.00 to $373.00

LONDON ARMORY 3-BAND 1853 ENFIELD

Caliber: 58 (.577" Minie, .575" round ball, .580" maxi ball). **Barrel:** 39". **Weight:** 9-1/2 lbs. **Length:** 54" overall. **Stock:** European walnut. **Sights:** Inverted "V" front, traditional Enfield folding ladder rear. **Features:** Recreation of the famed London Armory Company Pattern 1853 Enfield Musket. One-piece walnut stock, brass buttplate, trigger guard and nosecap. Lockplate marked "London Armoury Co." and with a British crown. Blued Baddeley barrel bands. From Dixie Gun Works, Euroarms of America, Navy Arms.
Price: About .... $350.00 to $495.00
Price: Assembled kit (Dixie, Euroarms of America) .. $425.00 to $431.00

LYMAN COUGAR IN-LINE RIFLE

Caliber: 50 or 54. **Barrel:** 22"; 1:24" twist. **Weight:** NA. **Length:** NA. **Stock:** Smooth walnut; swivel studs. **Sights:** Bead on ramp front, folding adjustable rear. Drilled and tapped for Lyman 57WTR receiver sight and Weaver scope bases. **Features:** Blued barrel and receiver. Has bolt safety notch and trigger safety. Rubber recoil pad. Delrin ramrod. Introduced 1996. From Lyman.
Price: $299.95
Price: Stainless steel $382.95

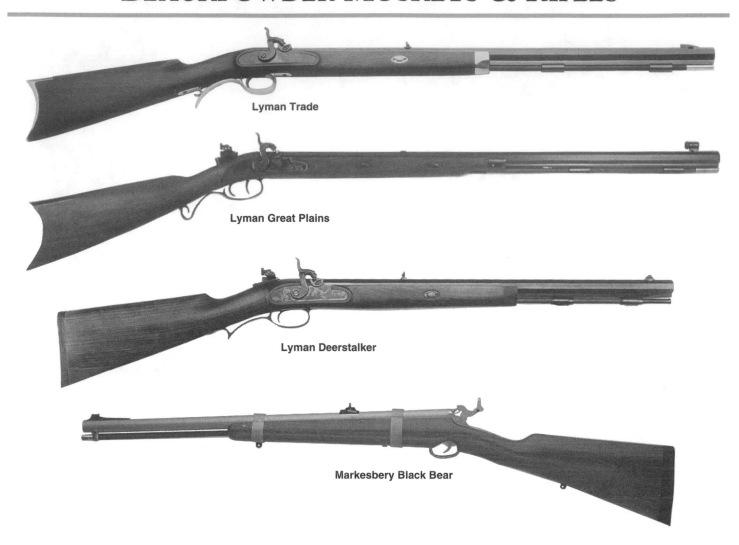

Lyman Trade

Lyman Great Plains

Lyman Deerstalker

Markesbery Black Bear

Lyman Great Plains Hunter Rifle
Similar to the Great Plains model except has 1:32" twist shallow-groove barrel and comes drilled and tapped for the Lyman 57GPR peep sight.
Price: **$429.95**

LYMAN TRADE RIFLE
Caliber: 50, 54. **Barrel:** 28" octagon;1:48" twist. **Weight:** 8-3/4 lbs. **Length:** 45" overall. **Stock:** European walnut. **Sights:** Blade front, open rear adjustable for windage or optional fixed sights. **Features:** Fast twist rifling for conical bullets. Polished brass furniture with blue steel parts, stainless steel nipple. Hook breech, single trigger, coil spring percussion lock. Steel barrel rib and ramrod ferrules. Introduced 1980. From Lyman.
Price: Percussion **$299.95**
Price: Flintlock **$324.95**

LYMAN DEERSTALKER RIFLE
Caliber: 50, 54. **Barrel:** 24", octagonal; 1:48" rifling. **Weight:** 7-1/2 lbs. **Stock:** Walnut with black rubber buttpad. **Sights:** Lyman #37MA beaded front, fully adjustable fold-down Lyman #16A rear. **Features:** Stock has less drop for quick sighting. All metal parts are blackened, with color case-hardened lock; single trigger. Comes with sling and swivels. Available in flint or percussion. Introduced 1990. From Lyman.
Price: 50- or 54-cal., percussion.......................... **$304.95**
Price: 50- or 54-cal., flintlock......................... **$329.95**
Price: 50- or 54-cal., percussion, left-hand.................. **$319.95**
Price: 50-cal., flintlock, left-hand......................... **$344.95**
Price: Stainless steel **$384.95**

LYMAN GREAT PLAINS RIFLE
Caliber: 50- or 54-cal. **Barrel:** 32"; 1:60" twist. **Weight:** 9 lbs. **Stock:** Walnut. **Sights:** Steel blade front, buckhorn rear adjustable for windage and elevation and fixed notch primitive sight included. **Features:** Blued steel furniture. Stainless steel nipple. Coil spring lock, Hawken-style trigger guard and double-set triggers. Round thimbles recessed and sweated into rib. Steel wedge plates and toe plate. Introduced 1979. From Lyman.
Price: Percussion **$429.95**
Price: Flintlock **$454.95**
Price: Percussion kit.................................... **$349.95**
Price: Flintlock kit **$374.95**
Price: Left-hand percussion **$439.95**
Price: Left-hand flintlock................................ **$464.95**

MARKESBERY KM BLACK BEAR M/L RIFLE
Caliber: 36, 45, 50, 54. **Barrel:** 24"; 1:26" twist. **Weight:** 6-1/2 lbs. **Length:** 38-1/2" overall. **Stock:** Two-piece American hardwood, walnut, black laminate, green laminate, black composition, X-Tra or Mossy Oak Break-Up camouflage. **Sights:** Bead front, open fully adjustable rear. **Features:** Interchangeable barrels; exposed hammer; Outer-Line Magnum ignition system uses small rifle primer or standard No. 11 cap and nipple. Blue, black matte, or stainless. Made in U.S. by Markesbery Muzzle Loaders.
Price: American hardwood walnut, blue finish **$536.63**
Price: American hardwood walnut, stainless **$553.09**
Price: Black laminate, blue finish **$539.67**
Price: Camouflage stock, blue finish **$556.46**
Price: Black composite, blue finish........................ **$532.65**

BLACKPOWDER MUSKETS & RIFLES

Markesbery KM Colorado

Markesbery KM Grizzly Bear

Markesbery KM Brown Bear

Marlin Model MLS-50

MARKESBERY KM COLORADO ROCKY MOUNTAIN M/L RIFLE
Caliber: 36, 45, 50, 54. **Barrel:** 24"; 1:26" twist. **Weight:** 6-1/2 lbs. **Length:** 38-1/2" overall. **Stock:** American hardwood walnut, green or black laminate. **Sights:** Firesight bead on ramp front, fully adjustable open rear. **Features:** Replicates Reed/Watson rifle of 1851. Straight grip stock with or without two barrel bands, rubber recoil pad, large-spur hammer. Made in U.S. by Markesbery Muzzel Loaders, Inc.
Price: American hardwood walnut, blue finish $545.92
Price: Black or green laminate, blue finish $548.30
Price: American hardwood walnut, stainless $563.17
Price: Black or green laminate, stainless $566.34

Marksbery KM Brown Bear M/L Rifle
Similar to the KM Black Bear except has one-piece thumbhole stock with Monte Carlo comb. Stock available in Crotch Walnut composite, green or black laminate, black composite or X-Tra or Mossy Oak Break-Up camouflage. Contact maker for complete price listing. Made in U.S. by Markesbery Muzzle Loaders, Inc.
Price: Black composite, blue finish $658.83
Price: Crotch Walnut composite, stainless $676.11
Price: Green laminate, stainless $680.07

Marksbery KM Grizzly Bear M/L Rifle
Similar to the KM Black Bear except has thumbhole buttstock with Monte Carlo comb. Stock available in Crotch Walnut composite, green or black laminate, black composite or X-Tra or Mossy Oak Break-Up camouflage.

Contact maker for complete price listing. Made in U.S. by Markesbery Muzzle Loaders, Inc.
Price: Black composite, blue finish $642.96
Price: Crotch Walnut composite, stainless $660.98
Price: Camouflage composite, blue finish $666.67

Marksbery KM Polar Bear M/L Rifle
Similar to the KM Black Bear except has one-piece stock with Monte Carlo comb. Stock available in American Hardwood walnut, green or black laminate, black composite, or X-Tra or Mossy Oak Break-Up camouflage. Has interchangeable barrel system, Outer-Line ignition system, cross-bolt double safety. Available in 36, 45, 50, 54 caliber. Contact maker for full price listing. Made in U.S. by Markesbery Muzzle Loaders, Inc.
Price: American Hardwood walnut , blue finish $539.01
Price: Black composite, blue finish $536.63
Price: Black laminate, blue finish $541.17
Price: Camouflage, stainless $573.94

MARLIN MODELS MLS-50, MLS-54 IN-LINE RIFLES
Caliber: 50, 54. **Barrel:** 22"; 1:28" twist. **Weight:** 6-1/2 lbs. **Length:** 41" overall. **Stock:** Black fiberglass-reinforced Rynite with moulded-in checkering, rubber buttpad, swivel studs. **Sights:** Ramp front with brass bead, adjustable Marble open rear. Receiver drilled and tapped for scope mounting. **Features:** All stainless steel construction. Reversible cocking handle for right- or left-hand shooters; automatic tang safety; one-piece barrel/receiver. Introduced 1997. Made in U.S. by Marlin Firearms Co.
Price: $419.00

Navy Arms 1763

Navy Arms Whitworth

Navy Arms 1859 Sharps

Navy Arms Berdan

1841 Mississippi

Mississippi 1841 Percussion Rifle
Similar to Zouave rifle but patterned after U.S. Model 1841. Imported by Dixie Gun Works, Euroarms of America, Navy Arms.
Price: About .... $430.00 to $500.00

NAVY ARMS HAWKEN HUNTER RIFLE/CARBINE
Caliber: 50, 54, 58. **Barrel:** 22-1/2" or 28"; 1:48" twist. **Weight:** 6 lbs., 12 oz. **Length:** 39" overall. **Stock:** Walnut with cheekpiece. **Sights:** Blade front, fully adjustable rear. **Features:** Double-set triggers; all metal has matte black finish; rubber recoil pad; detachable sling swivels. Imported by Navy Arms.
Price: Rifle or Carbine $240.00

NAVY ARMS 1763 CHARLEVILLE
Caliber: 69. **Barrel:** 44-5/8". **Weight:** 8 lbs., 12 oz. **Length:** 59-3/8" overall. **Stock:** Walnut. **Sights:** Brass blade front. **Features:** Replica of the French musket used by American troops during the Revolution. Imported by Navy Arms.
Price: $925.00

NAVY ARMS PARKER-HALE VOLUNTEER RIFLE
Caliber: .451. **Barrel:** 32". **Weight:** 9-1/2 lbs. **Length:** 49" overall. **Stock:** Walnut, checkered wrist and forend. **Sights:** Globe front, adjustable ladder-type rear. **Features:** Recreation of the type of gun issued to volunteer regiments during the 1860s. Rigby-pattern rifling, patent breech, detented lock. Stock is glass bedded for accuracy. Imported by Navy Arms.
Price: $850.00

NAVY ARMS 1859 SHARPS CAVALRY CARBINE
Caliber: 54. **Barrel:** 22". **Weight:** 7-3/4 lbs. **Length:** 39" overall. **Stock:** Walnut. **Sights:** Blade front, military ladder-type rear. **Features:** Color case-hardened action, blued barrel. Has saddle ring. Introduced 1991. Imported from Navy Arms.
Price: $885.00

NAVY ARMS BERDAN 1859 SHARPS RIFLE
Caliber: 54. **Barrel:** 30". **Weight:** 8 lbs., 8 oz. **Length:** 46-3/4" overall. **Stock:** Walnut. **Sights:** Blade front, folding military ladder-type rear. **Features:** Replica of the Union sniper rifle used by Berdan's 1st and 2nd Sharpshooter regiments. Color case-hardened receiver, patchbox, furniture. Double-set triggers. Imported by Navy Arms.
Price: $1,095.00
Price: 1859 Sharps Infantry Rifle (three-band)............. $1,030.00

NAVY ARMS PENNSYLVANIA LONG RIFLE
Caliber: 32, 45. **Barrel:** 40-1/2". **Weight:** 7-1/2 lbs. **Length:** 56-1/2" overall. **Stock:** Walnut. **Sights:** Blade front, fully adjustable rear. **Features:** Browned barrel, brass furniture, polished lock with double-set triggers. Imported by Navy Arms.
Price: Percussion $490.00
Price: Flintlock $505.00

NAVY ARMS PARKER-HALE WHITWORTH MILITARY TARGET RIFLE
Caliber: 45. **Barrel:** 36". **Weight:** 9-1/4 lbs. **Length:** 52-1/2" overall. **Stock:** Walnut. Checkered at wrist and forend. **Sights:** Hooded post front, open

Navy Arms Smith Carbine

Navy Arms 1863

Pacific Model 1837 Zephyr

Prairie River Arms Classic

step-adjustable rear. **Features:** Faithful reproduction of the Whitworth rifle, only bored for 45-cal. Trigger has a detented lock, capable of being adjusted very finely without risk of the sear nose catching on the half-cock bent and damaging both parts. Introduced 1978. Imported by Navy Arms.
Price: $875.00

NAVY ARMS SMITH CARBINE

Caliber: 50. **Barrel:** 21-1/2". **Weight:** 7-3/4 lbs. **Length:** 39" overall. **Stock:** American walnut. **Sights:** Brass blade front, folding ladder-type rear. **Features:** Replica of the breech-loading Civil War carbine. Color case-hardened receiver, rest blued. Cavalry model has saddle ring and bar, Artillery model has sling swivels. Imported by Navy Arms.
Price: Cavalry model $600.00
Price: Artillery model. $600.00

NAVY ARMS 1863 C.S. RICHMOND RIFLE

Caliber: 58. **Barrel:** 40". **Weight:** 10 lbs. **Length:** NA. **Stocks:** Walnut. **Sights:** Blade front, adjustable rear. **Features:** Copy of the three-band rifle musket made at Richmond Armory for the Confederacy. All steel polished bright. Imported by Navy Arms.
Price: $550.00

NAVY ARMS 1863 SPRINGFIELD

Caliber: 58, uses .575 Minie. **Barrel:** 40", rifled. **Weight:** 9-1/2 lbs. **Length:** 56" overall. **Stock:** Walnut. **Sights:** Open rear adjustable for elevation. **Features:** Full-size, three-band musket. Polished bright metal, including lock. From Navy Arms.
Price: Finished rifle. $550.00

NAVY ARMS 1861 SPRINGFIELD RIFLE

Caliber: 58. **Barrel:** 40" **Weight:** 10 lbs., 4 oz. **Length:** 56" overall. **Stock:** Walnut. **Sights:** Blade front, military leaf rear. **Features:** Steel barrel, lock and all furniture have polished bright finish. Has 1855-style hammer. Imported by Navy Arms.
Price: $550.00

PACIFIC RIFLE MODEL 1837 ZEPHYR

Caliber: 62. **Barrel:** 30", tapered octagon. **Weight:** 7-3/4 lbs. **Length:** NA. **Stock:** Oil-finished fancy walnut. **Sights:** German silver blade front, semi-buckhorn rear. Options available. **Features:** Improved underhammer action. First production rifle to offer Forsyth rifle, with narrow lands and shallow rifling with 1:144" pitch for high-velocity round balls. Metal finish is slow rust brown with nitre blue accents. Optional sights, finishes and integral muzzle brake available. Introduced 1995. Made in U.S. by Pacific Rifle Co.
Price: From. $995.00

Pacific Rifle Big Bore, African Rifles

Similar to the 1837 Zephyr except in 72-caliber and 8-bore. The 72-caliber is available in standard form with 28" barrel, or as the African with flat buttplate, checkered upgraded wood; weight is 9 lbs. The 8-bore African has dual-cap ignition, 24" barrel, weighs 12 lbs., checkered English walnut, engraving, gold inlays. Introduced 1998. Made in U.S. by Pacific Rifle Co.
Price: 72-caliber, from $1,150.00
Price: 8-bore from. $2,500.00

PRAIRIE RIVER ARMS PRA CLASSIC RIFLE

Caliber: 50, 54. **Barrel:** 26"; 1:28" twist. **Weight:** 7-1/2 lbs. **Length:** 40-1/2" overall. **Stock:** Hardwood or black all-weather. **Sights:** Blade front, open adjustable rear. **Features:** Patented internal percussion ignition system. Drilled and tapped for scope mount. Introduced 1995. Made in U.S. by Prairie River Arms, Ltd.
Price: 4140 alloy barrel, hardwood stock $375.00
Price: As above, stainless barrel $425.00
Price: 4140 alloy barrel, black all-weather stock $390.00
Price: As above, stainless barrel $440.00

PRAIRIE RIVER ARMS PRA BULLPUP RIFLE

Caliber: 50, 54. **Barrel:** 28"; 1:28" twist. **Weight:** 7-1/2 lbs. **Length:** 31-1/2" overall. **Stock:** Hardwood or black all-weather. **Sights:** Blade front, open adjustable rear. **Features:** Bullpup design thumbhole stock. Patented inter-

BLACKPOWDER MUSKETS & RIFLES

Prairie River Bullpup

Peifer TS-93

Remington Model 700 ML

C.S. Richmond 1863

Ruger K77/50RSZB

nal percussion ignition system. Left-hand model available. Dovetailed for scope mount. Introduced 1995. Made in U.S. by Prairie River Arms, Ltd.

Price: 4140 alloy barrel, hardwood stock **$375.00**
Price: As above, black stock. **$390.00**
Price: Stainless barrel, hardwood stock **$425.00**
Price: As above, black stock. **$440.00**

PEIFER MODEL TS-93 RIFLE

Caliber: 45, 50. **Barrel:** 24" Douglas premium; 1:20" twist in 45; 1:28" in 50. **Weight:** 7 lbs. **Length:** 43-1/4" overall. **Stock:** Bell & Carlson solid composite, with recoil pad, swivel studs. **Sights:** Williams bead front on ramp, fully adjustable open rear. Drilled and tapped for Weaver scope mounts with dovetail for rear peep. **Features:** In-line ignition uses #209 shotshell primer; extremely fast lock time; fully enclosed breech; adjustable trigger; automatic safety; removable primer holder. Blue or stainless. Made in U.S. by Peifer Rifle Co. Introduced 1996.

Price: Blue, black stock **$730.00**
Price: Blue, wood or camouflage composite stock, or stainless with black composite stock **$803.00**
Price: Stainless, wood or camouflage composite stock **$876.00**

C.S. RICHMOND 1863 MUSKET

Caliber: 58. **Barrel:** 40". **Weight:** 11 lbs. **Length:** 56-1/4" overall. **Stock:** European walnut with oil finish. **Sights:** Blade front, adjustable folding leaf rear. **Features:** Reproduction of the three-band Civil War musket. Sling swivels attached to trigger guard and middle barrel band. Lockplate

marked "1863" and "C.S. Richmond." All metal left in the white. Brass buttplate and forend cap. Imported by Euroarms of America, Navy Arms.

Price: **$530.00**

RUGER 77/50 IN-LINE PERCUSSION RIFLE

Caliber: 50. **Barrel:** 22"; 1:28" twist. **Weight:** 6-1/2 lbs. **Length:** 41-1/2" overall. **Stock:** Birch with rubber buttpad and swivel studs. **Sights:** Gold bead front, folding leaf rear. Comes with Ruger scope mounts. **Features:** Shares design features with the Ruger 77/22 rifle. Stainless steel bolt and nipple/breech plug; uses #11 caps; three-position safety; blued steel ramrod. Introduced 1997. Made in U.S. by Sturm, Ruger & Co.

Price: 77/50RS **$429.00**
Price: 77/50RSO Officers (straight-grip checkered walnut stock, blued) **$550.00**
Price: K77/50RSBBZ All-Weather (stainless steel, black laminated stock) **$596.00**
Price: K77/50RSP (stainless steel, synthetic stock) **$575.00**

REMINGTON MODEL 700 ML, MLS RIFLES

Caliber: 50, 54. **Barrel:** 24"; 1:28" twist. **Weight:** 7-3/4 lbs. **Length:** 44-1/2" overall. **Stock:** Black fiberglass-reinforced synthetic with checkered grip and forend; magnum-style buttpad. **Sights:** Ramped bead front, open fully adjustable rear. Drilled and tapped for scope mounts. **Features:** Uses the Remington 700 bolt action, stock design, safety and trigger mechanisms; removable stainelss steel breech plug, No. 11 nipple; solid aluminum ramrod. Comes with cleaning tools and accessories.

BLACKPOWDER MUSKETS & RIFLES

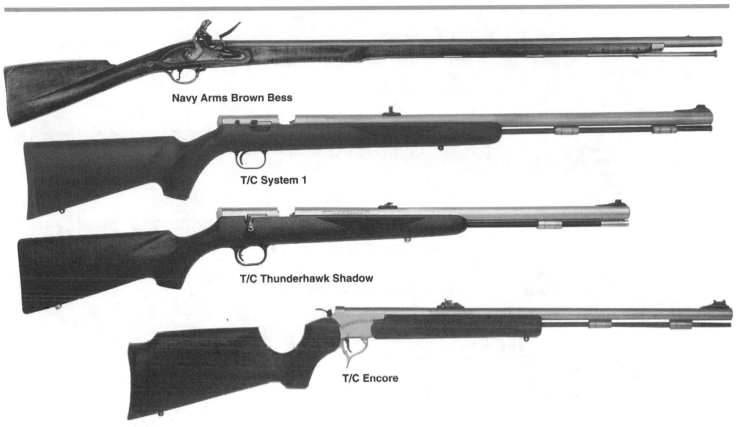

Navy Arms Brown Bess

T/C System 1

T/C Thunderhawk Shadow

T/C Encore

Price: ML, blued, 50-caliber only **$372.00**
Price: MLS, stainless, 50- or 54-caliber **$469.00**
Price: ML, blued, Mossy Oak Break-Up camo stock **$405.00**
Price: MLS, stainless, Mossy Oak Break-Up camo stock....... **$503.00**
Price: ML Youth (12-3/8" length of pull, 21" barrel) **$372.00**

SECOND MODEL BROWN BESS MUSKET
Caliber: 75, uses .735" round ball. **Barrel:** 42", smoothbore. **Weight:** 9-1/2 lbs. **Length:** 59" overall. **Stock:** Walnut (Navy), walnut-stained hardwood (Dixie). **Sights:** Fixed **Features:** Polished barrel and lock with brass trigger guard and buttplate. Bayonet and scabbard available. From Navy Arms, Dixie Gun Works, Cabela's.
Price: Finished .... **$475.00** to **$850.00**
Price: Kit (Dixie Gun Works, Navy Arms).......... **$575.00** to **$625.00**
Price: Carbine (Navy Arms) **$835.00**

STONE MOUNTAIN SILVER EAGLE RIFLE
Caliber: 50. **Barrel:** 26", octagonal; 15/16" flats; 1:48" twist. **Weight:** About 6-1/2 lbs. **Length:** 40" overall. **Stock:** DuraGrip synthetic; checkered grip and forend. **Sights:** Blade front, fixed rear. **Features:** Weatherguard nickel finish on metal; oversize trigger guard. Introduced 1995. From Stone Mountain Arms.
Price: **$139.95**

THOMPSON/CENTER BLACK MOUNTAIN MAGNUM RIFLE
Caliber: 50, 54. **Barrel:** 26"; 1:28" twist. **Weight:** 7 lbs. **Length:** 4-3/4" overall. **Stock:** American Walnut or black composite. **Sights:** Ramp front with Tru-Glo fiber optic inseat, click adjustable open rear with Tru-Glo fiber optic inserts. **Features:** Side lock percussion with breeech designed for Pyrodex Pellets, loose blackpowder and Pyrodex. blued steel. Uses QLA muzzle system. Introduced 1999. Made in U.S. by Thompson/Center Arms.
Price: Blue, composite stock, 50-cal. **$347.00**
Price: Blue, walnut stock, 50- or 54-cal. (westraner) **$369.00**

THOMPSON/CENTER PENNSYLVANIA HUNTER RIFLE
Caliber: 50. **Barrel:** 28", octagonal. **Weight:** About 7-1/2 lbs. **Length:** 48" overall. **Stock:** Black walnut. **Sights:** Open, adjustable. **Features:** Rifled 1:66" for round-ball shooting. Available in flintlock only. From Thompson/Center.
Price: **$417.00**

THOMPSON/CENTER SYSTEM 1 IN-LINE RIFLE
Caliber: 32, 50, 54, 58; 12-gauge. **Barrel:** 26" round; 1:38" twlst. **Weight:** About 7-1/2lbs. **Length:** 44" overall. **Stock:** American black walnut or composite. **Sights:** Ramp front with white bead, adjustable leaf rear. **Features:** In-line ignition. Interchangeable barrels; removable breech plug allows cleaning from the breech; fully adjustable trigger; sliding thumb safety; QLA muzzle system; rubber recoil pad; sling swivel studs. Introduced 1997. Made in U.S. by Thompson/Center Arms.
Price: Blue, walnut stock **$396.00**
Price: Stainless, composite stock, 50-, 54-caliber **$440.00**
Price: Stainless, camo composite stock, 50-caliber **$479.00**
Price: Extra barrels, blue **$176.00**
Price: Extra barrels, stainless, 50-, 54-caliber **$220.00**

Thompson/Center Pennsylvania Hunter Carbine
Similar to the Pennsylvania Hunter except has 21" barrel, weighs 6.5 lbs., and has an overall length of 38". Designed for shooting patched round balls. Available in flintlock only. Introduced 1992. From Thompson/Center.
Price: **$406.00**

THOMPSON/CENTER ENCORE 209x50 MAGNUM
Caliber: 50. **Barrel:** 26"; interchangeable with centerfire calibers. **Weight:** 7 lbs. **Length:** 40-1/2" overall. **Stock:** American walnut butt and forend, or black composite. **Sights:** Tru-Glo Fiber Optic front, Tru-Glo Fiber Optic rear. **Features:** Blue or stainless steel. Uses the stock, frame and forend of the Encore centerfire pistol; break-open design using trigger guard spur; stainless steel universal breech plug; uses #209 shotshell primers. Introduced 1998. Made in U.S. by Thompson/Center Arms.
Price: **$581.00**
Price: Blue, walnut stock and forend **$581.00**
Price: Blue, composite stock and forend **$562.00**
Price: Stainless, composite stock and forend................ **$634.00**

BLACKPOWDER MUSKETS & RIFLES

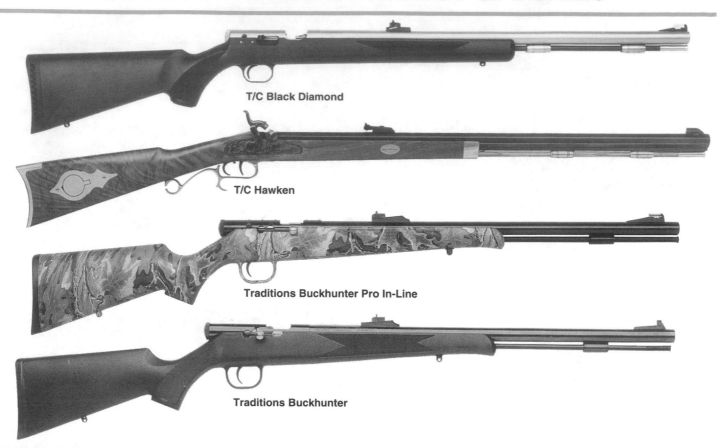

T/C Black Diamond

T/C Hawken

Traditions Buckhunter Pro In-Line

Traditions Buckhunter

THOMPSON/CENTER THUNDERHAWK SHADOW
Caliber: 50, 54. **Barrel:** 24"; 1:38" twist. **Weight:** 7 lbs. **Length:** 41-3/4" overall. **Stock:** American walnut or black composite with rubber recoil pad. **Sights:** Bead on ramp front, adjustable leaf rear. **Features:** Uses modern in-line ignition system, adjustable trigger. Knurled striker handle indicators for Safe and Fire. Black wood ramrod, Drilled and tapped for T/C scope mounts. Introduced 1996. From Thompson/Center Arms.
Price: Blued **$294.00**

THOMPSON/CENTER BLACK DIAMOND RIFLE
Caliber: 50. **Barrel:** 22-1/2" with QLA; 1:28" twist. **Weight:** 6 lbs., 9 oz. **Length:** 41-1/2" overall. **Stock:** Black Rynite with moulded-in checkering and grip cap, or walnut. **Sights:** Tru-Glo Fiber Optic ramp-style front, Tru-Glo Fiber Optic open rear. **Features:** In-line ignition system for musket cap, No. 11 cap, or 209 shotshell primer; removable universal breech plug; stainless steel construction. Introduced 1998. Made in U.S. by Thompson/Center Arms.
Price: **$362.00**
Price: With walnut stock **$333.00**

THOMPSON/CENTER HAWKEN RIFLE
Caliber: 45, 50 or 54. **Barrel:** 28" octagon, hooked breech. **Stock:** American walnut. **Sights:** Blade front, rear adjustable for windage and elevation. **Features:** Solid brass furniture, double-set triggers, button rifled barrel, coil-type mainspring. From Thompson/Center Arms.
Price: Percussion model (45-, 50- or 54-cal.) **$461.00**
Price: Flintlock model (50-cal.) **$472.00**

TRADITIONS BUCKHUNTER PRO IN-LINE RIFLES
Caliber: 50 (1:32" twist); 54 (1:48" twist). **Barrel:** 24" tapered round. **Weight:** 7-1/2 lbs. **Length:** 42" overall. **Stock:** Beech, composite or laminated; thumbhole available in black, Break-Up or Realtree® Advantage camouflage. **Sights:** Beaded blade front, fully adjustable open rear. Drilled and tapped for scope mounting. **Features:** In-line percussion ignition system; adjustable trigger; manual thumb safety; removable stainless steel breech plug. Eleven models available. Introduced 1996. From Traditions.
Price: . . . . **$175.00** to **$299.00**

TRADITIONS BUCKSKINNER CARBINE
Caliber: 50. **Barrel:** 21"; 15/16" flats, half octagon, half round; 1:20" or 1:66" twist. **Weight:** 6 lbs. **Length:** 37" overall. **Stock:** Beech or black laminated. **Sights:** Beaded blade front, hunting-style open rear click adjustable for windage and elevation. **Features:** Uses V-type mainspring, single trigger. Non-glare hardware. From Traditions.
Price: Flintlock **$204.00**
Price: Flintlock, laminated stock **$279.00**

Traditions Deerhunter Composite Rifle
Similar to the Deerhunter except has black composite stock with checkered grip and forend. Blued barrel, C-Nickel or Advantage camouflage finish, 50-caliber flintlock. Introduced 1996. Imported by Traditions.
Price: Blued, flintlock, 50-cal. **$160.00**
Price: Blued or Advantage camo, 50-cal. **$175.00**

TRADITIONS HAWKEN WOODSMAN RIFLE
Caliber: 50 and 54. **Barrel:** 28"; 15/16" flats. **Weight:** 7 lbs., 11 oz. **Length:** 44-1/2" overall. **Stock:** Walnut-stained hardwood. **Sights:** Beaded blade front, hunting-style open rear adjustable for windage and elevation. **Features:** Percussion only. Brass patchbox and furniture. Double triggers. From Traditions.
Price: 50 or 54 . . . . **$219.00**
Price: 50-cal., left-hand **$233.00**
Price: 50-caliber, flintlock **$248.00**

TRADITIONS IN-LINE BUCKHUNTER SERIES RIFLES
Caliber: 50, 54. **Barrel:** 24", round; 1:32" (50); 1:48" (54) twist. **Weight:** 7 lbs., 6 oz. to 8 lbs. **Length:** 41" overall. **Stock:** All-Weather composite. **Sights:** Fiber Optic blade front, click adjustable rear. Drilled and tapped for scope mounting. **Features:** Removable breech plug; PVC ramrod; sling swivels. Introduced 1995. From Traditions.
Price: **$175.00**
Price: With RS Redi-Pak (powder measure, powder flask, two fast loaders, 5-in-1 loader, capper, ball starter, ball puller, cleaning jag, nipple wrench, bullets) 50- and 54-caliber **$199.00**

BLACKPOWDER MUSKETS & RIFLES

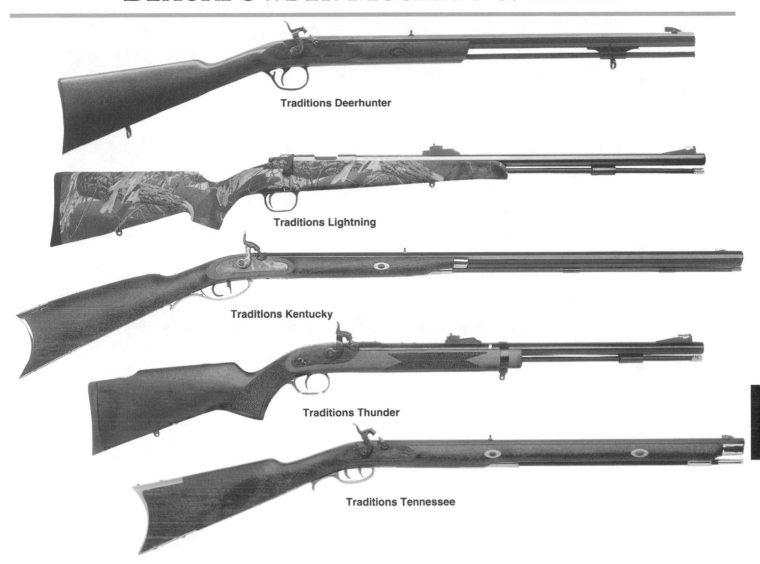

Traditions Deerhunter

Traditions Lightning

Traditions Kentucky

Traditions Thunder

Traditions Tennessee

TRADITIONS DEERHUNTER RIFLE SERIES

Caliber: 32, 50 or 54. **Barrel:** 24", octagonal; 15/16" flats; 1:48" or 1:66" twist. **Weight:** 6 lbs. **Length:** 40" overall. **Stock:** Stained hardwood and All-Weather composite with rubber buttpad, sling swivels. **Sights:** Blade front, fixed rear. **Features:** Flint or percussion with color case-hardened lock. Hooked breech, oversized trigger guard, blackened furniture, PVC ramrod. All-Weather has composite stock and C-Nickel barrel. Drilled and tapped for scope mounting. Imported by Traditions, Inc.

Price: Percussion, 50 or 54; 1:48" twist **$160.00**
Price: Flintlock, 50-caliber only; 1:66" twist **$182.00**
Price: Flintlock, All-Weather, 50-cal. **$160.00**
Price: Percussion, All-Weather, 50 or 54 . . . . **$152.00**

TRADITIONS KENTUCKY RIFLE

Caliber: 50. **Barrel:** 33-1/2"; 7/8" flats; 1:66" twist. **Weight:** 7 lbs. **Length:** 49" overall. **Stock:** Beech; inletted toe plate. **Sights:** Blade front, fixed rear. **Features:** Full-length, two-piece stock; brass furniture; color case-hardened lock. Introduced 1995. From Traditions.

Price: Finished **$219.00**
Price: Kit **$175.00**

TRADITIONS LIGHTNING BOLT-ACTION MUZZLELOADER

Caliber: 50, 54. **Barrel:** 24" round; blued, stainless, C-Nickel or Ultra Coat. **Weight:** 7 lbs. **Length:** 43" overall. **Stock:** Select hardwood, brown laminated, All-Weather composite, Advantage, X-Tra Brown or Break-Up camouflage. **Sights:** Fiber Optic blade front, fully adjustable open rear. **Features:** Twenty-one variations available. Field-removable stainless steel bolt; silent thumb safety; adjustable trigger, drilled and tapped for scope mounting. Introduced 1997. Imported by Traditions.

Price: Select hardwood stock **$219.00**
Price: Laminated stock, stainless steel barrel **$380.00**
Price: All Weather composite stock, blue finish **$262.00**
Price: All-weather composite, stainless steel **$307.00**
Price: Camouflage composite **$307.00**
Price: All-weather composite, Teflon finish **$307.00**
Price: Camouflage composite, Teflon finish **$351.00**
Price: Composite, with muzzle brake **$249.00**
Price: Composite, with muzzle brake, stainless, fluted barrel **$376.00**

TRADITIONS TENNESSEE RIFLE

Caliber: 50. **Barrel:** 24", octagon; 15/16" flats; 1:66" twist. **Weight:** 6 lbs. **Length:** 40-1/2" overall. **Stock:** Stained beech. **Sights:** Blade front, fixed rear. **Features:** One-piece stock has inletted brass furniture, cheekpiece; double-set trigger; V-type mainspring. Flint or percussion. Introduced 1995. From Traditions.

Price: Percussion **$270.00**
Price: Flintlock **$285.00**

TRADITIONS THUNDER MAGNUM RIFLE

Caliber: 50. **Barrel:** 24"; 1:32" twist. **Weight:** 7 lbs., 9 oz. **Length:** 42-1/2" overall. **Stock:** Hardwood or composite. **Sights:** Fiber optic front, adjustable rear. **Features:** Sidelock action with thumb-activated safety. Introduced 1999. From Traditions.

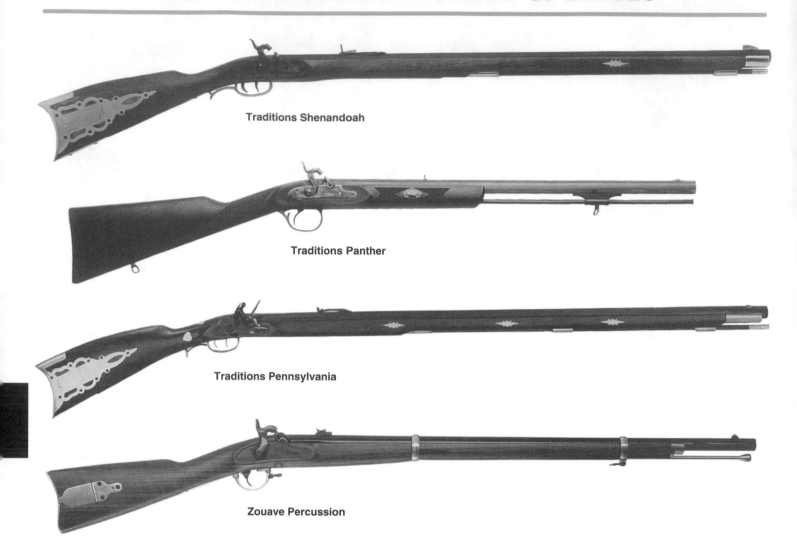

Traditions Shenandoah

Traditions Panther

Traditions Pennsylvania

Zouave Percussion

Price: Hardwood. **$359.00**
Price: Composite **$339.00**
Price: Composite, C-Nickel. **$359.00**

TRYON TRAILBLAZER RIFLE

Caliber: 50, 54. **Barrel:** 28", 30". **Weight:** 9 lbs. **Length:** 48" overall. **Stock:** European walnut with cheekpiece. **Sights:** Blade front, semi-buckhorn rear. **Features:** Reproduction of a rifle made by George Tryon about 1820. Double-set triggers, back action lock, hooked breech with long tang. From Armsport.
Price: About **$825.00**

TRADITIONS SHENANDOAH RIFLE

Caliber: 50. **Barrel:** 33-1/2" octagon; 1:66" twist. **Weight:** 7 lbs., 3 oz. **Length:** 49-1/2" overall. **Stock:** Walnut. **Sights:** Blade front, buckhorn rear. **Features:** V-type mainspring; double-set trigger; solid brass buttplate, patchbox, nosecap, thimbles, trigger guard. Introduced 1996. From Traditions.
Price: Flintlock **$351.00**
Price: Percussion **$337.00**

TRADITIONS PANTHER RIFLE

Caliber: 50. **Barrel:** 24" octagon (1:48" twist); 15/16" flats. **Weight:** 6 lbs. **Length:** 40" overall. **Stock:** All-Weather composite. **Sights:** Brass blade

front, fixed rear. **Features:** Percussion only; color case-hardened lock; blackened furniture; sling swivels; PVC ramrod. Introduced 1996. Imported by Traditions.
Price: **$116.00**
Price: With RS Redi-Pak (powder measure, flask, fast loaders, 5-in-1 loader, capper, ball starter, ball puller, cleaning jag, nipple wrench). **$169.00**

TRADITIONS PENNSYLVANIA RIFLE

Caliber: 50. **Barrel:** 40-1/4"; 7/8" flats; 1:66" twist, octagon. **Weight:** 9 lbs. **Length:** 57-1/2" overall. **Stock:** Walnut. **Sights:** Blade front, adjustable rear. **Features:** Brass patchbox and ornamentation. Double-set triggers. From Traditions.
Price: Flintlock **$469.00**
Price: Percussion **$462.00**

ZOUAVE PERCUSSION RIFLE

Caliber: 58, 59. **Barrel:** 32-1/2". **Weight:** 9-1/2 lbs. **Length:** 48-1/2" overall. **Stock:** Walnut finish, brass patchbox and buttplate. **Sights:** Fixed front, rear adjustable for elevation. **Features:** Color case-hardened lockplate, blued barrel. From Navy Arms, Dixie Gun Works, Euroarms of America (M1863), E.M.F., Cabela's.
Price: About . . . . $325.00 to **$465.00**
Price: Kit (Euroarms 58-cal. only). **$335.00**

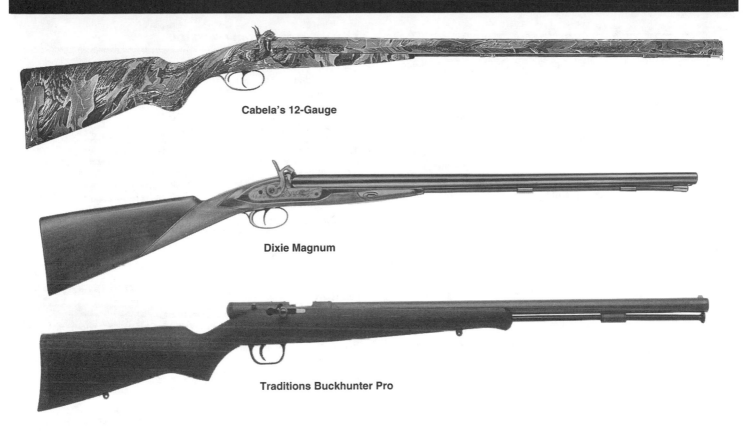

Cabela's 12-Gauge

Dixie Magnum

Traditions Buckhunter Pro

CABELA'S BLACKPOWDER SHOTGUNS

Gauge: 10, 12, 20. **Barrel:** 10-ga., 30"; 12-ga., 28-1/2" (Extra-Full, Mod., Imp. Cyl. choke tubes); 20-ga., 27-1/2" (Imp. Cyl. & Mod. fixed chokes). **Weight:** 6-1/2 to 7 lbs. **Length:** 45" overall (28-1/2" barrel). **Stock:** American walnut with checkered grip; 12- and 20-gauge have straight stock, 10-gauge has pistol grip. **Features:** Blued barrels, engraved, color case-hardened locks and hammers, brass ramrod tip. From Cabela's.

Price: 10-gauge **$499.99**
Price: 10-gauge, Advantage camo **$549.99**
Price: 12-gauge **$449.99**
Price: 12-gauge, Advantage camo **$499.99**
Price: 20-gauge **$429.99**

CVA TRAPPER PERCUSSION

Gauge: 12. **Barrel:** 28". **Weight:** 6 lbs. **Length:** 46" overall. **Stock:** English-style checkered straight grip of walnut-finished hardwood. **Sights:** Brass bead front. **Features:** Single-blued barrel; color case-hardened lockplate and hammer; screw adjustable sear engagements, V-type mainspring; brass wedge plates; color case-hardened and engraved trigger guard and tang. From CVA.

Price: Finished **$239.95**

DIXIE MAGNUM PERCUSSION SHOTGUN

Gauge: 10, 12, 20. **Barrel:** 30" (Imp. Cyl. & Mod.) in 10-gauge; 28" in 12-gauge. **Weight:** 6-1/4 lbs. **Length:** 45" overall. **Stock:** Hand-checkered walnut, 14" pull. **Features:** Double triggers; light hand engraving; case-hardened locks in 12-gauge, polished steel in 10-gauge; sling swivels. From Dixie Gun Works.

Price: Upland **$449.00**
Price: 12-ga. kit. **$375.00**

Price: 20-ga. **$495.00**
Price: 10-ga. **$495.00**
Price: 10-ga. kit **$395.00**

NAVY ARMS STEEL SHOT MAGNUM SHOTGUN

Gauge: 10. **Barrel:** 28" (Cyl. & Cyl.). **Weight:** 7 lbs., 9 oz. **Length:** 45-1/2" overall. **Stock:** Walnut, with cheekpiece. **Features:** Designed specifically for steel shot. Engraved, polished locks; sling swivels; blued barrels. Imported by Navy Arms.

Price: **$605.00**

NAVY ARMS T&T SHOTGUN

Gauge: 12. **Barrel:** 28" (Full & Full). **Weight:** 7-1/2 lbs. **Stock:** Walnut. **Sights:** Bead front. **Features:** Color case-hardened locks, double triggers, blued steel furniture. From Navy Arms.

Price: **$580.00**

TRADITIONS BUCKHUNTER PRO SHOTGUN

Gauge: 12. **Barrel:** 24", choke tube. **Weight:** 6 lbs., 4 oz. **Length:** 43" overall. **Stock:** Composite matte black, Break-Up or Advantage camouflage. **Features:** In-line action with removable stainless steel breech plug; thumb safety; adjustable trigger; rubber buttpad. Introduced 1996. From Traditions.

Price: **$235.00**
Price: With Advantage, Shadow Branch, or Break-Up camouflage stock. **$279.00**

THOMPSON/CENTER BLACK MOUNTAIN MAGNUM SHOTGUN

Gauge: 12. **Barrel:** 27" screw-in Turkey choke tube. **Weight:** 7 lbs. **Length:** 41-3/4" overall. **Stock:** Black composite. **Sights:** Bead front. **Features:** Sidelock percussion action. Polished blue finish. Introduced in 1999. Made in U.S. by Thompson/Center Arms.

Price: **$369.00**

Daisy/Power Line 717

ANICS A-101 SUBCOMPACT AIR PISTOL
Caliber: 177, 4.5mm, BB; 15-shot magazine. **Barrel:** 4" steel smoothbore. **Weight:** 35 oz. **Length:** 7" overall. **Power:** CO_2. **Stocks:** Ambidextrous black composite. **Sights:** Blade front, fixed rear. **Features:** Velocity to 450 fps. Semi-automatic action; double action only; cross-bolt safety; black and silver finish. Comes with two 15-shot magazines, case. Introduced 1996. Imported by Anics Corp.
Price: With case, about $72.00

Anics A-101 Magnum Air Pistol
Similar to the A-101 except has 5-1/3" barrel with compensator, gives about 490 fps. Introduced 1996. Imported by Anics Corp.
Price: With case, about $75.00

ANICS A-111 AIR PISTOL
Caliber: 177, 4.5mm, BB; 15-shot magazine. **Barrel:** 4" steel smoothbore. **Weight:** 35 oz. **Length:** 7" overall. **Power:** CO_2. **Stocks:** Black synthetic, wrap-around style. **Sights:** Blade front, fully adjustable rear. **Features:** Velocity about 450 fps. Semi-automatic action; double action only; cross-bolt safety; black finish. Comes with two magazines, case. Introduced 1998. Imported by Anics Corp.
Price: $74.00
Price: Magnum version (5-1/3" barrel, 490 fps) $77.00

ANICS A-201 AIR REVOLVER
Caliber: 177, 4.5mm, BB; 30-shot cylinder. **Barrel:** 4", steel smoothbore. **Weight:** 36 oz. **Length:** 9.75" overall. **Power:** CO_2. **Stocks:** Black synthetic. **Sights:** Blade front, fully adjustable rear. **Features:** Velocity about 410 fps. Fixed barrel; single/double action; black and silver finish. Introduced 1998. Imported by Anics Corp.
Price: $125.00
Price: Magnum version (6" barrel, 460 fps) $130.00

BEEMAN P1 MAGNUM AIR PISTOL
Caliber: 177, 5mm, single shot. **Barrel:** 8.4". **Weight:** 2.5 lbs. **Length:** 11" overall. **Power:** Top lever cocking; spring-piston. **Stocks:** Checkered walnut. **Sights:** Blade front, square notch rear with click micrometer adjustments for windage and elevation. Grooved for scope mounting. **Features:** Dual power for 177 and 20-cal.: low setting gives 350-400 fps; high setting 500-600 fps. Rearward expanding mainspring simulates firearm recoil. All Colt 45 auto grips fit gun. Dry-firing feature for practice. Optional wooden shoulder stock. Introduced 1985. Imported by Beeman.
Price: 177, 5mm $405.00

Beeman P2 Match Air Pistol
Similar to the Beeman P1 Magnum except shoots only 177 pellets; completely recoilless single-stroke pnuematic action. Weighs 2.2 lbs. Choice of thumbrest match grips or standard style. Introduced 1990.
Price: 177, 5mm, standard grip $445.00
Price: 177, match grip $480.00

BEEMAN/FEINWERKBAU 65 MKII AIR PISTOL
Caliber: 177, single shot. **Barrel:** 6.1", removable bbl. wgt. available. **Weight:** 42 oz. **Length:** 13.3" overall. **Power:** Spring, sidelever cocking. **Stocks:** Walnut, stippled thumbrest; adjustable or fixed. **Sights:** Front, interchangeable post element system, open rear, click adjustable for windage and elevation and for sighting notch width. Scope mount available. **Features:** New shorter barrel for better balance and control. Cocking effort 9 lbs. Two-stage trigger, four adjustments. Quiet firing, 525 fps. Programs instantly for recoil or recoilless operation. Permanently lubricated. Steel piston ring. Imported by Beeman.
Price: Right-hand $1,170.00
Price: Left-hand $1,230.00

BEEMAN/FEINWERKBAU 103 PISTOL
Caliber: 177, single shot. **Barrel:** 10.1", 12-groove rifling. **Weight:** 2.5 lbs. **Length:** 16.5" overall. **Power:** Single-stroke pneumatic, underlever cocking. **Stocks:** Stippled walnut with adjustable palm shelf. **Sights:** Blade front, open rear adjustable for windage and elevation. Notch size adjustable for width. Interchangeable front blades. **Features:** Velocity 510 fps. Fully adjustable trigger. Cocking effort of 2 lbs. Imported by Beeman.
Price: Right-hand $1,520.00
Price: Left-hand $1,580.00

BEEMAN/FWB P30 MATCH AIR PISTOL
Caliber: 177, single shot. **Barrel:** 10-5/16", with muzzlebrake. **Weight:** 2.4 lbs. **Length:** 16.5" overall. **Power:** Pre-charged pneumatic. **Stocks:** Stippled walnut; adjustable match type. **Sights:** Undercut blade front, fully adjustable match rear. **Features:** Velocity to 525 fps; up to 200 shots per CO_2 cartridge. Fully adjustable trigger; built-in muzzlebrake. Introduced 1995. Imported from Germany by Beeman.
Price: Right-hand $1,465.00
Price: Left-hand $1,520.00

BEEMAN/FWB C55 CO_2 RAPID FIRE PISTOL
Caliber: 177, single shot or 5-shot magazine. **Barrel:** 7.3". **Weight:** 2.5 lbs. **Length:** 15" overall. **Power:** Special CO_2 cylinder. **Stocks:** Anatomical, adjustable. **Sights:** Interchangeable front, fully adjustable open micro-click rear with adjustable notch size. **Features:** Velocity 510 fps. Has 11.75" sight radius. Built-in muzzlebrake. Introduced 1993. Imported by Beeman Precision Airguns.
Price: Right-hand $1,705.00
Price: Left-hand $1,755.00

BEEMAN HW70A AIR PISTOL
Caliber: 177, single shot. **Barrel:** 6-1/4", rifled. **Weight:** 38 oz. **Length:** 12-3/4" overall. **Power:** Spring, barrel cocking. **Stocks:** Plastic, with thumbrest. **Sights:** Hooded post front, square notch rear adjustable for windage and elevation. Comes with scope base. **Features:** Adjustable trigger, 31-lb. cocking effort, 440 fps MV; automatic barrel safety. Imported by Beeman.
Price: $225.00
Price: HW70S, black grip, silver finish $240.00

BEEMAN/WEBLEY TEMPEST AIR PISTOL
Caliber: 177, 22, single shot. **Barrel:** 6-7/8". **Weight:** 32 oz. **Length:** 8.9" overall. **Power:** Spring-piston, break barrel. **Stocks:** Checkered black plastic with thumbrest. **Sights:** Blade front, adjustable rear. **Features:** Velocity to 500 fps (177), 400 fps (22). Aluminum frame; black epoxy finish; manual safety. Imported from England by Beeman.
Price: $210.00

Beeman/Webley Hurricane Air Pistol
Similar to the Tempest except has extended frame in the rear for a click-adjustable rear sight; hooded front sight; comes with scope mount. Imported from England by Beeman.
Price: $240.00

BEEMAN/WEBLEY NEMESIS AIR PISTOL
Caliber: 177, single shot. **Barrel:** 7". **Weight:** 2.2 lbs. **Length:** 9.8" overall. **Power:** Single-stroke pneumatic. **Stocks:** Checkered black composition. **Sights:** Blade on ramp front, fully adjustable rear. Integral scope rail. **Features:** Velocity to 400 fps. Adjustable two-stage trigger, manual safety. Recoilless action. Introduced 1995. Imported from England by Beeman.
Price: $200.00

BENJAMIN SHERIDAN CO_2 PELLET PISTOLS
Caliber: 177, 20, 22, single shot. **Barrel:** 6-3/8", rifled brass. **Weight:** 29 oz. **Length:** 9.8" overall. **Power:** 12-gram CO_2 cylinder. **Stocks:** Walnut. **Sights:** High ramp front, fully adjustable notch rear. **Features:** Velocity to 500 fps. Turn-bolt action with cross-bolt safety. Gives about 40 shots per CO_2 cylinder. Black or nickel finish. Made in U.S. by Benjamin Sheridan Co.
Price: Black finish, EB17 (177), EB20 (20), EB22 (22), about $105.00
Price: Nickel finish, E17 (177), E20 (20), E22 (22), about $120.00

BENJAMIN SHERIDAN PNEUMATIC PELLET PISTOLS
Caliber: 177, 20, 22, single shot. **Barrel:** 9-3/8", rifled brass. **Weight:** 38 oz. **Length:** 13-1/8" overall. **Power:** Underlever pnuematic, hand pumped. **Stocks:** Walnut stocks and pump handle. **Sights:** High ramp front, fully adjustable notch rear. **Features:** Velocity to 525 fps (variable). Bolt action with cross-bolt safety. Choice of black or nickel finish. Made in U.S. by Benjamin Sheridan Co.
Price: Black finish, HB17 (177), HB20 (20), HB22 (22), about $115.00
Price: Nickel finish, H17 (177), H20 (20), H22 (22), about $120.00

BRNO TAU-7 CO_2 MATCH PISTOL
Caliber: 177. **Barrel:** 10.24". **Weight:** 37 oz. **Length:** 15.75" overall. **Power:** 12.5-gram CO_2 cartridge. **Stocks:** Stippled hardwood with adjustable palm rest. **Sights:** Blade front, open fully adjustable rear. **Features:** Comes with extra seals and counterweight. Blue finish. Imported by Great Lakes Airguns.
Price: About $379.50

BSA 240 MAGNUM AIR PISTOL
Caliber: 177, 22. **Barrel:** 6". **Weight:** 2 lbs. **Length:** 9" overall. **Power:** Spring-air, top-lever cocking. **Stocks:** Walnut. **Sights:** Blade front, micrometer adjustable rear. **Features:** Velocity 510 fps (177), 420 fps (22); crossbolt safety. Combat autoloader styling. Imported from U.K. by Precision Sales International, Inc.
Price: $293.00

COLT GOVERNMENT 1911 A1 AIR PISTOL
Caliber: 177, 8-shot cylinder magazine. **Barrel:** 5", rifled. **Weight:** 38 oz. **Length:** 8-1/2" overall. **Power:** CO_2 cylinder. **Stocks:** Checkered black plastic or smooth wood.

AIRGUNS—HANDGUNS

Sights: Post front, adjustable rear. **Features:** Velocity to 393 fps. Quick-loading cylinder magazine; single and double action; black or silver finish. Introduced 1998. Imported by Colt's Mfg. Co., Inc.
Price: Black finish... $199.00
Price: Silver finish.. $209.00

COPPERHEAD BLACK VENOM PISTOL
Caliber: 177 pellets, BB, 17-shot magazine; darts, single shot. **Barrel:** 4.75" smoothbore. **Weight:** 16 oz. **Length:** 10.8" overall. **Power:** Spring. **Stocks:** Checkered. **Sights:** Blade front, adjustable rear. **Features:** Velocity to 270 fps (BBs), 250 fps (pellets). Spring-fed magazine; cross-bolt safety. Introduced 1996. Made in U.S. by Crosman Corp.
Price: About.. $20.00

COPPERHEAD BLACK FANG PISTOL
Caliber: 177 BB, 17-shot magazine. **Barrel:** 4.75" smoothbore. **Weight:** 10 oz. **Length:** 10.8" overall. **Power:** Spring. **Stocks:** Checkered. **Sights:** Blade front, fixed notch rear. **Features:** Velocity to 250 fps. Spring-fed magazine; cross-bolt safety. Introduced 1996. Made in U.S. by Crosman Corp.
Price: About.. $16.00

CROSMAN MODEL 1322, 1377 AIR PISTOLS
Caliber: 177 (M1377), 22 (M1322), single shot. **Barrel:** 8", rifled steel. **Weight:** 39 oz. **Length:** 13-5/8". **Power:** Hand pumped. **Sights:** Blade front, rear adjustable for windage and elevation. **Features:** Moulded plastic grip, hand size pump forearm. Cross-bolt safety. Model 1377 also shoots BBs. From Crosman.
Price: About.. $60.00

CROSMAN AUTO AIR II PISTOL
Caliber: BB, 17-shot magazine, 177 pellet, single shot. **Barrel:** 8-5/8" steel, smoothbore. **Weight:** 13 oz. **Length:** 10-3/4" overall. **Power:** CO_2 Powerlet. **Stocks:** Grooved plastic. **Sights:** Blade front, adjustable rear; highlighted system. **Features:** Velocity to 480 fps (BBs), 430 fps (pellets). Semi-automatic action with BBs, single shot with pellets. Silvered finish. Introduced 1991. From Crosman.
Price: About.. $35.00

CROSMAN MODEL 357 SERIES AIR PISTOL
Caliber: 177, 6- and 10-shot pellet clips. **Barrel:** 4" (Model 3574GT), 6" (Model 3576GT). **Weight:** 32 oz. (6"). **Length:** 11-3/8" overall (357-6). **Power:** CO_2 Powerlet. **Stocks:** Checkered wood-grain plastic. **Sights:** Ramp front, fully adjustable rear. **Features:** Average 430 fps (Model 3574GT). Break-open barrel for easy loading. Single or double action. Vent. rib barrel. Wide, smooth trigger. Two cylinders come with each gun. Black and gold finish. From Crosman.
Price: 4" or 6", about.. $60.00

CROSMAN MODEL 1008 REPEAT AIR
Caliber: 177, 8-shot pellet clip. **Barrel:** 4.25", rifled steel. **Weight:** 17 oz. **Length:** 8.625" overall. **Power:** CO_2 Powerlet. **Stocks:** Checkered black plastic. **Sights:** Post front, adjustable rear. **Features:** Velocity about 430 fps. Break-open barrel for easy loading; single or double semi-automatic action; two 8-shot clips included. Optional carrying case available. Introduced 1992. From Crosman.
Price: About.. $60.00
Price: With case, about....................................... $65.00
Price: Model 1008SB (silver and black finish), about.......... $60.00

DAISY MODEL 2003 PELLET PISTOL
Caliber: 177 pellet, 35-shot clip. **Barrel:** Rifled steel. **Weight:** 2.2 lbs. **Length:** 11.7" overall. **Power:** CO_2. **Stocks:** Checkered plastic. **Sights:** Blade front, open rear. **Features:** Velocity to 400 fps. Crossbolt trigger-block safety. Made in U.S. by Daisy Mfg. Co.
Price: About.. $67.95

DAISY MODEL 454 AIR PISTOL
Caliber: 177 BB, 20-shot clip. **Barrel:** Smoothbore steel. **Weight:** 1.6 lbs. **Length:** 10.4" overall. **Power:** CO_2. **Stocks:** Moulded black, ribbed composition. **Sights:** Blade front, fixed rear. **Features:** Velocity to 420 fps. Semi-automatic action; cross-bolt safety; black finish. Introduced 1998. Made in U.S. by Dairy Mfg. Co.
Price: $61.95

DAISY/POWER LINE 717 PELLET PISTOL
Caliber: 177, single shot. **Barrel:** 9.61". **Weight:** 2.8 lbs. **Length:** 13-1/2" overall. **Stocks:** Moulded wood-grain plastic, with thumbrest. **Sights:** Blade and ramp front, micro-adjustable notch rear. **Features:** Single pump pneumatic pistol. Rifled steel barrel. Cross-bolt trigger block. Muzzle velocity 385 fps. From Daisy Mfg. Co. Introduced 1979.
Price: About.. $69.95

Daisy/Power Line 747 Pistol
Similar to the 717 pistol except has a 12-groove rifled steel barrel by Lothar Walther, and adjustable trigger pull weight. Velocity of 360 fps. Manual cross-bolt safety.
Price: About.. $140.00

DAISY/POWER LINE 1140 PELLET PISTOL
Caliber: 177, single shot. **Barrel:** Rifled steel. **Weight:** 1.3 lbs. **Length:** 11.7" overall. **Power:** Single-stroke barrel cocking. **Stocks:** Checkered resin. **Sights:** Hooded post front, open adjustable rear. **Features:** Velocity to 325 fps. Made of black lightweight engineering resin. Introduced 1995. From Daisy.
Price: About.. $38.95

DAISY/POWER LINE 44 REVOLVER
Caliber: 177 pellets, 6-shot. **Barrel:** 6", rifled steel; interchangeable 4" and 8". **Weight:** 2.7 lbs. **Stocks:** Moulded plastic with checkering. **Sights:** Blade on ramp front, fully adjustable notch rear. **Features:** Velocity up to 400 fps. Replica of 44 Magnum revolver. Has swingout cylinder and interchangeable barrels. Introduced 1987. From Daisy Mfg. Co.
Price: $60.95

DAISY/POWER LINE 1270 CO_2 AIR PISTOL
Caliber: BB, 60-shot magazine. **Barrel:** Smoothbore steel. **Weight:** 17 oz. **Length:** 11" overall. **Power:** CO_2 pump action. **Stocks:** Moulded black polymer. **Sights:** Blade on ramp front, adjustable rear. **Features:** Velocity to 420 fps. Crossbolt trigger block safety; plated finish. Introduced 1997. Made in U.S. by Daisy Mfg. Co.
Price: About.. $40.95

DAISY/POWER LINE 1700 AIR PISTOL
Caliber: 177 BB, 60-shot magazine. **Barrel:** Smoothbore steel. **Weight:** 1.4 lbs. **Length:** 11.2" overall. **Power:** CO_2. **Stocks:** Moulded checkered plastic. **Sights:** Blade front, adjustable rear. **Features:** Velocity to 420 fps. Cross-bolt trigger block safety; matte finish. Has 3/8" dovetail mount for scope or point sight. Introduced 1994. From Daisy Mfg. Co.
Price: About.. $34.95

DRULOV DU-10 CONDOR TARGET PISTOL
Caliber: 177, 5-shot magazine. **Barrel:** 7.09". **Weight:** 2.32 lbs. **Length:** 11.81" overall. **Power:** CO_2. **Stocks:** Target-type walnut with stippling. **Sights:** Blade front, fully adjustable open rear. **Features:** Velocity to 472 fps. Developed for Olympic Rapid Fire and 10-meter Sport Pistol events. Introduced 1997. Imported from the Czech Republic by Great Lakes Airguns.
Price: About.. $495.50

"GAT" AIR PISTOL
Caliber: 177, single shot. **Barrel:** 7-1/2" cocked, 9-1/2" extended. **Weight:** 22 oz. **Power:** Spring-piston. **Stocks:** Cast checkered metal. **Sights:** Fixed. **Features:** Shoots pellets, corks or darts. Matte black finish. Imported from England by Stone Enterprises, Inc.
Price: $24.95

HAMMERLI 480 MATCH AIR PISTOL
Caliber: 177, single shot. **Barrel:** 9.8". **Weight:** 37 oz. **Length:** 16.5" overall. **Power:** Air or CO_2. **Stocks:** Walnut with 7-degree rake adjustment. Stippled grip area. **Sights:** Undercut blade front, fully adjustable open match rear. **Features:** Under-barrel cannister charges with air or CO_2 for power supply; gives 320 shots per filling. Trigger adjustable for position. Introduced 1994. Imported from Switzerland by Hammerli Pistols U.S.A.
Price: $1,325.00

Hammerli 480k Match Air Pistol
Similar to the 480 except has a short, detachable aluminum air cylinder for use only with compressed air; can be filled while on the gun or off; special adjustable barrel weights. Muzzle velocity of 470 fps, gives about 180 shots. Has stippled black composition grip with adjustable palm shelf and rake angle. Comes with air pressure gauge. Introduced 1996. Imported from Switzerland by SIGARMS, Inc.
Price: $1,155.00

MARKSMAN 1010 REPEATER PISTOL
Caliber: 177, 18-shot BB repeater. **Barrel:** 2-1/2", smoothbore. **Weight:** 24 oz. **Length:** 8-1/4" overall. **Power:** Spring. **Features:** Velocity to 200 fps. Thumb safety. Black finish. Uses BBs, darts, bolts or pellets. Repeats with BBs only. From Marksman Products.
Price: Matte black finish...................................... $26.00
Price: Model 2000 (as above except silver-chrome finish)....... $27.00

MARKSMAN 2005 LASERHAWK SPECIAL EDITION AIR PISTOL
Caliber: 177, 24-shot magazine. **Barrel:** 3.8", smoothbore. **Weight:** 22 oz. **Length:** 10.3" overall. **Power:** Spring-air. **Stocks:** Checkered. **Sights:** Fixed fiber optic front sight. **Features:** Velocity to 300 fps with Hyper-Velocity pellets. Square trigger guard with skeletonized trigger; extended barrel for greater velocity and accuracy. Shoots BBs, pellets, darts or bolts. Made in the U.S. From Marksman Products.
Price: $32.00

MORINI 162E MATCH AIR PISTOL
Caliber: 177, single shot. **Barrel:** 9.4". **Weight:** 32 oz. **Length:** 16.1" overall. **Power:** Pre-charged CO_2. **Stocks:** Adjustable match type. **Sights:** Interchangeable blade front, fully adjustable match-type rear. **Features:** Power mechanism shuts down

when pressure drops to a pre-set level. Adjustable electronic trigger. Introduced 1995. Imported from Switzerland by Nygord Precision Products.
Price: $950.00

PARDINI K58 MATCH AIR PISTOL
Caliber: 177, single shot. Barrel: 9.0". Weight: 37.7 oz. Length: 15.5" overall. Power: Pre-charged compressed air; single-stroke cocking. Stocks: Adjustable match type; stippled walnut. Sights: Interchangeable post front, fully adjustable match rear. Features: Fully adjustable trigger. Introduced 1995. Imported from Italy by Nygord Precision Products.
Price: $650.00
Price: K60 model (CO$_2$) $650.00

RECORD JUMBO DELUXE AIR PISTOL
Caliber: 177, single shot. Barrel: 6", rifled. Weight: 1.9 lbs. Length: 7.25" overall. Power: Spring-air, lateral cocking lever. Stocks: Smooth walnut. Sights: Blade front, fully adjustable open rear. Features: Velocity to 322 fps. Thumb safety. Grip magazine compartment for extra pellet storage. Introduced 1983. Imported from Germany by Great Lakes Airguns.
Price: $127.61

RWS/Diana Model 6G Air Pistols
Similar to the Model 6M except does not have the movable barrel shroud. Has click micrometer rear sight, two-stage adjustable trigger, interchangeable tunnel front sight. Available in right- or left-hand models.
Price: Right-hand $450.00
Price: Left-hand $490.00

RWS MODEL C-357 AIR PISTOL
Caliber: 177, 8-shot cylinder. Barrel: 6", rifled. Weight: 1.75 lbs. Length: 11" overall. Power: CO$_2$. Stocks: Checkered black synthetic. Sights: Blade front, adjustable rear. Features: Velocity to 380 fps. Manual safety; black finish. Imported from Germany by Dynamit Nobel-RWS Inc.
Price: $175.00

RWS/DIANA MODEL 5G AIR PISTOL
Caliber: 177, single shot. Barrel: 7". Weight: 2-3/4 lbs. Length: 15" overall. Power: Spring-air, barrel cocking. Stocks: Plastic, thumbrest design. Sights: Tunnel front, micro-click open rear. Features: Velocity of 450 fps. Adjustable two-stage trigger with automatic safety. Imported from Germany by Dynamit Nobel-RWS, Inc.
Price: $260.00

RWS/DIANA MODEL 6M MATCH AIR PISTOL
Caliber: 177, single shot. Barrel: 7". Weight: 3 lbs. Length: 15" overall. Power: Spring-air, barrel cocking. Stocks: Walnut-finished hardwood with thumbrest. Sights: Adjustable front, micro. click open rear. Features: Velocity of 410 fps. Recoilless double piston system, movable barrel shroud to protect from sight during cocking. Imported from Germany by Dynamit Nobel-RWS, Inc.
Price: Right-hand $585.00
Price: Left-hand $640.00

RWS C-225 AIR PISTOLS
Caliber: 177, 8-shot rotary magazine. Barrel: 4", 6". Weight: NA. Length: NA. Power: CO$_2$. Stocks: Checkered black plastic. Sights: Post front, rear adjustable for windage. Features: Velocity to 385 fps. Semi-automatic fire; decocking lever. Imported from Germany by Dynamit Nobel-RWS.
Price: 4", blue $200.00
Price: 4", nickel $210.00
Price: 6", blue $210.00
Price: 6", nickel $235.00

STEYR LP5C MATCH PISTOL
Caliber: 177, 5-shot magazine. Barrel: NA. Weight: 40.2 oz. Length: 13.39" overall. Power: Refillable CO$_2$ cylinders. Stocks: Adjustable Morini match with palm shelf; stippled walnut. Sights: Movable 2.5mm blade front; 2-3mm interchangeable in .2mm increments; fully adjustable open match rear. Features: Velocity about 500 fps. Fully adjustable trigger; compensator; has dry-fire feature. Barrel and grip weights available. Introduced 1993. Imported from Austria by Nygord Precision Products.
Price: $1,350.00

STEYR LP 5CP MATCH AIR PISTOL
Caliber: 177, 5-shot magazine. Barrel: NA. Weight: 40.7 oz. Length: 15.2" overall. Power: Pre-charged air cylinder. Stocks: Adjustable match type. Sights: Interchangeable blade front, fully adjustable match rear. Features: Adjustable sight radius; fully adjustable trigger. Has barrel compensator. Introduced 1995. Imported from Austria by Nygord Precision Products.
Price: $1,395.00

STEYR CO$_2$ MATCH LP1C PISTOL
Caliber: 177, single shot. Barrel: 9". Weight: 38.7 oz. Length: 15.3" overall. Power: Refillable CO$_2$ cylinders. Stocks: Fully adjustable Morini match with palm shelf; stippled walnut. Sights: Interchangeable blade in 4mm, 4.5mm or 5mm widths, fully adjustable open rear with interchangeable 3.5mm or 4mm leaves. Features: Velocity about 500 fps. Adjustable trigger, adjustable sight radius from 12.4" to 13.2". With compensator. Imported from Austria by Nygord Precision Products.
Price: $1,250.00

WALTHER CP88 PELLET PISTOL
Caliber: 177, 8-shot rotary magazine. Barrel: 4", 6". Weight: 37 oz. (4" barrel) Length: 7" (4" barrel). Power: CO$_2$. Stocks: Checkered plastic. Sights: Blade front, fully adjustable rear. Features: Faithfully replicates size, weight and trigger pull of the 9mm Walther P88 compact pistol. Has SA/DA trigger mechanism; ambidextrous safety, levers. Comes with two magazines, 500 pellets, one CO2 cartridge. Introduced 1997. Imported from Germany by Interarms.
Price: Blue $179.00
Price: Nickel $189.00

WALTHER CPM-1 CO$_2$ MATCH PISTOL
Caliber: 177, single shot. Barrel: 8.66". Weight: NA. Length: 15.1" overall. Power: CO$_2$. Stocks: Orthopaedic target type. Sights: Undercut blade front, open match rear fully adjustable for windage and elevation. Features: Adjustable velocity; matte finish. Introduced 1995. Imported from Germany by Nygord Precision Products.
Price: $950.00

Walther CP88 Competition Pellet Pistol
Similar to the standard CP88 except has 6" match-grade barrel, muzzle weight, wood or plastic stocks. Weighs 41 oz., has overall length of 9". Introduced 1997. Imported from Germany by Interarms.
Price: Blue, plastic stocks $189.00
Price: Nickel, plastic stocks $199.00
Price: Blue, wood stocks $220.00
Price: Nickel, wood stocks $232.00

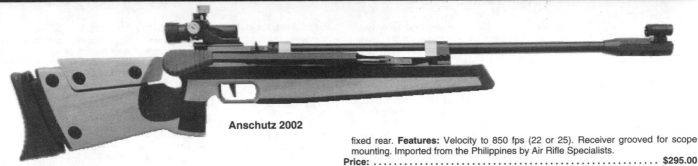

Anschutz 2002

AIR ARMS TX 200 AIR RIFLE
Caliber: 177; single shot. **Barrel:** 15.7". **Weight:** 9.3 lbs. **Length:** 41.5" overall. **Power:** Spring-air; underlever cocking. **Stock:** Oil-finished hardwood; checkered grip and forend; rubber buttpad. **Sights:** None furnished. **Features:** Velocity about 900 fps. Automatic safety; adjustable two-stage trigger. Imported from England by Great Lakes Airguns.
Price: $593.27

AIR ARMS S-300 HI-POWER AIR RIFLE
Caliber: 22. **Barrel:** 19-1/2". **Weight:** 6.4 lbs. **Length:** 38.5" overall. **Stock:** Stained European hardwood; ambidextrous. **Power:** Precharged pneumatic. **Sights:** None furnished. **Features:** Velocity about 750 fps. Two-stage trigger. Blue finish. Introduced 1997. Imported from England by Great Lakes Airarms.
Price: $764.07

AIRROW MODEL A-8SRB STEALTH AIR GUN
Caliber: 177, 22, 25, 38, 9-shot. **Barrel:** 19.7"; rifled. **Weight:** 6 lbs. **Length:** 34" overall. **Power:** CO_2 or compressed air; variable power. **Stock:** Telescoping CAR-15-type. **Sights:** Variable 3.5-10x scope. **Features:** Velocity 1100 fps in all calibers. Pneumatic air trigger. All aircraft aluminum and stainless steel construction. Mil-spec materials and finishes. Introduced 1992. From Swivel Machine Works, Inc.
Price: About $2,599.00

AIRROW MODEL A-8S1P STEALTH AIR GUN
Caliber: #2512 16" arrow. **Barrel:** 16". **Weight:** 4.4 lbs. **Length:** 30.1" overall. **Power:** CO_2 or compressed air; variable power. **Stock:** Telescoping CAR-15-type. **Sights:** Scope rings only. **Features:** Velocity to 650 fps with 260-grain arrow. Pneumatic air trigger. All aircraft aluminum and stainless steel construction. Mil-spec materials and finishes. Waterproof case. Introduced 1991. From Swivel Machine Works, Inc.
Price: About $1,699.00

ARS/KING HUNTING MASTER AIR RIFLE
Caliber: 22, 5-shot repeater. **Barrel:** 22-3/4". **Weight:** 7-3/4 lbs. **Length:** 42" overall. **Power:** Pre-compressed air from 3000 psi diving tank. **Stock:** Indonesian walnut with checkered grip and forend; rubber buttpad. **Sights:** Blade front, fully adjustable open rear. Receiver grooved for scope mounting. **Features:** Velocity over 1000 fps with 32-grain pellet. High and low power switch for hunting or target velocities. Slide lever cocks action and inserts pellet. Rotary magazine. Imported from Korea by Air Rifle Specialists.
Price: $580.00
Price: Hunting Master 900 (9mm, limited production) $1,000.00

ARS/Magnum 6 Air Rifle
Similar to the King Hunting Master except is 6-shot repeater with 23-3/4" barrel, weighs 8-1/4 lbs. Stock is walnut-stained hardwood with checkered grip and forend; rubber buttpad. Velocity of 1000+ fps with 32-grain pellet. Imported from Korea by Air Rifle Specialists.
Price: $500.00

ARS HUNTING MASTER AR6 AIR RIFLE
Caliber: 22, 6-shot repeater. **Barrel:** 25-1/2". **Weight:** 7 lbs. **Length:** 41-1/4" overall. **Power:** Pre-compressed air from 3000 psi diving tank. **Stock:** Indonesian walnut with checkered grip; rubber buttpad. **Sights:** Blade front, adjustable peep rear. **Features:** Velocity over 1000 fps with 32-grain pellet. Receiver grooved for scope mounting. Has 6-shot rotary magazine. Imported by Air Rifle Specialists.
Price: $580.00

ARS/CAREER 707 AIR RIFLE
Caliber: 22, 6-shot repeater. **Barrel:** 23". **Weight:** 7.75 lbs. **Length:** 40.5" overall. **Power:** Pre-compressed air; variable power. **Stock:** Indonesian walnut with checkered grip, gloss finish. **Sights:** Hooded post front with interchangeable inserts, fully adjustable diopter rear. **Features:** Velocity to 1000 fps. Lever-action with straight feed magazine; pressure gauge in lower front air reservoir; scope mounting rail included. Introduced 1996. Imported from the Philippines by Air Rifle Specialists.
Price: $580.00

ARS/FARCO FP SURVIVAL AIR RIFLE
Caliber: 22, 25, single shot. **Barrel:** 22-3/4". **Weight:** 5-3/4 lbs. **Length:** 42-3/4" overall. **Power:** Multi-pump foot pump. **Stock:** Philippine hardwood. **Sights:** Blade front,

fixed rear. **Features:** Velocity to 850 fps (22 or 25). Receiver grooved for scope mounting. Imported from the Philippines by Air Rifle Specialists.
Price: $295.00

ARS/FARCO CO_2 AIR SHOTGUN
Caliber: 51 (28-gauge). **Barrel:** 30". **Weight:** 7 lbs. **Length:** 48-1/2" overall. **Power:** 10-oz. refillable CO_2 tank. **Stock:** Hardwood. **Sights:** Blade front, fixed rear. **Features:** Gives over 100 ft. lbs. energy for taking small game. Imported from the Philippines by Air Rifle Specialists.
Price: $460.00

ARS/Farco CO_2 Stainless Steel Air Rifle
Similar to the ARS/Farco CO_2 shotgun except in 22- or 25-caliber with 21-1/2" barrel; weighs 6-3/4 lbs., 42-1/2" overall; Philippine hardwood stock with stippled grip and forend; blade front sight, adjustable rear, grooved for scope mount. Uses 10-oz. refillable CO_2 cylinder. Made of stainless steel. Imported from the Philippines by Air Rifle Specialists.
Price: Including CO_2 cylinder $460.00

ARS/QB77 DELUXE AIR RIFLE
Caliber: 177, 22, single shot. **Barrel:** 21-1/2". **Weight:** 5-1/2 lbs. **Length:** 40" overall. **Power:** Two 12-oz. CO_2 cylinders. **Stock:** Walnut-stained hardwood. **Sights:** Blade front, adjustable rear. **Features:** Velocity to 625 fps (22), 725 fps (177). Receiver grooved for scope mounting. Comes with bulk-fill valve. Imported by Air Rifle Specialists.
Price: $195.00

ANSCHUTZ 2002 MATCH AIR RIFLE
Caliber: 177, single shot. **Barrel:** 26". **Weight:** 10-1/2 lbs. **Length:** 44.5" overall. **Stock:** European walnut, blonde hardwood or colored laminated hardwood; stippled grip and forend. Also available with flat-forend walnut stock for benchrest shooting. **Sights:** Optional sight set #6834. **Features:** Muzzle velocity 575 fps. Balance, weight match the 1907 ISU smallbore rifle. Uses #5021 match trigger. Recoil and vibration free. Fully adjustable cheekpiece and buttplate; accessory rail under forend. Introduced 1988. Imported from Germany by Gunsmithing, Inc., Accuracy International.
Price: Right-hand, blonde hardwood stock . . . . $1,017.50 to $1,275.00
Price: Left-hand, blonde hardwood stock . . . . $1,070.60 to $1,365.00
Price: Right-hand, walnut stock . . . . $1,058.40 to $1,329.00
Price: Right-hand, color laminated stock . . . . $1,073.30 to $1,365.00
Price: Left-hand, color laminated stock $1,121.70
Price: Model 2002D-RT Running Target, right-hand, no sights $1,185.60
Price: #6834 Sight Set . . . . $210.00 to $225.00

BEEMAN BEARCUB AIR RIFLE
Caliber: 177, single shot. **Barrel:** 13". **Weight:** 7.2 lbs. **Length:** 37.8" overall. **Power:** Spring-piston, barrel cocking. **Stock:** Stained hardwood. **Sights:** Hooded post front, open fully adjustable rear. **Features:** Velocity to 915 fps. Polished blue finish; receiver dovetailed for scope mounting. Imported from England by Beeman Precision Airguns.
Price: $325.00

BEEMAN CROW MAGNUM AIR RIFLE
Caliber: 20, 22, 25, single shot. **Barrel:** 16"; 10-groove rifling. **Weight:** 8.5 lbs. **Length:** 46" overall. **Power:** Gas-spring; adjustable power to 32 foot pounds muzzle energy. Barrel-cocking. **Stock:** Classic-style hardwood; hand checkered. **Sights:** For scope use only; built-in base and 1" rings included. **Features:** Adjustable two-stage trigger. Automatic safety. Also available in 22-caliber on special order. Introduced 1992. Imported by Beeman.
Price: $1,220.00

BEEMAN KODIAK AIR RIFLE
Caliber: 25, single shot. **Barrel:** 17.6". **Weight:** 9 lbs. **Length:** 45.6" overall. **Power:** Spring-piston, barrel cocking. **Stock:** Stained hardwood. **Sights:** Blade front, open fully adjustable rear. **Features:** Velocity to 820 fps. Up to 30 foot pounds muzzle energy. Introduced 1993. Imported by Beeman.
Price: $625.00

BEEMAN MAKO AIR RIFLE
Caliber: 177, single shot. **Barrel:** 20", with compensator. **Weight:** 7.3 lbs. **Length:** 38.5" overall. **Power:** Pre-charged pneumatic. **Stock:** Stained beech; Monte Carlo cheekpiece; checkered grip. **Sights:** None furnished. **Features:** Velocity to 930 fps.

Gives over 50 shots per charge. Manual safety; brass trigger blade; vented rubber butt pad. Requires scuba tank for air. Introduced 1994. Imported from England by Beeman.

Price: **$1,000.00**
Price: Mako FT (thumbhole stock) **$1,350.00**

BEEMAN R1 AIR RIFLE

Caliber: 177, 20 or 22, single shot. **Barrel:** 19.6", 12-groove rifling. **Weight:** 8.5 lbs. **Length:** 45.2" overall. **Power:** Spring-piston, barrel cocking. **Stock:** Walnut-stained beech; cut-checkered pistol grip; Monte Carlo comb and cheekpiece; rubber buttpad. **Sights:** Tunnel front with interchangeable inserts, open rear click-adjustable for windage and elevation. Grooved for scope mounting. **Features:** Velocity of 940-1000 fps (177), 860 fps (20), 800 fps (22). Non-drying nylon piston and breech seals. Adjustable metal trigger. Milled steel safety. Right- or left-hand stock. Available with adjustable cheekpiece and buttplate at extra cost. Custom and Super Laser versions available. Imported by Beeman.

Price: Right-hand, 177, 20, 22 .... **$540.00**
Price: Left-hand, 177, 20, 22 .... **$575.00**

BEEMAN R6 AIR RIFLE

Caliber: 177, single shot. **Barrel:** NA. **Weight:** 7.1 lbs. **Length:** 41.8" overall. **Power:** Spring-piston, barrel cocking. **Stock:** Stained hardwood. **Sights:** Tunnel post front, open fully adjustable rear. **Features:** Velocity to 815 fps. Two-stage Rekord adjustable trigger; receiver dovetailed for scope mounting; automatic safety. Introduced 1996. Imported from Germany by Beeman Precision Airguns.

Price: **$325.00**

BEEMAN R1 LASER MK II AIR RIFLE

Caliber: 177, 20, 22, 25, single shot. **Barrel:** 16.1" or 19.6". **Weight:** 8.4 lbs. **Length:** 41.7" overall. **Power:** Spring-piston, barrel cocking. **Stock:** Laminated wood with high cheekpiece, ventilated recoil pad. **Sights:** Tunnel front with interchangeable inserts, open adjustable rear; receiver grooved for scope mounting. **Features:** Velocity to 1150 fps (177). Special powerplant components. Built from the Beeman R1 rifle by Beeman.

Price: **$995.00**

BEEMAN R7 AIR RIFLE

Caliber: 177, 20, single shot. **Barrel:** 17". **Weight:** 6.1 lbs. **Length:** 40.2" overall. **Power:** Spring piston. **Stock:** Stained beech. **Sights:** Hooded front, fully adjustable micrometer click open rear. **Features:** Velocity to 700 fps (177), 620 fps (20). Receiver grooved for scope mounting; double-jointed cocking lever; fully adjustable trigger; checkered grip. Imported by Beeman.

Price: **$325.00**

BEEMAN R9 AIR RIFLE

Caliber: 177, 20, single shot. **Barrel:** NA. **Weight:** 7.3 lbs. **Length:** 43" overall. **Power:** Spring-piston, barrel cocking. **Stock:** Stained hardwood. **Sights:** Tunnel post front, fully adjustable open rear. **Features:** Velocity to 1000 fps (177), 800 fps (20). Adjustable Rekord trigger; automatic safety; receiver dovetailed for scope mounting. Introduced 1996. Imported from Germany by Beeman Precision Airguns.

Price: **$350.00**

Beeman R9 Deluxe Air Rifle

Same as the R9 except has an extended forend stock, checkered pistol grip, grip cap, carved Monte Carlo cheekpiece. Globe front sight with inserts. Introduced 1997. Imported by Beeman.

Price: **$400.00**

BEEMAN R11 AIR RIFLE

Caliber: 177, single shot. **Barrel:** 19.6". **Weight:** 8.8 lbs. **Length:** 47" overall. **Power:** Spring-piston, barrel cocking. **Stock:** Walnut-stained beech; adjustable buttplate and cheekpiece. **Sights:** None furnished. Has dovetail for scope mounting. **Features:** Velocity 910-940 fps. All-steel barrel sleeve. Imported by Beeman.

Price: **$600.00**

BEEMAN SUPER 12 AIR RIFLE

Caliber: 22, 25, 12-shot magazine. **Barrel:** 19", 12-groove rifling. **Weight:** 7.8 lbs. **Length:** 41.7" overall. **Power:** Pre-charged pneumatic; external air reservoir. **Stock:** European walnut. **Sights:** None furnished; drilled and tapped for scope mounting; scope mount included. **Features:** Velocity to 850 fps (25-caliber). Adjustable power setting gives 30-70 shots per 400 cc air bottle. Requires scuba tank for air. Introduced 1995. Imported by Beeman.

Price: **$1,675.00**

BEEMAN S1 MAGNUM AIR RIFLE

Caliber: 177, single shot. **Barrel:** 19". **Weight:** 7.1 lbs. **Length:** 45.5" overall. **Power:** Spring-piston, barrel cocking. **Stock:** Stained beech with Monte Carlo cheekpiece; checkered grip. **Sights:** Hooded post front, fully adjustable micrometer click rear. **Features:** Velocity to 900 fps. Automatic safety; receiver grooved for scope mounting; two-stage adjustable trigger; curved rubber buttpad. Introduced 1995. Imported by Beeman.

Price: **$210.00**

BEEMAN RX-1 GAS-SPRING MAGNUM AIR RIFLE

Caliber: 177, 20, 22, 25, single shot. **Barrel:** 19.6", 12-groove rifling. **Weight:** 8.8 lbs. **Power:** Gas-spring piston air; single stroke barrel cocking. **Stock:** Walnut-finished hardwood, hand checkered, with cheekpiece. Adjustable cheekpiece and buttplate. **Sights:** Tunnel front, click-adjustable rear. **Features:** Velocity adjustable to about 1200 fps. Uses special sealed chamber of air as a mainspring. Gas-spring cannot take a set. Introduced 1990. Imported by Beeman.

Price: 177, 20, 22 or 25 regular, right-hand **$590.00**
Price: 177, 20, 22, 25, left-hand **$625.00**

BEEMAN R1 CARBINE

Caliber: 177, 20, 22, 25, single shot. **Barrel:** 16.1". **Weight:** 8.6 lbs. **Length:** 41.7" overall. **Power:** Spring-piston, barrel cocking. **Stock:** Stained beech; Monte Carlo comb and checkpiece; cut checkered pistol grip; rubber buttpad. **Sights:** Tunnel front with interchangeable inserts, open adjustable rear; receiver grooved for scope mounting. **Features:** Velocity up to 1000 fps (177). Non-drying nylon piston and breech seals. Adjustable metal trigger. Machined steel receiver end cap and safety. Right- or left-hand stock. Imported by Beeman.

Price: 177, 20, 22, 25, right-hand............................... **$540.00**
Price: As above, left-hand **$575.00**
Price: R1-AW (synthetic stock, nickel plating) **$705.00**

BEEMAN/FEINWERKBAU 300-S SERIES MATCH RIFLE

Caliber: 177, single shot. **Barrel:** 19.9", fixed solid with receiver. **Weight:** Approx. 10 lbs. with optional bbl. sleeve. **Length:** 42.8" overall. **Power:** Spring-piston, single stroke sidelever. **Stock:** Match model—walnut, deep forend, adjustable buttplate. **Sights:** Globe front with interchangeable inserts. Click micro. adjustable match aperture rear. Front and rear sights move as a single unit. **Features:** Recoilless, vibration free. Five-way adjustable match trigger. Grooved for scope mounts. Permanent lubrication, steel piston ring. Cocking effort 9 lbs. Optional 10-oz. barrel sleeve. Available from Beeman.

Price: Right-hand **$1,270.00**
Price: Left-hand **$1,370.00**

BEEMAN/FEINWERKBAU 603 AIR RIFLE

Caliber: 177, single shot. **Barrel:** 16.6". **Weight:** 10.8 lbs. **Length:** 43" overall. **Power:** Single stroke pneumatic. **Stock:** Special laminated hardwoods and hard rubber for stability. Multi-colored stock also available. **Sights:** Tunnel front with interchangeable inserts, click micrometer match aperture rear. **Features:** Velocity to 570 fps. Recoilless action; double supported barrel; special, short rifled area frees pellet form barrel faster so shooter's motion has minimum effect on accuracy. Fully adjustable match trigger with separately adjustable trigger and trigger slack weight. Trigger and sights blocked when loading latch is open. Introduced 1997. Imported by Beeman.

Price: **$1,755.00**

BEEMAN/FEINWERKBAU 300-S MINI-MATCH

Caliber: 177, single shot. **Barrel:** 17-1/8". **Weight:** 8.8 lbs. **Length:** 40" overall. **Power:** Spring-piston, single stroke sidelever cocking. **Stock:** Walnut. Stippled grip, adjustable buttplate. Scaled-down for youthful or slightly built shooters. **Sights:** Globe front with interchangeable inserts, micro. adjustable rear. Front and rear sights move as a single unit. **Features:** Recoilless, vibration free. Grooved for scope mounts. Steel piston ring. Cocking effort about 9-1/2 lbs. Barrel sleeve optional. Left-hand model available. Introduced 1978. Imported by Beeman.

Price: Right-hand **$1,270.00**
Price: Left-hand **$1,370.00**

BEEMAN/FEINWERKBAU P70 AIR RIFLE

Caliber: 177, single shot. **Barrel:** 16.6". **Weight:** 10.6 lbs. **Length:** 42.6" overall. **Power:** Precharged pneumatic. **Stock:** Laminated hardwoods and hard rubber for stability. Multi-colored stock also available. **Sights:** Tunnel front with interchangeable inserts, click micormeter match aperture rear. **Features:** Velocity to 570 fps. Recoilless action; double supported barrel; special short rifled area frees pellet from barrel faster so shooter's motion has minimum effect on accuracy. Fully adjustable match trigger with separately adjustable trigger and trigger slack weight. Trigger and sights blocked when loading latch is open. Introduced 1997. Imported by Beeman.

Price: **$1,975.00**

BEEMAN/HW 97 AIR RIFLE

Caliber: 177, 20, single shot. **Barrel:** 17.75". **Weight:** 9.2 lbs. **Length:** 44.1" overall. **Power:** Spring-piston, underlever cocking. **Stock:** Walnut-stained beech; rubber buttpad. **Sights:** None. Receiver grooved for scope mounting. **Features:** Velocity 830 fps (177). Fixed barrel with fully opening, direct loading breech. Adjustable trigger. Introduced 1994. Imported by Beeman Precision Airguns.

Price: Right-hand only **$550.00**

BENJAMIN SHERIDAN PNEUMATIC (PUMP-UP) AIR RIFLES

Caliber: 177 or 22, single shot. **Barrel:** 19-3/8", rifled brass. **Weight:** 5-1/2 lbs. **Length:** 36-1/4" overall. **Power:** Underlever pneumatic, hand pumped. **Stock:** American walnut stock and forend. **Sights:** High ramp front, fully adjustable notch rear. **Features:** Variable velocity to 800 fps. Bolt action with ambidextrous push-pull safety. Black or nickel finish. Introduced 1991. Made in the U.S. by Benjamin Sheridan Co.

Price: Black finish, Model 397 (177), Model 392 (22), about **$130.00**
Price: Nickel finish, Model S397 (177), Model S392 (22), about **$140.00**

BENJAMIN SHERIDAN W.F. AIR RIFLE
Caliber: 177, 20 or 22, single-shot. **Barrel:** 19-3/8", rifled brass. **Weight:** 5 lbs. **Length:** 36-1/2" overall. Power 12-gram CO_2 cylinder. **Stocks:** American walnut with buttplate. **Sights:** High ramp front, fully adjustable notch rear. **Features:** Velocity to 680 fps (177). Bolt action with ambidextrous push-pull safety. Gives about 40 shots per cylinder. Black or nickel finish. Introduced 1991. Made in the U.S. by Benjamin Sheridan Co.

Price: Black finish, Model G397 (177), Model G392 (22), about **$130.00**
Price: Black finish, Model FB9 (20), about........................... **$124.50**

Benjamin Sheridan 397C Pneumatic Carbine
Similar to the standard Model 397 except has 16-3/4" barrel, weighs 4 lbs., 3 oz. Velocity about 650 fps. Introduced 1995. Made in U.S. by Benjamin Sheridan Co.

Price: About **$125.00**

BENJAMIN SHERIDAN CO$_2$ AIR RIFLES
Caliber: 177, 20 or 22, single shot. **Barrel:** 19-3/8", rifled brass. **Weight:** 5 lbs. **Length:** 36-1/2" overall. **Power:** 12-gram CO_2 cylinder. **Stock:** American walnut with buttplate.

BRNO TAU-200 AIR RIFLE
Caliber: 177, single shot. **Barrel:** 19", rifled. **Weight:** 7-1/2 lbs. **Length:** 42" overall. **Power:** 6-oz. CO_2 cartridge. **Stock:** Wood match style with adjustable comb and buttplate. **Sights:** Globe front with interchangeable inserts, fully adjustable open rear. **Features:** Adjustable trigger. Comes with extra seals, large CO_2 bottle, counterweight. Introduced 1993. Imported by Century International Arms, Great Lakes Airguns.

Price: About **$446.50**

BSA MAGNUM SUPERSTAR™ MKII MAGNUM AIR RIFLE, CARBINE
Caliber: 177, 22, 25, single shot. **Barrel:** 18". **Weight:** 8 lbs., 8 oz. **Length:** 43" overall. **Power:** Spring-air, underlever cocking. **Stock:** Oil-finished hardwood; Monte Carlo with cheekpiece, checkered at grip; recoil pad. **Sights:** Ramp front, micrometer adjustable rear. Maxi-Grip scope rail. **Features:** Velocity 1020 fps (177), 800 fps (22), 675 fps (25). Patented rotating breech design. Maxi-Grip scope rail protects optics from recoil; automatic anti-beartrap plus manual safety. Imported from U.K. by Precision Sales International, Inc.

Price: **$540.00**
Price: MKII Carbine (14" barrel, 39-1/2" overall) **$540.00**

BSA MAGNUM SUPERSPORT™ AIR RIFLE
Caliber: 177, 22, 25, single shot. **Barrel:** 18". **Weight:** 6 lbs. 8 oz. **Length:** 41" overall. **Power:** Spring-air, barrel cocking. **Stock:** Oil-finished hardwood; Monte Carlo with cheekpiece, recoil pad. **Sights:** Ramp front, micrometer adjustable rear. Maxi-Grip scope rail. **Features:** Velocity 1020 fps (177), 800 fps (22), 675 fps (25). Patented Maxi-Grip scope rail protects optics from recoil; automatic anti-beartrap plus manual tang safety. Muzzle brake standard. Imported for U.K. by Precision Sales International, Inc.

Price: **$289.00**
Price: Carbine, 14" barrel, muzzle brake **$323.00**

BROLIN MAX VELOCITY SM1000 AIR RIFLE
Caliber: 177 or 22, single shot. **Barrel:** 19.5". **Weight:** 9.2 lbs. **Length:** 46" overall. **Stock:** Walnut-stained hardwood; smooth, checkered or adjustable styles. **Sights:** Adjustable blade front, fully adjustable rear. Comes with Weaver-style base mount. **Features:** Velocity 1100+ fps (177) 900+ fps (22). Telescoping side cocking lever; double locking safety system. Introduced 1997. Imported by Brolin Industries, Inc.

Price: 177 or 22, smooth stock...................................... **$199.95**
Price: 177 or 22, checkered stock **$219.95**
Price: 177 or 22, adjustable stock **$249.95**

BSA MAGNUM AIRSPORTER RB2 MAGNUM AIR RIFLE, CARBINE
Caliber: 177, 22, 25, single shot. **Barrel:** 18". **Weight:** 8 lbs., 4 oz. **Length:** 44-1/2" overall. **Power:** Spring-air, underlever cocking. **Stock:** Oil-finished hardwood; Monte Carlo with cheekpiece, checkered at grip; recoil pad. **Sights:** Ramp front, micrometer adjustable rear, comes with Maxi-Grip scope rail. **Features:** Velocity 1020 fps (177), 800 fps (22), 675 fps (25). Maxi-Grip scope rail protects optics from recoil; automatic anti-beartrap plus manual tang safety. Imported from U.K. by Precision Sales International, Inc.

Price: **$450.00**
Price: RB2 Carbine (14" barrel, 41" overall, muzzle brake) **$474.50**

BSA MAGNUM GOLDSTAR MAGNUM AIR RIFLE
Caliber: 177, 22, 10-shot repeater. **Barrel:** 18". **Weight:** 8 lbs., 8 oz. **Length:** 42.5" overall. **Power:** Spring-air, underlever cocking. **Stock:** Oil-finished hardwood; Monte Carlo with cheekpiece, checkered at grip; recoil pad. **Sights:** Ramp front, micrometer adjustable rear; comes with Maxi-Grip scope rail. **Features:** Velocity 1020 fps (177), 800 fps (22). Patented 10-shot indexing magazine; Maxi-Grip scope rail pro-

tects optics from recoil; automatic anti-beartrap plus manual safety; muzzlebrake standard. Imported from U.K. by Precision Sales International, Inc.

Price: **$847.00**

BSA MAGNUM SUPERTEN AIR RIFLE
Caliber: 177, 22 10-shot repeater. **Barrel:** 17-1/2". **Weight:** 7 lbs., 8 oz. **Length:** 37" overall. **Power:** Precharged pneumatic via buddy bottle. **Stock:** Oil-finished hardwood; Monte Carlo with cheekpiece, cut checkering at grip; adjustable recoil pad. **Sights:** No sights; intended for scope use. **Features:** Velocity 1300+ fps (177), 1000+ fps (22). Patented 10-shot indexing magazine, bolt-action loading. Left-hand version also available. Imported from U.K. by Precision Sales International, Inc.

Price: **$999.00**
Price: Left-hand **$1,069.00**

BSA MAGNUM STUTZEN RB2 AIR RIFLE
Caliber: 177, 22, 25, single shot. **Barrel:** 14". **Weight:** 8 lbs., 8 oz. **Length:** 37" overall. **Power:** Spring-air, underlever cocking. **Stock:** Oil-finished hardwood; Monte Carlo with cheekpiece; checkered at grip, recoil pad. **Sights:** Ramp front, adjustable leaf rear. Comes with Maxi-Grip scope rail. **Features:** Velocity 1020 fps (177), 800 fps (22), 675 fps (25). Maxi-Grip scope rail protects optics from recoil; automatic anti-beartrap plus manual tang safety. Imported from U.K. by Precision Sales International, Inc.

Price: **$698.00**

BSA METEOR MK6 AIR RIFLE
Caliber: 177, 22, single shot. **Barrel:** 18". **Weight:** 6 lbs. **Length:** 41" overall. **Power:** Spring-air, barrel cocking. **Stock:** Oil-finished hardwood. **Sights:** Ramp front, micrometer adjustable rear. **Features:** Velocity 650 fps (177), 500 fps (22). Automatic anti-beartrap; manual tang safety. Receiver grooved for scope mounting. Imported from U.K. by Precision Sales International, Inc.

Price: Rifle or carbine **$224.00**

COPPERHEAD BLACK FIRE RIFLE
Caliber: 177 BB only. **Barrel:** 14" smoothbore steel. **Weight:** 2 lbs., 7 oz. **Length:** 31-1/2" overall. **Power:** Pneumatic, hand pumped. **Stock:** Textured plastic. **Sights:** Blade front, open adjustable rear. **Features:** Velocity to 437 fps. Introduced 1996. Made in U.S. by Crosman Corp.

Price: About **$25.00**

COPPERHEAD BLACK SERPENT RIFLE
Caliber: 177 pellets, 5-shot, on BB, 195-shot magazine. **Barrel:** 19-1/2" smoothbore steel. **Weight:** 2 lbs., 14 oz. **Length:** 35-7/8" overall. **Power:** Pneumatic, single pump. **Stock:** Textured plastic. **Sights:** Blade front, open adjustable rear. **Features:** Velocity to 405 fps. Introduced 1996. Made in U.S. by Crosman Corp.

Price: About **$40.00**

COPPERHEAD BLACK LIGHTNING RIFLE
Caliber: 177 BB, 15-shot magazine. **Barrel:** 14" smoothbore. **Weight:** 2 lbs. **Length:** 32" overall. **Power:** Single-stroke pneumatic. **Stock:** Textured plastic. **Sights:** Bead front. **Features:** Velocity to 350 fps. Cross-bolt safety. Introduced 1996. Made in U.S. by Crosman Corp.

Price: About **$25.00**

CROSMAN MODEL 66 POWERMASTER
Caliber: 177 (single shot pellet) or BB, 200-shot reservoir. **Barrel:** 20", rifled steel. **Weight:** 3 lbs. **Length:** 38-1/2" overall. **Power:** Pneumatic; hand pumped. **Stock:** Wood-grained ABS plastic; checkered pistol grip and forend. **Sights:** Ramp front, fully adjustable open rear. **Features:** Velocity about 645 fps. Bolt action, cross-bolt safety. Introduced 1983. From Crosman.

Price: About **$55.00**
Price: Model 66RT (as above with Realtree® camo finish), about......... **$65.00**
Price: Model 664X (as above with 4x scope) **$70.00**
Price: Model 664SB (as above with silver and black finish), about **$70.00**
Price: Model 664GT (black and gold finish, 4x scope) about.............. **$70.00**

CROSMAN MODEL 760 PUMPMASTER
Caliber: 177 pellets (single shot) or BB (200-shot reservoir). **Barrel:** 19-1/2", rifled steel. **Weight:** 2 lbs., 12 oz. **Length:** 33.5" overall. **Power:** Pneumatic, hand pumped. **Stock:** Walnut-finished ABS plastic stock and forend. **Features:** Velocity to 590 fps (BBs, 10 pumps). Short stroke, power determined by number of strokes. Post front sight and adjustable rear sight. Cross-bolt safety. Introduced 1966. From Crosman.

Price: About **$36.00**
Price: Model 760SB (silver and black finish), about.................... **$50.00**

CROSMAN MODEL 782 BLACK DIAMOND AIR RIFLE
Caliber: 177 pellets (5-shot clip) or BB (195-shot reservoir). **Barrel:** 18", rifled steel. **Weight:** 3 lbs. **Power:** CO_2 Powerlet. **Stock:** Wood-grained ABS plastic; checkered grip and forend. **Sights:** Blade front, open adjustable rear. **Features:** Velocity up to 595 fps (pellets), 650 fps (BB). Black finish with white diamonds. Introduced 1990. From Crosman.

Price: About **$60.00**

CROSMAN MODEL 795 SPRING MASTER RIFLE
Caliber: 177, single shot. **Barrel:** Rifled steel. **Weight:** 4 lbs., 8 oz. **Length:** 42" overall. **Power:** Spring-piston. **Stock:** Black synthetic. **Sights:** Hooded front, fully adjustable rear. **Features:** Velocity about 550 fps. Introduced 1995. From Crosman.
Price: About $90.00

CROSMAN MODEL 1077 REPEATAIR RIFLE
Caliber: 177 pellets, 12-shot clip. **Barrel:** 20.3", rifled steel. **Weight:** 3 lbs., 11 oz. **Length:** 38.8" overall. **Power:** CO_2 Powerlet. **Stock:** Textured synthetic or American walnut. **Sights:** Blade front, fully adjustable rear. **Features:** Velocity 590 fps. Removable 12-shot clip. True semi-automatic action. Introduced 1993. From Crosman.
Price: About $62.75
Price: 1077SB Silver Series (black stock, silver bbl.). $65.00
Price: 1077W (walnut stock) $100.00

CROSMAN MODEL 1389 BACKPACKER RIFLE
Caliber: 177, single shot. **Barrel:** 14", rifled steel. **Weight:** 3 lbs. 3 oz. **Length:** 31" overall. **Power:** Hand pumped, pneumatic. **Stock:** Composition, skeletal type. **Sights:** Blade front, rear adjustable for windage and elevation. **Features:** Velocity to 560 fps. Detachable stock. Receiver grooved for scope mounting. Metal parts blued. From Crosman.
Price: About $70.00

CROSMAN MODEL 2100 CLASSIC AIR RIFLE
Caliber: 177 pellets (single shot), or BB (200-shot BB reservoir). **Barrel:** 21", rifled. **Weight:** 4 lbs., 13 oz. **Length:** 39-3/4" overall. **Power:** Pump-up, pneumatic. **Stock:** Wood-grained checkered ABS plastic. **Features:** Three pumps give about 450 fps, 10 pumps about 755 fps (BBs). Cross-bolt safety; concealed reservoir holds over 200 BBs. From Crosman.
Price: About $70.00
Price: Model 2100SB (silver and black finish), about. $80.00
Price: Model 2104GT (black and gold finish, 4x scope), about $80.00
Price: Model 2100W (walnut stock, pellets only), about. $100.00

CROSMAN MODEL 2200 MAGNUM AIR RIFLE
Caliber: 22, single shot. **Barrel:** 19", rifled steel. **Weight:** 4 lbs., 12 oz. **Length:** 39" overall. **Stock:** Full-size, wood-grained ABS plastic with checkered grip and forend or American walnut. **Sights:** Ramp front, open step-adjustable rear. **Features:** Variable pump power—three pumps give 395 fps, six pumps 530 fps, 10 pumps 595 fps (average). Full-size adult air rifle. Has white line spacers at pistol grip and buttplate. Introduced 1978. From Crosman.
Price: About $70.00
Price: 2200W, about. $100.00

DAISY MODEL 840
Caliber: 177 pellet single shot; or BB 350-shot. **Barrel:** 19", smoothbore, steel. **Weight:** 2.7 lbs. **Length:** 36.8" overall. **Power:** Pneumatic, single pump. **Stock:** Moulded wood-grain stock and forend. **Sights:** Ramp front, open, adjustable rear. **Features:** Muzzle velocity 335 fps (BB), 300 fps (pellet). Steel buttplate; straight pull bolt action; cross-bolt safety. Forend forms pump lever. Introduced 1978. From Daisy Mfg. Co.
Price: About $33.95

DAISY/POWER LINE 853
Caliber: 177 pellets. **Barrel:** 20.9"; 12-groove rifling, high-grade solid steel by Lothar Waltherô, precision crowned; bore size for precision match pellets. **Weight:** 5.08 lbs. **Length:** 38.9" overall. **Power:** Single-pump pneumatic. **Stock:** Full-length, select American hardwood, stained and finished; black buttplate with white spacers. **Sights:** Globe front with four aperture inserts; precision micrometer adjustable rear peep sight mounted on a standard 3/8" dovetail receiver mount. **Features:** Single shot. From Daisy Mfg. Co.
Price: About $225.00

DAISY/POWER LINE 856 PUMP-UP AIRGUN
Caliber: 177 pellets (single shot) or BB (100-shot reservoir). **Barrel:** Rifled steel with shroud. **Weight:** 2.7 lbs. **Length:** 37.4" overall. **Power:** Pneumatic pump-up. **Stock:** Moulded wood-grain with Monte Carlo cheekpiece. **Sights:** Ramp and blade front, open rear adjustable for elevation. **Features:** Velocity from 315 fps (two pumps) to 650 fps (10 pumps). Shoots BBs or pellets. Heavy die-cast metal receiver. Cross-bolt trigger-block safety. Introduced 1984. From Daisy Mfg. Co.
Price: About $39.95

DAISY MODEL 990 DUAL-POWER AIR RIFLE
Caliber: 177 pellets (single shot) or BB (100-shot magazine). **Barrel:** Rifled steel. **Weight:** 4.1 lbs. **Length:** 37.4" overall. **Power:** Pneumatic pump-up and 12-gram CO_2. **Stock:** Moulded woodgrain. **Sights:** Ramp and blade front, adjustable open rear. **Features:** Velocity to 650 fps (BB), 630 fps (pellet). Choice of pump or CO_2 power. Shoots BBs or pellets. Heavy die-cast receiver dovetailed for scope mount. Cross-bolt trigger block safety. Introduced 1993. From Daisy Mfg. Co.
Price: About $62.95

DAISY 1938 RED RYDER 60th ANNIVERSARY CLASSIC
Caliber: BB, 650-shot repeating action. **Barrel:** Smoothbore steel with shroud. **Weight:** 2.2 lbs. **Length:** 35.4" overall. **Stock:** Walnut stock burned with Red Ryder lariat signature. **Sights:** Post front, adjustable V-slot rear. **Features:** Walnut forend. Saddle ring with leather thong. Lever cocking. Gravity feed. Controlled velocity. One of Daisy's most popular guns. From Daisy Mfg. Co.
Price: About $40.95

DAISY/POWER LINE 1170 PELLET RIFLE
Caliber: 177, single shot. **Barrel:** Rifled steel. **Weight:** 5.5 lbs. **Length:** 42.5" overall. **Power:** Spring-air, barrel cocking. **Stock:** Hardwood. **Sights:** Hooded post front, micrometer adjustable open rear. **Features:** Velocity to 800 fps. Monte Carlo comb. Introduced 1995. From Daisy Mfg. Co.
Price: About $138.95
Price: Model 131 (velocity to 600 fps) $120.95
Price: Model 1150 (black copolymer stock, velocity to 600 fps) $77.95

DAISY/POWER LINE EAGLE 7856 PUMP-UP AIRGUN
Caliber: 177 (pellets), BB, 100-shot BB magazine. **Barrel:** Rifled steel with shroud. **Weight:** 2-3/4 lbs. **Length:** 37.4" overall. **Stock:** Moulded wood-grain plastic. **Sights:** Ramp and blade front, open rear adjustable for elevation. **Features:** Velocity from 315 fps (two pumps) to 650 fps (10 pumps). Finger grooved forend. Cross-bolt trigger-block safety. Introduced 1985. From Daisy Mfg. Co.
Price: With 4x scope, about $51.95

DAISY/POWER LINE 880
Caliber: 177 pellet or BB, 50-shot BB magazine, single shot for pellets. **Barrel:** Rifled steel. **Weight:** 3.7 lbs. **Length:** 37.6" overall. **Power:** Multi-pump pneumatic. **Stock:** Moulded wood grain; Monte Carlo comb. **Sights:** Hooded front, adjustable rear. **Features:** Velocity to 685 fps. (BB). Variable power (velocity and range) increase with pump strokes; resin receiver with dovetail scope mount. Introduced 1997. Made in U.S. by Daisy Mfg. Co.
Price: About $52.95
Price: Model 4880 with Glo-Point fiber optic sight $57.95

DAISY/POWER LINE 1000 AIR RIFLE
Caliber: 177, single shot. **Barrel:** NA. **Weight:** 6 lbs. **Length:** 43" overall. **Power:** Spring-air, barrel cocking. **Stock:** Stained hardwood. **Sights:** Hooded blade front on ramp, fully adjustable micrometer rear. **Features:** Velocity to 1000 fps. Blued finish; trigger block safety. Introduced 1997. From Daisy Mfg. Co.
Price: About $214.95

DAISY/YOUTHLINE MODEL 105 AIR RIFLE
Caliber: BB, 400-shot magazine. **Barrel:** 13-1/2". **Weight:** 1.6 lbs. **Length:** 29.8" overall. **Power:** Spring. **Stock:** Moulded woodgrain. **Sights:** Blade on ramp front, fixed rear. **Features:** Velocity to 275 fps. Blue finish. Cross-bolt trigger block safety. Made in U.S. by Daisy Mfg. Co.
Price: $24.95

DAISY/YOUTHLINE MODEL 95 AIR RIFLE
Caliber: BB, 700-shot magazine. **Barrel:** 18". **Weight:** 2.4 lbs. **Length:** 35.2" overall. **Power:** Spring. **Stock:** Stained hardwood. **Sights:** Blade on ramp front, open adjustable rear. **Features:** Velocity to 325 fps. Cross-bolt trigger block safety. Made in U.S. by Daisy Mfg. Co.
Price: $38.95

"GAT" AIR RIFLE
Caliber: 177, single shot. **Barrel:** 17-1/4" cocked, 23-1/4" extended. **Weight:** 3 lbs. **Power:** Spring-piston. **Stock:** Composition. **Sights:** Fixed. **Features:** Velocity about 450 fps. Shoots pellets, darts, corks. Imported from England by Stone Enterprises, Inc.
Price: $38.95

HAMMERLI AR 50 AIR RIFLE
Caliber: 177. **Barrel:** 19.8". **Weight:** 10 lbs. **Length:** 43.2" overall. **Power:** Compressed air. **Stock:** Anatomically-shaped universal and right-hand; match style; multi-colored laminated wood. **Sights:** Interchangeable element tunnel front, fully adjustable Hammerli peep rear. **Features:** Vibration-free firing release; fully adjustable match trigger and trigger stop; stainless air tank, built-in pressure gauge. Gives 270 shots per filling. Introduced 1998. Imported from Switzerland by Sigarms, Inc.
Price: .... NA

HAMMERLI MODEL 450 MATCH AIR RIFLE
Caliber: 177, single shot. **Barrel:** 19.5". **Weight:** 9.8 lbs. **Length:** 43.3" overall. **Power:** Pneumatic. **Stock:** Match style with stippled grip, rubber buttpad. Beach or walnut. **Sights:** Match tunnel front, Hammerli diopter rear. **Features:** Velocity about 560 fps. Removable sights; forend sling rail; adjustable trigger; adjustable comb. Introduced 1994. Imported from Switzerland by Sigarms, Inc.
Price: Beech stock $1,355.00
Price: Walnut stock. $1,395.00

MARKSMAN BB BUDDY AIR RIFLE
Caliber: 177, 20-shot magazine. **Barrel:** 10.5" smoothbore. **Weight:** 1.6 lbs. **Length:** 33" overall. **Power:** Spring-air. **Stock:** Moulded composition. **Sights:** Blade on ramp front, adjustable V-slot rear. **Features:** Velocity 275 fps. Positive feed; automatic

safety. Youth-sized lightweight design. Introduced 1998. Made in U.S. From Marksman Products.

Price: $27.95

MARKSMAN 1750 BB BIATHLON REPEATER RIFLE

Caliber: BB, 18-shot magazine. **Barrel:** 15", smoothbore. **Weight:** 4.7 lbs. **Power:** Spring-piston, barrel cocking. **Stock:** Moulded composition. **Sights:** Tunnel front, open adjustable rear. **Features:** Velocity of 450 fps. Automatic safety. Positive Feed System loads a BB each time gun is cocked. Introduced 1990. From Marksman Products.

Price: $59.75

MARKSMAN 1798 COMPETITION TRAINER AIR RIFLE

Caliber: 177, single shot. **Barrel:** 15", rifled. **Weight:** 4.7 lbs. **Power:** Spring-air, barrel cocking. **Stock:** Synthetic. **Sights:** Laserhawk fiber optic front, match-style diopter rear. **Features:** Velocity about 495 fps. Automatic safety. Introduced 1998. Made in U.S. From Marksman Products.

Price: $70.00

MARKSMAN 1710 PLAINSMAN AIR RIFLE

Caliber: 177, BB, 20-shot repeater. **Barrel:** Smoothbore steel with shroud. **Weight:** 2.25 lbs. **Length:** 34" overall. **Power:** Spring-air. **Stock:** Stained hardwood. **Sights:** Blade on ramp front, adjustable V-slot rear. **Features:** Velocity about 275 fps. Positive feed; automatic safety. Introduced 1994. Made in U.S. From Marksman Products.

Price: $36.45

MARKSMAN 1745 BB REPEATER AIR RIFLE

Caliber: 177 BB or pellet, 18-shot BB reservoir. **Barrel:** 15-1/2", rifled. **Weight:** 4.75 lbs. **Length:** 36" overall. **Power:** Spring-air. **Stock:** Moulded composition with ambidextrous Monte Carlo cheekpiece and rubber recoil pad. **Sights:** Hooded front, adjustable rear. **Features:** Velocity about 450 fps. Break-barrel action; automatic safety. Uses BBs, pellets, darts or bolts. Introduced 1997. Made in the U.S. From Marksman Products.

Price: $58.00
Price: Model 1745S (same as above except combo with #1804 4x20 scope) $73.00

MARKSMAN 1790 BIATHLON TRAINER

Caliber: 177, single shot. **Barrel:** 15", rifled. **Weight:** 4.7 lbs. **Power:** Spring-air, barrel cocking. **Stock:** Synthetic. **Sights:** Hooded front, match-style diopter rear. **Features:** Velocity of 450 fps. Endorsed by the U.S. Shooting Team. Introduced 1989. From Marksman Products.

Price: $70.00

MARKSMAN 2015 LASERHAWK™ BB REPEATER AIR RIFLE

Caliber: 177 BB, 20-shot magazine. **Barrel:** 10.5" smoothbore. **Weight:** 1.6 lbs. **Length:** Adjustable to 33", 34" or 35" overall. **Power:** Spring-air. **Stock:** Moulded composition. **Sights:** Fixed fiber optic front sight, adjustable elevation V-slot rear. **Features:** Velocity about 275 fps. Positive feed; automatic safety. Adjustable stock. Introduced 1997. Made in the U.S. From Marksman Products.

Price: $33.00

RWS MODEL 75S T01 MATCH

Caliber: 177, single shot. **Barrel:** 19".**Weight:** 11 lbs. **Length:** 43.7" overall. **Power:** Dual spring piston. **Stock:** Oil-finished beech with stippled grip; adjustable cheekpiece, buttplate. **Sights:** Globe front, fully adjustable match peep rear. **Features:** Velocity of 580 fps. Fully adjustable trigger; recoilless action. Introduced 1990. Imported from Germany by Dynamit Nobel-RWS.

Price: $1,650.00

RWS/DIANA MODEL 24 AIR RIFLE

Caliber: 177, 22, single shot. **Barrel:** 17", rifled. **Weight:** 6 lbs. **Length:** 42" overall. **Power:** Spring-air, barrel cocking. **Stock:** Beech. **Sights:** Hooded front, adjustable rear. **Features:** Velocity of 700 fps (177). Easy cocking effort; blue finish. Imported from Germany by Dynamit Nobel-RWS, Inc.

Price: $205.00
Price: Model 24C $205.00

RWS/Diana Model 34 Air Rifle

Similar to the Model 24 except has 19" barrel, weighs 7.5 lbs. Gives velocity of 1000 fps (177), 800 fps (22). Adjustable trigger, synthetic seals. Comes with scope rail.

Price: 177 or 22 .... $285.00
Price: Model 34N (nickel-plated metal, black epoxy-coated wood stock) ... $330.00
Price: Model 34BC (matte black metal, black stock, 4x32 scope, mounts) .. $485.00

RWS/DIANA MODEL 36 AIR RIFLE

Caliber: 177, 22, single shot. **Barrel:** 19", rifled. **Weight:** 8 lbs. **Length:** 45" overall. **Power:** Spring-air, barrel cocking. **Stock:** Beech. **Sights:** Hooded front (interchangeable inserts available), adjustable rear. **Features:** Velocity of 1000 fps (177-

cal.). Comes with scope mount; two-stage adjustable trigger. Imported from Germany by Dynamit Nobel-RWS, Inc.

Price: $415.00
Price: Model 36 Carbine (same as Model 36 rifle except has 15" barrel) $415.00

RWS/DIANA MODEL 52 AIR RIFLE

Caliber: 177, 22, single shot. **Barrel:** 17", rifled. **Weight:** 8-1/2 lbs. **Length:** 43" overall. **Power:** Spring-air, sidelever cocking. **Stock:** Beech, with Monte Carlo, cheekpiece, checkered grip and forend. **Sights:** Ramp front, adjustable rear. **Features:** Velocity of 1100 fps (177). Blue finish. Solid rubber buttpad. Imported from Germany by Dynamit Nobel-RWS, Inc.

Price: $535.00
Price: Model 52 Deluxe (select walnut stock, rosewood grip and forend caps, palm swell grip) $775.00
Price: Model 48B (as above except matte black metal, black stock) $535.00
Price: Model 48 (same as Model 52 except no Monte Carlo, cheekpiece or checkering) $530.00

RWS MODEL CA 100 AIR RIFLE

Caliber: 177, single shot. **Barrel:** 22". **Weight:** 11.4 lbs. **Length:** 44" overall. **Power:** Compressed air; interchangeable cylinders. **Stock:** Laminated hardwood with adjustable cheekpiece and buttplate. **Sights:** Tunnel front, match rear. **Features:** Gives 250 shots per full charge. Double-sided power regulator. Introduced 1995. Imported from England by Dynamit Nobel-RWS, Inc.

Price: $2,200.00

RWS/DIANA MODEL 45 AIR RIFLE

Caliber: 177, single shot. **Weight:** 8 lbs. **Length:** 45" overall. **Power:** Spring-air, barrel cocking. **Stock:** Walnut-finished hardwood with rubber recoil pad. **Sights:** Globe front with interchangeable inserts, micro. click open rear with four-way blade. **Features:** Velocity of 820 fps. Dovetail base for either micrometer peep sight or scope mounting. Automatic safety. Imported from Germany by Dynamit Nobel-RWS, Inc.

Price: $330.00

RWS/DIANA MODEL 54 AIR KING RIFLE

Caliber: 177, 22, single shot. **Barrel:** 17". **Weight:** 9 lbs. **Length:** 43" overall.**Power:** Spring-air, sidelever cocking. **Stock:** Walnut with Monte Carlo cheekpiece, checkered grip and forend. **Sights:** Ramp front, fully adjustable rear. **Features:** Velocity to 1000 fps (177), 900 fps (22). Totally recoilless system; floating action absorbs recoil. Imported from Germany by Dynamit Nobel-RWS, Inc.

Price: $750.00

SLAVIA MODEL 631 AIR RIFLE

Caliber: 177, single shot. **Barrel:** 21". **Weight:** 6.8 lbs. **Length:** 45.5" overall. **Power:** Spring-air; barrel cocking. **Stock:** Oil-finished European hardwood; checkered forend. **Sights:** Hooded post front, fully adjustable open rear. **Features:** Velocity to 720 fps. Adjustable two-stage trigger; receiver grooved for scope mounting; automatic safety. Introduced 1996. Imported from the Czech Republic by Great Lakes Airguns.

Price: $114.40

STEYR LG1P AIR RIFLE

Caliber: 177, single shot. **Barrel:** 20.75", (10.75" rifled). **Weight:** 10.5 lbs. **Length:** 51.7" overall. **Power:** Precharged air. **Stock:** Match. Laminated wood. Adjustable buttplate and cheekpiece. **Sights:** Precision diopter. **Features:** Velocity 577 fps. Air cylinders are refillable; about 320 shots per cylinder. Designed for 10-meter shooting. Introduced 1996. Imported from Austria by Nygord Precision Products.

Price: About $1,295.00
Price: Left-hand, about $1,350.00

WEBLEY PATRIOT AIR RIFLE

Caliber: 22, single shot. **Barrel:** 17.5". **Weight:** 9 lbs. **Length:** 45.6" overall. **Power:** Spring-air; barrel cocking. **Stock:** Walnut-stained beech; checkered grip; rubber buttpad. **Sights:** Post front, fully adjustable open rear. **Features:** Velocity to 932 fps. Automatic safety; receiver grooved for scope mounting. Imported from England by Great Lakes Airguns.

Price: $561.12

WHISCOMBE JW SERIES AIR RIFLES

Caliber: 177, 20, 22, 25, single shot. **Barrel:** 17", Lothar Walther. Polygonal rifling. **Weight:** 9 lbs., 8 oz. **Length:** 39" overall. **Power:** Dual spring-piston, multi-stroke; underlever cocking. **Stock:** Walnut with adjustable buttplate and cheekpiece. **Sights:** None furnished; grooved scope rail. **Features:** Velocity 660-1000 (JW80) fps (22-caliber, fixed barrel) depending upon model. Interchangeable barrels; automatic safety; muzzle weight; semi-floating action; twin opposed pistons with counterwound springs; adjustable trigger. All models include H.O.T. System (Harmonic Optimization Tunable System). Introduced 1995. Imported from England by Pelaire Products.

Price: JW50, MKII fixed barrel only $1,895.00
Price: JW60, MKII fixed barrel only $1,895.00
Price: JW70, MKII fixed barrel only $1,950.00
Price: JW80, MKII $1,995.00

C-H/4-D Heavyweight Champion

Frame: Cast iron
Frame Type: O-frame
Die Thread: 7/8-14 or 1-14
Avg. Rounds Per Hour: NA
Ram Stroke: 3-1/4"
Weight: 26 lbs.
Features: 1.185" diameter ram with 16 square inches of bearing surface; ram drilled to allow passage of spent primers; solid steel handle; toggle that slightly breaks over the top dead center. Includes universal primer arm with large and small punches. From C-H Tool & Die/4-D Custom Die.
Price: **$220.00**

C-H/4-D No. 444

Frame: Aluminum alloy
Frame Type: H-frame
Die Thread: 7/8-14
Avg. Rounds Per Hour: 200
Ram Stroke: 3-3/4"
Weight: 12 lbs.
Features: Two 7/8" solid steel shaft "H" supports; platen rides on permanently lubed bronze bushings; loads smallest pistol to largest magnum rifle cases and has strength to full-length resize. Includes four rams, large and small primer arm and primer catcher. From C-H Tool & Die/4-D Custom Die.
Price: **$214.50**

C-H/4-D No. 444

C-H/4-D No. 444-X Pistol Champ

Frame: Aluminum alloy
Frame Type: H-frame
Die Thread: 7/8-14
Avg. Rounds Per Hour: 200
Ram Stroke: 3-3/4"
Weight: 12 lbs.
Features: Tungsten carbide sizing die; Speed Seater seating die with tapered entrance to automatically align bullet on case mouth; automatic primer feed for large or small primers; push-button powder measure with easily changed bushings for 215 powder/load combinations; taper crimp die. Conversion kit for caliber changeover available. From C-H Tool & Die/4-D Custom Die.
Price: .... **See chart for pricing.**

C-H/4-D 444-X
Pistol Champ

FORSTER Co-Ax Press B-2

Frame: Cast iron
Frame Type: Modified O-frame
Die Thread: 7/8-14
Avg. Rounds Per Hour: 120
Ram Stroke: 4"
Weight: 18 lbs.
Features: Snap in/snap out die change; spent primer catcher with drop tube threaded into carrier below shellholder; automatic, handle-activated, cammed shellholder with opposing spring-loaded jaws to contact extractor groove; floating guide rods for alignment and reduced friction; no torque on the head due to design of linkage and pivots; shellholder jaws that float with die permitting case to center in the die; right- or left-hand operation; priming device for seating to factory specifications. "S" shellholder jaws included. From Forster Products.
Price: **$294.00**
Price: Extra shellholder jaws **$24.00**

Forster Co-Ax

HOLLYWOOD Senior Press

Frame: Ductile iron
Frame Type: O-frame
Die Thread: 7/8-14
Avg. Rounds Per Hour: 50-100
Ram Stroke: 6-1/2"
Weight: 50 lbs.
Features: Leverage and bearing surfaces ample for reloading cartridges or swaging bullets. Precision ground one-piece 2-1/2" pillar with base; operating

METALLIC CARTRIDGE PRESSES

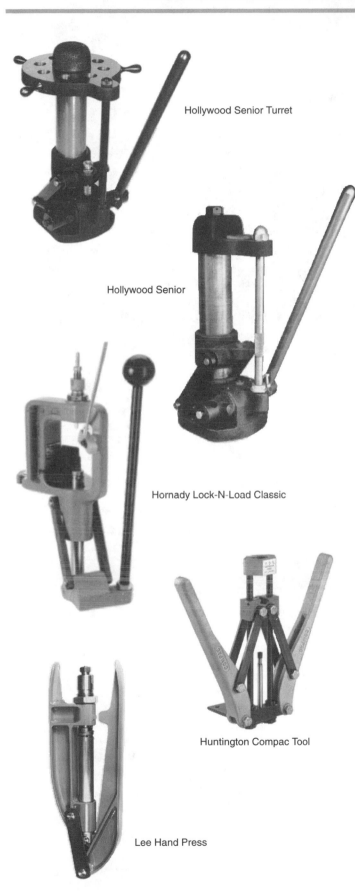

Hollywood Senior Turret

Hollywood Senior

Hornady Lock-N-Load Classic

Huntington Compac Tool

Lee Hand Press

handle of 3/4" steel and 15" long; 5/8" steel tie-down rod fro added strength when swaging; heavy steel toggle and camming arms held by 1/2" steel pins in reamed holes. The 1-1/2" steel die bushing takes standard threaded dies; removed, it allows use of Hollywood shotshell dies. From Hollywood Engineering.

Price: **$500.00**

HOLLYWOOD Senior Turret Press

Frame: Ductile iron
Frame Type: H-frame
Die Thread: 7/8-14
Avg. Rounds Per Hour: 50-100
Ram Stroke: 6-1/2"
Weight: 50 lbs.
Features: Same features as Senior press except has three-position turret head; holes in turret may be tapped 1-1/2" or 7/8" or four of each. Height, 15". Comes complete with one turret indexing handle; one 1-1/2" to 7/8" die hole buching; one 5/8" tie down bar for swaging. From Hollywood Engineering.

Price: **$600.00**

HORNADY Lock-N-Load Classic

Frame: Die cast heat-treated aluminum alloy
Frame Type: O-frame
Die Thread: 7/8-14
Avg. Rounds Per Hour: NA
Ram Stroke: 3-5/8"
Weight: 14 lbs.
Features: Features Lock-N-Load bushing system that allows instant die changeovers. Solid steel linkage arms that rotate on otool pins; 30° angled frame design for improved visibility and accessibility; primer arm automatically moves in and out of ram for primer pickup and solid seating; two primer arms for large and small primers; long offset handle for increased leverage and unobstructed reloading; lifetime warranty. Comes as a package with primer catcher, PPS automatic primer feed and three Lock-N-Load die bushings. Dies and shellholder available separately or as a kit with primer catcher, positive priming system, automatic primer feed, three die bushings and reloading accessories. From Hornady Mfg. Co.

Price: Classic Reloading Package **$99.95**
Price: Classic Reloading Kit **$229.95**

HUNTINGTON Compac Tool

Frame: Aircraft aluminum
Frame Type: NA
Die Thread: 7/8-14
Avg. Rounds Per Hour: NA
Ram Stroke: NA
Weight: 37 oz.
Features: Small and lightweight for portability; performs all standard reloading operations; sufficient leverage to full-length resize, decap military brass and case-form. Accepts standard shellholders. Is bench mountable. Dimensions: 3-1/2" x 9". From Huntington Die Specialties.

Price: **$74.98**

LEE Hand Press

Frame: ASTM 380 aluminum
Frame Type: NA
Die Thread: 7/8-14
Avg. Rounds Per Hour: 100
Ram Stroke: 3-1/4"
Weight: 1 lb., 8 oz.
Features: Small and lightweight for portability; compound linkage for handling up to 375 H&H and case forming. Dies and shellholder not included. From Lee Precision, Inc.

Price: **$22.98**

METALLIC CARTRIDGE PRESSES

LEE Challenger Press

Frame: ASTM 380 aluminum
Frame Type: O-frame
Die Thread: 7/8-14
Avg. Rounds Per Hour: 100
Ram Stroke: 3-1/2"
Weight: 4 lbs., 1 oz.
Features: Larger than average opening with 30˚ offset for maximum hand clearance; steel connecting pins; spent primer catcher; handle adjustable for start and stop positions; handle repositions for left- or right-hand use; shortened handle travel to prevent springing the frame from alignment. Dies and shellholders not included. From Lee Precision, Inc.
Price: **$43.00**

LEE Loader

Kit consists of reloading dies to be used with mallet or soft hammer. Neck sizes only. Comes with powder charge cup. From Lee Precision, Inc.
Price: **$19.98**

LEE Reloader Press

Frame: ASTM 380 aluminum
Frame Type: C-frame
Die Thread: 7/8-14
Avg. Rounds Per Hour: 100
Ram Stroke: 3"
Weight: 1 lb., 12 oz.
Features: Balanced lever to prevent pinching fingers; unlimited hand clearance; left- or right-hand use. Dies and shellholders not included. From Lee Precision, Inc.
Price: **$24.98**

LEE Turret Press

Frame: ASTM 380 aluminum
Frame Type: O-frame
Die Thread: 7/8-14
Avg. Rounds Per Hour: 300
Ram Stroke: 3"
Weight: 7 lbs., 2 oz.
Features: Replaceable turret lifts out by rotating 30˚; T-primer arm reverses for large or small primers; built-in primer catcher; adjustable handle for right- or left-hand use or changing angle of down stroke; accessory mounting hole for Lee Auto-Disk powder measure. Optional Auto-Index rotates die turret to next station for semi-progressive use. Safety override prevents overstressing should turret not turn. From Lee Precision, Inc.
Price: **$69.98**
Price: With Auto-Index **$83.98**
Price: Extra turret **$10.98**

LYMAN 310 Tool

Frame: Stainless steel
Frame Type: NA
Die Thread: 7/8-14
Avg. Rounds Per Hour: NA
Ram Stroke: NA
Weight: 10 oz.
Features: Compact, portable reloading tool for pistol or rifle cartridges. Adapter allows loading rimmed or rimless cases. Die set includes neck resizing/decapping die, primer seating chamber; neck expanding die; bullet seating die; and case head adapter. From Lyman Products Corporation.
Price: Dies **$39.95**
Price: Press **$39.95**
Price: Carrying pouch.................................... **$9.95**

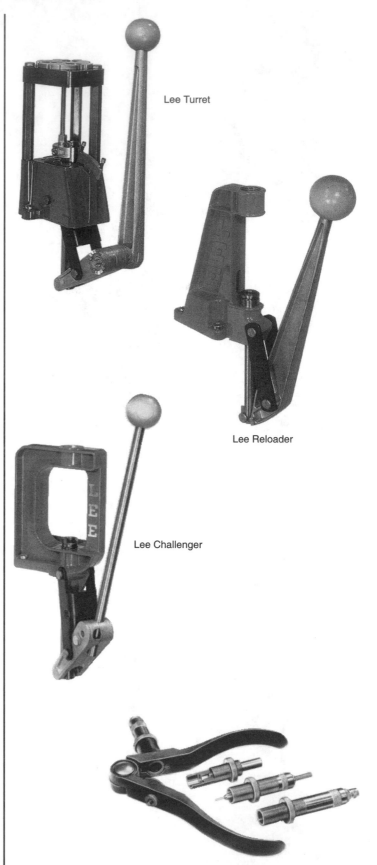

Lee Turret

Lee Reloader

Lee Challenger

Lyman 310

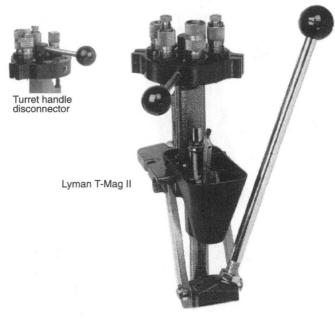

Turret handle
disconnector

Lyman T-Mag II

Lyman Crusher II

Ponsness/Warren
Metal-Matic P-200

LYMAN AccuPress

Frame: Die cast
Frame Type: C-frame
Die Thread: 7/8-14
Avg. Rounds Per Hour: 75
Ram Stroke: 3.4"
Weight: 4 lbs.
Features: Reversible, contoured handle for bench mount or hand-held use; for rifle or pistol; compound leverage; Delta frame design. Accepts all standard powder measures. From Lyman Products Corporation.
Price: $33.25

LYMAN Crusher II

Frame: Cast iron
Frame Type: O-frame
Die Thread: 7/8-14
Avg. Rounds Per Hour: 75
Ram Stroke: 3-7/8"
Weight: 19 lbs.
Features: Reloads both pistol and rifle cartridges; 1" diameter ram; 4-1/2" press opening for loading magnum cartridges; direct torque design; right- or left-hand use. New base design with 14 square inches of flat mounting surface with three bolt holes. Comes with priming arm and primer catcher. Dies and shellholders not included. From Lyman Products Corporation.
Price: $112.50

LYMAN T-Mag II

Frame: Cast iron with silver metalflake powder finish
Frame Type: Turret
Die Thread: 7/8-14
Avg. Rounds Per Hour: 125
Ram Stroke: 3-13/16"
Weight: 18 lbs.
Features: Reengineered and upgraded with new turret system for ease of indexing and tool-free turret removal for caliber changeover; new flat machined base for bench mounting; new nickel-plated non-rust handle and links; and new silver hammertone powder coat finish for durability. Right- or left-hand operation, handles all rifle or pistol dies. Comes with priming arm and primer catcher. Dies and shellholders not included. From Lyman Products Corporation.
Price: $154.95
Price: Extra turret $36.00

PONSNESS/WARREN Metal-Matic P-200

Frame: Die cast aluminum
Frame Type: Unconventional
Die Thread: 7/8-14
Avg. Rounds Per Hour: 200+
Weight: 18 lbs.
Features: Designed for straight-wall cartridges; die head with 10 tapped holes for holding dies and accessories for two calibers at one time; removable spent primer box; pivoting arm moves case from station to station. Comes with large and small primer tool. Optional accessories include primer feed, extra die head, primer speed feeder, powder measure extension and dust cover. Dies, powder measure and shellholder not included. From Ponsness/Warren.
Price: $195.00
Price: Extra die head. $42.95
Price: Powder measure extension $24.95
Price: Primer feed. $39.95
Price: Primer speed feed. $12.95
Price: Dust cover. $20.95

RCBS Partner

Frame: Aluminum
Frame Type: O-frame
Die Thread: 7/8-14
Avg. Rounds Per Hour: 50-60
Ram Stroke: 3-5/8"
Weight: 5 lbs.
Features: Designed for the beginning reloader. Comes with primer arm equipped with interchangeable primer plugs and sleeves for seating large and small primers. Shellholder and dies not included. Available in kit form (see Metallic Presses—Accessories). From RCBS.
Price: $54.95

RCBS Partner

RCBS AmmoMaster Single

Frame: Aluminum base; cast iron top plate connected by three steel posts.
Frame Type: NA
Die Thread: 1-1/4"-12 bushing; 7/8-14 threads
Avg. Rounds Per Hour: 50-60
Ram Stroke: 5-1/4"
Weight: 19 lbs.
Features: Single-stage press convertible to progressive. Will form cases or swage bullets. Case detection system to disengage powder measure when no case is present in powder charging station; five-station shellplate; Uniflow Powder measure with clear powder measure adaptor to make bridged powders visible and correctable. 50-cal. conversion kit allows reloading 50 BMG. Kit includes top plate to accommodate either 1-3/8" x 12 or 1-1/2" x 12 reloading dies. Piggyback die plate for quick caliber change-overs available. Reloading dies not included. From RCBS.
Price: $186.95
Price: 50 conversion kit $74.95
Price: Piggyback/AmmoMaster die plate $22.95
Price: Piggyback/AmmoMaster shellplate $27.95
Price: Press cover $7.95

RCBS AmmoMaster Single

RCBS Reloader Special-5

Frame: Aluminum
Frame Type: 30˚ offset O-frame
Die Thread: 1-1/4"-12 bushing; 7/8-14 threads
Avg. Rounds Per Hour: 50-60
Ram Stroke: 3-1/16"
Weight: 7.5 lbs.
Features: Single-stage press convertible to progressive with RCBS Piggyback II. Primes cases during resizing operation. Will accept RCBS shotshell dies. From RCBS.
Price: $103.95

RCBS Reloader Special-5

RCBS Rock Chucker

Frame: Cast iron
Frame Type: O-frame
Die Thread: 1-1/4"-12 bushing; 7/8-14 threads
Avg. Rounds Per Hour: 50-60
Ram Stroke: 3-1/16"
Weight: 17 lbs.
Features: Designed for heavy-duty reloading, case forming and bullet swaging. Provides 4" of ram-bearing surface to support 1" ram and ensure alignment; ductile iron toggle blocks; hardened steel pins. Comes standard with Universal Primer Arm and primer catcher. Can be converted from single-stage to progressive with Piggyback II conversion unit. From RCBS.
Price: $130.95

RCBS Rock Chucker

METALLIC CARTRIDGE PRESSES

Redding Model 25

REDDING Turret Press

Frame: Cast iron
Frame Type: Turret
Die Thread: 7/8-14
Avg. Rounds Per Hour: NA
Ram Stroke: 3.4"
Weight: 23 lbs., 2 oz.
Features: Strength to reload pistol and magnum rifle, case form and bullet swage; linkage pins heat-treated, precision ground and in double shear; hollow ram to collect spent primers; removable turret head for caliber changes; progressive linkage for increased power as ram nears die; slight frame tilt for comfortable operation; rear turret support for stability and precise alignment; six-station turret head; priming arm for both large and small primers. Also available in kit form with shellholder, primer catcher and one die set. From Redding Reloading Equipment.
Price: $298.50
Price: Kit $334.50

REDDING Boss

Frame: Cast iron
Frame Type: O-frame
Die Thread: 7/8-14
Avg. Rounds Per Hour: NA
Ram Stroke: 3.4"
Weight: 11 lbs., 8 oz.
Features: 36° frame offset for visibility and accessibility; primer arm positioned at bottom ram travel; positive ram travel stop machined to hit exactly top-dead-center. Also available in kit form with shellholder and set of Redding A dies. From Redding Reloading Equipment.
Price: $129.00
Price: Kit $165.00

REDDING Ultramag

Frame: Cast iron
Frame Type: Non-conventional
Die Thread: 7/8-14
Avg. Rounds Per Hour: NA
Ram Stroke: 4-1/8"
Weight: 23 lbs., 6 oz.
Features: Unique compound leverage system connected to top of press for tons of ram pressure; large 4-3/4" frame opening for loading outsized cartridges; hollow ram for spent primers. Kit available with shellholder and one set Redding A dies. From Redding Reloading Equipment.
Price: $298.50
Price: Kit $334.50

ROCK CRUSHER Press

Frame: Cast iron
Frame Type: O-frame
Die Thread: 2-3/4"-12 with bushing reduced to 1-1/2"-12
Avg. Rounds Per Hour: 50
Ram Stroke: 6"
Weight: 67 lbs.
Features: Designed to load and form ammunition from 50 BMG up to 23x115 Soviet. Frame opening of 8-1/2"x3-1/2"; 1-1/2"x12"; bushing can be removed and bushings of any size substituted; ram pressure can exceed 10,000 lbs. with normal body weight; 40mm diameter ram. Angle block for bench mounting and reduction bushing for RCBS dies available. Accessories for Rock crusher include powder measure, dies, shellholder, bullet puller, priming tool, case gauge and other accessories found elsewhere in this catalog. From The Old Western Scrounger.
Price: $785.00
Price: Angle block $57.95
Price: Reduction bushing $21.00
Price: Shellholder, 50 BMG, 12.7, 55 Boyes..........$36.75
Price: Shellholder, 23 Soviet........................$65.00
Price: Shellholder, all others $47.95
Price: Priming tool, 50 BMG, 20 Lahti...............$65.10

Redding Boss

Rock Crusher

Redding Ultramag

SHARP SHOOTER Port-A-Press

Frame: 6061 aluminum
Frame Type: O-frame
Die Thread: 7/8-14
Avg. Rounds Per Hour: NA
Ram Stroke: 2-1/2"
Weight: 8 lbs.
Features: Lightweight, compact three-station turret press; measures 12" high, 5" wide and 6-1/2" deep; built-in bench clamp to attach to any bench; removable turret. From Sharp Shooter Supply.
Price: $225.00
Price: Extra turret $10.50

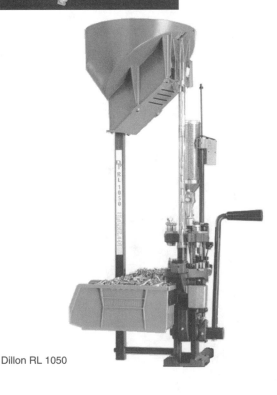

Sharp Shooter Port-A-Press

PROGRESSIVE PRESSES

DILLON AT 500

Frame: Aluminum alloy
Frame Type: NA
Die Thread: 7/8-14
Avg. Rounds Per Hour: 200-300
Ram Stroke: 3-7/8"
Weight: NA
Features: Four stations; removable tool head to hold dies in alignment and allow caliber changes without die adjustment; manual indexing; capacity to be upgraded to progressive RL 550B. Comes with universal shellplate to accept 223, 22-250, 243, 30-06, 9mm, 38/357, 40 S&W, 45 ACP. Dies not included. From Dillon Precision Products.
Price: $191.95

DILLON RL 550B

Frame: Aluminum alloy
Frame Type: NA
Die Thread: 7/8-14
Avg. Rounds Per Hour: 500-600
Ram Stroke: 3-7/8"
Weight: 25 lbs.
Features: Four stations; removable tool head to hold dies in alignment and allow caliber changes without die adjustment; auto priming system that emits audible warning when primer tube is low; a 100-primer capacity magazine contained in DOM steel tube for protection; new auto powder measure system with simple mechanical connection between measure and loading platform for positive powder bar return; a separate station for crimping with star-indexing system; 220 ejected-round capacity bin; 3/4-lb. capacity powder measure. Height above bench, 35"; requires 3/4" bench overhang. Will reload 120 different rifle and pistol calibers. Comes with one caliber conversion kit. Dies not included. From Dillon Precision Products, Inc.
Price: $319.95

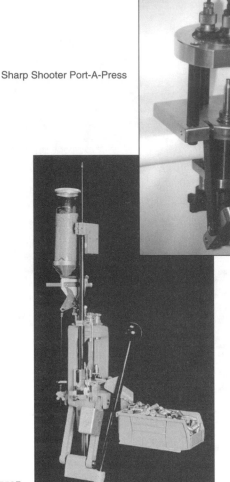

Dillon RL 550B

DILLON RL 1050

Frame: Ductile iron
Frame Type: Platform type
Die Thread: 7/8-14
Avg. Rounds Per Hour: 1000-1200
Ram Stroke: 2-5/16"
Weight: 62 lbs.
Features: Eight stations; auto case feed; primer pocket swager for military cartridge cases; auto indexing; removable tool head; auto prime system with 100-primer capacity; low primer supply alarm; positive powder bar return; auto powder measure; 515 ejected round bin capacity; 500-600 case feed capacity; 3/4-lb. capacity powder measure. Loads all pistol rounds as well as 30 M1 Carbine, 223, and 7.62x39 rifle rounds. Height above the bench, 43". Dies not included. From Dillon Precision Products, Inc.
Price: $1189.95

Dillon RL 1050

Dillon Square Deal B

Dillon XL 650

Lee Load-Master

Hornady Lock-N-Load AP

DILLON Square Deal B

Frame: Zinc alloy
Frame Type: NA
Die Thread: None (unique Dillon design)
Avg. Rounds Per Hour: 400-500
Ram Stroke: 2-5/16"
Weight: 17 lbs.
Features: Four stations; auto indexing; removable tool head; auto prime system with 100-primer capacity; low primer supply alarm; auto powder measure; positive powder bar return; 170 ejected round capacity bin; 3/4-lb. capacity powder measure. Height above the bench, 34". Comes complete with factory adjusted carbide die set. From Dillon Precision Products, Inc.
Price:. **$249.95**

DILLON XL 650

Frame: Aluminum alloy
Frame Type: NA
Die Thread: 7/8-14
Avg. Rounds Per Hour: 800-1000
Ram Stroke: 4-9/16"
Weight: 46 lbs.
Features: Five stations; auto indexing; auto case feed; removable tool head; auto prime system with 100-primer capacity; low primer supply alarm; auto powder measure; positive powder bar return; 220 ejected round capacity bin; 3/4-lb. capacity powder measure. 500-600 case feed capacity with optional auto case feed. Loads all pistol/rifle calibers less than 3-1/2" in length. Height above the bench, 44"; 3/4" bench overhang required. From Dillon Precision Products, Inc.
Price: Less dies. **$438.95**

HORNADY Lock-N-Load AP

Frame: Die cast heat-treated aluminum alloy
Frame Type: O-frame
Die Thread: 7/8-14
Avg. Rounds Per Hour: NA
Ram Stroke: 3-3/4"
Weight: 26 lbs.
Features: Features Lock-N-Load bushing system that allows instant die changeovers; five-station die platform with option of seating and crimping separately or adding taper-crimp die; auto prime with large and small primer tubes with 100-primer capacity and protective housing; brass kicker to eject loaded rounds into 80-round capacity cartridge catcher; offset operating handle for leverage and unobstructed operation; 2" diameter ram driven by heavy duty cast linkage arms rotating on steel pins. Comes with five Lock-N-Load die bushings, shellplate, deluxe powder measure, auto powder drop, and auto primer feed and shut-off, brass kicker and primer catcher. Lifetime warranty. From Hornady Mfg. Co.
Price: **$349.95**

LEE Load-Master

Frame: ASTM 380 aluminum
Frame Type: O-frame
Die Thread: 7/8-14
Avg. Rounds Per Hour: 600
Ram Stroke: 3-1/4"
Weight: 8 lbs., 4 oz.
Features: Available in kit form only. A 1-3/4" diameter hard chrome ram for handling largest magnum cases; loads rifle or pistol rounds; five station press to factory crimp and post size; auto indexing with wedge lock mechanism to hold one ton; auto priming; removable turrets; four-tube case feeder with optional case collator and bullet feeder (late 1995); loaded round ejector with chute to optional loaded round catcher; quick change shellplate; primer catcher. Dies and shellholder for one caliber included. From Lee Precision, Inc.
Price: Rifle. **$320.00**
Price: Pistol **$330.00**
Price: Extra turret **$14.98**
Price: Adjustable charge bar. **$9.98**

LEE Pro 1000

Frame: ASTM 380 aluminum and steel
Frame Type: O-frame
Die Thread: 7/8-14
Avg. Rounds Per Hour: 600
Ram Stroke: 3-1/4"
Weight: 8 lbs., 7 oz.
Features: Optional transparent large/small or rifle case feeder; deluxe auto-disk case-activated powder measure; case sensor for primer feed. Comes complete with carbide die set (steel dies for rifle) for one caliber. Optional accessories include: case feeder for large/small pistol cases or rifle cases; shell plate carrier with auto prime, case ejector, auto-index and spare parts; case collator for case feeder. From Lee Precision, Inc.
Price: **$199.98**

PONSNESS/WARREN Metallic II

Frame: Die cast aluminum
Frame Type: H-frame
Die Thread: 7/8-14
Avg. Rounds Per Hour: 150+
Ram Stroke: NA
Weight: 32 lbs.
Features: Die head with five tapped 7/8-14 holes for dies, powder measure or other accessories; pivoting die arm moves case from station to station; depriming tube for removal of spent primers; auto primer feed; interchangeable die head. Optional accessories include additional die heads, powder measure extension tube to accommodate any standard powder measure, primer speed feeder to feed press primer tube without disassembly. Comes with small and large primer seating tools. Dies, powder measure and shellholder not included. From Ponsness/Warren.
Price: **$339.00**
Price: Extra die head **$49.95**
Price: Primer speed feeder. **$12.95**
Price: Powder measure extension **$24.95**
Price: Dust cover **$27.95**

RCBS AmmoMaster-Auto

Frame: Aluminum base; cast iron top plate connected by three steel posts.
Frame Type: NA
Die Thread: 1-1/4-12 bushing; 7/8-14 threads
Avg. Rounds Per Hour: 400-500
Ram Stroke: 5-1/4"
Weight: 19 lbs.
Features: Progressive press convertible to single-stage. Features include: 1-1/2" solid ram; automatic indexing, priming, powder charging and loaded round ejection. Case detection system disengages powder measure when no case is present in powder charging station. Comes with five-station shellplate and Uniflow powder measure with clear powder measure adaptor to make bridged powders visible and correctable. Piggyback die plate for quick caliber change-over available. Reloading dies not included. From RCBS.
Price: **$394.95**
Price: Piggyback/AmmoMaster die plate **$22.95**
Price: Piggyback/AmmoMaster shellplate **$27.95**
Price: Press cover **$10.95**

STAR Universal Pistol Press

Frame: Cast iron with aluminum base
Frame Type: Unconventional
Die Thread: 11/16-24 or 7/8-14
Avg. Rounds Per Hour: 300
Ram Stroke: NA
Weight: 27 lbs.
Features: Four or five-station press depending on need to taper crimp; handles all popular handgun calibers from 32 Long to 45 Colt. Comes completely assembled and adjusted with carbide dies (except 30 Carbine) and shellholder to load one caliber. Prices slightly higher for 9mm and 30 Carbine. From Star Machine Works.
Price: With taper crimp **$950.00**
Price: Without taper crimp **$925.00**
Price: Extra tool head, taper crimp **$381.00**
Price: Extra tool head, w/o taper crimp **$356.00**

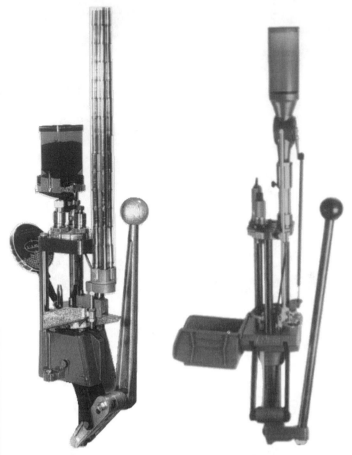

Lee Pro 1000   RCBS AmmoMaster

Fully-automated Star Universal

Dillon SL 900

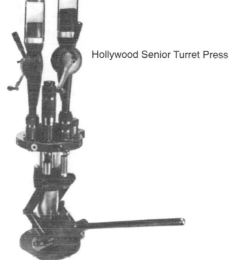

Hollywood Automatic

Hollywood Senior Turret Press

Hornady 366 Auto

Hornady Apex 3.1
Gas-Assist Auto

DILLON SL 900

Press Type: Progressive
Avg. Rounds Per Hour: 700-900
Weight: 51 lbs.
Features: 12-ga. only; factory adjusted to load AA hulls; extra large 25-pound capacity shot hopper; fully-adjustable case-activated shot system; hardened steel starter crimp die; dual-action final crimp and taper die; tilt-out wad guide; auto prime; auto index; strong mount machine stand. From Dillon Precision Products.
Price: **$799.95**

HOLLYWOOD Automatic Shotshell Press

Press Type: Progressive
Avg. Rounds Per Hour: 1,800
Weight: 100 lbs.
Features: Ductile iron frame; fully automated press with shell pickup and ejector; comes completely set up for one gauge; one starter crimp; one finish crimp; wad guide for plastic wads; decap and powder dispenser unit; one wrench for inside die lock screw; one medium and one large spanner wrench for spanner nuts; one shellholder; powder and shot measures. Available for 10, 12, 20, 28 or 410. From Hollywood Engineering.
Price: **$3,600.00**

HOLLYWOOD Senior Turret Press

Press Type: Turret
Avg. Rounds Per Hour: 200
Weight: 50 lbs.
Features: Multi-stage press constructed of ductile iron comes completely equipped to reload one gauge; one starter crimp; one finish crimp; wad guide for plastic wads; decap and powder dispenser unit; one wrench for inside die lock screw; one medium and one large spanner wrench for spanner nuts; one shellholder; powder and shot measures. Available for 10, 12, 16, 20, 28 or 410. From Hollywood Engineering.
Price: Press with die set. **$875.00**
Price: Press only **$600.00**
Price: Senior Single-Stage Press. **$500.00**

HORNADY 366 Auto

Press Type: Progressive
Avg. Rounds Per Hour: NA
Weight: 25 lbs.
Features: Heavy-duty die cast and machined steel body and components; auto primer feed system; large capacity shot and powder tubes; adjustable for right- or left-hand use; automatic charge bar with shutoff; swing-out wad guide; primer catcher at base of press; interchangeable shot and powder bushings; life-time warranty. Available for 12, 20, 28 2-3/4 and 410 2-1/2 . From Hornady Mfg. Co.
Price: **$390.00**
Price: Die set, 12, 20, 28 . . . . **$96.50**
Price: Magnum conversion dies, 12, 20. . . . . **$21.20**

HORNADY Apex 3.1 Gas-Assist Auto

Press Type: Auto
Avg. Rounds Per Hour: NA
Weight: 15 lbs.
Features: Features shell retainer system; full-length collet size die to automatically size the full length of brass; shell-actuated auto primer feed; shell-actuated automatic powder/shot drop with shell detect; cam-activated dual-action crimp/taper die; auto index converts single stage shellplate to progressive. Includes a gas-assist indexing assembly which rotates the shellplate

smoothly regardless of handle speed. Available for 12, 20, 28 gauges or 410 bore. From Hornady Mfg. Co.

Price: 12, 20 .... **$399.95**
Price: 28, 410 .... **$399.95**

LEE Load-All II

Press Type: Single stage
Avg. Rounds Per Hour: 100
Weight: 3 lbs., 3 oz.
Features: Loads steel or lead shot; built-in primer catcher at base with door in front for emptying; recesses at each station for shell positioning; optional primer feed. Comes with safety charge bar with 24 shot and powder bushings. Available for 12-, 16- or 20-gauge. From Lee Precision, Inc.
Price: **$49.98**

MEC 600 Jr. Mark V

Press Type: Single stage
Avg. Rounds Per Hour: 200
Weight: 10 lbs.
Features: Spindex crimp starter for shell alignment during crimping; a cam-action crimp die; Pro-Check to keep charge bar properly positioned; adjustable for three shells. Available in 10, 12, 16, 20, 28 gauges and 410 bore. Die set not included. From Mayville Engineering Company, Inc.
Price: **$167.50**
Price: Die set **$59.38**

MEC 650

Press Type: Progressive
Avg. Rounds Per Hour: 400
Weight: NA
Features: Six-station press; does not resize except as separate operation; auto primer feed standard; three crimping stations for starting, closing and tapering crimp. Die sets not available. Available in 12, 16, 20, 28 and 410. From Mayville Engineering Company, Inc.
Price: **$329.39**

MEC 8567 Grabber

Press Type: Progressive
Avg. Rounds Per Hour: 400
Weight: 15 lbs.
Features: Ten-station press; auto primer feed; auto-cycle charging; three-stage crimp; power ring resizer returns base to factory specs; resizes high and low base shells; optional kits to reload three shells and steel shot. Available in 12, 16, 20, 28 gauge and 410 bore. From Mayville Engineering Company, Inc.
Price: **$472.54**
Price: 3" kit, 12-ga. **$39.19**
Price: 3" kit, 20-ga. **$24.00**
Price: Steel shot kit. **$23.22**

MEC 9000G

Press Type: Progressive
Avg. Rounds Per Hour: 400
Weight: 18 lbs.
Features: All same features as the MEC Grabber, but with auto-indexing and auto-eject. Finished shells automatically ejected from shell carrier to drop chute for boxing. Available in 12, 16, 20, 28 and 410. From Mayville Engineering Company, Inc.
Price: **$573.73**
Price: 3" kit, 12-ga. **$39.19**
Price: 3" kit, 20-ga. **$24.00**
Price: Steel shot kit. **$23.22**

MEC 600 Jr. Mark V

Lee Load-All II

MEC 8567 Grabber

MEC 650

MEC 9000G

MEC 9000H

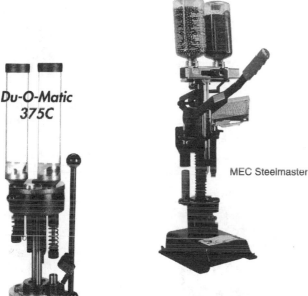

Ponsness/Warren
Du-O-Matic 375C

Ponsness/Warren
Hyddro-Multispeed

MEC Sizemaster

MEC Steelmaster

MEC 9000H

Press Type: Progressive
Avg. Rounds Per Hour: 400
Weight: 23 lbs.
Features: Same features as 9000G with addition of foot pedal-operated hydraulic system for complete automation. Operates on standard 110V household current. Comes with bushing-type charge bar and three bushings. Available in 12, 16, 20, 28 gauge and 410 bore. From Mayville Engineering Company, Inc.
Price: $1,386.09
Price: Steel shot kit $23.22

MEC Sizemaster

Press Type: Single stage
Avg. Rounds Per Hour: 150
Weight: 13 lbs.
Features: Power ring eight-fingered collet resizer returns base to factory specs; handles brass or steel, high or low base heads; auto primer feed; adjustable for three shells. Available in 10, 12, 16, 20, 28 gauges and 410 bore. From Mayville Engineering Company, Inc.
Price: $252.39
Price: Die set, 12, 16, 20, 28, 410 ....$88.67
Price: Die set, 10-ga. $104.06
Price: Steel shot kit $14.34
Price: Steel shot kit, 12-ga. 31/2 ....$70.27

MEC Steelmaster

Press Type: Single stage
Avg. Rounds Per Hour: 150
Weight: 13 lbs.
Features: Same features as Sizemaster except can load steel shot. Press is available for 3-1/2 10-ga. and 12-ga. 2-3/4 ,3 or 3-1/2. For loading lead shot, die sets available in 10, 12, 16, 20, 28 and 410. From Mayville Engineering Company, Inc.
Price: $262.65
Price: 10 ga. 3-1/2 " $289.08

PONSNESS/WARREN Du-O-Matic 375C

Press Type: Progressive
Avg. Rounds Per Hour: NA
Weight: 31 lbs.
Features: Steel or lead shot reloader; large shot and powder reservoirs; bushing access plug for dropping in shot buffer or buckshot; positive lock charging ring to prevent accidental flow of powder; double-post construction for greater leverage; removable spent primer box; spring-loaded ball check for centering size die at each station; tip-out wad guide; two-gauge capacity tool head. Available in 10 (extra charge), 12, 16, 20, 28 and 410 with case lengths of 2-1/2, 2-3/4, 3 and 3-1/2 inches. From Ponsness/ Warren.
Price: $269.00
Price: 12-ga. 3-1/2 ; 3 12, 20, 410. ....$285.00
Price: 12, 20 2-3/4 ....$358.95
Price: 10-ga. press...$295.00

PONSNESS/WARREN Hydro-Multispeed

Hydraulic system developed for the Ponsness/Warren L/S-1000. Also usable for the 950, 900 and 800 series presses. Three reloading speed settings operated with variable foot pedal control. Features stop/reverse at any station; automatic shutdown with pedal control release; fully adjustable hydraulic cylinder rod to prevent racking or bending of machine; quick disconnect hoses for ease of installation. Comes preassembled with step-by-step instructions. From Ponsness/Warren.

Price: **$849.00**
Price: Cylinder kit **$379.95**

PONSNESS/WARREN L/S-1000

Frame: Die cast aluminum
Avg. Rounds Per Hour: NA
Weight: 55 lbs.
Features: Fully progressive press to reload steel, bismuth or lead shot. Equipped with new Uni-Drop shot measuring and dispensing system which allows the use of all makes of shot in any size. Shells automatically resized and deprimed with new Auto-Size and De-Primer system. Loaded rounds drop out of shellholders when completed. Each shell pre-crimped and final crimped with Tru-Crimp system. Available in 10-gauge 3-1/2 or 12-gauge 2-3/4 and 3 . 12-gauge 3-1/2 conversion kit also available. 20-gauge 2-3/4 and 3 special order only. From Ponsness/Warren.

Price: 12 ga. **$755.00**
Price: 10 ga. **$799.00**
Price: Conversion kit. **$44.95**

PONSNESS/WARREN Size-O-Matic 900 Elite

Press Type: Progressive
Avg. Rounds Per Hour: 500-800
Weight: 49 lbs.
Features: Progressive eight-station press; frame of die cast aluminum; center post design index system ensures positive indexing; timing factory set, drilled and pinned. Automatic features include index, deprime, reprime, powder and shot drop, crimp start, tapered final crimp, finished shell ejection. Available in 12, 20, 28 and 410. 16-ga. special order. Conversion kit converts the 900 press to the new 950 Elite. Kit includes the new shellholders, seating port, resize/primer knockout assembly and new crimp assembly. From Ponsness/Warren.

Price: **$679.00**
Price: Tooling, 12, 20, 28, 410 . . . . **$177.00**

PONSNESS/WARREN Platinum 2000

Press Type: Progressive
Avg. Rounds Per Hour: 500-800
Weight: 52 lbs.
Features: Progressive eight-station press is similar to the 900 and 950 except has die removal system that allows removal of any die component during the reloading cycle. Comes standard with 25-lb. shot tube, 19" powder tube, brass adjustable priming feed allows adjustment of primer seating depth. From Ponsness/Warren.

Price . . . . **Contact manufacturer**

PONSNESS/WARREN 950 Elite

Press Type: Progressive
Avg. Rounds Per Hour: 500-800
Weight: 55 lbs.
Features: Same as the 900 Elite, but comes with the L/S 1000 shellholder and resizing system which automatically seats shells into new shellholders and resizes them in primer knockout station. Conversion kit allows converting 900 Elite to 950. Handles both high and low brass with no alteration. Available in 12, 20 and 28 gauges. From Ponsness/Warren.

Price: **$679.00**
Price: Tooling 12 ga. **$195.00**
Price: Conversion kit. **$169.00**

Ponsness/Warren
L/S-1000

Ponsness/Warren
Size-O-Matic 900 Elite

NEW!
Platinum 2000
Series

Ponsness/Warren
Platinum 2000

950 Elite

Ponsness/Warren 950 Elite

Maker and Model	Magn.	Field at 100 Yds. (feet)	Eye Relief (in.)	Length (in.)	Tube Dia. (in.)	W & E Adjustments	Weight (ozs.)	Price	Other Data
ADCO									
Magnum 45 mm[5]	0	—	—	4.1	45 mm	Int.	6.8	$279.00	[1]Multi-Color Dot system changes from red to green. [2]For airguns, paintball, rimfires. Uses common lithium water battery. [3]Comes with standard dovetail mount. [4].75" dovetail mount; poly body; adj. intensity diode. [5]10 MOA dot; black or nickel. [6]Square format; with mount battery. From ADCO Sales.
MIRAGE Ranger 1"	0	—	—	5.2	1	Int.	3.9	159.00	
MIRAGE Ranger 30mm	0	—	—	5.5	30mm	Int.	5	179.00	
MIRAGE Sportsman[1]	0	—	—	5.2	1	Int.	4.5	229.00	
MIRAGE Competitor	0	—	—	5.5	30mm	Int.	5.5	229.00	
IMP Sight[2]	0	—	—	4.5	—	Int.	1.3	17.95	
Square Shooter[3]	0	—	—	5	—	Int.	5	125.00	
MIRAGE Eclipse[1]	0	—	—	5.5	30mm	Int.	5.5	229.00	
MIRAGE Champ Red Dot	0	—	—	4.5	—	Int.	2	33.95	
Vantage 1"	0	—	—	3.9	1	Int.	3.9	129.00	
Vantage 30mm	0	—	—	4.2	30mm	Int.	4.9	132.00	
Vision 2000[6]	0	60	—	4.7	—	Int.	6.2	79.00	
AIMPOINT									
Comp	0	—	—	4.6	30mm	Int.	4.3	317.00	Illuminates red dot in field of view. Noparallax (dot does not need to be centered). Unlimited field of view and eye relief. On/off, adj. intensity. Dot covers 3" @100 yds. [1]Comes with 30mm rings, battery, lense cloth. [2]Requires 1" rings. AP Comp avail. in black, blue, SS, camo. [3]Black finish (AP 5000-B) ; avail. with regular 3-min. or 10-min. Mag Dot as B2 or S2. [4]Band pass reflection coating for compatibility with night vision equipment; U.S. Army contract model; with anti-reflex coated lenses (Comp ML), $359.00. From Aimpoint U.S.A.
Comp M[4]	0	—	—	5	30mm	Int.	6.1	392.00	
Series 5000[3]	0	—	—	6	30mm	Int.	6	285.00	
Series 3000 Universal[2]	0	—	—	6.25	1	Int.	6	232.00	
Series 5000/2x[1]	2	—	—	7	30mm	Int.	9	378.00	
ARMSON O.E.G.									
Standard	0	—	—	5.125	1	Int.	4.3	202.00	Shown red dot aiming point. No batteries needed. Standard model fits 1" ring mounts (not incl.). Other O.E.G. models for shotguns and rifles can be special ordered. [1]Daylight Only Sight with .375" dovetail mount for 22s. Does not contain tritium. From Trijicon, Inc.
22 DOS[1]	0	—	—	3.75	—	Int.	3	127.00	
22 Day/Night	0	—	—	3.75	—	Int.	3	169.00	
M16/AR-15	0	—	—	5.125	—	Int.	5.5	220.00	
ARTEMIS 2000									
4x32	4	34.4	3.15	10.7	1	Int.	17.5	215.00	Click-stop windage and elevation adjustments; constantly centered reticle; rubber eyepiece ring; nitrogen filled. Imported from the Czech Republic by CZ-USA.
6x42	6	23	3.15	13.7	1	Int.	17.5	317.00	
7x50	7	18.7	3.15	13.9	1	Int.	17.5	329.00	
1.5-6x42	1.5-6	40-12.8	2.95	12.4	30mm	Int.	19.4	522.00	
2-8x42	2-8	31-9.5	2.95	13.1	30mm	Int.	21.1	525.00	
3-9x42	3-9	24.6-8.5	2.95	12.4	30mm	Int.	19.4	400.00	
3-12x50	3-12	20.6-6.2	2.95	14	30mm	Int.	22.9	574.00	
BAUSCH & LOMB									
Elite 4200 RainGuard									
40-6244A[1]	6-24	18-6	3	16.9	1	Int.	20.2	672.95	[1]Adj. objective, sunshade; also in matte and with 1/4-MOA dot reticle. [2]Also in matte and silver finish. [3]Only in matte finish. [4]Also in matte and silver finish. [5]Adjustable objective. [6]50mm objective; also in matte finish. [7]Also in silver finish. **Partial listings shown. Contact Bushnell Sports Optics for details.**
40-2104G[2]	2.5-10	41.5-10.8	3	13.5	1	Int.	16	592.95	
40-1636M[3]	1.5-6	61.8-16.1	3	12.8	1	Int.	15.4	560.95	
42-3640A	36	3	3	15	1	Int.	17.0	800.95	
42-4165M[5]	4-16	26-7	3	*	15.6	Int.	22	768.95	
Elite 3000									
30-5155M	5-15	21-7	3	15.9	1	Int.	24	471.95	
30-4124A[1]	4-12	26.9-9	3	13.2	1	Int.	15	417.95	
30-3940G[4]	3-9	33.8-11.5	3	12.6	1	Int.	13	319.95	
30-2732M[5]	2-7	44.6-12.7	3	11.6	1	Int.	12	303.05	
30-3950G[6]	3-9	31.5-10.5	3	15.7	1	Int.	19	382.95	
30-3956E	3-9	31.5-10.5	3	15.6	30mm	Int.	22	592.95	
Elite 3000 Handgun									
30-2032G[7]	2-6	10-4	20	9	1	Int.	10	417.95	
30-2632G	2-6	10-4	20	9	1	Int.	10	417.95	
BEC									
EuroLux									
EL2510x56	2.5-10	39.4-11.5	3.25-2	15.1	30mm	Int.	25.4	249.90	Black matte finish. Multi-coated lenses; 1/4-MOA click adjustments (1/2-MOA on EL4x25, AR4x22WA); fog and water-proof. [1]For AR-15;bullet drop compensator; q.d. mount. [2]Rubber armored. Imported by BEC Inc.
EL39x42	3-9	34.1-13.2	3.5-3	12.3	30mm	Int.	17.7	99.80	
EL28x36	2-8	44.9-11.5	3.8-3	12.2	30mm	Int.	15.9	149.50	
ELA39x40RB[2]	3-9	39-13	3	12.7	30mm	Int.	14.3	95.95	
EL6x42	6	21	3	12.6	30mm	Int.	14.8	69.00	
EL4x42	4	29	3	12.6	30mm	Int.	14.8	59.60	
EL4x36	4	29	3	12	30mm	Int.	14	49.90	
EL4x25	4	26	3	7	30mm	Int.	7.6	37.00	
AR4x22WA[1]	4	24	3	7	34mm	Int.	13.6	109.97	
BEEMAN									
Rifle Scopes									
5045[1]	4-12	26.9-9	3	13.2	1	Int.	15	NA	All scopes have 5 point reticle, all glass fully coated lenses. [1]Parallel adjustable. [2]Reticle lighted by ambient light. [3]Available with lighted Electro-Dot reticle. Imported by Beeman.
5046[1]	6-24	18-4.5	3	16.9	1	Int.	20.2	NA	
5050[1]	4	26	3.5	11.7	1	Int.	11	NA	
5055[1]	3-9	38-13	3.5	10.75	1	Int.	11.2	NA	
5060[1]	4-12	30-10	3	12.5	1	Int.	16.2	NA	
5065[1]	6-18	17-6	3	14.7	1	Int.	17.3	NA	
5066RL[2]	2-7	58-15	3	11.4	1	Int.	17	380.00	
5047L[2]	4	25	3.5	7	1	Int.	13.7	NA	
Pistol Scopes									
5025	2	19	10-24	9.1	1	Int.	7.4	NA	
5020	1.5	14	11-16	8.3	.75	Int.	3.6	NA	

Maker and Model	Magn.	Field at 100 Yds. (feet)	Eye Relief (in.)	Length (in.)	Tube Dia. (in.)	W & E Adjustments	Weight (ozs.)	Price	Other Data
BSA									
Catseye[1]									
CE1545x32	1.5-4.5	78-23	4	11.25	1	Int.	12	89.95	[1]Waterproof, fogproof; multi-coated lenses; finger-adjustable knobs. [2]Waterproof, fogproof; matte black finish. [3]With 4" sunshade; target knobs; 1/8-MOA click adjustments. [4]Adjustable for parallax; with sunshades; target knobs, 1/8-MOA adjustments. Imported by BSA.
CE4x44	4	32	3.25	12.75	1	Int.	13.5	139.95	
CE310x44	3-10	39-12	3.25	12.75	1	Int.	16	149.95	
CE3510x50	3.5-10	30-10.5	3.25	13.25	1	Int.	17.25	169.95	
CE416x50	4-16	25-6	3	15.25	1	Int.	22	189.95	
CE624x50	6-24	16-3	3	16	1	Int.	23	219.95	
Deer Hunter[2]									
DH25x20	2.5	72	6	7.5	1	Int.	7.5	59.95	
DH4x32	4	32	3	12	1	Int.	12.5	49.95	
DH39x32	3-9	39-13	3	12	1	Int.	11	69.95	
DH39x40	3-9	39-13	3	13	1	Int.	12.1	89.95	
DH39x50	3-9	41-15	3	12.75	1	Int.	13	109.95	
DH2510x44	2.5-10	42-12	3	13	1	Int.	12.5	99.95	
DH4x40	4	36	3	13	1	Int.	12	69.95	
DH6x40	6	25	3	13	1	Int.	12	89.95	
Contender[3]									
CT24x40TS	24	6	3	15	1	Int.	18	129.95	
CT36x40TS	36	3	3	15.25	1	Int.	19	139.95	
CT312x40TS	3-12	28-7	3	13	1	Int.	17.5	119.95	
CT416x40TS	4-16	21-5	3	13.5	1	Int.	18	129.95	
CT624x40TS	6-24	16-4	3	15.5	1	Int.	20	144.95	
CT832x40TS	8-32	11-3	3	15.5	1	Int.	20	169.95	
CT24x50TS	24	6	3	15	1	Int.	22	149.95	
CT36x50TS	36	3	3	15.25	1	Int.	23	159.95	
CT312x50TS	3-12	28-7	3	13.75	1	Int.	21	129.95	
CT416x50TS	4-16	21-5	3	15.25	1	Int.	22	149.95	
CT624x50TS	6-24	16-4	3	16	1	Int.	23	169.95	
CT832x50TS	8-32	11-3	3	16.5	1	Int.	24	189.95	
Platinum[4]									
PT24x44TS	24	4.5	3	16.25	1	Int.	17.9	189.55	
PT36x44TS	36	3	3	14.9	1	Int.	17.9	199.95	
PT624x44TS	6-24	15-4.5	3	15.25	1	Int.	18.5	219.95	
PT832x44TS	8-32	11-3.5	3	17.25	1	Int.	19.5	239.95	
PT1050x60TS	10-50	7-2	3	18	1	Int.	22	399.95	
.22 Special									
S25x20WR	2.5	58	3	8	1	Int.	7	39.95	
S4x32WR	4	26	3	10.75	1	Int.	9	49.95	
Air Rifle									
AR4x32	4	33	3	13	1	Int.	14	69.95	
AR27x32	2-7	48	3	12.25	1	Int.	14	79.95	
AR312x44	3-12	36	3	12.25	1	Int.	15	109.95	
AR612x44	6-24	18	3	15.5	1	Int.	17	144.95	
BURRIS									
Black Diamond									
3-12x50[3,4,6]	3.2-11.9	34-12	3.5-4	13.8	30mm	Int.	25	854.00	**Black Diamond & Fullfield:** All scopes avail. with Plex reticle. Steel-on-steel click adjustments. [1]Dot reticle on some models. [2]Post crosshair reticle extra. [3]Matte satin finish. [4]Available with parallax adjustment (standard on 10x, 12x, 4-12x, 6-12x, 6-18x, 6x HBR and 3-12x Signature). [5]Silver matte finish extra. [6]Target knobs extra, standard on silhouette models. LER and XER with P.A., 6x HBR. [7]Sunshade avail. [8]Avail. with Fine Plex reticle. [9]Available with Heavy Plex reticle. [10]Available with Posi-Lock. [11]Available with Peep Plex reticle. [12]Also avail. for rimfires, airguns. [13]Selected models available with camo finish.
6-24x50	6-24	18-6	3.5-4	16.2	30mm	Int.	25	926.00	
Fullfield									**Signature Series:** LER=Long Eye Relief; IER=Intermediate Eye Relief; XER=Extra Eye Relief.
1.5x[9]	1.6	62	3.5-3.75	10.25	1	Int.	9	299.00	
2.5x[9]	2.5	55	3.5-3.75	10.25	1	Int.	9	308.00	**Speeddot 135:** [13]Waterproof, fogproof, coated lenses, 11 brightness settings;3-MOA or 11-MOA dot size; includes Weaver-style rings and battery **Partial listing shown.** Contact Burris for complete details..
4x[1,2,3]	3.75	36	3.5-3.75	11.25	1	Int.	11.5	314.00	
6x[1,3]	5.8	23	3.5-3.75	13	1	Int.	12	343.00	
12x[1,4,6,7,8]	11.8	10.5	3.5-3.75	15	1	Int.	15	463.00	
1.75-5x[1,2,9,10]	1.7-4.6	66-25	3.5-3.75	10.875	1	Int.	13	374.00	
2-7x[1,2,3]	2.5-6.8	47-18	3.5-3.75	12	1	Int.	14	399.00	
3-9x38[1,2,3,10]	3.3-8.7	38-15	3.5-3.75	12.625	1	Int.	15	356.00	
3-9x50	3-9	35-15	3.5-3.75	13	1	Int.	18	427.00	
3.5-10x50mm[3,5,10]	3.7-9.7	29.5-11	3.5-3.75	14	1	Int.	19	496.00	
4-12x[1,4,8,11]	4.4-11.8	27-10	3.5-3.75	15	1	Int.	18	503.00	
6-18x[1,3,4,6,7,8]	6.5-17.6	16.7	3.5-3.75	15.8	1	Int.	18.5	527.00	
Compact Scopes									
1x XER[3]	1	51	4.5-20	8.8	1	Int.	7.9	290.00	
4x[4,5]	3.6	24	3.75-5	8.25	1	Int.	7.8	263.00	
6x[1,4]	5.5	17	3.75-5	9	1	Int.	8.2	279.00	
6x HBR[1,5,8]	6	13	4.5	11.25	1	Int.	13	438.00	
1-4x XER[3]	1-3.8	53-15	4.25-30	8.8	1	Int.	10.3	377.00	
3-9x[4,5]	3.6-8.8	25-11	3.75-5	12.625	1	Int.	11.5	368.00	
4-12x[1,4,6]	4.5-11.6	19-8	3.75-4	15	1	Int.	15	485.00	
Signature Series									
1.5-6x[2,3,5,9,10]	1.7-5.8	70-20	3.5-4	10.8	1	Int.	13	494.00	
4x[3]	4	30	3.5-4	12.125	1	Int.	14	366.00	
6x[3]	6	20	3.5-4	12.125	1	Int.	14	405.00	
2-8x[3,5,11]	2.1-7.7	53-17	3.5-4	11.75	1	Int.	14	547.00	
3-9x[3,5,10,13]	3.3-8.8	36-14	3.5-4	12.875	1	Int.	15.5	560.00	
2.50-10x[3,5,10]	2.7-9.5	37-10.5	3.5-4	14	1	Int.	19	682.00	
3-12x[3,10]	3.3-11.7	34-9	3.5-4	14.25	1	Int.	21	677.00	
4-16x[1,3,5,6,8,10]	4.3-15.7	33-9	3.5-4	15.4	1	Int.	23.7	709.00	
6-24x[1,3,5,6,8,10,13]	6.6-23.8	17-6	3.5-4	16	1	Int.	22.7	727.00	
8-32x[8,10,12]	8.6-31.4	13-3.8	3.5-4	17	1	Int.	24	782.00	
Speeddot 135[13]									
Red Dot	1	—	—	4.85	35mm	Int.	5	282.00	

Plex   Fine Plex

Heavy Plex & Electro-Dot Plex   Peep Plex   Ballistic Mil-Dot

Target Dot   Mil-Dot

SCOPES & MOUNTS

Maker and Model	Magn.	Field at 100 Yds. (feet)	Eye Relief (in.)	Length (in.)	Tube Dia. (in.)	W & E Adjustments	Weight (ozs.)	Price	Other Data
BURRIS (cont'd.)									
Handgun									
1.50-4x LER[1,5,10]	1.6-3.	16-11	11-25	10.25	1	Int.	11	352.00	
2-7x LER[3,4,5,10]	2-6.5	21-7	7-27	9.5	1	Int.	12.6	390.00	
3-9x LER[4,5,10]	3.4-8.4	12-5	22-14	11	1	Int.	14	440.00	
2x LER[4,5,6]	1.7	21	10-24	8.75	1	Int.	6.8	257.00	
4x LER[1,4,5,6,10]	3.7	11	10-22	9.625	1	Int.	9	288.00	
10x LER[1,4,6]	9.5	4	8-12	13.5	1	Int.	14	447.00	
Scout Scope									
1.50 XER[3,9]	1.5	22	7-18	9	1	Int.	7.3	301.00	
2.75x XER[3,9]	2.7	15	7-14	9.375	1	Int.	7.5	301.00	
BUSHNELL									
Scopechief									
70-1563M[4]	1.5-6	74-20	3.5	10.7	1	Int.	14.4	337.95	
70-3104M[4]	3.5-10	43-15	3.5	13	1	Int.	17	293.95	
70-3940M[4]	3-9	42-14	3.5	11.5	1	Int.	16	255.95	
70-4145A[12]	4-14	31-9	3.5	14.1	1	Int.	23	408.95	
70-6204A[12]	6-20	21-6	3.5	15.75	1	Int.	21	583.95	
Trophy									
73-1420	1.75-4	73-30	3.5	10.8	1	Int.	10.9	237.95	
73-1500[1]	1.75-5	60-23	3.6	10.8	1	Int.	12.3	243.95	
73-4124[1]	4-12	32-11	3	12.5	1	Int.	16.1	285.95	
73-3940	3-9	42-14	3	11.7	1	Int.	13.2	159.95	
73-6184	6-18	17.3-6	3	14.8	1	Int.	17.9	360.95	
73-4154M	4-15	26-7.7	3	13.7	1	Int.	18.7	337.95	
73-3941[5]	3-9	37-12.5	3	13	1	Int.	16	410.95	
Turkey & Brush									
73-1420	1.75-4	73-30	3.5	10.8	32mm	Int.	10.9	237.95	
HOLOsight Model 400[8]	1	—	—	6	—	Int.	8.7	562.95	
Trophy Handgun									
73-0232[2]	2	20	9-26	8.7	1	Int.	7.7	262.95	
73-2632[3]	2-6	21-7	9-26	9.1	1	Int.	9.6	268.95	
Banner									
71-1545	1.5-4.5	67-23	3.5	10.5	1	Int.	10.5	116.95	
71-3944[9]	3-9	30-10	4	11.5	1	Int.	12.5	120.95	
71-3950[10]	3-9	31-10	3	16	1	Int.	19	186.95	
71-4124[7]	4-12	29-11	3	12	1	Int.	15	157.95	
71-4228	4	26.5	3	11.75	1	Int.	10	81.95	
71-6185[10]	6-18	17-6	3	16	1	Int.	18	209.95	
Sportview									
79-0428	4	25	3	7.6	1	Int.	8.5	75.95	
79-0004	4	31	4	11.7	1	Int.	11.2	97.95	
79-0039	3-9	38-13	3.5	10.75	1	Int.	11.2	116.95	
79-0412[7]	4-12	27-9	3.2	13.1	1	Int.	14.6	141.95	
79-1393[6]	3-9	35-12	3.5	11.75	1	Int	10	68.95	
79-1545	1.5-4.5	69-24	3	10.7	1	Int.	8.6	86.95	
79-1548[11]	1.5-4.5	71-25	3.5	10.4	1	Int.	11.8	104.95	
79-2538[11]	2.5	45	3	11	1	Int.	10	76.95	
79-1403	4	29	4	11.75	1	Int.	9.2	56.95	
79-6184	6-18	19.1-6.8	3	14.5	1	Int.	15.9	170.95	
79-3940M	3-9	42-14	3	12.7	1	Int.	12.5	95.95	
C-MORE SYSTEMS									
Classic AR[1]	4	225	3	7.2	35mm	Int.	14.6	249.00	
SSE[2]	6	159	3.3	12.8	30mm	Int	22.8	499.00	
Tactical Elite[3]	6	159	3.38	13	30mm	Int.	22.6	469.00	
Compact 1-5x20[4]	1-5	301-62	3.45	9.5	30mm	Int.	14.2	359.00	
Tactical[5]	6	157	3.35	12.2	30mm	Int.	13.8	449.00	
Handgun 1.5x20[6]	1.5	183	11-22	5.4	1	Int.	6.8	159.00	
Handgun 4x32	4	91	11-22	8.6	1	Int.	7.6	165.00	
Handgun 1.5-4.5x20	1.5-4.5	190-88	11-22	7.7	1	Int.	7.6	215.00	
Handgun 2.5-7x28	2.5-7	135-52	11-22	9.3	1	Int.	8.6	245.00	
Red Dots									
Railway[1]	1	—	—	4.8	—	Int.	5	299.00	
Colt Scout[2]	1	—	—	11	—	Int.	7.5	368.00	
Serendipity[4]	1	—	—	5.3	—	Int.	3.75	299.00	
Slide Ride[5]	1	—	—	4.8	—	Int.	3	249.00	
Colt Tactical[3]	1	—	—	8	—	Int.	12	444.00	
DOCTER OPTIC									
Fixed Power									
4x32	4	31	3	10.7	26mm	Int.	10	898.00	
6x42	6	20	3	12.8	26mm	Int.	12.7	1,004.00	
8x56[1]	8	15	3	14.7	26mm	Int.	15.6	1,240.00	
Variables									
1-4x24	1-4	79.7-31.3	3	10.8	30mm	Int.	13	1,300.00	
1.2-5x32	1.2-5	65-25	3	11.6	30mm	Int.	15.4	1,345.00	
1.5-6x42	1.5-6	41.3-20.6	3	12.7	30mm	Int.	16.8	1,378.00	
2.5-10x48	2.5-10	36.6-12.4	3	13.7	30mm	Int.	18.6	1,378.00	
2-12x56	3-12	44.2-13.8	3	14.8	30mm	Int.	20.3	1,425.00	
3-10x40	3-10	34.4-11.7	3	13	1	Int.	18	795.00	

[1]Wide Angle. [2]Also silver finish. [3]Also silver finish. [4]Matte finish. [5]Selective red L.E.D. dot for low light hunting. [6]Also silver finish. [7]Adj. obj. [8]Variable intensity; interchangeable extra reticles (Dual Rings, Open Cross Hairs) **$111.95**; fits Weaver-style base. Comp model 430 with diamond reticle and 1911 No-hole or 5-hole pattern mount, or STI mount, **$631.00**. (2x magnification adapter **$248.95**). [9]Blackpowder scope; extended eye relief, Circle-X reticle. [10]50mm objective. [11]With Circle-X reticle, matte finish. [12]Matte finish, adjustable objective.

HOLOSIGHT RETICLES

Ring

MOA Dot

Inner Ring

Diamond

Dual Ring

Open Cross

Standard

Tombstone

SCOPE RETICLES

CP2

Multi

Euro

Circle-X

[1]All Weaver and Picatinny-style rail mounts. [2]Carry handle mount for A1/A2-style receivers. [3]Flattop mount for A3-style receivers. [4]Most popular auto pistols. [5]Mounts to any flat surface, custom mounts, shotgun ribs; Glock adapter plate for direct slide mounting. From C-More Systems, Inc.

Matte black and matte silver finish available. All lenses multi-coated. Illuminated reticle avail., choice of reticles. [1]Rail mount, aspherical lenses avail. Aspherical lens model, **$1,375.00**. Imported from Germany by Docter Optic Technologies, Inc.

SCOPES & MOUNTS

Maker and Model	Magn.	Field at 100 Yds. (feet)	Eye Relief (in.)	Length (in.)	Tube Dia. (in.)	W & E Adjustments	Weight (ozs.)	Price	Other Data
EUROPTIK SUPREME									
4x36K	4	39	3.5	11.6	26mm	Int.	14	795.00	[1]Military scope with adjustable parallax. Fixed powers have 26mm tubes,
6x42K	6	21	3.5	13	26mm	Int.	15	875.00	variables have 30mm tubes. Some models avail. with steel tubes. All
8x56K	8	18	3.5	14.4	26mm	Int.	20	925.00	lenses multi-coated. Dust and water tight. From Europtik.
1.5-6x42K	1.5-6	61.7-23	3.5	12.6	30mm	Int.	17	1,095.00	
2-8x42K	2-8	52-17	3.5	13.3	30mm	Int.	17	1,150.00	
2.5-10x56K	2.5-10	40-13.6	3.5	15	30mm	Int.	21	1,295.00	
3-12x56 Super	3-12	10.8-34.7	3.5-2.5	15.2	30mm	Int.	24	1,495.00	
4-16x56 Super	4-16	9.8-3.9	3.1	18	30mm	Int.	26	1,575.00	
3-9x40 Micro	3-9	3.2-12.1	2.7	13	1	Int.	14	1,450.00	
2.5-10x46 Micro	2.5-10	13.7-33.4	2.7	14	30mm	Int.	20	1,395.00	
4-16x56 EDP[1]	4-16	22.3-7.5	3.1	18	30mm	Int.	29	1,995.00	
7-12x50 Target	7-12	8.8-5.5	3.5	15	30mm	Int.	21	1,495.00	
KAHLES									
4x36	4	34.5	3.25	11.2	1	Int.	12.7	555.50	Aluminum tube. Multi-coated, waterproof. [1]Also available with illuminated
6x42	6	23	3.25	12.4	1	Int.	14.4	699.94	reticle. Imported from Austria by Swarovski Optik.
8x50[1]	8	17.3	3.25	13	1	Int.	16.5	755.50	
1.1-4.5x20	1.1-4.5	72-27	3.25	10.6	30mm	Int.	12.7	699.94	
1.5-6x42[1]	1.5-6	61-21	3.25	12.5	30mm	Int.	15.8	772.72	
2.2-9x42	2.2-9	39.5-15	3.25	13.3	30mm	Int.	15.8	955.50	
3-9x42	3-9	43-16	3.25	12	1	Int.	13	611.06	
3-9x42AH	3-9	43-16	3.5	12.36	1	Int.	12.7	549.00	
3-12x56[1]	3-12	30-11	3.25	15.4	30mm	Int.	18	999.04	

No. 4A   **No. 7A**   **Plex**   **Illuminated No. 4N**   **Illuminated Plex N**   **TD Smith**

Maker and Model	Magn.	Field at 100 Yds. (feet)	Eye Relief (in.)	Length (in.)	Tube Dia. (in.)	W & E Adjustments	Weight (ozs.)	Price	Other Data
KILHAM									
Hutson Handgunner II	1.7	8	—	5.5	.875	Int.	5.1	119.95	Unlimited eye relief; internal click adjustments; crosshair reticle. Fits Thompson/Center rail mounts, for S&W K, N, Ruger Blackhawk, Super,
Hutson Handgunner	3	8	10-12	6	.875	Int.	5.3	119.95	Super Single-Six, Contender.
LEICA									
Ultravid 1.75-6x32	1.75-6	47-18	4.8-3.7	11.25	30mm	Int.	14	749.00	Aluminum tube with hard anodized matte black finish with titanium
Ultravid 3.5-10x42	3.5-10	29.5-10.7	4.6-3.6	12.62	30mm	Int.	16	849.00	accents; finger-adjustable windage and elevation with 1/4-MOA clicks.
Ultravid 4.5-14x42	4.5-14	20.5-7.4	5-3.7	12.28	30mm	Int.	18	949.00	Made in U.S. From Leica.

Leicaplex Standard   **Leica Dot**   **Standard Dot**   **Crosshair**   **Euro**   **Post & Plex**

Maker and Model	Magn.	Field at 100 Yds. (feet)	Eye Relief (in.)	Length (in.)	Tube Dia. (in.)	W & E Adjustments	Weight (ozs.)	Price	Other Data
LEUPOLD									
Vari-X III 3.5x10 Tactical	3.5-10	29.5-10.7	3.6-4.6	12.5	1	Int.	13.5	771.40	Constantly centered reticles, choice of Duplex, tapered CPC, Leupold Dot, Crosshair and Dot. CPC and Dot reticles extra. [1]2x and 4x scopes
M8-2X EER[1]	1.7	21.2	12-24	7.9	1	Int.	6	300.00	have from 12"-24" of eye relief and are suitable for handguns, top ejection
M8-2X EER Silver[1]	1.7	21.2	12-24	7.9	1	Int.	6	321.40	arms and muzzleloaders. [2]3x9 Compact, 6x Compact, 12x, 3x9, and
M8-2.5x28 IER Scout	2.3	22	9.3	10.1	1	Int.	7.5	389.30	6.5x20 come with adjustable objective. Sunshade available for all adjust-
M8-4X EER[1]	3.7	9	12-24	8.4	1	Int.	7	405.40	able objective scopes, **$23.20-$41.10.** [3]Silver finish about **$15.00** extra.
M8-4X EER Silver[1]	3.7	9	12-24	8.4	1	Int.	7	405.40	[4]Long Range scopes have side focus parallax adjustment, additional
Vari-X 2.5-8 EER	2.5-8	13-4.4	11.7-12	9.7	1	Int.	10.9	639.30	windage and elevation travel. Partial listing shown. **Contact Leupold for**
M8-4X Compact	3.6	25.5	4.5	9.2	1	Int.	7.5	367.90	**complete details.**
Vari-X 2-7x Compact	2.5-6.6	41.7-16.5	5-3.7	9.9	1	Int.	8.5	460.70	
Vari-X 3-9x Compact	3.2-8.6	34-13.5	4-3	11-11.3	1	Int.	11	498.20	
M8-4X	4	24	4	10.7	1	Int.	9.3	371.40	
M8-6X36mm	5.9	17.7	4.3	11.4	1	Int.	10	394.60	
M8-6x 42mm	6	17	4.5	12	1	Int.	11.3	491.10	
M8-6x42 A.O. Tactical	6	17	4.2	12.1	1	Int.	11.3	628.60	
M8-12x A.O. Varmint	11.6	9.1	4.2	13	1	Int.	13.5	550.00	
Vari-X 3-9x Compact EFR A.O.	3.8-8.6	34-13.5	4-3	11	1	Int.	11	532.10	
Vari-X-II 1x4	1.6-4.2	70.5-28.5	4.3-3.8	9.2	1	Int.	9	380.40	
Vari-X-II 2x7	2.5-6.6	42.5-17.8	4.9-3.8	11	1	Int.	10.5	412.50	
Vari-X-II 3x9[1,3]	3.3-8.6	32.3-14	4.1-3.7	12.3	1	Int.	13.5	416.10	
Vari-X-II 3-9x50mm	3.3-8.6	32.3-14	4.7-3.7	12	1	Int.	13.6	494.60	
Vari-X II 3-9x40 Tactical	3-9	32.3-14	4.7-3.7	12.2	1	Int.	13	516.10	
Vari-X-II 4-12 A.O. Matte	4.4-11.6	22.8-11	5-3.3	12.3	1	Int.	13.5	573.20	
Vari-X-III 1.5-5x20	1.5-4.5	66-23	5.3-3.7	9.4	1	Int.	9.5	610.70	
Vari-X-III 1.75-6x32	1.9-5.6	47-18	4.8-3.7	9.8	1	Int.	11	653.60	
Vari-X-III 2.5x8	2.6-7.8	37-13.5	4.7-3.7	11.3	1	Int.	11.5	651.80	
Vari-X-III 3.5-10x40 Long Range M3[4]	3.9-9.7	29.8-11	4-3.5	13.5	30mm	Int.	19.5	1,108.90	

Duplex   **CPC**   **Post & Duplex**   **Leupold Dot**   **Dot**

SCOPES & MOUNTS

Maker and Model	Magn.	Field at 100 Yds. (feet)	Eye Relief (in.)	Length (in.)	Tube Dia. (in.)	W & E Adjustments	Weight (ozs.)	Price	Other Data
LEUPOLD (cont'd.)									
Vari-X-III 3.5-10x50	3.3-9.7	29.5-10.7	4.6-3.6	12.4	1	Int.	13	769.60	
Vari-X-III 4.5-14 A.O.	4.7-13.7	20.8-7.4	5-3.7	12.4	1	Int.	14.5	750.00	
Vari-X-III 4.5-14x50 A.O.	4.7-13.7	20.8-7.4	5-3.7	12.4	1	Int.	14.5	869.60	
Vari-X 4.5-14x 50 Long Range Tactical[4]	4.9-14.3	19-6	5-3.7	12.1	30mm	Int.	17.5	1,037.50	
Vari-X-III 6.5-20 A.O. Varmint	6.5-19.2	14.2-5.5	5.3-3.6	14.2	1	Int.	17.5	892.90	
Vari-X-III 6.5x20xTarget EFR A.O.	6.5-19.2	—	5.3-3.6	14.2	1	Int.	16.5	910.70	
Vari-X III 6.5-20x 50 Long Range Target[4]	6.8-19.2	14.7-5.4	4.9-3.7	14.3	30mm	Int.	19	1,117.90	
Vari-X III 8.5-25x40 A.O. Target	8.5-25	10.86-4.2	5.3	14.3	1	Int.	17.5	900.00	
Vari-X III 8.5-25x 50 Long Range Target[4]	8.3-24.2	11.4-4.3	4.4-3.6	14.3	30mm	Int.	19	1,208.90	
Mark 4 M1-10x	10	11.1	3.6	13.125	30mm	Int.	21	1,735.70	
Mark 4 M1-16x	16	6.6	4.1	12.875	30mm	Int.	22	1,735.70	
Mark 4 M3-10x	10	11.1	3.6	13.125	30mm	Int.	21	1,735.70	
Vari-X III 6.5x20[2] A.O.	6.5-19.2	14.2-5.5	5.3-3.6	14.2	1	Int.	16	812.50	
BR-D 24x40 A.O. Target	24	4.7	3.2	13.6	1	Int.	15.3	992.90	
BR-D 36x-40 A.O. Target	36	3.2	3.4	14.1	1	Int.	15.6	1,039.30	
LPS 1.5-6x42	1.5-6	58.7-15.7	4	11.2	30mm	Int.	16	1,476.80	
LPS 3.5-14x52 A.O.	3.5-14	28-7.2	4	13.1	30mm	Int.	22	1,569.60	
Rimfire									
Vari-X II 2-7x RF Special	3.6	25.5	4.5	9.2	1	Int.	7.5	460.70	
Shotgun									
M8 4x	3.7	9	12-24	8.4	1	Int.	6	392.90	
Vari-X II 1x4	1.6-4.2	70.5-28.5	4.3-3.8	9.2	1	Int.	9	401.80	
Vari-X-II 2x7	2.5-6.6	42.5-17.8	4.9-3.8	11	1	Int.	9	433.90	
LYMAN									
Super TargetSpot[1]	10, 12, 15, 20, 25, 30	5.5	2	24.3	.75	Int.	27.5	685.00	Made under license from Lyman to Lyman's orig. specs. Blue steel. Three-point suspension rear mount with .25-min. click adj. Data listed are for 20x model. [1]Price approximate. Made in U.S. by Parsons Optical Mfg. Co.
McMILLAN									
Vision Master 2.5-10x	2.5-10	14.2-4.4	4.3-3.3	13.3	30mm	Int.	17	1,250.00	42mm obj. lens; .25-MOA clicks; nitrogen filled, fogproof, waterproof; etched duplex-type reticle. [1]Tactical Scope with external adj. knobs, military reticle; 60+ min. adj.
Vision Master Model 1[1]	2.5-10	14.2-4.4	4.3-3.3	13.3	30mm	Int.	17	1,250.00	
MILLETT									
Buck 3-9x44	3-9	38-14	3.25-4	13	1	Int.	16.2	549.00	[1]3-MOA dot. [2]5 MOA dot. [3]3-, 5-, 8-, 10-MOA dots. [4]10-MOA dot. All have click adjustments; waterproof, shockproof; 11 dot intensity settings. All avail. in matte/black or silver finish. From Millett Sights.
SP 1 Compact[1] Red Dot	1	36.65	—	4.1	1	Int.	3.2	149.95	
SP-2 Compact[2] Red Dot	1	58	—	4.5	30mm	Int.	4.3	149.95	
MultiDot SP[3]	1	50	—	4.8	30mm	Int.	5.3	289.95	
30mm Wide View[4]	1	60	—	5.5	30mm	Int.	5	289.95	
MIRADOR									
RXW 4x40[1]	4	37	3.8	12.4	1	Int.	12	179.95	[1]Wide angle scope. Multi-coated objective lens. Nitrogen filled; waterproof; shockproof. From Mirador Optical Corp.
RXW 1.5-5x20[1]	1.5-5	46-17.4	4.3	11.1	1	Int.	10	188.95	
RXW 3-9x40	3-9	43-14.5	3.1	12.9	1	Int.	13.4	251.95	
NIGHTFORCE									
2.5-10x50	2.5-10	31.4-9.4	3.3	13.9	30mm	Int.	28	847.87	Lighted reticles with eleven intensity levels. Most scopes have choice of reticles. From Lightforce U.S.A.
3.5-15x56	3.5-15	24.5-6.9	3	15.8	30mm	Int.	32	507.78	
5.5-22x56	5.5-22	15.7-4.4	3	19.4	30mm	Int.	38.5	965.53	
8-32x56	8-32	9.4-3.1	3	16.6	30mm	Int.	36	997.90	
12-42x56	12-42	6.7-2.3	3	17	30mm	Int.	36	1,053.64	
NIKON									
Monarch UCC									
4x40[2]	4	26.7	3.5	11.7	1	Int.	11.7	322.95	Super multi-coated lenses and blackening of all internal metal parts for maximum light gathering capability; positive .25-MOA; fogproof; waterproof; shockproof; luster and matte finish. [1]Also available in matte silver finish. [2]Available in silver matte finish. [3]Available with TurkeyPro or Nikoplex reticle. [4]Silver Shadow finish; black matte $296.95. From Nikon, Inc.
1.5-4.5x20[3]	1.5-4.5	67.8-22.5	3.7-3.2	10.1	1	Int.	9.5	356.95	
2-7x32	2-7	46.7-13.7	3.9-3.3	11.3	1	Int.	11.3	416.95	
3-9x40[1]	3-9	33.8-11.3	3.6-3.2	12.5	1	Int.	12.5	420.95	
3.5-10x50	3.5-10	25.5-8.9	3.9-3.8	13.7	1	Int.	15.5	630.95	
4-12x40 A.O.	4-12	25.7-8.6	3.6-3.2	14	1	Int.	16.6	540.95	
6.5-20x44	6.5-19.4	16.2-5.4	3.5-3.1	14.8	1	Int.	19.6	670.95	
2x20 EER	2	22	26.4	8.1	1	Int.	6.3	242.95	
Buckmasters									
4x40	4	30.4	3.3	12.7	1	Int.	11.8	238.95	
3-9x40[4]	3.3-8.6	33.8-11.3	3.5-3.4	12.7	1	Int.	13.4	316.95	
3-9x50	3.3-8.6	33.8-11.3	3.5-3.4	12.9	1	Int.	18.2	442.95	

German #1 German #2 Turkey Reticle

3/4-Mil. Dot Crosshair

SCOPES & MOUNTS

Maker and Model	Magn.	Field at 100 Yds. (feet)	Eye Relief (in.)	Length (in.)	Tube Dia. (in.)	W & E Adjustments	Weight (ozs.)	Price	Other Data
NORINCO									
N2520	2.5	44.1	4	—	1	Int.	—	52.28	Partial listing shown. Some with Ruby Lens coating, blue/black and matte finish. Imported by Nic Max, Inc.
N420	4	29.3	3.7	—	1	Int.	—	52.70	
N640	6	20	3.1	—	1	Int.	—	67.88	
N154520	1.5-4.5	63.9-23.6	4.1-3.2	—	1	Int.	—	80.14	
N251042	2.5-10	27-11	3.5-2.8	—	1	Int.	—	206.60	
N3956	3-9	35.1-6.3	3.7-2.6	—	1	Int.	—	231.88	
N31256	3-12	26-10	3.5-2.8	—	1	Int.	—	290.92	
NC2836M	2-8	50.8-14.8	3.6-2.7	—	1	Int.	—	255.60	
PARSONS									
Parsons Long Scope	6	10	2	28-34+	.75	Ext.	13	475.00-525.00	Adjustable for parallax, focus. Micrometer rear mount with .25-min. click adjustments. Price is approximate. Made in U.S. by Parsons Optical Mfg. Co.
PENTAX									
Lightseeker 1.75-6x[1]	1.75-6	71-20	3.5-4	10.8	1	Int.	13	526.00	[1]Glossy finish; Matte finish, Heavy Plex or Penta-Plex, **$546.00**. [2]Glossy finish; Matte finish, **$594.00**. [3]Glossy finish; Matte finish, **$628.00**; Heavy Plex, add **$20.00**. [4]Matte finish; Mil-Dot, **$798.00**. [5]Glossy finish; Matte finish, **$652.00**; Heavy Plex, add **$10.00**. [6]Glossy finish; Matte finish, **$816.00**; with Heavy Plex, **$830.00**; with Mil-Dot, **$978.00**. [7]Matte finish; with Mil-Dot, **$1,018.00**. [8]Matte finish, with Mil-Dot, **$1098.00**. [9]Lightseeker II, Matte finish, **$844.00**. [10]Lightseeker II, Glossy finish, **$636.00**. [11]Lightseeker II, Matte finish, **$660.00**. [12]Lightseeker II, Matte finish, **$878.00**. [13]Matte finish; Advantage finish, Break-up Mossy Oak finish, Treestand Mossy Oak finish, **$364.00**. From Pentax Corp.
Lightseeker 2-8x[2]	2-8	53-17	3.5-4	11.7	1	Int.	14	560.00	
Lightseeker 3-9x [3, 4, 10, 11]	3-9	36-14	3.5-4	12.7	1	Int.	15	594.00	
Lightseeker 3.5-10x[5]	3.5-10	29.5-11	3.5-4	14	1	Int.	19.5	630.00	
Lightseeker 4-16x[6, 9]	4-16	33-9	3.5-4	15.4	1	Int.	22.7	796.00	
Lightseeker 6-24x [7, 12]	6-24	18-5.5	3.5-4	16	1	Int.	23.7	856.00	
Lightseeker 8.5-32x[8]	8.5-32	13-3.8	3.5-4	17.2	1	Int.	24	944.00	
Shotgun									
Lightseeker 2.5x[13]	2.5	55	3.5-4	10	1	Int.	9	350.00	
Lightseeker Zero-X SG Plus	0	51	4.5-15	8.9	1	Int.	7.9	372.00	
Lightseeker Zero-X/V Still-Target	0-4	53.8-15	3.5-7	8.9	1	Int.	10.3	476.00	
Lightseeker Zero X/V	0-4	53.8-15	3.5-7	8.9	1	Int.	10.3	454.00	
RWS									
300	4	36	3.5	11.75	1	Int.	13.2	170.00	
400[1]	2-7	55-16	3.5	11.75	1	Int.	13.2	190.00	
450	3-9	43-14	3.5	12	1	Int.	14.3	215.00	
500	4	36	3.5	12.25	1	Int.	13.9	225.00	
550	2-7	55-16	3.5	12.75	1	Int.	14.3	235.00	
600	3-9	43-14	3.5	13	1	Int.	16.5	260.00	
SCHMIDT & BENDER									
Fixed									
4x36	4	30	3.25	11	1	Int.	14	725.00	All scopes have 30-yr. warranty, click adjustments, centered reticles, rotation indicators. [1]Glass reticle; aluminum. Available in aluminum with mounting rail. [2]Aluminum only. [3]Aluminum tube. Choice of two bullet drop compensators, choice of two sunshades, two range finding reticles. From Schmidt & Bender, Inc. [4]Parallax adjustment in third turret; extremely fine crosshairs. [5]Available with illuminated reticle that glows red; third turret houses on/off switch, dimmer and battery. Also with Long Eye Relief. From Schmidt & Bender, Inc.
6x42	6	21	3.25	13	1	Int.	17	795.00	
8x56	8	16.5	3.25	14	1	Int.	22	915.00	
10x42	10	10.5	3.25	13	1	Int.	18	910.00	
Variables									
1.25-4x20[1]	1.25-4	96-16	3.25	10	30mm	Int.	15.5	945.00	
1.25-4x20 Safari[5]	1.25-4	96-16	3.75	10	30mm	Int.	15.5	990.00	
1.5-6x42[1, 5]	1.5-6	60-19.5	3.25	12	30mm	Int.	19.7	1,073.00	
2.5-10x56[1, 5]	2.5-10	37.5-12	3.25	14	30mm	Int.	24.6	1,298.00	
3-12x42[2]	3-12	34.5-11.5	3.25	13.5	30mm	Int.	19	1,222.00	
3-12x50[1, 5]	3-12	33.3-12.6	3.25	13.5	30mm	Int.	22.9	1,262.00	
4-16x50 Varmint[4, 6]	4-16	22.5-7.5	3.25	14	30mm	Int.	26	1,495.00	
Police/Marksman Fixed									
6x42[1]	6	21	3.25	13	30mm	Int.	17	900.00	
10x42[3]	10	10.5	3.25	13	30mm	Int.	18	950.00	
Variables									
1.5-6x42[3]	1.5-6	60-19.5	3.25	12	30mm	Int.	NA	1,200.00	
3-12x42[3]	3-12	34.5-11.5	3.25	13.5	30mm	Int.	NA	1,360.00	
3-12x50[3]	3-12	33.3-12.6	3.25	13.5	30mm	Int.	NA	1,400.00	
SHEPHERD									
3940-E	3-9	43.5-15	3.3	13	1	Int.	17	1,039.40	[1]Also avail. as 310-P, 310-PE, **$524.25**. [2]Also avail. as 310-P1, 310-P2, 310-P3, 310-Pla, 310-PE1, 310-P22, 310-P22 Mag., 310-PE, **$524.95**. All have patented Dual Reticle system with range finder bullet drop compensation; multi-coated lenses, waterproof, shock-proof, nitrogen filled, matte finish. From Shepherd Scope, Ltd.
310-2[1, 2]	3-10	35.3-11.6	3-3.75	12.8	1	Int.	18	524.25	
SIGHTRON									
Variables									
SII 1.56x42	1.5-6	50-15	3.8-4	11.69	1	Int.	15.35	259.95	[1]Adjustable objective. [2]3MOA dot; also with 5 or 10 MOA dot. [3]Variable 3, 5, 10 MOA dot; black finish; also stainless. [4]Satin black; also stainless. Electronic Red Dot scopes come with ring mount, front and rear extension tubes, polarizing filter, battery, haze filter caps, wrench. Rifle, pistol, shotgun scopes have aluminum tubes, Exac Trak adjustments, Lifetime warranty. From Sightron, Inc. [5]3" sun shade. [6]Mil Dot or Plex reticle. [7]Dot or Plex reticle. [8]Double Diamond reticle.
SII 2.5-7x32SG[8]	2.5-7	26-7	4.3	10.9	1	Int.	8.46	199.95	
SII 2.58x42	2.5-8	36-12	3.6-4.2	11.89	1	Int.	12.82	233.95	
SII 39x42[4, 6, 7]	3-9	34-12	3.6-4.2	12.00	1	Int.	13.22	246.95	
SII 312x42[6]	3-12	32-9	3.6-4.2	11.89	1	Int.	12.99	261.95	
SII 3.510x42	3.5-10	32-11	3.6	11.89	1	Int.	13.16	261.95	
SII 4.514x42[1]	4.5-14	22-7.9	3.6	13.88	1	Int.	16.07	340.95	
Target									
SII6x42HBR	6	20	4	12.48	1	Int.	12.3	259.95	
SII 24x44	24	4.1	4.33	13.30	1	Int.	15.87	279.95	
SII 416x42[1, 4, 5,6, 7]	4-16	26-7	3.6	13.62	1	Int.	16	317.95	
SII 624-42[1, 4, 5, 7]	6-24	16-5	3.6	14.6	1	Int.	18.7	334.95	

Pentax reticle illustrations:

Heavy Plex   **Fine Plex**   **Penta-Plex**

SCOPES & MOUNTS

Maker and Model	Magn.	Field at 100 Yds. (feet)	Eye Relief (in.)	Length (in.)	Tube Dia. (in.)	W & E Adjustments	Weight (ozs.)	Price	Other Data
SIGHTRON (cont'd.)									
SII1040x42	10-40	8.9-4	3.6	16.1	1	Int.	19	399.95	
Compact									
SII 4x32	4	25	4.5	9.69	1	Int.	9.34	123.95	
SII2.5-10x32	2.5-10	41-10.5	3.75-3.5	10.9	1	Int.	10.39	233.95	
Shotgun									
SII 2.5x20SG	2.5	41	4.3	10.28	1	Int.	8.46	133.95	
Pistol									
SII 1x28P[4]	1	30	9-24	9.49	1	Int.	8.46	135.95	
SII 2x28P[4]	2	16-10	9-24	9.49	1	Int.	8.28	135.95	
SIMMONS									
AETEC									
2100[8]	2.8-10	44-14	5	11.9	1	Int.	15.5	315.95	
2104[16]	3.8-12	33-11	4	13.5	1	Int.	20	343.95	
44Mag									
M-1044	3-10	34-10.5	3	12.75	1	Int.	15.5	224.95	
M-1045	4-12	29.5-9.5	3	13.2	1	Int.	18.25	274.95	
M-1047	6.5-20	14-.5	2.6-3.4	12.8	1	Int.	19.5	284.95	
1048[20]	6.5-20	16-5.5	2.6-3.4	14.5	1	Int.	20	325.95	
M-1050M[19]	3.8-12	26-9	3	13.08	1	Int.	16.75	315.95	
Prohunter									
7700	2-7	53-16.25	3	11.5	1	Int.	12.5	121.95	
7710[2]	3-9	36-13	3	12.6	1	Int.	13.5	131.95	
7716	4-12	26-9	3	12.6	1	Int.	14	155.95	
7721[3]	6-18	18.5-6	3	13.75	1	Int.	12	172.95	
7740[3]	6	21.75	3	12.5	1	Int.	12	114.95	
Prohunter Handgun									
7732[18]	2	22	9-17	8.75	1	Int.	7	131.95	
7738[18]	4	15	10.5-26.4	8.5	1	Int.	8	141.95	
Whitetail Classic									
WTC I1	1.5-5	75-23	3.4-3.2	9.3	1	Int.	9.7	176.95	
WTC12	2.5-8	45-14	3.2-3	11.3	1	Int.	13	192.95	
WTC13	3.5-10	30-10.5	3.2-3	12.4	1	Int.	10.5	203.95	
WTC 15	3.5-10	29.5-11.5	3.2	12.75	1	Int.	13.5	274.95	
WTC 45	4.5-14	22.5-8.6	3.2	13.2	1	Int.	14	253.95	
Pro50									
8800[10]	4-12	27-9	3.5	13.2	1	Int.	18.25	210.95	
8810[10]	6-18	17-5.8	3.6	13.2	1	Int.	18.25	229.95	
8830[3]	2.5-10	30.5-11	3	12.75		Int.	17	142.95	
Deerfield									
21006	4	29.5	3.3	11.5	1	Int.	10	40.95	
21029	3-9	37-13	3.4-3	12.1	1	Int.	12.25	73.95	
21031	4-12	27-9	3-2.8	13.25	1	Int.	14.6	108.95	
Gold Medal Silhoutte									
23002	6-20	18-5.4	2.6-3.4	14.75	1	Int.	19.75	570.95	
Gold Medal Handgun									
22002[6]	2.5-7	11-4	15.7-19.7	9.25	1	Int.	9	264.95	
22004[6]	2	21.5	10.5-20.4	7.8	1	Int.	5.75	202.95	
22008	1.5-4	14-6.3	10-26	8.7	1	Int.	7.25	253.95	
Shotgun									
21004	4	16	5.5	8.8	1	Int.	9.1	80.95	
21005	2.5	24	6	7.4	1	Int.	7	59.95	
7789D	2	31	5.5	8.8	1	Int.	8.75	100.95	
7700D	4	17	5.5	8.5	1	Int.	8.75	110.95	
7791D	1.5-5	76-23.5	3.4	9.5	1	Int.	10.75	131.95	
Rimfire									
1031[18]	4	23.5	3	7.25		Int.	8.25	74.95	
1022[7]	4	29.5	3	11.75	1	Int.	11	67.95	
1022T	3-9	42-14	3.5	11.5	1	Int.	12	161.95	
1039[18]	3-9	38-13	3.3-2.9	11.6	1	Int.	13	78.95	
Blackpowder									
BP0420M[17]	4	19.5	4	7.5	1	Int.	8.3	110.95	
BP2732M[12]	2-7	57.7-16.6	3	11.6	1	Int.	12.4	131.95	
Red Dot									
51004[21]	1	—	—	4.8	1	Int.	4.7	58.95	
51112[22]	1	—	—	5.25	30mm	Int.	6	93.95	
Pro Air Gun									
21608 A.O.	4	25	3.5	12	1	Int.	11.3	108.95	
21613 A.O.	4-12	25-9	3.1-2.9	13.1	1	Int.	15.8	188.95	
21619 A.O.	6-18	18-7	2.9-2.7	13.8	1	Int.	18.2	303.95	
SPRINGFIELD ARMORY									
6x40 Government Model 7.62mm[1]	6	—	3.5	13	1	Int.	14.7	339.00	
4-14x70 Tactical Government Model[2]	4-14	—	3.5	14.25	1	Int.	15.8	339.00	
4-14x56 1st Gen. Government Model[3]	4-14	—	3.5	14.75	30mm	Int.	23	466.00	
10x56 Mil Dot Government Model[4]	10	—	3.5	14.75	30mm	Int.	28	659.00	
6-20x56 Mil Dot Government Model	6-20	—	3.5	18.25	30mm	Int.	33	769.00	

[1]Matte; also polished finish. [2]Silver; also black matte or polished. [3]Black matte finish. [4]Granite finish; black polish **$216.95**; silver **$218.95**; also with 50mm obj., black granite **$336.95**. [5]Camouflage. [6]Black polish. [7]With ring mounts. [8]Silver; black polish avail. [9]Lighted reticle, Black Granite finish. [10]50mm obj.; black matte. [11]Black or silver matte. [12]75-yd. parallax; black or silver matte. [13]TV view. [14]Adj. obj. [15]Silver matte. [16]Adj. objective; 4" sunshade; black matte. [17]Octagon body; rings included; black matte or silver finish. [18]Black matte finish; also available in silver. [19]Smart reticle. [20]Target turrets. [21]With dovetail rings. [23]With 3V lithium battery, extension tube, polarizing filter, Weaver rings. **Only selected models shown.** Contact Simmons Outdoor Corp. for complete details.

[1]Range finding reticle with automatic bullet drop compensator for 308 match ammo to 700 yds. [2]Range finding reticle with automatic bullet drop compensator for 223 match ammo to 700 yds. [3]Also avail. as 2nd Gen. with target knobs and adj. obj., **$549.00**; as 3rd Gen. with illuminated reticle, **$698.00**; as Mil Dot model with illuminated Target Tracking reticle, target knobs, adj. obj., **$698.00**. [4]Unlimited range finding, target knobs, adj. obj., illuminated Target Tracking green reticle. All scopes have matte black finish, internal bubble level, 1/4-MOA clicks. From Springfield, Inc.

SCOPES & MOUNTS

Maker and Model	Magn.	Field at 100 Yds. (feet)	Eye Relief (in.)	Length (in.)	Tube Dia. (in.)	W & E Adjustments	Weight (ozs.)	Price	Other Data
STEINER									
Hunting Z									Waterproof, fogproof, nitrogen filled. [1]Heavy-Duplex, Duplex or European
1.5-5x20[1]	1.5-5	32-12	4.3	9.6	30mm	Int.	11.7	1,399.00	#4 reticle. Aluminum tubes; matte black finish. From Pioneer Research.
2.5-8x36[1]	2.5-8	40-15	4	11.6	30mm	Int.	13.4	1,599.00	
3.5-10x50[1]	3.5-10	77-25	4	12.4	30mm	Int.	16.9	1,799.00	
SWAROVSKI OPTIK									
PF Series									[1]Also in aluminum. [2]Also with 56mm obj., **$1,398.89**. [3]Also available with
8x50[1, 3]	8	17	3.15	13.9	30mm	Int.	21.5	1,343.33	illuminated reticle. [4]Aluminum only. Imported from Austria by Swarovski
8x56[1, 3]	8	17	3.15	14.29	30mm	Int.	24	1,388.88	Optik.
PV Series									
1.25-4x24[1]	1.25-4	98.4-31.2	3.15	10.63	30mm	Int.	16.2	998.89	
1.5-6x42[1]	1.5-6	65.4-21	3.15	12.99	30mm	Int.	20.8	1,132.22	
2.5-10x42[1, 2]	2.5-10	39.6-12.6	3.15	13.23	30mm	Int.	19.8	1,298.89	
3-12x50[1]	3-12	33-10.5	3.15	14.33	30mm	Int.	22.4	1,376.67	
PV-S									
6-24x50[4]	6-24	18.6-5.4	3.15	15.4	30mm	Int.	23.6	1,665.56	
American Series									
3-9x36AV[4]	3-9	39-13.5	3.35	11.8	1	Int.	11.7	754.44	
3-10x42AV[4]	3-10	33-11.7	3.35	12.44	1	Int.	12.7	798.89	
4-12x50AV[4]	4-12	29.1-9.9	3.35	13.5	1	Int.	13.9	821.11	

No. 1   No. 1A   No. 2   No. 4   No. 4A   No. 7A

Maker and Model	Magn.	Field at 100 Yds. (feet)	Eye Relief (in.)	Length (in.)	Tube Dia. (in.)	W & E Adjustments	Weight (ozs.)	Price	Other Data
SWIFT									
600 4x15	4	17	2.8	10.6	.75	Int.	3.5	20.00	All Swift scopes, with the exception of the 4x15, have Quadraplex reticles
601 3-7x20	3-7	25-12	3-2.9	11	.75	Int.	5.6	53.00	and are fogproof and waterproof. The 4x15 has crosshair reticle and is
650 4x32	4	26	4	12	1	Int.	9.1	88.00	non-waterproof. [1]Available in regular matte black or silver finish. [2]Comes
653 4x40WA[1]	4	35	4	12.2	1	Int.	12.6	116.00	with ring mounts, wrench, lens caps, extension tubes, filter, battery.
654 3-9x32	3-9	35-12	3.4-2.9	12	1	Int.	9.8	116.00	[3]Regular and matte black finish. [4]Speed Focus scopes. From Swift Instru-
656 3-9x40WA[1]	3-9	40-14	3.4-2.8	12.6	1	Int.	12.3	126.00	ments.
657 6x40	6	28	4	12.6	1	Int.	10.4	116.00	
658 2-7x40WA[3]	2-7	55-18	3.3-3	11.6	1	Int.	12.5	151.00	
659 3.5-10x44WA	3.5-10	34-12	3-2.8	12.8	1	Int.	13.5	226.00	
665 1.5-4.5x21	1.5-4.5	69-24.5	3.5-3	10.9	1	Int.	9.6	123.00	
665M 1.5-4.5x21	1.5-4.5	69-24.5	3.5-3	10.9	1	Int.	9.6	123.00	
666M Shotgun 1x20	1	113	3.2	7.5	1	Int.	9.6	126.00	
667 Fire-Fly[2]	1	40	—	5.4	30mm	Int.	5	220.00	
668M 4x32	4	25	4	10	1	Int.	8.9	116.00	
669M 6-18x44	6-18	18-6.5	2.8	14.5	1	Int.	17.6	216.00	
Premier[4]									
649R 4-12x50WA[3]	4-12	29.5-9.5	3.2-3	13.8	1	Int.	17.8	235.00	
671M 3-9x50WA	3-9	35-12	3.24-3.12	15.5	1	Int.	18.2	245.00	
672M 6-18x50WA	6-18	19.4-6.7	3.25-3	15.8	1	Int.	20.9	255.00	
673M 2.5-10x50WA	2.5-10	33-9	4-3.5	11.8	30mm	Int.	18.9	290.00	
674M 3-5x40WA	3-9	40-14.2	3.6-2.9	12	1	Int.	13.1	160.00	
676 4-12x40WA[1]	4-12	29.3-10.5	3.15-2.9	12.4	1	Int.	15.4	170.00	
Pistol									
679M 1.25-4x28	1.25-4	23-9	23-15	9.3	1	Int.	8.2	212.00	
Pistol Scopes									
661 4x32	4	90	10-22	9.2	1	Int.	9.5	126.00	
663 2x20[1]	2	18.3	9-21	7.2	1	Int.	8.4	126.00	
TASCO									
Titan									[1]Water, fog & shockproof; fully coated optics; .25-min. click stops; haze
T1.25-4.5x26NG	1.25-4.5	59-20	3.5	12	30mm	Int.	16.4	623.90	filter caps; 30-day/limited lifetime warranty. [2]30/30 range finding reticle.
T1.56x42N	1.5-6	59-20	3.5	12	30mm	Int.	16.4	713.00	[3]Fits most popular auto pistols, MP5, AR-15/M16. [4]1/3 greater zoom
T39x42N	3-9	37-13	3.5	12.5	30mm	Int.	16.8	677.35	range. [5]Trajectory compensating scopes, Opti-Centered® stadia reticle.
T312x52N	3-12	27-10	4.5	14	30mm	Int.	20.7	802.15	[6]Black gloss or stainless. [7]True one-power scope. [8]Coated optics;
Electronic Reticle									crosshair reticle; ring mounts included to fit most 22, 10mm receivers.
ERD39x40WA	3-9	41-14	3	12.75	1	Int.	16	338.70	[9]Red dot; also with switchable red/green dot (EZ02, **$42.05**). [10]Also matte
World Class TS									aluminum finish. [11]11-position rheostat, 10-MOA dot; built-in dovetail-
TS24x44[16]	24	4.5	3	14	1	Int.	17.9	407.00	style mount. Also with crosshair reticle. [12]Also 30/30 reticle. [13]Also in
TS36x44[16]	36	3	3	14	1	Int.	17.9	441.00	stainless finish. [14]Black matte or stainless finish. [15]Also with stainless
TS832x44[16]	8-24	11-3.5	3	14	1	Int.	19.5	492.00	finish. [16]Also in matte black. [17]Available with 5-min., or 10-min. dot. [18]Red
TS624x44[16]	6-24	15-4.5	3	14	1	Int.	18.5	475.00	dot device; can be used on rifles, shotguns, handguns; 3.5 or 7 MOA dot.
TS832x44[16]	8-32	11-3.5	4.5	17	1	Int.	19.5	1,127.00	Available with 10, 15, 20-min. dot. [19]20-min. dot. [20]20mm; also 32mm. [21]20mm; black
Mag IV									matte; also stainless steel; also 32mm. [21]Pro-Shot reticle. [22]Has 4, 8, 12,
W312x40[1, 2, 4]	3-12	35-9	3	12.25	1	Int.	12	160.45	16MOA dots (switchable). [23]Available with BDC. **Contact Tasco for**
W416x40[1, 2, 4, 13, 14]	4-16	26-7	3	14.25	1	Int.	15.6	221.55	**details on complete line.**
W416x50	4-16	31-8	4	13.5	1	Int.	16	410.00	
W520x50[23]	5-20	24-6	4	13.5	1	Int.	16	463.45	
Golden Antler									
GA4x32TV	4	32	3	13	1	Int.	12.7	82.65	
GA39x32TV[1]	3-9	39-13	3	—	1	Int.	12.2	106.75	
GA39x40TV	3-9	39-13	3	12.5	1	Int.	13	160.15	
Silver Antler									
SA2.5x32	2.5	42	3.25	11	1	Int.	10	82.65	
SA4x40	4	32	3	12	1	Int.	12.5	89.15	
SA39x32	3-9	39-13	3	13.25	1	Int.	12.2	106.75	
SA39x40WA[10]	3-9	41-15	3	12.75	1	Int.	13	160.15	

SCOPES & MOUNTS

Maker and Model	Magn.	Field at 100 Yds. (feet)	Eye Relief (in.)	Length (in.)	Tube Dia. (in.)	W & E Adjustments	Weight (ozs.)	Price	Other Data
TASCO (cont'd.)									
Pronghorn									
PH4x32	4	32	3	12	1	Int.	12.5	61.15	
PH39x32	3-9	39-13	3	12	1	Int.	11	83.20	
PH39x40	3-9	39-13	3	13	1	Int.	12.1	110.35	
TR Scopes									
TR416x40	4-16	26-7	3	14.25	1	Int.	16.8	392.15	
TR624x40	6-24	17.4	3	15.5	1	Int.	17.5	427.80	
Bantam									
S1.5-45x20A[19, 21]	1.5-4.5	69.5-23	4	10.25	1	Int.	10	106.95	
S1.54x32A[21]	1.5-4.5	69.5-23	4	11.25	1	Int.	12	115.90	
S2.5x20A[20, 21]	2.5	22	6	7.5	1	Int.	7.5	83.70	
SA2.5x32A	2.5	32	6	8.5	1	Int.	8.5	91.85	
Airgun									
AG4x20	4	20	2.5	10.75	.75	Int.	5	42.80	
AG4x32N	4	30	3	—	1	Int.	12.25	151.55	
AG27x32	2-7	48-17	3	12.25	1	Int.	14	187.20	
Rimfire									
RF4x15[8]	4	22.5	2.5	11	.75	Int.	4	16.15	
RF4x20WA	4	23	2.5	10.5	.75	Int.	3.8	23.80	
RF4x32[16]	4	31	3	12.25	1	Int.	12.6	77.45	
RF37x20	3-7	24-11	2.5	11.5	.75	Int.	6.7	45.85	
Propoint									
PDP2[10, 17]	1	40	Unltd.	5	30mm	Int.	5	267.40	
PDP3[10, 17]	1	52	Unltd.	5	30mm	Int.	5	320.85	
PDP3CMP	1	68	Unltd.	4.75	33mm	Int.	—	410.00	
PDP5CMP[22]	1	82	Unltd.	4	47mm	Int.	8	410.00	
Optima 2000									
OPP2000-3.5[3, 20]	1	—	—	1.5	—	Int.	1/2	625.70	
OPP2000-7[3, 20]	1	—	—	1.5	—	Int.	1.2	625.70	
Pistol Scopes									
PX20[10]	2	21	10-23	8	1	Int.	6.5	160.45	
P1.254x28[10]	1.25-4	23-9	15-23	9.25	1	Int.	8.2	356.50	
Tactical & Target									
CU840x56M	8-40	11.5-2.6	3	16	30mm	Int.	31.5	1,324.15	
CU1050x56M	10-50	7.8-2.6	3	18	30mm	Int.	32	1,426.00	
CU1250x56M	12-50	5.7-1.6	3	20	30mm	Int.	00	1,510.00	
SS10x42M	10	13	4	14.25	30mm	Int.	26	1,283.40	
EZ01	1	35	—	4.75	1	Int.	2.5	34.00	
World Class Plus									
WCP4x44	4	32	3.25	12.75	1	Int.	13.5	249.55	
WCP3.510x50[18]	3.5-10	30-10.5	3.75	13	1	Int.	17.1	356.50	
WCP39x44[1,16]	3-9	39-14	3.5	12.75	1	Int.	15.8	288.80	
DWC832x50 Target	8-32	13-4	3	14.5	1	Int.	25.1	588.25	
DWCP1040x50 Target	10-40	11-2.5	3	14.5	1	Int.	25.3	541.70	
THOMPSON/CENTER RECOIL PROOF SERIES									
Pistol Scopes									[1]Black finish; silver optional. [2]Black, lighted reticle. From Thompson/Center Arms.
8315[2]	2.5-7	15-5	8-21, 8-11	9.25	1	Int.	9.2	299.00	
8322	2.5	15	9-21	7.4	1	Int.	7.2	289.00	
8326[4]	2.5-7	15-5	8-21, 8-11	9.25	1	Int.	10.5	349.00	
Muzzleloader Scopes									
8658	1	60	3.8	9.125	1	Int.	10.2	119.00	
8662	4	16	3	8.8	1	Int.	9.1	119.00	
TRIJICON									
Reflex 1x24	1	—	—	4.25	1	Int.	4.6	299.00	[1]Advanced Combat Optical Gunsight for AR-15, M-16, with Intergral mount. Other mounts available. From Trijicon, Inc.
TA44 1.5x16[1]	1.5	43.8	2.4	4.1	—	Int.	3.5	595.00	
TA45 1.5x24[1]	1.5	28.9	3.6	5.6	—	Int.	3.9	595.00	
TA47 2x20[1]	2	33.1	2.1	4.5	—	Int.	3.8	595.00	
TA50 3x24[1]	3	28.9	1.4	4.8	—	Int.	3.9	619.00	
TA11 3.5x35[1]	3.5	28.9	2.4	8	—	Int.	14	1,295.00	
TAO1 4x32[1]	4	36.8	1.5	5.8	—	Int.	9.9	895.00	
Variable AccuPoint									
3-9x40	3-9	—	3.2-3.6	12.2	1	Int.	12.8	649.00	
ULTRA DOT									
Micro-Dot Scopes[1]									[1]Brightness-adjustable fiber optic red dot reticle. Waterproof, nitrogen-filled one-piece tube. Tinted see-through lens covers and battery included. [2]Parallax adjustable. [3]Ultra Dot sights include rings, battery, polarized filter, and 5-year warranty. All models available in black or satin finish. [4]Illuminated red dot has eleven brightness settings. Shock-proof aluminum tube. From Ultra Dot Distribution.
1.5-4.5x20 Rifle	1.5-4.5	80-26	3	9.8	1	Int.	10.5	297.00	
2-7x32	2-7	54-18	3	11	1	Int.	12.1	308.00	
3-9x40	3-9	40-14	3	12.2	1	Int.	13.3	327.00	
4x-12x56[2]	4-12	30-10	3	14.3	1	Int.	18.3	417.00	
Ultra-Dot Sights[3]									
Ultra-Dot 25[4]	1	—	—	5.1	1	Int.	3.9	159.00	
Ultra-Dot 30[4]	1	—	—	5.1	30mm	Int.	4	179.00	
UNERTL									
1" Target	6, 8, 10	16-10	2	21.5	.75	Ext.	21	358.00	[1]Dural .25-MOA click mounts. Hard coated lenses. Non-rotating objective lens focusing. [2].25-MOA click mounts. [3]With target mounts. [4]With calibrated head. [5]Same as 1" Target but without objective lens focusing. [6]With new Posa mounts. [7]Range focus unit near rear of tube. Price is with Posa or standard mounts. Magnum clamp. From Unertl.
1.25: Target[1]	8, 10, 12, 14	12-16	2	25	.75	Ext.	21	466.00	
1.5" Target	10, 12, 14, 16, 18, 20	11.5-3.2	2.25	25.5	.75	Ext.	31	487.00	

SCOPES & MOUNTS

Maker and Model	Magn.	Field at 100 Yds. (feet)	Eye Relief (in.)	Length (in.)	Tube Dia. (in.)	W & E Adjustments	Weight (ozs.)	Price	Other Data
UNERTL (cont'd.)									
2" Target[2]	10, 12, 14, 16, 18, 24, 30, 32, 36,	8	2.25	26.25	1	Ext.	44	642.00	
Varmint, 1.25"[3]	6, 8, 10, 12 8, 10, 12,	1-7	2.50	19.50	.875	Ext.	26	466.00	
Ultra Varmint, 2"[4]	15	12.6-7	2.25	24	1	Ext.	34	630.00	
Small Game[5]	3, 4, 6	25-17	2.25	18	.75	Ext.	16	284.00	
Programmer 200[7]	10, 12, 14, 16, 18, 20, 24, 30, 36	11.3-4	—	26.5	1	Ext.	45	805.00	
BV-20[8]	2	8	4.4	17.875	1	Ext.	21.25	595.00	
Tube Sight	—	—	—	17	—	Ext.	—	262.50	
U.S. OPTICS									
SN-1/TAR Fixed Power System									Prices shown are estimates; scopes built as ordered, to order; choice of reticles; choice of front or rear focal plane; extra-heavy MIL-SPEC construction; extra-long turrets; individual w&e rebound springs; up to 88mm dia. objectives; up to 50mm tubes; all lenses multi-coated. Made in U.S. by U.S. Optics.
16.2x	15	8.6	4.3	16.5	30mm	Int.	27	1,700.00	
22.4x	20	5.8	3.8	18	30mm	Int.	29	1,800.00	
26x	24	5	3.4	18	30mm	Int.	31	1,900.00	
31x	30	4.6	3.5	18	30mm	Int.	32	2,100.00	
37x	36	4	3.6	18	30mm	Int.	32	2,300.00	
48x	50	3	3.8	18	30mm	Int.	32	2,500.00	
Variables									
SN-2	4-22	26.8-5.8	5.4-3.8	18	30mm	Int.	24	1,762.00	
SN-3	1.6-8		4.4-4.8	18.4	30mm	Int.	36	1,435.00	
SN-4	1-4	116-31.2	4.6-4.9	18	30mm	Int.	35	1,065.00	
Fixed Power									
SN-6	4, 6, 8, 10	—	4.2-4.8	9.2	30mm	Int.	18	1,195.00	
SN-8	4, 10, 20, 40	32	3.3	7.5	30mm	Int.	11.1	890.00- 4,000.00	
WEAVER									
Riflescopes									[1]Gloss black, [2]Matte black, [3]Silver, [4]Satin, [5]Silver and black (slightly higher in price). [6]Field of view measured at 18" eye relief..25 MOA click adjustments, except T-Series which vary from .125 to .25 clicks. One-piece tubes with multi-coated lenses. All scopes are shock-proof, water-proof, and fogproof. Dual-X reticle available in all except V24 which has a fine X-hair and ot; T-Series in which certain models are available in fine X-hair and dots; Qwik-Point red dot scopes which are available in fixed 4 or 12 MOA, or variable 4-8-12 MOA. V16 also available with fine X-hair, dot or Dual-X reticle. T-Series scopes have Micro-Trac® adjustments. From Weaver Products.
K2.5[1]	2.5	35	3.7	9.5	1	Int.	7.3	171.75	
K4[1-2]	3.7	26.5	3.3	11.3	1	Int.	10	179.95	
K6[1]	5.7	18.5	3.3	11.4	1	Int.	10	191.95	
KT15[1]	14.6	7.5	3.2	12.9	1	Int.	14.7	363.95	
V3[1-2]	1.1-2.8	88-32	3.9-3.7	9.2	1	Int.	8.5	216.95	
V9[1-2]	2.8-8.7	33-11	3.5-3.4	12.1	1	Int.	11.1	227.95	
V9x50[1-2]	3-9	29.4-9.9	3.6-3	13.1	1	Int.	14.5	307.95	
V10[1-2-3]	2.2-9.6	38.5-9.5	3.4-3.3	12.2	1	Int.	11.2	252.95	
V10-50[1-2-3]	2.3-9.7	40.2-9.2	2.9-2.8	13.75	1	Int.	15.2	346.95	
V16 MDX[2-3]	3.8-15.5	26.8-6.8	3.1	13.9	1	Int.	16.5	424.95	
V16 MFC[2-3]	3.8-15.5	26.8-6.8	3.1	13.9	1	Int.	16.5	424.95	
V16 MDT[2-3]	3.8-15.5	26.8-6.8	3.1	13.9	1	Int.	16.5	424.95	
V24 Varmint[2]	6-24	15.3-4	3.15	14.3	1	Int.	17.5	494.95	
Handgun									
H2[1-3]	2	21	4-29	8.5	1	Int.	6.7	208.95	
H4[1-3]	4	18	11.5-18	8.5	1	Int.	6.7	226.95	
VH4[1-3]	1.5-4	13.6-5.8	11-17	8.6	1	Int.	8.1	278.95	
VH8[1-2-3]	2.5-8	8.5-3.7	12.16	9.3	1	Int.	8.3	290.95	
Rimfire									
R4[2-3]	3.9	29	3.9	9.7	1	Int.	8.8	148.95	
RV7[2-3]	2.5-7	37-13	3.7-3.3	10.75	1	Int.	10.7	171.95	
T-Series									
T-6[4]	614	14	3.58	12.75	1	Int.	14.9	424.95	
T-10[4]	10	9.3	3	15.1	1	Int.	16.7	774.95	
T16[4]	16	6.5	3	15.1	1	Int.	16.7	780.95	
T-24[4]	24	4.4	3	15.1	1	Int.	16.7	787.95	
T-36[3-4]	36	3	3	15.1	1	Int.	16.7	793.95	
ZEISS									
Z/ZM									[1]Also avail. with illuminated reticle. [2]Illuminated Vari-point reticle. Black matte finish. All scopes have .25-min. click-stop adjustments. Choice of Z-Plex or fine crosshair reticles. Rubber armored objective bell, rubber eyepiece ring. Lenses have T-Star coating for highest light transmission. VM/V scopes avail. with rail mount. From Carl Zeiss Optical, Inc.
6x42MC	6	22.9	3.2	12.7	1	Int.	13.4	799.00	
8x56MC	8	18	3.2	13.8	1	Int.	17.6	899.00	
1.25-4x24MC	1.25-4	105-33	3.2	11.46	30mm	Int.	17.3	949.00	
1.5-6x42MC	1.5-6	65.5-22.9	3.2	12.4	30mm	Int.	18.5	1,049.00	
2.5-10x48MC[1]	2.5-10	33-11.7	3.2	14.5	30mm	Int.	24	1,249.00	
3-12x56MC[1]	3-12	27.6-9.9	3.2	15.3	30mm	Int.	25.8	1,399.00	
Diavari									
3-9x36MC	3-9	36-13	3.5	11.9	1	Int.	15	615.00	
VM/V									
1.1-4x24[2]	1.1-4	120-34	3.5	11.8	30mm	Int.	15.8	1,799.00	
1.5-6x42T*	1.5-6	65.5-22.9	3.2	12.4	30mm	Int.	18.5	1,349.00	
2.5-10x50T*[1]	2.5-10	47.1-13	3.5	12.5	30mm	Int.	16.25	1,549.00	
3-12x56T*	3-12	37.5-10.5	3.5	13.5	30mm	Int.	19.5	1,599.00	
3-9x42T*	3-9	42-15	3.74	13.3	1	Int.	15.3	1,249.00	
5-15x42T*	5-15	25.7-8.5	3.74	13.3	1	Int.	15.4	1,499.00	

Hunting scopes in general are furnished with a choice of reticle—crosshairs, post with crosshairs, tapered or blunt post, or dot crosshairs, etc. The great majority of target and varmint scopes have medium or fine crosshairs but post or dot reticles may be ordered. W—Windage E—Elevation MOA—Minute of Angle or 1" (approx.) at 100 yards, etc.

LASER SIGHTS

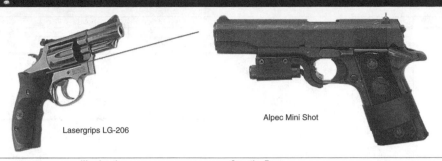

Lasergrips LG-206

Alpec Mini Shot

Laser Devices ULS 2001 with TLS 8R light

Maker and Model	Wavelength (nm)	Beam Color	Lens	Operating Temp. (degrees F.)	Weight (ozs.)	Price	Other Data
ALPEC							[1]Range 1000 yards. [2]Range 300 yards. Mini Shot II range 500 yards, output 650mm, **$129.95**. [3]Range 300 yards; Laser Shot II 500 yards; Super Laser Shot 1000 yards. Black or stainless finish aluminum; removable pressure or push-button switch. Mounts for most handguns, many rifles and shotguns. From Alpec Team, Inc.
Power Shot[1]	635	Red	Glass	NA	2.5	$199.95	
Mini Shot[2]	670	Red	Glass	NA	2.5	99.95	
Laser Shot[3]	670	Red	Glass	NA	3.0	99.95	
BEAMSHOT							[1]Black or silver finish; adj. for windage and elevation; 300-yd. range; also M1000/S (500-yd. range), M1000/u (800-yd.). [2]Black finish; 300-, 500-, 800-yd. models. All come with removable touch pad switch, 5" cable. Mounts to fit virtually any firearm. From Quarton USA Co.
1000[1]	670	Red	Glass	—	3.8	—	
3000[2]	635/670	Red	Glass	—	2	—	
1001/u	635	Red	Glass	—	3.8	—	
780	780	Red	Glass	—	3.8	—	
LASERAIM							[1]Red dot/laser combo; 300-yd. range: LA3xHD Hotdot has 500-yd. range **$249.00**; 4 MOA dot size, laser gives 2" dot size at 100 yds. [2]30mm obj. lens: 4 MOA dot at 100 yds; fits Weaver base. [3]300-yd range; 2" dot at 100 yds.; rechargeable Nicad battery [4]1.5-mile range; 1" dot at 100 yds.; 20+ hrs. batt. life. [5]1.5-mile range; 1" dot at 100 yds; rechargeable Nicad battery (comes with in-field charger); [6]Black or satin finish. With mount, **$169.00**. [7]Laser projects 2" dot at 100 yds.: with rotary switch; with Hotdot **$237.00**; with Hotdot touch switch **$357.00**. [8]For Glock 17-27; G1 Hotdot **$299.00**; price installed. [10]Fits std. Weaver base, no rings required; 6-MOA dot; seven brightness settings. All have w&e adj.; black or satin silver finish. From Laseraim Technologies, Inc.
LA3X Dualdot[1]	—	—	—	—	12	199.00	
LA5[3]	—	—	—	—	1.2	150.00	
LA10 Hotdot[4]	—	—	—	—	NA	199.00	
LA11 Hotdot[5]	—	—	—	—	NA	199.00	
LA16 Hotdot Mighty Sight [6]	—	—	—	—	1.5	149.00	
Red Dot Sights							
LA93 Illusion III[2]	—	—	—	—	5.0	99.00	
LA9750 Grand Illusion[10]	—	—	—	—	7.0	199.00	
Lasers							
MA3 Mini Aimer[7]	—	—	—	—	1.0	99.00	
G1 Laser[8]	—	—	—	—	2.0	229.00	
LASER DEVICES							[1]For semi-auto pistols; also BA-2, 5 oz., **$339.00**. [2]For revolvers. [3]For HK, Walther P99. [4]For semi-autos. [5]For rifles; also FA-4/ULS, 2.5 oz., **$325.00**. [6]For HK sub guns. [7]For military rifles. [8]For shotguns. [9]For SIG-Pro pistol. [10]Universal, semi-autos. [11]For AR-15 variants. All avail. with Magnum Power Point (650nM) or daytime-visible Super Power Point (632nM) diode. Infrared diodes avail. for law enforcement. From Laser Devices, Inc.
BA-1[1]	632	Red	Glass	—	2.5	371.50	
BA-3[2]	632	Red	Glass	—	2.5	332.50	
BA-5[3]	632	Red	Glass	—	3.0	372.00	
Duty-Grade[4]	632	Red	Glass	—	3.5	372.00	
FA-4[5]	632	Red	Glass	—	2.5	350.00	
LasTac[1]	002	Red	Glass	—	5.5	293.00	
MP-5 [6]	632	Red	Glass	—	2.5	495.00	
MR-2[7]	632	Red	Glass	—	3.5	405.00	
SA-2[8]	632	Red	Glass	—	3.0	360.00	
SIG-Pro[9]	632	Red	Glass	—	2.0	398.00	
ULS-2001[10]	632	Red	Glass	—	4.5	210.95	
Universal AR-2[11]	632	Red	Glass	—	4.5	337.00	
LASERGRIPS							Replaces existing grips with built-in laser high in the right grip panel. Integrated pressure sensitive pad in grip activates the laser. Also has master on/off switch. [1]For Beretta 92, 96, Colt 1911/Commander, Ruger MkII, S&W J-frames, SIG Sauer P228, P229. [2]For all Glock models. Option on/off switch. Requires factory installation. [3]For S&W K, L, N frames, round or square butt (LG-207); [4]For Taurus small-frame revolvers. [5]For Ruger SP-101. [6]For SIG Sauer P226. From Crimson Trace Corp.
LG-201[1]	633	Red-Orange	Glass	NA	—	349.00	
LG-206[3]	633	Red-Orange	Glass	NA	—	289.00	
LG-085[4]	633	Red-Orange	Glass	NA	—	279.00	
LG-101[5]	633	Red-Orange	Glass	NA	—	289.00	
LG-226[6]	633	Red-Orange	Glass	NA	—	379.00	
GLS-630[2]	633	Red-Orange	Glass	NA	—	595.00	
LASERLYTE							[1]Dot/circle or dot/crosshair projection; black or stainless. [2]Also 635/645mm model. From TacStar Laserlyte.
LLX-0006-140/090[1]	635/645	Red	—	—	1.4	159.95	
WPL-0004-140/090[2]	670	Red	—	—	1.2	109.95	
TPL-0004-140/090[2]	670	Red	—	—	1.2	109.95	
T7S-0004-140[2]	670	Red	—	—	0.8	109.95	
LASERMAX							Replaces the recoil spring guide rod; includes a customized takedown lever that serves as the laser's instant on/off switch. For Glock, Smith & Wesson, Sigarms, Beretta and select Taurus models. [2]For SIG 2340 pistol. [3]For SIG Sauer P220, P226, P228, P229; accepts laser or flashlight. [4]Allows interchange of laser and flashlight; for Beretta, Glock, USP, SIG Sauer, Walther P99, AR-15/M-16, Uzi Mini. [5]For most popular pistols. From LaserMax.
Guide Rod	635	Red-Orange	Glass	40-120	.25	From 394.95	
SIG Pro laser[2]	635	Red	Glass	—	1.8	NA	
SIG Laser[3]	635, 650, 670, 835	Red	Glass	—	5.6	NA	
LAS/TAC[4]	635, 650	Red	Glass	—	1.8	NA	
ULS-2001[5]	635, 650	Red	Glass	—	NA	NA	
NIGHT STALKER							Waterproof; LCD panel displays power remaining; programmable blink rate; constant or memory on. From Wilcox Industries Corp.
S0 Smart	635	Red	NA	NA	2.46	515.00	

CAUTION: PRICES SHOWN ARE SUPPLIED BY THE MANUFACTURER OR IMPORTER. CHECK YOUR LOCAL GUNSHOP.

54th EDITION, 2000 **461**

SCOPE RINGS & BASES

Maker, Model, Type	Adjust.	Scopes	Price
AIMTECH			
Handguns			
AMT Auto Mag II 22 Mag.	No	Weaver rail	$56.99
AMT Auto Mag III 30 Carb.	No	Weaver rail	64.95
Auto Mag IV 45WM	No	Weaver rail	64.95
Astra 44 Mag Revolver	No	Weaver rail	63.25
Beretta/Taurus 92/99	No	Weaver rail	63.25
Browning Buckmark/Challenger II	No	Weaver rail	56.99
Browning Hi-Power	No	Weaver rail	63.25
CZ75	No	Weaver rail	63.25
EA9/P9 Tanfoglio frame	No	Weaver rail	63.25
Glock 17, 17L, 19, 22, 23	No	Weaver rail	63.25
Glock 20, 21	No	Weaver rail	63.25
Govt. 45 Auto/38 Super	No	Weaver rail	63.25
Hi-Standard 22 all makes	No	Weaver rail	63.25
Rossi 85/851/951 Revolvers	No	Weaver rail	63.25
Ruger Mk I, Mk II	No	Weaver rail	49.95
Ruger P89	No	Weaver rail	63.25
S&W K, L, N frames	No	Weaver rail	63.25
S&W K, L, N with tapped top strap[1]	No	Weaver rail	69.95
S&W Model 41 Target 22	No	Weaver rail	63.25
S&W Model 52 Target 38	No	Weaver rail	63.25
S&W 2nd Gen. 59/459/659	No	Weaver rail	56.99
S&W 3rd Gen. 59 Series	No	Weaver rail	69.95
S&W 422/622/2206/2206TGT	No	Weaver rail	56.99
S&W 645/745	No	Weaver rail	56.99
S&W Sigma	No	Weaver rail	64.95
Taurus PT908	No	Weaver rail	63.25
Taurus 44 6.5" bbl.	No	Weaver rail	69.95
Shotguns			
Benelli M-1 Super 90	No	Weaver rail	40.95
Benelli Montefeltro 12-ga.	No	Weaver rail	40.95
Benelli Super Black Eagle	No	Weaver rail	49.95
Browning Auto-5 12-ga.	No	Weaver rail	40.95
Browning BPS	No	Weaver rail	40.95
Ithaca 37/87 12-ga.	No	Weaver rail	40.95
Mossberg 500/Maverick 12-ga.[2]	No	Weaver rail	40.95
Mossberg 500/Maverick 20-ga.[2]	No	Weaver rail	40.95
Mossberg 835 Ulti-Mag [2]	No	Weaver rail	40.95
Mossberg 5500/9200[2]	No	Weaver rail	40.95
Remington 1100/1187 12-ga.[2]	No	Weaver rail	40.95
Remington 1100/1187 12-ga. LH	No	Weaver rail	40.95
Remington 1100/1187 20-ga.	No	Weaver rail	40.95
Remington 1100/1187 20-ga. LH	No	Weaver rail	40.95
Remington 870 12-ga.[2]	No	Weaver rail	40.95
Remington 870 12-ga. LH	No	Weaver rail	40.95
Remington 870 20-ga.	No	Weaver rail	40.95
Remington 870 20-ga. LH	No	Weaver rail	40.95
Winchester 1300[2]	No	Weaver rail	40.95
Winchester 1400[2]	No	Weaver rail	40.95
Rifles			
AR-15/M16	No	Weaver rail	21.95
Browning A-Bolt	No	Weaver rail	21.95
Browning BAR	No	Weaver rail	21.95
Browning BLR	No	Weaver rail	21.95
CVA Apollo	No	Weaver rail	21.95
Marlin 336	No	Weaver rail	21.95
Mauser Mark X	No	Weaver rail	21.95
Modern Muzzleloading MK85	No	Weaver rail	21.95
Remington 700 Short	No	Weaver rail	21.95
Remington 700 Long	No	Weaver rail	21.95
Remington 7400/7600	No	Weaver rail	21.95
Ruger 10/22	No	Weaver rail	21.95
Savage 110, 111, 113, 114, 115, 116	No	Weaver rail	21.95
Thompson/Center Thunderhawk	No	Weaver rail	21.95
Traditions Buckhunter	No	Weaver rail	21.95
White W Series	No	Weaver rail	21.95
White G Series	No	Weaver rail	21.95
White WG Series	No	Weaver rail	21.95
Winchester Model 70	No	Weaver rail	21.95
Winchester 94 AE	No	Weaver rail	21.95

All mounts no-gunsmithing, see-through/iron sight usable. Rifle mounts are solid see-through bases. All mounts accommodate standard split rings of all makes. From Aimtech, L&S Technologies, Inc. [1]3-blade sight and mount combination. [2]These models also available in RSP camouflage.

Maker, Model, Type	Adjust.	Scopes	Price
A.R.M.S.			
M16A1,A2,AR-15	No	Weaver rail	59.95
Multibase	No	Weaver rail	59.95
#19 ACOG Throw Lever Mt.	No	Weaver rail	150.00
#19 Weaver/STANAG Throw Lever Rail	No	Weaver rail	140.00
STANAG Rings	No	30mm	75.00
Throw Lever Rings	No	Weaver rail	95.00
Ring Inserts	No	1", 30mm	29.00
#22M68 Aimpoint Comp	No	Weaver rail	89.00
Ring Throw Lever			
#38 Std. Swan Sleeve[1]	No	—	150.00

Maker, Model, Type	Adjust.	Scopes	Price
#39 A2 Plus Mod. Mt.	No	#39T rail	125.00
[1]Avail. in three lengths. From A.R.M.S., Inc.			
ARMSON			
AR-15[1]	No	1"	45.00
Mini-14[2]	No	1"	66.00
H&K[3]	No	1"	82.00
[1]Fastens with one nut. [2]Models 181, 182, 183, 184, etc. [3]Claw mount. From Trijicon, Inc.			
ARMSPORT			
100 Series [1]	No	1" rings, Low, med., high	10.75
104 22-cal.	No	1"	10.75
201 See-Thru	No	1"	13.00
1-Piece Base[2]	No	—	5.50
2-Piece Base[2]	No	—	2.75
[1]Weaver-type ring. [2]Weaver-type base; most popular rifles. Made in U.S. From Armsport.			
ASHLEY			
Ashley/Clifton Scout Scope	No	Weaver rail	60.00
Some gunsmithing required; surrounds barrel shank; 6" long; low profile. Ashley Outdoors, Inc.			
B-SQUARE			
Pistols (centerfire)			
Beretta 92/Taurus 99	No	Weaver rail	64.95
Colt M1911	E only	Weaver rail	64.95
Desert Eagle	No	Weaver rail	64.95
Glock	No	Weaver rail	64.95
H&K USP, 9mm and 40 S&W	No	Weaver rail	64.95
Ruger P85/89	E only	Weaver rail	64.95
SIG Sauer P226	E only	Weaver rail	64.95
Pistols (rimfire)			
Browning Buck Mark	No	Weaver rail	49.95
Colt 22	No	Weaver rail	49.95
Ruger Mk I/II, bull or taper	No	Weaver rail	49.95
Smith & Wesson 41, 2206	No	Weaver rail	49.95
Revolvers			
Colt Anaconda/Python	No	Weaver rail	64.95
Ruger Single-Six	No	Weaver rail	64.95
Ruger GP-100	No	Weaver rail	64.95
Ruger Blackhawk, Super	No	Weaver rail	64.95
Ruger Redhawk, Super	No	Weaver rail	64.95
Smith & Wesson K, L, N	No	Weaver rail	64.95
Taurus 66, 669, 689	No	Weaver rail	64.95
Rifles (sporting)			
Browning BAR, A-Bolt	No	Weaver rail	39.95
Marlin MR7	No	Weaver rail	39.95
Mauser 98 Large Ring	No	Weaver rail	39.95
Mauser 91/93/95/96 Small Ring	No	Weaver rail	39.95
Remington 700, 740, 742, 760	No	Weaver rail	39.95
Remington 7400, 7600	No	Weaver rail	39.95
Remington Seven	No	Weaver rail	39.95
Rossi 22 Pump	No	Weaver rail	39.95
Ruger Mini-14	W&E	Weaver rail	64.95
Ruger 96/22	No	Weaver rail	54.95
Ruger M77 (short and long)	No	Weaver rail	69.96
Ruger 10/22 (reg. and See-Thru)	No	Weaver rail	39.95
Savage 110-116, 10-16	No	Weaver rail	39.95
Modern Military (rings incl.)			
AK-47/MAC 90	No	Weaver rail	64.95
Colt AR-15 (See-Thru & Flat Top)	No	Weaver rail	74.95
FN/FAL/LAR (See-Thru rings)	No	Weaver rail	99.95
Classic Military (rings incl.)			
FN 49	No	Weaver rail	69.95
Hakim	No	Weaver rail	69.95
Mauser 38, 94, 96, 98	E only	Weaver rail	64.95
Mosin-Nagant 91	E only	Weaver rail	64.95
Air Rifles			
RWS, Diana, BSA, Gamo	W&E	11mm rail	59.95
Weihrauch, Anschutz, Beeman	W&E	11mm rail	59.95
Shotguns/Slug Guns			
Benelli Super 90 (See-Thru)	No	Weaver rail	49.95
Browning BPS, A-5 9 (See-Thru)	No	Weaver rail	49.95
Browning Gold 10/12/20-ga. (See-Thru)	No	Weaver rail	49.95
Ithaca 37, 87	No	Weaver rail	49.95
Mossberg 500/Mav. 88	No	Weaver rail	49.95
Mossberg 835/Mav. 91	No	Weaver rail	49.95
Remington 870/1100/11-87	No	Weaver rail	49.95
Remington SP10	No	Weaver rail	49.95
Winchester 1200-1500	No	Weaver rail	49.95
Prices shown for anodized black finish; add $10 for stainless finish. Partial listing of mounts shown here. Contact B-Square for complete listing and details.			
BEEMAN			
Two-Piece, Med.	No	1"	31.50
Deluxe Two-Piece, High	No	1"	33.00

SCOPE RINGS & BASES

Maker, Model, Type	Adjust.	Scopes	Price
BEEMAN (cont'd.)			
Deluxe Two-Piece	No	30mm	41.00
Deluxe One-Piece	No	1"	50.00
Dampa Mount	No	1"	120.00
All grooved receivers and scope bases on all known air rifles and 22-cal. rimfire rifles (1/2" to 5/8"—6mm to 15mm).			
BOCK			
Swing ALK[1]	W&E	1", 26mm, 30mm	349.00
Safari KEMEL[2]	W&E	1", 26mm, 30mm	149.00
Claw KEMKA[3]	W&E	1", 26mm, 30mm	224.00
ProHunter Fixed[4]	No	1", 26mm, 30mm	95.00

[1]Q.D.: pivots right for removal. For Steyr-Mannlicher, Win. 70, Rem. 700, Mauser 98, Dakota, Sako, Sauer 80, 90. Magnum has extra-wide rings, same price. [2]Heavy-duty claw-type reversible for front or rear removal. For Steyr-Mannlicher rifles. [3]True claw mount for bolt-action rifles. Also in extended model. For Steyr-Mannlicher, Win. 70, Rem. 700. Also avail. as Gunsmith Bases—bases not drilled or contoured—same price. [4]Extra-wide rings. Imported from Germany by GSI, Inc.

Maker, Model, Type	Adjust.	Scopes	Price
BURRIS			
Supreme (SU) One-Piece (T)[1]	W only	1" split rings, 3 heights	1-piece base - 23.00 -27.00
Trumount (TU) Two-Piece (T)	W only	1" split rings, 3 heights	2-piece base - 21.00 -30.00
Trumount (TU) Two-Piece Ext.	W only	1" split rings	26.00
Browning 22-cal. Auto Mount[2]	No	1" split rings	20.00
1" 22-cal. Ring Mounts[3]	No	1" split rings	1" rings - 24.00 -41.00
L.E.R. (LU) Mount Bases[4]	W only	1" split rings	24.00 -52.00
L.E.R. No Drill-No Tap Bases[4,7,8]	W only	1" split rings	48.00 -52.00
Extension Rings[5]	No	1" scopes	28.00 -46.00
Ruger Ring Mount[6,9]	W only	1" split rings	50.00 -68.00
Std. 1" Rings[9]	—	Low, medium, high heights	29.00 -43.00
Zee Rings[9]	—	Fit Weaver bases; medium and high heights	29.00 -44.00
Signature Rings	No	30mm split rings	68.00
Rimfire/Airgun Rings	W only	1" split rings, med. & high	24.00 -41.00
Double Dovetail (DD) Bases	No	30mm Signature	23.00 -26.00

[1]Most popular rifles. Universal rings, mounts fit Burris, Universal, Redfield, Leupold and Browning bases. Comparable prices. [2]Browning Standard 22 Auto rifle. [3]Grooved receivers. [4]Universal dovetail: accepts Burris, Universal, Redfield, Leupold bases. For Dan Wesson, S&W, Virginian, Ruger Blackhawk, Win. 94. [5]Medium standard front, extension rear, per pair. Low standard front, extension rear per pair. [6]Compact scopes, scopes with 2" bell for M77R. [7]Selected rings and bases available with matte Safari or silver finish. [8]For S&W K, L, N frames, Colt Python, Dan Wesson with 6" or longer barrels. [9]Also in 30mm.

Maker, Model, Type	Adjust.	Scopes	Price
CATCO			
Enfield Drop-In	No	1"	39.95
Uses Weaver-style rings (not incl.). No gunsmithing required. See-Thru design. From CATCO.			
CLEAR VIEW			
Universal Rings, Mod. 101[1]	No	1" split rings	21.95
Standard Model[2]	No	1" split rings	21.95
Broad View[3]	No	1"	21.95
22 Model[4]	No	3/4", 7/8", 1"	13.95
SM-94 Winchester[5]	No	1" split rings	23.95
94 EJ[6]	No	1" split rings	21.95

[1]Most rifles by using Weaver-type base; allows use of iron sights. [2]Most popular rifles; allows use of iron sights. [3]Most popular rifles; low profile, wide field of view. [4]22 rifles with grooved receiver. [5]Side mount. [6]For Win. A.E. From Clear View Mfg.

Maker, Model, Type	Adjust.	Scopes	Price
CONETROL			
Huntur[1]	W only	1", split rings, 3 heights	79.92
Gunnur[2]	W only	1", split rings, 3 heights	99.96
Custom[3]	W only	1", split rings, 3 heights	119.88
One-Piece Side Mount Base[4]	W only	1", 26mm, 26.5mm solid or split rings, 3 heights	—
DapTar Bases[5]	W only	1", 26mm, 26.5mm solid or split rings, 3 heights	—
Pistol Bases, 2-or 3-ring[6]	W only	—	—
Fluted Bases[7]	W only	Standard Conetrol rings	119.88
Metric Rings[8]	W only	26mm, 26.5mm, 30mm	79.92 -119.88

[1]All popular rifles, including metric-drilled foreign guns. Price shown for base, two rings. Matte finish. [2]Gunnur grade has mirror-finished rings to match scopes. Satin-finish base to match guns. Price shown for base, two rings. [3]Custom grade has mirror-finished rings and mirror-finished, streamlined base. Price shown for base, two rings. [4]Win. 94, Krag, older split-bridge Mannlicher-Schoenauer, Mini-14, etc. Prices same as above. [5]For all popular guns with integral mounting provision, including Sako. BSA Ithacagun, Ruger, Tikka, H&K, BRNO—**$39.96-$59.94**—and many others. Also for grooved-receiver rimfires and air rifles. Prices same as above. [6]For XP-100, T/C Contender, Colt SAA, Ruger Blackhawk, S&W and others. [7]Sculptured two-piece bases as found on fine custom rifles. Price shown is for base alone. Also available unfinished—**$79.92**, or finished but unblued—**$99.96**. [8]26mm, 26.5mm, and 30mm rings made in projectionless style, in three heights. Three-ring mount for T/C Contender and other pistols in Conetrol's three grades. Any Conetrol mount available in stainless or Teflon for double regular cost of grade.

Maker, Model, Type	Adjust.	Scopes	Price
CUSTOM QUALITY			
Custom See-Thru	No	Up to 44mm	29.95
Dovetail 101-1 See-Thru	No	1"	29.95
Removable Rings	No	1"	29.95
Solid Dovetail	No	1", 30mm vertically split	29.95
Dovetail 22 See-Thru	No	1"	29.95
Mounts for many popular rifles. From Custom Quality Products, Inc.			
EAW			
Quick-Loc Mount	W&E	1", 26mm	253.00
	W&E	30mm	291.00
Magnum Fixed Mount	W&E	1", 26mm	198.00
	W&E	30mm	215.00
Fit most popular rifles. Avail. in 4 heights, 4 extensions. Reliable return to zero. Stress-free mounting. Imported by New England Custom Gun Svc.			
GENTRY			
Feather-Light Rings and Bases	No	1", 30mm	90.00 -125.00
Bases for Rem. Seven, 700, Mauser 98, Browning A-Bolt, Weatherby Mk. V, Win. 70, HVA, Dakota. Two-piece base for Rem. Seven, chrome moly or stainless. Rings in matte or regular blue, or stainless gray; four heights. From David Gentry.			
GRIFFIN & HOWE			
Topmount[1]	No	1", 30mm	625.00
Sidemount[2]	No	1", 30mm	255.00
Garand Mount[3]	No	1", 30mm	255.00

[1]Quick-detachable, double-lever mount with 1" rings, installed; with 30mm rings **$875.00**. [2]Quick-detachable, double-lever mount with 1" rings; with 30mm rings **$375.00**; installed, 1" rings. **$405.00**; installed, 30mm rings **$525.00**. [3]Price installed, with 1" rings **$405.00**. From Griffin & Howe.

Maker, Model, Type	Adjust.	Scopes	Price
G. G. & G.			
Remington 700 Rail	No	Weaver base	115.00
Sniper Grade Rings	No	1", 30mm	145.00
M16/AR15 F.I.R.E. Std.[1]	No	Weaver rail	65.00
M16/AR15 F.I.R.E. Scout	No	Weaver rail	75.00
Aimpoint Single Ring[2]	No	—	155.00
Galil Side Mount	No	Weaver rail	NA
H&K MP-5 Low Boy Mount[3]	No	Weaver rail	NA

[1]For M16/A3, AR15 flat top receivers; also in extended length. [2]For Aimpoint 5000 and Comp; quick detachable; spare battery compartment. [3]Low profile; quick release. From G. G. & G.

Maker, Model, Type	Adjust.	Scopes	Price
IRONSIGHTER			
Wide Ironsighter™	No	1" split rings	35.98
Ironsighter Center Fire[1]	No	1" split rings	32.95
Ironsighter S-94	No	1" split rings	39.95
Ironsighter AR-15/M-16[8]	No	1", 30mm	103.95
Ironsighter 22-Cal.Rimfire[2]			
Model #570[9]	No	1" split rings	32.95
Model #573[9]	No	30mm split rings	32.95
Model #722	No	1" split rings	17.75
Model #727[3]	No	.875" split rings	17.75
Model #700[5]	No	1" split rings	32.95
Ruger Base Mounts[6]	No	1" split rings	83.95
Ironsighter Handguns[4]	No	1" split rings	83.95
Blackpowder Mount[7]	No	1"	32.95 -76.95

[1]Most popular rifles, including Ruger Mini-14, H&R M700, and muzzleloaders. Rings have oval holes to permit use of iron sights. [2]For 1" dia. scopes. [3]For .875 dia. scopes. [4]For 1" dia. extended eye relief scopes. [5]702—Browning A-Bolt; 709—Marlin 39A. [6]732—Ruger 77/22 R&RS, No. 1, Ranch Rifle; 778 fits Ruger 77R, RS. Both 733, 778 fit Ruger Integral bases. Fits most popular blackpowder rifles, one model for Holden Ironsighter mounts, one for Weaver rings. [8]Model 716 with 1" #540 rings; Model 717 with 30mm #530 rings. [9]Fits mount rail on Rem. 522 Viper. Adj. rear sight is integral. Some models in stainless finish. From Ironsighter Co.

Maker, Model, Type	Adjust.	Scopes	Price
K MOUNT By KENPATABLE			
Shotgun Mount	No	1", laser or red dot device	49.95

SCOPE RINGS & BASES

Maker, Model, Type	Adjust.	Scopes	Price
K MOUNT By KENPATABLE (cont'd.)			
SKS[1]	No	1"	39.95

Wrap-around design; no gunsmithing required. Models for Browning BPS, A-5 12-ga., Sweet 16, 20, Rem. 870/1100 (LTW, and L.H.), S&W 916, Mossberg 500, Ithaca 37 & 51 12-ga., S&W 1000/3000, Win. 1400. [1]Requires simple modification to gun. From KenPatable Ent.

KRIS MOUNTS			
Side-Saddle[1]	No	1",26mm split rings	12.98
Two-Piece (T)[2]	No	1", 26mm split rings	8.98
One Piece (T)[3]	No	1", 26mm split rings	12.98

[1]One-piece mount for Win. 94. [2]Most popular rifles and Ruger. [3]Blackhawk revolver. Mounts have oval hole to permit use of iron sights.

KWIK-SITE			
KS-See-Thru[1]	No	1"	31.95
KS-22 See-Thru[2]	No	1"	23.95
KS-W94[3]	No	1"	39.95
Kwik-Site (cont.)			
Bench Rest	No	1"	31.95
KS-WEV	No	1"	31.95
KS-WEV-HIGH	No	1"	37.95
KS-T22 1"[4]	No	1"	23.95
KS-FL Flashlite[5]	No	Mini or C cell flashlight	49.95
KS-T88[6]	No	1"	11.95
KS-T89	No	30mm	14.95
KSN 22 See-Thru	No	1", 7/8"	20.95
KSN-T22	No	1", 7/8"	20.95
KSN-M-16 See-Thru	No	1"	99.95
KS-202[1]	No	1"	31.95
KS-203	No	30mm	43.95
KSBP[7]	No	Intergral	76.95
KSSM8	No	1"	31.95
KSB Base Set	—	—	5.95
Combo Bases & Rings	No	1"	31.95

Bases interchangeable with Weaver bases. [1]Most rifles. Allows use of iron sights. [2]22-cal. rifles with grooved receivers. Allows use of iron sights. [3]Model 94, 94 Big Bore. No drilling or tapping. Also in adjustable model $49.95. [4]Non-See-Thru model for grooved receivers. [5]Allows Mag Lite or C or D, Mini Mag Lites to be mounted atop See-Thru mounts. [6]Fits any Redfield, Tasco, Weaver or Universal-style Kwik-Site dovetail base. [7]Blackpowder mount with integral rings and sights. [8]Shotgun side mount. Bright blue, black matte or satin finish. Standard, high heights.

LASER AIM	No	Laser Aim	19.99 -69.00

Mounts Laser Aim above or below barrel. Avail. for most popular handguns, rifles, shotguns, including militaries. From Laser Aim Technologies, Inc.

LEUPOLD			
STD Bases[1]	W only	One- or two-piece bases	24.20
STD Rings[2]	—	1" super low, low, medium, high	31.80
DD RBH Handgun Mounts[2]	No	—	58.40
Dual Dovetail Bases[3]	No	—	24.20
Dual Dovetail Rings[8]	—	1", super low, low, low	31.80
Ring Mounts[4,5,6]	No	7/8", 1"	79.80
22 Rimfire[8]	No	7/8", 1"	58.20
Gunmaker Base[7]	W only	1"	16.50
Quick Release Rings	—	1", low, med., high	32.40 -69.90
Quick Release Bases[9]	No	1", one- or two-piece	70.30

Base and two rings; Casull, Ruger, S&W, T/C; add $5.00 for silver finish. Rem. 700, Win. 70-type actions. For Ruger No. 1, 77, 77/22; interchangeable with Ruger units. For dovetailed rimfire rifles. Sako; high, medium, low. Must be drilled, tapped for each action. [8]13mm dovetail receiver. [9]BSA Monarch, Rem. 40x, 700, 721, 725, Ruger M77, S&W 1500, Weatherby Mark V, Vanguard, Win. M70.

MARLIN			
One-Piece QD (T)	No	1" split rings	10.10
Most Marlin lever actions.			

MILLETT			
Black Onyx Smooth	—	1", low, medium, high	31.15
Chaparral Engraved	—	engraved	46.15
One-Piece Bases[6]	Yes	1"	23.95
Universal Two-Piece Bases			
700 Series	W only	Two-piece bases	25.15
FN Series	W only	Two-piece bases	25.15
70 Series[1]	W only	1", two-piece bases	25.15
Angle-Loc Rings[2]	W only	1", low, medium, high	32.20 -47.20
Ruger 77 Rings[3]	—	1"	47.20
Shotgun Rings[4]	—	1"	28.29
Handgun Bases, Rings[5]	—	1"	34.60 -69.15
30mm Rings[7]	—	30mm	37.75 -42.95
Extension Rings[8]	—	1"	35.65
See-Thru Mounts[9]	No	1"	27.95 -32.95

Maker, Model, Type	Adjust.	Scopes	Price
Shotgun Mounts[10]	No	1"	49.95
Timber Mount	No	1"	78.00

BRNO, Rem. 40x, 700, 722, 725, 7400 Ruger 77 (round top), Marlin, Weatherby, FN Mauser, FN Brownings, Colt 57, Interarms Mark X, Parker-Hale, Savage 110, Sako (round receiver), many others. [1]Fits Win. M70 70XTR, 670, Browning BBR, BAR, BLR, A-Bolt, Rem. 7400/7600, Four, Six, Marlin 336, Win. 94 A. E., Sav. 110. [2]To fit Weaver-type bases. [3]Engraved. Smooth $34.60. [4]For Rem. 870, 1100; smooth. [5]Two- and three-ring sets for Colt Python, Trooper, Diamondback, Peacekeeper, Dan Wesson, Ruger Redhawk, Super Redhawk. [6]Turn-in bases and Weaver-style for most popular rifles and T/C Contender, XP-100 pistols. [7]Both Weaver and turn-in styles; three heights. [8]Med. or high; ext. front—std. rear, ext. rear—std. front, ext. front—ext. rear; $40.90 for double extension. [9]Many popular rifles, Knight MK-85, T/C Hawken, Renegade, Mossberg 500 Slugster, 835 slug. [10]For Rem. 879/1100, Win. 1200, 1300/1400, 1500, Mossberg 500. Some models available in nickel at extra cost. [11]For T/C Hawken and Renegade; See-Thru with adj. open sight inside. From Millett Sights.

MMC			
AK[1]	No	—	39.95
FN FAL/LAR[2]	No	—	59.95

[1]Fits all AK derivative receivers; Weaver-style base; low-profile scope position. [2]Fits all FAL versions; Weaver-style base. From MMC.

PEM'S			
22T Mount[1]	No	1"	17.95
The Mount[2]	Yes	1"	29.50

[1]Fits all 3/8" dovetail on rimfire rifles. [2]Base and ring set; for over 100 popular rifles; low, medium rings. From Pem's.

RAM-LINE			
Mini-14 Mount	Yes	1"	24.97

No drilling or tapping. Uses std. dovetail rings. Has built-in shell deflector. Made of solid black polymer. From Ram-Line, Inc.

REDFIELD			
NGS	No	Weaver rail	30.95 -78.95
American Rings[6]	No	1", low, med., high	27.95 -37.95
All American Aluminum Rings	No	1"	8.95-12.95
American Bases[6]	No	—	4.95-10.95
American Widefield See-Thru[7]	No	1"	15.95
JR-SR (T)[1]. One/two-piece bases.	W only	3/4", 1", 26mm, 30mm	JR-23.95 -52.95 SR-18.95 -22.95
Ring (T)[2]	No	3/4" and 1"	27.95 -29.95
Three-Ring Pistol System SMP[3]	No	1", split rings (three)	49.95 -52.95
Widefield See-Thru Mounts	No	1"	15.95
Ruger Rings[4]	No	1", med., high	34.95 -36.95
Ruger 30mm[5]	No	1"	42.95
Midline Ext. Rings	No	1"	24.95

[1]Low, med. & high, split rings. Reversible extension front rings for 1". 2-piece bases for Sako. Colt Sauer bases $39.95. Med. Top Access JR rings nickel-plated, $28.95. SR two-piece ABN mount nickel-plated $22.95. [2]Split rings for grooved 22s; 30mm, black matte $42.95. [3]Used with MP scopes for; S&W K, L or N frame, XP-100, T/C Contender, Ruger receivers. [4]For Ruger Model 77 rifles, medium and high; medium only for M77/22. [5]For Model 77. Also in matte finish $45.95. [6]Aluminum 22 groove mount $14.95; base and medium rings $18.95. [7]Fits American or Weaver-style base. Non-Gunsmithing mount system. For many popular shotguns, rifles, handguns and blackpowder rifles. Uses existing screw holes.

S&K			
Insta-Mount (T) Bases and Rings[1]	W only	Uses S&K rings only	47.00 -117.00
Conventional Rings and Bases[2]	W only	1" split rings	From 65.00
Sculptured Bases, Rings[2]	W only	1", 26mm, 30mm	From 65.00
Smooth Contoured Rings[3]	Yes	1", 26mm, 30mm	90.00 -120.00

[1]1903, A3, M1 Carbine, Lee Enfield #1. Mk.III, #4, #5, M1917, M98 Mauser, AR-15, AR-180, M-14, M-1, Ger. K-43, Mini-14, M1-A, Krag, AKM, Win. 94, SKS Type 56, Daewoo, H&K. [2]Most popular rifles already drilled and tapped and Sako, Tikka dovetails. [3]No projections; weigh 1/2-oz. each; matte or gloss finish. Horizontally and vertically split rings, matte or high gloss.

SSK INDUSTRIES			
T'SOB	No	1"	65.00 -145.00
T'SOB AR-15/M-16[1]	No	1", 30mm	125.00
Quick Detachable	No	1"	From 160.00

[1] Price includes altering carrying handle, mount and installation; allows use of iron sights. Custom installation using from two to four rings (included). For T/C Contender, most 22 auto pistols, Ruger and other S.A. revolvers, Dan Wesson, S&W, Colt DA revolvers. Black or white finish. Uses Kimber rings in two- or three-ring sets. In blue or SSK chrome. For T/C Contender or most popular revolvers. Standard, non-detachable model also available, from $65.00.

SCOPE RINGS & BASES

Maker, Model, Type	Adjust.	Scopes	Price
SAKO			
QD Dovetail	W only	1"	70.00 -155.00
Sako, or any rifle using Sako action, 3 heights available. Stoeger, importer.			
SPRINGFIELD, INC.			
M1A Third Generation	No	1" or 30mm	123.00
M1A Standard	N0	1" or 30mm	77.00
M6 Scout Mount	No	—	29.00
Weaver-style bases. From Springfield, Inc.			
TALBOT			
QD Bases	No	—	180.00 -190.00
Rings	No	1", 30mm	50.00 -70.00
Blue or stainless steel; standard or extended bases; rings in three heights. For most popular rifles. From Talbot QD Mounts.			
TASCO			
World Class			
Aluminum Ringsets	Yes	1", 30mm	12.00 -17.00
See-Thru	No	1"	19.00
Shotgun Bases	Yes	—	34.00
From Tasco.			
THOMPSON/CENTER			
Duo-Ring Mount[1]	No	1"	60.00
Weaver-Style Bases[2]	No	—	14.00
Weaver-Style Rings[3]	No	1"	28.00 -39.00
Weaver-Style See-Thru Rings[4]	No	1"	26.00
[1]Attaches directly to T/C Contender bbl.; no drilling/tapping; also for T/C M/L rifles, needs base adapter; blue or stainless; for M/L guns **$59.80**. [2]For T/C ThunderHawk, FireHawk rifles; blue; silver **$37.00**. [3]Medium and high; blue or silver finish. [4]For T.C Firel lawk, ThunderHawk; blue; silver **$29.00**. From Thompson/Center.			
UNERTL			
1/4 Click[1]	Yes	3/4", 1" target scopes	Per set 196.00
[1]Unertl target or varmint scopes. Posa or standard mounts, less bases. From Unertl.			
WARNE			
Premier Series (all steel)			
T.P.A. (Permanently Attached)	No	1", 4 heights	78.00
		30mm, 2 heights	87.60
Sako	No	1", 4 heights	78.00
		30mm, 3 heights	87.60
Premier Series Rings fit Premier Series Bases			
Premier Series (all-steel Q.D. rings)			
Premier Series (all steel).	No	1", 4 heights	111.00
Quick detachable lever.		26mm, 2 heights	115.50
		30mm, 3 heights	121.50
Brno 19mm	No	1", 3 heights	111.50
		30mm, 2 heights	121.50
Brno 16mm	No	1", 3 heights	111.50
Ruger	No	1", 4 heights	111.50
		30mm, 3 heights	121.50
Ruger M77	No	1", 3 heights	111.50
		30mm, 2 heights	121.50
Sako Medium & Long Action	No	1", 4 heights	111.50
		30mm, 3 heights	121.50
Sako Short Action	No	1", 3 heights	111.50
All-Steel One-Piece Base, ea.			35.00
All-Steel Two-Piece Base, ea.			12.50
Maxima Series (fits all Weaver-style bases)			
Permanently Attached[1]	No	1", 3 heights	31.40
		30mm, 3 heights	45.50
Adjustable Double Lever[2]	No	1", 3 heights	66.00
		30mm, 3 heights	73.40
Thumb Knob	No	1", 3 heights	54.50
		39mm, 3 heights	62.00
All-Steel Two-Piece Base, ea.			12.50
Vertically split rings with dovetail clamp, precise return to zero. Fit most popular rifles, handguns. Regular blue, matte blue, silver finish. [1]All-Steel, non-Q.D. rings. [2]All-steel, Q.D. rings. From Warne Mfg. Co.			
WEAVER			
Detachable Mounts			
Top Mount	No	7/8", 1", 30mm, 33mm	24.95 -38.95
Side Mount	No	1", 1" long	14.95 -34.95
Tip-Off Rings	No	7/8", 1"	24.95 -32.95
Pivot Mounts	No	1"	38.95
Complete Mount Systems			
Pistol	No	1"	75.00 -105.00

Maker, Model, Type	Adjust.	Scopes	Price
Rifle	No	1"	32.95
SKS Mount System	No	1"	49.95
Pro-View (no base required)	No	1"	13.95 -15.95
Converta-Mount, 12-ga. (Rem. 870, Moss. 500)	No	1", 30mm	74.95
See-Thru Mounts			
Detachable	No	1"	27.00 -32.00
System (no base required)	No	1"	15.00 -35.00
Tip-Off	No	1"	15.00
Nearly all modern rifles, pistols, and shotguns. Detachable rings in standard, See-Thru, and extension styles, in Low, Medium, High or X-High heights; gloss (blued), silver and matte finishes to match scopes. Extension rings are only available in 1" High style and See-Thru X-tensions only in gloss finish. Tip-Off rings only for 3/8" grooved receivers or 3/8"grooved adaptor bases; no base required. See-Thru & Pro-View mounts for most modern big bore rifles, some in silver. No Drill & Tap Pistol systems in gloss or silver for: Colt Python, Trooper, 357, Officer's Model; Ruger Single-Six, Security-Six (gloss finish only), Blackhawk, Super Blackhawk, Blackhawk SRM 357, Redhawk, Mini-14 Series (not Ranch), Ruger 22 Auto Pistols, Mark II; Smith & Wesson I- and current K-frames with adj. rear sights. Converta-Mount Systems in Standard and See-Under for: Mossberg 500 (12- and 20-ga.); Remington 870, 11-87 (12- and 20-ga. lightweight); Winchester 1200, 1300, 1400, 1500. Converta Brackets, Bases, Rings also avail. for Beretta A303 and A390; Browning A-5, BPS Pump; Ithaca 37, 87. From Weaver.			
WEIGAND			
Browning Buck Mark[1]	No	—	29.95
Colt 22 Automatic[1]	No	—	19.95
Integra Mounts[2]	No	—	39.95 -69.00
S&W Revolver[3]	No	—	29.95
Ruger 10/22[4]	No	—	14.95 -39.95
Ruger Revolver[5]	No	—	29.95
Taurus Revolver[4]	No	—	29.95 -65.00
T/C Encore Monster Mount	No	—	69.00
T/C Contender Monster Mount	No	—	69.00
Lightweight Rings	No	1", 30mm	29.95 -39.95
1911, P-9 Scopemounts			
SM3[6]	No	Weaver rail	99.95
SRS 1911-2[7]	No	30mm	59.95
APCMNT[8]	No	1"	69.95
[1]No gunsmithing. [2] S&W K, L, N frames; Taurus vent rib models; Colt Anaconda/Python; Ruger Redhawk; Ruger 10/22. [3]K, L, N frames. [4]Three models. [5] Redhawk, Blackhawk, GP-100. [6]3rd Gen.; drill and tap; without slots **$59.95**. [7]Ringless design, silver only. [8]For Aimpoint Comp. Red Dot scope, silver only. From Weigand Combat Handguns, Inc.			
WIDEVIEW			
Premium 94 Angle Eject	No	1"	18.70
Premium See-Thru	No	1"	18.70
22 Premium See-Thru	No	3/4", 1"	13.60
Universal Ring Angle Cut	No	1"	18.70
Universal Ring Straight Cut	No	1"	18.70
Solid Mounts			
Lo Ring Solid[1]	No	1"	13.60
Hi Ring Solid[1]	No	1"	13.60
SR Rings	—	1", 30mm	13.60
22 Grooved Receiver	No	1"	13.60
94 Side Mount	No	1"	18.70
Blackpowder Mounts[2]	No	1"	18.70 -37.40
[1]For Weaver-type base. Models for many popular rifles. Low ring, high ring and grooved receiver types. [2]No drilling, tapping, for T/C Renegade, Hawken, CVA, Knight Traditions guns. From Wideview Scope Mount Corp.			
WILLIAMS			
Side Mount with HCO Rings[1]	No	1", split or extension rings	74.21
Side Mount, Offset Rings[2]	No	Same	61.08
Sight-Thru Mounts[3]	No	1", 7/8" sleeves	18.95
Streamline Mounts	No	1" (bases form rings)	25.70
Guideline Handgun[4]	No	1" split rings	61.75
[1]Most rifles, Br. S.M.L.E. (round rec.) **$14.41** extra. [2]Most rifles incl. Win. 94 Big Bore. [3]Many modern rifles, including CVA Apollo, others with 1" octagon barrels. [4]No drilling, tapping required; heat treated alloy. For Ruger Mk II Bull Barrel (**$61.75**); Streamline Top Mount for T.C Contender (**$14.15**), Scout Rifle (**$24.00**), High Top Mount with sub-base (**$51.45**). From Williams Gunsight Co.			
YORK			
M-1 Garand	Yes	1"	39.95
Centers scope over the action. No drilling, tapping or gunsmithing. Uses standard dovetail rings. From York M-1 Conversions.			
NOTES			
(S)—Side Mount; (T)—Top Mount; 22mm=.866"; 25.4mm=1.024"; 26.5mm=1.045"; 30mm=1.81".			

Swift M700T Scout

Nikon
Fieldscope 78mm

BAUSCH & LOMB PREMIER HDR 60mm objective, 15x-45x zoom. Straight or 45° eyepiece. Field at 1000 yds. 125 ft. (15x), 68 ft. (45x). Length 13.0"; weight 38 oz. Interchangeable bayonet-style eyepieces.
Price: Straight, 15-45x $590.95
Price: Angled, 15-45x with 45° eyepiece............................. $638.95
Price: 22x wide angle eyepiece $86.95
Price: 30x long eye relief eyepiece $136.95

BAUSCH & LOMB DISCOVERER 15x to 60x zoom, 60mm objective. Constant focus throughout range. Field at 1000 yds. 38 ft (60x), 150 ft. (15x). Comes with lens caps. Length 17 1/2"; weight 48.5 oz.
Price: $391.95

BAUSCH & LOMB ELITE 15x to 45x zoom, 60mm objective. Field at 1000 yds., 125-65 ft. Length is 12.2"; weight, 26.5 oz. Waterproof, armored. Tripod mount. Comes with black case.
Price: $766.95

BAUSCH & LOMB ELITE ZOOM 20x-60x, 70mm objective. Roof prism. Field at 1000 yds. 90-50 ft. Length is 16"; weight 40 oz. Waterproof, armored. Tripod mount. Comes with black case.
Price: $877.95

BAUSCH & LOMB 77MM ELITE 20x-60x zoom, 77mm objective. Field of view at 1000 yds. 108-62 ft. (zoom). Weight 51 oz. (20x, 30x), 54 oz. (zoom); length 16.8". Interchangeable bayonet-style eyepieces. Built-in peep sight.
Price: With EDPrime Glass $1,251.95
Price: 20-60x zoom eyepiece $335.95

BURRIS 18-45x SPOTTER 60mm objective, 18x-45x, constant focus, Field at 1000 yds. 112-63 ft.; weighs 29oz.; length 12.6". Camera adapters available.
Price: $795.00

BURRIS 20x SPOTTER 20x, 50mm objective. Straight type. Field at 100 yds. 15 ft. Length 10"; weight 21 oz. Rubber armor coating, multi-coated lenses, 22mm eye relief. Recessed focus adjustment. Nitrogen filled. Retractable sunshade.
Price: 24x 60mm $598.00
Price: 30x 60mm $625.00

BUSHNELL TROPHY 63mm objective, 20x-60x zoom. Field at 1000 yds. 90ft. (20x), 45 ft. (60x). Length 12.7"; weight 20 oz. Black rubber armored, waterproof. Case included.
Price: $407.95

BUSHNELL COMPACT TROPHY 50mm objective, 20x-50x zoom. Field at 1000 yds. 92 ft. (20x), 52 ft. (50x). Length 12.2"; weight 17 oz. Black rubber armored, waterproof. Case included.
Price: $325.95

BUSHNELL BANNER SENTRY 18x-36x zoom, 50mm objective. Field at 1000 yds. 115-78 ft. Length 14.5"; weight 27 oz. Black rubber armored. Built-in peep sight. Comes with tripod and hardcase.
Price: $180.95
Price: With 45 field eyepiece, includes tripod........................... $202.95

BUSHNELL SPACEMASTER 20x-45x zoom. Long eye relief. Rubber armored, prismatic. 60mm objective. Field at 1000 yds. 98-58 ft. Minimum focus 20 ft. Length 12.7"; weight 43 oz.
Price: With tripod, carrying case and 20x-45x LER eyepiece. $560.95

BUSHNELL SPORTVIEW 12x-36x 200m, 50mm objective. Field at 100 yds. 160 ft. (12x), 90 ft. (36x). Length 14.6"; weight 25 oz.
Price: With tripod and carrying case $159.95

HERMES 1 70mm objective, 16x, 25x, 40x. Field at 1000 meters 160 ft. (16x), 75ft. (40x). Length 12.2"; weight 33 oz. From CZ-USA.
Price: Body $359.00
Price: 25x eyepiece $86.00
Price: 40x eyepiece $128.00

KOWA TSN SERIES Offset 45 or straight body. 77mm objective, 20x WA, 25x, 25x LER, 30x WA, 40x, 60x, 77x and 20-60x zoom. Field at 1000 yds. 179 ft. (20xWA), 52 ft. (60x). Available with flourite lens.
Price: TSN-1 (without eyepiece) 45 offset scope........................ $696.00
Price: TSN-2 (without eyepiece) Straight scope $660.00
Price: 20x W.A. (wide angle) eyepiece................................ $230.00
Price: 25x eyepiece... $143.00
Price: 25x LER (long eye relief) eyepiece $214.00
Price: 30x W.A. (wide angle) eyepiece................................ $266.00
Price: 40x eyepiece... $159.00
Price: 60x W.A. (wide angle) eyepiece................................ $230.00
Price: 77x eyepiece... $235.00
Price: 20-60x zoom eyepiece $302.00

KOWA TS-610 SERIES Offset 45 or straight body. 60mm objective, 20x WA, 25x, 25x LER, 27x WA, 40x and 20x-60x zoom. Field at 1000 yds. 162 ft. (20x WA), 51 ft. (60x). Available with ED lens.
Price: TS-611 (without eyepiece) 45 offset scope....................... $510.00

Price: TS-612 (without eyepiece) Straight scope $462.00
Price: 20x W.A. (wide angle) eyepiece................................ $111.00
Price: 25x eyepiece... $95.00
Price: 25x LER (long eye relief) eyepiece $214.00
Price: 27x W.A. (wide angle) eyepiece................................ $166.00
Price: 40x eyepiece... $98.00
Price: 20-60x zoom eyepiece $207.00

KOWA TS-9 SERIES Offset 45, straight or rubber armored (straight only). 50mm objective, 15x, 20x and 11-33x zoom. Field at 1000 yds. 188 ft. (15x), 99 ft. (33x).
Price: TS-9B (without eyepiece) 45 offset scope........................ $223.00
Price: TS-9C (without eyepiece) straight scope........................ $176.00
Price: TS-9R (without eyepiece) straight rubber armored scope/black... $197.00
Price: 15x eyepiece... $38.00
Price: 20x eyepiece... $36.00
Price: 11-33x zoom eyepiece $122.00

LEUPOLD 12-40x60 VARIABLE 60mm objective, 12-40x. Field at 100 yds. 17.5-5.3 ft.; eye relief 1.2" (20x). Overall length 11.5", weight 32 oz. Rubber armored.
Price: $1,171.40

LEUPOLD 25x50 COMPACT 50mm objective, 25x. Field at 100 yds. 8.3 ft.; eye relief 1"; length overall 9.4"; weight 20.5 oz.
Price: Armored model $816.10
Price: Packer Tripod $96.40

MIRADOR TTB SERIES Draw tube armored spotting scopes. Available with 75mm or 80mm objective. Zoom model (28x-62x, 80mm) is 11 7/8" (closed), weighs 50 oz. Field at 1000 yds. 70-42 ft. Comes with lens covers.
Price: 28-62x80mm $1,133.95
Price: 32x80mm $971.95
Price: 26-58x75mm $989.95
Price: 30x75mm $827.95

MIRADOR SSD SPOTTING SCOPES 60mm objective, 15x, 20x, 22x, 25x, 40x, 60x, 20-60x; field at 1000 yds. 37 ft.; length 10 1/4"; weight 33 oz.
Price: 25x $575.95
Price: 22x Wide Angle.. $593.95
Price: 20-60x Zoom... $746.95
Price: As above, with tripod, case................................ $944.95

MIRADOR SIA SPOTTING SCOPES Similar to the SSD scopes except with 45° eyepiece. Length 12 1/4"; weight 39 oz.
Price: 25x $809.95
Price: 22x Wide Angle.. $827.95
Price: 20-60x Zoom... $980.95

MIRADOR SSR SPOTTING SCOPES 50mm or 60mm objective. Similar to SSD except rubber armored in black or camouflage. Length 11 1/8"; weight 31 oz.
Price: Black, 20x $521.95
Price: Black, 18x Wide Angle $539.95
Price: Black, 16-48x Zoom $692.95
Price: Black, 20x, 60mm, EER $692.95
Price: Black, 22x Wide Angle, 60mm $701.95
Price: Black, 20-60x Zoom $854.95

MIRADOR SSF FIELD SCOPES Fixed or variable power, choice of 50mm, 60mm, 75mm objective lens. Length 9 3/4"; weight 20 oz. (15-32x50).
Price: 20x50mm $359.95
Price: 25x60mm $440.95
Price: 30x75mm $584.95
Price: 15-32x50mm Zoom $548.95

Price: 18-40x60mm Zoom **$629.95**
Price: 22-47x75mm Zoom **$773.95**

MIRADOR SRA MULTI ANGLE SCOPES Similar to SSF Series except eyepiece head rotates for viewing from any angle.
Price: 20x50mm **$503.95**
Price: 25x60mm **$647.95**
Price: 30x75mm **$764.95**
Price: 15-32x50mm Zoom **$692.95**
Price: 18-40x60mm Zoom **$836.95**
Price: 22-47x75mm Zoom **$953.95**

MIRADOR SIB FIELD SCOPES Short-tube, 45° scopes with porro prism design. 50mm and 60mm objective. Length 10 1/4″; weight 18.5 oz. (15-32x50mm); field at 1000 yds. 129-81 ft.
Price: 20x50mm **$386.95**
Price: 25x60mm **$449.95**
Price: 15-32x50mm Zoom **$575.95**
Price: 18-40x60mm Zoom **$638.95**

NIKON FIELDSCOPES 60mm and 78mm lens. Field at 1000 yds. 105 ft. (60mm, 20x), 126 ft. (78mm, 25x). Length 12.8″ (straight 60mm), 12.6″ (straight 78mm); weight 34.5-47.5 oz. Eyepieces available separately.
Price: 60mm straight body **$690.95**
Price: 60mm angled body **$796.95**
Price: 60mm straight ED body **$1,200.95**
Price: 60mm angled ED body **$1,314.95**
Price: 78mm straight ED body **$2,038.95**
Price: 78mm angled ED body **$2,170.95**
Price: Eyepieces (15x to 60x) . . . . **$146.95** to **$324.95**
Price: 20-45x eyepiece (25-56x for 78mm) **$318.95**

NIKON SPOTTING SCOPE 60mm objective, 20x fixed power or 15-45x zoom. Field at 1000 yds. 145 ft. (20x). Gray rubber armored. Straight or angled eyepiece. Weighs 44.2 oz., length 12.1″ (20x).
Price: 20x60 fixed (with eyepiece) **$368.95**
Price: 15-45x zoom (with case, tripod, eyepiece) **$578.95**

SIGHTRON SII 2050X63 63mm objective lens, 20x-50x zoom. Field at 1000 yds 91.9 ft. (20x), 52.5 ft. (50x). Length 14″; weight 30.8 oz. Black rubber finish. Also available with 80mm objective lens.
Price: 63mm or 80mm **$339.95**

SIMMONS 1280 50mm objective, 15-45x zoom. Black matte finish. Ocular focus. Peep finder sight. Waterproof.
Price: With tripod **$255.95**

SIMMONS 1281 60mm objective, 20-60x zoom. Black matte finish. Ocular focus. Peep finder sight. Waterproof.
Price: With tripod **$282.95**

SIMMONS 77206 PROHUNTER 50mm objectives, 25x fixed power. Field at 1000 yds. 113 ft.; length 10.25″; weighs 32oz. Black rubber armored.
Price: With tripod case **$152.95**

SIMMONS 41200 EUROSTYLE 50mm objective, 15x-45x zoom. Field at 1000 yds. 104-41 ft.; length 16.75″; weighs 32.75 oz.
Price: With hard case and tripod **$91.95**
Price: 20-60x, Model 41201 . . . . **$126.95**

STEINER FIELD TELESCOPE 24x, 80mm objective. Field at 1000 yds. 105 ft. Weight 44 oz. Tripod mounts. Rubber armored.
Price: **$1,299.00**

SWAROVSKI CT EXTENDIBLE SCOPES 75mm or 85mm objective, 20-60x zoom, or fixed 15x, 22x, 30x, 32x eyepieces. Field at 1000 yds. 135 ft. (15x), 99 ft. (32x); 99 ft. (20x), 5.2 ft. (60x) for zoom. Length 12.4″ (closed), 17.2″ (open) for the CT75; 9.7″/17.2″ for CT85. Weight 40.6 oz. (CT75), 49.4 oz. (CT85). Green rubber armored.
Price: CT75 body **$765.56**
Price: CT85 body **$1,094.44**
Price: 20-60x eyepiece **$343.33**
Price: 15x, 22x eyepiece **$232.22**
Price: 30x eyepiece **$265.55**

SWAROVSKI AT-80/ST-80 SPOTTING SCOPES 80mm objective, 20-60x zoom, or fixed 15x, 22x, 30x, 32x eyepieces. Field at 1000 yds. 135 ft. (15x), 99 ft. (32x); 99 ft. (20x), 52.5 ft. (60x) for zoom. Length 16″ (AT-80), 15.6″ (ST-80); weight 51.8 oz. Available with HD (high density) glass.
Price: AT-80 (angled) body **$1,094.44**
Price: ST-80 (straight) body **$1,094.44**
Price: With HD glass **$1,555.00**
Price: 20-60x eyepiece **$343.33**
Price: 15x, 22x eyepiece **$232.22**
Price: 30x eyepiece **$265.55**

SWIFT LYNX M836 15x-45x zoom, 60mm objective. Weight 7 lbs., length 14″. Has 45° eyepiece, sunshade.
Price: **$315.00**

SWIFT NIGHTHAWK M849U 80mm objective, 20x-60x zoom, or fixed 19, 25x, 31x, 50x, 75x eyepieces. Has rubber armored body, 1.8x optical finder, retractable lens hood, 45° eyepiece. Field at 1000 yds. 60 ft. (28x), 41 ft. (75x). Length 13.4 oz.; weight 39 oz.
Price: Body only **$870.00**
Price: 20-68x eyepiece **$370.00**
Price: Fixed eyepieces . . . . **$130.00** to **$240.00**
Price: Model 849 (straight) body **$795.00**

SWIFT NIGHTHAWK M850U 65mm objective, 16x-48x zoom, or fixed 19x, 20x, 25x, 40x, 60x eyepieces. Rubber armored with a 1.8x optical finder, retractable lens hood. Field at 1000 yds. 83 ft. (22x), 52 ft. (60x). Length 12.3″; weight 30 oz. Has 45° eyepiece.
Price: Body only **$650.00**
Price: 16x-48x eyepiece **$370.00**
Price: Fixed eyepieces . . . . **$130.00** to **$240.00**
Price: Model 850 (straight) body **$575.00**

SWIFT LEOPARD M837 50mm objective, 25x. Length 9 11/16″ to 10 1/2″. Weight with tripod 28 oz. Rubber armored. Comes with tripod.
Price: **$160.00**

SWIFT TELEMASTER M841 60mm objective. 15x to 60x variable power. Field at 1000 yds. 160 feet (15x) to 40 feet (60x). Weight 3.25 lbs.; length 18″ overall.
Price: **$399.50**

SWIFT PANTHER M844 15x-45x zoom or 22x WA, 15x, 20x, 40x. 60mm objective. Field at 1000 yds. 141 ft. (15x), 68 ft. (40x), 95-58 ft. (20x-45x).
Price: Body only **$380.00**
Price: 15x-45x zoom eyepiece **$120.00**
Price: 20x-45x zoom (long eye relief) eyepiece **$140.00**
Price: 15x, 20x, 40x eyepiece **$65.00**
Price: 22x WA eyepiece **$80.00**

SWIFT M700T 12x-36x, 50mm objective. Field of view at 100 yds. 16 ft. (12x), 9 ft. (36x). Length 14″; weight with tripod 3.22 lbs.
Price: **$225.00**

SWIFT SEARCHER M839 60mm objective, 20x, 40x. Field at 1000 yds. 118 ft. (30x), 59 ft. (40x). Length 12.6″; weight 3 lbs. Rotating eyepiece head for straight or 45° viewing.
Price: **$580.00**
Price: 30x, 50x eyepieces, each **$67.00**

TASCO 29TZBWP WATERPROOF SPOTTER 60mm objective lens, 20x-60x zoom. Field at 100 yds. 7 ft., 4 in. to 3 ft., 8 in. Black rubber armored. Comes with tripod, hard case.
Price: **$356.50**

TASCO WC28TZ WORLD CLASS SPOTTING SCOPE 50mm objective, 12-36x zoom. Field at 100 yds. World Class. 13-3.8 ft. Comes with tripod and case.
Price: **$220.00**

TASCO CW5001 COMPACT ZOOM 50mm objective, 12x-36x zoom. Field at 100 yds. 16 ft., 9 in. Includes photo adapter tube, tripod with panhead lever, case.
Price: **$280.00**

TASCO 3700WP WATERPROOF SPOTTER 50mm objective, 18x-36x zoom. Field at 100 yds. 12ft., 6 in. to 7 ft., 9 in. Black rubber armored. Comes with tripod, hard case.
Price: **$288.60**

TASCO 3700, 3701 SPOTTING SCOPE 50mm objective. 18x-36x zoom. Field at 100 yds. 12 ft., 6 in. to 7 ft., 9 in. Black rubber armored.
Price: Model 3700 (black, with tripod, case) **$237.00**
Price: Model 3701 (as above, brown camo) **$237.00**

TASCO 21EB ZOOM 50mm objective lens, 15x-45x zoom. Field at 100 yds. 11 ft. (15x). Weight 22 oz.; length 18.3″ overall. Comes with panhead lever tripod.
Price: **$119.00**

TASCO 22EB ZOOM 60mm objective lens, 20x-60x zoom. Field at 100 yds. 7 ft., 2 in. (20x). Weight 28 oz.; length 21.5″ overall. Comes with micro-adjustable tripod.
Price: **$183.00**

UNERTL "FORTY-FIVE" 54mm objective. 20x (single fixed power). Field at 100 yds. 10′,10″; eye relief 1″; focusing range infinity to 33 ft. Weight about 32 oz.; overall length 153/4″. With lens covers.
Price: With multi-layer lens coating **$662.00**
Price: With mono-layer magnesium coating **$572.00**

UNERTL STRAIGHT PRISMATIC 63.5mm objective, 24x. Field at 100 yds., 7 ft. Relative brightness, 6.96. Eye relief 1/2″. Weight 40 oz.; length closed 19″. Push-pull and screw-focus eyepiece. 16x and 32x eyepieces **$125.00** each.
Price: **$515.00**

UNERTL 20x STRAIGHT PRISMATIC 54mm objective, 20x. Field at 100 yds. 8.5 ft. Relative brightness 6.1. Eye relief 1/2″. Weight 36 oz.; length closed 13 1/2″. Complete with lens covers.
Price: **$477.00**

UNERTL TEAM SCOPE 100mm objective. 15x, 24x, 32x eyepieces. Field at 100 yds. 13 to 7.5 ft. Relative brightness, 39.06 to 9.79. Eye relief 2″ to 11/2″. Weight 13 lbs.; length 29 7/8″ overall. Metal tripod, yoke and wood carrying case furnished (total weight 80 lbs.).
Price: **$2,810.00**

WEAVER 20x50 50mm objective. Field of view 12.4 ft. at 100 yds. Eye relief .85″; weighs 21 oz.; overall length 10″. Waterproof, armored.
Price: **$363.95**

WEAVER 15-40x60 ZOOM 60mm objective. 15x-40x zoom. Field at 100 yds. 119 ft. (15x), 66 ft. (60x). Overall length 12.5″, weighs 26 oz. Waterproof, armored.
Price: **$544.95**

CHOKES & BRAKES

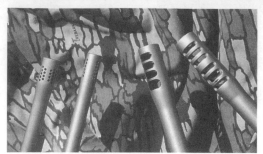

SSK Arrestor muzzle brakes.

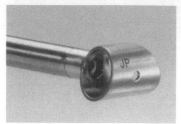

JP Muzzle Brake

Briley Screw-In Chokes

Installation of these choke tubes requires that all traces of the original choking be removed, the barrel threaded internally with square threads and then the tubes are custom fitted to the specific barrel diameter. The tubes are thin and, therefore, made of stainless steel. Cost of installation for single-barrel guns (pumps, autos), lead shot, 12-gauge, **$149.00**, 20-gauge **$159.00**; steel shot **$179.00** and **$189.00**, all with three chokes; un-single target guns run **$219.00**; over/unders and side-by-sides, lead shot, 12-gauge, **$369.00**, 20-gauge **$389.00**; steel shot **$469.00** and **$489.00**, all with five chokes. For 10-gauge auto or pump with two steel shot chokes, **$189.00**; over/unders, side-by-sides with three steel shot chokes, **$349.00**. For 16-gauge auto or pump, three lead shot chokes, **$179.00**; over/unders, side-by-sides with five lead shot chokes, **$449.00**. The 28 and 410-bore run **$179.00** for autos and pumps with three lead shot chokes, **$449.00** for over/unders and side-by-sides with five lead shot chokes.

Cutts Compensator

The Cutts Compensator is one of the oldest variable choke devices available. Manufactured by Lyman Gunsight Corporation, it is available with a steel body. A series of vents allows gas to escape upward and downward. For the 12-ga. Comp body, six fixed-choke tubes are available: the Spreader—popular with Skeet shooters; Improved Cylinder; Modified; Full; Superfull, and Magnum Full. Full, Modified and Spreader tubes are available for 12 or 20. Cutts Compensator, complete with wrench, adaptor and any single tube **$87.50**. All single choke tubes **$26.00** each. No factory installation available.

Dayson Automatic Brake System

This system fits most single barrel shotguns threaded for choke tubes, and cuts away 30 grooves on the exterior of a standard one-piece wad as it exits the muzzle. This slows the wad, allowing shot and wad to separate faster, reducing shot distortion and tightening patterns. The A.B.S. Choke Tube is claimed to reduce recoil by about 25 percent, and with the Muzzle Brake up to 60 percent. Ventilated Choke Tubes available from .685" to .725", in .005" increments. Model I Ventilated Choke Tube for use with A.B.S. Muzzle Brake, **$49.95**; for use without Muzzle Brake, **$52.95**; A.B.S. Muzzle Brake, from **$69.95**. Contact Dayson Arms for more data.

Gentry Quiet Muzzle Brake

Developed by gunmaker David Gentry, the "Quiet Muzzle Brake" is said to reduce recoil by up to 85 percent with no loss of accuracy or velocity. There is no increase in noise level because the noise and gases are directed away from the shooter. The barrel is threaded for installation and the unit is blued to match the barrel finish. Price, installed, is **$150.00**. Add **$15.00** for stainless steel, **$45.00** for knurled cap to protect threads. Shipping extra.

JP Muzzle Brake

Designed for single shot handguns, AR-15, Ruger Mini-14, Ruger Mini Thirty and other sporting rifles, the JP Muzzle Brake redirects high pressure gases against a large frontal surface which applies forward thrust to the gun. All gases are directed up, rearward and to the sides. Priced at **$79.95** (AR-15 or sporting rifles), **$89.95** (bull barrel and SKS, AK models), **$89.95** (Ruger Minis), Dual Chamber model **$79.95**. From JP Enterprises, Inc.

KDF Slim Line Muzzle Brake

This threaded muzzle brake has 30 pressure ports that direct combustion gases in all directions to reduce felt recoil up to a claimed 80 percent without affecting accuracy or ballistics. It is said to reduce felt recoil of a 30-06 to that of a 243. Price, installed, is **$179.00**. From KDF, Inc.

Mag-Na-Port

Electrical Discharge Machining works on any firearm except those having non-conductive shrouded barrels. EDM is a metal erosion technique using carbon electrodes that control the area to be processed. The Mag-Na-Port venting process utilizes small trapezoidal openings to direct powder gases upward and outward to reduce recoil. No effect is had on bluing or nickeling outside the Mag-Na-Port area so no refinishing is needed. Rifle-style porting on single shot or large caliber handguns with barrels 7 1/2" or longer is **$110.00**; Dual Trapezoidal porting on most handguns with minimum barrel length of 3", **$100.00**; standard revolver porting, **$78.50**; porting through the slide and barrel for semi-autos, **$115.00**; traditional rifle porting, **$125.00**. Prices do not include shipping, handling and insurance. From Mag-Na-Port International.

Mag-Na-Brake

A screw-on brake under 2" long with progressive integrated exhaust chambers to neutralize expanding gases. Gases dissipate with an opposite twist to prevent the brake from unscrewing, and with a 5-degree forward angle to minimize sound pressure level. Available in blue, satin blue, bright or satin stainless. Standard and Light Contour installation cost **$179.00** for bolt-action rifles, many single action and single shot handguns. A knurled thread protector supplied at extra cost. Also available in Varmint style with exhaust chambers covering 220 degrees for prone-position shooters. From Mag-Na-Port International.

Poly-Choke

Marble Arms Corp., manufacturer of the Poly-Choke adjustable shotgun choke, now offers two models in 12-, 16-, 20-, and 28-gauge—the Ventilated and Standard style chokes. Each provides nine choke settings including Xtra-Full and Slug. The Ventilated model reduces 20 percent of a shotgun's recoil, the company claims, and is priced at **$105.00**. The Standard Model is **$95.00**. Postage not included. Contact Marble Arms for more data.

Pro-port

A compound ellipsoid muzzle venting process similar to Mag-Na-Porting, only exclusively applied to shotguns. Like Mag-Na-Porting, this system reduces felt recoil, muzzle jump, and shooter fatigue. Very helpful for trap doubles shooters. Pro-Port is a patented process and installation is available in both the U.S. and Canada. Cost for the Pro-Port process is **$129.50** for over/unders (both barrels); **$99.50** for only the top or bottom barrel; and **$78.50** for single-barrel shotguns. Optional pigeon porting costs **$25.00** extra per barrel. Prices do not include shipping and handling. From Pro-port Ltd.

SSK Arrestor Brake

This is a true muzzle brake with an expansion chamber. It takes up about 1" of barrel and reduces velocity accordingly. Some Arrestors are added to a barrel, increasing its length. Said to reduce the felt recoil of a 458 to that approaching a 30-06. Can be set up to give zero muzzle rise in any caliber, and can be added to most guns. For handgun or rifle. Prices start at **$95.00**. Contact SSK Industries for full data.

Sporting Leaf and Open Sights

ERA EXPRESS SIGHTS A wide variety of open sights and bases for custom installation. Partial listing shown. From New England Custom Gun Service.
Price: One-leaf express **$66.00**
Price: Two-leaf express **$71.50**
Price: Three-leaf express **$77.00**
Price: Bases for above. **$27.50**
Price: Standing rear sight, straight. **$13.25**
Price: Base for above. **$16.50**

ERA PROFESSIONAL EXPRESS SIGHTS Standing or folding leaf sights are securely locked to the base with the ERA Magnum Clamp, but can be loosened for sighting in. Base can be attached with two socket-head cap screws or soldered. Finished and blued. Barrel diameters from .600" to .930".
Price: Standing leaf **$54.00**
Price: One-leaf express **$96.00**
Price: Two-leaf express **$101.00**
Price: Three-leaf express **$109.00**

ERA MASTERPIECE REAR SIGHT Adjustable for windage and elevation, and adjusted and locked with a small screwdriver. Comes with 8-36 socket-head cap screw and wrench. Barrel diameters from .600" to .930".
Price: **$75.00**

G.G. & G. SAME PLANE APERTURE M-16/AR-15 A2-style dual aperture rear sight with both large and small apertures centered on the same plane.
Price: **$45.00**

Williams Ruger Fire Sight

LYMAN No.16 Middle sight for barrel dovetail slot mounting. Folds flat when scope or peep sight is used. Sight notch plate adjustable for elevation. White triangle for quick aiming. 3 heights: A-.400" to.500", B-.345" to .445", C-.500" to .600".
Price: **$12.25**

MARBLE FALSE BASE #76, #77, #78 New screw-on base for most rifles replaces factory base. 3/8" dovetail slot permits installation of any folding rear sight. Can be had in sweat-on models also.
Price: **$7.95**

MARBLE FOLDING LEAF Flat-top or semi-buckhorn style. Folds down when scope or peep sights are used. Reversible plate gives choice of "U" or "V" notch. Adjustable for elevation.
Price: **$14.95**
Price: Also available with both windage and elevation adjustment **$16.95**

MARBLE SPORTING REAR With white enamel diamond, gives choice of two "U" and two "V" notches of different sizes. Adjustment in height by means of double step elevator and sliding notch piece. For all rifles; screw or dovetail installation.
Price: . . . . **$14.95-$16.95**

MARBLE #20 UNIVERSAL New screw or sweat-on base. Both have .100" elevation adjustment. In five base sizes. Three styles of U-notch, square notch, peep. Adjustable for windage and elevation.
Price: Screw-on **$23.00**
Price: Sweat-on **$21.00**

MILLETT SPORTING & BLACKPOWDER RIFLE Open click adjustable rear fits 3/8" dovetail cut in barrel. Choice of white outline, target black or open express V rear blades. Also available is a replacement screw-on sight with express V, .562" hole centers. Dovetail fronts in white or blaze orange in seven heights (.157"-.540").
Price: Dovetail or screw-on rear. **$55.60**
Price: Front sight **$12.34**

MILLETT SCOPE-SITE Open, adjustable or fixed rear sights dovetail into a base integral with the top scope-mounting ring. Blaze orange front ramp sight is integral with the front ring half. Rear sights have white outline aperture. Provides fast, short-radius, Patridge-type open sights on the top of the scope. Can be used with all Millett rings, Weaver-style bases, Ruger 77 (also fits Redhawk), Ruger Ranch Rifle, No. 1, No. 3, Rem. 870, 1100; Burris, Leupold and Redfield bases.
Price: Scope-Site top only, windage only. **$31.15**
Price: As above, fully adjustable **$66.10**
Price: Scope-Site Hi-Turret, fully adjustable, low, medium, high **$66.10**

WICHITA MULTI RANGE SIGHT SYSTEM Designed for silhouette shooting. System allows you to adjust the rear sight to four repeatable range settings, once it is pre-set. Sight clicks to any of the settings by turning a serrated wheel. Front sight is adjustable for weather and light conditions with one adjustment. Specify gun when ordering.
Price: Rear sight **$120.00**
Price: Front sight **$90.00**

WILLIAMS DOVETAIL OPEN SIGHT (WDOS) Open rear sight with windage and elevation adjustment. Furnished with "U" notch or choice of blades. Slips into dovetail and locks with gib lock. Heights from .281" to .531".
Price: With blade **$15.86**
Price: Less Blade. **$9.92**

WILLIAMS GUIDE OPEN SIGHT (WGOS) Open rear sight with windage and elevation adjustment. Bases to fit most military and commercial barrels. Choice of square "U" or "V" notch blade, 3/16", 1/4", 5/16", or 3/8" high.
Price: Less blade **$16.34**
Price: Extra blades, each. **$6.37**

WILLIAMS WGOS OCTAGON Open rear sight for 1" octagon barrels. Installs with two 6-48 screws and uses same hole spacing as most T/C muzzleloading rifles. Four heights, choice of square, U, V, B blade.
Price: **$21.80**

WILLIAMS WSKS, WAK47 Replaces original military-type rear sight. Adjustable for windage and elevation. No drilling or tapping. Peep aperture or open. For SKS carbines, AK-47.
Price: Aperture **$24.67**
Price: Open **$22.61**

WILLIAMS WM-96 Fits Mauser 96-type military rifles, replaces original rear sight with open blade or aperture. Fully adjustable for windage and elevation. No drilling; tapping.
Price: Aperture **$24.67**
Price: Open **$22.61**

WILLIAMS FIRE RIFLE SETS Replacement front and rear fiber optic sights, red bead front, two green elements in the fully adjustable rear. Made of CNC-machined metal.
Price: For Ruger 10/22. . . . . **$34.95**
Price: For most Marlin and Win. (3/8" dovetail) **$29.95**
Price: For Remington (newer style sight base) **$24.95**

Aperture and Micrometer Receiver Sights

ASHLEY GHOST RING HUNTING SIGHT Fully adjustable for windage and elevation. Available for most rifles, including blackpowder guns. Minimum gunsmithing required for most installations; matches most mounting holes. From Ashley Outdoors, Inc.
Price: **$60.00**
Price: White Stripe front post **$30.00**

ASHLEY AR-15/M-16 APERTURE Drop-in replacement of factory sights. Both apertures are on the same plane. Large ghost ring has .230" inside diameter; small ghost ring has .100" inside diameter. From Ashley Outdoors, Inc.
Price: **$30.00**

BEEMAN/FEINWERKBAU 5454 MATCH APERTURE SIGHT Small size, new-design sight uses constant-pressure flat springs to eliminate point of impact shifts.
Price: **$350.00**

BEEMAN SPORT APERTURE SIGHT Positive click micrometer adjustments. Standard units with flush surface screwdriver adjustments. Deluxe version has target knobs. For air rifles with grooved receivers.
Price: Standard **$40.00**
Price: Deluxe **$50.00**

Williams Fire Sight Peep Set

EAW RECEIVER SIGHT A fully adjustable aperture sight that locks securely into the EAW quick-detachable scope mount rear base. Made by New England Custom Gun Service.
Price: **$95.00**

G.G.&G. MAD IRIS Multiple Aperture Device is a four sight, rotating aperture disk with small and large apertures on the same plane. Mounts on M-16/AR-15 flat top receiver. Fully adjustable.
Price: **$129.00**
Price: A2 IRIS, two apertures, full windage adjustments **$120.00**

LYMAN NO. 2 TANG SIGHT Designed for the Winchester Model 94. Has high index marks on aperture post; comes with both .093" quick sighting aperture, .040" large disk aperture, and replacement mounting screws.
Price: **$69.95**
Price: For Marlin lever actions **$71.56**

Lyman No. 57 GPR

LYMAN No. 57 1/4-minute clicks. Stayset knobs. Quick release slide, adjustable zero scales. Made for almost all modern rifles.

Price: $62.50
Price: No. 57SME, 57SMET (for White Systems Model 91 and Whitetail rifles) $62.50
LYMAN 57GPR Designed especially for the Lyman Great Plains Rifle. Mounts directly onto the tang of the rifle and has 1/4-minute micrometer click adjustments.
Price: $62.50
LYMAN No. 66 Fits close to the rear of flat-sided receivers, furnished with Stayset knobs. Quick release slide, 1/4-min. adjustments. For most lever or slide action or flat-sided automatic rifles.
Price: $62.50
Price: No. 66MK (for all current versions of the Knight MK-85 in-line rifle with flat-sided receiver) $62.50
Price: No. 66 SKS fits Russian and Chinese SKS rifles; large and small apertures $62.50
LYMAN No. 66U Light weight, designed for most modern shotguns with a flat-sided, round-top receiver. 1/4-minute clicks. Requires drilling, tapping. Not for Browning A-5, Rem. M11.
Price: $71.50
LYMAN 90MJT RECEIVER SIGHT Mounts on standard Lyman and Williams FP bases. Has 1/4-minute audible micrometer click adjustments, target knobs with direction indicators. Adjustable zero scales, quick release slide. Large 7/8" diameter aperture disk.
Price: Right- or left-hand $72.50
MARBLE PEEP TANG SIGHT All-steel construction. Micrometer-like click adjustments for windage and elevation. For most popular old and new lever-action rifles.
Price: $99.00
MILLETT PEEP RIFLE SIGHTS Fully adjustable, heat-treated nickel steel peep aperture receiver sight for the Mini-14. Has fine windage and elevation adjustments; replaces original.
Price: Rear sight, Mini-14 ....$49.00
Price: Front sight, Mini-14 ....$18.75
Price: Front and rear combo with hood $64.00
WILLIAMS FIRE SIGHT PEEP SETS Combines the Fire Sight front bead with Williams fully adjustable metallic peep rear.
Price: For SKS $39.95
Price: For Ruger 10/22 ....$39.95
Price: For Marlin or Winchester lever actions $73.95

WILLIAMS FP Internal click adjustments. Positive locks. For virtually all rifles, T/C Contender, Heckler & Koch HK-91, Ruger Mini-14, plus Win., Rem. and Ithaca shotguns.
Price: From $59.95
Price: With Target Knobs $71.20
Price: With Square Notched Blade $63.03
Price: With Target Knobs & Square Notched Blade $74.45
Price: FP-GR (for dovetail-grooved receivers, 22s and air guns) $59.95
Price: FP-94BBSE (for Win. 94 Big Bore A.E.; uses top rear scope mount holes) $59.95
WILLIAMS TARGET FP Similar to the FP series but developed for most bolt-action rimfire rifles. Target FP High adjustable from 1.250" to 1.750" above centerline of bore; Target FP Low adjustable from .750" to 1.250". Attaching bases for Rem. 540X, 541-S, 580, 581, 582 (#540); Rem. 510, 511, 512, 513-T, 521-T (#510); Win. 75 (#75); Savage/Anschutz 64 and Mark 12 (#64). Some rifles require drilling, tapping.
Price: High or Low $77.15
Price: Base only $12.98
Price: FP-T/C Scout rifle, from $59.95
Price: FP-94BBSE (for Win. 94 Big Bore A.E.; uses top rear scope mount holes) $59.95
WILLIAMS 5-D SIGHT Low cost sight for shotguns, 22s and the more popular big game rifles. Adjustment for windage and elevation. Fits most guns without drilling and tapping. Also for British SMLE, Winchester M94 Side Eject.
Price: From $31.47
Price: With Shotgun Aperture $31.47
WILLIAMS GUIDE (WGRS) Receiver sight for 30 M1 Carbine, M1903A3 Springfield, Savage 24s, Savage-Anschutz and Weatherby XXII. Utilizes military dovetail; no drilling. Double-dovetail windage adjustment, sliding dovetail adjustment for elevation.
Price: $30.85
Price: WGRS-CVA (for rifles with octagon barrels, receivers) $30.85

Front Sights

ASHLEY AR-15/M-16 FRONT SIGHTS Drop-in replacement sight post. Double faced so it can be rotated 180 degrees for 2.5 MOA elevation adjustment. Available in .080" width with .030" white stripe, or .100" with .040" stripe. From Ashley Outdoors, Inc.
Price: $30.00
Price: Tritium Dot Express $60.00
ERA FRONT SIGHTS European-type front sights inserted from the front. Various heights available. From New England Custom Gun Service.
Price: 1/16" silver bead $11.50
Price: 3/32" silver bead $16.00
Price: Sourdough bead $14.50
Price: Tritium night sight $44.00
Price: Folding night sight with ivory bead $39.50
LYMAN HUNTING SIGHTS Made with gold or white beads 1/16" to 3/32" wide and in varying heights for most military and commercial rifles. Dovetail bases.
Price: $8.75

MARBLE STANDARD Ivory, red, or gold bead. For all American-made rifles, 1/16" wide bead with semi-flat face which does not reflect light. Specify type of rifle when ordering.
Price: $8.95
MARBLE CONTOURED Has 3/8" dovetail base, .090" deep, is 5/8" long. Uses standard 1/16" or 3/32" bead, ivory, red, or gold. Specify rifle type.
Price: $10.50
WILLIAMS RISER BLOCKS For adding .250" height to front sights when using a receiver sight. Two widths available: .250" for Williams Streamlined Ramp or .340" on all standard ramps having this base width. Uses standard 3/8" dovetail.
Price: $5.46

Globe Target Front Sights

LYMAN 20 MJT TARGET FRONT Has 7/8" diameter, one-piece steel globe with 3/8" dovetail base. Height is .700" from bottom of dovetail to center of aperture; height on 20 LJT is .750". Comes with seven Anschutz-size steel inserts—two posts and five apertures .126" through .177".
Price: 20 MJT or 20 LJT $31.50
LYMAN No. 17A TARGET Includes seven interchangeable inserts: four apertures, one transparent amber and two posts .50" and .100" in width.
Price: $26.00
Price: Insert set $9.00

Lyman 17AEU

LYMAN 17AEU Similar to the Lyman 17A except has a special dovetail design to mount easily onto European muzzleloaders such as CVA, Traditions and Investarm. All steel, comes with eight inserts.
Price: $26.00
LYMAN No. 93 MATCH Has 7/8" diameter, fits any rifle with a standard dovetail mounting block. Comes with seven target inserts and accepts most Anschutz accessories. Hooked locking bolt and nut allows quick removal, installation. Base available in .860" (European) and .562" (American) hole spacing.
Price: $41.25
WILLIAMS TARGET GLOBE FRONT Adapts to many rifles. Mounts to the base with a knurled locking screw. Height is .545" from center, not including base. Comes with inserts.
Price: $30.85
Price: Dovetail base (low) .220" $17.00
Price: Dovetail base (high) .465" $17.00
Price: Screw-on base, .300" height, .300" radius $15.45
Price: Screw-on base, .450" height, .350" radius $15.45
Price: Screw-on base, .215" height, .400" radius $15.45

Ramp Sights

ERA MASTERPIECE Banded ramps; 21 sizes; hand-detachable beads and hood; beads inserted from the front. Various heights available. From New England Custom Gun Service.
Price: Banded ramp $54.00
Price: Hood $10.50
Price: 1/16" silver bead $11.50
Price: 3/32" silver bead $16.00
Price: Sourdough bead $14.50
Price: Tritium night sight $47.00
Price: Folding night sight with ivory bead $39.50
LYMAN NO. 18 SCREW-ON RAMP Used with 8-40 screws but may also be brazed on. Heights from .10" to .350". Ramp without sight.
Price: $13.75
MARBLE FRONT RAMPS Available in polished or dull matte finish or serrated style. Standard 3/8x.090" dovetail slot. Made for MR-width (.340") front sights. Can be used as screw-on or sweat-on. Heights: .100", .150", .300".
Price: Polished or matte $14.00
Price: Serrated $10.00
WILLIAMS SHORTY RAMP Companion to "Streamlined" ramp, about 1/2" shorter. Screw-on or sweat-on. It is furnished in 1/8", 3/16", 9/32", and 3/8" heights without hood only. Also for shotguns.
Price: $15.90

Price: With dovetail lock $18.55
WILLIAMS STREAMLINED RAMP Available in screw-on or sweat-on models. Furnished in 9/16″, 7/16″, 3/8″, 5/16″, 3/16″ heights.
Price: $17.35
Price: Sight hood $3.95
WILLIAMS STREAMLINED FRONT SIGHTS Narrow (.250″ width) for Williams Streamlined ramps and others with 1/4″ top width; medium (.340″ width) for all standard factory ramps. Available with white, gold or flourescent beads, 1/16″ or 3/32″.
Price: . . . .$8.93 to $9.25

Handgun Sights

ASHLEY EXPRESS SIGHTS Low-profile, snag-free express-type sights. Shallow V rear with white vertical line, white dot front. All-steel, matte black finish. Rear is available in different heights. Made for most pistols, many with double set-screws. From Ashley Outdoors, Inc.
Price: Standard Set, front and rear $60.00
Price: Big Dot Set, front and rear $60.00
Price: Tritium Set, Standard or Big Dot $90.00
BO-MAR DELUXE BMCS Gives 3/8″ windage and elevation adjustment at 50 yards on Colt Gov't 45; sight radius under 7″. For GM and Commander models only. Uses existing dovetail slot. Has shield-type rear blade.
Price: $65.95
Price: BMCS-2 (for GM and 9mm) $68.95
Price: Flat bottom $65.95
Price: BMGC (for Colt Gold Cup), angled serrated blade, rear $68.95
Price: BMGC front sight $12.95
Price: BMCZ-75 (for CZ-75,TZ-75, P-9 and most clones).
    Works with factory front $68.95
BO-MAR FRONT SIGHTS Dovetail style for S&W 4506, 4516, 1076; undercut style (.250″, .280″, 5/16″ high); Fast Draw style (.210″, .250″, .230″ high).
Price $12.95
BO-MAR BMU XP-100/T/C CONTENDER No gunsmithing required; has .080″ notch.
Price: $77.00
BO-MAR BMML For muzzleloaders; has .062″ notch, flat bottom.
Price: $65.95
Price: With 3/8″ dovetail $65.95
BO-MAR RUGER "P" ADJUSTABLE SIGHT Replaces factory front and rear sights.
Price: Rear sight $65.95
Price: Front sight $12.00

Ashley Ghost Ring

BO-MAR BMR Fully adjustable rear sight for Ruger MKI, MKII Bull barrel autos.
Price: Rear $65.95
Price: Undercut front sight $12.00
BO-MAR GLOCK Fully adjustable, all-steel replacement sights. Sight fits factory dovetail. Longer sight radius. Uses Novak Glock .275″ high, .135″ wide front, or similar.
Price: Rear sight $68.95
Price: Front sight $20.95
BO-MAR LOW PROFILE RIB & ACCURACY TUNER Streamlined rib with front and rear sights; 7 1/8″ sight radius. Brings sight line closer to the bore than standard or extended sight and ramp. Weight 5 oz. Made for Colt Gov't 45, Super 38, and Gold Cup 45 and 38.
Price: $140.00
BO-MAR COMBAT RIB For S&W Model 19 revolver with 4″ barrel. Sight radius 5 3/4″, weight 5 1/2 oz.
Price: $127.00

Williams Fire Sight Set

BO-MAR WINGED RIB For S&W 4″ and 6″ length barrels—K-38, M10, HB 14 and 19. Weight for the 6″ model is about 7 1/4 oz.
Price: $140.00
BO-MAR COVER-UP RIB Adjustable rear sight, winged front guards. Fits right over revolver's original front sight. For S&W 4″ M-10HB, M-13, M-58, M-64 & 65, Ruger 4″ models SDA-34, SDA-84, SS-34, SS-84, GF-34, GF-84.
Price: $130.00
C-MORE SIGHTS Replacement front sight blades offered in two types and five styles. Made of Du Pont Acetal, they come in a set of five high-contrast colors: blue, green, pink, red and yellow. Easy to install. Patridge style for Colt Python (all barrels), Ruger Super Blackhawk (7 1/2″), Ruger Blackhawk (4 5/8″); ramp style for Python (all barrels), Blackhawk (4 5/8″), Super Blackhawk (7 1/2″ and 10 1/2″). From C-More Systems.
Price: Per set $19.95
G.G. & G. GHOST RINGS Replaces the factory rear sight without gunsmithing. Black phosphate finish. Available for Colt M1911 and Commander, Beretta M92F, Glock, S&W, SIG Sauer.
Price: $65.00
JP GHOST RING Replacement bead front, ghost ring rear for Glock and M1911 pistols. From JP Enterprises.
Price: $79.95
Price: Bo-Mar replacement leaf with JP dovetail front bead $99.95
MMC TACTICAL ADJUSTABLE SIGHTS Low-profile, snag free design. Twenty-two click positions for elevation, drift adjustable for windage. Machined from 4140 steel and heat treated to 40 RC. Tritium and non-tritium. Ten different configurations and colors. Three different finishes. For 1911s, all Glock, HK USP, S&W, Browning Hi-Power.
Price: Sight set, tritium $144.92
Price: Sight set, white outline or white dot $99.90
Price: Sight set, black $93.90
MEPROLIGHT TRITIUM NIGHT SIGHTS Replacement sight assemblies for use in low-light conditions. Available for rifles, shotguns, handguns and bows. TRU-DOT models carry a 12-year warranty on the useable illumination, while non-TRU-DOT have a 5-year warranty. Contact Hesco, Inc. for complete list of available models.
Price: Kahr K9, K40, fixed, TRU-DOT $100.00
Price: Ruger P85, P89, P94, adjustable, TRU-DOT $156.00
Price: Ruger Mini-14R sights $140.00
Price: SIG Sauer P220, P225, P226, P228, adjustable, TRU-DOT $156.00
Price: Smith&Wesson autos, fixed or adjustable, TRU-DOT $100.00
Price: Taurus PT92, PT100, adjustable, TRU-DOT $166.00
Price: Walther P-99, fixed, TRU-DOT $100.00
Price: Shotgun bead $32.00
Price: Beretta M92, Cougar, Brigadier, fixed, TRU-DOT $100.00
Price: Browning Hi-Power, adjustable, TRU-DOT $156.00
Price: Colt M1911 Govt., adjustable, TRU-DOT $156.00
MILLETT SERIES 100 REAR SIGHTS All-steel highly visible, click adjustable. Blades in white outline, target black, silhouette, 3-dot, and tritium bars. Fit most popular revolvers and autos.
Price: . . . . $49.30 to $80.00
MILLETT BAR-DOT-BAR TRITIUM NIGHT SIGHTS Replacement front and rear combos fit most automatics. Horizontal tritium bars on rear, dot front sight.
Price: $145.00
MILLETT 3-DOT SYSTEM SIGHTS The 3-Dot System sights use a single white dot on the front blade and two dots flanking the rear notch. Fronts available in Dual-Crimp and Wide Stake-On styles, as well as special applications. Adjustable rear sight available for most popular auto pistols and revolvers.
Price: Front, from $16.00
Price: Adjustable rear $55.60
MILLETT REVOLVER FRONT SIGHTS All-steel replacement front sights with either white or orange bar. Easy to install. For Ruger GP-100, Redhawk, Security-Six, Police-Six, Speed-Six, Colt Trooper, Diamondback, King Cobra, Peacemaker, Python, Dan Wesson 22 and 15-2.
Price: . . . . $13.60 to $16.00
MILLETT DUAL-CRIMP FRONT SIGHT Replacement front sight for automatic pistols. Dual-Crimp uses an all-steel two-point hollow rivet system. Available in eight heights and four styles. Has a skirted base that covers the front sight pad. Easily installed with the Millett Installation Tool Set. Available in Blaze Orange Bar, White Bar, Serrated Ramp, Plain Post.
Price: $16.00
MILLETT STAKE-ON FRONT SIGHT Replacement front sight for automatic pistols. Stake-On sights have skirted base that covers the front sight pad. Easily installed with the Millet Installation Tool Set. Available in seven heights and four styles—Blaze Orange Bar, White Bar, Serrated Ramp, Plain Post.
Price: $16.00
OMEGA OUTLINE SIGHT BLADES Replacement rear sight blades for Colt and Ruger single action guns and the Interarms Virginian Dragoon. Standard Outline available in gold or white notch outline on blue metal. From Omega Sales, Inc.
Price: $8.95
OMEGA MAVERICK SIGHT BLADES Replacement "peep-sight" blades for Colt, Ruger SAs, Virginian Dragoon. Three models available—No. 1, Plain; No. 2, Single Bar; No. 3, Double Bar Rangefinder. From Omega Sales, Inc.
Price: Each $6.95
PACHMAYR ACCU-SET Low-profile, fully adjustable rear sight to be used with existing front sight. Available with target, white outline or 3-dot blade. Blue finish. Uses factory dovetail and locking screw. For Browning, Colt, Glock, SIG Sauer, S&W and Ruger autos. From Pachmayr.
Price: . . . . NA

P-T TRITIUM NIGHT SIGHTS Self-luminous tritium sights for most popular handguns, Colt AR-15, H&K rifles and shotguns. Replacement handgun sight sets available in 3-Dot style (green/green, green/yellow, green/orange) with bold outlines around inserts; Bar-Dot available in green/green with or without white outline rear sight. Functional life exceeds 15 years. From Innovative Weaponry, Inc.
Price: Handgun sight sets...**$99.95**
Price: Rifle sight sets...**$99.95**
Price: Rifle, front only..**$49.95**
Price: Shotgun, front only...**$49.95**

TRIJICON NIGHT SIGHTS Three-dot night sight system uses tritium lamps in the front and rear sights. Tritium "lamps" are mounted in silicone rubber inside a metal cylinder. A polished crystal sapphire provides protection and clarity. Inlaid white outlines provide 3-dot aiming in daylight also. Available for most popular handguns. From Trijicon, Inc.
Price:...**$50.00 to $175.00**

Wichita Series 70/80

WICHITA SERIES 70/80 SIGHT Provides click windage and elevation adjustments with precise repeatability of settings. Sight blade is grooved and angled back at the top to reduce glare. Available in Low Mount Combat or Low Mount Target styles for Colt 45s and their copies, S&W 645, Hi-Power, CZ 75 and others.
Price: Rear sight, target or combat......................................**$75.00**
Price: Front sight, Patridge or ramp.....................................**$15.00**

WICHITA GRAND MASTER DELUXE RIBS Ventilated rib has wings machined into it for better sight acquisition and is relieved for Mag-Na-Porting. Milled to accept Weaver see-thru-style rings. Made of stainless or blued steel; front and rear sights blued. Has Wichita Multi-Range rear sight system, adjustable front sight. Made for revolvers with 6" barrel.
Price: Model 301S, 301B (adj. sight K frames with custom bbl. of 1" to 1.032" dia. L and N frame with 1.062" to 1.100" dia. bbl.)........................**$180.00**
Price: Model 303S, 303B (adj. sight K, L, N frames with factory barrel).....**$180.00**

WILLIAMS FIRE SIGHT SETS Red fiber optic metallic sight replaces the original. Rear sight has two green fiber optic elements. Made of CNC-machined aluminum. Fits all Glocks, Ruger P-85, S&W 910, Colt Gov't. Model Series 80, Ruger GP 100 and Redhawk, and SIG Sauer (front only).
Price: Front and rear set..**$39.95**
Price: SIG Sauer front..**$19.95**

Shotgun Sights

ACCURA-SITE For shooting shotgun slugs. Three models to fit most shotguns—"A" for vent. rib barrels, "B" for solid ribs, "C" for plain barrels. Rear sight has windage and elevation provisions. Easily removed and replaced. Includes front and rear sights. From All's, The Jim Tembeils Co.
Price:...**$27.95 to $34.95**

FIRE FLY EM-109 SL SHOTGUN SIGHT Made of aircraft-grade aluminum, this 1/4-oz. "channel" sight has a thick, sturdy hollowed post between the side rails to give a Patridge sight picture. All shooting is done with both eyes open, allowing the shooter to concentrate on the target, not the sights. The hole in the sight post gives reduced-light shooting capability and allows for fast, precise aiming. For sport or combat shooting. Model EM-109 fits all vent. rib and double barrel shotguns and muzzleloaders with octagon barrel. Model MOC-110 fits all plain barrel shotguns without screw-in chokes. From JAS, Inc.
Price:...**$35.00**

LYMAN Three sights of over-sized ivory beads. No. 10 Front (press fit) for double barrel or ribbed single barrel guns..**$4.50**; No. 10D Front (screw fit) for non-ribbed single barrel guns (comes with wrench)...**$5.50**; No. 11 Middle (press fit) for double and ribbed single barrel guns...**$4.75**.

MMC M&P COMBAT SHOTGUN SIGHT SET A durable, protected ghost ring aperture, combat sight made of steel. Fully adjustable for windage and elevation.
Price: M&P Sight Set (front and rear).....................................**$73.45**
Price: As above, installed...**$83.95**

MMC TACTICAL GHOST RING SIGHT Click adjustable for elevation with 30 MOA total adjustment in 3 MOA increments. Click windage adjustment. Machined from 4140 steel, heat treated to 40 RC. Front sight available in banded tactical or serrated ramp. Front and rear sights available with or without tritium. Available in three different finishes.

Price: Rear Ghost Ring with tritium..**$119.95**
Price: Rear Ghost Ring without tritium......................................**$99.95**
Price: Front Banded Tactical with tritium....................................**$59.95**
Price: Front Banded Tactical without tritium.................................**$39.95**
Price: Front serrated ramp...**$24.95**

MARBLE SHOTGUN BEAD SIGHTS No. 214—Ivory front bead, 11/64", tapered shank...**$4.40**; No. 223—Ivory rear bead, .080", tapered shank...**$4.40**; No. 217—Ivory front bead, 11/64", threaded shank...**$4.75**; No. 223-T—Ivory rear bead, .080", threaded shank...**$5.95**. Reamers, taps and wrenches available from Marble Arms.

MILLETT SHURSHOT SHOTGUN SIGHT A sight system for shotguns with ventilated rib. Rear sight attaches to the rib, front sight replaces the front bead. Front has an orange face, rear has two orange bars. For 870, 1100 or other models.
Price: Rear **$13.15**
Price: Adjustable front and rear set.......................................**$31.00**
Price: Front **$12.95**

POLY-CHOKE Replacement front shotgun sights in four styles—Xpert, Poly Bead, Xpert Mid Rib sights, and Bev-L-Block. Xpert Front available in 3x56, 6x48 thread, 3/32" or 5/32" shank length, gold, ivory...**$4.70**; or Sun Spot orange bead...**$5.95**; Poly Bead is standard replacement 1/8" bead, 6x48...**$2.95**; Xpert Mid Rib in tapered carrier (ivory only) …**$5.95**, or 3x56 threaded shank (gold only)...**$2.95**; Hi and Lo Blok sights with 6x48 thread, gold or ivory...**$5.25**. From Marble Arms.

SLUG SIGHTS Made of non-marring black nylon, front and rear sights stretch over and lock onto the barrel. Sights are low profile with blaze orange front blade. Adjustable for windage and elevation. For plain-barrel (non-ribbed) guns in 12-, 16- and 20-gauge, and for shotguns with 5/16" and 3/8" ventilated ribs. From Innovision Ent.
Price:...**$11.95**

WILLIAMS GUIDE BEAD SIGHT Fits all shotguns, 1/8" ivory, red or gold bead. Screws into existing sight hole. Various thread sizes and shank lengths.
Price:..**$4.77**

WILLIAMS SLUGGER SIGHTS Removable aluminum sights attach to the shotgun rib. High profile front, fully adjustable rear. Fits 1/4", 5/16" or 3/8" (special) ribs.
Price:...**$34.95**

WILLIAMS FIRE SIGHTS Fiber optic light gathering front sights in red or yellow, glow with natural light. Fit 1/4", 5/16" or 3/8" vent. ribs, most popular shotguns.
Price:...**$13.95**

Sight Attachments

MERIT ADJUSTABLE APERTURES Eleven clicks give 12 different apertures. No. 3 Disc and Master, primarily target types, 0.22" to .125"; No. 4, 1/2" dia. hunting type, .025" to .155". Available for all popular sights. The Master, with flexible rubber light shield, is particularly adapted to extension, scope height, and tang sights. All models have internal click springs; are hand fitted to minimum tolerance.
Price: No. 3 Master Disk..**$66.00**
Price: No. 3 Target Disc (Plain Face).....................................**$56.00**
Price: No. 4 Hunting Disc...**$48.00**

MERIT LENS DISC Similar to Merit Iris Shutter (Model 3 or Master) but incorporates provision for mounting prescription lens integrally. Lens may be obtained locally from your optician. Sight disc is 7/16" wide (Model 3), or 3/4" wide (Master).
Price: No. 3 Target Lens Disk...**$68.00**
Price: No. 3 Master Lens Disk...**$78.00**

Merit Optical Attachment

MERIT OPTICAL ATTACHMENT For iron sight shooting with handgun or rifle. Instantly attached by rubber suction cup to prescription or shooting glasses. Swings aside. Aperture adjustable from .020" to .156".
Price:...**$65.00**

WILLIAMS APERTURES Standard thread, fits most sights. Regular series 3/8" to 1/2" O.D., .050" to .125" hole. "Twilight" series has white reflector ring.
Price: Regular series...**$4.97**
Price: Twilight series...**$6.79**
Price: Wide open 5/16" aperture for shotguns fits 5-D or Foolproof sights (specify model) **$8.77**

THE ARMS LIBRARY

FOR COLLECTOR ◆ HUNTER ◆ SHOOTER ◆ OUTDOORSMAN

IMPORTANT NOTICE TO BOOK BUYERS

Books listed here may be bought from Ray Riling Arms Books Co., 6844 Gorsten St., P.O. Box 18925, Philadelphia, PA 19119, phone 215/438-2456; FAX: 215-438-5395. Joe Riling is the researcher and compiler of "The Arms Library" and a seller of gun books for over 30 years.

The Riling stock includes books classic and modern, many hard-to-find items, and many not obtainable elsewhere. These pages list a portion of the current stock. They offer prompt, complete service, with delayed shipments occurring only on out-of-print or out-of-stock books.

NOTICE FOR ALL CUSTOMERS: Remittance in U.S. funds must accompany all orders. For U.S. add $2.00 per book for postage and insurance. Minimum order $10.00. For UPS add 50% to mailing costs.

All foreign countries add $5.00 per book. All foreign orders are shipped at the buyer's risk unless an additional $5 for insurance is included.

Payments in excess of order or for "Backorders" are credited or fully refunded at request. Books "As-Ordered" are not returnable except by permission and a handling charge on these of $2.00 per book is deducted from refund or credit. Only Pennsylvania customers must include current sales tax.

A full variety of arms books also available from Rutgers Book Center, 127 Raritan Ave., Highland Park, NJ 08904/908-545-4344; FAX: 908-545-6686 or I.D.S.A. Books, 1324 Stratford Drive, Piqua, OH 45356/937-773-4203; FAX: 937-778-1922.

BALLISTICS AND HANDLOADING

ABC's of Reloading, 6th Edition, by C. Rodney James and the editors of *Handloader's Digest*, DBI Books, a division of Krause Publications, Iola, WI, 1997. 288 pp., illus. Paper covers. $21.95.
The definitive guide to every facet of cartridge and shotshell reloading.

Ammunition Making, by George E. Frost, National Rifle Association of America, Washington, D.C., 1990. 160 pp., illus. Paper covers. $17.95.
Reflects the perspective of "an insider" with half a century's experience in successful management of ammunition manufacturing operations.

Barnes Reloading Manual #1, Barnes Bullets, American Fork, UT, 1995. 350 pp., illus. $24.95.
Data for more than 65 cartridges from 243 to 50 BMG.

Basic Handloading, by George C. Nonte, Jr., Outdoor Life Books, New York, NY, 1982. 192 pp., illus. Paper covers. $6.95.
How to produce high-quality ammunition using the safest, most efficient methods.

Big Bore Rifles And Cartridges, Wolfe Publishing Co., Prescott, AZ, 1991. Paper covers. $26.00.
This book covers cartridges from 8mm to .600 Nitro with loading tables.

Black Powder Guide, 2nd Edition, by George C. Nonte, Jr., Stoeger Publishing Co., So. Hackensack, NJ, 1991. 288 pp., illus. Paper covers. $14.95.
How-to instructions for selection, repair and maintenance of muzzleloaders, making your own bullets, restoring and refinishing, shooting techniques.

Blackpowder Loading Manual, 3rd Edition, by Sam Fadala, DDI Books, a division of Krause Publications, Iola, WI, 1995. 368 pp., illus. Paper covers. $19.95.
Revised and expanded edition of this landmark blackpowder loading book. Covers hundreds of loads for most of the popular blackpowder rifles, handguns and shotguns.

The Bullet Swage Manual, by Ted Smith, Corbin Manufacturing and Supply Co., White City, OR, 1988. 45 pp., illus. Paper covers. $10.00.
A book that fills the need for information on bullet swaging.

Cartridges of the World, 8th Edition, by Frank Barnes, edited by M. L. McPherson, DBI Books, a division of Krause Publications, Iola, WI, 1997. 480 pp., illus. Paper covers. $24.95.
Completely revised edition of the general purpose reference work for which collectors, police, scientists and laymen reach first for answers to cartridge identification questions.

Cartridge Reloading Tools of the Past, by R.H. Chamberlain and Tom Quigley, Tom Quigley, Castle Rock, WA, 1998. 167 pp., illustrated. Paper covers. $25.00.
A detailed treatment of the extensive Winchester and Ideal line of handloading tools and bullet molds, plus Remington, Marlin, Ballard, Browning, Maynard, and many others.

Cast Bullets for the Black Powder Rifle, by Paul A. Matthews, Wolfe Publishing Co., Prescott, AZ, 1996. 133 pp., illus. Paper covers. $22.50.
The tools and techniques used to make your cast bullet shooting a success.

Complete Blackpowder Handbook, 3rd Edition, by Sam Fadala, DBI Books, a division of Krause Publications, Iola, WI, 1997. 400 pp., illus. Paper covers. $21.95.
Expanded and completely rewritten edition of the definitive book on the subject of blackpowder.

The Complete Handloader for Rifles, Handguns and Shotguns, by John Wootters, Stackpole Books, Harrisburg, PA, 1988. 214 pp., $29.95.
Loading-bench know-how.

Complete Reloading Guide, by Robert & John Traister, Stoeger Publishing Co., Wayne, NJ, 1997. 608 pp., illus. Paper covers. $34.95
Perhaps the finest, most comprehensive work ever published on the subject of reloading.

Designing and Forming Custom Cartridges, by Ken Howell, Ken Howell, Stevensville, MT, 1995. 596 pp., illus. $59.95.
Covers cartridge dimensions and includes complete introductory material on cartridge manufacture and appendices on finding loading data and equipment.

Game Loads and Practical Ballistics for the American Hunter, by Bob Hagel, Wolfe Publishing Co., Prescott, AZ, 1992. 310 pp., illus. $27.90.
Hagel's knowledge gained as a hunter, guide and gun enthusiast is gathered in this informative text.

Handbook of Bullet Swaging No. 7, by David R. Corbin, Corbin Manufacturing and Supply Co., White City, OR, 1986. 199 pp., illus. Paper covers. $10.00.
This handbook explains the most precise method of making quality bullets.

Handbook for Shooters and Reloaders, by P.O. Ackley, Salt Lake City, UT, 1970, (Vol. I), 567 pp., illus. (Vol. II), a new printing with specific new material. 495 pp., illus. $18.95 each.

Handbook of Metallic Cartridge Reloading, by Edward Matunas, Winchester Press, Piscataway, NJ, 1981. 272 pp., illus. $19.95.
Up-to-date, comprehensive loading tables prepared by four major powder manufacturers.

Handgun Reloading, The Gun Digest Book of, by Dean A. Grennell and Wiley M. Clapp, DBI Books, a division of Krause Publications, Iola, WI, 1987. 256 pp., illus. Paper covers. $16.95.
Detailed discussions of all aspects of reloading for handguns, from basic to complex. New loading data.

Handloader's Digest, 17th Edition, edited by Bob Bell. DBI Books, a division of Krause Publications, Iola, WI, 1997. 480 pp., illustrated. Paper covers. $27.95.
Top writers in the field contribute helpful information on techniques and components. Greatly expanded and fully indexed catalog of all currently available tools, accessories and components for metallic, blackpowder cartridge, shotgun reloading and swaging.

Handloader's Guide, by Stanley W. Trzoniec, Stoeger Publishing Co., So. Hackensack, NJ, 1985. 256 pp., illus. Paper covers. $14.95.
The complete step-by-step fully illustrated guide to handloading ammunition.

Handloader's Manual of Cartridge Conversions, by John J. Donnelly, Stoeger Publishing Co., So. Hackensack, NJ, 1986. Unpaginated. $49.95.
From 14 Jones to 70-150 Winchester in English and American cartridges, and from 4.85 U.K. to 15.2x28R Gevelot in metric cartridges. Over 900 cartridges described in detail.

Handloading, by Bill Davis, Jr., NRA Books, Wash., D.C., 1980. 400 pp., illus. Paper covers. $15.95.
A complete update and expansion of the NRA Handloader's Guide.

Handloading for Hunters, by Don Zutz, Winchester Press, Piscataway, NJ, 1977. 288 pp., illus. $30.00.
Precise mixes and loads for different types of game and for various hunting situations with rifle and shotgun.

Hatcher's Notebook, by S. Julian Hatcher, Stackpole Books, Harrisburg, PA, 1992. 488 pp., illus. $39.95.
A reference work for shooters, gunsmiths, ballisticians, historians, hunters and collectors.

Hodgdon Data Manual No. 26, Hodgdon Powder Co., Shawnee Mission, KS, 1993. 797 pp. $25.00.
Includes Hercules, Winchester and Dupont powders; data on cartridge cases; loads; silhouette; shotshell; pyrodex and blackpowder; conversion factors; weight equivalents, etc.

The Home Guide to Cartridge Conversions, by Maj. George C. Nonte Jr., The Gun Room Press, Highland Park, NJ, 1976. 404 pp., illus. $24.95.
Revised and updated version of Nonte's definitive work on the alteration of cartridge cases for use in guns for which they were not intended.

Hornady Handbook of Cartridge Reloading, 4th Edition, Vol. I and II, Hornady Mfg. Co., Grand Island, NE, 1991. 1200 pp., illus. $34.95.
New edition of this famous reloading handbook. Latest loads, ballistic information, etc.

Hornady Handbook of Cartridge Reloading, Abridged Edition, Hornady Mfg. Co., Grand Island, NE, 1991. $19.95.
Ballistic data for 25 of the most popular cartridges.

Hornady Load Notes, Hornady Mfg. Co., Grand Island, NE, 1991. $4.95.
Complete load data and ballistics for a single caliber. Eight pistol 9mm-45ACP; 16 rifle, 222-45-70.

How-To's for the Black Powder Cartridge Rifle Shooter, by Paul A. Matthews, Wolfe Publishing Co., Prescott, AZ, 1995. 45 pp. Paper covers. $22.50.

THE ARMS LIBRARY

Covers lube recipes, good bore cleaners and over-powder wads. Tips include compressing powder charges, combating wind resistance, improving ignition and much more.

The Illustrated Reference of Cartridge Dimensions, edited by Dave Scovill, Wolfe Publishing Co., Prescott, AZ, 1994. 343 pp., illus. Paper covers. $19.00

A comprehensive volume with over 300 cartridges. Standard and metric dimensions have been taken from SAAMI drawings and/or fired cartridges.

Loading the Black Powder Rifle Cartridge, by Paul A Matthews, Wolfe Publishing Co., Prescott, AZ, 1993. 121 pp., illus. Paper covers. $22.50.

Author Matthews brings the blackpowder cartridge shooter valuable information on the basics, including cartridge care, lubes and moulds, powder charges and developing and testing loads in his usual authoritative style.

Loading the Peacemaker—Colt's Model P, by Dave Scovill, Wolfe Publishing Co., Prescott, AZ, 1996. 227 pp., illus. $24.95.

A comprehensive work about the history, maintenance and repair of the most famous revolver ever made, including the most extensive load data ever published.

Lyman Cast Bullet Handbook, 3rd Edition, edited by C. Kenneth Ramage, Lyman Publications, Middlefield, CT, 1980. 416 pp., illus. Paper covers. $19.95.

Information on more than 5000 tested cast bullet loads and 19 pages of trajectory and wind drift tables for cast bullets.

Lyman Black Powder Handbook, edited by C. Kenneth Ramage, Lyman Products for Shooters, Middlefield, CT, 1975. 239 pp., illus. Paper covers. $14.95.

Comprehensive load information for the modern blackpowder shooter.

Lyman Pistol & Revolver Handbook, 2nd Edition, edited by Thomas J. Griffin, Lyman Products Co., Middlefield, CT, 1996. 287 pp., illus. Paper covers. $18.95.

The most up-to-date loading data available including the hottest new calibers, like 40 S&W, 9x21, 9mm Makarov, 9x25 Dillon and 454 Casull.

Lyman Reloading Handbook No. 47, edited by Edward A. Matunas, Lyman Publications, Middlefield, CT, 1992. 480 pp., illus. Paper covers. $24.95.

A comprehensive reloading manual complete with "How to Reload" information. Expanded data section with all the newest rifle and pistol calibers.

Lyman Shotshell Handbook, 4th Edition, edited by Edward A. Matunas, Lyman Products Co., Middlefield, CT, 1996. 330 pp., illus. Paper covers. $24.95.

Has 9000 loads, including slugs and buckshot, plus feature articles and a full color I.D. section.

Lyman's Guide to Big Game Cartridges & Rifles, by Edward Matunas, Lyman Publishing Corporation, Middlefield, CT, 1994. 287 pp., illus. Paper covers. $17.95.

A selection guide to cartridges and rifles for big game—antelope to elephant.

Making Loading Dies and Bullet Molds, by Harold Hoffman, H&P Publishing, San Angelo, TX, 1993. 230 pp., illus. Paper covers. $24.95.

A good book for learning tool and die making.

Metallic Cartridge Reloading, 3rd Edition, by M.L. McPherson, DBI Books, a division of Krause Publications, Iola, WI., 1996. 352 pp., illus. Paper covers. $21.95.

A true reloading manual with over 10,000 loads for all popular metallic cartridges and a wealth of invaluable technical data provided by a recognized expert.

Modern Handloading, by Maj. Geo. C. Nonte, Winchester Press, Piscataway, NJ, 1972. 416 pp., illus. $15.00.

Covers all aspects of metallic and shotshell ammunition loading, plus more loads than any book in print.

Modern Reloading, by Richard Lee, Inland Press, 1996. 510 pp., illus. $24.98.

The how-tos of rifle, pistol amd shotgun reloading plus load data for rifle and pistol calibers.

Modern Practical Ballistics, by Art Pejsa, Pejsa Ballistics, Minneapolis, MN, 1990. 150 pp., illus. $24.95.

Covers all aspects of ballistics and new, simplified methods. Clear examples illustrate new, easy but very accurate formulas.

Mr. Single Shot's Cartridge Handbook, by Frank de Haas, Mark de Haas, Orange City, IA, 1996. 116 pp., illus. Paper covers. $21.50.

This book covers most of the cartridges, both commercial and wildcat, that the author has known and used.

Nick Harvey's Practical Reloading Manual, by Nick Harvey, Australian Print Group, Maryborough, Victoria, Australia, 1995. 235 pp., illus. Paper covers. $24.95.

Contains data for rifle and handgun including many popular wildcat and improved cartridges. Tools, powders, components and techniques for assembling optimum reloads with particular application to North America.

Nosler Reloading Manual #4, edited by Gail Root, Nosler Bullets, Inc., Bend, OR, 1996. 516 pp., illus. $24.99.

Combines information on their Ballistic Tip, Partition and Handgun bullets with traditional powders and new powders never before used, plus trajectory information from 100 to 500 yards.

The Paper Jacket, by Paul Matthews, Wolfe Publishing Co., Prescott, AZ, 1991. Paper covers. $13.50.

Up-to-date and accurate information about paper-patched bullets.

Precision Handloading, by John Withers, Stoeger Publishing Co., So. Hackensack, NJ, 1985. 224 pp., illus. Paper covers. $14.95.

An entirely new approach to handloading ammunition.

Propellant Profiles New and Expanded, 3rd Edition, Wolfe Publishing Co., Prescott, AZ, 1991. Paper covers. $16.95.

Reloader's Guide, 3rd Edition, by R.A. Steindler, Stoeger Publishing Co., So. Hackensack, NJ, 1984. 224 pp., illus. Paper covers. $11.95.

Complete, fully illustrated step-by-step guide to handloading ammunition.

Reloading for Shotgunners, 4th Edition, by Kurt D. Fackler and M.L. McPherson, DBI Books, a division of Krause Publications, Iola, WI, 1997. 320 pp., illus. Paper covers. $19.95.

Expanded reloading tables with over 11,000 loads. Bushing charts for every major press and component maker. All new presentation on all aspects of shotshell reloading by two of the top experts in the field.

Sierra 50th Anniversary, 4th Edition Rifle Manual, edited by Ken Ramage, Sierra Bullets, Santa Fe Springs, CA, 1997. 800 pp., illus. $26.99.

New cartridge introductions, etc.

Sierra 50th Anniversary, 4th Edition Handgun Manual, edited by Ken Ramage, Sierra Bullets, Santa Fe, CA, 1997. 700 pp., illus. $21.99

Histories, reloading recommendations, bullets, powders and sections on the reloading process, etc.

Sixgun Cartridges and Loads, by Elmer Keith, The Gun Room Press, Highland Park, NJ, 1986. 151 pp., illus. $24.95.

A manual covering the selection, uses and loading of the most suitable and popular revolver cartridges. Originally published in 1936. Reprint.

Speer Reloading Manual Number 12, edited by members of the Speer research staff, Omark Industries, Lewiston, ID, 1987. 621 pp., illus. $18.95.

Reloading manual for rifles and pistols.

Understanding Ballistics, by Robert A. Rinker, Mulberry House Publishing Co., Corydon, IN, 1997. 373 pp., illus Paper covers. $19.95.

Explains basic to advanced firearm ballistics in understandable terms.

Why Not Load Your Own?, by Col. T. Whelen, A. S. Barnes, New York, 1957, 4th ed., rev. 237 pp., illus. $20.00.

A basic reference on handloading, describing each step, materials and equipment. Includes loads for popular cartridges.

Wildcat Cartridges Volumes 1 & 2 Combination, by the editors of Handloaders magazine, Wolfe Publishing Co., Prescott, AZ, 1997. 350 pp., illus. Paper covers. $39.95.

A profile of the most popular information on wildcat cartridges that appeared in the Handloader magazine.

The Winchester Lever Legacy, by Clyde "Snooky" Williamson, Buffalo Press, Zachary, LA, 1988. 664 pp., illustrated. $39.95.

A book on reloading for the different calibers of the Winchester lever action rifle.

Yours Truly, Harvey Donaldson, by Harvey Donaldson, Wolfe Publ. Co., Inc., Prescott, AZ, 1980. 288 pp., illus. $19.50.

Reprint of the famous columns by Harvey Donaldson which appeared in "Handloader" from May 1966 through December 1972.

COLLECTORS

Air Guns, by Eldon G. Wolff, Duckett's Publishing Co., Tempe, AZ, 1997. 204 pp., illus Paper covers. $35.00

Historical reference covering many makers, European and American guns, canes and more.

The American B.B. Gun, by Arni Dunathan, R&R Books, Livonia, N.Y. 1997. 154 pp., illus. $30.00.

A collector's guide.

The American Cartridge, by Charles R. Suydam, Borden Publishing Co., Alhambra, CA, 1986. 184 pp., illus. $24.95.

An illustrated study of the rimfire cartridge in the United States.

Ammunition: Grenades and Projectile Munitions, by Ian V. Hogg, Stackpole Books, Mechanicsburg, PA, 1998. 144 pp., illus. $22.95

Concise guide to modern ammunition. International coverage with detailed specifications and illustrations.

Antique Guns, the Collector's Guide, 2nd Edition, edited by John Traister, Stoeger Publishing Co., So. Hackensack, NJ, 1994. 320 pp., illus. Paper covers. $19.95.

Covers a vast spectrum of pre-1900 firearms: those manufactured by U.S. gunmakers as well as Canadian, French, German, Belgian, Spanish and other foreign firms.

Arms & Accoutrements of the Mounted Police 1873-1973, by Roger F. Phillips and Donald J. Klancher, Museum Restoration Service, Ont., Canada, 1982. 224 pp., illus. $49.95.

A definitive history of the revolvers, rifles, machine guns, cannons, ammunition, swords, etc. used by the NWMP, the RNWMP and the RCMP during the first 100 years of the Force.

Arms Makers of Maryland, by Daniel D. Hartzler, George Shumway, York, PA, 1975. 200 pp., illus. $50.00.

A thorough study of the gunsmiths of Maryland who worked during the late 18th and early 19th centuries.

Arming the Dragon, Mauser Rifle Production in China 1895-1950, by Dolf L. Goldsmith, Dolf L. Goldsmith, San Antonio, TX, 1998. 47 pp., illustrated. Spiral bound Paper covers. $15.00.

Details the manufacture and history of the Mauser rifle China.

Artistry in Arms: The Guns of Smith & Wesson, by Roy G. Jinks, Smith & Wesson, Springfield, MA, 1991. 85 pp., illus. Paper covers. $19.95.

Catalog of the Smith & Wesson International Museum Tour 1991-1995 organized by the Connecticut Valley Historical Museum and Springfield Library and Museum Association.

Assault Weapons, 4th Edition, The Gun Digest Book of, edited by Jack Lewis, DBI Books, a division of Krause Publications, Iola, WI, 1996. 256 pp., illus. Paper covers. $19.95.

An in-depth look at the history and uses of these arms.

Astra Automatic Pistols, by Leonardo M. Antaris, FIRAC Publishing Co., Sterling, CO, 1989. 248 pp., illus. $45.00.

Charts, tables, serial ranges, etc. The definitive work on Astra pistols.

THE ARMS LIBRARY

Basic Documents on U.S. Martial Arms, commentary by Col. B. R. Lewis, reissue by Ray Riling, Phila., PA, 1956 and 1960. *Rifle Musket Model 1855*. The first issue rifle of musket caliber, a muzzle loader equipped with the Maynard Primer, 32 pp. *Rifle Musket Model 1863*. The typical Union muzzle-loader of the Civil War, 26 pp. *Breech-Loading Rifle Musket Model 1866*. The first of our 50-caliber breechloading rifles, 12 pp. *Remington Navy Rifle Model 1870*. A commercial type breech-loader made at Springfield, 16 pp. *Lee Straight Pull Navy Rifle Model 1895*. A magazine cartridge arm of 6mm caliber. 23 pp. *Breech-Loading Arms* (five models) 27 pp. *Ward-Burton Rifle Musket 1871*-16 pp. Each $10.00.

Battle Weapons of the American Revolution, by George C. Neuman, Scurlock Publishing Co., Texarkana, TX, 1998. 400 pp. Illus. $65.00.
> The most extensive photographic collection of Revolutionary War weapons ever in one volume. More than 1,600 photos of over 500 muskets, rifles, swords, bayonets, knives and other arms used by both sides in America's War for Independence.

Behold, the Longrifle Again, by James B. Whisker, Old Bedford Village Press, Bedford, PA, 1997. 176 pp., illus. $45.00
> Excellent reference work for the ocllector profusely illustrated with photographs of some of the finest Kentucky rifles showing front and back profiles and overall view.

Beretta Automatic Pistols, by J.B. Wood, Stackpole Books, Harrisburg, PA, 1985. 192 pp., illus. $24.95.
> Only English-language book devoted to the Beretta line. Includes all important models.

Birmingham Gunmakers, by Douglas Tate, Safari Press, Inc., Huntington Beach, CA, 1997. 300 pp., illus. $50.00.
> An invaluable work for anybody interested in the fine sporting arms crafted in this famous British gunmakers' city.

Blacksmith Guide to Ruger Flat-Top & Super Blackhawks, by H.W. Ross, Jr., Blacksmith Corp., Chino Valley, AZ, 1990. 96 pp., illus. Paper covers. $9.95.
> A key source on the extensively collected Ruger Blackhawk revolvers.

Blue Book of Gun Values, 19th Edition, edited by S.P. Fjestad, Blue Book Publications, Inc., Minneapolis, MN, 1998. 1301 pp., illus. Paper covers. $29.95
> Covers all new 1998 firearm prices. Gives technical data on both new and discontinued domestic and foreign commercial and military guns.

The Blunderbuss 1500-1900, by James D. Forman, Museum Restoration Service, Bloomfield, Ont., Canada, 1995. 40 pp., illus. Paper covers. $4.95.
> The guns that had no peer as an anti-personal weapon throughout the flintlock era.

Boarders Away, Volume II: Firearms of the Age of Fighting Sail, by William Gilkerson, Andrew Mowbray, Inc. Publishers, Lincoln, RI, 1993. 331 pp., illus. $65.00.
> Covers the pistols, muskets, combustibles and small cannon used aboard American and European fighting ships, 1626-1826.

Boothroyd's Revised Directory of British Gunmakers, by Geoffrey and Susan Boothroyd, Sand Lake Press, Amity, OR, 1997. 412 pp., illus. $34.95.
> A new revised and enlarged edition. Lists all makers in alphabetical order.

Breech-Loading Carbines of the United States Civil War Period, by Brig. Gen. John Pitman, Armory Publications, Tacoma, WA, 1987. 94 pp., illus. $29.95.
> The first in a series of previously unpublished manuscripts originated by the late Brigadier General John Putnam. Exploded drawings showing parts actual size follow each sectioned illustration.

The Breech-Loading Single-Shot Rifle, by Major Ned H. Roberts and Kenneth L. Waters, Wolfe Publishing Co., Prescott, AZ, 1995. 333 pp., illus. $28.50.
> A comprehensive and complete history of the evolution of the Schutzen and single-shot rifle.

The British Enfield Rifles, Volume 1, The SMLE Mk I and Mk III Rifles, by Charles R. Stratton, North Cape Publications, Tustin, CA, 1997. 150 pp., illus. Paper covers. $19.95.
> A systematic and thorough examination on a part-by-part basis of the famous British battle rifle that endured for nearly 70 years as the British Army's number one battle rifle.

The British Falling Block Breechloading Rifle from 1865, by Jonathan Kirton, Tom Rowe Books, Maynardsville, TN, 2nd edition, 1997. 380 pp., illus. $70.00.
> Expanded 2nd edition of a comprehensive work on the British falling block rifle.

British Military Firearms 1650-1850, by Howard L. Blackmore, Stackpole Books, Mechanicsburg, PA, 1994. 224 pp., illus. $50.00.
> The definitive work on British military firearms.

British Service Rifles and Carbines 1888-1900, by Alan M. Petrillo, Excaliber Publications, Latham, NY, 1994. 72 pp., illus, Paper covers. $11.95.
> A complete review of the Lee-Metford and Lee-Enfield rifles and carbines.

British Single Shot Rifles, Volume 1, Alexander Henry, by Wal Einfer, Tom Rowe, Manardville, TN, 1998, 200 pp., illus. $50.00.
> Detailed Study of the single shot rifles made by Henry. Illustrated with hundreds of photographs and drawings.

British Single Shot Rifles Volume 2, George Gibbs, by Wal Winfer, Tom Rowe, Maynardville, TN, 1998. 177 pp., illus. $50.00
> Detailed study of the Farquharson as made by Gibbs. Hundreds of photos.

British Single Shot Rifles, Volume 3, Jeffery, by Wal Winfer, Rowe Publications, Rochester, N.Y., 1999. 260 pp., illustrated. $60.00.
> The Farquharson as made by Jeffery and his competitors, H&H Bland, Westley, Manton, etc. Large section on the development of nitro cartridges including the .600.

The British Soldier's Firearms from Smoothbore to Rifled Arms, 1850-1864, by Dr. C.H. Roads, R&R Books, Livonia, NY, 1994. 332 pp., illus. $49.00.
> A reprint of the classic text covering the development of British military hand and shoulder firearms in the crucial years between 1850 and 1864.

British Sporting Guns & Rifles, compiled by George Hoyem, Armory Publications, Coeur d'Alene, ID, 1997. 1024 pp., illus. In two volumes. $240.00.
> Eighteen old sporting firearms trade catalogs and a rare book reproduced with their color covers in a limited, signed and numbered edition.

British Sporting Rifle Cartridges, by Bill Fleming, Armory Publications, Oceanside, CA, 1994. 302 pp., illus. $75.00.
> An expanded study of volume three of *The History & Development of Small Arms Ammunition*. Includes pertinent trade catalog pages, etc.

Browning Dates of Manufacture, compiled by George Madis, Art and Reference House, Brownsboro, TX, 1989. 48 pp. $5.00.
> Gives the date codes and product codes for all models from 1824 to the present.

Browning Sporting Arms of Distinction 1903-1992, by Matt Eastman, Matt Eastman Publications, Fitzgerald, GA, 1995. 450 pp., illus. $49.95.
> The most recognized publication on Browning sporting arms; covers all models.

Bullard Arms, by G. Scott Jamieson, The Boston Mills Press, Ontario, Canada, 1989. 244 pp., illus. $35.00.
> The story of a mechanical genius whose rifles and cartridges were the equal to any made in America in the 1880s.

Burning Powder, compiled by Major D.B. Wesson, Wolfe Publishing Company, Prescott, AZ, 1992. 110 pp. Soft cover. $10.95.
> A rare booklet from 1932 for Smith & Wesson collectors.

The Burnside Breech Loading Carbines, by Edward A. Hull, Andrew Mowbray, Inc., Lincoln, RI, 1986. 95 pp., illus. $16.00.
> No. 1 in the "Man at Arms Monograph Series." A model-by-model historical/technical examination of one of the most widely used cavalry weapons of the American Civil War based upon important and previously unpublished research.

California Gunsmiths 1846-1900, by Lawrence P. Sheldon, Far Far West Publ., Fair Oaks, CA, 1977. 289 pp., illus. $30.00.
> A study of early California gunsmiths and the firearms they made.

Canadian Military Handguns 1855-1985, by Clive M. Law, Museum Restoration Service, Bloomfield, Ont. Canada, 1994. 130pp., illus. $40.00.
> A long-awaited and important history for arms historians and pistol collectors.

Cap Guns, by James Dundas, Schiffer Publishing, Atglen, PA, 1996. 160 pp., illus. Paper covers. $29.95.
> Over 600 full-color photos of cap guns and gun accessories with a current value guide.

Carbines of the Civil War, by John D. McAulay, Pioneer Press, Union City, TN, 1981. 123 pp., illus. Paper covers. $7.95.
> A guide for the student and collector of the colorful arms used by the Federal cavalry.

Carbines of the U.S. Cavalry 1861-1905, by John D. McAulay, Andrew Mowbray Publishers, Lincoln, RI, 1996. $35.00.
> Covers the crucial use of carbines from the beginning of the Civil War to the end of the cavalry carbine era in 1905.

Cartridge Catalogues, compiled by George Hoyem, Armory Publications, Coeur d'Alene, ID., 1997. 504 pp., illus. $125.00.
> Fourteen old ammunition makers' and designers' catalogs reproduced with their color covers in a limited, signed and numbered edition.

Cartridges for Breechloading Rifles, by A. Mattenheimer, Armory Publications, Oceanside, CA, 1989. 90 pp. with two 15"x19" color lithos containing 163 drawings of cartridges and firearms mechanisms. $29.95.
> Reprinting of this German work on cartridges. Text in German and English.

Cartridges of the World, 8th Edition, by Frank Barnes, edited by M. L. McPherson, DBI Books, a division of Krause Publications, Iola, WI, 1997. 480 pp., illus. Paper covers. $24.95.
> Completely revised edition of the general purpose reference work for which collectors, police, scientists and laymen reach first for answers to cartridge identification questions. Available October, 1996.

Civil War Arms Makers and Their Contracts, edited by Stuart C. Mowbray and Jennifer Heroux, Andrew Mowbray Publishing, Lincoln, RI, 1998. 595 pp. $39.50.
> A facsimile reprint of the Report by the Commissioner of Ordnance and Ordnance Stores, 1862.

Civil War Breech Loading Rifles, by John D. McAulay, Andrew Mowbray, Inc., Lincoln, RI, 1991. 144 pp., illus. Paper covers. $15.00.
> All the major breech-loading rifles of the Civil War and most, if not all, of the obscure types are detailed, illustrated and set in their historical context.

Civil War Carbines Volume 2: The Early Years, by John D. McAulay, Andrew Mowbray, Inc., Lincoln, RI, 1991. 144 pp., illus. Paper covers. $15.00.
> Covers the carbines made during the exciting years leading up to the outbreak of war and used by the North and South in the conflict.

Civil War Cartridge Boxes of the Union Infantryman, by Paul Johnson, Andrew Mowbray, Inc., Lincoln, RI, 1998. 352 pp., illustrated. $45.00.
> There were four patterns of infantry cartridge boxes used by Union forces during the Civil War. The author describes the development and subsequent pattern changes to these cartridge boxes.

Civil War Firearms, by Joseph G. Bilby, Combined Books, Conshohocken, PA, 1996. 252 pp., illus. $34.95.
> A unique work combining background data on each firearm including its battlefield use, and a guide to collecting and firing surviving relics and modern reproductions.

Civil War Guns, by William B. Edwards, Thomas Publications, Gerrysburg, PA, 1997. 444 pp., illus. $40.00.
> The complete story of Federal and Confederate small arms; design, manufacture, identifications, procurement issue, employment, effectiveness, and postwar disposal by the recognized expert.

Civil War Pistols, by John D. McAulay, Andrew Mowbray Inc., Lincoln, RI, 1992. 166 pp., illus. $38.50.
> A survey of the handguns used during the American Civil War.

Civil War Sharps Carbines and Rifles, by Earl J. Coates and John D. McAulay, Thomas Publications, Gettysburg, PA, 1996. 108 pp., illus. Paper covers. $12.95.
> Traces the history and development of the firearms including short histories of specific serial numbers and the soldiers who received them.

THE ARMS LIBRARY

The W.F. Cody Buffalo Bill Collector's Guide with Values, by James W. Wojtowicz, Collector Books, Paducah, KY, 1998. 271 pp., illustrated. $24.95.
A profusion of colorful collectibles including lithographs, programs, photographs, books, medals, sheet music, guns, etc. and today's values.

Col. Burton's Spiller & Burr Revolver, by Matthew W. Norman, Mercer University Press, Macon, GA, 1997. 152 pp., illus. $22.95.
A remarkable archival research project on the arm together with a comprehensive story of the establishment and running of the factory.

Collecting Western Toy Guns Identification and Value Guide, by Jim Schleyer, Books of Americana, Krause Publications, Iola, WI, 1996. 452 pp., illus. Paper covers. $29.95.
Includes toy pistols, rifles, boxes, derringers, holsters, spurs, wrist cuffs, kerchiefs, hats, gloves, clothing, laiats, ammunition, badges, rubber knives and cowboy character sets.

Collector's Guide to Colt .45 Service Pistols Models of 1911 and 1911A1, Enlarged and revised edition, by Charles W. Clawson, Clawson Publications, Fort Wayne, IN, 1998. 130 pp., illustrated. $29.95.
Complete military identification, including all contractors from 1911 to the end of production in 1945.

A Collector's Guide to United States Combat Shotguns, by Bruce N. Canfield, Andrew Mowbray Inc., Lincoln, RI, 1992. 184 pp., illus. Paper covers. $24.00
This book provides full coverage of combat shotguns, from the earliest examples right up to the Gulf War and beyond.

A Collector's Guide to Winchester in the Service, by Bruce N. Canfield, Andrew Mowbray, Inc., Lincoln, RI, 1991. 192 pp., illus. Paper covers. $22.00.
The firearms produced by Winchester for the national defense. From Hotchkiss to the M14, each firearm is examined and illustrated.

A Collector's Guide to the M1 Garand and the M1 Carbine, by Bruce N. Canfield, Andrew Mowbray, Inc., Publisher, Lincoln, RI, 1988. 144 pp., illus., paper covers. $22.00.
A comprehensive guide to the most important and ubiquitous American arms of WWII and Korea.

A Collector's Guide to the '03 Springfield, by Bruce N. Canfield, Andrew Mowbray Inc, Lincoln, RI, 1989. 160 pp., illus. Paper covers. $22.00.
A comprehensive guide follows the '03 through its unparalleled tenure of service. Covers all of the interesting variations, modifications and accessories of this highly collectible military rifle.

Collector's Illustrated Encyclopedia of the American Revolution, by George C. Neumann and Frank J. Kravic, Rebel Publishing Co., Inc., Texarkana, TX, 1989. 286 pp., illus. $29.95.
A showcase of more than 2,300 artifacts made, worn, and used by those who fought in the War for Independence.

Colonial Frontier Guns, by T.M. Hamilton, Pioneer Press, Union City, TN, 1988. 176 pp., illus. Paper covers. $13.95.
A complete study of early flint muskets of this country.

Colt .45 Government Models (Commercial Series), by Charles W. Clawson, Charles W. Clawson, Fort Wayne, IN, 1996. 230 pp., illustrated. $45.00.
A study of Colt's caliber .45 Government Model and other pistols built on the same size receiver.

The Colt Armory, by Ellsworth Grant, Man-at-Arms Bookshelf, Lincoln, RI, 1996. 232 pp., illus. $35.00.
A history of Colt's Manufacturing Company.

Colt Heritage, by R.L. Wilson, Simon & Schuster, 1979. 358 pp., illus. $75.00.
The official history of Colt firearms 1836 to the present.

Colt Memorabilia Price Guide, by John Ogle, Krause Publications, Iola, WI, 1998. 256 pp., illus. Paper covers. $29.95
The first book ever compiled about the vast array of non-gun merchandise produced by Sam Colt's companies, and other companies using the Colt name.

The Colt Model 1905 Automatic Pistol, by John Potocki, Andrew Mowbray Publishing, Lincoln, RI, 1998. 191 pp., illus. $28.00.
Covers all aspects of the Colt Model 1905 Automatic Pistol, from its invention by the legendary John Browning to its numerous production variations.

Colt Peacemaker British Model, by Keith Cochran, Cochran Publishing Co., Rapid City, SD, 1989. 160 pp., illus. $35.00.
Covers those revolvers Colt squeezed in while completing a large order of revolvers for the U.S. Cavalry in early 1874, to those magnificent cased target revolvers used in the pistol competitions at Bisley Commons in the 1890s.

Colt Peacemaker Encyclopedia, by Keith Cochran, Keith Cochran, Rapid City, SD, 1986. 434 pp., illus. $60.00.
A must book for the Peacemaker collector.

Colt Peacemaker Encyclopedia, Volume 2, by Keith Cochran, Cochran Publishing Co., SD, 1992. 416 pp., illus. $60.00.
Included in this volume are extensive notes on engraved, inscribed, historical and noted revolvers, as well as those revolvers used by outlaws, lawmen, movie and television stars.

Colt Percussion Accoutrements 1834-1873, by Robin Rapley, Robin Rapley, Newport Beach, CA, 1994. 432 pp., illus. Paper covers. $39.95.
The complete collector's guide to the identification of Colt percussion accoutrements; including Colt conversions and their values.

Colt Pocket Hammerless Pistols, by Dr. John W. Brunner, Phillips Publications, Williamstown, NJ, 1998. 212 pp., illustrated. $59.95.
You will never again have to question a .25, .32 or .380 with this well illustrated, definitive reference guide at hand.

Colt Revolvers and the Tower of London, by Joseph G. Rosa, Royal Armouries of the Tower of London, London, England, 1988. 72 pp., illus. Soft covers. $15.00.
Details the story of Colt in London through the early cartridge period.

Colt Rifles and Muskets from 1847-1870, by Herbert Houze, Krause Publications, Iola, WI, 1996. 192 pp., illus. $34.95.
Discover previously unknown Colt models along with an extensive list of production figures for all models.

Colt's SAA Post War Models, by George Garton, The Gun Room Press, Highland Park, NJ, 1995. 166 pp., illus. $39.95.
Complete facts on the post-war Single Action Army revolvers. Information on calibers, production numbers and variations taken from factory records.

Colt Single Action Army Revolvers and the London Agency, by C. Kenneth Moore, Andrew Mowbray Publishers, Lincoln, RI, 1990. 144 pp., illus. $35.00.
Drawing on vast documentary sources, this work chronicles the relationship between the London Agency and the Hartford home office.

The Colt U.S. General Officers' Pistols, by Horace Greeley IV, Andrew Mowbray Inc., Lincoln, RI, 1990. 199 pp., illus. $38.00.
These unique weapons, issued as a badge of rank to General Officers in the U.S. Army from WWII onward, remain highly personal artifacts of the military leaders who carried them. Includes serial numbers and dates of issue.

Colts from the William M. Locke Collection, by Frank Sellers, Andrew Mowbray Publishers, Lincoln, RI, 1996. 192 pp., illus. $35.00.
This important book illustrates all of the famous Locke Colts, with captions by arms authority Frank Sellers.

Colt's Dates of Manufacture 1837-1978, by R.L. Wilson, published by Maurie Albert, Coburg, Australia; N.A. distributor I.D.S.A. Books, Hamilton, OH, 1983. 61 pp. $10.00.
An invaluable pocket guide to the dates of manufacture of Colt firearms up to 1978.

Colt's 100th Anniversary Firearms Manual 1836-1936: A Century of Achievement, Wolfe Publishing Co., Prescott, AZ, 1992. 100 pp., illus. Paper covers. $12.95.
Originally published by the Colt Patent Firearms Co., this booklet covers the history, manufacturing procedures and the guns of the first 100 years of the genius of Samuel Colt.

Complete Guide to the M1 Garand and the M1 Carbine, by Bruce N. Canfield, Andrew Mowbray Publishing, Lincoln, RI, 1998. 296 pp., illus. $39.50.
Expanded and updated coverage of both the M1 Garand and the M1 Carbine, with more than twice as much information as the author's previous book on this topic.

The Complete Guide to U.S. Infantry Weapons of World War Two, by Bruce Canfield, Andrew Mowbray, Publisher, Lincoln, RI, 1995. 303 pp., illus. $35.00.
A definitive work on the weapons used by the United States Armed Forces in WWII.

Compliments of Col. Ruger: A Study of Factory Engraved Single Action Revolvers, by John C. Dougan, Taylor Publishing Co., El Paso, TX, 1992. 238 pp., illus. $46.50.
Clearly detailed black and white photographs and a precise text present an accurate history of the Sturm, Ruger & Co. single-action revolver engraving project.

Cowboy Collectibles and Western Memorabilia, by Bob Bell and Edward Vebell, Schiffer Publishing, Atglen, PA, 1992. 160 pp., illus. Paper covers. $29.95.
The exciting era of the cowboy and the wild west collectibles including rifles, pistols, gun rigs, etc.

Cowboy and Gunfighter Collectible, by Bill Mackin, Mountain Press Publishing Co., Missoula, MT, 1995. 178 pp., illus. Paper covers. $25.00.
A photographic encyclopedia with price guide and makers' index.

Cowboy Hero Cap Pistols, by Rudy D'Angelo, Antique Trader Books, Dubuque, IA, 1998. 196 pp., illus. Paper covers. $34.95.
Aimed at collectors of cap pistols created and named for famous film and television cowboy heros, this in-depth guide hits all the marks. Current values are given.

Czech Firearms and Ammunition Past and Present, 1919-1995, by Vladimir Dolinek & V. Karlicky, 190 pp., illus. in black & white and color. $49.95.
Covers Czech firearms from the earliest to the present day.

The Deringer in America, Volume 1, The Percussion Period, by R.L. Wilson and L.D. Eberhart, Andrew Mowbray Inc., Lincoln, RI, 1985. 271 pp., illus. $48.00.
A long awaited book on the American percussion deringer.

The Deringer in America, Volume 2, The Cartridge Period, by L.D. Eberhart and R.L. Wilson, Andrew Mowbray Inc., Publishers, Lincoln, RI, 1993. 284 pp., illus. $65.00.
Comprehensive coverage of cartridge deringers organized alphabetically by maker. Includes all types of deringers known by the authors to have been offered to the American market.

The Devil's Paintbrush: Sir Hiram Maxim's Gun, by Dolf Goldsmith, 2nd Edition, expanded and revised, Collector Grade Publications, Toronto, Canada, 1993. 384 pp., illus. $69.95
The classic work on the world's first true automatic machine gun.

Dr. Josephus Requa Civil War Dentist and the Billinghurst-Requa Volley Gun, by John M. Hyson, Jr., & Margaret Requa DeFrancisco, Museum Restoration Service, Bloomfield, Ont., Canada, 1999. 36 pp., illus. Paper covers. $6.95.
The story of the inventor of the first practical rapid-fire gun to be used during the American Civil War.

Drums A'beating Trumpets Sounding, by William H. Guthman, The Connecticut Historical Society, Westport, CT, 1993. 232 pp., illus. $75.00.
Artistically carved powder horns in the provincial manner, 1746-1781.

The Dutch Luger (Parabellum) A Complete History, by Bas J. Martens and Guus de Vries, Ironside International Publishers, Inc., Alexandria, VA, 1995. 268 pp., illus. $49.95.
The history of the Luger in the Netherlands. An extensive description of the Dutch pistol and trials and the different models of the Luger in the Dutch service.

The Eagle on U.S. Firearms, by John W. Jordan, Pioneer Press, Union City, TN, 1992. 140 pp., illus. Paper covers. $14.95.
Stylized eagles have been stamped on government owned or manufactured firearms in the U.S. since the beginning of our country. This book lists and illustrates these various eagles in an informative and refreshing manner.

Early Indian Trade Guns: 1625-1775, by T.M. Hamilton, Museum of the Great Plains, Lawton, OK, 1968. 34 pp., illus. Paper covers. $12.95.
Detailed descriptions of subject arms, compiled from early records and from the study of remnants found in Indian country.

Encyclopedia of Rifles & Handguns, edited by Sean Connolly, Book Sales, Inc., Edison, NJ, 1997. 160 pp., illus. $12.95.
A lavishly illustrated book providing a comprehensive history of military and civilian personal firepower.

Encyclopedia of Ruger Rimfire Semi-Automatic Pistols: 1949-1992, by Chad Hiddleson, Krause Publications, Iola, WI, 1993. 250 pp., illus. $29.95.
Covers all physical aspects of Ruger 22-caliber pistols including important features such as boxes, grips, muzzlebrakes, instruction manuals, serial numbers, etc.

Encyclopedia of Ruger Semi-Automatic Rimfire Pistols 1949-1992, by Chad Hiddleson, Krause Publications, Iola, WI, 1994. 304 pp., illus. $29.95.
This book is a compilation of years of research, outstanding photographs and technical data on Ruger.

Eprouvettes: A Comprehensive Study of Early Devices for the Testing of Gunpowder, by R.T.W. Kempers, Royal Armouries Museum, Leeds, England, 1998. 352 pp., illustrated with 240 black & white and 28 color plates. $125.00.
A survey of gunpowder testing through the ages precedes a proposal for an eprouvette typology, and the core of the book is an illustrated survey of types.

European Firearms in Swedish Castles, by Kaa Wennberg, Bohuslaningens Boktryckeri AB, Uddevalla, Sweden, 1986. 156 pp., illus. $50.00.
The famous collection of Count Keller, the Ettersburg Castle collection, and others. English text.

European Sporting Cartridges, Part 1, by W.B. Dixon, Armory Publications, Inc., Coeur d'Alene, ID, 1997. 250 pp., illus. $63.00
Photographs and drawings of over 550 centerfire cartridge case types in 1,300 illustrations produced in German and Austria from 1875 to 1995.

Fifteen Years in the Hawken Lode, by John D. Baird, The Gun Room Press, Highland Park, NJ, 1976. 120 pp., illus. $24.95.
A collection of thoughts and observations gained from many years of intensive study of the guns from the shop of the Hawken brothers.

'51 Colt Navies, by Nathan L. Swayze, The Gun Room Press, Highland Park, NJ, 1993. 243 pp., illus. $59.95.
The Model 1851 Colt Navy, its variations and markings.

Firearms and Tackle Memorabilia, by John Delph, Schiffer Publishing, Ltd., West Chester, PA, 1991. 124 pp., illus. $39.95.
A collector's guide to signs and posters, calendars, trade cards, boxes, envelopes, and other highly sought after memorabilia. With a value guide.

Firearms of the American West 1803-1865, Volume 1, by Louis A. Garavaglia and Charles Worman, University of Colorado Press, Niwot, CO, 1998. 402 pp., illustrated. $59.95.
Traces the development and uses of firearms on the frontier during this period.

Firearms of the American West 1866-1894, by Louis A. Garavaglia and Charles G. Worman, University of Colorado Press, Niwot, CO, 1998. 416 pp., illus. $59.95.
A monumental work that offers both technical information on all of the important firearms used in the West during this period and a highly entertaining history of how they were used, who used them, and why.

Flayderman's Guide to Antique American Firearms and Their Values, 7th Edition, edited by Norm Flayderman, DBI books, a division of Krause Publications, Iola, WI, 1998. 656 pp., illus. Paper covers. $32.95.
A completely updated and new edition with more than 3,600 models and variants extensively described with all marks and specifications necessary for quick identification.

The .45-70 Springfield, by Joe Poyer and Craig Riesch, North Cape Publications, Tustin, CA, 1996. 150 pp., illus. Paper covers. $15.95.
A revised and expanded second edition of a best-selling reference work organized by serial number and date of production to aid the collector in identifying popular "Trapdoor" rifles and carbines.

Frank and George Freund and the Sharps Rifle, by Gerald O. Kelver, Gerald O. Kelver, Brighton, CO, 1986. 60 pp., illus. Paper covers. $12.00.
Pioneer gunmakers of Wyoming Territory and Colorado.

The French 1935 Pistols, by Eugene Medlin and Colin Doane, Eugene Medlin, El Paso, TX, 1995. 172 pp., illus. Paper covers. $25.95.
The development and identification of successive models, fakes and variants, holsters and accessories, and serial numbers by dates of production.

Freund & Bro. Pioneer Gunmakers to the West, by F.J. Pablo Balentine, Graphic Publishers, Newport Beach, CA, 1997. 380 pp., illustrated $69.95.
The story of Frank W. and George Freund, skilled German gunsmiths who plied their trade on the Western American frontier during the final three decades of the nineteenth century.

From the Kingdom of Lilliput: The Miniature Firearms of David Kucer, by K. Corey Keeble and **The Making of Miniatures,** by David Kucer, Museum Restoration Service, Ontario, Canada, 1994. 51 pp., illus, $25.00.
An overview of the subject of miniatures in general combined with an outline by the artist himself on the way he makes a miniature firearm.

Frontier Pistols and Revolvers, by Dominique Venner, Book Sales Inc., Edison, N.J., 1998. 144 pp., illus. $19.95.
Colt, Smith & Wesson, Remington and other early-brand revolvers which tamed the American frontier are shown amid vintage photographs, etchings and paintings to evoke the wild West.

The Fusil de Tulole in New France, 1691-1741, by Russel Bouchard, Museum Restorations Service, Bloomfield, Ontario, Canada, 1997. 36 pp., illus. Paper covers. $6.95
The development of the company and the identification of their arms.

Game Guns & Rifles: Percussion to Hammerless Ejector in Britain, by Richard Akehurst, Trafalgar Square, N. Pomfret, VT, 1993. 192 pp., illus. $39.95.

Long considered a classic this important reprint covers the period of British gunmaking between 1830-1900.

George Schreyer, Sr. and Jr., Gunmakers of Hanover, Pennsylvania, by George Shumway, George Shumway Publishers, York, PA, 1990. 160pp., illus. $50.00.
This monograph is a detailed photographic study of almost all known surviving long rifles and smoothbore guns made by highly regarded gunsmiths George Schreyer, Sr. and Jr.

The German Assault Rifle 1935-1945, by Peter R. Senich, Paladin Press, Boulder, CO, 1987. 328 pp., illus. $49.95.
A complete review of machine carbines, machine pistols and assault rifles employed by Hitler's Wehrmacht during WWII.

The German K98k Rifle, 1934-1945: The Backbone of the Wehrmacht, by Richard D. Law, Collector Grade Publications, Inc., Toronto, Canada, 1993. 336 pp., illus. $69.95.
The most comprehensive study ever published on the 14,000,000 bolt-action K98k rifles produced in Germany between 1934 and 1945.

German Machineguns, by Daniel D. Musgrave, Revised edition, Ironside International Publishers, Inc. Alexandria, VA, 1992. 586 pp., 650 illus. $49.95.
The most definitive book ever written on German machineguns. Covers the introduction and development of machineguns in Germany from 1899 to the rearmament period after WWII.

German Military Rifles and Machine Pistols, 1871-1945, by Hans Dieter Gotz, Schiffer Publishing Co., West Chester, PA, 1990. 245 pp., illus. $35.00.
This book portrays in words and pictures the development of the modern German weapons and their ammunition including the scarcely known experimental types.

German 7.9mm Military Ammunition, by Daniel W. Kent, Daniel W. Kent, Ann Arbor, MI, 1991. 244 pp., illus. $35.00.
The long-awaited revised edition of a classic among books devoted to ammunition.

German Pistols and Holsters, 1934-1945, Volume 4, by Lt. Col. Robert D. Whittington, 3rd, U.S.A.R., Brownlee Books, Hooks, TX, 1991. 208 pp. $30.00.
Pistols and holsters issued in 412 selected armed forces, army and Waffen-SS units including information on personnel, other weapons and transportation.

The Golden Age of Remington, by Robert W.D. Ball, Krause publications, Iola, WI, 1995. 194 pp., illus. $29.95.
For Remington collectors or firearms historians, this book provides a pictorial history of Remington through World War I. Includes value guide.

The Government Models, by William H.D. Goddard, Andrew Mowbray Publishing, Lincoln, RI, 1998. 296 pp., illustrated. $58.50.
The most authoritative source on the development of the Colt model of 1911.

A Guide to Ballard Breechloaders, by George J. Layman, Pioneer Press, Union City, TN, 1997. 261 pp., illus. Paper covers. $19.95
Documents the saga of this fine rifle from the first models made by Ball & Williams of Worchester, to its production by the Marlin Firearms Co, to the cessation of 19th century manufacture in 1891, and finally to the modern reproductions made in the 1990's.

A Guide to the Maynard Breechloader, by George J. Layman, George J. Layman, Ayer, MA, 1993. 125 pp., illus. Paper covers. $17.95.
The first book dedicated entirely to the Maynard family of breech-loading firearms. Coverage of the arms is given from the 1850s through the 1880s.

Guide to Ruger Single Action Revolvers Production Dates, 1953-73, by John C. Dougan, Blacksmith Corp., Chino Valley, AZ, 1991. 22 pp., illus. Paper covers. $9.95.
A unique pocket-sized handbook providing production information for the popular Ruger single-action revolvers manufactured during the first 20 years.

Gun Collecting, by Geoffrey Boothroyd, Sportsman's Press, London, 1989. 208 pp., illus. $29.95.
The most comprehensive list of 19th century British gunmakers and gunsmiths ever published.

Gun Collector's Digest, 5th Edition, edited by Joseph J. Schroeder, DBI Books, a division of Krause Publications, Iola, WI, 1989. 224 pp., illus. Paper covers. $17.95.
The latest edition of this sought-after series.

Gunmakers of Illinois, 1683-1900, Vol. 1, by Curtis L. Johnson, George Shumway Publisher, York, PA, 1997. 200 pp., illus. $30.00
This first volume covering the alphabet from A to F of a projected three-volume series, records the available names, dates, biographical details, and illustrates the work undertaken, by almost 1600 Illinois gunsmiths and gunmakers.

Gunmakers of London 1350-1850, by Howard L. Blackmore, George Shumway Publisher, York, PA, 1986. 222 pp., illus. $35.00.
A listing of all the known workmen of gun making in the first 500 years, plus a history of the guilds, cutlers, armourers, founders, blacksmiths, etc. 260 gunmarks are illustrated.

Gunsmiths of Illinois, by Curtis L. Johnson, George Shumway Publishers, York, PA, 1995. 160 pp., illus. $50.00.
Genealogical information is provided for nearly one thousand gunsmiths. Contains hundreds of illustrations of rifles and other guns, of handmade origin, from Illinois.

The Gunsmiths of Manhattan, 1625-1900: A Checklist of Tradesmen, by Michael H. Lewis, Museum Restoration Service, Bloomfield, Ont., Canada, 1991. 40 pp., illus. Paper covers. $4.95.
This listing of more than 700 men in the arms trade in New York City prior to about the end of the 19th century will provide a guide for identification and further research.

The Guns of Dagenham: Lanchester, Patchett, Sterling, by Peter Laidler and David Howroyd, Collector Grade Publications, Inc., Cobourg, Ont., Canada, 1995. 310 pp., illus. $39.95.
An in-depth history of the small arms made by the Sterling Company of Dagenham, Essex, England, from 1940 until Sterling was purchased by British Aerospace in 1989 and closed.

THE ARMS LIBRARY

Guns of the Western Indian War, by R. Stephen Dorsey, Collector's Library, Eugene, OR, 1997. 220 pp., illus. Paper covers. $30.00.
The full story of the guns and ammunition that made western history in the turbulent period of 1865-1890.

Gun Powder Cans & Kegs, by Ted & David Bacyk and Tom Rowe, Rowe Publications, Rochester, NY, 1999. 150 pp., illus. $65.00.
The first book devoted to powder tins and kegs. All cans and kegs in full color. With a price guide and rarity scale.

Gun Tools, Their History and Identification by James B. Shaffer, Lee A. Rutledge and R. Stephen Dorsey, Collector's Library, Eugene, OR, 1992. 375 pp., illus. $32.00.
Written history of foreign and domestic gun tools from the flintlock period to WWII.

Gun Tools, Their History and Identifications, Volume 2, by Stephen Dorsey and James B. Shaffer, Collectors' Library, Eugene, OR, 1997. 396 pp., illus. Paper covers. $30.00.
Gun tools from the Royal Armouries Museum in England, Pattern Room, Royal Ordnance Reference Collection in Nottingham and from major private collections.

The Guns of Remington: Historic Firearms Spanning Two Centuries, compiled by Howard M. Madaus, Biplane Productions, Publisher, in cooperation with Buffalo Bill Historical Center, Cody, WY, 1998. 352 pp., illustrated with over 800 color photos. $79.95.
A complete catalog of the firearms in the exhibition, "It Never Failed Me: The Arms & Art of Remington Arms Company" at the Buffalo Bill Historical Center, Cody, Wyoming.

Gunsmiths of Maryland, by Daniel D. Hartzler and James B. Whisker, Old Bedford Village Press, Bedford, PA, 1998. 208 pp., illustrated. $45.00.
Covers firelock Colonial period through the breech-loading patent models. Featuring longrifles.

Hall's Military Breechloaders, by Peter A. Schmidt, Andrew Mowbray Publishers, Lincoln, RI, 1996. 232 pp., illus. $55.00.
The whole story behind these bold and innovative firearms.

Handbook of Military Rifle Marks 1870-1950, by Richard A. Hoffman and Noel P. Schott, Mapleleaf Militaria Publishing, St. Louis, MO, 1995. 42 pp., illus. Spiral bound. $15.00.
An illustrated guide to identifying military rifle and marks.

The Handgun, by Geoffrey Boothroyd, David and Charles, North Pomfret, VT, 1989. 566 pp., illus. $60.00.
Every chapter deals with an important period in handgun history from the 14th century to the present.

The Hawken Rifle: Its Place in History, by Charles E. Hanson, Jr., The Fur Press, Chadron, NE, 1979. 104 pp., illus. Paper covers. $15.00.
A definitive work on this famous rifle.

Hawken Rifles, The Mountain Man's Choice, by John D. Baird, The Gun Room Press, Highland Park, NJ, 1976. 95 pp., illus. $29.95.
Covers the rifles developed for the Western fur trade. Numerous specimens are described and shown in photographs.

High Standard: A Collector's Guide to the Hamden & Hartford Target Pistols, by Tom Dance, Andrew Mowbray, Inc., Lincoln, RI, 1991. 192 pp., illus. Paper covers. $24.00.
From Citation to Supermatic, all of the production models and specials made from 1951 to 1984 are covered according to model number or series.

Historic Pistols: The American Martial Flintlock 1760-1845, by Samuel E. Smith and Edwin W. Bitter, The Gun Room Press, Highland Park, NJ, 1986. 353 pp., illus. $45.00.
Covers over 70 makers and 163 models of American martial arms.

Historical Hartford Hardware, by William W. Dalrymple, Colt Collector Press, Rapid City, SD, 1976. 42 pp., illus. Paper covers. $10.00.
Historically associated Colt revolvers.

The History and Development of Small Arms Ammunition, Volume 1, by George A. Hoyem, Armory Publications, Oceanside, CA, 1991. 230 pp., illus. $65.00.
Military musket, rifle, carbine and primitive machine gun cartridges of the 18th and 19th centuries, together with the firearms that chambered them.

The History and Development of Small Arms Ammunition, Volume 2, by George A. Hoyem, Armory Publications, Oceanside, CA, 1991. 303 pp., illus. $65.00.
Covers the blackpowder military centerfire rifle, carbine, machine gun and volley gun ammunition used in 28 nations and dominions, together with the firearms that chambered them.

The History and Development of Small Arms Ammunition, Volume 4, by George A. Hoyem, Armory Publications, Seattle, WA, 1998. 200 pp., illustrated $60.00.
A comprehensive book on American black powder and early smokeless rifle cartridges.

History of Modern U.S. Military Small Arms Ammunition. Volume 1, 1880-1939, revised by F.W. Hackley, W.H. Woodin and E.L. Scranton, Thomas Publications, Gettysburg, PA, 1998. 328 pp., illus. $49.95.
This revised edition incorporates all publicly available information concerning military small arms ammunition for the period 1880 through 1939 in a single volume.

The History of Smith and Wesson, by Roy G. Jinks, Willowbrook Enterprises, Springfield, MA, 1988. 290 pp., illus. $27.95.
Revised 10th Anniversary edition of the definite book on S&W firearms.

The History of Winchester Firearms 1866-1992, sixth edition, updated, expanded, and revised by Thomas Henshaw, New Win Publishing, Clinton, NJ, 1993. 280 pp., illus. $27.95.
This classic is the standard reference for all collectors and others seeking the facts about any Winchester firearm, old or new.

History of Winchester Repeating Arms Company, by Herbert G. Houze, Krause Publications, Iola, WI, 1994. 800 pp., illus. $50.00.
The complete Winchester history from 1856-1981.

Honour Bound: The Chauchat Machine Rifle, by Gerard Demaison and Yves Buffetaut, Collector Grade Publications, Inc., Cobourg, Ont., Canada, 1995. $39.95.
The story of the CSRG (Chauchat) machine rifle, the most manufactured automatic weapon of World War One.

Hopkins & Allen Revolvers & Pistols, by Charles E. Carder, Avil Onze Publishing, Delphos, OH, 1998, illustrated. Paper covers. $24.95.
Covers over 165 photos, graphics and patent drawings.

How to Buy and Sell Used Guns, by John Traister, Stoeger Publishing Co., So. Hackensack, NJ, 1984. 192 pp., illus. Paper covers. $10.95.
A new guide to buying and selling guns.

Identification Manual on the .303 British Service Cartridge, No. 1-Ball Ammunition, by B.A. Temple, I.D.S.A. Books, Piqua, OH, 1986. 84 pp., 57 illus. $12.50

Identification Manual on the .303 British Service Cartridge, No. 2-Blank Ammunition, by B.A. Temple, I.D.S.A. Books, Piqua, OH, 1986. 95 pp., 59 illus. $12.50

Identification Manual on the .303 British Service Cartridge, No. 3-Special Purpose Ammunition, by B.A. Temple, I.D.S.A. Books, Piqua, OH, 1987. 82 pp., 49 illus. $12.50

Identification Manual on the .303 British Service Cartridge, No. 4-Dummy Cartridges Henry 1869-c.1900, by B.A. Temple, I.D.S.A. Books, Piqua, OH, 1988. 84 pp., 70 illus. $12.50

Identification Manual on the .303 British Service Cartridge, No. 5-Dummy Cartridges (2), by B.A. Temple, I.D.S.A. Books, Piqua, OH, 1994. 78 pp. $12.50

The Illustrated Encyclopedia of Civil War Collectibles, by Chuck Lawliss, Henry Holt and Co., New York, NY, 1997. 316 pp., illus. Paper covers. $22.95.
A comprehensive guide to Union and Confederate arms, equipment, uniforms, and other memorabilia.

Illustrations of United States Military Arms 1776-1903 and Their Inspector's Marks, compiled by Turner Kirkland, Pioneer Press, Union City, TN, 1988. 37 pp., illus. Paper covers. $4.95.
Reprinted from the 1949 Bannerman catalog. Valuable information for both the advanced and beginning collector.

Indian War Cartridge Pouches, Boxes and Carbine Boots, by R. Stephen Dorsey, Collector's Library, Eugene, OR, 1993. 156 pp., illus. Paper Covers. $25.00.
The key reference work to the cartridge pouches, boxes, carbine sockets and boots of the Indian War period 1865-1890.

An Introduction to the Civil War Small Arms, by Earl J. Coates and Dean S. Thomas, Thomas Publishing Co., Gettysburg, PA, 1990. 96 pp., illus. Paper covers. $10.00.
The small arms carried by the individual soldier during the Civil War.

Iver Johnson's Arms & Cycle Works Handguns, 1871-1964, by W.E. "Bill" Goforth, Blacksmith Corp., Chino Valley, AZ, 1991. 160 pp., illus. Paper covers. $14.95.
Covers all of the famous Iver Johnson handguns from the early solid-frame pistols and revolvers to optional accessories, special orders and patents.

Jaeger Rifles, by George Shumway, George Shumway Publisher, York, PA, 1994. 108 pp., illus. Paper covers. $30.00.
Thirty-six articles previously published in *Muzzle Blasts* are reproduced here. They deal with late-17th, and 18th century rifles from Vienna, Carlsbad, Bavaria, Saxony, Brandenburg, Suhl, North-Central Germany, and the Rhine Valley.

Japanese Rifles of World War Two, by Duncan O. McCollum, Excalibur Publications, Latham, NY, 1996. 64 pp., illus. Paper covers. $18.95.
A sweeping view of the rifles and carbines that made up Japan's arsenal during the conflict.

Kalashnikov Arms, compiled by Alexei Nedelin, Design Military Parade, Ltd., Moscow, Russia, 1997. 240 pp., illus. $49.95.
Weapons versions stored in the St. Petersburg Military Historical Museum of Artillery, Engineer Troops and Communications and in the Izhmash JSC.

The Kentucky Pistol, by Roy Chandler and James Whisker, Old Bedford Village Press, Bedford, PA, 1997. 225 pp., illus. $45.00
A photographic study of Kentucky pistols from famous collections.

The Kentucky Rifle, by Captain John G.W. Dillin, George Shumway Publisher, York, PA, 1993. 221 pp., illus. $50.00.
This well-known book was the first attempt to tell the story of the American longrifle. This edition retains the original text and illustrations with supplemental footnotes provided by Dr. George Shumway.

The Kentucky Rifle, a True American Heritage in Picture, by the Kentucky Rifle Associations, Washington, D.C., 1997. Published by the Forte Group, Alexandria, VA. 109 pp., illus. $35.00.
This photographic essay reveals both the beauty and the decorative nature of the Kentucky by providing detailed photos of some of the most significant examples of American rifles, pistols and accoutrements.

Know Your Broomhandle Mausers, by R.J. Berger, Blacksmith Corp., Southport, CT, 1985. 96 pp., illus. Paper covers. $9.95.
An interesting story on the big Mauser pistol and its variations.

Krag Rifles, by William S. Brophy, The Gun Room Press, Highland Park, NJ, 1980. 200 pp., illus. $50.00.
The first comprehensive work detailing the evolution and various models, both military and civilian.

The Krieghoff Parabellum, by Randall Gibson, Midland, TX, 1988. 279 pp., illus. $40.00.
A comprehensive text pertaining to the Lugers manufactured by H. Krieghoff Waffenfabrik.

Las Pistolas Espanolas Tipo "Mauser," by Artemio Mortera Perez, Quiron Ediciones, Valladolid, Spain, 1998. 71 pp., illustrated. Paper covers. $34.95.
This book covers in detail Spanish machine pistols and C96 copies made in Spain. Covers all Astra "Mauser" pistol series and the complete line of Beistegui C96 type pistols. Spanish text.

The Lee-Enfield Story, by Ian Skennerton, Ian Skennerton, Ashmore City, Australia, 1993. 503 pp., illus. $59.95.

THE ARMS LIBRARY

The Lee-Metford, Lee-Enfield, S.M.L.E. and No. 4 series rifles and carbines from 1880 to the present.

LeMat, the Man, the Gun, by Valmore J. Forgett and Alain F. and Marie-Antoinette Serpette, Navy Arms Co., Ridgefield, NJ, 1996. 218 pp., illus. $49.95.
The first definitive study of the Confederate revolvers invention, development and delivery by Francois Alexandre LeMat.

Les Pistolets Automatiques Francaise 1890-1990, by Jean Huon, Combined Books, Inc., Conshohocken, PA, 1997. 160 pp., illus. French text. $34.95
French automatic pistols from the earliest experiments through the World Wars and Indo-China to modern security forces.

Levine's Guide to Knives And Their Values, 4th Edition, by Bernard Levine, DBI Books, a division of Krause Publications, Iola, WI, 1997. 512 pp., illus. Paper covers. $27.95
All the basic tools for identifying, valuing and collecting folding and fixed blade knives.

The London Gunmakers and the English Duelling Pistol, 1770-1830, by Keith R. Dill, Museum Restoration Service, Bloomfield, Ontario, Canada, 1997. 36 pp., illus. Paper covers. $6.95
Ten gunmakers made London one of the major gunmaking centers of the world. This book examines how the design and construction of their pistols contributed to that reputation and how these characteristics may be used to date flintlock arms.

Longrifles of North Carolina, by John Bivens, George Shumway Publisher, York, PA, 1988. 256 pp., illus. $50.00.
Covers art and evolution of the rifle, immigration and trade movements. Committee of Safety gunsmiths, characteristics of the North Carolina rifle.

Longrifles of Pennsylvania, Volume 1, Jefferson, Clarion & Elk Counties, by Russel H. Harringer, George Shumway Publisher, York, PA, 1984. 200 pp., illus. $50.00.
First in series that will treat in great detail the longrifles and gunsmiths of Pennsylvania.

The Luger Handbook, by Aarron Davis, Krause Publications, Iola, WI, 1997. 112 pp., illus. Paper covers. $9.95.
Quick reference to classify Luger models and variations with complete details including proofmarks.

Lugers at Random, by Charles Kenyon, Jr., Handgun Press, Glenview, IL, 1990. 420 pp., illus. $49.95.
A new printing of this classic, comprehensive reference for all Luger collectors.

The Luger Story, by John Walter, Stackpole Books, Mechanicsburg, PA, 1995. 256 pp., illus. $39.95.
The standard history of the world's most famous handgun.

The M1 Garand Serial Numbers and Data Sheets, by Scott A. Duff, Export, PA, 1995. 101 pp., illus. Paper covers. $9.95.
Provides the reader with serial numbers related to dates of manufacture and a large sampling of data sheets to aid in identification or restoration.

The M1 Garand: Owner's Guide, by Scott A. Duff, Scott A. Duff, Export, PA, 1997. 126 pp., illus. Paper covers. $16.95.
This book answers the questions M1 owners most often ask concerning maintenance activities not encountered by military users.

Machine Guns of World War 1, by Robert Bruce, Combined Publishing, Conshohocken, PA, 1998. 128 pp., illus. $39.95.
Live firing classic military weapons in color photographs.

Maine Made Guns and Their Makers, by Dwight B. Demeritt Jr., Maine State Museum, Augusta, ME, 1998. 209 pp., illustrated. $55.00.
An authoritative, biographical study of Maine gunsmiths.

Marlin Firearms: A History of the Guns and the Company That Made Them, by Lt. Col. William S. Brophy, USAR, Ret., Stackpole Books, Harrisburg, PA, 1989. 672 pp., illus. $75.00.
The definitive book on the Marlin Firearms Co. and their products.

Martini-Henry .450 Rifles & Carbines, by Dennis Lewis, Excalibur Publications, Latham, NY, 1996. 72 pp., illus. Paper covers. $11.95.
The stories of the rifles and carbines that were the mainstay of the British soldier through the Victorian wars.

Matt Eastman's Guide to Browning Belgium Firearms 1903-1994, by Matt Eastman, Matt Eastman Publications, Fitzgerald, GA, 1995. 150 pp. Paper covers. $14.95.
Covers all Belgium models through 1994. Manufacturing production figures on the Auto-5 and Safari rifles.

Mauser Bolt Rifles, by Ludwig Olson, F. Brownell & Son, Inc., Montezuma, IA, 1976. 364 pp., illus. $51.95.
The most complete, detailed, authoritative and comprehensive work ever done on Mauser bolt rifles.

Mauser Military Rifles of the World, by Robert W.D. Ball, Krause Publications, Iola, WI, 1996. 272 pp., illus. $39.95.
The rifles produced by the Mauser Co. for their international market with complete production quantities, rarity and technical specifications.

Military Handguns of France 1858-1958, by Eugene Medlin and Jean Huon, Excalibur Publications, Latham, NY, 1994. 124 pp., illus. Paper covers. $24.95.
The first book written in English that provides students of arms with a thorough history of French military handguns.

Military Holsters of World War 2, by Eugene J. Bender, Rowe Publications, Rochester, NY, 1998. 200 pp., illustrated. $45.00.
A revised edition with a new price guide of the most definitive book on this subject.

Military Pistols of Japan, by Fred L. Honeycutt, Jr., Julin Books, Palm Beach Gardens, FL, 1991. 168 pp., illus. $42.00.
Covers every aspect of military pistol production in Japan through WWII.

The Military Remington Rolling Block Rifle, by George Layman, George Layman, Ayer, MA, 1996. 146 pp., illus. Paper covers. $24.95.

A standard reference for those with an interest in the Remington rolling block family of firearms.

Military Rifles of Japan, 4th Edition, by F.L. Honeycutt, Julin Books, Lake Park, FL, 1989. 208 pp., illus. $42.00.
A new revised and updated edition. Includes the early Murata-period markings, etc.

Military Small Arms of the 20th Century, 6th Edition, by Ian V. Hogg, DBI Books, a division of Krause Publications, Iola, WI, 1991. 352 pp., illus. Paper covers. $20.95.
Fully revised and updated edition of the standard reference in its field.

M1 Carbine, by Larry Ruth, Gun room Press, Highland Park, NJ, 1987. 291 pp., illus. Paper $19.95.
The origin, development, manufacture and use of this famous carbine of World War II.

The M1 Garand 1936 to 1957, by Joe Poyer and Craig Riesch, North Cape Publications, Tustin, CA, 1996. 216 pp., illus. Paper covers. $19.95.
Describes the entire range of M1 Garand production in text and quick-scan charts.

The M1 Garand: Post World War, by Scott A. Duff, Scott A. Duff, Export, PA, 1990. 139 pp., illus. Soft covers. $19.95.
A detailed account of the activities at Springfield Armory through this period. International Harvester, H&R, Korean War production and quantities delivered. Serial numbers.

The M1 Garand: World War 2, by Scott A. Duff, Scott A. Duff, Export, PA, 1993. 210 pp., illus. Paper covers. $39.95.
The most comprehensive study available to the collector and historian on the M1 Garand of World War II.

Modern Beretta Firearms, by Gene Gangarosa, Jr., Stoeger Publishing Co., So. Hackensack, NJ, 1994. 288 pp., illus. Paper covers. $16.95.
Traces all models of modern Beretta pistols, rifles, machine guns and combat shotguns.

Modern Gun Values, The Gun Digest Book of, 10th Edition, by the Editors of Gun Digest, DBI Books, a division of Krause Publications, Iola, WI, 1996. 560 pp. illus. Paper covers. $21.95.
Greatly updated and expanded edition describing and valuing over 7,000 firearms manufactured from 1900 to 1996. The standard for valuing modern firearms.

Modern Guns Identification & Value Guide, Eleventh Edition, by Russell and Steve Quertermous, Collector Books, Paducah, KY, 1996. 504 pp., illus. Paper covers. $12.95.
A popular guidebook featuring 2500 models of rifle, handgun and shotgun from 1900 to the present with detailed descriptions and prices.

Modern Gun Identification & Value Guide, Twelfth Edition, by Russell and Steve Quertermous, Collector Books, Paducah, KY, 1998. 504 pp., illus. Paper covers. $12.95.
Features current values for over 2,500 models of rifles, shotguns and handguns, with over 1,800 illustrations.

More Single Shot Rifles, by James C. Grant, The Gun Room Press, Highland Park, NJ, 1976. 324 pp., illus. $29.95.
Details the guns made by Frank Wesson, Milt Farrow, Holden, Borchardt, Stevens, Remington, Winchester, Ballard and Peabody-Martini

Mortimer, the Gunmakers, 1753-1923, by H. Lee Munson, Andrew Mowbray Inc., Lincoln, RI, 1992. 320 pp., illus. $65.00.
Seen through a single, dominant, English gunmaking dynasty this fascinating study provides a window into the classical era of firearms artistry.

The Mosin-Nagant Rifle, by Terence W. Lapin, North Cape Publications, Tustin, CA, 1998. 30 pp., illustrated. Paper covers. $19.95.
The first ever complete book on the Mosin Nagant rifle written in English Covers every variation.

Mossberg: More Gun for the Money, by V. and C. Havlin, Investment Rarities, Inc., Minneapolis, MN, 1995. 304 pp., illus. Paper covers. $24.95.
The history of O. F. Mossberg and Sons, Inc.

The Muzzle-Loading Cap Lock Rifle, by Ned H. Roberts, reprinted by Wolfe Publishing Co., Prescott, AZ, 1991. 432 pp., illus. $30.00.
Originally published in 1940, this fascinating study of the muzzle-loading cap lock rifle covers rifles on the frontier to hunting rifles, including the famous Hawken.

The Navy Luger, by Joachim Gortz and John Walter, Handgun Press, Glenview, IL, 1988. 128 pp., illus. $24.95.
The 9mm Pistole 1904 and the Imperial German Navy. A concise illustrated history.

The New World of Russian Small Arms and Ammunition, by Charlie Cutshaw, Paladin Press, Boulder, CO, 1998. 160 pp., illustrated. $39.95.
Detailed descriptions, specifications and first-class illustrations of the AN-94, PSS silent pistol, Bizon SMG, Saifa-12 tactical shotgun, the GP-25 grenade launcher and more cutting edge Russian weapons.

The Number 5 Jungle Carbine, by Alan M. Petrillo, Excalibur Publications, Latham, NY, 1994. 32 pp., illus. Paper covers. $7.95.
A comprehensive treatment of the rifle that collectors have come to call the "Jungle Carbine"—the Lee-Enfield Number 5, Mark 1.

The '03 Era: When Smokeless Revolutionized U.S. Riflery, by Clark S. Campbell, Collector Grade Publications, Inc., Ontario, Canada, 1994. 334 pp., illus. $44.50.
A much-expanded version of Campbell's The '03 Springfields, representing forty years of in-depth research into "all things '03."

Observations on Colt's Second Contract, November 2, 1847, by G. Maxwell Longfield and David T. Basnett, Museum Restoration Service, Bloomfield, Ontario, Canada, 1997. 36 pp., illus. Paper covers. $6.95.
This study traces the history and the construction of the Second Model Colt Dragoon supplied in 1848 to the U.S. Cavalry.

Official Guide to Gunmarks, 3rd Edition, by Robert H. Balderson, House of Collectibles, New York, NY, 1996. 367 pp., illus. Paper covers. $15.00.
Identifies manufacturers' marks that appear on American and foreign pistols, rifles and shotguns.

Official Price Guide to Antique and Modern Firearms, by Robert H. Balderson, House of Collectibles, New York, NY, 1996. 300 pp., illus. Paper covers. $17.00.
More than 30,000 updated prices for firearms manufactured from the 1600's to the present.

Official Price Guide to Civil War Collectibles, by Richard Friz, House of Collectibles, New York, NY, 1995. 375 pp., illus. Paper covers. $17.00.
Price listings and current market values for thousands of Civil War items.

Official Price Guide to Gun Collecting, by R.L. Wilson, Ballantine/House of Collectibles, New York, NY, 1998. 450 pp., illus. Paper covers. $21.50.
Covers more than 30,000 prices from Colt revolvers to Winchester rifles and shotguns to German Lugers and British sporting rifles and game guns.

Official Price Guide to Military Collectibles, 6th Edition, by Richard J. Austin, Random House, Inc., New York, NY, 1998. 200 pp., illus. Paper cover. $20.00.
Covers weapons and other collectibles from wars of the distant and recent past. More than 4,000 prices are listed. Illustrated with 400 black & white photos plus a full-color insert.

Old Gunsights: A Collector's Guide, 1850 to 2000, by Nicholas Stroebel, Krause Publications, Iola, WI, 1998. 320 pp., illus. Paper covers. $29.95
An in-depth and comprehensive examination of old gunsights and the rifles on which they were used to get accurate feel for prices in this expanding market.

The P-08 Parabellum Luger Automatic Pistol, edited by J. David McFarland, Desert Publications, Cornville, AZ, 1982. 20 pp., illus. Paper covers. $11.95.
Covers every facet of the Luger, plus a listing of all known Luger models.

Packing Iron, by Richard C. Rattenbury, Zon International Publishing, Millwood, NY, 1993. 216 pp., illus. $45.00.
The best book yet produced on pistol holsters and rifle scabbards. Over 300 variations of holster and scabbards are illustrated in large, clear plates.

Patents for Inventions, Class 119 (Small Arms), 1855-1930. British Patent Office, Armory Publications, Oceanside, CA, 1993. 7 volume set. $350.00.
Contains 7980 abridged patent descriptions and their sectioned line drawings, plus a 37-page alphabetical index of the patentees.

Pattern Dates for British Ordnance Small Arms, 1718-1783, by DeWitt Bailey, Thomas Publications, Gettysburg, PA, 1997. 116 pp., illus. Paper covers. $20.00
The weapons discussed in this work are those carried by troops sent to North America between 1737 and 1783, or shipped to them as replacement arms while in America.

Pistols of the World, 3rd Edition, by Ian Hogg and John Weeks, DBI Books, a division of Krause Publications, Iola, WI, 1992. 320 pp., illus. Paper covers. $20.95.
A totally revised edition of one of the leading studies of small arms.

The Pitman Notes on U.S. Martial Small Arms and Ammunition, 1776-1933, Volume 2, Revolvers and Automatic Pistols, by Brig. Gen. John Pitman, Thomas Publications, Gettysburg, PA, 1990. 192 pp., illus. $29.95.
A most important primary source of information on United States military small arms and ammunition.

The Plains Rifle, by Charles Hanson, Gun Room Press, Highland Park, NJ, 1989. 169 pp., illus. $35.00.
All rifles that were made with the plainsman in mind, including pistols.

Powder and Ball Small Arms, by Martin Pegler, Windrow & Green, London, 1998. 128 pp., illus. $39.95.
Part of the new "Live Firing Classic Weapons" series featuring full color photos of experienced shooters dressed in authentic costumes handling, loading and firing historic weapons.

The Powder Flask Book, by Ray Riling, R&R Books, Livonia, NY, 1993. 514 pp., illus. $70.00.
The complete book on flasks of the 19th century. Exactly scaled pictures of 1,600 flasks are illustrated.

Proud Promise: French Autoloading Rifles, 1898-1979, by Jean Huon, Collector Grade Publications, Inc., Cobourg, Ont., Canada, 1995. 216 pp., illus. $39.95.
The author has finally set the record straight about the importance of French contributions to modern arms design.

E. C. Prudhomme's Gun Engraving Review, by E. C. Prudhomme, R&R Books, Livonia, NY, 1994. 164 pp., illus. $60.00.
As a source for engravers and collectors, this book is an indispensable guide to styles and techniques of the world's foremost engravers.

Reloading Tools, Sights and Telescopes for Single Shot Rifles, by Gerald O. Kelver, Brighton, CO, 1982. 163 pp., illus. Paper covers. $15.00.
A listing of most of the famous makers of reloading tools, sights and telescopes with a brief description of the products they manufactured.

The Remington-Lee Rifle, by Eugene F. Myszkowski, Excalibur Publications, Latham, NY, 1995. 100 pp., illus. Paper covers. $22.50.
Features detailed descriptions, including serial number ranges, of each model from the first Lee Magazine Rifle produced for the U.S. Navy to the last Remington-Lee Small Bores shipped to the Cuban Rural Guard.

Revolvers of the British Services 1854-1954, by W.H.J. Chamberlain and A.W.F. Taylerson, Museum Restoration Service, Ottawa, Canada, 1989. 80 pp., illus. $27.50.
Covers the types issued among many of the United Kingdom's naval, land or air services.

Rhode Island Arms Makers & Gunsmiths, by William O. Archibald, Andrew Mowbray, Inc., Lincoln, RI, 1990. 108 pp., illus. $16.50.
A serious and informative study of an important area of American arms making.

Rifles of the World, by Jean-Noel Mouret, Book Sales, Edison, NJ, 1998. 144 pp., illus. $17.99.
This highly illustrated book recounts the fascinating story of the rifle and its development. Military, sporting and hunting.

Rifles of the World, 2nd Edition, by John Walter, DBI Books, a division of Krause Publications, Iola, WI. 512 pp., illus. Paper covers. $24.95.

Rifles of the World, by Oliver Achard, Chartwell Books, Inc., Edison, NJ, 141 pp., illus. $18.95.
A unique insight into the world of long guns, not just rifles, but also shotguns, carbines and all the usual multi-barreled guns that once were so popular with European hunters, especially in Germany and Austria.

The Rock Island '03, by C.S. Ferris, C.S. Ferris, Arvada, CO, 1993. 58 pp., illus. Paper covers. $12.50.
A monograph of interest to the collector or historian concentrating on the U.S. M1903 rifle made by the less publicized of our two producing facilities.

Round Ball to Rimfire, Vol. 1, by Dean Thomas, Thomas Publications, Gerrysburg, PA, 1997. 144 pp., illus. $40.00.
The first of a two-volume set of the most complete history and guide for all small arms ammunition used in the Civil War. The information includes data from research and development to the arsenals that created it.

Ruger and his Guns, by R.L. Wilson, Simon & Schuster, New York, NY, 1996. 358 pp., illus. $65.00.
A history of the man, the company and their firearms.

Russell M. Catron and His Pistols, by Warren H. Buxton, Ucross Books, Los Alamos, NM, 1998. 210 pp., illustrated. Paper covers. $35.00.
An unknown American firearms inventor and manufacturer of the mid twentieth century. Military, commerical ammunition.

The SAFN-49 and The FAL, by Joe Poyer and Dr. Richard Feirman, North Cape Publications, Tustin, CA, 1998. 160 pp., illus. Paper covers $14.95.
The first complete overview of the SAFN-49 battle rifle, from its pre-World War 2 beginnings to its military service in countries as diverse as the Belgian Congo and Argentina. The FAL was "light" version of the SAFN-49 and it became the Free World's most adopted battle rifle.

Sam Colt's Own Record 1847, by John Parsons, Wolfe Publishing Co., Prescott, AZ, 1992. 167 pp., illus. $24.50.
Chronologically presented, the correspondence published here completes the account of the manufacture, in 1847, of the Walker Model Colt revolver.

J.P. Sauer & Sohn, Suhl, by Jim Cate & Nico Van Gun, CBC Book Co., Chattanooga, TN, 1998. 406 pp., illus. $65.00.
A historical study of Sauer automatic pistols. Over 500 photos showing the different variations of pistols, grips, magazines and holsters.

Scottish Firearms, by Claude Blair and Robert Woosnam-Savage, Museum Restoration Service, Bloomfield, Ont., Canada, 1995. 52 pp., illus. Paper covers. $4.95.
This revision of the first book devoted entirely to Scottish firearms is supplemented by a register of surviving Scottish long guns.

The Scottish Pistol, by Martin Kelvin, Fairleigh Dickinson University Press, Dist. By Associated University Presses, Cranbury, NJ, 1997. 256 pp., illus. $49.50.
The Scottish pistol, its history, manufacture and design.

Scouts, Peacemakers and New Frontiers in .22 Caliber, by Don Wilkerson, Cherokee Publications, Kansas City, MO, 1995. 224 pp., illus. $40.00.
Covers the 48 variations and numerous subvariants of the later rimfire Single Actions.

Sharps Firearms, by Frank Seller, Frank M. Seller, Denver, CO, 1982. 358 pp., illus. $50.00.
Traces the development of Sharps firearms with full range of guns made including all martial variations.

Simeon North: First Official Pistol Maker of the United States, by S. North and R. North, The Gun Room Press, Highland Park, NJ, 1972. 207 pp., illus. $15.95.
Reprint of the rare first edition.

The SKS Carbine, by Steve Kehaya and Joe Poyer, North Cape Publications, Tustin, CA, 1997. 150 pp., illus. Paper covers. $16.95.
The first comprehensive examination of a major historical firearm used through the Vietnam conflict to the diamond fields of Angola.

The SKS Type 45 Carbines, by Duncan Long, Desert Publications, El Dorado, AZ, 1992. 110 pp., illus. Paper covers.
Covers the history and practical aspects of operating, maintaining and modifying this abundantly available rifle.

Small Arms of the East India Company 1600-1856, by D. F. Harding, Volume 1 & 2, Foresight Books, London, England, $185.00.
Over 100 patterns of East India Company muskets, fusils, rifles, carbines, pistols, blunderbusses, wallpieces and bayonets identified for the first time in print.

Smith & Wesson 1857-1945, by Robert J. Neal and Roy G. Jinks, R&R Books, Livonia, NY, 1996. 434 pp., illus. $50.00.
The bible for all existing and aspiring Smith & Wesson collectors.

Sniper Variations of the German K98k Rifle, by Richard D. Law, Collector Grade Publications, Ontario, Canada, 1997. 240 pp., illus. $47.50.
Volume 2 of "Backbone of the Wehrmacht" the author's in-depth study of the German K98k rifle. This volume concentrates on the telescopic-sighted rifle of choice for most German snipers during World War 2.

Southern Derringers of the Mississippi Valley, by Turner Kirkland, Pioneer Press, Tenn., 1971. 80 pp., illus., paper covers. $10.00.
A guide for the collector, and a much-needed study.

Soviet Russian Postwar Military Pistols and Cartridges, by Fred A. Datig, Handgun Press, Glenview, IL, 1988. 152 pp., illus. $29.95.
Thoroughly researched, this definitive sourcebook covers the development and adoption of the Makarov, Stechkin and the new PSM pistols. Also included in this source book is coverage on Russian clandestine weapons and pistol cartridges.

Soviet Russian Tokarev "TT" Pistols and Cartridges 1929-1953, by Fred Datig, Graphic Publishers, Santa Ana, CA, 1993. 168 pp., illus. $39.95.
Details of rare arms and their accessories are shown in hundreds of photos. It also contains a complete bibliography and index.

THE ARMS LIBRARY

Soviet Small-Arms and Ammunition, by David Bolotin, Handgun Press, Glenview, IL, 1996. 264 pp., illus. $49.95.
An authoritative and complete book on Soviet small arms.

Sporting Collectibles, by Jim and Vivian Karsnitz, Schiffer Publishing Ltd., West Chester, PA, 1992. 160 pp., illus. Paper covers. $29.95.
The fascinating world of hunting related collectibles presented in an informative text.

The Springfield 1903 Rifles, by Lt. Col. William S. Brophy, USAR, Ret., Stackpole Books Inc., Harrisburg, PA, 1985. 608 pp., illus. $75.00.
The illustrated, documented story of the design, development, and production of all the models, appendages, and accessories.

Springfield Armory Shoulder Weapons 1795-1968, by Robert W.D. Ball, Antique Trader Books, Dubuque, IA, 1998. 264 pp., illus. $34.95.
This book documents the 255 basic models of rifles, including test and trial rifles, produced by the Springfield Armory. It features the entire history of rifles and carbines manufactured at the Armory, the development of each weapon with specific operating characteristics and procedures.

Springfield Model 1903 Service Rifle Production and Lateration, 1905-1910, by C.S. Ferris and John Beard, Arvada, CO, 1995. 66 pp., illus. Paper covers. $12.50.
A highly recommended work for any serious student of the Springfield Model 1903 rifle.

Springfield Shoulder Arms 1795-1865, by Claud E. Fuller, S. & S. Firearms, Glendale, NY, 1986. 76 pp., illus. Paper covers. $17.95.
Exact reprint of the scarce 1930 edition of one of the most definitive works on Springfield flintlock and percussion muskets ever published.

Standard Catalog of Smith and Wesson, by Jim Supica and Richard Nahas, Krause Publications, Iola, WI, 1996. 240 pp., illus. $29.95.
Clearly details hundreds of products by the legendary manufacturer. How to identify, evaluate the condition and assess the value of 752 Smith & Wesson models and variations.

Steel Canvas: The Art of American Arms, by R.L. Wilson, Random House, NY, 1995. 384 pp., illus. $65.00.
Presented here for the first time is the breathtaking panorama of America's extraordinary engravers and embellishers of arms, from the 1700s to modern times.

Stevens Pistols & Pocket Rifles, by K.L. Cope, Museum Restoration Service, Alexandria Bay, NY, 1992. 114 pp., illus. $24.50.
This is the story of the guns and the man who designed them and the company which he founded to make them.

A Study of Colt Conversions and Other Percussion Revolvers, by R. Bruce McDowell, Krause Publications, Iola, WI, 1997. 464 pp., illus. $39.95.
The ultimate reference detailing Colt revolvers that have been converted from percussion to cartridge.

The Sumptuous Flaske, by Herbert G. Houze, Andrew Mowbray, Inc., Lincoln, RI, 1989. 158 pp., illus. Soft covers. $35.00.
Catalog of a recent show at the Buffalo Bill Historical Center bringing together some of the finest European and American powder flasks of the 16th to 19th centuries.

Textbook of Automatic Pistols, by R.K. Wilson, Wolfe Publishing Co., Prescott, AZ, 1990. 349 pp., illus. $54.00.
Reprint of the 1943 classic being a treatise on the history, development and functioning of modern military self-loading pistols.

Thompson: The American Legend, by Tracie L. Hill, Collector Grade Publications, Ontario, Canada, 1996. 584 pp., illus. $85.00.
The story of the first American submachine gun. All models are featured and discussed.

Toys That Shoot and Other Neat Stuff, by James Dundas, Schiffer Books, Atglen, PA, 1999. 112 pp., illustrated. Paper covers. $24.95.
Shooting toys from the twentieth century, especially 1920's to 1960's, in over 420 color photographs of BB guns, cap shooters, marble shooters, squirt guns and more. Complete with a price guide.

Trade Guns of the Hudson's Bay Company, 1670-1870, by S. James Gooding, Museum Restoration Service, Bloomfield, Ontario, Canada, 1998. 35 pp., illus. Paper covers. $6.95.
The various styles and patterns of muzzle loading guns brought by the Hudson Bay Co. to North America to trade with the Indians.

The Trapdoor Springfield, by M.D. Waite and B.D. Ernst, The Gun Room Press, Highland Park, NJ, 1983. 250 pp., illus. $39.95.
The first comprehensive book on the famous standard military rifle of the 1873-92 period.

U.S. Breech-Loading Rifles and Carbines, Cal. 45, by Gen. John Pitman, Thomas Publications, Gettysburg, PA, 1992. 192 pp., illus. $29.95.
The third volume in the Pitman Notes on U.S. Martial Small Arms and Ammunition, 1776-1933. This book centers on the "Trapdoor Springfield" models.

U.S. Handguns of World War 2: The Secondary Pistols and Revolvers, by Charles W. Pate, Andrew Mowbray, Inc., Lincoln, RI, 1998. 515 pp., illus. $39.00.
This indispensable new book covers all of the American military handguns of World War 2 except for the M1911A1 Colt automatic.

United States Martial Flintlocks, by Robert M. Reilly, Mowbray Publishing Co., Lincoln, RI, 1997. 264 pp., illus. $40.00.
A comprehensive history of American flintlock longarms and handguns (mostly military) c. 1775 to c. 1840.

U.S. Martial Single Shot Pistols, by Daniel D. Hartzler and James B. Whisker, Old Bedford Village Pess, Bedford, PA, 1998. 128 pp., illus. $45.00.
A photographic chronicle of military and semi-martial pistols supplied to the U.S. Government and the several States.

U.S. Military Arms Dates of Manufacture from 1795, by George Madis, David Madis, Dallas, TX, 1989. 64 pp. Soft covers. $5.00.

Lists all U.S. military arms of collector interest alphabetically, covering about 250 models.

U.S. Military Small Arms 1816-1865, by Robert M. Reilly, The Gun Room Press, Highland Park, NJ, 1983. 270 pp., illus. $39.95.
Covers every known type of primary and secondary martial firearms used by Federal forces.

U.S. M1 Carbines: Wartime Production, by Craig Riesch, North Cape Publications, Tustin, CA, 1994. 72 pp., illus. Paper covers. $15.95.
Presents only verifiable and accurate information. Each part of the M1 Carbine is discussed fully in its own section; including markings and finishes.

U.S. Naval Handguns, 1808-1911, by Fredrick R. Winter, Andrew Mowbray Publishers, Lincoln, RI, 1990. 128 pp., illus. $26.00.
The story of U.S. Naval Handguns spans an entire century—included are sections on each of the important naval handguns within the period.

Walther Models PP and PPK, 1929-1945, by James L. Rankin, assisted by Gary Green, James L. Rankin, Coral Gables, FL, 1974. 142 pp., illus. $35.00.
Complete coverage on the subject as to finish, proofmarks and Nazi Party inscriptions.

Walther P-38 Pistol, by Maj. George Nonte, Desert Publications, Cornville, AZ, 1982. 100 pp., illus. Paper covers. $11.95.
Complete volume on one of the most famous handguns to come out of WWII. All models covered.

Walther Volume II, Engraved, Presentation and Standard Models, by James L. Rankin, J.L. Rankin, Coral Gables, FL, 1977. 112 pp., illus. $35.00.
The new Walther book on embellished versions and standard models. Has 88 photographs, including many color plates.

Walther, Volume III, 1908-1980, by James L. Rankin, Coral Gables, FL, 1981. 226 pp., illus. $35.00.
Covers all models of Walther handguns from 1908 to date, includes holsters, grips and magazines.

The Whitney Firearms, by Claud Fuller, Standard Publications, Huntington, WV, 1946, 334 pp., many plates and drawings, $50.00.
An authoritative history of all Whitney arms and their maker. Highly recommended. An exclusive with Ray Riling Arms Books Co.

Winchester: An American Legend, by R.L. Wilson, Random House, New York, NY, 1991. 403 pp., illus. $65.00.
The official history of Winchester firearms from 1849 to the present.

Winchester Bolt Action Military & Sporting Rifles 1877 to 1937, by Herbert G. Houze, Andrew Mowbray Publishing, Lincoln, RI, 1998. 295 pp., illus. $45.00.
Winchester was the first American arms maker to commercially manufacture a bolt action repeating rifle, and this book tells the exciting story of these Winchester bolt actions.

The Winchester Book, by George Madis, David Madis Gun Book Distributor, Dallas, TX, 1986. 650 pp., illus. $49.50.
A new, revised 25th anniversary edition of this classic book on Winchester firearms. Complete serial ranges have been added.

Winchester Dates of Manufacture 1849-1984, by George Madis, Art & Reference House, Brownsboro, TX, 1984. 59 pp. $5.95.
A most useful work, compiled from records of the Winchester factory.

Winchester Engraving, by R.L. Wilson, Beinfeld Books, Springs, CA, 1989. 500 pp., illus. $125.00.
A classic reference work of value to all arms collectors.

The Winchester Handbook, by George Madis, Art & Reference House, Lancaster, TX, 1982. 287 pp., illus. $19.95.
The complete line of Winchester guns, with dates of manufacture, serial numbers, etc.

Winchester Lever Action Repeating Firearms, Vol. 1, The Models of 1866, 1873 and 1876, by Arthur Pirkle, North Cape Publications, Tustin, CA, 1995. 112 pp., illus. Paper covers. $19.95.
Complete, part-by-part description, including dimensions, finishes, markings and variations throughout the production run of these fine, collectible guns.

Winchester Lever Action Repeating Rifles, Vol. 2, The Models of 1886 and 1892, by Arthur Pirkle, North Cape Publications, Tustin, CA, 1996. 150 pp. Paper covers. $19.95.
Describes each model on a part-by-part basis by serial number range complete with finishes, markings and changes.

Winchester Lever Action Repeating Rifles, Volume 3, The Model of 1894, by Arthur Pirkle, North Cape Publications, Tustin, CA, 1998. 150 pp., illus. Paper covers. $16.95.
The first book ever to provide a detailed description of the Model 1894 rifle and carbine.

The Winchester Model 94: The First 100 Years, by Robert C. Renneberg, Krause Publications, Iola, WI, 1991. 208 pp., illus. $34.95.
Covers the design and evolution from the early years up to the many different editions that exist today.

Winchester Shotguns and Shotshells, by Ronald W. Stadt, Krause Publications, Iola, WI, 1995. 256 pp., illus. $34.95.
The definitive book on collectible Winchester shotguns and shotshells manufactured through 1961.

The Winchester Single-Shot, by John Cambell, Andrew Mowbray, Inc., Lincoln RI, 1995. 272 pp., illus. $55.00.
Covers every important aspect of this highly-collectible firearm.

Winchester Slide-Action Rifles, Volume 1: Model 1890 & 1906, by Ned Schwing, Krause Publications, Iola, WI, 1992. 352 pp., illus. $39.95.
First book length treatment of models 1890 & 1906 with over 50 charts and tables showing significant new information about caliber style and rarity.

Winchester Slide-Action Rifles, Volume 2: Model 61 & Model 62, by Ned Schwing, Krause Publications, Iola, WI, 1993. 256 pp., illus. $34.95.
A complete historic look into the Model 61 and the Model 62. These favorite slide-action guns receive a thorough presentation which takes you to the

factory to explore receivers, barrels, markings, stocks, stampings and engraving in complete detail.
Winchester's 30-30, Model 94, by Sam Fadala, Stackpole Books, Inc., Harrisburg, PA, 1986. 223 pp., illus. $24.95.
The story of the rifle America loves.

EDGED WEAPONS

The American Blade Collectors Association Price Guide to Antique Knives, by J. Bruce Voyles, Krause Publications, Iola, WI, 1995. 480 pp., illus. Paper covers. $16.95.
In this complete guide to pocketknives there are 40,000 current values in six grades of condition for knives produced from 1800-1970.
The American Eagle Pommel Sword: The Early Years 1794-1830, by Andrew Mowbray, Manrat Arms Publications, Lincoln, RI, 1997. 244 pp., illus. $65.00.
The standard guide to the most popular style of American sword.
American Indian Tomahawks, by Harold L. Peterson, The Gun Room Press, Highland Park, NJ, 1993. 142 pp., illus. $49.95.
The tomahawk of the American Indian, in all its forms, as a weapon and as a tool.
American Knives; The First History and Collector's Guide, by Harold L. Peterson, The Gun Room Press, Highland Park, NJ, 1980. 178 pp., illus. $24.95.
A reprint of this 1958 classic. Covers all types of American knives.
American Military Bayonets of the 20th Century, by Gary M. Cunningham, Scott A. Duff Publications, Export, PA, 1997. 116 pp., illus. Paper covers. $19.95.
A guide for collectors, including notes on makers, markings, finishes, variations, scabbards, and production data.
American Premium Guide to Pocket Knives and Razors, Identification and Value Guide, 4th Edition, by Jim Sargent, Books Americana, a division of Krause Publications, Iola, WI, 1996. Paper covers. $22.95.
Hundreds of rare photos have been added to the huge sections on Case, Remington, Pal and Browning knives and sheaths.
American Primitive Knives 1770-1870, by G.B. Minnes, Museum Restoration Service, Ottawa, Canada, 1983. 112 pp., illus. $24.95.
Origins of the knives, outstanding specimens, structural details, etc.
American Socket Bayonets and Scabbards, by Robert M. Reilly, 2nd printing, Andrew Mowbray, Inc., Lincoln, RI, 1998. 208 pp., illustrated. $45.00.
Full coverage of the socket bayonet in America, from Colonial times through the post-Civil War.
The American Sword, 1775-1945, by Harold L. Peterson, Ray Riling Arms Books, Co., Phila., PA, 1980. 286 pp. plus 60 pp. of illus. $45.00.
1977 reprint of a survey of swords worn by U.S. uniformed forces, plus the rare "American Silver Mounted Swords, (1700-1815)."
American Swords and Sword Makers, by Richard H. Bezdek, Paladin Press, Boulder, CO, 1994. 648 pp., illus. $79.95.
The long-awaited definitive reference volume to American swords, sword makers and sword dealers from Colonial times to the present.
American Swords & Sword Makers Volume 2, by Richard H. Bezdek, Paladin Press, Boulder, CO, 1998. 384 pp., illus. $64.95.
Features a bonanza of new information on makers of swords, bowie knives, and tomahawks as well as sword dealers, silver and even early gun makers and dealers.
American Swords from the Philip Medicus Collection, edited by Stuart C. Mowbray, with photographs and an introduction by Norm Flayderman, Andrew Mowbray Publishers, Lincoln, RI, 1998. 272 pp., with 604 swords illustrated. $55.00.
Covers all areas of American sword collecting.
The Ames Sword Company, 1829-1935, by John D. Hamilton, Andrew Mowbray Publisher, Linclon, RI, 1995. 255 pp., illus. $45.00.
An exhaustively researched and comprehensive history of America's foremost sword manufacturer and arms supplier during the Civil War.
Battle Blades: A Professional's Guide to Combat/Fighting Knives, by Greg Walker; Foreword by Al Mar, Paladin Press, Boulder, CO, 1993. 168 pp., illus. $30.00.
The author evaluates daggers, Bowies, switchblades and utility blades according to their design, performance, reliability and cost.
Bayonets from Janzen's Notebook, by Jerry L. Janzen, Cedar Ridge Publications, Broken Arrow, OK, 1994. 512 pp., illus. $34.50.
A very popular reference book covering bayonets of the World.
The Bayonet in New France, 1665-1760, by Erik Goldstein, Museum Restoration Service, Bloomfield, Ontario, Canada, 1997. 36 pp., illus. Paper covers. $6.95.
Traces bayonets from the recently developed plug bayonet, through the regulation socket bayonets which saw service in North America.
Bayonets of the Remington Cartridge Period, by Jerry L. Janzen, Cedar Ridge Publications, Broken Arrow, OK, 1994. 200 pp., illus. $39.95.
The story of the bayonets which accompanied the Remington Rolling Block and its many successors. Included are the rifles, the countries who used them, pictures of the bayonets in use and detailed descriptions of each bayonet.
Bayonets, Knives & Scabbards, edited by Frank Trzaska, Knife Books, Deptford, NJ, 1998. 80 pp., illus. Paper covers. $15.95.
A reprint of the United States Army edged weapons report 1917 through 1945. Covers manufacturers involved, dates, numbers produced, problems encountered, and production data.
The Book of the Sword, by Richard F. Burton, Dover Publications, New York, NY, 1987. 199 pp., illus. Paper covers. $12.95.
Traces the swords origin from its birth as a charged and sharpened stick through diverse stages of development.
Borders Away, Volume 1: With Steel, by William Gilkerson, Andrew Mowbray, Inc., Lincoln, RI, 1991. 184 pp., illus. $48.00.

A comprehensive study of naval armament under fighting sail. This first voume covers axes, pikes and fighting blades in use between 1626-1826.
The Bowie Knife, by Raymond Thorp, Phillips Publications, Williamstown, NJ, 1992. 167 pp., illus. $9.95.
After forty-five years, the classic work on the Bowie knife is once again available.
British & Commonwealth Bayonets, by Ian D. Skennerton and Robert Richardson, I.D.S.A. Books, Piqua, OH, 1986. 404 pp., 1300 illus. $40.00.
Civil War Knives, by Marc Newman, Paladin Press, Boulder, CO, 1998. 120 pp., illus. $39.95.
Here are the stories behind the many knives carried by soldiers and sailors during the U.S. Civil War.
Collecting the Edged Weapons of Imperial Germany, by Thomas M. Johnson and Thomas T. Wittmann, Johnson Reference Books, Fredricksburg, VA, 1989. 363 pp., illus. $39.50.
An in-depth study of the many ornate military, civilian, and government daggers and swords of the Imperial era.
Collecting North American Indian Knives, by Lara Hothem, Books Americana, a division of Krause Publications, Iola, WI, 1996. 152 pp., illus. Paper covers. $41.95.
A complete guide to the identification and value of sharp-edged weapons and ceremonial knives of the Native Americans from every region.
Collector's Guide to Ames U.S. Contract Military Edged Weapons: 1832-1906, by Ron G. Hickox, Pioneer Press, Union City, IN, 1993. 70 pp., illus. Paper covers. $14.95.
While this book deals primarily with edged weapons made by the Ames Manufacturing Company, this guide refers to other manufactureres of United States swords.
Collector's Guide to Swords, Daggers and Cutlasses, by Gerald Weland, Book Sales Inc., Edison, NJ, 1998. 128 pp., illustrated. $12.99
After an introduction that analyzes the evolution and historical significance of edged weapons this volume considers swords, daggers, and cutlasses and Oriental edged weapons.
Collector's Handbook of World War 2 German Daggers, by LtC. Thomas M. Johnson, Johnson Reference Books, Fredricksburg, VA, 2nd edition, 1991. 252 pp., illus. Paper covers. $25.00.
Concise pocket reference guide to Third Reich daggers and accoutrements in a convenient format. With value guide.
Collins Machetes and Bowies 1845-1965, by Danial E. Henry, Krause Publications, Iola, WI, 1996. 232 pp., illus. Paper covers. $19.95.
A comprehensive history of Collins machetes and bowies including more than 1200 blade instruments and accessories.
The Complete Bladesmith: Forging Your Way to Perfection, by Jim Hrisoulas, Paladin Press, Boulder, CO, 1987. 192 pp., illus. $25.00.
Novice as well as experienced bladesmith will benefit from this definitive guide to smithing world-class blades.
The Complete Book of Pocketknife Repair, by Ben Kelly, Jr., Krause Publications, Iola, WI, 1995. 130 pp., illus. Paper covers. $10.95.
Everything you need to know about repairing knives can be found in this step-by-step guide to knife repair.
Confederate Edged Weapons, by W.A. Albaugh, R&R Books, Lavonia, NY, 1994. 198 pp., illus. $30.00.
The master reference to edged weapons of the Confederate forces. Features precise line drawings and an extensive text.
The Craft of the Japanese Sword, by Leon and Hiroko Kapp, Yoshindo Yoshihara, Kodanska International, Tokyo, Japan, 1990. 167 pp., illus. $39.00.
The first book in English devoted to contemporary sword manufacturing in Japan.
Eickhorn Edged Weapons Exports, Vol. 1: Latin America, by A.M. de Quesada, Jr. And Ron G. Hicock, Pioneer Press, Union City, TN, 1996. 120 pp., illus. Paper covers. $15.00.
This research studies the various Eickhorn edged weapons and accessories manufactured for various countries outside of Germany.
Exploring the Dress Daggers of the German Army, by Thomas T. Wittmann, Johnson Reference Books, Fredricksburg, VA, 1995. 350 pp., illus. $59.95.
The first in-depth analysis of the dress daggers worn by the German Army.
The First Commando Knives, by Prof. Kelly Yeaton and Col. Rex Applegate, Phillips Publications, Williamstown, NJ, 1996. 115 pp., illus. Paper covers. $12.95.
Here is the full story of the Shanghai origins of the world's best known dagger.
German Clamshells and Other Bayonets, by G. Walker and R.J. Weinard, Johnson Reference Books, Fredricksburg, VA, 1994. 157 pp., illus. $22.95.
Includes unusual bayonets, many of which are shown for the first time. Current market values are listed.
German Military Fighting Knives 1914-1945, by Gordon A. Hughes, Johnson Reference Books, Fredricksburg, VA, 1994. 64 pp., illus. Paper covers. $24.50.
Documents the different types of German military fighting knives used during WWI and WWII. Makers' proofmarks are shown as well as details of blade inscriptions, etc.
The Halberd and other European Polearms 1300-1650, by George Snook, Museum Restoration Service, Bloomfield, Ontario, Canada, 1998. 40 pp., illus. Paper covers. $6.95.
A comprehensive introduction to the history, use, and identification of the staff weapons of Europe.
The Handbook of British Bayonets, by Ian D. Skennerton, I.D.S.A. Books, Piqua, OH. 64 pp. $4.95
The Hand Forged Knife, Krause Publications, Iola, WI. 136 pp., illus., $12.95.
Explains the techniques for forging, hardening and tempering knives and other stainless steel tools.
How to Make Folding Knives, by Ron Lake, Frank Centofante and Wayne Clay, Krause Publications, Iola, WI, 1995. 193 pp., illus. Paper covers. $13.95.

With step-by-step instructions, learn how to make your own folding knife from three top custom makers.

How to Make Knives, by Richard W. Barney and Robert W. Loveless, Krause Publications, Iola, WI, 1995. 182 pp., illus. Paper covers. $13.95.
Complete instructions from two premier knife makers on making high-quality, handmade knives.

How to Make Multi-Blade Folding Knives, by Eugene Shadley & Terry Davis, Krause Publications, Iola, WI, 1997. 192 pp., illus. Paper covers. $19.95.
This step-by-step instructional guide teaches knifemakers how to craft these complex folding knives.

IBCA Price Guide to Commemorative Knives 1960-1990 by Bruce Voyles, Krause Publications, Iola, WI. 256 pp., illus., $16.95.

IBCA Price Guide to Antique Knives edited by Bruce Voyles, Krause Publications, Iola, WI. 480 pp., illus., $17.95.

Japanese Military and Civil Swords and Dirks, by Richard Fuller and Ron Gregory, Howell Press, Charlottesville, VA, 1997. 288 pp., illus. $49.95.
This essential reference covers both military and civil Japanese swords and dirks from 1868 to 1945. More than 110 sword and dirk patterns are described and illustrated.

Kentucky Knife Traders Manual No. 6, by R.B. Ritchie, Hindman, KY, 1980. 217 pp., illus. Paper covers. $10.00.
Guide for dealers, collectors and traders listing pocket knives and razor values.

Knife and Tomahawk Throwing: The Art of the Experts, by Harry K. McEvoy, Charles E. Tuttle, Rutland, VT, 1989. 150 pp., illus. Soft covers. $8.95.
The first book to employ side-by-side the fascinating art and science of knives and tomahawks.

Knife Talk, the Art and Science of Knifemaking, by Ed. Fowler, Krause Publications, Iola, WI, 1998. 158 pp., illus. Paper covers. $14.95.
Valuable how-to advice on knife design and construction plus 20 years of memorable articles from the pages of "Blade" Magazine.

Knifemakers of Old San Francisco, by Bernard Levine, 2nd edition, Paladin Press, Boulder, CO, 1998. 150 pp., illus. $39.95.
The definitive history of the knives and knife makers of 19th century San Francisco.

Knifemaking, The Gun Digest Book of, by Jack Lewis and Roger Combs, DBI Books, a division of Krause Publications, Iola, WI, 1989. 256 pp., illus. Paper covers. $16.95.
All the ins and outs from the world of knifemaking in a brand new book.

Knives, 5th Edition, The Gun Digest Book of, edited by Jack Lewis and Roger Combs, DBI Books, a division of Krause Publications, Iola, WI, 1997. 256 pp., illus. Paper covers. $19.95.
Covers practically every aspect of the knife world.

Knives 2000, 20th Annual Edition, edited by Ken Warner, DBI Books a division of Krause Publications, Iola, WI, 1999. 304 pp., illustrated. Paper covers. $21.95.
More than 1,000 photos and listings of new knives plus articles from top writers in the field.

Levine's Guide to Knives And Their Values, 4th Edition, by Bernard Levine, DBI Books, a division of Krause Publications, Iola, WI, 1997. 512 pp., illus. Paper covers. $27.95.
All the basic tools for identifying, valuing and collecting folding and fixed blade knives.

The Master Bladesmith: Advanced Studies in Steel, by Jim Hrisoulas, Paladin Press, Boulder, CO, 1990. 296 pp., illus. $45.00.
The author reveals the forging secrets that for centuries have been protected by guilds.

Medieval Swordsmanship, Illustrated Methods and Techniques, by John Clements, Paladin Press, Boulder, CO, 1998. 344 pp., illustrated. $40.00.
The most comprehensive and historically accurate view ever written of the lost fighting arts of Medieval knights.

Military Swords of Japan 1868-1945, by Richard Fuller and Ron Gregory, Arms and Armour Press, London, England, 1986. 127 pp., illus. Paper covers. $18.95.
A wide-ranging survey of the swords and dirks worn by the armed forces of Japan until the end of World War II.

Modern Combat Blades, by Duncan Long, Paladin Press, Boulder, CO, 1993. 128 pp., illus. $25.00.
Long discusses the pros and cons of bowies, bayonets, commando daggers, kukris, switchblades, butterfly knives, belt-buckle blades and many more.

Official Price Guide to Collector Knives, 11th Edition, by C. Houston Price, Krause Publications, Iola, WI, 1996. 531 pp., illus. $17.00
Invaluable information on grading, buying, selling, age determination, and how to spot fakes. More than 13,000 price lists.

On Damascus Steel, by Dr. Leo S. Figiel, Atlantis Arts Press, Atlantis, FL, 1991. 145 pp., illus. $65.00.
The historic, technical and artistic aspects of Oriental and mechanical Damascus. Persian and Indian sword blades, from 1600-1800, which have never been published, are illustrated.

The Pattern-Welded Blade: Artistry in Iron, by Jim Hrisoulas, Paladin Press, Boulder, CO, 1994. 120 pp., illus. $35.00.
Reveals the secrets of this craft—from the welding of the starting billet to the final assembly of the complete blade.

Randall Made Knives, Krause Publications, Iola, WI. 292 pp., illus. $50.00.
Plots the designs of all 24 of Randall's unique knives.

Randall Made Knives: The History of the Man and the Blades, by Robert L. Gaddis, Paladin Press, Boulder, CO, 1993. 304 pp., illus. $50.00.
The authorized history of Bo Randall and his blades, told in his own words and those of the people who knew him best.

Renaissance Swordsmanship, by John Clements, Paladin Press, Boulder, CO, 1997. 152 pp., illus. Paper covers. $25.00.
The illustrated use of rapiers and cut-and-thrust swords.

Rice's Trowel Bayonet, reprinted by Ray Riling Arms Books, Co., Phila., PA, 1968. 8 pp., illus. Paper covers. $3.00.
A facsimile reprint of a rare circular originally published by the U.S. government in 1875 for the information of U.S. troops.

The Samurai Sword, by John M. Yumoto, Charles E. Tuttle Co., Rutland, VT, 1958. 191 pp., illus. $23.95.
A must for anyone interested in Japanese blades, and the first book on this subject written in English.

The Scottish Dirk, by James D. Forman, Museum Restoration Service, Bloomfield, Ont., Canada, 1991. 60 pp., illus. Paper covers. $5.95.
More than 100 dirks are illustrated with a text that sets the dirk and Sgian Dubh in their socio-historic content following design changes through more than 300 years of evolution.

Scottish Swords from the Battlefield at Culloden, by Lord Archibald Campbell, The Mowbray Co., Providence, RI, 1973. 63 pp., illus. $15.00.
A modern reprint of an exceedingly rare 1894 privately printed edition.

The Sheffield Knife Book, by Geoffrey Tweedale, Krause Publications, Iola, WI. 320 pp., illus., $50.00.

Small Arms Identification Series, No. 6-British Service Sword & Lance Patterns, by Ian Skennerton, I.D.S.A. Books, Piqua, OH, 1994. 48 pp. $9.50.

Small Arms Series, No. 2. The British Spike Bayonet, by Ian Skennerton, I.D.S.A. Books, Piqua, OH, 1982. 32 pp., 30 illus. $9.00.

Sure Defence, The Bowie Knife Book, by Kenneth J. Burton, I.D.S.A. Books, Piqua, OH, 1988. 100 pp., 115 illus. $37.50.

The Standard Knife Collector's Guide, 3rd Edition, by Roy Ritchie and Ron Stewart, Collector Books, Paducah, KY, 1996. 688 pp., illus. Paper covers. $12.95.
Includes virtually all knife manufacturers both old and new, plus custom made and commemorative knives.

Swords and Sword Makers of the War of 1812, by Richard Bezdek, Paladin Press, Boulder, CO, 1997. 104 pp., illus. $40.00.
The complete history of the men and companies that made swords during and before the war. Includes examples of cavalry and artillery sabers.

Swords of Imperial Japan 1868-1845, by Jim Dawson, Krause Publications, Inc. 160 pp., illus. $29.95.
Details the military, civilian, diplomatic and civil, police and colonial swords of post-Samurai era.

Sword of the Samurai, by George R. Parulski, Jr., Paladin Press, Boulder, CO, 1985. 144 pp., illus. $34.95.
The classical art of Japanese swordsmanship.

Swords from Public Collections in the Commonwealth of Pennsylvania, edited by Bruce S. Bazelon, Andrew Mowbray Inc., Lincoln, RI, 1987. 127 pp., illus. Paper covers. $12.00.
Contains new information regarding swordmakers of the Philadelphia area.

Swords and Blades of the American Revolution, by George C. Neumann, Rebel Publishing Co., Inc., Texarkana, TX, 1991. 288 pp., illus. $35.95.
The encyclopedia of bladed weapons—swords, bayonets, spontoons, halberds, pikes, knives, daggers, axes—used by both sides, on land and sea, in America's struggle for independence.

Tomahawks Illustrated, by Robert Kuck, Robert Kuck, New Knoxville, OH, 1977. 112 pp., illus. Paper covers. $5.95.
A pictorial record to provide a reference in selecting and evaluating tomahawks.

The Working Folding Knife, by Steven Dick, Stoeger Publishing Co., Wayne, NJ, 1998. 280 pp., illus. Paper covers. $21.95
From the classic American Barlow to exotic folders like the spanish Navaja this book has it all.

GENERAL

Advanced Muzzleloader's Guide, by Toby Bridges, Stoeger Publishing Co., So. Hackensack, NJ, 1985. 256 pp., illus. Paper covers. $14.95.
The complete guide to muzzle-loading rifles, pistols and shotguns—flintlock and percussion.

Aids to Musketry for Officers & NCOs, by Capt. B.J. Friend, Excalibur Publications, Latham, NY, 1996. 40 pp., illus. Paper covers. $7.95.
A facsimile edition of a pre-WWI British manual filled with useful information for training the common soldier.

Air Gun Digest, 3rd Edition, by J.I. Galan, DBI Books, a division of Krause Publications, Iola, WI, 1995. 258 pp., illus. Paper covers. $19.95
Everything from A to Z on air gun history, trends and technology.

American Gunsmiths, by Frank M. Sellers, The Gun Room Press, Highland Park, NJ, 1983. 349 pp. $39.95.
A comprehensive listing of the American gun maker, patentee, gunsmith and entrepreneur.

American and Imported Arms, Ammunition and Shooting Accessories, Catalog No. 18 of the Shooter's Bible, Stoeger, Inc., reprinted by Fayette Arsenal, Fayetteville, NC, 1988. 142 pp., illus. Paper covers. $10.95.
A facsimile reprint of the 1932 Stoeger's Shooter's Bible.

America's Great Gunmakers, by Wayne van Zwoll, Stoeger Publishing Co., So. Hackensack, NJ, 1992. 288 pp., illus. Paper covers. $16.95.
This book traces in great detail the evolution of guns and ammunition in America and the men who formed the companies that produced them.

Armed and Female, by Paxton Quigley, E.P. Dutton, New York, NY, 1989. 237 pp., illus. $16.95.
The first complete book on one of the hottest subjects in the media today, the arming of the American woman.

THE ARMS LIBRARY

Arming the Glorious Cause: Weapons of the Second War for Independence, by James B. Whisker, Daniel D. Hartzler and Larry W. Yantz, R&R Books, Livonia, NY, 1998. 175 pp., illustrated. $45.00.

A photographic study of Confederate weapons.

Arms and Armour in Antiquity and the Middle Ages, by Charles Boutell, Stackpole Books, Mechanicsburg, PA, 1996. 352 pp., illus. $22.95.

Detailed descriptions of arms and armor, the development of tactics and the outcome of specific battles.

Arms & Armor in the Art Institute of Chicago, by Walter J. Karcheski, Jr., Bulfinch Press, Boston, MA, 1995. 128 pp., illus. $35.00.

Now, for the first time, the Art Institute of Chicago's arms and armor collection is presented in the visual delight of 103 color illustrations.

Arms for the Nation: Springfield Longarms, edited by David C. Clark, Scott A. Duff, Export, PA, 1994. 73 pp., illus. Paper covers. $9.95.

A brief history of the Springfield Armory and the arms made there.

Arsenal of Freedom, The Springfield Armory, 1890-1948: A Year-by-Year Account Drawn from Official Records, compiled and edited by Lt. Col, William S. Brophy, USAR Ret., Andrew Mowbray, Inc., Lincoln, RI, 1991. 400 pp., illus. Soft covers. $29.95.

A "must buy" for all students of American military weapons, equipment and accoutrements.

Assault Weapons, 4th Edition, The Gun Digest Book of, edited by Jack Lewis, DBI Books, a division of Krause Publications, Iola, WI. 256 pp. illus. Paper covers. $19.95.

An in-depth look at the history and uses of these arms.

The Belgian Rattlesnake: The Lewis Automatic Machine Gun, by William M. Easterly, Collector Grade Publications, Inc., Cobourg, Ont. Canada, 1998. 542 pp., illus. $79.95.

A social and technical biography of the Lewis automatic machine gun and its inventors.

The Big Bang: A History of Explosives, by G.I. Brown, Sutton Publishing, Herndon, VA, 1998. 240 pp., illustrated. $35.00.

The first scientific history of explosives from gunpowder to the nuclear bomb.

The Big Guns: Civil War Siege, Seacoast, and Naval Cannon, by Edwin Olmstead, Wayne E. Stark and Spencer C. Tucker, Museum Restoration Service, Bloomfield, Ontario, Canada, 1997. 360 pp., illus. $80.00.

This book is designed to identify and record the heavy guns available to both sides during the Civil War.

Blackpowder Loading Manual, 3rd Edition, by Sam Fadala, DBI Books, a division of Krause Publications, Iola, WI, 1995. 368 pp., illus. Paper covers. $20.95.

Revised and expanded edition of this landmark blackpowder loading book. Covers hundreds of loads for most of the popular blackpowder rifles, handguns and shotguns.

The Blackpowder Notebook, by Sam Fadala, Wolfe Publishing Co., Prescott, AZ, 1994. 212 pp., illus. $22.50.

For anyone interested in shooting muzzleloaders, this book will help improve scores and obtain accuracy and reliability.

Bolt Action Rifles, 3rd Edition, by Frank de Haas, DBI Books, a division of Krause Publications, Iola, WI, 1995. 528 pp., illus. Paper covers. $24.95.

A revised edition of the most definitive work on all major bolt-action rifle designs.

The Book of the Crossbow, by Sir Ralph Payne-Gallwey, Dover Publications, Mineola, NY, 1996. 416 pp., illus. Paper covers. $14.95.

Unabridged republication of the scarce 1907 London edition of the book on one of the most devastating hand weapons of the Middle Ages.

Bows and Arrows of the Native Americans, by Jim Hamm, Lyons & Burford Publishers, New York, NY, 1991. 156 pp., illus. $19.95.

A complete step-by-step guide to wooden bows, sinew-backed bows, composite bows, strings, arrows and quivers.

Bowhunter's Digest, 3rd Edition, by Chuck Adams, DBI Books, a division of Krause Publications, Iola, WI, 1990. 288 pp., illus. Soft covers. $17.95.

All-new edition covers all the necessary equipment and how to use it, plus the fine points on how to improve your skill.

British Small Arms of World War 2, by Ian D. Skennerton, I.D.S.A. Books, Piqua, OH, 1988. 110 pp., 37 illus. $25.00.

British Sniper, by Ian Skennerton, I.D.S.A. Books, Piqua, OH, 1983. 26 pp., over 375 illus. $40.00.

"Carbine," the Story of David Marshall Williams, by Ross E. Beard, Jr. Phillips Publications, Williamstown, NJ, 1999. 225 pp., illus. $29.95.

The story of the firearms genius, David Marshall "Carbine" Williams. From prison to the pinnacles of fame, the tale of this North Carolinian is inspiring. The author details many of Williams' firearms inventions and developments.

Cartridges of the World, 8th Edition, by Frank Barnes, edited by M. L. McPherson, DBI Books, a division of Krause Publications, Iola, WI, 1997. 480 pp., illus. Paper covers. $24.95.

Completely revised edition of the general purpose reference work for which collectors, police, scientists and laymen reach first for answers to cartridge identification questions.

Combat Handgunnery, 4th Edition, The Gun Digest Book of, by Chuck Taylor, DBI Books, a division of Krause Publications, Iola, WI, 1997. 256 pp., illus. Paper covers. $18.95.

This edition looks at real world combat handgunnery from three different perspectives—military, police and civilian.

The Complete Blackpowder Handbook, 3rd Edition, by Sam Fadala, DBI Books, a division of Krause Publications, Iola, WI, 1997. 400 pp., illus. Paper covers. $21.95.

Expanded and completely rewritten edition of the definitive book on the subject of blackpowder.

The Complete Guide to Game Care and Cookery, 3rd Edition, by Sam Fadala, DBI Books, a division of Krause Publications, Iola, WI, 1994. 320 pp., illus. Paper covers. $18.95.

Over 500 photos illustrating the care of wild game in the field and at home with a separate recipe section providing over 400 tested recipes.

Complete Guide to Guns & Shooting, by John Malloy, DBI Books, a division of Krause Publications, Iola, WI, 1995. 256 pp., illus. Paper covers. $18.95.

What every shooter and gun owner should know about firearms, ammunition, shooting techniques, safety, collecting and much more.

Cowboy Action Shooting, by Charly Gullett, Wolfe Publishing Co., Prescott, AZ, 1995. 400 pp., illus. Paper covers. $24.50.

The fast growing of the shooting sports is comprehensively covered in this text—the guns, loads, tactics and the fun and flavor of this Old West era competition.

Crossbows, edited by Roger Combs, DBI Books, a division of Krause Publications, Iola, WI, 1986. 192 pp., illus. Paper covers. $15.95.

Complete, up-to-date coverage of the hottest bow going—and the most controversial.

Dead On, by Tony Noblitt and Warren Gabrilska, Paladin Press, Boulder, CO, 1998. 176 pp., illustrated. Paper covers. $20.00

The long-range marksman's guide to extreme accuracy.

Death from Above: The German FG42 Paratrooper Rifle, by Thomas B. Dugelby and R. Blake Stevens, Collector Grade Publications, Toronto, Canada, 1990. 147 pp., illus. $39.95.

The first comprehensive study of all seven models of the FG42.

The Emma Gees, by H.W. McBride, Lancer Militaria, Mt. Ida, AR, 1998. 220 pp., illustrated. Paper cover. $19.95

Originally published in 1918, this was McBride's first book about his service with the machine gun section in World War One.

Encyclopedia of Modern Firearms, Vol. 1, compiled and publ. by Bob Brownell, Montezuma, IA, 1959. 1057 pp. plus index, illus. $60.00. Dist. By Bob Brownell, Montezuma, IA 50171.

Massive accumulation of basic information of nearly all modern arms pertaining to "parts and assembly." Replete with arms photographs, exploded drawings, manufacturers' lists of parts, etc.

Exploded Handgun Drawings, The Gun Digest Book of, edited by Harold A. Murtz, DBI Books, a division of Krause Publications, Iola, WI, 1992. 512 pp., illus. Paper covers. $20.95.

Exploded or isometric drawings for 494 of the most popular handguns.

Exploded Long Gun Drawings, The Gun Digest Book of, edited by Harold A. Murtz, DBI Books, a division of Krause Publications, Iola, WI, 512 pp., illus. Paper covers. $20.95.

Containing almost 500 rifle and shotgun exploded drawings.

Firearms Engraving as Decorative Art, by Dr. Fredric A. Harris, Barbara R. Harris, Seattle, WA, 1989. 172 pp., illus. $115.00.

The origin of American firearms engraving motifs in the decorative art of the Middle East. Illustrated with magnificent color photographs.

Fireworks: A Gunsight Anthology, by Jeff Cooper, Paladin Press, Boulder, CO, 1998. 192 pp., illus. Paper cover. $25.00

A collection of wild, hilarious, shocking and always meaningful tales from the remarkable life of an American firearms legend.

Firing Back, by Clayton E. Cramer, Krause Publications, Iola, WI, 1995. 208 pp., Paper covers. $9.95.

Proposes answers and arguments to counter the popular anti-gun sentiments.

Frank Pachmayr: The Story of America's Master Gunsmith and his Guns, by John Lachuk, Safari Press, Huntington Beach, CA, 1996. 254 pp., illus. First edition, limited, signed and slipcased. $85.00; Second printing trade edition. $50.00.

The colorful and historically significant biography of Frank A. Pachmayr, America's own gunsmith emeritus.

The Frontier Rifleman, by H.B. LaCrosse Jr., Pioneer Press, Union City, TN, 1989. 183 pp., illus. Soft covers. $14.95.

The Frontier rifleman's clothing and equipment during the era of the American Revolution, 1760-1800.

The Gatling Gun: 19th Century Machine Gun to 21st Century Vulcan, by Joseph Berk, Paladin Press, Boulder, CO, 1991. 136 pp., illus. $29.95.

Here is the fascinating on-going story of a truly timeless weapon, from its beginnings during the Civil War to its current role as a state-of-the-art modern combat system.

German Artillery of World War Two, by Ian V. Hogg, Stackpole Books, Mechanicsburg, PA, 1997. 304 pp., illus. $44.95.

Complete details of German artillery use in WWII.

Good Guns Again, by Stephen Bodio, Wilderness Adventures Press, Bozeman, MT, 1994. 183 pp., illus. $29.00.

A celebration of fine sporting arms.

Grand Old Lady of No Man's Land: The Vickers Machine Gun, by Dolf L. Goldsmith, Collector Grade Publications, Cobourg, Canada, 1994. 600 pp., illus. $79.95.

Goldsmith brings his years of experience as a U.S. Army armourer, machine gun collector and shooter to bear on the Vickers, in a book sure to become a classic in its field.

Great Shooters of the World, by Sam Fadala, Stoeger Publishing Co., So. Hackensack, NJ, 1991. 288 pp., illus. Paper covers. $18.95.

This book offers gun enthusiasts an overview of the men and women who have forged the history of firearms over the past 150 years.

The Grenade Recognition Manual, Volume 1, U.S. Grenades & Accessories, by Darryl W. Lynn, Service Publications, Ottawa, Canada, 1998. 112 pp., illus. Paper covers. $29.95.

This new book examines the hand grenades of the United States beginning with the hand grenades of the U.S. Civil War and continues through to the present.

THE ARMS LIBRARY

Gun Digest Treasury, 7th Edition, edited by Harold A. Murtz, DBI Books, a division of Krause Publications, Iola, WI, 1994. 320 pp., illus. Paper covers. $17.95.
A collection of some of the most interesting articles which have appeared in Gun Digest over its first 45 years.

Gun Digest 2000, 54th Edition, edited by Ken Warner, DBI Books a division of Krause Publications, Iola, WI, 1999. 544 pp., illustrated. Paper covers. $24.95.
This all new 54th edition continues the editorial excellence, quality, content and comprehensive cataloguing that firearms enthusiasts have come to know and expect. The most read gun book in the world for the last half century.

Gun Engraving, by C. Austyn, Safari Press Publication, Huntington Beach, CA, 1998. 128 pp., plus 24 pages of color photos. $50.00.
A well-illustrated book on fine English and European gun engravers. Includes a fantastic pictorial section that lists types of engravings and prices.

Gun Notes, Volume 2, by Elmer Keith, Safari Press, Huntington Beach, CA, 1997. 292 pp., illus. Limited 1st edition, numbered and signed by Keith's son. Slipcased. $75.00. Second edition. $35.00.
Covers articles from Keith's monthly column in "Guns & Ammo" magazine during the period from 1971 through Keith's passing in 1982.

Gunshot Injuries: How They Are Inflicted, Their Complications and Treatment, by Col. Louis A. La Garde, 2nd revised edition, Lancer Militaria, Mt. Ida, AR, 1991. 480 pp., illus. $34.95.
A classic work which was the standard textbook on the subject at the time of WWI.

Gun Talk, edited by Dave Moreton, Winchester Press, Piscataway, NJ, 1973. 256 pp., illus. $9.95.
A treasury of original writing by the top gun writers and editors in America. Practical advice about every aspect of the shooting sports.

The Gun That Made the Twenties Roar, by Wm. J. Helmer, rev. and enlarged by George C. Nonte, Jr., The Gun Room Press, Highland Park, NJ, 1977. Over 300 pp., illus. $24.95.
Historical account of John T. Thompson and his invention, the infamous "Tommy Gun."

Gun Trader's Guide, 22nd Edition, published by Stoeger Publishing Co., Wayne, NJ, 1999. 592 pp., illus. Paper covers. $23.95.
Complete specifications and current prices for used guns. Prices of over 5,000 handguns, rifles and shotguns both foreign and domestic.

Gun Writers of Yesteryear, compiled by James Foral, Wolfe Publishing Co., Prescott, AZ, 1993. 449 pp. $35.00.
Here, from the pre-American rifleman days of 1898-1920, are collected some 80 articles by 34 writers from eight magazines.

The Gunfighter, Man or Myth? by Joseph G. Rosa, Oklahoma Press, Norman, OK, 1969. 229 pp., illus. (including weapons). Paper covers. $14.95.
A well-documented work on gunfights and gunfighters of the West and elsewhere. Great treat for all gunfighter buffs.

Gunfitting: The Quest for Perfection, by Michael Yardley, Safari Press, Huntington Beach, CA, 1995. 128 pp., illus. $24.95.
The author, a very experienced shooting instructor, examines gun stocks and gunfitting in depth.

Guns Illustrated 2000, 32nd Edition, edited by Harold A. Murtz, DBI Books a division of Krause Publications, Iola, WI, 1999. 352 pp., illustrated. Paper covers. $22.95.
Highly informative, technical articles on a wide range of shooting topics by some of the top writers in the industry. A catalog section lists more than 3,000 firearms currently manufactured in or imported to the U.S.

Guns in Combat, edited by Chris Bishop, Book Sales Inc., Edison, NJ, 1998. 192 pp., illustrated. $19.95.
Here the most used and important small arms - pistols, rifles, machine guns, and submachine guns - are each illustrated by a large, full-color cutaway, annotated artwork showing the gun's working parts to full effect. Along with a detailed and accurate text.

Guns of the Wild West, by George Markham, Sterling Publishing Co., New York, NY, 1993. 160 pp., illus. Paper covers. $19.95.
Firearms of the American Frontier, 1849-1917.

Guns, Who Should Have Them, edited by David B. Kopel, Prometheus Books, Amherst, NY, 1995. 475 pp., illustrated. $26.95.
Topics include the increasing rates of gun ownership and use; arms and women; background checks and waiting periods; the 2nd amendment "Assault Weapons"; and children and guns.

Guns & Shooting: A Selected Bibliography, by Ray Riling, Ray Riling Arms Books Co., Phila., PA, 1982. 434 pp., illus. Limited, numbered edition. $75.
A limited edition of this superb bibliographical work, the only modern listing of books devoted to guns and shooting.

Guns, Bullets, and Gunfighters, by Jim Cirillo, Paladin Press, Boulder, CO, 1996. 119 pp., illus. Paper covers. $15.00.
Lessons and tales from a modern-day gunfighter.

Guns, Loads, and Hunting Tips, by Bob Hagel, Wolfe Publishing Co., Prescott, AZ, 1986. 509 pp., illus. $19.95.
A large hardcover book packed with shooting, hunting and handloading wisdom.

Handgun Digest, 3rd Edition, edited by Chris Christian, DBI Books, a division of Krause Publications, Iola, WI, 1995. 256 pp., illus. Paper covers. $18.95.
Full coverage of all aspects of handguns and handgunning from a highly readable and knowledgeable author.

HK Assault Rifle Systems, by Duncan Long, Paladin Press, Boulder, CO, 1995. 110 pp., illus. Paper covers. $27.95.
The little known history behind this fascinating family of weapons tracing its beginnings from the ashes of World War Two to the present time.

I Remember Skeeter, compiled by Sally Jim Skelton, Wolfe Publishing Co., Prescott, AZ, 1998. 401 pp., illus. Paper covers. $19.95.

A collection of some of the beloved storyteller's famous works interspersed with anecdotes and tales from the people who knew best.

Jim Dougherty's Guide to Bowhunting Deer, by Jim Dougherty, DBI Books, a division of Krause Publications, Iola, WI, 1992. 256 pp., illus. Paper covers. $17.95.
Dougherty sets down some important guidelines for bowhunting and bowhunting equipment.

Kill or Get Killed, by Col. Rex Applegate, Paladin Press, Boulder, CO, 1996. 400 pp., illus. $29.95.
The best and longest-selling book on close combat in history.

The Long-Range War: Sniping in Vietnam, by Peter R. Senich, Paladin Press, Boulder, CO, 1994. 280 pp., illus. $39.95.
The most complete report on Vietnam-era sniping ever documented.

Machine Guns of World War I, by Robert Bruce, Windrow & Greene, London, 1997. 128 pp., illustrated. $39.95.
Seven classic automatic weapons of W.W.I. are illustrated in some 250 color photographs. Detailed sequences show them in close-up during field stripping and handling.

Manual for H&R Reising Submachine Gun and Semi-Auto Rifle, edited by George P. Dillman, Desert Publications, El Dorado, AZ, 1994. 81 pp., illus. Paper covers. $12.95.
A reprint of the Harrington & Richardson 1943 factory manual and the rare military manual on the H&R submachine gun and semi-auto rifle.

The Manufacture of Gunflints, by Sydney B.J. Skertchly, facsimile reprint with new introduction by Seymour de Lotbiniere, Museum Restoration Service, Ontario, Canada, 1984. 90 pp., illus. $24.50.
Limited edition reprinting of the very scarce London edition of 1879.

Master Tips, by J. Winokur, Potshot Press, Pacific Palisades, CA, 1985. 96 pp., illus. Paper covers. $11.95.
Basics of practical shooting.

The Military and Police Sniper, by Mike R. Lau, Precision Shooting, Inc., Manchester, CT, 1998. 352 pp., illustrated. Paper covers. $39.95.
Advanced precision shooting for combat and law enforcement.

Military Rifle & Machine Gun Cartridges, by Jean Huon, Paladin Press, Boulder, CO, 1990. 392 pp., illus. $34.95.
Describes the primary types of military cartridges and their principal loadings, as well as their characteristics, origin and use.

Military Small Arms of the 20th Century, 6th Edition, by Ian V. Hogg, DBI Books, a division of Krause Publications, Iola, WI, 1991. 352 pp., illus. Paper covers. $21.95.
Fully revised and updated edition of the standard reference in its field.

Modern Custom Guns, Walnut, Steel, and Uncommon Artistry, by Tom Turpin, Krause Publications, Iola, WI, 1997. 206 pp., illus. $49.95.
From exquisite engraving to breathtaking exotic woods, the mystique of today's custom guns is expertly detailed in word and awe-inspiring color photos of rifles, shotguns and handguns.

Modern Guns Identification & Values, 13th Edition, by Russell & Steve Quertermous, Collector Books, Paducah, KY, 1999. 516 pp., illus. Paper covers. $12.95.
A standard reference for over 20 years. Over 1,800 illustrations of over 2,500 models with their current values.

Modern Law Enforcement Weapons & Tactics, 2nd Edition, by Tom Ferguson, DBI Books, a division of Krause Publications, Iola, WI, 1991. 256 pp., illus. Paper covers. $18.95.
An in-depth look at the weapons and equipment used by law enforcement agencies of today.

Modern Sporting Guns, by Christopher Austyn, Safari Press, Huntington Beach, CA, 1994. 128 pp., illus. $40.00.
A discussion of the "best" English guns; round action, over-and-under, boxlocks, hammer guns, bolt action and double rifles as well as accessories.

The More Complete Cannoneer, by M.C. Switlik, Museum & Collectors Specialties Co., Monroe, MI, 1990. 199 pp., illus. $19.95.
Compiled agreeably to the regulations for the U.S. War Department, 1861, and containing current observations on the use of antique cannons.

The MP-40 Machine Gun, Desert Publications, El Dorado, AZ, 1995. 32 pp., illus. Paper covers. $11.95.
A reprint of the hard-to-find operating and maintenance manual for one of the most famous machine guns of World War II.

Naval Percussion Locks and Primers, by Lt. J. A. Dahlgren, Museum Restoration Service, Bloomfield, Canada, 1996. 140 pp., illus. $35.00
First published as an Ordnance Memoranda in 1853, this is the finest existing study of percussion locks and primers origin and development.

L.D. Nimschke Firearms Engraver, by R.L. Wilson, R&R Books, Livonia, NY, 1992. 108 pp., illus. $100.00.
The personal work record of one of the 19th century America's foremost engravers. Augmented by a comprehensive text, photographs of deluxe-engraved firearms, and detailed indexes.

1999 Standard Catalog of Firearms, the Collector's Price & Reference Guide, 9th Edition, by Ned Schwing, Krause Publications, Iola, WI, 1999. 1,248 pp., illus. Paper covers. $29.95.
40,000 updated gun prices with more than 4,600 photos. Easy to use master index listing every firearm model.

The Official Soviet AKM Manual, translated by Maj. James F. Gebhardt (Ret.), Paladin Press, Boulder, CO, 1999. 120 pp., illustrated. Paper covers. $16.00.
This official military manual, available in English for the first time, was originally published by the Soviet Ministry of Defence.
Covers the history, function, maintenance, assembly and disassembly, etc. of the 7.62mm AKM assault rifle.

The One-Round War: U.S.M.C. Scout-Snipers in Vietnam, by Peter Senich, Paladin Press, Boulder, CO, 1996. 384 pp., illus. $59.95.
Sniping in Vietnam focusing specifically on the Marine Corps program.

OSS Weapons, by Dr. John W. Brunner, Phillips Publications, Williamstown, NJ, 1996. 224 pp., illus. $44.95.

The most definitive book ever written on the weapons and equipment used by the supersecret warriors of the Office of Strategic Services.

Pin Shooting: A Complete Guide, by Mitchell A. Ota, Wolfe Publishing Co., Prescott, AZ, 1992. 145 pp., illus. Paper covers. $14.95.

Traces the sport from its humble origins to today's thoroughly enjoyable social event, including the mammoth eight-day Second Chance Pin Shoot in Michigan.

Powder and Ball Small Arms, by Martin Pegler, Windrow & Greene Publishing, London, 1998. 128 pp., illustrated with 200 color photos. $39.95.

Part of the new "Live Firing Classic Weapons" series. Full-color photos of experienced shooters dressed in authentic costumes handling, loading and firing historic weapons.

E.C. Prudhomme, Master Gun Engraver, A Retrospective Exhibition: 1946-1973, intro. by John T. Amber, The R. W. Norton Art Gallery, Shreveport, LA, 1973. 32 pp., illus. Paper covers. $9.95.

Examples of master gun engravings by Jack Prudhomme.

A Rifleman Went to War, by H. W. McBride, Lancer Militaria, Mt. Ida, AR, 1987. 398 pp., illus. $24.95.

The classic account of practical marksmanship on the battlefields of World War I.

Sharpshooting for Sport and War, by W.W. Greener, Wolfe Publishing Co., Prescott, AZ, 1995. 192 pp., illus. $30.00.

This classic reprint explores the *first* expanding bullet; service rifles; shooting positions; trajectories; recoil; external ballistics; and other valuable information.

The Shooter's Bible 2000, No. 91, edited by William S. Jarrett, Stoeger Publishing Co., Wayne, NJ, 1999. 576 pp., illustrated. Paper covers. $23.95.

Over 3,000 firearms currently offered by major American and foreign gunmakers. Represented are handguns, rifles, shotguns and black powder arms with complete specifications and retail prices.

Shooting, by J.H. FitzGerald, Wolfe Publishing Co., Prescott, AZ, 1993. 421 pp., illus. $29.00.

A classic book and reference for anyone interested in pistol and revolver shooting.

Shooting Sixguns of the Old West, by Mike Venturino, MLV Enterprises, Livingston, MT, 1997. 221 pp., illus. Paper covers. $26.50.

A comprehensive look at the guns of the early West: Colts, Smith & Wesson and Remingtons, plus blackpowder and reloading specs.

Sniper: The World of Combat Sniping, by Adrian Gilbert, St Martin's Press, NY, 1995. 290 pp., illus. $24.95.

The skills, the weapons and the experiences.

Sniper Training, FM 23-10, Reprint of the U.S. Army field manual of August, 1994, Paladin Press, Boulder, CO, 1995. 352pp., illus. Paper covers. $25.00

The most up-to-date U.S. military sniping information and doctrine.

Sniping in France, by Major H. Hesketh-Prichard, Lancer Militaria, Mt. Ida, AR, 1993. 224 pp., illus. $24.95.

The author was a well-known British adventurer and big game hunter. He was called upon in the early days of "The Great War" to develop a program to offset an initial German advantage in sniping. How the British forces came to overcome this advantage.

Special Warfare: Special Weapons, by Kevin Dockery, Emperor's Press, Chicago, IL, 1997. 192 pp., illus. $29.95.

The arms and equipment of the UDT and SEALS from 1943 to the present.

Sporting Collectibles, by Dr. Stephen R. Irwin, Stoeger Publishing Co., Wayne, NJ, 1997. 256 pp., illus. Paper covers. $19.95.

A must book for serious collectors and admirers of sporting collectibles.

The Sporting Craftsmen: A Complete Guide to Contemporary Makers of Custom-Built Sporting Equipment, by Art Carter, Countrysport Press, Traverse City, MI, 1994. 240 pp., illus. $49.50.

Profiles leading makers of centerfire rifles; muzzleloading rifles; bamboo fly rods; fly reels; flies; waterfowl calls; decoys; handmade knives; and traditional longbows and recurves.

Sporting Rifle Takedown & Reassembly Guide, 2nd Edition, by J.B. Wood, DBI Books, a division of Krause Publications, Iola, WI, 1997. 480 pp., illus. $19.95.

An updated edition of the reference guide for anyone who wants to properly care for their sporting rifle. (Available September 1997)

The Street Smart Gun Book, by John Farnam, Police Bookshelf, Concord, NH, 1986. 45 pp., illus. Paper covers. $11.95.

Weapon selection, defensive shooting techniques, and gunfight-winning tactics from one of the world's leading authorities.

Stress Fire, Vol. 1: Stress Fighting for Police, by Massad Ayoob, Police Bookshelf, Concord, NH, 1984. 149 pp., illus. Paper covers. $9.95.

Gunfighting for police, advanced tactics and techniques.

Survival Guns, by Mel Tappan, Desert Publications, El Dorado, AZ, 1993. 456 pp., illus. Paper covers. $21.95.

Discusses in a frank and forthright manner which handguns, rifles and shotguns to buy for personal defense and securing food, and the ones to avoid.

The Tactical Advantage, by Gabriel Suarez, Paladin Press, Boulder, CO, 1998. 216 pp., illustrated. Paper covers. $20.00.

Learn combat tactics that have been tested in the world's toughest schools.

Tactical Marksman, by Dave M. Lauch, Paladin Press, Boulder, CO, 1996. 165 pp., illus. Paper covers. $35.00.

A complete training manual for police and practical shooters.

Thompson Guns 1921-1945, Anubis Press, Houston, TX, 1980. 215 pp., illus. Paper covers. $15.95.

Facsimile reprinting of five complete manuals on the Thompson submachine gun.

Trailriders Guide to Cowboy Action Shooting, by James W. Barnard, Pioneer Press, Union City, TN, 1998. 134 pp., plus 91 photos, drawings and charts. Paper covers. $24.95.

Covers the complete spectrum of this shooting discipline, from how to dress to authentic leather goods, which guns are legal, calibers, loads and ballistics.

The Ultimate Sniper, by Major John L. Plaster, Paladin Press, Boulder, CO, 1994. 464 pp., illus. Paper covers. $39.95.

An advanced training manual for military and police snipers.

U.S. Marine Corp Rifle and Pistol Marksmanship, 1935, reprinting of a government publication, Lancer Militaria, Mt. Ida, AR, 1991. 99 pp., illus. Paper covers. $11.95.

The old corps method of precision shooting.

U.S. Marine Corps Scout/Sniper Training Manual, Lancer Militaria, Mt. Ida, AR, 1989. Soft covers. $14.95.

Reprint of the original sniper training manual used by the Marksmanship Training Unit of the Marine Corps Development and Education Command in Quantico, Virginia.

U.S. Marine Corps Scout-Sniper, World War II and Korea, by Peter R. Senich, Paladin Press, Boulder, CO, 1994. 236 pp., illus. $39.95.

The most thorough and accurate account ever printed on the training, equipment and combat experiences of the U.S. Marine Corps Scout-Snipers.

U.S. Marine Corps Sniping, Lancer Militaria, Mt. Ida, AR, 1989. Irregular pagination. Soft covers. $14.95.

A reprint of the official Marine Corps FMFM1-3B.

Unrepentant Sinner, by Charles Askins, Tejano Publications, San Antonio, TX, 1985. 322 pp., illus. Soft covers. $19.95.

The autobiography of Colonel Charles Askins.

Weapons of the Waffen-SS, by Bruce Quarrie, Sterling Publishing Co., Inc., 1991. 168 pp., illus. $24.95.

An in-depth look at the weapons that made Hitler's Waffen-SS the fearsome fighting machine it was.

Weatherby: The Man, The Gun, The Legend, by Grits and Tom Gresham, Cane River Publishing Co., Natchitoches, LA, 1992. 290 pp., illus. $24.95.

A fascinating look at the life of the man who changed the course of firearms development in America.

The Winchester Era, by David Madis, Art & Reference House, Brownsville, TX, 1984. 100 pp., illus. $14.95.

Story of the Winchester company, management, employees, etc.

Winchester Repeating Arms Company by Herbert Houze, Krause Publications, Iola, WI. 512 pp., illus. $50.00.

With British Snipers to the Reich, by Capt. C. Shore, Lander Militaria, Mt. Ida, AR, 1988. 420 pp., illus. $24.95.

One of the greatest books ever written on the art of combat sniping.

The World's Sniping Rifles, by Ian V. Hogg, Paladin Press, Boulder, CO, 1998. 144 pp., illustrated. Paper covers. $22.95.

A detailed manual with descriptions and illustrations of more than 50 high-precision rifles from 14 countries and a complete analysis of sights and systems.

You Can't Miss, by John Shaw and Michael Bane, John Shaw, Memphis, TN, 1983. 152 pp., illus. Paper covers. $12.95.

The secrets of a successful combat shooter; how to better defensive shooting skills.

GUNSMITHING

Advanced Rebarreling of the Sporting Rifle, by Willis H. Fowler, Jr., Willis H. Fowler, Jr., Anchorage, AK, 1994. 127 pp., illus. Paper covers. $32.50.

A manual outlining a superior method of fitting barrels and doing chamber work on the sporting rifle.

The Art of Engraving, by James B. Meek, F. Brownell & Son, Montezuma, IA, 1973. 196 pp., illus. $33.95.

A complete, authoritative, imaginative and detailed study in training for gun engraving. The first book of its kind—and a great one.

Artistry in Arms, The R. W. Norton Gallery, Shreveport, LA, 1970. 42 pp., illus. Paper covers. $9.95.

The art of gunsmithing and engraving.

Barrels & Actions, by Harold Hoffman, H&P Publishers, San Angelo, TX, 1990. 309 pp., illus. Sprial bound. $27.95.

A manual on barrel making.

Black Powder Hobby Gunsmithing, by Sam Fadala and Dale Storey, DBI Books, a division of Krause Publications, Iola, WI., 1994. 256 pp., illus. Paper covers. $18.95.

A how-to guide for gunsmithing blackpowder pistols, rifles and shotguns from two men at the top of their respective fields.

Checkering and Carving of Gun Stocks, by Monte Kennedy, Stackpole Books, Harrisburg, PA, 1962. 175 pp., illus. $39.95.

Revised, enlarged cloth-bound edition of a much sought-after, dependable work.

The Complete Metal Finishing Book, by Harold Hoffman, H&P Publishers, San Angelo, TX, 1992. 364 pp., illus. Paper covers. $29.95.

Instructions for the different metal finishing operations that the normal craftsman or shop will use. Primarily firearm related.

Custom Gunstock Carving, by Philip Eck, Stackpole Books, Mechanicsburg, PA, 1995. 232 pp., illus. $34.95.

Featuring a gallery of more than 100 full-size patterns for buttstocks, grips, accents and borders that carvers can use for their own projects.

Exploded Handgun Drawings, The Gun Digest Book of, edited by Harold A. Murtz, DBI Books, a division of Krause Publications, Iola, WI. 1992. 512 pp., illus. Paper covers. $20.95.
Exploded or isometric drawings for 494 of the most popular handguns.

Exploded Long Gun Drawings, The Gun Digest Book of, edited by Harold A. Murtz, DBI Books, a division of Krause Publications, Iola, WI. 512 pp., illus. Paper covers. $20.95.
Containing almost 500 rifle and shotgun exploded drawings. An invaluable aid to both professionals and hobbyists.

The Finishing of Gun Stocks, by Harold Hoffman, H&P Publishers, San Angelo, TX, 1994. 98 pp., illus. Paper covers. $17.95.
Covers different types of finishing methods and finishes.

Firearms Assembly/Disassembly, Part I: Automatic Pistols, Revised Edition, The Gun Digest Book of, by J.B. Wood, DBI Books, a division of Krause Publications, Iola, WI, 1990. 480 pp., illus. Paper covers. $19.95.
Covers 58 popular autoloading pistols plus nearly 200 variants of those models integrated into the text and completely cross-referenced in the index.

Firearms Assembly/Disassembly Part II: Revolvers, Revised Edition, The Gun Digest Book of, by J.B. Wood, DBI Books, a division of Krause Publications, Iola, WI, 1990. 480 pp., illus. Paper covers. $19.95.
Covers 49 popular revolvers plus 130 variants. The most comprehensive and professional presentation available to either hobbyist or gunsmith.

Firearms Assembly/Disassembly Part III: Rimfire Rifles, Revised Edition, The Gun Digest Book of, by J. B. Wood, DBI Books, a division of Krause Publications, Iola, WI., 1994. 480 pp., illus. Paper covers. $19.95.
Greatly expanded edition covering 65 popular rimfire rifles plus over 100 variants all completely cross-referenced in the index.

Firearms Assembly/Disassembly Part IV: Centerfire Rifles, Revised Edition, The Gun Digest Book of, by J.B. Wood, DBI Books, a division of Krause Publications, Iola, WI, 1991. 480 pp., illus. Paper covers. $19.95.
Covers 54 popular centerfire rifles plus 300 variants. The most comprehensive and professional presentation available to either hobbyist or gunsmith.

Firearms Assembly/Disassembly, Part V: Shotguns, Revised Edition, The Gun Digest Book of, by J.B. Wood, DBI Books, a division of Krause Publications, Iola, WI, 1992. 480 pp., illus. Paper covers. $19.95.
Covers 46 popular shotguns plus over 250 variants with step-by-step instructions on how to dismantle and reassemble each. The most comprehensive and professional presentation available to either hobbyist or gunsmith.

Firearms Assembly/Disassembly Part VI: Law Enforcement Weapons, The Gun Digest Book of, by J.B. Wood, DBI Books, a division of Krause Publications, Iola, WI, 1981. 288 pp., illus. Paper covers. $16.95.
Step-by-step instructions on how to completely dismantle and reassemble the most commonly used firearms found in law enforcement arsenals.

Firearms Assembly 3: The NRA Guide to Rifle and Shotguns, NRA Books, Wash., DC, 1980. 264 pp., illus. Paper covers. $13.95.
Text and illustrations explaining the takedown of 125 rifles and shotguns, domestic and foreign.

Firearms Assembly 4: The NRA Guide to Pistols and Revolvers, NRA Books, Wash., DC, 1980. 253 pp., illus. Paper covers. $13.95.
Text and illustrations explaining the takedown of 124 pistol and revolver models, domestic and foreign.

Firearms Bluing and Browning, By R.H. Angier, Stackpole Books, Harrisburg, PA. 151 pp., illus. $19.95.
A world master gunsmith reveals his secrets of building, repairing and renewing a gun, quite literally, lock, stock and barrel. A useful, concise text on chemical coloring methods for the gunsmith and mechanic.

Firearms Disassembly With Exploded Views, by John A. Karns & John E. Traister, Stoeger Publishing Co., S. Hackensack, NJ, 1995. 320 pp., illus. Paper covers. $19.95.
Provides the do's and don'ts of firearms disassembly. Enables owners and gunsmiths to disassemble firearms in a professional manner.

Guns and Gunmaking Tools of Southern Appalachia, by John Rice Irwin, Schiffer Publishing Ltd., 1983. 118 pp., illus. Paper covers. $9.95.
The story of the Kentucky rifle.

Gunsmithing Tips and Projects, a collection of the best articles from the *Handloader* and *Rifle* magazines, by various authors, Wolfe Publishing Co., Prescott, AZ, 1992. 443 pp., illus. Paper covers. $25.00.
Includes such subjects as shop, stocks, actions, tuning, triggers, barrels, customizing, etc.

Gunsmith Kinks, by F.R. (Bob) Brownell, F. Brownell & Son, Montezuma, IA, 1st ed., 1969. 496 pp., well illus. $18.95.
A widely useful accumulation of shop kinks, short cuts, techniques and pertinent comments by practicing gunsmiths from all over the world.

Gunsmith Kinks 2, by Bob Brownell, F. Brownell & Son, Publishers, Montezuma, IA, 1983. 496 pp., illus. $18.95.
A collection of gunsmithing knowledge, shop kinks, new and old techniques, shortcuts and general know-how straight from those who do them best—the gunsmiths.

Gunsmith Kinks 3, edited by Frank Brownell, Brownells Inc., Montezuma, IA, 1993. 504 pp., illus. $19.95.
Tricks, knacks and "kinks" by professional gunsmiths and gun tinkerers. Hundreds of valuable ideas are given in this volume.

Gunsmithing, by Roy F. Dunlap, Stackpole Books, Harrisburg, PA, 1990. 742 pp., illus. $34.95.
A manual of firearm design, construction, alteration and remodeling. For amateur and professional gunsmiths and users of modern firearms.

Gunsmithing at Home: Lock, Stock and Barrel, by John Traister, Stoeger Publishing Co., Wayne, NJ, 1997. 320 pp., illus. Paper covers. $19.95.
A Complete step-by-step fully illustrated guide to the art of gunsmithing.

Gunsmithing: Pistols & Revolvers, by Patrick Sweeney, DBI Books, a division of Krause Publications, Iola, WI, 1998. 352 pp., illus. Paper covers. $24.95.
Do-it-Yourself projects, diagnosis and repair for pistols and revolvers.

The Gunsmith's Manual, by J.P. Stelle and Wm. B. Harrison, The Gun Room Press, Highland Park, NJ, 1982. 376 pp., illus. $19.95.
For the gunsmith in all branches of the trade.

Handbook of Hard-to-Find Guns Parts Drawings, by LeeRoy Wisner, Brownells, Inc., Montezuma, IA, 1997. Unpaginated. Deluxe edition. $54.95.
Over 2901 dimensioned drawings covering 147 guns from 36 manufacturers. The most valuable tool you'll ever buy for your shop.

Home Gunsmithing the Colt Single Action Revolvers, by Loren W. Smith, Ray Riling Arms Books, Co., Phila., PA, 1995. 119 pp., illus. $24.95.
Affords the Colt Single Action owner detailed, pertinent information on the operating and servicing of this famous and historic handgun.

How to Convert Military Rifles, Williams Gun Sight Co., Davision, MI, new and enlarged seventh edition, 1997. 76 pp., illus. Paper covers. $13.95.
This latest edition updated the changes that have occured over the past thirty years. Tips, instructions and illustratons on how to convert popular military rifles as the Enfield, Mauser 96 nad SKS just to name a few are presented.

Mr. Single Shot's Gunsmithing-Idea-Book, by Frank de Haas, Mark de Haas, Orange City, IA, 1996. 168 pp., illus. Paper covers. $21.50.
Offers easy to follow, step-by-step instructions for a wide variety of gunsmithing procedures all reinforced by plenty of photos.

The NRA Gunsmithing Guide—Updated, by Ken Raynor and Brad Fenton, National Rifle Association, Wash., DC, 1984. 336 pp., illus. Paper covers. $19.95.
Material includes chapters and articles on all facets of the gunsmithing art.

Pistolsmithing, The Gun Digest Book of, by Jack Mitchell, DBI Books, a division of Krause Publications, Iola, WI, 1980. 256 pp., illus. Paper covers. $16.95.
An expert's guide to the operation of each of the handgun actions with all the major functions of pistolsmithing explained.

Pistolsmithing, by George C. Nonte, Jr., Stackpole Books, Harrisburg, PA, 1974. 560 pp., illus. $29.95.
A single source reference to handgun maintenance, repair, and modification at home, unequaled in value.

Practical Gunsmithing, by the editors of American Gunsmith, DBI Books, a division of Krause Publications, Iola, WI, 1996. 256 pp., illus. Paper covers. $19.95.
A book intended primarily for home gunsmithing, but one that will be extremely helpful to professionals as well.

Professional Stockmaking, by D. Wesbrook, Wolfe Publishing Co., Prescott AZ, 1995. 308 pp., illus. $54.00.
A step-by-step how-to with complete photographic support for every detail of the art of working wood into riflestocks.

Riflesmithing, The Gun Digest Book of, by Jack Mitchell, DBI Books, a division of Krause Publications, Iola, WI, 1982. 256 pp., illus. Paper covers. $16.95.
The art and science of rifle gunsmithing. Covers tools, techniques, designs, finishing wood and metal, custom alterations.

Shotgun Gunsmithing, The Gun Digest Book of, by Ralph Walker, DBI Books, a division of Krause Publications, Iola, WI, 1983. 256 pp., illus. Paper covers. $16.95.
The principles and practices of repairing, individualizing and accurizing modern shotguns by one of the world's premier shotgun gunsmiths.

Sporting Rifle Take Down & reassembly Guide, 2nd Edition, by J.B. Wood, Krause Publications, Iola, WI, 1997. 480 pp., illus. Paper covers. $19.95.
Hunters and shooting enthusiasts must have this reference featuring 52 of the most popular and widely used sporting centerfire and rimfire rifles.

The Story of Pope's Barrels, by Ray M. Smith, R&R Books, Livonia, NY, 1993. 203 pp., illus. $39.00.
A reissue of a 1960 book whose author knew Pope personally. It will be of special interest to Schuetzen rifle fans, since Pope's greatest days were at the height of the Schuetzen-era before WWI.

Survival Gunsmithing, by J.B. Wood, Desert Publications, Cornville, AZ, 1986. 92 pp., illus. Paper covers. $11.95.
A guide to repair and maintenance of the most popular rifles, shotguns and handguns.

The Tactical 1911, by Dave Lauck, Paladin Press, Boulder, CO, 1998. 137 pp., illus. Paper covers. $20.00.
Here is the only book you will ever need to teach you how to select, modify, employ and maintain your Colt.

The Trade Rifle Sketchbook, by Charles E. Hanson, The Fur Press, Chadron, NE, 1979. 48 pp., illus. Paper covers. $9.95.
Includes full-scale plans for 10 rifles made for Indian and mountain men; from 1790 to 1860, plus plans for building three pistols.

HANDGUNS

Advanced Master Handgunning, by Charles Stephens, Paladin Press, Boulder, CO., 1994. 72 pp., illus. Paper covers. $10.00.
Secrets and surefire techniques for winning handgun competitions.

The Ayoob Files: The Book, by Massad Ayoob, Police Bookshelf, Concord, NH, 1995. 223 pp., illus. Paper covers. $14.95.
The best of Massad Ayoob's acclaimed series in American Handgunner magazine.

Big Bore Sixguns, by John Taffin, Krause Publications, Iola, WI, 1997. 336 pp., illus. $39.95.
The author takes aim on the entire range of big bores from .357 Magnums to .500 Maximums, single actions and cap-and-ball sixguns to custom touches for big bores..

THE ARMS LIBRARY

Black Powder Hobby Gunsmithing, by Sam Fadala and Dale Storey, DBI Books, a division of Krause Publications, Iola, WI., 1994. 256 pp., illus. Paper covers. $18.95.
A how-to guide for gunsmithing blackpowder pistols, rifles and shotguns from two men at the top of their respective fields.

Browning Hi-Power Pistols, Desert Publications, Cornville, AZ, 1982. 20 pp., illus. Paper covers. $9.95.
Covers all facets of the various military and civilian models of the Browning Hi-Power pistol.

The Colt .45 Auto Pistol, compiled from U.S. War Dept. Technical Manuals, and reprinted by Desert Publications, Cornville, AZ, 1978. 80 pp., illus. Paper covers. $9.95.
Covers every facet of this famous pistol from mechanical training, manual of arms, disassembly, repair and replacement of parts.

Combat Handgunnery, 4th Edition, by Chuck Taylor, DBI Books, a division of Krause Publications, Iola, WI, 1997. 256 pp., illus. Paper covers. $18.95.
This all-new edition looks at real world combat handgunnery from three different perspectives—military, police and civilian. Available, October, 1996.

Combat Raceguns, by J.M. Ramos, Paladin Press, Boulder, CO, 1994. 168 pp., illus. Paper covers. $25.00.
Learn how to put together precision combat raceguns with the best compensators, frames, controls, sights and custom accessories.

Competitive Pistol Shooting, by Dr. Laslo Antal, A&C Black, London, England, 2nd edition, 1995. 176 pp., illus. Paper covers. $24.95.
Covers the basic principles followed in each case by a well illustrated and detailed discussion of the rules, technique, and training as well as the choice and maintenance of weapons.

The Complete Book of Combat Handgunning, by Chuck Taylor, Desert Publications, Cornville, AZ, 1982. 168 pp., illus. Paper covers. $20.00.
Covers virtually every aspect of combat handgunning.

Complete Guide to Compact Handguns, by Gene Gangarosa, Jr., Stoeger Publishing Co., Wayne, NJ, 1997. 228 pp., illus. Paper covers. $22.95.
Includes hundreds of compact firearms, along with text results conducted by the author.

Complete Guide to Service Handguns, by Gene Gangarosa, Jr., Stoeger Publishing Co., Wayne, NJ, 1998. 320 pp., illus. Paper covers. $22.95.
The author explores the revolvers and pistols that are used around the globe by military, law enforcement and civilians.

The Custom Government Model Pistol, by Layne Simpson, Wolfe Publishing Co., Prescott, AZ, 1994. 639 pp., illus. Paper covers. $24.50.
The book about one of the world's greatest firearms and the things pistolsmiths do to make it even greater.

The CZ-75 Family: The Ultimate Combat Handgun, by J.M. Ramos, Paladin Press, Boulder, CO, 1990. 100 pp., illus. Soft covers. $21.00.
An in-depth discussion of the early-and-late model CZ-75s, as well as the many newest additions to the Czech pistol family.

Encyclopedia of Pistols & Revolvers, by A.E. Hartnik, Knickerbocker Press, New York, NY, 1997. 272 pp., illus. $19.95.
A comprehensive encyclopedia specially written for collectors and owners of pistols and revolvers.

Experiments of a Handgunner, by Walter Roper, Wolfe Publishing Co., Prescott, AZ, 1989. 202 pp., illus. $37.00.
A limited edition reprint. A listing of experiments with functioning parts of handguns, with targets, stocks, rests, handloading, etc.

Exploded Handgun Drawings, The Gun Digest Book of, edited by Harold A. Murtz, DBI Books, a division of Krause Publications, Iola, WI. 1992. 512 pp., illus. Paper covers. $20.95.
Exploded or isometric drawings for 494 of the most popular handguns.

The Farnam Method of Defensive Handgunning, by John S. Farnam, DTI, Inc., Seattle, WA, 1994. 191 pp., illus. Paper covers. $13.95.
A book intended to not only educate the new shooter, but also to serve as a guide and textbook for his and his instructor's training courses.

Fast and Fancy Revolver Shooting, by Ed. McGivern, Anniversary Edition, Winchester Press, Piscataway, NJ, 1984. 484 pp., illus. $18.95.
A fascinating volume, packed with handgun lore and solid information by the acknowledged dean of revolver shooters.

Firearms Assembly/Disassembly, Part I: Automatic Pistols, Revised Edition, The Gun Digest Book of, by J.B. Wood, DBI Books, a division of Krause Publications, Iola, WI, 1990. 480 pp., illus. Soft covers. $19.95.
Covers 58 popular autoloading pistols plus nearly 200 variants of those models integrated into the text and completely cross-referenced in the index.

Firearms Assembly/Disassembly Part II: Revolvers, Revised Edition, The Gun Digest Book of, by J.B. Wood, DBI Books, a division of Krause Publications, Iola, WI, 1990. 480 pp., illus. Soft covers. $19.95.
Covers 49 popular revolvers plus 130 variants. The most comprehensive and professional presentation available to either hobbyist or gunsmith.

.45 ACP Super Guns, by J.M. Ramos, Paladin Press, Boulder, CO, 1991. 144 pp., illus. Paper covers. $24.00.
Modified .45 automatic pistols for competition, hunting and personal defense.

The .45, The Gun Digest Book of, by Dean A. Grennell, DBI Books, a division of Krause Publications, Iola, WI, 1989. 256 pp., illus. Paper covers. $17.95.
Definitive work on one of America's favorite calibers.

Glock: The New Wave in Combat Handguns, by Peter Alan Kasler, Paladin Press, Boulder, CO, 1993. 304 pp., illus. $25.00.
Kasler debunks the myths that surround what is the most innovative handgun to be introduced in some time.

Glock's Handguns, by Duncan Long, Desert Publications, El Dorado, AR, 1996. 180 pp., illus. Paper covers. $18.95.
An outstanding volume on one of the world's newest and most successful firearms of the century.

Hand Cannons: The World's Most Powerful Handguns, by Duncan Long, Paladin Press, Boulder, CO, 1995. 208 pp., illus. Paper covers. $20.00.
Long describes and evaluates each powerful gun according to their features.

Handguns 2000, 12th Edition, edited by Harold A. Murtz, DBI Books a division of Krause Publications, Iola, WI, 1999. 352 pp., illustrated. Paper covers. $22.95.
Top writers in the handgun industry give you a complete report on new handgun developments, testfire reports on the newest introductions and previews on what's ahead.

Handgun Digest, 3rd Edition, edited by Chris Christian, DBI Books, a division of Krause Publications, Iola, WI, 1995. 256 pp., illus. Paper covers. $18.95.
Full coverage of all aspects of handguns and handgunning from a highly readable and knowledgeable author.

Handgun Reloading, The Gun Digest Book of, by Dean A. Grennell and Wiley M. Clapp, DBI Books, a division of Krause Publications, Iola, WI, 1987. 256 pp., illus. Paper covers. $16.95.
Detailed discussions of all aspects of reloading for handguns, from basic to complex. New loading data.

Heckler & Koch's Handguns, by Duncan Long, Desert Publications, El Dorado, AR, 1996. 142 pp., illus. Paper covers. $18.95.
Traces the history and the evolution of H&K's pistols from the company's beginning at the end of WWII to the present.

Hidden in Plain Sight, by Trey Bloodworth & Mike Raley, Professional Press, Chapel Hill, NC, 1995. Paper covers. $13.00.
A practical guide to concealed handgun carry.

High Standard Automatic Pistols 1932-1950, by Charles E. Petty, The Gunroom Press, Highland Park, NJ, 1989. 124 pp., illus. $19.95.
A definitive source of information for the collector of High Standard arms.

The Hi-Standard Pistol Guide, by Burr Leyson, Duckett's Sporting Books, Tempe AZ, 1995. 128 pp., illus. Paper covers. $22.00.
Complete information on selection, care and repair, ammunition, parts, and accessories.

How to Become a Master Handgunner: The Mechanics of X-Count Shooting, by Charles Stephens, Paladin Press, Boulder, CO, 1993. 64 pp., illus. Paper covers. $12.00.
Offers a simple formula for success to the handgunner who strives to master the technique of shooting accurately.

Hunting for Handgunners, by Larry Kelly and J.D. Jones, DBI Books, a division of Krause Publications, Iola, WI, 1990. 256 pp., illus. Paper covers. $16.95.
Covers the entire spectrum of hunting with handguns in an amusing, easy-flowing manner that combines entertainment with solid information.

Illustrated Encyclopedia of Handguns, by A.B. Zhuk, Stackpole Books, Mechanicsburg, PA, 1994. 256 pp., illus. Cloth cover, $49.95; paper cover, $29.95.
Identifies more than 2,000 military and commercial pistols and revolvers with details of more than 100 popular handgun cartridges.

Instinct Combat Shooting, by Chuck Klein, Chuck Klein, The Goose Creek, IN, 1989. 49 pp., illus. Paper covers. $12.00.
Defensive handgunning for police.

Know Your Czechoslovakian Pistols, by R.J. Berger, Blacksmith Corp., Chino Valley, AZ, 1989. 96 pp., illus. Soft covers. $9.95.
A comprehensive reference which presents the fascinating story of Czech pistols.

Know Your 45 Auto Pistols—Models 1911 & A1, by E.J. Hoffschmidt, Blacksmith Corp., Southport, CT, 1974. 58 pp., illus. Paper covers. $9.95.
A concise history of the gun with a wide variety of types and copies.

Know Your Walther P38 Pistols, by E.J. Hoffschmidt, Blacksmith Corp., Southport, CT, 1974. 77 pp., illus. Paper covers. $9.95.
Covers the Walther models Armee, M.P., H.P., P.38—history and variations.

Know Your Walther PP & PPK Pistols, by E.J. Hoffschmidt, Blacksmith Corp., Southport, CT, 1975. 87 pp., illus. Paper covers. $9.95.
A concise history of the guns with a guide to the variety and types.

The Gordon Macquarrie Treasury, with introduction and commentary by Zack Taylor, Willow Creek Press, Minocqua, WI, 1998. $29.50.
This new treasury draws 20 of the very best of Macquarrie's best stories that appeared in his trilogy plus 19 newly discovered stories never before published in book form.

The Mauser Self-Loading Pistol, by Belford & Dunlap, Borden Publ. Co., Alhambra, CA. Over 200 pp., 300 illus., large format. $24.95.
The long-awaited book on the "Broom Handles," covering their inception in 1894 to the end of production. Complete and in detail: pocket pistols, Chinese and Spanish copies, etc.

Modern American Pistols and Revolvers, by A.C. Gould, Wolfe Publishing Co., Prescott, AZ, 1988. 222 pp., illus. $37.00.
A limited edition reprint. An account of the development of those arms as well as the manner of shooting them.

The Modern Technique of the Pistol, by Gregory Boyce Morrison, Gunsite Press, Paulden, AZ, 1991. 153 pp., illus. $45.00.
The theory of effective defensive use of modern handguns.

9mm Handguns, 2nd Edition, The Gun Digest Book of, edited by Steve Comus, DBI Books, a division of Krause Publications, Iola, WI, 1993. 256 pp., illus. Paper covers. $18.95.
Covers the 9mmP cartridge and the guns that have been made for it in greater depth than any other work available.

9mm Parabellum; The History & Developement of the World's 9mm Pistols & Ammunition, by Klaus-Peter Konig and Martin Hugo, Schiffer Publishing Ltd., Atglen, PA, 1993. 304 pp., illus. $39.95.
Detailed history of 9mm weapons from Belguim, Italy, Germany, Israel, France, USA, Czechoslovakia, Hungary, Poland, Brazil, Finland and Spain.

The Official 9mm Markarov Pistol Manual, translated into English by Major James Gebhardt, U.S. Army (Ret.), Desert Publications, El Dorado, AR, 1996. 84 pp., illus. Paper covers. $12.95.

The information found in this book will be of enormous benefit and interest to the owner or a prospective owner of one of these pistols.

The 100 Greatest Combat Pistols, by Timothy J. Mullin, Paladin Press, Boulder, CO, 1994. 409 pp., illus. Paper covers. $40.00.
  Hands-on tests and evaluations of handguns from around the world.

P-38 Automatic Pistol, by Gene Gangarosa, Jr., Stoeger Publishing Co., S. Hackensack, NJ, 1993. 272 pp., illus. Paper covers. $16.95
  This book traces the origins and development of the P-38, including the momentous political forces of the World War II era that caused its near demise and, later, its rebirth.

Pistol & Revolver Guide, 3rd Ed., by George C. Nonte, Stoeger Publ. Co., So. Hackensack, NJ, 1975. 224 pp., illus. Paper covers. $11.95.
  The standard reference work on military and sporting handguns.

Pistol Guide, by George C. Nonte, Jr., Stoeger Publishing Co., So. Hackensack, NJ, 1991. 280 pp., illus. Paper covers. $13.95.
  Covers handling, care and maintenance, pistol ammunition, how to buy a used gun, military pistols, air pistols and repairs.

Pistols of the World, 3rd Edition, by Ian Hogg and John Weeks, DBI Books, a division of Krause Publications, Iola, WI, 1992. 352 pp., illus. Paper covers. $20.95.
  A totally revised edtion of one of the leading studies of small arms.

Pistolsmithing, The Gun Digest Book of, by Jack Mitchell, DBI Books, a division of Krause Publications, Iola, WI, 1980, 288 pp., illus. Paper covers. $16.95.
  An expert's guide to the operation of each of the handgun actions with all the major functions of pistolsmithing explained.

Practical Shooting: Beyond Fundamentals, by Brian Enos, Zediker Publishing, Clifton, CO, 1997. 201 pp., illus. $27.95.
  This prize-winning master covers technique of combat shooting in all its aspects.

Report of Board on Tests of Revolvers and Automatic Pistols, From the Annual Report of the Chief of Ordnance, 1907. Reprinted by J.C. Tillinghast, Marlow, NH, 1969. 34 pp., 7 plates, paper covers. $9.95.
  A comparison of handguns, including Luger, Savage, Colt, Webley-Fosbery and other makes.

Revolver Guide, by George C. Nonte, Jr., Stoeger Publishing Co., So. Hackensack, NJ, 1991. 288 pp., illus. Paper covers. $10.95.
  A detailed and practical encyclopedia of the revolver, the most common handgun to be found.

Ruger Automatic Pistols and Single Action Revolvers, by Hugo A. Lueders, edited by Don Findley, Blacksmith Corp., Chino Valley, AZ, 1993. 79 pp., illus. Paper covers. $14.95.
  The definitive work on Ruger automatic pistols and single action revolvers.

The Ruger "P" Family of Handguns, by Duncan Long, Desert Publications, El Dorado, AZ, 1993. 128 pp., illus. Paper covers. $14.95.
  A full-fledged documentary on a remarkable series of Sturm Ruger handguns.

The Ruger .22 Automatic Pistol, Standard/Mark I/Mark II Series, by Duncan Long, Paladin Press, Boulder, CO, 1989. 168 pp., illus. Paper covers. $12.00.
  The definitive book about the pistol that has served more than 1 million owners so well.

The Semiautomatic Pistols in Police Service and Self Defense, by Massad Ayoob, Police Bookshelf, Concord, NH, 1990. 25 pp., illus. Soft covers. $9.95.
  First quantitative, documented look at actual police experience with 9mm and 45 police service automatics.

The Sharpshooter—How to Stand and Shoot Handgun Metallic Silhouettes, by Charles Stephens, Yucca Tree Press, Las Cruces, NM, 1993. 86 pp., illus. Paper covers. $10.00.
  A narration of some of the author's early experiences in silhouette shooting, plus how to information.

Shoot to Win, by John Shaw, Blacksmith Corp., Southport, CT, 1985. 160 pp., illus. Paper covers. $15.50.
  The lessons taught here are of interest and value to all handgun shooters.

Shooting, by J.H. FitzGerald, Wolfe Publishing Co., Prescott, AZ, 1993. 421 pp., illus. $29.00
  Exhaustive coverage of handguns and their use for target shooting, defense, trick shooting, and in police work by a noted firearms expert.

Shooting Colt Single Actions, by Mike Venturino, Livingston, MT, 1995.
  A definitive work on the famous Colt SAA and the ammunition it shoots.

Sig/Sauer Handguns, by Duncan Long, Desert Publications, El Dorado, AZ, 1995. 150 pp., illus. Paper covers. $16.95.
  The history of Sig/Sauer handguns, including Sig, Sig-Hammerli and Sig/Sauer variants.

Sixgun Cartridges and Loads, by Elmer Keith, reprint edition by The Gun Room Press, Highland Park, NJ, 1984. 151 pp., illus. $24.95.
  A manual covering the selection, use and loading of the most suitable and popular revolver cartridges.

Sixguns, by Elmer Keith, Wolfe Publishing Company, Prescott, AZ, 1992. 336 pp. Paper covers. $29.95.
  The history, selection, repair, care, loading, and use of this historic frontiersman's friend—the one-hand firearm.

Smith & Wesson's Automatics, by Larry Combs, Desert Publications, El Dorado, AZ, 1994. 143 pp., illus. Paper covers. $19.95.
  A must for every S&W auto owner or prospective owner.

Standard Catalog of Smith and Wesson by Jim Supica and Richard Nahas, Krause Publications, Inc. Iola, WI, 1996. 240 pp., illus. $29.95.
  Clearly details hundreds of products by the legendary manufacturer. How to identify, evaluate the conditions and assesses the value of 752 Smith & Wesson models and variations.

Street Stoppers: The Latest Handgun Stopping Power Street Results, by Evan P. Marshall & Edwin J. Sandow, Paladin Press, Boulder, CO, 1997. 392 pp., illus. Paper covers. $39.95.

Compilation of the results of real-life shooting incidents involving every major handgun caliber.

The Tactical Pistol, by Gabriel Suarez with a foreword by Jeff Cooper, Paladin Press, Boulder, CO, 1996. 216 pp., illus. Paper covers. $25.00.
  Advanced gunfighting concepts and techniques.

The Thompson/Center Contender Pistol, by Charles Tephens, Paladin Press, Boulder, CO, 1997. 58 pp., illus. Paper covers. $12.00.
  How to tune and time, load and shoot accurately with the Contender pistol.

The .380 Enfield No. 2 Revolver, by Mark Stamps and Ian Skennerton, I.D.S.A. Books, Piqua, OH, 1993. 124 pp., 80 illus. Paper covers. $19.95.

The Truth About Handguns, by Duane Thomas, Paladin Press, Boulder, CO, 1997. 136 pp., illus. Paper covers. $14.00.
  Exploding the myths, hype, and misinformation about handguns.

U.S. Handguns of World War 2, The Secondary Pistols and Revolvers, by Charles W. Pate, Mowbray Publishers, Lincoln, RI, 1997. 368 pp., illus. $39.00.
  This indispensable new book covers all of the American military handguns of W.W.2 except for the M1911A1.

World's Deadliest Rimfire Battleguns, by J.M. Ramos, Paladin Press, Boulder, CO, 1990. 184 pp., illus. Paper covers. $14.00.
  This heavily illustrated book shows international rimfire assault weapon innovations from World War II to the present.

HUNTING

NORTH AMERICA

Advanced Black Powder Hunting, by Toby Bridges, Stoeger Publishing Co., Wayne, NJ, 1998. 288 pp., illus. Paper covers. $21.95.
  The first modern day publication to be filled from cover to cover with guns, loads, projectiles, accessories and the techniques to get the most from today's front loading guns.

Advanced Strategies for Trophy Whitetails, by David Morris, Safari Press, Inc., Huntington Beach, CA, 1998. 399 pp., illustrated. $29.95.
  An in-depth look into the critical where-to and when-to strategies, covering exactly where in North America the great trophies are found and how to pick the best time to hunt.

Advanced Wild Turkey Hunting & World Records, by Dave Harbour, Winchester Press, Piscataway, NJ, 1983. 264 pp., illus. $10.95.
  The definitive book, written by an authority who has studied turkeys and turkey calling for over 40 years.

After the Hunt With Lovett Williams, by Lovett Williams, Krause Publications, Iola, WI, 1996. 256 pp., illus. Paper covers. $15.95.
  The author carefully instructs you on how to prepare your trophy turkey for a trip to the taxidermist. Plus help on planning a grand slam hunt.

Aggressive Whitetail Hunting, by Greg Miller, Krause Publications, Iola, WI, 1995. 208 pp., illus. Paper covers. $14.95.
  Learn how to hunt trophy bucks in public forests, private farmlands and exclusive hunting grounds from one of America's foremost hunters.

Alaskan Adventures, Volume 2, by Russell Annabel, Safari Press, Inc., Huntington Beach, CA, 1997. 351 pp., illus. $50.00.
  More of this famous writer's previously unpublished magazine articles in book form.

All About Bears, by Duncan Gilchrist, Stoneydale Press Publishing Co., Stevensville, MT, 1989 176 pp., illus. $19.95.
  Covers all kinds of bears - black, grizzly, Alaskan brown, polar and leans on a lifetime of hunting and guiding experiences to explore proper hunting techniques.

All-American Deer Hunter's Guide, edited by Jim Zumbo and Robert Elman, Winchester Press, Piscataway, NJ, 1983. 320 pp., illus. $29.95.
  The most comprehensive, thorough book yet published on American deer hunting.

American Duck Shooting, by George Bird Grinnell, Stackpole Books, Harrisburg, PA, 1991. 640 pp., illus. Paper covers. $19.95.
  First published in 1901 at the height of the author's career. Describes 50 species of waterfowl, and discusses hunting methods common at the turn of the century.

American Hunting and Fishing Books, 1800-1970, Volume 1, by Morris Heller, Nimrod and Piscator Press, Mesilla, NM, 1997. 220 pp., illus. A limited, numbered edition. $125.00.
  An up-to-date, profusely illustrated, annotated bibliography on American hunting and fishing books and booklets.

The Art of Super-Accurate Hunting with Scoped Rifles, by Don Judd, Wolfe Publishing Co., Prescott, AZ, 1996. 99 pp., illus. Paper covers. $14.95.
  The philosophy of super-accurate hunting and the rewards of making your shot a trophy.

Autumn Passages, Compiled by the editors of Ducks Unlimited Magazine, Willow Creek Press, Minocqua, WI, 1997. 320 pp. $27.50.
  An exceptional collection of duck hunting stories.

Awesome Antlers of North America, by Odie Sudbeck, HTW Publications, Seneca, KS, 1993. 150 pp., illus. $35.00.
  500 world-class bucks in color and black and white. This book starts up where the Boone & Crockett recordbook leaves off.

Bare November Days, by George Bird Evans et al, Countrysport Press, Traverse City, MI, 1992. 136 pp., illus. $39.50.
  A new, original anthology, a tribute to ruffed grouse, king of upland birds.

THE ARMS LIBRARY

Bear Attacks, by K. Etling, Safari Press, Long Beach, CA, 1998. 574 pp., illus. In 2 volumes. $80.00.
Classic tales of dangerous North American bears.

The Bear Hunter's Century, by Paul Schullery, Stackpole Books, Harrisburg, PA, 1989. 240 pp., illus. $19.95.
Thrilling tales of the bygone days of wilderness hunting.

The Best of Babcock, by Havilah Babcock, selected and with an introduction by Hugh Grey, The Gunnerman Press, Auburn Hills, MI, 1985. 262 pp., illus. $19.95.
A treasury of memorable pieces, 21 of which have never before appeared in book form.

The Best of Nash Buckingham, by Nash Buckingham, selected, edited and annotated by George Bird Evans, Winchester Press, Piscataway, NJ, 1973. 320 pp., illus. $35.00.
Thirty pieces that represent the very cream of Nash's output on his whole range of outdoor interests—upland shooting, duck hunting, even fishing.

The Best of Sheep Hunting, by John Batten, Amwell Press, Clinton, NJ, 1992. 616 pp., illus. $47.50.
This "Memorial Edition" is a collection of 40 articles and appendices covering sheep hunting in the North American area of Canada, Alaska, the West and Midwest as well as Africa and Europe.

Better on a Rising Tide, by Tom Kelly, Lyons & Burford Publishers, New York, NY, 1995. 184 pp. $22.95.
Tales of wild turkeys, turkey hunting and Southern folk.

Big Bucks the Benoit Way, by Bryce Towsley, Krause Publications Iola, WI, 1998. 208 pp., illus. $24.95.
Secrets from America's first family of whitetail hunting.

Big December Canvasbacks, by Worth Mathewson, Sand Lake Press, Amity, OR, 1997. 171 pp., illus. By David Hagenbaumer. Limited, signed and numbered edition. $29.95.
Duck hunting stories.

Big Woods, by William Faulkner, wilderness adventures, Gallatin Gateway, MT, 1998. 208 pp., illus. Slipcased. $60.00.
A collection of Faulkner's best hunting stories that belongs in the library of every sportsman.

Birdhunter, by Richard S. Grozik, Safari Press, Huntington Beach, CA, 1998. 180 pp., illus. Limited, numbered and signed edition. Slipcased. $60.00.
An entertaining salute to the closeness between man and his dog, man and his gun, and man and the great outdoors.

Bird Dog Days, Wingshooting Ways, by Archibald Rutledge, edited by Jim Casada, Wilderness Adventure Press, Gallatin Gateway, MT, 1998. 200 pp., illus. $35.00.
One of the most popular and enduring outdoor writers of this century, the poet laureate of South Carolina.

Birds on the Horizon, by Stuart Williams, Countrysport Press, Traverse City, MI, 1993. 288 pp., illus. $49.50.
Wingshooting adventures around the world.

Blacktail Trophy Tactics, by Boyd Iverson, Stoneydale Press, Stevensville, MI, 1992. 166 pp., illus. Paper covers. $14.95.
A comprehensive analysis of blacktail deer habits, describing a deer's and man's use of scents, still hunting, tree techniques, etc.

Bowhunter's Digest, 3rd Edition, by Chuck Adams, DBI Books, a division of Krause Publications, Iola, WI, 1990. 288 pp., illus. Soft covers. $17.95.
All-new edition covers all the necessary equipment and how to use it, plus the fine points on how to improve your skill.

Bowhunter's Handbook, Expert Strategies and Techniques, by M.R. James with Fred Asbell, Dave Holt, Dwight Schuh & Dave Samuel, DBI Books, a division of Krause Publications, Iola, WI, 1997. 256 pp., illus. Paper covers. $19.95.
Tips from the top on taking your bowhunting skills to the next level.

The Buffalo Harvest, by Frank Mayer as told to Charles Roth, Pioneer Press, Union City, TN, 1995. 96 pp., illus. Paper covers. $7.50.
The story of a hide hunter during his buffalo hunting days on the plains.

Bugling for Elk, by Dwight Schuh, Stoneydale Press Publishing Co., Stevensville, MT, 1983. 162 pp., illus. $18.95.
A complete guide to early season elk hunting.

Call of the Quail: A Tribute to the Gentleman Game Bird, by Michael McIntosh, et al., Countrysport Press, Traverse City, MI, 1990. 175 pp., illus. $39.50.
A new anthology on quail hunting.

Calling All Elk, by Jim Zumbo, Cody, WY, 1989. 169 pp., illus. Paper covers. $14.95.
The only book on the subject of elk hunting that covers every aspect of elk vocalization.

Campfires and Game Trails: Hunting North American Big Game, by Craig Boddington, Winchester Press, Piscataway, NJ, 1985. 295 pp., illus. $23.95.
How to hunt North America's big game species.

Come October, by Gene Hill et al, Countrysport Press, Inc., Traverse City, MI, 1991. 176 pp., illus. $39.50.
A new and all-original anthology on the woodcock and woodcock hunting.

The Complete Guide to Bird Dog Training, by John R. Falk, Lyons & Burford, New York, NY, 1994. 288 pp., illus. $22.95.
The latest on live-game field training techniques using released quail and recall pens. A new chapter on the services available for entering field trials and other bird dog competitions.

The Complete Guide to Bowhunting Deer, by Chuck Adams, DBI Books, a division of Krause Publications, Iola, WI, 1984. 256 pp., illus. Paper covers. $16.95.
Plenty on equipment, bows, sights, quivers, arrows, clothes, lures and scents, stands and blinds, etc.

The Complete Guide to Game Care & Cookery, 3rd Edition, by Sam Fadala, DBI Books, a division of Krause Publications, Iola, WI, 1994. 320 pp., illus. Paper covers. $18.95.

Over 500 photos illustrating the care of wild game in the field and at home with a separate recipe section providing over 400 tested recipes.

The Complete Smoothbore Hunter, by Brook Elliot, Winchester Press, Piscataway, NJ, 1986. 240 pp., illus. $16.95.
Advice and information on guns and gunning for all varieties of game.

The Complete Venison Cookbook from Field to Table, by Jim & Ann Casada, Krause Publications, Iola, WI, 1996. 208 pp., Comb-bound. $12.95.
More than 200 kitchen tested recipes make this book the answer to a table full of hungry hunters or guests.

Covey Rises and Other Pleasures, by David H. Henderson, Amwell Press, Clinton, NJ, 1983. 155 pp., illus. $17.50.
A collection of essays and stories concerned with field sports.

Coveys and Singles: The Handbook of Quail Hunting, by Robert Gooch, A.S. Barnes, San Diego, CA, 1981. 196 pp., illus. $11.95.
The story of the quail in North America.

Coyote Hunting, by Phil Simonski, Stoneydale Press, Stevensville, MT, 1994. 126 pp., illus. Paper covers. $12.95.
Probably the most thorough "How-to-do-it" book on coyote hunting ever written.

Dabblers & Divers: A Duck Hunter's Book, compiled by the editors of Ducks Unlimited Magazine, Willow Creek Press, Minocqua, WI, 1997. 160 pp., illus. $39.95.
A word-and-photographic portrayal of waterfowl hunter's singular intimacy with, and passion for, watery haunts and wildfowl.

Dancers in the Sunset Sky, by Robert F. Jones, The Lyons Press, New York, NY, 1997. 192 pp., illus. $22.95.
The musings of a bird hunter.

Deer & Deer Hunting, by Al Hofacker, Krause Publications, Iola, WI, 1993. 208 pp., illus. $34.95.
Coffee-table volume packed full of how-to-information that will guide hunts for years to come.

Deer and Deer Hunting: The Serious Hunter's Guide, by Dr. Robert Wegner, Stackpole Books, Harrisburg, PA, 1984. 384 pp., illus. Paper covers. $18.95.
In-depth information from the editor of "Deer & Deer Hunting" magazine. Major bibliography of English language books on deer and deer hunting from 1838-1984.

Deer and Deer Hunting Book 2, by Dr. Robert Wegner, Stackpole Books, Harrisburg, PA, 1987. 400 pp., illus. Paper covers. $18.95.
Strategies and tactics for the advanced hunter.

Deer and Deer Hunting, Book 3, by Dr. Robert Wegner, Stackpole Books, Harrisburg, PA, 1990. 368 pp., ilus. $29.95.
This comprehensive volume covers natural history, deer hunting lore, profiles of deer hunters, and discussion of important issues facing deer hunters today.

Deer Hunter's Guide to Guns, Ammunition, and Equipment, by Edward A. Matunas, an Outdoor Life Book, distributed by Stackpole Books, Harrisburg, PA, 1983. 352 pp., illus. $24.95.
Where to hunt for North American deer. An authoritative guide that will help every deer hunter get maximum enjoyment and satisfaction from his sport.

The Deer Hunters: The Tactics, Lore, Legacy and Allure of American Deer Hunting, Edited by Patrick Durkin, Krause Publications, Iola, WI, 1997. 208 pp., illus. $29.95.
More than twenty years of research from America's top whitetail hunters, researchers, and photographers have gone in to the making of this book.

Deer Hunting, by R. Smith, Stackpole Books, Harrisburg, PA, 1978. 224 pp., illus. Paper covers. $14.95.
A professional guide leads the hunt for North America's most popular big game animal.

Deer Hunting Coast to Coast, by C. Boddington and R. Robb, Safari Press, Long Beach, CA, 1989. 248 pp., illus. $24.95.
Join the authors as they hunt whitetail deer in eastern woodlot, southern swamps, midwestern prairies, and western river bottom; mule deer in badland, deserts, and high alpine basins; blacktails in oak grasslands and coastal jungles.

Doves and Dove Shooting, by Byron W. Dalrymple, New Win Publishing, Inc., Hampton, NJ, 1992. 256 pp., illus. $17.95.
The author reveals in this classic book his penchant for observing, hunting, and photographing this elegantly fashioned bird.

Dove Hunting, by Charley Dickey, Galahad Books, NY, 1976. 112 pp., illus. $10.00.
This indispensable guide for hunters deals with equipment, techniques, types of dove shooting, hunting dogs, etc.

Dreaming the Lion, by Thomas McIntyre, Countrysport Press, Traverse City, MI, 1994. 309 pp., illus. $35.00.
Reflections on hunting, fishing and a search for the wild. Twenty-three stories by *Sports Afield* editor, Tom McIntyre.

Drummer in the Woods, by Burton L. Spiller, Stackpole Books, Harrisburg, PA, 1990. 240 pp., illus. Soft covers. $16.95.
Twenty-one wonderful stories on grouse shooting by "the Poet Laureate of Grouse."

Duck Decoys and How to Rig Them, by Ralf Coykendall, revised by Ralf Coykendall, Jr., Nick Lyons Books, New York, NY, 1990. 137 pp., illus. Paper covers. $14.95.
Sage and practical advice on the art of decoying ducks and geese.

The Duck Hunter's Handbook, by Bob Hinman, revised, expanded, updated edition, Winchester Press, Piscataway, NJ, 1985. 288 pp., illus. $15.95.
The duck hunting book that has it all.

Eastern Upland Shooting, by Dr. Charles C. Norris, Countrysport Press, Traverse City, MI, 1990. 424 pp., illus. $29.50.
A new printing of this 1946 classic with a new, original Foreword by the author's friend and hunting companion, renowned author George Bird Evans.

THE ARMS LIBRARY

Elk and Elk Hunting, by Hart Wixom, Stackpole Books, Harrisburg, PA, 1986. 288 pp., illus. $34.95.
Your practical guide to fundamentals and fine points of elk hunting.

Elk Hunting in the Northern Rockies, by Ed. Wolff, Stoneydale Press, Stevensville, MT, 1984. 162 pp., illus. $18.95.
Helpful information about hunting the premier elk country of the northern Rocky Mountain states—Wyoming, Montana and Idaho.

Elk Hunting with the Experts, by Bob Robb, Stoneydale Press, Stevensville, MT, 1992. 176 pp., illus. Paper covers. $15.95.
A complete guide to elk hunting in North America by America's top elk hunting expert.

Elk Rifles, Cartridges and Hunting Tactics, by Wayne van Zwoll, Larsen's Outdoor Publishing, Lakeland, FL, 1992. 414 pp., illus. $24.95.
The definitive work on which rifles and cartridges are proper for hunting elk plus the tactics for hunting them.

Encyclopedia of Deer, by G. Kenneth Whitehead, Safari Press, Huntington, CA, 1993. 704 pp., illus. $130.00.
This massive tome will be the reference work on deer for well into the next century.

Fair Chase, by Jim Rikhoff, Amwell Press, Clinton, NJ, 1984. 323 pp., illus. $25.00.
A collection of hunting experiences from the Arctic to Africa, Mongolia to Montana, taken from over 25 years of writing.

A Fall of Woodcock, by Tom Huggler, Countrysport Press, Selman, AL, 1997. 256 pp., illus. $39.00.
A book devoted to the woodcock and to those who await his return to their favorite converts each autumn.

Firelight, by Burton L. Spiller, Gunnerman Press, Auburn Hills, MI, 1990. 196 pp., illus. $19.95.
Enjoyable tales of the outdoors and stalwart companions.

The Formidable Game, by John H. Batten, Amwell Press, Clinton, NJ. 1983. 264 pp., illus. $40.00.
Big game hunting in India, Africa and North America by a world famous hunter.

Fresh Looks at Deer Hunting, by Byron W. Dalrymple, New Win Publishing, Inc., Hampton, NJ, 1993. 288 pp., illus. $24.95.
Tips and techniques abound throughout the pages of this latest work by Mr. Dalrymple whose name is synonymous with hunting proficiency.

From the Peace to the Fraser, by Prentis N. Gray, Boone and Crockett Club, Missoula, MT, 1995. 400 pp., illus. $49.95.
Newly discovered North American hunting and exploration journals from 1900 to 1930.

Fur Trapping in North America, by Steven Geary, Winchester Press, Piscataway, NJ, 1985. 160 pp., illus. Paper covers. $19.95.
A comprehensive guide to techniques and equipment, together with fascinating facts about fur bearers.

A Gallery of Waterfowl and Upland Birds, by Gene Hill, with illustrations by David Maass, Petersen Prints, Los Angeles, CA, 1978. 132 pp., illus. $44.95.
Gene Hill at his best. Liberally illustrated with 51 full-color reproductions of David Maass' finest paintings.

Game in the Desert Revisited, by Jack O'Connor, Amwell Press, Clinton, NJ, 1984. 306 pp., illus. $27.50.
Reprint of a Derrydale Press classic on hunting in the Southwest

Getting the Most Out of Modern Waterfowling, by John O. Cartier, St. Martin's Press, NY, 1974. 396 pp., illus. $22.50.
The most comprehensive, up-to-date book on waterfowling imaginable.

Getting a Stand, by Miles Gilbert, Pioneer Press, Union City, TN, 1993. 204 pp., illus. Paper covers. $10.95.
An anthology of 18 short personal experiences by buffalo hunters of the late 1800s, specifically from 1870-1882.

Gordon MacQuarrie Trilogy: Stories of the Old Duck Hunters, by Gordon MacQuarrie, Willow Creek Press, Minocqua, WI, 1994. $49.00.
A slip-cased three volume set of masterpieces by one of America's finest outdoor writers.

The Grand Passage: A Chronicle of North American Waterfowling, by Gene Hill, et al., Countrysport Press, Traverse City, MI, 1990. 175 pp., illus. $39.50.
A new original anthology by renowned sporting authors on our world of waterfowling.

Grouse and Woodcock, A Gunner's Guide, by Don Johnson, Krause Publications, Iola, WI, 1995. 256 pp., illus. Paper covers. $14.95.
Find out what you need in guns, ammo, equipment, dogs and terrain.

Grouse of North America, by Tom Huggler, NorthWord Press, Inc., Minocqua, WI, 1990. 160 pp., illus. $29.95.
A cross-continental hunting guide.

Grouse Hunter's Guide, by Dennis Walrod, Stackpole Books, Harrisburg, PA, 1985. 192 pp., illus. $18.95.
Solid facts, observations, and insights on how to hunt the ruffed grouse.

Gunning for Sea Ducks, by George Howard Gillelan, Tidewater Publishers, Centreville, MD, 1988. 144 pp., illus. $14.95.
A book that introduces you to a practically untouched arena of waterfowling.

Heartland Trophy Whitetails, by Odie Sudbeck, HTW Publications, Seneca, KS, 1992. 130 pp., illus. $35.00.
A completely revised and expanded edition which includes over 500 photos of Boone & Crockett class whitetail, major mulies and unusual racks.

The Heck with Moose Hunting, by Jim Zumbo, Wapiti Valley Publishing Co., Cody, WY, 1996. 199 pp., illus. $17.95.
Jim's hunts around the continent including encounters with moose, caribou, sheep, antelope and mountain goats.

High Pressure Elk Hunting, by Mike Lapinski, Stoneydale Press Publishing Co., Stevensville, MT, 1996. 192 pp., illus. $19.95.
The secrets of hunting educated elk revealed.

Hill Country, by Gene Hill, Countrysport Press, Traverse City, MI, 1996. 180 pp., illus. $25.00.
Stories about hunting, fishing, dogs and guns.

Home from the Hill, by Fred Webb, Safari Press, Huntington Beach, CA, 1997. 283 pp., illus. Limited edition, signed and numbered. In a slipcase. $50.00.
The story of a big-game guide in the Canadian wilderness.

Horns in the High Country, by Andy Russell, Alfred A. Knopf, NY, 1973. 259 pp., illus. Paper covers. $12.95.
A many-sided view of wild sheep and their natural world.

How to Hunt, by Dave Bowring, Winchester Press, Piscataway, NJ, 1982. 208 pp., illus. Paper covers. $10.95; cloth, $15.00.
A basic guide to hunting big game, small game, upland birds, and waterfowl.

Hunt Alaska Now: Self-Guiding for Trophy Moose & Caribou, by Dennis W. Confer, Wily Ventures, Anchorage, AK, 1997. 309 pp., illus. Paper covers. $26.95.
How to plan affordable, successfull, safe hunts you can do yourself.

The Hunters and the Hunted, by George Laycock, Outdoor Life Books, New York, NY, 1990. 280 pp., illus. $34.95.
The pursuit of game in America from Indian times to the present.

A Hunter's Fireside Book, by Gene Hill, Winchester Press, Piscataway, NJ, 1972. 192 pp., illus. $16.95.
An outdoor book that will appeal to every person who spends time in the field—or who wishes he could.

A Hunter's Road, by Jim Fergus, Henry Holt & Co., NY, 1992. 290 pp. $22.50
A journey with gun and dog across the American uplands.

Hunt High for Rocky Mountain Goats, Bighorn Sheep, Chamois & Tahr, by Duncan Gilchrist, Stoneydale Press, Stevensville, MT, 1992. 192 pp., illus. Paper covers. $19.95.
The source book for hunting mountain goats.

The Hunter's Shooting Guide, by Jack O'Connor, Outdoor Life Books, New York, NY, 1982. 176 pp., illus. Paper covers. $5.95.
A classic covering rifles, cartridges, shooting techniques for shotguns/rifles/handguns.

The Hunter's World, by Charles F. Waterman, Winchester Press, Piscataway, NJ, 1983. 250 pp., illus. $29.95.
A classic. One of the most beautiful hunting books that has ever been produced.

Hunting Adventure of Me and Joe, by Walt Prothero, Safari Press, Huntington Beach, CA, 1995. 220 pp., illus. $22.50.
A collection of the author's best and favorite stories.

Hunting America's Game Animals and Birds, by Robert Elman and George Peper, Winchester Press, Piscataway, NJ, 1975. 368 pp., illus. $16.95.
A how-to, where-to, when-to guide by 40 top experts—covering the continent's big, small, upland game and waterfowl.

Hunting Ducks and Geese, by Steven Smith, Stackpole Books, Harrisburg, PA, 1984. 160 pp., illus. $19.95.
Hard facts, good bets, and serious advice from a duck hunter you can trust.

Hunting for Handgunners, by Larry Kelly and J.D. Jones, DBI Books, a division of Krause Publications, Iola, WI, 1990. 256 pp., illus. Soft covers. $16.95.
A definitive work on an increasingly popular sport.

Hunting in Many Lands, edited by Theodore Roosevelt and George Bird Grinnell, et al., Boone & Crockett Club, Dumphries, VA, 1990. 447 pp., illus. $40.00.
A limited edition reprinting of the original Boone & Crockett Club 1895 printing.

Hunting Mature Bucks, by Larry L. Weishuhn, Krause Publications, Iola, WI, 1995. 256 pp., illus. Paper covers. $14.95.
One of North America's top white-tailed deer authorities shares his expertise on hunting those big, smart and elusive bucks.

Hunting Open-Country Mule Deer, by Dwight Schuh, Sage Press, Nampa, ID, 1989. 160 pp., illus. $16.50.
A guide taking Western bucks with rifle and bow.

Hunting Predators for Hides and Profits, by Wilf E. Pyle, Stoeger Publishing Co., So. Hackensack, NJ, 1985. 224 pp., illus. Paper covers. $11.95.
The author takes the hunter through every step of the hunting/marketing process.

Hunting the American Wild Turkey, by Dave Harbour, Stackpole Books, Harrisburg, PA, 1975. 256 pp., illus. $24.95.
The techniques and tactics of hunting North America's largest, and most popular, woodland game bird.

Hunting the Rockies, Home of the Giants, by Kirk Darner, Marceline, MO, 1996. 291 pp., illus. $25.00.
Understand how and where to hunt Western game in the Rockies.

Hunting the Sun, by Ted Nelson Lundrigan, Countrysport Press, Selma, AL, 1997. 240 pp., illus. $30.00.
One of the best books on grouse and woodcock ever published.

Hunting Trips in North America, by F.C. Selous, Wolfe Publishing Co., Prescott, AZ, 1988. 395 pp., illus. $52.00.
A limited edition reprint. Coverage of caribou, moose and other big game hunting in virgin wilds.

Hunting Trophy Deer, by John Wootters, The Lyons Press, New York, NY, 1997. 272 pp., illus. $24.95.
A revised edition of the definitive manual for identifying, scouting, and successfully hunting a deer of a lifetime.

Hunting Trophy Whitetails, by David Morris, Stoneydale Press, Stevensville, MT, 1993. 483 pp., illus. $29.95.
This is one of the best whitetail books published in the last two decades. The author is the former editor of *North American Whitetail* magazine.

Hunting Upland Birds, by Charles F. Waterman, Countrysport Press, Selma, AL, 1997. 220 pp., illus. $30.00.
Originally published a quarter of a century ago, this classic has been newly updated with the latest information for today's wingshooter.

Hunting Western Deer, by Jim and Wes Brown, Stoneydale Press, Stevensville, MT, 1994. 174 pp., illus. Paper covers. $14.95.
A pair of expert Oregon hunters provide insight into hunting mule deer and blacktail deer in the western states.

Hunting Wild Turkeys in the West, by John Higley, Stoneydale Press, Stevensville, MT, 1992. 154 pp., illus. Paper covers. $12.95.
Covers the basics of calling, locating and hunting turkeys in the western states.

Hunting with the Twenty-two, by Charles Singer Landis, R&R Books, Livonia, NY, 1994. 429 pp., illus. $45.00.
A miscellany of articles touching on the hunting and shooting of small game.

I Don't Want to Shoot an Elephant, by Havilah Babcock, The Gunnerman Press, Auburn Hills, MI, 1985. 184 pp., illus. $19.95.
Eighteen delightful stories that will enthrall the upland gunner for many pleasureable hours.

In Search of the Buffalo, by Charles G. Anderson, Pioneer Press, Union City, TN, 1996. 144 pp., illus. Paper covers. $13.95.
The primary study of the life of J. Wright Mooar, one of the few hunters fortunate enough to kill a white buffalo.

In Search of the Wild Turkey, by Bob Gooch, Greatlakes Living Press, Ltd., Waukegan, IL, 1978. 182 pp., illus. $9.95.
A state-by-state guide to wild turkey hot spots, with tips on gear and methods for bagging your bird.

Indian Hunts and Indian Hunters of the Old West, by Dr. Frank C. Hibben, Safari Press, Long Beach, CA, 1989. 228 pp., illus. $24.95.
Tales of some of the most famous American Indian hunters of the Old West as told to the author by an old Navajo hunter.

Jack O'Connor's Gun Book, by Jack O'Connor, Wolfe Publishing Company, Prescott, AZ, 1992. 208 pp. Hardcover. $26.00.
Jack O'Connor imparts a cross-section of his knowledge on guns and hunting. Brings back some of his writings that have here-to-fore been lost.

Jaybirds Go to Hell on Friday, by Havilah Babcock, The Gunnerman Press, Auburn Hills, MI, 1985. 149 pp., illus. $19.95.
Sixteen jewels that reestablish the lost art of good old-fashioned yarn telling.

Jim Dougherty's Guide to Bowhunting Deer, by Jim Dougherty, DBI Books, a division of Krause Publications, Iola, WI, 1992. 256 pp., illus. Paper covers. $17.95.
Dougherty sets down some important guidelines for bowhunting and bowhunting equipment.

Last Casts and Stolen Hunts, edited by Jim Casada and Chuck Wechsler, Countrysport Press, Traverse City, MI, 1994. 270 pp., illus. $29.95.
The world's best hunting and fishing stories by writers such as Zane Grey, Jim Corbett, Jack O'Connor, Archibald Rutledge and others.

A Listening Walk...and Other Stories, by Gene Hill, Winchester Press, Piscataway, NJ, 1985. 208 pp., illus. $15.95.
Vintage Hill. Over 60 stories.

Longbows in the Far North, by E. Donnall Thomas, Jr. Stackpole Books, Mechanicsburg, PA, 1994. 200 pp., illus. $18.95.
An archer's adventures in Alaska and Siberia.

The Longwalkers: 25 Years of Tracking the Northern Cougar, by Jerry A. Lewis, Wolfe Publishing Co., Prescott, AZ, 1996. 140 pp., illus. Paper covers. $24.95.
Trek the snow-covered mountain forests of Idaho, Montana, British Columbia, and Alberta with the author as he follows cougars/mountain lions on foot, guided by his keen hounds.

Mammoth Monarchs of North America, by Odie Sudbeck, HTW Publications, Seneca, KA, 1995. 288 pp., illus. $35.00.
This book reveals eye-opening big buck secrets.

Matching the Gun to the Game, by Clair Rees, Winchester Press, Piscataway, NJ, 1982. 272 pp., illus. $17.95.
Covers selection and use of handguns, blackpowder firearms for hunting, matching rifle type to the hunter, calibers for multiple use, tailoring factory loads to the game.

Measuring and Scoring North American Big Game Trophies, by Wm. H. Nesbitt and Philip L. Wright, The Boone and Crockett Club, Alexandria, VA, 1986. 176 pp., illus. $15.00.
The Boone and Crockett Club official scoring system, with tips for trophy evaluation.

Meditation on Hunting, by Jose Ortego y Gasset, Wilderness Adventures Press, Bozeman, MT, 1996. 140 pp., illus. In a slipcase. $60.00.
The classic work on the philosophy of hunting.

Mixed Bag, by Jim Rikhoff, National Rifle Association of America, Wash., DC, 1981. 284 pp., illus. Paper covers. $9.95.
Reminiscences of a master raconteur.

Modern Pheasant Hunting, by Steve Grooms, Stackpole Books, Harrisburg, PA, 1982. 224 pp., illus. Paper covers. $10.95.
New look at pheasants and hunters from an experienced hunter who respects this splendid gamebird.

Modern Waterfowl Guns and Gunning, by Don Zutz, Stoeger Publishing Co., So. Hackensack, NJ, 1985. 224 pp., illus. Paper covers. $11.95.
Up-to-date information on the fast-changing world of waterfowl guns and loads.

Montana—Land of Giant Rams, by Duncan Gilchrist, Stoneydale Press Publishing Co., Stevensville, MT, 1990. 208 pp., illus. $19.95.
Latest information on Montana bighorn sheep and why so many Montana bighorn rams are growing to trophy size.

Montana—Land of Giant Rams, Volume 2, by Duncan Gilchrist, Outdoor Expeditions and Books, Corvallis, MT, 1992. 208 pp., illus. $34.95.
The reader will find stories of how many of the top-scoring trophies were taken.

More and Better Pheasant Hunting, by Steve Smith, Winchester Press, Piscataway, NJ, 1986. 192 pp., illus. $15.95.
Complete, fully illustrated, expert coverage of the bird itself, the dogs, the hunt, the guns, and the best places to hunt.

More Grouse Feathers, by Burton L. Spiller, Crown Publ., NY, 1972. 238 pp., illus. $25.00.
Facsimile of the original Derrydale Press issue of 1938. Guns and dogs, the habits and shooting of grouse, woodcock, ducks, etc. Illus. by Lynn Bogue Hunt.

More Tracks: 78 Years of Mountains, People & Happinesss, by Howard Copenhaver, Stoneydale Press, Stevensville, MT, 1992. 150 pp., illus. $18.95.
A collection of stories by one of the back country's best storytellers about the people who shared with Howard his great adventure in the high places and wild Montana country.

Moss, Mallards and Mules, by Robert Brister, Countrysport Books, Selma, AL, 1998. 216 pp., illustrated by David Maass. $30.00.
Twenty-seven short stories on hunting and fishing on the Gulf Coast.

Mostly Huntin', by Bill Jordan, Everett Publishing Co., Bossier City, LA, 1987. 254 pp., illus. $21.95.
Jordan's hunting adventures in North America, Africa, Australia, South America and Mexico.

Mostly Tailfeathers, by Gene Hill, Winchester Press, Piscataway, NJ, 1975. 192 pp., illus. $15.95.
An interesting, general book about bird hunting.

"Mr. Buck": The Autobiography of Nash Buckingham, by Nash Buckingham, Countrysport Press, Traverse City, MI, 1990. 288 pp., illus. $39.50.
A lifetime of shooting, hunting, dogs, guns, and Nash's reflections on the sporting life, along with previously unknown pictures and stories written especially for this book.

Mule Deer: Hunting Today's Trophies, by Tom Carpenter and Jim Van Norman, Krause Publications, Iola, WI, 1998. 256 pp., illustrated. Paper covers. $19.95.
A tribute to both the deer and the people who hunt them. Includes info on where to look for big deer, prime mule deer habitat and effective weapons for the hunt.

Murry Burnham's Hunting Secrets, by Murry Burnham with Russell Tinsley, Winchester Press, Piscataway, NJ, 1984. 244 pp., illus. $17.95.
One of the great hunters of our time gives the reasons for his success in the field.

My Health is Better in November, by Havilah Babcock, University of S. Carolina Press, Columbia, SC, 1985. 284 pp., illus. $19.95.
Adventures in the field set in the plantation country and backwater streams of SC.

North American Big Game Animals, by Byron W. Dalrymple and Erwin Bauer, Outdoor Life Books/Stackpole Books, Harrisburg, PA, 1985. 258 pp., illus. $29.95.
Complete illustrated natural histories. Habitat, movements, breeding, birth and development, signs, and hunting.

North American Elk: Ecology and Management, edited by Jack Ward Thomas and Dale E. Toweill, Stackpole Books, Harrisburg, PA, 1982. 576 pp., illus. $39.95.
The definitive, exhaustive, classic work on the North American elk.

The North American Waterfowler, by Paul S. Bernsen, Superior Publ. Co., Seattle, WA, 1972. 206 pp. Paper covers. $9.95.
The complete inside and outside story of duck and goose shooting. Big and colorful, illustrations by Les Kouba.

Of Bears and Man, by Mike Cramond, University of Oklahoma Press, Norman, OK, 1986. 433 pp., illus. $29.95.
The author's lifetime association with bears of North America. Interviews with survivors of bear attacks.

The Old Man and the Boy, by Robert Ruark, Henry Holt & Co., New York, NY, 303 pp., illus. $24.95.
A timeless classic, telling the story of a remarkable friendship between a young boy and his grandfather as they hunt and fish together.

The Old Man's Boy Grows Older, by Robert Ruark, Henry Holt & Co., Inc., New York, NY, 1993. 300 pp., illus. $24.95.
The heartwarming sequel to the best-selling *The Old Man and the Boy.*

Old Wildfowling Tales, Volume 2, edited by Worth Mathewson, Sand Lake Press, Amity, OR, 1996. 240 pp. $21.95.
A collection of duck and geese hunting stories based around accounts from the past.

Once Upon a Time, by Nash Buckingham, Beaver Dam Press, Brentwood, TN, 1995. 170 pp., illus. $29.50.

161 Waterfowling Secrets, edited by Matt Young, Willow Creek Press, Minocqua, WI, 1997. 78 pp., Paper covers. $10.95.
Time-honored, field-tested waterfowling tips and advice.

The Only Good Bear is a Dead Bear, by Jeanette Hortick Prodgers, Falcon Press, Helena, MT, 1986. 204 pp. Paper covers. $12.50.
A collection of the West's best bear stories.

Outdoor Pastimes of an American Hunter, by Theodore Roosevelt, Stackpole Books, Mechanicsburg, PA, 1994. 480 pp., illus. Paper covers. $18.95.
Stories of hunting big game in the West and notes about animals pursued and observed.

Outdoor Yarns & Outright Lies, by Gene Hill and Steve Smith, Stackpole Books, Harrisburg, PA, 1984. 168 pp., illus. $18.95.
Fifty or so stories by two good sports.

The Outlaw Gunner, by Harry M. Walsh, Tidewater Publishers, Cambridge, MD, 1973. 178 pp., illus. $22.95.
A colorful story of market gunning in both its legal and illegal phases.

Passing a Good Time, by Gene Hill, Countrysport Press, Traverse City, MI, 1996. 200 pp., illus. $25.00.
Filled with insights and observations of guns, dogs and fly rods that make Gene Hill a master essayist.

Pear Flat Philosophies, by Larry Weishuhn, Safari Press, Huntington Beach, CA, 1995. 234 pp., illus. $24.95.
The author describes his more lighthearted adventures and funny anecdotes while out hunting.

THE ARMS LIBRARY

Pheasant Days, by Chris Dorsey, Voyageur Press, Stillwater, MN, 1992. 233 pp., illus. $24.95.

The definitive resource on ringnecks. Includes everything from basic hunting techniques to the life cycle of the bird.

Pheasant Hunter's Harvest, by Steve Grooms, Lyons & Burford Publishers, New York, NY, 1990. 180 pp. $22.95.

A celebration of pheasant, pheasant dogs and pheasant hunting. Practical advice from a passionate hunter.

Pheasant Tales, by Gene Hill et al, Countrysport Press, Traverse City, MI, 1996. 202 pp., illus. $39.00.

Charley Waterman, Michael McIntosh and Phil Bourjaily join the author to tell some of the stories that illustrate why the pheasant is America's favorite game bird.

Pheasants of the Mind, by Datus Proper, Wilderness Adventures Press, Bozeman, MT, 1994. 154 pp., illus. $25.00.

No single title sums up the life of the solitary pheasant hunter like this masterful work.

Pinnell and Talifson: Last of the Great Brown Bear Men, by Marvin H. Clark, Jr., Great Northwest Publishing and Distributing Co., Spokane, WA, 19880. 224 pp., Illus. $39.95

The story of these famous Alaskan guides and some of the record bears taken by both of them.

Predator Calling with Gerry Blair, by Gerry Blair, Krause Publications, Iola, WI, 1996. 208 pp., illus. Paper covers. $14.95.

Time-tested secrets lure predators closer to your camera or gun.

Proven Whitetail Tactics, by Greg Miller, Krause Publications, Iola, WI, 1997. 224 pp., illus. Paper covers. $19.95.

Proven tactics for scouting, calling and still-hunting whitetail.

Quail Hunting in America, by Tom Huggler, Stackpole Books, Harrisburg, PA, 1987. 288 pp., illus. $19.95.

Tactics for finding and taking bobwhite, valleys, Gambel's Mountain, scaled-blue, and Mearn's quail by season and habitat.

Quest for Dall Rams, by Duncan Gilchrist, Duncan Gilchrist Outdoor Expeditions and Books, Corvallis, MT, 1997. 224 pp., illus. Limited numbered edition. $34.95.

The most complete book of Dall sheep ever written. Covers information on Alaska and provinces with Dall sheep and explains hunting techniques, equipment, etc.

Quest for Giant Bighorns, by Duncan Gilchrist, Outdoor Expeditions and Books, Corvallis, MT, 1994. 224 pp., illus. Paper covers. $19.95.

How some of the most successful sheep hunters hunt and how some of the best bighorns were taken.

Radical Elk Hunting Strategies, by Mike Lapinski, Stoneydale Press Publishing Co., Stevensville, MT, 1988. 161 pp., illus. $18.95.

Secrets of calling elk in close.

Records of North American Big Game 1932, by Prentis N. Grey, Boone and Crockett Club, Dumfries, VA, 1988. 178 pp., illus. $79.95.

A reprint of the book that started the Club's record keeping for native North American big game.

Records of North American Caribou and Moose, Craig Boddington et al, The Boone & Crockett Club, Missoula, MT, 1997. 250 pp., illus. $24.95.

More than 1,800 caribou listings and more than 1,500 moose listings, organized by the state or Canadian province where they were taken.

Records of North American Elk and Mule Deer, 2nd Edition, edited by Jack and Susan Reneau, Boone & Crockett Club, Missoula, MT, 1996. 360 pp., illus. Paper cover, $18.95; hardcover, $24.95.

Updated and expanded edition featuring more than 150 trophy, field and historical photos of the finest elk and mule deer trophies ever recorded.

Records of North American Sheep, Rocky Mountain Goats and Pronghorn edited by Jack and Susan Reneau, Boone & Crockett Club, Missoula, MT, 1996. 400 pp., illus. Paper cover, $18.95; hardcover, $24.95.

The first B&C Club records book featuring all 3941 accepted wild sheep, Rocky Mountain goats and pronghorn trophies.

The Rifles, the Cartridges, and the Game, by Clay Harvey, Stackpole Books, Harrisburg, PA, 1991. 254 pp., illus. $32.95.

Engaging reading combines with exciting photos to present the hunt with an intense level of awareness and respect.

Ringneck! Pheasants & Pheasant Hunting, by Ted Janes, Crown Publ., NY, 1975. 120 pp., illus. $15.95.

A thorough study of one of our more popular game birds.

Ruffed Grouse, edited by Sally Atwater and Judith Schnell, Stackpole Books, Harrisburg, PA, 1989. 370 pp., illus. $59.95.

Everything you ever wanted to know about the ruffed grouse. More than 25 wildlife professionals provided in-depth information on every aspect of this popular game bird's life. Lavishly illustrated with over 300 full-color photos. The Russell Annabel Adventure Series, by Russell Anabel, Safari Press, Huntington Beach, CA: Vol. 1, Alaskan Adventure, The Early Years..$35.00, Vol. 2, Adventure is My Business, 1951-1955..$35.00, Vol. 3, Adventure is in My Blood, 1957-1964..$35.00, Vol. 4, High Road to Adventure, 1964-1970..$35.00, Vol. 5, The Way We Were, 1970-1979..$35.00.

A complete collection of previously unpublished magazine articles in book form by this gifted outdoor writer.

The Season, by Tom Kelly, Lyons & Burford, New York, NY, 1997. 160 pp., illus. $22.95.

The delight and challenges of a turkey hunter's Spring season.

Secret Strategies from North America's Top Whitetail Hunters, compiled by Nick Sisley, Krause Publications, Iola, WI, 1995. 256 pp., illus. Paper covers. $14.95.

Bow and gun hunters share their success stories.

Sheep Hunting in Alaska—The Dall Sheep Hunter's Guide, by Tony Russ, Outdoor Expeditions and Books, Corvallis, MT, 1994. 160 pp., illus. Paper covers. $19.95.

A how-to guide for the Dall sheep hunter.

Shorebirds: The Birds, The Hunters, The Decoys, by John M. Levinson & Somers G. Headley, Tidewater Publishers, Centreville, MD, 1991. 160 pp., illus. $49.95.

A thorough study of shorebirds and the decoys used to hunt them. Photographs of more than 200 of the decoys created by prominent carvers are shown.

Shots at Big Game, by Craig Boddington, Stackpole Books, Harrisburg, PA, 1989. 198 pp., illus. $24.95.

How to shoot a rifle accurately under hunting conditions.

Some Bears Kill!: True-Life Tales of Terror, by Larry Kanuit, Safari Press, Huntington Beach, CA, 1997. 313 pp., illus. $24.95.

A collection of 38 stories as told by the victims, and in the case of fatality, recounted by the author from institutional records, episodes involve all three species of North American bears.

Southern Deer & Deer Hunting, by Larry Weishuhn and Bill Bynum, Krause Publications, Iola, WI, 1995. 256 pp., illus. $14.95.

Mount a trophy southern whitetail on your wall with this firsthand account of stalking big bucks below the Mason-Dixon line.

Spring Gobbler Fever, by Michael Hanback, Krause Publications, Iola, WI, 1996. 256 pp., illus. Paper covers. $15.95.

Your complete guide to spring turkey hunting.

Spirit of the Wilderness, Compiled by Theodore J. Holsten, Jr., Susan C. Reneau and Jack Reneau, the Boone & Crockett Club, Missoula, MT, 1997 300 pp., illus. $29.95.

Stalking wild sheep, tracking a trophy cougar, hiking the back country of British Columbia, fishing for striped bass and coming face-to-face with a grizzly bear are some of the adventures found in this book.

Stand Hunting for Whitetails, by Richard P. Smith, Krause Publications, Iola, WI, 1996. 256 pp., illus. Paper covers. $14.95.

The author explains the tricks and strategies for successful stand hunting.

Successful Goose Hunting, by Charles L. Cadieux, Stone Wall Press, Inc., Washington, DC, 1986. 223 pp., illus. $24.95.

Here is a complete book on modern goose hunting by a lifetime waterfowler and professional wildlifer.

The Sultan of Spring: A Hunter's Odyssey Through the World of the Wild Turkey, by Bob Sailo, The Lyons Press, New York, NY, 1998. 176 pp., illus. $22.95.

A literary salute to the magic and mysticism of spring turkey hunting.

Taking Big Bucks, by Ed Wolff, Stoneydale Press, Stevensville, MT, 1987. 169 pp., illus. $18.95

Solving the whitetail riddle.

Taking Chances in the High Country, compiled and with an introduction by Jim Rikhoff, The Amwell Press, Clinton, NJ, 1995. 411 pp., illus. In a slipcase. $85.00.

An anthology by some thirty stories by different authors on hunting sheep in the high country.

Taking More Birds, by Dan Carlisle and Dolph Adams, Lyons & Burford Publishers, New York, NY, 1993. 160 pp., illus. Paper covers. $15.95.

A practical handbook for success at Sporting Clays and wing shooting.

Tales of Alaska's Big Bears, by Jim Rearden, Wolfe Publishing Co., Prescott, AZ, 1989. 125 pp., illus. Soft covers. $12.95.

A collection of bear yarns covering nearly three-quarters of a century.

Tales of Quails 'n Such, by Havilah Babcock, University of S. Carolina Press, Columbia, SC, 1985. 237 pp. $19.95.

A group of hunting stories, told in informal style, on field experiences in the South in quest of small game.

Tears and Laughter, by Gene Hill, Countrysport Press, Traverse City, MI, 1996. 176 pp., illus. $25.00.

In twenty-six stories, Gene Hill explores the ancient and honored bond between man and dog.

Tenth Legion, by Tom Kelly, the Lyons Press, New York, NY, 1998. 128 pp., illus. $21.95.

The classic work on that frustrating, yet wonderful sport of turkey hunting.

They Left Their Tracks, by Howard Coperhaver, Stoneydale Press Publishing Co., Stevensville, MT, 1990. 190 pp., illus. $18.95.

Recollections of 60 years as an outfitter in the Bob Marshall Wilderness.

Timberdoodle, by Frank Woolner, Nick Lyons Books, N. Y., NY, 1987. 168 pp., illus. $18.95.

The classic guide to woodcock and woodcock hunting.

Timberdoodle Tales, by T. Waters, Safari Press, Inc., Huntington Beach, CA, 1997. 220 pp., illus. $30.00.

A fresh appreciation of this captivating bird and the ethics of its hunt.

Timberdoodle Tales: Adventures of a Minnesota Woodcock Hunter, Safari Press, Huntington Beach, CA, 1997. 220 pp., illus. $35.00.

The life history and hunt of the American woodcock by the author.

To Heck with Moose Hunting, by Jim Zumbo, Wapiti Publishing Co., Cody, WY, 1996. 199 pp., illus. $17.95.

Jim's hunts around the continent and even an African adventure.

Trail and Campfire, edited by George Bird Grinnel and Theodore Roosevelt, The Boone and Crockett Club, Dumfries, VA, 1989. 357 pp., illus. $39.50.

Reprint of the Boone and Crockett Club's 3rd book published in 1897.

Trailing a Bear, by Robert S. Munger, The Munger Foundation, Albion, MI, 1997. 352 pp., illus. Paper covers. $19.95.

An exciting and humorous account of hunting with legendary archer Fred Bear.

The Trickiest Thing in Feathers, by Corey Ford; compiled and edited by Laurie Morrow and illustrated by Christopher Smith, Wilderness Adventures, Gallatin Gateway, MT, 1998. 208 pp., illus. $29.95.

Here is a collection of Corey Ford's best wing-shooting stories, many of them previously unpublished.

Trophy Mule Deer: Finding & Evaluating Your Trophy, by Lance Stapleton, Outdoor Experiences Unlimited, Salem, OR, 1993. 290 pp., illus. Paper covers. $24.95.
The most comprehensive reference book on mule deer.

The Turkey Hunter's Book, by John M. McDaniel, Amwell Press, Clinton, NJ, 1980. 147 pp., illus. Paper covers. $11.95.
One of the most original turkey hunting books to be published in many years.

Turkey Hunter's Digest, Revised Edition, by Dwain Bland, DBI Books, a division of Krause Publications, Iola, WI, 1994. 256 pp., illus. Paper covers. $17.95.
A no-nonsense approach to hunting all five sub-species of the North American wild turkey that make up the Royal Grand Slam.

Turkey Hunting with Gerry Blair, by Gerry Blair, Krause Publications, Iola, WI, 1993. 280 pp., illus. $19.95.
Novice and veteran turkey hunters alike will enjoy this complete examination of the varied wild turkey subspecies, their environments, equipment needed to pursue them and the tactics to outwit them.

The Upland Equation: A Modern Bird-Hunter's Code, by Charles Fergus, Lyons & Burford Publishers, New York, NY, 1996. 86 pp. $18.00
A book that deserves space in every sportsman's library. Observations based on firsthand experience.

The Upland Gunner's Book, edited by George Bird Evans, The Amwell Press, Clinton, NJ, 1985. 263 pp., illus. In slipcase. $27.50.
An anthology of the finest stories ever written on the sport of upland game hunting.

Upland Tales, by Worth Mathewson (Ed.), Sand Lake Press, Amity, OR, 1996. 271 pp., illus. $21.95.
A collection of articles on grouse, snipe and quail.

Varmint and Small Game Rifles and Cartridges, by various authors, Wolfe Publishing Co., Prescott, AZ, 1993. 228 pp., illus. Paper covers. $26.00.
This is a collection of reprints of articles originally appearing in Wolfe's *Rifle* and *Handloader* magazines from 1966 through 1990.

Waterfowling Horizons: Shooting Ducks and Geese in the 21st Century, by Chris and Jason Smith, Wilderness Adventures, Gallatin Gateway, MT, 1998. 320 pp., illus. $49.95.
A compendium of the very latest in everything for the duck and goose hunter today.

Waterfowling These Past 50 Years, Especially Brant, by David Hagerbaumer, Sand Lake Press, Amity, OR, 1998. 182 pp., illustrated. $35.00.
The author's autobiography from the time he mustered out of the Marines in 1946 to the present day. Dave has done 209 pencil drawings, plus a color frontispiece for the book.

Wegner's Bibliography on Dear and Deer Hunting, by Robert Wegner, St. Hubert's Press, Deforest, WI, 1993. 333 pp., 16 full-page illustrations. $45.00.
A comprehensive annotated compilation of books in English pertaining to deer and their hunting 1413-1991.

Western Hunting Guide, by Mike Lapinski, Stoneydale Press Publishing Co., Stevensville, MT, 1989. 168 pp., illus. $18.95.
A complete where-to-go and how-to-do-it guide to Western hunting.

Whispering Wings of Autumn, by Gene Hill and Steve Smith, Wilderness Adventures Press, Bozeman, MT, 1994. 150 pp., illus. $29.00.
Hill and Smith, masters of hunting literature, treat the reader to the best stories of grouse and woodcock hunting.

Whitetail: Behavior Through the Seasons, by Charles J. Alsheimer, Krause Publications, Iola, WI, 1996. 208 pp., illus. $34.95.
In-depth coverage of whitetail behavior presented through striking portraits of the whitetail in every season.

Whitetail: The Ultimate Challenge, by Charles J. Alsheimer, Krause Publications, Iola, WI, 1995. 228 pp., illus. Paper covers. $14.95.
Learn deer hunting's most intriguing secrets—fooling deer using decoys, scents and calls—from America's premier authority.

Wildfowlers Season, by Chris Dorsey, Lyons & Burford Publishers, New York, NY, 1998. 224 pp., illus. $37.95.
Modern methods for a classic sport.

The Wild Turkey Book, edited and with special commentary by J. Wayne Fears, Amwell Press, Clinton, NJ, 1982. 303 pp., illus. $22.50.
An anthology of the finest stories on wild turkey ever assembled under one cover.

The Wilderness Hunter, by Theodore Roosevelt, Wolfe Publishing Co., Prescott, AZ, 1994. 200 pp., illus. $25.00.
Reprint of a classic by one of America's most famous big game hunters.

Wildfowling Tales 1888-1913, Volume One, edited by Worth Mathewson, Sand Lake Press, Amity, OR, 1998. 186 pp., illustrated by David Hagerbaumer. $22.50.
A collection of some of the best accounts from our literary heritage.

Windward Crossings: A Treasury of Original Waterfowling Tales, edited and with a foreword by Chuck Petrie et al, Willow Creek Press, Minocqua, WI, 1998. $35.00.
An illustrated, modern anthology of previously unpublished waterfowl hunting (fiction and creative non-fiction) stories by America's finest outdoor journalists.

Wings of Thunder: New Grouse Hunting Revisited, by Steven Mulak, Countrysport Books, Selma, AL, 1998. 168 pp. illustrated. $30.00.
The author examines every aspect of New England grouse hunting as it is today - the bird and its habits, the hunter and his dog, guns and loads, shooting and hunting techniques, practice on clay targets, clothing and equipment.

Wings for the Heart, by Jerry A. Lewis, West River Press, Corvallis, MT, 1991. 324 pp., illus. Paper covers. $14.95.
A delightful book on hunting Montana's upland birds and waterfowl.

Wisconsin Hunting, by Brian Lovett, Krause Publications, Iola, WI, 1997. 208 pp., illus. Paper covers. $16.95.
A comprehensive guide to Wisconsin's public hunting lands.

The Woodchuck Hunter, by Paul C. Estey, R&R Books, Livonia, NY, 1994. 135 pp., illus. $25.00.

This book contains information on woodchuck equipment, the rifle, telescopic sights and includes interesting stories.

Woodcock Shooting, by Steve Smith, Stackpole Books, Inc., Harrisburg, PA, 1988. 142 pp., illus. $16.95.
A definitive book on woodcock hunting and the characteristics of a good woodcock dog.

World Record Whitetail: The Hanson Buck Story, by Milo Hanson with Ian McMurchy, Krause Publications, Iola, WI, 1995. 144 pp., illus. Paper covers. $9.95.
How do you top a deer hunting record that stood for 80 years? Milo Hanson shares in his firsthand account of bagging the largest whitetail ever scored in the history of B&C measurements.

The Working Retrievers, Tom Quinn, The Lyons Press, New York, NY, 1998. 257 pp., illus. $40.00.
The author covers every aspect of the training of dogs for hunting and field trials - from the beginning to the most advanced levels - for Labradors, Chesapeakes, Goldens and others.

World Record Whitetails, by Gordon Whittington, Safari Press Books, Inc., Huntington Beach, CA, 1998. 246 pp., illustrated. $39.95.
The first and only complete chronicle of all the bucks that have ever held the title "World Record Whitetail." Covers the greatest trophies ever recorded in their categories, typical, non-typical, gun, bow, and muzzleloader.

AFRICA/ASIA/ELSEWHERE

African Adventures, by J.F. Burger, Safari Press, Huntington Beach, CA, 1993. 222 pp., illus. $35.00.
The reader shares adventures on the trail of the lion, the elephant and buffalo.

The African Adventures: A Return to the Silent Places, by Peter Hathaway Capstick, St. Martin's Press, New York, NY, 1992. 220 pp., illus. $22.95.
This book brings to life four turn-of-the-century adventurers and the savage frontier they braved. Frederick Selous, Constantine "Iodine" Ionides, Johnny Boyes and Jim Sutherland.

African Camp-fire Nights, by J.E. Burger, Safari Press, Huntington Beach, CA, 1993. 192 pp., illus. $32.50.
In this book the author writes of the men who made hunting their life's profession.

African Game Trails, by Theodore Roosevelt, Peter Capstick, Series Editor, St. Martin's Press, New York, NY 1988. 583 pp., illustrated. $24.95.
The famed safari of the noted sportsman, conservationist, and President.

African Hunter, by James Mellon, Safari Press, Huntington Beach, CA, 1996. 522 pp., illus. Clothbound, $125.00; paper covers, $75.00.
Regarded as the most comprehensive title ever published on African hunting.

African Hunting and Adventure, by William Charles Baldwin, Books of Zimbabwe, Bulawayo, 1981. 451 pp., illus. $75.00.
Facsimile reprint of the scarce 1863 London edition. African hunting and adventure from Natal to the Zambezi.

African Jungle Memories, by J.F. Burger, Safari Press, Huntington Beach, CA, 1993. 192 pp., illus. $32.50.
A book of reminiscences in which the reader is taken on many exciting adventures on the trail of the buffalo, lion, elephant and leopard.

African Rifles & Cartridges, by John Taylor, The Gun Room Press, Highland Park, NJ, 1977. 431 pp., illus. $35.00.
Experiences and opinions of a professional ivory hunter in Africa describing his knowledge of numerous arms and cartridges for big game. A reprint.

African Safaris, by Major G.H. Anderson, Safari Press, Long Beach, CA, 1997. 173 pp., illus. $35.00.
A reprinting of one of the rarest books on African hunting, with a foreword by Tony Sanchez.

African Twilight, by Robert F. Jones, Wilderness Adventure Press, Bozeman, MT, 1994. 208 pp., illus. $36.00.
Details the hunt, danger and changing face of Africa over a span of three decades.

After Big Game in Central Africa, by Edouard Foa, St. Martin's Press, New York, NY, 1989. 400 pp., illus. $16.95.
Reprint of the scarce 1899 edition. This sportsman covered 7200 miles, mostly on foot—from Zambezi delta on the east coast to the mouth of the Congo on the west.

A Man Called Lion: The Life and Times of John Howar "Pondoro" Taylor, by P.H. Capstick, Safari Press, Huntington Beach, CA, 1994. 240 pp., illus. $24.95.
With the help of Brian Marsh, an old Taylor acquaintance, Peter Capstick has accumulated over ten years of research into the life of this mysterious man.

Argali: High-Mountain Hunting, by Ricardo Medem, Safari Press, Huntington Beach, CA, 1995. 304 pp., illus. Limited, signed edition. $150.00.
Medem describes hunting seven different countries in the pursuit of sheep and other mountain game.

Baron in Africa, by W. Alvensleben, Safari Press, Inc., Huntington Beach, CA, 1997. 100 pp., illus. $60.00.
A must-read adventure story on one of the most interesting characters to have come out of Africa after WWII.

The Best of Big Game, by Terry Wieland, John Culler and Sons, Camden, SC, 1996. 200 pp., illus. $49.95.
Twenty detailed accounts of the best hunters from around the world.

The Big Five, by Tony Dyer, Trophy Room Books, Angoura, CA, 1996. 224 pp., illus. Limited, numbered edition signed by both the artist and author. $100.00.
A new edition of this classic study of the big five by two of the men who know them best.

Big Game and Big Game Rifles, by John Taylor, Safari Press, Huntington Beach, CA, 1993. 215 pp., illus. $24.95.
A classic by the man who probably knew more about ammunition and rifles for African game than any other hunter.

Big Game Hunting and Collecting in East Africa 1903-1926, by Kalman Kittenberger, St. Martin's Press, New York, NY, 1989. 496 pp., illus. $16.95.
   One of the most heart stopping, charming and funny accounts of adventure in the Kenya Colony ever penned.

Big Game Hunting Around the World, by Bert Klineburger and Vernon W. Hurst, Exposition Press, Jericho, NY, 1969. 376 pp., illus. $30.00.
   The first book that takes you on a safari all over the world.

Big Game Hunting in Asia, Africa, and Elsewhere, by Jacques Vettier, Trophy Room Books, Agoura, CA, 1993. 400 pp., illus. Limited, numbered edition. $150.00.
   The first English language edition of the book that set a new standard in big game hunting book literature.

Big Game Hunting in North-Eastern Rhodesia, by Owen Letcher, St. Martin's Press, New York, NY, 1986. 272 pp., illus. $15.95.
   A classic reprint and one of the very few books to concentrate on this fascinating area, a region that today is still very much safari country.

Big Game Shooting in Cooch Behar, the Duars and Assam, by The Maharajah of Cooch Behar, Wolfe Publishing Co., Prescott, AZ, 1993. 461 pp., illus. $49.50.
   A reprinting of the book that has become legendary. This is the Maharajah's personal diary of killing 365 tigers.

The Book of the Lion, by Sir Alfred E. Pease, St. Martin's Press, New York, NY, 1986. 305 pp., illus. $15.95.
   Reprint of the finest book ever published on the subject. The author describes all aspects of lion history and lion hunting, drawing heavily on his own experiences in British East Africa.

Bwana Cotton, by Cotton Gordon, Trophy Room Books, Agoura, CA, 1996. 300 pp., illus. Limited, numbered and signed edition. $85.00.
   Rambling, witty, wonderful reminiscences of an African hunter.

Chui! A Guide to Hunting the African Leopard, by Lou Hallamore and Bruce Woods, Trophy Room Books, Agoura, CA, 1994. 239 pp., illus. $75.00.
   Tales of exciting leopard encounters by one of today's most respected pros.

A Country Boy in Africa, by George Hoffman, Trophy Room Books, Agoura, CA, 1998. 267 pp., illustrated with over 100 photos. Limited, numbered edition signed by the author. $85.00.
   In addition to the author's long and successful hunting career, he is known for developing a most effective big game cartridge, the .416 Hoffman.

Death in a Lonely Land, by Peter Capstick, St. Martin's Press, New York, NY, 1990. 284 pp., illus. $22.95.
   Twenty-three stories of hunting as only the master can tell them.

Death in the Dark Continent, by Peter Capstick, St. Martin's Press, New York, NY, 1983. 238 pp., illus $22.95.
   A book that brings to life the suspense, fear and exhilaration of stalking ferocious killers under primitive, savage conditions, with the ever present threat of death.

Death in the Long Grass, by Peter Hathaway Capstick, St. Martin's Press, New York, NY, 1977. 297 pp., illus. $22.95.
   A big game hunter's adventures in the African bush.

Death in the Silent Places, by Peter Capstick, St. Martin's Press, New York, NY, 1981. 243 pp., illus. $22.95.
   The author recalls the extraordinary careers of legendary hunters such as Corbett, Karamojo Bell, Stigand and others.

Duck Hunting in Australia, by Dick Eussen, Australia Outdoor Publishers Pty Ltd., Victoria, Australia, 1994. 106 pp., illus. Paper covers. $17.95.
   Covers the many aspects of duck hunting from blinds to hunting methods.

East Africa and its Big Game, by Captain Sir John C. Willowghby, Wolfe Publishing Co., Prescott, AZ, 1990. 312 pp., illus. $52.00.
   A deluxe limited reprint of the very scarce 1889 edition of a narrative of a sporting trip from Zanzibar to the borders of the Masai.

East of the Sun and West of the Moon, by Theodore and Kermit Roosevelt, Wolfe Publishing Co., Prescott, AZ, 1988. 284 pp., illus. $25.00.
   A limited edition reprint. A classic on Marco Polo sheep hunting. A life experience unique to hunters of big game.

Elephant Hunting in East Equatorial Africa, by A. Neumann, St. Martin's Press, New York, NY, 1994. 455 pp., illus. $26.95.
   This is a reprint of one of the rarest elephant hunting titles ever.

Elephants of Africa, by Dr. Anthony Hall-Martin, New Holland Publishers, London, England, 1987. 120 pp., illus. $75.00.
   A superbly illustrated overview of the African elephant with reproductions of paintings by the internationally acclaimed wildlife artist Paul Bosman.

Encounters with Lions, by Jan Hemsing, Trophy Room books, Agoura, CA, 1995. 302 pp., illus. $75.00.
   Some stories fierce, fatal, frightening and even humorous of when man and lion meet.

First Wheel, by Bunny Allen, Amwell Press, Clinton, NJ, 1984. Limited, signed and numbered edition in the NSFL "African Hunting Heritage Series." 292 pp., illus. $100.00.
   A white hunter's diary, 1927-47.

The Formidable Game, by John Batten, The Amwell Press, Clinton, NJ, 1994. 336 pp., illus. $40.00.
   Batten and his wife cover the globe in search of the world's dangerous game. Includes a section on the development of the big bore rifle for formidable game.

"For the Honour of a Hunter....", by A.M.D. (Tony) Seth-Smith, Trophy Room Books, Agoura, CA, 1996. 320 pp., illus. Limited, numbered and signed edition. $85.00.
   Autobiography of one of the breed of "hard safari men" whose lives are full of changes and charges.

Fourteen Years in the African Bush, by A. Marsh, Safari Press Publication, Huntington Beach, CA, 1998. 312 pp., illus. Limited signed, numbered, slipcased. $70.00.
   An account of a Kenyan game warden. A graphic and well-written story.

From Sailor to Professional Hunter: The Autobigraphy of John Northcote, Trophy Room Books, Agoura, CA, 1997. 400 pp., illus. Limited edition, signed and numbered. $125.00.
   Only a handfull of men can boast of having a fifty-year professional hunting career throughout Africa as John Northcote has had.

Glory Days of Baja, by Larry Stanton, John Culler and Sons, Camden, SC, 1996. 184 pp., illus. $21.95.
   This book represents twenty-five years of hunting in Mexico's Baja.

The Great Arc of the Wild Sheep, by J.L. Clark, Safari Press, Huntington Beach, CA, 1994. 247 pp., illus. $24.95.
   Perhaps the most complete work done on all the species and subspecies of the wild sheep of the world.

Horned Death, by John F. Burger, Safari Press, Huntington Beach, CA, 1992. 343 pp.illus. $35.00.
   The classic work on hunting the African buffalo.

Great Hunters: Their Trophy Rooms and Collections, Volume 1, compiled and published by Safari Press, Inc., Huntington Beach, CA, 1997. 172 pp., illustrated in color. $60.00.
   A rare glimpse into the trophy rooms of top international hunters. A few of these trophy rooms are museums.

Great Hunters: Their Trophy Rooms & Collections, Volume 2, compiled and published by Safari Press, Inc., Huntington Beach, CA, 1998. 224 pp., illustrated with 260 full-color photographs. $60.00.
   Volume two of the world's finest, best produced series of books on trophy rooms and game collections. 46 sportsmen sharing sights you'll never forget on this guided tour.

Horn of the Hunter, by Robert Ruark, Safari Press, Long Beach, CA, 1987. 315 pp., illus. $35.00.
   Ruark's most sought-after title on African hunting, here in reprint.

Hunter, by J.A. Hunter, Safari Press Publications, Huntington Beach, CA, 1999. 263 pp., illus. $24.95.
   Hunter's best known book on African big-game hunting. Internationally recognized as being one of the all-time African hunting classics.

A Hunter's Africa, by Gordon Cundill, Trophy Room Books, Agoura, CA, 1998. 298 pp., over 125 photographic illustrations. Limited numbered edition signed by the author. $125.00.
   A good look by the author at the African safari experience - elephant, lion, spiral-horned antelope, firearms, people and events, as well as the clients that make it worthwhile.

Hunter's Tracks, by J.A. Hunter, Safari Press Publications, Huntington Beach, CA, 1999. 240 pp., illustrated. $24.95.
   One of the most well-written stories of East African hunting, big game, and eccentric characters.

Hunters of Man, by Capt. J. Brandt, Safari Press, Huntington Beach, CA, 1997. 242 pp., illus. Paper covers. $18.95.
   True stories of man-eaters, man killers and rogues in Southeast Asia.

Hunting Adventures Worldwide, by Jack Atcheson, Jack Atcheson & Sons, Butte, MT, 1995. 256 pp., illus. $29.95.
   The author chronicles the richest adventures of a lifetime spent in quest of big game across the world – including Africa, North America and Asia.

Hunting in Ethiopia, An Anthology, by Tony Sanchez-Arino, Safari Press, Huntington Beach, CA, 1996. 350 pp., illus. Limited, signed and numbered edition. $135.00.
   The finest selection of hunting stories ever compiled on hunting in this great game country.

Hunting in Many Lands, by Theodore Roosevelt and George Bird Grinnel, The Boone and Crockett Club, Dumfries, VA, 1987. 447 pp., illus. $40.00.
   Limited edition reprint of this 1895 classic work on hunting in Africa, India, Mongolia, etc.

Hunting in the Sudan, An Anthology, compiled by Tony Sanchez-Arino, Safari Press, Huntington Beach, CA, 1992. 350 pp., illus. Limited, signed and numbered edition in a slipcase. $125.00.
   The finest selection of hunting stories ever compiled on hunting in this great game country.

Hunting, Settling and Remembering, by Philip H. Percival, Trophy Room Books, Agoura, CA, 1997. 230 pp., illus. Limited, numbered and signed edition. $85.00
   If Philip Percival is to come alive again, it will be through this, the first edition of his easy, intricate and magical book illustrated with some of the best historical big game hunting photos ever taken.

Hunting the Dangerous Game of Africa, by John Kingsley-Heath, Sycamore Island Books, Boulder, CO, 1998. 477 pp., illustrated. $95.00.
   Written by one of the most respected, successful, and ethical P.H.'s to trek the sunlit plains of Botswana, Kenya, Uganda, Tanganyika, Somaliland, Eritrea, Ethiopia, and Mozambique. Filled with some of the most gripping and terrifying tales ever to come out of Africa.

Hunting the Elephant in Africa, by Captain C.H. Stigand, St. Martin's Press, New York, NY, 1986. 379 pp., illus. $14.95.
   A reprint of the scarce 1913 edition; vintage Africana at its best.

Jaguar Hunting in the Mato Grosso and Bolivia, by T. Almedia, Safari Press, Long Beach, CA, 1989. 256 pp., illus. $35.00.
   Not since Sacha Siemel has there been a book on jaguar hunting like this one.

Jim Corbett, Master of the Jungle, by Tim Werling, Safari Press, Huntington Beach, CA, 1998. 215 pp., illus. $30.00
   A biography of India's most famous hunter of man-eating tigers and leopards.

King of the Wa-Kikuyu, by John Boyes, St. Martin Press, New York, NY, 1993. 240 pp., illus. $19.95.
   In the 19th and 20th centuries, Africa drew to it a large number of great hunters, explorers, adventurers and rogues. Many have become legendary, but John Boyes (1874-1951) was the most legendary of them all.

Lake Ngami, by Charles Anderson, New Holland Press, London, England, 1987. 576 pp., illus. $35.00.
Originally published in 1856. Describes two expeditions into what is now Botswana, depicting every detail of landscape and wildlife.

Last Horizons: Hunting, Fishing and Shooting on Five Continents, by Peter Capstick, St. Martin's Press, New York, NY, 1989. 288 pp., illus. $19.95.
The first in a two volume collection of hunting, fishing and shooting tales from the selected pages of The American Hunter, Guns & Ammo and Outdoor Life.

Last of the Few: Forty-Two Years of African Hunting, by Tony Sanchez-Arino, Safari Press, Huntington Beach, CA, 1996. 250 pp., illus. $85.00.
The story of the author's career with all the highlights that come from pursuing the unusual and dangerous animals that are native to Africa.

Last of the Ivory Hunters, by John Taylor, Safari Press, Long Beach, CA, 1990. 354 pp., illus. $29.95.
Reprint of the classic book "Pondoro" by one of the most famous elephant hunters of all time.

Legends of the Field: More Early Hunters in Africa, by W.R. Foran, Trophy Room Press, Agoura, CA, 1997. 319 pp., illus. Limited edition. $100.00.
This book contains the biographies of some very famous hunters: William Cotton Oswell, F.C. Selous, Sir Samuel Baker, Arthur Neumann, Jim Sutherland, W.D.M. Bell and others.

The Lost Classics, by Robert Ruark, Safari Press, Huntington Beach, CA, 1996. 260 pp., illus. $35.00.
The magazine stories that Ruark wrote in the 1950s and 1960s finally in print in book form.

The Magic of Big Games, by Terry Wieland, Countrysport Books, Selma, AL, 1998. 200 pp., illus. $39.00.
Original essays on hunting big game around the world.

Mahohboh, by Ron Thomson, African Safari Press, Hartbeespoort, South Africa, 1997. 312 pp., illustrated. Limited edition, signed and numbered. $70.00.
Elephants and elephant hunting in South Central Africa.

The Man-Eaters of Tsavo, by Lt. Colonel J.H. Patterson, Peter Capstick, series editor, St. Martin's Press, New York, NY, 1986, 5th printing. 346 pp., illus. $22.95.
The classic man-eating story of the lions that halted construction of a railway line and reportedly killed one hundred people, told by the man who risked his life to successfully shoot them.

Memoirs of an African Hunter, by Terry Irwin, Safari Press Publications, Huntington Beach, CA, 1998. 421 pp., illustrated. Limited numbered, signed and slipcased. $125.00.
A narrative of a professional hunter's experiences in Africa.

Men for all Seasons: The Hunters and Pioneers, by Tony Dyers, Trophy Room Books, Agoura, CA, 1996. 440 pp., illus. Limited, numbered and signed edition. $125.00.
The men, women and warriors who created the great Safari Industry of East Africa.

Months of the Sun; Forty Years of Elephant Hunting in the Zambezi Valley, by Ian Nyschens, Safari Press, Huntington Beach, CA, 1998. 420 pp., illus. Limited signed and numbered edition. Slipcased. $85.00.
The author has shot equally as many elephants as Walter Bell, and under much more difficult circumstances. His book will rank, or surpass, the best elephant-ivory hunting books published this century.

Mundjamba: The Life Story of an African Hunter, by Hugo Seia, Trophy Room Books, Agoura, CA, 1996. 400 pp., illus. Limited, numbered and signed by the author. $125.00.
An autobiography of one of the most respected and appreciated professional African hunters.

My Last Kambaku, by Leo Kroger, Safari Press, Huntington Beach, CA, 1997. 272 pp., illus. Limited edition signed and numbered and slipcased. $60.00.
One of the most engaging hunting memoirs ever published.

The Nature of the Game, by Ben Hoskyns, Quiller Press, Ltd., London, England, 1994. 160 pp., illus. $37.50.
The first complete guide to British, European and North American game.

One Happy Hunter, by George Barrington, Safari Press, Huntington Beach, CA, 1994. 240 pp., illus. $40.00.
A candid, straightforward look at safari hunting.

One Long Safari, by Peter Hay, Trophy Room Books, Agoura, CA, 1998. 350 pp., with over 200 photographic illustrations and 7 maps. Limited numbered edition signed by the author. $100.00.
Contains hunts for leopards, sitatunga, hippo, rhino, snakes and, of course, the general African big game bag.

The Path of a Hunter, by Gilles Tre-Hardy, Trophy Room Books, Agoura, CA, 1997. 318 pp., illus. Limited Edition, signed and numbered. $85.00.
A most unusual hunting autobiography with much about elephant hunting in Africa.

Peter Capstick's Africa: A Return to the Long Grass, by Peter Hathaway Capstick, St. Martin's Press, N. Y., NY, 1987. 213 pp., illus. $29.95.
A first-person adventure in which the author returns to the long grass for his own dangerous and very personal excursion.

The Recollections of an Elephant Hunter 1864-1875, by William Finaughty, Books of Zimbabwe, Bulawayo, Zimbabwe, 1980. 244 pp., illus. $85.00.
Reprint of the scarce 1916 privately published edition. The early game hunting exploits of William Finaughty in Matabeleland and Nashonaland.

Safari: A Chronicle of Adventure, by Bartle Bull, Viking/Penguin, London, England, 1989. 383 pp., illus. $40.00.
The thrilling history of the African safari, highlighting some of Africa's best-known personalities.

Safari Rifles: Double, Magazine Rifles and Cartridges for African Hunting, by Craig Boddington, Safari Press, Huntington Beach, CA, 1990. 416 pp., illus. $24.95.

A wealth of knowledge on the safari rifle. Historical and present double-rifle makers, ballistics for the large bores, and much, much more.

Safari: The Last Adventure, by Peter Capstick, St. Martin's Press, New York, NY, 1984. 291 pp., illus. $19.95.
A modern comprehensive guide to the African Safari.

Sands of Silence, by Peter H. Capstick, Saint Martin's Press, New York, NY, 1991. 224 pp., illus. $35.00.
Join the author on safari in Nambia for his latest big-game hunting adventures.

Shoot Straight and Stay Alive: A Lifetime of Hunting Experiences, by Fred Bartlett, Trophy Room Books, Argoura, CA, 1994. 262 pp., illus. $85.00.
A book written by a man who has left his mark on the maps of Africa's great gamelands.

Skyline Pursuits, by John Batten, The Amwell Press, Clinton, NJ, 1994. 372 pp., illus. $40.00.
A chronicle of Batten's own hunting adventures in the high country on four continents since 1928, traces a sheep hunting career that has accounted for both North American and International Grand Slams.

Solo Safari, by T. Cacek, Safari Press, Huntington Beach, CA, 1995. 270 pp., illus. $30.00.
Here is the story of Terry Cacek who hunted elephant, buffalo, leopard and plains game in Zimbabwe and Botswana on his own.

South Pacific Trophy Hunter, by Murray Thomas, Safari Press, Long Beach, CA, 1988. 181 pp., illus. $37.50.
A record of a hunter's search for a trophy of each of the 15 major game species in the South Pacific region.

Spiral-Horn Dreams, by Terry Wieland, Trophy Room Books, Agoura, CA, 1996. 362 pp., illus. Limited, numbered and signed by the author. $85.00.
Everyone who goes to hunt in Africa is looking for something; this is for those who go to hunt the spiral-horned antelope—the bongo, myala, mountain nyala, greater and lesser kudu, etc.

Sport on the Pamirs and Turkestan Steppes, by Major C.S. Cumberland, Moncrieff & Smith, Victoria, Autralia, 1992. 278 pp., illus. $45.00.
The first in a series of facsimile reprints of great trophy hunting books by Moncrieff & Smith.

Tales of the African Frontier, by J.A. Hunter, Safari Press Publications, Huntington Beach, CA, 1999. 308 pp., illus. $24.95.
The early days of East Africa is the subject of this powerful John Hunter book.

Theodore Roosevelt Outdoorsman, by R.L. Wilson, Trophy Room Books, Agoura, CA, 1994. 326 pp., illus. $85.00.
This book presents Theodore Roosevelt as a rancher, Rough Rider, Governor, President, naturalist and international big game hunter.

Those Were the Days, by Rudolf Sand, Safari Press, Huntington Beach, CA, 1993. 300 pp., illus. $100.00.
Travel with Rudolf Sand to the pinnacles of the world in his pursuit of wild sheep and goats.

Through the Brazilian Wilderness, by Theodore Roosevelt, Stackpole Books, Mechanicsburg, PA, 1994. 448 pp., illus. Paper covers. $16.95.
Adventure and drama in the South American jungle.

Trophy Hunter in Africa, by Elgin Gates, Safari Press, Huntington Beach, CA, 1994. 315 pp., illus. $29.95.
This is the story of one man's adventure in Africa's wildlife paradise.

Uganda Safaris, by Brian Herne, Winchester Press, Piscataway, NJ, 1979. 236 pp., illus. $12.95.
The chronicle of a professional hunter's adventures in Africa.

Under the Shadow of Man Eaters, by Jerry Jaleel, The Jim Corbett Foundation, Edmonton, Alberta, Canada, 1997. 152 pp., illus. A limited, numbered and signed edition. Paper covers. $35.00.
The life and legend of Jim Corbett of Kumaon.

Use Enough Gun, by Robert Ruark, Safari Press, Huntington Beach, CA, 1997. 333 pp., illus. $35.00.
Robert Ruark on big game hunting.

Warrior: The Legend of Col. Richard Meinertzhagen, by Peter H. Capstick, St. Martins Press, New York, NY, 1998. 320 pp., illus. $23.95.
A stirring and vivid biography of the famous British colonial officer Richard Meinertzhagen, whose exploits earned him fame and notoriety as one of the most daring and ruthless men to serve during the glory days of the British Empire.

Where Lions Roar: Ten More Years of African Hunting, by Craig Boddington, Safari Press, Huntington Beach, CA, 1997. 250 pp., illus. Limited edition, signed and numbered. In a slipcase. $60.00.
The story of Boddington's hunts in the Dark Continent during the last ten years.

White Hunter, by J.A. Hunter, Safari Press Publications, Huntington Beach, CA, 1999. 282 pp., illustrated. $24.95.
This book is a seldom-seen account of John Hunter's adventures in pre-WW2 Africa.

A White Hunters Life, by Angus MacLagan, an African Heritage Book, published by Amwell Press, Clinton, NJ, 1983. 283 pp. Limited, signed, and numbered deluxe edition, in slipcase. $100.00.
True to life, a sometimes harsh yet intriguing story.

Wild Sports of Southern Africa, by William Cornwallis Harris, New Holland Press, London, England, 1987. 376 pp., illus. $35.00.
Originally published in 1863, describes the author's travels in Southern Africa.

With a Gun in Good Country, by Ian Manning, Trophy Room Books, Agoura, CA, 1996. Limited, numbered and signed by the author. $85.00.
A book written about that splendid period before the poaching onslaught which almost closed Zambia and continues to the granting of her independence. It

then goes on to recount Manning's experiences in Botswana, Congo, and briefly in South Africa.

RIFLES

The Accurate Varmint Rifle, by Boyd Mace, Precision Shooting, Inc., Whitehall, NY, 1991. 184 pp., illus. $15.00.
A long overdue and long needed work on what factors go into the selection of components for and the subsequent assembly of...the accurate varmint rifle.

The AK-47 Assault Rifle, Desert Publications, Cornville, AZ, 1981. 150 pp., illus. Paper covers. $13.95.
Complete and practical technical information on the only weapon in history to be produced in an estimated 30,000,000 units.

American Hunting Rifles: Their Application in the Field for Practical Shooting, by Craig Boddington, Safari Press, Huntington Beach, CA, 1996. 446 pp., illus. First edition, limited, signed and slipcased. $85.00. Second printing trade edition. $35.00.
Covers all the hunting rifles and calibers that are needed for North America's diverse game.

The AR-15/M16, A Practical Guide, by Duncan Long. Paladin Press, Boulder, CO, 1985. 168 pp., illus. Paper covers. $20.00.
The definitive book on the rifle that has been the inspiration for so many modern assault rifles.

The Art of Shooting With the Rifle, by Col. Sir H. St. John Halford, Excalibur Publications, Latham, NY, 1996. 96 pp., illus. Paper covers. $12.95.
A facsimile edition of the 1888 book by a respected rifleman providing a wealth of detailed information.

The Art of the Rifle, by Jeff Cooper, Paladin Press, Boulder, CO, 1997. 104 pp., illus. $29.95.
Everthing you need to know about the rifle whether you use it for security, meat or target shooting.

Assault Weapons, 4th Edition, by Jack Lewis, DBI Books, a division of Krause Publications, Iola, WI, 1996. 256 pp., illus. Paper covers. $19.95.
An in-depth look at the history and uses of these arms.

Australian Military Rifles & Bayonets, 200 Years of, by Ian Skennerton, I.D.S.A. Books, Piqua, OH, 1988. 124 pp., 198 illus. Paper covers. $19.50.

Australian Service Machineguns, 100 Years of, by Ian Skennerton, I.D.S.A. Books, Piqua, OH, 1989. 122 pp., 150 illus. Paper covers. $19.50.

The Big Game Rifle, by Jack O'Connor, Safari Press, Huntington Beach, CA, 1994. 370 pp., illus. $37.50.
An outstanding description of every detail of construction, purpose and use of the big game rifle.

Big Game Rifles and Cartridges, by Elmer Keith, reprint edition by The Gun Room Press, Highland Park, NJ, 1984. 161 pp., illus. $29.95.
Reprint of Elmer Keith's first book, a most original and accurate work on big game rifles and cartridges.

Black Magic: The Ultra Accurate AR-15, by John Feamster, Precision Shooting, Manchester, CT, 1998. 300 pp., illustrated. $29.95.
The author has compiled his experiences pushing the accuracy envelope of the AR-15 to its maximum potential. A wealth of advice on AR-15 loads, modifications and accessories for everything from NRA Highpower and Service Rifle competitions to benchrest and varmint shooting.

The Black Rifle, M16 Retrospective, R. Blake Stevens and Edward C. Ezell, Collector Grade Publications, Toronto, Canada, 1987. 400 pp., illus. $59.95
The complete story of the M16 rifle and its development.

Bolt Action Rifles, 3rd Edition, by Frank de Haas, DBI Books, a division of Krause Publications, Iola, WI, 1995. 528 pp., illus. Paper covers. $24.95.
A revised edition of the most definitive work on all major bolt-action rifle designs.

The Book of the Garand, by Maj. Gen. J.S. Hatcher, The Gun Room Press, Highland Park, NJ, 1977. 292 pp., illus. $26.95.
A new printing of the standard reference work on the U.S. Army M1 rifle.

The Book of the Twenty-Two: The All American Caliber, by Sam Fadala, Stoeger Publishing Co., So. Hackensack, NJ, 1989. 288 pp., illus. Soft covers. $16.95.
The All American Caliber from BB caps up to the powerful 226 Barnes. It's about ammo history, plinking, target shooting, and the quest for the one-hole group.

British Military Martini, Treatise on the, Vol. 1, by B.A. Temple and Ian Skennerton, I.D.S.A. Books, Piqua, OH, 1983. 256 pp., 114 illus. $40.00.

British Military Martini, Treatise on the, Vol. 2, by B.A. Temple and Ian Skennerton, I.D.S.A. Books, Piqua, OH, 1989. 213 pp., 135 illus. $40.00.

British .22RF Training Rifles, by Dennis Lewis and Robert Washburn, Excalibur Publications, Latham, NY, 1993. 64 pp., illus. Paper covers. $10.95.
The story of Britain's training rifles from the early Aiming Tube models to the post-WWII trainers.

Classic Sporting Rifles, by Christopher Austyn, Safari Press, Huntington Beach, CA, 1997. 128 pp., illus. $50.00.
As the head of the gun department at Christie's Auction House the author examines the "best" rifles built over the last 150 years.

Combat Rifles of the 21st Century, by Duncan Long, Paladin Press, Boulder, CO, 1991. 115 pp., illus. Paper covers. $16.50.
An inside look at the U.S. Army's program to develop a super advanced combat rifle to replace the M16.

The Complete AR15/M16 Sourcebook, by Duncan Long, Paladin Press, Boulder, CO, 1993. 232 pp., illus. Paper covers. $35.00.

The latest development of the AR15/M16 and the many spin-offs now available, selective-fire conversion systems for the 1990s, the vast selection of new accessories.

The Complete M1 Garand, by Jim Thompson, Paladin Press, Boulder, CO, 1998. 160 pp., illustrated. Paper cover. $25.00.
A guide for the shooter and collector, heavily illustrated.

Exploded Long Gun Drawings, The Gun Digest Book of, edited by Harold A. Murtz, DBI Books, a division of Krause Publications, Iola, WI, 512 pp., illus. Paper covers. $20.95.
Containing almost 500 rifle and shotgun exploded drawings. An invaluable aid to both professionals and hobbyists.

The FAL Rifle, by R. Blake Stevens and Jean van Rutten, Collector Grade Publications, Cobourg, Canada, 1993. 848 pp., illus. $129.95.
Originally published in three volumes, this classic edition covers North American, UK and Commonwealth and the metric FAL's.

The Fighting Rifle, by Chuck Taylor, Paladin Press, Boulder, CO, 1983. 184 pp., illus. Paper covers. $25.00.
The difference between assault and battle rifles and auto and light machine guns.

Firearms Assembly/Disassembly Part III: Rimfire Rifles, Revised Edition, The Gun Digest Book of, by J. B. Wood, DBI Books, a division of Krause Publications, Iola, WI., 1994. 480 pp., illus. Paper covers. $19.95.
Covers 65 popular rimfires plus over 100 variants, all cross-referenced in the index.

Firearms Assembly/Disassembly Part IV: Centerfire Rifles, Revised Edition, The Gun Digest Book of, by J.B. Wood, DBI Books, a division of Krause Publications, Iola, WI, 1991. 480 pp., illus. Paper covers. $19.95.
Covers 54 popular centerfire rifles plus 300 variants. The most comprehensive and professional presentation available to either hobbyist or gunsmith.

The FN-FAL Rifle, et al, by Duncan Lond, Delta Press, El Dorado, AR, 1998. 148 pp., illustrated. Paper covers. $18.95.
A comprehensive study of one of the classic assault weapons of all times. Detailed descriptions of the basic models plus the myriad of variants that evolved as a result of its universal acceptance.

Forty Years with the .45-70, second edition, revised and expanded, by Paul A. Matthews, Wolfe Publishing Co., Prescott, AZ, 1997. 184 pp., illus. Paper covers. $14.95.
This book is pure gun lore-lore of the .45-70. It not only contains a history of the cartridge, but also years of the author's personal experiences.

F.N.-F.A.L. Auto Rifles, Desert Publications, Cornville, AZ, 1981. 130 pp., illus. Paper covers. $13.95.
A definitive study of one of the free world's finest combat rifles.

The Hammerless Double Rifle, by Alexander Gray, Wolfe Publishing Co., Prescott, AZ, 1994. 154 pp., illus. $39.50.
The history, design, construction and maintenance are explored for a better understanding of these firearms.

Hints and Advice on Rifle-Shooting, by Private R. McVittie with new introductory material by W.S. Curtis, W.S. Curtis Publishers, Ltd., Clwyd, England, 1993. 32 pp. Paper covers. $10.00.
A reprint of the original 1886 London edition.

How-To's for the Black Powder Cartridge Rifle Shooter, by Paul A. Matthews, Wolfe Publishing Co., Prescott, AZ, 1996. 136 pp., illus. Paper covers. $22.50.
Practices and procedures used in the reloading and shooting of blackpowder cartridges.

Hunting with the .22, by C.S. Landis, R&R Books, Livonia, NY, 1995. 429 pp., illus. $45.00.
A reprinting of the classical work on .22 rifles.

Illustrated Handbook of Rifle Shooting, by A.L. Russell, Museum Restoration Service, Alexandria Bay, NY, 1992. 194 pp., illus. $24.50.
A new printing of the 1869 edition by one of the leading military marksman of the day.

Know Your M1 Garand, by E. J. Hoffschmidt, Blacksmith Corp., Southport, CT, 1975, 84 pp., illus. Paper covers. $9.95.
Facts about America's most famous infantry weapon. Covers test and experimental models, Japanese and Italian copies, National Match models.

Know Your Ruger 10/22 Carbine, by William E. Workman, Blacksmith Corp., Chino Valley, AZ, 1991. 96 pp., illus. Paper covers. $9.95.
The story and facts about the most popular 22 autoloader ever made.

The Lee Enfield No. 1 Rifles, by Alan M. Petrillo, Excalibur Publications, Latham, NY, 1992. 64 pp., illus. Paper covers. $10.95.
Highlights the SMLE rifles from the Mark 1-VI.

The Lee Enfield Number 4 Rifles, by Alan M. Petrillo, Excalibur Publications, Latham, NY, 1992. 64 pp., illus. Paper covers. $10.95.
A pocket-sized, bare-bones reference devoted entirely to the .303 World War II and Korean War vintage service rifle.

The Lee Enfield Story, by Ian Skennerton, I.D.S.A. Books, Piqua, OH, 1993. 504 pp., nearly 1,000 illus. $59.95.

Legendary Sporting Rifles, by Sam Fadala, Stoeger Publishing Co., So. Hackensack, NJ, 1992. 288 pp., illus. Paper covers. $16.95.
Covers a vast span of time and technology beginning with the Kentucky Long-rifle.

The Li'l M1 .30 Cal. Carbine, by Duncan Long, Desert Publications, El Dorado, AZ, 1995. 203 pp., illus. Paper covers. $14.95.
Traces the history of this little giant from its original creation.

Make It Accurate: Get the Maximum Performance from Your Hunting Rifle, by Craig Boddington, Safari Press Publications, Huntington Beach, CA, 1999. 224 pp., illustrated. $24.95.
Tips on how to select the rifle, cartridge, and scope best suited to your needs. A must-have for any hunter who wants to improve his shot.

THE ARMS LIBRARY

Mauser Smallbore Sporting, Target and Training Rifles, by Jon Speed, Collector Grade Publications, Inc., Cobourg, Ont., Canada, 1998. 372 pp., illustrated. $67.50.

The history of all the smallbore sporting, target and training rifles produced by the legendary Mauser-Werke of Obendorf am Neckar.

Mauser: Original-Oberndorf Sporting Rifles, by Jon Speed, Collector Grade Publications, Inc., Cobourg, Ont., Canada, 1997. 508 pp., illustrated. $89.95.

The most exhaustive study ever published of the design origins and manufacturing history of the original Oberndorf Mauser Sporter.

M14/M14A1 Rifles and Rifle Markmanship, Desert Publications, El Dorado, AZ, 1995. 236 pp., illus. Paper covers. $18.95.

Contains a detailed description of the M14 and M14A1 rifles and their general characteristics, procedures for disassembly and assembly, operating and functioning of the rifles, etc.

The M14 Owner's Guide and Match Conditioning Instructions, by Scott A. Duff and John M. Miller, Scott A. Duff Publications, Export, PA, 1996. 180 pp., illus. Paper covers. $19.95.

Traces the history and development from the T44 through the adoption and production of the M14 rifle.

The M-14 Rifle, facsimile reprint of FM 23-8, Desert Publications, Cornville, AZ, 50 pp., illus. Paper $11.95.

Well illustrated and informative reprint covering the M-14 and M-14E2.

The M14-Type Rifle: A Shooter's and Collector's Guide, by Joe Poyer, North Cape Publications, Tustin, CA, 1997. 82 pp., illus. Paper covers. $18.95.

covers the history and development, commercial copies, cleaning and maintenance instructions, and targeting and shooting.

The M16/AR15 Rifle, by Joe Poyer, North Cape Publications, Tustin, CA, 1998. 150 pp., illustrated. Paper covers. $19.95.

From its inception as the first American assault battle rifle to the firing lines of the National Matches, the M16/AR15 rifle in all its various models and guises has made a significant impact on the American rifleman.

Military Bolt Action Rifles, 1841-1918, by Donald B. Webster, Museum Restoration Service, Alexander Bay, NY, 1993. 150 pp., illus. $34.50.

A photographic survey of the principal rifles and carbines of the European and Asiatic powers of the last half of the 19th century and the first years of the 20th century.

Military and Sporting Rifle Shooting, by Captain E.C. Crossman, Wolfe Publishing Co., Prescott, AZ, 1988. 449 pp., illus. $45.00.

A limited edition reprint. A complete and practical treatise covering the use of rifles.

The Mini-14, by Duncan Long, Paladin Press, Boulder, CO, 1987. 120 pp., illus. Paper covers. $15.00.

History of the Mini-14, the factory-produced models, specifications, accessories, suppliers, and much more.

Mr. Single Shot's Book of Rifle Plans, by Frank de Haas, Mark de Haas, Orange City, IA, 1996. 85 pp., illus. Paper covers. $22.50.

Contains complete and detailed drawings, plans and instructions on how to build four different and unique breech-loading single shot rifles of the author's own proven design.

M1 Carbine Owner's Manual, M1, M2 & M3 .30 Caliber Carbines, Firepower Publications, Cornville, AZ, 1984. 102 pp., illus. Paper covers. $16.95.

The complete book for the owner of an M1 Carbine.

The M1 Garand Serial Numbers & Data Sheets, by Scott A. Duff, Scott A. Duff, Export, PA, 1995. 101 pp. Paper covers. $9.95.

This pocket reference book includes serial number tables and data sheets on the Springfield Armory, Gas Trap Rifles, Gas Port Rifles, Winchester Repeating Arms, International Harvester and H&R Arms Co. and more.

More Single Shot Rifles and Actions, by Frank de Haas, Mark de Haas, Orange City, IA, 1996. 146 pp., illus. Paper covers. $22.50.

Covers 45 different single shot rifles. Includes the history plus photos, drawings and personal comments.

The Muzzle-Loading Rifle...Then and Now, by Walter M. Cline, National Muzzle Loading Rifle Association, Friendship, IN, 1991. 161 pp., illus. $32.00.

This extensive compilation of the muzzleloading rifle exhibits accumulative preserved data concerning the development of the "hallowed old arms of the Southern highlands."

The No. 4 (T) Sniper Rifle: An Armourer's Perspective, by Peter Laidler with Ian Skennerton, I.D.S.A. Books, Piqua, OH, 1993. 125 pp., 75 illus. Paper covers. $19.95.

Notes on Rifle-Shooting, by Henry William Heaton, reprinted with a new introduction by W.S. Curtis, W.S. Curtis Publishers, Ltd., Clwyd, England, 1993. 89 pp. $19.95.

A reprint of the 1864 London edition. Captain Heaton was one of the great rifle shots from the earliest days of the Volunteer Movement.

The Official SKS Manual, Translation by Major James F. Gebhardt (Ret.), Paladin Press, Boulder, CO, 1997. 96 pp., illus. Paper covers. $15.00.

This Soviet military manual covering the widely distributed SKS is now available in English.

The Pennsylvania Rifle, by Samuel E. Dyke, Sutter House, Lititz, PA, 1975. 61 pp., illus. Paper covers. $10.00.

History and development, from the hunting rifle of the Germans who settled the area. Contains a full listing of all known Lancaster, PA, gunsmiths from 1729 through 1815.

Police Rifles, by Richard Fairburn, Paladin Press, Boulder, CO, 1994. 248 pp., illus. Paper covers. $30.00.

Selecting the right rifle for street patrol and special tactical situations.

The Poor Man's Sniper Rifle, by D. Boone, Paladin Press, Boulder, CO, 1995. 152 pp., illus. Paper covers. $14.95.

Here is a complete plan for converting readily available surplus military rifles to high-performance sniper weapons.

A Potpourri of Single Shot Rifles and Actions, by Frank de Haas, Mark de Haas, Ridgeway, MO, 1993. 153 pp., illus. Paper covers. $22.50.

The author's 6th book on non-bolt-action single shots. Covers more than 40 single-shot rifles in historical and technical detail.

The Remington 700, by John F. Lacy, Taylor Publishing Co., Dallas, TX, 1990. 208 pp., illus. $44.95.

Covers the different models, limited editions, chamberings, proofmarks, serial numbers, military models, and much more.

The Revolving Rifles, by Edsall James, Pioneer Press, Union City, TN, 1975. 23 pp., illus. Paper covers. $2.50.

Valuable information on revolving cylinder rifles, from the earliest matchlock forms to the latest models of Colt and Remington.

Rifle Guide, by Sam Fadala, Stoeger Publishing Co., S. Hackensack, NJ, 1993. 288 pp., illus. Paper covers. $16.95.

This comprehensive, fact-filled book beckons to both the seasoned rifleman as well as the novice shooter.

The Rifle: Its Development for Big-Game Hunting, by S.R. Truesdell, Safari Press, Huntington Beach, CA, 1992. 274 pp., illus. $35.00.

The full story of the development of the big-game rifle from 1834-1946.

Rifleman's Handbook: A Shooter's Guide to Rifles, Reloading & Results, by Rick Jamison, NRA Publications, Washington, DC, 1990. 303 pp., illus. $21.95.

Helpful tips on precision reloading, how to squeeze incredible accuracy out of an "everyday" rifle, etc.

Riflesmithing, The Gun Digest Book of, by Jack Mitchell, DBI Books, a division of Krause Publications, Iola, WI, 1982. 256 pp., illus. Paper covers. $16.95.

Covers tools, techniques, designs, finishing wood and metal, custom alterations.

Rifles of the World, 2nd Edition, edited by John Walter, DBI Books, a division of Krause Publications, Iola, WI, 1998. 384 pp., illus. $24.95.

The definitive guide to the world's centerfire and rimfire rifles.

Ned H. Roberts and the Schuetzen Rifle, edited by Gerald O. Kelver, Brighton, CO, 1982. 99 pp., illus. $15.00.

A compilation of the writings of Major Ned H. Roberts which appeared in various gun magazines.

The Ruger 10/22, by William E. Workman, Krause Publications, Iola, WI, 1994. 320 pp., illus. Paper covers. $19.95.

Learn all about the most popular, best-selling and perhaps best-built 22 caliber semi-automatic rifles of all time.

Schuetzen Rifles, History and Loading, by Gerald O. Kelver, Gerald O. Kelver, Publisher, Brighton, CO, 1972. Illus. $15.00.

Reference work on these rifles, their bullets, loading, telescopic sights, accuracy, etc. A limited, numbered ed.

Semi-Auto Rifles: Data and Comment, edited by Robert W. Hunnicutt, The National Rifle Association, Washington, DC, 1988. 156 pp., illus. Paper covers. $15.95.

A book for those who find military-style self-loading rifles interesting for their history, intriguing for the engineering that goes into their design, and a pleasure to shoot.

Shooting the Blackpowder Cartridge Rifle, by Paul A. Matthews, Wolfe Publishing Co., Prescott, AZ, 1994. 129 pp., illus. Paper covers. $22.50.

A general discourse on shooting the blackpowder cartridge rifle and the procedure required to make a particular rifle perform.

Single Shot Rifles and Actions, by Frank de Haas, Orange City, IA, 1990. 352 pp., illus. Soft covers. $27.00.

The definitive book on over 60 single shot rifles and actions.

Sixty Years of Rifles, by Paul A. Matthews, Wolfe Publishing Co., Prescott, AZ, 1991. 224 pp., illus. $19.50.

About rifles and the author's experience and love affair with shooting and hunting.

S.L.R.—Australia's F.N. F.A.L. by Ian Skennerton and David Balmer, I.D.S.A. Books, Piqua, OH, 1989. 124 pp., 100 illus. Paper covers. $19.50.

Small Arms Identification Series, No. 2—.303 Rifle, No. 4 Marks I, & I*, Marks 1/2, 1/3 & 2, by Ian Skennerton, I.D.S.A. Books, Piqua, OH, 1994. 48 pp. $9.50.

Small Arms Identification Series, No. 3—9mm Austen Mk I & 9mm Owen Mk I Sub-Machine Guns, by Ian Skennerton, I.D.S.A. Books, Piqua, OH, 1994. 48 pp. $9.50.

Small Arms Identification Series, No. 4—.303 Rifle, No. 5 Mk I, by Ian Skennerton, I.D.S.A. Books, Piqua, OH, 1994. 48 pp. $9.50.

Small Arms Identification Series, No. 5—.303-in. Bren Light Machine Gun, by Ian Skennerton, I.D.S.A. Books, Piqua, OH, 1994. 48 pp. $9.50.

Small Arms Series, No. 1 DeLisle's Commando Carbine, by Ian Skennerton, I.D.S.A. Books, Piqua, OH, 1981. 32 pp., 24 illus. $9.00.

Small Arms Identification Series, No. 1—.303 Rifle, No. 1 S.M.L.E. Marks III and III*, by Ian Skennerton, I.D.S.A. Books, Piqua, OH, 1994. 48 pp. $9.50.

Sporting Rifle Takedown & Reassembly Guide, 2nd Edition, by J.B. Wood, DBI Books, a division of Krause Publications, Iola, WI, 1997. 480 pp., illus. $19.95.

An updated edition of the reference guide for anyone who wants to properly care for their sporting rifle. (Available September 1997)

The Springfield Rifle M1903, M1903A1, M1903A3, M1903A4, Desert Publications, Cornville, AZ, 1982. 100 pp., illus. Paper covers. $12.00.

Covers every aspect of disassembly and assembly, inspection, repair and maintenance.

Still More Single Shot Rifles, by James J. Grant, Pioneer Press, Union City, TN, 1995. 211 pp., illus. $27.50.

This is Volume Four in a series of Single-Shot Rifles by America's foremost authority. It gives more in-depth information on those single-shot rifles which were presented in the first three books.

The Sturm, Ruger 10/22 Rifle and .44 Magnum Carbine, by Duncan Long, Paladin Press, Boulder, CO, 1988. 108 pp., illus. Paper covers. $12.00.

THE ARMS LIBRARY

An in-depth look at both weapons detailing the elegant simplicity of the Ruger design. Offers specifications, troubleshooting procedures and ammunition recommendations.

Target Rifle in Australia, by J.E. Corcoran, R&R, Livonia, NY, 1996. 160 pp., illus. $40.00.
A most interesting study of the evolution of these rifles from 1860 - 1900. British rifles from the percussion period through the early smokeless era are discussed.

To the Dreams of Youth: The .22 Caliber Single Shot Winchester Rifle, by Herbert Houze, Krause Publications, Iola, WI, 1993. 192 pp., illus. $34.95.
A thoroughly researched history of the 22-caliber Winchester single shot rifle, including interesting photographs.

U.S. Marine Corps AR15/M16 A2 Manual, reprinted by Desert Publications, El Dorado, AZ, 1993. 262 pp., illus. Paper covers. $16.95.
A reprint of TM05538C-23&P/2, August, 1987. The A-2 manual for the Colt AR15/M16.

U.S. Rifle M14—From John Garand to the M21, by R. Blake Stevens, Collector Grade Publications, Inc., Toronto, Canada, revised second edition, 1991. 350 pp., illus. $49.50.
A classic, in-depth examination of the development, manufacture and fielding of the last wood-and-metal ("lock, stock, and barrel") battle rifle to be issued to U.S. troops.

War Baby!: The U.S. Caliber 30 Carbine, Volume I, by Larry Ruth, Collector Grade Publications, Toronto, Canada, 1992. 512 pp., illus. $69.95.
Volume 1 of the in-depth story of the phenomenally popular U.S. caliber 30 carbine. Concentrates on design and production of the military 30 carbine during World War II.

War Baby Comes Home: The U.S. Caliber 30 Carbine, Volume 2, by Larry Ruth, Collector Grade Pulications, Toronto, Canada, 1993. 386 pp., illus. $49.95.
The triumphant competion of Larry Ruth's two-volume in-depth series on the most popular U.S. military small arm in history.

The Winchester Model 52, Perfection in Design, by Herbert G. Houze, Krause Publicaitons, Iola, WI, 1997. 192 pp., illus. $34.95.
This book covers the complete story of this technically superior gun.

The Winchester Model 94: The First 100 Years, by Robert C. Renneberg, Krause Publications, Iola, WI, 1991. 208 pp., illus. $34.95.
Covers the design and evolution from the early years up to today.

Winchester Slide-Action Rifles, Volume I: Model 1890 and Model 1906 by Ned Schwing, Krause Publications, Iola, WI. 352 pp., illus. $39.95
Traces the history through word and picture in this chronolgy of the Model 1890 and 1906.

Winchester Slide-Action Rifles, Volume II: Model 61 & Model 62 by Ned Schwing, Krause Publications, Iola, WI. 256 pp., illus. $34.95
Historical look complete with markings, stampings and engraving.

SHOTGUNS

Advanced Combat Shotgun: The Stress Fire Concept, by Massad Ayoob, Police Bookshelf, Concord, NH, 1993. 197 pp., illus. Paper covers. $9.95.
Advanced combat shotgun fighting for police.

The American Shotgun, by Charles Askins, Wolfe Publishing Co., Prescott, AZ, 1988. 321 pp., illus. $39.00.
A limited edition reprint. Askins covers shotguns and patterning extremely well.

The American Shotgun, by David F. Butler, edited by C. Kenneth Ramage, Lyman Publications, Middlefield, CT, 1973. 243 pp., illus. Paper covers. $14.95.
A comprehensive history of the American smoothbore's evolution from Colonial times to the present day.

Best Guns, by Michael McIntosh, Countrysport, Inc., Traverse City, MI, 1989. 288 pp., illus. $39.50.
Devoted to the best shotguns ever made in the United States and the best presently being made in the world.

The Better Shot, by Ken Davies, Quiller Press, London, England, 1992. 136 pp., illus. $39.95.
Step-by-step shotgun technique with Holland and Holland.

Black Powder Hobby Gunsmithing, by Sam Fadala and Dale Storey, DBI Books, a division of Krause Publications, Iola, WI, 1994. 256 pp., illus. Paper covers. $18.95
A how-to-guide for gunsmithing blackpowder pistols, rifles and shotguns from two men at the top of their respective fields.

The British Shotgun, Volume 1, 1850-1870, by I.M. Crudington and D.J. Baker, Barrie & Jenkins, London, England, 1979. 256 pp., illus. $65.00.
An attempt to trace, as accurately as is now possible, the evolution of the shotgun during its formative years in Great Britain.

Boothroyd on British Shotguns, by Geoffrey Boothroyd, Sand Lake Press, Amity, OR, 1996. 221 pp., illus. plus a 32 page reproduction of the 1914 Webley & Scott catalog. A limited, numbered edition. $34.95.
Based on articles by the author that appeared in the British Publication *Shooting Times & Country Magazine.*

The British Over-and-Under Shotgun, by Geoffrey and Susan Boothroyd, Sand Lake Press, Amity, OR, 1996. 137 pp., illus. $34.95.
Historical outline of the development of the O/U shotgun with individual chapters devoted to the twenty-two British makers.

Boss & Co. Builders of Best Guns Only, by Donald Dallas, Safari Press, Huntington Beach, CA, 1996. 336 pp., illus. $75.00

The Browning Superposed: John M. Browning's Last Legacy, by Ned Schwing, Krause Publications, Iola, WI, 1996. 496 pp., illus. $49.95.
An exclusive story of the man, the company and the best-selling over-and-under shotgun in North America.

Clay Pigeon Shooting for Beginners and Enthusiasts, by John King, The Sportsman's Press, London, England, 1991. 94 pp., illus. $24.95.
John King has devised this splendid guide to clay pigeon shooting in the same direct style in which he teaches at his popular Barbury Shooting School near Swindon.

Clay Shooting, by Peter Croft, Ward Lock, London, England, 1990. 160 pp., illus, $29.95.
A complete guide to Skeet, trap and sporting shooting.

Clay Target Handbook, by Jerry Meyer, Lyons & Buford, Publisher, New York, NY, 1993. 182 pp., illus. $22.95.
Contains in-depth, how-to-do-it information on trap, skeet, sporting clays, international trap, international skeet and clay target games played around the country.

Clay Target Shooting, by Paul Bentley, A&C Black, London, England, 1987. 144 pp., illus. $25.00.
Practical book on clay target shooting written by a very successful international competitor, providing valuable professional advice and instruction for shooters of all disciplines.

A Collector's Guide to United States Combat Shotguns, by Bruce N. Canfield, Andrew Mowbray Inc., Publishers, Lincoln, RI, 1993. 184 pp., illus. Paper covers. $24.00.
Full coverage of the combat shotgun, from the earliest examples to the Gulf War and beyond.

The Complete Clay Shot, by Mike Barnes, Trafalgar Square, N. Pomfret, VT, 1993. 192 pp., illus. $39.95.
The latest compendium on the clay sports by Mike Barnes, a well-known figure in shotgunning in the U.S. and England.

Cradock on Shotguns, by Chris Cradock, Banford Press, London, England, 1989. 200 pp., illus. $45.00.
A definitive work on the shotgun by a British expert on shotguns.

The Defensive Shotgun, by Louis Awerbuck, S.W.A.T. Publications, Cornville, AZ, 1989. 77 pp., illus. Soft covers. $14.95.
Cuts through the myths concerning the shotgun and its attendant ballistic effects.

The Double Shotgun, by Don Zutz, Winchester Press, Piscataway, NJ, 1985. 304 pp., illus. $20.95.
Revised, updated, expanded edition of the history and development of the world's classic sporting firearms.

Exploded Long Gun Drawings, The Gun Digest Book of, edited by Harold A. Murtz, DBI Books, a division of Krause Publications, Iola, WI. 512 pp., illus. Paper covers. $20.95.
Containing almost 500 rifle and shotgun exploded drawings. An invaluable aid to both professionals and hobbyists.

Field, Cover and Trap Shooting, by Adam H. Bogardus, Wolfe Publishing Co., Prescott, AZ, 1988. 446 pp., illus. $45.00.
A limited edition reprint. Hints for skilled marksmen as well as young sportsmen. Includes haunts and habits of game birds and waterfowl.

Finding the Extra Target, by Coach John R. Linn & Stephen A. Blumenthal, Shotgun Sports, Inc., Auburn, CA, 1989. 126 pp., illus. Paper covers. $14.95.
The ultimate training guide for all the clay target sports.

Fine Gunmaking: Double Shotguns, by Steven Dodd Hughes, Krause Publications Iola, WI, 1998. 167 pp., illustrated. $34.95.
An in-depth look at the creation of fine shotguns.

Firearms Assembly/Disassembly, Part V: Shotguns, Revised Edition, The Gun Digest Book of, by J.B. Wood, DBI Books, a division of Krause Publications, Iola, WI, 1992. 480 pp., illus. Paper covers. $19.95.
Covers 46 popular shotguns plus over 250 variants. The most comprehensive and professional presentation available to either hobbyist or gunsmith.

A.H. Fox "The Finest Gun in the World", revised and enlarged edition, by Michael McIntosh, Countrysport, Inc., New Albany, OH, 1995. 408 pp., illus. $49.00.
The first detailed history of one of America's finest shotguns.

Game Gun, by Richard Grozik, Country Sport Press, Traverse City, MI, 1997. 203 pp., illus. $39.00.
A revision of a classic on the craftsmanship and function of double guns.

Game Shooting, by Robert Churchill, Countrysport Press, Selma, AL, 1998. 258 pp., illus. $34.95.
The basis for every shotgun instructional technique devised and the foundation for all wingshooting and the game of sporting clays.

The Golden Age of Shotgunning, by Bob Hinman, Wolfe Publishing Co., Inc., Prescott, AZ, 1982. $22.50.
A valuable history of the late 1800s detailing that fabulous period of development in shotguns, shotshells and shotgunning.

Grand Old Shotguns, by Don Zutz, Shotgun Sports Magazine, Auburn, CA, 1995. 136 pp., illus. Paper covers. $19.95
A study of the great smoothbores, their history and how and why they were discontinued. Find out the most sought-after and which were the best shooters.

Gun Digest Book of Sporting Clays, 2nd Edition, edited by Harold A. Murtz, Krause Publications, Iola, WI, 1999. 256 pp., illus. Paper covers. $21.95.
A concise Gun Digest book that covers guns, ammo, chokes, targets and course layouts so you'll stay a step ahead.

Hartman on Skeet, by Barney Hartman, Stackpole Books, Harrisburg, PA, 1973. 143 pp., illus. $19.95.
A definitive book on Skeet shooting by a pro.

The Italian Gun, by Steve Smith & Laurie Morrow, wilderness Adventures, Gallatin Gateway, MT, 1997. 325 pp., illus. $49.95.
The first book ever written entirely in English for American enthusiasts who own, aspire to own, or simply admire Italian guns.

The Ithaca Featherlight Repeater; the Best Gun Going, by Walter C. Snyder, Southern Pines, NC, 1998. 300 pp., illus. $89.95.

Describes the complete history of each model of the legendary Ithaca Model 37 and Model 87 Repeaters from their conception in 1930 throught 1997.

L.C. Smith Shotguns, by Lt. Col. William S. Brophy, The Gun Room Press, Highland Park, NJ, 1979. 244 pp., illus. $35.00.
The first work on this very important American gun and manufacturing company.

The Little Trapshooting Book, by Frank Little, Shotgun Sports Magazine, Auburn, CA, 1994. 168 pp., illus. Paper covers. $19.95.
Packed with know-how from one of the greatest trapshooters of all time.

Lock, Stock, and Barrel, by C. Adams & R. Braden, Safari Press, Huntington Beach, CA, 1996. 254 pp., illus. $24.95.
The process of making a best grade English gun from a lump of steel and a walnut tree trunk to the ultimate product plus practical advise on consistent field shooting with a double gun.

A Manual of Clayshooting, by Chris Cradock, Hippocrene Books, Inc., New York, NY, 1983. 192 pp., illus. $39.95.
Covers everything from building a range to buying a shotgun, with lots of illus. & dia.

Mental Training for the Shotgun Sports, by Michael J. Keyes, Shotgun Sports, Auburn, CA, 1996. 160 pp., illus. Paper covers. $24.95.
The most comprehensive book ever published on what it takes to shoot winning scores at trap, Skeet and Sporting Clays.

The Model 12, 1912-1964, by Dave Riffle, Dave Riffle, Ft. Meyers, FL, 1995. 274 pp., illus. $49.95.
The story of the greatest hammerless repeating shotgun ever built.

More Shotguns and Shooting, by Michael McIntosh, Countrysport Books, Selma, AL, 1998. 256 pp., illustrated. $30.00.
From specifics of shotguns to shooting your way out of a slump, it's McIntosh at his best.

The Mysteries of Shotgun Patterns, by George G. Oberfell and Charles E. Thompson, Oklahoma State University Press, Stillwater, OK, 1982. 164 pp., illus. Paper covers. $25.00.
Shotgun ballistics for the hunter in non-technical language.

The Orvis Wing-Shooting Handbook, by Bruce Bowlen, Nick Lyons Books, New York, NY, 1985. 83 pp., illus. Paper covers. $10.95.
Proven techniques for better shooting.

Parker Guns "The Old Reliable", by Ed Muderiak, Safari Press, Inc., Huntington Beach, CA, 1997. 325 pp., illus. $40.00.
A look at the small beginnings, the golden years, and the ultimate decline of the most famous of all American shotgun manufacturers.

Positive Shooting, by Michael Yardley, Safari Press, Huntington Beach, CA, 1995. 160 pp., illus. $30.00.
This book will provide the shooter with a sound foundation from which to develop an effective, personal technique that can dramatically improve shooting performance.

Purdey's, the Guns and the Family, by Richard Beaumont, David and Charles, Pomfret, VT, 1984. 248 pp., illus. $39.95.
Records the history of the Purdey family from 1814 to today, how the guns were and are built and daily functioning of the factory.

Reloading for Shotgunners, 4th Edition, by Kurt D. Fackler and M.L. McPherson, DBI Books, a division of Krause Publications, Iola, WI, 1997. 320 pp., illus. Paper covers. $19.95.
Expanded reloading tables with over 11,000 loads. Bushing charts for every major press and component maker. All new presentation on all aspects of shotshell reloading by two of the top experts in the field. (Available October 1997.)

Remington Double Shotguns, by Charles G. Semer, Denver, CO, 1997. 617 pp., illus. $60.00.
This book deals with the entire production and all grades of double shotguns made by Remington during the period of their production 1873-1910.

75 Years with the Shotgun, by C.T. (Buck) Buckman, Valley Publ., Fresno, CA, 1974. 141 pp., illus. $10.00.
An expert hunter and trapshooter shares experiences of a lifetime.

The Shooting Field with Holland & Holland, by Peter King, Quiller Press, London, England, new & enlarged edition, 1990. 184 pp., illus. $49.95.
The story of a company which has produced excellence in all aspects of gunmaking.

The Shotgun in Combat, by Tony Lesce, Desert Publications, Cornville, AZ, 1979. 148 pp., illus. Paper covers. $10.00.
A history of the shotgun and its use in combat.

Shotgun Digest, 4th Edition, edited by Jack Lewis, DBI Books, a division of Krause Publications, Iola, WI, 1993. 256 pp., illus. Paper covers. $17.95.
A look at what's happening with shotguns and shotgunning today.

Shotgun Gunsmithing, The Gun Digest Book of, by Ralph Walker, DBI Books, a division of Krause Publications, Iola, WI, 1983. 256 pp., illus. Paper covers. $16.95.
The principles and practices of repairing, individualizing and accurizing modern shotguns by one of the world's premier shotgun gunsmiths.

The Shotgun: History and Development, by Geoffrey Boothroyd, Safari Press, Huntington Beach, CA, 1995. 240 pp., illus. $35.00.
The first volume in a series that traces the development of the British shotgun from the 17th century onward.

The Shotgun Handbook, by Mike George, The Croswood Press, London, England, 1999. 128 pp., illus. $35.00.
For all shotgun enthusiasts, this detailed guide ranges from design and selection of a gun to adjustment, cleaning, and maintenance.

Shotgun Stuff, by Don Zutz, Shotgun Sports, Inc., Auburn, CA, 1991. 172 pp., illus. Paper covers. $19.95.
This book gives shotgunners all the "stuff" they need to achieve better performance and get more enjoyment from their favorite smoothbore.

Shotgunner's Notebook: The Advice and Reflections of a Wingshooter, by Gene Hill, Countrysport Press, Traverse City, MI, 1990. 192 pp., illus. $24.50.
Covers the shooting, the guns and the miscellany of the sport.

Shotgunning: The Art and the Science, by Bob Brister, Winchester Press, Piscataway, NJ, 1976. 321 pp., illus. $18.95.
Hundreds of specific tips and truly novel techniques to improve the field and target shooting of every shotgunner.

Shotgunning Trends in Transition, by Don Zutz, Wolfe Publishing Co., Prescott, AZ, 1990. 314 pp., illus. $29.50.
This book updates American shotgunning from post WWII to present.

Shotguns and Cartridges for Game and Clays, by Gough Thomas, edited by Nigel Brown, A & C Black, Ltd., Cambs, England, 1989. 256 pp., illus. Soft covers. $24.95.
Gough Thomas' well-known and respected book for game and clay pigeon shooters in a thoroughly up-dated edition.

Shotguns and Gunsmiths: The Vintage Years, by Geoffrey Boothroyd, Safari Press, Huntington Beach, CA, 1995. 240 pp., illus. $35.00.
A fascinating insight into the lives and skilled work of gunsmiths who helped develop the British shotgun during the Victorian and Edwardian eras.

Shotguns and Shooting, by Michael McIntosh, Countrysport Press, New Albany, OH, 1995. 258 pp., illus. $30.00.
The art of guns and gunmaking, this book is a celebration no lover of fine doubles should miss.

Sidelocks & Boxlocks, by Geoffrey Boothroyd, Sand Lake Press, Amity, OR, 1991. 271 pp., illus. $35.00.
The story of the classic British shotgun.

Spanish Best: The Fine Shotguns of Spain, by Terry Wieland, Countrysport, Inc., Traverse City, MI, 1994. 264 pp., illus. $49.50.
A practical source of information for owners of Spanish shotguns and a guide for those considering buying a used shotgun.

The Sporting Clay Handbook, by Jerry Meyer, Lyons and Burford Publishers, New York, NY, 1990. 140 pp., illus. Soft covers. $17.95.
Introduction to the fastest growing, and most exciting, gun game in America.

Sporting Clays, by Michael Pearce, Stackpole Books, Harrisburg, PA, 1991. 192 pp., illus. $18.95.
Expert techniques for every kind of clays course.

Successful Clay Pigeon Shooting, compiled by T. Hoare, Trafalgar Square, N. Pomfret, VT, 1993. 176 pp., illus. $39.95.
This comprehensive guide has been written by ten leading personalities for all aspiring clay pigeon shooters.

The Tactical Shotgun, by Gabriel Suzrez, Paladin Press, Boulder, CO, 1996. 232 pp., illus. Paper covers. $25.00.
The best techniques and tactics for employing the shotgun in personal combat.

Taking More Birds, by Dan Carlisle & Dolph Adams, Lyons & Burford, New York, NY, 1993. 120 pp., illus. $19.95.
A practical guide to greater success at sporting clays and wing shooting.

Trap & Skeet Shooting, 3rd Edition, by Chris Christian, DBI Books, a division of Krause Publications, Iola, WI, 1994. 288 pp., illus. Paper covers. $17.95.
A detailed look at the contemporary world of Trap, Skeet and Sporting Clays.

Trapshooting is a Game of Opposites, by Dick Bennett, Shotgun Sports, Inc., Auburn, CA, 1996. 129 pp., illus. Paper covers. $19.95.
Discover everything you need to know about shooting trap like the pros.

Turkey Hunter's Digest, Revised Edition, by Dwain Bland, DBI Books, a division of Krause Publications, Iola, WI, 1994. 256 pp., illus. Paper covers. $17.95.
Presents no-nonsense approach to hunting all five sub-species of the North American wild turkey.

U.S. Shotguns, All Types, reprint of TM9-285, Desert Publications, Cornville, AZ, 1987. 257 pp., illus. Paper covers. $9.95.
Covers operation, assembly and disassembly of nine shotguns used by the U.S. armed forces.

U.S. Winchester Trench and Riot Guns and Other U.S. Military Combat Shotguns, by Joe Poyer, North Cape Publications, Tustin, CA, 1992. 124 pp., illus. Paper covers. $15.95.
A detailed history of the use of military shotguns, and the acquisition procedures used by the U.S. Army's Ordnance Department in both World Wars.

The Winchester Model Twelve, by George Madis, David Madis, Dallas, TX, 1984. 176 pp., illus. $19.95.
A definitive work on this famous American shotgun.

The Winchester Model 42, by Ned Schwing, Krause Pub., Iola, WI, 1990. 160 pp., illus. $34.95.
Behind-the-scenes story of the model 42's invention and its early development. Production totals and manufacturing dates; reference work.

Winchester Shotguns and Shotshells, by Ron Stadt, Krause Pub., Iola, WI. 288 pp., illus. $34.95.
Must-have for Winchester collectors of shotguns manufactured through 1961.

Winchester's Finest, the Model 21, by Ned Schwing, Krause Publicatons, Iola, WI, 1990. 360 pp., illus. $49.95.
The classic beauty and the interesting history of the Model 21 Winchester shotgun.

The World's Fighting Shotguns, by Thomas F. Swearengen, T.B.N. Enterprises, Alexandria, VA, 1979. 500 pp., illus. $34.95.
The complete military and police reference work from the shotgun's inception to date, with up-to-date developments.

ARMS ASSOCIATIONS

UNITED STATES

ALABAMA
Alabama Gun Collectors Assn.
Secretary, P.O. Box 70965, Tuscaloosa, AL 35407

ALASKA
Alaska Gun Collectors Assn., Inc.
C.W. Floyd, Pres., 5240 Little Tree, Anchorage, AK 99507

ARIZONA
Arizona Arms Assn.
Don DeBusk, President, 4837 Bryce Ave., Glendale, AZ 85301

CALIFORNIA
California Cartridge Collectors Assn.
Rick Montgomery, 1729 Christina, Stockton, CA 95204/209-463-7216 evs.

California Waterfowl Assn.
4630 Northgate Blvd., #150, Sacramento, CA 95834

Greater Calif. Arms & Collectors Assn.
Donald L. Bullock, 8291 Carburton St., Long Beach, CA 90808-3302

Los Angeles Gun Ctg. Collectors Assn.
F.H. Ruffra, 20810 Amie Ave., Apt. #9, Torrance, CA 90503

Stock Gun Players Assn.
6038 Appian Way, Long Beach, CA, 90803

COLORADO
Colorado Gun Collectors Assn.
L.E.(Bud) Greenwald, 2553 S. Quitman St., Denver, CO 80219/303-935-3850

Rocky Mountain Cartridge Collectors Assn.
John Roth, P.O. Box 757, Conifer, CO 80433

CONNECTICUT
Ye Connecticut Gun Guild, Inc.
Dick Fraser, P.O. Box 425, Windsor, CT 06095

FLORIDA
Unified Sportsmen of Florida
P.O. Box 6565, Tallahassee, FL 32314

GEORGIA
Georgia Arms Collectors Assn., Inc.
Michael Kindberg, President, P.O. Box 277, Alpharetta, GA 30239-0277

ILLINOIS
Illinois State Rifle Assn.
P.O. Box 637, Chatsworth, IL 60921

Mississippi Valley Gun & Cartridge Coll. Assn.
Bob Filbert, P.O. Box 61, Port Byron, IL 61275/309-523-2593

Sauk Trail Gun Collectors
Gordell M. Matson, P.O. Box 1113, Milan, IL 61264

Wabash Valley Gun Collectors Assn., Inc.
Roger L. Dorsett, 2601 Willow Rd., Urbana, IL 61801/217-384-7302

INDIANA
Indiana State Rifle & Pistol Assn.
Thos. Glancy, P.O. Box 552, Chesterton, IN 46304

Southern Indiana Gun Collectors Assn., Inc.
Sheila McClary, 309 W. Monroe St., Boonville, IN 47601/812-897-3742

IOWA
Beaver Creek Plainsmen Inc.
Steve Murphy, Secy., P.O. Box 298, Bondurant, IA 50035

Central States Gun Collectors Assn.
Dennis Greischar, Box 841, Mason City, IA 50402-0841

KANSAS
Kansas Cartridge Collectors Assn.
Bob Linder, Box 84, Plainville, KS 67663

KENTUCKY
Kentuckiana Arms Collectors Assn.
Charles Billips, President, Box 1776, Louisville, KY 40201

Kentucky Gun Collectors Assn., Inc.
Ruth Johnson, Box 64, Owensboro, KY 42302/502-729-4197

LOUISIANA
Washitaw River Renegades
Sandra Rushing, P.O. Box 256, Main St., Grayson, LA 71435

MARYLAND
Baltimore Antique Arms Assn.
Mr. Cillo, 1034 Main St., Darlington, MD 21304

MASSACHUSETTS
Bay Colony Weapons Collectors, Inc.
John Brandt, Box 111, Hingham, MA 02043

Massachusetts Arms Collectors
Bruce E. Skinner, P.O. Box 31, No. Carver, MA 02355/508-866-5259

MICHIGAN
Association for the Study and Research of .22 Calibor Rimfire Cartridges
George Kass, 4512 Nakoma Dr., Okemos, MI 48864

MINNESOTA
Sioux Empire Cartridge Collectors Assn.
Bob Cameron, 14597 Glendale Ave. SE, Prior Lake, MN 55372

MISSISSIPPI
Mississippi Gun Collectors Assn.
Jack E. Swinney, P.O. Box 16323, Hattiesburg, MS 39402

MISSOURI
Greater St. Louis Cartridge Collectors Assn.
Don MacChesney, 634 Scottsdale Rd., Kirkwood, MO 63122-1109

Mineral Belt Gun Collectors Assn.
D.F. Saunders, 1110 Cleveland Ave., Monett, MO 65708

Missouri Valley Arms Collectors Assn., Inc.
L.P Brammer II, Membership Secy., P.O. Box 33033, Kansas City, MO 64114

MONTANA
Montana Arms Collectors Assn.
Dean E. Yearout, Sr., Exec. Secy., 1516 21st Ave. S., Great Falls, MT 59405

Weapons Collectors Society of Montana
R.G. Schipf, Ex. Secy., 3100 Bancroft St., Missoula, MT 59801/406-728-2995

NEBRASKA
Nebraska Cartridge Collectors Club
Gary Muckel, P.O. Box 84442, Lincoln, NE 68501

NEW HAMPSHIRE
New Hampshire Arms Collectors, Inc.
James Stamatelos, Secy., P.O. Box 5, Cambridge, MA 02139

NEW JERSEY
Englishtown Benchrest Shooters Assn.
Michael Toth, 64 Cooke Ave., Carteret, NJ 07008

Jersey Shore Antique Arms Collectors
Joe Sisia, P.O. Box 100, Bayville, NJ 08721-0100

New Jersey Arms Collectors Club, Inc.
Angus Laidlaw, Vice President, 230 Valley Rd., Montclair, NJ 07042/201-746-0939; e-mail: acclaidlaw@juno.com

NEW YORK
Iroquois Arms Collectors Assn.
Bonnie Robinson, Show Secy., P.O. Box 142, Ransomville, NY 14131/716-791-4096

Mid-State Arms Coll. & Shooters Club
Jack Ackerman, 24 S. Mountain Terr., Dinghamton, NY 13903

NORTH CAROLINA
North Carolina Gun Collectors Assn.
Jerry Ledford, 3231-7th St. Dr. NE, Hickory, NC 28601

OHIO
Ohio Gun Collectors Assn.
P.O. Box 9007, Maumee, OH 43537-9007/419-897-0861; Fax:419-897-0860

Shotshell Historical and Collectors Society
Madeline Bruemmer, 3886 Dawley Rd., Ravenna, OH 44266

The Stark Gun Collectors, Inc.
William I. Gann, 5666 Waynesburg Dr., Waynesburg, OH 44688

OREGON
Oregon Arms Collectors Assn., Inc.
Phil Bailey, P.O. Box 13000-A, Portland, OR 97213-0017/503-281-6864; off.:503-281-0918

Oregon Cartridge Collectors Assn.
Boyd Northrup, P.O. Box 285, Rhododendron, OR 97049

PENNSYLVANIA
Presque Isle Gun Collectors Assn.
James Welch, 156 E. 37 St., Erie, PA 16504

SOUTH CAROLINA
Belton Gun Club, Inc.
J.K. Phillips, 195 Phillips Dr., Belton, SC 29627

Gun Owners of South Carolina
Membership Div.: William Strozier, Secretary, P.O. Box 70, Johns Island, SC 29457-0070/803-762-3240; Fax:803-795-0711; e-mail:76053.222@compuserve.com

SOUTH DAKOTA
Dakota Territory Gun Coll. Assn., Inc.
Curt Carter, Castlewood, SD 57223

TENNESSEE
Smoky Mountain Gun Coll. Assn., Inc.
Hugh W. Yabro, President, P.O. Box 23225, Knoxville, TN 37933

Tennessee Gun Collectors Assn., Inc.
M.H. Parks, 3556 Pleasant Valley Rd., Nashville, TN 37204-3419

TEXAS
Houston Gun Collectors Assn., Inc.
P.O. Box 741429, Houston, TX 77274-1429

Texas Cartridge Collectors Assn., Inc.
Robert Mellichamp, Memb. Contact, 907 Shirkmere, Houston, TX 77008/713-869-0558

Texas Gun Collectors Assn.
Bob Eder, Pres., P.O. Box 12067, El Paso, TX 79913/915-584-8183

Texas State Rifle Assn.
1131 Rockingham Dr., Suite 101, Richardson, TX 75080-4326

VIRGINIA
Virginia Gun Collectors Assn., Inc.
Addison Hurst, Secy., 38802 Charlestown Height, Waterford, VA 20197/540-882-3543

WASHINGTON
Association of Cartridge Collectors on the Pacific Northwest
Robert Jardin, 14214 Meadowlark Drive KPN, Gig Harbor, WA 98329

Washington Arms Collectors, Inc.
Joyce Boss, P.O. Box 389, Renton, WA, 98057-0389/206-255-8410

WISCONSIN
Great Lakes Arms Collectors Assn., Inc.
Edward C. Warnke, 2913 Woodridge Lane, Waukesha, WI 53188

Wisconsin Gun Collectors Assn., Inc.
Lulita Zellmer, P.O. Box 181, Sussex, WI 53089

WYOMING
Wyoming Weapons Collectors
P.O. Box 284, Laramie, WY 82070/307-745-4652 or 745-9530

NATIONAL ORGANIZATIONS

Amateur Trapshooting Assn.
David D. Bopp, Exec. Director, 601 W. National Rd., Vandalia, OH 45377/937-898-4638; Fax:937-898-5472

American Airgun Field Target Assn.
5911 Cherokee Ave., Tampa, FL 33604

American Coon Hunters Assn.
Opal Johnston, P.O. Cadet, Route 1, Box 492, Old Mines, MO 63630

American Custom Gunmakers Guild
Jan Billeb, Exec. Director, P.O. Box 812, Burlington, IA 52601-0812/319-752-6114 (Phone or Fax)

American Defense Preparedness Assn.
Two Colonial Place, 2101 Wilson Blvd., Suite 400, Arlington, VA 22201-3061

American Paintball League
P.O. Box 3561, Johnson City, TN 37602/800-541-9169

American Pistolsmiths Guild
Alex B. Hamilton, Pres., 1449 Blue Crest Lane, San Antonio, TX 78232/210-494-3063

American Police Pistol & Rifle Assn.
3801 Biscayne Blvd., Miami, FL 33137

American Single Shot Rifle Assn.
Gary Staup, Secy., 709 Carolyn Dr., Delphos, OH 45833/419-692-3866

American Society of Arms Collectors
George E. Weatherly, P.O. Box 2567, Waxahachie, TX 75165

American Tactical Shooting Assn.(A.T.S.A.)
c/o Skip Gochenour, 2600 N. Third St., Harrisburg, PA 17110/717-233-0402; Fax:717-233-5340

Association of Firearm and Tool Mark Examiners
Lannie G. Emanuel, Secy., Southwest Institute of Forensic Sciences, P.O. Box 35728, Dallas, TX 75235/214-920-5979; Fax:214-920-5928; Membership Secy., Ann D. Jones, VA Div. of Forensic Science, P.O. Box 999, Richmond, VA 23208/804-786-4706; Fax:804-371-8328

Boone & Crockett Club
250 Station Dr., Missoula, MT 59801-2753

Browning Collectors Assn.
Secretary:Scherrie L. Brennac, 2749 Keith Dr., Villa Ridge, MO 63089/314-742-0571

The Cast Bullet Assn., Inc.
Ralland J. Fortier, Editor, 4103 Foxcraft Dr., Traverse City, MI 49684

Citizens Committee for the Right to Keep and Bear Arms
Natl. Hq., Liberty Park, 12500 NE Tenth Pl., Bellevue, WA 98005

Colt Collectors Assn.
25000 Highland Way, Los Gatos, CA 95030

Ducks Unlimited, Inc.
Natl. Headquarters, One Waterfowl Way, Memphis, TN 38120

Fifty Caliber Shooters Assn.
11469 Olive St. Rd., Suite 50, St. Louis, MO 63141/601-475-7545;Fax:601-475-0452

Firearms Coalition/Neal Knox Associates
Box 6537, Silver Spring, MD 20906/301-871-3006

Firearms Engravers Guild of America
Rex C. Pedersen, Secy., 511 N. Rath Ave., Lundington, MI 49431/616-845-7695(Phone and Fax)

ARMS ASSOCIATIONS

Foundation for North American Wild Sheep
720 Allen Ave., Cody, WY 82414-3402/web site: http://iigi.com/os/non/fnaws/fnaws.htm; e-mail: fnaws@wyoming.com

Freedom Arms Collectors Assn.
P.O. Box 160302, Miami, FL 33116-0302

Garand Collectors Assn.
P.O. Box 181, Richmond, KY 40475

Golden Eagle Collectors Assn. (G.E.C.A.)
Chris Showler, 11144 Slate Creek Rd., Grass Valley, CA 95945

Gun Owners of America
8001 Forbes Place, Suite 102, Springfield, VA 22151/703-321-8585

Handgun Hunters International
J.D. Jones, Director, P.O. Box 357 MAG, Bloomingdale, OH 43910

Harrington & Richardson Gun Coll. Assn.
George L. Cardet, 330 S.W. 27th Ave., Suite 603, Miami, FL 33135

High Standard Collectors' Assn.
John J. Stimson, Jr., Pres., 540 W. 92nd St., Indianapolis, IN 46260

Hopkins & Allen Arms & Memorabilia Society (HAAMS)
P.O. Box 187, Delphos, OH 45833

International Ammunition Association, Inc.
C.R. Punnett, Secy., 8 Hillock Lane, Chadds Ford, PA 19317/610-358-1285;Fax:610-358-1560

International Benchrest Shooters
Joan Borden, RR1, Box 250BB, Springville, PA 18844/717-965-2366

International Blackpowder Hunting Assn.
P.O. Box 1180, Glenrock, WY 82637/307-436-9817

IHMSA (Intl. Handgun Metallic Silhouette Assn.)
Frank Scotto, P.O. Box 5038, Meriden, CT 06451

International Society of Mauser Arms Collectors
Michael Kindberg, Pres., P.O. Box 277, Alpharetta, GA 30239-0277

Jews for the Preservation of Firearms Ownership (JPFO) 501(c)(3)
2872 S. Wentworth Ave., Milwaukee, WI 53207/414-769-0760; Fax:414-483-8435

The Mannlicher Collectors Assn.
Thomas Seefeldt, Membership Secy., P.O. Box 1455, Kalispell, MT 59903

Marlin Firearms Collectors Assn., Ltd.
Dick Paterson, Secy., 407 Lincoln Bldg., 44 Main St., Champaign, IL 61820

Miniature Arms Collectors/Makers Society, Ltd.
Ralph Koebbeman, Pres., 4910 Kilburn Ave., Rockford, IL 61101/815-964-2569

M1 Carbine Collectors Assn. (M1-CCA)
623 Apaloosa Ln., Gardnerville, NV 89410-7840

National Association of Buckskinners (NAB)
Territorial Dispatch—1800s Historical Publication, 4701 Marion St., Suite 324, Livestock Exchange Bldg., Denver, CO 80216/303-297-9671

The National Association of Derringer Collectors
P.O. Box 20572, San Jose, CA 95160

National Assn. of Federally Licensed Firearms Dealers
Andrew Molchan, 2455 E. Sunrise, Ft. Lauderdale, FL 33304

National Association to Keep and Bear Arms
P.O. Box 78336, Seattle, WA 98178

National Automatic Pistol Collectors Assn.
Tom Knox, P.O. Box 15738, Tower Grove Station, St. Louis, MO 63163

National Bench Rest Shooters Assn., Inc.
Pat Ferrell, 2835 Guilford Lane, Oklahoma City, OK 73120-4404/405-842-9585; Fax: 405-842-9575

National Muzzle Loading Rifle Assn.
Box 67, Friendship, IN 47021

National Professional Paintball League (NPPL)
540 Main St., Mount Kisco, NY 10549/914-241-7400

National Reloading Manufacturers Assn.
One Centerpointe Dr., Suite 300, Lake Oswego, OR 97035

National Rifle Assn. of America
11250 Waples Mill Rd., Fairfax, VA 22030

National Shooting Sports Foundation, Inc.
Robert T. Delfay, President, Flintlock Ridge Office Center, 11 Mile Hill Rd., Newtown, CT 06470-2359/203-426-1320; FAX: 203-426-1087

National Skeet Shooting Assn.
Mike Hampton, Exec. Director, 5931 Roft Road, San Antonio, TX 78253-9261

National Sporting Clays Association
5931 Roft Road, San Antonio, TX 78253-9261/800-877-5338

National Wild Turkey Federation, Inc.
P.O. Box 530, 770 Augusta Rd., Edgefield, SC 29824

North American Hunting Club
P.O. Box 3401, Minnetonka, MN 55343/612-936-9333; Fax: 612-936-9755

North American Paintball Referees Association (NAPRA)
584 Cestaric Dr., Milpitas, CA 95035

North-South Skirmish Assn., Inc.
Stevan F. Meserve, Exec. Secretary, 507 N. Brighton Court, Sterling, VA 20164-3919

Remington Society of America
Leon W. Wier Jr., President, 8268 Lone Feather Ln., Las Vegas, NV 89123

Rocky Mountain Elk Foundation
P.O. Box 8249, Missoula, MT 59807-8249/406-523-4500;Fax: 406-523-4581

Ruger Collector's Assn., Inc.
P.O. Box 240, Greens Farms, CT 06436

Safari Club International
Philip DeLone, Executive Dir., 4800 W. Gates Pass Rd., Tucson, AZ 85745/602-620-1220

Sako Collectors Assn., Inc.
Jim Lutes, 202 N. Locust, Whitewater, KS 67154

Second Amendment Foundation
James Madison Building, 12500 NE 10th Pl., Bellevue, WA 98005

Single Action Shooting Society
1938 North Batavia St., Suite M, Orange, CA 92865/714-998-1899; Fax:714-998-1992

Smith & Wesson Collectors Assn.
George Linne, 2711 Miami St., St. Louis, MO 63118

The Society of American Bayonet Collectors
P.O. Box 234, East Islip, NY 11730-0234

Southern California Schuetzen Society
Dean Lillard, 34657 Ave. E., Yucaipa, CA 92399

Sporting Arms and Ammunition Manufacturers' Institute (SAAMI)
Flintlock Ridge Office Center, 11 Mile Hill Rd., Newtown, CT 06470-2359/203-426-4358; FAX: 203-426-1087

Sporting Clays of America (SCA)
Ron L. Blosser, Pres., 9257 Buckeye Rd., Sugar Grove, OH 43155-9632/614-746-8334; Fax: 614-746-8605

The Thompson/Center Assn.
Joe Wright, President, Box 792, Northboro, MA 01532/508-845-6960

U.S. Practical Shooting Assn./IPSC
Dave Thomas, P.O. Box 811, Sedro Woolley, WA 98284/360-855-2245

U.S. Revolver Assn.
Brian J. Barer, 40 Larchmont Ave., Taunton, MA 02780/508-824-4836

U.S. Shooting Team
U.S. Olympic Shooting Center, One Olympic Plaza, Colorado Springs, CO 80909/719-578-4670

The Varmint Hunters Assn., Inc.
Box 759, Pierre, SD 57501/Member Services 800-528-4868

Weatherby Collectors Assn., Inc.
P.O. Box 888, Ozark, MO 65721

The Wildcatters
P.O. Box 170, Greenville, WI 54942

Winchester Arms Collectors Assn.
Richard Berg, Executive Secy., P.O. Box 6754, Great Falls, MT 59406

The Women's Shooting Sports Foundation (WSSF)
1505 Highway 6 South, Suite 101, Houston, TX 77077

ARGENTINA

Asociacion Argentina de Coleccionistas de Armes y Municiones
Castilla de Correos No. 28, Succursal I B, 1401 Buenos Aires, Republica Argentina

AUSTRALIA

Antique & Historical Arms Collectors of Australia
P.O. Box 5654, GCMC Queensland 9726, Australia

The Arms Collector's Guild of Queensland Inc.
Ian Skennerton, P.O. Box 433, Ashmore City 4214, Queensland, Australia

Australian Cartridge Collectors Assn., Inc.
Bob Bennett, 126 Landscape Dr., E. Doncaster 3109, Victoria, Ausrtalia

Sporting Shooters Assn. of Australia, Inc.
P.O. Box 2066, Kent Town, SA 5071, Australia

CANADA

ALBERTA

Canadian Historical Arms Society
P.O. Box 901, Edmonton, Alb., Canada T5J 2L8

National Firearms Assn.
Natl. Hq: P.O. Box 1779, Edmonton, Alb., Canada T5J 2P1

BRITISH COLUMBIA

The Historical Arms Collectors of B.C. (Canada)
Harry Moon, Pres., P.O. Box 50117, South Slope RPO, Burnaby, BC V5J 5G3, Canada/604-438-0950; Fax:604-277-3646

ONTARIO

Association of Canadian Cartridge Collectors
Monica Wright, RR 1, Millgrove, ON, L0R 1V0, Canada

Tri-County Antique Arms Fair
P.O. Box 122, RR #1, North Lancaster, Ont., Canada K0C 1Z0

EUROPE

BELGIUM

European Catridge Research Assn.
Graham Irving, 21 Rue Schaltin, 4900 Spa, Belgium/32.87.77.43.40; Fax:32.87.77.27.51

CZECHOSLOVAKIA

Spolecnost Pro Studium Naboju (Czech Cartridge Research Assn.)
JUDr. Jaroslav Bubak, Pod Homolko 1439, 26601 Beroun 2, Czech Republic

DENMARK

Aquila Dansk Jagtpatron Historic Forening (Danish Historical Cartridge Collectors Club)
Steen Elgaard Møller, Ulriksdalsvej 7, 4840 Nr. Alslev, Denmark 10045-53846218;Fax:00455384 6209

ENGLAND

Arms and Armour Society
Hon. Secretary A. Dove, P.O. Box 10232, London, 5W19 2ZD, England

Dutch Paintball Federation
Aceville Publ., Castle House 97 High Street, Colchester, Essex C01 1TH, England/011-44-206-564840

European Paintball Sports Foundation
c/o Aceville Publ., Castle House 97 High St., Colchester, Essex, C01 1TH, England

Historical Breechloading Smallarms Assn.
D.J. Penn M.A., Secy., P.O. Box 12778, London SE1 6BX, England. Journal and newsletter are $23 a yr., including airmail.

National Rifle Assn.
(Great Britain) Bisley Camp, Brookwood, Woking Surrey GU24 OPB, England/01483.797777; Fax: 014730686275

United Kingdom Cartridge Club
Ian Southgate, 20 Millfield, Elmley Castle, Nr. Pershore, Worcestershire, WR10 3HR, England

FRANCE

STAC-Western Co.
3 Ave. Paul Doumer (N.311); 78360 Montesson, France/01.30.53-43-65; Fax: 01.30.53.19.10

GERMANY

Bund Deutscher Sportschützen e.v. (BDS)
Borsigallee 10, 53125 Bonn 1, Germany

Deutscher Schützenbund
Lahnstrasse 120, 65195 Wiesbaden, Germany

SPAIN

Asociacion Espanola de Colleccionistas de Cartuchos (A.E.C.C.)
Secretary: Apdo. Correos No. 1086, 2880-Alcala de Henares (Madrid), Spain. President: Apdo. Correos No. 682, 50080 Zaragoza, Spain

SWEDEN

Scandinavian Ammunition Research Assn.
Box 107, 77622 Hedemora, Sweden

NEW ZEALAND

New Zealand Cartridge Collectors Club
Terry Castle, 70 Tiraumea Dr., Pakuranga, Auckland, New Zealand

New Zealand Deerstalkers Assn.
P.O. Box 6514 TE ARO, Wellington, New Zealand

SOUTH AFRICA

Historical Firearms Soc. of South Africa
P.O. Box 145, 7725 Newlands, Republic of South Africa

Republic of South Africa Cartridge Collectors Assn.
Arno Klee, 20 Eugene St., Malanshof Randburg, Gauteng 2194, Republic of South Africa

S.A.A.C.A. (Southern Africa Arms and Ammunition Assn.)
Gauteng Office: P.O. Box 7597, Weltevreden Park, 1715, Republic of South Africa/011-679-1151; Fax: 011-679-1131; e-mail: saaaca@iafrica.com. Kwa-Zulu Natal office: P.O. Box 4065, Northway, Kwazulu-Natal 4065, Republic of South Africa

SAGA (S.A. Gunowners' Assn.)
P.O. Box 35203, Northway, Kwazulu-Natal 4065, Republic of South Africa

2000
GUN DIGEST
DIRECTORY OF THE
ARMS TRADE

The **Product Directory** contains 78 product categories. Note that in the Product Directory, a black bullet preceding a manufacturer's name indicates the availability of a Warranty Service Center address, which can be found on page 437.

The **Manufacturers' Directory** alphabetically lists the manufacturers with their addresses, phone numbers, FAX numbers and Internet addresses, if available.

DIRECTORY OF THE ARMS TRADE INDEX

AMMUNITION COMPONENTS, SHOTSHELL

Garcia National Gun Traders, Inc.
Precision Reloading, Inc.
Tar-Hunt Custom Rifles, Inc.
Vitt/Boos

AMMUNITION COMPONENTS-- BULLETS, POWDER, PRIMERS, CASES

3-D Ammunition & Bullets
4W Ammunition (See Hunters Supply)
A-Square Co.,Inc.
Acadian Ballistic Specialties
Accuracy Unlimited
Accurate Arms Co., Inc.
Action Bullets & Alloy Inc
ADCO Sales, Inc.
Alaska Bullet Works, Inc.
Alliant Techsystems Smokeless Powder Group
Allred Bullet Co.
Alpha LaFranck Enterprises
American Bullet
American Products, Inc.
Arco Powder
Armfield Custom Bullets
Atlantic Rose, Inc.
Baer's Hollows
Ballard Rifle & Cartridge Co., LLC
Ballistic Product, Inc.
Barnes Bullets, Inc.
Beartooth Bullets
Beeline Custom Bullets Limited
Bell Reloading, Inc.
Berger Bullets Ltd.
Berry's Mfg., Inc.
Big Bore Bullets of Alaska
Big Bore Express
Bitterroot Bullet Co.
Black Belt Bullets (See Big Bore Express)
Black Hills Shooters Supply
Black Powder Products
Blount, Inc., Sporting Equipment Div.
Brenneke KG, Wilhelm
Briese Bullet Co., Inc.
Brown Co, E. Arthur
Brown Dog Ent.
BRP, Inc. High Performance Cast Bullets
Buck Stix--SOS Products Co.
Buckeye Custom Bullets
Buckskin Bullet Co.
Buffalo Arms Co.
Buffalo Rock Shooters Supply
Bull-X, Inc.
Bullet, Inc.
Bullseye Bullets
Butler Enterprises
Buzztail Brass (See Grayback Wildcats)
Cambos Outdoorsman
Canyon Cartridge Corp.
Carnahan Bullets
Cascade Bullet Co., Inc.
Cast Performance Bullet Company
Casull Arms Corp.
CCI Div. of Blount, Inc.
Champion's Choice, Inc.
Cheddite France S.A.
CheVron Bullets
Clean Shot Technologies
Colorado Sutlers Arsenal (See Cumberland States Ar

Competitor Corp. Inc.
Cook Engineering Service
Cor-Bon Bullet & Ammo Co.
Cumberland States Arsenal
Cummings Bullets
Curtis Cast Bullets
Curtis Gun Shop (See Curtis Cast Bullets)
Custom Bullets by Hoffman
D&J Bullet Co. & Custom Gun Shop, Inc.
Dakota Arms, Inc.
Dick Marple & Associates
Dixie Gun Works, Inc.
DKT, Inc.
Dohring Bullets
Double A Ltd.
Eichelberger Bullets, Wm
Eldorado Cartridge Corp (See PMC/Eldorado Cartridg
Elkhorn Bullets
Epps, Ellwood (See "Gramps" Antique
Federal Cartridge Co.
Fiocchi of America Inc.
Fish Mfg. Gunsmith Sptg. Co., Marshall F
Forkin Arms
Forkin, Ben (See Belt MTN Arms)
Fowler Bullets
Fowler, Bob (See Black Powder Products)
Foy Custom Bullets
Freedom Arms, Inc.
Fusilier Bullets
G&C Bullet Co., Inc.
Garcia National Gun Traders, Inc.
Gehmann, Walter (See Huntington Die Specialties)
GOEX Inc.
Golden Bear Bullets
Gotz Bullets
Grayback Wildcats
Green Mountain Rifle Barrel Co., Inc.
Grier's Hard Cast Bullets
GTB
Gun City
Hammets VLD Bullets
Hardin Specialty Dist.
Harris Enterprises
Harrison Bullets
Hart & Son, Inc.
Hawk Laboratories, Inc. (See Hawk, Inc.)
Hawk, Inc.
Haydon Shooters Supply, Russ
Heidenstrom Bullets
Hercules, Inc. (See Alliant Techsystems, Smokeless
Hi-Performance Ammunition Company
Hirtenberger Aktiengesellschaft
Hobson Precision Mfg. Co.
Hodgdon Powder Co.
Hornady Mfg. Co.
HT Bullets
Hunters Supply
Huntington Die Specialties
IMI Services USA, Inc.
Imperial Magnum Corp.
IMR Powder Co.
J&D Components
J&L Superior Bullets (See Huntington Die Specialis
J-4 Inc.
J.R. Williams Bullet Co.
James Calhoon Mfg.
Jensen Bullets
Jensen's Firearms Academy
Jericho Tool & Die Co., Inc.
Jester Bullets
JLK Bullets

JRP Custom Bullets
Ka Pu Kapili
Kasmarsik Bullets
Kaswer Custom, Inc.
Keith's Bullets
Ken's Kustom Kartridges
Keng's Firearms Specialty, Inc./US Tactical Systems
Kent Cartridge Mfg. Co. Ltd.
KLA Enterprises
Knight Rifles
Knight Rifles (See Modern Muzzle Loading, Inc.)
Lage Uniwad
Lapua Ltd.
Lawrence Brand Shot (See Precision Reloading, Inc.)
Legend Products Corp.
Liberty Shooting Supplies
Lightfield Ammunition Corp. (See Slug Group, Inc.)
Lightning Performance Innovations, Inc.
Lindsley Arms Cartridge Co.
Littleton, J. F.
Lomont Precision Bullets
Loweth, Richard H.R.
M & D Munitions Ltd.
Magnus Bullets
Maine Custom Bullets
Maionchi-L.M.I.
Marchmon Bullets
Markesbery Muzzle Loaders, Inc.
MarMik, Inc.
MAST Technology
McMurdo, Lynn (See Specialty Gunsmithing)
Meister Bullets (See Gander Mountain)
Men-Metallwerk Elisenhuette GmbH
Merkuria Ltd.
MI-TE Bullets
Michael's Antiques
Mitchell Bullets, R.F.
Montana Armory, Inc (See C. Sharps Arms Co. Inc.)
Montana Precision Swaging
Mountain State Muzzleloading Supplies, Inc.
Mt. Baldy Bullet Co.
Mulhern, Rick
Murmur Corp.
Mushroom Express Bullet Co.
Nagel's Custom Bullets
National Bullet Co.
Naval Ordnance Works
Necromancer Industries, Inc.
North American Shooting Systems
North Devon Firearms Services
Northern Precision Custom Swaged Bullets
Nosler, Inc.
Oklahoma Ammunition Co.
Old Wagon Bullets
Old Western Scrounger,Inc.
Ordnance Works, The
Oregon Trail Bullet Company
Pacific Cartridge, Inc.
Pacific Rifle Co.
Page Custom Bullets
Patrick Bullets
Pease Accuracy
Penn Bullets
Petro-Explo Inc.
Phillippi Custom Bullets, Justin
Pinetree Bullets
PMC/Eldorado Cartridge Corp.
Polywad, Inc.
Pomeroy, Robert
Precision Components
Precision Components and Guns

Precision Delta Corp.
Precision Munitions, Inc.
Prescott Projectile Co.
Price Bullets, Patrick W.
PRL Bullets, c/o Blackburn Enterprises
Professional Hunter Supplies (See Star Custom Bull
Proofmark Corp.
R.I.S. Co., Inc.
R.M. Precision
Rainier Ballistics Corp.
Ramon B. Gonzalez Guns
Ranger Products
Red Cedar Precision Mfg.
Redwood Bullet Works
Reloading Specialties, Inc.
Remington Arms Co., Inc.
Rhino
Robinson H.V. Bullets
Rubright Bullets
SAECO (See Redding Reloading Equipment)
Scharch Mfg., Inc.
Schmidtman Custom Ammunition
Schneider Bullets
Schroeder Bullets
Scot Powder
Seebeck Assoc., R.E.
Shappy Bullets
Sharps Arms Co., Inc., C.
Shilen, Inc.
Sierra Bullets
SOS Products Co. (See Buck Stix-SOS Products Co.)
Southern Ammunition Co., Inc.
Specialty Gunsmithing
Speer Products Div. of Blount Inc. Sporting Equipm
Spencer's Custom Guns
Stanley Bullets
Star Ammunition, Inc.
Star Custom Bullets
Stark's Bullet Mfg.
Starke Bullet Company
Stewart's Gunsmithing
Swift Bullet Co.
T.F.C. S.p.A.
Talon Mfg. Co., Inc.
Taracorp Industries, Inc.
TCCI
TCSR
Thompson Precision
TMI Products (See Haselbauer Products, Jerry)
Traditions Performance Firearms
Trico Plastics
Trophy Bonded Bullets, Inc.
True Flight Bullet Co.
Tucson Mold, Inc.
Unmussig Bullets, D. L.
USAC
Vann Custom Bullets
Vihtavuori Oy/Kaltron-Pettibone
Vincent's Shop
Viper Bullet and Brass Works
Vom Hoffe (See Old Western Scrounger, Inc., The)
Warren Muzzleloading Co., Inc.
Watson Trophy Match Bullets
Weatherby, Inc.
Western Nevada West Coast Bullets
Widener's Reloading & Shooting Supply, Inc.
Winchester Div. Olin Corp.
Windjammer Tournament Wads Inc.
Winkle Bullets
Woodleigh (See Huntington Die Specialties)
Worthy Products, Inc.

Wosenitz VHP, Inc.
Wyant Bullets
Wyoming Bonded Bullets
Wyoming Custom Bullets
Yukon Arms Classic Ammunition
Zero Ammunition Co., Inc.

AMMUNITION, COMMERCIAL

3-D Ammunition & Bullets
3-Ten Corp.
4W Ammunition (See Hunters Supply)
A-Square Co.,Inc.
Ace Custom 45's, Inc.
American Ammunition
Arizona Ammunition, Inc.
Arms Corporation of the Philippines
Arundel Arms & Ammunition, Inc., A.
Atlantic Rose, Inc.
Badger Shooters Supply, Inc.
Ben William's Gun Shop
Big Bear Arms & Sporting Goods, Inc.
Black Hills Ammunition, Inc.
Blammo Ammo
Blount, Inc., Sporting Equipment Div.
Brown Dog Ent.
Buffalo Bullet Co., Inc..
Bull-X, Inc.
BulletMakers Workshop, The
Cambos Outdoorsman
Casull Arms Corp.
CBC
Champion's Choice, Inc.
Cor-Bon Bullet & Ammo Co.
Creekside Gun Shop Inc.
Cubic Shot Shell Co., Inc.
Cumberland States Arsenal
Daisy Mfg. Co.
Dead Eye's Sport Center
Delta Arms Ltd.
Diana (See U.S. Importer - Dynamit Nobel-RWS, Inc.
Dynamit Nobel-RWS, Inc.
Effebi SNC-Dr. Franco Beretta
Eley Ltd.
Elite Ammunition
Estate Cartridge, Inc.
Executive Protection Institute
Federal Cartridge Co.
Fiocchi of America Inc.
Fish Mfg. Gunsmith Sptg. Co., Marshall F
Garcia National Gun Traders, Inc.
Garrett Cartridges Inc.
Garthwaite Pistolsmith, Inc., Jim
Gibbs Rifle Co., Inc.
Glaser Safety Slug, Inc.
Groenewold, John
Gun City
Gun Hunter Trading Co.
Gun Room Press, The
Hansen & Co. (See Hansen Cartridge Co.)
Hart & Son, Inc.
Hi-Performance Ammunition Company
Hirtenberger Aktiengesellschaft
Hornady Mfg. Co.
Hunters Supply
IMI
Ion Industries, Inc
Israel Military Industries Ltd. (See IMI)
Jones, J.D./SSK Industries
Keng's Firearms Specialty, Inc./US Tactical Systems
Kent Cartridge America, Inc

Kent Cartridge Mfg. Co. Ltd.
Knight Rifles
Lapua Ltd.
Lightfield Ammunition Corp. (See Slug Group, Inc.)
Lock's Philadelphia Gun Exchange
M & D Munitions Ltd.
Magnum Research, Inc.
MagSafe Ammo Co.
Maionchi-L.M.I.
Markell,Inc.
McBros Rifle Co.
Men-Metallwerk Elisenhuette GmbH
Mullins Ammunition
New England Ammunition Co.
Oklahoma Ammunition Co.
Omark Industries,Div. of Blount,Inc.
Outdoor Sports Headquarters,Inc.
Pacific Cartridge, Inc.
Paragon Sales & Services, Inc.
Parker & Sons Shooting Supply
PMC/Eldorado Cartridge Corp.
Pulywad, Inc.
Pony Express Reloaders
Precision Delta Corp.
Pro Load Ammunition, Inc.
R.E.I.
Remington Arms Co., Inc.
Rucker Dist. Inc.
RWS (See US Importer-Dynamit Nobel-RWS, Inc.)
Sellier & Bellot, USA Inc
Slug Group, Inc.
Southern Ammunition Co., Inc.
Talon Mfg. Co., Inc.
TCCI
Thompson Bullet Lube Co.
USAC
Valor Corp.
Victory USA
Vihtavuori Oy/Kaltron-Pettibone
Voere-KGH m.b.H.
Vom Hoffe (See Old Western Scrounger, Inc., The)
Weatherby, Ino.
Westley Richards & Co.
Widener's Reloading & Shooting Supply, Inc.
Winchester Div. Olin Corp.
Zero Ammunition Co., Inc.

AMMUNITION, CUSTOM

3-D Ammunition & Bullets
3-Ten Corp.
4W Ammunition (See Hunters Supply)
A-Square Co.,Inc.
Accuracy Unlimited
AFSCO Ammunition
Allred Bullet Co.
American Derringer Corp.
Arizona Ammunition, Inc.
Arms Corporation of the Philippines
Atlantic Rose, Inc.
Ballard Rifle & Cartridge Co., LLC
Belding's Custom Gun Shop
Berger Bullets Ltd.
Big Bore Bullets of Alaska
Black Hills Ammunition, Inc.
Blue Mountain Bullets
Brynin, Milton
Buckskin Bullet Co.
BulletMakers Workshop, The
CBC
Country Armourer, The
Cubic Shot Shell Co., Inc.

Custom Tackle and Ammo
Dakota Arms, Inc.
Dead Eye's Sport Center
Delta Frangible Ammunition LLC
DKT, Inc.
Elite Ammunition
Estate Cartridge, Inc.
Freedom Arms, Inc.
GDL Enterprises
Glaser Safety Slug, Inc.
GOEX Inc.
Gonzalez Guns, Ramon B
Grayback Wildcats
Gun Accessories (See Glaser Safety Slug, Inc.)
Hirtenberger Aktiengesellschaft
Hoelscher, Virgil
Horizons Unlimited
Hornady Mfg. Co.
Hunters Supply
IMI
Israel Military Industries Ltd. (See IMI)
James Calhoon Mfg.
Jensen Bullets
Jensen's Custom Ammunition
Jensen's Firearms Academy
Kaswer Custom, Inc.
Keeler, R. H.
Kent Cartridge Mfg. Co. Ltd.
L.A.R. Mfg., Inc.
Lindsley Arms Cartridge Co.
Linebaugh Custom Sixguns
MagSafe Ammo Co.
MAST Technology
McBros Rifle Co.
McKillen & Heyer, Inc.
McMurdo, Lynn (See Specialty Gunsmithing)
Men-Metallwerk Elisenhuette GmbH
Milstor Corp.
Mountain Rifles, Inc.
Mullins Ammunition
Naval Ordnance Works
Northern Precision Custom Swaged Bullets
Nygord Precision Products
Oklahoma Ammunition Co.
Old Western Scrounger,Inc.
Phillippi Custom Bullets, Justin
Precision Delta Corp.
Precision Munitions, Inc.
Precision Reloading, Inc.
Professional Hunter Supplies (See Star Custom Bull
R.E.I.
Ramon B. Gonzalez Guns
Sanders Custom Gun Service
Sandia Die & Cartridge Co.
SOS Products Co. (See Buck Stix-SOS Products Co.)
Specialty Gunsmithing
Spencer's Custom Guns
Star Custom Bullets
State Arms Gun Co.
Stewart's Gunsmithing
Talon Mfg. Co., Inc.
Unmussig Bullets, D. L.
Vitt/Boos
Vom Hoffe (See Old Western Scrounger, Inc., The)
Vulpes Ventures, Inc. Fox Cartridge Division
Walters, John
Warren Muzzleloading Co., Inc.
Weaver Arms Corp. Gun Shop
Worthy Products, Inc.
Yukon Arms Classic Ammunition
Zero Ammunition Co., Inc.

AMMUNITION, FOREIGN

A-Square Co.,Inc.
AFSCO Ammunition
Armscorp USA , Inc.
Atlantic Rose, Inc.
B & P America
B-West Imports, Inc.
Beeman Precision Airguns
BulletMakers Workshop, The
CBC
Cheddite France S.A.
Cubic Shot Shell Co., Inc.
Dead Eye's Sport Center
Diana (See U.S. Importer - Dynamit Nobel-RWS, Inc.
DKT, Inc.
Dynamit Nobel-RWS, Inc.
E. Arthur Brown Co.
Fiocchi of America Inc.
First Inc, Jack
Fisher Enterprises, Inc.
Fisher, R. Kermit (See Fisher Enterprises, Inc)
FN Herstal
Forgett Jr., Valmore J.
Gamebore Division, Polywad Inc
Gibbs Rifle Co., Inc.
GOEX Inc.
Gunsmithing, Inc.
Hansen & Co. (See Hansen Cartridge Co.)
Heidenstrom Bullets
Hirtenberger Aktiengesellschaft
Hornady Mfg. Co.
IMI
IMI Services USA, Inc.
Israel Military Industries Ltd. (See IMI)
Johnson's Gunsmithing, Inc, Neal
K.B.I. Inc
MagSafe Ammo Co.
Magtech Ammunition Co.
Maionchi-L.M.I.
Marksman Products
MAST Technology
Merkuria Ltd.
Mullins Ammunition
Naval Ordnance Works
Navy Arms Co
Neal Johnson's Gunsmithing, Inc.
Oklahoma Ammunition Co.
Old Western Scrounger,Inc.
Paragon Sales & Services, Inc.
Paul Co., The
Petro-Explo Inc.
Precision Delta Corp.
R.E.T. Enterprises
RWS (See US Importer-Dynamit Nobel-RWS, Inc.)
Samco Global Arms, Inc.
Sentinel Arms
Southern Ammunition Co., Inc.
Stratco, Inc.
SwaroSports, Inc. (See JagerSport Ltd
T.F.C. S.p.A.
Victory Ammunition
Vihtavuori Oy/Kaltron-Pettibone
Vom Hoffe (See Old Western Scrounger, Inc., The)
Yukon Arms Classic Ammunition

ANTIQUE ARMS DEALER

Ackerman & Co.
Ad Hominem
Antique American Firearms
Antique Arms Co.
Aplan Antiques & Art, James O.
Armoury, Inc., The

Arundel Arms & Ammunition, Inc., A.
Ballard Rifle & Cartridge Co., LLC
Bear Mountain Gun & Tool
Bill Johns Master Engraver
Bob's Tactical Indoor Shooting Range & Gun Shop
British Antiques
Buckskin Machine Works, A. Hunkeler
Buffalo Arms Co.
Bustani, Leo
Cape Outfitters
Carlson, Douglas R, Antique American Firearms
CBC-BRAZIL
Chadick's Ltd.
Chambers Flintlocks Ltd., Jim
Champlin Firearms, Inc.
Chuck's Gun Shop
Classic Guns, Inc., Frank S. Wood
Clements' Custom Leathercraft, Chas
Cole's Gun Works
Collectors Firearms Etc
D&D Gunsmiths, Ltd.
Dixie Gun Works, Inc.
Dixon Muzzleloading Shop, Inc.
Duffy, Charles E (See Guns Antique & Modern DBA)
Enguix Import-Export
Fagan & Co.Inc
Fanzoj GmbH
Fish Mfg. Gunsmith Sptg. Co., Marshall F
Forgett Jr., Valmore J.
Frielich Police Equipment
Fulmer's Antique Firearms, Chet
Getz Barrel Co.
Glass, Herb
Goergen's Gun Shop, Inc.
Golden Age Arms Co.
Goodwin, Fred
Gun Hunter Trading Co.
Gun Room Press, The
Gun Room, The
Gun Works, The
Guncraft Sports Inc.
Guns Antique & Modern DBA/Charles E. Duffy
Hallowell & Co.
Hamilton, Jim
HandCrafts Unltd (See Clements' Custom Leathercrat
Handgun Press
Hansen & Co. (See Hansen Cartridge Co.)
Hunkeler, A (See Buckskin Machine Works
Kelley's
Knight's Mfg. Co.
Ledbetter Airguns, Riley
LeFever Arms Co., Inc.
Lever Arms Service Ltd.
Lock's Philadelphia Gun Exchange
Log Cabin Sport Shop
Mandell Shooting Supplies Inc.
Martin's Gun Shop
Montana Outfitters, Lewis E. Yearout
Museum of Historical Arms, Inc.
Muzzleloaders Etcetera, Inc.
N. Flayderman & Co., Inc.
New England Arms Co.
Pony Express Sport Shop
Powder Horn Antiques
Retting, Inc., Martin B
Samco Global Arms, Inc.
Sarco, Inc.
Scott Fine Guns Inc., Thad
Shootin' Shack, Inc.

Sportsmen's Exchange & Western Gun Traders, Inc.
Steves House of Guns
Stott's Creek Armory, Inc.
Strawbridge, Victor W.
Vic's Gun Refinishing
Vintage Arms, Inc.
Wallace, Terry
Westley Richards & Co.
Wiest, M. C.
Winchester Sutler, Inc., The
Wood, Frank (See Classic Guns, Inc.)
Yearout, Lewis E. (See Montana Outfitters)

APPRAISER - GUNS, ETC.

Antique Arms Co.
Armoury, Inc., The
Arundel Arms & Ammunition, Inc., A.
Barta's Gunsmithing
Beitzinger, George
Blue Book Publications, Inc.
Bob's Tactical Indoor Shooting Range & Gun Shop
British Antiques
Bustani, Leo
Butterfield & Butterfield
Camilli, Lou
Cannon's
Cape Outfitters
Chadick's Ltd.
Champlin Firearms, Inc.
Christie's East
Clark Firearms Engraving
Classic Guns, Inc., Frank S. Wood
Clements' Custom Leathercraft, Chas
Cole's Gun Works
Collectors Firearms Etc
Colonial Arms, Inc.
Colonial Repair
Corry, John
Creekside Gun Shop Inc.
Custom Tackle and Ammo
D&D Gunsmiths, Ltd.
DGR Custom Rifles
Dilliott Gunsmithing, Inc.
Dixon Muzzleloading Shop, Inc.
Duane's Gun Repair (See DGR Custom Rifles)
Epps, Ellwood (See "Gramps" Antique
Evercull Co., Inc., K.
Fagan & Co.Inc
Ferris Firearms
Fish Mfg. Gunsmith Sptg. Co., Marshall F
Forgett Jr., Valmore J.
Forty Five Ranch Enterprises
Francotte & Cie S.A. Auguste
Frontier Arms Co.,Inc.
Gene's Custom Guns
George E. Mathews & Son, Inc.
Getz Barrel Co.
Gillmann, Edwin
Goergen's Gun Shop, Inc.
Golden Age Arms Co.
Gonzalez Guns, Ramon B
Goodwin, Fred
Griffin & Howe, Inc.
Gun City
Gun Hunter Trading Co.
Gun Room Press, The
Gun Shop, The
Guncraft Sports Inc.
Guns
Hallberg Gunsmith, Fritz
Hallowell & Co.
Hammans, Charles E.

PRODUCT DIRECTORY

HandCrafts Unltd (See Clements'
    Custom Leathercraf
Handgun Press
Hank's Gun Shop
Hansen & Co. (See Hansen
    Cartridge Co.)
Hughes, Steven Dodd
Irwin, Campbell H.
Island Pond Gun Shop
Jackalope Gun Shop
Jensen's Custom Ammunition
Kelley's
L.L. Bean, Inc.
Lampert, Ron
LaRocca Gun Works
Ledbetter Airguns, Riley
LeFever Arms Co., Inc.
Lock's Philadelphia Gun
    Exchange
Log Cabin Sport Shop
Mac's .45 Shop
Madis, George
Mandell Shooting Supplies Inc.
Martin's Gun Shop
Mathews & Son, Inc., George E.
McCann Industries
McCann's Machine & Gun Shop
McCann's Muzzle-Gun Works
Montana Outfitters, Lewis E.
    Yearout
Museum of Historical Arms, Inc.
Muzzleloaders Etcetera, Inc.
N. Flayderman & Co., Inc.
New England Arms Co.
Nitex, Inc.
Orvis Co., The
Pasadena Gun Center
Pentheny de Pentheny
Perazzi USA, Inc.
Peterson Gun Shop, Inc., A.W.
Pettinger Books, Gerald
Pony Express Sport Shop
Powder Horn Antiques
R.A. Wells Custom Gunsmith
R.E.T. Enterprises
Ramon B. Gonzalez Guns
Retting, Inc., Martin B
River Road Sporting Clays
Rogers Gunsmithing, Bob
Safari Outfitters Ltd.
Scott Fine Guns Inc., Thad
Shootin' Shack, Inc.
Spencer Reblue Service
Sportsmen's Exchange &
    Western Gun Traders, Inc.
Steger, James R.
Stott's Creek Armory, Inc.
Stratco, Inc.
Strawbridge, Victor W.
Swampfire Shop (See Peterson
    Gun Shop, Inc.), The
Thurston Sports, Inc.
Valade Engraving, Robert
Vic's Gun Refinishing
Walker Arms Co., Inc.
Wasmundt, Jim
Wayne Firearms for Collectors
    and Investors, James
Werth, T. W.
Whildin & Sons Ltd, E.H.
Wichita Arms, Inc.
Wiest, M. C.
Williams Shootin' Iron Service,
    The Lynx-Line
Winchester Sutler, Inc., The
Wood, Frank (See Classic Guns,
    Inc.)
Yearout, Lewis E. (See Montana
    Outfitters)
Yee, Mike

AUCTIONEER - GUNS, ETC.

"Little John's" Antique Arms
Buck Stix--SOS Products Co.
Butterfield & Butterfield
Christie's East
Fagan & Co.Inc
Kelley's
Sotheby's

BOOKS & MANUALS (PUBLISHERS & DEALERS)

"Su-Press-On",Inc.
Accurate Arms Co., Inc.
Alpha 1 Drop Zone
American Handgunner Magazine
Armory Publications, Inc.
Arms & Armour Press
Ballistic Product, Inc.
Barnes Bullets, Inc.
Beeman Precision Airguns
Blacksmith Corp.
Blacktail Mountain Books
Blue Book Publications, Inc.
Blue Ridge Machinery & Tools,
    Inc.
Boone's Custom Ivory Grips, Inc.
Brown Co, E. Arthur
Brownells, Inc.
Bullet'n Press
Calibre Press, Inc.
Cape Outfitters
Colonial Repair
Colorado Sutlers Arsenal (See
    Cumberland States Ar
Corbin Mfg. & Supply, Inc.
Cumberland States Arsenal
DBI Books Division of Krause
    Publications (Edito
Dixie Gun Works, Inc.
Dixon Muzzleloading Shop, Inc.
Ed~ Brown Products, Inc.
Executive Protection Institute
Flores Publications Inc, J (See
    Action Direct Inc)
Forgett Jr., Valmore J.
Galati International
Golden Age Arms Co.
Gun City
Gun Hunter Books (See Gun
    Hunter Trading Co)
Gun Hunter Trading Co.
Gun List (See Krause
    Publications)
Gun Parts Corp., The
Gun Room Press, The
Gun Works, The
Guncraft Books (See Guncraft
    Sports Inc)
Guncraft Sports Inc.
Gunnerman Books
GUNS Magazine
Gunsmithing, Inc.
H&P Publishing
Handgun Press
Harris Publications
Hawk Laboratories, Inc. (See
    Hawk, Inc.)
Hawk, Inc.
Heritage/VSP Gun Books
High North Products, Inc.
Hodgdon Powder Co.
Home Shop Machinist The Village
    Press Publications
Hornady Mfg. Co.
Hungry Horse Books
Huntington Die Specialties
I.D.S.A. Books
Info-Arm

Ironside International Publishers,
    Inc.
J Martin Inc
Jantz Supply
Kelley's
Koval Knives
Krause Publications, Inc.
Lapua Ltd.
Lethal Force Institute (See Police
    Bookshelf)
Load From A Disk
Lyman Products Corp.
Madis Books
Magma Engineering Co.
MarMik, Inc.
McKee Publications
Milberry House Publishing
Montana Armory, Inc (See C.
    Sharps Arms Co. Inc.)
Mountain South
New Win Publishing, Inc.
NgraveR Co., The
OK Weber,Inc.
Outdoor Sports
    Headquarters,Inc.
Outdoorsman's Bookstore, The
Paintball Games International
    Magazine (Aceville P
Pejsa Ballistics
Petersen Publishing Co.
Pettinger Books, Gerald
Police Bookshelf
Precision Shooting,Inc.
PWL Gunleather
Ray Riling Arms Books Co.
Remington Double Shotguns
Riling Arms Books Co., Ray
Rocky Mountain Wildlife
    Products
Rutgers Book Center
S&S Firearms
Safari Press, Inc.
Saunders Gun & Machine Shop
Scharch Mfg., Inc.
Semmer, Charles (See
    Remington Double
    Shotguns)
Sharps Arms Co., Inc., C.
Shootin' Accessories, Ltd.
Sierra Bullets
SPG LLC
Stackpole Books
Stewart Game Calls, Inc., Johnny
Stoeger Industries
Stoeger Publishing Co. (See
    Stoeger Industries)
Thomas, Charles C.
Track of the Wolf, Inc.
Trafalgar Square
Trotman, Ken
Tru-Balance Knife Co.
Vintage Industries, Inc.
VSP Publishers (See
    Heritage/VSP Gun Books)
W. Square Enterprises
W.E. Brownell Checkering Tools
WAMCO--New Mexico
Wells Creek Knife & Gun Works
Wilderness Sound Products Ltd.
Williams Gun Sight Co.
Winchester Press (See New Win
    Publishing, Inc.)
Wolf's Western Traders
Wolfe Publishing Co.

BULLET CASTING, ACCESSORIES

Ferguson, Bill

BULLET CASTING, FURNACES & POTS

Ferguson, Bill

BULLET CASTING, LEAD

Action Bullets & Alloy Inc
Belltown Ltd.
Buckskin Bullet Co.
Bullseye Bullets
Jericho Tool & Die Co., Inc.
Muzzleloading Technologies, Inc
Penn Bullets
SPG LLC

BULLET TOOLS

Brynin, Milton
Bullet Swaging Supply Inc.
Camdex, Inc.
Corbin Mfg. & Supply, Inc.
Cumberland Arms
Eagan, Donald V.
Holland's Gunsmithing
Hollywood Engineering
Necromancer Industries, Inc.
Niemi Engineering, W. B.
North Devon Firearms Services
Rorschach Precision Products
Sport Flite Manufacturing Co.
WTA Manufacturing

BULLET, CASE & DIE LUBRICANTS

4-D Custom Die Co.
Bonanza (See Forster Products)
Brown Co, E. Arthur
Buckskin Bullet Co.
Camp-Cap Products
CH Tool & Die Co (See 4-D
    Custom Die Co)
Chem-Pak Inc.
Cooper-Woodward
CVA
E-Z-Way Systems
Elkhorn Bullets
Ferguson, Bill
Forster Products
Guardsman Products
HEBB Resources
Heidenstrom Bullets
Hollywood Engineering
Hornady Mfg. Co.
Imperial (See E-Z-Way Systems)
Knoell, Doug
Le Clear Industries (See E-Z-Way
    Systems)
Lee Precision, Inc.
Lestrom Laboratories, Inc.
Lithi Bee Bullet Lube
MI-TE Bullets
Michaels of Oregon Co.
Paco's (See Small Custom Mould
    & Bullet Co)
RCBS Div. of Blount
Reardon Products
Rooster Laboratories
Shay's Gunsmithing
Small Custom Mould & Bullet Co.
Tamarack Products, Inc.
Uncle Mike's (See Michaels of
    Oregon Co)
Warren Muzzleloading Co., Inc.
Widener's Reloading & Shooting
    Supply, Inc.
Young Country Arms

CARTRIDGES FOR COLLECTORS

"Gramps" Antique Cartridges

Ad Hominem
British Antiques
Cameron's
Campbell, Dick
Cartridge Transfer Group, Pete de
    Coux
Cole's Gun Works
Collectors Firearms Etc
Colonial Repair
Country Armourer, The
de Coux, Pete (See Cartridge
    Transfer Group)
Duane's Gun Repair (See DGR
    Custom Rifles)
Enguix Import-Export
Epps, Ellwood (See "Gramps"
    Antique
First Inc, Jack
Fitz Pistol Grip Co.
Forty Five Ranch Enterprises
Grayback Wildcats
Gun City
Gun Parts Corp., The
Liberty Shooting Supplies
Mandell Shooting Supplies Inc.
MAST Technology
Michael's Antiques
Montana Outfitters, Lewis E.
    Yearout
Pasadena Gun Center
San Francisco Gun Exchange
SOS Products Co. (See Buck Stix-
    SOS Products Co.)
Stone Enterprises Ltd.
Ward & Van Valkenburg
Yearout, Lewis E. (See Montana
    Outfitters)

CASE & AMMUNITION PROCESSORS, INSPECTORS, BOXERS

Ben's Machines
Scharch Mfg., Inc.

CASE CLEANERS & POLISHING MEDIA

G96 Products Co., Inc.
Penn Bullets
VibraShine, Inc.

CASE PREPARATION TOOLS

Hoehn Sales, Inc.
Match Prep--Doyle Gracey

CASE TRIMMERS, TRIM DIES & ACCESSORIES

Match Prep--Doyle Gracey
Ozark Gun Works

CASE TUMBLERS, VIBRATORS, MEDIA & ACCESSORIES

Penn Bullets
VibraShine, Inc.

CASES, CABINETS, RACKS & SAFES - GUN

Alco Carrying Cases
All Rite Products, Inc.
Allen Co., Bob
Allen Co., Inc.
Allen Sportswear, Bob (See Allen
    Co., Bob)

PRODUCT DIRECTORY

Alumna Sport by Dee Zee
American Display Co.
American Security Products Co.
Americase
Art Jewel Enterprises Ltd.
Ashby Turkey Calls
Bagmaster Mfg., Inc.
Barramundi Corp.
BEC, Inc.
Berry's Mfg., Inc.
Big Sky Racks, Inc.
Big Spring Enterprises "Bore
    Stores"
Bill's Custom Cases
Bison Studios
Black Sheep Brand
Brauer Bros. Mfg. Co.
Brown, H. R. (See Silhouette
    Leathers)
Browning Arms Co.
Bushmaster Hunting & Fishing
Cannon Safe, Inc.
Chipmunk (See Oregon Arms,
    Inc.)
Cobalt Mfg., Inc.
CONKKO
Connecticut Shotgun Mfg. Co.
D&L Industries (See D.J.
    Marketing)
D.J. Marketing
Dara-Nes, Inc. (See Nesci
    Enterprises, Inc.)
Deepeeka Exports Pvt. Ltd.
Doskocil Mfg. Co., Inc.
DTM International, Inc.
Elk River, Inc.
English, Inc., A.G.
Enhanced Presentations, Inc.
Eutaw Co., Inc., The
Eversull Co., Inc., K.
Fort Knox Security Products
Frontier Safe Co.
Galati International
GALCO International Ltd.
Gun Locker Div. of Airmold W.R.
    Grace & Co.-Conn.
Gun-Ho Sports Cases
Hafner Creations, Inc.
Hall Plastics, Inc., John
Hastings Barrels
Homak
Hoppe's Div. Penguin Industries,
    Inc.
Huey Gun Cases
Hugger Hooks Co.
Hunter Co., Inc.
Hydrosorbent Products
Impact Case Co.
Johanssons Vapentillbehor, Bert
Johnston Bros. (See C&T Corp.
    TA Johnson Brothers)
Jumbo Sports Products
Kalispel Case Line
Kane Products, Inc.
KK Air International (See Impact
    Case Co.)
Knock on Wood Antiques
Kolpin Mfg., Inc.
Lakewood Products LLC
Liberty Safe
Marsh, Mike
Maximum Security Corp.
McWelco Products
Morton Booth Co.
MPC
MTM Molded Products Co., Inc.
Nalpak
National Security Safe Co., Inc.
Necessary Concepts, Inc.
Nesci Enterprises Inc.
Oregon Arms, Inc. (See Rogue
    Rifle Co., Inc.)
Outa-Site Gun Carriers

Outdoor Connection,Inc., The
Palmer Security Products
Perazzi USA, Inc.
Pflumm Mfg. Co.
Poburka, Philip (See Bison
    Studios)
Powell & Son (Gunmakers) Ltd.,
    William
Prototech Industries, Inc.
Quality Arms, Inc.
Schulz Industries
Silhouette Leathers
Southern Security
Sportsman's Communicators
Sun Welding Safe Co.
Surecase Co., The
Sweet Home, Inc.
Tinks & Ben Lee Hunting
    Products (See Wellington O
Universal Sports
W. Waller & Son, Inc.
WAMCO, Inc.
Wilson Case, Inc.
Woodstream
Zanotti Armor, Inc.
Ziegel Engineering

CHOKE DEVICES, RECOIL ABSORBERS & RECOIL PADS

3-Ten Corp.
Accuright
Action Products, Inc.
Allen Co., Bob
Allen Sportswear, Bob (See Allen
    Co., Bob)
Answer Products Co.
Arms Ingenuity Co.
B-Square Company, Inc.
Baer Custom, Inc, Les
Baker, Stan
Bansner's Gunsmithing
    Specialties
Bartlett Engineering
Briley Mfg. Inc.
Brooks Tactical Systems
Brownells, Inc.
Buffer Technologies
Bull Mountain Rifle Co.
C&H Research
Cape Outfitters
Cation
Chuck's Gun Shop
Clearview Products
Colonial Arms, Inc.
Connecticut Shotgun Mfg. Co.
CRR , Inc./Marble's Inc.
Danuser Machine Co.
Dina Arms Corporation
Elsen Inc., Pete
Frank Custom Classic Arms, Ron
Graybill's Gun Shop
Gruning Precision Inc
Guns
Hammans, Charles E.
Harry Lawson Co.
Hogue Grips
Holland's Gunsmithing
I.N.C. Inc (See Kick Eez)
J.P. Enterprises Inc.
Jackalope Gun Shop
Jenkins Recoil Pads, Inc.
Kick Eez
Lawson Co., Harry
London Guns Ltd.
Mag-Na-Port International, Inc.
Marble Arms (See CRR,
    Inc./Marble's Inc.)
Meadow Industries
Menck, Gunsmith Inc., T.W.
Michaels of Oregon Co.
Middlebrooks Custom Shop

Morrow, Bud
Nelson/Weather-Rite, Inc.
Nu-Line Guns,Inc.
One Of A Kind
Original Box, nc.
Palsa Outdoor Products
PAST Sporting Goods,Inc.
Pro-Port Ltd.
Protektor Model
Que Industries, Inc.
R.M. Precision
Shotguns Unlimited
Simmons Gun Repair, Inc.
Spencer's Custom Guns
Stone Enterprises Ltd.
Trulock Tool
Uncle Mike's (See Michaels of
    Oregon Co)
Universal Sports
Vortek Products, Inc.
Wise Guns, Dale

CHRONOGRAPHS & PRESSURE TOOLS

Air Rifle Specialists
Brown Co, E. Arthur
Canons Delcour
Clearview Products
Competition Electronics, Inc.
Custom Chronograph, Inc.
D&H Precision Tooling
Hege Jagd-u. Sporthandels
    GmbH
Hornady Mfg. Co.
Hutton Rifle Ranch
Kent Cartridge Mfg. Co. Ltd.
Oehler Research,Inc.
P.A.C.T., Inc.
Romain's Custom Guns, Inc.
Savage Arms, Inc.
Shooting Chrony, Inc.
SKAN A.R.
Stratco, Inc.
Tepeco

CLEANERS & DEGREASERS

G96 Products Co., Inc.

CLEANING & REFINISHING SUPPLIES

AC Dyna-tite Corp.
Accupro Gun Care
Alpha 1 Drop Zone
American Gas & Chemical Co.,
    Ltd
Answer Products Co.
Armite Laboratories
Armsport, Inc.
Atlantic Mills , Inc.
Atsko/Sno-Seal, Inc.
Barnes Bullets, Inc.
Beeman Precision Airguns
Belltown Ltd.
Bill's Gun Repair
Birchwood Casey
Blackhawk East
Blount, Inc., Sporting Equipment
    Div.
Blue and Gray Products Inc (See
    Ox-Yoke Originals
Break-Free, Inc.
Bridgers Best
Brown Co, E. Arthur
Brownells, Inc.
C.S. Van Gorden & Son, Inc.
Camp-Cap Products
Cape Outfitters
Chem-Pak Inc.

CONKKO
Connecticut Shotgun Mfg. Co.
Creedmoor Sports, Inc.
CRR , Inc./Marble's Inc.
Custom Products (See Jones
    Custom Products)
Cylinder & Slide, Inc., William R.
    Laughridge
D&H Prods. Co., Inc.
Dara-Nes, Inc. (See Nesci
    Enterprises, Inc.)
Decker Shooting Products
Deepeeka Exports Pvt. Ltd.
Desert Mountain Mfg.
Dever Co, Jack
Dewey Mfg. Co., Inc., J.
Du-Lite Corp.
Dutchman's Firearms, Inc., The
Dykstra, Doug
E&L Mfg., Inc.
Eezox, Inc.
Ekol Leather Care
Faith Associates, Inc.
Flashette Co
Flitz International Ltd.
Fluoramics, Inc.
Frontier Products Co.
G96 Products Co., Inc.
Golden Age Arms Co.
Gozon Corp. U.S.A.
Great Lakes Airguns
Guardsman Products
Gunsmithing, Inc.
Healbath Corp.
Heckler & Koch, Inc.
Hoppe's Div. Penguin Industries,
    Inc.
Hornady Mfg. Co.
Hydrosorbent Products
Iosso Products
Jantz Supply
Johnston Bros. (See C&T Corp.
    TA Johnson Brothers)
Jonad Corp.
K&M Industries, Inc.
Kellogg's Professional Products
Kent Cartridge Mfg. Co. Ltd.
Kesselring Gun Shop
Kleen-Bore,Inc.
Knight Rifles
Laurel Mountain Forge
Lee Supplies, Mark
LEM Gun Specialties Inc. The
    Lewin Lead Remover
Lewis Lead Remover (See LEM
    Gun Specialties,, The
List Precision Engineering
LPS Laboratories, Inc.
Marble Arms (See CRR,
    Inc./Marble's Inc.)
Mark Lee Supplies
Micro Sight Co.
Minute Man High Tech Industries
Mountain View Sports, Inc.
MTM Molded Products Co., Inc.
Muscle Products Corp.
Muzzleloading Technologies, Inc
Neal Johnson's Gunsmithing, Inc.
Nesci Enterprises Inc.
Northern Precision Custom
    Swaged Bullets
Now Products, Inc.
October Country Muzzleloading
Old World Oil Products
Omark Industries,Div. of
    Blount,Inc.
Original Mink Oil,Inc.
Otis Technology, Inc
Outers Laboratories Div. of
    Blount, Inc.Sporting E
Ox-Yoke Originals, Inc.
P&M Sales and Service
Parker & Sons Shooting Supply

Parker Gun Finishes
Paul Co., The
Pendleton Royal, c/o Swingler
    Buckland Ltd.
Pete Rickard, Inc.
Precision Reloading, Inc.
Pro-Shot Products, Inc.
Prolixr Lubricants
R&S Industries Corp.
Radiator Specialty Co.
Rickard, Inc., Pete
Rooster Laboratories
Rusteprufe Laboratories
Rusty Duck Premium Gun Care
    Products
Saunders Gun & Machine Shop
Shiloh Creek
Shooter's Choice
Shootin' Accessories, Ltd.
Silencio/Safety Direct
Sinclair International, Inc.
Sno-Seal, Inc. (See Atsko/Sno-
    Seal)
Southern Bloomer Mfg. Co.
Spencer's Custom Guns
Starr Trading Co., Jedediah
Stoney Point Products, Inc.
Svon Corp.
T.F.C. S.p.A.
TDP Industries, Inc.
Tetra Gun Lubricants (See FTI,
    Inc.)
Texas Platers Supply Co.
Thompson Bullet Lube Co.
Thompson/Center Arms
Track of the Wolf, Inc.
United States Products Co.
Venco Industries, Inc. (See
    Shooter's Choice)
Volquartsen Custom Ltd.
Warren Muzzleloading Co., Inc.
WD-40 Co.
Wick, David E.
Willow Bend
Wolf's Western Traders
Young Country Arms

COMPUTER SOFTWARE - BALLISTICS

Action Target, Inc.
AmBr Software Group Ltd.
Arms Software
Arms, Programming Solutions
    (See Arms Software)
Ballistic Engineering & Software,
    Inc.
Ballistic Program Co., Inc., The
Barnes Bullets, Inc.
Beartooth Bullets
Canons Delcour
Corbin Mfg. & Supply, Inc.
Country Armourer
Data Tech Software Systems
Exe, Inc.
Gun Hunter Trading Co.
Hodgdon Powder Co.
Huntington Die Specialties
J.I.T. Ltd.
Jensen Bullets
Kent Cartridge Mfg. Co. Ltd.
Load From A Disk
Maionchi-L.M.I.
Oehler Research,Inc.
Outdoor Sports
    Headquarters,Inc.
P.A.C.T., Inc.
Pejsa Ballistics
Powley Computer (See Hutton
    Rifle Ranch)
Sierra Bullets
Tioga Engineering Co., Inc.

Vancini, Carl (See Bestload, Inc.)
W. Square Enterprises

CUSTOM GUNSMITH

300 Gunsmith Service, Inc.
A&W Repair
A.A. Arms, Inc.
Acadian Ballistic Specialties
Accuracy Unlimited
Ace Custom 45's, Inc.
Ackerman & Co.
Acra-Bond Laminates
Actions by "T" Teddy Jacobson
Ad Hominem
Adair Custom Shop, Bill
Ahlman Guns
Aldis Gunsmithing & Shooting
   Supply
Alpha Gunsmith Division
Alpine's Precision Gunsmithing &
   Indoor Shooting R
Amrine's Gun Shop
Answer Products Co.
Antique Arms Co.
Armament Gunsmithing Co., Inc.
Arms Craft Gunsmithing
Arms Ingenuity Co.
Arnold Arms Co., Inc.
Art's Gun & Sport Shop, Inc.
Arundel Arms & Ammunition,
   Inc., A.
Autauga Arms, Inc.
Baelder, Harry
Baer Custom, Inc, Les
Bain & Davis, Inc.
Ballard Rifle & Cartridge Co., LLC
Bansner's Gunsmithing
   Specialties
Barnes Bullets, Inc.
Barta's Gunsmithing
Bear Arms
Bear Mountain Gun & Tool
Beaver Lodge (See Fellowes, Ted)
Behlert Precision, Inc.
Beitzinger, George
Belding's Custom Gun Shop
Bellm Contenders
Ben William's Gun Shop
Benchmark Guns
Bengtson Arms Co., L.
Biesen, Al
Biesen, Roger
Bill Adair Custom Shop
Billeb, Stephen L.
Billings Gunsmiths Inc.
BlackStar AccuMax Barrels
BlackStar Barrel Accurizing (See
   BlackStar AccuMax
Boltin, John M.
Bond Custom Firearms
Borden's Accuracy
Borovnik KG, Ludwig
Bowen Classic Arms Corp.
Brace, Larry D.
Briese Bullet Co., Inc.
Briganti, A.J.
Briley Mfg. Inc.
Broad Creek Rifle Works
Brockman's Custom
   Gunsmithing
Broken Gun Ranch
Brown Precision,Inc.
Buckhorn Gun Works
Buckskin Machine Works, A.
   Hunkeler
Budin, Dave
Bull Mountain Rifle Co.
Bullberry Barrel Works, Ltd.
Burkhart Gunsmithing, Don
Cache La Poudre Rifleworks
Cambos Outdoorsman
Camilli, Lou

Cannon's
Carolina Precision Rifles
Carter's Gun Shop
Caywood, Shane J.
CBC-BRAZIL
Chambers Flintlocks Ltd., Jim
Champlin Firearms, Inc.
Chicasaw Gun Works
Chuck's Gun Shop
Clark Custom Guns, Inc.
Clark Firearms Engraving
Classic Arms Company
Classic Arms Corp.
Classic Guns, Inc., Frank S. Wood
Clearview Products
Cleland's Outdoor World, Inc
Cloward's Gun Shop
Cogar's Gunsmithing
Cole's Gun Works
Coleman's Custom Repair
Colonial Arms, Inc.
Colonial Repair
Colorado Gunsmithing Academy
Colorado School of Trades
Colt's Mfg. Co., Inc.
Competitive Pistol Shop, The
Conrad, C. A.
Corkys Gun Clinic
Cox, Ed. C.
Craig Custom Ltd., Research &
   Development
Creekside Gun Shop Inc.
Cullity Restoration
Curtis Custom Shop
Custom Checkering Service,
   Kathy Forster
Custom Gun Products
Custom Gun Stocks
Custom Gunsmiths
Custom Shop, The
Cylinder & Slide, Inc., William R.
   Laughridge
D&D Gunsmiths, Ltd.
D&J Bullet Co. & Custom Gun
   Shop, Inc.
Dangler, Homer L.
Darlington Gun Works, Inc.
Dave's Gun Shop
David Miller Co.
David W. Schwartz Custom Guns
Davis, Don
Del-Sports, Inc.
Delorge, Ed
Dever Co, Jack
DGR Custom Rifles
DGS, Inc., Dale A. Storey
Dietz Gun Shop & Range, Inc.
Dilliott Gunsmithing, Inc.
Donnelly, C. P.
Duane A. Hobbie Gunsmithing
Duane's Gun Repair (See DGR
   Custom Rifles)
Duffy, Charles E (See Guns
   Antique & Modern DBA)
Duncan's Gun Works, Inc.
E. Arthur Brown Co.
Echols & Co., D'Arcy
Eckelman Gunsmithing
Ed~ Brown Products, Inc.
Eggleston, Jere D.
EGW Evolution Gun Works
Entre'prise Arms, Inc.
Erhardt, Dennis
Eskridge Rifles
Eversull Co., Inc., K.
Eyster Heritage Gunsmiths, Inc.,
   Ken
Fanzoj GmbH
Ferris Firearms
Fish Mfg. Gunsmith Sptg. Co.,
   Marshall F
Fisher Custom Firearms
Fisher, Jerry A.

Fleming Firearms
Flynn's Custom Guns
Forkin Arms
Forkin, Ben (See Belt MTN Arms)
Forster, Kathy (See Custom
   Checkering S
Forster, Larry L.
Forthofer's Gunsmithing &
   Knifemaking
Francesca, Inc.
Francotte & Cie S.A. Auguste
Frank Custom Classic Arms, Ron
Fred F. Wells/Wells Sport Store
Frontier Arms Co.,Inc.
Fullmer, Geo. M.
G.G. & G.
Gary Reeder Custom Guns
Gator Guns & Repair
Genecco Gun Works, K
Gentry Custom Gunmaker, David
George E. Mathews & Son, Inc.
Gilkes, Anthony W.
Gillmann, Edwin
Gilman-Mayfield, Inc.
Giron, Robert E.
Goens, Dale W.
Gonic Arms/North American Arm
Gonzalez Guns, Ramon B
Goodling's Gunsmithing
Goodwin, Fred
Gordie's Gun Shop
Grace, Charles E.
Grayback Wildcats
Graybill's Gun Shop
GrE-Tan Rifles
Green, Roger M.
Greg Gunsmithing Repair
Griffin & Howe, Inc.
Griffin & Howe, Inc.
Gruning Precision Inc
Gun Shop, The
Gun Works, The
Guncraft Sports Inc.
Guns Antique & Modern
   DBA/Charles E. Duffy
Gunsite Custom Shop
Gunsite Gunsmithy (See Gunsite
   Custom Shop)
Gunsite Training Center
Gunsmithing Ltd.
Hagn Rifles & Actions, Martin
Hallberg Gunsmith, Fritz
Halstead, Rick
Hamilton, Alex B (See Ten-Ring
   Precision, Inc)
Hamilton, Jim
Hammans, Charles E.
Hammond Custom Guns Ltd.
Hank's Gun Shop
Hanson's Gun Center, Dick
Hanus Birdguns Bill
Harold's Custom Gun Shop Inc.
   Broughton Rifle Barr
Harris Gunworks
Harry Lawson Co.
Hart & Son, Inc.
Hart Rifle Barrels,Inc.
Hartmann & Weiss GmbH
Harwood, Jack O.
Hawken Shop, The (See Dayton
   Traister)
Hecht, Hubert J, Waffen-Hecht
Heilmann, Stephen
Heinie Specialty Products
Hensler, Jerry
Hensley, Gunmaker, Darwin
Heppler's Machining
Heppler, Keith M, Keith's Custom
   Gunstocks
Heydenberk, Warren R.
High Bridge Arms, Inc
High Performance International

Highline Machine Co.
Hill, Loring F.
Hiptmayer, Armurier
Hiptmayer, Klaus
Hoag, James W.
Hodgson, Richard
Hoehn Sales, Inc.
Hoelscher, Virgil
Hoenig & Rodman
Hofer Jagdwaffen, P.
Holland's Gunsmithing
Hollis Gun Shop
Huebner, Corey O.
Hughes, Steven Dodd
Hunkeler, A (See Buckskin
   Machine Works
Hyper-Single, Inc.
Imperial Magnum Corp.
Irwin, Campbell H.
Island Pond Gun Shop
Ivanoff, Thomas G (See Tom's
   Gun Repair)
J&S Heat Treat
J.J. Roberts/Engraver
Jackalope Gun Shop
Jamison's Forge Works
Jarrett Rifles, Inc.
Jarvis, Inc.
Jeffredo Gunsight
Jensen's Custom Ammunition
Jim Norman Custom Gunstocks
Jim's Gun Shop (See Spradlin's)
Jim's Precision, Jim Ketchum
John Norrell Arms
Johnston, James (See North Fork
   Custom Gunsmithing
Jones, J.D./SSK Industries
Juenke, Vern
Jungkind, Reeves C.
Jurras, L. E.
K-D, Inc.
KDF, Inc.
Keith M. Heppler, Keith's Custom
   Gunstocks
Keith's Custom Gunstocks (See
   Heppler, Keith M)
Ken Eyster Heritage Gunsmiths,
   Inc.
Ken Starnes Gunmaker
Ken's Gun Specialties
Ketchum, Jim (See Jim's
   Precision)
Kilham & Co.
Kimball, Gary
King's Gun Works
KLA Enterprises
Klein Custom Guns, Don
Kleinendorst, K. W.
Kneiper, James
Knippel, Richard
KOGOT
Korzinek Riflesmith, J
LaFrance Specialties
Lair, Sam
Lampert, Ron
LaRocca Gun Works
Larry Lyons Gunworks
Lathrop's, Inc.
Laughridge, William R (See
   Cylinder & Slide Inc)
Lawson Co., Harry
Lazzeroni Arms Co.
Lee's Red Ramps
LeFever Arms Co., Inc.
Liberty Antique Gunworks
Lind Custom Guns, Al
Linebaugh Custom Sixguns
List Precision Engineering
Lock's Philadelphia Gun
   Exchange
Long, George F.
Mac's .45 Shop
Mag-Na-Port International, Inc.

Mahony, Philip Bruce
Mahovsky's Metalife
Makinson, Nicholas
Mandell Shooting Supplies Inc.
Martin's Gun Shop
Martz, John V.
Mathews & Son, Inc., George E.
Mazur Restoration, Pete
McCament, Jay
McCann Industries
McCann's Muzzle-Gun Works
McCluskey Precision Rifles
McFarland, Stan
McGowen Rifle Barrels
McKinney, R.P. (See Schuetzen
   Gun Co.)
McMillan Rifle Barrels
MCS, Inc.
Mercer Custom Stocks, R. M.
Michael's Antiques
Mid-America Recreation, Inc.
Middlebrooks Custom Shop
Miller Arms, Inc.
Miller Custom
Mills Jr., Hugh B.
Mo's Competitor Supplies (See
   MCS Inc)
Moeller, Steve
Monell Custom Guns
Morrison Custom Rifles, J. W.
Morrow, Bud
Mowrey's Guns & Gunsmithing
Mullis Guncraft
Muzzleloading Technologies, Inc
Nastoff's 45 Shop, Inc., Steve
NCP Products, Inc.
Nelson, Stephen
Nettestad Gun Works
New England Arms Co.
New England Custom Gun
   Service
Newman Gunshop
Nicholson Custom
Nickels, Paul R.
Nicklas, Ted
Nitex, Inc.
North American Shooting
   Systems
North Fork Custom Gunsmithing,
   James Johnston
Nu-Line Guns,Inc.
Oakland Custom Arms,Inc.
Old World Gunsmithing
Olson, Vic
Orvis Co., The
Ottmar, Maurice
Ozark Gun Works
P.S.M.G. Gun Co.
Pagel Gun Works, Inc.
Parker Gun Finishes
Pasadena Gun Center
Paterson Gunsmithing
PEM's Mfg. Co.
Pence Precision Barrels
Penrod Precision
Pentheny de Pentheny
Perazone-Gunsmith, Brian
Performance Specialists
Pete Mazur Restoration
Peterson Gun Shop, Inc., A.W.
Powell & Son (Gunmakers) Ltd.,
   William
Power Custom, Inc.
Professional Hunter Supplies
   (See Star Custom Bull
Quality Firearms of Idaho, Inc.
R&J Gun Shop
R.A. Wells Custom Gunsmith
Ramon B. Gonzalez Guns
Ray's Gunsmith Shop
Renfrew Guns & Supplies
Ridgetop Sporting Goods
Ries, Chuck

Rifles, Inc.
Rigby & Co., John
River Road Sporting Clays
RMS Custom Gunsmithing
Robar Co.'s, Inc., The
Robinson, Don
Rocky Mountain Arms, Inc.
Rocky Mountain Rifle Works Ltd.
Rogers Gunsmithing, Bob
Romain's Custom Guns, Inc.
RPM
Rupert's Gun Shop
Ryan, Chad L.
Sanders Custom Gun Service
Savage Arms, Inc.
Schiffman, Mike
Schumakers Gun Shop
Score High Gunsmithing
Scott McDougall & Associates
Scott, Dwight
Sharp Shooter Supply
Shaw, Inc., E. R. (See Small Arms Mfg. Co.)
Shay's Gunsmithing
Shockley, Harold H.
Shooters Supply
Shootin' Shack, Inc.
Shooting Specialties (See Titus, Daniel)
Shotguns Unlimited
Sile Distributors, Inc.
Silver Ridge Gun Shop (See Goodwin, Fred)
Simmons Gun Repair, Inc.
Singletary, Kent
Sipes Gun Shop
Sickiyou Gun Works (See Donnelly, C. P.)
Skeoch, Brian R.
Slezak, Jerome F.
Small Arms Mfg. Co.
Smith, Art
Smith, Sharmon
Snapp's Gunshop
Speiser, Fred D.
Spencer Reblue Service
Spencer's Custom Guns
Sportsmen's Exchange & Western Gun Traders, Inc.
Springfield, Inc.
SSK Industries
Star Custom Bullets
Steelman's Gun Shop
Steffens, Ron
Steger, James R.
Stiles Custom Guns
Storey, Dale A. (See DGS Inc.)
Stott's Creek Armory, Inc.
Strawbridge, Victor W.
Sturgeon Valley Sporters, K. Ide
Sullivan, David S .(See Westwind Rifles Inc.)
Swampfire Shop (See Peterson Gun Shop, Inc.), The
Swann, D. J.
Swenson's 45 Shop, A. D.
Swift River Gunworks
Szweda, Robert (See RMS Custom Gunsmithing)
Taconic Firearms Ltd., Perry Lane
Talmage, William G.
Tank's Rifle Shop
Tar-Hunt Custom Rifles, Inc.
Tarnhelm Supply Co., Inc.
Taylor & Robbins
Ten-Ring Precision, Inc.
Terry K. Kopp Professional Gunsmithing
Thompson, Randall (See Highline Machine Co.)
Thurston Sports, Inc.
Time Precision, Inc.

Titus, Daniel, Shooting Specialties
Tom's Gun Repair, Thomas G. Ivanoff
Tom's Gunshop
Tooley Custom Rifles
Trevallion Gunstocks
Trulock Tool
Tucker, James C.
Unmussig Bullets, D. L.
Upper Missouri Trading Co.
Valade Engraving, Robert
Van Horn, Gil
Van Patten, J. W.
Van's Gunsmith Service
Vest, John
Vic's Gun Refinishing
Vintage Arms, Inc.
Volquartsen Custom Ltd.
Von Minden Gunsmithing Services
Walker Arms Co., Inc.
Wallace, Terry
Wasmundt, Jim
Weaver Arms Corp. Gun Shop
Weber & Markin Custom Gunsmiths
Weems, Cecil
Weigand Combat Handguns, Inc.
Welch, Bud
Wenig Custom Gunstocks
Werth, T. W.
Wessinger Custom Guns & Engraving
Western Design (See Alpha Gunsmith Division)
Westley Richards & Co.
Westwind Rifles, Inc., David S. Sullivan
White Shooting Systems, Inc. (See White Muzzleload
Wichita Arms, Inc.
Wiebe, Duane
Wiest, M. C.
Wild West Guns
Williams Gun Sight Co.
Williams Shootin' Iron Service, The Lynx-Line
Williamson Precision Gunsmithing
Wilson Gun Shop
Winter, Robert M.
Wise Guns, Dale
Wiseman and Co., Bill
Wood, Frank (See Classic Guns, Inc.)
Working Guns
Wright's Hardwood Gunstock Blanks
Yankee Gunsmith
Yee, Mike
Zeeryp, Russ

CUSTOM METALSMITH

A&W Repair
Ahlman Guns
Aldis Gunsmithing & Shooting Supply
Amrine's Gun Shop
Answer Products Co.
Arnold Arms Co., Inc.
Baer Custom, Inc, Les
Bansner's Gunsmithing Specialties
Baron Technology
Bear Mountain Gun & Tool
Behlert Precision, Inc.
Beitzinger, George
Benchmark Guns
Bengtson Arms Co., L.
Biesen, Al

Bill Adair Custom Shop
Billings Gunsmiths Inc.
Billingsley & Brownell
Bone Engraving, Ralph
Brace, Larry D.
Briganti, A.J.
Broad Creek Rifle Works
Brown Precision,Inc.
Buckhorn Gun Works
Bull Mountain Rifle Co.
Bullberry Barrel Works, Ltd.
Burkhart Gunsmithing, Don
Bustani, Leo
Campbell, Dick
Carter's Gun Shop
Caywood, Shane J.
Champlin Firearms, Inc.
Checkmate Refinishing
Chicasaw Gun Works
Classic Guns, Inc., Frank S. Wood
Cleland's Outdoor World, Inc
Colonial Repair
Colorado Gunsmithing Academy
Craftguard
Crandall Tool & Machine Co.
Cullity Restoration
Custom Gun Products
Custom Gunsmiths
Custom Shop, The
D&D Gunsmiths, Ltd.
D&H Precision Tooling
Dave's Gun Shop
Delorge, Ed
DGR Custom Rifles
DGS, Inc., Dale A. Storey
Duane's Gun Repair (See DGR Custom Rifles)
Duncan's Gun Works, Inc.
Eversull Co., Inc., K.
Eyster Heritage Gunsmiths, Inc., Ken
Ferris Firearms
Forster, Larry L.
Forthofer's Gunsmithing & Knifemaking
Francesca, Inc.
Frank Custom Classic Arms, Ron
Fred F. Wells/Wells Sport Store
Fullmer, Geo. M.
Gene's Custom Guns
Genecco Gun Works, K
Gentry Custom Gunmaker, David
Gilkes, Anthony W.
Gordie's Gun Shop
Grace, Charles E.
Graybill's Gun Shop
Green, Roger M.
Griffin & Howe, Inc.
Gun Shop, The
Guns
Gunsmithing Ltd.
Hagn Rifles & Actions, Martin
Hallberg Gunsmith, Fritz
Hamilton, Alex B (See Ten-Ring Precision, Inc)
Harry Lawson Co.
Hart & Son, Inc.
Hartmann & Weiss GmbH
Harwood, Jack O.
Hecht, Hubert J, Waffen-Hecht
Heilmann, Stephen
Heppler's Machining
Heritage Wildlife Carvings
Highline Machine Co.
Hiptmayer, Armurier
Hiptmayer, Klaus
Hoag, James W.
Hoelscher, Virgil
Holland's Gunsmithing
Hollis Gun Shop
Hyper-Single, Inc.
Island Pond Gun Shop

Ivanoff, Thomas G (See Tom's Gun Repair)
J&S Heat Treat
Jamison's Forge Works
Jeffredo Gunsight
Johnston, James (See North Fork Custom Gunsmithing
KDF, Inc.
Ken Eyster Heritage Gunsmiths, Inc.
Ken Starnes Gunmaker
Ken's Gun Specialties
Kilham & Co.
Klein Custom Guns, Don
Kleinendorst, K. W.
Lampert, Ron
Larry Lyons Gunworks
Lawson Co., Harry
List Precision Engineering
Mac's .45 Shop
Mahovsky's Metalife
Makinson, Nicholas
Mazur Restoration, Pete
McCament, Jay
McCann Industries
McCann's Machine & Gun Shop
McFarland, Stan
Mid-America Recreation, Inc.
Miller Arms, Inc.
Morrison Custom Rifles, J. W.
Morrow, Bud
Mullis Guncraft
Nelson, Stephen
Nettestad Gun Works
New England Custom Gun Service
Nicholson Custom
Nitex, Inc.
Noreen, Peter H.
North Fork Custom Gunsmithing, James Johnston
Nu-Line Guns,Inc.
Olson, Vic
Ozark Gun Works
Pagel Gun Works, Inc.
Parker Gun Finishes
Pasadena Gun Center
Penrod Precision
Pete Mazur Restoration
Precise Metalsmithing Enterprises
Precision Metal Finishing, John Westrom
Precision Specialties
R.A. Wells Custom Gunsmith
Rice, Keith (See White Rock Tool & Die)
Rifles, Inc.
River Road Sporting Clays
Robar Co.'s, Inc., The
Rocky Mountain Arms, Inc.
Rogers Gunsmithing, Bob
Score High Gunsmithing
Simmons Gun Repair, Inc.
Sipes Gun Shop
Skeoch, Brian R.
Smith, Art
Smith, Sharmon
Snapp's Gunshop
Spencer Reblue Service
Spencer's Custom Guns
Sportsmen's Exchange & Western Gun Traders, Inc.
Steffens, Ron
Steger, James R.
Stiles Custom Guns
Storey, Dale A. (See DGS Inc.)
Strawbridge, Victor W.
Taylor & Robbins
Ten-Ring Precision, Inc.
Terry K. Kopp Professional Gunsmithing

Thompson, Randall (See Highline Machine Co.)
Tom's Gun Repair, Thomas G. Ivanoff
Tooley Custom Rifles
Valade Engraving, Robert
Van Horn, Gil
Van Patten, J. W.
Von Minden Gunsmithing Services
Waldron, Herman
Wallace, Terry
Weber & Markin Custom Gunsmiths
Werth, T. W.
Wessinger Custom Guns & Engraving
Westrom, John (See Precision Metal Finishing)
White Rock Tool & Die
Wiebe, Duane
Wild West Guns
Williams Gun Sight Co.
Williams Shootin' Iron Service, The Lynx-Line
Williamson Precision Gunsmithing
Winter, Robert M.
Wise Guns, Dale
Wood, Frank (See Classic Guns, Inc.)
Wright's Hardwood Gunstock Blanks
Zufall, Joseph F.

DECOYS

A&M Waterfowl ,Inc.
Baekgaard Ltd.
Belding's Custom Gun Shop
Boyds' Gunstock Industries, Inc.
Carry-Lite, Inc.
Deer Me Products Co.
Fair Game International
Farm Form Decoys, Inc.
Feather, Flex Decoys
Flambeau Products Corp.
G&H Decoys,Inc.
Herter's Manufacturing, Inc.
Hiti-Schuch, Atelier Wilma
Klingler Woodcarving
L.L. Bean, Inc.
Molin Industries, Tru-Nord Division
North Wind Decoy Co.
Penn's Woods Products, Inc.
Quack Decoy & Sporting Clays
Russ Trading Post
Sports Innovations Inc.
Tanglefree Industries
Waterfield Sports, Inc.
Woods Wise Products

DIES, METALLIC

Carbide Die & Mfg. Co., Inc.
Ozark Gun Works
Redding Reloading Equipment

DIES, SHOTSHELL

MEC, Inc.

ENGRAVER, ENGRAVING TOOLS

Ackerman & Co.
Adair Custom Shop, Bill
Adams & Son Engravers, John J
Adams Jr., John J.
Ahlman Guns
Alfano, Sam
Allard, Gary/Creek Side Metal & Woodcrafters

PRODUCT DIRECTORY

Allen Firearm Engraving
Altamont Co.
American Pioneer Video
Anthony and George Ltd.
Baron Technology
Barraclough, John K.
Bates Engraving, Billy
Bill Johns Master Engraver
Blair Engraving, J. R.
Bleile, C. Roger
Boessler, Erich
Bone Engraving, Ralph
Bratcher, Dan
Brooker, Dennis
Burgess, Byron
Churchill, Winston
Clark Firearms Engraving
Collings, Ronald
Creek Side Metal & Woodcrafters
Cullity Restoration
Cupp, Alana, Custom Engraver
Davidson, Jere
Dayton Traister
Delorge, Ed
Dolbare, Elizabeth
Drain, Mark
Dremel Mfg. Co.
Dubber, Michael W.
Engraving Artistry
Evans Engraving, Robert
Eversull Co., Inc., K.
Eyster Heritage Gunsmiths, Inc.,
    Ken
Firearms Engraver's Guild of
    America
Flannery Engraving Co., Jeff W
Forty Five Ranch Enterprises
Fountain Products
Francotte & Cie S.A. Auguste
Frank E. Hendricks Master
    Engravers, Inc.
Frank Knives
French, Artistic Engraving, J. R.
Gene's Custom Guns
George, Tim
Glimm, Jerome C.
Golden Age Arms Co.
Gournet, Geoffroy
Grant, Howard V.
Griffin & Howe, Inc.
Gun Room, The
Guns
Gurney, F. R.
Gwinnell, Bryson J.
Hale, Engraver, Peter
Hamilton, Jim
Hands Engraving, Barry Lee
Harris Gunworks
Harris Hand Engraving, Paul A.
Harwood, Jack O.
Hawken Shop, The (See Dayton
    Traister)
Hendricks, Frank E. Inc., Master
    Engravers
Heritage Wildlife Carvings
Hiptmayer, Armurier
Hiptmayer, Heidemarie
Ingle, Ralph W.
J.J. Roberts/Engraver
J.R. Blair Engraving
Jantz Supply
John J. Adams & Son Engravers
Kamyk Engraving Co., Steve
Kane, Edward
Kehr, Roger
Kelly, Lance
Ken Eyster Heritage Gunsmiths,
    Inc.
Klingler Woodcarving
Koevenig's Engraving Service
Kudlas, John M.
Larry Lyons Gunworks
LeFever Arms Co., Inc.

Leibowitz, Leonard
Lindsay, Steve
Little Trees Ramble (See Scott
    Pilkington, Little
Lutz Engraving, Ron E.
Master Engravers, Inc. (See
    Hendricks, Frank E)
McCombs, Leo
McDonald, Dennis
McKenzie, Lynton
Mele, Frank
Metals Hand Engraver/European
    Hand Engraving
Mid-America Recreation, Inc.
Mittermeier, Inc., Frank
Montgomery Community College
Mountain States Engraving,
    Kenneth W. Warren
Nelson, Gary K.
New England Custom Gun
    Service
New Orleans Jewelers Supply Co.
NgraveR Co., The
Oker's Engraving
Pedersen, C. R.
Pedersen, Rex C.
Pilgrim Pewter,Inc. (See Bell
    Originals Inc. Sid)
Pilkington, Scott (See Little Trees
    Ramble)
Piquette, Paul R.
Potts, Wayne E.
Rabeno, Martin
Reed, Dave
Reno, Wayne
Riggs, Jim
Roberts/Engraver, J J
Rohner, Hans
Rohner, John
Rosser, Bob
Rundell's Gun Shop
Runge, Robert P.
Sampson, Roger
Schiffman, Mike
Sherwood, George
Singletary, Kent
Smith, Mark A.
Smith, Ron
Smokey Valley Rifles (See Lutz
    Engraving, Ron E)
Theis, Terry
Thiewes, George W.
Thirion Gun Engraving, Denise
Thompson/Center Arms
Valade Engraving, Robert
Vest, John
Viramontez, Ray
Vorhes, David
W.E. Brownell Checkering Tools
Wagoner, Vernon G.
Wallace, Terry
Warenski, Julie
Warren, Kenneth W. (See
    Mountain States Engraving)
Weber & Markin Custom
    Gunsmiths
Welch, Sam
Wells, Rachel
Wessinger Custom Guns &
    Engraving
Wood, Mel
Yee, Mike
Ziegel Engineering

GAME CALLS

Adventure Game Calls
Arkansas Mallard Duck Calls
Ashby Turkey Calls
Bostick Wildlife Calls, Inc.
Cedar Hill Game Calls Inc.
Creative Concepts USA, Inc.

Crit'R Call (See Rocky Mountain
    Wildlife Products)
Custom Calls
D&H Prods. Co., Inc.
D-Boone Ent., Inc.
Deepeeka Exports Pvt. Ltd.
Dr. O's Products Ltd.
Duck Call Specialists
Eddie Salter Calls, Inc.
Faulhaber Wildlocker
Faulk's Game Call Co., Inc.
Fibron Products, Inc.
Glynn Scobey Duck & Goose
    Calls
Green Head Game Call Co.
Hally Caller
Haydel's Game Calls, Inc.
Herter's Manufacturing, Inc.
Hunter's Specialties Inc.
Keowee Game Calls
Kingyon, Paul L. (See Custom
    Calls)
Knight & Hale Game Calls
Lohman Mfg. Co., Inc.
Mallardtone Game Calls
Marsh, Johnny
Moss Double Tone, Inc.
Mountain Hollow Game Calls
Oakman Turkey Calls
Outdoor Sports
    Headquarters,Inc.
Penn's Woods Products, Inc.
Pete Rickard, Inc.
Philip S. Olt Co.
Primos, Inc.
Quaker Boy, Inc.
Rickard, Inc., Pete
Rocky Mountain Wildlife
    Products
Russ Trading Post
Sceery Game Calls
Sports Innovations Inc.
Stanley Scruggs' Game Calls
Stewart Game Calls, Inc., Johnny
Sure-Shot Game Calls, Inc.
Tanglefree Industries
Tink's Safariland Hunting Corp.
Tinks & Ben Lee Hunting
    Products (See Wellington O
Wellington Outdoors
Wilderness Sound Products Ltd.
Woods Wise Products
Wyant's Outdoor Products, Inc.

GAUGES, CALIPERS & MICROMETERS

Starrett Co., L. S.

GUN PARTS, U.S. & FOREIGN

"Su-Press-On",Inc.
A.A. Arms, Inc.
Actions by "T" Teddy Jacobson
Ahlman Guns
Amherst Arms
Armscorp USA , Inc.
Auto-Ordnance Corp.
Badger Shooters Supply, Inc.
Bar-Sto Precision Machine
Bear Mountain Gun & Tool
Bill's Gun Repair
Billings Gunsmiths Inc.
Bob's Gun Shop
Bohemia Arms Co.
Briese Bullet Co., Inc.
British Antiques
Brown Products, Inc., Ed
Buffer Technologies
Bushmaster Firearms (See
    Quality Parts Co/Bushmast
Bustani, Leo

Cape Outfitters
Caspian Arms, Ltd.
CBC-BRAZIL
Ciener Inc., Jonathan Arthur
Cole's Gun Works
Colonial Arms, Inc.
Colonial Repair
Cryo-Accurizing
Cylinder & Slide, Inc., William R.
    Laughridge
Delta Arms Ltd.
DGR Custom Rifles
Dibble, Derek A.
Duane's Gun Repair (See DGR
    Custom Rifles)
Duffy, Charles E (See Guns
    Antique & Modern DBA)
E.A.A. Corp.
EGW Evolution Gun Works
Elliott Inc., G. W.
EMF Co., Inc.
Enguix Import-Export
Entre'prise Arms, Inc.
European American Armory Corp
    (See E.A.A. Corp)
Federal Arms Corp. of America
Fleming Firearms
Forrest Inc., Tom
Glimm, Jerome C.
Goodwin, Fred
Granite Mountain Arms, Inc
Greider Precision
Groenewold, John
Gun Parts Corp., The
Gun Shop, The
Gun-Tec
Guns Antique & Modern
    DBA/Charles E. Duffy
Hastings Barrels
Hawken Shop, The (See Dayton
    Traister)
High Performance International
Hines Co, S C
I.S.S.
Irwin, Campbell H.
Jamison's Forge Works
Johnson's Gunsmithing, Inc, Neal
K&T Co. Div. of T&S Industries,
    Inc.
K.K. Arms Co.
Kimber of America, Inc.
Knight's Mfg. Co.
Krico Jagd-und Sportwaffen
    GmbH
Lampert, Ron
Laughridge, William R (See
    Cylinder & Slide Inc)
List Precision Engineering
Lodewick, Walter H.
Long, George F.
Mac's .45 Shop
Mandell Shooting Supplies Inc.
Markell,Inc.
Martin's Gun Shop
McCormick Corp., Chip
MCS, Inc.
Merkuria Ltd.
Mid-America Recreation, Inc.
Mo's Competitor Supplies (See
    MCS Inc)
Morrow, Bud
North Star West
Northwest Arms
Nu-Line Guns,Inc.
Nygord Precision Products
Olympic Arms Inc.
P.S.M.G. Gun Co.
Parts & Surplus
Pennsylvania Gun Parts Inc
Perazone-Gunsmith, Brian
Perazzi USA, Inc.
Performance Specialists
Peterson Gun Shop, Inc., A.W.

Pre-Winchester 92-90-62 Parts
    Co.
Quality Firearms of Idaho, Inc.
Quality Parts Co./Bushmaster
    Firearms
Ranch Products
Randco UK
Raptor Arms Co., Inc.
Ravell Ltd.
Retting, Inc., Martin B
Romain's Custom Guns, Inc.
Ruger (See Sturm, Ruger & Co.,
    Inc.)
S&S Firearms
Sabatti S.r.l.
Samco Global Arms, Inc.
Sarco, Inc.
Savage Arms (Canada), Inc.
Scherer
Shockley, Harold H.
Shootin' Shack, Inc.
Silver Ridge Gun Shop (See
    Goodwin, Fred)
Simmons Gun Repair, Inc.
Sipes Gun Shop
Smires, C. L.
Smith & Wesson
Southern Ammunition Co., Inc.
Southern Armory, The
Sportsmen's Exchange &
    Western Gun Traders, Inc.
Springfield Sporters, Inc.
Springfield, Inc.
Steyr Mannlicher AG & CO KG
STI International
Strayer-Voigt, Inc
Sturm Ruger & Co. Inc.
Sunny Hill Enterprises, Inc.
Swampfire Shop (See Peterson
    Gun Shop, Inc.), The
Tank's Rifle Shop
Tarnhelm Supply Co., Inc.
Triple-K Mfg. Co., Inc.
VAM Distribution Co LLC
Vektor USA
Vintage Arms, Inc.
W. Waller & Son, Inc.
W.C. Wolff Co.
Walker Arms Co., Inc.
Weaver Arms Corp. Gun Shop
Wescombe, Bill (See North Star
    West)
Whitestone Lumber Corp.
Williams Mfg. of Oregon
Winchester Sutler, Inc., The
Wise Guns, Dale
Wisners Inc/Twin Pine Armory

GUNS & GUN PARTS, REPLICA & ANTIQUE

Ahlman Guns
Armi San Paolo
Auto-Ordnance Corp.
Ballard Rifle & Cartridge Co., LLC
Bear Mountain Gun & Tool
Billings Gunsmiths Inc.
Bob's Gun Shop
British Antiques
Buckskin Machine Works, A.
    Hunkeler
Buffalo Arms Co.
Cache La Poudre Rifleworks
Cape Outfitters
CBC-BRAZIL
CCL Security Products
Chambers Flintlocks Ltd., Jim
Cogar's Gunsmithing
Cole's Gun Works
Collectors Firearms Etc
Colonial Repair
Custom Riflestocks, Inc., Michael
    M. Kokolus

PRODUCT DIRECTORY

D.B.A. Flintlocks, Etc
Dangler, Homer L.
Delhi Gun House
Delta Arms Ltd.
Dilliott Gunsmithing, Inc.
Euroarms of America, Inc.
Flintlocks Etc.
Forgett Jr., Valmore J.
Galaxy Imports Ltd.,Inc.
George E. Mathews & Son, Inc.
Getz Barrel Co.
Golden Age Arms Co.
Goodwin, Fred
Groenewold, John
Gun Parts Corp., The
Gun Works, The
Gun-Tec
Guns
Hastings Barrels
Hunkeler, A (See Buckskin
   Machine Works
IAR Inc.
Ken Starnes Gunmaker
Kokolus, Michael M. (See Custom
   Riflestocks, In
L&R Lock Co.
Leonard Day & Sons Inc.
Liberty Antique Gunworks
List Precision Engineering
Lock's Philadelphia Gun
   Exchange
Lucas, Edward E
Mandell Shooting Supplies Inc.
Martin's Gun Shop
Mathews & Son, Inc., George E.
McKee Publications
McKinney, R.P. (See Schuetzen
   Gun Co.)
Mountain State Muzzleloading
   Supplies, Inc.
Mowrey Gun Works
Museum of Historical Arms, Inc.
Muzzleloaders Etcetera, Inc.
Navy Arms Co.
Neumann GmbH
North Star West
Nu-Line Guns,Inc.
Pasadena Gun Center
Pecatonica River Longrifle
PEM's Mfg. Co.
Pennsylvania Gun Parts Inc
Pony Express Sport Shop
Precise Metalsmithing
   Enterprises
Quality Firearms of Idaho, Inc.
R.A. Wells Custom Gunsmith
Randco UK
Ravell Ltd.
Retting, Inc., Martin B
S&S Firearms
Samco Global Arms, Inc.
Sarco, Inc.
Shootin' Shack, Inc.
Silver Ridge Gun Shop (See
   Goodwin, Fred)
Simmons Gun Repair, Inc.
Southern Ammunition Co., Inc.
Starr Trading Co., Jedediah
Stott's Creek Armory, Inc.
Taylor's & Co., Inc.
Tennessee Valley Mfg.
Tiger-Hunt Gunstocks
Triple-K Mfg. Co., Inc.
Uberti USA, Inc.
Upper Missouri Trading Co.
Vintage Industries, Inc.
Vortek Products, Inc.
Weisz Parts
Wescombe, Bill (See North Star
   West)
Winchester Sutler, Inc., The

GUNS, AIR

Air Arms
Air Rifle Specialists
Air Venture Airguns
Airrow
Allred Bullet Co.
Anschutz GmbH
Arms Corporation of the
   Philippines
Beeman Precision Airguns
Benjamin/Sheridan Co.,
   Crossman
Bohemia Arms Co.
Brass Eagle, Inc.
Brocock Ltd.
Bryan & Assoc
BSA Guns Ltd.
Compasseco, Ltd.
Component Concepts, Inc.
Conetrol Scope Mounts
Creedmoor Sports, Inc.
Crosman Airguns
Crosman Products of Canada Ltd.
Daisy Mfg. Co.
Daystate Ltd.
Diana (See U.S. Importer -
   Dynamit Nobel-RWS, Inc.
Domino
Dynamit Nobel-RWS, Inc.
European American Armory Corp
   (See E.A.A. Corp)
Frankonia Jagd Hofmann & Co.
FWB
Gamo USA, Inc.
Gaucher Armes, S.A.
Great Lakes Airguns
Groenewold, John
Gun Room Press, The
Hebard Guns, Gil
Interarms/Howa
Israel Arms International, Inc.
Labanu, Inc.
Leapers, Inc.
List Precision Engineering
Loch Leven Industries
Mac-1 Airgun Distributors
Marksman Products
Maryland Paintball Supply
Merkuria Ltd.
Neal Johnson's Gunsmithing, Inc.
Nygord Precision Products
Pardini Armi Srl
Park Rifle Co., Ltd., The
Precision Airgun Sales, Inc.
Precision Sales International, Inc.
Ripley Rifles
Robinson, Don
RWS (See US Importer-Dynamit
   Nobel-RWS, Inc.)
S.G.S. Sporting Guns Srl.
Savage Arms, Inc.
SKAN A.R.
Smart Parts
Smith & Wesson
Snapp's Gunshop
Steyr Mannlicher AG & CO KG
Stone Enterprises Ltd.
Theoben Engineering
Tippman Pneumatics, Inc.
Tristar Sporting Arms, Ltd.
Trooper Walsh
UltraSport Arms, Inc.
Valor Corp.
Vortek Products, Inc.
Walther GmbH, Carl
Webley and Scott Ltd.
Weihrauch KG, Hermann
Whiscombe (See U.S. Importer-
   Pelaire Products)
World Class Airguns

GUNS, FOREIGN MANUFACTURER U.S. IMPORTER

Accuracy Int'l. North America,
   Inc.
Accuracy Internationl Precision
   Rifles (See U.S. I
Air Arms
Armas Kemen S. A. (See U.S.
   Importers)
Armi Perazzi S.p.A.
Armi San Marco (See U.S.
   Importers-Taylor's & Co I
Armi Sport (See U.S. Importers-
   Cape Outfitters)
Arms Corporation of the
   Philippines
Armscorp USA , Inc.
Arrieta S.L.
Astra Sport , S.A.
Atamec-Bretton
AYA (See U.S. Importer-New
   England Custom Gun Serv
B.C. Outdoors
BEC, Inc.
Benelli Armi S.p.A.
Beretta S.p.A., Pietro
Beretta U.S.A. Corp.
Bernardelli S.p.A., Vincenzo
Bersa S.A.
Bertuzzi (See U.S. Importer-New
   England Arms Co)
Bill Hanus Birdguns LLC
Blaser Jagdwaffen GmbH
Bohemia Arms Co.
Borovnik KG, Ludwig
Bosis (See U.S. Importer-New
   England Arms Co.)
Brenneke KG, Wilhelm
BRNO (See U.S. Importers-
   Bohemia Arms Co.)
Brocock Ltd.
Browning Arms Co.
BSA Guns Ltd.
Cabanas (See U.S. Importer-
   Mandall Shooting Suppli
CBC
Chapuis Armes
Churchill (See U.S. Importer-
   Ellett Bros)
Cosmi Americo & Figlio s.n.c.
Crucelegui Hermanos (See U.S.
   Importer-Mandall Sh
Cryo-Accurizing
Daewoo Precision Industries Ltd.
Dakota (See U.S. Importer-EMF
   Co., Inc.)
Davide Pedersoli and Co.
Diana (See U.S. Importer -
   Dynamit Nobel-RWS, Inc.
Domino
Dumoulin, Ernest
EAW (See U.S. Importer-New
   England Custom Gun Serv
Effebi SNC-Dr. Franco Beretta
Euro-Imports
F.A.I.R. Techni-Mec s.n.c. di
   Isidoro Rizzini & C.
Fabarm S.p.A.
Fanzoj GmbH
Fausti Cav. Stefano & Figlie snc
FEG
Felk, Inc.
FERLIB
Fiocchi Munizioni S.p.A. (See
   U.S. Importer-Fiocch
Firearms Co Ltd/Alpine (See U.S.
   Importer-Mandall
Firearms International
FN Herstal
Franchi S.p.A.

FWB
Galaxy Imports Ltd.,Inc.
Gamba S.p.A. Societa Armi
   Bresciane Srl
Gamo (See U.S. Importers-Arms
   United Corp, Daisy M
Garbi, Armas Urki
Gaucher Armes, S.A.
Gibbs Rifle Co., Inc.
Glock GmbH
Grulla Armes
Hammans, Charles E.
Hammerli Ltd.
Hartford (See U.S. Importer-EMF
   Co. Inc.)
Hartmann & Weiss GmbH
Heckler & Koch, Inc.
Hege Jagd-u. Sporthandels
   GmbH
Helwan (See U.S. Importer-
   Interarms)
Holland & Holland Ltd.
Howa Machinery, Ltd.
I.A.B. (See U.S. Importer-Taylor's
   & Co. Inc.)
IGA (See U.S. Importer-Stoeger
   Industries)
IMI
Imperial Magnum Corp.
Inter Ordnance of America LP
Interarms/I Iowa
JSL Ltd (See U.S. Importer-
   Specialty Shooters Supp
Kimar (See U.S. Importer-IAR
   ,Inc)
Korth
Krico Jagd-und Sportwaffen
   GmbH
Krieghoff Gun Co., H.
KSN Industries Ltd (See U.S.
   Importer-Israel Arms
Lakefield Arms Ltd (See Savage
   Arms Inc)
Lanber Armas, S.A.
Lapua Ltd.
Laurona Armas Eibar, S.A.L.
Lebeau-Courally
Lever Arms Service Ltd.
Llama Gabilondo Y Cia
London Guns Ltd.
M. Thys (See U.S. Importer-
   Champlin Firearms Inc)
Madis, George
Magtech Ammunition Co
Mandell Shooting Supplies Inc.
Marocchi F.lli S.p.A
Mauser Werke Oberndorf
   Waffensysteme GmbH
MEC-Gar S.r.l.
Merkel Freres
Miltex, Inc
Miroku, B C/Daly, Charles (See
   U.S. Importer-Bell'
Morini (See U.S. Importers-
   Mandall Shooting Suppli
Navy Arms Co.
New SKB Arms Co.
Norica, Avnda Otaola
Norinco
Norma Precision AB (See U.S.
   Importers-Dynamit Nob
Para-Ordnance Mfg., Inc.
Pardini Armi Srl
Pease International
Perugini Visini & Co. S.r.l.
Peters Stahl GmbH
Pietta (See U.S. Importers-Navy
   Arms Co, Taylor's
Piotti (See U.S. Importer-Moore
   & Co, Wm. Larkin)
Powell & Son (Gunmakers) Ltd.,
   William
Prairie Gun Works

Rigby & Co., John
Rizzini F.lli (See U.S. Importers-
   Moore & C Englan
Rizzini SNC
Rossi Firearms, Braztech
Rutten (See U.S. Importer-
   Labanu Inc)
RWS (See US Importer-Dynamit
   Nobel-RWS, Inc.)
S.A.R.L. G. Granger
S.I.A.C.E. (See U.S. Importer-IAR
   Inc)
Sabatti S.r.l.
Sako Ltd (See U.S. Importers-
   Stoeger Industries)
San Marco (See U.S. Importers-
   Cape Outfitters-EMF
Sauer (See U.S. Importers-Paul
   Co., The, Sigarms I
SIG
SIG-Sauer (See U.S. Importer-
   Sigarms Inc.)
Societa Armi Bresciane Srl (See
   U.S. Importer-Cape
Sphinx Engineering SA
Springfield, Inc.
Star Bonifacio Echeverria S.A.
Steyr Mannlicher AG & CO KG
T.F.C. S.p.A.
Tanfoglio Fratelli S.r.l.
Tanner (See U.S. Importer-
   Mandall Shooting Supplie
Taurus International Firearms
   (See U.S. Importer-T
Taurus S.A. Forjas
Techno Arms (See U.S. Importer-
   Auto-Ordnance Corp
Tikka (See U.S. Importer-Stoeger
   Industries)
TOZ (See U.S. Importer-Nygord
   Precision Products)
Turkish Firearms Corp.
Uberti, Aldo
Ugartechea S. A., Ignacio
Ultralux (See U.S. Importer-
   Keng's Firearms Specia
Unique/M.A.P.F.
Valtro USA, Inc
Voere-KGH m.b.H.
Walther GmbH, Carl
Weatherby, Inc.
Webley and Scott Ltd.
Weihrauch KG, Hermann
Westley Richards & Co
Whiscombe (See U.S. Importer-
   Pelaire Products)
Wolf (See J.R. Distributing)
Zabala Hermanos S.A.
Zanoletti, Pietro
Zoli, Antonio

GUNS, FOREIGN-IMPORTER

Accuracy International
AcuSport Corporation
Air Rifle Specialists
American Arms Inc.
American Frontier Firearms Mfg.,
   Inc
Amtec 2000, Inc.
Armsport, Inc.
Auto-Ordnance Corp.
B-West Imports, Inc.
Bell's Legendary Country Wear
Benelli USA Corp
Big Bear Arms & Sporting Goods,
   Inc.
Bill Hanus Birdguns LLC
Bohemia Arms Co.
Bridgeman Products
British Sporting Arms
Browning Arms Co.

Cabela's
Cape Outfitters
Century International Arms, Inc.
Champion Shooters' Supply
Champion's Choice, Inc.
Champlin Firearms, Inc.
Chapuis USA
Cimarron F.A. Co.
CVA
CZ USA
D.B.A. Flintlocks, Etc
Dynamit Nobel-RWS, Inc.
E&L Mfg., Inc.
E.A.A. Corp.
Eagle Imports, Inc.
Ellett Bros.
EMF Co., Inc.
Euroarms of America, Inc.
Eversull Co., Inc., K.
Fiocchi of America Inc.
Fisher, Jerry A.
Forgett Jr., Valmore J.
Franzen International,Inc (See
    U.S. Importer for P
G.U. Inc (See U.S. Importer for
    New SKB Arms Co)
Galaxy Imports Ltd.,Inc.
Gamba, USA
Gamo USA, Inc.
Giacomo Sporting USA
Glock, Inc.
Great Lakes Airguns
Gremmel Enterprises
Griffin & Howe, Inc.
GSI, Inc.
Gun Shop, The
Gunsite Custom Shop
Gunsite Training Center
Hammerli USA
Hanus Birdguns Bill
Heckler & Koch, Inc.
I.S.S.
IAR Inc.
Imperial Magnum Corp.
Import Sports Inc.
Interarms/Howa
Israel Arms International, Inc.
Ithaca Gun Co. LLC
Johnson's Gunsmithing, Inc, Neal
K-Sports Imports Inc.
K.B.I. Inc
Kemen America
Keng's Firearms Specialty,
    Inc./US Tactical Systems
Krieghoff International,Inc.
Labanu, Inc.
Lion Country Supply
London Guns Ltd.
Magnum Research, Inc.
Magtech Ammunition Co.
Mandell Shooting Supplies Inc.
Marx, Harry (See U.S. Importer
    for FERLIB)
MCS, Inc.
MEC-Gar U.S.A., Inc.
Nationwide Sports Distributors,
    Inc.
Neal Johnson's Gunsmithing, Inc.
New England Arms Co.
New England Custom Gun
    Service
Nygord Precision Products
OK Weber,Inc.
Orvis Co., The
P.S.M.G. Gun Co.
Para-Ordnance, Inc.
Paul Co., The
Pelaire Products
Perazzi USA, Inc.
Powell Agency, William
Precision Sales International, Inc.
Quality Arms, Inc.
Savage Arms, Inc.

Schuetzen Pistol Works
Scott Fine Guns Inc., Thad
Sigarms, Inc.
SKB Shotguns
Southern Ammunition Co., Inc.
Specialty Shooters Supply, Inc.
Springfield, Inc.
Stoeger Industries
Stone Enterprises Ltd.
Swarovski Optik North America
    Ltd.
Taurus Firearms, Inc.
Taylor's & Co., Inc.
Track of the Wolf, Inc.
Tradewinds, Inc.
Traditions Performance Firearms
Tristar Sporting Arms, Ltd.
Trooper Walsh
Turkish Firearms Corp.
Uberti USA, Inc.
VAM Distribution Co LLC
Vektor USA
Vintage Arms, Inc.
Weatherby, Inc.
Westley Richards Agency USA
    (See U.S. Importer for
    Whitestone Lumber Corp.
Wingshooting Adventures
World Class Airguns

GUNS, SURPLUS, PARTS & AMMUNITION

Ad Hominem
Ahlman Guns
Alpha 1 Drop Zone
Armscorp USA , Inc.
Arundel Arms & Ammunition,
    Inc., A.
Bondini Paolo
Cambos Outdoorsman
Century International Arms, Inc.
Chuck's Gun Shop
Cole's Gun Works
Combat Military Ordnance Ltd.
Delta Arms Ltd.
First Inc, Jack
Fleming Firearms
Forgett Jr., Valmore J.
Forrest Inc., Tom
Frankonia Jagd Hofmann & Co.
Garcia National Gun Traders, Inc.
Gun City
Gun Parts Corp., The
Hallberg Gunsmith, Fritz
Hank's Gun Shop
Hart & Son, Inc.
Hege Jagd-u. Sporthandels
    GmbH
Interarms/Howa
Jackalope Gun Shop
Ken Starnes Gunmaker
LaRocca Gun Works
Lever Arms Service Ltd.
Log Cabin Sport Shop
Lomont Precision Bullets
Mandell Shooting Supplies Inc.
Martin's Gun Shop
Navy Arms Co.
Nevada Pistol Academy, Inc.
Northwest Arms
Oil Rod and Gun Shop
Paragon Sales & Services, Inc.
Parts & Surplus
Pasadena Gun Center
Perazone-Gunsmith, Brian
Quality Firearms of Idaho, Inc.
Ravell Ltd.
Retting, Inc., Martin B
Samco Global Arms, Inc.
San Francisco Gun Exchange
Sarco, Inc.

Shootin' Shack, Inc.
Silver Ridge Gun Shop (See
    Goodwin, Fred)
Simmons Gun Repair, Inc.
Sportsmen's Exchange &
    Western Gun Traders, Inc.
Springfield Sporters, Inc.
T.F.C. S.p.A.
Tarnhelm Supply Co., Inc.
Thurston Sports, Inc.
Whitestone Lumber Corp.
Williams Shootin' Iron Service,
    The Lynx-Line

GUNS, U.S. MADE

3-Ten Corp.
A-Square Co.,Inc.
A.A. Arms, Inc.
Accu-Tek
Ace Custom 45's, Inc.
Acra-Bond Laminates
Airrow
Allred Bullet Co.
American Arms Inc.
American Derringer Corp.
American Frontier Firearms Mfg.,
    Inc
Angel Arms, Inc.
AR-7 Industries, LLC
ArmaLite, Inc.
Armscorp USA , Inc.
Austin & Halleck
Autauga Arms, Inc.
Auto-Ordnance Corp.
Baer Custom, Inc, Les
Ballard Rifle & Cartridge Co., LLC
Bar-Sto Precision Machine
Barrett Firearms Manufacturer,
    Inc.
Beretta S.p.A., Pietro
Beretta U.S.A. Corp.
Big Bear Arms & Sporting Goods,
    Inc.
Bond Arms, Inc.
Brockman's Custom
    Gunsmithing
Brown Co, E. Arthur
Brown Products, Inc., Ed
Browning Arms Co.
Bushmaster Firearms (See
    Quality Parts Co/Bushmast
Calico Light Weapon Systems
Cambos Outdoorsman
Cape Outfitters
Casull Arms Corp.
CCL Security Products
Century Gun Dist. Inc.
Champlin Firearms, Inc.
Charter 2000
Colt's Mfg. Co., Inc.
Competitor Corp. Inc.
Conetrol Scope Mounts
Connecticut Shotgun Mfg. Co.
Connecticut Valley Classics (See
    CVC)
Coonan Arms (JS Worldwide
    DBA)
Cooper Arms
Creekside Gun Shop Inc.
Crossfire, L.L.C.
Cryo-Accurizing
Cumberland Arms
Cumberland Mountain Arms
CVA
CVC
Daisy Mfg. Co.
Dakota Arms, Inc.
DAN WESSON FIREARMS
Dangler, Homer L.
Davis Industries
Dayton Traister
Downsizer Corp.

E&L Mfg., Inc.
E. Arthur Brown Co.
Eagle Arms, Inc. (See ArmaLite,
    Inc.)
Ed~ Brown Products, Inc.
Emerging Technologies, Inc. (See
    Laseraim Technolo
Entre'prise Arms, Inc.
Essex Arms
FN Herstal
Forgett Jr., Valmore J.
Fort Worth Firearms
Frank Custom Classic Arms, Ron
Freedom Arms, Inc.
Fulton Armory
Galena Industries AMT
Garcia National Gun Traders, Inc.
Genecco Gun Works, K
Gentry Custom Gunmaker, David
Gibbs Rifle Co., Inc.
Gilbert Equipment Co., Inc.
Goergen's Gun Shop, Inc.
Granite Mountain Arms, Inc
Griffin & Howe, Inc.
Gun Room Press, The
Gunsite Custom Shop
Gunsite Gunsmithy (See Gunsite
    Custom Shop)
H&R 1871, Inc.
H-S Precision, Inc.
Hammans, Charles E.
Harrington & Richardson (See
    H&R 1871, Inc.)
Harris Gunworks
Hawken Shop, The (See Dayton
    Traister)
Heritage Firearms (See Heritage
    Mfg., Inc.)
Heritage Manufacturing, Inc.
Hesco-Meprolight
Hi-Point Firearms
HJS Arms,Inc.
Hutton Rifle Ranch
IAR Inc.
Imperial Miniature Armory
Intratec
Ithaca Classic Doubles
Ithaca Gun Co. LLC
J.P. Enterprises Inc.
J.P. Gunstocks, Inc.
James Calhoon Mfg.
Jones, J.D./SSK Industries
JS Worldwide DBA (See Coonan
    Arms)
K.K. Arms Co.
Kahr Arms
Kel-Tec CNC Industries, Inc.
Kelbly, Inc.
Kimber of America, Inc.
Knight Rifles
Knight's Mfg. Co.
Kolar
L.A.R. Mfg., Inc.
L.W. Seecamp Co., Inc.
LaFrance Specialties
Lakefield Arms Ltd (See Savage
    Arms Inc)
Laseraim Technologies, Inc.
Lever Arms Service Ltd.
Ljutic Industries, Inc.
Lock's Philadelphia Gun
    Exchange
Lone Star Rifle Company
Lorcin Engineering Co. Inc.
M.O.A. Corp.
Madis, George
Mag-Na-Port International, Inc.
Magnum Research, Inc.
Mandell Shooting Supplies Inc.
Marlin Firearms Co.
Maverick Arms, Inc.
McBros Rifle Co.
Miller Arms, Inc.

MKS Supply, Inc. (See Hi-Point
    Firearms)
Montana Armory, Inc (See C.
    Sharps Arms Co. Inc.)
Mountain Rifles, Inc.
MPI Stocks
NCP Products, Inc.
New England Firearms
Noreen, Peter H.
North American Arms, Inc.
North Star West
Northwest Arms
Nowlin Mfg. Co.
October Country Muzzleloading
Olympic Arms Inc.
Oregon Arms, Inc. (See Rogue
    Rifle Co., Inc.)
Parker & Sons Shooting Supply
Phoenix Arms
Professional Ordnance, Inc.
ProWare, Inc.
Quality Parts Co./Bushmaster
    Firearms
Rapine Bullet Mould Mfg. Co.
Raptor Arms Co., Inc.
Remington Arms Co., Inc.
Republic Arms, Inc.
Rocky Mountain Arms, Inc.
Rogue Rifle Co., Inc.
Rogue River Rifleworks
RPM
Ruger (See Sturm, Ruger & Co.,
    Inc.)
Savage Arms (Canada), Inc.
Scattergun Technologies, Inc.
Sharps Arms Co., Inc., C.
Shiloh Rifle Mfg.
Small Arms Specialties
Smith & Wesson
Sporting Arms Mfg., Inc.
Springfield, Inc.
STI International
Stoeger Industries
Strayer-Voigt, Inc
Sturm Ruger & Co. Inc.
Sunny Hill Enterprises, Inc.
Taconic Firearms Ltd., Perry Lane
Tar-Hunt Custom Rifles, Inc.
Taurus Firearms, Inc.
Texas Armory (See Bond Arms,
    Inc.)
Thompson/Center Arms
Time Precision, Inc.
Tristar Sporting Arms, Ltd.
U.S. Repeating Arms Co., Inc.
UFA, Inc.
Ultra Light Arms, Inc.
Volquartsen Custom Ltd.
Wallace, Terry
Weatherby, Inc.
Wescombe, Bill (See North Star
    West)
Whildin & Sons Ltd, E.H.
Wichita Arms, Inc.
Wildey, Inc.
Wilson Gun Shop
Z-M Weapons

GUNSMITH SCHOOL

American Gunsmithing Institute
Bull Mountain Rifle Co.
Colorado Gunsmithing Academy
Colorado School of Trades
Cylinder & Slide, Inc., William R.
    Laughridge
Lassen Community College,
    Gunsmithing Dept.
Laughridge, William R (See
    Cylinder & Slide Inc)
Log Cabin Sport Shop
Modern Gun Repair School
Montgomery Community College

PRODUCT DIRECTORY

Murray State College
North American Correspondence
 Schools The Gun Pro
Nowlin Mfg. Co.
NRI Gunsmith School
Pennsylvania Gunsmith School
Piedmont Community College
Pine Technical College
Professional Gunsmiths of
 America,Inc.
Smith & Wesson
Southeastern Community College
Spencer's Custom Guns
Trinidad St. Jr Col Gunsmith Dept
Wright's Hardwood Gunstock
 Blanks
Yavapai College

GUNSMITH SUPPLIES, TOOLS & SERVICES

Ace Custom 45's, Inc.
Actions by "T" Teddy Jacobson
Aldis Gunsmithing & Shooting
 Supply
Alley Supply Co.
Allred Bullet Co.
American Frontier Firearms Mfg.,
 Inc
B-Square Company, Inc
Baer Custom, Inc, Les
Bar-Sto Precision Machine
Bear Mountain Gun & Tool
Bengtson Arms Co., L.
Biesen, Al
Biesen, Roger
Bill Johns Master Engraver
Bill's Gun Repair
Blue Ridge Machinery & Tools,
 Inc.
Break-Free, Inc.
Briley Mfg. Inc.
Brockman's Custom
 Gunsmithing
Brown Products, Inc., Ed
Brownells, Inc.
Buffer Technologies
Bull Mountain Rifle Co.
Burkhart Gunsmithing, Don
C.S. Van Gorden & Son, Inc.
Carbide Checkoring Tools (See
 J&R Engineering)
Caywood, Shane J.
CBC-BRAZIL
Chapman Manufacturing Co.
Chem-Pak Inc.
Chicasaw Gun Works
Choate Machine & Tool Co., Inc.
Chopie Mfg.,Inc.
Chuck's Gun Shop
Ciener Inc., Jonathan Arthur
Colonial Arms, Inc.
Colorado School of Trades
Conetrol Scope Mounts
Craig Custom Ltd., Research &
 Development
Creekside Gun Shop Inc.
CRR , Inc./Marble's Inc.
Cumberland Arms
Cumberland Mountain Arms
Custom Checkering Service,
 Kathy Forster
Custom Gun Products
D&J Bullet Co. & Custom Gun
 Shop, Inc.
Decker Shooting Products
Dem-Bart Checkering Tools, Inc.
Dewey Mfg. Co., Inc., J.
Dixie Gun Works, Inc.
Dremel Mfg. Co.
Du-Lite Corp.
Dutchman's Firearms, Inc., The
Echols & Co., D'Arcy

EGW Evolution Gun Works
Entre'prise Arms, Inc.
Erhardt, Dennis
Faith Associates, Inc.
FERLIB
Fisher, Jerry A.
Forgreens Tool Mfg., Inc.
Forkin Arms
Forkin, Ben (See Belt MTN Arms)
Forster, Kathy (See Custom
 Checkering S
Fred F. Wells/Wells Sport Store
Gentry Custom Gunmaker, David
Gilkes, Anthony W.
Grace Metal Products
GrE-Tan Rifles
Greider Precision
Groenewold, John
GRS Corp., Glendo
Gruning Precision Inc
Gun Hunter Trading Co.
Gun-Tec
Gunline Tools
Half Moon Rifle Shop
Halstead, Rick
Hammond Custom Guns Ltd.
Hastings Barrels
Henriksen Tool Co., Inc.
High Performance International
Hines Co, S C
Hoelscher, Virgil
Holland's Gunsmithing
Huey Gun Cases
Ivanoff, Thomas G (See Tom's
 Gun Repair)
J&R Engineering
J&S Heat Treat
Jantz Supply
JGS Precision Tool Mfg.
Kasenit Co., Inc.
Kimball, Gary
Kleinendorst, K. W.
Kmount
Korzinek Riflesmith, J
Kwik Mount Corp.
LaBounty Precision Reboring, Inc
Lea Mfg. Co.
Lee Supplies, Mark
Lee's Red Ramps
List Precision Engineering
London Guns Ltd.
Mahovsky's Metalife
Marble Arms (See CRR,
 Inc./Marble's Inc.)
Marsh, Mike
Martin's Gun Shop
McKillen & Heyer, Inc.
Menck, Gunsmith Inc., T.W.
Metalife Industries (See
 Mahovsky's Metalife)
Metaloy, Inc.
Michael's Antiques
MMC
Mo's Competitor Supplies (See
 MCS Inc)
Morrow, Bud
Mowrey's Guns & Gunsmithing
N&J Sales
New England Custom Gun
 Service
NgraveR Co., The
Nowlin Mfg. Co.
Nu-Line Guns,Inc.
Ole Frontier Gunsmith Shop
P.M. Enterprises, Inc.
Parker Gun Finishes
PEM's Mfg. Co.
Perazone-Gunsmith, Brian
Power Custom, Inc.
Practical Tools, Inc.
Precision Metal Finishing, John
 Westrom
Precision Specialties

Professional Gunsmiths of
 America,Inc.
Prolixr Lubricants
Ranch Products
Ransom International Corp.
Reardon Products
Rice, Keith (See White Rock Tool
 & Die)
Robar Co.'s, Inc., The
Rocky Mountain Arms, Inc.
Rogers Gunsmithing, Bob
Romain's Custom Guns, Inc.
Roto Carve
Royal Arms Gunstocks
Rusteprufe Laboratories
Scott McDougall & Associates
Sharp Shooter Supply
Shooter's Choice
Simmons Gun Repair, Inc.
Smith Abrasives, Inc.
Southern Bloomer Mfg. Co.
Spradlin's
Starr Trading Co., Jedediah
Starrett Co., L. S.
Stiles Custom Guns
Sullivan, David S .(See Westwind
 Rifles Inc.)
Sunny Hill Enterprises, Inc.
Terry K. Kopp Professional
 Gunsmithing
Texas Platers Supply Co.
Theis, Terry
Tom's Gun Repair, Thomas G.
 Ivanoff
Track of the Wolf, Inc.
Trinidad St. Jr Col Gunsmith Dept
Trulock Tool
Turnbull Restoration, Doug
United States Products Co.
Van Gorden & Son Inc., C. S.
Venco Industries, Inc. (See
 Shooter's Choice)
W.C. Wolff Co.
Warne Manufacturing Co.
Washita Mountain Whetstone Co.
Weaver Arms Corp. Gun Shop
Weigand Combat Handguns, Inc.
Welsh, Bud
Westrom, John (See Precision
 Metal Finishing)
Westwind Rifles, Inc., David S
 Sullivan
White Rock Tool & Die
Wilcox All-Pro Tools & Supply
Will-Burt Co.
Williams Gun Sight Co.
Williams Shootin' Iron Service,
 The Lynx-Line
Willow Bend
Windish, Jim
Winter, Robert M.
Wise Guns, Dale
Wright's Hardwood Gunstock
 Blanks
Yavapai College

HANDGUN ACCESSORIES

"Su-Press-On",Inc.
4-D Custom Die Co.
A.A. Arms, Inc.
Ace Custom 45's, Inc.
Action Direct, Inc.
ADCO Sales, Inc.
Adventurer's Outpost
African Import Co.
Aimpoint c/o Springfield, Inc.
Aimtech Mount Systems
Ajax Custom Grips, Inc.
Alpha 1 Drop Zone
Alpha Gunsmith Division
American Derringer Corp.

American Frontier Firearms Mfg.,
 Inc
Arms Corporation of the
 Philippines
Aro-Tek Ltd.
Astra Sport , S.A.
Autauga Arms, Inc.
Baer Custom, Inc, Les
Bagmaster Mfg., Inc.
Bar-Sto Precision Machine
BEC, Inc.
Behlert Precision, Inc.
Berry's Mfg., Inc.
Bill's Custom Cases
Blue and Gray Products Inc (See
 Ox-Yoke Originals
Bond Custom Firearms
Bridgeman Products
Broken Gun Ranch
Brooks Tactical Systems
Brown Products, Inc., Ed
Bucheimer, J. M. (See Jumbo
 Sports Products)
Bushmaster Firearms (See
 Quality Parts Co/Bushmast
Bushmaster Hunting & Fishing
Butler Creek Corp.
Cannon Safe, Inc.
Catco-Ambush, Inc.
Centaur Systems, Inc.
Central Specialties Ltd (See
 Trigger Lock Division
Charter 2000
Ciener Inc., Jonathan Arthur
Clark Custom Guns, Inc.
Classic Arms Company
Conetrol Scope Mounts
Craig Custom Ltd., Research &
 Development
CRR , Inc./Marble's Inc.
Cylinder & Slide, Inc., William R.
 Laughridge
D&L Industries (See D.J.
 Marketing)
D.J. Marketing
Dade Screw Machine Products
Delhi Gun House
DeSantis Holster & Leather
 Goods, Inc.
Doskocil Mfg. Co., Inc.
E&L Mfg., Inc.
E. Arthur Brown Co.
E.A.A. Corp.
Ed- Brown Products, Inc.
Essex Arms
Euroarms of America, Inc.
European American Armory Corp
 (See E.A.A. Corp)
Faith Associates, Inc.
Federal Arms Corp. of America
Feminine Protection, Inc.
Fisher Custom Firearms
Fleming Firearms
Flores Publications Inc, J (See
 Action Direct Inc)
Frielich Police Equipment
FWB
G.G. & G.
Galati International
GALCO International Ltd.
Garcia National Gun Traders, Inc.
Garthwaite Pistolsmith, Inc., Jim
Glock, Inc.
Gould & Goodrich
Greider Precision
Gremmel Enterprises
Gun Parts Corp., The
Gun-Alert
Gun-Ho Sports Cases
H-S Precision, Inc.
H.K.S. Products
Hebard Guns, Gil
Heckler & Koch, Inc.

Heinie Specialty Products
Henigson & Associates, Steve
Hi-Point Firearms
Hill Speed Leather, Ernie
Hines Co, S C
Hoppe's Div. Penguin Industries,
 Inc.
Hunter Co., Inc.
Impact Case Co.
Israel Arms International, Inc.
J.P. Enterprises Inc.
Jarvis, Inc.
JB Custom
Jeffredo Gunsight
Jim Noble Co.
Jones, J.D./SSK Industries
Jumbo Sports Products
K.K. Arms Co.
Kalispel Case Line
KeeCo Impressions, Inc.
Keller Co., The
King's Gun Works
KK Air International (See Impact
 Case Co.)
L&S Technologies Inc (See
 Aimtech Mount Systems)
LaserMax, Inc.
Lee's Red Ramps
Loch Leven Industries
Lohman Mfg. Co., Inc.
Mac's .45 Shop
Mag-Na-Port International, Inc.
Magnolia Sports,Inc.
Marble Arms (See CRR,
 Inc./Marble's Inc.)
Markell,Inc.
Maxi-Mount
McCormick Corp., Chip
MEC-Gar S.r.l.
Menck, Gunsmith Inc., T.W.
Merkuria Ltd.
Michaels of Oregon Co.
Mid-America Guns and Ammo
Middlebrooks Custom Shop
Millett Sights
MTM Molded Products Co., Inc.
No-Sho Mfg. Co.
Omega Sales
Outdoor Sports
 Headquarters,Inc.
Ox-Yoke Originals, Inc.
Pachmayr Div. Lyman Products
Paser Pal
PAST Sporting Goods,Inc.
Pearce Grip, Inc.
Phoenix Arms
Practical Tools, Inc.
Precision Small Arms
Protector Mfg. Co., Inc., The
Quality Parts Co./Bushmaster
 Firearms
Ram-Line Blount, Inc.
Ranch Products
Ransom International Corp.
Redfield, Inc
Ringler Custom Leather Co.
Round Edge, Inc.
RPM
Simmons Gun Repair, Inc.
Southern Bloomer Mfg. Co.
Southwind Sanctions
Springfield, Inc.
Sturm Ruger & Co. Inc.
T.F.C. S.p.A.
TacStar
TacTell, Inc.
Tactical Defense Institute
Tanfoglio Fratelli S.r.l.
Thompson/Center Arms
Trigger Lock Division/Central
 Specialties Ltd.
Trijicon, Inc.
Triple-K Mfg. Co., Inc.

Truglo, Inc
Tyler Manufacturing & Distributing
Universal Sports
Valor Corp.
W. Waller & Son, Inc.
W.C. Wolff Co.
Weigand Combat Handguns, Inc.
Western Design (See Alpha Gunsmith Division)
Wilson Gun Shop

HANDGUN GRIPS

A.A. Arms, Inc.
Ahrends, Kim (See Custom Firearms, Inc)
Ajax Custom Grips, Inc.
Altamont Co.
American Derringer Corp.
American Frontier Firearms Mfg., Inc
American Gripcraft
Arms Corporation of the Philippines
Aro-Tek Ltd.
Art Jewel Enterprises Ltd.
Baelder, Harry
Baer Custom, Inc, Les
Bear Hug Grip, Inc.
Big Bear Arms & Sporting Goods, Inc.
Bob's Gun Shop
Boone Trading Co., Inc.
Boone's Custom Ivory Grips, Inc.
Boyds' Gunstock Industries, Inc.
Brooks Tactical Systems
Brown Products, Inc., Ed
Clark Custom Guns, Inc.
Cole-Grip
Colonial Repair
Crimson Trace Lasers
Custom Firearms (See Ahrends, Kim)
E.A.A. Corp.
EMF Co., Inc.
Essex Arms
European American Armory Corp (See E.A.A. Corp)
Fibron Products, Inc.
Fisher Custom Firearms
Fitz Pistol Grip Co.
Forrest Inc., Tom
FWB
Garthwaite Pistolsmith, Inc., Jim
H-S Precision, Inc.
Herrett's Stocks, Inc.
HIP-GRIP Barami Corp.
Hogue Grips
Huebner, Corey O.
Jim Norman Custom Gunstocks
John Masen Co. Inc.
KeeCo Impressions, Inc.
Kim Ahrends Custom Firearms, Inc.
Korth
Lee's Red Ramps
Lett Custom Grips
Linebaugh Custom Sixguns
Mac's .45 Shop
Michaels of Oregon Co.
Mid-America Guns and Ammo
Millett Sights
N.C. Ordnance Co.
Newell, Robert H.
Northern Precision Custom Swaged Bullets
Pachmayr Div. Lyman Products
Pardini Armi Srl
Peacemaker Specialists
Pilgrim Pewter,Inc. (See Bell Originals Inc. Sid)
Precision Small Arms

Radical Concepts
Rosenberg & Son, Jack A
Roy's Custom Grips
Sile Distributors, Inc.
Spegel, Craig
Stoeger Industries
Sunny Hill Enterprises, Inc.
Tactical Defense Institute
Taurus Firearms, Inc.
Tyler Manufacturing & Distributing
Uncle Mike's (See Michaels of Oregon Co)
Vintage Industries, Inc.
Volquartsen Custom Ltd.
Western Gunstock Mfg. Co.
Wright's Hardwood Gunstock Blanks

HEARING PROTECTORS

Aero Peltor
Ajax Custom Grips, Inc.
Brown Co, E. Arthur
Brown Products, Inc., Ed
Browning Arms Co.
David Clark Co., Inc.
Dick Marple & Associates
Dillon Precision Products, Inc.
E-A-R, Inc.
Electronic Shooters Protection, Inc.
Faith Associates, Inc.
Flents Products Co., Inc.
Gentex Corp.
Gun Room Press, The
Gunsmithing, Inc.
Hoppe's Div. Penguin Industries, Inc.
Huntington Die Specialties
Kesselring Gun Shop
North Specialty Products
Paterson Gunsmithing
Peltor, Inc. (See Aero Peltor)
R.E.T. Enterprises
Ridgeline, Inc
Rucker Dist. Inc.
Silencio/Safety Direct
Tactical Defense Institute
Willson Safety Prods. Div.

HOLSTERS & LEATHER GOODS

A&B Industries,Inc (See Top-Line USA Inc)
A.A. Arms, Inc.
Action Direct, Inc.
Action Products, Inc.
Alessi Holsters, Inc.
American Sales & Mfg. Co.
Arratoonian, Andy (See Horseshoe Leather Products)
Autauga Arms, Inc.
Bagmaster Mfg., Inc.
Baker's Leather Goods, Roy
Bandcor Industries , Div. of Man-Sew Corp.
Bang-Bang Boutique (See Holster Shop, The)
Bear Hug Grip, Inc.
Beretta S.p.A., Pietro
Bianchi International, Inc.
Brauer Bros. Mfg. Co.
Brooks Tactical Systems
Brown, H. R. (See Silhouette Leathers)
Browning Arms Co.
Bucheimer, J. M. (See Jumbo Sports Products)
Bull-X, Inc.

Bushwacker Backpack & Supply Co (See Counter Assau
Cathey Enterprises, Inc.
Chace Leather Products
Churchill Glove Co., James
Cimarron F.A. Co.
Classic Old West Styles
Clements' Custom Leathercraft, Chas
Cobra Sport S.r.l.
Colonial Repair
Counter Assault
Creedmoor Sports, Inc.
Davis Leather Co., Gordon Wm.
Delhi Gun House
DeSantis Holster & Leather Goods, Inc.
Dillon Precision Products, Inc.
Ekol Leather Care
El Dorado Leather (c/o Dill)
El Paso Saddlery Co.
EMF Co., Inc.
Eutaw Co., Inc., The
F&A Inc. (See ShurKatch Corporation)
Faust Inc., T. G.
Feminine Protection, Inc.
Flores Publications Inc, J (See Action Direct Inc)
Fobus International Ltd.
Forgett Jr., Valmore J.
Frankonia Jagd Hofmann & Co.
Gage Manufacturing
GALCO International Ltd.
Garcia National Gun Traders, Inc.
GML Products, Inc.
Gould & Goodrich
Gun Leather Limited
Gun Works, The
Gunfitters
Hafner Creations, Inc.
HandCrafts Unltd (See Clements' Custom Leathercraf
Hank's Gun Shop
Hebard Guns, Gil
Heinie Specialty Products
Hellweg Ltd.
Henigson & Associates, Steve
High North Products, Inc.
Hill Speed Leather, Ernie
HIP-GRIP Barami Corp.
Hogue Grips
Holster Shop, The
Horseshoe Leather Products
Hoyt Holster Co., Inc.
Hume, Don
Hunter Co., Inc.
Israel Arms International, Inc.
Jim Noble Co.
John's Custom Leather
Jumbo Sports Products
K.L. Null Holsters Ltd.
Kane Products, Inc.
Keller Co., The
Kirkpatrick Leather Co.
Kolpin Mfg., Inc.
Korth
Kramer Handgun Leather
L.A.R. Mfg., Inc.
Lawrence Leather Co.
Lock's Philadelphia Gun Exchange
Lone Star Gunleather
Magnolia Sports,Inc.
Markell,Inc.
Marksman Products
Michaels of Oregon Co.
Minute Man High Tech Industries
Nikolai leather
No-Sho Mfg. Co.
Null Holsters Ltd. K.L.
October Country Muzzleloading
Ojala Holsters, Arvo

Oklahoma Leather Products,Inc.
Old West Reproductions,Inc.
R.M. Bachman
Paser Pal
Pathfinder Sports Leather
Peacemaker Specialists
PWL Gunleather
Renegade
Ringler Custom Leather Co.
Rumanya Inc.
Safariland Ltd., Inc.
Safety Speed Holster, Inc.
Schulz Industries
Second Chance Body Armor
Shoemaker & Sons Inc., Tex
ShurKatch Corporation
Sile Distributors, Inc.
Silhouette Leathers
Smith Saddlery, Jesse W.
Southwind Sanctions
Sparks, Milt
Stalker, Inc.
Starr Trading Co., Jedediah
Strong Holster Co.
Stuart, V. Pat
Tabler Marketing
Tactical Defense Institute
Ted Blocker Holsters, Inc.
Thad Rybka Custom Leather Equipment
Top-Line USA, Inc.
Torel, Inc.
Triple-K Mfg. Co., Inc.
Tristar Sporting Arms, Ltd.
Tyler Manufacturing & Distributing
Uncle Mike's (See Michaels of Oregon Co)
Valor Corp.
Venus Industries
Viking Leathercraft, Inc.
Walt's Custom Leather, Walt Whinnery
Westley Richards & Co.
Whinnery, Walt (See Walt's Custom Leather)
Wild Bill's Originals
Wilson Gun Shop

HUNTING & CAMP GEAR, CLOTHING, ETC.

A&M Waterfowl ,Inc.
Ace Sportswear, Inc.
Action Direct, Inc.
Action Products, Inc.
Adventure 16, Inc.
Adventure Game Calls
Allen Co., Bob
Allen Sportswear, Bob (See Allen Co., Bob)
Alpha 1 Drop Zone
Armor (See Buck Stop Lure Co., Inc.)
Atlanta Cutlery Corp.
Atsko/Sno-Seal, Inc.
B.B. Walker Co.
Baekgaard Ltd.
Bagmaster Mfg., Inc.
Barbour, Inc.
Bauer, Eddie
Bear Archery
Beaver Park Product, Inc.
Beretta S.p.A., Pietro
Better Concepts Co.
Bill Johns Master Engraver
Boss Manufacturing Co.
Brown Manufacturing
Brown, H. R. (See Silhouette Leathers)
Browning Arms Co.
Buck Stop Lure Co., Inc.

Bushmaster Hunting & Fishing
C.W. Erickson's Mfg. Inc.
Camp-Cap Products
Carhartt ,Inc.
Churchill Glove Co., James
Clarkfield Enterprises, Inc.
Classic Old West Styles
Coghlan's Ltd.
Cold Steel Inc.
Coleman Co., Inc.
Coulston Products, Inc.
Creative Concepts USA, Inc.
Creedmoor Sports, Inc.
D&H Prods. Co., Inc.
Dakota Corp.
Danner Shoe Mfg. Co.
Deer Me Products Co.
Dr. O's Products Ltd.
Dunham Boots
Duofold, Inc.
Dynalite Products, Inc.
E-A-R, Inc.
Ekol Leather Care
Eutaw Co., Inc., The
F&A Inc. (See ShurKatch Corporation)
Flores Publications Inc, J (See Action Direct Inc)
Forrest Tool Co.
Fortune Products, Inc.
Fox River Mills, Inc.
Frontier
G&H Decoys,Inc.
Gerber Legendary Blades
Glacier Glove
Gozon Corp. U.S.A.
Hafner Creations, Inc.
Heritage Wildlife Carvings
Hinman Outfitters, Bob
Hodgman, Inc.
Houtz & Barwick
Hunter's Specialties Inc.
John's Custom Leather
K&M Industries, Inc.
Kamik Outdoor Footwear
Kolpin Mfg., Inc.
L.L. Bean, Inc.
LaCrosse Footwear, Inc.
Langenberg Hat Co.
Leapers, Inc.
Lectro Science, Inc.
Liberty Trouser Co.
MAG Instrument, Inc.
Mag-Na-Port International, Inc.
Marathon Rubber Prods. Co., Inc.
McCann Industries
McCann's Machine & Gun Shop
Melton Shirt Co., Inc.
Molin Industries, Tru-Nord Division
Mountain Hollow Game Calls
Nelson/Weather-Rite, Inc.
North Specialty Products
Northlake Outdoor Footwear
Original Mink Oil,Inc.
Orvis Co., The
Outdoor Connection,Inc., The
Palsa Outdoor Products
Partridge Sales Ltd., John
Pointing Dog Journal, Village Press Publications
Powell & Son (Gunmakers) Ltd., William
Pro-Mark Div. of Wells Lamont
Pyramid, Inc.
Randolph Engineering, Inc.
Ranging, Inc.
Red Ball
Ringler Custom Leather Co.
Rocky Shoes & Boots
Scansport, Inc.
Sceery Game Calls
Servus Footwear Co.

ShurKatch Corporation
Simmons Outdoor Corp.
Sno-Seal, Inc. (See Atsko/Sno-Seal)
Streamlight, Inc.
Swanndri New Zealand
T.H.U. Enterprises, Inc.
TEN-X Products Group
Thompson, Norm
Thompson/Center Arms
Tink's Safariland Hunting Corp.
Torel, Inc.
Triple-K Mfg. Co., Inc.
United Cutlery Corp.
Venus Industries
Wakina by Pic
Walls Industries, Inc.
Wideview Scope Mount Corp.
Wilderness Sound Products Ltd.
Willson Safety Prods. Div.
Winchester Sutler, Inc., The
Wolverine Footwear Group
Woolrich, Inc.
Wyoming Knife Corp.
Yellowstone Wilderness Supply

KNIVES & KNIFEMAKER'S SUPPLIES

A.G. Russell Knives,Inc.
Action Direct, Inc.
Adventure 16, Inc.
Aitor-Cuchilleria Del Norte S.A.
Al Mar Knives, Inc.
All Rite Products, Inc.
American Target Knives
Art Jewel Enterprises Ltd.
Atlanta Cutlery Corp.
B&D Trading Co., Inc.
Barteaux Machete
Belltown Ltd.
Benchmark Knives (See Gerber Legendary Blades)
Beretta S.p.A., Pietro
Beretta U.S.A. Corp.
Big Bear Arms & Sporting Goods, Inc.
Bill Johns Master Engraver
Bill's Custom Cases
Bob Schrimsher's Custom Knifemaker's Supply
Boker USA , Inc.
Boone Trading Co., Inc.
Boone's Custom Ivory Grips, Inc.
Bowen Knife Co., Inc.
Brooks Tactical Systems
Brown, H. R. (See Silhouette Leathers)
Browning Arms Co.
Buck Knives, Inc.
Buster's Custom Knives
Camillus Cutlery Co.
Campbell, Dick
Case & Sons Cutlery Co., W R
Chicago Cutlery Co.
Clements' Custom Leathercraft, Chas
Cold Steel Inc.
Coleman Co., Inc.
Colonial Knife Co., Inc.
Compass Industries , Inc.
Creative Craftsman, Inc., The
Crosman Blades (See Coleman Co., Inc.)
CRR , Inc./Marble's Inc.
Cutco Cutlery
DAMASCUS-U.S.A.
Dan's Whetstone Co., Inc.
Degen Inc. (See Aristocrat Knives)
Delhi Gun House

DeSantis Holster & Leather Goods, Inc.
Diamond Machining Technology, Inc. (See DMT)
EdgeCraft Corp., P.B. Tuminello
Empire Cutlery Corp.
Eze-Lap Diamond Prods.
Flitz International Ltd.
Flores Publications Inc, J (See Action Direct Inc)
Forrest Tool Co.
Forthofer's Gunsmithing & Knifemaking
Fortune Products, Inc.
Frank Knives
Frost Cutlery Co.
George Ibberson (Sheffield) Ltd.
Gerber Legendary Blades
Gibbs Rifle Co., Inc.
Glock, Inc.
Golden Age Arms Co.
Gun Room, The
H&B Forge Co.
HandCrafts Unltd (See Clements' Custom Leathercraf
Harris Publications
High North Products, Inc.
Hoppe's Div. Penguin Industries, Inc.
Hubertus Schneidwarenfabrik
Hunter Co., Inc.
Hunting Classics Ltd.
Imperial Schrade Corp.
J.A. Blades, Inc. (See Christopher Firearms Co.)
J.A. Henckels Zwillingswerk Inc.
Jackalope Gun Shop
Jantz Supply
Jenco Sales, Inc.
Johnson Wood Products
KA-BAR Knives
Kasenit Co., Inc.
Kershaw Knives
Knife Importers, Inc.
Koval Knives
Lamson & Goodnow Mfg. Co.
Lansky Sharpeners
Leapers, Inc.
Leatherman Tool Group, Inc.
Linder Solingen Knives
Marble Arms (See CRR, Inc./Marble's Inc.)
Matthews Cutlery
McCann Industries
McCann's Machine & Gun Shop
Molin Industries, Tru-Nord Division
Mountain State Muzzleloading Supplies, Inc.
Normark Corp.
October Country Muzzleloading
Outdoor Edge Cutlery Corp.
Pilgrim Pewter,Inc. (See Bell Originals Inc. Sid)
Plaza Cutlery, Inc.
Queen Cutlery Co.
R&C Knives & Such
R. Murphy Co., Inc.
Randall-Made Knives
Rodgers & Sons Ltd., Joseph (See George Ibberson
Scansport, Inc.
Schiffman, Mike
Sheffield Knifemakers Supply, Inc.
Smith Saddlery, Jesse W.
Spyderco, Inc.
T.F.C. S.p.A.
Theis, Terry
Traditions Performance Firearms
Tru-Balance Knife Co.
United Cutlery Corp.
Utica Cutlery Co.

Valade Engraving, Robert
Venus Industries
Washita Mountain Whetstone Co.
Weber Jr., Rudolf
Wells Creek Knife & Gun Works
Wenger North America/Precise Int'l
Western Cutlery (See Camillus Cutlery Co.)
Whinnery, Walt (See Walt's Custom Leather)
Wideview Scope Mount Corp.
Wostenholm (See Ibberson [Sheffield] Ltd., George)
Wyoming Knife Corp.

LABELS, BOXES & CARTRIDGE HOLDERS

Ballistic Product, Inc.
Berry's Mfg., Inc.
Blackhawk East
Brown Co, E. Arthur
Cabinet Mtn. Outfitters Scents & Lures
Cheyenne Crt'g Boxes
Del Rey Products
DeSantis Holster & Leather Goods, Inc.
Fitz Pistol Grip Co.
Flambeau Products Corp.
J&J Products, Inc.
Kolpin Mfg., Inc.
Liberty Shooting Supplies
Midway Arms, Inc.
MTM Molded Products Co., Inc.
Pendleton Royal, c/o Swingler Buckland Ltd.
Precision Reloading, Inc.
Ziegel Engineering

LEAD WIRES & WIRE CUTTERS

Unmussig Bullets, D. L.

LOAD TESTING & PRODUCT TESTING

Ballistic Research
Briese Bullet Co., Inc.
Buckskin Bullet Co.
CFVentures
Clearview Products
D&H Precision Tooling
Defense Training International, Inc.
Duane's Gun Repair (See DGR Custom Rifles)
H.P. White Laboratory, Inc.
Henigson & Associates, Steve
Hensler, Jerry
Hoelscher, Virgil
Hutton Rifle Ranch
Jackalope Gun Shop
Jensen Bullets
Jurras, L. E.
Liberty Shooting Supplies
Linebaugh Custom Sixguns
Lomont Precision Bullets
Maionchi-L.M.I.
MAST Technology
McMurdo, Lynn (See Specialty Gunsmithing)
Middlebrooks Custom Shop
Multiplex International
Oil Rod and Gun Shop
Precision Reloading, Inc.
R.A. Wells Custom Gunsmith
Rupert's Gun Shop
SOS Products Co. (See Buck Stix-SOS Products Co.)

Spencer's Custom Guns
Tar-Hunt Custom Rifles, Inc.
Tioga Engineering Co., Inc.
Vancini, Carl (See Bestload, Inc.)
Vulpes Ventures, Inc. Fox Cartridge Division
X-Spand Target Systems

LOADING BLOCKS, METALLIC & SHOTSHELL

Jericho Tool & Die Co., Inc.

LUBRISIZERS, DIES & ACCESSORIES

Ben's Machines
SPG LLC
WTA Manufacturing

MISCELLANEOUS

Actions, Rifle
Hall Manufacturing

Adapters, Cartridge
Alex, Inc.

Adapters, Shotshell
PC Co.

Airgun Accessories
BSA Guns Ltd.

Airgun Repair
Airgun Repair Centre

Assault Rifle Accessories
Ram-Line Blount, Inc.

Barrel Stress Relieving
300 Below Services (See Cryo-Accurizing)

Bi-Pods
B.M.F. Activator , Inc.

Body Armor
A&B Industries,Inc (See Top-Line USA Inc)
Faust Inc., T. G.
Second Chance Body Armor
Top-Line USA, Inc.

Bore Illuminator
Flashette Co.

Bore Lights
MDS

Brass Catcher
Bridgeman Products
Gage Manufacturing

Bullets, Moly Coat
Starke Bullet Company

Bullets, Rubber
CIDCO

Cannons, Miniature Replicas
Furr Arms

Dehumidifiers
Buenger Enterprises/Goldenrod Dehumidifier
Hydrosorbent Products

Dryers
Peet Shoe Dryer, Inc.

E-Z Loader
Del Rey Products

FFL Record Keeping
Basics Information Systems, Inc.
PFRB Co.
R.E.T. Enterprises

Firearm Refinishers
Armoloy Co. of Ft. Worth

Firearm Restoration
Adair Custom Shop, Bill
Mazur Restoration, Pete
Moeller, Steve
Nicholson Custom

Hunting Trips
J/B Adventures & Safaris Inc.
Professional Hunter Supplies (See Star Custom Bull
Wild West Guns

Hypodermic Rifles/Pistols
Multipropulseurs

Industrial Dessicants
WAMCO--New Mexico

Lettering Restoration System
Pranger, Ed G.

Locks, Gun
Brown Manufacturing
Central Specialties Ltd (See Trigger Lock Division
L&R Lock Co.
Master Lock Co.
Trigger Lock Division/Central Specialties Ltd.
Voere-KGH m.b.H.

Magazines
Mag-Pack Corp.
Mech-Tech Systems, Inc.

Mats
Brigade Quartermasters

Military Equipment/Accessories
Amherst Arms

Photographers, Gun
Bilal, Mustafa
Hanusin, John
Macbean, Stan
Payne Photography, Robert
Radack Photography
Smith, Michael
Weyer International
White Pine Photographic Services

Pistol Barrel Maker
Bar-Sto Precision Machine

Power Tools, Rotary Flexible Shaft
Foredom Electric Co.

RF Barrel Vibration Reducer
Hoehn Sales, Inc.

RF Device
B.M.F. Activator , Inc.

Saddle Rings, Studs
Silver Ridge Gun Shop (See Goodwin, Fred)

Safeties
P.M. Enterprises, Inc.

Safety Devices
P&M Sales and Service

Scents and Lures
Buck Stop Lure Co., Inc.
Cabinet Mtn. Outfitters Scents & Lures
Dr. O's Products Ltd.
Mountain Hollow Game Calls
Russ Trading Post
Tink's Safariland Hunting Corp.
Tinks & Ben Lee Hunting Products (See Wellington O
Wellington Outdoors

PRODUCT DIRECTORY

Wildlife Research Center, Inc.
Wyant's Outdoor Products, Inc.

Scrimshaw
Dolbare, Elizabeth
Hoover, Harvey
Reno, Wayne

Shooting Range Equipment
Caswell Detroit Armor Companies

Shotgun Barrel Maker
Baker, Stan
Eyster Heritage Gunsmiths, Inc., Ken

Shotgun Conversion Tubes
Dina Arms Corporation

Silencers
AWC Systems Technology
DLO Mfg.
Fleming Firearms
S.C.R.C.
Sound Technology
Ward Machine

Silver Sportsmen's Art
Heritage Wildlife Carvings

Slings and Swivels
DTM International, Inc.
Pathfinder Sports Leather
Schulz Industries
Torel, Inc.

Treestands and Steps
Dr. O's Products Ltd.
Russ Trading Post
Silent Hunter
Summit Specialties, Inc.
Trax America, Inc.
Treemaster
Warren & Sweat Mfg. Co.

Trophies
V.H. Blackinton & Co., Inc.

Ventilated Rib
Simmons Gun Repair, Inc.

Ventilation
Scanco Environmental Systems

Video Tapes
American Pioneer Video
Calibre Press, Inc.
Cedar Hill Game Calls Inc.
Clements' Custom Leathercraft, Chas
Foothills Video Productions, Inc.
HandCrafts Unltd (See Clements' Custom Leathercraf
Lethal Force Institute (See Police Bookshelf)
Police Bookshelf
Primos, Inc.
R.T. Eastman Products
Trail Visions
Wilderness Sound Products Ltd.

Wind Flags
Time Precision, Inc.

Xythos-Miniature Revolver
Andres & Dworsky

MOULDS & MOULD ACCESSORIES

Buffalo Arms Co.
Gun Hunter Trading Co.
Old West Bullet Moulds
Penn Bullets
Redding Reloading Equipment

MUZZLE-LOADING GUNS, BARRELS & EQUIPMENT

Accuracy Unlimited
Adkins, Luther
Allen Mfg.
Armi San Paolo
Armoury, Inc., The
Austin & Halleck
Bauska Barrels
Beaver Lodge (See Fellowes, Ted)
Bentley, John
Big Bore Bullets of Alaska
Birdsong & Assoc, W. E.
Black Powder Products
Blackhawk East
Blue and Gray Products Inc (See Ox-Yoke Originals)
Bridgers Best
Buckskin Bullet Co.
Buckskin Machine Works, A. Hunkeler
Butler Creek Corp.
Cache La Poudre Rifleworks
California Sights (See Fautheree, Andy)
Cash Mfg. Co., Inc.
CBC-BRAZIL
Chambers Flintlocks Ltd., Jim
Chopie Mfg.,Inc.
Cimarron F.A. Co.
Cogar's Gunsmithing
Colonial Repair
Colt Blackpowder Arms Co.
Conetrol Scope Mounts
Cousin Bob's Mountain Products
Cumberland Arms
Cumberland Mountain Arms
Curly Maple Stock Blanks (See Tiger-Hunt)
CVA
D.B.A. Flintlocks, Etc
Dangler, Homer L.
Davide Pedersoli and Co.
Day & Sons Inc., Leonard
Dayton Traister
deHaas Barrels
Delhi Gun House
DGS, Inc., Dale A. Storey
Dixie Gun Works, Inc.
Dixon Muzzleloading Shop, Inc.
EMF Co., Inc.
Euroarms of America, Inc.
Eutaw Co., Inc., The
Feken, Dennis
Fellowes, Ted
Flintlocks Etc.
Forgett Jr., Valmore J.
Fort Hill Gunstocks
Fowler, Bob (See Black Powder Products)
Frankonia Jagd Hofmann & Co.
Frontier
Getz Barrel Co.
Goergen's Gun Shop, Inc.
Golden Age Arms Co.
Gonic Arms/North American Arm
Green Mountain Rifle Barrel Co., Inc.
Gun Works, The
Hastings Barrels
Hawken Shop, The (See Dayton Traister)
Hege Jagd-u. Sporthandels GmbH
Hodgdon Powder Co.
Hoppe's Div. Penguin Industries, Inc.
Hornady Mfg. Co.
House of Muskets, Inc., The

Hunkeler, A (See Buckskin Machine Works
Impact Case Co.
J.P. Gunstocks, Inc.
Jamison's Forge Works
Jones Co., Dale
K&M Industries, Inc.
Kalispel Case Line
Kennedy Firearms
Knight Rifles
Knight Rifles (See Modern Muzzle Loading, Inc.)
Kolar
L&R Lock Co.
L&S Technologies Inc (See Aimtech Mount Systems)
Legend Products Corp.
Lestrom Laboratories, Inc.
Lothar Walther Precision Tool Inc.
Lutz Engraving, Ron E.
Lyman Products Corp.
Lyman Products Corporation
Markesbery Muzzle Loaders, Inc.
Marlin Firearms Co.
McCann's Muzzle-Gun Works
Michaels of Oregon Co.
Millennium Designed Muzzleloaders
MMP
Modern Muzzleloading, Inc
Montana Precision Swaging
Mountain State Muzzleloading Supplies, Inc.
Mowrey Gun Works
MSC Industrial Supply Co.
Mt. Alto Outdoor Products
Mushroom Express Bullet Co.
Muzzleloading Technologies, Inc
Naval Ordnance Works
Navy Arms Co.
Newman Gunshop
North Star West
October Country Muzzleloading
Oklahoma Leather Products,Inc.
Olson, Myron
Orion Rifle Barrel Co.
Ox-Yoke Originals, Inc.
Pacific Rifle Co.
Parker & Sons Shooting Supply
Parker Gun Finishes
Pecatonica River Longrifle
Pioneer Arms Co.
Prairie River Arms
Prolixr Lubricants
Rusty Duck Premium Gun Care Products
S&B Industries
S&S Firearms
Selsi Co., Inc.
Shiloh Creek
Shooter's Choice
Simmons Gun Repair, Inc.
Sklany's Machine Shop
Smokey Valley Rifles (See Lutz Engraving, Ron E)
South Bend Replicas, Inc.
Southern Bloomer Mfg. Co.
Starr Trading Co., Jedediah
Starr Trading Co., Jedediah
Stone Mountain Arms
Sturm Ruger & Co. Inc.
Taylor's & Co., Inc.
Tennessee Valley Mfg.
Thompson Bullet Lube Co.
Thompson/Center Arms
Thunder Mountain Arms
Tiger-Hunt Gunstocks
Track of the Wolf, Inc.
Traditions Performance Firearms
Treso, Inc.
Uberti, Aldo
UFA, Inc.

Uncle Mike's (See Michaels of Oregon Co)
Upper Missouri Trading Co.
Venco Industries, Inc. (See Shooter's Choice)
Voere-KGH m.b.H.
W.E. Birdsong & Assoc.
Walters, John
Warne Manufacturing Co.
Warren Muzzleloading Co., Inc.
Wescombe, Bill (See North Star West)
White Owl Enterprises
White Shooting Systems, Inc. (See White Muzzleload
Williams Gun Sight Co.
Woodworker's Supply
Wright's Hardwood Gunstock Blanks
Young Country Arms
Ziegel Engineering

PISTOLSMITH

300 Gunsmith Service, Inc.
Acadian Ballistic Specialties
Accuracy Unlimited
Ace Custom 45's, Inc.
Actions by "T" Teddy Jacobson
Adair Custom Shop, Bill
Ahlman Guns
Ahrends, Kim (See Custom Firearms, Inc)
Aldis Gunsmithing & Shooting Supply
Alpha Precision, Inc.
Alpine's Precision Gunsmithing & Indoor Shooting R
Armament Gunsmithing Co., Inc.
Arundel Arms & Ammunition, Inc., A.
Baer Custom, Inc, Les
Bain & Davis, Inc.
Banks, Ed
Bar-Sto Precision Machine
Behlert Precision, Inc.
Bellm Contenders
Ben William's Gun Shop
Bengtson Arms Co., L.
Bill Adair Custom Shop
Bowen Classic Arms Corp.
Broken Gun Ranch
Burkhart Gunsmithing, Don
Cannon's
Caraville Manufacturing
Carter's Gun Shop
Chicasaw Gun Works
Clark Custom Guns, Inc.
Cleland's Outdoor World, Inc
Colonial Repair
Colorado School of Trades
Coonan Arms (JS Worldwide DBA)
Corkys Gun Clinic
Craig Custom Ltd., Research & Development
Curtis Custom Shop
Custom Firearms (See Ahrends, Kim)
Custom Gunsmiths
Cylinder & Slide, Inc., William R. Laughridge
D&D Gunsmiths, Ltd.
D&L Sports
Dayton Traister
Ed~ Brown Products, Inc.
EGW Evolution Gun Works
Ellicott Arms, Inc./Woods Pistolsmithing
Ferris Firearms
Fisher Custom Firearms
Forkin Arms
Forkin, Ben (See Belt MTN Arms)

Francesca, Inc.
Frielich Police Equipment
G.G. & G.
Garthwaite Pistolsmith, Inc., Jim
Genecco Gun Works, K
Gentry Custom Gunmaker, David
George E. Mathews & Son, Inc.
Greider Precision
Guncraft Sports Inc.
Gunsite Custom Shop
Gunsite Gunsmithy (See Gunsite Custom Shop)
Gunsite Training Center
Hallberg Gunsmith, Fritz
Hamilton, Alex B (See Ten-Ring Precision, Inc)
Hammond Custom Guns Ltd.
Hank's Gun Shop
Hanson's Gun Center, Dick
Harris Gunworks
Harwood, Jack O.
Hawken Shop, The (See Dayton Traister)
Hebard Guns, Gil
Heinie Specialty Products
High Bridge Arms, Inc
Highline Machine Co.
Hoag, James W.
Irwin, Campbell H.
Island Pond Gun Shop
Ivanoff, Thomas G (See Tom's Gun Repair)
J&S Heat Treat
Jarvis, Inc.
Jeffredo Gunsight
Jensen's Custom Ammunition
Johnston, James (See North Fork Custom Gunsmithing
Jones, J.D./SSK Industries
Jungkind, Reeves C.
K-D, Inc.
Kaswer Custom, Inc.
Ken Starnes Gunmaker
Ken's Gun Specialties
Kilham & Co.
Kim Ahrends Custom Firearms, Inc.
Kimball, Gary
La Clinique du .45
LaFrance Specialties
LaRocca Gun Works
Lathrop's, Inc.
Lawson, John G (See Sight Shop, The)
Leckie Professional Gunsmithing
Lee's Red Ramps
Liberty Antique Gunworks
Linebaugh Custom Sixguns
List Precision Engineering
Long, George F.
Mac's .45 Shop
Mag-Na-Port International, Inc.
Mahony, Philip Bruce
Mahovsky's Metalife
Mandell Shooting Supplies Inc.
Marent, Rudolf
Marvel, Alan
Mathews & Son, Inc., George E.
Maxi-Mount
McCann Industries
McCann's Machine & Gun Shop
MCS, Inc.
Middlebrooks Custom Shop
Miller Custom
Mitchell's Accuracy Shop
MJK Gunsmithing, Inc.
Mo's Competitor Supplies (See MCS Inc)
Mowrey's Guns & Gunsmithing
Mullis Guncraft
Nastoff's 45 Shop, Inc., Steve
NCP Products, Inc.

PRODUCT DIRECTORY

North Fork Custom Gunsmithing, James Johnston
Novak's, Inc.
Nygord Precision Products
Pace Marketing, Inc.
Paris, Frank J.
Pasadena Gun Center
Peacemaker Specialists
PEM's Mfg. Co.
Performance Specialists
Pierce Pistols
Plaxco, J. Michael
Power Custom, Inc.
Precision Specialties
Randco UK
Ries, Chuck
Rim Pac Sports, Inc.
Robar Co.'s, Inc., The
Rocky Mountain Arms, Inc.
Rogers Gunsmithing, Bob
RPM
Score High Gunsmithing
Scott McDougall & Associates
Seecamp Co. Inc., L. W.
Shooters Supply
Shootin' Shack, Inc.
Sight Shop, The
Singletary, Kent
Sipes Gun Shop
Spokhandguns, Inc.
Springfield, Inc.
SSK Industries
Steger, James R.
Swenson's 45 Shop, A. D.
Swift River Gunworks
Ten-Ring Precision, Inc.
Terry K. Kopp Professional Gunsmithing
Thompson, Randall (See Highline Machine Co.)
Thurston Sports, Inc.
Tom's Gun Repair, Thomas G. Ivanoff
Vic's Gun Refinishing
Walters Industries
Wardell Precision Handguns Ltd.
Weigand Combat Handguns, Inc.
Wessinger Custom Guns & Engraving
Wichita Arms, Inc.
Wild West Guns
Williams Gun Sight Co.
Williamson Precision Gunsmithing
Wilson Gun Shop
Wright's Hardwood Gunstock Blanks

POWDER MEASURES, SCALES, FUNNELS & ACCESSORIES

Frontier
Redding Reloading Equipment
VibraShine, Inc.

PRESS ACCESSORIES, METALLIC

R.E.I.

PRESS ACCESSORIES, SHOTSHELL

Precision Reloading, Inc.
R.E.I.

PRESSES, METALLIC

Redding Reloading Equipment

PRESSES, SHOTSHELL

MEC, Inc.

PRIMING TOOLS & ACCESSORIES

Simmons, Jerry

REBORING & RERIFLING

300 Gunsmith Service, Inc.
Ahlman Guns
Bauska Barrels
BlackStar AccuMax Barrels
BlackStar Barrel Accurizing (See BlackStar AccuMax
Chicasaw Gun Works
Collectors Firearms Etc
Gun Works, The
H&S Liner Service
IAI (See A.M.T.)
Ivanoff, Thomas G (See Tom's Gun Repair)
Jackalope Gun Shop
K-D, Inc.
LaBounty Precision Reboring, Inc
Matco, Inc.
NCP Products, Inc.
Pence Precision Barrels
Pro-Port Ltd.
Redman's Rifling & Reboring
Rice, Keith (See White Rock Tool & Die)
Ridgetop Sporting Goods
Savage Arms, Inc.
Shaw, Inc., E. R. (See Small Arms Mfg. Co.)
Siegrist Gun Shop
Simmons Gun Repair, Inc.
Stratco, Inc.
Terry K. Kopp Professional Gunsmithing
Time Precision, Inc.
Tom's Gun Repair, Thomas G. Ivanoff
Van Patten, J. W.
White Rock Tool & Die
Zufall, Joseph F.

RELOADING TOOLS AND ACCESSORIES

"Gramps" Antique Cartridges
4 D Custom Die Co.
4W Ammunition (See Hunters Supply)
Accurate Arms Co., Inc.
Advance Car Mover Co., Rowell Div.
Alaska Bullet Works, Inc.
American Products, Inc.
Ames Metal Products
Ammo Load, Inc.
Armfield Custom Bullets
Armite Laboratories
Arms Corporation of the Philippines
Atlantic Rose, Inc.
Atsko/Sno-Seal, Inc.
B-Square Company, Inc.
Bald Eagle Precision Machine Co.
Ballistic Product, Inc.
Belltown Ltd.
Ben William's Gun Shop
Ben's Machines
Berger Bullets Ltd.
Berry's Mfg., Inc.
Blackhawk East
Blount, Inc., Sporting Equipment Div.
Blue Mountain Bullets

Blue Ridge Machinery & Tools, Inc.
Bonanza (See Forster Products)
Break-Free, Inc.
Brown Co, E. Arthur
BRP, Inc. High Performance Cast Bullets
Brynin, Milton
Buck Stix--SOS Products Co.
Bull Mountain Rifle Co.
Bullet Swaging Supply Inc.
Bullseye Bullets
C&D Special Products (See Claybuster Wads & Harves
Camdex, Inc.
Camp-Cap Products
Canyon Cartridge Corp.
Carbide Die & Mfg. Co., Inc.
Case Sorting System
CFVentures
CH Tool & Die Co (See 4-D Custom Die Co)
Chem-Pak Inc.
CheVron Bullets
Claybuster Wads & Harvester Bullets
Clymer Manufacturing Co. Inc.
CONKKO
Cook Engineering Service
Cooper-Woodward
Crouse's Country Cover
Cumberland Arms
Curtis Cast Bullets
Custom Products (See Jones Custom Products)
CVA
D.C.C. Enterprises
Dale Wise Guns
Davide Pedersoli and Co.
Davis Products, Mike
Davis, Don
Denver Instrument Co.
Dever Co, Jack
Dewey Mfg. Co., Inc., J.
Dillon Precision Products, Inc.
Dropkick
Dutchman's Firearms, Inc., The
E&L Mfg., Inc.
E-Z-Way Systems
Eagan, Donald V.
Eezox, Inc.
Efficient Machinery Co
Eichelberger Bullets, Wm
Elkhorn Bullets
Enguix Import-Export
Euroarms of America, Inc.
F&A Inc. (See ShurKatch Corporation)
Federated-Fry (See Fry Metals)
Feken, Dennis
Ferguson, Bill
First Inc, Jack
Fisher Custom Firearms
Fitz Pistol Grip Co.
Flambeau Products Corp.
Flitz International Ltd.
Forgett Jr., Valmore J.
Forster Products
Fremont Tool Works
Fry Metals
Fusilier Bullets
G&C Bullet Co., Inc.
GAR
Gehmann, Walter (See Huntington Die Specialties)
Gozon Corp. U.S.A.
Graf & Sons
Graphics Direct
Graves Co.
Green, Arthur S.
Greenwood Precision
GTB
Gun City

Gun Works, The
Hanned Line, The
Hanned Precision (See Hanned Line, The)
Harrell's Precision
Harris Enterprises
Harrison Bullets
Haydon Shooters Supply, Russ
Heidenstrom Bullets
Hensley & Gibbs
Hirtenberger Aktiengesellschaft
Hobson Precision Mfg. Co.
Hoch Custom Bullet Moulds (See Colorado Shooter's
Hodgdon Powder Co.
Hoehn Sales, Inc.
Hoelscher, Virgil
Holland's Gunsmithing
Hollywood Engineering
Hondo Ind.
Hornady Mfg. Co.
Howell Machine
Hunters Supply
Huntington Die Specialties
Hutton Rifle Ranch
Image Ind. Inc.
IMI Services USA, Inc.
Imperial Magnum Corp.
INTEC International, Inc.
Iosso Products
J&L Superior Bullets (See Huntington Die Specialis
Javelina Lube Products
JGS Precision Tool Mfg.
JLK Bullets
Jonad Corp.
Jones Custom Products, Neil A.
Jones Moulds, Paul
K&M Services
Kapro Mfg.Co. Inc. (See R.E.I.)
King & Co.
Kleen-Bore,Inc.
Knoell, Doug
Korzinek Riflesmith, J
L.A.R. Mfg., Inc.
L.E. Wilson, Inc.
Lapua Ltd.
LBT
Le Clear Industries (See E Z Way Systems)
Lee Precision, Inc.
Legend Products Corp.
Liberty Metals
Liberty Shooting Supplies
Lightning Performance Innovations, Inc.
Lithi Bee Bullet Lube
Littleton, J. F.
Lock's Philadelphia Gun Exchange
Lortone Inc.
Loweth, Richard H.R.
Lyman Instant Targets, Inc. (See Lyman Products, C
Lyman Products Corp.
M & D Munitions Ltd.
MA Systems
Magma Engineering Co.
MarMik, Inc.
Marquart Precision Co.
MAST Technology
Match Prep--Doyle Gracey
Mayville Engineering Co. (See MEC, Inc.)
McKillen & Heyer, Inc.
MCRW Associates Shooting Supplies
MCS, Inc.
MEC, Inc.
MI-TE Bullets
Midway Arms, Inc.
MMP

Mo's Competitor Supplies (See MCS Inc)
Montana Armory, Inc (See C. Sharps Arms Co. Inc.)
Mountain South
Mountain State Muzzleloading Supplies, Inc.
Mt. Baldy Bullet Co.
MTM Molded Products Co., Inc.
Multi-Scale Charge Ltd.
MWG Co.
Necromancer Industries, Inc.
NEI Handtools, Inc.
Newman Gunshop
North Devon Firearms Services
Northern Precision Custom Swaged Bullets
October Country Muzzleloading
Old West Bullet Moulds
Omark Industries,Div. of Blount,Inc.
Original Box, nc.
Outdoor Sports Headquarters,Inc.
Paco's (See Small Custom Mould & Bullet Co)
Paragon Sales & Services, Inc.
Pease Accuracy
Peerless Alloy, Inc.
Pinetree Bullets
Plum City Ballistic Range
Pomeroy, Robert
Ponsness/Warren
Prairie River Arms
Precision Castings & Equipment
Precision Reloading, Inc.
Prime Reloading
Pro-Shot Products, Inc.
Professional Hunter Supplies (See Star Custom Bull
Prolixr Lubricants
Protector Mfg. Co., Inc., The
R.A. Wells Custom Gunsmith
R.E.I.
R.I.S. Co., Inc.
Rapine Bullet Mould Mfg. Co.
Redding Reloading Equipment
Reloading Specialties, Inc.
Rice, Keith (See White Rock Tool & Die)
Roberts Products
Rochester Lead Works
Rooster Laboratories
Rorschach Precision Products
Rosenthal, Brad and Sallie
Royal Arms Gunstocks
S.L.A.P. Industries
SAECO (See Redding Reloading Equipment)
Sandia Die & Cartridge Co.
Saunders Gun & Machine Shop
Saville Iron Co. (See Greenwood Precision)
Scharch Mfg., Inc.
Scot Powder Co. of Ohio, Inc.
Scott, Dwight
Seebeck Assoc., R.E.
Sharp Shooter Supply
Sharps Arms Co., Inc., C.
Shiloh Creek
Shiloh Rifle Mfg.
Shooter's Choice
ShurKatch Corporation
Sierra Specialty Prod. Co.
Silver Eagle Machining
Simmons, Jerry
Sinclair International, Inc.
Skip's Machine
Small Custom Mould & Bullet Co.
Sno-Seal, Inc. (See Atsko/Sno-Seal)
SOS Products Co. (See Buck Stix-SOS Products Co.)

Spencer's Custom Guns
SPG LLC
Sport Flite Manufacturing Co.
Sportsman Supply Co.
SSK Industries
Stalwart Corporation
Star Custom Bullets
Starr Trading Co., Jedediah
Starr Trading Co., Jedediah
Stillwell, Robert
Stoney Point Products, Inc.
Stratco, Inc.
Tamarack Products, Inc.
Taracorp Industries, Inc.
TCCI
TCSR
TDP Industries, Inc.
Tetra Gun Lubricants (See FTI, Inc.)
Thompson Bullet Lube Co.
Thompson/Center Arms
Timber Heirloom Products
Time Precision, Inc.
TMI Products (See Haselbauer Products, Jerry)
Trammco
Tru-Square Metal Prods., Inc.
TTM
United States Products Co.
Vega Tool Co.
Venco Industries, Inc. (See Shooter's Choice)
Vibra-Tek Co.
VibraShine, Inc.
Vihtavuori Oy/Kaltron-Pettibone
Vitt/Boos
Von Minden Gunsmithing Services
W.B. Niemi Engineering
W.J. Riebe Co.
Walters, John
WD-40 Co.
Webster Scale Mfg. Co.
Welsh, Bud
White Rock Tool & Die
Whitetail Design & Engineering Ltd.
Widener's Reloading & Shooting Supply, Inc.
Wolf's Western Traders
Woodleigh (See Huntington Die Specialties)
WTA Manufacturing
Yesteryear Armory & Supply
Young Country Arms

RESTS BENCH, PORTABLE AND ACCESSORIES

Accuright
Adventure 16, Inc.
Armor Metal Products
B-Square Company, Inc.
Bald Eagle Precision Machine Co.
Bartlett Engineering
Borden's Accuracy
Browning Arms Co.
Bull Mountain Rifle Co.
C.W. Erickson's Mfg. Inc.
Canons Delcour
Chem-Pak Inc.
Clift Mfg., L. R.
Clift Welding Supply & Cases
Decker Shooting Products
Desert Mountain Mfg.
F&A Inc. (See ShurKatch Corporation)
Greenwood Precision
Harris Engineering Inc.
Hidalgo, Tony
Hoehn Sales, Inc.
Hoelscher, Virgil

Hoppe's Div. Penguin Industries, Inc.
Keng's Firearms Specialty, Inc./US Tactical Systems
Kolpin Mfg., Inc.
Kramer Designs
Midway Arms, Inc.
Millett Sights
MJM Mfg.
Outdoor Connection,Inc., The
PAST Sporting Goods,Inc.
Protektor Model
Ransom International Corp.
Saville Iron Co. (See Greenwood Precision)
ShurKatch Corporation
Sinclair International, Inc.
Stoney Point Products, Inc.
T.H.U. Enterprises, Inc.
Thompson Target Technology
Tonoloway Tack Drives
Varmint Masters, LLC
Wichita Arms, Inc.
Zanotti Armor, Inc.

RIFLE BARREL MAKER

Airrow
American Safe Arms, Inc.
Bauska Barrels
BlackStar AccuMax Barrels
BlackStar Barrel Accurizing (See BlackStar AccuMax
Border Barrels Ltd.
Broad Creek Rifle Works
Brown Co, E. Arthur
Bullberry Barrel Works, Ltd.
Canons Delcour
Carter's Gun Shop
Christensen Arms
Cincinnati Swaging
Cryo-Accurizing
D&J Bullet Co. & Custom Gun Shop, Inc.
deHaas Barrels
DKT, Inc.
Donnelly, C. P.
Douglas Barrels Inc.
Fanzoj GmbH
Fred F. Wells/Wells Sport Store
Gaillard Barrels
Gary Schneider Rifle Barrels Inc.
Getz Barrel Co.
Granite Mountain Arms, Inc
Green Mountain Rifle Barrel Co., Inc.
Gruning Precision Inc
Gun Works, The
H-S Precision, Inc.
Half Moon Rifle Shop
Harold's Custom Gun Shop Inc. Broughton Rifle Barr
Harris Gunworks
Hart Rifle Barrels,Inc.
Hastings Barrels
Hoelscher, Virgil
IAI (See A.M.T.)
Jackalope Gun Shop
K-D, Inc.
KOGOT
Krieger Barrels, Inc.
LaBounty Precision Reboring, Inc
Lilja Precision Rifle Barrels
Lothar Walther Precision Tool Inc.
Mac's .45 Shop
Matco, Inc.
McGowen Rifle Barrels
McMillan Rifle Barrels
Mid-America Recreation, Inc.
Nowlin Mfg. Co.
Obermeyer Rifled Barrels

Olympic Arms Inc.
Orion Rifle Barrel Co.
Pac-Nor Barreling
Pell, John T. (See KOGOT)
Pence Precision Barrels
Perazone-Gunsmith, Brian
Raptor Arms Co., Inc.
Rocky Mountain Rifle Works Ltd.
Rosenthal, Brad and Sallie
Sabatti S.r.l.
Sanders Custom Gun Service
Savage Arms, Inc.
Schneider Rifle Barrels, Inc, Gary
Shaw, Inc., E. R. (See Small Arms Mfg. Co.)
Shilen, Inc.
Siskiyou Gun Works (See Donnelly, C. P.)
Small Arms Mfg. Co.
Specialty Shooters Supply, Inc.
Strutz Rifle Barrels, Inc., W. C.
Swift River Gunworks
Terry K. Kopp Professional Gunsmithing
Unmussig Bullets, D. L.
Verney-Carron
W.C. Strutz Rifle Barrels, Inc.
Wilson Arms Co., The
Wiseman and Co., Bill

SCOPES, MOUNTS, ACCESSORIES, OPTICAL EQUIPMENT

A.R.M.S., Inc.
ABO (USA) Inc
Accuracy Innovations, Inc.
Ackerman, Bill (See Optical Services Co)
ADCO Sales, Inc.
Adventurer's Outpost
Aimpoint c/o Springfield, Inc.
Aimtech Mount Systems
Air Rifle Specialists
Air Venture Airguns
Alley Supply Co.
Apel GmbH, Ernst
ArmaLite, Inc.
Arundel Arms & Ammunition, Inc., A.
B-Square Company, Inc.
Baer Custom, Inc, Les
Barrett Firearms Manufacturer, Inc.
Beaver Park Product, Inc.
BEC, Inc.
Beeman Precision Airguns
Ben William's Gun Shop
BKL Technologies
Blount, Inc., Sporting Equipment Div.
Bohemia Arms Co.
Boonie Packer Products
Borden's Accuracy
Brockman's Custom Gunsmithing
Brown Co, E. Arthur
Brownells, Inc.
Brunton U.S.A.
BSA Optics
Bull Mountain Rifle Co.
Burris Co., Inc.
Bushnell Sports Optics Worldwide
Butler Creek Corp.
Carl Zeiss Optical
Catco-Ambush, Inc.
Celestron International
Center Lock Scope Rings
Clark Custom Guns, Inc.
Clearview Mfg. Co., Inc.
Combat Military Ordnance Ltd.
Compass Industries , Inc.

Concept Development Corp.
Conetrol Scope Mounts
Creedmoor Sports, Inc.
Crimson Trace Lasers
Custom Quality Products, Inc.
D&H Prods. Co., Inc.
D.C.C. Enterprises
Daisy Mfg. Co.
Del-Sports, Inc.
DHB Products
E. Arthur Brown Co.
Eclectic Technologies, Inc.
Edmund Scientific Co.
Ednar, Inc.
Eggleston, Jere D.
EGW Evolution Gun Works
Emerging Technologies, Inc. (See Laseraim Technolo
Entre'prise Arms, Inc.
Excalibur Electro Optics Inc
Farr Studio,Inc.
Federal Arms Corp. of America
Forgett Jr., Valmore J.
Frankonia Jagd Hofmann & Co.
Fujinon, Inc.
G.G. & G.
Galati International
Glaser Safety Slug, Inc.
Great Lakes Airguns
Groenewold, John
GSI, Inc.
Gun South, Inc. (See GSI, Inc.)
Guns
Guns Div. of D.C. Engineering, Inc.
Gunsmithing, Inc.
Hakko Co. Ltd.
Hammerli USA
Harris Gunworks
Harvey, Frank
Heckler & Koch, Inc.
Hertel & Reuss
Hines Co, S C
Hiptmayer, Armurier
Hiptmayer, Klaus
HiTek International
Holland's Gunsmithing
Ironsighter Co.
Jeffredo Gunsight
Jerry Phillips Optics
Jewell Triggers, Inc.
John Masen Co. Inc.
Johnson's Gunsmithing, Inc, Neal
Kahles A Swarovski Company
Kalispel Case Line
KDF, Inc.
Keng's Firearms Specialty, Inc./US Tactical Systems
KenPatable Ent., Inc.
Kesselring Gun Shop
Kimber of America, Inc.
Kmount
Kowa Optimed, Inc.
Kris Mounts
KVH Industries, Inc.
Kwik Mount Corp.
Kwik-Site Co.
L&S Technologies Inc (See Aimtech Mount Systems)
L.A.R. Mfg., Inc.
Laser Devices, Inc.
Laseraim Technologies, Inc.
Laserlyte
LaserMax, Inc.
Leapers, Inc.
Lectro Science, Inc.
Lee Co., T. K.
Leica USA, Inc.
Leupold & Stevens, Inc.
Lightforce U.S.A. Inc.
List Precision Engineering
Lohman Mfg. Co., Inc.
London Guns Ltd.

Lyte Optronics (See TracStar Industries Inc)
Mac's .45 Shop
Mac-1 Airgun Distributors
Mag-Na-Port International, Inc.
Marksman Products
Maxi-Mount
McBros Rifle Co.
McCann Industries
McCann's Machine & Gun Shop
McMillan Optical Gunsight Co.
MCS, Inc.
MDS
Merit Corp.
Michaels of Oregon Co.
Military Armament Corp.
Millett Sights
Mirador Optical Corp.
Mitchell Optics, Inc.
Mo's Competitor Supplies (See MCS Inc)
Mountain Rifles, Inc.
Muzzleloading Technologies, Inc
MWG Co.
Neal Johnson's Gunsmithing, Inc.
New England Custom Gun Service
Nic Max, Inc.
Nightforce (See Lightforce USA Inc)
Nikon, Inc.
Norincoptics (See BEC, Inc.)
Nygord Precision Products
Olympic Optical Co.
Optical Services Co.
Orchard Park Enterprise
Oregon Arms, Inc. (See Rogue Rifle Co., Inc.)
Outdoor Connection,Inc., The
Ozark Gun Works
P.M. Enterprises, Inc.
Parsons Optical Mfg. Co.
PECAR Herbert Schwarz GmbH
PEM's Mfg. Co.
Pentax Corp.
Perazone-Gunsmith, Brian
Precise Metalsmithing Enterprises
Precision Sport Optics
Premier Reticles
Quarton USA, Ltd. Co.
R.A. Wells Custom Gunsmith
Ram-Line Blount, Inc.
Ramon B. Gonzalez Guns
Ranch Products
Randolph Engineering, Inc.
Ranging, Inc.
Redfield, Inc
Redfield/Blount
Rice, Keith (See White Rock Tool & Die)
Rocky Mountain High Sports Glasses
Rogue Rifle Co., Inc.
Romain's Custom Guns, Inc.
S&K Mfg. Co.
Sanders Custom Gun Service
Sanders Gun and Machine Shop
Schmidt & Bender, Inc.
Scope Control, Inc.
ScopLevel
Score High Gunsmithing
Segway Industries
Selsi Co., Inc.
Sharp Shooter Supply
Shepherd Enterprises, Inc.
Sightron, Inc.
Simmons Outdoor Corp.
Sinclair International, Inc.
Six Enterprises
SKAN A.R.
SKB Shotguns
Slug Group, Inc.

Southern Bloomer Mfg. Co.
Sportsmatch U.K. Ltd.
Springfield, Inc.
SSK Industries
Stiles Custom Guns
Stoeger Industries
Sunny Hill Enterprises, Inc.
SwaroSports, Inc. (See JagerSport Ltd
Swarovski Optik North America Ltd.
Swift Instruments, Inc.
T.K. Lee Co.
TacStar
Talley, Dave
Tele-Optics
Thompson/Center Arms
Trijicon, Inc.
Ultra Dot Distribution
Uncle Mike's (See Michaels of Oregon Co)
Unertl Optical Co. Inc., John
United Binocular Co.
United States Optics Technologies, Inc.
Valor Corp.
Voere-KGH m.b.H.
Warne Manufacturing Co.
Warren Muzzleloading Co., Inc.
WASP Shooting Systems
Weatherby, Inc.
Weaver Products
Weaver Scope Repair Service
Weigand Combat Handguns, Inc.
Westley Richards & Co.
White Rock Tool & Die
White Shooting Systems, Inc. (See White Muzzleload
Wideview Scope Mount Corp.
Wilcox Industries Corp
Wild West Guns
Williams Gun Sight Co.
York M-1 Conversions
Zanotti Armor, Inc.

SHELLHOLDERS

Redding Reloading Equipment

SHOOTING/TRAINING SCHOOL

300 Gunsmith Service, Inc.
Alpine's Precision Gunsmithing & Indoor Shooting R
American Gunsmithing Institute
American Small Arms Academy
Auto Arms
Beretta U.S.A. Corp.
Bob's Tactical Indoor Shooting Range & Gun Shop
Bridgeman Products
Cannon's
Chapman Academy of Practical Shooting
Chelsea Gun Club of New York City Inc.
CQB Training
Defense Training International, Inc.
Executive Protection Institute
Feminine Protection, Inc.
Ferris Firearms
Firearm Training Center, The
Front Sight Firearms Training Institute
G.H. Enterprises Ltd.
Gene's Custom Guns
Griffin & Howe, Inc.
Guncraft Sports Inc.
Gunsite Training Center
Henigson & Associates, Steve
Israel Arms International, Inc.

Jensen's Custom Ammunition
Jensen's Firearms Academy
L.L. Bean, Inc.
Lethal Force Institute (See Police Bookshelf)
Ljutic Industries, Inc.
McMurdo, Lynn (See Specialty Gunsmithing)
Mendez, John A.
Montgomery Community College
NCP Products, Inc.
Nevada Pistol Academy, Inc.
North American Shooting Systems
North Mountain Pine Training Center (See Executive
Paxton Quigley's Personal Protection Strategies
Pentheny de Pentheny
Performance Specialists
River Road Sporting Clays
SAFE
Shoot Where You Look
Shooter's World
Shooting Gallery, The
Smith & Wesson
Specialty Gunsmithing
Starlight Training Center, Inc.
Steger, James R.
Tactical Defense Institute
Thunder Ranch
Western Missouri Shooters Alliance
Yankee Gunsmith
Yavapai Firearms Academy Ltd.

SHOTSHELL MISCELLANY

Bridgeman Products
MEC, Inc.
Precision Reloading, Inc.
Vitt/Boos

SIGHTS, METALLIC

Accura-Site (See All's, The Jim Tembells Co., Inc.
All's, The Jim J. Tembells Co., Inc.
Alley Supply Co.
Alpec Team, Inc.
Andela Tool & Machine, Inc.
Anschutz GmbH
Armsport, Inc.
Ashley Outdoors, Inc
Aspen Outfitting Co
Baer Custom, Inc, Les
BEC, Inc.
Bo-Mar Tool & Mfg. Co.
Bob's Gun Shop
Bond Custom Firearms
Bowen Classic Arms Corp.
Bradley Gunsight Co.
Brockman's Custom Gunsmithing
Brown Co, E. Arthur
Brown Products, Inc., Ed
Brownells, Inc.
C-More Systems
California Sights (See Fautheree, Andy)
Cape Outfitters
Center Lock Scope Rings
Champion's Choice, Inc.
Colonial Repair
CRR , Inc./Marble's Inc.
D.B.A. Flintlocks, Etc
DGS, Inc., Dale A. Storey
DHB Products
E. Arthur Brown Co.
Evans Gunsmithing (See Evans, Andrew)

Evans, Andrew
Farr Studio,Inc.
Forgett Jr., Valmore J.
Forkin Arms
G.G. & G.
Garthwaite Pistolsmith, Inc., Jim
Goergen's Gun Shop, Inc.
Gun Doctor, The
Gun Works, The
Gunsmithing, Inc.
Hank's Gun Shop
Heidenstrom Bullets
Heinie Specialty Products
Hesco-Meprolight
Hines Co, S C
Hiptmayer, Armurier
Hiptmayer, Klaus
Innovision Enterprises
J.P. Enterprises Inc.
Johnson's Gunsmithing, Inc, Neal
Keng's Firearms Specialty, Inc./US Tactical Systems
Knight Rifles
Kris Mounts
L.P.A. Snc
Leapers, Inc.
Lee's Red Ramps
List Precision Engineering
London Guns Ltd.
Lyman Instant Targets, Inc. (See Lyman Products, C
Mac's .45 Shop
Madis, George
Marble Arms (See CRR, Inc./Marble's Inc.)
MCS, Inc.
MEC-Gar S.r.l.
Meprolight (See Hesco Meprolight)
Merit Corp.
Middlebrooks Custom Shop
Millett Sights
MMC
Mo's Competitor Supplies (See MCS Inc)
Montana Armory, Inc (See C. Sharps Arms Co. Inc.)
Montana Vintage Arms
New England Custom Gun Service
Newman Gunshop
North Pass
Novak's, Inc.
UK Weber,Inc.
P.M. Enterprises, Inc.
PFM's Mfg. Co.
Quarton USA, Ltd. Co.
Redfield, Inc
RPM
Sharps Arms Co., Inc., C.
Slug Site
STI International
T.F.C. S.p.A.
Talley, Dave
Thompson/Center Arms
Time Precision, Inc.
Trijicon, Inc.
Truglo, Inc
United States Optics Technologies, Inc.
Warne Manufacturing Co.
WASP Shooting Systems
Wichita Arms, Inc.
Wild West Guns
Williams Gun Sight Co.
Wilson Gun Shop

STOCK MAKER

Amrine's Gun Shop
Aspen Outfitting Co
Belding's Custom Gun Shop
Boltin, John M.

Bone Engraving, Ralph
Broad Creek Rifle Works
Caywood, Shane J.
Claro Walnut Gunstock Co.
Clear Creek Outdoors
Coffin, Charles H.
Colorado Gunsmithing Academy
D.D. Custom Stocks, R.H. "Dick" Devereaux
Dever Co, Jack
DGR Custom Rifles
DGS, Inc., Dale A. Storey
Fieldsport Ltd
Fisher, Jerry A.
Genecco Gun Works, K
George E. Mathews & Son, Inc.
Gillmann, Edwin
Great American Gunstock Co.
Gunsmithing Ltd.
Harper's Custom Stocks
Harry Lawson Co.
Heilmann, Stephen
Heydenberk, Warren R.
Jurras, L. E.
Keith M. Heppler, Keith's Custom Gunstocks
Larry Lyons Gunworks
Mathews & Son, Inc., George E.
McCament, Jay
Mid-America Recreation, Inc.
Mitchell, Jack
Morrow, Dud
Nelson, Stephen
Nettestad Gun Works
Nickels, Paul R.
Pawling Mountain Club
Pentheny de Pentheny
Royal Arms Gunstocks
Smith, Art
Smith, Sharmon
Talmage, William G.
Tiger-Hunt Gunstocks
Walker Arms Co., Inc.
Williamson Precision Gunsmithing
Winter, Robert M.
Working Guns
Yee, Mike

STOCKS (COMMERCIAL)

3-Ten Corp.
Accuracy Unlimited
Ackerman & Co.
Acra-Bond Laminates
Ahlman Guns
Amrine's Gun Shop
Arms Ingenuity Co.
Arundel Arms & Ammunition, Inc., A.
Aspen Outfitting Co
Baelder, Harry
Bain & Davis, Inc.
Balickie, Joe
Bansner's Gunsmithing Specialties
Barnes Bullets, Inc.
Beitzinger, George
Belding's Custom Gun Shop
Bell & Carlson, Inc.
Benchmark Guns
Biesen, Al
Biesen, Roger
Billeb, Stephen L.
Billings Gunsmiths Inc.
Blount, Inc., Sporting Equipment Div.
Bob's Gun Shop
Bohemia Arms Co.
Boltin, John M.
Borden's Accuracy
Bowerly, Kent

Boyds' Gunstock Industries, Inc.
Brace, Larry D.
Briganti, A.J.
Broad Creek Rifle Works
Brockman's Custom Gunsmithing
Brown Co, E. Arthur
Brown Precision,Inc.
Buckhorn Gun Works
Bull Mountain Rifle Co.
Bullberry Barrel Works, Ltd.
Burkhart Gunsmithing, Don
Butler Creek Corp.
Cali'co Hardwoods, Inc.
Camilli, Lou
Campbell, Dick
Cape Outfitters
Carter's Gun Shop
Caywood, Shane J.
Chambers Flintlocks Ltd., Jim
Chicasaw Gun Works
Churchill, Winston
Claro Walnut Gunstock Co.
Clear Creek Outdoors
Cloward's Gun Shop
Coffin, Charles H.
Coffin, Jim (See Working Guns)
Colonial Repair
Colorado Gunsmithing Academy
Colorado School of Trades
Conrad, C. A.
Creedmoor Sports, Inc
Curly Maple Stock Blanks (See Tiger-Hunt)
Custom Checkering Service, Kathy Forster
Custom Gun Products
Custom Gun Stocks
Custom Riflestocks, Inc., Michael M. Kokolus
D&D Gunsmiths, Ltd.
D&G Precision Duplicators (See Greene Precision Du
D&J Bullet Co. & Custom Gun Shop, Inc
D.D. Custom Stocks, R.H. "Dick" Devereaux
Dakota Arms, Inc.
Dangler, Homer L.
David W. Schwartz Custom Guns
Dever Co, Jack
Devereaux, R.H. "Dick" (See D.D. Custom S
DGR Custom Rifles
DGS, Inc., Dale A. Storey
Dick Marple & Associates
Dillon, Ed
Dressel Jr., Paul G.
Duane's Gun Repair (See DGR Custom Rifles)
Duncan's Gun Works, Inc.
Echols & Co., D'Arcy
Eggleston, Jere D.
Erhardt, Dennis
Eversull Co., Inc., K.
Farmer-Dressel, Sharon
Fibron Products, Inc.
Fieldsport Ltd
Fisher, Jerry A.
Folks, Donald E.
Forster, Kathy (See Custom Checkering S
Forster, Larry L.
Forthofer's Gunsmithing & Knifemaking
Francotte & Cie S.A. Auguste
Frank Custom Classic Arms, Ron
Fred F. Wells/Wells Sport Store
Game Haven Gunstocks
Gary Goudy Classic Stocks
Gene's Custom Guns
Gervais, Mike
Gillmann, Edwin

Giron, Robert E.
Glaser Safety Slug, Inc.
Goens, Dale W.
Golden Age Arms Co.
Gordie's Gun Shop
Grace, Charles E.
Great American Gunstock Co.
Green, Roger M.
Greenwood Precision
Griffin & Howe, Inc.
Gun Shop, The
Guns
Gunsmithing Ltd.
H-S Precision, Inc.
Hallberg Gunsmith, Fritz
Halstead, Rick
Hamilton, Jim
Hanson's Gun Center, Dick
Harper's Custom Stocks
Harris Gunworks
Harry Lawson Co.
Hart & Son, Inc.
Harwood, Jack O.
Hastings Barrels
Hecht, Hubert J, Waffen-Hecht
Heilmann, Stephen
Hensley, Gunmaker, Darwin
Heppler, Keith M, Keith's Custom
    Gunstocks
Heydenberk, Warren R.
High Tech Specialties, Inc.
Hines Co, S C
Hiptmayer, Armurier
Hiptmayer, Klaus
Hoelscher, Virgil
Hoenig & Rodman
Hogue Grips
Huebner, Corey O.
Hughes, Steven Dodd
Island Pond Gun Shop
Ivanoff, Thomas G (See Tom's
    Gun Repair)
J.P. Gunstocks, Inc.
Jackalope Gun Shop
Jamison's Forge Works
Jarrett Rifles, Inc.
Jim Norman Custom Gunstocks
John Masen Co. Inc.
Johnson Wood Products
KDF, Inc.
Keith's Custom Gunstocks (See
    Heppler, Keith M)
Kelbly, Inc.
Ken's Rifle Blanks
Kilham & Co.
Klein Custom Guns, Don
Klingler Woodcarving
Knippel, Richard
Kokolus, Michael M. (See Custom
    Riflestocks, In
Larry Lyons Gunworks
Lawson Co., Harry
Lind Custom Guns, Al
Mac's .45 Shop
Mazur Restoration, Pete
McBros Rifle Co.
McCament, Jay
McCann's Muzzle-Gun Works
McCullough, Ken (See Ken's Rifle
    Blanks)
McDonald, Dennis
McFarland, Stan
McGowen Rifle Barrels
McGuire, Bill
McKinney, R.P. (See Schuetzen
    Gun Co.)
McMillan Fiberglass Stocks, Inc.
Mercer Custom Stocks, R. M.
Michaels of Oregon Co.
Mid-America Recreation, Inc.

Miller Arms, Inc.
Mitchell, Jack
Morrison Custom Rifles, J. W.
MPI Stocks
MWG Co.
NCP Products, Inc.
Nelson, Stephen
Nettestad Gun Works
New England Arms Co.
New England Custom Gun
    Service
Newman Gunshop
Nickels, Paul R.
Oakland Custom Arms,Inc.
Oil Rod and Gun Shop
OK Weber,Inc.
Old World Gunsmithing
One Of A Kind
Orvis Co., The
Ottmar, Maurice
Pacific Research Laboratories,
    Inc. (See Rimrock R
Pagel Gun Works, Inc.
Paragon Sales & Services, Inc.
Paul D. Hillmer Custom
    Gunstocks
Paulsen Gunstocks
Pawling Mountain Club
Pecatonica River Longrifle
PEM's Mfg. Co.
Perazone-Gunsmith, Brian
Perazzi USA, Inc.
Pohl, Henry A. (See Great
    American Gun Co.
Powell & Son (Gunmakers) Ltd.,
    William
Precision Gun Works
R&J Gun Shop
R.A. Wells Custom Gunsmith
Ram-Line Blount, Inc.
Rampart International
Reagent Chemical & Research,
    Inc. (See Calico Hard
Reiswig, Wallace E. (See Claro
    Walnut Gunstock
Richards Micro-Fit Stocks
Rimrock Rifle Stocks
RMS Custom Gunsmithing
Robinson Firearms Mfg. Ltd.
Robinson, Don
Rogers Gunsmithing, Bob
Romain's Custom Guns, Inc.
Roto Carve
Ryan, Chad L.
Sanders Custom Gun Service
Saville Iron Co. (See Greenwood
    Precision)
Schiffman, Curt
Schiffman, Mike
Schiffman, Norman
Schumakers Gun Shop
Score High Gunsmithing
Sile Distributors, Inc.
Simmons Gun Repair, Inc.
Six Enterprises
Skeoch, Brian R.
Smith, Sharmon
Speiser, Fred D.
Stan de Treville & Co.
Stiles Custom Guns
Storey, Dale A. (See DGS Inc.)
Stott's Creek Armory, Inc.
Strawbridge, Victor W.
Sturgeon Valley Sporters, K. Ide
Swann, D. J.
Swift River Gunworks
Szweda, Robert (See RMS
    Custom Gunsmithing)
T.F.C. S.p.A.
Talmage, William G.

Taylor & Robbins
Tecnolegno S.p.A.
Thompson/Center Arms
Tiger-Hunt Gunstocks
Tirelli
Tom's Gun Repair, Thomas G.
    Ivanoff
Track of the Wolf, Inc.
Trevallion Gunstocks
Tucker, James C.
Turkish Firearms Corp.
Tuttle, Dale
Vest, John
Vic's Gun Refinishing
Vintage Industries, Inc.
Volquartsen Custom Ltd.
Von Minden Gunsmithing
    Services
Walker Arms Co., Inc.
Walnut Factory, The
Weber & Markin Custom
    Gunsmiths
Weems, Cecil
Wenig Custom Gunstocks
Werth, T. W.
Wessinger Custom Guns &
    Engraving
Western Gunstock Mfg. Co.
Williams Gun Sight Co.
Windish, Jim
Winter, Robert M.
Working Guns
Wright's Hardwood Gunstock
    Blanks
Yee, Mike
York M-1 Conversions
Zeeryp, Russ

TARGETS, BULLET & CLAYBIRD TRAPS

A-Tech Corp.
Action Target, Inc.
American Target
American Whitetail Target
    Systems
Autauga Arms, Inc.
Beeman Precision Airguns
Beomat of America, Inc.
Birchwood Casey
Blount, Inc., Sporting Equipment
    Div.
Blue and Gray Products Inc (See
    Ox-Yoke Originals
Brown Manufacturing
Bull-X, Inc.
Caswell Detroit Armor Companies
Champion Target Co.
D.C.C. Enterprises
Datumtech Corp.
Detroit-Armor Corp.
Diamond Mfg. Co.
Federal Champion Target Co.
Freeman Animal Targets
G.H. Enterprises Ltd.
Gozon Corp. U.S.A.
H-S Precision, Inc.
Hiti-Schuch, Atelier Wilma
Hunterjohn
Innovision Enterprises
J.G. Dapkus Co., Inc.
Kennebec Journal
Kleen-Bore,Inc.
Lakefield Arms Ltd (See Savage
    Arms Inc)
Littler Sales Co.
Lyman Instant Targets, Inc. (See
    Lyman Products, C
Lyman Products Corp.
M & D Munitions Ltd.

Marksman Products
Mendez, John A.
MSR Targets
N.B.B., Inc.
National Target Co.
North American Shooting
    Systems
Outers Laboratories Div. of
    Blount, Inc.Sporting E
Ox-Yoke Originals, Inc.
Palsa Outdoor Products
Passive Bullet Traps, Inc. (See
    Savage Range Syste
PlumFire Press, Inc.
Quack Decoy & Sporting Clays
Redfield, Inc
Remington Arms Co., Inc.
Rockwood Corp.
Rocky Mountain Target Co.
Savage Arms (Canada), Inc.
Savage Range Systems, Inc.
Schaefer Shooting Sports
Seligman Shooting Products
Shoot-N-C Targets (See
    Birchwood Casey)
Shooters Supply
Target Shooting, Inc.
Thompson Target Technology
Trius Traps, Inc.
Universal Sports
White Flyer Targets
World of Targets (See Birchwood
    Casey)
X-Spand Target Systems
Z's Metal Targets & Frames
Zriny's Metal Targets (See Z's
    Metal Targets & Fra

TAXIDERMY

African Import Co.
Jack Jonas Appraisals &
    Taxidermy
Kulis Freeze Dry Taxidermy
Montgomery Community College
World Trek, Inc.

TRAP & SKEET SHOOTER'S EQUIPMENT

Accurate Arms Co., Inc.
Allen Co., Bob
Allen Sportswear, Bob (See Allen
    Co., Bob)
Bagmaster Mfg., Inc.
Baker, Stan
Beomat of America, Inc.
Beretta S.p.A., Pietro
Bridgeman Products
Cape Outfitters
Clymer Manufacturing Co. Inc.
F&A Inc. (See ShurKatch
    Corporation)
Fiocchi of America Inc.
G.H. Enterprises Ltd.
Game Winner, Inc.
Hastings Barrels
Hoppe's Div. Penguin Industries,
    Inc.
Hunter Co., Inc.
Jenkins Recoil Pads, Inc.
Jim Noble Co.
K&T Co. Div. of T&S Industries,
    Inc.
Kalispel Case Line
Kolar
Lakewood Products LLC
Ljutic Industries, Inc.
Mag-Na-Port International, Inc.

Maionchi-L.M.I.
Meadow Industries
MEC, Inc.
Moneymaker Guncraft Corp.
MTM Molded Products Co., Inc.
NCP Products, Inc.
Pachmayr Div. Lyman Products
Palsa Outdoor Products
PAST Sporting Goods,Inc.
Paul D. Hillmer Custom
    Gunstocks
Perazzi USA, Inc.
Pro-Port Ltd.
Protektor Model
Quack Decoy & Sporting Clays
Remington Arms Co., Inc.
Rhodeside, Inc.
Shootin' Accessories, Ltd.
Shooting Specialties (See Titus,
    Daniel)
ShurKatch Corporation
Titus, Daniel, Shooting
    Specialties
Trius Traps, Inc.
Universal Sports
Warne Manufacturing Co.
X-Spand Target Systems
Ziegel Engineering

TRIGGERS, RELATED EQUIPMENT

Actions by "T" Teddy Jacobson
B&D Trading Co., Inc.
Baer Custom, Inc, Les
Behlert Precision, Inc.
Bond Custom Firearms
Boyds' Gunstock Industries, Inc.
Bull Mountain Rifle Co.
Dayton Traister
Electronic Trigger Systems, Inc.
Eversull Co., Inc., K.
FWB
Galati International
Guns
Hawken Shop, The (See Dayton
    Traister)
Hoehn Sales, Inc.
Hoelscher, Virgil
Holland's Gunsmithing
IAI (See A.M.T.)
Impact Case Co.
J.P. Enterprises Inc.
Jewell Triggers, Inc.
John Masen Co. Inc.
KK Air International (See Impact
    Case Co.)
L&R Lock Co.
List Precision Engineering
London Guns Ltd.
M.H. Canjar Co.
Mahony, Philip Bruce
Master Lock Co.
Miller Single Trigger Mfg. Co.
NCP Products, Inc.
OK Weber,Inc.
PEM's Mfg. Co.
Penrod Precision
Perazone-Gunsmith, Brian
Perazzi USA, Inc.
S&B Industries
Sharp Shooter Supply
Shilen, Inc.
Simmons Gun Repair, Inc.
Slug Group, Inc.
Target Shooting, Inc.

MANUFACTURER'S DIRECTORY

A

A Zone Bullets, 2039 Walter Rd., Billings, MT 59105 / 800-252-3111; FAX: 406-248-1961

A&B Industries,Inc (See Top-Line USA Inc)

A&J Products, Inc., 5791 Hall Rd., Muskegon, MI 49442-1964

A&M Waterfowl ,Inc., P.O. Box 102, Ripley, TN 38063 / 901-635-4003; FAX: 901-635-2320

A&W Repair, 2930 Schneider Dr., Arnold, MO 63010 / 314-287-3725

A-Square Co.,Inc., One Industrial Park, Bedford, KY 40006-9667 / 502-255-7456; FAX: 502-255-7657

A-Tech Corp., P.O. Box 1281, Cottage Grove, OR 97424

A.A. Arms, Inc., 4811 Persimmont Ct., Monroe, NC 28110 / 704-289-5356 or 800-935-1119; FAX: 704-289-5859

A.B.S. III, 9238 St. Morritz Dr., Fern Creek, KY 40291

A.G. Russell Knives,Inc., 1705 Hwy. 71B North, Springdale, AR 72764 / 501-751-7341

A.R.M.S., Inc., 230 W. Center St., West Bridgewater, MA 02379-1620 / 508-584-7816; FAX: 508-588-8045

A.W. Peterson Gun Shop, Inc., 4255 W. Old U.S. 441, Mt. Dora, FL 32757-3299 / 352-383-4258; FAX: 352-735-1001

ABO (USA) Inc, 615 SW 2nd Avenue, Miami, FL 33130 / 305-859-2010 FAX: 305-859-2099

AC Dyna-tite Corp., 155 Kelly St., P.O. Box 0984, Elk Grove Village, IL 60007 / 847-593-5566; FAX: 847-593-1304

Acadian Ballistic Specialties, P.O. Box 787, folsom, LA 70437 / 504-796-0078

Accu-Tek, 4510 Carter Ct., Chino, CA 91710 / 909-627-2404; FAX: 909-627-7817

Accupro Gun Care, 15512-109 Ave., Surrey, BC U3R 7E8 CANADA / 604-583-7807

Accura-Site (See All's, The Jim Tembelis Co., Inc.

Accuracy Den, The, 25 Bitterbrush Rd., Reno, NV 89523 / 702-345-0225

Accuracy Innovations, Inc., P.O. Box 376, New Paris, PA 15554 / 814-839-4517; FAX: 814-839-2601

Accuracy Int'l. North America, Inc., PO Box 5267, Oak Ridge, TN 37831 / 423-482-0330; FAX: 423-482-0336

Accuracy International, 9115 Trooper Trail, P.O. Box 2019, Bozeman, MT 59715 / 406-587-7922; FAX: 406-585-9434

Accuracy Internationl Precision Rifles (See U.S. I)

Accuracy Unlimited, 7479 S. DePew St., Littleton, CO 80123

Accuracy Unlimited, 16036 N. 49 Ave., Glendale, AZ 85306 / 602-978-9089; FAX: 602-978-9089

Accurate Arms Co., Inc., 5891 Hwy. 230 West, McEwen, TN 37101 / 800-416-3006 FAX: 931-729-4211

Accuright, RR 2 Box 397, Sebeka, MN 56477 / 218-472-3383

Ace Custom 45's, Inc., 1880 1/2 Upper Turtle Creek Rd., Kerrville, TX 78028 / 830-257-4290; FAX: 830-257-5724

Ace Sportswear, Inc., 700 Quality Rd., Fayetteville, NC 28306 / 919-323-1223; FAX: 919-323-5392

Ackerman & Co., 16 Cortez St., Westfield, MA 01085 / 413-568-8008

Ackerman, Bill (See Optical Services Co)

Acra-Bond Laminates, 134 Zimmerman Rd., Kalispell, MT 59901 / 406-257-9003; FAX: 406-257-9003

Action Bullets & Alloy Inc, RR 1, P.O. Box 189, Quinter, KS 67752 / 913-754-3609; FAX: 913-754-3629

Action Direct, Inc., P.O. Box 830760, Miami, FL 33283 / 305-559-4652; FAX: 305-559-4652

Action Products, Inc., 22 N. Mulberry St., Hagerstown, MD 21740 / 301-797-1414; FAX: 301-733-2073

Action Target, Inc., P.O. Box 636, Provo, UT 84603 / 801-377-8033; FAX: 801-377-8096

Actions by "T" Teddy Jacobson, 16315 Redwood Forest Ct., Sugar Land, TX 77478 / 281-277-4008

AcuSport Corporation, 1 Hunter Place, Bellefontaine, OH 43311-3001 / 513-593-7010 FAX: 513-592-5625

Ad Hominem, 3130 Gun Club Lane, RR, Orillia, ON L3V 6H3 CANADA / 705-689-5303; FAX: 705-689-5303

Adair Custom Shop, Bill, 2886 Westridge, Carrollton, TX 75006

Adams & Son Engravers, John J, 87 Acorn Rd, Dennis, MA 02638 / 508-385-7971

Adams Jr., John J., 87 Acorn Rd., Dennis, MA 02638 / 508-385-7971

ADCO Sales, Inc., 4 Draper St. #A, Woburn, MA 01801 / 781-935-1799; FAX: 781-935-1011

Adkins, Luther, 1292 E. McKay Rd., Shelbyville, IN 46176-8706 / 317-392-3795

Advance Car Mover Co., Rowell Div., P.O. Box 1, 240 N. Depot St., Juneau, WI 53039 / 414-386-4464; FAX: 414-386-4416

Adventure 16, Inc., 4620 Alvarado Canyon Rd., San Diego, CA 92120 / 619-283-6314

Adventure Game Calls, R.D. 1, Leonard Rd., Spencer, NY 14883 / 607-589-4611

Adventurer's Outpost, P.O. Box 547, Cottonwood, AZ 86326-0547 / 800-762-7471; FAX: 602-634-8781

Aero Peltor, 90 Mechanic St, Southbridge, MA 01550 / 508-764-5500; FAX: 508-764-0188

African Import Co., 20 Braunecker Rd., Plymouth, MA 02360 / 508-746-8552

AFSCO Ammunition, 731 W. Third St., P.O. Box L, Owen, WI 54460 / 715-229-2516

Ahlman Guns, 9525 W. 230th St., Morristown, MN 55052 / 507-685-4243; FAX: 507-685-4280

Ahrends, Kim (See Custom Firearms, Inc), Box 203, Clarion, IA 50525 / 515-532-3449; FAX: 515-532-3926

Aimpoint c/o Springfield, Inc., 420 W. Main St, .Geneseo, IL 61254 / 309-944-1702

Aimtech Mount Systems, P.O. Box 1638, 101 Inwood Acres, Thomasville, GA 31799-1638 / 912-226-4313; FAX: 912-227-0222

Air Arms, Hailsham Industrial Park, Diplocks Way, Hailsham, E. Sussex, BN27 3JF ENGLAND / 011-0323-845853

Air Rifle Specialists, P.O. Box 138, 130 Holden Rd., Pine City, NY 14871-0138 / 607-734-7340; FAX: 607-733-3261

Air Venture Airguns, 9752 E. Flower St., Bellflower, CA 90706 / 310-867-6355

Airgun Repair Centre, 3227 Garden Meadows, Lawrenceburg, IN 47025 / 812-637-1463; FAX: 812-637-1463

Airrow, 11 Monitor Hill Rd, Newtown, CT 06470 / 203-270-6343

Aitor-Cuchilleria Del Norte S.A., Izelaieta, 17, 48260, Ermua, S SPAIN / 43-17-08-50

Ajax Custom Grips, Inc., 9130 Viscount Row, Dallas, TX 75247 / 214-630-8893; FAX: 214-630-4942

Aker International, Inc., 2248 Main St., Suite 6, Chula Vista, CA 91911 / 619-423-5182; FAX: 619-423-1363

Al Lind Custom Guns, 7821 76th Ave. SW, Tacoma, WA 98498 / 206-584-6361

Al Mar Knives, Inc., 5755 SW Jean Rd., Suite 101, Lake Oswego, OR 97035 / 503-635-9229; FAX: 503-223-0467

Alana Cupp Custom Engraver, P.O. Box 207, Annabella, UT 84711 / 801-896-4834

Alaska Bullet Works, Inc., 9978 Crazy Horse Drive, Juneau, AK 99801 / 907 789 3834; FAX: 907-789-3433

Alco Carrying Cases, 601 W. 26th St., New York, NY 10001 / 212-675-5820; FAX: 212-691-5935

Aldis Gunsmithing & Shooting Supply, 502 S. Montezuma St., Prescott, AZ 86303 / 602-445-6723; FAX: 602-445-6763

Alessi Holsters, Inc., 2465 Niagara Falls Blvd., Amherst, NY 14228-3527 / 716-691-5615

Alex, Inc., Box 3034, Bozeman, MT 59772 / 406-282-7396; FAX: 406-282-7396

Alfano, Sam, 36180 Henry Gaines Rd., Pearl River, LA 70452 / 504-863-3364; FAX: 504-863-7715

All American Lead Shot Corp., P.O. Box 224566, Dallas, TX 75062

All Rite Products, Inc., 5752 N. Silverstone Circle, Mountain Green, UT 84050 / 801-876-3330; FAX: 801-876-2216

All's, The Jim J. Tembelis Co., Inc., 216 Loper Ct., Neenah, WI 54956 / 920-725-5251; FAX: 920-725-5251

Allard, Gary/Creek Side Metal & Woodcrafters, Fishers Hill, VA 22626 / 703-465-3903

Allen Co., Bob, 214 SW Jackson, P.O. Box 477, Des Moines, IA 50315 / 515-283-2191 or 800-685-7020; FAX: 515-283-0779

Allen Co., Inc., 525 Burbank St., Broomfield, CO 80020 / 303-469-1857 or 800-876-8600; FAX: 303-466-7437

Allen Firearm Engraving, 339 Grove Ave., Prescott, AZ 86301 / 520-778-1237

Allen Mfg., 6449 Hodgson Rd., Circle Pines, MN 55014 / 612-429-8231

Allen Sportswear, Bob (See Allen Co., Bob)

Alley Supply Co., P.O. Box 848, Gardnerville, NV 89410 / 702-782-3800

Alliant Techsystems Smokeless Powder Group, 200 Valley Rd., Suite 305, Mt. Arlington, NJ 07856 / 800-276-9337; FAX: 201-770-2528

Allred Bullet Co., 932 Evergreen Drive, Logan, UT 84321 / 435-752-6983; FAX: 435-752-6983

Alpec Team, Inc., 201 Ricken Backer Cir., Livermore, CA 94550 / 510-606-8245; FAX: 510-606-4279

Alpha 1 Drop Zone, 2121 N. Tyler, Wichita, KS 67212 / 316-729-0800

Alpha Gunsmith Division, 1629 Via Monserate, Fallbrook, CA 92028 / 619-723-9279 or 619-728-2663

Alpha LaFranck Enterprises, P.O. Box 81072, Lincoln, NE 68501 / 402-466-3193

Alpha Precision, Inc., 2765-B Preston Rd. NE, Good Hope, GA 30641 / 770-267-6163

Alpine's Precision Gunsmithing & Indoor Shooting R, 2401 Government Way, Coeur d'Alene, ID 83814 / 208-765-3559; FAX: 208-765-3559

Altamont Co., 901 N. Church St., P.O. Box 309, Thomasboro, IL 61878 / 217-643-3125 or 800-626-5774; FAX: 217-643-7973

Alumna Sport by Dee Zee, 1572 NE 58th Ave., P.O. Box 3090, Des Moines, IA 50316 / 800-798-9899

Amadeo Rossi S.A., Rua: Amadeo Rossi, 143, Sao Leopoldo, RS 93030-220 BRAZIL / 051-592-5566

AmBr Software Group Ltd., P.O. Box 301, Reistertown, MD 21136-0301 / 800-888-1917; FAX: 410-526-7212

American Ammunition, 3545 NW 71st St., Miami, FL 33147 / 305-835-7400; FAX: 305-694-0037

American Arms Inc., 715 Armour Rd., N. Kansas City, MO 64116 / 816-474-3161; FAX: 816-474-1225

American Bullet, 1512 W Chester Pike #298, West Chester, PA 19382-7754 / 610-399-6584

American Custom Gunmakers Guild, PO Box 812, Burlington, IA 52601 / 318-752-6114; FAX: 319-752-6114

American Derringer Corp., 127 N. Lacy Dr., Waco, TX 76705 / 800-642-7817 or 817-799-9111; FAX: 817-799-7935

American Display Co., 55 Cromwell St., Providence, RI 02907 / 401-331-2464; FAX: 401-421-1264

American Frontier Firearms Mfg., Inc, PO Box 744, Aguanga, CA 92536 / 909-763-0014; FAX: 909-763-0014

American Gas & Chemical Co., Ltd, 220 Pegasus Ave, Northvale, NJ 07647 / 201-767-7300

American Gripcraft, 3230 S Dodge 2, Tucson, AZ 85713 / 602-790-1222

American Gunsmithing Institute, 1325 Imola Ave #504, Napa, CA 94559 / 707-253-0462; FAX: 707-253-7149

American Handgunner Magazine, 591 Camino de la Reina, Ste 200, San Diego, CA 92108 / 619-297-5350; FAX: 619-297-5353

American Pioneer Video, PO Box 50049, Bowling Green, KY 42102-2649 / 800-743-4675

American Products, Inc., 14729 Spring Valley Road, Morrison, IL 61270 / 815-772-3336; FAX: 815-772-8046

American Safe Arms, Inc., 1240 Riverview Dr., Garland, UT 84312 / 801-257-7472; FAX: 801-785-8156

American Sales & Kirkpatrick Mfg. Co., P.O. Box 677, Laredo, TX 78042 / 210-723-6893; FAX: 210-725-0672

American Sales & Mfg. Co., PO Box 677, Laredo, TX 78042 / 956-723-6893; FAX: 956-725-0672

American Security Products Co., 11925 Pacific Ave., Fontana, CA 92337 / 909-685-9680 or 800-421-6142; FAX: 909-685-9685

American Small Arms Academy, P.O. Box 12111, Prescott, AZ 86304 / 602-778-5623

American Target, 1328 S. Jason St., Denver, CO 80223 / 303-733-0433; FAX: 303-777-0311

American Target Knives, 1030 Brownwood NW, Grand Rapids, MI 49504 / 616-453-1998

American Whitetail Target Systems, P.O. Box 41, 106 S. Church St., Tennyson, IN 47637 / 812-567-4527

Americase, P.O. Box 271, 1610 E. Main, Waxahachie, TX 75165 / 800-880-3629; FAX: 214-937-8373

Ames Metal Products, 4323 S. Western Blvd., Chicago, IL 60609 / 773-523-3230; FAX: 773-523-3854

Amherst Arms, P.O. Box 1457, Englewood, FL 34295 / 941-475-2020; FAX: 941-473-1212

Ammo Load, Inc., 1560 E. Edinger, Suite G, Santa Ana, CA 92705 / 714-558-8858; FAX: 714-569-0319

Amrine's Gun Shop, 937 La Luna, Ojai, CA 93023 / 805-646-2376

Amsec, 11925 Pacific Ave., Fontana, CA 92337

Amtec 2000, Inc., 84 Industrial Rowe, Gardner, MA 01440 / 508-632-9608; FAX: 508-632-2300

Analog Devices, Box 9106, Norwood, MA 02062

Andela Tool & Machine, Inc., RD3, Box 246, Richfield Springs, NY 13439

Anderson Manufacturing Co., Inc., 22602 53rd Ave. SE, Bothell, WA 98021 / 206-481-1858; FAX: 206-481-7839

Andres & Dworsky, Bergstrasse 18, A-3822 Karlstein, Thaya, AUSTRIA / 0 28 44-285

Angel Arms, Inc., 1825 Addison Way, Haywood, CA 94545 / 510-783-7122

Angelo & Little Custom Gun Stock Blanks, P.O. Box 240046, Dell, MT 59724-0046

Anics Firm Inc3 Commerce Park Square, 23200 Chagrin Blvd. Suite 240, Beechwood, OH 44122 / 800-556-1582; FAX: 216-292-2588

Anschutz GmbH, Postfach 1128, D-89001 Ulm, Donau, GERMANY / 731-40120

Answer Products Co., 1519 Westbury Drive, Davison, MI 48423 / 810-653-2911

Anthony and George Ltd., Rt. 1, P.O. Box 45, Evington, VA 24550 / 804-821-8117

Antique American Firearms, P.O. Box 71035, Dept. GD, Des Moines, IA 50325 / 515-224-6552

Antique Arms Co., 1110 Cleveland Ave., Monett, MO 65708 / 417-235-6501

Apel GmbH, Ernst, Am Kirschberg 3, D-97218, Gerbrunn, GERMANY / 0 (931) 707192

Aplan Antiques & Art, James O., James O. , HC 80, Box 793-25, Piedmont, SD 57769 / 605-347-5016

AR-7 Industries, LLC, 998 N. Colony Rd., Meriden, CT 06450 / 203-630-3536; FAX: 203-630-3637

Arco Powder, HC-Rt. 1 P.O. Box 102, County Rd. 357, Mayo, FL 32066 / 904-294-3882; FAX: 904-294-1498

Arizona Ammunition, Inc., 21421 No. 14th Ave., Suite E, Phoenix, AZ 85727 / 602-516-9004; FAX: 602-516-9012

Arkansas Mallard Duck Calls, Rt. Box 182, England, AR 72046 / 501-842-3597

ArmaLite, Inc., P.O. Box 299, Geneseo, IL 61254 / 309-944-6939; FAX: 309-944-6949

Armament Gunsmithing Co., Inc., 525 Rt. 22, Hillside, NJ 07205 / 908-686-0960

MANUFACTURER'S DIRECTORY

Armas Kemen S. A. (See U.S. Importers)
Armas Urki Garbi, 12-14 20.600, Eibar (Guipuzcoa), / 43-11 38 73
Armfield Custom Bullets, 4775 Caroline Drive, San Diego, CA 92115 / 619-582-7188; FAX: 619-287-3238
Armi Perazzi S.p.A., Via Fontanelle 1/3, 1-25080, Botticino Mattina, / 030-2692591; FAX: 030 2692594+
Armi San Marco (See U.S. Importers-Taylor's & Co I
Armi San Paolo, 172-A, I-25062, via Europa, ITALY / 030-2751725
Armi Sport (See U.S. Importers-Cape Outfitters)
Armite Laboratories, 1845 Randolph St., Los Angeles, CA 90001 / 213-587-7768; FAX: 213-587-5075
Armoloy Co. of Ft. Worth, 204 E. Daggett St., Fort Worth, TX 76104 / 817-332-5604; FAX: 817-335-6517
Armor (See Buck Stop Lure Co., Inc.)
Armor Metal Products, P.O. Box 4609, Helena, MT 59604 / 406-442-5560; FAX: 406-442-5650
Armory Publications, Inc., 17171 Bothall Way NE, #276, Seattle, WA 98155 / 208-664-5061; FAX: 208-664-9906
Armoury, Inc., The, Rt. 202, Box 2340, New Preston, CT 06777 / 860-868-0001; FAX: 860-868-2919
Arms & Armour Press, Wellington House, 125 Strand, London, WC2R 0BB ENGLAND / 0171-420-5555; FAX: 0171-240-7265
Arms Corporation of the Philippines, Bo. Parang Marikina, Metro Manila, PHILIPPINES / 632-941-6243 or 632-941-6244; FAX: 632-942-0682
Arms Craft Gunsmithing, 1106 Linda Dr., Arroyo Grande, CA 93420 / 805-481-2830
Arms Ingenuity Co., P.O. Box 1, 51 Canal St., Weatogue, CT 06089 / 203-658-5624
Arms Software, P.O. Box 1526, Lake Oswego, OR 97035 / 800-366-5559 or 503-697-0533; FAX: 503-697-3337
Arms, Programming Solutions (See Arms Software)
Armscorp USA , Inc., 4424 John Ave., Baltimore, MD 21227 / 410-247-6200; FAX: 410-247-6205
Armsport, Inc., 3950 NW 49th St., Miami, FL 33142 / 305-635-7850; FAX: 305-633-2877
Arnold Arms Co., Inc., P.O. Box 1011, Arlington, WA 98223 / 800-371-1011 or 360-435-1011; FAX: 360-435-7304
Aro-Tek Ltd., 206 Frontage Rd. North, Suite C, Pacific, WA 98047 / 206-351-2984; FAX: 206-833-4483
Arratoonian, Andy (See Horseshoe Leather Products)
Arrieta S.L., Morkaiko 5, 20870, Elgoibar, SPAIN / 34-43-743150; FAX: 34-43-743154+
Art Jewel Enterprises Ltd., Eagle Business Ctr., 460 Randy Rd., Carol Stream, IL 60188 / 708-260-0400
Art's Gun & Sport Shop, Inc., 6008 Hwy. Y, Hillsboro, MO 63050
Artistry in Wood, 134 Zimmerman Rd., Kalispell, MT 59901 / 406-257-9003
Arundel Arms & Ammunition, Inc., A., 24A Defense St., Annapolis, MD 21401 / 410-224-8683
Arvo Ojala Holsters, P.O. Box 98, N. Hollywood, CA 91603 / 818-222-9700; FAX: 818-222-0401
Ashby Turkey Calls, P.O. Box 1466, Ava, MO 65608-1466 / 417-967-3787
Ashley Outdoors, Inc, 2401 Ludelle St, Fort Worth, TX 76105 / 888-744-4880; FAX: 800-734-7939
Aspen Outfitting Co, Jon Hollinger , 9 Dean St, Aspen, CO 81611 / 970-925-3406
Astra Sport , S.A., Apartado 3, 48300 Guernica, Espagne, SPAIN / 34-4-6250100; FAX: 34-4-6255186+
Atamec-Bretton, 19 rue Victor Grignard, F-42026, St.-Etienne (Cedex 1, / 77-93-54-69; FAX: 33-77-93-57-98+
Atlanta Cutlery Corp., 2143 Gees Mill Rd., Box 839 CIS, Conyers, GA 30207 / 800-883-0300; FAX: 404-388-0246
Atlantic Mills , Inc., 1295 Towbin Ave., Lakewood, NJ 08701-5934 / 800-242-7374
Atlantic Rose, Inc., P.O. Box 10717, Bradenton, FL 34282-0717
Atsko/Sno-Seal, Inc., 2664 Russell St., Orangeburg, SC 29115 / 803-531-1820; FAX: 803-531-2139
Auguste Francotte & Cie S.A., rue du Trois Juin 109, 4400 Herstal-Liege, BELGIUM / 32-4-248-13-18; FAX: 32-4-948-11-79
Austin & Halleck, 1099 Welt, Weston, MO 64098 / 816-386-2176; FAX: 816-386-2177
Austin Sheridan USA, Inc., P.O. Box 577, 36 Haddam Quarter Rd., Durham, CT 06422 / 203-349-1772; FAX: 203-349-1771
Autauga Arms, Inc., Pratt Plaza Mall No. 13, Prattville, AL 36067 / 800-262-9563; FAX: 334-361-2961
Auto Arms, 738 Clearview, San Antonio, TX 78228 / 512-434-5450
Auto-Ordnance Corp., PO Box 220, Blauvelt, NY 10913 / 914-353-7770
Automatic Equipment Sales, 627 E. Railroad Ave., Salesburg, MD 21801
Autumn Sales, Inc. (Blaser), 1320 Lake St., Fort Worth, TX 76102 / 817-335-1634; FAX: 817-338-0119
Avnda Otaola Norica, 16 Apartado 68, 20600, Eibar,
AWC Systems Technology, P.O. Box 41938, Phoenix, AZ 85080-1938 / 602-780-1050 FAX: 602-780-2967
AYA (See U.S. Importer-New England Custom Gun Serv

B

B & P America, 12321 Brittany Cir, Dallas, TX 75230 / 972-726-9069
B&D Trading Co., Inc., 3935 Fair Hill Rd., Fair Oaks, CA 95628 / 800-334-3790 or 916-967-9366; FAX: 916-967-4873
B-Square Company, Inc., ; , P.O. Box 11281, 2708 St. Louis Ave., Ft. Worth, TX 76110 / 817-923-0964 or 800-433-2909 FAX: 817-926-7012
B-West Imports, Inc., 2425 N. Huachuca Dr., Tucson, AZ 85745-1201 / 602-628-1990; FAX: 602-628-3602
B.B. Walker Co., PO Box 1167, 414 E Dixie Dr, Asheboro, NC 27203 / 910-625-1380; FAX: 910-625-8125
B.C. Outdoors, Larry McGhee , PO Box 61497, Boulder City, NV 89006 / 702-294-0025
B.M.F. Activator , Inc., 803 Mill Creek Run, Plantersville, TX 77363 / 409-894-2005 or 800-527-2881
Badger Shooters Supply, Inc., P.O. Box 397, Owen, WI 54460 / 800-424-9069; FAX: 715-229-2332
Baekgaard Ltd., 1855 Janke Dr., Northbrook, IL 60062 / 708-498-3040; FAX: 708-493-3106
Baelder, Harry, Alte Goennebeker Strasse 5, 24635, Rickling, GERMANY / 04328-722732; FAX: 04328-722733
Baer Custom, Inc, Les, 29601 34th Ave, Hillsdale, IL 61257 / 309-658-2716; FAX: 309-658-2610
Baer's Hollows, P.O. Box 284, Eads, CO 81036 / 719-438-5718
Bagmaster Mfg., Inc., 2731 Sutton Ave., St. Louis, MO 63143 / 314-781-8002; FAX: 314-781-3363
Bain & Davis, Inc., 307 E. Valley Blvd., San Gabriel, CA 91776-3522 / 818-573-4241 or 213-283-7449
Baker's Leather Goods, Roy, PO Box 893, Magnolia, AR 71753 / 501-234-0344
Baker, Stan, 10000 Lake City Way, Seattle, WA 98125 / 206-522-4575
Balaance Co., 340-39 Ave., S.E., Box 505, Calgary, AB T2G 1X6 CANADA
Bald Eagle Precision Machine Co., 101-A Allison St., Lock Haven, PA 17745 / 570-748-6772; FAX: 570-748-4443
Balickie, Joe, 408 Trelawney Lane, Apex, NC 27502 / 919-362-5185
Ballard Industries, 10271 Lockwood Dr., Suite B, Cupertino, CA 95014 / 408-996-0957; FAX: 408-257-6828
Ballard Rifle & Cartridge Co., LLC, 113 W Yellowstone Ave, Cody, WY 82414 / 307-587-4914; FAX: 307-527-6097
Ballisti-Cast , Inc., 6347 49th St. NW, Plaza, ND 58771 / 701-497-3333; FAX: 701-497-3335
Ballistic Engineering & Software, Inc., 185 N. Park Blvd., Suite 330, Lake Orion, MI 48362 / 313-391-1074
Ballistic Product, Inc., 20015 75th Ave. North, Corcoran, MN 55340-9456 / 612-494-9237; FAX: 612-494-9236
Ballistic Program Co., Inc., The, 2417 N. Patterson St., Thomasville, GA 31792 / 912-228-5739 or 800-368-0835
Ballistic Research, 1108 W. May Ave., McHenry, IL 60050 / 815-385-0037
Bandcor Industries , Div. of Man-Sew Corp., 6108 Sherwin Dr., Port Richey, FL 34668 / 813-848-0432
Bang-Bang Boutique (See Holster Shop, The)
Banks, Ed, 2762 Hwy. 41 N., Ft. Valley, GA 31030 / 912-987-4665
Bansner's Gunsmithing Specialties, 261 East Main St. Box VH, Adamstown, PA 19501 / 800-368-2379; FAX: 717-484-0523
Bar-Sto Precision Machine, 73377 Sullivan Rd., P.O. Box 1838, Twentynine Palms, CA 92277 / 760-367-2747; FAX: 760-367-2407
Barbour, Inc., 55 Meadowbrook Dr., Milford, NH 03055 / 603-673-1313; FAX: 603-673-6510
Barnes Bullets, Inc., P.O. Box 215, American Fork, UT 84003 / 801-756-4222 or 800-574-9200; FAX: 801-756-2465
Baron Technology, 62 Spring Hill Rd., Trumbull, CT 06611 / 203-452-0515; FAX: 203-452-0663
Barraclough, John K., 55 Merit Park Dr., Gardena, CA 90247 / 310-324-2574
Barramundi Corp., P.O. Drawer 4259, Homosassa Springs, FL 32687 / 904-628-0200
Barrett Firearms Manufacturer, Inc., P.O. Box 1077, Murfreesboro, TN 37133 / 615-896-2938; FAX: 615-896-7313
Barry Lee Hands Engraving, 26192 E. Shore Route, Bigfork, MT 59911 / 406-837-0035
Barta's Gunsmithing, 10231 US Hwy. 10, Cato, WI 54206 / 920-732-4472
Barteaux Machete, 1916 SE 50th Ave., Portland, OR 97215-3238 / 503-233-5880
Bartlett Engineering, 40 South 200 East, Smithfield, UT 84335-1645 / 801-563-5910
Basics Information Systems, Inc., 1141 Georgia Ave., Suite 515, Wheaton, MD 20902 / 301-949-1070; FAX: 301-949-5326
Bates Engraving, Billy, 2302 Winthrop Dr, Decatur, AL 35603 / 256-355-3690
Bauer, Eddie, 15010 NE 36th St., Redmond, WA 98052
Baumgartner Bullets, 3011 S. Alane St., W. Valley City, UT 84120
Bauska Barrels, 105 9th Ave. W., Kalispell, MT 59901 / 406-752-7706
Bear Archery, RR 4, 4600 Southwest 41st Blvd., Gainesville, FL 32601 / 904-376-2327
Bear Arms, 121 Rhodes St., Jackson, SC 29831 / 803-471-9859
Bear Hug Grip, Inc., P.O. Box 16649, Colorado Springs, CO 80935-6649 / 800-232-7710
Bear Mountain Gun & Tool, 120 N. Plymouth, New Plymouth, ID 83655 / 208-278-5221; FAX: 208-278-5221
Beartooth Bullets, P.O. Box 491, Dept. HLD, Dover, ID 83825-0491 / 208-448-1865
Beaver Lodge (See Fellowes, Ted)
Beaver Park Product, Inc., 840 J St., Penrose, CO 81240 / 719-372-6744
BEC, Inc., 1227 W. Valley Blvd., Suite 204, Alhambra, CA 91803 / 818-281-5751; FAX: 818-293-7073
Beeline Custom Bullets Limited, P.O. Box 85, Yarmouth, NS B5A 4B1 CANADA / 902-648-3494; FAX: 902-648-0253
Beeman Precision Airguns, 5454 Argosy Dr., Huntington Beach, CA 92649 / 714-890-4800; FAX: 714-890-4808
Behlert Precision, Inc., P.O. Box 288, 7067 Easton Rd., Pipersville, PA 18947 / 215-766-8681 or 215-766-7301; FAX: 215-766-8681
Beitzinger, George, 116-20 Atlantic Ave, Richmond Hill, NY 11419 / 718-847-7661
Belding's Custom Gun Shop, 10691 Sayers Rd., Munith, MI 49259 / 517-596-2388
Bell & Carlson, Inc., Dodge City Industrial Park, 101 Allen Rd., Dodge City, KS 67801 / 800-634-8586 or 316-225-6688; FAX: 316-225-9095
Bell Reloading, Inc., 1725 Harlin Lane Rd., Villa Rica, GA 30180
Bell's Gun & Sport Shop, 3309-19 Mannheim Rd, Franklin Park, IL 60131
Bell's Legendary Country Wear, 22 Circle Dr., Bellmore, NY 11710 / 516-679-1158
Bellm Contenders, P.O. Box 459, Cleveland, UT 84518 / 801-653-2530
Belltown Ltd., 11 Camps Rd., Kent, CT 06757 / 860-354-5750 FAX: 860-354-6764
Ben William's Gun Shop, 1151 S. Cedar Ridge, Duncanville, TX 75137 / 214-780-1807
Ben's Machines, 1151 S. Cedar Ridge, Duncanville, TX 75137 / 214-780-1807 FAX: 214-780-0316
Benchmark Guns, 12593 S. Ave. 5 East, Yuma, AZ 85365
Benchmark Knives (See Gerber Legendary Blades)
Benelli Armi S.p.A., Via della Stazione, 61029, Urbino, ITALY / 39-722-307-1; FAX: 39-722-327427+
Benelli USA Corp, 17603 Indian Head Hwy, Accokeek, MD 20607 / 301-283-6981; FAX: 301-283-6988
Bengtson Arms Co., L., 6345-B E. Akron St., Mesa, AZ 85205 / 602-981-6375
Benjamin/Sheridan Co., Crossman, Rts. 5 and 20, E. Bloomfield, NY 14443 / 716-657-6161; FAX: 716-657-5405
Bentley, John, 128-D Watson Dr., Turtle Creek, PA 15145
Beomat of America, Inc., 300 Railway Ave., Campbell, CA 95008 / 408-379-4829
Beretta S.p.A., Pietro, Via Beretta, 18-25063, Gardone V.T., ITALY / 39-30-8341-1 FAX: 39-30-8341-421
Beretta U.S.A. Corp., 17601 Beretta Drive, Accokeek, MD 20607 / 301-283-2191; FAX: 301-283-0435
Berger Bullets Ltd., 5342 W. Camelback Rd., Suite 200, Glendale, AZ 85301 / 602-842-4001; FAX: 602-934-9083
Bernardelli S.p.A., Vincenzo, 125 Via Matteotti, PO Box 74, Brescia, ITALY / 39-30-8912851-2-3; FAX: 39-30-8910249
Berry's Mfg., Inc., 401 North 3050 East St., St. George, UT 84770 / 801-634-1682; FAX: 801-634-1683
Bersa S.A., Gonzales Castillo 312, 1704, Ramos Mejia, ARGENTINA / 541-656-2377; FAX: 541-656-2093+
Bert Johanssons Vapentillbehor, S-430 20 Veddige, SWEDEN,
Bertuzzi (See U.S. Importer-New England Arms Co)
Better Concepts Co., 663 New Castle Rd., Butler, PA 16001 / 412-285-9000
Beverly, Mary, 3201 Horseshoe Trail, Tallahassee, FL 32312
Bianchi International, Inc., 100 Calle Cortez, Temecula, CA 92590 / 909-676-5621; FAX: 909-676-6777
Biesen, Al, 5021 Rosewood, Spokane, WA 99208 / 509-328-9340
Biesen, Roger, 5021 W. Rosewood, Spokane, WA 99208 / 509-328-9340
Big Bear Arms & Sporting Goods, Inc., 1112 Milam Way, Carrollton, TX 75006 / 972-416-8051 or 800-400-BEAR; FAX: 972-416-0771
Big Bore Bullets of Alaska, P.O. Box 872785, Wasilla, AK 99687 / 907-373-2673; FAX: 907-373-2673
Big Bore Express, 7154 W. State St., Boise, ID 83703 / 800-376-4010; FAX: 208-376-4020
Big Sky Racks, Inc., P.O. Box 729, Bozeman, MT 59771-0729 / 406-586-9393; FAX: 406-585-7378
Big Spring Enterprises "Bore Stores", P.O. Box 1115, Big Spring Rd., Yellville, AR 72687 / 870-449-5297; FAX: 870-449-4446
Bilal, Mustafa, 908 NW 50th St., Seattle, WA 98107-3634 / 206-782-4164
Bilinski, Bryan. See: FIELDSPORT LTD
Bill Austin's Calls, Box 284, Kaycee, WY 82639 / 307-738-2552

MANUFACTURER'S DIRECTORY

Bill Adair Custom Shop, 2886 Westridge, Carrollton, TX 75006 / 972-418-0950
Bill Hanus Birdguns LLC, P.O. Box 533, Newport, OR 97365 / 541-265-7433; FAX: 541-265-7400
Bill Johns Master Engraver, 7927 Ranch Roach 965, Fredericksburg, TX 78624-9545 / 830-997-6795
Bill Wiseman and Co., P.O. Box 3427, Bryan, TX 77805 / 409-690-3456; FAX: 409-690-0156
Bill's Custom Cases, P.O. Box 2, Dunsmuir, CA 96025 / 530-235-0177; FAX: 530-235-4959
Bill's Gun Repair, 1007 Burlington St., Mendota, IL 61342 / 815-539-5786
Billeb, Stephen L., 1101 N. 7th St., Burlington, IA 52601 / 319-753-2110
Billings Gunsmiths Inc., 1841 Grand Ave., Billings, MT 59102 / 406-256-8390
Billingsley & Brownell, P.O. Box 25, Dayton, WY 82836 / 307-655-9344
Billy Bates Engraving, 2302 Winthrop Dr., Decatur, AL 35603 / 205-355-3690
Birchwood Casey, 7900 Fuller Rd., Eden Prairie, MN 55344 / 800-328-6156 or 612-937-7933; FAX: 612-937-7979
Birdsong & Assoc, W. E., 1435 Monterey Rd, Florence, MS 39073-9748 / 601-366-8270
Bismuth Cartridge Co., 3500 Maple Ave., Suite 1650, Dallas, TX 75219 / 214-521-5880; FAX: 214-521-9035
Bison Studios, 1409 South Commerce St., Las Vegas, NV 89102 / 702-388-2891; FAX: 702-383-9967
Bitterroot Bullet Co., PO Box 412, Lewiston, ID 83501-0412 / 208-743-5635 FAX: 208-743-5635
BKL Technologies, PO Box 5237, Brownsville, TX 78523
Black Belt Bullets (See Big Bore Express)
Black Hills Ammunition, Inc., P.O. Box 3090, Rapid City, SD 57709-3090 / 605-348-5150; FAX: 605-348-9827
Black Hills Shooters Supply, P.O. Box 4220, Rapid City, SD 57709 / 800-289-2506
Black Powder Products, 67 Township Rd. 1411, Chesapeake, OH 45619 / 614-867-8047
Black Sheep Brand, 3220 W. Gentry Parkway, Tyler, TX 75702 / 903-592-3853; FAX: 903-592-0527
Blackhawk East, Box 2274, Loves Park, IL 61131
Blacksmith Corp., PO Box 280, North Hampton, OH 45349 / 800-531-2665; FAX: 937-969-8299
BlackStar AccuMax Barrels, 11501 Brittmoore Park Drive, Houston, TX 77041 / 281-721-6040; FAX: 281-721-6041
BlackStar Barrel Accurizing (See BlackStar AccuMax
Blacktail Mountain Books, 42 First Ave. W., Kalispell, MT 59901 / 406-257-5573
Blair Engraving, J. R., PO Box 64, Glenrock, WY 82637 / 307-436-8115
Blammo Ammo, P.O. Box 1677, Seneca, SC 29679 / 803-882-1768
Blaser Jagdwaffen GmbH, D-88316, Isny Im Allgau, GERMANY
Bleile, C. Roger, 5040 Ralph Ave., Cincinnati, OH 45238 / 513-251-0249
Blount, Inc., Sporting Equipment Div., 2299 Snake River Ave., P.O. Box 856, Lewiston, ID 83501 / 800-627-3640 or 208-746-2351; FAX: 208-799-3904
Blue and Gray Products Inc (See Ox-Yoke Originals
Blue Book Publications, Inc., One Appletree Square, 8009 34th Ave. S. Suite 175, Minneapolis, MN 55425 / 800-877-4867 or 612-854-5229; FAX: 612-853-1486
Blue Mountain Bullets, HCR 77, P.O. Box 231, John Day, OR 97845 / 541-820-4594
Blue Ridge Machinery & Tools, Inc., P.O. Box 536-GD, Hurricane, WV 25526 / 800-872-6500; FAX: 304-562-5311
BMC Supply, Inc., 26051 - 179th Ave. S.E., Kent, WA 98042
Bo-Mar Tool & Mfg. Co., Rt. 8, Box 405, Longview, TX 75604 / 903-759-4784; FAX: 903-759-9141
Bob Allen Co.214 SW Jackson, P.O. Box 477, Des Moines, IA 50315 / 800-685-7020 FAX: 515-283-0779
Bob Schrimsher's Custom Knifemaker's Supply, P.O. Box 308, Emory, TX 75440 / 903-473-3330; FAX: 903-473-2235
Bob's Gun Shop, P.O. Box 200, Royal, AR 71968 / 501-767-1970; FAX: 501-767-1970
Bob's Tactical Indoor Shooting Range & Gun Shop, 90 Lafayette Rd., Salisbury, MA 01952 / 508-465-5561
Boessler, Erich, Am Vogeltal 3, 97702, Munnerstadt, GERMANY
Bohemia Arms Co., 17101 Los Modelos St., Fountain Valley, CA 92708 / 619-442-7005; FAX: 619-442-7005
Boker USA , Inc., 1550 Balsam Street, Lakewood, CO 80215 / 303-462-0662; FAX: 303-462-0668
Boltin, John M., P.O. Box 644, Estill, SC 29918 / 803-625-2185
Bonanza (See Forster Products), 310 E Lanark Ave, Lanark, IL 61046 / 815-493-6360; FAX: 815-493-2371
Bond Arms, Inc., P.O. Box 1296, Granbury, TX 76048 / 817-573-4445; FAX: 817-573-5636
Bond Custom Firearms, 8954 N. Lewis Ln., Bloomington, IN 47408 / 812-332-4519
Bondini Paolo, Via Sorrento 345, San Carlo di Cesena, ITALY / 0547-663-240; FAX: 0547-663-780
Bone Engraving, Ralph, 718 N Atlanta, Owasso, OK 74055 / 918-272-9745
Boone Trading Co., Inc., P.O. Box BB, Brinnan, WA 98320
Boone's Custom Ivory Grips, Inc., 562 Coyote Rd., Brinnon, WA 98320 / 206-796-4330
Boonie Packer Products, P.O. Box 12204, Salem, OR 97309 / 800-477-3244 or 503-581-3244; FAX: 503-581-3191
Borden's Accuracy, RD 1, Box 250BC, Springville, PA 18844 / 717-965-2505; FAX: 717-965-2328
Border Barrels Ltd., Riccarton Farm, Newcastleton, SCOTLAND UK
Borovnik KG, Ludwig, 9170 Ferlach, Bahnhofstrasse 7, AUSTRIA / 042 27 24 42; FAX: 042 26 43 49
Bosis (See U.S. Importer-New England Arms Co.)
Boss Manufacturing Co., 221 W. First St., Kewanee, IL 61443 / 309-852-2131 or 800-447-4581; FAX: 309-852-0848
Bostick Wildlife Calls, Inc., P.O. Box 728, Estill, SC 29918 / 803-625-2210 or 803-625-4512
Bowen Classic Arms Corp., P.O. Box 67, Louisville, TN 37777 / 423-984-3583
Bowen Knife Co., Inc., P.O. Box 590, Blackshear, GA 31516 / 912-449-4794
Bowerly, Kent, 710 Golden Pheasant Dr, Redmond, OR 97756 / 541-595-6028
Boyds' Gunstock Industries, Inc., 25376 403RD AVE, MITCHELL, SD 57301 / 605-996-5011; FAX: 605-996-9878
Brace, Larry D., 771 Blackfoot Ave., Eugene, OR 97404 / 541-688-1278; FAX: 541-607-5833
Bradley Gunsight Co., P.O. Box 340, Plymouth, VT 05056 / 860-589-0531; FAX: 860-582-6294
Brass and Bullet Alloys, P.O. Box 1238, Sierra Vista, AZ 85636 / 602-458-5321; FAX: 602-458-9125
Brass Eagle, Inc., 7050A Bramalea Rd., Unit 19, Mississauga,, ON L4Z 1C7 CANADA / 416-848-4844
Bratcher, Dan, 311 Belle Air Pl., Carthage, MO 64836 / 417-358-1518
Brauer Bros. Mfg. Co., 2020 Delman Blvd., St. Louis, MO 63103 / 314-231-2864; FAX: 314-249-4952
Break-Free, Inc., P.O. Box 25020, Santa Ana, CA 92799 / 714-953-1900; FAX: 714-953-0402
Brenneke KG, Wilhelm, Ilmenauweg 2, 30851 Langenhagen, GERMANY / 0511-97262-0; FAX: 0511-97262-62
Brian Perazone-Gunsmith, Cold Spring Rd., Roxbury, NY 12474 / 607-326-4088; FAX: 607-326-3140
Bridgeman Products, Harry Jaffin , 153 B Cross Slope Court, Englishtown, NJ 07726 / 732-536-3604; FAX: 732-972-1004
Bridgers Best, P.O. Box 1410, Berthoud, CO 80513
Briese Bullet Co., Inc., RR1, Box 108, Tappen, ND 58487 / 701-327-4578; FAX: 701-327-4579
Brigade Quartermasters, 1025 Cobb International Blvd., Dept. VH, Kennesaw, GA 30144-4300 / 404-428-1248 or 800-241-3125; FAX: 404-426-7726
Briganti, A.J., 512 Rt. 32, Highland Mills, NY 10930 / 914-928-9573
Briley Mfg. Inc., 1230 Lumpkin, Houston, TX 77043 / 800-331-5718 or 713-932-6995; FAX: 713-932-1043
British Antiques, P.O. Box 35369, Tucson, AZ 85740 / 518-783-0773
British Sporting Arms, RR1, Box 130, Millbrook, NY 12545 / 914-677-8303
BRNO (See U.S. Importers-Bohemia Arms Co.)
Broad Creek Rifle Works, 120 Horsey Ave., Laurel, DE 19956 / 302-875-5446; FAX: 302-875-1449
Brockman's Custom Gunsmithing, P.O. Box 357, Gooding, ID 83330 / 208-934-5050
Brocock Ltd., 43 River Street, Digbeth, Birmingham, B5 5SA ENGLAND / 011-021-773-1200
Broken Gun Ranch, 10739 126 Rd., Spearville, KS 67876 / 316-385-2587; FAX: 316-385-2597
Brolin Arms, 2755 Thompson Creek Rd., Pomona, CA 91767 / 909-392-7822; FAX: 909-392-7824
Brooker, Dennis, Rt. 1, Box 12A, Derby, IA 50068 / 515-533-2103
Brooks Tactical Systems, 279-C Shorewood Ct., Fox Island, WA 98333 / 800-410-4747; FAX: 206-572-6797
Brown Co, E. Arthur, 3404 Pawnee Dr, Alexandria, MN 56308 / 320-762-8847
Brown Dog Ent., 2200 Calle Camelia, 1000 Oaks, CA 91360 / 805-497-2318; FAX: 805-497-1618
Brown Manufacturing, P.O. Box 9219, Akron, OH 44305 / 800-837-GUNS
Brown Precision,Inc., 7786 Molinos Ave., Los Molinos, CA 96055 FAX: 916-384-1638
Brown Products, Inc., Ed, 43825 Muldrow Trail, Perry, MO 63462 / 573-565-3261; FAX: 573-565-2791
Brown, H. R. (See Silhouette Leathers)
Brownells, Inc., 200 S. Front St., Montezuma, IA 50171 / 515-623-5401; FAX: 515-623-3896
Browning Arms Co., One Browning Place, Morgan, UT 84050 / 801-876-2711; FAX: 801-876-3331
Browning Arms Co. (Parts & Service), 3005 Arnold Tenbrook Rd., Arnold, MO 63010 / 314-287-6800; FAX: 314-287-9751
BRP, Inc. High Performance Cast Bullets, 1210 Alexander Rd., Colorado Springs, CO 80909 / 719-633-0658
Brunton U.S.A., 620 E. Monroe Ave., Riverton, WY 82501 / 307-856-6559; FAX: 307-856-1840
Bryan & Assoc, R D Sauls , PO Box 5772, Anderson, SC 29623-5772 / 864-261-6810
Brynin, Milton, P.O. Box 383, Yonkers, NY 10710 / 914-779-4333
BSA Guns Ltd., Armoury Rd. Small Heath, Birmingham, ENGLAND / 011-021-772-8543; FAX: 011-021-773-084
BSA Optics, 3911 SW 47th Ave #914, Ft Lauderdale, FL 33314 / 954-581-2144 FAX: 954-581-3165
Bucheimer, J. See: JUMBO SPORTS PRODUCTS
Bucheimer, J. M. (See Jumbo Sports Products), 721 N 20th St, St Louis, MO 63103 / 314-241-1020
Buck Knives, Inc., 1900 Weld Blvd., P.O. Box 1267, El Cajon, CA 92020 / 619-449-1100 or 800-326-2825; FAX: 619-562-5774 8
Buck Stix--SOS Products Co., Box 3, Neenah, WI 54956
Buck Stop Lure Co., Inc., 3600 Grow Rd. NW, P.O. Box 636, Stanton, MI 48888 / 517-762-5091; FAX: 517-762-5124
Buckeye Custom Bullets, 6490 Stewart Rd., Elida, OH 45807 / 419-641-4463
Buckhorn Gun Works, 8109 Woodland Dr., Black Hawk, SD 57718 / 605-787-6472
Buckskin Bullet Co., P.O. Box 1893, Cedar City, UT 84721 / 435-586-3286
Buckskin Machine Works, A. Hunkeler, 3235 S. 358th St., Auburn, WA 98001 / 206-927-5412
Budin, Dave, Main St., Margaretville, NY 12455 / 914-568-4103; FAX: 914-586-4105
Buenger Enterprises/Goldenrod Dehumidifier, 3600 S. Harbor Blvd., Oxnard, CA 93035 / 800-451-6797 or 805-985-5828; FAX: 805-985-1534
Buffalo Arms Co., 99 Raven Ridge, Samuels, ID 83864 / 208-263-6953; FAX: 208-265-2096
Buffalo Bullet Co., Inc.., 12637 Los Nietos Rd., Unit A., Santa Fe Springs, CA 90670 FAX: 562-944-5054
Buffalo Rock Shooters Supply, R.R. 1, Ottawa, IL 61350 / 815-433-2471
Buffer Technologies, P.O. Box 104930, Jefferson City, MO 65110 / 573-634-8529; FAX: 573-634-8522
Bull Mountain Rifle Co., 6327 Golden West Terrace, Billings, MT 59106 / 406-656-0778
Bull-X, Inc., 520 N. Main, Farmer City, IL 61842 / 309-928-2574 or 800-248-3845; FAX: 309-928-2130
Bullberry Barrel Works, Ltd., 2430 W. Bullberry Ln. 67-5, Hurricane, UT 84737 / 435-635-9866; FAX: 435-635-0348
Bullet Swaging Supply Inc., P.O. Box 1056, 303 McMillan Rd, West Monroe, LA 71291 / 318-387-3266; FAX: 318-387-7779
Bullet'n Press, 19 Key St., Eastport, ME 04631 / 207-853-4116
Bullet, Inc., 3745 Hiram Alworth Rd., Dallas, GA 30132
BulletMakers Workshop, The, RFD 1 Box 1755, Brooks, ME 04921
Bullseye Bullets, 1610 State Road 60, No. 12, Valrico, FL 33594 / 813-654-6563
Burgess, Byron, PO Box 6853, Los Osos, CA 93412 / 805-528-1005
Burkhart Gunsmithing, Don, P.O. Box 852, Rawlins, WY 82301 / 307-324-6007
Burnham Bros., P.O. Box 1148, Menard, TX 78659 / 915-396-4572; FAX: 915-396-4574
Burris Co., Inc., P.O. Box 1747, 331 E. 8th St., Greeley, CO 80631 / 970-356-1670; FAX: 970-356-8702
Bushmann Hunters & Safaris, P.O. Box 293088, Lewisville, TX 75029 / 214-317-0768
Bushmaster Firearms (See Quality Parts Co/Bushmast
Bushmaster Hunting & Fishing, 451 Alliance Ave., Toronto, ON M6N 2J1 Canada / 416-763-4040; FAX: 416-763-0623
Bushnell Sports Optics Worldwide, 9200 Cody, Overland Park, KS 66214 / 913-752-3400 or 800-423-3537; FAX: 913-752-3550
Bushwacker Backpack & Supply Co (See Counter Assau
Bustani, Leo, P.O. Box 8125, W. Palm Beach, FL 33410 / 305-622-2710
Buster's Custom Knives, P.O. Box 214, Richfield, UT 84701 / 801-896-5319
Butler Creek Corp., 290 Arden Dr., Belgrade, MT 59714 / 800-423-8327 or 406-388-1356; FAX: 406-388-7204
Butler Enterprises, 834 Oberting Rd., Lawrenceburg, IN 47025 / 812-537-3584
Butterfield & Butterfield, 220 San Bruno Ave., San Francisco, CA 94103 / 415-861-7500
Buzztail Brass (See Grayback Wildcats)
Byron Burgess, P.O. Box 6853, Los Osos, CA 93412 / 805-528-1005

C

C&D Special Products (See Claybuster Wads & Harves
C&H Research, 115 Sunnyside Dr., Box 351, Lewis, KS 67552 / 316-324-5445
C-More Systems, P.O. Box 1750, 7553 Gary Rd., Manassas, VA 20108 / 703-361-2663; FAX: 703-361-5881
C. Palmer Manufacturing Co., Inc., P.O. Box 220, West Newton, PA 15089 / 412-872-8200; FAX: 412-872-8302

MANUFACTURER'S DIRECTORY

C. Sharps Arms Co. Inc., 100 Centennial, Box 885, Big Timber, MT 59011 / 406-932-4353; FAX: 406-932-4443
C.S. Van Gorden & Son, Inc., 1815 Main St., Bloomer, WI 54724 / 715-568-2612
C.W. Erickson's Mfg. Inc., 530 Garrison Ave NE, PO Box 522, Buffalo, MN 55313 / 612-682-3665; FAX: 612-682-4328
Cabanas (See U.S. Importer-Mandall Shooting Suppli
Cabela's, 812-13th Ave., Sidney, NE 69160 / 308-254-6644 or 800-237-4444; FAX: 308-254-6745
Cabinet Mtn. Outfitters Scents & Lures, P.O. Box 766, Plains, MT 59859 / 406-826-3970
Cache La Poudre Rifleworks, 140 N. College, Ft. Collins, CO 80524 / 303-482-6913
Cali'co Hardwoods, Inc., 3580 Westwind Blvd., Santa Rosa, CA 95403 / 707-546-4045; FAX: 707-546-4027
Calibre Press, Inc., 666 Dundee Rd., Suite 1607, Northbrook, IL 60062 / 800-323-0037; FAX: 708-498-6869
Calico Light Weapon Systems, 405 E. 19th St., Bakersfield, CA 93305 / 805-835-9605; FAX: 805-835-9605
California Sights (See Fautheree, Andy)
Cambos Outdoorsman, 532 E. Idaho Ave., Ontario, OR 97914 / 541-889-3138 FAX: 541-889-2633
Camdex, Inc., 2330 Alger, Troy, ML 48083 / 810-528-2300; FAX: 810-528-0989
Cameron's, 16690 W. 11th Ave., Golden, CO 80401 / 303-279-7365; FAX: 303-628-5413
Camilli, Lou, 600 Sandtree Dr., Suite 212, Lake Park, FL 33403
Camillus Cutlery Co., 54 Main St., Camillus, NY 13031 / 315-672-8111; FAX: 315-672-8832
Camp-Cap Products, P.O. Box 3805, Chesterfield, MO 63006 / 314-532-4340; FAX: 314-532-4340
Campbell, Dick, 20000 Silver Ranch Rd., Conifer, CO 80433 / 303-697-0150; FAX: 303-697-0150
Cannon, Andy. See: CANNON'S
Cannon Safe, Inc., 9358 Stephens St., Pico Rivera, CA 90660 / 310-692-0636 or 800-242-1055; FAX: 310-692-7252
Cannon's, Andy Cannon , Box 1026, 320 Main St., Polson, MT 59860 / 406-887-2048
Canons Delcour, Rue J.B. Cools, B-4040, Herstal, BELGIUM / +32.(0)42.40.61.40; FAX: +32(0)42.40.22.88
Canyon Cartridge Corp., P.O. Box 152, Albertson, NY 11507 FAX: 516-294-8946
Cape Outfitters, 599 County Rd. 206, Cape Girardeau, MO 63701 / 573-335-4103; FAX: 573-335-1555
Caraville Manufacturing, P.O. Box 4545, Thousand Oaks, CA 91359 / 805-499-1234
Carbide Checkering Tools (See J&R Engineering)
Carbide Die & Mfg. Co., Inc., 15615 E. Arrow Hwy., Irwindale, CA 91706 / 818-337-2518
Carhartt ,Inc., P.O. Box 600, 3 Parklane Blvd., Dearborn, MI 48121 / 800-358-3825 or 313-271-8460; FAX: 313-271-3455
Carl Walther GmbH, B.P. 4325, D-89033, Ulm, GERMANY
Carl Walther USA, PO Box 208, Ten Prince St, Alexandria, VA 22313 / 703-548-1400; FAX: 703-549-7826
Carl Zeiss Optical, 1015 Commerce St., Petersburg, VA 23803 / 804-861-0033 or 800-388-2984; FAX: 804-733-4024
Carlson, Douglas R, Antique American Firearms, PO Box 71035, Dept GD, Des Moines, IA 50325 / 515-224-6552
Carnahan Bullets, 17645 110th Ave. SE, Renton, WA 98055
Carolina Precision Rifles, 1200 Old Jackson Hwy., Jackson, SC 29831 / 803-827-2069
Carrell's Precision Firearms, 643 Clark Ave., Billings, MT 59101-1614 / 406-962-3593
Carry-Lite, Inc., 5203 W. Clinton Ave., Milwaukee, WI 53223 / 414-355-3520; FAX: 414-355-4775
Carter's Gun Shop, 225 G St., Penrose, CO 81240 / 719-372-6240
Cartridge Transfer Group, Pete de Coux, 235 Oak St., Butler, PA 16001 / 412-282-3426
Cascade Bullet Co., Inc., 2355 South 6th St., Klamath Falls, OR 97601 / 503-884-9316
Cascade Shooters, 2155 N.W. 12th St., Redwood, OR 97756
Case & Sons Cutlery Co., W R, Owens Way, Bradford, PA 16701 / 814-368-4123 or 800-523-6350; FAX: 814-768-5369
Case Sorting System, 12695 Cobblestone Creek Rd., Poway, CA 92064 / 619-486-9340
Cash Mfg. Co., Inc., P.O. Box 130, 201 S. Klein Dr., Waunakee, WI 53597-0130 / 608-849-5664; FAX: 608-849-5664
Caspian Arms, Ltd., 14 North Main St., Hardwick, VT 05843 / 802-472-6454; FAX: 802-472-6709
Cast Performance Bullet Company, 113 Riggs Rd, Shoshoni, WY 82649 / 307-856-4347
Casull Arms Corp., P.O. Box 1629, Afton, WY 83110 / 307-886-0200
Caswell Detroit Armor Companies, 1221 Marshall St. NE, Minneapolis, MN 55413-1055 / 612-379-2000; FAX: 612-379-2367
Catco-Ambush, Inc., P.O.Box 300, Corte Madera, CA 94926
Cathey Enterprises, Inc., P.O. Box 2202, Brownwood, TX 76804 / 915-643-2553; FAX: 915-643-3653
Cation, 2341 Alger St., Troy, MI 48083 / 810-689-0658; FAX: 810-689-7558
Caywood, Shane J., P.O. Box 321, Minocqua, WI 54548 / 715-277-3866
CBC, Avenida Humberto de Campos 3220, 09400-000, Ribeirao Pires, SP, BRAZIL / 55-11-742-7500; FAX: 55-11-459-7385
CBC-BRAZIL, 3 Cuckoo Lane, Honley, Yorkshire HD7 2BR, ENGLAND / 44-1484-661062; FAX: 44-1484-663709
CCG Enterprises, 5217 E. Belknap St., Halton City, TX 76117 / 800-819-7464
CCI Div. of Blount, Inc., Sporting Equipment Div.2299 Sn, P.O. Box 856, Lewiston, ID 83501 / 800-627-3640 or 208-746-2351; FAX: 208-746-2915
CCL Security Products, 199 Whiting St, New Britain, CT 06051 / 800-733-8588
Cedar Hill Game Calls Inc., 238 Vic Allen Rd, Downsville, LA 71234 / 318-982-5632; FAX: 318-368-2245
Celestron International, P.O. Box 3578, 2835 Columbia St., Torrance, CA 90503 / 310-328-9560; FAX: 310-212-5835
Centaur Systems, Inc., 1602 Foothill Rd., Kalispell, MT 59901 / 406-755-8609; FAX: 406-755-8609
Center Lock Scope Rings, 9901 France Ct., Lakeville, MN 55044 / 612-461-2114
Central Specialties Ltd (See Trigger Lock Division
Century Gun Dist. Inc., 1467 Jason Rd., Greenfield, IN 46140 / 317-462-4524
Century International Arms, Inc., P.O. Box 714, St. Albans, VT 05478-0714 / 802-527-1252 or 800-527-1252; FAX: 802-527-0470
CFVentures, 509 Harvey Dr., Bloomington, IN 47403-1715
CH Tool & Die Co (See 4-D Custom Die Co), 711 N Sandusky St, PO Box 889, Mt Vernon, OH 43050-0889 / 740-397-7214; FAX: 740-397-6600
Chace Leather Products, 507 Alden St., Fall River, MA 02722 / 508-678-7556; FAX: 508-675-9666
Chadick's Ltd., P.O. Box 100, Terrell, TX 75160 / 214-563-7577
Chambers Flintlocks Ltd., Jim, 116 Sams Branch Rd, Candler, NC 28715 / 828-667-8361 FAX: 828-665-0852
Champion Shooters' Supply, P.O. Box 303, New Albany, OH 43054 / 614-855-1603; FAX: 614-855-1209
Champion Target Co., 232 Industrial Parkway, Richmond, IN 47374 / 800-441-4971
Champion's Choice, Inc., 201 International Blvd., LaVergne, TN 37086 / 615-793-4066; FAX: 615-793-4070
Champlin Firearms, Inc., P.O. Box 3191, Woodring Airport, Enid, OK 73701 / 580-237-7388; FAX: 580-242-6922
Chapman Academy of Practical Shooting, 4350 Academy Rd., Hallsville, MO 65255 / 573-696-5544 or 573-696-2266
Chapman, J Ken. See: OLD WEST BULLET MOULDS
Chapman Manufacturing Co., 471 New Haven Rd., P.O. Box 250, Durham, CT 06422 / 860-349-9228; FAX: 860-349-0084
Chapuis Armes, 21 La Gravoux, BP15, 42380, St. Bonnet-le-Chatea, FRANCE / (33)77.50.06.96+
Chapuis USA, 416 Business Park, Bedford, KY 40006
Charter 2000, 273 Canal St, Shelton, CT 06484 / 203-922-1652
Checkmate Refinishing, 370 Champion Dr., Brooksville, FL 34601 / 904-799-5774
Cheddite France S.A., 99 Route de Lyon, F-26501, Bourg-les-Valence, FRANCE / 33-75-56-4545; FAX: 33-75-56-3587
Chelsea Gun Club of New York City Inc., 237 Ovington Ave., Apt. D53, Brooklyn, NY 11209 / 718-836-9422 or 718-833-2704
Chem-Pak Inc., 11 Oates Ave., P.O. Box 1685, Winchester, VA 22604 / 800-336-9828 or 703-667-1341 FAX: 703-722-3993
Chet Fulmer's Antique Firearms, P.O. Box 792, Rt. 2 Buffalo Lake, Detroit Lakes, MN 56501 / 218-847-7712
CheVron Bullets, RR1, Ottawa, IL 61350 / 815-433-2471
Cheyenne Crt'g Boxes, PO Box 28425, Kansas City, MO 64188 / 816-413-9196
Chicago Cutlery Co., 1536 Beech St., Terre Haute, IN 47804 / 800-457-2665
Chicasaw Gun Works, 4 Mi. Mkr., Pluto Rd. Box 868, Shady Spring, WV 25918-0868 / 304-763-2848 FAX: 304-763-3725
Chipmunk (See Oregon Arms, Inc.)
Choate Machine & Tool Co., Inc., P.O. Box 218, 116 Lovers Ln., Bald Knob, AR 72010 / 501-724-6193 or 800-972-6390; FAX: 501-724-5873
Chopie Mfg.,Inc., 700 Copeland Ave., LaCrosse, WI 54603 / 608-784-0926
Christensen Arms, 385 N. 3050 E., St. George, UT 84790 / 435-624-9535; FAX: 435-674-9293
Christie's East, 219 E. 67th St., New York, NY 10021 / 212-606-0400
Chu Tani Ind., Inc., P.O. Box 2064, Cody, WY 82414-2064
Chuck's Gun Shop, P.O. Box 597, Waldo, FL 32694 / 904-468-2264
Churchill (See U.S. Importer-Ellett Bros)
Churchill Glove Co., James, PO Box 298, Centralia, WA 98531 / 360-736-2816 FAX: 360-330-0151
Churchill, Winston, Twenty Mile Stream Rd., RFD P.O. Box 29B, Proctorsville, VT 05153 / 802-226-7772
CIDCO, 21480 Pacific Blvd., Sterling, VA 22170 / 703-444-5353
Ciener Inc., Jonathan Arthur, 8700 Commerce St., Cape Canaveral, FL 32920 / 407-868-2200; FAX: 407-868-2201
Cimarron F.A. Co., P.O. Box 906, Fredericksburg, TX 78624-0906 / 210-997-9090; FAX: 210-997-0802
Cincinnati Swaging, 2605 Marlington Ave., Cincinnati, OH 45208
Clark Custom Guns, Inc., 336 Shootout Lane, Princeton, LA 71067 / 318-949-9884; FAX: 318-949-9829
Clark Firearms Engraving, P.O. Box 80746, San Marino, CA 91118 / 818-287-1652
Clarkfield Enterprises, Inc., 1032 10th Ave., Clarkfield, MN 56223 / 612-669-7140
Claro Walnut Gunstock Co., 1235 Stanley Ave., Chico, CA 95928 / 530-342-5188; FAX: 530-342-5199
Classic Arms Company, Rt 1 Box 120F, Burnet, TX 78611 / 512-756-4001
Classic Arms Corp., P.O. Box 106, Dunsmuir, CA 96025-0106 / 916-235-2000
Classic Guns, Inc., Frank S. Wood, 3230 Medlock Bridge Rd., Suite 110, Norcross, GA 30092 / 404-242-7944
Classic Old West Styles, 1060 Doniphan Park Circle C, El Paso, TX 79936 / 915-587-0684
Claybuster Wads & Harvester Bullets, 309 Sequoya Dr., Hopkinsville, KY 42240 / 800-922-6287 or 800-284-1746; FAX: 502-885-8088 50
Clean Shot Technologies, 21218 St. Andrews Blvd. Ste 504, Boca Raton, FL 33433 / 888-866-2532
Clear Creek Outdoors, Pat LaBoone , 2550 Hwy 23, Wrenshall, MN 55797 / 218-384-3670
Clearview Mfg. Co., Inc., 413 S. Oakley St., Fordyce, AR 71742 / 501-352-8557; FAX: 501-352-7120
Clearview Products, 3021 N. Portland, Oklahoma City, OK 73107
Cleland's Outdoor World, Inc, 10306 Airport Hwy, Swanton, OH 43558 / 419-865-4713; FAX: 419-865-5865
Clements' Custom Leathercraft, Chas, 1741 Dallas St., Aurora, CO 80010-2018 / 303-364-0403; FAX: 303-739-9824
Clenzoil Corp., P.O. Box 80226, Sta. C, Canton, OH 44708-0226 / 330-833-9758; FAX: 330-833-4724
Clift Mfg., L. R., 3821 hammonton Rd, Marysville, CA 95901 / 916-755-3390; FAX: 916-755-3393
Clift Welding Supply & Cases, 1332-A Colusa Hwy., Yuba City, CA 95993 / 916-755-3390 FAX: 916-755-3393
Cloward's Gun Shop, 4023 Aurora Ave. N, Seattle, WA 98103 / 206-632-2072
Clymer Manufacturing Co. Inc., 1645 W. Hamlin Rd., Rochester Hills, MI 48309-3312 / 248-853-5555; FAX: 248-853-1530
Cobalt Mfg., Inc., 4020 Mcewen Rd Ste 180, Dallas, TX 75244-5090 / 817-382-8986 FAX: 817-383-4281
Cobra Sport S.r.l., Via Caduti Nei Lager No. 1, 56020 San Romano, Montopoli v/Arno (Pi, ITALY / 0039-571-450490; FAX: 0039-571-450492
Coffin, Jim. See: WORKING GUNS
Coffin, Charles H., 3719 Scarlet Ave., Odessa, TX 79762 / 915-366-4729 FAX: 915-366-4729
Coffin, Jim (See Working Guns)
Cogar's Gunsmithing, P.O. Box 755, Houghton Lake, MI 48629 / 517-422-4591
Coghlan's Ltd., 121 Irene St., Winnipeg, MB R3T 4C7 CANADA / 204-284-9550; FAX: 204-475-4127
Cold Steel Inc., 2128-D Knoll Dr., Ventura, CA 93003 / 800-255-4716 or 800-624-2363 FAX: 805-642-9727
Cole's Gun Works, Old Bank Building, Rt. 4 Box 250, Moyock, NC 27958 / 919-435-2345
Cole-Grip, 16135 Cohasset St., Van Nuys, CA 91406 / 818-782-4424
Coleman Co., Inc., 250 N. St. Francis, Wichita, KS 67201
Coleman's Custom Repair, 4035 N. 20th Rd., Arlington, VA 22207 / 703-528-4486
Collectors Firearms Etc, P.O. Box 62, Minnesota City, MN 55959 / 507-689-2925
Collings, Ronald, 1006 Cielta Linda, Vista, CA 92083
Colonial Arms, Inc., P.O. Box 636, Selma, AL 36702-0636 / 334-872-9455; FAX: 334-872-9540
Colonial Knife Co., Inc., P.O. Box 3327, Providence, RI 02909 / 401-421-1600; FAX: 401-421-2047
Colonial Repair, 47 NAVARRE ST, ROSLINDALE, MA 02131-4725 / 617-469-4951
Colorado Gunsmithing Academy, 27533 Highway 287 South, Lamar, CO 81052 / 719-336-4099 or 800-754-2046; FAX: 719-336-9642
Colorado School of Trades, 1575 Hoyt St., Lakewood, CO 80215 / 800-234-4594; FAX: 303-233-4723
Colorado Sutlers Arsenal (See Cumberland States Ar
Colt Blackpowder Arms Co., 110 8th Street, Brooklyn, NY 11215 / 212-925-2159; FAX: 212-966-4986
Colt's Mfg. Co., Inc., P.O. Box 1868, Hartford, CT 06144-1868 / 800-962-COLT or 860-236-6311; FAX: 860-244-1449
Combat Military Ordnance Ltd., 3900 Hopkins St., Savannah, GA 31405 / 912-238-1900; FAX: 912-236-7570
Compass Industries , Inc., 104 East 25th St., New York, NY 10010 / 212-473-2614 or 800-221-9904; FAX: 212-353-0826
Compasseco, Ltd., 151 Atkinson Hill Ave., Bardtown, KY 40004 / 502-349-0910
Competition Electronics, Inc., 3469 Precision Dr., Rockford, IL 61109 / 815-874-8001; FAX: 815-874-8181

MANUFACTURER'S DIRECTORY

Competitive Pistol Shop, The, 5233 Palmer Dr., Ft. Worth, TX 76117-2433 / 817-834-8479
Competitor Corp. Inc., Appleton Business Center, 30 Tricnit Road Unit 16, New Ipswich, NH 03071 / 603-878-3891; FAX: 603-878-3950
Component Concepts, Inc., 530 S Springbrook Dr, Newberg, OR 97132-7056 / 503-554-8095 FAX: 503-554-9370
Concept Development Corp., 14715 N. 78th Way, Suite 300, Scottsdale, AZ 85260 / 800-472-4405; FAX: 602-948-7560
Conetrol Scope Mounts, 10225 Hwy. 123 S., Seguin, TX 78155 / 210-379-3030 or 800-CONETROL; FAX: 210-379-3030
CONKKO, P.O. Box 40, Broomall, PA 19008 / 215-356-0711
Connecticut Shotgun Mfg. Co., P.O. Box 1692, 35 Woodland St., New Britain, CT 06051 / 860-225-6581; FAX: 860-832-8707
Connecticut Valley Classics (See CVC)
Conrad, C. A., 3964 Ebert St., Winston-Salem, NC 27127 / 919-788-5469
Cook Engineering Service, 891 Highbury Rd., Vict, 3133 AUSTRALIA
Coonan Arms (JS Worldwide DBA), 1745 Hwy. 36 E., Maplewood, MN 55109 / 612-777-3156; FAX: 612-777-3683
Cooper Arms, P.O. Box 114, Stevensville, MT 59870 / 406-777-5534; FAX: 406-777-5228
Cooper-Woodward, 3800 Pelican Rd., Helena, MT 59602 / 406-458-3800
Cor-Bon Bullet & Ammo Co., 1311 Industry Rd., Sturgis, SD 57785 / 800-626-7266; FAX: 800-923-2666
Corbin Mfg. & Supply, Inc., 600 Industrial Circle, P.O. Box 2659, White City, OR 97503 / 541-826-5211; FAX: 541-826-8669
Corkys Gun Clinic, 4401 Hot Springs Dr., Greeley, CO 80634-9226 / 970-330-0516
Corry, John, 861 Princeton Ct., Neshanic Station, NJ 08853 / 908-369-8019
Cosmi Americo & Figlio s.n.c., Via Flaminia 307, Ancona, ITALY / 071-888208; FAX: 39-071-887008+
Coulston Products, Inc., P.O. Box 30, 201 Ferry St. Suite 212, Easton, PA 18044-0030 / 215-253-0167 or 800-445-9927; FAX: 215-252-1511
Counter Assault, Box 4721, Missoula, MT 59806 / 406-728-6241 FAX: 406-728-8800
Country Armourer, The, P.O. Box 308, Ashby, MA 01431-0308 / 508-827-6797; FAX: 508-827-4845
Cousin Bob's Mountain Products, 7119 Ohio River Blvd., Ben Avon, PA 15202 / 412-766-5114 FAX: 412-766-5114
Cox, Ed. C., RD 2, Box 192, Prosperity, PA 15329 / 412-228-4984
CP Bullets, 1310 Industrial Hwy #5-6, South Hampton, PA 18966 / 215-953-7264; FAX: 215-953-7275
CQB Training, P.O. Box 1739, Manchester, MO 63011
Craftguard, 3624 Logan Ave., Waterloo, IA 50703 / 319-232-2959 FAX: 319-234-0804
Craig Custom Ltd., Research & Development, 629 E. 10th, Hutchinson, KS 67501 / 316 669-0601
Craig, Spegel, P.O. Box 3108, Bay City, OR 97107 / 503-377-2697
Crandall Tool & Machine Co., 19163 21 Mile Rd., Tustin, MI 49688 / 616-829-4430
Creative Concepts USA, Inc., P.O. Box 1705, Dickson, TN 37056 / 615-446-8346 or 800-874-6965 FAX: 615-446-0646
Creative Craftsman, Inc., The, 95 Highway 29 North, P.O. Box 331, Lawrenceville, GA 30246 / 404-963-2112; FAX: 404-513-9488
Creedmoor Sports, Inc., P.O. Box 1040, Oceanside, CA 92051 / 619-757-5529
Creek Side Metal & Woodcrafters, Fishers Hill, VA 22626 / 703-465-3903
Creekside Gun Shop Inc., Main St., Holcomb, NY 14469 / 716-657-6338 FAX: 716-657-7900
Creighton Audette, 19 Highland Circle, Springfield, VT 05156 / 802-885-2331
Crimson Trace Lasers, 1433 N.W. Quimby, Portland, OR 97209 / 503-295-2406; FAX: 503-295-2225
Crit'R Call (See Rocky Mountain Wildlife Products)
Crosman Airguns, Rts. 5 and 20, E. Bloomfield, NY 14443 / 716-657-6161 FAX: 716-657-5405
Crosman Blades (See Coleman Co., Inc.)
Crosman Products of Canada Ltd., 1173 N. Service Rd. West, Oakville, ON L6M 2V9 CANADA / 905-827-1822
Crossfire, L.L.C., 2169 Greenville Rd., La Grange, GA 30241 / 706-882-8070 FAX: 706-882-9050
Crouse's Country Cover, P.O. Box 160, Storrs, CT 06268 / 860-423-8736
CRR , Inc./Marble's Inc., 420 Industrial Park, P.O. Box 111, Gladstone, MI 49837 / 906-428-3710; FAX: 906-428-3711
Crucelegui, Hermanos (See U.S. Importer-Mandall Sh
Cryo-Accurizing, 2101 East Olive, Decatur, IL 62526 / 217-423-3070 FAX: 217-423-3075
Cubic Shot Shell Co., Inc., 98 Fatima Dr., Campbell, OH 44405 / 330-755-0349
Cullity Restoration, 209 Old Country Rd., East Sandwich, MA 02537 / 508-888-1147
Cumberland Arms, 514 Shafer Road, Manchester, TN 37355 / 800-797-8414
Cumberland Mountain Arms, P.O. Box 710, Winchester, TN 37398 / 615-967-8414; FAX: 615-967-9199
Cumberland States Arsenal, 1124 Palmyra Road, Clarksville, TN 37040
Cummings Bullets, 1417 Esperanza Way, Escondido, CA 92027
Cupp, Alana, Custom Engraver, PO Box 207, Annabella, UT 84711 / 801-896-4834
Curly Maple Stock Blanks (See Tiger-Hunt)
Curtis Cast Bullets, 527 W. Babcock St., Bozeman, MT 59715 / 406-587-8117; FAX: 406-587-8117
Curtis Custom Shop, RR1, Box 193A, Wallingford, KY 41093 / 703-659-4265
Curtis Gun Shop (See Curtis Cast Bullets)
Custom Bullets by Hoffman, 2604 Peconic Ave., Seaford, NY 11783
Custom Calls, 607 N. 5th St., Burlington, IA 52601 / 319-752-4465
Custom Checkering Service, Kathy Forster, 2124 SE Yamhill St., Portland, OR 97214 / 503-236-5874
Custom Chronograph, Inc., 5305 Reese Hill Rd., Sumas, WA 98295 / 360-988-7801
Custom Firearms (See Ahrends, Kim)
Custom Gun Products, 5021 W. Rosewood, Spokane, WA 99208 / 509-328-9340
Custom Gun Stocks, 3062 Turners Bend Rd, P.O. Box 177, McMinnville, TN 37110 / 615-668-3912
Custom Gunsmiths, 4303 Friar Lane, Colorado Springs, CO 80907 / 719-599-3366
Custom Products (See Jones Custom Products)
Custom Quality Products, Inc., 345 W. Girard Ave., P.O. Box 71129, Madison Heights, MI 48071 / 810-585-1616; FAX: 810-585-0644
Custom Riflestocks, Inc., Michael M. Kokolus, 7005 Herber Rd., New Tripoli, PA 18066 / 610-298-3013
Custom Shop, The, 890 Cochrane Crescent, Peterborough, ON K0H 5N3 CANADA / 705-742-6693
Custom Tackle and Ammo, P.O. Box 1886, Farmington, NM 87499 / 505-632-3539
Cutco Cutlery, P.O. Box 810, Olean, NY 14760 / 716-372-3111
CVA, 5988 Peachtree Corners East, Norcross, GA 30071 / 800-251-9412; FAX: 404-242-8546
CVC, 48 Commercial Street, Holyoke, MA 01040 / 413-552-3184; FAX: 413-552-3276
Cylinder & Slide, Inc., William R. Laughridge, 245 E. 4th St., Fremont, NE 68025 / 402-721-4277; FAX: 402-721-0263
CZ USA, 1401 Fairfax Traffic WYA, B119, Kansas City, KS 66115 / 913-321-1811; FAX: 913-321-4901

D

D&D Gunsmiths, Ltd., 363 E. Elmwood, Troy, MI 48083 / 810-583-1512; FAX: 810-583-1524
D&G Precision Duplicators (See Greene Precision Du
D&H Precision Tooling, 7522 Barnard Mill Rd., Ringwood, IL 60072 / 815-653-4011
D&H Prods. Co., Inc., 465 Denny Rd., Valencia, PA 16059 / 412-898-2840 or 800-776-0281; FAX: 412-898-2013
D&J Bullet Co. & Custom Gun Shop, Inc., 426 Ferry St., Russell, KY 41169 / 606-836-2663; FAX: 606-836-2663
D&L Industries (See D.J. Marketing)
D&L Sports, P.O. Box 651, Gillette, WY 82717 / 307-686-4008
D&R Distributing, 308 S.E. Valley St., Myrtle Creek, OR 97457 / 503-863-6850
D-Boone Ent., Inc., 5900 Colwyn Dr., Harrisburg, PA 17109
D.B.A. Flintlocks, Etc, 160 Rossiter Rd., P.O. Box 181, Richmond, MA 01254 / 413-698-3822; FAX: 413-698-3866
D.C.C. Enterprises, 259 Wynburn Ave., Athens, GA 30601
D.D. Custom Stocks, R.H. "Dick" Devereaux, 5240 Mule Deer Dr., Colorado Springs, CO 80919 / 719-548-8468
D.J. Marketing, 10602 Horton Ave., Downey, CA 90241 / 310-806-0891; FAX: 310-806-6231
Dade Screw Machine Products, 2319 NW 7th Ave., Miami, FL 33127 / 305-573-5050
Daewoo Precision Industries Ltd., 34-3 Yeoeuido-Dong, Yeongdeungoo-GU 15th Fl., Seoul, KOREA
Daisy Mfg. Co., PO Box 220, Rogers, AR 72757 / 501-621-4210; FAX: 501-636-0573
Dakota (See U.S. Importer-EMF Co., Inc.)
Dakota Arms, Inc., HC 55, Box 326, Sturgis, SD 57785 / 605-347-4686; FAX: 605-347-4459
Dakota Corp., 77 Wales St., P.O. Box 543, Rutland, VT 05701 / 802-775-6062 or 800-451-4167; FAX: 802-773-3919
Dale Wise Guns, 333 W. Olmos Dr., San Antonio, TX 78212 / 210-828-3388
DAMASCUS-U.S.A., 149 Deans Farm Rd., Tyner, NC 27980 / 252-221-2010; FAX: 252-221-2009
DAN WESSON FIREARMS, 119 Kemper Lane, Norwich, NY 13815 / 607-336-1174; FAX: FAX:607-336-2730
Dan's Whetstone Co., Inc., 130 Timbs Place, Hot Springs, AR 71913 / 501-767-1616; FAX: 501-767-9598
Danforth, Mikael. See: VEKTOR USA
Dangler, Homer L., Box 254, Addison, MI 49220 / 517-547-6745
Danner Shoe Mfg. Co., 12722 NE Airport Way, Portland, OR 97230 / 503-251-1100 or 800-345-0430; FAX: 503-251-1119
Danuser Machine Co., 550 E. Third St., P.O. Box 368, Fulton, MO 65251 / 573-642-2246; FAX: 573-642-2240
Dara-Nes, Inc. (See Nesci Enterprises, Inc.)
Darlington Gun Works, Inc., P.O. Box 698, 516 S. 52 Bypass, Darlington, SC 29532 / 803-393-3931
Darwin Hensley Gunmaker, P.O. Box 329, Brightwood, OR 97011 / 503-622-5411
Data Tech Software Systems, 19312 East Eldorado Drive, Aurora, CO 80013
Datumtech Corp., 2275 Wehrle Dr., Buffalo, NY 14221
Dave Norin Schrank's Smoke & Gun, 2010 Washington St., Waukegan, IL 60085 / 708-662-4034
Dave's Gun Shop, 555 Wood Street, Powell, WY 82435 / 307-754-9724
David Clark Co., Inc., PO Box 15054, Worcester, MA 01615-0054 / 508-756-6216; FAX: 508-753-5827
David Condon, Inc., 109 E. Washington St., Middleburg, VA 22117 / 703-687-5642
David Miller Co., 3131 E Greenlee Rd, Tucson, AZ 85716 / 520-326-3117
David W. Schwartz Custom Guns, 2505 Waller St, Eau Claire, WI 54703 / 715-832-1735
Davide Pedersoli and Co., Via Artigiani 57, Gardone VT, Brescia 25063, ITALY / 030-8912402; FAX: 030-8911019
Davidson, Jere, Rt. 1, Box 132, Rustburg, VA 24588 / 804-821-3637
Davis Industries, 15150 Sierra Bonita Ln., Chino, CA 91710 / 909-597-4726; FAX: 909-393-9771
Davis Leather Co., Gordon Wm., PO Box 2270, Walnut, CA 91788 / 909-598-5620
Davis Products, Mike, 643 Loop Dr., Moses Lake, WA 98837 / 509-765-6178 or 509-766-7281
Davis, Don, 1619 Heights, Katy, TX 77493 / 713-391-3090
Day & Sons Inc., Leonard, PO Box 122, Flagg Hill Rd., Heath, MA 01346 / 413-337-8369
Daystate Ltd., Birch House Lanee, Cotes Heath Staffs, ST15.022, ENGLAND / 01782-791755; FAX: 01782-791617
Dayton Traister, 4778 N. Monkey Hill Rd., P.O. Box 593, Oak Harbor, WA 98277 / 360-679-4657; FAX: 360-675-1114
DBI Books Division of Krause Publications (Edito, 700 E State St, Iola, WI 54990-0001 / 630-759-1229
de Coux, Pete (See Cartridge Transfer Group)
Dead Eye's Sport Center, RD 1, Box 147B, Shickshinny, PA 18655 / 570-256-7432
Decker Shooting Products, 1729 Laguna Ave., Schofield, WI 54476 / 715-359-5873
Deepeeka Exports Pvt. Ltd., D-78, Saket, Meerut-250-006, INDIA / 011-91-121-512889 or 011-91-121-545363; FAX: 011-91-121-542988
Deer Me Products Co., Box 34, 1208 Park St., Anoka, MN 55303 / 612-421-8971; FAX: 612-422-0526
Defense Training International, Inc., 749 S. Lemay, Ste. A3-337, Ft. Collins, CO 80524 / 303-482-2520; FAX: 303-482-0548
Degen Inc. (See Aristocrat Knives)
deHaas Barrels, RR 3, Box 77, Ridgeway, MO 64481 / 816-872-6308
Del Rey Products, P.O. Box 5134, Playa Del Rey, CA 90296-5134 / 213-823-0494
Del-Sports, Inc., Box 685, Main St., Margaretville, NY 12455 / 914-586-4103; FAX: 914-586-4105
Delhi Gun House, 1374 Kashmere Gate, Delhi, 0110 006 INDIA FAX: 91-11-2917344
Delorge, Ed, 2231 Hwy. 308, Thibodaux, LA 70301 / 504-447-1633
Delta Arms Ltd., P.O. Box 1000, Delta, VT 84624-1000
Delta Enterprises, 284 Hagemann Drive, Livermore, CA 94550
Delta Frangible Ammunition LLC, P.O. Box 2350, Stafford, VA 22555-2350 / 540-720-5778 or 800-339-1933; FAX: 540-720-5667
Dem-Bart Checkering Tools, Inc., 6807 Bickford Ave., Old Hwy. 2, Snohomish, WA 98290 / 360-568-7356; FAX: 360-568-1798
Denver Instrument Co., 6542 Fig St., Arvada, CO 80004 / 800-321-1135 or 303-431-7255; FAX: 303-423-4831
DeSantis Holster & Leather Goods, Inc., P.O. Box 2039, 149 Denton Ave., New Hyde Park, NY 11040-0701 / 516-354-8000; FAX: 516-354-7501
Desert Mountain Mfg., P.O. Box 130184, Coram, MT 59913 / 800-477-0762 or 406-387-5361; FAX: 406-387-5361
Detroit-Armor Corp., 720 Industrial Dr. No. 112, Cary, IL 60013 / 708-639-7666; FAX: 708-639-7694
Dever Co, Jack, 8590 NW 90, Oklahoma City, OK 73132 / 405-721-6393
Devereaux, R.H. "Dick" (See D.D. Custom S
Dewey Mfg. Co., Inc., J., P.O. Box 2014, Southbury, CT 06488 / 203-264-3064; FAX: 203-262-6907
DGR Custom Rifles, 4191 37th Ave SE, Tappen, ND 58487 / 701-327-8135
DGS, Inc., Dale A. Storey, 1117 E. 12th, Casper, WY 82601
DHB Products, P.O. Box 3092, Alexandria, VA 22302 / 703-836-2648
Diamond Machining Technology, Inc. (See DMT)

Manufacturer's Directory

Diamond Mfg. Co., P.O. Box 174, Wyoming, PA 18644 / 800-233-9601
Diana (See U.S. Importer - Dynamit Nobel-RWS, Inc., 81 Ruckman Rd., Closter, NJ 07624 / 201-767-7971; FAX: 201-767-1589
Dibble, Derek A., 555 John Downey Dr., New Britain, CT 06051 / 203-224-2630
Dick Marple & Associates, 21 Dartmouth St, Hooksett, NH 03106 / 603-627-1837; FAX: 603-627-1837
Dietz Gun Shop & Range, Inc., 421 Range Rd., New Braunfels, TX 78132 / 210-885-4662
Dilliott Gunsmithing, Inc., 657 Scarlett Rd., Dandridge, TN 37725 / 423-397-9204
Dillon Precision Products, Inc., 8009 East Dillon's Way, Scottsdale, AZ 85260 / 602-948-8009 or 800-762-3845; FAX: 602-998-2786
Dillon, Ed, 1035 War Eagle Dr. N., Colorado Springs, CO 80919 / 719-598-4929; FAX: 719-598-4929
Dina Arms Corporation, P.O. Box 46, Royersford, PA 19468 / 610-287-0266; FAX: 610-287-0266
Division Lead Co., 7742 W. 61st Pl., Summit, IL 60502
Dixie Gun Works, Inc., Hwy. 51 South, Union City, TN 38261 / order 800-238-6785;
Dixon Muzzleloading Shop, Inc., 9952 Kunkels Mill Rd., Kempton, PA 19529 / 610-756-6271
DKT, Inc., 14623 Vera Drive, Union, MI 49130-9744 / 800-741-7083 orders; FAX: 616-641-2015
DLO Mfg., 10807 SE Foster Ave., Arcadia, FL 33821-7304
DMT--Diamond Machining Technology Inc., 85 Hayes Memorial Dr., Marlborough, MA 01752 FAX: 508-485-3924
Doctor Optic Technologies, Inc., 4685 Boulder Highway, Suite A, Las Vegas, NV 89121 / 800-290-3634 or 702-898-7161; FAX: 702-898-3737
Dogtown Varmint Supplies, 1048 Irvine Ave. No. 333, Newport Beach, CA 92660 / 714-642-3997
Dohring Bullets, 100 W. 8 Mile Rd., Ferndale, MI 48220
Dolbare, Elizabeth, P.O. Box 222, Sunburst, MT 59482-0222
Domino, PO Box 108, 20019 Settimo Milanese, Milano, ITALY / 1-39-2-33512040; FAX: 1-39-2-33511587
Donnelly, C. P., 405 Kubli Rd., Grants Pass, OR 97527 / 541-846-6604
Doskocil Mfg. Co., Inc., P.O. Box 1246, 4209 Barnett, Arlington, TX 76017 / 817-467-5116; FAX: 817-472-9810
Double A Ltd., P.O. Box 11306, Minneapolis, MN 55411 / 612-522-0306
Douglas Barrels Inc., 5504 Big Tyler Rd., Charleston, WV 25313-1398 / 304-776-1341; FAX: 304-776-8560
Downsizer Corp., P.O. Box 710316, Santee, CA 92072-0316 / 619-448-5510; FAX: 619-448-5780
Dr. O's Products Ltd., P.O. Box 111, Niverville, NY 12130 / 518-784-3333; FAX: 518-784-2800
Drain, Mark, SE 3211 Kamilche Point Rd., Shelton, WA 98584 / 206-426-5452
Dremel Mfg. Co., 4915-21st St., Racine, WI 53406
Dressel Jr., Paul G., 209 N. 92nd Ave., Yakima, WA 98908 / 509-966-9233; FAX: 509-966-3365
Dri-Slide, Inc., 411 N. Darling, Fremont, MI 49412 / 616-924-3950
Dropkick, 1460 Washington Blvd., Williamsport, PA 17701 / 717-326-6561; FAX: 717-326-4950
DTM International, Inc., 40 Joslyn Rd., P.O. Box 5, Lake Orion, MI 48362 / 313-693-6670
Du-Lite Corp., 171 River Rd., Middletown, CT 06457 / 203-347-2505; FAX: 203-347-9404
Duane A. Hobbie Gunsmithing, 2412 Pattie Ave, Wichita, KS 67216 / 316-264-8266
Duane's Gun Repair (See DGR Custom Rifles)
Dubber, Michael W., P.O. Box 312, Evansville, IN 47702 / 812-424-9000; FAX: 812-424-6551
Duck Call Specialists, P.O. Box 124, Jerseyville, IL 62052 / 618-498-9855
Duffy, Charles E (See Guns Antique & Modern DBA), Williams Lane, PO Box 2, West Hurley, NY 12491 / 914-679-2997
Dumoulin, Ernest, Rue Florent Boclinville 8-10, 13-4041, Votten, BELGIUM / 41 27 78 92
Duncan's Gun Works, Inc., 1619 Grand Ave., San Marcos, CA 92069 / 619-727-0515
Dunham Boots, 1 Keuka business Park #300, Penn Yan, NY 14527-8995 / 802-254-2316
Duofold, Inc., RD 3 Rt. 309, Valley Square Mall, Tamaqua, PA 18252 / 717-386-2666; FAX: 717-386-3652
Dutchman's Firearms, Inc., The, 4143 Taylor Blvd., Louisville, KY 40215 / 502-366-0555
Dybala Gun Shop, P.O. Box 1024, FM 3156, Bay City, TX 77414 / 409-245-0866
Dykstra, Doug, 411 N. Darling, Fremont, MI 49412 / 616-924-3950
Dynalite Products, Inc., 215 S. Washington St., Greenfield, OH 45123 / 513-981-2124
Dynamit Nobel-RWS, Inc., 81 Ruckman Rd., Closter, NJ 07624 / 201-767-7971; FAX: 201-767-1589

E

E&L Mfg., Inc., 4177 Riddle By Pass Rd., Riddle, OR 97469 / 541-874-2137; FAX: 541-874-3107
E-A-R, Inc., Div. of Cabot Safety Corp., 5457 W. 79th St., Indianapolis, IN 46268 / 800-327-3431; FAX: 800-488-8007
E-Z-Way Systems, P.O. Box 4310, Newark, OH 43058-4310 / 614-345-6645 or 800-848-2072; FAX: 614-345-6600
E. Arthur Brown Co., 3404 Pawnee Dr., Alexandria, MN 56308 / 320-762-8847
E.A.A. Corp., P.O. Box 1299, Sharpes, FL 32959 / 407-639-4842 or 800-536-4442; FAX: 407-639-7006
Eagan, Donald V., P.O. Box 196, Benton, PA 17814 / 717-925-6134
Eagle Arms, Inc. (See ArmaLite, Inc.)
Eagle Grips, Eagle Business Center, 460 Randy Rd., Carol Stream, IL 60188 / 800-323-6144 or 708-260-0400; FAX: 708-260-0486
Eagle Imports, Inc., 1750 Brielle Ave., Unit B1, Wanamassa, NJ 07712 / 908-493-0333
EAW (See U.S. Importer-New England Custom Gun Serv
Echols & Co., D'Arcy, 164 W. 580 S., Providence, UT 84332 / 801-753-2367
Eckelman Gunsmithing, 3125 133rd St. SW, Fort Ripley, MN 56449 / 218-829-3176
Eclectic Technologies, Inc., 45 Grandview Dr., Suite A, Farmington, CT 06034
Ed~ Brown Products, Inc., 43825 Muldrow Trail, Perry, MO 63462 / 573-565-3261; FAX: 573-565-2791
Eddie Salter Calls, Inc., Hwy. 31 South-Brewton Industrial, Park, Brewton, AL 36426 / 205-867-2584; FAX: 206-867-9005
Edenpine, Inc. c/o Six Enterprises, Inc., 320 D Turtle Creek Ct., San Jose, CA 95125 / 408-999-0201; FAX: 408-999-0216
EdgeCraft Corp., P.B. Tuminello, 825 Southwood Road, Avondale, PA 19311 / 610-268-0500 or 800-342-3255; FAX: 610-268-3545
Edmisten Co., P.O. Box 1293, Boone, NC 28607
Edmund Scientific Co., 101 E. Gloucester Pike, Barrington, NJ 08033 / 609-543-6250
Ednar, Inc., 2-4-8 Kayabacho, Nihonbashi Chuo-ku, Tokyo, JAPAN / 81(Japan)-3-3667-1651; FAX: 81-3-3661-8113
Eezox, Inc., P.O. Box 772, Waterford, CT 06385-0772 / 800-462-3331; FAX: 860-447-3484
Effebi SNC-Dr. Franco Beretta, via Rossa, 4, 25062, ITALY / 030-2751955; FAX: 030-2180414
Efficient Machinery Co, 12878 NE 15th Pl, Bellevue, WA 98005
Eggleston, Jere D., 400 Saluda Ave., Columbia, SC 29205 / 803-799-3402
EGW Evolution Gun Works, 4050 B-8 Skyron Dr., Doylestown, PA 18901 / 215-348-9892; FAX: 215-348-1056
Eichelberger Bullets, Wm, 158 Crossfield Rd., King Of Prussia, PA 19406
Ekol Leather Care, P.O. Box 2652, West Lafayette, IN 47906 / 317-463-2250; FAX: 317-463-7004
El Dorado Leather (c/o Dill), P.O. Box 566, Benson, AZ 85602 / 520-586-4791; FAX: 520-586-4791
El Paso Saddlery Co., P.O. Box 27194, El Paso, TX 79926 / 915-544-2233; FAX: 915-544-2535
Eldorado Cartridge Corp (See PMC/Eldorado Cartridg
Electro Prismatic Collimators, Inc., 1441 Manatt St., Lincoln, NE 68521
Electronic Shooters Protection, Inc., 11997 West 85th Place, Arvada, CO 80005 / 800-797-7791; FAX: 303-456-7179
Electronic Trigger Systems, Inc., P.O. Box 13, 230 Main St. S., Hector, MN 55342 / 320-848-2760; FAX: 320-848-2760
Eley Ltd., P.O. Box 705, Witton, Birmingham, B6 7UT ENGLAND / 021-356-8899; FAX: 021-331-4173
Elite Ammunition, P.O. Box 3251, Oakbrook, IL 60522 / 708-366-9006
Elk River, Inc., 1225 Paonia St., Colorado Springs, CO 80915 / 719-574-4407
Elkhorn Bullets, P.O. Box 5293, Central Point, OR 97502 / 541-826-7440
Ellett Bros., 267 Columbia Ave., P.O. Box 128, Chapin, SC 29036 / 803-345-3751 or 800-845-3711; FAX: 803-345-1820
Ellicott Arms, Inc./Woods Pistolsmithing, 3840 Dahlgren Ct., Ellicott City, MD 21042 / 410-465-7979
Elliott Inc., G. W., 514 Burnside Ave, East Hartford, CT 06108 / 203-289-5741; FAX: 203-289-3137
Elsen Inc., Pete, 1529 S 113th St, West Allis, WI 53214
Emerging Technologies, Inc. (See Laseraim Technolo
EMF Co., Inc., 1900 E. Warner Ave., Suite 1-D, Santa Ana, CA 92705 / 714-261-6611; FAX: 714-756-0133
Empire Cutlery Corp., 12 Kruger Ct., Clifton, NJ 07013 / 201-472-5155; FAX: 201-779-0759
English, Inc., A.G., 708 S. 12th St., Broken Arrow, OK 74012 / 918-251-3399
Englishtown Sporting Goods Co., Inc., 38 Main St., Englishtown, NJ 07726 / 201-446-7717
Engraving Artistry, 36 Alto Rd., RFD 2, Burlington, CT 06013 / 203-673-6837
Enguix Import-Export, Alpujarras 58, Alzira, Valencia, SPAIN / (96) 241 43 95; FAX: (96) (241 43 95
Enhanced Presentations, Inc., 5929 Market St., Wilmington, NC 28405 / 910-799-1622; FAX: 910-799-5004
Enlow, Charles, 895 Box, Beaver, OK 73932 / 405-625-4487
Ensign-Bickford Co., The, 660 Hopmeadow St., Simsbury, CT 06070
Entre'prise Arms, Inc., 15861 Business Center Dr., Irwindale, CA 91706
EPC, 1441 Manatt St., Lincoln, NE 68521 / 402-476-3946
Epps, Ellwood (See "Gramps" Antique, Box 341, Washago, ON L0K 2B0 CANADA / 705-689-5348
Erhardt, Dennis, 3280 Green Meadow Dr., Helena, MT 59601 / 406-442-4533
Erma Werke GmbH, Johan Ziegler St., 13/15/FeldiglSt., D-8060 Dachau, GERMANY
Eskridge Rifles, Steven Eskridge , 218 N. Emerson, Mart, TX 76664 / 817-876-3544
Eskridge, Steven. See: ESKRIDGE RIFLES
Essex Arms, P.O. Box 363, Island Pond, VT 05846 / 802-723-6203 FAX: 802-723-6203
Essex Metals, 1000 Brighton St., Union, NJ 07083 / 800-282-8369
Estate Cartridge, Inc., 12161 FM 830, Willis, TX 77378 / 409-856-7277; FAX: 409-856-5486
Euber Bullets, No. Orwell Rd., Orwell, VT 05760 / 802-948-2621
Euro-Imports, 905 West Main St Ste E, El Cajon, CA 92020 / 619-442-7005; FAX: 619-442-7005
Euroarms of America, Inc., P.O. Box 3277, Winchester, VA 22604 / 540-662-1863; FAX: 540-662-4464
European American Armory Corp (See E.A.A. Corp)
Eutaw Co., Inc., The, P.O. Box 608, U.S. Hwy. 176 West, Holly Hill, SC 29059 / 803-496-3341
Evans Engraving, Robert, 332 Vine St, Oregon City, OR 97045 / 503-656-5693
Evans Gunsmithing (See Evans, Andrew)
Evans, Andrew, 2325 NW Squire St., Albany, OR 97321 / 541-928-3190; FAX: 541-928-4128
Eversull Co., Inc., K., 1 Tracemont, Boyce, LA 71409 / 318-793-8728; FAX: 318-793-5483
Excalibur Electro Optics Inc, P.O. Box 400, Fogelsville, PA 18051-0400 / 610-391-9105; FAX: 610-391-9220
Exe, Inc., 18830 Partridge Circle, Eden Prairie, MN 55346 / 612-944-7662
Executive Protection Institute, PO Box 802, Berryville, VA 22611 / 540-955-1128
Eyster Heritage Gunsmiths, Inc., Ken, 6441 Bishop Rd., Centerburg, OH 43011 / 614-625-6131
Eze-Lap Diamond Prods., P.O. Box 2229, 15164 West State St., Westminster, CA 92683 / 714-847-1555; FAX: 714-897-0280

F

F&A Inc. (See ShurKatch Corporation)
F.A.I.R. Techni-Mec s.n.c. di Isidoro Rizzini & C., Via Gitti, 41 Zona Industrial, 25060 Marcheno (Bres, ITALY / 030/861162-8610344; FAX: 030/8610179
Fabarm S.p.A., Via Averolda 31, 25039 Travagliato, Brescia, ITALY / 030-6863629; FAX: 030-6863684
Fagan & Co.Inc, 22952 15 Mile Rd, Clinton Township, MI 48035 / 810-465-4637; FAX: 810-792-6996
Fair Game International, P.O. Box 77234-34053, Houston, TX 77234 / 713-941-6269
Faith Associates, Inc., PO Box 549, Flat Rock, NC 28731-0549 / 828-692-1916; FAX: 828-697-6827
Fanzoj GmbH, Griesgasse 1, 9170 Ferlach, 9170 AUSTRIA / (43) 04227-2283; FAX: (43) 04227-2867
Far North Outfitters, Box 1252, Bethel, AK 99559
Farm Form Decoys, Inc., 1602 Biovu, P.O. Box 748, Galveston, TX 77553 / 409-744-0762 or 409-765-6361; FAX: 409-765-8513
Farmer-Dressel, Sharon, 209 N. 92nd Ave., Yakima, WA 98908 / 509-966-9233; FAX: 509-966-3365
Farr Studio,Inc., 1231 Robinhood Rd., Greeneville, TN 37743 / 615-638-8825
Farrar Tool Co., Inc., 12150 Bloomfield Ave., Suite E, Santa Fe Springs, CA 90670 / 310-863-4367; FAX: 310-863-5123
Faulhaber Wildlocker, Dipl.-Ing. Norbert Wittasek, Seilergasse 2, A-1010 Wien, AUSTRIA / OM-43-1-5137001; FAX: OM-43-1-5137001
Faulk's Game Call Co., Inc., 616 18th St., Lake Charles, LA 70601 / 318-436-9726 FAX: 318-494-7205
Faust Inc., T. G., 544 minor St, Reading, PA 19602 / 610-375-8549; FAX: 610-375-4488
Fausti Cav. Stefano & Figlie snc, Via Martiri Dell Indipendenza, 70, Marcheno, 25060 ITALY
Fautheree, Andy, P.O. Box 4607, Pagosa Springs, CO 81157 / 970-731-5003; FAX: 970-731-5009
Feather, Flex Decoys, 1655 Swan Lake Rd., Bossier City, LA 71111 / 318-746-8596; FAX: 318-742-4815
Federal Arms Corp. of America, 7928 University Ave, Fridley, MN 55432 / 612-780-8780; FAX: 612-780-8780
Federal Cartridge Co., 900 Ehlen Dr., Anoka, MN 55303 / 612-323-2300; FAX: 612-323-2506
Federal Champion Target Co., 232 Industrial Parkway, Richmond, IN 47374 / 800-441-4971; FAX: 317-966-7747
Federated-Fry (See Fry Metals)
FEG, Budapest, Soroksariut 158, H-1095, HUNGARY

Feken, Dennis, Rt. 2, Box 124, Perry, OK 73077 / 405-336-5611
Felk, Inc., 2121 Castlebridge Rd., Midlothian, VA 23113 / 804-794-3744
Fellowes, Ted, Beaver Lodge, 9245 16th Ave. SW, Seattle, WA 98106 / 206-763-1698
Feminine Protection, Inc., 949 W. Kearney Ste. 100, Mesquite, TX 75149 / 972-289-8997 FAX: 972-289-4410
Ferguson, Bill, P.O. Box 1238, Sierra Vista, AZ 85636 / 520-458-5321; FAX: 520-458-9125
FERLIB, Via Costa 46, 25063, Gardone V.T., ITALY / 30-89-12-586; FAX: 30-89-12-586
Ferris Firearms, 7110 F.M. 1863, Bulverde, TX 78163 / 210-980-4424
Fibron Products, Inc., P.O. Box 430, Buffalo, NY 14209-0430 / 716-886-2378; FAX: 716-886-2394
Fieldsport Ltd, Bryan Bilinski , 3313 W South Airport Rd, Traverse Vity, MI 49684 / 616-933-0767
Fiocchi Munizioni S.p.A. (See U.S. Importer-Fiocch
Fiocchi of America Inc., 5030 Fremont Rd., Ozark, MO 65721 / 417-725-4118 or 800-721-2666 FAX: 417-725-1039
Firearm Training Center, The, 9555 Blandville Rd., West Paducah, KY 42086 / 502-554-5886
Firearms Co Ltd/Alpine (See U.S. Importer-Mandall
Firearms Engraver's Guild of America, 332 Vine St., Oregon City, OR 97045 / 503-656-5693
Firearms International, 5709 Hartsdale, Houston, TX 77036 / 713-460-2447
First Inc, Jack, 1201 Turbine Dr., Rapid City, SD 57701 / 605-343-9544; FAX: 605-343-9420
Fish Mfg. Gunsmith Sptg. Co., Marshall F, Rd. Box 2439, Rt. 22 N, Westport, NY 12993 / 518-962-4897 FAX: 518-962-4897
Fisher Custom Firearms, 2199 S. Kittredge Way, Aurora, CO 80013 / 303-755-3710
Fisher Enterprises, Inc., 1071 4th Ave. S., Suite 303, Edmonds, WA 98020-4143 / 206-771-5382
Fisher, Jerry A., 553 Crane Mt. Rd., Big Fork, MT 59911 / 406-837-2722
Fisher, R. Kermit (See Fisher Enterprises, Inc), 1071 4th Ave S Ste 303, Edmonds, WA 98020-4143 / 206-771-5382
Fitz Pistol Grip Co., P.O. Box 744, LEWISTON, CA 96052-0744 / 916-778-0240
Flambeau Products Corp., 15981 Valplast Rd., Middlefield, OH 44062 / 216-632-1631; FAX: 216-632-1581
Flannery Engraving Co., Jeff W, 11034 Riddles Run Rd, Union, KY 41091 / 606-384 3127
Flashette Co., 4725 S. Kolin Ave., Chicago, IL 60632 FAX: 773-927-3083
Fleming Firearms, 7720 E 126th St. N, Collinsville, OK 74021 7016 / 918-665-3624
Flents Products Co., Inc., P.O. Box 2109, Norwalk, CT 06852 / 203-866-2581; FAX: 203-854-9322
Flintlocks Etc., 160 Rositter Rd, Richmond, MA 01254 / 413-698-3822
Flitz International Ltd., 821 Mohr Ave., Waterford, WI 53185 / 414 534 5808; FAX: 414-534-2991
Flores Publications Inc, J (See Action Direct Inc), PO Box 030760, Miami, FL 33283 / 305-559-4652; FAX: 305 559-4652
Fluoramics, Inc., 18 Industrial Ave., Mahwah, NJ 07430 / 800-922-0075, FAX: 201 825 7035
Flynn's Custom Guns, P.O. Box 7461, Alexandria, LA 71306 / 318-455-7130
FN Herstal, Voie de Liege 33, Herstal, 4040 Belgium / (32)41.40.82.83; FAX: (32)41.40.86.79
Fobus International Ltd., P.O. Box 64, Kfar Hess, 40692 ISRAEL / 972-9-7964170; FAX: 972-9-7964169
Folks, Donald E., 205 W. Lincoln St., Pontiac, IL 61764 / 815-844-7901
Foothills Video Productions, Inc., P.O. Box 651, Spartanburg, SC 29304 / 803-573-7023 or 800-782-5358
Foredom Electric Co., Rt. 6, 16 Stony Hill Rd., Bethel, CT 06801 / 203-792-8622
Forgett Jr., Valmore J., 689 Bergen Blvd., Ridgefield, NJ 07657 / 201-945-2500; FAX: 201-945-6859
Forgreens Tool Mfg., Inc., P.O. Box 990, 723 Austin St., Robert Lee, TX 76945 / 915-453-2800; FAX: 915-453-2460
Forkin Arms, 205 10th Ave SW, White Sulphur Spring, MT 59645 / 406-547-2344; FAX: 406-547-2456
Forkin, Ben (See Belt MTN Arms)
Forrest Inc., Tom, PO Box 326, Lakeside, CA 92040 / 619-561-5800; FAX: 619-561-0227
Forrest Tool Co., P.O. Box 768, 44380 Gordon Lane, Mendocino, CA 95460 / 707-937-2141; FAX: 717-937-1817
Forster Products, 310 E Lanark Ave, Lanark, IL 61046 / 815-493-6360; FAX: 815-493-2371
Forster, Kathy (See Custom Checkering S
Forster, Larry L., P.O. Box 212, 220 First St. NE, Gwinner, ND 58040-0212 / 701-678-2475
Fort Hill Gunstocks, 12807 Fort Hill Rd., Hillsboro, OH 45133 / 513-466-2763
Fort Knox Security Products, 1051 N. Industrial Park Rd., Orem, UT 84057 / 801-224-7233 or 800-821-5216; FAX: 801-226-5493
Fort Worth Firearms, 2006-B, Martin Luther King Fwy., Ft. Worth, TX 76104-6303 / 817-536-0718; FAX: 817-535-0290
Forthofer's Gunsmithing & Knifemaking, 5535 U.S. Hwy 93S, Whitefish, MT 59937-8411 / 406-862-2674
Fortune Products, Inc., HC04, Box 303, Marble Falls, TX 78654 / 210-693-6111; FAX: 210-693-6394
4-D Custom Die Co., 711 N. Sandusky St., P.O. Box 889, Mt. Vernon, OH 43050-0889 / 740-397-7214; FAX: 740-397-6600
4W Ammunition (See Hunters Supply), Rt. 1 PO Box 313, Tioga, TX 76271 / 800-868-6612; FAX: 817-437-2228
Forty Five Ranch Enterprises, Box 1080, Miami, OK 74355-1080 / 918-542-5875
Fouling Shot, The, 6465 Parfet St., Arvada, CO 80004
Fountain Products, 492 Prospect Ave., West Springfield, MA 01089 / 413-781-4651; FAX: 413-733-8217
Fowler Bullets, 806 Dogwood Dr., Gastonia, NC 28054 / 704-867-3259
Fowler, Bob (See Black Powder Products)
Fox River Mills, Inc., P.O. Box 298, 227 Poplar St., Osage, IA 50461 / 515-732-3798; FAX: 515-732-5128
Foy Custom Bullets, 104 Wells Ave., Daleville, AL 36322
Francesca, Inc., 3115 Old Ranch Rd., San Antonio, TX 78217 / 512-826-2584; FAX: 512-826-8211
Franchi S.p.A., Via del Serpente 12, 25131, Brescia, ITALY / 030-3581833; FAX: 030-3581554
Francotte & Cie S.A. Auguste, rue de Trois Juin 109, 4400 Herstal-Liege, BELGIUM / 32-4-248-13-18; FAX: 32-4-948-11-79
Frank Custom Classic Arms, Ron, 7131 Richland Rd, Ft Worth, TX 76118 / 817-284-9300; FAX: 817-284-9300
Frank E. Hendricks Master Engravers, Inc., HC03, Box 434, Dripping Springs, TX 78620 / 512-858-7828
Frank Knives, 13868 NW Keleka Pl., Seal Rock, OR 97376 / 541-563 3041; FAX: 541-563-3041
Frank Mittermeier, Inc., P.O. Box 2G, 3577 E. Tremont Ave., Bronx, NY 10465 / 718-828-3843
Frankonia Jagd Hofmann & Co., D-97064 Wurzburg, Wurzburg, GERMANY / 09302-200; FAX: 09302-20200
Franzen International,Inc (See U.S. Importer for P
Fred F. Wells/Wells Sport Store, 110 N Summit St, Prescott, AZ 86301 / 520-445-3655
Freedom Arms, Inc., P.O. Box 1776, Freedom, WY 83120 / 307-883-2468 or 800-833-4432; FAX: 307-883-2005
Freeman Animal Targets, 5519 East County Road, 100 South, Plainsfield, IN 46168 / 317-272-2663; FAX: 317-272-2674
Fremont Tool Works, 1214 Prairie, Ford, KS 67842 / 316-369-2327
French, Artistic Engraving, J. R., 1712 Creek Ridge Ct, Irving, TX 75060 / 214-254-2654
Frielich Police Equipment, 211 East 21st St., New York, NY 10010 / 212 254-3045
Front Sight Firearms Training Institute, P.O. Box 2619, Aptos, CA 95001 / 800-987 7719; FAX: 408-684-2137
Frontier, 2910 San Bernardo, Laredo, TX 78040 / 956-723-5409; FAX: 956-723-1774
Frontier Arms Co.,Inc., 401 W. Rio Santa Cruz, Green Valley, AZ 85614-3932
Frontier Products Co., 164 E. Longview Ave., Columbus, OH 43202 / 614-262-9357
Frontier Safe Co., 3201 S. Clinton St., Fort Wayne, IN 46806 / 219-744-7233; FAX: 219-744-6678
Frost Cutlery Co., P.O. Box 22636, Chattanooga, TN 37422 / 615-894-6079; FAX: 615-894-9576
Fry Metals, 4100 6th Ave., Altoona, PA 16602 / 814-946-1611
Fujinon, Inc., 10 High Point Dr., Wayne, NJ 07470 / 201-633-5600; FAX: 201-633-5216
Fullmer, Geo. M., 2499 Mavis St., Oakland, CA 94601 / 510-533-4193
Fulmer's Antique Firearms, Chet, PO Box 792, Rt 2 Buffalo Lake, Detroit Lakes, MN 56501 / 218-847-7712
Fulton Armory, 8725 Bollman Place No. 1, Savage, MD 20763 / 301-490-9485; FAX: 301-490-9547
Furr Arms, 91 N. 970 W., Orem, UT 84057 / 801-226-3877; FAX: 801-226-3877
Fusilier Bullets, 10010 N. 6000 W., Highland, UT 84003 / 801-756-6813
FWB, Neckarstrasse 43, 78727, Oberndorf a. N., GERMANY / 07423-814-0; FAX: 07423-814-89

G

G&C Bullet Co., Inc., 8835 Thornton Rd., Stockton, CA 95209 / 209-477-6479; FAX: 209-477-2813
G&H Decoys,Inc., P.O. Box 1208, Hwy. 75 North, Henryetta, OK 74437 / 918-652-3314; FAX: 918-652-3400
G.C.C.T., 4455 Torrance Blvd., Ste. 453, Torrance, CA 90503-4398
G.G. & G., 3602 E. 42nd Stravenue, Tucson, AZ 85713 / 520-748-7167; FAX: 520-748-7583
G.H. Enterprises Ltd., Bag 10, Okotoks, AB TOL 1TO CANADA / 403-938-6070
G.U. Inc (See U.S. Importer for New SKB Arms Co)
G.W. Elliott, Inc., 514 Burnside Ave., East Hartford, CT 06108 / 203-289-5741; FAX: 203-289-3137
G96 Products Co., Inc., 85 5th Ave, Bldg #6, Paterson, NJ 07544 / 973-684-4050 FAX: 973-684-4050
Gage Manufacturing, 663 W. 7th St., A, San Pedro, CA 90731 / 310-832-3546
Gaillard Barrels, P.O. Box 21, Pathlow, SK S0K 3B0 CANADA / 306-752-3769; FAX: 306-752-5969
Gain Twist Barrel Co. Rifle Works and Armory, 707 12th Street, Cody, WY 82414 / 307-587-4919; FAX: 307-527-6097
Galati International, PO Box 10, Wesco, MO 65586 / 314-257-4837; FAX: 314-257-2268
Galaxy Imports Ltd.,Inc., P.O. Box 3361, Victoria, TX 77903 / 512-573-4867; FAX: 512-576-9622
GALCO International Ltd., 2019 W. Quail Ave., Phoenix, AZ 85027 / 602-258-8295 or 800-874-2526; FAX: 602-582-6854
Galena Industries AMT, 5463 Diaz St, Irwindale, CA 91706 / 626-856-8883; FAX: 626-856-8878
Gamba S.p.A. Societa Armi Bresciane Srl, Renato, Via Artigiani 93, ITALY / 30-8911640; FAX: 30-8911648
Gamba, USA, P.O. Box 60452, Colorado Springs, CO 80960 / 719-578-1145; FAX: 719-444-0731
Game Haven Gunstocks, 13750 Shire Rd., Wolverine, MI 49799 / 616-525-8257
Game Winner, Inc., 2625 Cumberland Parkway, Suite 220, Atlanta, GA 30339 / 770-434-9210; FAX: 770-434-9215
Gamebore Division, Polywad Inc, PO Box 7916, Macon, GA 31209 / 912-477-0669
Gamo (See U.S. Importers-Arms United Corp, Daisy M
Gamo USA, Inc., 3911 SW 47th Ave., Suite 914, Ft. Lauderdale, FL 33314 / 954-581-5822; FAX: 954-581-3165
Gander Mountain, Inc., 12400 Fox River Rd., Wilmont, WI 53192 / 414-862-6848
GAR, 590 McBride Avenue, West Paterson, NJ 07424 / 973-754-1114; FAX: 973-754-1114
Garbi, Armas Urki, 12-14 20.600 Elbar, Guipuzcoa, SPAIN
Garcia National Gun Traders, Inc., 225 SW 22nd Ave., Miami, FL 33135 / 305-642-2355
Garrett Cartridges Inc., P.O. Box 178, Chehalis, WA 98532 / 360-736-0702
Garthwaite Pistolsmith, Inc., Jim, Rt 2 Box 310, Watsontown, PA 17777 / 570-538-1566; FAX: 570-538-2965
Gary Goudy Classic Stocks, 263 Hedge Rd., Menlo Park, CA 94025 1711 / 415-322-1338
Gary Reeder Custom Guns, 2710 N Steves Blvd. #22, Flagstaff, AZ 86004 / 520-526-3313; FAX: 520-527-0840
Gary Schneider Rifle Barrels Inc., 12202 N. 62nd Pl., Scottsdale, AZ 85254 / 602-948-2525
Gator Guns & Repair, 6255 Spur Hwy., Kenai, AK 99611 / 907-283-7947
Gaucher Armes, S.A., 46 rue Desjoyaux, 42000, Saint-Etienne, FRANCE / 04-77-33-38-92; FAX: 04-77-61-95-72
GDL Enterprises, 409 Le Gardeur, Slidell, LA 70460 / 504-649-0693
Gehmann, Walter (See Huntington Die Specialties)
Genco, P.O. Box 5704, Asheville, NC 28803
Gene's Custom Guns, P.O. Box 10534, White Bear Lake, MN 55110 / 612-429-5105
Genecco Gun Works, K, 10512 Lower Sacramento Rd., Stockton, CA 95210 / 209-951-0706 FAX: 209-931-3872
Gentex Corp., 5 Tinkham Ave., Derry, NH 03038 / 603-434-0311; FAX: 603-434-3002
Gontner Bullets, 109 Woodlawn Ave., Upper Darby, PA 19082 / 610-352-9396
Gentry Custom Gunmaker, David, 314 N Hoffman, Belgrade, MT 59714 / 406-388-GUNS
George & Roy's, PO Box 2125, Sisters, OR 97759-2125 / 503-228-5424 or 800-553-3022; FAX: 503-225-9409
George E. Mathews & Son, Inc., 10224 S. Paramount Blvd., Downey, CA 90241 / 562-862-6719; FAX: 562-862-6719
George Ibberson (Sheffield) Ltd., 25-31 Allen St., Sheffield, S3 7AW ENGLAND / 0114-2766123; FAX: 0114-2738465
George, Tim, Rt. 1, P.O. Box 45, Evington, VA 24550 / 804-821-8117
Gerald Pettinger Books, see Pettinger Books, G, Rt. 2, Box 125, Russell, IA 50238 / 515-535-2239
Gerber Legendary Blades, 14200 SW 72nd Ave., Portland, OR 97223 / 503-639-6161 or 800-950-6161; FAX: 503-684-7008
Gervais, Mike, 3804 S. Cruise Dr., Salt Lake City, UT 84109 / 801-277-7729
Getz Barrel Co., P.O. Box 88, Beavertown, PA 17813 / 717-658-7263
Giacomo Sporting USA, 6234 Stokes Lee Center Rd., Lee Center, NY 13363
Gibbs Rifle Co., Inc., 211 Lawn St, Martinsburg, WV 25401 / 304-262-1651; FAX: 304-262-1658
Gil Hebard Guns, 125-129 Public Square, Knoxville, IL 61448
Gilbert Equipment Co., Inc., 960 Downtowner Rd., Mobile, AL 36609 / 205-344-3322
Gilkes, Anthony W., 26574 HILLMAN HWY, MEADOWVIEW, VA 24361-3142 / 303-657-1873; FAX: 303-657-1885
Gillmann, Edwin, 33 Valley View Dr., Hanover, PA 17331 / 717-632-1662

Gilman-Mayfield, Inc., 3279 E. Shields, Fresno, CA 93703 / 209-221-9415; FAX: 209-221-9419

Gilmore Sports Concepts, 5949 S. Garnett, Tulsa, OK 74146 / 918-250-4867; FAX: 918-250-3845

Giron, Robert E., 1328 Pocono St., Pittsburgh, PA 15218 / 412-731-6041

Glacier Glove, 4890 Aircenter Circle, Suite 210, Reno, NV 89502 / 702-825-8225; FAX: 702-825-6544

Glaser Safety Slug, Inc., P.O. Box 8223, Foster City, CA 94404 / 800-221-3489; FAX: 510-785-6685

Glass, Herb, P.O. Box 25, Bullville, NY 10915 / 914-361-3021

Glimm, Jerome C., 19 S. Maryland, Conrad, MT 59425 / 406-278-3574

Glock GmbH, P.O. Box 50, A-2232, Deutsch Wagram, AUSTRIA

Glock, Inc., PO Box 369, Smyrna, GA 30081 / 770-432-1202; FAX: 770-433-8719

Glynn Scobey Duck & Goose Calls, Rt. 3, Box 37, Newbern, TN 38059 / 901-643-6241

GML Products, Inc., 394 Laredo Dr., Birmingham, AL 35226 / 205-979-4867

Gner's Hard Cast Bullets, 1107 11th St., LaGrande, OR 97850 / 503-963-8796

Goens, Dale W., P.O. Box 224, Cedar Crest, NM 87008 / 505-281-5419

Goergen's Gun Shop, Inc., Rt. 2, Box 182BB, Austin, MN 55912 / 507-433-9280 FAX: 507-433-9280

GOEX Inc., PO Box 659, Doyline, LA 71023-0659 / 318-382-9300; FAX: 318-382-9303

Golden Age Arms Co., 115 E. High St., Ashley, OH 43003 / 614-747-2488

Golden Bear Bullets, 3065 Fairfax Ave., San Jose, CA 95148 / 408-238-9515

Gonic Arms/North American Arm, 134 Flagg Rd., Gonic, NH 03839 / 603-332-8456 or 603-332-8457

Gonzalez Guns, Ramon B, PO Box 370, 93 St. Joseph's Hill Rd, Monticello, NY 12701 / 914-794-4515

Goodling's Gunsmithing, R.D. 1, Box 1097, Spring Grove, PA 17362 / 717-225-3350

Goodwin, Fred, Silver Ridge Gun Shop, Sherman Mills, ME 04776 / 207-365-4451

Gordie's Gun Shop, 1401 Fulton St., Streator, IL 61364 / 815-672-7202

Gordon Wm. Davis Leather Co., P.O. Box 2270, Walnut, CA 91788 / 909-598-5620

Gotz Bullets, 7313 Rogers St., Rockford, IL 61111

Gould & Goodrich, 709 E. McNeil, Lillington, NC 27546 / 910-893-2071; FAX: 910-893-4742

Gournet, Geoffroy, 820 Paxinosa Ave., Easton, PA 18042 / 610-559-0710

Gozon Corp. U.S.A., P.O. Box 6278, Folson, CA 95763 / 916-983-2026; FAX: 916-983-9500

Grace Metal Products, P.O. Box 67, Elk Rapids, MI 49629 / 616-264-8133

Grace, Charles E., 1305 Arizona Ave., Trinidad, CO 81082 / 719-846-9435

Graf & Sons, 4050 S Clark St, Mexico, MO 65265 / 573-581-2266 FAX: 573-581-2875

"Gramps" Antique Cartridges, Box 341, Washago, ON L0K 2B0 CANADA / 705-689-5348

Granite Mountain Arms, Inc, 100 N Summit Ave, Ste A, Prescott, AZ 86301 / 520-541-9758; FAX: 520-541-9758

Grant, Howard V., Hiawatha 15, Woodruff, WI 54568 / 715-356-7146

Graphics Direct, P.O. Box 372421, Reseda, CA 91337-2421 / 818-344-9002

Graves Co., 1800 Andrews Ave., Pompano Beach, FL 33069 / 800-327-9103; FAX: 305-960-0301

Grayback Wildcats, 5306 Bryant Ave., Klamath Falls, OR 97603 / 541-884-1072

Graybill's Gun Shop, 1035 Ironville Pike, Columbia, PA 17512 / 717-684-2739

GrE-Tan Rifles, 29742 W.C.R. 50, Kersey, CO 80644 / 970-353-6176; FAX: 970-356-9133

Great American Gunstock Co., 3420 Industrial Drive, Yuba City, CA 95993 / 530-671-4570; FAX: 530-671-3906

Great Lakes Airguns, 6175 S. Park Ave, New York, NY 14075 / 716-648-6666; FAX: 716-648-5279

Green Genie, Box 114, Cusseta, GA 31805

Green Head Game Call Co., RR 1, Box 33, Lacon, IL 61540 / 309-246-2155

Green Mountain Rifle Barrel Co., Inc., P.O. Box 2670, 153 West Main St., Conway, NH 03818 / 603-447-1095; FAX: 603-447-1099

Green, Arthur S., 485 S. Robertson Blvd., Beverly Hills, CA 90211 / 310-274-1283

Green, Roger M., P.O. Box 984, 435 E. Birch, Glenrock, WY 82637 / 307-436-9804

Greenwood Precision, P.O. Box 468, Nixa, MO 65714-0468 / 417-725-2330

Greg Gunsmithing Repair, 3732 26th Ave. North, Robbinsdale, MN 55422 / 612-529-8103

Greg's Superior Products, P.O. Box 46219, Seattle, WA 98146

Greider Precision, 431 Santa Marina Ct., Escondido, CA 92029 / 619-480-8892; FAX: 619-480-9800

Gremmel Enterprises, 2111 Carriage Drive, Eugene, OR 97408-7537 / 541-302-3000

Grier's Hard Cast Bullets, 1107 11th St., LaGrande, OR 97850 / 503-963-8796

Griffin & Howe, Inc., 33 Claremont Rd., Bernardsville, NJ 07924 / 908-766-2287

Griffin & Howe, Inc., 36 W. 44th St., Suite 1011, New York, NY 10036 / 212-921-0980

Grifon, Inc., 58 Guinam St., Waltham, MS 02154

Groenewold, John, P.O. Box 830, Mundelein, IL 60060 / 847-566-2365

GRS Corp., Glendo, P.O. Box 1153, 900 Overlander St., Emporia, KS 66801 / 316-343-1084 or 800-835-3519

Grulla Armes, Apartado 453, Avda Otaloa 12, Eiber, SPAIN

Gruning Precision Inc, 7101 Jurupa Ave., No. 12, Riverside, CA 92504 / 909-689-6692 FAX: 909-689-7791

GSI, Inc., 108 Morrow Ave., P.O. Box 129, Trussville, AL 35173 / 205-655-8299

GTB, 482 Comerwood Court, San Francisco, CA 94080 / 650-583-1550

Guarasi, Robert. See: WILCOX INDUSTRIES CORP

Guardsman Products, 411 N. Darling, Fremont, MI 49412 / 616-924-3950

Gun Accessories (See Glaser Safety Slug, Inc.), PO Box 8223, Foster City, CA 94404 / 800-221-3489; FAX: 510-785-6685

Gun City, 212 W. Main Ave., Bismarck, ND 58501 / 701-223-2304

Gun Doctor, The, P.O. Box 39242, Downey, CA 90242 / 310-862-3158

Gun Doctor, The, 435 East Maple, Roselle, IL 60172 / 708-894-0668

Gun Hunter Books (See Gun Hunter Trading Co), 5075 Heisig St, Beaumont, TX 77705 / 409-835-3006

Gun Hunter Trading Co., 5075 Heisig St., Beaumont, TX 77705 / 409-835-3006

Gun Leather Limited, 116 Lipscomb, Ft. Worth, TX 76104 / 817-334-0225; FAX: 800-247-0609

Gun List (See Krause Publications), 700 E State St, Iola, WI 54945 / 715-445-2214; FAX: 715-445-4087

Gun Locker Div. of Airmold W.R. Grace & Co.-Conn., Becker Farms Ind. Park, P.O. Box 610, Roanoke Rapids, NC 27870 / 800-344-5716; FAX: 919-536-2201

Gun Parts Corp., The, 226 Williams Lane, West Hurley, NY 12491 / 914-679-2417; FAX: 914-679-5849

Gun Room Press, The, 127 Raritan Ave., Highland Park, NJ 08904 / 732-545-4344; FAX: 732-545-4344

Gun Room, The, 1121 Burlington, Muncie, IN 47302 / 317-282-9073; FAX: 317-282-5270

Gun Shop, The, 5550 S. 900 East, Salt Lake City, UT 84117 / 801-263-3633

Gun Shop, The, 716-A South Rogers Road, Olathe, KS 66062

Gun Shop, The, 62778 Spring Creek Rd., Montrose, CO 81401

Gun South, Inc. (See GSI, Inc.)

Gun Vault, 7339 E Acoma Dr., Ste. 7, Scottsdale, AZ 85260 / 602-951-6855

Gun Works, The, 247 S. 2nd, Springfield, OR 97477 / 541-741-4118; FAX: 541-988-1097

Gun-Alert, 1010 N. Maclay Ave., San Fernando, CA 91340 / 818-365-0864; FAX: 818-365-1308

Gun-Ho Sports Cases, 110 E. 10th St., St. Paul, MN 55101 / 612-224-9491

Gun-Tec, P.O. Box 8125, W. Palm Beach, FL 33407

Guncraft Books (See Guncraft Sports Inc), 10737 Dutchtown Rd, Knoxville, TN 37932 / 423-966-4545; FAX: 423-966-4500

Guncraft Sports Inc., 10737 Dutchtown Rd., Knoxville, TN 37932 / 423-966-4545; FAX: 423-966-4500

Gunfitters, P.O. 426, Cambridge, WI 53523-0426 / 608-764-8128

Gunline Tools, 2950 Saturn St., "O", Brea, CA 92821 / 714-993-5100; FAX: 714-572-4128

Gunnerman Books, P.O. Box 217, Owosso, MI 48867 / 517-729-7018; FAX: 517-725-9391

Guns, 81 E. Streetsboro St., Hudson, OH 44236 / 330-650-4563

Guns Antique & Modern DBA/Charles E. Duffy, Williams Lane, West Hurley, NY 12491 / 914-679-2997

Guns Div. of D.C. Engineering, Inc., 8633 Southfield Fwy., Detroit, MI 48228 / 313-271-7111 or 800-886-7623; FAX: 313-271-7112

GUNS Magazine, 591 Camino de la Reina, Suite 200, San Diego, CA 92108 / 619-297-5350 FAX: 619-297-5353

Gunsight, The, 1712 North Placentia Ave., Fullerton, CA 92631

Gunsite Custom Shop, P.O. Box 451, Paulden, AZ 86334 / 520-636-4104; FAX: 520-636-1236

Gunsite Gunsmithy (See Gunsite Custom Shop)

Gunsite Training Center, P.O. Box 700, Paulden, AZ 86334 / 520-636-4565; FAX: 520-636-1236

Gunsmith in Elk River, The, 14021 Victoria Lane, Elk River, MN 55330 / 612-441-7761

Gunsmithing Ltd., 57 Unquowa Rd., Fairfield, CT 06430 / 203-254-0436; FAX: 203-254-1535

Gunsmithing, Inc., 208 West Buchanan St., Colorado Springs, CO 80907 / 719-632-3795; FAX: 719-632-3493

Gurney, F. R., Box 13, Sooke, BC V0S 1N0 CANADA / 604-642-5282; FAX: 604-642-7859

Gwinnell, Bryson J., P.O. Box 248C, Maple Hill Rd., Rochester, VT 05767 / 802-767-3664

H

H&B Forge Co., Rt. 2, Geisinger Rd., Shiloh, OH 44878 / 419-895-1856

H&P Publishing, 7174 Hoffman Rd., San Angelo, TX 76905 / 915-655-5953

H&R 1871, Inc., 60 Industrial Rowe, Gardner, MA 01440 / 978-632-9393; FAX: 978-632-2300

H&S Liner Service, 515 E. 8th, Odessa, TX 79761 / 915-332-1021

H-S Precision, Inc., 1301 Turbine Dr., Rapid City, SD 57701 / 605-341-3006; FAX: 605-342-8964

H. Krieghoff Gun Co., Boschstrasse 22, D-89079, Ulm, GERMANY / 731-401820; FAX: 731-4018270

H.K.S. Products, 7841 Founion Dr., Florence, KY 41042 / 606-342-7841 or 800-354-9814; FAX: 606-342-5865

H.P. White Laboratory, Inc., 3114 Scarboro Rd., Street, MD 21154 / 410-838-6550; FAX: 410-838-2802

Hafner Creations, Inc., P.O. Box 1987, Lake City, FL 32055 / 904-755-6481; FAX: 904-755-6595

Hagn Rifles & Actions, Martin, PO Box 444, Cranbrook, BC V1C 4H9 CANDA / 604-489-4861

Hakko Co. Ltd., 1-13-12, Narimasu, Itabashiku Tokyo, JAPAN / 03-5997-7870/2; FAX: 81-3-5997-7840

Hale, Engraver, Peter, 800 E Canyon Rd., Spanish Fork, UT 84660 / 801-798-8215

Half Moon Rifle Shop, 490 Halfmoon Rd., Columbia Falls, MT 59912 / 406-892-4409

Hall Manufacturing, 142 CR 406, Clanton, AL 35045 / 205-755-4094

Hall Plastics, Inc., John, P.O. Box 1526, Alvin, TX 77512 / 713-489-8709

Hallberg Gunsmith, Fritz, 532 E. Idaho Ave, Ontario, OR 97914 / 541-889-3135; FAX: 541-889-2633

Hallowell & Co., PO Box 1445, Livingston, MT 59047 / 406-222-4770 FAX: 406-222-4792

Hally Caller, 443 Wells Rd., Doylestown, PA 18901 / 215-345-6354

Halstead, Rick, 313 TURF ST, CARL JUNCTION, MO 64834-9658 / 918-540-0933

Hamilton, Alex B (See Ten-Ring Precision, Inc)

Hamilton, Jim, Rte. 5, Box 278, Guthrie, OK 73044 / 405-282-3634

Hammans, Charles E., P.O. Box 788, 2022 McCracken, Stuttgart, AR 72106 / 870-673-1388

Hammerli Ltd., Seonerstrasse 37, CH-5600, SWITZERLAND / 064-50 11 44; FAX: 064-51 38 27

Hammerli USA, 19296 Oak Grove Circle, Groveland, CA 95321 FAX: 209-962-5311

Hammets VLD Bullets, P.O. Box 479, Rayville, LA 71269 / 318-728-2019

Hammond Custom Guns Ltd., 619 S. Pandora, Gilbert, AZ 85234 / 602-892-3437

Hammonds Rifles, RD 4, Box 504, Red Lion, PA 17356 / 717-244-7879

HandCrafts Unltd (See Clements' Custom Leathercraf, 1741 Dallas St, Aurora, CO 80010-2018 / 303-364-0403; FAX: 303-739-9824

Handgun Press, P.O. Box 406, Glenview, IL 60025 / 847-657-6500; FAX: 847-724-8831

Hands Engraving, Barry Lee, 26192 E Shore Route, Bigfork, MT 59911 / 406-837-0035

Hank's Gun Shop, Box 370, 50 West 100 South, Monroe, UT 84754 / 801-527-4456

Hanned Line, The, P.O. Box 2387, Cupertino, CA 95015-2387

Hanned Precision (See Hanned Line, The)

Hansen & Co. (See Hansen Cartridge Co.), 244-246 Old Post Rd, Southport, CT 06490 / 203-259-6222; FAX: 203-254-3832

Hanson's Gun Center, Dick, 233 Everett Dr, Colorado Springs, CO 80911

Hanus Birdguns Bill, PO Box 533, Newport, OR 97365 / 541-265-7433; FAX: 541-265-7400

Hanusin, John, 3306 Commercial, Northbrook, IL 60062 / 708-564-2706

Hardin Specialty Dist., P.O. Box 338, Radcliff, KY 40159-0338 / 502-351-6649

Harford (See U.S. Importer-EMF Co. Inc.)

Harold's Custom Gun Shop Inc. Broughton Rifle Barr, Rt. 1, Box 447, Big Spring, TX 79720 / 915-394-4430

Harper's Custom Stocks, 928 Lombrano St., San Antonio, TX 78207 / 210-732-5780

Harrell's Precision, 5756 Hickory Dr., Salem, VA 24133 / 703-380-2683

Harrington & Richardson (See H&R 1871, Inc.)

Harris Engineering Inc., Dept GD54, Barlow, KY 42024 / 502-334-3633 FAX: 502-334-3000

Harris Enterprises, P.O. Box 105, Bly, OR 97622 / 503-353-2625

Harris Gunworks, 20813 N. 19th Ave., PO Box 9249, Phoenix, AZ 85027 / 602-582-9627; FAX: 602-582-5178
Harris Hand Engraving, Paul A., 113 Rusty Ln, Boerne, TX 78006-5746 / 512-391-5121
Harris Publications, 1115 Broadway, New York, NY 10010 / 212-807-7100 FAX: 212-627-4678
Harrison Bullets, 6437 E. Hobart St., Mesa, AZ 85205
Harry Lawson Co., 3328 N. Richey Blvd., Tucson, AZ 85716 / 520-326-1117
Hart & Son, Inc., Robert W. , 401 Montgomery St, Nescopeck, PA 18635 / 717-752-3655; FAX: 717-752-1088
Hart Rifle Barrels,Inc., P.O. Box 182, 1690 Apulia Rd., Lafayette, NY 13084 / 315-677-9841; FAX: 315-677-9610
Hartford (See U.S. Importer-EMF Co. Inc.)
Hartmann & Weiss GmbH, Rahlstedter Bahnhofstr. 47, 22143, Hamburg, GERMANY / (40) 677 55 85; FAX: (40) 677 55 92
Harvey, Frank, 218 Nightfall, Terrace, NV 89015 / 702-558-6998
Harwood, Jack O., 1191 S. Pendlebury Lane, Blackfoot, ID 83221 / 208-785-5368
Hastings Barrels, 320 Court St., Clay Center, KS 67432 / 913-632-3169; FAX: 913-632-6554
Hawk Laboratories, Inc. (See Hawk, Inc.), 849 Hawks Bridge Rd, Salem, NJ 08079 / 609-299-2700; FAX: 609-299-2800
Hawk, Inc., 849 Hawks Bridge Rd., Salem, NJ 08079 / 609-299-2700; FAX: 609-299-2800
Hawken Shop, The (See Dayton Traister)
Haydel's Game Calls, Inc., 5018 Hazel Jones Rd., Bossier City, LA 71111 / 800-HAYDELS; FAX: 318-746-3711
Haydon Shooters Supply, Russ, 15018 Goodrich Dr NW, Gig Harbor, WA 98329-9738 / 253-857-7557; FAX: 253-857-7884
Heatbath Corp., P.O. Box 2978, Springfield, MA 01101 / 413-543-3381
Hebard Guns, Gil, 125-129 Public Square, Knoxville, IL 61448
HEBB Resources, P.O. Box 999, Mead, WA 99021-0999 / 509-466-1292
Hecht, Hubert J, Waffen-Hecht, PO Box 2635, Fair Oaks, CA 95628 / 916-966-1020
Heckler & Koch GmbH, P.O. Box 1329, 78722 Oberndorf, Neckar, GERMANY / 49-7423179-0; FAX: 49-7423179-2406
Heckler & Koch, Inc., 21480 Pacific Blvd., Sterling, VA 20166-8900 / 703-450-1900; FAX: 703-450-8160
Hege Jagd u. Sporthandels GmbH, P.O. Box 101461, W-7770, Ueberlingen a. Boden, GERMANY
Heidenstrom Bullets, Urdngt 1, 3937 Heroya, NORWAY,
Heilmann, Stephen, P.O. Box 657, Grass Valley, CA 95945 / 530-272-8758
Heinie Specialty Products, 301 Oak St., Quincy, IL 62301-2500 / 309-543-4535; FAX: 309-543-2521
Hellweg Ltd., 40356 Oak Park Way, Suite W, Oakhurst, CA 93644 / 209-683-3030; FAX: 209-683-3422
Helwan (See U.S. Importer-Interarms)
Hendricks, Frank E. Inc., Master Engravers, HC 03, Box 434, Dripping Springs, TX 78620 / 512-858-7828
Henigson & Associates, Steve, PO Box 2726, Culver City, CA 90231 / 310-305-8288; FAX: 310-305-1905
Henriksen Tool Co., Inc., 8515 Wagner Creek Rd., Talent, OR 97540 / 541-535-2300
Henry Repeating Arms Co., 110 8th St., Brooklyn, NY 11215 / 718-499-5600
Hensler, Jerry, 6614 Country Field, San Antonio, TX 78240 / 210-690-7491
Hensley & Gibbs, Box 10, Murphy, OR 97533 / 541-862-2341
Hensley, Gunmaker, Darwin, PO Box 329, Brightwood, OR 97011 / 503-622-5411
Heppler's Machining, 2240 Calle Del Mundo, Santa Clara, CA 95054 / 408-748-9166; FAX: 408-988-7711
Heppler, Keith M, Keith's Custom Gunstocks, 540 Banyan Cir, Walnut Creek, CA 94598 / 510-934-3509; FAX: 510-934-3143
Hercules, Inc. (See Alliant Techsystems, Smokeless
Heritage Firearms (See Heritage Mfg., Inc.)
Heritage Manufacturing, Inc., 4600 NW 135th St., Opa Locka, FL 33054 or 305-685-5966; FAX: 305-687-6721
Heritage Wildlife Carvings, 2145 Wagner Hollow Rd., Fort Plain, NY 13339 / 518-993-3983
Heritage/VSP Gun Books, P.O. Box 887, McCall, ID 83638 / 208-634-4104; FAX: 208-634-3101
Herrett's Stocks, Inc., P.O. Box 741, Twin Falls, ID 83303 / 208-733-1498
Hertel & Reuss, Werk fr Optik und Feinmechanik GmbH, Quellhofstrasse 67, 34 127, GERMANY / 0561-83006; FAX: 0561-893308
Herter's Manufacturing, Inc., 111 E. Burnett St., P.O. Box 518, Beaver Dam, WI 53916 / 414-887-1765; FAX: 414-887-8444
Hesco-Meprolight, 2139 Greenville Rd., LaGrange, GA 30241 / 706-884-7967; FAX: 706-882-4683
Heydenberk, Warren R., 1059 W. Sawmill Rd., Quakertown, PA 18951 / 215-538-2682
Hi-Grade Imports, 8655 Monterey Rd., Gilroy, CA 95021 / 408-842-9301; FAX: 408-842-2374
Hi-Performance Ammunition Company, 484 State Route 366, Apollo, PA 15613 / 412-327-8100
Hi-Point Firearms, 5990 Philadelphia Dr., Dayton, OH 45415 / 513-275-4991; FAX: 513-522-8330
Hickman, Jaclyn, Box 1900, Glenrock, WY 82637
Hidalgo, Tony, 12701 SW 9th Pl., Davie, FL 33325 / 954-476-7645
High Bridge Arms, Inc, 3185 Mission St., San Francisco, CA 94110 / 415-282-8358
High North Products, Inc., P.O. Box 2, Antigo, WI 54409 / 715-627-2331 FAX: 715-623-5451
High Performance International, 5734 W. Florist Ave., Milwaukee, WI 53218 / 414-466-9040
High Standard Mfg. Co., Inc., 4601 S. Pinemont, Suite 144, Houston, TX 77041 / 713-462-4200; FAX: 713-462-6437
High Tech Specialties, Inc., P.O. Box 387R, Adamstown, PA 19501 / 215-484-0405 or 800-231-9385
Highline Machine Co., 654 Lela Place, Grand Junction, CO 81504 / 970-434-4971
Hill Speed Leather, Ernie, 4507 N 195th Ave, Litchfield Park, AZ 85340 / 602-853-9222; FAX: 602-853-9235
Hill, Loring F., 304 Cedar Rd., Elkins Park, PA 19027
Hines Co, S C, PO Box 423, Tijeras, NM 87059 / 505-281-3783
Hinman Outfitters, Bob, 107 N Sanderson Ave, Bartonville, IL 61607-1839 / 309-691-8132
HIP-GRIP Barami Corp., 6689 Orchard Lake Rd. No. 148, West Bloomfield, MI 48322 / 248-738-0462; FAX: 248-738-2542
Hiptmayer, Armurier, RR 112 750, P.O. Box 136, Eastman, PQ J0E 1P0 CANADA / 514-297-2492
Hiptmayer, Heidemarie, RR 112 750, P.O. Box 136, Eastman, PQ J0E 1P0 CANADA / 514-297-2492
Hiptmayer, Klaus, RR 112 750, P.O. Box 136, Eastman, PQ J0E 1P0 CANADA / 514-297-2492
Hirtenberger Aktiengesellschaft, Leobersdorferstrasse 31, A-2552, Hirtenberg, / 43(0)2256 81184; FAX: 43(0)2256 81807
HiTek International, 484 El Camino Real, Redwood City, CA 94063 / 415-363-1404 or 800-54-NIGHT FAX: 415-363-1408
Hiti-Schuch, Atelier Wilma, A-8863 Predlitz, Pirming, Y1 AUSTRIA / 0353418278
HJS Arms,Inc., P.O. Box 3711, Brownsville, TX 78523-3711 / 800-453-2767; FAX: 210-542-2767
Hoag, James W., 8523 Canoga Ave., Suite C, Canoga Park, CA 91304 / 818-998-1510
Hobson Precision Mfg. Co., Rt. 1, Box 220-C, Brent, AL 35034 / 205-926-4662
Hoch Custom Bullet Moulds (See Colorado Shooter's
Hodgdon Powder Co., 6231 Robinson, Shawnee Mission, KS 66202 / 913-362-9455; FAX: 913-362-1307
Hodgman, Inc., 1750 Orchard Rd., Montgomery, IL 60538 / 708-897-7555; FAX: 708-897-7558
Hodgson, Richard, 9081 Tahoe Lane, Boulder, CO 80301
Hoehn Sales, Inc., 2045 Kohn Road, Wright City, MO 63390 / 314-745-8144; FAX: 314-745-8144
Hoelscher, Virgil, 8230 Hillrose St, Sunland, CA 91040-2404 / 310-631-8545
Hoenig & Rodman, 6521 Morton Dr., Boise, ID 83704 / 208-375-1116
Hofer Jagdwaffen, P., Buchsenmachermeister, Kirchgasse 24, A-9170 Ferlach, AUSTRIA
Hoffman New Ideas, 821 Northmoor Rd., Lake Forest, IL 60045 / 312-234-4075
Hogue Grips, P.O. Box 1138, Paso Robles, CA 93447 / 800-438-4747 or 805-239-1440; FAX: 805-239-2553
Holland & Holland Ltd., 33 Bruton St., London, ENGLAND / 44-171-499-4411; FAX: 44-171-408-7962
Holland's Gunsmithing, P.O. Box 69, Powers, OR 97466 / 541-439-5155; FAX: 541-439-5155
Hollinger, Jon. See: ASPEN OUTFITTING CO
Hollis Gun Shop, 917 Rex St., Carlsbad, NM 88220 / 505-885-3782
Hollywood Engineering, 10642 Arminta St., Sun Valley, CA 91352 / 818-842-8376
Holster Shop, The, 720 N. Flagler Dr., Ft. Lauderdale, FL 33304 / 305-463-7910; FAX: 305-761-1483
Homak, 5151 W. 73rd St., Chicago, IL 60638-6613 / 312-523-3100; FAX: 312-523-9455
Home Shop Machinist The Village Press Publications, P.O. Box 1810, Traverse City, MI 49685 / 800-447-7367; FAX: 616-946-3289
Hondo Ind., 510 S. 52nd St., I04, Tempe, AZ 85281
Hoover, Harvey, 5750 Pearl Dr., Paradise, CA 95969-4829
Hoppe's Div. Penguin Industries, Inc., Airport Industrial Mall, Coatesville, PA 19320 / 610-384-6000
Horizons Unlimited, P.O. Box 426, Warm Springs, GA 31830 / 706-655-3603; FAX: 706-655-3603
Hornady Mfg. Co., P.O. Box 1848, Grand Island, NE 68802 / 800-338-3220 or 308-382-1390; FAX: 308-382-5761
Horseshoe Leather Products, Andy Arratoonian, The Cottage Sharow, Ripon, ENGLAND / 44-1765-605858
House of Muskets, Inc., The, P.O. Box 4640, Pagosa Springs, CO 81157 / 970-731-2295
Houtz & Barwick, P.O. Box 435, W. Church St., Elizabeth City, NC 27909 / 800-775-0337 or 919-335-4191; FAX: 919-335-1152
Howa Machinery, Ltd., Sukaguchi, Shinkawa-cho Nishikasugai-gun, Aichi 452, JAPAN
Howell Machine, 815 1/2 D St., Lewiston, ID 83501 / 208-743-7418
Hoyt Holster Co., Inc., P.O. Box 69, Coupeville, WA 98239-0069 / 360-678-6640; FAX: 360-678-6549
HT Bullets, 244 Belleville Rd., New Bedford, MA 02745 / 508-999-3338
Hubert J. Hecht Waffen-Hecht, P.O. Box 2635, Fair Oaks, CA 95628 / 916-966-1020
Hubertus Schneidwarenfabrik, P.O. Box 180 106, D-42626, Solingen, GERMANY / 01149-212-59-19-94; FAX: 01149-212-59-19-92
Huebner, Corey O., P.O. Box 2074, Missoula, MT 59806-2074 / 406-721-7168
Huey Gun Cases, P.O. Box 22456, Kansas City, MO 64113 / 816-444-1637; FAX: 816-444-1637
Hugger Hooks Co., 3900 Easley Way, Golden, CO 80403 / 303-279-0600
Hughes, Steven Dodd, P.O. Box 545, Livingston, MT 59047 / 406-222-9377; FAX: 406-222-9377
Hume, Don, P.O. Box 351, Miami, OK 74355 / 800-331-2686 FAX: 918-542-4340
Hungry Horse Books, 4605 Hwy. 93 South, Whitefish, MT 59937 / 406-862-7997
Hunkeler, A (See Buckskin Machine Works, 3235 S 358th St., Auburn, WA 98001 / 206-927-5412
Hunter Co., Inc., 3300 W. 71st Ave., Westminster, CO 80030 / 303-427-4626; FAX: 303-428-3980
Hunter's Specialties Inc., 6000 Huntington Ct. NE, Cedar Rapids, IA 52402-1268 / 319-395-0321; FAX: 319-395-0326
Hunterjohn, P.O. Box 771457, St. Louis, MO 63177 / 314-531-7250
Hunters Supply, Rt. 1, P.O. Box 313, Tioga, TX 76271 / 800-868-6612; FAX: 817-437-2228
Hunting Classics Ltd., P.O. Box 2089, Gastonia, NC 28053 / 704-867-1307; FAX: 704-867-0491
Huntington Die Specialties, 601 Oro Dam Blvd., Oroville, CA 95965 / 530-534-1210; FAX: 530-534-1212
Hutton Rifle Ranch, P.O. Box 45236, Boise, ID 83711 / 208-345-8781
Hydrosorbent Products, P.O. Box 437, Ashley Falls, MA 01222 / 413-229-2967; FAX: 413-229-8743
Hyper-Single, Inc., 520 E. Beaver, Jenks, OK 74037 / 918-299-2391

I

I.A.B. (See U.S. Importer-Taylor's & Co. Inc.)
I.D.S.A. Books, 1324 Stratford Drive, Piqua, OH 45356 / 937-773-4203; FAX: 937-778-1922
I.N.C. Inc (See Kick Eez)
I.S.S., P.O. Box 185234, Ft. Worth, TX 76181 / 817-595-2090
I.S.W., 106 E. Cairo Dr., Tempe, AZ 85282
IAI (See A.M.T.)
IAR Inc., 33171 Camino Capistrano, San Juan Capistrano, CA 92675 / 949-443-3642; FAX: 949-443-3647
IGA (See U.S. Importer-Stoeger Industries)
Ignacio Ugartechea S.A., Chonta 26, Eibar, 20600 SPAIN / 43-121257; FAX: 43-121669
Illinois Lead Shop, 7742 W. 61st Place, Summit, IL 60501
Image Ind. Inc., 382 Balm Court, Wood Dale, IL 60191 / 630-766-2402; FAX: 630-766-7373
IMI, P.O. Box 1044, Ramat Hasharon, 47100 ISRAEL / 972-3-5485617; FAX: 972-3-5406908
IMI Services USA, Inc., 2 Wisconsin Circle, Suite 420, Chevy Chase, MD 20815 / 301-215-4800; FAX: 301-657-1446
Impact Case Co., P.O. Box 9912, Spokane, WA 99209-0912 / 800-262-3322 or 509-467-3303; FAX: 509-326-5436
Imperial (See E-Z-Way Systems), PO Box 4310, Newark, OH 43058-4310 / 614-345-6645; FAX: 614-345-6600
Imperial Magnum Corp., P.O. Box 249, Oroville, WA 98844 / 604-495-3131; FAX: 604-495-2816
Imperial Miniature Armory, 10547 S. Post Oak, Houston, TX 77035 / 713-729-8428 FAX: 713-729-2274
Imperial Schrade Corp., 7 Schrade Ct., Box 7000, Ellenville, NY 12428 / 914-647-7601; FAX: 914-647-8701
Import Sports Inc., 1750 Brielle Ave., Unit B1, Wanamassa, NJ 07712 / 908-493-0302; FAX: 908-493-0301
IMR Powder Co., 1080 Military Turnpike, Suite 2, Plattsburgh, NY 12901 / 518-563-2253; FAX: 518-563-6916
Info-Arm, P.O. Box 1262, Champlain, NY 12919 / 514-955-0355; FAX: 514-955-0357
Ingle, Ralph W., Engraver, 112 Manchester Ct., Centerville, GA 31028 / 912-953-5824
Innovision Enterprises, 728 Skinner Dr., Kalamazoo, MI 49001 / 616-382-1681 FAX: 616-382-1830
INTEC International, Inc., P.O. Box 5708, Scottsdale, AZ 85261 / 602-483-1708
Inter Ordnance of America LP, 3904-B Sardis Church Rd, Monroe, NC 28110 / 704-821-8337; FAX: 704-821-8523

Interarms/Howa, PO Box 208, Ten Prince St, Alexandria, VA 22313 / 703-548-1400; FAX: 703-549-7826
Intratec, 12405 SW 130th St., Miami, FL 33186-6224 / 305-232-1821; FAX: 305-253-7207
Ion Industries, Inc, 3508 E Allerton Ave, Cudahy, WI 53110 / 414-486-2007; FAX: 414-486-2017
Iosso Products, 1485 Lively Blvd., Elk Grove Village, IL 60007 / 847-437-8400; FAX: 847-437-8478
Iron Bench, 12619 Bailey Rd., Redding, CA 96003 / 916-241-4623
Ironside International Publishers, Inc., P.O. Box 55, 800 Slaters Lane, Alexandria, VA 22313 / 703-684-6111; FAX: 703-683-5486
Ironsighter Co., P.O. Box 85070, Westland, MI 48185 / 734-326-8731; FAX: 734-326-3378
Irwin, Campbell H., 140 Hartland Blvd., East Hartland, CT 06027 / 203-653-3901
Island Pond Gun Shop, P.O. Box 428, Cross St., Island Pond, VT 05846 / 802-723-4546
Israel Arms International, Inc., 5709 Hartsdale, Houston, TX 77036 / 713-789-0745; FAX: 713-789-7513
Israel Military Industries Ltd. (See IMI), PO Box 1044, Ramat Hasharon, ISRAEL / 972-3-5485617; FAX: 972-3-5406908
Ithaca Classic Doubles, Stephen Lamboy, PO Box 665, Mendon, NY 14506 / 706-569-6760; FAX: 706-561-9248
Ithaca Gun Co. LLC, 891 Route 34-B, King Ferry, NY 13081 / 888-9ITHACA; FAX: 315-364-5134
Ivanoff, Thomas G (See Tom's Gun Repair)

J

J Martin Inc, PO Drawer AP, Beckley, WV 25802 / 304-255-4073; FAX: 304-255-4077
J&D Components, 75 East 350 North, Orem, UT 84057-4719 / 801-225-7007
J&J Products, Inc., 9240 Whitmore, El Monte, CA 91731 / 818-571-5228; FAX: 800-927-8361
J&J Sales, 1501 21st Ave. S., Great Falls, MT 59405 / 406-453-7549
J&L Superior Bullets (See Huntington Die Specialis
J&R Engineering, Po Box 77, 200 Lyons Hill Rd., Athol, MA 01331 / 508-249-9241
J&R Enterprises, 4550 Scotts Valley Rd., Lakeport, CA 95453
J&S Heat Treat, 803 S. 16th St., Blue Springs, MO 64015 / 816-229-2149; FAX: 816-228-1135
J-4 Inc., 1700 Via Burton, Anaheim, CA 92806 / 714-254-8315; FAX: 714-956-4421
J-Gar Co., 183 Turnpike Rd., Dept. 3, Petersham, MA 01366-9604
J. Dewey Mfg. Co., Inc., P.O. Box 2014, Southbury, CT 06488 / 203-264-3064; FAX: 203-262-6907
J. Korzinek Riflesmith, RD 2, Box 73D, Canton, PA 17724 / 717-673-8512
J.A. Blades, Inc. (See Christopher Firearms Co.,
J.A. Henckels Zwillingswerk Inc., 9 Skyline Dr., Hawthorne, NY 10532 / 914-592-7370
J.G. Dapkus Co., Inc., Commerce Circle, P.O. Box 293, Durham, CT 06422
J.I.T. Ltd., P.O. Box 230, Freedom, WY 83120 / 708-494-0937
J.J. Roberts/Engraver, 7808 Lake Dr., Manassas, VA 22111 / 703-330-0448
J.M. Bucheimer Jumbo Sports Products, 721 N. 20th St., St. Louis, MO 63103 / 314-241-1020
J.P. Enterprises Inc., P.O. Box 26324, Shoreview, MN 55126 / 612-486-9064; FAX: 612-482-0970
J.P. Gunstocks, Inc., 4508 San Miguel Ave., North Las Vegas, NV 89030 / 702-645-0718
J.R. Blair Engraving, P.O. Box 64, Glenrock, WY 82637 / 307-436-8115
J.R. Williams Bullet Co., 2008 Tucker Rd., Perry, GA 31069 / 912-987-0274
J.W. Morrison Custom Rifles, 4015 W. Sharon, Phoenix, AZ 85029 / 602-978-3754
J/B Adventures & Safaris Inc., 2275 E. Arapahoe Rd., Ste. 109, Littleton, CO 80122-1521 / 303-771-0977
Jack Dever Co., 8590 NW 90, Oklahoma City, OK 73132 / 405-721-6393
Jack A. Rosenberg & Sons, 12229 Cox Ln., Dallas, TX 75234 / 214-241-6302
Jack First, Inc., 1201 Turbine Dr., Rapid City, SD 57701 / 605-343-9544; FAX: 605-343-9420
Jack Jonas Appraisals & Taxidermy, 1675 S. Birch, Suite 506, Denver, CO 80222 / 303-757-7347; FAX: 303-639-9655
Jackalope Gun Shop, 1048 S. 5th St., Douglas, WY 82633 / 307-358-3441
Jaffin, Harry. See: BRIDGEMAN PRODUCTS
Jagdwaffen, P. Hofer, Buchsenmachermeister, Kirchgasse 24 A-9170, Ferlach, AUSTRIA / 04227-3683
James Calhoon Varmint Bullets, Shambo Rt., 304, Havre, MT 59501 / 406-395-4079
James Churchill Glove Co., P.O. Box 298, Centralia, WA 98531
James Calhoon Mfg., Rt. 304, Havre, MT 59501 / 406-395-4079
James Wayne Firearms for Collectors and Investors, 2608 N. Laurent, Victoria, TX 77901 / 512-578-1258; FAX: 512-578-3559

Jamison's Forge Works, 4527 Rd. 6.5 NE, Moses Lake, WA 98837 / 509-762-2659
Jantz Supply, P.O. Box 584-GD, Davis, OK 73030-0584 / 580-369-2316; FAX: 580-369-3082
Jarrett Rifles, Inc., 383 Brown Rd., Jackson, SC 29831 / 803-471-3616
Jarvis, Inc., 1123 Cherry Orchard Lane, Hamilton, MT 59840 / 406-961-4392
JAS, Inc., P.O. Box 0, Rosemount, MN 55068 / 612-890-7631
Javelina Lube Products, PO Box 337, San Bernardino, CA 92402 / 714-882-5847; FAX: 714-434-9787
JB Custom, P.O. Box 6912, Leawood, KS 66206 / 913-381-2329
Jeff W. Flannery Engraving Co., 11034 Riddles Run Rd., Union, KY 41091 / 606-384-3127
Jeffredo Gunsight, P.O. Box 669, San Marcos, CA 92079 / 619-728-2695
Jenco Sales, Inc., P.O. Box 1000, Manchaca, TX 78652 / 800-531-5301 FAX: 800-266-2373
Jenkins Recoil Pads, Inc., 5438 E. Frontage Ln., Olney, IL 62450 / 618-395-3416
Jensen Bullets, 86 North, 400 West, Blackfoot, ID 83221 / 208-785-5590
Jensen's Custom Ammunition, 5146 E. Pima, Tucson, AZ 85712 / 602-325-3346 FAX: 602-322-5704
Jensen's Firearms Academy, 1280 W. Prince, Tucson, AZ 85705 / 602-293-8516
Jericho Tool & Die Co., Inc., RD 3 Box 70, Route 7, Bainbridge, NY 13733-9496 / 607-563-8222; FAX: 607-563-8560
Jerry Phillips Optics, P.O. Box L632, Langhorne, PA 19047 / 215-757-5037 FAX: 215-757-7097
Jesse W. Smith Saddlery, 16909 E. Jackson Road, Elk, WA 99009-9600 / 509-325-0622
Jester Bullets, Rt. 1 Box 27, Orienta, OK 73737
Jewell Triggers, Inc., 3620 Hwy. 123, San Marcos, TX 78666 / 512-353-2999
JGS Precision Tool Mfg., 100 Main Sumner, Coos Bay, OR 97420 / 541-267-4331 FAX: 541-267-5996
Jim Chambers Flintlocks Ltd., Rt. 1, Box 513-A, Candler, NC 28715 / 704-667-8361
Jim Garthwaite Pistolsmith, Inc., Rt. 2 Box 310, Watsontown, PA 17777 / 717-538-1566
Jim Noble Co., 1305 Columbia St, Vancouver, WA 98660 / 360-695-1309; FAX: 360-695-6835
Jim Norman Custom Gunstocks, 14281 Cane Rd, Valley Center, CA 92082 / 619-749-6252
Jim's Gun Shop (See Spradlin's)
Jim's Precision, Jim Ketchum, 1725 Moclips Dr., Petaluma, CA 94952 / 707-762-3014
JLK Bullets, 414 Turner Rd., Dover, AR 72837 / 501-331-4194
Johanssons Vapentillbehor, Bert, S-430 20, Veddige, SWEDEN
John Hall Plastics, Inc., Inc., P.O. Box 1526, Alvin, TX 77512 / 713-489-8709
John J. Adams & Son Engravers, PO Box 66, Vershire, VT 05079 / 802-685-0019
John Masen Co. Inc., 1305 Jelmak, Grand Prairie, TX 75050 / 817-430-8732; FAX: 817-430-1715
John Norrell Arms, 2608 Grist Mill Rd, Little Rock, AR 72207 / 501-225-7864
John Partridge Sales Ltd., Trent Meadows Rugeley, Staffordshire, WS15 2HS ENGLAND
John Rigby & Co., 66 Great Suffolk St., London, SE1 OBU ENGLAND / 0171-620-0690; FAX: 0171-928-9205
John Unertl Optical Co., Inc., 308 Clay Ave., P.O. Box 818, Mars, PA 16046-0818 / 412-625-3810
John's Custom Leather, 523 S. Liberty St., Blairsville, PA 15717 / 412-459-6802
Johnny Stewart Game Calls, Inc., P.O. Box 7954, 5100 Fort Ave., Waco, TX 76714 / 817-772-3261; FAX: 817-772-3670
Johnson Wood Products, 34968 Crystal Road, Strawberry Point, IA 52076 / 319-933-4930
Johnson's Gunsmithing, Inc, Neal, 208 W Buchanan St, Ste B, Colorado Springs, CO 80907 / 800-284-8671; FAX: 719-632-3493
Johnston Bros. (See C&T Corp. TA Johnson Brothers)
Johnston, James (See North Fork Custom Gunsmithing
Jonad Corp., 2091 Lakeland Ave., Lakewood, OH 44107 / 216-226-3161
Jonathan Arthur Ciener, Inc., 8700 Commerce St., Cape Canaveral, FL 32920 / 407-868-2200; FAX: 407-868-2201
Jones Co., Dale, 680 Hoffman Draw, Kila, MT 59920 / 406-755-4684
Jones Custom Products, Neil A., 17217 Brookhouser Rd , Saegertown, PA 16433 / 814-763-2769; FAX: 814-763-4228
Jones Moulds, Paul, 4901 Telegraph Rd, Los Angeles, CA 90022 / 213-262-1510
Jones, J.D./SSK Industries, 590 Woodvue Ln., Wintersville, OH 43953 / 740-264-0176; FAX: 740-264-2257
JP Sales, Box 307, Anderson, TX 77830
JRP Custom Bullets, RR2 2233 Carlton Rd., Whitehall, NY 12887 / 518-282-0084 or 802-438-5548
JS Worldwide DBA (See Coonan Arms)
JSL Ltd (See U.S. Importer-Specialty Shooters Supp

Juenke, Vern, 25 Bitterbush Rd., Reno, NV 89523 / 702-345-0225
Jumbo Sports Products, J. M. Bucheimer , 721 N. 20th St., St. Louis, MO 63103 / 314-241-1020
Jungkind, Reeves C., 5001 Buckskin Pass, Austin, TX 78745-2841 / 512-442-1094
Jurras, L. E., P.O. Box 680, Washington, IN 47501 / 812-254-7698
Justin Phillippi Custom Bullets, P.O. Box 773, Ligonier, PA 15658 / 412-238-9671

K

K&M Industries, Inc., Box 66, 510 S. Main, Troy, ID 83871 / 208-835-2281; FAX: 208-835-5211
K&M Services, 5430 Salmon Run Rd., Dover, PA 17315 / 717-292-3175; FAX: 717-292-3175
K&T Co. Div. of T&S Industries, Inc., 1027 Skyview Dr., W. Carrollton, OH 45449 / 513-859-8414
K-D, Inc., Box 459, 585 N. Hwy. 155, Cleveland, UT 84518 / 801-653-2530
K-Sports Imports Inc., 2755 Thompson Creek Rd., Pomona, CA 91767 / 909-392-2345 FAX: 909-392-2354
K. Eversull Co., inc., 1 Tracemont, Boyce, LA 71409 / 318-793-8728
K.B.I. Inc, PO Box 6625, Harrisburg, PA 17112 / 717-540-8518; FAX: 717-540-8567
K.K. Arms Co., Star Route Box 671, Kerrville, TX 78028 / 210-257-4718 FAX: 210-257-4891
K.L. Null Holsters Ltd., 161 School St. NW, Hill City Station, Reseca, GA 30735 / 706-625-5643; FAX: 706-625-9392
Ka Pu Kapili, P.O. Box 745, Honokaa, HI 96727 / 808-776-1644; FAX: 808-776-1731
KA-BAR Knives, 1116 E. State St., Olean, NY 14760 / 800-282-0130; FAX: 716-373-6245
Kahles A Swarovski Company, 1 Wholesale Way, Cranston, RI 02920-5540 / 401-946-2220; FAX: 401-946-2587
Kahr Arms, P.O. Box 220, 630 Route 303, Blauvelt, NY 10913 / 914-353-5996; FAX: 914-353-7833
Kalispel Case Line, P.O. Box 267, Cusick, WA 99119 / 509-445-1121
Kamik Outdoor Footwear, 554 Montee de Liesse, Montreal, PQ H4T 1P1 CANADA / 514-341-3950; FAX: 514-341-1861
Kamyk Engraving Co., Steve, 9 Grandview Dr, Westfield, MA 01085-1810 / 413-568-0457
Kane Products, Inc., 5572 Brecksville Rd., Cleveland, OH 44131 / 216-524-9962
Kane, Edward, P.O. Box 385, Ukiah, CA 95482 / 707-462-2937
Kapro Mfg.Co. Inc. (See R.E.I.)
Kasenit Co., Inc., 13 Park Ave., Highland Mills, NY 10930 / 914-928-9595; FAX: 914-928-7292
Kasmarsik Bullets, 4016 7th Ave. SW, Puyallup, WA 98373
Kaswer Custom, Inc., 13 Surrey Drive, Brookfield, CT 06804 / 203-775-0564; FAX: 203-775-6872
KDF, Inc., 2485 Hwy. 46 N., Seguin, TX 78155 / 210-379-8141; FAX: 210-379-5420
KeeCo Impressions, Inc., 346 Wood Ave., North Brunswick, NJ 08902 / 800-468-0546
Keeler, R. H., 817 "N" St., Port Angeles, WA 98362 / 206-457-4702
Kehr, Roger, 2131 Agate Ct. SE, Lacy, WA 98503 / 360-456-0831
Keith M. Heppler, Keith's Custom Gunstocks, 540 Banyan Circle, Walnut Creek, CA 94598 / 925-934-3509; FAX: 925-934-3143
Keith's Bullets, 942 Twisted Oak, Algonquin, IL 60102 / 708-658-3520
Keith's Custom Gunstocks (See Heppler, Keith M)
Kel-Tec CNC Industries, Inc., P.O. Box 3427, Cocoa, FL 32924 / 407-631-0068; FAX: 407-631-1169
Kelbly, Inc., 7222 Dalton Fox Lake Rd., North Lawrence, OH 44666 / 216-683-4674; FAX: 216-683-7349
Keller Co., The, 4215 McEwen Rd., Dallas, TX 75244 / 214-770-8585
Kelley's, P.O. Box 125, Woburn, MA 01801 / 617-935-3389
Kellogg's Professional Products, 325 Pearl St., Sandusky, OH 44870 / 419-625-6551; FAX: 419-625-6167
Kelly, Lance, 1723 Willow Oak Dr., Edgewater, FL 32132 / 904-423-4933
Kemen America, 2550 Hwy. 23, Wrenshall, MN 55797
Ken Eyster Heritage Gunsmiths, Inc., 6441 Bishop Rd., Centerburg, OH 43011 / 614-625-6131
Ken Starnes Gunmaker, 15940 SW Holly Hill Rd, Hillsboro, OR 97123-9033 / 503-628-0705; FAX: 503-628-6005
Ken's Gun Specialties, Rt. 1, Box 147, Lakeview, AR 72642 / 501-431-5606
Ken's Kustom Kartridges, 331 Jacobs Rd., Hubbard, OH 44425 / 216-534-4595
Ken's Rifle Blanks, Ken McCullough , Rt. 2, P.O. Box 85B, Weston, OR 97886 / 503-566-3879
Keng's Firearms Specialty, Inc./US Tactical Systems, 875 Wharton Dr., P.O. Box 44405, Atlanta, GA 30336-1405 / 404-691-7611; FAX: 404-505-8445
Kennebec Journal, 274 Western Ave., Augusta, ME 04330 / 207-622-6288

MANUFACTURER'S DIRECTORY

Kennedy Firearms, 10 N. Market St., Muncy, PA 17756 / 717-546-6695
KenPatable Ent., Inc., P.O. Box 19422, Louisville, KY 40259 / 502-239-5447
Kent Cartridge America, Inc, PO Box 849, 1000 Zigor Rd, Kearneysville, WV 25430
Kent Cartridge Mfg. Co. Ltd., Unit 16 Branbridges Industrial Esta, Tonbridge, Kent, ENGLAND / 622-872255; FAX: 622-872645
Keowee Game Calls, 608 Hwy. 25 North, Travelers Rest, SC 29690 / 864-834-7204; FAX: 864-834-7831
Kershaw Knives, 25300 SW Parkway Ave., Wilsonville, OR 97070 / 503-682-1966 or 800-325-2891; FAX: 503-682-7168
Kesselring Gun Shop, 400 Hwy. 99 North, Burlington, WA 98233 / 206-724-3113; FAX: 206-724-7003
Ketchum, Jim (See Jim's Precision)
Kick Eez, P.O. Box 12767, Wichita, KS 67277 / 316-721-9570; FAX: 316-721-5260
Kilham & Co., Main St., P.O. Box 37, Lyme, NH 03768 / 603-795-4112
Kim Ahrends Custom Firearms, Inc., Box 203, Clarion, IA 50525 / 515-532-3449; FAX: 515-532-3926
Kimar (See U.S. Importer-IAR, Inc)
Kimball, Gary, 1526 N. Circle Dr., Colorado Springs, CO 80909 / 719-634-1274
Kimber of America, Inc., 1 Lawton St., Yonkers, NY 10705 / 800-880-2418; FAX: 914-964-9340
King & Co., P.O. Box 1242, Bloomington, IL 61702 / 309-473-2161
King's Gun Works, 1837 W. Glenoaks Blvd., Glendale, CA 91201 / 818-956-6010; FAX: 818-548-8606
Kingyon, Paul L. (See Custom Calls)
Kirkpatrick Leather Co., PO Box 677, Laredo, TX 78040 / 956-723-6631; FAX: 956-725-0672
KK Air International (See Impact Case Co.)
KLA Enterprises, P.O. Box 2028, Eaton Park, FL 33840 / 941-682-2829 FAX: 941-682-2829
Kleen-Bore,Inc., 16 Industrial Pkwy., Easthampton, MA 01027 / 413-527-0300; FAX: 413-527-2522
Klein Custom Guns, Don, 433 Murray Park Dr, Ripon, WI 54971 / 920-748-2931
Kleinendorst, K. W., RR 1, Box 1500, Hop Bottom, PA 18824 / 717-289-4687
Klingler Woodcarving, P.O. Box 141, Thistle Hill, Cabot, VT 05647 / 802-426-3811
Kmount, P.O. Box 19422, Louisville, KY 40259 / 502-239-5447
Kneiper, James, P.O. Box 1516, Basalt, CO 81621-1516 / 303-963-9880
Knife Importers, Inc., P.O. Box 1000, Manchaca, TX 78652 / 512-282-6860
Knight & Hale Game Calls, Box 468, Industrial Park, Cadiz, KY 42211 / 502-924-1755; FAX: 502-924-1763
Knight Rifles, 21852 hwy j46, P.O. Box 130, Centerville, IA 52544 / 515-856-2626; FAX: 515-856-2628
Knight Rifles (See Modern Muzzle Loading, Inc.)
Knight's Mfg. Co., 7750 9th St. SW, Vero Beach, FL 32960 / 561-562-5697; FAX: 561-569-2955
Knippel, Richard, 500 Gayle Ave Apt 213, Modesto, CA 95350-4241 / 209-869-1469
Knock on Wood Antiques, 355 Post Rd., Darien, CT 06820 / 203-655-9031
Knoell, Doug, 9737 McCardle Way, Santee, CA 92071
Koevenig's Engraving Service, Box 55 Rabbit Gulch, Hill City, SD 57745
KOGOT, 410 College, Trinidad, CO 81082 / 719-846-9406 FAX: 719-846-9406
Kokolus, Michael M. (See Custom Riflestocks, In
Kolar, 1925 Roosevelt Ave, Racine, WI 53406 / 414-554-0800; FAX: 414-554-9093
Kolpin Mfg., Inc., P.O. Box 107, 205 Depot St., Fox Lake, WI 53933 / 414-928-3118; FAX: 414-928-3687
Korth, Robert-Bosch-Str. 4, P.O. Box 1320, 23909 Ratzeburg, GERMANY / 451-4991497; FAX: 451-4993230
Korzinek Riflesmith, J, RD 2 Box 73D, Canton, PA 17724 / 717-673-8512
Koval Knives, 5819 Zarley St., Suite A, New Albany, OH 43054 / 614-855-0777; FAX: 614-855-0945
Kowa Optimed, Inc., 20001 S. Vermont Ave., Torrance, CA 90502 / 310-327-1913; FAX: 310-327-4177
Kramer Designs, P.O. Box 129, Clancy, MT 59634 / 406-933-8658; FAX: 406-933-8658
Kramer Handgun Leather, P.O. Box 112154, Tacoma, WA 98411 / 206-564-6652; FAX: 206-564-1214
Krause Publications, Inc., 700 E. State St., Iola, WI 54990 / 715-445-2214; FAX: 715-445-4087
Krico Jagd-und Sportwaffen GmbH, Nurnbergerstrasse 6, D-90602, Pyrbaum, GERMANY / 09180-2780; FAX: 09180-2661
Krieger Barrels, Inc., N114 W18697 Clinton Dr., Germantown, WI 53022 / 414-255-9593; FAX: 414-255-9586
Krieghoff Gun Co., H., Boschstrasse 22, D-89079 Elm, GERMANY or 731-4018270
Krieghoff International,Inc., 7528 Easton Rd., Ottsville, PA 18942 / 610-847-5173; FAX: 610-847-8691
Kris Mounts, 108 Lehigh St., Johnstown, PA 15905 / 814-539-9751
KSN Industries Ltd (See U.S. Importer-Israel Arms
Kudlas, John M., 622 14th St. SE, Rochester, MN 55904 / 507-288-5579
Kulis Freeze Dry Taxidermy, 725 Broadway Ave., Bedford, OH 44146 / 216-232-8352; FAX: 216-232-7305
KVH Industries, Inc., 110 Enterprise Center, Middletown, RI 02842 / 401-847-3327; FAX: 401-849-0045
Kwik Mount Corp., P.O. Box 19422, Louisville, KY 40259 / 502-239-5447
Kwik-Site Co., 5555 Treadwell, Wayne, MI 48184 / 734-326-1500; FAX: 734-326-4120

L

L&R Lock Co., 1137 Pocalla Rd., Sumter, SC 29150 / 803-775-6127 FAX: 803-775-5171
L&S Technologies Inc (See Aimtech Mount Systems)
L. Bengtson Arms Co., 6345-B E. Akron St., Mesa, AZ 85205 / 602-981-6375
L.A.R. Mfg., Inc., 4133 W. Farm Rd., West Jordan, UT 84088 / 801-280-3505; FAX: 801-280-1972
L.E. Wilson, Inc., Box 324, 404 Pioneer Ave., Cashmere, WA 98815 / 509-782-1328; FAX: 509-782-7200
L.L. Bean, Inc., Freeport, ME 04032 / 207-865-4761; FAX: 207-552-2802
L.P.A. Snc, Via Alfieri 26, Gardone V.T., Brescia, ITALY / 30-891-14-81; FAX: 30-891-09-51
L.R. Clift Mfg., 3821 Hammonton Rd., Marysville, CA 95901 / 916-755-3390; FAX: 916-755-3393
L.S. Starrett Co., 121 Crescent St., Athol, MA 01331 / 617-249-3551
L.W. Seecamp Co., Inc., P.O. Box 255, New Haven, CT 06502 / 203-877-3429
La Clinique du .45, 1432 Rougemont, Chambly,, PQ J3L 2L8 CANADA / 514-658-1144
Labanu, Inc., 2201-F Fifth Ave., Ronkonkoma, NY 11779 / 516-467-6197; FAX: 516-981-4112
LaBoone, Pat. See: CLEAR CREEK OUTDOORS
LaBounty Precision Reboring, Inc, 7968 Silver Lake Rd., PO Box 186, Maple Falls, WA 98266 / 360-599-2047 FAX: 360-599-3018
LaCrosse Footwear, Inc., P.O. Box 1328, La Crosse, WI 54602 / 608-782-3020 or 800-323-2668; FAX: 800-658-9444
LaFrance Specialties, P.O. Box 87933, San Diego, CA 92138-7933 / 619-293-3373; FAX: 619-293-7087
Lage Uniwad, P.O. Box 2302, Davenport, IA 52809 / 319-388-LAGE; FAX: 319-388-LAGE
Lair, Sam, 520 E. Beaver, Jenks, OK 74037 / 918-299-2391
Lake Center, P.O. Box 38, St. Charles, MO 63302 / 314-946-7500
Lakefield Arms Ltd (See Savage Arms Inc)
Lakewood Products LLC, 275 June St., Berlin, WI 54923 / 800-872-8458; FAX: 920-361-7719
Lamboy, Stephen. See: ITHACA CLASSIC DOUBLES
Lampert, Ron, Rt. 1, Box 177, Guthrie, MN 56461 / 218-854-7345
Lamson & Goodnow Mfg. Co., 45 Conway St., Shelburne Falls, MA 03170 / 413-625-6331; FAX: 413-625-9816
Lanber Armas, S.A., Zubiaurre 5, Zaldibar, 48250 SPAIN / 34-4-6827702; FAX: 34-4-6827999
Langenberg Hat Co., P.O. Box 1860, Washington, MO 63090 / 800-428-1860; FAX: 314-239-3151
Lanphert, Paul, P.O. Box 1985, Wenatchee, WA 98807
Lansky Levine, Arthur. See: LANSKY SHARPENERS
Lansky Sharpeners, Arthur Lansky Levine , PO Box 50830, Las Vegas, NV 89016 / 702-361-7511; FAX: 702-896-9511
Lapua Ltd., P.O. Box 5, Lapua, FINLAND / 6-310111; FAX: 6-4388991
LaRocca Gun Works, 51 Union Place, Worcester, MA 01608 / 508-754-2887; FAX: 508-754-2887
Larry Lyons Gunworks, 110 Hamilton St., Dowagiac, MI 49047 / 616-782-9478
Laser Devices, Inc., 2 Harris Ct. A-4, Monterey, CA 93940 / 408-373-0701; FAX: 408-373-0903
Laseraim Technologies, Inc., P.O. Box 3548, Little Rock, AR 72203 / 501-375-2227
Laserlyte, 3015 Main St #300, Santa Monica, CA 90405 / 800-255-9133; FAX: 310-392-1754
LaserMax, Inc., 3495 Winton Place, Bldg. B, Rochester, NY 14623-2807 / 800-527-3703 FAX: 716-272-5427
Lassen Community College, Gunsmithing Dept., P.O. Box 3000, Hwy. 139, Susanville, CA 96130 / 916-251-8800; FAX: 916-251-8838
Lathrop's, Inc., Inc., 5146 E. Pima, Tucson, AZ 85712 / 520-881-0266 or 800-875-4867; FAX: 520-322-5704
Laughridge, William R (See Cylinder & Slide Inc)
Laurel Mountain Forge, P.O. Box 224C, Romeo, MI 48065 / 810-749-5742
Laurona Armas Eibar, S.A.L., Avenida de Otaola 25, P.O. Box 260, Eibar 20600, SPAIN / 34-43-700600; FAX: 34-43-700616
Lawrence Brand Shot (See Precision Reloading, Inc.
Lawrence Leather Co., P.O. Box 1479, Lillington, NC 27546 / 910-893-2071; FAX: 910-893-4742
Lawson Co., Harry, 3328 N Richey Blvd., Tucson, AZ 85716 / 520-326-1117
Lawson, John. See: THE SIGHT SHOP
Lawson, John G (See Sight Shop, The)
Lazzeroni Arms Co., PO Box 26696, Tucson, AZ 85726 / 888-492-7247; FAX: 520-624-4250
LBT, HCR 62, Box 145, Moyie Springs, ID 83845 / 208-267-3588
Le Clear Industries (See E-Z-Way Systems), PO Box 4310, Newark, OH 43058-4310 / 614-345-6645; FAX: 614-345-6600
Lea Mfg. Co., 237 E. Aurora St., Waterbury, CT 06720 / 203-753-5116
Leapers, Inc., 7675 Five Mile Rd., Northville, MI 48167 / 248-486-1231; FAX: 248-486-1430
Leatherman Tool Group, Inc., 12106 NE Ainsworth Cir., P.O. Box 20595, Portland, OR 97294 / 503-253-7826; FAX: 503-253-7830
Lebeau-Courally, Rue St. Gilles, 386 4000, Liege, BELGIUM / 042-52-48-43; FAX: 32-042-52-20-08
Leckie Professional Gunsmithing, 546 Quarry Rd., Ottsville, PA 18942 / 215-847-8594
Lectro Science, Inc., 6410 W. Ridge Rd., Erie, PA 16506 / 814-833-6487; FAX: 814-833-0447
Ledbetter Airguns, Riley, 1804 E Sprague St, Winston Salem, NC 27107-3521 / 919-784-0676
Lee Co., T. K., 1282 Branchwater Ln, Birmingham, AL 35216 / 205-913-5222
Lee Precision, Inc., 4275 Hwy. U, Hartford, WI 53027 / 414-673-3075; FAX: 414-673-9273
Lee Supplies, Mark, 9901 France Ct., Lakeville, MN 55044 / 612-461-2114
Lee's Red Ramps, 4 Kristine Ln., Silver City, NM 88061 / 505-538-8529
LeFever Arms Co., Inc., 6234 Stokes, Lee Center Rd., Lee Center, NY 13363 / 315-337-6722; FAX: 315-337-1543
Legend Products Corp., 21218 Saint Andrews Blvd., Boca Raton, FL 33433-2435
Leibowitz, Leonard, 1205 Murrayhill Ave., Pittsburgh, PA 15217 / 412-361-5455
Leica USA, Inc., 156 Ludlow Ave., Northvale, NJ 07647 / 201-767-7500; FAX: 201-767-8666
LEM Gun Specialties Inc. The Lewis Lead Remover, P.O. Box 2855, Peachtree City, GA 30269-2024
Leonard Day & Sons Inc., P.O. Box 122, Flagg Hill Rd., Heath, MA 01346 / 413-337-8369
Les Baer Custom,Inc., 29601 34th Ave., Hillsdale, IL 61257 / 309-658-2716; FAX: 309-658-2610
Lestrom Laboratories, Inc., P.O. Box 628, Mexico, NY 13114-0628 / 315-343-3076; FAX: 315-592-3370
Lethal Force Institute (See Police Bookshelf), PO Box 122, Concord, NH 03301 / 603-224-6814; FAX: 603-226-3554
Lett Custom Grips, 672 Currier Rd., Hopkinton, NH 03229-2652 / 800-421-5388 FAX: 603-226-4580
Leupold & Stevens, Inc., P.O. Box 688, Beaverton, OR 97075 / 503-646-9171; FAX: 503-526-1455
Lever Arms Service Ltd., 2131 Burrard St., Vancouver, BC V6J 3H7 CANADA / 604-736-2711; FAX: 604-738-3503
Lew Horton Dist. Co., Inc., 15 Walkup Dr., Westboro, MA 01581 / 508-366-7400; FAX: 508-366-5332
Lewis Lead Remover (See LEM Gun Specialties,, The
Liberty Antique Gunworks, 19 Key St., P.O. Box 183, Eastport, ME 04631 / 207-853-4116
Liberty Metals, 2233 East 16th St., Los Angeles, CA 90021 / 213-581-9171; FAX: 213-581-9351
Liberty Safe, 1060 N. Spring Creek Pl., Springville, UT 84663 / 800-247-5625; FAX: 801-489-6409
Liberty Shooting Supplies, P.O. Box 357, Hillsboro, OR 97123 / 503-640-5518; FAX: 503-640-5518
Liberty Trouser Co., 3500 6 Ave S., Birmingham, AL 35222-2406 / 205-251-9143
Lightfield Ammunition Corp. (See Slug Group, Inc.), PO Box 376, New Paris, PA 15554 / 814-839-4517; FAX: 814-839-2601
Lightforce U.S.A. Inc., 19226 66th Ave. So., L-103, Kent, WA 98032 / 206-656-1577; FAX: 206-656-1578
Lightning Performance Innovations, Inc., RD1 Box 555, Mohawk, NY 13407 / 800-242-5873; FAX: 315-866-1578
Lilja Precision Rifle Barrels, P.O. Box 372, Plains, MT 59859 / 406-826-3084; FAX: 406-826-3083
Lincoln, Dean, Box 1886, Farmington, NM 87401
Lind Custom Guns, Al, 7821 76th Ave SW, Tacoma, WA 98498 / 253-584-6361
Linder Solingen Knives, 4401 Sentry Dr., Tucker, GA 30084 / 770-939-6915; FAX: 770-939-6738
Lindsay, Steve, RR 2 Cedar Hills, Kearney, NE 68847 / 308-236-7885
Lindsley Arms Cartridge Co., P.O. Box 757, 20 College Hill Rd., Henniker, NH 03242 / 603-428-3127
Linebaugh Custom Sixguns, Route 2, Box 100, Maryville, MO 64468 / 816-562-3031
Lion Country Supply, P.O. Box 480, Port Matilda, PA 16870
List Precision Engineering, Unit 1 Ingley Works, 13 River Road, Barking, ENGLAND / 011-081-594-1686

MANUFACTURER'S DIRECTORY

Lithi Bee Bullet Lube, 1728 Carr Rd., Muskegon, MI 49442 / 616-788-4479

"Little John's" Antique Arms, 1740 W. Laveta, Orange, CA 92668

Little Trees Ramble (See Scott Pilkington, Little

Littler Sales Co., 20815 W. Chicago, Detroit, MI 48228 / 313-273-6888; FAX: 313-273-1099

Littleton, J. F., 275 Pinedale Ave., Oroville, CA 95966 / 916-533-6084

Ljutic Industries, Inc., 732 N. 16th Ave., Suite 22, Yakima, WA 98907 / 509-248-0476; FAX: 509-576-8233

Llama Gabilondo Y Cia, Apartado 290, E-01080, Victoria, spain, SPAIN

Load From A Disk, 9826 Sagedale, Houston, TX 77089 / 713-484-0935; FAX: 281-484-0935

Loch Leven Industries, P.O. Box 2751, Santa Rosa, CA 95405 / 707-573-8735; FAX: 707-573-0369

Lock's Philadelphia Gun Exchange, 6700 Rowland Ave., Philadelphia, PA 19149 / 215-332-6225; FAX: 215-332-4800

Lodewick, Walter H., 2816 NE Halsey St., Portland, OR 97232 / 503-284-2554

Log Cabin Sport Shop, 8010 Lafayette Rd., Lodi, OH 44254 / 330-948-1082; FAX: 330-948-4307

Logan, Harry M., Box 745, Honokaa, HI 96727 / 808-776-1644

Lohman Mfg. Co., Inc., 4500 Doniphan Dr., P.O. Box 220, Neosho, MO 64850 / 417-451-4438; FAX: 417-451-2576

Lomont Precision Bullets, RR 1, Box 34, Salmon, ID 83467 / 208-756-6819; FAX: 208-756-6824

London Guns Ltd., Box 3750, Santa Barbara, CA 93130 / 805-683-4141; FAX: 805-683-1712

Lone Star Gunleather, 1301 Brushy Bend Dr., Round Rock, TX 78681 / 512-255-1805

Lone Star Rifle Company, 11231 Rose Road, Conroe, TX 77303 / 409-856-3363

Long, George F., 1500 Rogue River Hwy., Ste. F, Grants Pass, OR 97527 / 541-476-7552

Lorcin Engineering Co. Inc., 10427 San Sevaine Way, Ste. A, Mira Loma, CA 91752 / 909-360-1406; FAX: 909-360-0623

Lortone Inc., 2856 NW Market St., Seattle, WA 98107

Lothar Walther Precision Tool Inc., 3425 Hutchinson Rd., Cumming, GA 30040 / 770-889-9998; FAX: 770-889-4918

Loweth, Richard H.R., 29 Hedgegrow Lane, Kirby Muxloe, Leics, LE9 2BN ENGLAND / (0) 116 238 6295

LPS Laboratories, Inc., 4647 Hugh Howell Rd., P.O. Box 3050, Tucker, GA 30084 / 404-934-7800

Lucas, Edward E, 32 Garfield Ave., East Brunswick, NJ 08816 / 201-251-5526

Lucas, Mike, 1631 Jessamine Rd., Lexington, SC 29073

Lupton, Keith. See: PAWLING MOUNTAIN CLUB

Lutz Engraving, Ron E., E1998 Smokey Valley Rd, Scandinavia, WI 54977 / 715-467-2674

Lyman Instant Targets, Inc. (See Lyman Products, C

Lyman Products Corp., 475 Smith Street, Middletown, CT 06457-1541 / 860-632-2020 or 800-22-LYMAN FAX: 860-632-1699

Lyman Products Corporation, 475 Smith Street, Middletown, CT 06457-1529 / 800-22-LYMAN or 860-632-2020; FAX: 860-632-1699

Lyte Optronics (See TracStar Industries Inc)

M

M & D Munitions Ltd., 66 Birch Ln, Massapequa Park, NY 11762-3911 / 800-878-2788 or 516-752-1038; FAX: 516-752-1905

M. Thys (See U.S. Importer-Champlin Firearms Inc)

M.H. Canjar Co., 500 E. 45th Ave., Denver, CO 80216 / 303-295-2638; FAX: 303-295-2638

M.O.A. Corp., 2451 Old Camden Pike, Eaton, OH 45320 / 513-456-3669

MA Systems, P.O. Box 1143, Chouteau, OK 74337 / 918-479-6378

Mac's .45 Shop, P.O. Box 2028, Seal Beach, CA 90740 / 310-438-5046

Mac-1 Airgun Distributors, 13974 Van Ness Ave., Gardena, CA 90249 / 310-327-3581; FAX: 310-327-0238

Macbean, Stan, 754 North 1200 West, Orem, UT 84057 / 801-224-6446

Madis Books, 2453 West Five Mile Pkwy., Dallas, TX 75233 / 214-330-7168

Madis, George, P.O. Box 545, Brownsboro, TX 75756 / 903-852-6480

MAG Instrument, Inc., 1635 S. Sacramento Ave., Ontario, CA 91761 / 909-947-1006; FAX: 909-947-3116

Mag-Na-Port International, Inc., 41302 Executive Dr., Harrison Twp., MI 48045-1306 / 810-469-6727; FAX: 810-469-0425

Mag-Pack Corp., P.O. Box 846, Chesterland, OH 44026

Magma Engineering Co., P.O. Box 161, 20955 E. Ocotillo Rd., Queen Creek, AZ 85242 / 602-987-9008 FAX: 602-987-0148

Magnolia Sports,Inc., 211 W. Main, Magnolia, AR 71753 / 501-234-8410 or 800-530-7816; FAX: 501-234-8117

Magnum Grips, 16356 N Thompson Peak Pkwy, Apt 1147, Scottsdale, AZ 85260-2106

Magnum Power Products, Inc., P.O. Box 17768, Fountain Hills, AZ 85268

Magnum Research, Inc., 7110 University Ave. NE, Minneapolis, MN 55432 / 800-772-6168 or 612-574-1868; FAX: 612-574-0109

Magnus Bullets, P.O. Box 239, Toney, AL 35773 / 256-420-8359; FAX: 256-420-8360

MagSafe Ammo Co., 4700 S US Highway 17/92, Casselberry, FL 32707-3814 / 407-834-9966; FAX: 407-834-8185

Magtech Ammunition Co., 5030 Paradise Rd., Suite A104, Las Vegas, NV 89119 / 702-736-2043; FAX: 702-736-2140

Mahony, Philip Bruce, 67 White Hollow Rd., Lime Rock, CT 06039-2418 / 203-435-9341

Mahovsky's Metalife, R.D. 1, Box 149a Eureka Road, Grand Valley, PA 16420 / 814-436-7747

Maine Custom Bullets, RFD 1, Box 1755, Brooks, ME 04921

Maionchi-L.M.I., Via Di Coselli-Zona, Industriale Di Guamo 55060, Lucca, ITALY / 011 39-583 94291

Makinson, Nicholas, RR 3, Komoka, ON N0L 1R0 CANADA / 519-471-5462

Malcolm Enterprises, 1023 E. Prien Lake Rd., Lake Charles, LA 70601

Mallardtone Game Calls, 2901 16th St., Moline, IL 61265 / 309-762-8089

Mandell Shooting Supplies Inc., 3616 N. Scottsdale Rd., Scottsdale, AZ 85252 / 602-945-2553; FAX: 602-949-0734

Marathon Rubber Prods. Co., Inc., 510 Sherman St., Wausau, WI 54401 / 715-845-6255

Marble Arms (See CRR, Inc./Marble's Inc.)

Marchmon Bullets, 8191 Woodland Shore Dr., Brighton, MI 48116

Marent, Rudolf, 9711 Tiltree St., Houston, TX 77075 / 713-946-7028

Mark Lee Supplies, 9901 France Ct., Lakeville, MN 55044 / 612-461-2114

Markell,Inc., 422 Larkfield Center 235, Santa Rosa, CA 95403 / 707-573-0792; FAX: 707-573-9867

Markesbery Muzzle Loaders, Inc., 7785 Foundation Dr., Ste. 6, Florence, KY 41042 / 606-342-5553; or 606-342-2380

Marksman Products, 5482 Argosy Dr., Huntington Beach, CA 92649 / 714-898-7535 or 800-822-8005; FAX: 714-891-0782

Marlin Firearms Co., 100 Kenna Dr., North Haven, CT 06473 / 203-239-5621; FAX: 203-234-7991

MarMik, Inc., 2116 S. Woodland Ave., Michigan City, IN 46360 / 219-872-7231; FAX: 219-872-7231

Marocchi F.lli S.p.A, Via Galileo Galilei 8, I-25068 Zanano, ITALY

Marquart Precision Co., P.O. Box 1740, Prescott, AZ 86302 / 520-445-5646

Marsh, Johnny, 1007 Drummond Dr., Nashville, TN 37211 / 615-833-3259

Marsh, Mike, Croft Cottage, Main St., Derbyshire, DE4 2BY ENGLAND / 01629 650 669

Marshall Enterprises, 792 Canyon Rd., Redwood City, CA 94062

Marshall F. Fish Mfg. Gunsmith Sptg. Co., Rd. Box 2439, Rt. 22 North, Westport, NY 12993 / 518-962-4897 FAX: 518-962-4897

Martin B. Retting Inc., 11029 Washington, Culver City, CA 90232 / 213-837-2412

Martin Hagn Rifles & Actions, P.O. Box 444, Cranbrook, BC V1C 4H9 CANADA / 604-489-4861

Martin's Gun Shop, 937 S. Sheridan Blvd., Lakewood, CO 80226 / 303-922-2184

Martz, John V., 8060 Lakeview Lane, Lincoln, CA 95648 FAX: 916-645-3815

Marvel, Alan, 3922 Madonna Rd., Jarretsville, MD 21084 / 301-557-6545

Marx, Harry (See U.S. Importer for FERLIB)

Maryland Paintball Supply, 8507 Harford Rd., Parkville, MD 21234 / 410-882-5607

MAST Technology, 4350 S. Arville, Suite 3, Las Vegas, NV 89103 / 702-362-5043; FAX: 702-362-9554

Master Engravers, Inc. (See Hendricks, Frank E)

Master Lock Co., 2600 N. 32nd St., Milwaukee, WI 53245 / 414-444-2800

Match Prep--Doyle Gracey, P.O. Box 155, Tehachapi, CA 93581 / 661-822-5383; FAX: 661-823-8680

Matco, Inc., 1003-2nd St., N. Manchester, IN 46962 / 219-982-8282

Mathews & Son, Inc., George E., 10224 S Paramount Blvd, Downey, CA 90241 / 562-862-6719; FAX: 562-862-6719

Matthews Cutlery, 4401 Sentry Dr., Tucker, GA 30084 / 770-939-6915

Mauser Werke Oberndorf Waffensysteme GmbH, Postfach 1349, 78722, Oberndorf/N., GERMANY

Maverick Arms, Inc., 7 Grasso Ave., P.O. Box 497, North Haven, CT 06473 / 203-230-5300; FAX: 203-230-5420

Maxi-Mount, P.O. Box 291, Willoughby Hills, OH 44094-0291 / 216-944-9456; FAX: 216-944-9456

Maximum Security Corp., 32841 Calle Perfecto, San Juan Capistrano, CA 92675 / 714-493-3684; FAX: 714-496-7733

Mayville Engineering Co. (See MEC, Inc.)

Mazur Restoration, Pete, 13083 Drummer Way, Grass Valley, CA 95949 / 530-268-2412

McBros Rifle Co., P.O. Box 86549, Phoenix, AZ 85080 / 602-582-3713; FAX: 602-581-3825

McCament, Jay, 1730-134th St. Ct. S., Tacoma, WA 98444 / 253-531-8832

McCann Industries, P.O. Box 641, Spanaway, WA 98387 / 253-537-6919; FAX: 253-537-6919

McCann's Machine & Gun Shop, P.O. Box 641, Spanaway, WA 98387 / 253-537-6919; FAX: 253-537-6993

McCann's Muzzle-Gun Works, 14 Walton Dr., New Hope, PA 18938 / 215-862-2728

McCluskey Precision Rifles, 10502 14th Ave. NW, Seattle, WA 98177 / 206-781-2776

McCombs, Leo, 1862 White Cemetery Rd., Patriot, OH 45658 / 614-256-1714

McCormick Corp., Chip, 1825 Fortview Rd Ste 115, Austin, TX 78704 / 800-328-CHIP; FAX: 512-462-0009

McCullough, Ken. See: KEN'S RIFLE BLANKS

McCullough, Ken (See Ken's Rifle Blanks)

McDonald, Dennis, 8359 Brady St., Peosta, IA 52068 / 319-556-7940

McFarland, Stan, 2221 Idella Ct., Grand Junction, CO 81505 / 970-243-4704

McGhee, Larry. See: B.C. OUTDOORS

McGowen Rifle Barrels, 5961 Spruce Lane, St. Anne, IL 60964 / 815-937-9816; FAX: 815-937-4024

McGuire, Bill, 1600 N. Eastmont Ave., East Wenatchee, WA 98802 / 509-884-6021

Mchalik, Gary. See: ROSSI FIREARMS, BRAZTECH

McKee Publications, 121 Eatons Neck Rd., Northport, NY 11768 / 516-575-8850

McKenzie, Lynton, 6940 N. Alvernon Way, Tucson, AZ 85718 / 520-299-5090

McKillen & Heyer, Inc., 35535 Euclid Ave., Suite 11, Willoughby, OH 44094 / 216-942-2044

McKinney, R.P. (See Schuetzen Gun Co.)

McMillan Fiberglass Stocks, Inc., 21421 N. 14th Ave., Suite B, Phoenix, AZ 85027 / 602-582-9635; FAX: 602-581-3825

McMillan Optical Gunsight Co., 28638 N. 42nd St., Cave Creek, AZ 85331 / 602-585-7868; FAX: 602-585-7872

McMillan Rifle Barrels, P.O. Box 3427, Bryan, TX 77805 / 409-690-3456; FAX: 409-690-0156

McMurdo, Lynn (See Specialty Gunsmithing), PO Box 404, Afton, WY 83110 / 307-886-5535

MCRW Associates Shooting Supplies, R.R. 1, Box 1425, Sweet Valley, PA 18656 / 717-864-3967; FAX: 717-864-2669

MCS, Inc., 34 Delmar Dr., Brookfield, CT 06804 / 203-775-1013; FAX: 203-775-9462

McWelco Products, 6730 Santa Fe Ave., Hesperia, CA 92345 / 619-244-8876; FAX: 619-244-9398

MDS, P.O. Box 1441, Brandon, FL 33509-1441 / 813-653-1180; FAX: 813-684-5953

Meadow Industries, 24 Club Lane, Palmyra, VA 22963 / 804-589-7672; FAX: 804-589-7672

Measurement Group Inc., Box 27777, Raleigh, NC 27611

Measures, Leon. See: SHOOT WHERE YOU LOOK

MEC, Inc., 715 South St., Mayville, WI 53050 / 414-387-4500; FAX: 414-387-5802

MEC-Gar S.r.l., Via Madonnina 64, Gardone V.T. Brescia, ITALY / 39-30-8912687; FAX: 39-30-8910065

MEC-Gar U.S.A., Inc., Box 112, 500B Monroe Turnpike, Monroe, CT 06468 / 203-635-8662; FAX: 203-635-8662

Mech-Tech Systems, Inc., 1602 Foothill Rd., Kalispell, MT 59901 / 406-755-8055

Meister Bullets (See Gander Mountain)

Mele, Frank, 201 S. Wellow Ave., Cookeville, TN 38501 / 615-526-4860

Melton Shirt Co., Inc., 56 Harvester Ave., Batavia, NY 14020 / 716-343-8750; FAX: 716-343-6887

Men-Metallwerk Elisenhuette GmbH, P.O. Box 1263, Nassau/Lahn, D-56372 GERMANY / 2604-7819

Menck, Gunsmith Inc., T.W., 5703 S 77th St, Ralston, NE 68127

Mendez, John A., P.O. Box 620984, Orlando, FL 32862 / 407-344-2791

Meprolight (See Hesco-Meprolight)

Mercer Custom Stocks, R. M., 216 S Whitewater Ave, Jefferson, WI 53549 / 414-674-5130

Merit Corp., Box 9044, Schenectady, NY 12309 / 518-346-1420

Merkel Freres, Strasse 7 October, 10, Suhl, GERMANY

Merkuria Ltd., Argentinska 38, 17005, Praha 7 CZECH, REPUBLIC / 422-875117; FAX: 422-809152

Metal Merchants, PO Box 186, Walled Lake, MI 48390-0186

Metalife Industries (See Mahovsky's Metalife)

Metaloy, Inc., Rt. 5, Box 595, Berryville, AR 72616 / 501-545-3611

Metals Hand Engraver/European Hand Engraving, Ste. 216, 12 South First St., San Jose, CA 95113 / 408-293-6559

MI-TE Bullets, 1396 Ave. K, Ellsworth, KS 67439 / 785-472-4575; FAX: 785-472-5579

Michael's Antiques, Box 591, Waldoboro, ME 04572

Michaels of Oregon Co., P.O. Box 1690, Portland, OR 97045 / 503-557-0536; FAX: 503-655-7546

Micro Sight Co., 242 Harbor Blvd., Belmont, CA 94002 / 415-591-0769; FAX: 415-591-7531

MANUFACTURER'S DIRECTORY

Microfusion Alfa S.A., Paseo San Andres N8, P.O. Box 271, Eibar, 20600 SPAIN / 34-43-11-89-16; FAX: 34-43-11-40-38
Mid-America Guns and Ammo, 1205 W. Jefferson, Suite E, Effingham, IL 62401 / 800-820-5177
Mid-America Recreation, Inc., 1328 5th Ave., Moline, IL 61265 / 309-764-5089; FAX: 309-764-2722
Middlebrooks Custom Shop, 7366 Colonial Trail East, Surry, VA 23883 / 757-357-0881; FAX: 757-365-0442
Midway Arms, Inc., 5875 W. Van Horn Tavern Rd., Columbia, MO 65203 / 800-243-3220 or 573-445-6363; FAX: 573-446-1018
Midwest Gun Sport, 1108 Herbert Dr., Zebulon, NC 27597 / 919-269-5570
Midwest Sport Distributors, Box 129, Fayette, MO 65248
Mike Davis Products, 643 Loop Dr., Moses Lake, WA 98837 / 509-765-6178 or 509-766-7281
Milberry House Publishing, PO Box 575, Corydon, IN 47112 / 888-738-1567; FAX: 888-738-1567
Military Armament Corp., P.O. Box 120, Mt. Zion Rd., Lingleville, TX 76461 / 817-965-3253
Millennium Designed Muzzleloaders, PO Box 536, Routes 11 & 25, Limington, ME 04049 / 207-637-2316
Miller Arms, Inc., P.O. Box 260 Purl St., St. Onge, SD 57779 / 605-642-5160; FAX: 605-642-5160
Miller Custom, 210 E. Julia, Clinton, IL 61727 / 217-935-9362
Miller Single Trigger Mfg. Co., Rt. 209, Box 1275, Millersburg, PA 17061 / 717-692-3704
Millett Sights, 7275 Murdy Circle, Adm. Office, Huntington Beach, CA 92647 / 714-842-5575 or 800-645-5388; FAX: 714-843-5707
Mills Jr., Hugh B., 3615 Canterbury Rd., New Bern, NC 28560 / 919-637-4631
Milstor Corp., 80-975 Indio Blvd., Indio, CA 92201 / 760-775-9998; FAX: 760-772 4990
Miltex, Inc, 700 S Lee St, Alexandria, VA 22314-4332 / 888-642-9123; FAX: 301-645-1430
Minute Man High Tech Industries, 10611 Canyon Rd. E., Suite 151, Puyallup, WA 98373 / 800-233-2734
Mirador Optical Corp., P.O. Box 11614, Marina Del Rey, CA 90295-7614 / 310-821-5587; FAX: 310-305-0386
Miroku, B C/Daly, Charles (See U.S. Importer-Bell'
Mitchell Bullets, R.F., 430 Walnut St, Westernport, MD 21562
Mitchell Optics, Inc., 2072 CR 1100 N, Sidney, IL 61877 / 217-688-2219 or 217-621-3018; FAX: 217-688-2505
Mitchell's Accuracy Shop, 68 Greenridge Dr., Stafford, VA 22554 / 703-659-0165
Mitchell, Jack, c/o Geoff Gaebe, Addieville East Farm, 200 Pheasant Dr, Mapleville, RI 02839 / 401-568-3185
Mittermeier, Inc., Frank, PO Box 2G, 3577 E Tremont Ave, Bronx, NY 10465 / 718-828-3843
Mixson Corp., 7635 W. 28th Ave., Hialeah, FL 33016 / 305-821-5190 or 800-327-0078; FAX: 305 558-9318
MJK Gunsmithing, Inc., 417 N. Huber Ct., E. Wenatchee, WA 98802 / 509-884-7683
MJM Mfg., 3283 Rocky Water Ln., Suite B, San Jose, CA 95148 / 408 270-4207
MKS Supply, Inc. (See Hi-Point Firearms)
MMC, 2513 East Loop 820 North, Ft. Worth, TX 76118 / 817-595-0404; FAX: 817 595-3074
MMP, Rt. 6, Box 384, Harrison, AR 72601 / 501-741-5019; FAX: 501-741-3104
Mo's Competitor Supplies (See MCS Inc)
Modern Gun Repair School, P.O. Box 92577, Southlake, TX 76092 / 800-493-4114; FAX: 800-556-5112
Modern Muzzleloading, Inc, PO Box 130, Centerville, IA 52544 / 515-856-2626
Moeller, Steve, 1213 4th St., Fulton, IL 61252 / 815-589-2300
Molin Industries, Tru-Nord Division, P.O. Box 365, 204 North 9th St., Brainerd, MN 56401 / 218-829-2870
Monell Custom Guns, 228 Red Mills Rd., Pine Bush, NY 12566 / 914-744-3021
Moneymaker Guncraft Corp., 1420 Military Ave., Omaha, NE 68131 / 402-556-0226
Montana Armory, Inc (See C. Sharps Arms Co. Inc.), 100 Centennial, Box 885, Big Timber, MT 59011 / 406-932-4353
Montana Outfitters, Lewis E. Yearout, 308 Riverview Dr. E., Great Falls, MT 59404 / 406-761-0859
Montana Precision Swaging, P.O. Box 4746, Butte, MT 59702 / 406-782-7502
Montana Vintage Arms, 2354 Bear Canyon Rd., Bozeman, MT 59715
Montgomery Community College, P.O. Box 787-GD, Troy, NC 27371 / 910-576-6222 or 800-839-6222; FAX: 910-576-2176
Morini (See U.S. Importers-Mandall Shooting Suppli
Morrison Custom Rifles, J. W., 4015 W Sharon, Phoenix, AZ 85029 / 602-978-3754
Morrow, Bud, 11 Hillside Lane, Sheridan, WY 82801-9729 / 307-674-8360
Morton Booth Co., P.O. Box 123, Joplin, MO 64802 / 417-673-1962; FAX: 417-673-3642
Moss Double Tone, Inc., P.O. Box 1112, 2101 S. Kentucky, Sedalia, MO 65301 / 816-827-0827
Mountain Hollow Game Calls, Box 121, Cascade, MD 21719 / 301-241-3282
Mountain Plains, Inc., 244 Glass Hollow Rd., Alton, VA 22920 / 800-687-3000
Mountain Rifles, Inc., P.O. Box 2789, Palmer, AK 99645 / 907-373-4194; FAX: 907-373-4195
Mountain South, P.O. Box 381, Barnwell, SC 29812 / FAX: 803-259-3227
Mountain State Muzzleloading Supplies, Inc., Box 154-1, Rt. 2, Williamstown, WV 26187 / 304-375-7842; FAX: 304-375-3737
Mountain States Engraving, Kenneth W. Warren, P.O. Box 2842, Wenatchee, WA 98807 / 509-663-6123 FAX: 509-665-6123
Mountain View Sports, Inc., Box 188, Troy, NH 03465 / 603-357-9690; FAX: 603-357-9691
Mowrey Gun Works, P.O. Box 246, Waldron, IN 46182 / 317-525-6181; FAX: 317-525-9595
Mowrey's Guns & Gunsmithing, 119 Fredericks St., Canajoharie, NY 13317 / 518-673-3483
MPC, P.O. Box 450, McMinnville, TN 37110-0450 / 615-473-5513; FAX: 615-473-5516
MPI Stocks, PO Box 83266, Portland, OR 97283 / 503-226-1215; FAX: 503-226-2661
MSC Industrial Supply Co., 151 Sunnyside Blvd., Plainview, NY 11803-9915 / 516-349-0330
MSR Targets, P.O. Box 1042, West Covina, CA 91793 / 818-331-7840
Mt. Alto Outdoor Products, Rt. 735, Howardsville, VA 24562
Mt. Baldy Bullet Co., 12981 Old Hill City Rd., Keystone, SD 57751-6623 / 605-666-4725
MTM Molded Products Co., Inc., 3370 Obco Ct., Dayton, OH 45414 / 937-890-7461; FAX: 937-890-1747
Mulhern, Rick, Rt. 5, Box 152, Rayville, LA 71269 / 318-728-2688
Mullins Ammunition, Rt. 2, Box 304K, Clintwood, VA 24228 / 540-926-6772; FAX: 540-926-6092
Mullis Guncraft, 3523 Lawyers Road E., Monroe, NC 28110 / 704-283-6683
Multi-Scale Charge Ltd., 3269 Niagara Falls Blvd., N. Tonawanda, NY 14120 / 905-566-1255; FAX: 905-276-6295
Multiplex International, 26 S. Main St., Concord, NH 03301 / FAX: 603-796-2223
Multipropulseurs, La Bertrandiere, 42580, FRANCE / 77 74 01 30; FAX: 77 93 19 34
Mundy, Thomas A., 69 Robbins Road, Somerville, NJ 08876 / 201-722-2199
Murmur Corp., 2823 N. Westmoreland Ave., Dallas, TX 75222 / 214-630-5400
Murray State College, 1 Murray Campus St., Tishomingo, OK 73460 / 508-371-2371
Muscle Products Corp., 112 Fennell Dr., Butler, PA 16001 / 800-227-7049 or 412-283-0567; FAX: 412-283-8310
Museum of Historical Arms, Inc., 2750 Coral Way, Suite 204, Miami, FL 33145 / 305-444-9199
Mushroom Express Bullet Co., 601 W. 6th St., Greenfield, IN 46140-1728 / 317-462-6332
Muzzleloaders Etcetera, Inc., 9901 Lyndale Ave. S., Bloomington, MN 55420 / 612-884-1161
Muzzleloading Technologies, Inc, 25 E. Hwy. 40, Suite 330-12, Roosevelt, UT 84066 / 801-722-5996; FAX: 801-722-5909
MWG Co., P.O. Box 971202, Miami, FL 33197 / 800-428-9394 or 305 253 8393; FAX: 305-232-1247

N

N&J Sales, Lime Kiln Rd., Northford, CT 06472 / 203-484-0247
N. Flayderman & Co., Inc., PO Box 2446, Ft Lauderdale, FL 33303 / 954-761-8855
N.B.B., Inc., 24 Elliot Rd., Sterling, MA 01564 / 508-422-7538 or 800-942-9444
N.C. Ordnance Co., P.O. Box 3254, Wilson, NC 27895 / 919-237-2440; FAX: 919-243-9845
Nagel's Custom Bullets, 100 Scott St., Baytown, TX 77520-2849
Nalpak, 1937-C Friendship Drive, El Cajon, CA 92020 / 619-258-1200
Nastoff's 45 Shop, Inc., Steve, 12288 Mahoning Ave, PO Box 446, North Jackson, OH 44451 / 330-538-2977
National Bullet Co., 1585 E. 361 St., Eastlake, OH 44095 / 216-951-1854; FAX: 216-951-7761
National Security Safe Co., Inc., P.O. Box 39, 620 S. 380 E., American Fork, UT 84003 / 801-756-7706 or 800-544-3829; FAX: 801-756-8043
National Target Co., 4690 Wyaconda Rd., Rockville, MD 20852 / 800-827-7060 or 301-770-7060; FAX: 301-770-7892
Nationwide Sports Distributors, Inc., 70 James Way, Southampton, PA 18966 / 800-355-3006; FAX: 215-322-2050
Naval Ordnance Works, Rt. 2, Box 919, Sheperdstown, WV 25443 / 304-876-0998
Navy Arms Co., 689 Bergen Blvd., Ridgefield, NJ 07657 / 201-945-2500; FAX: 201-945-6859
NCP Products, Inc., 3500 12th St. N.W., Canton, OH 44708 / 330-456-5130; FAX: 330-456-5234
Neal Johnson's Gunsmithing, Inc., 208 W. Buchanan St., Suite B, Colorado Springs, CO 80907 / 800-284-8671; FAX: 719-632-3493
Necessary Concepts, Inc., P.O. Box 571, Deer Park, NY 11729 / 516-667-8509; FAX: 516-667-8588
Necromancer Industries, Inc., 14 Communications Way, West Newton, PA 15089 / 412-872-8722
NEI Handtools, Inc., 51583 Columbia River Hwy., Scappoose, OR 97056 / 503-543-6776; FAX: 503-543-6799
Neil A. Jones Custom Products, 17217 Brookhouser Road, Saegertown, PA 16433 / 814-763-2769; FAX: 814-763-4228
Nelson, Gary K., 975 Terrace Dr., Oakdale, CA 95361 / 209-847-4590
Nelson, Stephen, 7365 NW Spring Creek Dr., Corvallis, OR 97330 / 541-745-5232
Nelson/Weather-Rite, Inc., 14760 Santa Fe Trail Dr., Lenexa, KS 66215 / 913-492-3200; FAX: 913-492-8749
Nesci Enterprises Inc., P.O. Box 119, Summit St., East Hampton, CT 06424 / 203-267-2588
Nesika Bay Precision, 22239 Big Valley Rd., Poulsbo, WA 98370 / 206-697-3830
Nettestad Gun Works, RR 1, Box 160, Pelican Rapids, MN 56572 / 218-863-4301
Neumann GmbH, Am Galgenberg 6, 90575, GERMANY / 09101/8258; FAX: 09101/6356
Nevada Pistol Academy, Inc., 4610 Blue Diamond Rd., Las Vegas, NV 89139 / 702-897-1100
New England Ammunition Co., 1771 Post Rd. East, Suite 223, Westport, CT 06880 / 203-254-8048
New England Arms Co., Box 278, Lawrence Lane, Kittery Point, ME 03905 / 207-439-0593; FAX: 207-439-6726
New England Custom Gun Service, 438 Willow Brook Rd., Plainfield, NH 03781 / 603-469-3450; FAX: 603-469-3471
New England Firearms, 60 Industrial Rowe, Gardner, MA 01440 / 508-632-9393; FAX: 508-632-2300
New Orleans Jewelers Supply Co., 206 Charters St., New Orleans, LA 70130 / 504-523-3839; FAX: 504-523-3836
New SKB Arms Co., C.P.O. Box 1401, Tokyo, JAPAN / 81-3-3943-9550; FAX: 81-3-3943-0695
New Win Publishing, Inc., 186 Center St., Clinton, NJ 08809 / 908-735-9701; FAX: 908-735-9703
Newark Electronics, 4801 N. Ravenswood Ave., Chicago, IL 60640
Newell, Robert H., 55 Coyote, Los Alamos, NM 87544 / 505-662-7135
Newman Gunshop, 119 Miller Rd., Agency, IA 52530 / 515-937-5775
NgraveR Co., The, 67 Wawecus Hill Rd., Bozrah, CT 06334 / 860-823-1533
Nic Max, Inc., 535 Midland Ave., Garfield, NJ 07026 / 201-546-7191; FAX: 201-546-7419
Nicholson Custom, 17285 Thornlay Road, Hughesville, MO 65334 / 816-826-8746
Nickels, Paul R., 4789 Summerhill Rd., Las Vegas, NV 89121 / 702-435-5318
Nicklas, Ted, 5504 Hegel Rd., Goodrich, MI 48438 / 810-797-4493
Niemi Engineering, W. B., Box 126 Center Rd, Greensboro, VT 05041 / 802-533-7180; FAX: 802-533-7141
Nightforce (See Lightforce USA Inc)
Nikolai leather, 15451 Electronic ln, Huntington Beach, CA 92649 / 714-373-2721 FAX: 714 373 2723
Nikon, Inc., 1300 Walt Whitman Rd., Melville, NY 11747 / 516-547-8623; FAX: 516-547-0309
Nitex, Inc., P.O. Box 1706, Uvalde, TX 78801 / 888-543-8843
No-Sho Mfg. Co., 10727 Glenfield Ct., Houston, TX 77096 / 713-723-5332
Noreen, Peter H., 5075 Buena Vista Dr., Belgrade, MT 59714 / 406-586-7383
Norica, Avnda Otaola, 16 Apartado 68, Eibar, SPAIN
Norinco, 7A Yun Tan N, Beijing, CHINA
Norincoptics (See BEC, Inc.)
Norma Precision AB (See U.S. Importers-Dynamit Nob
Normark Corp., 10395 Yellow Circle Dr., Minnetonka, MN 55343-9101 / 612-933-7060 FAX: 612-933-0046
North American Arms, Inc., 2150 South 950 East, Provo, UT 84606-6285 / 800-821-5783 or 801-374-9990; FAX: 801-374-9998
North American Correspondence Schools The Gun Pro, Oak & Pawney St., Scranton, PA 18515 / 717-342-7701
North American Shooting Systems, P.O. Box 306, Osoyoos, BC V0H 1V0 CANADA / 604-495-3131; FAX: 604-495-2816
North Devon Firearms Services, 3 North St., Braunton, EX33 1AJ ENGLAND / 01271 813624; FAX: 01271 813624
North Fork Custom Gunsmithing, James Johnston, 428 Del Rio Rd., Roseburg, OR 97470 / 503-673-4467
North Mountain Pine Training Center (See Executive
North Pass, 425 South Bowen St., Ste. 6, Longmount, CO 80501 / 303-682-4315; FAX: 303-678-7109
North Specialty Products, 2664-B Saturn St., Brea, CA 92621 / 714-524-1665
North Star West, P.O. Box 488, Glencoe, CA 95232 / 209-293-7010

MANUFACTURER'S DIRECTORY

North Wind Decoy Co., 1005 N. Tower Rd., Fergus Falls, MN 56537 / 218-736-4378; FAX: 218-736-7060
Northern Precision Custom Swaged Bullets, 329 S. James St., Carthage, NY 13619 / 315-493-1711
Northlake Outdoor Footwear, P.O. Box 10, Franklin, TN 37065-0010 / 615-794-1556; FAX: 615-790-8005
Northside Gun Shop, 2725 NW 109th, Oklahoma City, OK 73120 / 405-840-2353
Northwest Arms, 26884 Pearl Rd., Parma, ID 83660 / 208-722-6771; FAX: 208-722-1062
Nosler, Inc., P.O. Box 671, Bend, OR 97709 / 800-285-3701 or 541-382-3921; FAX: 541-388-4667
Novak's, Inc., 1206 1/2 30th St., P.O. Box 4045, Parkersburg, WV 26101 / 304-485-9295; FAX: 304-428-6722
Now Products, Inc., PO Box 27608, Tempe, AZ 85285 / 800-662-6063: FAX: 480-966-0890
Nowlin Mfg. Co., 20622 S 4092 Rd, Claremore, OK 74017 / 918-342-0689; FAX: 918-342-0624
NRI Gunsmith School, 4401 Connecticut Ave. NW, Washington, DC 20008
Nu-Line Guns,Inc., 1053 Caulks Hill Rd., Harvester, MO 63304 / 314-441-4500 or 314-447-4501; FAX: 314-447-5018
Null Holsters Ltd. K.L., 161 School St NW, Resaca, GA 30735 / 706-625-5643; FAX: 706-625-9392
Numrich Arms Corp., 203 Broadway, W. Hurley, NY 12491
NW Sinker and Tackle, 380 Valley Dr., Myrtle Creek, OR 97457-9717
Nygord Precision Products, P.O. Box 12578, Prescott, AZ 86304 / 520-717-2315; FAX: 520-717-2198

O

O.F. Mossberg & Sons,Inc., 7 Grasso Ave., North Haven, CT 06473 / 203-230-5300; FAX: 203-230-5420
Oakland Custom Arms,Inc., 4690 W. Walton Blvd., Waterford, MI 48329 / 810-674-8261
Oakman Turkey Calls, RD 1, Box 825, Harrisonville, PA 17228 / 717-485-4620
Obermeyer Rifled Barrels, 23122 60th St., Bristol, WI 53104 / 262-843-3537; FAX: 262-843-2129
October Country Muzzleloading, P.O. Box 969, Dept. GD, Hayden, ID 83835 / 208-772-2068; FAX: 208-772-9230
Oehler Research,Inc., P.O. Box 9135, Austin, TX 78766 / 512-327-6900 or 800-531-5125; FAX: 512-327-6903
Oil Rod and Gun Shop, 69 Oak St., East Douglas, MA 01516 / 508-476-3687
Ojala Holsters, Arvo, PO Box 98, N Hollywood, CA 91603 / 503-669-1404
OK Weber,Inc., P.O. Box 7485, Eugene, OR 97401 / 541-747-0458; FAX: 541-747-5927
Oker's Engraving, 365 Bell Rd., P.O. Box 126, Shawnee, CO 80475 / 303-838-6042
Oklahoma Ammunition Co., 3701A S. Harvard Ave., No. 367, Tulsa, OK 74135-2265 / 918-396-3187; FAX: 918-396-4270
Oklahoma Leather Products,Inc., 500 26th NW, Miami, OK 74354 / 918-542-6651; FAX: 918-542-6653
Old Wagon Bullets, 32 Old Wagon Rd., Wilton, CT 06897
Old West Bullet Moulds, J Ken Chapman , P.O. Box 519, Flora Vista, NM 87415 / 505-334-6970
Old West Reproductions,Inc. R.M. Bachman, 446 Florence S. Loop, Florence, MT 59833 / 406-273-2615; FAX: 406-273-2615
Old Western Scrounger,Inc., 12924 Hwy. A-l2, Montague, CA 96064 / 916-459-5445; FAX: 916-459-3944
Old World Gunsmithing, 2901 SE 122nd St., Portland, OR 97236 / 503-760-7681
Old World Oil Products, 3827 Queen Ave. N., Minneapolis, MN 55412 / 612-522-5037
Ole Frontier Gunsmith Shop, 2617 Hwy. 29 S., Cantonment, FL 32533 / 904-477-8074
Olson, Myron, 989 W. Kemp, Watertown, SD 57201 / 605-886-9787
Olson, Vic, 5002 Countryside Dr., Imperial, MO 63052 / 314-296-8086
Olympic Arms Inc., 620-626 Old Pacific Hwy. SE, Olympia, WA 98513 / 360-491-3447; FAX: 360-491-3447
Olympic Optical Co., P.O. Box 752377, Memphis, TN 38175-2377 / 901-794-3890 or 800-238-7120; FAX: 901-794-0676 80
Omark Industries,Div. of Blount,Inc., 2299 Snake River Ave., P.O. Box 856, Lewiston, ID 83501 / 800-627-3640 or 208-746-2351
Omega Sales, P.O. Box 1066, Mt. Clemens, MI 48043 / 810-469-7323; FAX: 810-469-0425
One Of A Kind, 15610 Purple Sage, San Antonio, TX 78255 / 512-695-3364
Op-Tec, P.O. Box L632, Langhorn, PA 19047 / 215-757-5037
Optical Services Co., P.O. Box 1174, Santa Teresa, NM 88008-1174 / 505-589-3833
Orchard Park Enterprise, P.O. Box 563, Orchard Park, NY 14227 / 616-656-0356
Ordnance Works, The, 2969 Pidgeon Point Road, Eureka, CA 95501 / 707-443-3252
Oregon Arms, Inc. (See Rogue Rifle Co., Inc.)
Oregon Trail Bullet Company, P.O. Box 529, Dept. P, Baker City, OR 97814 / 800-811-0548; FAX: 514-523-1803
Original Box, nc., 700 Linden Ave., York, PA 17404 / 717-854-2897; FAX: 717-845-4276
Original Mink Oil,Inc., 10652 NE Holman, Portland, OR 97220 / 503-255-2814 or 800-547-5895; FAX: 503-255-2487
Orion Rifle Barrel Co., RR2, 137 Cobler Village, Kalispell, MT 59901 / 406-257-5649
Orvis Co., The, Rt. 7, Manchester, VT 05254 / 802-362-3622; FAX: 802-362-3525
Otis Technology, Inc, RR 1 Box 84, Boonville, NY 13309 / 315-942-3320
Ottmar, Maurice, Box 657, 113 E. Fir, Coulee City, WA 99115 / 509-632-5717
Outa-Site Gun Carriers, 219 Market St., Laredo, TX 78040 / 210-722-4678 or 800-880-9715; FAX: 210-726-4858
Outdoor Connection,Inc., The, 201 Cotton Dr., P.O. Box 7751, Waco, TX 76714-7751 / 800-533-6076 or 817-772-5575; FAX: 817-776-3553
Outdoor Edge Cutlery Corp., 2888 Bluff St., Suite 130, Boulder, CO 80301 / 303-652-8212; FAX: 303-652-8238
Outdoor Enthusiast, 3784 W. Woodland, Springfield, MO 65807 / 417-883-9841
Outdoor Sports Headquarters,Inc., 967 Watertower Ln., West Carrollton, OH 45449 / 513-865-5855; FAX: 513-865-5962
Outdoorsman's Bookstore, The, Llangorse, Brecon, LD3 7UE U.K. / 44-1874-658-660; FAX: 44-1874-658-650
Outers Laboratories Div. of Blount, Inc.Sporting E, Route 2, P.O. Box 39, Onalaska, WI 54650 / 608-781-5800; FAX: 608-781-0368
Ox-Yoke Originals, Inc., 34 Main St., Milo, ME 04463 / 800-231-8313 or 207-943-7351; FAX: 207-943-2416
Ozark Gun Works, 11830 Cemetery Rd., Rogers, AR 72756 / 501-631-6944; FAX: 501-631-6944

P

P&M Sales and Service, 5724 Gainsborough Pl., Oak Forest, IL 60452 / 708-687-7149
P.A.C.T., Inc., P.O. Box 531525, Grand Prairie, TX 75053 / 214-641-0049
P.M. Enterprises, Inc., 146 Curtis Hill Rd., Chehalis, WA 98532 / 360-748-3743; FAX: 360-748-1802
P.S.M.G. Gun Co., 10 Park Ave., Arlington, MA 02174 / 617-646-8845; FAX: 617-646-2133
Pac-Nor Barreling, 99299 Overlook Rd., P.O. Box 6188, Brookings, OR 97415 / 503-469-7330; FAX: 503-469-7331
Pace Marketing, Inc., P.O. Box 2039, Stuart, FL 34995 / 561-871-9682; FAX: 561-871-6552
Pachmayr Div. Lyman Products, 1875 S. Mountain Ave., Monrovia, CA 91016 / 626-357-7771
Pacific Cartridge, Inc., 2425 Salashan Loop Road, Ferndale, WA 98248 / 360-366-4444; FAX: 360-366-4445
Pacific Research Laboratories, Inc. (See Rimrock R
Pacific Rifle Co., PO Box 11, Newberg, OR 97132 / 503-538-7437
Paco's (See Small Custom Mould & Bullet Co)
Page Custom Bullets, P.O. Box 25, Port Moresby, NEW GUINEA
Pagel Gun Works, Inc., 1407 4th St. NW, Grand Rapids, MN 55744 / 218-326-3003
Paintball Games International Magazine (Aceville P, Castle House 97 High St., Essex, ENGLAND / 011-44-206-564840
Palmer Security Products, 2930 N. Campbell Ave., Chicago, IL 60618 / 800-788-7725; FAX: 773-267-8080
Palsa Outdoor Products, P.O. Box 81336, Lincoln, NE 68501 / 402-488-5288; FAX: 402-488-2321
Para-Ordnance Mfg., Inc., 980 Tapscott Rd., Scarborough, ON M1X 1E7 CANADA / 416-297-7855; FAX: 416-297-1289
Para-Ordnance, Inc., 1919 NE 45th St., Ste 215, Ft. Lauderdale, FL 33308
Paragon Sales & Services, Inc., P.O. Box 2022, Joliet, IL 60434 / 815-725-9212; FAX: 815-725-8974
Pardini Armi Srl, Via Italica 154, 55043, Lido Di Camaiore Lu, ITALY / 584-90121; FAX: 584-90122
Paris, Frank J., 17417 Pershing St., Livonia, MI 48152-3822
Park Rifle Co., Ltd., The, Unit 6a Dartford Trade Park, Power Mill Lane, Dartford DA7 7NX, ENGLAND / 011-0322-222512
Parker & Sons Shooting Supply, 9337 Smoky Row Rd, Straw Plains, TN 97871-1257
Parker Gun Finishes, 9337 Smokey Row Rd., Strawberry Plains, TN 37871 / 423-933-3286
Parker Reproductions, 124 River Rd., Middlesex, NJ 08846 / 908-469-0100 FAX: 908-469-9692
Parsons Optical Mfg. Co., P.O. Box 192, Ross, OH 45061 / 513-867-0820; FAX: 513-867-8380
Partridge Sales Ltd., John, Trent Meadows, Rugeley, ENGLAND
Parts & Surplus, P.O. Box 22074, Memphis, TN 38122 / 901-683-4007
Pasadena Gun Center, 206 E. Shaw, Pasadena, TX 77506 / 713-472-0417; FAX: 713-472-1322
Paser Pal, 200 W Pleasantview, Hurst, TX 76054 / 800-561-1603 FAX: 817-285-8769
Passive Bullet Traps, Inc. (See Savage Range Syste
PAST Sporting Goods,Inc., P.O. Box 1035, Columbia, MO 65205 / 314-445-9200; FAX: 314-446-6606
Paterson Gunsmithing, 438 Main St., Paterson, NJ 07502 / 201-345-4100
Pathfinder Sports Leather, 2920 E. Chambers St., Phoenix, AZ 85040 / 602-276-0016
Patrick Bullets, P.O. Box 172, Warwick, QSLD, 4370 AUSTRALIA
Patrick W. Price Bullets, 16520 Worthley Drive, San Lorenzo, CA 94580 / 510-278-1547
Pattern Control, 114 N. Third St., P.O. Box 462105, Garland, TX 75046 / 214-494-3551; FAX: 214-272-8447
Paul A. Harris Hand Engraving, 113 Rusty Lane, Boerne, TX 78006-5746 / 512-391-5121
Paul Co., The, 27385 Pressonville Rd., Wellsville, KS 66092 / 785-883-4444; FAX: 785-883-2525
Paul D. Hillmer Custom Gunstocks, 7251 Hudson Heights, Hudson, IA 50643 / 319-988-3941
Paul Jones Moulds, 4901 Telegraph Rd., Los Angeles, CA 90022 / 213-262-1510
Paulsen Gunstocks, Rt. 71, Box 11, Chinook, MT 59523 / 406-357-3403
Pawling Mountain Club, Keith Lupton , PO Box 573, Pawling, NY 12564 / 914-855-3825
Paxton Quigley's Personal Protection Strategies, 9903 Santa Monica Blvd., 300, Beverly Hills, CA 90212 / 310-281-1762
Payne Photography, Robert, Robert , P.O. Box 141471, Austin, TX 78714 / 512-272-4554
PC Co., 5942 Secor Rd., Toledo, OH 43623 / 419-472-6222
Peacemaker Specialists, P.O. Box 157, Whitmore, CA 96096 / 916-472-3438
Pearce Grip, Inc., P.O. Box 187, Bothell, WA 98041-0187 / 206-485-5488; FAX: 206-488-9497
Pease Accuracy, Bob , P.O. Box 310787, New Braunfels, TX 78131 / 210-625-1342
Pease International, 53 Durham St, Portsmouth, NH 03801 / 603-431-1331; FAX: 603-431-1221
PECAR Herbert Schwarz GmbH, Kreuzbergstrasse 6, 10965, Berlin, GERMANY / 004930-785-7383; FAX: 004930-785-1934
Pecatonica River Longrifle, 5205 Nottingham Dr., Rockford, IL 61111 / 815-968-1995 FAX: 815-968-1996
Pedersen, C. R., 2717 S. Pere Marquette Hwy., Ludington, MI 49431 / 616-843-2061
Pedersen, Rex C., 2717 S. Pere Marquette Hwy., Ludington, MI 49431 / 616-843-2061
Peerless Alloy, Inc., 1445 Osage St., Denver, CO 80204-2439 / 303-825-6394 or 800-253-1278
Peet Shoe Dryer, Inc., 130 S. 5th St., P.O. Box 618, St. Maries, ID 83861 / 208-245-2095 or 800-222-PEET; FAX: 208-245-5441
Peifer Rifle Co., P.O. Box 192, Nokomis, IL 62075-0192 / 217-563-7050; FAX: 217-563-7060
Pejsa Ballistics, 2120 Kenwood Pkwy., Minneapolis, MN 55405 / 612-374-3337; FAX: 612-374-5383
Pelaire Products, 5346 Bonky Ct., W. Palm Beach, FL 33415 / 561-439-0691; FAX: 561-967-0052
Pell, John T. (See KOGOT)
Peltor, Inc. (See Aero Peltor)
PEM's Mfg. Co., 5063 Waterloo Rd., Atwater, OH 44201 / 216-947-3721
Pence Precision Barrels, 7567 E. 900 S., S. Whitley, IN 46787 / 219-839-4745
Pendleton Royal, c/o Swingler Buckland Ltd., 4/7 Highgate St., Birmingham, ENGLAND / 44 121 440 3060 or 44 121 446 5898; FAX: 44 121 446 4165
Pendleton Woolen Mills, P.O. Box 3030, 220 N.W. Broadway, Portland, OR 97208 / 503-226-4801
Penn Bullets, P.O. Box 756, Indianola, PA 15051
Penn's Woods Products, Inc., 19 W. Pittsburgh St., Delmont, PA 15626 / 412-468-8311; FAX: 412-468-8975
Pennsylvania Gun Parts Inc, 1701 Mud Run Rd., York Springs, PA 17372 / 717-259-8010; FAX: 717-259-0057
Pennsylvania Gunsmith School, 812 Ohio River Blvd., Avalon, Pittsburgh, PA 15202 / 412-766-1812
Penrod Precision, 312 College Ave., P.O. Box 307, N. Manchester, IN 46962 / 219-982-8385
Pentax Corp., 35 Inverness Dr. E., Englewood, CO 80112 / 303-799-8000; FAX: 303-790-1131
Pentheny de Pentheny, 108 Petaluma Ave #202, Sebastopol, CA 95472-4220 / 707-573-1390; FAX: 707-573-1390
Perazone-Gunsmith, Brian, Cold Spring Rd, Roxbury, NY 12474 / 607-326-4088; FAX: 607-326-3140
Perazzi USA, Inc., 1207 S. Shamrock Ave., Monrovia, CA 91016 / 626-303-0068; FAX: 626-303-2081
Performance Specialists, 308 Eanes School Rd., Austin, TX 78746 / 512-327-0119
Perugini Visini & Co. S.r.l., Via Camprelle, 126, 25080 Nuvolera, ITALY / 30-6897535; FAX: 30-6897821
Pete Elsen, Inc., 1529 S. 113th St., West Allis, WI 53214
Pete Mazur Restoration, 13083 Drummer Way, Grass Valley, CA 95949 / 916-268-2412
Pete Rickard, Inc., RD 1, Box 292, Cobleskill, NY 12043 / 518-234-2731; FAX: 518-234-2454
Peter Dyson & Son Ltd., 3 Cuckoo Lane, Honley Huddersfield, Yorkshire, HD7 2BR ENGLAND / 44-1484-661062; FAX: 44-1484-663709

MANUFACTURER'S DIRECTORY

Peter Hale/Engraver, 800 E. Canyon Rd., Spanish Fork, UT 84660 / 801-798-8215
Peters Stahl GmbH, Stettiner Strasse 42, D-33106, Paderborn, / 05251-750025; FAX: 05251-75611
Petersen Publishing Co., 6420 Wilshire Blvd., Los Angeles, CA 90048 / 213-782-2000; FAX: 213-782-2867
Peterson Gun Shop, Inc., A.W., 4255 W. Old U.S. 441, Mt. Dora, FL 32757-3299 / 352-383-4258; FAX: 352-735-1001
Petro-Explo Inc., 7650 U.S. Hwy. 287, Suite 100, Arlington, TX 76017 / 817-478-8888
Pettinger Books, Gerald, Rt. 2, Box 125, Russell, IA 50238 / 515-535-2239
Pflumm Mfg. Co., 10662 Widmer Rd., Lenexa, KS 66215 / 800-888-4867; FAX: 913-451-7857
PFRB Co., P.O. Box 1242, Bloomington, IL 61702 / 309-473-3964; FAX: 309-473-2161
Philip S. Olt Co., P.O. Box 550, 12662 Fifth St., Pekin, IL 61554 / 309-348-3633; FAX: 309-348-3300
Phillippi Custom Bullets, Justin, P.O. Box 773, Ligonier, PA 15658 / 724-238-2962; FAX: 724-238-9671
Phoenix Arms, 1420 S. Archibald Ave., Ontario, CA 91761 / 909-947-4843; FAX: 909-947-6798
Photronic Systems Engineering Company, 6731 Via De La Reina, Bonsall, CA 92003 / 619-758-8000
Piedmont Community College, P.O. Box 1197, Roxboro, NC 27573 / 336-599-1181
Pierce Pistols, 55 Sorrellwood Lane, Sharpsburg, GA 30277-9523 / 404-253-8192
Pietta (See U.S. Importers-Navy Arms Co, Taylor's
Pilgrim Pewter,Inc. (See Bell Originals Inc. Sid)
Pilkington, Scott (See Little Trees Ramble)
Pine Technical College, 1100 4th St., Pine City, MN 55063 / 800-521-7463; FAX: 612-629-6766
Pinetree Bullets, 133 Skeena St., Kitimat, BC V8C 1Z1 CANADA / 604-632-3768; FAX: 604-632-3768
Pioneer Arms Co., 355 Lawrence Rd., Broomall, PA 19008 / 215-356-5203
Piotti (See U.S. Importer-Moore & Co, Wm. Larkin)
Piquotto, Paul R., 80 Bradford Dr., Feeding Hills, MA 01030 / 413-786-8118; or 413-789-4582
Plaxco, J. Michael, Rt. 1, P.O. Box 203, Roland, AR 72135 / 501-868-9787
Plaza Cutlery, Inc., 3333 Bristol, 161 South Coast Plaza, Costa Mesa, CA 92626 / 714-549-3932
Plum City Ballistic Range, N2162 80th St., Plum City, WI 54761 / 715-647-2539
PlumFire Press, Inc., 30-A Grove Ave., Patchogue, NY 11772-4112 / 800-695-7246; FAX: 516-758-4071
PMC/Eldorado Cartridge Corp., P.O. Box 62508, 12801 U.S. Hwy. 95 S., Boulder City, NV 89005 / 702-294-0025; FAX: 702-294-0121
Poburka, Philip (See Bison Studios)
Pohl, Henry A. (See Great American Gun Co.
Pointing Dog Journal, Village Press Publications, P.O. Box 968, Dept. PGD, Traverse City, MI 49685 / 800-272-3246; FAX: 616-946-3289
Police Bookshelf, P.O. Box 122, Concord, NH 03301 / 603-224-6814; FAX: 603-226-3554
Polywad, Inc., P.O. Box 7916, Macon, GA 31209 / 912-477-0669
Pomeroy, Robert, RR1, Box 50, E. Corinth, ME 04427 / 207-285-7721
Ponsness/Warren, P.O. Box 8, Rathdrum, ID 83858 / 208-687-2231; FAX: 208-687-2233
Pony Express Reloaders, 608 E. Co. Rd. D, Suite 3, St. Paul, MN 55117 / 612-483-9406; FAX: 612-483-9884
Pony Express Sport Shop, 16606 Schoenborn St., North Hills, CA 91343 / 818-895-1231
Potts, Wayne E., 912 Poplar St., Denver, CO 80220 / 303-355-5462
Powder Horn Antiques, P.O. Box 4196, Ft. Lauderdale, FL 33338 / 305-565-6060
Powder Horn, Inc., The, P.O. Box 114 Patty Drive, Cusseta, GA 31805 / 404-989-3257
Powell & Son (Gunmakers) Ltd., William, 35-37 Carrs Lane, Birmingham, B4 7SX ENGLAND / 121-643-0689; FAX: 121-631-3504
Powell Agency, William, 22 Circle Dr., Bellmore, NY 11710 / 516-679-1158
Power Custom, Inc., 29739 Hwy. J, Gravois Mills, MO 65037 / 513-372-5684; FAX: 573-372-5799
Powley Computer (See Hutton Rifle Ranch)
Practical Tools, Inc., 7067 Easton Rd., P.O. Box 133, Pipersville, PA 18947 / 215-766-7301; FAX: 215-766-8681
Prairie Gun Works, 1-761 Marion St., Winnipeq, MB R2J 0K6 Canada / 204-231-2976; FAX: 204-231-8566
Prairie River Arms, 1220 N. Sixth St., Princeton, IL 61356 / 815-875-1616 or 800-445-1541; FAX: 815-875-1402
Pranger, Ed G., 1414 7th St., Anacortes, WA 98221 / 206-293-3488
Pre-Winchester 92-90-62 Parts Co., P.O. Box 8125, W. Palm Beach, FL 33407
Precise Metalsmithing Enterprises, 146 Curtis Hill Rd., Chehalis, WA 98532 / 206-748-3743; FAX: 206-748-8102
Precision Airgun Sales, Inc., 5247 Warrensville Ctr Rd, Maple Hts., OH 44137 / 216-587-5005 or 216-587-5005
Precision Cartridge, 176 Eastside Rd., Deer Lodge, MT 59722 / 800-397-3901 or 406-846-3900
Precision Cast Bullets, 101 Mud Creek Lane, Ronan, MT 59864 / 406-676-5135
Precision Castings & Equipment, P.O. Box 326, Jasper, IN 47547-0135 / 812-634-9167
Precision Components, 3177 Sunrise Lake, Milford, PA 18337 / 717-686-4414
Precision Components and Guns, Rt. 55, P.O. Box 337, Pawling, NY 12564 / 914-855-3040
Precision Delta Corp., P.O. Box 128, Ruleville, MS 38771 / 601-756-2810; FAX: 601-756-2590
Precision Gun Works, 104 Sierra Rd Dept. GD, Kerrville, TX 78028 / 830-367-4587
Precision Metal Finishing, John Westrom, P.O. Box 3186, Des Moines, IA 50316 / 515-288-8680; FAX: 515-244-3925
Precision Munitions, Inc., P.O. Box 326, Jasper, IN 47547
Precision Reloading, Inc., P.O. Box 122, Stafford Springs, CT 06076 / 860-684-5680 FAX: 860-684-6788
Precision Sales International, Inc., P.O. Box 1776, Westfield, MA 01086 / 413-562-5055; FAX: 413-562-5056
Precision Shooting,Inc., 222 McKee St., Manchester, CT 06040 / 860-645-8776; FAX: 860-643-8215
Precision Small Arms, 9777 Wilshire Blvd., Suite 1005, Beverly Hills, CA 90212 / 310-859-4867; FAX: 310-859-2868
Precision Small Arms Inc, 9272 Jeronimo Rd, Ste 121, Irvine, CA 92618 / 800-554-5515; FAX: 949-768-4808
Precision Specialties, 131 Hendom Dr., Feeding Hills, MA 01030 / 413-786-3365; FAX: 413-786-3365
Precision Sport Optics, 15571 Producer Lane, Unit G, Huntington Beach, CA 92649 / 714-891-1309; FAX: 714-892-6920
Premier Reticles, 920 Breckinridge Lane, Winchester, VA 22601-6707 / 540-722-0601; FAX: 540-722-3522
Prescott Projectile Co., 1808 Meadowbrook Road, Prescott, AZ 86303
Preslik's Gunstocks, 4245 Keith Ln., Chico, CA 95926 / 916-891-8236
Price Bullets, Patrick W., 16520 Worthley Dr., San Lorenzo, CA 94580 / 510-278-1547
Prime Reloading, 30 Chiswick End, Meldreth, ROYSTON UK / 0763-260636
Primos, Inc., P.O. Box 12785, Jackson, MS 39236-2785 / 601-366-1288; FAX: 601-362-3274
PRL Bullets, c/o Blackburn Enterprises, 114 Stuart Rd., Ste. 110, Cleveland, TN 37312 / 423-559-0340
Pro Load Ammunition, Inc., 5180 E. Seltice Way, Post Falls, ID 83854 / 208-773-9444; FAX: 208-773-9441
Pro-Mark Div. of Wells Lamont, 6640 W. Touhy, Chicago, IL 60648 / 312-647-8200
Pro-Port Ltd., 41302 Executive Dr., Harrison Twp., MI 48045-1306 / 810-469-6727 FAX: 810-469-0425
Pro-Shot Products, Inc., P.O. Box 763, Taylorville, IL 62568 / 217-824-9133; FAX: 217-824-8861
Professional Gunsmiths of America,Inc., Route 1, Box 224F, Lexington, MO 64067 / 816-259-2636
Professional Hunter Supplies (See Star Custom Bull, PO Box 608, 468 Main St, Ferndale, CA 95536 / 707-786-9140; FAX: 707-786-9117
Professional Ordnance, Inc., 1215 E. Airport Dr., Box 182, Ontario, CA 91761 / 909-923-5559; FAX: 909-923-0899
Prolixr Lubricants, P.O. Box 1348, Victorville, CA 92393 / 800-248-5823 or 760-243-3129; FAX: 760-241-0148
Proofmark Corp., P.O. Box 610, Burgess, VA 22432 / 804-453-4337; FAX: 804-453-4337
Protector Mfg. Co., Inc., The, 443 Ashwood Place, Boca Raton, FL 33431 / 407-394-6011
Protektor Model, 1-11 Bridge St., Galeton, PA 16922 / 814-435-2442
Prototech Industries, Inc., Rt. 1, Box 81, Delia, KS 66418 / 913-771-3571; FAX: 913-771-2531
ProWare, Inc., 15847 NE Hancock St., Portland, OR 97230 / 503-239-0159
PWL Gunleather, P.O. Box 450432, Atlanta, GA 31145 / 770-822-1640; FAX: 770-822-1704
Pyromid, Inc., 3292 S. Highway 97, Redmond, OR 97756 / 503-548-1041; FAX: 503-923-1004

Q

Quack Decoy & Sporting Clays, 4 Ann & Hope Way, P.O. Box 98, Cumberland, RI 02864 / 401-723-8202; FAX: 401-722-5910
Quaker Boy, Inc., 5455 Webster Rd., Orchard Parks, NY 14127 / 716-662-3979; FAX: 716-662-9426
Quality Arms, Inc., Box 19477, Dept. GD, Houston, TX 77224 / 281-870-8377; FAX: 281-870-8524
Quality Firearms of Idaho, Inc., 659 Harmon Way, Middleton, ID 83644-3065 / 208-466-1631
Quality Parts Co./Bushmaster Firearms, 999 Roosevelt Trail Bldg. 3, Windham, ME 04062 / 207-892-2005; FAX: 207-892-8068
Quarton USA, Ltd. Co., 7042 Alamo Downs Pkwy., Suite 370, San Antonio, TX 78238-4518 / 800-520-8435 or 210-520-8430; FAX: 210-520-8433
Que Industries, Inc., P.O. Box 2471, Everett, WA 98203 / 800-769-6930 or 206-347-9843; FAX: 206-514-3266
Queen Cutlery Co., P.O. Box 500, Franklinville, NY 14737 / 800-222-5233; FAX: 800-299-2618

R

R&C Knives & Such, 2136 CANDY CANE WALK, Manteca, CA 95336-9501 / 209-239-3722; FAX: 209-825-6947
R&D Gun Repair, Kenny Howell, RR1 Box 283, Beloit, WI 53511
R&J Gun Shop, 337 S Humbolt St, Canyon City, OR 97820 / 541-575-2130
R&S Industries Corp., 8255 Brentwood Industrial Dr., St. Louis, MO 63144 / 314-781-5400
R. Murphy Co., Inc., 13 Groton-Harvard Rd., P.O. Box 376, Ayer, MA 01432 / 617-772-3481
R.A. Wells Custom Gunsmith, 3452 1st Ave., Racine, WI 53402 / 414-639-5223
R.E. Seebeck Assoc., P.O. Box 59752, Dallas, TX 75229
R.E.I., P.O. Box 88, Tallevast, FL 34270 / 813-755-0085
R.E.T. Enterprises, 2608 S. Chestnut, Broken Arrow, OK 74012 / 918-251-GUNS; FAX: 918-251-0587
R.F. Mitchell Bullets, 430 Walnut St., Westernport, MD 21562
R.F.D. Rifles, 8230 Wilson Dr., Ralston, NE 68127 / 402-331-9529
R.I.S. Co., Inc., 718 Timberlake Circle, Richardson, TX 75080 / 214-235-0933
R.M. Mercer Custom Stocks, 216 S. Whitewater Ave., Jefferson, WI 53549 / 414-674-5130
R.M. Precision, P.O. Box 210, LaVerkin, UT 84745 / 801-635-4656; FAX: 801-635-4430
R.T. Eastman Products, P.O. Box 1531, Jackson, WY 83001 / 307-733-3217 or 800-624-4311
Rabeno, Martin, 92 Spook Hole Rd., Ellenville, NY 12428 / 914-647-4567; FAX: 914-647-2129
Radack Photography, Lauren , 21140 Jib Court L-12, Aventura, FL 33180 / 305 931 3110
Radiator Specialty Co., 1900 Wilkinson Blvd., P.O. Box 34689, Charlotte, NC 28234 / 800-438-6947; FAX: 800-421-9525
Radical Concepts, P.O. Box 1473, Lake Grove, OR 97035 / 503-538-7437
Rainier Ballistics Corp., 4500 15th St. East, Tacoma, WA 98424 / 800-638-8722 or 206-922-7589; FAX: 206-922-7854
Ralph Bono Engraving, 718 N. Atlanta, Owasso, OK 74055 / 918-272-9745
Ram-Line Blount, Inc., P.O. Box 39, Onalaska, WI 54650
Ramon B. Gonzalez Guns, P.O. Box 370, 93 St. Joseph's Hill Road, Monticello, NY 12701 / 914-794-4515
Rampart International, 2781 W. MacArthur Blvd., B-283, Santa Ana, CA 92704 / 800-976-7240 or 714-557-6405
Ranch Products, P.O. Box 145, Malinta, OH 43535 / 313-277-3118; FAX: 313-565-8536
Randall-Made Knives, P.O. Box 1988, Orlando, FL 32802 / 407-855-8075
Randco UK, 286 Gipsy Rd., Welling, DA16 1JJ ENGLAND / 44 81 303 4118
Randolph Engineering, Inc., 26 Thomas Patten Dr., Randolph, MA 02368 / 800-541-1405; FAX: 800-875-4200
Randy Duane Custom Stocks, 110 W. North Ave., Winchester, VA 22601 / 703-667-9461; FAX: 703-722-3993
Range Brass Products Company, P.O. Box 218, Rockport, TX 78381
Ranger Products, 2623 Grand Blvd., Suite 209, Holiday, FL 34609 / 813-942-4652 or 800-407-7007; FAX: 813-942-6221
Ranger Shooting Glasses, 26 Thomas Patten Dr., Randolph, MA 02368 / 800-541-1405; FAX: 617-986-0337
Ranging, Inc., Routes 5 & 20, East Bloomfield, NY 14443 / 716-657-6161; FAX: 716-657-5405
Ransom International Corp., 1027 Spire Dr, Prescott, AZ 86302 / 520-778-7899; FAX: 520-778-7993
Rapine Bullet Mould Mfg. Co., 9503 Landis Lane, East Greenville, PA 18041 / 215-679-5413; FAX: 215-679-9795
Raptor Arms Co., Inc., 273 Canal St, #179, Shelton, CT 06484 / 203-924-7618; FAX: 203-924-7624
Ravell Ltd., 289 Diputacion St., 08009, Barcelona, SPAIN / 34(3) 4874486; FAX: 34(3) 4881394
Ray Riling Arms Books Co., 6844 Gorsten St., P.O. Box 18925, Philadelphia, PA 19119 / 215-438-2456; FAX: 215-438-5395
Ray's Gunsmith Shop, 3199 Elm Ave., Grand Junction, CO 81504 / 970-434-6162; FAX: 970-434-6162
Raytech Div. of Lyman Products Corp., 475 Smith Street, Middletown, CT 06457-1541 / 860-632-2020; FAX: 860-632-1699
RCBS Div. of Blount, 605 Oro Dam Blvd., Oroville, CA 95965 / 800-533-5000 or 916-533-5191; FAX: 916-533-1647
Reagent Chemical & Research, Inc. (See Calico Hard
Reardon Products, P.O. Box 126, Morrison, IL 61270 / 815-772-3155
Red Ball, 100 Factory St., Nashua, NH 03060 / 603-881-4420
Red Cedar Precision Mfg., W. 485 Spruce Dr., Brodhead, WI 53520 / 608-897-8416
Red Diamond Dist. Co., 1304 Snowdon Dr., Knoxville, TN 37912

Manufacturer's Directory

Redding Reloading Equipment, 1089 Starr Rd., Cortland, NY 13045 / 607-753-3331; FAX: 607-756-8445
Redfield Media Resource Center, 4607 N.E. Cedar Creek Rd., Woodland, WA 98674 / 360-225-5000 FAX: 360-225-7616
Redfield, Inc, 5800 E Jewell Ave, Denver, CO 80224 / 303-757-6411; FAX: 303-756-2338
Redfield/Blount, PO Box 39, Onalaska, WI 54650 / 800-635-7656
Redman's Rifling & Reboring, 189 Nichols Rd., Omak, WA 98841 / 509-826-5512
Redwood Bullet Works, 3559 Bay Rd., Redwood City, CA 94063 / 415-367-6741
Reed, Dave, Rt. 1, Box 374, Minnesota City, MN 55959 / 507-689-2944
Reiswig, Wallace E. (See Claro Walnut Gunstock
Reloaders Equipment Co., 4680 High St., Ecorse, ML 48229
Reloading Specialties, Inc., Box 1130, Pine Island, MN 55463 / 507-356-8500; FAX: 507-356-8800
Remington Arms Co., Inc., 870 Remington Drive, P.O. Box 700, Madison, NC 27025-0700 / 800-243-9700; FAX: 910-548-8700
Remington Double Shotguns, 7885 Cyd Dr., Denver, CO 80221 / 303-429-6947
Renato Gamba S.p.A.-Societa Armi Bresciane Srl., Via Artigiani 93, 25063 Gardone, Val Trompia (BS), ITALY / 30-8911640; FAX: 30-8911648
Renegade, P.O. Box 31546, Phoenix, AZ 85046 / 602-482-6777; FAX: 602-482-1952
Renfrew Guns & Supplies, R.R. 4, Renfrew, ON K7V 3Z7 CANADA / 613-432-7080
Reno, Wayne, 2808 Stagestop Rd, Jefferson, CO 80456 / 719-836-3452
Republic Arms, Inc., 15167 Sierra Bonita Lane, Chino, CA 91710 / 909-597-3873; FAX: 909-597-2612
Retting, Inc., Martin B, 11029 Washington, Culver City, CA 90232 / 213-837-2412
RG-G, Inc., PO Box 935, Trinidad, CO 81082 / 719-845-1436
Rhino, P.O. Box 787, Locust, NC 28097 / 704-753-2198
Rhodeside, Inc., 1704 Commerce Dr., Piqua, OH 45356 / 513-773-5781
Rice, Keith (See White Rock Tool & Die)
Richard H.R. Loweth (Firearms), 29 Hedgegrow Lane, Kirby Muxloe, Leics. LE9 2BN, ENGLAND
Richards Micro-Fit Stocks, 8331 N. San Fernando Ave., Sun Valley, CA 91352 / 818-767-6097; FAX: 818-767-7121
Rickard, Inc., Pete, RD 1, Box 292, Cobleskill, NY 12043 / 800-282-5663; FAX: 518-234-2454
Ridgeline, Inc, Bruce Sheldon, PO Box 930, Dewey, AZ 86327-0930 / 800-632-5900; FAX: 520-632-5900
Ridgetop Sporting Goods, P.O. Box 306, 42907 Hilligoss Ln. East, Eatonville, WA 98328 / 360-832-6422; FAX: 360-832-6422
Ries, Chuck, 415 Ridgecrest Dr., Grants Pass, OR 97527 / 503-476-5623
Rifles, Inc., 873 W. 5400 N., Cedar City, UT 84720 / 801-586-5996; FAX: 801-586-5996
Rigby & Co., John, 66 Great Suffolk St, London, ENGLAND / 0171-620-0690; FAX: 0171-928-9205
Riggs, Jim, 206 Azalea, Boerne, TX 78006 / 210-249-8567
Riley Ledbetter Airguns, 1804 E. Sprague St., Winston Salem, NC 27107-3521 / 919-784-0676
Riling Arms Books Co., Ray, 6844 Gorsten St, PO Box 18925, Philadelphia, PA 19119 / 215-438-2456; FAX: 215-438-5395
Rim Pac Sports, Inc., 1034 N. Soldano Ave., Azusa, CA 91702-2135
Rimrock Rifle Stocks, P.O. Box 589, Vashon Island, WA 98070 / 206-463-5551 FAX: 206-463-2526
Ringler Custom Leather Co., 31 Shining Mtn. Rd., Powell, WY 82435 / 307-645-3255
Ripley Rifles, 42 Fletcher Street, Ripley, Derbyshire, DE5 3LP ENGLAND / 011-0773-748353
River Road Sporting Clays, Bruce Barsotti, P.O. Box 3016, Gonzales, CA 93926 / 408-675-2473
Rizzini F.lli (See U.S. Importers-Moore & C Englan
Rizzini SNC, Via 2 Giugno, 7/7Bis-25060, Marcheno (Brescia), ITALY
RLCM Enterprises, 110 Hill Crest Drive, Burleson, TX 76028
RMS Custom Gunsmithing, 4120 N. Bitterwell, Prescott Valley, AZ 86314 / 520-772-7626
Robar Co.'s, Inc., The, 21438 N. 7th Ave., Suite B, Phoenix, AZ 85027 / 602-581-2648; FAX: 602-582-0059
Robert Evans Engraving, 332 Vine St., Oregon City, OR 97045 / 503-656-5693
Robert Valade Engraving, 931 3rd Ave., Seaside, OR 97138 / 503-738-7672
Robert W. Hart & Son, Inc., 401 Montgomery St., Nescopeck, PA 18635 / 717-752-3655 or 800-368-3656; FAX: 717-752-1800
Roberts Products, 25328 SE Iss. Beaver Lk. Rd., Issaquah, WA 98029 / 206-392-8172
Roberts/Engraver, J J, 7808 Lake Dr, Manassas, VA 22111 / 703-330-0448
Robinett, R. G., P.O. Box 72, Madrid, IA 50156 / 515-795-2906
Robinson Firearms Mfg. Ltd., 1699 Blondeaux Crescent, Kelowna, BC V1Y 4J8 CANADA / 604-868-9596
Robinson H.V. Bullets, 3145 Church St., Zachary, LA 70791 / 504-654-4029
Robinson, Don, Pennsylvaia Hse, 36 Fairfax Crescent, W Yorkshire, ENGLAND / 0422-364458
Rochester Lead Works, 76 Anderson Ave., Rochester, NY 14607 / 716-442-8500; FAX: 716-442-4712
Rockwood Corp., Speedwell Division, 136 Lincoln Blvd., Middlesex, NJ 08846 / 800-243-8274; FAX: 980-560-7475
Rocky Mountain Arms, Inc., 1813 Sunset Pl, Unit D, Longmont, CO 80501 / 800-375-0846; FAX: 303-678-8766
Rocky Mountain High Sports Glasses, 8121 N. Central Park Ave., Skokie, IL 60076 / 847-679-1012 or 800-323-1418; FAX: 847-679-0184
Rocky Mountain Rifle Works Ltd., 1707 14th St., Boulder, CO 80302 / 303-443-9189
Rocky Mountain Target Co., 3 Aloe Way, Leesburg, FL 34788 / 352-365-9598
Rocky Mountain Wildlife Products, P.O. Box 999, La Porte, CO 80535 / 970-484-2768; FAX: 970-484-0807
Rocky Shoes & Boots, 294 Harper St., Nelsonville, OH 45764 / 800-848-9452 or 614-753-1951; FAX: 614-753-4024
Rodgers & Sons Ltd., Joseph (See George Ibberson
Rogers Gunsmithing, Bob, P.O. Box 305, 344 S. Walnut St., Franklin Grove, IL 61031 / 888-639-0666; FAX: 815-288-7142
Rogue Rifle Co., Inc., P.O. Box 20, Prospect, OR 97536 / 541-560-4040; FAX: 541-560-4041
Rogue River Rifleworks, 1317 Spring St., Paso Robles, CA 93446 / 805-227-4706; FAX: FAX:805-227-4723
Rohner, Hans, 1148 Twin Sisters Ranch Rd., Nederland, CO 80466-9600
Rohner, John, 186 Virginia Ave, Asheville, NC 28806 / 303-444-3841
Romain's Custom Guns, Inc., RD 1, Whetstone Rd., Brockport, PA 15823 / 814-265-1948
Ron Frank Custom Classic Arms, 7131 Richland Rd., Ft. Worth, TX 76118 / 817-284-9300; FAX: 817-284-9300
Ron Lutz Engraving, E. 1998 Smokey Valley Rd., Scandinavia, WI 54977 / 715-467-2674
Rooster Laboratories, P.O. Box 412514, Kansas City, MO 64141 / 816-474-1622; FAX: 816-474-1307
Rorschach Precision Products, P.O. Box 151613, Irving, TX 75015 / 214-790-3487
Rosenberg & Son, Jack A, 12229 Cox Ln, Dallas, TX 75234 / 214-241-6302
Rosenthal, Brad and Sallie, 19303 Ossenfort Ct., St. Louis, MO 63038 / 314-273-5159; FAX: 314-273-5149
Ross, Don, 12813 West 83 Terrace, Lenexa, KS 66215 / 913-492-6982
Rosser, Bob, 1824 29th Ave., Suite 214, Birmingham, AL 35209 / 205-870-4422; FAX: 205-870-4421
Rossi Firearms, Braztech, Gary Mchalik, 16175 NW 49th Ave, Miami, FL 33014-6314 / 305-474-0401
Roto Carve, 2754 Garden Ave., Janesville, IA 50647
Round Edge, Inc., P.O. Box 723, Lansdale, PA 19446 / 215-361-0859
Roy Baker's Leather Goods, P.O. Box 893, Magnolia, AR 71753 / 501-234-0344
Roy's Custom Grips, Rt. 3, Box 174-E, Lynchburg, VA 24504 / 804-993-3470
Royal Arms Gunstocks, 919 8th Ave. NW, Great Falls, MT 59404 / 406-453-1149
RPM, 15481 N. Twin Lakes Dr., Tucson, AZ 85739 / 520-825-1233; FAX: 520-825-3333
Rubright Bullets, 1008 S. Quince Rd., Walnutport, PA 18088 / 215-767-1339
Rucker Dist. Inc., P.O. Box 479, Terrell, TX 75160 / 214-563-2094
Ruger (See Sturm, Ruger & Co., Inc.)
Rumanya Inc., 11513 Piney Lodge Rd, Gaithersburg, MD 20878-2443 / 281-345-2077; FAX: 281-345-2005
Rundell's Gun Shop, 6198 Frances Rd., Clio, MI 48420 / 313-687-0559
Runge, Robert P., 94 Grove St., Ilion, NY 13357 / 315-894-3036
Rupert's Gun Shop, 2202 Dick Rd., Suite B, Fenwick, MI 48834 / 517-248-3252
Russ Haydon Shooters' Supply, 15018 Goodrich Dr. NW, Gig Harbor, WA 98329 / 253-857-7557; FAX: 253-857-7884
Russ Trading Post, William A. Russ, 23 William St., Addison, NY 14801-1326 / 607-359-3896
Russ, William. See: RUSS TRADING POST
Rusteprufe Laboratories, 1319 Jefferson Ave., Sparta, WI 54656 / 608-269-4144
Rusty Duck Premium Gun Care Products, 7785 Foundation Dr., Suite 6, Florence, KY 41042 / 606-342-5553; FAX: 606-342-5556
Rutgers Book Center, 127 Raritan Ave., Highland Park, NJ 08904 / 732-545-4344 FAX: 732-545-6686
Rutten (See U.S. Importer-Labanu Inc)
RWS (See US Importer-Dynamit Nobel-RWS, Inc.), 81 Ruckman Rd, Closter, NJ 07624 / 201-767-7971; FAX: 201-767-1589
Ryan, Chad L., RR 3, Box 72, Cresco, IA 52136 / 319-547-4384

S

S&B Industries, 11238 McKinley Rd., Montrose, MI 48457 / 810-639-5491
S&K Mfg. Co., P.O. Box 247, Pittsfield, PA 16340 / 814-563-7808; FAX: 814-563-4067
S&S Firearms, 74-11 Myrtle Ave., Glendale, NY 11385 / 718-497-1100; FAX: 718-497-1105
S.A.R.L. G. Granger, 66 cours Fauriel, 42100, Saint Etienne, FRANCE / 04 77 25 14 73; FAX: 04 77 38 66 99
S.C.R.C., P.O. Box 660, Katy, TX 77492-0660 FAX: 713-578-2124
S.G.S. Sporting Guns Srl., Via Della Resistenza, 37 20090, Buccinasco, ITALY / 2-45702446; FAX: 2-45702464
S.I.A.C.E. (See U.S. Importer-IAR Inc)
S.L.A.P. Industries, P.O. Box 1121, Parklands, 02121 SOUTH AFRICA / 27-11-788-0030; FAX: 27-11-788-0030
Sabatti S.r.l., via Alessandro Volta 90, 25063 Gardone V.T., Brescia, ITALY / 030-8912207-831312; FAX: 030-8912059
SAECO (See Redding Reloading Equipment)
Saf-T-Lok, 5713 Corporate Way, Suite 100, W. Palm Beach, FL 33407
Safari Outfitters Ltd., 71 Ethan Allan Hwy., Ridgefield, CT 06877 / 203-544-9505
Safari Press, Inc., 15621 Chemical Lane B, Huntington Beach, CA 92649 / 714-894-9080; FAX: 714-894-4949
Safariland Ltd., Inc., 3120 E. Mission Blvd., P.O. Box 51478, Ontario, CA 91761 / 909-923-7300; FAX: 909-923-7400
SAFE, P.O. Box 864, Post Falls, ID 83854 / 208-773-3624
Safety Speed Holster, Inc., 910 S. Vail Ave., Montebello, CA 90640 / 323-723-4140; FAX: 323-726-6973
Sako Ltd (See U.S. Importer-Stoeger Industries)
Samco Global Arms, Inc., 6995 NW 43rd St., Miami, FL 33166 / 305-593-9782 FAX: 305-593-1014
Sampson, Roger, 2316 Mahogany St., Mora, MN 55051 / 612-679-4868
San Francisco Gun Exchange, 124 Second St., San Francisco, CA 94105 / 415-982-6097
San Marco (See U.S. Importers-Cape Outfitters-EMF
Sanders Custom Gun Service, 2358 Tyler Lane, Louisville, KY 40205 / 502-454-3338; FAX: 502-451-8857
Sanders Gun and Machine Shop, 145 Delhi Road, Manchester, IA 52057
Sandia Die & Cartridge Co., 37 Atancacio Rd. NE, Auquerque, NM 87123 / 505-298-5729
Sarco, Inc., 323 Union St., Stirling, NJ 07980 / 908-647-3800; FAX: 908-647-9413
Sauer (See U.S. Importers-Paul Co., The, Sigarms I
Sauls, R. See: BRYAN & ASSOC
Saunders Gun & Machine Shop, R.R. 2, Delhi Road, Manchester, IA 52057
Savage Arms (Canada), Inc., 248 Water St., P.O. Box 1240, Lakefield, ON K0L 2H0 CANADA / 705-652-8000; FAX: 705-652-8431
Savage Arms, Inc., 100 Springdale Rd., Westfield, MA 01085 / 413-568-7001; FAX: 413-562-7764
Savage Range Systems, Inc., 100 Springdale RD., Westfield, MA 01085 / 413-568-7001; FAX: 413-562-1152
Saville Iron Co. (See Greenwood Precision)
Savino, Barbara J., P.O. Box 51, West Burke, VT 05871-0051
Scanco Environmental Systems, 5000 Highlands Parkway, Suite 180, Atlanta, GA 30082 / 770-431-0025; FAX: 770-431-0028
Scansport, Inc., P.O. Box 700, Enfield, NH 03748 / 603-632-7654
Scattergun Technologies, Inc., 620 8th Ave. South, Nashville, TN 37203 / 615-254-1441; FAX: 615-254-1449
Sceery Game Calls, P.O. Box 6520, Sante Fe, NM 87502 / 505-471-9110; FAX: 505-471-3476
Schaefer Shooting Sports, P.O. Box 1515, Melville, NY 11747-0515 / 516-379-4900; FAX: 516-379-6701
Scharch Mfg., Inc., 10325 CR 120, Salida, CO 81201 / 719-539-7242 or 800-836-4683; FAX: 719-539-3021
Scherer, Box 250, Ewing, VA 24240 / 615-733-2615; FAX: 615-733-2073
Schiffman, Curt, 3017 Kevin Cr., Idaho Falls, ID 83402 / 208-524-4684
Schiffman, Mike, 8233 S. Crystal Springs, McCammon, ID 83250 / 208-254-9114
Schiffman, Norman, 3017 Kevin Cr., Idaho Falls, ID 83402 / 208-524-4684
Schmidt & Bender, Inc., 438 Willow Brook Rd., Meriden, NH 03770 / 800-468-3450 or 800-468-3450; FAX: 603-469-3471
Schmidtke Group, 17050 W. Salentine Dr., New Berlin, WI 53151-7349
Schmidtman Custom Ammunition, 6 Gilbert Court, Cotati, CA 94931
Schneider Bullets, 3655 West 214th St., Fairview Park, OH 44126
Schneider Rifle Barrels, Inc, Gary, 12202 N 62nd Pl, Scottsdale, AZ 85254 / 602-948-2525
School of Gunsmithing, The, 6065 Roswell Rd., Atlanta, GA 30328 / 800-223-4542

Schroeder Bullets, 1421 Thermal Ave., San Diego, CA 92154 / 619-423-3523; FAX: 619-423-8124

Schuetzen Pistol Works, 620-626 Old Pacific Hwy. SE, Olympia, WA 98513 / 360-459-3471; FAX: 360-491-3447

Schulz Industries, 16247 Minnesota Ave., Paramount, CA 90723 / 213-439-5903

Schumakers Gun Shop, 512 Prouty Corner Lp. A, Colville, WA 99114 / 509-684-4848

Scope Control, Inc., 5775 Co. Rd. 23 SE, Alexandria, MN 56308 / 612-762-7295

ScopLevel, 151 Lindbergh Ave., Suite C, Livermore, CA 94550 / 925-449-5052; FAX: 925-373-0861

Score High Gunsmithing, 9812-A, Cochiti SE, Albuquerque, NM 087123 / 800-326-5632 or 505-292-5532; FAX: 505-292-2592

Scot Powder, Rt.1 Box 167, McEwen, TN 37101 / 800-416-3006; FAX: 615-729-4211

Scot Powder Co. of Ohio, Inc., Box GD96, Only, TN 37140 / 615-729-4207 or 800-416-3006; FAX: 615-729-4217

Scott Fine Guns Inc., Thad, PO Box 412, Indianola, MS 38751 / 601-887-5929

Scott McDougall & Associates, 7950 Redwood Dr., Cotati, CA 94931 / 707-546-2264; FAX: 707-795-1911

Scott, Dwight, 23089 Englehardt St., Clair Shores, MI 48080 / 313-779-4735

Second Chance Body Armor, P.O. Box 578, Central Lake, MI 49622 / 616-544-5721; FAX: 616-544-9824

Seebeck Assoc., R.E., P. O. Box 59752, Dallas, TX 75229

Seecamp Co. Inc., L. W., PO Box 255, New Haven, CT 06502 / 203-877-3429

Segway Industries, P.O. Box 783, Suffern, NY 10901-0783 / 914-357-5510

Seligman Shooting Products, Box 133, Seligman, AZ 86337 / 602-422-3607

Sellier & Bellot, USA Inc, PO Box 27006, Shawnee Mission, KS 66225 / 913-685-0916; FAX: 913-685-0917

Selsi Co., Inc., P.O. Box 10, Midland Park, NJ 07432-0010 / 201-935-0388; FAX: 201-935-5851

Semmer, Charles (See Remington Double Shotguns), 7885 Cyd Dr, Denver, CO 80221 / 303-429-6947

Sentinel Arms, P.O. Box 57, Detroit, MI 48231 / 313-331-1951; FAX: 313-331-1456

Service Armament, 689 Bergen Blvd., Ridgefield, NJ 07657

Servus Footwear Co., 1136 2nd St., Rock Island, IL 61204 / 309-786-7741; FAX: 309-786-9808

Shappy Bullets, 76 Milldale Ave., Plantsville, CT 06479 / 203-621-3704

Sharp Shooter Supply, 4970 Lehman Road, Delphos, OH 45833 / 419-695-3179

Sharps Arms Co., Inc., C., 100 Centennial, Box 885, Big Timber, MT 59011 / 406-932-4353

Shaw, Inc., E. R. (See Small Arms Mfg. Co.)

Shay's Gunsmithing, 931 Marvin Ave., Lebanon, PA 17042

Sheffield Knifemakers Supply, Inc., P.O. Box 741107, Orange City, FL 32774-1107 / 904-775-6453; FAX: 904-774-5754

Sheldon, Bruce. See: RIDGELINE, INC

Shepherd Enterprises, Inc., Box 189, Waterloo, NE 68069 / 402-779-2424; FAX: 402-779-4010

Sherwood, George, 46 N. River Dr., Roseburg, OR 97470 / 541-672-3159

Shilen, Inc., 205 Metro Park Blvd., Ennis, TX 75119 / 972-875-5318; FAX: 972-875-5402

Shiloh Creek, Box 357, Cottleville, MO 63338 / 314-925-1842; FAX: 314-925-1842

Shiloh Rifle Mfg., 201 Centennial Dr., Big Timber, MT 59011 / 406-932-4454; FAX: 406-932-5627

Shockley, Harold H., 204 E. Farmington Rd., Hanna City, IL 61536 / 309-565-4524

Shoemaker & Sons Inc., Tex, 714 W Cienega Ave, San Dimas, CA 91773 / 909-592-2071; FAX: 909-592-2378

Shoot Where You Look, Leon Measures , Dept GD, 408 Fair, Livingston, TX 77351

Shoot-N-C Targets (See Birchwood Casey)

Shooter's Choice, 16770 Hilltop Park Place, Chagrin Falls, OH 44023 / 216-543-8808; FAX: 216-543-8811

Shooter's Edge Inc., P.O.Box 769, Trinidad, CO 81082

Shooter's World, 3828 N. 28th Ave., Phoenix, AZ 85017 / 602-266-0170

Shooters Supply, 1120 Tieton Dr., Yakima, WA 98902 / 509-452-1181

Shootin' Accessories, Ltd., P.O. Box 6810, Auburn, CA 95604 / 916-889-2220

Shootin' Shack, Inc., 1065 Silver Beach Rd., Riviera Beach, FL 33403 / 561-842-0990

Shooting Chrony, Inc., 3269 Niagara Falls Blvd., N. Tonawanda, NY 14120 / 905-276-6292; FAX: 416-276-6295

Shooting Gallery, The, 8070 Southern Blvd., Boardman, OH 44512 / 216-726-7788

Shooting Specialties (See Titus, Daniel)

Shooting Star, 1715 FM 1626 Ste 105, Manchaca, TX 78652 / 512-462-0009

Shotgun Sports, PO Box 6810, Auburn, CA 95604 / 530-889-2220; FAX: 530-889-9106

Shotguns Unlimited, 2307 Fon Du Lac Rd., Richmond, VA 23229 / 804-752-7115

ShurKatch Corporation, 50 Elm St., Richfield Springs, NY 13439 / 315-858-1470; FAX: 315-858-2969

Siegrist Gun Shop, 8754 Turtle Road, Whittemore, MI 48770

Sierra Bullets, 1400 W. Henry St., Sedalia, MO 65301 / 816-827-6300; FAX: 816-827-6300

Sierra Specialty Prod. Co., 1344 Oakhurst Ave., Los Altos, CA 94024 FAX: 415-965-1536

SIG, CH-8212 Neuhausen, SWITZERLAND

SIG-Sauer (See U.S. Importer-Sigarms Inc.)

Sigarms, Inc., Corporate Park, Exeter, NH 03833 / 603-772-2302; FAX: 603-772-9082

Sight Shop, The, John G. Lawson , 1802 E. Columbia Ave., Tacoma, WA 98404 / 206-474-5465

Sightron, Inc., 1672B Hwy. 96, Franklinton, NC 27525 / 919-528-8783; FAX: 919-528-0995

Signet Metal Corp., 551 Stewart Ave., Brooklyn, NY 11222 / 718-384-5400; FAX: 718-388-7488

Sile Distributors, Inc., 7 Centre Market Pl., New York, NY 10013 / 212-925-4111; FAX: 212-925-3149

Silencio/Safety Direct, 56 Coney Island Dr., Sparks, NV 89431 / 800-648-1812 or 702-354-4451; FAX: 702-359-1074

Silent Hunter, 1100 Newton Ave., W. Collingswood, NJ 08107 / 609-854-3276

Silhouette Leathers, P.O. Box 1161, Gunnison, CO 81230 / 303-641-6639

Silver Eagle Machining, 18007 N. 69th Ave., Glendale, AZ 85308

Silver Ridge Gun Shop (See Goodwin, Fred)

Simmons Gun Repair, Inc., 700 S. Rogers Rd., Olathe, KS 66062 / 913-782-3131; FAX: 913-782-4189

Simmons Outdoor Corp., 201 Plantation Oak Parkway, Thomasville, GA 31792 / 912-227-9053; FAX: 912-227-9054

Simmons, Jerry, 715 Middlebury St., Goshen, IN 46526 / 219-533-8546

Sinclair International, Inc., 2330 Wayne Haven St., Fort Wayne, IN 46803 / 219-493-1858; FAX: 219-493-2530

Singletary, Kent, 2915 W. Ross, Phoenix, AZ 85027 / 602-582-4900

Sipes Gun Shop, 7415 Asher Ave., Little Rock, AR 72204 / 501-565-8480

Siskiyou Gun Works (See Donnelly, C. P.)

Six Enterprises, 320-D Turtle Creek Ct., San Jose, CA 95125 / 408-999-0201; FAX: 408-999-0216

SKAN A.R., 4 St. Catherines Road, Long Melford, Suffolk, 010 9JU ENGLAND / 011-0787-312942

SKB Shotguns, 4325 S. 120th St., P.O. Box 37669, Omaha, NE 68137 / 800-752-2767; FAX: 402-330-8029

Skeoch, Brian R., P.O. Box 279, Glenrock, WY 82637 / 307-436-9655 FAX: 307-436-9034

Skip's Machine, 364 29 Road, Grand Junction, CO 81501 / 303-245-5417

Sklany's Machine Shop, 566 Birch Grove Dr., Kalispell, MT 59901 / 406-755-4257

Slezak, Jerome F., 1290 Marlowe, Lakewood (Cleveland), OH 44107 / 216-221-1668

Slug Group, Inc., P.O. Box 376, New Paris, PA 15554 / 814-839-4517; FAX: 814-839-2601

Slug Site, Ozark Wilds, 21300 Hwy. 5, Versailles, MO 65084 / 573-378-6430

Small Arms Mfg. Co., 5312 Thoms Run Rd., Bridgeville, PA 15017 / 412-221-4343; FAX: 412-221-4303

Small Arms Specialties, 29 Bernice Ave., Leominster, MA 01453 / 800-635-9290

Small Custom Mould & Bullet Co., Box 17211, Tucson, AZ 85731

Smart Parts, 1203 Spring St., Latrobe, PA 15650 / 412-539-2660; FAX: 412-539-2298

Smires, C. L., 5222 Windmill Lane, Columbia, MD 21044-1328

Smith & Wesson, 2100 Roosevelt Ave., Springfield, MA 01104 / 413-781-8300; FAX: 413-731-8980

Smith Abrasives, Inc., 1700 Sleepy Valley Rd., P.O. Box 5095, Hot Springs, AR 71902-5095 / 501-321-2244; FAX: 501-321-9232

Smith Saddlery, Jesse W., 16909 E Jackson Rd, Elk, WA 99009-9600 / 509-325-0622

Smith, Art, 230 Main St. S., Hector, MN 55342 / 320-848-2760; FAX: 320-848-2760

Smith, Mark A., P.O. Box 182, Sinclair, WY 82334 / 307-324-7929

Smith, Michael, 620 Nye Circle, Chattanooga, TN 37405 / 615-267-8341

Smith, Ron, 5869 Straley, Ft. Worth, TX 76114 / 817-732-6768

Smith, Sharmon, 4545 Speas Rd., Fruitland, ID 83619 / 208-452-6329

Smokey Valley Rifles (See Lutz Engraving, Ron E)

Snapp's Gunshop, 6911 E. Washington Rd., Clare, MI 48617 / 517-386-9226

Sno-Seal, Inc. (See Atsko/Sno-Seal)

Societa Armi Bresciane Srl (See U.S. Importer-Cape

SOS Products Co. (See Buck Stix-SOS Products Co.), Box 3, Neenah, WI 54956

Sotheby's, 1334 York Ave. at 72nd St., New York, NY 10021 / 212-606-7260

Sound Technology, Box 391, Pelham, AL 35124 / 205-664-5860 or 907-486-2825

South Bend Replicas, Inc., 61650 Oak Rd.., South Bend, IN 46614 / 219-289-4500

Southeastern Community College, 1015 S. Gear Ave., West Burlington, IA 52655 / 319-752-2731

Southern Ammunition Co., Inc., 4232 Meadow St., Loris, SC 29569-3124 / 803-756-3262; FAX: 803-756-3583

Southern Armory, The, 25 Millstone Road, Woodlawn, VA 24381 / 703-238-1343; FAX: 703-238-1453

Southern Bloomer Mfg. Co., P.O. Box 1621, Bristol, TN 37620 / 615-878-6660; FAX: 615-878-8761

Southern Security, 1700 Oak Hills Dr., Kingston, TN 37763 / 423-376-6297; FAX: 800-251-9992

Southwind Sanctions, P.O. Box 445, Aledo, TX 76008 / 817-441-8917

Sparks, Milt, 605 E. 44th St. No. 2, Boise, ID 83714-4800

Spartan-Realtree Products, Inc., 1390 Box Circle, Columbus, GA 31907 / 706-569-9101; FAX: 706-569-0042

Specialty Gunsmithing, Lynn McMurdo, P.O. Box 404, Afton, WY 83110 / 307-886-5535

Specialty Shooters Supply, Inc., 3325 Griffin Rd., Suite 9mm, Fort Lauderdale, FL 33317

Speedfeed Inc., PO Box 1146, Rocklin, CA 95677 / 916-630-7720; FAX: 916-630-7719

Speer Products Div. of Blount Inc. Sporting Equipm, P.O. Box 856, Lewiston, ID 83501 / 208-746-2351; FAX: 208-746-2915

Spegel, Craig, PO Box 387, Nehalem, OR 97131 / 503-368-5653

Speiser, Fred D., 2229 Dearborn, Missoula, MT 59801 / 406-549-8133

Spencer Reblue Service, 1820 Tupelo Trail, Holt, MI 48842 / 517-694-7474

Spencer's Custom Guns, Rt. 1, Box 546, Scottsville, VA 24590 / 804-293-6836

SPC LLC, P.O. Box 1625, Cody, WY 82414 / 307-587-7621; FAX 307-587-7695

Sphinx Engineering SA, Ch. des Grandex-Vies 2, CH-2900, Porrentruy, SWITZERLAND FAX: 41 66 66 30 90

Spokhandguns, Inc., 1206 Fig St., Benton City, WA 99320 / 509-588-5255

Sport Flite Manufacturing Co., P.O. Box 1082, Bloomfield Hills, MI 48303 / 248-647-3747

Sporting Arms Mfg., Inc., 801 Hall Ave., Littlefield, TX 79339 / 806-385-5665; FAX: 806-385-3394

Sporting Clays Of America, 9257 Bluckeye Rd, Sugar Grove, OH 43155-9632 / 740-746-8334; FAX: 740-746-8605

Sports Innovations Inc., P.O. Box 5181, 8505 Jacksboro Hwy., Wichita Falls, TX 76307 / 817-723-6015

Sportsman Safe Mfg. Co., 6309-6311 Paramount Blvd., Long Beach, CA 90805 / 800-266-7150 or 310-984-5445

Sportsman Supply Co., 714 E. Eastwood, P.O. Box 650, Marshall, MO 65340 / 816-886-9393

Sportsman's Communicators, 588 Radcliffe Ave., Pacific Palisades, CA 90272 / 800-538-3752

Sportsmatch U.K. Ltd., 16 Summer St., Leighton Buzzard, Bedfordshire, LU7 8HT ENGLAND / 01525-381638; FAX: 01525-851236

Sportsmen's Exchange & Western Gun Traders, Inc., 560 S. C St., Oxnard, CA 93030 / 805-483-1917

Spradlin's, 457 Shannon Rd, Texas Creek, CO 81223 / 719-275-7105

Springfield Sporters, Inc., RD 1, Penn Run, PA 15765 / 412-254-2626; FAX: 412-254-9173

Springfield, Inc., 420 W. Main St., Geneseo, IL 61254 / 309-944-5631; FAX: 309-944-3676

Spyderco, Inc., 4565 N. Hwy. 93, P.O. Box 800, Golden, CO 80403 / 303-279-8383 or 800-525-7770; FAX: 303-278-2229

SSK Industries, 590 Woodvue Lane, Wintersville, OH 43953 / 740-264-0176; FAX: 740-264-2257

Stackpole Books, 5067 Ritter Rd., Mechanicsburg, PA 17055-6921 / 717-796-0411; FAX: 717-796-0412

Stalker, Inc., P.O. Box 21, Fishermans Wharf Rd., Malakoff, TX 75148 / 903-489-1010

Stalwart Corporation, 76 Imperial, Unit A, Evanston, WY 82930 / 307-789-7687; FAX: 307-789-7688

Stan de Treville & Co., 4129 Normal St., San Diego, CA 92103 / 619-298-3393

Stan de Treville & Co., 4129 Normal St., San Diego, CA 92103 / 619-298-3393

Stanley Bullets, 2085 Heatheridge Ln., Reno, NV 89509

Stanley Scruggs' Game Calls, Rt. 1, Hwy. 661, Cullen, VA 23934 / 804-542-4241 or 800-323-4828

Star Ammunition, Inc., 5520 Rock Hampton Ct., Indianapolis, IN 46268 / 800-221-5927; FAX: 317-872-5847

Star Bonifacio Echeverria S.A., Torrekva 3, Eibar, 20600 SPAIN / 43-107340;

Star Custom Bullets, P.O. Box 608, 468 Main St., Ferndale, CA 95536 / 707-786-9140; FAX: 707-786-9117

Star Machine Works, PO Box 1872, Pioneer, CA 95666 / 209-295-5000

Stark's Bullet Mfg., 2580 Monroe St., Eugene, OR 97405

MANUFACTURER'S DIRECTORY

Starke Bullet Company, P.O. Box 400, 605 6th St. NW, Cooperstown, ND 58425 / 888-797-3431
Starkey Labs, 6700 Washington Ave. S., Eden Prairie, MN 55344
Starkey's Gun Shop, 9430 McCombs, El Paso, TX 79924 / 915-751-3030
Starlight Training Center, Inc., Rt. 1, P.O. Box 88, Bronaugh, MO 64728 / 417-843-3555
Starline, 1300 W. Henry St., Sedalia, MO 65301 / 816-827-6640 FAX: 816-827-6650
Starr Trading Co., Jedediah, P.O. Box 2007, Farmington Hills, MI 48333 / 810-683-4343; FAX: 810-683-3282
Starr Trading Co., Jedediah, PO Box 2007, Farmington Hill, MI 48333 / 810-683-4343; FAX: 810-683-3282
Starrett Co., L. S., 121 Crescent St, Athol, MA 01331 / 978-249-3551 FAX: 978-249-8495
State Arms Gun Co., 815 S. Division St., Waunakee, WI 53597 / 608-849-5800
Steelman's Gun Shop, 10465 Beers Rd., Swartz Creek, MI 48473 / 810-735-4884
Steffens, Ron, 18396 Mariposa Creek Rd., Willits, CA 95490 / 707-485-0873
Stegall, James B., 26 Forest Rd., Wallkill, NY 12589
Steger, James R., 1131 Dorsey Pl., Plainfield, NJ 07062
Steve Henigson & Associates, P.O. Box 2726, Culver City, CA 90231 / 310-305-8288; FAX: 310-305-1905
Steve Kamyk Engraving Co., 9 Grandview Dr., Westfield, MA 01085-1810 / 413-568-0457
Steve Nastoff's 45 Shop, Inc., 12288 Mahoning Ave., P.O. Box 446, North Jackson, OH 44451 / 330-538-2977
Steves House of Guns, Rt. 1, Minnesota City, MN 55959 / 507-689-2573
Stewart Game Calls, Inc., Johnny, PO Box 7954, 5100 Fort Ave, Waco, TX 76714 / 817-772-3261; FAX: 817-772-3670
Stewart's Gunsmithing, P.O. Box 5854, Pietersburg North 0750, Transvaal, SOUTH AFRICA / 01521-89401
Steyr Mannlicher AG & CO KG, Mannlicherstrasse 1, A-4400, Steyr, AUSTRIA / 0043-7252-78621; FAX: 0043-7252-68621
STI International, 114 Halmar Cove, Georgetown, TX 78628 / 800-959-8201; FAX: 512-819-0465
Stiles Custom Guns, 76 Cherry Run Rd, Box 1605, Homer City, PA 15748 / 712-479-9945
Stillwell, Robert, 421 Judith Ann Dr., Schertz, TX 78154
Stoeger Industries, 5 Mansard Ct., Wayne, NJ 07470 / 201-872-9500 or 800-631-0722; FAX: 201-872-2230
Stoeger Publishing Co. (See Stoeger Industries)
Stone Enterprises Ltd., Rt. 609, P.O. Box 335, Wicomico Church, VA 22579 / 804-580-5114; FAX: 804-580-8421
Stone Mountain Arms, 5988 Peachtree Corners E., Norcross, GA 30071 / 800-251-9412
Stoney Point Products, Inc., P.O. Box 234, 1815 North Spring Street, New Ulm, MN 56073-0234 / 507-354-3360; FAX: 507-354-7236
Storage Tech, 1254 Morris Ave., N. Huntingdon, PA 15642 / 800-437-9393
Storey, Dale A. (See DGS Inc.)
Storm, Gary, P.O. Box 5211, Richardson, TX 75083 / 214-385-0862
Stott's Creek Armory, Inc., 2526 S. 475W, Morgantown, IN 46160 / 317-878-5489; FAX: 317-878-9489
Stratco, Inc., P.O. Box 2270, Kalispell, MT 59901 / 406-755-1221; FAX: 406-755-1226
Strawbridge, Victor W., 6 Pineview Dr., Dover, NH 03820 / 603-742-0013
Strayer, Sandy. See: STRAYER-VOIGT, INC
Strayer-Voigt, Inc, Sandy Strayer , 3435 Ray Orr Blvd, Grand Prairie, TX 75050 / 972-513-0575
Streamlight, Inc., 1030 W. Germantown Pike, Norristown, PA 19403 / 215-631-0600; FAX: 610-631-0712
Strong Holster Co., 39 Grove St., Gloucester, MA 01930 / 508-281-3300; FAX: 508-281-6321
Strutz Rifle Barrels, Inc., W. C., PO Box 611, Eagle River, WI 54521 / 715-479-4766
Stuart, V. Pat, Rt.1, Box 447-S, Greenville, VA 24440 / 804-556-3845
Sturgeon Valley Sporters, K. Ide, P.O. Box 283, Vanderbilt, MI 49795 / 517-983-4338
Sturm Ruger & Co. Inc., 200 Ruger Rd., Prescott, AZ 86301 / 520-541-8820; FAX: 520-541-8850
Sullivan, David S .(See Westwind Rifles Inc.)
"Su-Press-On",Inc., P.O. Box 09161, Detroit, MI 48209 / 313-842-4222
Summit Specialties, Inc., P.O. Box 786, Decatur, AL 35602 / 205-353-0634; FAX: 205-353-9818
Sun Welding Safe Co., 290 Easy St. No.3, Simi Valley, CA 93065 / 805-584-6678 or 800-729-SAFE FAX: 805-584-6169
Sunny Hill Enterprises, Inc., W1790 Cty. HHH, Malone, WI 53049 / 920-795-4722 FAX: 920-795-4822
Sure-Shot Game Calls, Inc., P.O. Box 816, 6835 Capitol, Groves, TX 77619 / 409-962-1636; FAX: 409-962-5465
Surecase Co., The, 233 Wilshire Blvd., Ste. 900, Santa Monica, CA 90401 / 800-92ARMLOC
Survival Arms, Inc., 273 Canal St., Shelton, CT 06484-3173 / 203-924-6533; FAX: 203-924-2581
Svon Corp., 280 Eliot St., Ashland, MA 01721 / 508-881-8852
Swampfire Shop (See Peterson Gun Shop, Inc.), The
Swann, D. J., 5 Orsova Close, Eltham North Vic., 3095 AUSTRALIA / 03-431-0323
Swanndri New Zealand, 152 Elm Ave., Burlingame, CA 94010 / 415-347-6158
SwaroSports, Inc. (See JagerSport Ltd, One Wholesale Way, Cranston, RI 02920 / 800-962-4867; FAX: 401-946-2587
Swarovski Optik North America Ltd., One Wholesale Way, Cranston, RI 02920 / 401-946-2220 or 800-426-3089 FAX: 401-946-2587
Sweet Home, Inc., P.O. Box 900, Orrville, OH 44667-0900
Swenson's 45 Shop, A. D., 3839 Ladera Vista Rd, Fallbrook, CA 92028-9431
Swift Bullet Co., P.O. Box 27, 201 Main St., Quinter, KS 67752 / 913-754-3959; FAX: 913-754-2359
Swift Instruments, Inc., 952 Dorchester Ave., Boston, MA 02125 / 617-436-2960; FAX: 617-436-3232
Swift River Gunworks, 450 State St., Belchertown, MA 01007 / 413-323-4052
Szweda, Robert (See RMS Custom Gunsmithing)

T

T.F.C. S.p.A., Via G. Marconi 118, B, Villa Carcina 25069, ITALY / 030-881271; FAX: 030-881826
T.G. Faust , Inc., 544 Minor St., Reading, PA 19602 / 610-375-8549; FAX: 610-375-4488
T.H.U. Enterprises, Inc., P.O. Box 418, Lederach, PA 19450 / 215-256-1665; FAX: 215-256-9718
T.K. Lee Co., 1282 Branchwater Ln., Birmingham, AL 35216 / 205-913-5222
T.W. Menck Gunsmith Inc., 5703 S. 77th St., Ralston, NE 68127
Tabler Marketing, 2554 Lincoln Blvd., Suite 555, Marina Del Rey, CA 90291 / 818-755-4565; FAX: 818-755-0972
Taconic Firearms Ltd., Perry Lane, PO Box 553, Cambridge, NY 12816 / 518-677-2704; FAX: 518-677-5974
TacStar, PO Box 547, Cottonwood, AZ 86326-0547 / 602-639-0072; FAX: 602-634-8781
TacTell, Inc., P.O. Box 5654, Maryville, TN 37802 / 615-982-7855; FAX: 615-558-8294
Tactical Defense Institute, 574 Miami Bluff Ct., Loveland, OH 45140 / 513-677-8229 FAX: 513-677-0447
Tag Distributors
Talley, Dave, P.O. Box 821, Glenrock, WY 82637 / 307-436-8724 or 307-436-9315
Talmage, William G., 10208 N. County Rd. 425 W., Brazil, IN 47834 / 812-442-0804
Talon Mfg. Co., Inc., 621 W. King St., Martinsburg, WV 25401 / 304-264-9714; FAX: 304-264-9725
Tamarack Products, Inc., P.O. Box 625, Wauconda, IL 60084 / 708-526-9333; FAX: 708-526-9353
Tanfoglio Fratelli S.r.l., via Valtrompia 39, 41, Brescia, ITALY / 30-8910361; FAX: 30-8910183
Tanglefree Industries, 1261 Heavenly Dr., Martinez, CA 94553 / 800-982-4868; FAX: 510-825-3874
Tank's Rifle Shop, P.O. Box 474, Fremont, NE 68026-0474 / 402-727-1317; FAX: 402-721-2573
Tanner (See U.S. Importer-Mandall Shooting Supplie
Tar-Hunt Custom Rifles, Inc., RR3, P.O. Box 572, Bloomsburg, PA 17815-9351 / 717-784-6368; FAX: 717-784-6368
Taracorp Industries, Inc., 1200 Sixteenth St., Granite City, IL 62040 / 618-451-4400
Target Shooting, Inc., PO Box 773, Watertown, SD 57201 / 605-882-6955; FAX: 605-882-8840
Tarnhelm Supply Co., Inc., 431 High St., Boscawen, NH 03303 / 603-796-2551; FAX: 603-796-2918
Taurus Firearms, Inc., 16175 NW 49th Ave., Miami, FL 33014 / 305-624-1115; FAX: 305-623-7506
Taurus International Firearms (See U.S. Importer-T
Taurus S.A. Forjas, Avenida Do Forte 511, Porto Alegre, RS BRAZIL 91360 / 55-51-347-4050; FAX: 55-51-347-3065
Taylor & Robbins, P.O. Box 164, Rixford, PA 16745 / 814-966-3233
Taylor's & Co., Inc., 304 Lenoir Dr., Winchester, VA 22603 / 540-722-2017; FAX: 540-722-2018
TCCI, P.O. Box 302, Phoenix, AZ 85001 / 602-237-3823; FAX: 602-237-3858
TCSR, 3998 Hoffman Rd., White Bear Lake, MN 55110-4626 / 800-328-5323; FAX: 612-429-0526
TDP Industries, Inc., 606 Airport Blvd., Doylestown, PA 18901 / 215-345-8687; FAX: 215-345-6057
Techno Arms (See U.S. Importer- Auto-Ordnance Corp
Tecnolegno S.p.A., Via A. Locatelli, 6 10, 24019 Zogno, I ITALY / 0345-55111; FAX: 0345-55155
Ted Blocker Holsters, Inc., Clackamas Business Park Bldg A, 14787 SE 82nd Dr, Clackamas, OR 97015 / 503-557-7757; FAX: 503-557-3771
Tele-Optics, 630 E. Rockland Rd., PO Box 6313, Libertyville, IL 60048 / 847-362-7757
Ten-Ring Precision, Inc., Alex B. Hamilton, 1449 Blue Crest Lane, San Antonio, TX 78232 / 210-494-3063; FAX: 210-494-3066
TEN-X Products Group, 1905 N Main St, Suite 133, Cleburne, TX 76031-1305 / 972-243-4016 or 800-433-2225; FAX: 972-243-4112
Tennessee Valley Mfg., P.O. Box 1175, Corinth, MS 38834 / 601-286-5014
Tepeco, P.O. Box 342, Friendswood, TX 77546 / 713-482-2702
Terry K. Kopp Professional Gunsmithing, Rt 1 Box 224F, Lexington, MO 64067 / 816-259-2636
Testing Systems, Inc., 220 Pegasus Ave., Northvale, NJ 07647
Teton Arms, Inc., P.O. Box 411, Wilson, WY 83014 / 307-733-3395
Tetra Gun Lubricants (See FTI, Inc.)
Tex Shoemaker & Sons, Inc., 714 W. Cienega Ave., San Dimas, CA 91773 / 909-592-2071; FAX: 909-592-2378
Texas Armory (See Bond Arms, Inc.)
Texas Platers Supply Co., 2453 W. Five Mile Parkway, Dallas, TX 75233 / 214-330-7168
Thad Rybka Custom Leather Equipment, 134 Havilah Hill, Odenville, AL 35120
Thad Scott Fine Guns, Inc., P.O. Box 412, Indianola, MS 38751 / 601-887-5929
Theis, Terry, HC 63 Box 213, Harper, TX 78631 / 830-864-4438
Theoben Engineering, Stephenson Road, St. Ives Huntingdon, Cambs., PE17 4WJ ENGLAND / 011-0480-461718
Thiewes, George W., 14329 W. Parada Dr., Sun City West, AZ 85375
Things Unlimited, 235 N. Kimbau, Casper, WY 82601 / 307-234-5277
Thirion Gun Engraving, Denise, PO Box 408, Graton, CA 95444 / 707-829-1876
Thomas, Charles C., 2600 S. First St., Springfield, IL 62794 / 217-789-8980; FAX: 217-789-9130
Thompson Bullet Lube Co., P.O. Box 472343, Garland, TX 75047-2343 / 972-271-8063; FAX: 972-840-6743
Thompson Precision, 110 Mary St., P.O. Box 251, Warren, IL 61087 / 815-745-3625
Thompson Target Technology, 618 Roslyn Ave., SW, Canton, OH 44710 / 216-453-7707; FAX: 216-478-4723
Thompson, Norm, 18905 NW Thurman St., Portland, OR 97209
Thompson, Randall (See Highline Machine Co.)
Thompson/Center Arms, P.O. Box 5002, Rochester, NH 03867 / 603-332-2394; FAX: 603-332-5133
3-D Ammunition & Bullets, PO Box 433, Doniphan, NE 68832 / 402-845-2285 or 800-255-6712; FAX: 402-845-6546
3-Ten Corp., P.O. Box 269, Feeding Hills, MA 01030 / 413-789-2086; FAX: 413-789-1549
300 Below Services (See Cryo-Accurizing)
300 Gunsmith Service, Inc., Cherry Creek State Park Shooting Ce, 12500 E. Belleview Ave., Englewood, CO 80111 / 303-690-3300
Thunden Ranch, HCR 1, Box 53, Mt. Home, TX 78058 / 830-640-3138
Thunder Mountain Arms, P.O. Box 593, Oak Harbor, WA 98277 / 206-679-4657; FAX: 206-675-1114
Thurston Sports, Inc., RD 3 Donovan Rd., Auburn, NY 13021 / 315-253-0966
Tiger-Hunt Gunstocks, Box 379, Beaverdale, PA 15921 / 814-472-5161
Tikka (See U.S. Importer-Stoeger Industries)
Timber Heirloom Products, 618 Roslyn Ave. SW, Canton, OH 44710 / 216-453-7707; FAX: 216-478-4723
Time Precision, Inc., 640 Federal Rd., Brookfield, CT 06804 / 203-775-8343
Tink's Safariland Hunting Corp., P.O. Box 244, 1140 Monticello Rd., Madison, GA 30650 / 706-342-4915; FAX: 706-342-7568
Tinks & Ben Lee Hunting Products (See Wellington O
Tioga Engineering Co., Inc., P.O. Box 913, 13 Cone St., Wellsboro, PA 16901 / 717-724-3533; FAX: 717-662-3347
Tippman Pneumatics, Inc., 3518 Adams Center Rd., Fort Wayne, IN 46806 / 219-749-6022; FAX: 219-749-6619
Tirelli, Snc Di Tirelli Primo E.C., Via Matteotti No. 359, Gardone V.T. Brescia, I ITALY / 030-8912819; FAX: 030-832240
Titus, Daniel, Shooting Specialties, 119 Morlyn Ave, Bryn Mawr, PA 19010-3737 / 215-525-8829
TM Stockworks, 6355 Maplecrest Rd., Fort Wayne, IN 46835 / 219-485-5389
TMI Products (See Haselbauer Products, Jerry)
Tom Forrest, Inc., P.O. Box 326, Lakeside, CA 92040 / 619-561-5800; FAX: 619-561-0227
Tom's Gun Repair, Thomas G. Ivanoff, 76-6 Rt. Southfork Rd., Cody, WY 82414 / 307-587-6949
Tom's Gunshop, 3601 Central Ave., Hot Springs, AR 71913 / 501-624-3856
Tombstone Smoke'n' Deals, 3218 East Bell Road, Phoenix, AZ 85032 / 602-905-7013; FAX: 602-443-1998
Tonoloway Tack Drives, HCR 81, Box 100, Needmore, PA 17238
Tooley Custom Rifles, 516 Creek Meadow Dr., Gastonia, NC 28054 / 704-864-7525
Top-Line USA, Inc., 7920-28 Hamilton Ave., Cincinnati, OH 45231 / 513-522-2992 or 800-346-6699; FAX: 513-522-0916

MANUFACTURER'S DIRECTORY

Torel, Inc., 1708 N. South St., P.O. Box 592, Yoakum, TX 77995 / 512-293-2341; FAX: 512-293-3413
TOZ (See U.S. Importer-Nygord Precision Products)
Track of the Wolf, Inc., P.O. Box 6, Osseo, MN 55369-0006 / 612-424-2500; FAX: 612-424-9860
TracStar Industries, Inc., 218 Justin Dr., Cottonwood, AZ 86326 / 520-639-0072; FAX: 520-634-8781
Tradewinds, Inc., P.O. Box 1191, 2339-41 Tacoma Ave. S., Tacoma, WA 98401 / 206-272-4887
Traditions Performance Firearms, P.O. Box 776, 1375 Boston Post Rd., Old Saybrook, CT 06475 / 860-388-4656; FAX: 860-388-4657
Trafalgar Square, P.O. Box 257, N. Pomfret, VT 05053 / 802-457-1911
Traft Gunshop, P.O. Box 1078, Buena Vista, CO 81211
Trail Visions, 5800 N. Ames Terrace, Glendale, WI 53209 / 414-228-1328
Trammco, 839 Gold Run Rd., Boulder, CO 80302
Trax America, Inc., P.O. Box 898, 1150 Eldridge, Forrest City, AR 72335 / 870-633-0410 or 800-232-2327; FAX: 870-633-4788
Treadlok Gun Safe, Inc., 1764 Granby St. NE, Roanoke, VA 24012 / 800-729-8732 or 703-982-6881; FAX: 703-982-1059
Treemaster, P.O. Box 247, Guntersville, AL 35976 / 205-878-3597
Treso, Inc., P.O. Box 4640, Pagosa Springs, CO 81157 / 303-731-2295
Trevallion Gunstocks, 9 Old Mountain Rd., Cape Neddick, ME 03902 / 207-361-1130
Trico Plastics, 590 S. Vincent Ave., Azusa, CA 91702
Trigger Lock Division/Central Specialties Ltd., 1122 Silver Lake Road, Cary, IL 60013 / 847-639-3900; FAX: 847-639-3972
Trijicon, Inc., 49385 Shafer Ave., P.O. Box 930059, Wixom, MI 48393-0059 / 810-960-7700; FAX: 810-960-7725
Trilux, Inc., P.O. Box 24608, Winston-Salem, NC 27114 / 910-659-9438; FAX: 910-768-7720
Trinidad St. Jr Col Gunsmith Dept, 600 Prospect St., Trinidad, CO 81082 / 719-846-5631; FAX: 719-846-5667
Triple-K Mfg. Co., Inc., 2222 Commercial St., San Diego, CA 92113 / 619-232-2066; FAX: 619-232-7675
Tristar Sporting Arms, Ltd., 1814-16 Linn St., P.O. Box 7496, N. Kansas City, MO 64116 / 816-421-1400; FAX: 816-421-4182
Trius Traps, Inc., P.O. Box 471, 221 S. Miami Ave., Cleves, OH 45002 / 513-941-5682; FAX: 513-941-7970
Trooper Walsh, 2393 N Edgewood St, Arlington, VA 22207
Trophy Bonded Bullets, Inc., 900 S. Loop W., Suite 190, Houston, TX 77054 / 713-645-4499 or 888-308-3006; FAX: 713-741-6393
Trotman, Ken, 135 Ditton Walk, Unit 11, Cambridge, CB5 8PY ENGLAND / 01223-211030; FAX: 01223 212317
Tru-Balance Knife Co., P.O. Box 140555, Grand Rapids, MI 49514 / 616-453-3679
Tru-Square Metal Prods., Inc., 640 First St. SW, P.O. Box 585, Auburn, WA 98071 / 206-833-2310; FAX: 206-833-2349
True Flight Bullet Co., 5581 Roosevelt St., Whitehall, PA 18052 / 610-262-7630; FAX: 610-262-7806
Truglo, Inc, PO Box 1612, McKinna, TX 75070 / 972-488-8999
Trulock Tool, Broad St., Whigham, GA 31797 / 912-762-4678
TTM, 1550 Solomon Rd., Santa Maria, CA 93455 / 805-934-1281
Tucker, James C., P.O. Box 1212, Paso Robles, CA 93447-1212
Tucson Mold, Inc., 930 S. Plumer Ave., Tucson, AZ 85719 / 520-792-1075; FAX: 520-792-1075
Turkish Firearms Corp., 522 W. Maple St., Allentown, PA 18101 / 610-821-8660; FAX: 610-821-9049
Turnbull Restoration, Doug, 6680 Rt 58 & 20 Dept. SM 2000, PO Box 471, Bloomfield, NY 14469 / 716-657-6338
Tuttle, Dale, 4046 Russell Rd., Muskegon, MI 49445 / 616-766-2250
Tyler Manufacturing & Distributing, 3804 S. Eastern, Oklahoma City, OK 73129 / 405-677-1487 or 800-654-8415

U

U.S. Patent Fire Arms, No. 25-55 Van Dyke Ave., Hartford, CT 06106 / 800-877-2832; FAX: 800-644-7265
U.S. Repeating Arms Co., Inc., 275 Winchester Ave., Morgan, UT 84050-9333 / 801-876-3440; FAX: 801-876-3737
U.S. Tactical Systems (See Keng's Firearms Specialty)
U.S.A. Magazines, Inc., P.O. Box 39115, Downey, CA 90241 / 800-872-2577
Uberti USA, Inc., P.O. Box 469, Lakeville, CT 06039 / 860-435-8068; FAX: 860-435-8146
Uberti, Aldo, Casella Postale 43, I-25063 Gardone V.T., ITALY
UFA, Inc., 6927 E. Grandview Dr., Scottsdale, AZ 85254 / 800-616-2776
Ugartechea S. A., Ignacio, Chonta 26, Eibar, SPAIN / 43-121257; FAX: 43-121669
Ultimate Accuracy, 121 John Shelton Rd., Jacksonville, AR 72076 / 501-985-2530
Ultra Dot Distribution, 2316 N.E. 8th Rd., Ocala, FL 34470
Ultra Light Arms, Inc., P.O. Box 1270, 214 Price St., Granville, WV 26505 / 304-599-5687; FAX: 304-599-5687
Ultralux (See U.S. Importer-Keng's Firearms Specia
UltraSport Arms, Inc., 1955 Norwood Ct., Racine, WI 53403 / 414-554-3237; FAX: 414-554-9731
Uncle Bud's, HCR 81, Box 100, Needmore, PA 17238 / 717-294-6000; FAX: 717-294-6005
Uncle Mike's (See Michaels of Oregon Co)
Unertl Optical Co. Inc., John, 308 Clay Ave, PO Box 818, Mars, PA 16046-0818 / 412-625-3810
Unique/M.A.P.F., 10 Les Allees, 64700, Hendaye, FRANCE / 33-59 20 71 93
UniTec, 1250 Bedford SW, Canton, OH 44710 / 216-452-4017
United Binocular Co., 9043 S. Western Ave., Chicago, IL 60620
United Cutlery Corp., 1425 United Blvd., Sevierville, TN 37876 / 423-428-2532 or 800-548-0835 FAX: 423-428-2267
United States Optics Technologies, Inc., 5900 Dale St., Buena Park, CA 90621 / 714-994-4901; FAX: 714-994-4904
United States Products Co., 518 Melwood Ave., Pittsburgh, PA 15213 / 412-621-2130; FAX: 412-621-8740
Universal Sports, P.O. Box 532, Vincennes, IN 47591 / 812-882-8680; FAX: 812-882-8680
Unmussig Bullets, D. L., 7862 Brentford Dr., Richmond, VA 23225 / 804-320-1165
Upper Missouri Trading Co., 304 Harold St., Crofton, NE 68730 / 402-388-4844
USAC, 4500-15th St. East, Tacoma, WA 98424 / 206-922-7589
Utica Cutlery Co., 820 Noyes St., Utica, NY 13503 / 315-733-4663; FAX: 315-733-6602

V

V.H. Blackinton & Co., Inc., 221 John L. Dietsch, Attleboro Falls, MA 02763-0300 / 508-699-4436; FAX: 508-695-5349
Valade Engraving, Robert, 931 3rd Ave, Seaside, OR 97138 / 503-738-7672
Valor Corp., 5555 NW 36th Ave., Miami, FL 33142 / 305-633-0127; FAX: 305-634-4536
Valtro USA, Inc, 1281 Andersen Dr., San Rafael, CA 94901 / 415-256-2575; FAX: 415-256-2576
VAM Distribution Co LLC, 1141-B Mechanicsburg Rd, Wooster, OH 44691
Van Gorden & Son Inc., C. S., 1815 Main St., Bloomer, WI 54724 / 715-568-2612
Van Horn, Gil, P.O. Box 207, Llano, CA 93544
Van Patten, J. W., P.O. Box 145, Foster Hill, Milford, PA 18337 / 717-296-7069
Van's Gunsmith Service, 224 Route 69-A, Parish, NY 13131 / 315-625-7251
Vancini, Carl (See Bestload, Inc.)
Vann Custom Bullets, 330 Grandview Ave., Novato, CA 94947
Varmint Masters, LLC, Rick Vecqueray , PO Box 6724, Bend, OR 97708 / 541-318-7306; FAX: 541-318-7306
Vecqueray, Rick. See: VARMINT MASTERS, LLC
Vega Tool Co., c/o T.R. Ross, 4865 Tanglewood Ct., Boulder, CO 80301 / 303-530-0174
Vektor USA, Mikael Danforth , 5139 Stanart St, Norfolk, VA 23502 / 888-740-0837; or 757-455-8895; FAX: 757-461-9155
Venco Industries, Inc. (See Shooter's Choice)
Venus Industries, P.O. Box 240, Sialkot-1, PAKISTAN FAX: 92 432 85579
Verney-Carron, B.P. 72, 54 Boulevard Thiers, 42002, FRANCE / 33-477791500; FAX: 33-477790702
Vest, John, P.O. Box 1552, Susanville, CA 96130 / 916-257-7228
Vibra-Tek Co., 1844 Arroya Rd., Colorado Springs, CO 80906 / 719-634-8611; FAX: 719-634-6886
VibraShine, Inc., P.O. Box 577, Taylorsville, MS 39168 / 601-785-9854; FAX: 601-785-9874
Vic's Gun Refinishing, 6 Pineview Dr., Dover, NH 03820-6422 / 603-742-0013
Victory Ammunition, PO Box 1022, Milford, PA 18337 / 717-296-5768; FAX: 717-296-9298
Victory USA, P.O. Box 1021, Pine Bush, NY 12566 / 914-744-2060; FAX: 914-744-5181
Vihtavuori Oy, FIN-41330 Vihtavuori, FINLAND, / 358-41-3779211; FAX: 358-41-3771643
Vihtavuori Oy/Kaltron-Pettibone, 1241 Ellis St., Bensenville, IL 60106 / 708-350-1116; FAX: 708-350-1606
Viking Leathercraft, Inc., 1579A Jayken Way, Chula Vista, CA 91911 / 800-262-6666; FAX: 619-429-8268
Viking Video Productions, P.O. Box 251, Roseburg, OR 97470
Vincent's Shop, 210 Antoinette, Fairbanks, AK 99701
Vincenzo Bernardelli S.p.A., 125 Via Matteotti, P.O. Box 74, Gardone V.T., Bresci, 25063 ITALY / 39-30-8912851-2-3; FAX: 39-30-8910249+
Vintage Arms, Inc., 6003 Saddle Horse, Fairfax, VA 22030 / 703-968-0779; FAX: 703-968-0780
Vintage Industries, Inc., 781 Big Tree Dr., Longwood, FL 32750 / 407-831-8949; FAX: 407-831-5346
Viper Bullet and Brass Works, 11 Brock St., Box 582, Norwich, ON N0J 1P0 CANADA
Viramontez, Ray, 601 Springfield Dr., Albany, GA 31707 / 912-432-9683
Visible Impact Targets, Rts. 5 & 20, E. Bloomfield, NY 14443 / 716-657-6161; FAX: 716-657-5405
Vitt/Boos, 2178 Nichols Ave., Stratford, CT 06614 / 203-375-6859
Voere-KGH m.b.H., P.O. Box 416, A-6333 Kufstein, Tirol, AUSTRIA / 0043-5372-62547; FAX: 0043-5372-65752
Volquartsen Custom Ltd., 24276 240th Street, P.O. Box 397, Carroll, IA 51401 / 712-792-4238; FAX: 712-792-2542
Vom Hoffe (See Old Western Scrounger, Inc., The), 12924 Hwy A-12, Montague, CA 96064 / 916-459-5445; FAX: 916-459-3944
Von Minden Gunsmithing Services, 2403 SW 39 Terrace, Cape Coral, FL 33914 / 813-542-8946
Vorhes, David, 3042 Beecham St., Napa, CA 94558 / 707-226-9116
Vortek Products, Inc., P.O. Box 871181, Canton, MI 48187-6181 / 313-397-5656; FAX: 313-397-5656
VSP Publishers (See Heritage/VSP Gun Books), PO Box 887, McCall, ID 83638 / 208-634-4104; FAX: 208-634-3101
Vulpes Ventures, Inc. Fox Cartridge Division, P.O. Box 1363, Bolingbrook, IL 60440-7363 / 708-759-1229

W

W. Square Enterprises, 9826 Sagedale, Houston, TX 77089 / 713-484-0935; FAX: 281-484-0935
W. Waller & Son, Inc., 2221 Stoney Brook Rd., Grantham, NH 03753-7706 / 603-863-4177
W.B. Niemi Engineering, Box 126 Center Road, Greensboro, VT 05841 / 802-533-7180 or 802-533-7141
W.C. Strutz Rifle Barrels, Inc., P.O. Box 611, Eagle River, WI 54521 / 715-479-4766
W.C. Wolff Co., PO Box 458, Newtown Square, PA 19073 / 610-359-9600; FAX: 610-359-9496
W.E. Birdsong & Assoc., 1435 Monterey Rd., Florence, MS 39073-9748 / 601-366-8270
W.E. Brownell Checkering Tools, 9390 Twin Mountain Cir, San Diego, CA 92126 / 619-695-2479; FAX: 619-695-2479
W.J. Riebe Co., 3434 Tucker Rd., Boise, ID 83703
W.R. Case & Sons Cutlery Co., Owens Way, Bradford, PA 16701 / 814-368-4123 or 800-523-6350; FAX: 814-768-5369
Wagoner, Vernon G., 2325 E. Encanto, Mesa, AZ 85213 / 602-835-1307
Wakina by Pic, 24813 Alderbrook Dr., Santa Clarita, CA 91321 / 800-295-8194
Waldron, Herman, Box 475, 80 N. 17th St., Pomeroy, WA 99347 / 509-843-1404
Walker Arms Co., Inc., 499 County Rd. 820, Selma, AL 36701 / 334-872-6231; FAX: 334-872-6262
Walker Mfg., Inc., 8296 S. Channel, Harsen's Island, ML 48028
Wallace, Terry, 385 San Marino, Vallejo, CA 94589 / 707-642-7041
Walls Industries, Inc., P.O. Box 98, 1905 N. Main, Cleburne, TX 76031 / 817-645-4366; FAX: 817-645-7946
Walnut Factory, The, 235 West Rd. No. 1, Portsmouth, NH 03801 / 603-436-2225; FAX: 603-433-7003
Walt's Custom Leather, Walt Whinnery, 1947 Meadow Creek Dr., Louisville, KY 40218 / 502-458-4361
Walters Industries, 6226 Park Lane, Dallas, TX 75225 / 214-691-6973
Walters, John, 500 N. Avery Dr., Moore, OK 73160 / 405-799-0376
Walther GmbH, Carl, B.P. 4325, D-89033 Ulm, GERMANY
WAMCO, Inc., Mingo Loop, P.O. Box 337, Oquossoc, ME 04964-0337 / 207-864-3344
WAMCO--New Mexico, P.O. Box 205, Peralta, NM 87042-0205 / 505-869-0826
Ward & Van Valkenburg, 114 32nd Ave. N., Fargo, ND 58102 / 701-232-2351
Ward Machine, 5620 Lexington Rd., Corpus Christi, TX 78412 / 512-992-1221
Wardell Precision Handguns Ltd., 48851 N. Fig Springs Rd., New River, AZ 85027-8513 / 602-465-7995
Warenski, Julie, 590 E. 500 N., Richfield, UT 84701 / 801-896-5319; FAX: 801-896-5319
Warne Manufacturing Co., 9039 SE Jannsen Rd., Clackamas, OR 97015 / 503-657-5590 or 800-683-5590; FAX: 503-657-5695
Warren & Sweat Mfg. Co., P.O. Box 350440, Grand Island, FL 32784 / 904-669-3166; FAX: 904-669-7272
Warren Muzzleloading Co., Inc., Hwy. 21 North, P.O. Box 100, Ozone, AR 72854 / 501-292-3268
Warren, Kenneth W. (See Mountain States Engraving)
Washita Mountain Whetstone Co., P.O. Box 378, Lake Hamilton, AR 71951 / 501-525-3914
Wasmundt, Jim, P.O. Box 511, Fossil, OR 97830
WASP Shooting Systems, Rt. 1, Box 147, Lakeview, AR 72642 / 501-431-5606
Waterfield Sports, Inc., 13611 Country Lane, Burnsville, MN 55337 / 612-435-8339
Watson Bros., 39 Redcross Way, London Bridge, LONDON U.K. FAX: 44-171-403-336
Watson Trophy Match Bullets, 2404 Wade Hampton Blvd., Greenville, SC 29615 / 864-244-7948 or 941-635-7948
Wayne E. Schwartz Custom Guns, 970 E. Britton Rd., Morrice, MI 48857 / 517-625-4079
Wayne Firearms for Collectors and Investors, James, 2608 N. Laurent, Victoria, TX 77901 / 512-578-1258; FAX: 512-578-3559

Manufacturer's Directory

Wayne Reno, 2808 Stagestop Rd., Jefferson, CO 80456 / 719-836-3452

Wayne Specialty Services, 260 Waterford Drive, Florissant, MO 63033 / 413-831-7083

WD-40 Co., 1061 Cudahy Pl., San Diego, CA 92110 / 619-275-1400; FAX: 619-275-5823

Weatherby, Inc., 3100 El Camino Real, Atascadero, CA 93422 / 805-466-1767 or 800-227-2016; FAX: 805-466-2527

Weaver Arms Corp. Gun Shop, RR 3, P.O. Box 266, Bloomfield, MO 63825-9528

Weaver Products, P.O. Box 39, Onalaska, WI 54650 / 800-648-9624 or 608-781-5800; FAX: 608-781-0368

Weaver Scope Repair Service, 1121 Larry Mahan Dr., Suite B, El Paso, TX 79925 / 915-593-1005

Webb, Bill, 6504 North Bellefontaine, Kansas City, MO 64119 / 816-453-7431

Weber & Markin Custom Gunsmiths, 4-1691 Powick Rd., Kelowna, BC V1X 4L1 CANADA / 250-762-7575; FAX: 250-861-3655

Weber Jr., Rudolf, P.O. Box 160106, D-5650, GERMANY / 0212-592136

Webley and Scott Ltd., Frankley Industrial Park, Tay Rd., Birmingham, B45 0PA ENGLAND / 011-021-453-1864; FAX: 021-457-7846

Webster Scale Mfg. Co., P.O. Box 188, Sebring, FL 33870 / 813-385-6362

Weems, Cecil, 510 W Hubbard St, Mineral Wells, TX 76067-4847 / 817-325-1462

Weigand Combat Handguns, Inc., 685 South Main Rd., Mountain Top, PA 18707 / 570-868-8358; FAX: 570-868-5218

Weihrauch KG, Hermann, Industriestrasse 11, 8744 Mellrichstadt, Mellrichstadt, GERMANY

Weisz Parts, P.O. Box 20038, Columbus, OH 43220-0038 / 614-45-70-500; FAX: 614-846-8585

Welch, Sam, CVSR 2110, Moab, UT 84532 / 801-259-8131

Wellington Outdoors, P.O. Box 244, 1140 Monticello Rd., Madison, GA 30650 / 706-342-4915; FAX: 706-342-7568

Wells Creek Knife & Gun Works, 32956 State Hwy. 38, Scottsburg, OR 97473 / 541-587-4202; FAX: 541-587-4223

Wells, Rachel, 110 N. Summit St., Prescott, AZ 86301 / 520-445-3655

Welsh, Bud, 80 New Road, E. Amherst, NY 14051 / 716-688-6344

Wenger North America/Precise Int'l, 15 Corporate Dr., Orangeburg, NY 10962 / 800-431-2996 FAX: 914-425-4700

Wenig Custom Gunstocks, 103 N. Market St., P.O. Box 249, Lincoln, MO 65338 / 816-547-3334; FAX: 816-547-2881

Werth, T. W., 1203 Woodlawn Rd., Lincoln, IL 62656 / 217-732-1300

Wescombe, Bill (See North Star West)

Wessinger Custom Guns & Engraving, 268 Limestone Rd., Chapin, SC 29036 / 803-345-5677

West, Jack L., 1220 W. Fifth, P.O. Box 427, Arlington, OR 97812

Western Cutlery (See Camillus Cutlery Co.)

Western Design (See Alpha Gunsmith Division)

Western Gunstock Mfg. Co., 550 Valencia School Rd., Aptos, CA 95003 / 408-688-5884

Western Missouri Shooters Alliance, P.O. Box 11144, Kansas City, MO 64119 / 816-597-3950; FAX: 816-229-7350

Western Nevada West Coast Bullets, PO BOX 2270, DAYTON, NV 89403-2270 / 702-246-3941; FAX: 702-246-0836

Westley Richards & Co., 40 Grange Rd., Birmingham, ENGLAND / 010-214722953

Westley Richards Agency USA (See U.S. Importer for Westrom, John (See Precision Metal Finishing)

Westwind Rifles, Inc., David S. Sullivan, P.O. Box 261, 640 Briggs St., Erie, CO 80516 / 303-828-3823

Weyer International, 2740 Nebraska Ave., Toledo, OH 43607 / 419-534-2020; FAX: 419-534-2697

Whildin & Sons Ltd, E.H., RR 2 Box 119, Tamaqua, PA 18252 / 717-668-6743; FAX: 717-668-6745

Whinnery, Walt (See Walt's Custom Leather)

Whiscombe (See U.S. Importer-Pelaire Products)

White Flyer Targets, 124 River Road, Middlesex, NJ 08846 / 908-469-0100 or 602-972-7528 FAX: 908-469-9692

White Owl Enterprises, 2583 Flag Rd., Abilene, KS 67410 / 913-263-2613; FAX: 913-263-2613

White Pine Photographic Services, Hwy. 60, General Delivery, Wilno, ON K0J 2N0 CANADA / 613-756-3452

White Rock Tool & Die, 6400 N. Brighton Ave., Kansas City, MO 64119 / 816-454-0478

White Shooting Systems, Inc. (See White Muzzleload

Whitestone Lumber Corp., 148-02 14th Ave., Whitestone, NY 11357 / 718-746-4400; FAX: 718-767-1748

Whitetail Design & Engineering Ltd., 9421 E. Mannsiding Rd., Clare, MI 48617 / 517-386-3932

Wichita Arms, Inc., 923 E. Gilbert, P.O. Box 11371, Wichita, KS 67211 / 316-265-0661; FAX: 316-265-0760

Wick, David E., 1504 Michigan Ave., Columbus, IN 47201 / 812-376-6960

Widener's Reloading & Shooting Supply, Inc., P.O. Box 3009 CRS, Johnson City, TN 37602 / 615-282-6786; FAX: 615-282-6651

Wideview Scope Mount Corp., 13535 S. Hwy. 16, Rapid City, SD 57701 / 605-341-3220; FAX: 605-341-9142

Wiebe, Duane, 846 Holly WYA, Placerville, CA 95667-3415

Wiest, M. C., 10737 Dutchtown Rd., Knoxville, TN 37932 / 423-966-4545

Wilcox All-Pro Tools & Supply, 4880 147th St., Montezuma, IA 50171 / 515-623-3138; FAX: 515-623-3104

Wilcox Industries Corp, Robert F Guarasi , 53 Durham St, Portsmouth, NH 03801 / 603-431-1331; FAX: 603-431-1221

Wild Bill's Originals, P.O. Box 13037, Burton, WA 98013 / 206-463-5738; FAX: 206-465-5925

Wild West Guns, 7521 Old Seward Hwy, Unit A, Anchorage, AK 99518 / 800-992-4570 or 907-344-4500; FAX: 907-344-4005

Wilderness Sound Products Ltd., 4015 Main St. A, Springfield, OR 97478 / 503-741-0263 or 800-437-0006; FAX: 503-741-7648

Wildey, Inc., 458 Danbury Rd #6, New Milford, CT 06776-4345 / 203-355-9000; FAX: 203-354-7759

Wildlife Research Center, Inc., 1050 McKinley St., Anoka, MN 55303 / 612-427-3350 or 800-USE-LURE; FAX: 612-427-8354

Wilhelm Brenneke KG, Ilmenauweg 2, 30851, Langenhagen, GERMANY / 0511/97262-0; FAX: 0511/97262-62

Will-Burt Co., 169 S. Main, Orrville, OH 44667

William Fagan & Co., 22952 15 Mile Rd., Clinton Township, MI 48035 / 810-465-4637; FAX: 810-792-6996

William Powell & Son (Gunmakers) Ltd., 35-37 Carrs Lane, Birmingham, B4 7SX ENGLAND / 121-643-0689; FAX: 121-631-3504

William Powell Agency, 22 Circle Dr., Bellmore, NY 11710 / 516-679-1158

Williams Gun Sight Co., 7389 Lapeer Rd., Box 329, Davison, MI 48423 / 810-653-2131 or 800-530-9028; FAX: 810-658-2140

Williams Mfg. of Oregon, 110 East B St., Drain, OR 97435 / 503-836-7461; FAX: 503-836-7245

Williams Shootin' Iron Service, The Lynx-Line, Rt 2 Box 223A, Mountain Grove, MO 65711 / 417-948-0902 FAX: 417-948-0902

Williamson Precision Gunsmithing, 117 W. Pipeline, Hurst, TX 76053 / 817-285-0064; FAX: 817-280-0044

Willow Bend, P.O. Box 203, Chelmsford, MA 01824 / 508-256-8508; FAX: 508-256-8508

Willson Safety Prods. Div., PO Box 622, Reading, PA 19603-0622 / 610-376-6161; FAX: 610-371-7725

Wilson Arms Co., The, 63 Leetes Island Rd., Branford, CT 06405 / 203-488-7297; FAX: 203-488-0135

Wilson Case, Inc., P.O. Box 1106, Hastings, NE 68902-1106 / 800-322-5493; FAX: 402-463-5276

Wilson Gun Shop, Box 578, Rt. 3, Berryville, AR 72616 / 870-545-3618; FAX: 870-545-3310

Winchester Div. Olin Corp., 427 N. Shamrock, E. Alton, IL 62024 / 618-258-3566; FAX: 618-258-3599

Winchester Press (See New Win Publishing, Inc.), 186 Center St, Clinton, NJ 08809 / 908-735-9701; FAX: 908-735-9703

Winchester Sutler, Inc., The, 270 Shadow Brook Lane, Winchester, VA 22603 / 540-888-3595; FAX: 540-888-4632

Windish, Jim, 2510 Dawn Dr., Alexandria, VA 22306 / 703-765-1994

Windjammer Tournament Wads Inc., 750 W. Hampden Ave., Suite 170, Englewood, CO 80110 / 303-781-6329

Wingshooting Adventures, 0-1845 W. Leonard, Grand Rapids, MI 49544 / 616-677-1980; FAX: 616-677-1986

Winkle Bullets, R.R. 1, Box 316, Heyworth, IL 61745

Winter, Robert M., P.O. Box 484, 42975-287th St., Menno, SD 57045 / 605-387-5322

Wise Guns, Dale, 333 W Olmos Dr, San Antonio, TX 78212 / 210-828-3388

Wiseman and Co., Bill, PO Box 3427, Bryan, TX 77805 / 409-690-3456; FAX: 409-690-0156

Wisners Inc/Twin Pine Armory, P.O. Box 58, Hwy. 6, Adna, WA 98522 / 360-748-4590; FAX: 360-748-1802

Wolf (See J.R. Distributing)

Wolf's Western Traders, 40 E. Works, No. 3F, Sheridan, WY 82801 / 307-674-5352

Wolfe Publishing Co., 6471 Airpark Dr., Prescott, AZ 86301 / 520-445-7810 or 800-899-7810; FAX: 520-778-5124

Wolverine Footwear Group, 9341 Courtland Dr. NE, Rockford, MI 49351 / 616-866-5500; FAX: 616-866-5658

Wood, Frank (See Classic Guns, Inc.), 3230 Medlock Bridge Rd, Ste 110, Norcross, GA 30092 / 404-242-7944

Wood, Mel, P.O. Box 1255, Sierra Vista, AZ 85636 / 602-455-5541

Woodleigh (See Huntington Die Specialties)

Woods Wise Products, P.O. Box 681552, 2200 Bowman Rd., Franklin, TN 37068 / 800-735-8182; FAX: 615-726-2637

Woodstream, P.O. Box 327, Lititz, PA 17543 / 717-626-2125 FAX: 717-626-1912

Woodworker's Supply, 1108 North Glenn Rd., Casper, WY 82601 / 307-237-5354

Woolrich, Inc., Mill St., Woolrich, PA 17701 / 800-995-1299; FAX: 717-769-6234/6259

Working Guns, Jim Coffin , 1224 NW Fernwood Cir, Corvallis, OR 97330-2909 / 541-928-4391

World Class Airguns, 2736 Morningstar Dr., Indianapolis, IN 46229 / 317-897-5548

World of Targets (See Birchwood Casey)

World Trek, Inc., 7170 Turkey Creek Rd., Pueblo, CO 81007-1046 / 719-546-2121; FAX: 719-543-6886

Worthy Products, Inc., RR 1, P.O. Box 213, Martville, NY 13111 / 315-324-5298

Wosenitz VHP, Inc., Box 741, Dania, FL 33004 / 305-923-3748; FAX: 305-925-2217

Wostenholm (See Ibberson [Sheffield] Ltd., George)

Wright's Hardwood Gunstock Blanks, 8540 SE Kane Rd., Gresham, OR 97080 / 503-666-1705

WTA Manufacturing, P.O. Box 164, Kit Carson, CO 80825 / 800-700-3054; FAX: 719-962-3570

Wyant Bullets, Gen. Del., Swan Lake, MT 59911

Wyant's Outdoor Products, Inc., P.O. Box 9, Broadway, VA 22815

Wyoming Bonded Bullets, Box 91, Sheridan, WY 82801 / 307-674-8091

Wyoming Custom Bullets, 1626 21st St., Cody, WY 82414

Wyoming Knife Corp., 101 Commerce Dr., Ft. Collins, CO 80524 / 303-224-3454

X

X-Spand Target Systems, 26-10th St. SE, Medicine Hat, AB T1A 1P7 CANADA / 403-526-7997; FAX: 403-528-2362

Y

Yankee Gunsmith, 2901 Deer Flat Dr., Copperas Cove, TX 76522 / 817-547-8433

Yavapai College, 1100 E. Sheldon St., Prescott, AZ 86301 / 520-776-2353 FAX: 520-776-2355

Yavapai Firearms Academy Ltd., P.O. Box 27290, Prescott Valley, AZ 86312 / 520-772-8262

Yearout, Lewis E. (See Montana Outfitters), 308 Riverview Dr E, Great Falls, MT 59404 / 406-761-0859

Yee, Mike, 29927 56 Pl. S., Auburn, WA 98001 / 206-839-3991

Yellowstone Wilderness Supply, P.O. Box 129, W. Yellowstone, MT 59758 / 406-646-7613

Yesteryear Armory & Supply, P.O. Box 408, Carthage, TN 37030

York M-1 Conversions, 803 Mill Creek Run, Plantersville, TX 77363 / 800-527-2881 or 713-477-8442

Young Country Arms, William , 1409 Kuehner Dr #13, Simi Valley, CA 93063-4478

Yukon Arms Classic Ammunition, 1916 Brooks, P.O. Box 223, Missoula, MT 59801 / 406-543-9614

Z

Z's Metal Targets & Frames, P.O. Box 78, South Newbury, NH 03255 / 603-938-2826

Z-M Weapons, 203 South St., Bernardston, MA 01337 / 413-648-9501; FAX: 413-648-0219

Zabala Hermanos S.A., P.O. Box 97, Eibar, 20600 SPAIN / 43-768085 or 43-768076; FAX: 34-43-768201

Zander's Sporting Goods, 7525 Hwy 154 West, Baldwin, IL 62217-9706 / 800-851-4373 FAX: 618-785-2320

Zanoletti, Pietro, Via Monte Gugielpo, 4, I-25063 Gardone V.T., ITALY

Zanotti Armor, Inc., 123 W. Lone Tree Rd., Cedar Falls, IA 50613 / 319-232-9650

ZDF Import Export, Inc., 2975 South 300 West, Salt Lake City, UT 84115 / 801-485-1012; FAX: 801-484-4363

Zeeryp, Russ, 1601 Foard Dr., Lynn Ross Manor, Morristown, TN 37814 / 615-586-2357

Zero Ammunition Co., Inc., 1601 22nd St. SE, P.O. Box 1188, Cullman, AL 35056-1188 / 800-545-9376; FAX: 205-739-4683

Ziegel Engineering, 2108 Lomina Ave., Long Beach, CA 90815 / 562-596-9481; FAX: 562-598-4734

Zim's, Inc., 4370 S. 3rd West, Salt Lake City, UT 84107 / 801-268-2505

Zoli, Antonio, Via Zanardelli 39, Casier Postal 21, I-25063 Gardone V.T., ITALY

Zriny's Metal Targets (See Z's Metal Targets & Fra

Zufall, Joseph F., P.O. Box 304, Golden, CO 80402-0304

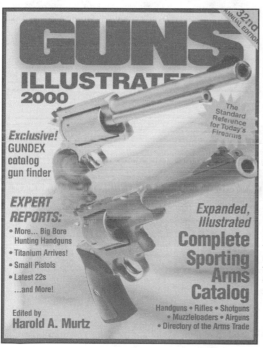

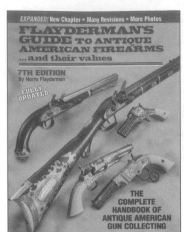
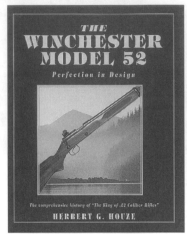
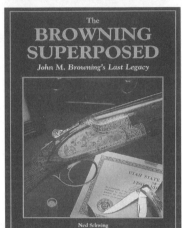

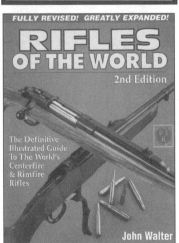
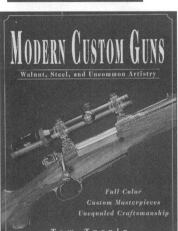